T0343404

HANDBOOKS IN OPERATIONS RESEARCH
AND MANAGEMENT SCIENCE
VOLUME 6

Handbooks in Operations Research and Management Science

Volume 6

NORTH-HOLLAND
AMSTERDAM · LONDON · NEW YORK · TOKYO

Operations Research and the Public Sector

Edited by

S.M. Pollock
The University of Michigan

M.H. Rothkopf
Rutgers University

A. Barnett
Massachusetts Institute of Technology

1994
NORTH-HOLLAND
AMSTERDAM · LONDON · NEW YORK · TOKYO

ELSEVIER SCIENCE B.V.

P.O. Box 211, 1000 AE Amsterdam, The Netherlands

Library of Congress Cataloging-in-Publication Data
Operations research and the public sector / edited by S. M. Pollock, M. H. Rothkopf, A. Barnett.
   p.   cm. – (Handbooks in operations research and management science; v. 6)
  Includes bibliographical references (p.   ) and index.
  ISBN 0-444-89204-4 (acid-free paper)
  1. Operations research. 2. Public administration. I. Pollock, S. M. (Stephen M.) II. Rothkopf,
M. H. (Michael H.) III. Barnett, Arnold. IV. Series
JF1525.06058 1994
350'.0001'1--dc20   94-14930
                                                    CIP

ISBN: 0 444 89204 4

Transferred to digital print 2008

Printed and bound in Great Britain by CPI Antony Rowe, Eastbourne

Preface

This volume represents a departure from its companions in the series *Handbooks in Operations Research and Management Science*. Rather than concentrating on methodology or techniques (such as optimization or computing) or specific application areas (production and inventory, or marketing), we have chosen to present the reader with a compendium of techniques, methods, models and approaches to analyzing operational problems found in the Public Sector (broadly defined). For this reason, our audience is assumed to be eclectic and heterogeneous, including:

(a) practitioners whose day-to-day activities involve modeling and decision making within the public sector;

(b) policy makers with responsibilities for managing the production of and/or understanding the results of analysis;

(c) graduate (and advanced undergraduate) students in non-OR/MS programs (such as natural resources, urban and regional planning, geography, criminology, political science);

(d) operations research students who have interests in applications in the public sector.

This is also why the level of treatment of the topics within this volume may appear to vary widely – a natural phenomenon when one considers that each reader is bound to bring to his or her perusal an equally wide variation of backgrounds, education and technical skills.

The first chapter, by Pollock and Maltz, sets the stage by discussing the suggested boundaries for what we mean by the 'public sector', 'operations research' and 'management science'. It also presents a brief history of the applications of the latter two to the former.

In Chapter 2, Gass provides a different kind of introduction, in which he discusses the nature of an 'application' in the public sector and how it differs from one in the private sector. He examines ways that public sector applications can be improved and presents the ethical issues that arise in the context of model use for public sector advocacy.

"Everyone concedes that models can fail, but many modelers appear furtively to believe that their own efforts are invulnerable to that fate." So says Barnett in his 'admonitional' Chapter 3, in which he also contends that the creativity so often apparent in the construction of models is less evident when the need arises to validate them. This serious omission can have particularly serious consequences when dealing with issues involving human life and welfare. Some readers will be surprised at his re-telling of the argument that the R^2 measure, so pervasive in regression analysis, may be the most overrated statistic in the history of mathematics.

It is well established that the first organized use of operations research as a 'discipline' was in the analysis of military operations. No one doubts that analytical capabilities continue to be vital in both tactical and strategic aspects warfare. As Washburn makes clear in Chapter 4, it continues to be an important, if not infallible, contributor to national defense. He also presents arguments as to why military planners are well advised to use these capabilities to ferret out the implications of imperfect (and thus often probabilistic) information.

Operations research has especially strong links to the transportation field; it is no accident that *Transportation Science* was the first of ORSA's specialized journals. Beyond solving myriad problems in scheduling and routing by land, sea, and air, OR can help in such unexpected areas as designing airport terminal buildings. Odoni, Rousseau and Wilson offer, in Chapter 5, a vivid spectacle of OR-in-motion.

Problems in planning for and operating emergency services (e.g. police, fire, and ambulances) have proved highly amenable to such techniques as queuing analysis and mathematical programming. OR studies have generated a clearer understanding about the allocation of critical resources to such services. They have also made the case for such unsettling decisions as delaying the response to a current fire alarm to prevent a far greater delay for 'the fire next time'. In Chapter 6, Swersey surveys developments in this area in which OR models have doubtless influenced many lives.

In Chapter 7 on Crime and Justice, Maltz points out that Poisson derived his seminal probability distribution – practically the 'union label' of operations research – during the course of modeling jury behavior. More recent OR activities in this area have focused on the stochastic processes that underlie data about the commission and punishment of crime. This work has deepened and sometimes radically transformed the public understanding of criminal activity, leading to the observation that operations researchers have had an influence on criminology far exceeding the proportion of their numbers.

The energy industry has seen extensive *private* sector application of operations research modeling. In Chapter 8, Weyant, the director of Stanford's Energy Modeling Forum, describes the use of models to analyze energy policy choices. These models, spanning the range from engineering to economics, are crucial to understanding the impact of various alternative energy generation and distribution strategies on the general public.

In bitter forest-usage debates in the Pacific Northwest, it has sometimes seemed unclear whether the endangered species is the spotted owl or the lumberjack. Operations research cannot provide moral guidance in such matters but, as Golden and Wasil explain in Chapter 9, it can explicate tradeoffs between particular policy choices. In a parallel fashion, they also present the application of appropriate models to the understanding of impacts of various actions on the availability and usage of other natural resources: fisheries, wildlife and water.

In Chapter 10, ReVelle and Ellis consider a different but related concern: modelling the effects of management decisions on air and water *quality*. Different methods of generating energy, producing goods or extracting raw materials cost differing amounts and yield different levels of air and water pollution. Understanding the appropriate balance of such activities naturally produces problems in constrained optimization, one of the classical tools of OR.

Nobody wants a garbage dump located near his or her home, but no one wants to live in a society that has no garbage dumps. Kleindorfer and Kunreuther deal with conundrums of this kind in Chapter 11, where they present the analyses behind rational approaches to siting hazardous or other noxious facilities. They describe the important features of this 'facilities siting' problem, discuss approaches for improving structuring of the problem, and review research devoted to siting (and related route selection) problems.

The Delaney Amendment made everything seem easy when it passed the U.S. Congress: a substance would be banned if it had even the slightest carcinogenic potential. Taken literally, the amendment would indeed have eliminated cancer because we would have starved to death in a few weeks. But defining, estimating and managing risk is a more subtle business, as Lave makes clear in a wide-ranging Chapter 12.

Pierskalla and Brailer's Chapter 13, on the use of operations research in analyzing health care delivery, is particularly timely now that the United States is embarked upon a national debate over changing the way health care is delivered. Dealing with death and physical impairment as possible decision outcomes, within the constructs of formal operations research models, is a challenge that can be met in dealing with health care analysis. The discussion evaluates these methods, and provides extensive references to an extensive body of relevant literature.

The analysis of sports and athletic competitions may not be considered to fit easily within the rubric of understanding a 'public sector' activity. It does share at least one factor in common, however: the use of a *financial* 'bottom line' is often an inadequate way of characterizing the more interesting problems. Moreover, anything that contributes to the fairness and excitement of sporting activities has far-reaching economic and social implications for the public sector. (The Olympics are watched by half the people in the world.) Gerchak reminds us in Chapter 14 that operations research is by no means absent from the sporting arenas, and may have had more influence (or at least may deserve more) than is commonly recognized.

Suppose the Census reveals that, over the previous decade, your state's population has grown while all other states had no change in their populations. A reapportionment method, supposedly rooted in the 'one person, one vote' principle, could wind up reducing your state's representation in Congress! In Chapter 15, Balinski and Young subject various apportionment rules to deep scrutiny, identifying the axioms implicit in each system and suggesting anomalies to which they can lead.

In Chapter 16, Anderson addresses the ubiquitous public-sector concern about how to reach decisions among many parties who have conflicting preferences. The obvious application is to voting as a means of electing public officers, but generalizations to other group selection processes are also covered. In Chapter 17 he presents the principles by which one can understand ranking and pairwise comparisons, analyses that encompass a wide spectrum of activities, ranging from weapon system evaluation to college football and basketball polls.

The last two chapters deal with methodological issues (in contrast to the previous chapters' arena-based materials) of particular concern in the public sector.

In analyzing public sector problems, management scientists and operations research analysts are immediately faced with the task of defining scales of measurement related to the phenomena they are studying. In Chapter 18, Roberts spells out the issues that arise when analysts create such measurement scales and indicates the kinds of difficulties that can arise if these scales are not chosen appropriately.

In seeking a politically acceptable way to purchase property for the government, or to transfer government rights, governments often turn to the use of auctions. In the final Chapter 19, Rothkopf surveys critically the wide variety of mathematical models of auctions, and analyses their use in the design of competitive systems.

Initiating and organizing the material in this volume, and dealing with the authors over the past few years, has been a challenging and rewarding experience for us. We hope the reader will find the breadth and depth of the applications and methods presented here as exciting and provocative as we did. With some irony we recognize that, due to the obvious success in applying operations research methods and approaches to the 'public sector', there is a good possibility that within the next few decades there will be little need to single them out as anything but accepted 'good practice' in this important arena.

Stephen Pollock
Michael Rothkopf
Arnold Barnett

1994

Contents

CHAPTER 4
Military Operations Research
A. Washburn   67

CHAPTER 5
Models in Urban and Air Transportation
A.R. Odoni, J.-M. Rousseau and N.H.M. Wilson   107

CHAPTER 6
The Deployment of Police, Fire, and Emergency Medical Units
A.J. Swersey   151

CHAPTER 7
Operations Research in Studying Crime and Justice: Its History and Accomplishments
M.D. Maltz

CHAPTER 8
Energy Policy Applications of Operations Research
J.P. Weyant

CHAPTER 19

Models of Auctions and Competitive Bidding
M.H. Rothkopf   673

S.M. Pollock et al., Eds., *Handbooks in OR & MS, Vol. 6*

Chapter 1

Operations Research in the Public Sector: An Introduction and a Brief History

Stephen M. Pollock

Department of Industrial and Operations Engineering, University of Michigan,
1205 Beal Avenue, Ann Arbor, MI 48109-2117, U.S.A.

Michael D. Maltz

Department of Criminal Justice and Department of Information and Decision Sciences,
University of Illinois at Chicago, Chicago, IL, U.S.A.

This Handbook is intended to provide the reader with an exposure to the methods and applications of operations research in the public sector. In this chapter we provide an overview of these applications and place them in a historical context. We have attempted to cover the major areas in which operations research and associated modelling activities are not only applicable, but also have shown evidence of application and – to various degrees – acceptance.

To accomplish this, however, our first obligation is to make an effort to explain what we mean by 'operations research' and 'public sector'. These are terms that have evolved over the years according to the predilections of their practitioners, champions and critics, and have naturally been subject to the vagaries of historical events.

1. What is operations research?

Perhaps the most serviceable and wide-spread definitions of operations research have been promulgated by the Operations Research Society of America [ORSA, 1990] in its educational materials:

(1) Operations research is a scientific approach to decision making.

(2) Operations research is concerned with scientifically deciding how best to design and operate systems, usually under conditions requiring the allocation of scarce resources.

The British Operational Research Society in 1962 defined operational research (as it is called in the U.K.) to be the use of formal mathematical models to investigate '... complex problems arising in the direction and management of large systems of men, machines, materials and money in industry, business, government and defense.'

1

None of these definitions, unfortunately, are sufficiently specific to distinguish it from related fields. To complicate matters, the field of management science is so close to operations research that the main professional societies of these two disciplines – The Institute of Management Sciences, and The Operations Research Society of America – have all but merged; in this Handbook we make no distinction between the two.

Thus, a consensus definition of 'Operations Research' is, by all the evidence in the introspective articles that have appeared in *Operations Research* and *Management Science* since the mid 1950's, still sorely lacking. Whether one means the term to be a professional designation, a label for a body of methods, an approach to problem solving or, as has been apocryphally suggested 'the re-invention of applied economics by a bunch of physicists and chemical engineers',[1] it seems almost easier to describe operations research by example than by formal definition.

Yet we do present here an attempt to distinguish between operations research and other related quantitative fields, even while bearing in mind Quade's [1975] observation that 'the distinctions among operations research, cost–effectiveness analysis, cost–benefit analysis, and systems analysis are rather arbitrary'. Yet there are differences, which we describe below.

Economics and operations research both attempt to quantify processes, and search for policies which will improve or optimize a specified output. In economics, however, the phenomena under consideration are exclusively those in which such entities as markets, personal predilections toward consumption, information gathering, etc. are the forces governing the behavior under study. Thus the system is usually restricted to goods, services and resources which are produced, consumed and exchanged. Mainstream economics is concerned with descriptive and/or predictive analysis of such systems; most economists *assume* that economic agents act optimally (or else they would be replaced in the market place by those who do).

Insofar as economics research focuses on determining the underlying character-istics of a process, the two are very similar. Operations research methods indeed are relevant in the study of economic systems. In fact, both Kenneth Arrow, a Nobel Laureate in economics, and George Dantzig, a winner of the National Medal of Science for his work in economics, are operations researchers. But there are some limitations to taking models and techniques originally developed to study economic behavior, and applying these to other fields. Maltz (Chapter 7) and Barnett (Chapter 3) provide some examples of this problem.

Systems Analysis has often been used to describe an analytic process devoted to 'higher-level' issues, wherein the 'systems' nature of an activity is thoroughly explored, rather than concentrating on the reductionist pieces needed for an operations research approach. It frequently implies taking a step back from the specifics of the situation and attempting to place it in a broader context.

---

[1] Indeed, Philip Morse and George Kimball, two undisputable founders of the field, were respectively a physicist and a chemist.

But one person's (or agency's) 'system' is another's small piece of a bigger picture. Thus systems analysis may not be a useful term, except perhaps outside of the professional community where the appeal of being concerned about a 'system' might carry political or persuasive weight. Moreover, the growth of computer systems in the last two decades, and the associated use of the term Systems Analysis to mean, more often than not, *computer* systems analysis, does not clarify the situation.

Cost–Effectiveness and *Cost–Benefit Analyses* refer to specific techniques used to address issues involving multiple criteria of performance. Imbedded in a historical context (mostly having to do with the military, for the first of these terms, and extension to non-military public sector analyses for the second), they have more to say about specific *measures of performance* than about a fundamental approach or method. One of the more difficult aspects of structuring an operational problem is in fact *determining* the appropriate cost, effectiveness, or benefit to use to characterize a system or process. Thus, using these terms to describe general methods of analysis adds little to the discussion.

In the context of this handbook, we have tried to emphasize that it is *operations* or *phenomena* that are being researched, not *algorithms* or *methods*.[2] In this spirit, we define operations research as an analytic process that includes the following steps:

• Studying the process under investigation in sufficient detail, in order to understand its characteristics and how its different elements interrelate. This often means spending a great deal of time in determining what *actually* happens, not what is *supposed* to happen, and observing the interactions among the people who are involved in the process as well as observing the process itself. (Rarely is a cloistered ivory tower the best vantage point for making these observations.)

• Using information obtained by such a study to develop a tentative model of the process. This model is often (but not exclusively) a mathematical or statistical representation, one that incorporates the salient features of the process being studied, as well as those of the communication links between the various actors.

• Measuring the characteristics (input, output, and internal variables) of the process. Here again, observation of what actually occurs, instead of what is supposed to occur, is an important step.

• Incorporating these measurements and observations into the model, and adjusting some of the model's characteristics in order to determine their effect on the process output.

• If optimization is appropriate for the process, determining the configuration that provides the 'best' output according to appropriate criteria.

• If possible, verifying to see if the model is accurate by testing it with actual data. In any event, a verification of its construct validity, and logical consistency (internal validity) are also called for. It is the concern for eventual implementation

---

[2] White [1991] makes much the same point in his observation that 'the desire to become distanced from reality, to avoid direct connections with the real world, has infected OR/MS'.

that might represent the best distinction between operations research and applied mathematics.

• Repeating this sequence of steps a number of times, since the first model developed is rarely adequate, and the insights gained from the deficiencies of the first efforts help to improve the subsequent models.

Thus, our conception of operations research is as a *process* of developing mathematical models in order to understand (and possibly influence) complex operational systems. This view contrasts with other approaches to modelling which are found in the literature, wherein the focus is not on the extent to which the model exemplifies the process, but rather on the model's *output, tractability*, or *methods*. These other approaches, found in the OR literature as well as in the social sciences, economics, and statistics, ignore to a greater or lesser degree the goal of obtaining an understanding of the process under study.

Those who focus primarily on the *output* implicitly assume that the model is *defined* by the analytic method they are using (regression, linear programming, M/M/k queue, ARIMA, LISREL, survival analysis, factor analysis, etc.), and thus is *a priori* correct. In other words, a 'model' of a process becomes reduced to, for example, the beta weights in a linear regression equation.[3] These analysts rarely explore alternative models; the analytic question instead centers on which variables appear to be the most 'statistically significant'[4] This may be due to a lack of knowledge of other possible models that can be used.

By *tractability* we mean the inherent ease with which the model can be manipulated using standard mathematical, statistical or (more recently) computer-based techniques. While tractability is an important feature of a quantitative empirical analysis, it should be seen as neither necessary nor sufficient: intractability may merely be a signal to the analyst that the model underlying the method is inappropriate; and tractability alone may lull the analyst (and user) into a false sense of appropriateness.

Analysts who focus primarily on *methods* may initially have considered the applicability of the tools they develop to the solution of real problems. However, they may get caught up in the intricacies of the mathematics as distinct from the needs of the problem. In such cases, they sometimes appear to prefer honing sharper and sharper tools, irrespective of the tools' applicability to real problems. Thus they can lose sight of the real problem that inspired a new method in their desire to generalize or extend it.

---

[3] As Freedman [1985] notes, 'In social-science regression analysis, [u]sually the idea is to fit a curve to the data, rather than figuring out the process that generated the data. As a matter of fact, investigators often talk about "modelling the data". This is almost perverse: surely the object is to model the phenomenon, and the data are interesting only because they contain information about that phenomenon. Whatever it is that most social science investigators are doing when they construct regression models, discovering natural laws does not seem to be uppermost in their minds.'

[4] Cohen [1990] has an amusing example of the difference between statistical significance and substantive significance. He cites a study that demonstrated the statistical significance of a relationship between height and IQ and showed that 'for a 30-point increase in IQ it would take only enough growth hormone to produce a 3.5-ft increase in height'.

Restricting efforts to any one of these three aspects – output, tractability and methodology – should be avoided. In fact, our view is that successful analysts are those who pay attention to all of these concerns at different times. In order to study a problem, they may at first steep themselves in the process, developing a model along the way. They may then focus entirely on the output, ignoring inaccuracies and inappropriate assumptions along the way, to get an insight into the nature of the phenomenon under study. Still later they may consider the model by itself in greater depth, exploring its mathematical properties to their limits, perhaps discovering new theory as a by-product.

Good operations research, we suggest, requires one to continually go back to the basics, to recognize that the essence of operations research is the operation, not the algorithm, and that the goal of operations research is to understand the process in sufficient detail to determine how different conditions or inputs would affect its output. Thus, whatever operations research *is*, 'the proper use of the operational research approach reduces the area of hunch to an absolute minimum, showing where judgment is needed and where it is unnecessary' [Moore, 1966]. The reader should refer to Chapters 2 and 3 of this Handbook for more thorough discussions of these points.

2. What is the 'public sector'?

A definitional problem also exists with the term 'public sector' in an operations research context, particularly with regard to how decisions get made 'there', and the tools, methods, approaches or mechanisms one might use to help inform these decisions. For example, it is possible to consider the public sector to be that arena wherein:
- the public (or its representatives) make decisions;
- a public servant directs the organization within which the decision is made;
- the general public pays for the analysis and/or bears the major effects of the decision;
- the ultimate measure of the outcome of a decision or policy is non-monetary;
- analyses, or other methods used to inform decisions, are subject to public scrutiny.

Each of these possible criteria has its drawbacks. From our standpoint, it is not so much the type of decision, or the nature of the arena in which the decision is made, that determines the difference. For example, while all military organizations use various reliability modelling and inventory control methods to maintain and manage their equipment, these techniques are just as appropriate (and indeed were for the most part initially developed) for business purposes. Symmetrically, executives at General Motors are at this moment probably making decisions (possibly using operations research methods to do so!) that will have effects, material or otherwise, on the general public – at least on people outside their company, or even outside the automobile industry.

Perhaps a better way to characterize this sense of distributed responsibility for, and impact of, decisions is to note that in the public sector decision makers are almost always faced with the existence of multiple constituencies, each of which has its own notions and measures of costs, benefits, incentives, equity, etc. Moreover, with the obvious exception of true autocracies, there are *many* decision makers who (in some sense) represent the various affected groups.

Thus it may not be sufficient to limit ourselves to excluding analyses where the 'bottom line' criterion is monetary (we had, in fact, originally thought of subtitling this volume 'Beyond the Profit Motive'), since many public sector decisions, as defined above, contain reasonable notions of profitability – albeit profit to the public good. Conversely, simply because a steel mill in one of the (decreasingly common) socialized economies is owned and run by a government agency, its application of (say) modern *S-s* inventory policies to adjust production schedules would not lie within our purview.

That public funds were used to support the research or application in question is neither necessary nor sufficient for it to be considered 'public sector' operations research. Instead, one criterion used for this Handbook is based on what operations research technique was discovered, by whom, and how the technique was predominantly used. If a scheduling algorithm was first used to allocate police officers to shifts, then it is included in this volume. If it was originally developed to schedule factory shift workers, then it would not be included – unless the technique had to be modified to adapt to its new use.

We further note that, at least as currently conceived, there seem to be three general application areas for operations research: military, business, and 'other', where this last category includes most of the areas discussed in this Handbook. We also note that the military and business uses are very often not subject to public scrutiny for reasons of military security or good business sense. It is for this reason that the 'public sector' to which we refer in this Handbook relates not so much to the agency or to who is involved in (or benefits from) its decision-making, but rather to the fact that the analyses and results are open to and subject to public scrutiny. It is for this reason that we have included sports applications in this volume. Granted, sports is a 'big business' particularly in the United States, but the non-business aspects – strategies, training, descriptive and predictive studies, etc. – have aspects that rise above the idea of profit maximization or market analysis. What could be more public in terms of operational analyses than a debate on when to pull the goalie in the final minutes of a hockey game, or whether a basketball or baseball player or team's 'hot streak' is real or merely a statistical artifact?

3. A brief history

In this section we describe the application of mathematical and statistical models to a variety of public sector issues, problems, and systems. Its beginnings are traced to the works of early European statisticians, then early 20th-century models of population dynamics and congestion, followed by the growth of operations research – much of it in the military – in the years during and after World War II, culminating in the renaissance of public sector applications and developments that started in the 1960's and continued to the present.

This short history suffers from an obvious, but readily admitted, bias: the material dealing with the latter half of the 20th century is almost exclusively concerned with activities in the United States. Our excuse is that, to our American eyes, there is a more general blurring of distinctions between the public and private sectors in other countries. This certainly is *not* to say that operations research has not had its impact on, or paid attention to, important public sector problems in the rest of the world:

> The journal *Socio-Economic Planning Sciences* is a good source for work done over the last 25 years in various countries, including third world ones (where the public sector is dominant in most economies.)
>
> *Management Science* devoted its December 1973 issue to the achievements and applications of operations research in Canada.
>
> While the central planning efforts of the 'newly independent' Eastern bloc nations do not necessarily provide many success stories, their sheer magnitude brought about some OR-like developments, including the use of a rudimentary linear programming model by Kantorovich in the 30's.
>
> The short-lived Allende government in Chile engaged the talents of a high-profile team of British and Canadian operations researchers to advise them in economic planning.

Many of these activities in other countries certainly fall within the definitions of 'operations research' and 'public sector' we have described. Yet a lack of familiarity with the older literature in these areas has prevented us from including much of this material in our review.

3.1. The early years – 19th century social statistics

Although operations research as a profession dates from World War II, as a method of analysis it has been around a lot longer than that. In fact, some of the early statisticians practiced a type of operations research, and applied it to social problems. The 19th century saw, throughout Europe, the establishment of governmental agencies with charters to collect statistical data about citizens. For a variety of reasons, judicial data became an important part of this collection – and therefore analysis – activity.[5]

One cause of this 'avalanche of printed numbers' [Hacking, 1990] was the discovery of stable patterns in such data, and the consequent goal of governments to make use of them for planning. This movement had its roots in the 17th century, starting with John Graunt who in 1662 developed the first population mortality tables, which showed the relative constancy of the ratio of male to female births

---

[5] Those who would like to read further on the early history of probability, statistics, and stochastic models are referred to the books by Daston [1988], Gigerenzer, Zeno, Porter, Daston, Beatty & Kruger [1989], Hacking [1990], Kruger et al. [1987], Porter [1986], and Stigler [1986] listed in the references.

and how the death rate varied as a function of age. He then used these statistics to answer policy questions such as an estimation of the number of London males eligible for military duty. Thirty years later William Petty coined the term 'political arithmetic' to describe the use of quantitative thinking in developing governmental policies.

Statistical analyses also took on religious overtones, as statisticians (e.g., Abraham De Moivre, Jakob Bernoulli) and theologians marveled at the relative constancy of some statistics (e.g., gender ratios of newborns) from year to year and attributed it to a 'general, great, complete, and beautiful order' in the world. These numbers inspired John Arbuthnot to write, in 1710, a treatise entitled *An Argument for Divine Providence, taken from the Regularity Observed in the Birth of both Sexes* [Daston, 1988]. This growing belief in the relative constancy of nature was a forerunner of the development of moral statistics and the 'average man', discussed below.

The term 'statistics' (*Statistik* in German) was first used by Gottfried Achenwall in 1749, to describe the collection of 'remarkable facts about the state' [Hacking, 1990]. According to Porter [1986], this term replaced the term 'political arithmetic' at the beginning of the 19th century. In doing so it symbolized a shift in thinking. Whereas political arithmeticians placed their expertise in the service of the (centralized) state, for controlling the population, statists (who used statistics in service of *society*) sought to improve the lot of individuals, by bringing a measure of expertise to social questions; their unit of analysis was the individual rather than society [Gigerenzer, Zeno, Porter, Daston, Beatty & Kruger, 1989].

Adolphe Quetelet was the first to combine the use of statistics in the social sciences with the mathematical tools then being brought to bear on the measurement of astronomical observations [Stigler, 1986]. As described above, the stability of social statistics was held in reverence by many. Quetelet found the same regularity in crime statistics, or at least in the 'known and tried offenses', since 'the sum total of crimes committed will probably ever continue unknown' [Quetelet, 1835].[6] Based on this constancy, he argued that there was such a construct as *l'homme moyen* (the 'average man'); in fact, that one could extend this concept to *l'homme moyen moral*. He asserted that the average man had a statistically constant 'penchant for crime', one that would permit the 'social physicist' to calculate a trajectory over time that 'would reveal simple laws of motion and permit prediction of the future' [Gigerenzer, Zeno, Porter, Daston, Beatty & Kruger, 1989].

Quetelet felt that the statistical regularities were 'signs of a deeper social reality'. By analogizing crime statistics to the statistics of repeated independent measurements of a fixed but unknown quantity, he in effect inverted the logic of the central limit theorem: if such measurements (e.g., of the fixed position of a star) could be shown to follow a normal distribution, then should not a normal distribution (of crime rates, of heights) then be based on a single true value (i.e., a 'correct' height or crime rate), with different individuals exhibiting errors from

---

[6] Maltz [1977] suggests that there were other reasons for this apparent constancy: 'manpower limitations in law enforcement agencies, arrest quotas, a constant jail capacity.'

this value? This conjecture of his was in keeping with the *zeitgeist* of a belief in and a search for natural laws.

In some sense, this inference of Quetelet (that each characteristic of each individual is based on a fixed value, but may contain 'errors') may have contributed to the concept of a master race [Hacking, 1990]. That is, if deviations from the mean are seen as errors rather than as natural variation, it then seems plausible to attempt to 'purify' the genetic stock and free it from all errors and imperfections. This is not the only example during these years of proto-operations research in which a model from one field has been transplanted to another field lock, stock, and barrel with no concern for its relevance: in this case, because the probability distributions for error and for, e.g., human heights, both followed the same normal distribution – at that time called the 'error law'.

Simon-Denis Poisson, on the other hand, did not seem to view statistical constancy with the same awe. Rather, he saw it as a consequence of the fact that the law of large numbers applied to social as well as natural phenomena, is 'indicative of physical causes, not the veiled hand of God' [Daston, 1988]. He went on to develop models of juries and the judicial process that led to the development of what is now known as the Poisson distribution (see Chapter 7 for a discussion of how both Quetelet and Poisson took advantage of the criminal justice statistics that had begun to be collected in France.)

These 19th century attempts to analyze statistics to infer laws of human behavior also gave rise to a major branch of another discipline, sociology; specifically, statistical sociology [Hacking, 1991]. A French sociology textbook at the turn of the century crowed:

> 'True eloquence in sociology is the eloquence of numbers. By statistics sociology can foresee and forecast: the law of large numbers gives them an almost infallible character' [quoted in Hacking, 1991].

Emile Durkheim was one of the major forces in this movement and remains a key figure in sociology to this day; his book, *Suicide*, is still part of sociology's canon. It is important, however, to consider his contribution in the context of the thinking of the times. Following the lead of Quetelet, he believed that the normal distribution described errors rather than natural variation. For example, rather than chalk up the relative constancy of suicide statistics to the concatenation of many independent factors, Durkheim wrote about 'suicidogenetic currents' in society, as if there was an innate propensity of the same magnitude for suicide within every individual [Hacking, 1991].

In contrast, Francis Galton was critical of the penchant of statisticians to focus on the average as the 'true' value and to ignore the variation in the numbers:

> 'It is difficult to understand why statisticians commonly limit their inquiries to Averages, and do not revel in more comprehensive views. Their souls seem as dull to the charm of variety as that of the native of one of our flat English counties, whose retrospect of Switzerland was that, if its mountains could be thrown into its lakes, two nuisances would be got rid of at once' [quoted in Porter, 1986].

Hacking [1991] succinctly summarizes Durkheim's and Galton's differences in their conception of the normal as embodied in the mean of a distribution:

> 'Durkheim identified the moral with the normal. For Galton the normal was not good but mediocre .... For Durkheim, the abnormal was called the pathological. In the end the abnormal was sick. For Galton, the abnormal is exceptional, and may be the healthiest stock of the race.'

Galton's concern with natural variation had another beneficial outcome; it led him to invent correlation, and crime and justice figure prominently in its development [Hacking, 1990]. Alfonse Bertillon had proposed measuring the lengths of different parts of the body as a means of identifying criminals. Based on his work on anthropometry, Galton realized that these measurements were not independent [Porter, 1986], and by graphing two such measurements against each other (after first normalizing them to their respective standard units) was able to show their interdependence.

Areas other than social behavior and criminal activity also received some formal attention from early mathematical modellers by the end of the 19th century. In 1898 Gifford Pinchot, Chief of the Division of Forestry, United States Forest Service, argued for an organized and scientifically backed planning of forest resources. This encouraged economists and agronomists to develop embryonic mathematical models of forest growth and yield management.

One of the most public of processes – political representation and voting behavior – was also affected (or infected) by quantitative reasoning. Earlier in the century, a literature on apportionment and voting started to appear. Although not truly model- (or even mathematically-) oriented, this analysis set the philosophical framework (a process in which Daniel Webster became involved in the 1830's) for eventual formal analysis of the 'fairness' of representation schemes, and how the constitutional mandate of congressional seat allocations to the states could be satisfied. Of particular interest is the fact that even such formal approaches as a 'method' presented by Vinton in 1850 – essentially the same as one proposed earlier by Alexander Hamilton – was subject to the so called 'Alabama paradox' (see Chapter 15), an eminently practical defect that was not even *realized* until its manifestation appeared after the census of 1880.

3.2. The 20th century prior to World War II

In the early part of the 20th century there was a great deal of mathematical modelling activity that paved the way for many of the advances presented in this Handbook, including developments in military activity, forestry, voting, decision analysis and telecommunications. Perhaps one of the most important contributions in the early part of the 20th century was the work of Frederick William Lanchester, who in 1916 published his *Aircraft in Warfare, the Dawn of the Fourth Arm*. This analysis of the mathematics of warfare set the stage for a more formal understanding of conflict, and more importantly its logistics, that was the foundation of the burst of operations research activity a quarter century later.[7] Other analyses around this time, inspired by the desire to apply analytical thinking to the science of warfare, included work by Lord Tiverton in 1917 that argued for the concentration of aerial bombs on a single target on a given raid (a rationale leading ultimately to the massive 1000-plane raids by the British and American Airforces 25 years later), and analysis by the U.S. Naval Consulting Board (headed by Thomas A. Edison) leading to the acceptance of zig-zagging as a suitable method for surface ships to use to evade submarine attacks.

In the 1920's, the notion of 'working circles' as a unit within which analysis could be performed for forest planning was developed. By 1922 Hanzlik's formula for regulating timber cut and harvesting became available, a method used even up to the 1950's. This analytical activity spread to other application areas under the control of the U.S. Forest Service. In the mid 1920's, predator–prey models became the basis for some modest policy making regarding wildlife management, and differential equations describing oxygen concentration along rivers were presented [see, for example, Streeter & Phelps, 1925], in essentially the same form used today for policy analysis

In the arena of political analysis, Hill [1911] and Huntington [1921] provided the first truly 'formal' exposition of the apportionment of representation.

In economics, the notion of utility functions and value functions were introduced in the 1920's. These concepts eventually became important parts of operations research analyses in the 1950's with the formalization of decision analysis, and with specific application to problems in the public sector. Spatial analysis was applied to businesses, leading to Hotelling's [1929] results and Reilly's law of retail gravitation – modelling approaches that had natural extensions to public sector locational problems.

Also at this time, the origins of operations research's sister profession (industrial engineering) were evolving, with the work of Taylor and others concerned with production efficiency. Again, these intellectual roots – along with the seductive ideas of 'scientism' and reductionist analyses – helped set the stage for the burst of quantitative analytic activity during World War II.

In communications, Palme and Erlang had, by 1908, established the equations by which congestion in telephone systems could be forecast and designed for. Subsequent developments led to a general understanding of congestion phenomena by means of the theory of queues – one of the major branches of modern operations research.[8]

---

[7] For a complete and literate exposition of the contributions of this first professional operations researcher, see McCloskey [1956].

[8] This is perhaps the first important application of operations research to the public sector, since at that time telephone systems were a governmental responsibility in the European nations. However, in the context of this Handbook, these contributions are considered more in the realm of 'traditional' operations research, since the objectives of these systems (operating essentially as governmental monopolies) were perhaps more consistent with commercialization rather than the 'public good'.

3.3. 1940 through 1960: The birth of operations research as a profession, and public sector applications

Just as the primary impetus for improving processes came from the military during these war and cold-war years, so was the major thrust of applications of operations research. However, efficiency in military operations was not the only focus. Additional activity was apparent in such diverse areas as water storage, traffic control, forestry, aquaculture and bidding behavior.

Operations research became a recognizable discipline shortly before World War II. Its contributions to military tactical and strategic planning and decision-making are well documented elsewhere (for example, see the excellent three-part article by McCloskey [1987a,b,c]). Its birth in the operational use of early British anti-aircraft fire-control and radar systems, and the Anglo-American development of antisubmarine warfare methods, convoy sizing and routing, are well known and the objects of both historically accurate and apocryphal 'war stories'. The involvement of first-rate scientists (including seven Nobel laureates) from a variety of fields, including such luminaries as E.A. Appleton, P.M.S. Blackett, J. Cockcroft, A.V. Hill, A.F. Huxley, J.C. Kendrew, G. Kimball, B.G. Koopman, P.M. Morse, W. Shockley and C.H. Waddington, created an environment within which the results had to be taken seriously. An important set of desiderata for the embryonic discipline was also set down during this period: multi-disciplinary groups; direct and prolonged field-contact for analysts (the Navy's Operations Evaluation Group and the Army Air Force's Operations Analysis Section required their analysts to be connected to a fleet or wing 'client' for six months every year), and access to decision makers at the highest levels.

That operations research should have its professional beginnings in this quintessentially 'public sector' arena, only to see it develop for the next two decades primarily in the commercial/private realm, is an irony of history. During the fifteen years after the end of World War II, non-military public sector applications (even conceptual theoretical advancements) were few and far between. The bulk of the work (at least the majority of the publications) involved inventory, queueing (rather abstract), oil refining, product mix, production, etc. A perhaps even greater irony is that the adaptation of the methods and mathematics by the private sector did not often carry along two important features of the 'operational' aspects of the wartime work: empiricism, and access to high-level decision makers. In a letter to *Science*, Faberge [1974] reinforced Waddington's [1974] earlier remarks that operations research in World War II was recognized and rewarded by top levels of both military and civilian authorities. Yet in the private sector operations analysts often found themselves reporting to second- or third-level decision makers in the organizational hierarchy.

One spin-off from the military, however, *was* influential in transferring analytical and 'systems thinking' to the rest of the public sector. In 1948, the Rand Corporation was established (after a two year existence as the U.S. Army Air Force's Project RAND). Rand was designed to be an non-profit, non-governmental organization that would apply science and technology, using an interdisciplinary approach to major problems in the public sector. It was viewed as being at the center of a triangle whose vertices were government, industry and universities. In Rand's early days its major emphases were on military and international strategic policy analysis. Although this unique organization would eventually devote considerable resources to non-military public sector concerns, it was the U.S. federal government (via D.O.D., AEC, DARPA, NASA, etc.) that remained its sole sponsors until the mid 1960's. Because of its success in helping to clarify the difficult and complex issues facing policy makers in the 1950's, Rand and its employees and consultants became firmly identified with its practical philosophy of problem-solving variously known as Systems Analysis, the Systems Approach, or Policy Analysis.

During this period a number of other seminal events occurred: the publication of the first book with the words 'operations research' in its title (Morse and Kimball's *Methods of Operations Research* [1951]); the establishment of the Operational Research Club, London, in 1948 (which became the Operational Research Society in 1953); and the founding of the Operations Research Society of America (ORSA) in 1952. Early issues of these organization's journals contained few explicitly public-sector applications, other than those that were clearly military in nature, or dealing with road and aircraft traffic analysis. A noteworthy exception was J.D.C. Little's article in *Operations Research* [1955] on the optimization of the operation of water storage reservoirs. But even ostensibly 'military' subjects offered scientifically supported justification for decisions having ultimately profound impact on our society: Hausrath [1954], for example, presented a study that 'provided policy makers in the U.S. Army with objective arguments in favor of integrated units of Negro and White soldiers'.

Much of the applied work during this time was not appearing in the archival literature (as unfortunately true then as it is now!), but included studies performed for The Port Of New York Authority by Edie [1954], using queueing-theory based analyses of bridge and tunnel traffic, and associated policies for staffing toll booths, etc. The concept of 'sustained yield' in forestry management was being refined, with more and more detailed sets of equations. The same was true of fishery population models. Competitive bidding strategies ('... a government agency invites a large number of companies ... to bid for contracts.') of obvious interest to public sector financial agents, was the subject of an article in the fourth volume of *Operations Research* [Friedman, 1956]. The author was apparently the first to be awarded a Ph.D. in operations research (from Case Institute of Technology). The Shapley-Shubik index, a model-based measure of the strength of various individuals involved in voting systems, appeared in 1954. More generally, as early as 1946 Stevens [1946] introduced formal concepts of measurement and associated scales – a foundation that would be necessary for subsequent public (and private) sector data collection and assessment. The cognitive aspects of these scales and measurements – equally important for understanding our capability to *obtain* scale identities, levels and values – were addressed by Luce [1956].

Spatial models of voter attitudes and candidate positions were developed by Downs [1957], using mathematical abstractions perhaps more suited to market forces than political attraction – models that nonetheless are still used today in fancier, and embellished (if not more predictive) forms. And in a rather different arena, mathematical, model-driven (as contrasted to strictly statistically oriented) analyses of baseball began to appear [e.g. Bellman, 1964; Lindsey, 1959].

3.4. The renaissance of public sector operations research in the 1960's

In 1967, Philip M. Morse wrote:

> 'During the past five years an increasing number of experts have become persuaded that the procedures of operations research would be effective in solving some of the problems of the public sector ....'

This optimistic position was contained in the preface to a collection of papers presented at a program on 'Operations Research in Public Affairs' held at MIT in September, 1966. Twenty experts from the public sector met with twenty specialists with experience in public sector operations research applications. The meeting covered techniques for dealing with governmental buying policy, inventory control, school supplies, warehouse centralization, urban planning, traffic, transportation networks, medical and hospital practice, demands for services in hospitals, medical diagnosis, and crime and criminal justice. This meeting was symbolic of the reawakening, at least among academics, of the need for using the 'scientific method' for attacking problems in the public arena. As Moore [1966] put it, 'it is only relatively recently that interest has been shown in the application [of O.R.] in other areas, such as insurance and sociological studies.'

The decade saw a variety of public sector fields either refine earlier work or transfer (or innovate) methods from more commercial endeavors. The concept of 'maximum sustained ' forest yield received model-based support by the late 50's, along with the articulated need for planners to use both spatial and temporal analyses. Agencies responsible for other natural resource policy making found it important to develop multiple-use models of land, water and other shared resources. Although arguably more concerned with the profitability of operations, problems formulated in the mid 1950's dealt with lumber and paper trim. The resulting general 'cutting stock' problem, in fact was the basis of R. Gomory and P. Gilmore's being awarded the 1963 Lanchester Award, the premier recognition granted by ORSA for outstanding contributions to operations research.

Operations research was also contributing to health and medical systems. Johns Hopkins University and the University of Michigan's Hospital Systems Improvement Program extended classical work sampling methodology to the specifics of hospitals and medical care facilities. Patient classification systems were in use by the U.S. Public Health Service; the effective use of nursing resources was studied by inventory-like models and principles.

Civil engineers and geographers were the source of many operations research analyses during this period. These were part of a vanguard of scientists from a variety of application areas (within which appropriate models were seen to be both useful and potentially rewarding in research insights). The market potential was not lost on computer manufacturers: an early use of linear programming, to assess various air pollution amelioration strategies, appeared in an IBM symposium [Teller, 1968]. The specifics of effective uses of resources for the treatment of wastewater for removal of dissolved oxygen in rivers, the study of trade-offs among various factors in the treatment of drinking water and wastewater, location, sizing and timing of construction of facilities, air quality management, etc., all were vigorously being attacked by the mid to late 1960's.

This reaching out to other disciplines is well illustrated by the fact that, when it was shown [Banzhaf, 1965] that weighted voting does not have desirable properties, the details of the mathematical analysis were published in a Law Review. The early sixties also saw the start of the maturing of the formal analyses of auctions, so that by 1961 the Vickrey auction was explicated, along with the behavior of important practical procedures as 'second price' bidding. On the other hand, as late as 1966 it was claimed that bidding 'has been given very little attention in the literature' [Moore, 1966]

Then came the war in Vietnam. Suffice it to say that the use of operations research models saw the apex of its applications in this ultimate public-sector exercise of war, weapons and associated materiel. The Pentagon's 'whiz kids' were well versed in the application (if not the development) of operations research models, and used them with varying degrees of success in all areas of military activity, whether warranted or not. Some of this work still remains classified; some (such as the use of body counts as inputs into strategic as well as tactical models; a macabre example of 'G.I.G.O.'[9]) should be remembered, as Santayana cautions us, if only so as not to revisit past mistakes. It should be noted, however, that the 'successes' of the use of formal models for waging war were the impetus behind a call for the use of similar methods on less deadly applications in the following decade.

The application of operations research to problems of crime and criminal justice was also affected by national events. As a consequence of increases in crime during the 1960's, a Presidential Commission was established to investigate causes and operational problems in the criminal justice system, and to recommend policies. One of the more successful task forces of that commission was the Science and Technology Task Force [1967], which provided some preliminary quantitative analyses of criminal justice problems and set the direction for most of the subsequent operations research studies in this field.

In short, the sixties were a time when many academics, other scientists and policy makers, were imbued with the spirit and 'social action' ethic of the times. Whether Camelot or the 'Best and the Brightest' was the metaphor, a sense of the ability to apply the scientific method to a variety of public sector's problems seemed almost self-evident. Using a technology based on measurement capabilities, and emerging large-scale information systems, decisions would be made on a more rational basis, people and problems would no longer 'fall through the cracks' and the total system would function more effectively and efficiently.

---

[9] G.I.G.O: garbage in, garbage out.

These beliefs in the ultimate triumph of technology in curing urban ills should be seen from another historical context of the decade: we were about to put a man on the moon, and the cry from everyone was, 'If we can put a man on the moon, why can't we solve X?', where X was whatever urban problem was pressing at the moment.

Also during this time the attention of other organizations began to focus on these sorts of problems and issues. In particular, the Rand Corporation began to diversify its efforts beyond its prior exclusive commitment to military problems. A report on its 25th Anniversary [Rand Corporation, 1973] notes that ongoing research not only involved weapons studies, strategic material and Russian and Chinese economics, but that it also included '... the economics of health care, the effectiveness of education, the provision of police and fire services; and on the problems and prospects of cable television and of energy supply.'

In other words, analysts who had developed command-and-control systems for the military felt that the same techniques could be brought to bear on solving the urban problems. For example, 'crime in the streets' was a major focus of the Presidential campaign of 1964, and computers and other high-tech solutions – after all crime involved people with weapons doing bad things, just like in Vietnam – were just beginning to be seen (largely inappropriately, as it turned out) as the answer to social as well as technical problems. The combination of high hopes, poorly thought out objectives, bureaucratic control of resources, inappropriate (and naive) models led, unfortunately, to poor analysis, ineffective links of good analysis to decision makers, and even downright charlatanism. These deficiencies were scathingly denounced by critics such as Hoos [1972] (who unfortunately indicted by association many valid analyses along with the reprehensible example she identified) in her description of the uses and abuses, methodology and mythology, of the practice and practitioners of pubic sector systems analysis [Pollock, 1972]. Nevertheless, since the methodology clearly had much to say to policy makers who were able to evaluate competently done and relevant analyses, the scene was set for the rapid incorporation of operations research methods into the practice of public sector decision-making.

3.5. The early 1970's to 1985 – transferring techniques

In 1970, Blumstein, Kamrass & Weiss published the proceedings of a symposium on the use of 'Systems Analysis' in the analysis of social problems. Topics included: the management of housing stock, location of fire stations, human resources development (education, manpower), transportation, environmental quality, public order and safety, 'urban application', military and aerospace. That year the IEEE Transactions on Systems Science Cybernetics published a special issue on urban and public systems, covering the 'systems analysis' of urban planning, public safety, health, education, pollution and traffic control. These were perhaps the first compendia of public sector operations research results widely available in the open literature.

A few years later, a book written by Drake, Keeney & Morse [1972] appeared, based on results produced by analysts at MIT and NYC–RAND[10], with its origins in summer programs held as early as 1966. The authors observed that:

> 'There is far more experience and accomplishment in applying formal models and operations research to the military and private sectors than to the (nonmilitary) public sector'

and proceeded to present results involving The New York City Fire Project, emergency ambulance transportation, improving the effectiveness of New York's 911 emergency system, blood bank inventory control, library models, airport runways, post office operations, models of the 'total criminal justice system', water quality management, air pollution, health planning, university planning, and a case study of the use of decision analysis in airport development for Mexico City. At the same time, a volume of *Operations Research* was devoted to 'Urban Problems' [ORSA, 1972].

These were followed by the publication (in what might be considered a precursor to this Handbook) by Gass & Sisson [1975] of *A Guide to Models in Governmental Planning and Operations*. The areas covered were: Air Pollution, Water Resources, Solid Waste Management, Urban Development, Transportation, Law Enforcement and Criminal Justice, Educational Planning and Operations, Energy, Planning and Operating Health Services, and Economic Models for Policy Analysis. This survey of models then in use in government planning had the express intention of helping the user sort through what was available, and then be able to choose models appropriate to the situation.

It was not only urban and local governmental problems that were tackled at this time using analytic methods. Concerns about the world population and the Malthusian limits of natural resources led to the development of mathematical models that simulated the inexorable march toward overpopulation, scarcity, and pollution. The books by Forrester [1973], Meadows et al. [1972], Meadows, Richardson & Bruckmann [1982] – even though their methods are still controversial – alerted the general public to the possibility that we would not be able to continue along at our current pace of expanding the world population and squandering our natural resources without limit: the piper would eventually have to be paid. A special issue of the proceedings of the IEEE on Social Systems Engineering [1975] promised, in the introduction, '... far reaching implications

---

[10] The New York City–Rand Institute was established in 1969, true to the spirit of the times, in an attempt to apply the 'systems' technology and analytical skills nurtured by Rand to the solution of urban problems [Szanton, 1972]. While there were occasional successes, these were fewer than anticipated, often due to the inherently controversial nature of the social problems addressed. Moreover, their impacts were vitiated by the inertia of an entrenched bureaucracy and a political power structure devoted more to ensuring re-election than to solving problems. This situation made it difficult, at best, to implement all but the most non-threatening changes and resulted in the eventual dissolution of NYC-RAND in 1975. This innovative organization did, however, set the stage for later, more successful efforts in New York City and other parts of the nation, and provided training for a new generation of young researchers.

not only in engineering but also in the interdisciplinary approach to social problem solving.'

Within a few years textbooks (such as Dickey & Watts [1978] at the undergraduate level, or Helly [1975] for graduate students), aimed specifically at public policy and urban planning students, were appearing. These not only contained the usual statistics, calculus, systems dynamics (and the associated Dynamo language), and Delphi techniques, but also included linear programming, PERT, and goal programming. Even the 'softer' sciences were targeted by such texts as Lave & March [1975], which introduced social scientists to such concepts as decision analysis, Markov process, etc. Specialty texts subsequently appeared, noteworthy being Larson & Odoni's [1981], which evolved from a course 'Analysis of Urban Service Systems', taught at MIT from 1971 onwards, and covering both (by then 'standard') techniques and advanced methods.

The professionals were now convinced. The book edited by Goreux & Manne [1973], dealing with the interdependence of agencies involved in planning in Mexico, and how it is helped by the use of models – including large-scale LP's for energy, agriculture, and water use – was another Lanchester Award winner. In 1975 Quade wrote:

> 'The belief that policy analysis or related approaches such as ... operations research have the capability of being very helpful with public policy-making is by no means new. It has been fairly widespread for ten years or so.'

In 1972, the International Institute of Applied Systems Analysis was founded. Located in Vienna, IIASA is a truly international organization, supported by fifteen countries (including the United States, Great Britain, and the USSR) with the broad objective of initiating and supporting individual and collaborative research on transnational problems associated with social, economic, technological and environmental communities throughout the world. Its development and use of global-scale models to study such phenomena as air and water pollution or insect damage to crops, problems that clearly do not stop at national boundaries, was deemed important enough by sponsoring nations to be funded – and staffed – even through the most suspicious days of the cold war.

Both applications and theoretical developments flourished. In health care systems, demand forecasting, and locational analysis became routine, as did decision aids for such routine operations as nurse scheduling. Disease screening and surveillance (i.e. for breast cancer) were linked to sophisticated models of diseases. Analogues between machine maintenance and human breakdown prevention were explored. In 1971 an entire conference was devoted to the science of clinical decision-making [Jacquez, 1972].

In natural resources analyses, linear programming was explicitly applied to fisheries management. By the early 80's a number of books and symposia were devoted to *summarizing* Operations Research model use in fisheries. 'National Level' linear programming-based analysis models for forestry management – TREES, TIMBER and RAM – were approved by the USFS. The first working heuristics for mix of water treatment plants (regional and at-source), and allocations of efficiencies among them, appeared in 1972. By the mid-1970's, air quality optimization models started to appear in *other* than mainstream O.R. journals. Moreover there was even enough interesting and useful analysis of sports applications to result in two different books: Ladany & Machol [1977] and Machol, Ladany & Morrison [1976].

The 1970's and 1980's also witnessed the development of applications in a number of different criminal justice contexts. Queueing theory was applied to the allocation of police patrol cars and other emergency vehicles, and to the design of police beats; reliability theory was modified so that it could be applied to the study of offender recidivism; 'standard' but unsuitable analytical techniques were criticized for their inadequacies, and new techniques began to be accepted; police, prosecutorial and correctional agencies started to make use of efficiencies inherent in applying operations research techniques to their operations; and a new paradigm of offender behavior, based on stochastic models, made its way into the criminology literature and into widespread acceptance. In short, in the past few decades operations research left a fundamental mark on practitioners in the criminal justice field, from the cop on the beat to the theoretical criminologist.

However, it was the appearance of 'advice' books, such as those by House & Mcleod [1977] or Nagel & Neef [1976] that eventually made it clear that the use of models was firmly ensconced in the professional practice of public policy, political science, and similar tactical decision-making. In these and similar works, care is taken to impart to policy makers the value of mathematical, operations research-type models from the viewpoint of theory and methodology, data adequacy, and capability of being programmed, as well as issues of validity, utility and transferability. The appearance of courses, associated textbooks, and 'users manuals' has, perhaps more than anything else, demonstrated that 'Public Sector Operations Research' is a full-fledged discipline, and deserving of society's attention and resources.

3.6. 1985 to the present

There is little (or too much) we can say about events past the middle of the last decade. New journals are multiplying proportional to the numbers of researchers involved in improving our understanding of various phenomena and problem structures in the public arena. Intellectual links are being forged (and re-defined) between operations researchers, statisticians, political scientists, ecologists, civil engineers and city planners. (This outreach, of course, is simply a newly affirmed recognition of the value of doing operations research in interdisciplinary teams – a defining attribute among the early practitioners.)

Required courses in operations research (often called 'quantitative methods' or 'mathematical modelling') are more and more common in curricula ranging from natural resources planning to public administration. The June 1992 volume of *OR/ MS Today* was devoted to applications of operations research to the environment: analyses of acid rain, garbage disposal, logistics and pollution studies for the U.S. Antarctic Research Program. In the same issue, notice was made of the recognition given to the use of operations research modelling to help in policy formulation for countering aspects of the AIDS epidemic.

The revolution that has been effecting *all* sciences since the mid-1980's – the existence of high powered desktop mini- and micro-computers, and the consequent availability of data, computational power and communications – has of course had an immense impact on the practice of operations research, particularly in the public sector. The availability of user-friendly software at every public official's desk makes it possible to use mathematical models, in all varieties of problem areas, without a need for consultants, analysts or experts. Chapter 2 addresses some of the practical and professional issues related to such an inundation of data and software. From our perspective, the last decade of this century will be the most challenging – and potentially valuable – ten years in the short history of operations research and the public sector.

References

Banzhaf, J.F. (1965). Weighted voting doesn't work; A mathematical analysis. *Rutgers Law Rev.* 19, 317–343.

Bellman, R.E. (1964). Dynamic programming and Markovian decision processes with particular application to baseball and chess, in: E. Beckenbach (ed.), *Applied Combinatorial Mathematics*, Wiley, New York, pp. 221–234.

Blumstein, A., M. Kamrass and A. Weiss (eds.) (1970). *Systems Analysis for Social Problems*, Washington Operations Council.

Cohen, J. (1990). Things I have learned (so far). *American Psychologist* 45, 1304–1312.

Daston, L. (1988). *Classical Probability in the Enlightenment*, Princeton University Press, Princeton, NJ.

Dickey, J., and T. Watts (1978). *Analytical Techniques in Urban and Regional Planning*, McGraw-Hill, New York.

Downs, A. (1957). *An Economic Theory of Democracy*, Harper and Row, New York.

Drake, A., R. Keeney and P. Morse (eds.) (1972). *Analysis of Public Systems*, MIT Press, Cambridge, MA.

Edie, L.C. (1954). Traffic delays at toll booths. *Oper. Res.* 2, 107–138.

Faberge, A.C. (1974). Change in operations research. *Science*, 184, 1328.

Forrester, J.W. (1973). *World Dynamics*, Wright-Allen, Cambridge, MA.

Freedman, D.A. (1985). Statistics and the scientific method, in: W.M. Mason, and S.E. Fienberg (eds.), *Cohort Analysis in Social Research: Beyond the Identification Problem*, Springer-Verlag, New York, pp. 343–366.

Friedman, L. (1956). A competitive bidding strategy. *Oper. Res.* 4(1), 104–112.

Gass, S., and R. Sisson (1975). *A Guide to Models in Governmental Planning and Operations*, Sauger Books, Potomac, MD.

Gigerenzer, G., S. Zeno, T. Porter, L. Daston, J. Beatty and L. Kruger (1989). *The Empire of Chance*, Cambridge University Press, Cambridge.

Goreux, L.M., and A.S. Manne (1973). *Multi-Level Planning: Case Studies in Mexico*, North-Holland, Amsterdam.

Hacking, I. (1991). *The Taming of Chance*, Cambridge University Press, Cambridge.

Hausrath, A.H. (1954). Utilization of negro manpower in the army. *Oper. Res.* 2(1), 17–30.

Helly, W. (1975). *Urban System Models*, Academic Press, New York.

Hill, J. (1911). Letter in *House Report* 12, 62nd U.S. Congress, April 25.

Hoos, I. (1972). *Systems Analysis in Public Policy*, University of California Press, Berkeley, CA.

Hotelling, H. (1929). Stability in competition. *Econom. J.* 39(153), 41–57.

House, P., and J. Mcleod (1977). *Large Scale Models for Policy Evaluation*, John Wiley and Sons, New York.

Huntington, E.V. (1921). The mathematical theory of the apportionment of representatives. *Proc. National Academy Sci. USA* 7, 123–127.

Institute of Electrical and Electronics Engineers, Inc. (1970). *IEEE Trans. Syst. Sci. Cybernet.* 6(4).

Institute of Electrical and Electronics Engineers, Inc. (1975). *Proceedings of IEEE, Special Issue on Social Systems Engineering*, 63(3).

Jacquez, J. (1972). *Computer Diagnosis and Diagnostic Methods, Proceedings of a 1971 Conference.* Thomas Publishing Co, Springfield, IL.

Kruger, L., L.J. Daston and M. Heidelberger (eds.) (1987). *The Probabilistic Revolution*, M.I.I. Press, Cambridge, MA.

Ladany, S.P., and R.E. Machol (eds.) (1977). *Optimal Strategies in Sports*, North-Holland, Amsterdam.

Larson, R., and A. Odoni (1981). *Urban Operations Research*, Prentice-Hall, Englewood Cliffs, NJ.

Lave, C., and J. March (1975). *An Introduction to Models in the Social Sciences*, Harper and Row, New York.

Lindsey, G.R. (1959). Statistical data useful in the operations of a baseball team. *Oper. Res.* 7, 197–207.

Little, J.D.C. (1955). The use of storage water in a hydroelectric system. *Oper. Res.* 3, 187–189.

Luce, R.D. (1956). Semiorders and a theory of utility discrimination. *Econometrica* 24, 178–191.

Machol, R.E., S.P. Ladany and D.G. Morrison (eds.) (1976). *Management Science in Sports*, North-Holland, Amsterdam.

Maltz, M.D. (1977). Crime statistics: a historical perspective. *Crime and Delinquency*, 23, 32–40.

McCloskey, J.F. (1956). Of horseless carriages, flying machines and operations research: A tribute to Frederick William Lanchester. *Oper. Res.* 4, 141–147.

McCloskey, J.F. (1987a). The beginnings of operations research, 1934–1941. *Oper. Res.* 35, 143–152.

McCloskey, J.F. (1987b). British operational research in World War II. *Oper. Res.* 35, 453–470.

McCloskey, J.F. (1987c). U.S. operations research in World War II. *Oper. Res.* 35, 910–925.

Meadows, D.H., D.L. Meadows, J. Randers and W.W. Behrens (1972). *The Limits to Growth: A Report for the Club of Rome's Project on the Predicament of Mankind*, Universe Books, New York.

Meadows, D.H., J. Richardson and G. Bruckmann (1982). *Groping in the Dark: The First Decade of Global Modeling*, Wiley, New York.

Moore, P.G. (1966). A survey of operational research. *J. Roy. Statist. Soc.* 129, Part 3, 399–447.

Morse, P.M., and L. Bacon (eds.) (1967). *Operations Research for Public Systems*, MIT Press, Cambridge, MA.

Morse, P.M., and G. Kimball (1951). *Methods of Operations Research*, MIT Press, Cambridge, MA; John Wiley and Sons, Inc., New York.

Nagel, S. and M. Neef (1976). *Operations Research Methods: As Applied to Political Science and the Legal Process*, Sage Publications, Beverly Hills, CA.

ORSA (1972). Special Issue on Urban Planning, *Oper. Res.* 20(3), May–June.

ORSA (1990). *Careers in Operations Research*, p. 8.

Pack, A.N. (1933). *Forestry: An Economic Challenge*, Macmillan, New York, 161 pp.

Pollock, S.M. (1972). Review of systems analysis in public policy: A critique, by I.R. Hoos. *Science* 178, November 17, 739–740.

Porter, T.M. (1986). *The Rise of Statistical Thinking 1820–1900*, Princeton University Press, Princeton, NJ.

Quade, E. (1975). *Analysis for Public Decisions*, Elsevier, New York.

Quetelet, L.A.J. (1835). *A Treatise on Man*, Translated by S. Diamond, Scholars Facsimiles and Reprints, Gainesville, FL, 1969.

Rand Corporation (1973). *Rand 25th Anniversary Volume*, Rand Corporation, Santa Monica, CA.

Science and Technology Task Force (1967). *Task Force Report: Science and Technology*, US Government Printing Office, Washington, DC.

Stevens, S.S. (1946). On the theory of scales of measurements. *Science*, 103(1946), 677–680.

Stigler, S.M. (1986). *The History of Statistics: The Measurement of Uncertainty before 1900*, The Belknap Press of Harvard University Press, Cambridge, MA.

Streeter, H., and C. Phelps (1925). A study of the pollution and natural purification of the Ohio River. *U.S. Public Health Bulletin* 146, February.

Szanton, P.L. (1972). Research in 1970–1971; The New York City–Rand Institute. *Oper. Res.* 20, 474–515.

Teller, A. (1968). The use of linear programming to estimate the cost of some alternative air pollution abatement policies, *Proc. IBM Scientific Computing Symposium on Water and Air Resource Management*, pp. 345–353.

Waddington, C.H. (1974). Operations research. *Science*, 184, March, 1141.

White, J. (1991). An existence theorem for OR/MS. *Oper. Res.* 39, 183–193.

S.M. Pollock et al., Eds., *Handbooks in OR & MS, Vol. 6*

Chapter 2

Public Sector Analysis and Operations Research/Management Science

Saul I. Gass

College of Business and Management, University of Maryland, College Park, MD 20742, U.S.A.

1. Introduction

The philosophical and methodological foundations of Operations Research/ Management Science (OR/MS) are recognized as the precursors of the similar aspects that define the disciplines of systems analysis and policy (public-sector) analysis. The relationships between these fields have been well-documented by Majone [Chapter 2 of Miser & Quade, 1985] and by Quade [Chapter 2 of Quade, 1989]. The purpose of this chapter is: (1) to acquaint the non-public sector OR/MS professional with what policy analysis is all about; (2) to indicate the differences between doing analysis in the private and governmental sectors; (3) to indicate that, although there have been many successes by OR/MS in policy analysis (as evidenced by the applications in this Handbook), things could be better; (4) to describe approaches to improving OR/MS analysis in the public sector; and (5) to introduce the notion of model advocacy and related ethical concerns that OR/MS analysts can encounter when working in the public policy arena.

The reader can, of course, obtain much fuller descriptions of the public sector analysis field by consulting the books and papers devoted to this area that are listed in the references and bibliography sections at the end of this chapter. In particular, we cite the two-volume *Handbook of Systems Analysis* by Miser & Quade [1985, 1988], *Analysis for Public Decisions* by Quade [1989], and *Models in the Policy Process* by Greenberger, Crenson & Crissey [1976].

OR/MS can contribute much to the resolution of the social and political problems of this last decade of the 20th century. The OR/MS analyst who turns to the public sector will find theoretical and practical challenges of immense value and personal satisfaction.

2. Public sector analysis and Operations Research/Management Science

Operations Research/Management Science ideas and methods have proven to be of extreme value in their ability to aid decision makers from all facets of business and industry. Although this success stems mainly from the analysis of what may be termed operational decision problems, we also find OR/MS techniques being of critical importance in the understanding and solution of planning and policy problems. But what of governmental problems? How well has OR/MS fared?

Certainly, as it grew out of the urgent military problems of World War II, OR/MS has prospered and flourished in the military environment. The chapter on military OR by Washburn attests to this fact. In like manner, operational problems found at all levels of government have also been successful targets of OR/MS researchers. At the Federal government level, we cite the chapter by Odoni, Rousseau and Wilson on transportation and the chapter by Golden and Wasil on natural resources; at the local level, we have the chapter by Swersey on urban services, the chapter by Pierskalla and Brailer on health care, and the chapter by Maltz on crime and justice. A number of governmental planning and policy problems, which have different decision requirements than similarly named problems found in business and industry, have been successfully analyzed by a wide range of OR/MS procedures. The chapter by Weyant addresses energy applications and energy futures; the chapter by ReVelle and Ellis discusses air and water environmental issues; and the chapter by Kleindorfer and Kunreuther applies decision analysis to the selection of a site for radioactive waste. These public policy uses of OR/MS do indicate that OR/MS has been of some value to public sector decision makers. But, how wide is the acceptance of OR/MS for public sector analysis?

Looking back in time, let us say from the 1960's (when OR/MS came into its own) to the recent past, most OR/MS researchers and involved public sector officials would probably agree to the statement that the impact and value of OR/MS to public sector applications has not been extensive. Such agreement stems from two sources: (1) past failures that received extensive critical review, in contrast to the limited publicity concerning the successful inventive and novel approaches used by OR/MS researchers to solve difficult public sector problems, and (2) the lack of understanding by OR/MS researchers that public sector decision problems are different than those encountered in business and industry and, hence, OR/MS methodologies must be adapted and extended to fit the decision requirements of the public sector. This Handbook should improve the OR/MS image that is the concern of point (1), while this chapter should help clarify point (2).

What is public sector analysis or, as we shall term it here, policy analysis? The policy analysis description that we like best is due to Quade [1989, p. 4]: '... policy analysis is a form of applied research carried out to acquire a deeper understanding of sociotechnical issues and to bring about better solutions.' As with the general range of OR/MS applications, we are concerned with not only understanding, but with providing information that will aid decision makers to make better decisions. 'A public policy decision is a decision made by society for itself or for society by its elected representatives or their appointees' [Quade, 1989, p. 3]. From these statements, we see a striking difference between the decision environments of a public sector problem and one from business or industry.

3. Differences between decisions in public vs. private sectors

3.1. The impact of the decision will be felt by others than those making the decision

Where CEOs of private companies have to try and survive with their decisions, in contrast, governmental officials are often detached from the results of their acts. For example, a city official who decides to vote for the airport location away from where the official lives does not suffer the consequences of the resulting noise and traffic.

3.2. Political concerns are more extreme

All organizations are subject to political pressures. However, private company management does not have to measure its choices and decisions based on an election cycle (see Section 3.5). Governmental officials, either explicitly or implicitly, always include the political criterion when making decisions, even mundane ones, for example, the decision to place stop signs in a community that complains of too much through traffic.

3.3. Measures of outcomes are more difficult

The question of what is the 'bottom line' for governmental decisions is in sharp contrast to the obvious financial and related measures associated with business and industrial decisions. Of course, many public sector decisions are made with financial considerations being the determining factor, for example, the purchase of a new fleet of police patrol cars. But most critical public sector issues consider other measures, usually described by cost–benefit or cost–effectiveness ratios. These ratios try to measure imponderables such as the value of saving a life in the decision to maintain a 55 mile-per-hour limit on Federal highways.

3.4. Organizational structures – Bureaucracies vs. line organizations

How decision units are organized is critical to both the solving of a problem and the implementation of the results. A frequent complaint of OR/MS analysts working in the public sector is that it is difficult to keep track of who is in charge [the vanishing advocate phenomenon, Larson & Odoni, 1981], and that the bureaucracy (and the public-employee unions) can make-or-break the implementation aspects of an analysis [Beltrami, 1977; Walker, Chaiken & Ignall, 1979]. Private sector organizations structure themselves with clear lines of authority and can adapt rapidly to changes, especially when it concerns improving the 'bottom line'. Also, in contrast to city officials, private company management can take direct and timely actions to reduce bureaucratic inefficiencies by firing and reorganizations.

3.5. Elected officials' time horizon

When making decisions, elected officials have short time horizons whose length is measured from the current day to the date of the next election. At the local level, the timing of minor decisions, like when to fill the county's potholes, to major decisions, like when to raise the property tax, are often geared to election day. At the Federal level, we hear of 'election-year politics' and have seen Congress delay giving its members raises or postpone tax increases until after an election. Private company management does not have to measure its choices and decisions based on an election cycle. Certainly, the time to declare a dividend may be based on the date of the next stockholder's meeting, but the impact of such a decision is rather negligible in its importance when compared to putting off the decision to raise taxes until after the election. Industry and business management are basically there for the long term.

3.6. The issues of efficiency, effectiveness, and equity

Although we note that it is a simplification, a 'bottom line' single criterion mentality usually governs decisions in the private sector. Public sector decision makers have a multicriteria environment in which they have to address each problem in terms of at least the three measures of efficiency, effectiveness, and equity. Efficiency is usually concerned with the proper use of resources; effectiveness considers the attaining of goals and objectives; and equity means treating all citizens alike. These terms are illustrated by the following examples: a police patrol is efficient if its average response time to a call-for-service is four minutes; the effectiveness of a new police patrol policy is measured by the decrease in the number of street crimes; a police patrol policy is equitable if all areas in the city have the same average response time. In allocating patrol resources, one can see how these three criteria can conflict with one another. In the public sector, the benefits of initiating a new policy is often confused as some benefits can be measured by hard numbers, for example, the decrease in the number of persons on welfare, while others are intangibles and require surrogate measure(s), for example, improving the quality of life as measured by air quality, lower infant mortality rate, etc.

3.7. Who is in charge and legislative concerns

The management of a private sector company views its problems from a single perspective and, although they may need to confront a board-of-directors and stockholders, the management is in charge and usually gets its way. In contrast, a city official, such as the superintendent of schools who wants to close a school, must view the problem in terms of the school committee, the PTA, the mayor, and the city council. Each group will have its perspective on the decision and could cause the superintendent to be overruled. An effective superintendent is one who can cause all the views to merge into one, namely the superintendent's. A decision choice and the timing of the decision are often ruled by legislative concerns and tradeoffs between legislators. A school closing in one district may be accomplished if a new library is built in another district.

3.8. Was the correct decision made?

If a manufacturer brings out the wrong product and it does not sell, a feedback loop exists that soon indicates that wrong decisions were made in, say, product design and marketing strategy. Corrective, back-to-the-drawing-board actions can be taken, or, possibly, the company goes out of business. Also, private companies can test market products in different areas to see which one is most acceptable to the public and what is the best marketing strategy. As they are measured mainly by financial concerns, private sector companies know if their decisions were appropriate for the problem situations, although they will never know if they were the optimal ones. In turn, the public sector has difficulty measuring and evaluating the success of many of its policies. There is little ability to experiment, to try out different ideas on the public, and to see which one works the best. Alternative drug programs or welfare programs are difficult to run, control, measure, and justify. Alternatives that are not chosen cannot be evaluated.

3.9. MOST IMPORTANT: Review of public sector analyses

Unlike OR/MS analyses in the private sector, public sector studies are done in an open, 'freedom of information' environment. OR/MS employees or consultants in governmental agencies must perform and report their studies under the assumption that their work will be reviewed and evaluated by interested parties other than those who sponsored their work. Such interested parties may be advocates with objectives that are different from those of a study's sponsor. We shall discuss this topic in more detail below.

To this point of our discussion, we have highlighted the differences in the decision environments between the public and private sectors. However, from an OR/MS researcher's perspective, the objective of an analysis in either sector is the same: to aid the policy (decision) maker in choosing the best (or better) solution among competing alternatives.

Policy analysis includes and extends the full range of ideas and analytical techniques from OR/MS and systems analysis, cost–benefit analysis, economics, simulation, decision analysis, etc. *and* explicitly considers the political and social impacts. The latter aspects are best taken into account by relying heavily on the intuition, judgment and experience of the public sector officials. (To most researchers, the differences between policy analysis, OR/MS, and systems analysis is not very clear cut; we choose here not to pursue the elements that differentiate between the disciplines. The interested reader should consult Miser & Quade [1985] and Quade [1989].)

4. Policy analysis and policy problems

Policy analysis can be viewed as the systematic analysis of the processes and questions faced by governmental planning or decision-making units, conducted with the intention of affecting the outcomes of those units [Quade, 1989]. To our mind, the diversity of policy analysis applications forms a most challenging field for OR/MS. We agree with A. Blumstein (as quoted in *OR/MS Today*, December 1988, p. 36) that the public sector is the 'new frontier' whose problems OR/MS methodologies are most suitable to address. Much has been accomplished already. Many successful OR/MS applications which are discussed in this Handbook or in the bibliographic citations include, among others:
- School desegregation plans
- Fire department positioning and dispatching
- Police patrol and dispatching
- Garbage and snow removal vehicle routing
- Evaluation and selection of military weapons systems
- Energy policy analysis
- Selecting among alternative welfare programs
- Spreading and impact of the AIDS epidemic
- Blood bank operations
- Air traffic control
- Military manpower planning
- Positioning and deployment of emergency medical units
- Criminal justice and judicial operations
- Analysis of food stamp policy issues and program
- Urban transportation systems
- Urban planning
- Solid waste management
- Water (quality and quantity) resource management
- Air pollution
- Evaluation of Medicare operations
- Legislative redistricting
- Housing development and housing allowances and assistance
- Merger of public safety units

As is the case in the private sector, the wide range of public sector problems can be divided into broad classes of problem types: operational, planning, and policy. The distinction between problem types is often not clear. It comes as no surprise to note that while many public sector problems have straightforward statements, others do not. The former are mainly those that can be classified as operational. More generally, we can state that policy analysis problems are of two kinds: (1) well defined in that a problem has a clear-cut description and its solution is amenable to rigorous analysis, as the problem basically deals with technological or physical questions; and (2) ill-defined (squishy, messy, wicked) in that the problem description has a high behavioral content for which there is a lack of theory, and it is overlaid with strong political implications. Problems of the first kind include police patrol operations and blood bank inventory studies, while problems of the second kind include selection of a welfare program or energy policy. Policy analysis is difficult as public sector problems usually do not have a definitive, singular formulation. They are multi-objective, and solutions are either good or bad, not optimal. The final decision often rests on political judgment, hopefully aided by an objective and comprehensive OR/MS-based analysis.

In trying to determine and describe the process of policy analysis or systems analysis or OR/MS, one is struck by the similarity of such discussions in the literature. It is clear that the process includes a model or integrated set of models that form an abstraction of the problem, where the theoretical basis of the model(s) may be weak or strong. One extreme has the decision based only on the unknown and unstatable 'mental model' of the decision maker, while the other extreme includes detailed mathematical models whose technical sophistication often cause them to be understood by few.

A typical policy analysis view of the process is shown in Figure 1 [Quade, 1989, p. 50]. Such figures should be considered to be 'models of the modeling process' and like all such models are abstractions of the real world process. Statements that usually accompany such diagrams include 'The phases or steps are not necessarily sequential' and 'Successful analysis depends upon a continuous cycle

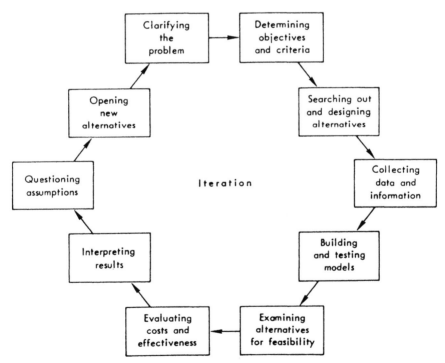

Fig. 1. The process of policy analysis. (From Quade [1988], reprinted by permission of the publisher.)

of formulating the problem, selecting objectives, designing alternatives, building better models, and so on, until the client is satisfied or lack of time or money forces a cutoff' [Quade, 1989, p. 50].

Our interests here cause us to review the analysis process in terms of one that includes a computer-based representation of the problem as an integral part. That is, the analysis of the problem is conducted by means of a computer-based model and its associated data files. This concept, which is not new to OR/MS analysts, is shown in Figure 2 [U.S. GAO, 1979]. The boxes and flow are self-explanatory and we do not go into details here. We shall modify this figure to take into account one of the critical differences between model-based analyses in the public and private sectors: the need for openness and review.

5. The extended role of the model in policy analysis

As we have tried to make clear, public sector problems are different from private sector ones in many aspects. As Quade [1989, p. 50] notes:

> 'In practice, things are seldom tidy. Too often the objectives are multiple, con-
> flicting, and obscure; no feasible alternative is adequate to attain the objectives;
> one's initial understanding of how the policy system works is inconsistent with the
> data; the predictions from the models are full of crucial uncertainties; and other
> criteria that look as plausible as the one chosen may lead to a different order
> of preference. When this happens, one must try again to obtain a satisfactory
> solution. A single attempt or pass at a problem is seldom enough.'

In other words, the problem situation is usually a mess!

Given that OR/MS analysts should be concerned with public sector problems, what can they do to improve the use and utility of their efforts? First, the good news: The analytical methodologies and the objective scientific training of the OR/MS analysts are most suitable for public sector studies. Second, the bad news: Public sector problems are not necessarily solved by objective means. How do we resolve this disparity in means and ends? In our view, the only way that OR/MS analysts can and should function in the public sector is to take an extended view at their analysis process, with this view encompassing a life-cycle approach to the modeling effort which assumes that an independent review of the model and its results will occur. Let us explain what we mean and why it is necessary.

As we noted earlier, because of their multicriteria structure and the political environment in which it is found, a decision–an answer–a resolution to most public sector problems is always open to debate and second-guessing. There is no one, correct answer. And, because such work is of a public nature, it has to be assumed that the results and the process by which the results were obtained have to be available for review. These considerations must be recognized by the OR/MS analysts and be addressed in a positive and satisfactory manner. This can only be accomplished by a process that results in a proper study being accomplished that is accompanied by clear and understandable documentation of the computer-based model and its use. This theme is captured in Figure 3 in which we modify the

BASIC STEPS IN THE MODELING PROCESS

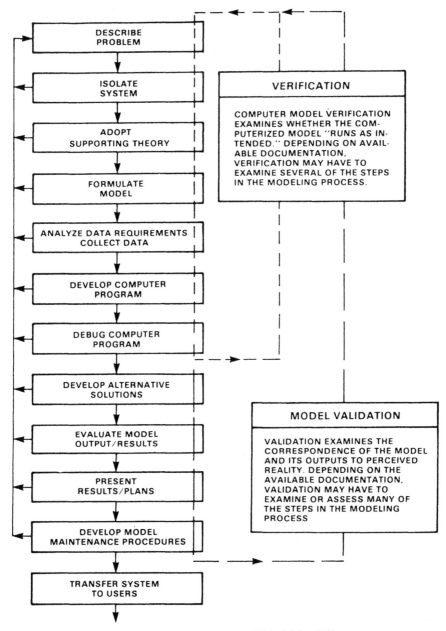

Fig. 2. The modeling process [U.S. GAO, 1979].

BASIC STEPS IN THE MODELING PROCESS

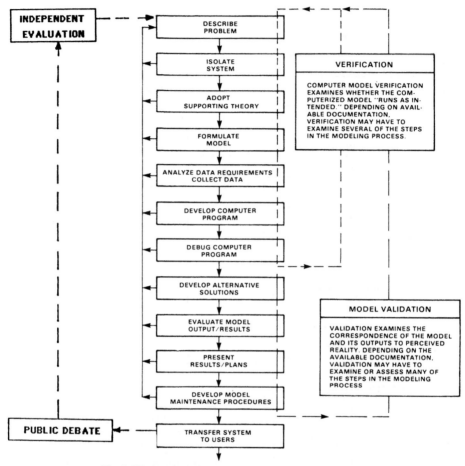

Fig. 3. The extended modeling process for policy analysis.

basic modeling approach (Figure 2) to include the substeps of public debate and evaluation by other analysts. Figure 3 is the computer-based policy model process that should be followed [adapted from Clark & Cole, 1975, p. 98].

The failures in policy analysis studies that have used the techniques of OR/ MS and systems analysis have one common feature: the processes by which the results were obtained and presented were suspect [Brewer & Shubik, 1979; Hoos, 1972]. By that we mean that the theories behind the modeling analysis were not established, the analyses were incomplete and had little validity content, the documentation of the results to the nontechnical clients was not clear or not available, and, we are sorry to say, the objectivity and abilities of many study teams were weak and their knowledge of public processes meager, at best. There is no magic elixir that will overcome such deficiencies, especially the latter one. But, with respect to OR/MS involvement, we do feel that the application of the concept of model evaluation and the model life-cycle process will help to avoid further failures. We next discuss the imbedding of the process of evaluation into the mainstream of model formulation, development and implementation that leads to the operational concept of a model life-cycle.

6. Model evaluation

Model evaluation has been a well-studied activity, but is not a well-known idea. Briefly, model evaluation is a process by which interested parties, who were not involved in a model's origins, development, and implementation, can assess the model's results in terms of its structure and data to determine, with some level of confidence, whether or not the results can be used to aid the decision maker. In other words, model evaluation equates to an independent assessment of the model and its use. Not all models need to be or should be evaluated. Our concern is with public sector modeling projects that are complex and involve critical decision components. A full discussion of model evaluation concepts, especially as applied to policy problems, is given in Gass [1983]. Here, we illustrate the essential features of one approach that involves the following five major evaluation criteria [U.S. GAO, 1979]:

  (1) DOCUMENTATION
  (2) VALIDITY
        Theoretical validity
        Data validity
        Operational validity
  (3) COMPUTER MODEL VERIFICATION
  (4) MAINTAINABILITY
        Updating
        Review
  (5) USABILITY

Briefly, these criteria are concerned with the following aspects of the modeling process:

  (1) *Documentation* – Documentation must describe what the developers have done, and why, and how; documentation should be sufficient enough to permit replication by independent evaluators of the model's results and claims [Gass, 1984].

  (2) *Validity* – There is no standard way to validate a decision model, but most investigators will agree that any such evaluation encompasses the concerns of theory (does the theory fit the problem environment?), data (are the data accurate, complete, impartial and appropriate?), and operations (how does the model diverge from the users' perception of the real-world?) [Landry, Malouin & Oral, 1983].

  (3) *Computer model verification* – Verification attempts to ensure that the computer-based model runs as intended; that is, the computer program accurately describes the model as designed.

(4) *Maintainability* – The long term use of many government models calls for a preplanned and regularly scheduled program for reviewing the accuracy of the model over its life-cycle, which includes a process for updating and changing model parameters and model structure.

(5) *Usability* – The usability of a model rests on the availability of data, the ability of the user to understand the model's output, model portability, and costs and resources required to run the model.

Evaluation is usually applied to a modeling project after the model has been developed and, more often then not, after implementation. The view that evaluation is done at the end of a project is how this issue was first addressed. Our current view is that the emphasis on performing evaluation activities at the end of a project is wrong. Post evaluation of a model is costly; it is difficult to accomplish, as many of the principal analysts are no longer available; and, as the implemented model is ever changing, the evaluation team usually ends up evaluating an outdated model. Post evaluation is like locking the stable door after the horse has been stolen; corrective actions should be ongoing and continual. The benefits from a post evaluation are not proportional to the cost. The funds and resources are better applied to what might be called 'ongoing evaluation'. This means that OR/MS analysts must carry out the project tasks under the assumption that they are operating under a continuing and ongoing evaluation. Working under that assumption would force them to perform verification and validation activities consistent with the aims and resources of the project, and to document the results. It would force them to insist on the correct level of funds and personnel to do the work properly the first time. What we are saying is that if OR/MS analysts conducted themselves as if they expected an independent evaluation to take place, they would necessarily do a more thorough and professional job. The need for a post evaluation would disappear, as the evidence that the analysts furnished would state explicitiy the assumptions, limitations, and the proper uses of the model. An evaluator would then only need be concerned with independent replication and extensions of the model to other problem areas. The concept of developing and implementing a model-based project under the framework of an ongoing evaluation protocol is an important message that must be taken to heart by public sector OR/MS analysts, and by the public sector administrators who are responsible for the funding of these projects.

(In passing, we note that although this discussion for an ongoing model evaluation protocol grew out of the concerns of governmental applications, such evaluation ideas also apply to business and industry.)

7. Model life-cycle process

By the concept of an OR/MS model life-cycle process, we mean a set of integrated steps that must be carried out to *develop and maintain* a decision-aiding model throughout its lifetime [see Gass, 1979, 1984, 1987, for details]. Briefly, our life-cycle approach includes the following steps:

- Initiation
- Feasibility
- Formulation
- Data
- Design
- Software development (including verification)
- Validation
- Training and education
- Implementation
- Maintenance and update
- Documentation and dissemination

We emphasize that the model life-cycle phases are interdependent and often blend together, that they do not necessarily coincide with fixed time periods, and that they are just convenient groupings of project activities that can be related to the documentation requirements of a modeling project. The life-cycle phases may seem a bit of overkill to one who just wants to knock-off a simple model (or even a complex one). The requirements of the phases can be adjusted to the needs of the analysis, but all OR/MS model developers must justify what they have done; the requirements of each phase cause that to happen. Special emphasis must be given to the data, design, verification, and validation phases, and surrounding the total process is the absolute requirement for documenting the model and related analyses. We stress that applying the principles of the model life-cycle and ongoing model evaluation to public sector problems are key to ensuring outcomes that have high utility.

8. Models, ethics and advocacy

OR/MS is a scientific endeavor which operates under the rules of science that includes objective and unbiased behavior in performing and reporting an experiment or an analysis. Such behavior is expected of all of us in all professions. Since OR/MS has been and will be used to resolve difficult and complex public policy issues, and since the OR/MS methodology is not easily grasped by nontechnical public administrators, OR/MS analysts working in the public sector must make special efforts to ensure that their work is not misconstrued (inadvertently or on purpose) and is not used in an unethical manner.

As noted above, the success of OR/MS decision-aiding models, as applied to a wide range of operational problems, has led many in the OR/MS profession to apply such models to nonoperational situations and/or to problem areas that have a human component whose analysis by mathematical models is open to question. For example, OR/MS-based models have been used in determining energy policy to the year 2000 and as a means for evaluating national welfare programs. As such problem areas often have a weak quantitative basis, referred to as 'squishy' problems, and are characterized by a strong political and behavioral content, the ability of OR/MS models to serve as objective decision aids is open to question.

Critical to the acceptance of the results from policy modeling efforts is the ability of the modelers to establish a basis for the users to believe that the models do replicate the users' decision situations; that is, demonstrating that the models have a strong validity content. This is usually most difficult to accomplish. The theoretical bases of these models is often rather weak (Do we really understand how the market forces will behave in the year 2000?). The structure of a particular policy model and the results that are generated are dependent on the model developers to an extent that is quite different from that of a model of an operational problem whose validity can be established by engineering or field tests. Thus, when any analyst, OR/MS or otherwise, works on a policy analysis problem, great care must be taken to ensure that the analyst's biases are not imbedded in the results. As Quade [1989, p. 28] notes: 'Ideally, policy analysis is unbiased, designed to consider the entire problem and to give all factors and all sides of the question proper weight.'

We all come to any problem with our individual biases and views. The beauty of scientific methodology is that there are procedural filters to control against our biases, plus the pride of objectivity and scientific training that we bring to our analysis. But things are not that straightforward. OR models for many policy analysis problems are quite complex, and when they are imbedded in a computer program, few, if any of the interested parties, can attest to the correctness and the objectivity of the results.

Where do ethics come in? Philosophically, ethics is a theoretical subject that attempts to abstract, clarify, and examine the ideas of good and evil, right and wrong, and duty and obligation. From this perspective, the problems of ethics tend to fall into three basic categories: problems about value and basic goods, problems about rightness and wrongness, and problems about moral obligations [McGreal, 1970; Stroll & Popkin, 1965]. From a professional work perspective, we usually think of these ethical categories in terms of a set of principles or a set of rules that sanction or forbid certain kinds of conduct. Many professions have such 'codes of conduct'. The Operations Research Society of America (ORSA), for example, has a set of 'Guidelines for Professional Conduct', which we will briefly discuss below [Caywood, Berger, Engel, Magee, Miser & Thrall, 1971]. Our interest, then, is with normative ethical rules as they apply to situations that arise in our profession. We have chosen to address this topic in this Handbook so as to give ethical issues of OR/MS practice in the public sector the high visibility that we feel it deserves. Next, we present a little history [Gass, 1991].

In 1969, the Nixon Administration was considering the deployment of an antiballistic missile system (ABM) called SAFEGUARD. A series of congressional hearings was held at which opponents and proponents of the ABM gave highly technical and contradictory testimony that relied greatly on what we would call military OR. The debate was heated and peppered with statements like '... (so and so) makes an assumption that is plainly absurd' [Caywood, Berger, Engel, Magee, Miser & Thrall, 1971, p. 1165]. One of the key participants in the debate, an ORSA member, wrote to the president of ORSA requesting '... ORSA to appoint a panel to consider some aspects of professional conduct during the

ABM debate...' and stated 'The question that I am raising is not whether the ABM decision was good or bad, but a question of professional standards and professional ethics' [Caywood, Berger, Engel, Magee, Miser & Thrall, 1971, pp. 1246–1247]. Such a panel was established. The panel's report was rather critical of the opponents of the ABM and concluded: 'The evidence strongly supports the disturbing conclusion that when prominent experts outside the Administration supported their opinions on SAFEGUARD deployment with arguments and results of an operations-research nature these analyses were often inappropriate, misleading, or factually in error. ... Failure to distinguish properly between the roles of the analyst and the advocate contributed to the lack of complete research to clarify the presentation' [Caywood, Berger, Engel, Magee, Miser & Thrall, 1971, p. 1176].

The panel's report includes a major section titled 'Guidelines for Professional Practice'. It is well done. It appeared in the September 1971 issue of *Operations Research*, volume 19, number 5. That issue contains the panel's complete report on the ABM debate. The 'Guidelines' are excellent and they apply to many of the professional practice issues encountered today (although some feel that there is a need to update them [Machol, 1982]). In particular, with policy analysis in mind, the 'Guidelines' address the issue of OR analysts as adversaries.

The professional practice 'how to' part of the 'Guidelines' is sectioned into six major headings:

(1) General – emphasizes the scientific spirit of openness, explicitness, and objectivity.

(2) In Beginning a Study – describes the initial procedural and cooperative elements that an analyst and the client must follow to establish an initial framework for the study.

(3) In Conducting a Study – describes the analytical aspects that must be carried out during the course of the study.

(4) In Reporting a Study – describes the items and procedural aspects required to ensure that the study findings are communicated, understood, and then acted upon.

(5) In Reviewing a Study – reviews the approach one should take when critiquing someone else's study.

(6) In Following Up Studies – stresses that the analyst must be particularly conscientious in recognizing and reporting unpredicted results and unpleasant surprises.

The OR/MS analyst usually serves in a consultative mode in which the requirements of the above six topics can be applied in a rather logical and objective fashion. However, as the panel's report notes, not all complex problems are amenable to solution by such logical means. A problem's actors and organizations will have different points of view, attitudes, value systems, roles, vested interests, and objectives. Such problems are often resolved by an adversarial process in which the presentation of one's case is an overt act of trying to influence the outcome of the decision and, in contrast to the rules of an OR/MS study, could include biased and slanted testimony [Caywood, Berger, Engel, Magee, Miser &

Thrall, 1971]. One immediately sees how ethical dilemmas for the OR/MS analyst can arise when the analyst serves as an adversary or as an expert witness.

There appear to be three views of a scientist's role in the analysis of public issues [Kalkstein, 1969]:

(1) The scientist is to present the facts in an unbiased manner and not advocate a particular position in attempting to influence the decision-making process (one works on nuclear plant siting and presents the results objectively).

(2) The scientist has a moral responsibility for the effects of his/her own involvement in the scientific endeavors of society (one does not work on site selection of a nuclear plant if one believes that all such plants are a menace to society and the environment).

(3) The scientist works openly as an advocate for a particular point of view (the best site for the nuclear plant is in location A).

As scientists, OR analysts usually find themselves in the first role: just presenting the facts. However, when working in the policy analysis area, we often find ourselves in the second role, facing a moral dilemma, or in the third role, working as an advocate. When we do, we usually rely on our personal code of ethics to guide us. But a code of ethics for policy scientists has been proposed [Dror, 1971]. They are concerned with:

(a) goals and values of the client – do they contradict basic values of democracy and human rights,

(b) relationship between the analyst's values and the clients – do the client's beliefs contradict the basic values of the analyst,

(c) presentation of all viable alternatives – the analysts should not hide an alternative because it contradicts his/her own personal values or preferences,

(d) increasing the judgment opportunities of the client – careful delineation of assumptions and the presentation of unbiased sensitivity studies,

(e) 'rubber stamping' a conclusion – a study should not be undertaken whose sole purpose is to support the client's conclusion that has been reached by other means,

(f) access to information – the analyst should not work for a client who does not provide the necessary information and opportunities for presentation of the study and its findings, and

(g) conflicts of interest – the analyst must avoid all such conflicts, including the use of the study for personal gain and the making of recommendations on matters in which the analyst has a personal and private interest.

An additional ethical consideration to the above deals with the use of the study [Quade, 1989, p. 381]:

> 'An analyst should try to keep his work from being misinterpreted or used to imply more than it should.'

Other informative discussions on ethical issues for policy analysts include that of Miser & Quade [1985, pp. 316–325] in their section 'Guidelines for Professional Behavior', and the book *Ethics, Government, and Public Policy* by Bowman & Elliston [1988]. A chapter in the latter book titled 'The Use of Quantitative

Analysis in the Public Sector' [Plant, 1988, pp. 247–265] concludes with the following message [p. 261]:

> 'Social and policy scientists trained in the application of quantitative methods will provide the body of experts needed to create a political dialogue that is knowledgeable of facts and sensitive to their limitation. It will help in the elevation of the general over the particular and the disinterested over the selfish, which is the proper goal of any public ethics.'

9. Examples of policy models in adversarial situations

We find that OR/MS models have a life of their own and are subject to use beyond the original intent. They are becoming tools of advocacy. We find the same policy analysis model being used by different organizations to develop conclusions that favor the specific objectives of each organization. When politicians are faced with competing solutions produced by the same OR/MS model, they rightly raise questions as to the efficacy of the methodology and the objectivity of the related scientific field. This was the case for the ABM debate, and, we feel, will be the case for most adversarial modeling situations. (A reading of Pirandello's play 'Right You Are (If You Think You Are)' offers insight into why adversaries, with or without models, always think they are correct.) We next describe two examples in which policy models supposedly had a role in adversarial situations [Gass, 1991].

9.1. Project Independence Evaluation System (PIES)

The Project Independence Evaluation System (PIES) was a large, computer-based model that integrated many economic and linear programming submodels. It was developed in the Nixon Administration to aid in determining a plan that would make the U.S. independent of foreign oil imports by 1980. PIES forecasted the state of the nation's energy system for an average day at the end of 5 to 15 year planning horizons.

During the 1970's, PIES was probably the most important and influential OR/MS public sector model used by the Federal government. Its development was a *tour de force* in that it addressed a most complex problem by applying new and novel ideas that combined the full range of methods from OR/MS, economics, computer programming, and statistics. Extensions of the system were used during the Ford and Carter Administrations. In the 1980's, as the Reagan Administration was not interested in developing an energy policy, PIES was ignored and eventually eliminated.

At first, the PIES model was developed and maintained by an independent agency, the Federal Energy Administration, and then by an independent unit within the new Department of Energy, the Office of Energy Information and Analysis. Independence here means Congressionally mandated separation from the executive branch of the government. This was done to shield the model and the analysis from political influences. However, according to a claim by

Commoner [1979], the Carter Administration was able to direct 21 changes in certain economic assumptions in the PIES model. The net impact of these changes was to increase the estimate of energy demand, while decreasing the supply. Such changes aided the President's energy policy in that the gap between supply and demand would have to be filled either by imports, something that Congress would not want to do, or by conservation measures, something that President Carter wanted to do. Before it was changed, the PIES model's results did not give much credence to a big push on conservation. Thus, the model, according to Commoner, was changed to reflect the desired outcome.

Our point in describing the PIES controversy is not to give credence to Commoner's interpretation of what happened. The point is that an external constituent felt, for whatever reasons, that PIES, a policy analysis model, was used incorrectly. The lesson for MS/OR policy analysts is that they must be explicit in their development and use of a model, document their actions concerning the structure of the model and the related analyses of its results, and be prepared for an external evaluation of their work. The use of a model life-cycle, evaluative approach, as described above, will certainly aid in addressing such challenges.

(The correctness of Commoner's assertions is debatable [Murphy, 1991]. Because of its independence, the PIES organization was able to control and carefully scrutinize all of the data and analyses so as to filter out the types of data manipulations that Commoner claims occurred. The PIES system was probably the most independently evaluated and checked computer-based system ever; likewise, its analyses were probably reviewed and replicated by more external agencies and groups than those of any other model-based system.)

9.2. Transfer Income Models (TRIM/MATH)

In the second situation in which a model was used as a tool for advocacy, we find the same model being used by different government groups to reach conclusions that bolstered the differing legislation that each was proposing. Again, we have a model in an adversarial role, but this situation also raised a different ethical issue [Kraemer, Dickhoven, Tierney & King, 1987].

The Transfer Income Models use microsimulation methodology for modeling the behavior of individuals (or households, or firms) in a larger system. Such models use survey data on population characteristics (income, family size, etc.) of a representative sample of individual units, along with models of behavior, to simulate the population's likely participation in some activity (childbearing, food stamps, tax liability). The basic models, called TRIM, and a subsequent variation, called MATH, were used by the Congressional Budget Office to project annual costs of all transfer-income programs to the year 2000, used by the Treasury Department to forecast tax implications of proposed changes in welfare and social service policies, and used by the Department of Agriculture to determine eligibility and participation rates in food stamp programs.

The Ford Administration proposed a reform of the food stamp bill and claimed that it would reduce food stamp use by 3.4 million recipients and save $ 1.2

billion. However, there were two Congressional bills, one more conservative and one more liberal. The conservative backers projected a savings of $ 2.5 billion, but an analysis of the conservative assumptions by the MATH model showed only a savings of $ 300 million. President Ford stuck with his bill. The House Agriculture Committee did not use the MATH model as the Republican members were convinced that the model was 'loaded' with liberal interests. The final bill had three cost savings estimates:

The Agriculture Committee, using a simple 'in-house' model, claimed a savings of $ 41 million.

The Department of Agriculture, using the MATH model, showed a savings of $ 43 million.

The Congressional Budget Office, also using the MATH model, claimed a savings of $ 38 million.

The bill never passed as time ran out and the Congressional session adjourned. But note that the use of the various models had savings estimates that were very close, with these savings much lower than the original estimates.

You might wonder about the ethical questions here. Why did the Republicans feel that the models were biased with liberal leanings? There was nothing in the descriptions of the models that indicated liberal assumptions. What happened was that a key member of the team that developed both TRIM and MATH had written an editorial for the *Washington Post* and had given Congressional testimony that she would support significant liberalizing policy changes in the food stamp program. The question then comes up as to how such a person, who takes an adversarial role for a policy issue, can claim to develop a bias-free model that evaluates programmatic changes of that issue. Should such a talented person be barred from such model developments in which she has a great deal of expertise? Should she not have acted as an adversary for liberal changes? Do we only work in areas where we do not have any biases? If so, we may not be able to work on any problems of value! How do you control against such biases? The OR/MS profession and individual analysts must address and resolve such questions if they want their models to be of any value in the important field of policy analysis.

The issues concerning the use of TRIM and MATH are still current. The Committee on National Statistics at the National Research Council was requested (in 1989) by the Department of Health and Human Services and the Department of Agriculture to evaluate the latest versions of TRIM and MATH. This two-year study culminated in the publication *Improving Information for Social Policy Decisions: The Uses of Microsimulation Modeling* [Citro & Hanushek, 1991]. Relative to the thrust of the policy model discussion in this chapter and to policy analysis in general, the study noted the following [Citro & Hanushek, 1991, pp. 2–3]:

> 'We identified two major deficiencies that demand attention if policy models, of whatever type, are to provide cost-effective information to the legislative debates of the future. The first problem (one of long standing) is lack of regular and systematic model validation. Ingrained patterns of behavior on the part of both decision makers and policy analysts have led to systematic underinvestment in the

validation task. The second problem (of more recent origin) is underinvestment and consequent deterioration in the scope and quality of needed input data for policy models.'

10. Examples of ethical situations in OR modeling

Next, we briefly describe other ethical situations that OR/MS analysts may encounter [Mulvey, 1981, 1982].

Let's get it done. Due to cost, time and ability, when developing and implementing a model, you do not or can not consider all the factors.

Give me this answer. Forcing a model to produce the user's desired outcome when such an outcome would not result if the model was used objectively.

Blow that whistle. Not going to authorities after determining that your company's model and/or its use has been rigged to produce a desired outcome.

Incomplete exposure. Using model-based results to state a position knowing that the position is sensitive to debatable hidden assumptions, is not really backed up by the data (which are uncertain), and that alternate positions could be justified using the same model.

I know I am objective. Working as a consultant in an area in which you have a personal or corporate interest and not divulging such information to the individuals who must use your analysis.

I know what's best. Not including an alternative as it may be better than the one you think the public should have.

Read my printouts. Not describing the model and its results in a clear fashion and attempting to 'snow' your audience by technical overkill.

Read my model. When using a model in an adversarial situation, you do not document the model and the analysis in a form that makes it readily available for evaluation and replication of results.

Over the past few years, some elements of the U.S. scientific establishment have been rocked by claims of fraud, data fabrication, and plagiarism. Such claims have occurred mainly in the medical and biological areas. Congressional committees have been formed to investigate specific situations. As OR/MS models and studies of public policy issues increase, our concern is with how do we ensure that such work does not make the headlines in a negative way. Certainly, following the code of ethics for policy scientists and the ORSA 'Guidelines' described above will help. In addition, we call your attention to the publication *Guidelines for the Conduct of Research at the National Institutes of Health* [National Institutes of Health, 1990]. It states principles of behavior that all scientists are expected to follow. However, as these *Guidelines* note: 'The formulation of these *Guidelines* is not meant to codify a set of rules, but to make explicit patterns of scientific practice that have been developed over many years and are followed by the vast majority of scientists, and to provide benchmarks when problems arise.' The *Guidelines* are quoted and summarized as follows:

Supervision of trainees. The scientist, as a mentor and supervisor of a trainee, must avoid the involvement of trainees in research activities that do not provide meaningful training experiences but which are designed mainly to further research or development activities in which the mentor has a potential monetary or other compelling interest; training must impart to the trainee appropriate standards of scientific conduct, as conveyed by the mentor; and, mentors have a responsibility to provide trainees with realistic appraisals of their performance.

Data management. The scientist must record research data and the results of research in a form that will allow continuous access for analysis and review; research data should always be immediately available to scientific collaborators and supervisors for review; research data should be retained for a sufficient period to allow analysis and repetition by others of published material from those data.

Publication practices. Timely publication of new and significant results is important, but fragmentary publications or multiple publications of the same or similar data are inappropriate; each paper should contain sufficient information for the informed reader to assess its validity with all the information that would enable scientific peers to repeat the experiment; tenure appointments and promotions should be based on scientific accomplishments and not on the number of publications.

Authorship. The privilege of authorship should be based on a significant contribution to the conceptualization, design, execution, and/or interpretation of the research study; each author should be willing to support the general conclusions of the study and be willing to defend the study.

Peer review and privileged information. Scientists have an obligation to participate in the peer review process (review of scientific paper, grant proposal, etc.); the reviewer should avoid any real or perceived conflict of interest; the review should be objective; all material under review is privileged information and should not be shared with anyone unless necessary to the review process.

11. Summary

The use of OR/MS for aiding public sector decision makers to make better decisions has not reached its full potential. In this chapter, we described some of the past difficulties and offered some suggestions for improving the role of OR/MS in policy analysis. A number of researchers has also been concerned with this aspect and, in particular, we cite the paper by Richels [1981] in which he combines the ideas of model evaluation (assessment) and user analysis into a concept of model analysis that is a bridge between the modeler and the policy maker. Information flows across this bridge in a continuous manner and reflects the fact that policy analysis, and its support by OR/MS, is a not a single-shot affair. We conclude with the flow diagram that Richels uses to illustrate his concept (Figure 4). We strongly suggest that the OR/MS analyst who wishes to work in the public sector, consult the original source of this figure and the other references on which this chapter is based.

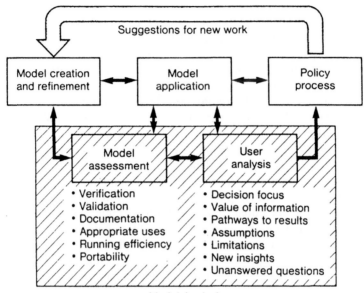

Model Analysis

Fig. 4. Model analysis. (From Richels [1981], reprinted by permission of the author; copyright 1981 by the Operations Research Society of America and The Institute of Management Science, 290 Westminster Street, Providence, Rhode Island 02903, USA.)

Acknowledgements

We are most appreciative of the invaluable work of the cited authors and the many others who wish to improve public sector analysis by the proper application of OR/MS. Their explicit and implicit contributions to this chapter are gratefully acknowledged.

References

Beltrami, E.J. (1977). *Models for Public Systems Analysis*, Academic Press, New York.

Bowman, J.S., and F.A. Elliston (eds.) (1988). *Ethics, Government, and Public Policy: A Reference Guide*, Greenwood Press, New York.

Brewer, G.D., and M. Shubik (1979). *The War Game*, Harvard University Press, Cambridge, MA.

Caywood, T.E., H.M. Berger, J.H. Engel, J.F. Magee, H.J. Miser and R.M. Thrall (1971). Guidelines for the practice of operations research. *Oper. Res.* 19, 1123–1258.

Citro, C.F., and E.A. Hanushek (1991). *Improving Information for Social Policy Decisions: The Uses of Microsimulation Modeling, Vol. I, Review and Recommendations*, National Academy Press, Washington, DC.

Clark, J., and S. Cole (1975). *Global Simulation Models*, John Wiley and Sons, New York.

Commoner, B. (1979). *The Politics of Energy*, Alfred H. Knopf, New York.

Dror, Y. (1971). *Design for Policy Sciences*, Elsevier, New York.

Gass, S.I. (1979). *Computer Model Documentation: A Review and an Approach*, National Bureau of Standards Special Publication 500-39, U.S. GPO Stock No. 033-003-02020-6, Washington, DC.

Gass, S.I. (1983). Decision-aiding models: Validation, assessment, and related issues for policy analysis. *Oper. Res.* 31, 603–631.

Gass, S.I. (1984). Documenting a computer-based model. *Interfaces* 14(3), 84–93.

Gass, S.I. (1987). Managing the modeling process: A personal perspective. *European J. Oper. Res.* 31, 1–8.

Gass, S.I. (1991). Model world: Models at the OK Corral. *Interfaces* 21(6), 80–86.

Greenberger, M., M.A. Crenson and B.L. Crissey (1976). *Models in the Policy Process*, Russell Sage Foundation, New York.

Hoos, I.R. (1972). *Systems Analysis in Public Policy*, University of California Press, Berkeley, CA.

Kalkstein, M. (1969). Personal involvement vs professional information in facing public issues, in: J. Mock (ed.), *The Engineer's Responsibility to Society*, The American Society of Mechanical Engineers, New York, pp. 21–23.

Kraemer, K.L., S. Dickhoven, S.F. Tierney and J.L. King (1987). *Datawars: The Politics of Modeling in Federal Policymaking*, Columbia University Press, New York.

Landry, M., J.-L. Malouin and M. Oral (1983). Model validation in operations research. *European J. Oper. Res.* 14, 207–220.

Larson, R.C., and A.R. Odoni (1981). *Urban Operations Research*, Prentice-Hall, Englewood Cliffs, NJ.

Machol, R.E. (1982). The ORSA guidelines report–A retrospective. *Interfaces* 12(3), 20–28.

McGreal, I.P. (1970). *Problems of Ethics*, Chandler Publishing Co., Scranton, PA.

Miser, H.J., and E.S. Quade (eds.) (1985). *Handbook of Systems Analysis: Overview of Uses, Procedures, Applications, and Practice*, Wiley, Chichester.

Miser, H.J., and E.S. Quade (eds.) (1988). *Handbook of Systems Analysis: Craft Issues and Procedural Choices*, Wiley, Chichester.

Mock, J. (ed.) (1969). *Responsibility to Society*, The American Society of Mechanical Engineers, New York.

Mulvey, J. (1981, 1982). Unpublished case studies and problems in ethics for OR analysts, Princeton University, Princeton, NJ.

Murphy, F.H. (1991). Policy analysis in a political environment. *Interfaces* 21(6), 87–91.

National Institutes of Health (1990). *Guidelines for the Conduct of Research*, Bethesda, MD.

Plant, J.F. (1988). The use of quantitative analysis in the public sector, in: J.S. Bowman, and F.A. Elliston (eds.), *Ethics, Government, and Public Policy: A Reference Guide*, Greenwood Press, New York, pp. 247–265.

Quade, E.S. (1989). *Analysis for Public Decisions, 3rd edition*, North-Holland, New York.

Richels, R. (1981). Building good models is not enough. *Interfaces* 11(4), 48–54.

Stroll, A., and R. Popkin (1965). *Introduction to Philosophy*, Holt, Rinehart and Winston, New York.

U.S. GAO (1979). *Guidelines for Model Evaluation*, PAD-79-17, Washington, DC.

Walker, W.E., J.M. Chaiken and E.J. Ignall (1979). *Fire Department Deployment Analysis*, North-Holland, New York.

Bibliography

Brewer, G.D. (1973). *Politicians, Bureaucrats, and the Consultant*, Basic Books, New York.

Brewer, G.D. (1978–79). Operational social systems modeling: Pitfalls and perspectives. *Policy Sci.* 10, 157–169.

Brill, E.D. Jr (1979). The use of optimization models in public-sector planning. *Management Sci.* 25, 413–422.

Drake, A.W., R.L. Keeney and P.M. Morse (1972). *Analysis of Public Systems*, The MIT Press, Cambridge, MA.

Gass, S.I. (ed.) (1977). Utility and use of large-scale mathematical models, National Bureau of Standards, Special Publication 534, Washington, DC.

Gass, S.I., and R.L. Sisson (eds.) (1975). *A Guide to Models in Governmental Planning and Operations*, Sauger Books, Potomac, MD.

Goeller, B.F. (1988). A framework for evaluating success in systems analysis, P-7454, The Rand Corporation, Santa Monica, CA.

Greenberger, M. (1980). A way of thinking about models. *Interfaces* 10(2), 91–96.

House, P.W., and J. McLeod (1977). *Large-Scale Models for Policy Evaluation*, John Wiley and Sons, New York.

Kraemer, K.L., and J.L. King (1986). Computer-based models for policy making: Uses and impacts in the U.S. Federal Government. *Oper. Res.* 34(4), 501–512.

Majone, G., and E.S. Quade (eds.) (1980). *Pitfalls of Analysis*, John Wiley and Sons, New York.

Miller, L., G. Fisher, W. Walker and C. Wolf (1988). Operations research and policy analysis at RAND, 1968–1988. *OR/MS Today*, December, 20–25.

Mulvey, J.M. (1989). Models in the public sector: Success, failure and ethical behavior, Report SOR-89-19, School of Engineering and Applied Science, Princeton University, Princeton, NJ.

S.M. Pollock et al., Eds., *Handbooks in OR & MS, Vol. 6*

Chapter 3

Models Fail

Arnold Barnett

Sloan School of Management, Operations Research Center, Massachusetts Institute of Technology, Cambridge, MA 02139, U.S.A.

Virtually every chapter in this volume (and, indeed, practically every chapter in this series of O.R. handbooks) discusses at least one mathematical model. When conditions are auspicious, such models show the way to clearer thinking, greater efficiency, higher standards of living, or a safer world. But trying to understand a process through mathematical modeling is not the same as achieving such understanding. If the assumptions of a model are incomplete and/or inaccurate, then its implications are compromised to an unknown and perhaps catastrophic extent.

Few users of mathematical models would dispute any of the statements above. If one examines actual modeling *behavior*, however, one sees great variability in the attention paid to issues of verification and validity. Everyone concedes that models can fail, but many modelers appear furtively to believe that their own efforts are invulnerable to that fate. Given such attitudes, an admonitional chapter about the success and failure of models is not superfluous in a book of this kind. I offer one below.

To be sure, we will not come up in this chapter with some highly precise concept of success, let alone some universal test of whether or not a given model is successful. What we will do is stress the importance of a middle path between pointless perfectionism and the insouciant belief that our models inevitably are illuminating. And, while we cannot show exactly how to plot that middle path on a map, we will argue that an attempt at such cartography is an essential part of serious modeling.

After some introductory discussion in the next section, we turn to a particular modeling effort that illustrates how crucial validity issues can arise. Then we spend much of the chapter pursuing an underappreciated point: no model-validity procedure now in use provides a simple 'litmus' test of a given model's adequacy. Thereafter we return to a few case studies, propose and explore a concept of successful modeling, and offer some final observations.

1. Some preliminaries

I should begin by limiting the scope of this enterprise. Our focus will be on *descriptive models*, by which we mean mathematical representations of phenomena that depend, at least implicitly, on some key starting assumptions. We further restrict ourselves to models that can be *falsified* against data, meaning those for which it can empirically be assessed whether they 'adequately' describe what they purport to describe. We do not explore whether the model was actually implemented or taken seriously; we simply inquire whether it deserved to be taken seriously.

We further limit ourselves to relatively *small* models that, roughly speaking, have (i) limited and well-defined objectives, (ii) a mathematical structure simple enough that it can be understood quickly, and (iii) comprehensible and finite data requirements. This emphasis seems desirable because excessive optimism about the adequacy of models seems inversely related to their size: we recognize that huge models focused on 'squishy' problems with strong 'political or behavioral content' are highly speculative [Strauch, 1974]; we may be unduly trusting, though, of smaller endeavors.

We could well start our quest for concept of successful modeling with two thoughtful observations, the first by a statistician and the second by an operations researcher:

> 'All models are wrong. Some are useful.' (George Box)

> 'Is the decision-making process enhanced in terms of scientific credibility by having this model and comparing alternatives? If so, the model is a good model.'
> (Richard C. Larson)

Both these comments remind us that no model is exactly correct, and that it is imprudent to hold models to standards of perfection that would never be applied to other sources of information. Yet the remarks provide no direct guidance about what lesser standards are appropriate. Box points out that some models are useful, but does not specify how we identify them. Larson notes that a good model can improve decision-making, but the question remains whether a particular model leads to better decisions or worse ones.

Perhaps a specific example could serve as a natural conduit to more detailed analysis. Here we turn to the study that did the most to stimulate my own interest in successes and failures among models.

2. The deterrent effect of capital punishment

In 1975, an article appeared in the *Stanford Law Review* about the deterrent effect of the death penalty. Its author Peter Passell was then on the Economics faculty at Columbia and is now an editor of *The New York Times*. At the time, the U.S. Supreme Court was deliberating on whether to authorize the resumption of capital punishment, and the argument was being advanced that, unless executions deter potential killers, performing them is an unconstitutional exercise in cruel and unusual punishment.

Passell (1975) tried to exploit the fact that death-penalty policy in the United States is decided at the state level. If executions act to deter killings then, all other factors being equal, states with relatively high execution rates should have fewer killings per capita than other states. But the phrase 'all other factors equal' is a weighty caveat. American states differ greatly on any number of dimensions that could affect their levels of homicide.

To weed out the effect of such large extraneous factors, Passell constructed a multivariate regression model. He hypothesized that a state's homicide rate was governed by seven primary determinants according to an approximate linear formula:

$$H = a_0 + a_1 P + a_2 T + a_3 E + a_4 A + a_5 I + a_6 M + a_7 S,$$

where

$H =$ killings per 100,000 residents,
$P =$ the fraction of killings that ended in criminal convictions,
$T =$ the median time spent in prison by convicted killers,
$E =$ the fraction of defendants convicted of homicide who were executed,
$A =$ the fraction of the residents in the age range 15–24,
$I =$ the fraction of families with incomes below the poverty level,
$M =$ the ratio of net non-white migration over the past ten years to the state's total population,
$S =$ a regional indicator variable (1 for Southern states, 0 for others) meant to reflect the greater 'tradition of violence' in the South than elsewhere,
$a_j =$ a numerical constant to be estimated from data ($j = 0, \ldots, 7$).

Using cross-sectional data from the various American states, Passell calibrated this model (and some slight variations of it) for the years 1950 and 1960. Under his main criterion for goodness-of-fit to the data (R^2, which is discussed in the next section), his most potent model arose for 1960:

$$H = -15.1 - 4.7P - 0.013T + 4.9E + 1.5A + 0.12I + 1.9M + 2.4S. \tag{1}$$

Note that a_3, the coefficient of the execution-rate variable, was +4.9 in (1). Taken literally, that outcome implies that executions stimulate killings (i.e. higher E-values induce higher H-values). Given imprecision in the parameter estimates, Passell did not claim the existence of such a counterdeterrent effect. But because of this outcome and some associated ones, he did conclude that there was 'no reasonable way of interpreting the cross-section data that would lend support to the deterrence hypothesis'.

I viewed Passell's work as unquestionably intelligent and extremely well written. I wondered, however, whether its findings were sufficiently reliable as to deserve major attention in the ongoing national debate. The issue seemed especially vexing

A. Barnett

Table 1

Estimated 1960 State homicide levels under Passell's Equation (1) and actual levels recorded

State	Predicted number	Actual number	State	Predicted number	Actual number
Alabama	354	422	Montana	17	26
Arizona	62	81	Nebraska	31	33
Arkansas	175	154	Nevada	20	26
California	1109	619	New Hampshire	6	8
Colorado	90	74	New Mexico	58	70
Connecticut	30	43	New York	392	488
Delaware	21	29	North Carolina	476	462
Florida	508	525	Ohio	317	321
Georgia	403	475	Oklahoma	117	175
Illinois	445	514	Oregon	40	43
Indiana	228	206	Pennsylvania	367	317
Iowa	2	17	Rhode Island	25	9
Kansas	74	70	South Carolina	299	318
Kentucky	207	207	South Dakota	23	14
Louisiana	294	284	Tennessee	278	304
Maine	21	17	Texas	968	837
Maryland	149	171	Utah	28	14
Massachusetts	84	77	Virginia	389	399
Michigan	303	337	Washington	113	60
Minnesota	9	45	West Virginia	106	82
Mississippi	256	218	Wisconsin	128	52
Missouri	220	199			

because of a point that Passell did not stress: in 1960, there were only 44 executions in the entire United States, which works out to fewer than one per state. Even if each of these executions had considerable deterrent power, their cumulative effect would be small and hard to detect. Why was Passell confident that, because he had found no deterrent effect, no 'reasonable' person was likely to do otherwise?

A natural first step in assessing the reliability of (1) is to turn to the 43 states used in calibrating the model, and to examine how closely the equation replicates their 1960 homicide levels. Table 1 presents the comparison. In no state except Kentucky did the actual number of killings correspond exactly to Passell's projection. To be sure, it would be farfetched to criticize Passell on this ground alone: quite apart from systematic factors, a state's annual murder toll is subject to roughly Poisson noise that no expected-value model could precisely capture [Barnett, 1981]. Thus, for example, the difference between the 175 homicides projected for Arkansas in 1960 and the 154 actually recorded does not represent a 'statistically significant' show of weakness.

Yet Poisson noise cannot possibly explain the larger disparities in Table 1, which include for California alone a difference of nearly 500 between projected and recorded homicide levels. Passell did not discuss such disparities in his paper; possible explanations for them include data inaccuracies, omitted or imperfectly defined variables, an inappropriate weighting scheme for the various data points, and an improper functional form. But an obvious question suggests itself: if we do not know what systematic problem caused the large discrepancies in Table 1, how can we be confident that the difficulty left unscathed the capital-deterrence coefficient in the model? Given the prevailing rarity of executions, that parameter estimate would have been volatile in the best of circumstances.

3. Testimonials to model validity

As we will discuss, Passell was not oblivious to the issue of validity and, indeed, few modelers expect us to treat their work as manifestly correct. But many analysts proceed as if validating a model were as simple as finding a hypotenuse via the Pythagorean theorem. The issue is more subtle than that, and the validity of a model is often unknown because the validity tests invoked in its behalf are themselves of dubious validity. I fear that much of the 'conventional wisdom' about verifying models reflects dangerous levels of sloganeering and, for that reason, postpone formal consideration of the notion of modeling success until after we have peered closely at some widely worn seals of approval.

Model validity is a multifaceted concept. If a model is used to glean information from data, there are the issues of whether the analysis was performed sensibly, how far the results can be generalized, and how closely the question the analysis considered related to the question one actually wanted to answer. Many more specialized concepts of model validity have been advanced; Gass [1983] offers a lucid survey on the topic, especially in conjunction with large-scale models.

The evidence offered in defense of falsifiable models comes in an enormous variety. Much of it, however, falls into one of four categories:

(1) standardized statistics;
(2) 'customized' statistics;
(3) tests against new data; and
(4) sensitivity analyses.

More stringent forms of stress testing – such as validating the model's main assumptions one-by-one – have also been applied.

All these approaches are potentially meritorious but, as we will see, their implementation in particular settings can be distressing. What sounds fine in the abstract may seem considerably less so when one looks at the rest of the paper.

3.1. Standardized statistics

By a *standard validity statistic* we mean a numerical measure that is widely construed as a 'success score' for any analysis of a given type. While such statistics are typically very easy to calculate, they pay no attention to the kind of data used, the specific question of interest, or the level of precision required of the answer. This last statement, of course, says a great deal in itself about the limits of such all-purpose indicators.

Like the soups that Goldilocks found too hot or too cold, standard validity statistics are far too flaccid in some contexts and far too taxing in others. And from the way such statistics are often discussed, it appears that their definitions (let alone rationales) are unfamiliar to many of their users. To make this point forcefully, we now examine in considerable detail perhaps the most widely used success score of all: the R^2-statistic of multivariate regression analysis. Then we move on to a commonly used gauge of the accuracy of a series of forecasts.

3.1.1. The R^2 measure

Because any regression analysis depends on a series of strong assumptions, there is a widespread yearning for some simple numerical measure of how 'good' a regression is. Probably the market leader among the indices now in use is the coefficient of determination, which is designated R^2. (The ORSA/TIMS journal *Interfaces* recently ran an article titled 'Validation Strategies for Multiple Regression Analyses: Using the Coefficient of Determination' [Sobol, 1991].) But there is a surprisingly weak relationship between the definition of R^2 and the statistic's public image.

3.1.1.1. Definition. In defining R^2, it is convenient to focus on the two-dimensional case with n data points of the form (x_i, y_i). One can imagine at least two linear representations of the variation of y over the data set:

$$\text{MODEL A:} \qquad y = c + e,$$

$$\text{MODEL B:} \qquad y = a + bx + e.$$

Here a, b, and c are numerical constants, while e is a random 'disturbance' term assumed to follow some zero-mean normal distribution and to take independent values at the various data points. (The e's are treated as inducing the data points to scatter vertically around the straight line that would join them in the absence of disturbances.) Of course, model A is but the special case of model B in which the y-to-x relationship has zero slope.

Under the standard least-squares criterion, one calibrates model A by finding the horizontal line which has the lowest sum of squares of vertical distances to the n data points. This least-squares line is simply $y = Y$, where Y is the arithmetical average of the y_i-values. For model B, least-squares analysis leads to the parameter estimates $\hat{b}$ and $\hat{a}$ of, respectively, the slope and intercept of the linear relationship:

$$\hat{b} = \frac{\sum (x_i - X)^2 y_i}{\sum (x_i - X)^2},$$

$$\hat{a} = Y - \hat{b}X,$$

where X = arithmetic average of the x_i-values.

Figure 1 presents the two least-squares linear portrayals of a hypothetical set of data points. Note that the tilted line seems to fit the points better; this outcome is

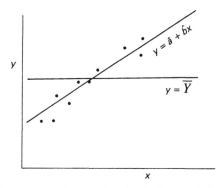

Fig. 1. Two least-squares linear portrayals of a hypothetical set of data points.

unsurprising because, while model A is constrained to be horizontal, model B can take on any slope and any intercept. To quantify the improvement of model B over model A, one could first compute the sum of squares of the n vertical distances by which each line 'missed' the data points, and then note the percentage reduction when B is used rather than A. R^2 is *defined* as this percentage reduction:

$$R^2 = \frac{\text{SS}(A) - \text{SS}(B)}{\text{SS}(A)} = 1 - \frac{\text{SS}(B)}{\text{SS}(A)},$$

where

$$\text{SS}(A) = \sum_1^n (Y_i - Y)^2, \quad \text{and} \quad \text{SS}(B) = \sum_1^n (y_i - [\hat{a} + \hat{b}x_i])^2.$$

When $R^2 = 0.762$, for example, the sum of squared vertical deviations drops 76.2% when the unconstrained least-squares line replaces the horizontal line $y = Y$.

Given its definition, R^2 can vary between 0 and 1. It assumes its maximum value when the data points fall perfectly along some line with non-zero slope. (In that case, $\text{SS}(A) > 0$ while $\text{SS}(B) = 0$.) It takes on its minimum when $\hat{b} = 0$ and thus $\hat{a} = Y$; in that case, tilting the line from the horizontal yields no gains whatsoever from a least-squares perspective.

3.1.1.2. Discussion. R^2 is not especially difficult to comprehend or to compute. But many of its users, having been exposed to opaque algebraic treatments and such unfortunate phrases as 'percentage of variance explained', misconstrue R^2 as a measure of viability of the linear model B. When computer printouts of regression results are scanned, R^2's near 1 can produce elation while those near 0 can provoke dismay. Such strong reactions are often misplaced.

Consider, for example, the situation depicted in Figure 2. The tilted line sustains far smaller squared vertical deviations from the data than does its horizontal counterpart; hence the calculated R^2 would be high. But the model B line still

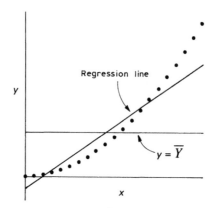

Fig. 2. The regression line attains a high R^2 but a less-than-ideal description of the data.

suffers appreciable deviations from the data, and fails to depict the apparent convexity in the y-to-x relationship. It is thus not clear that B constitutes an adequate representation of the underlying pattern.

The underlying problem is that R^2 is a *relative* and not an absolute measure of accuracy and that, in many settings, the baseline model A against which comparisons are made is something of a straw man. In such conditions, even a large amount of improvement over A could leave us short of a successful model. The danger is of a kind summarized by the proverb 'in the valley of the blind, the one-eyed man is king'.

At the same time, a low R^2-value need not imply that a model lacks credibility. When a horizontal line fits the data very well, model B has little opportunity to improve over model A. Hence a very low R^2 can be quite compatible with very small vertical deviations. It is one thing to be disappointed that x seems irrelevant to y, but quite another to impugn the regression analysis that accurately conveyed the information. To do the latter because of the low R^2 would be to blame the messenger for the content of the message.

Interestingly, it can be shown that R^2 in the two-dimensional case is simply the square of the coefficient of correlation of x and y. The correlation coefficient concerns itself solely with *directional* questions about the y vs. x relationship (e.g. do relatively high x-values tend to accompany relatively high y-values?). That R^2 is mathematically equivalent to the correlation coefficient pointedly suggests the weakness of its credentials as an arbiter of model validity.

3.1.2. *Relative improvement over chance*

Many models are used to generate forecasts of which members of a group will fall into each of two categories (e.g. which borrowers will default and which will pay back). On eventually learning what actually happened to each individual, one can go back to the earlier predictions and assess their accuracy. To summarize the findings of such a review, analysts frequently cite the statistic called *relative improvement over chance* (RIOC) [see Farrington & Loeber, 1989].

3.1.2.1. Definition. Suppose that N individuals have borrowed money, and that a model identifies P of them that it predicts will default on their loans. (It projects that the other $N - P$ will pay back.) Let A be the number of borrowers that ultimately do default, and let x be the number of borrowers who default *and* were (correctly) forecast to do so. RIOC is a linear function of x tied to outcomes in two special cases.

Given P and A, we can readily deduce how x behaves in situations favorable to and unfavorable to the model. (For simplicity, we assume here that $P > A$.) If the model has no discriminatory power, then its estimated proportion of defaulters among those A borrowers who subsequently did default will be the same as that among those who repaid their loans. (Both proportions would be P/N.) Then D, the *number* of defaulters identified as defaulters by the model, would follow:

$$D = A(P/N). \tag{2}$$

If, by contrast, all those who defaulted had been labelled defaulters by the model, then x would take on its maximum possible value, namely A.

RIOC is defined by:

$$\text{RIOC} = (x - D)/(A - D). \tag{3}$$

RIOC reaches its highest value of 1 when $x = A$, and equals zero when $x = D$ (the expected number of correct guesses if one picks P of the N people at random and proclaims them defaulters). RIOC is negative if the model forecasts a higher rate of defaulting among those who paid back than among those who actually defaulted. In that disheartening circumstance, one would have fared better under RIOC using the opposite of the model's predictions than using the predictions themselves.

3.1.2.2. Discussion. An anomaly in the definition of RIOC is made clear by two specific cases reflected in the contingency tables below.

Actual and predicted borrower behavior in two situations

Case 1		Actual		Case 2		Actual	
		DF	PB			DF	PB
Predicted	DF	10	70	Predicted	DF	7	3
	PB	0	20		PB	3	87

DF = default, PB = pay back.

In case 1, 80 of the 100 borrowers were predicted to default by the model (i.e. $P = 70 + 10 = 80$). In actuality, only 10 did so (i.e. $A = 10$). Thus, under Equation (2), $D = 10(80/100) = 8$. But because all 10 defaulters were on the list of 80 predicted ones, $x = 10$, and thus RIOC would assume under (3) the maximum value of 1. This despite the fact that only 30 (10 + 20) of the 100 individual forecasts were correct.

In case 2, the model correctly forecasts that the overall default rate would be 10% (both the predicted and actual rates were $[7+3]/100$). Its specific list of 10 defaulters, however, contained only 7 of the actual ones. In this situation, $P = 10$, $A = 10$, $D = 1$, and $x = 7$; therefore $D = 0.667$. In other words, even though 94 of the model's 100 predictions were accurate $(87 + 7)$, its RIOC is only 2/3.

What these outcomes highlight is that RIOC treats as *irrelevant* the difference between the predicted 'base' rate of defaulting (P/N) and the actual rate (A/N). The statistic views the discrepancy between P/N and A/N as a neutral input variable and, *conditioned on that difference*, suggests how successful were the individual forecasts. Thus, even though the case 1 model overestimated the default rate by a factor of eight, while the case 2 model hit the rate on the nose, RIOC is indifferent to that discrepancy and treats the case 1 model as superior.

Is such a convention sound? Doubtless, there are some circumstances in which the model should not be faulted for misspecifying the base rate of the activity under study. But it is hard to imagine that such circumstances are very common. Giving the ratio in (2) the all-encompassing name 'relative improvement over chance' obscures the ratio's overpowering lack of interest in the frequency of the phenomenon under study. Such inappropriate labeling may explain why many users seem unaware of the statistic's limitations.

As noted earlier, some standardized statistics may be excessively harsh to the models to which they are applied. If, for example, lots of data are available and a χ^2-test is performed, then even minor imperfections in the model can generate harrowing test statistics. Much as the best can be the enemy of the good, standardized statistics that scream 'failure!' at the model's first sign of infirmity can do more to demoralize than enlighten us.

And yet, a certain asymmetry may be at work. A model-builder who achieved an unnerving result in a χ^2-test might well report the outcome but make clear the artificiality of the test. Yet, following the natural inclination not to look gift horses in their mouths, a model-builder who attained a high R^2 or RIOC does not usually probe the outcome for evidence that it is too flattering. Thus, standardized tests seem less likely to cause a viable model to be discarded than to allow an inadequate one to be embraced.

3.2. Customized statistics

By a *customized* statistic we mean one that, in the context of a particular analysis, conveys information about the credibility of the associated model. Outside that analysis, the statistic might be utterly meaningless. Such 'parochialism' contrasts with the broad scope of standard statistics like R^2 or RIOC, which are used in highly diverse settings and essentially interpreted the same way in all.

A scientific theory, for example, might predict the numerical value of some physical quantity. Should subsequent experiments yield an estimate of that quantity very close to the prediction, the credibility of the theory is enhanced. Likewise, many mathematical models have highly specific implications of one sort or another; customized statistics indicate whether such implications are in harmony with available data.

Clearly, customized statistics can be helpful in model validation. Yet the consistency between a model and some customized statistic falls far short of demonstrating that the model is correct. Such consistency does not even preclude the catastrophic failure of the model, as a simple example makes clear.

Suppose that it is hypothesized that all the men in Mudville wear hats while none of the women do. If men and women are equally numerous, one would expect under the hypothesis that half those surveyed in a random sample of citizens would be hat-wearers. If the actual fraction who wear hats turns out to be (say) 0.496, one could report spectacular consistency between prediction and data. But that outcome could have arisen because all the *women* questioned wear hats while none of the men do.

In other words, even if the hypothesis was the exact opposite of the truth, that failing need not invalidate the estimate of the 'participation rate' in hat-wearing. It would be highly unfortunate, therefore, to use that estimate as the centerpiece of a test of the hypothesis. More generally, tests that are oblivious to a model's fundamental premises can hardly provide it with unequivocal support.

The example above is contrived, but consider a recent paper in *Criminology*, perhaps the world's most prestigious journal in its field. The article [Greenberg, 1991] posited the following mathematical model of arrest patterns for youths:

(i) Throughout the observation period (generally an age range like 10 to 25), a given offender sustains arrests under a Poisson process with constant rate λ.

(ii) The numerical value of λ can vary from individual to individual and, over the offender population, follows a gamma probability distribution.

Implicit in (i) is the assumption that all youthful 'criminal careers' were already in progress at the start of the observation period, and that no offenders 'retired' from their careers before the age at which observations ended.

The author calibrated his mixed-Poisson model with cohort data from several cities. To test the accuracy of the city-specific results, he applied only one criterion: how well the model predicted the number of cohort members with each given total number of arrests over the observation period. (For example, he estimated how many youths in a Philadelphia cohort would have exactly three arrests over the age range 10–18, and then compared that estimate with the actual number of 'three-timers'.) He concluded that all the predictions performed satisfactorily and, indeed, that one of his predicted distributions had achieved 'awesome' success.

One looks in vain, however, for any explanation why the distribution of total arrests should be the primary gauge of model validity. The model has a bold and startling central premise: each person's criminal career is already under way by age 10 and that, except for zero-mean fluctuations, the career proceeds with utter constancy far into adulthood. (Even time in detention was not excluded from the observation period.) To test that gloomily deterministic view of juvenile crime, one would presumably want to scrutinize individual-level data and see whether, as the model implies, arrests are uniformly scattered over the age range studied. Should the uniformity assumption be strongly contradicted by the data, the model's success in estimating the number of Philadelphia youths with exactly three juvenile arrests would be no more meaningful than the Mudville model's success with the hat-wearing rate.

Viewed in this light, the model quickly runs into serious empirical trouble. One thing all participants in the criminal-careers debate agree on is the age–crime relationship: aggregate arrest rates increase steadily with age until they reach a peak, after which they steadily decline. Data about the very cohorts studied in the *Criminology* paper make clear the colossal failure of the model's assumption of age-invariant arrest rates. In the East London cohort, for example, the annual apprehension rate per 100 youths was 2.6 at ages 10–12, 15.8 at ages 16–18, and 4.4 at ages 23–25.

The general problem is that customized statistics (such as the distribution of total arrests in the case above) often seem to arise in conjunction with lenient and/or eccentric tests of model validity. Such tests can be so uninformative that it might be charitable to treat them as irrelevant.

3.3. Tests against new data

Sometimes a model calibrated with one data set is tested against another set to which it is supposed to apply. Should the model fail to replicate relevant patterns in the new data, its credibility would be in great jeopardy. But should the model fare well with the new data, would its credibility therefore be appreciably enhanced?

The answer, of course, is 'it depends'. A model that performs impressively in a range of independent settings certainly has a claim to respect. But tests against new data are often less definitive than their architects believe. They often give short shrift, for example, to the concept of independence. Rather than use two different data sets, researchers commonly divide an existing set into two parts: a calibration set and a 'holdout sample' used for validation. The problem with this approach is that, should the full data set be eccentric in some important way, the holdout sample will likewise be so.

Suppose, for example, that a firm wants to estimate how sales of some product depend on the extent to which it is advertised. The firm could consciously vary advertising levels across N distinct geographic areas and then observe the data points (A_i, S_i), where A_i and S_i are per capita sales and advertising, respectively, in area i ($i = 1, \ldots, N$). If it believes that the S vs. A relationship is linear, the firm could use half the data to estimate the slope and intercept of the line $S = a + bA$; then it could see how well that line depicts per capita sales in that half of the data *not* used in approximating a and b.

If the line gives a splendid fit to both the calibration data and the holdout-sample, b would supposedly provide an excellent indicator of the economic benefits of advertising. That inference, however, could be highly misleading. Perhaps, unbeknownst to the firm's analyst, advertising and price are strongly correlated throughout the data set: wherever advertising is high, the product's price is low, and vice versa. Then an upsurge in sales in the high-advertising region might reflect not the power of the ads but rather the lure of lower prices.

The *S* vs. *A* model, in other words, may fit the data well because advertising improperly gets credit for the influence actually exerted by its omitted correlate: price. And the holdout sample, as thoroughly contaminated by the problem as the original data, can do nothing to bring the difficulty to our attention.

Returning to the general case, we face a fundamental question: what constitutes a satisfactory showing in the new data set? It is not unusual to see a relative standard: the model survives the test so long as its compatibility with the data does not substantially 'shrink' when the validation sample replaces the calibration one. But that criterion begs the key question of whether the model's performance with the calibration data was adequate to begin with. If not, then it is unclear why the model should be applauded for reproducing with the holdout sample the earlier disappointing result. Two wrongs, after all, do not make a right.

A recent article in an ORSA/TIMS journal inadvertently highlighted this last problem [Sobol, 1991]. The author wished to project a business school student's grade point average (GPA) on the basis of such prior information as her GMAT score and undergraduate GPA. Multiple regression analysis yielded a forecasting formula that attained an R^2-score of 0.18 within the data set used for calibration. When the formula was applied to a new data set for a later year, the resulting R^2 was 0.17. Because the latter coefficient of determination was only marginally lower than the original one, the analyst used a capital V in a key table to announce that the GPA-forecast formula had been 'validated'.

We have already discussed R^2 at length, but it is worth making explicit what the numbers above are saying. A simple approach for estimating the GPA's of individual students is to compute the school-wide mean GPA and use that number as the 'guess' about each student. Unless the student body is remarkably homogeneous, such a procedure is unlikely to produce very accurate forecasts. An R^2 of 0.18 means that the researcher's student-specific rule only slightly outperformed the simple one just stated, achieving only an 18% reduction in average squared forecasting error (and hence about a 10% drop in average absolute error). Suppose, for example, that mean GPA among the students was 3.2 (out of 4). Then the R^2-value suggests that, under the regression formula, an excellent student with a GPA of 3.7 might typically be projected to have a GPA around 3.25 (i.e. 10% closer to the true GPA than the overall mean of 3.2).

When the regression formula was tested against new data, it turned in a comparably weak performance. But the fact that matters had not become even worse was construed as a victory for the model! In the atmosphere of celebration, there was little incentive to ponder whether some other feasible formula might generate far better predictions.

4. Sensitivity analyses

Researchers sometimes defend their models by offering evidence that, even if key assumptions or parameters were altered in plausible ways, the conclusions of the analysis would scarcely be affected. Such demonstrations of 'robustness' are meant to imply that it would be picayune to criticize specific details of the modeling because nothing consequential depends on them. Such sensitivity analyses are often highly persuasive, and often deservedly so.

Yet one is reminded of Dorothy Parker's observation that 'there's less to this than meets the eye'. Varying the parameters of a model around the values initially chosen is not really a form of model validation, for the exercise *assumes* that the underlying model is correct. At most, one can learn whether the results of the modeling exercise are stable within the range of parameter variation. Even that limited objective can be thwarted when the parameters are altered one at a time, so that the potentially explosive consequences of changing several variables at once are never observed.

Moreover, even sensitivity assessments that focus directly on the model are of limited value. There are an infinite number of possible ways to model any partic- ular phenomenon, and even the most elaborate sensitivity assessment concerns a rather finite number. Arrayed against the full spectrum of possibilities, the models compared are often minor variants of one another. It is therefore conceivable that some common flaw could incapacitate all the models studied, in which case the fact that they reach similar conclusions is hardly decisive evidence that the consensus view is correct.

Passell, for example, tested the sensitivity of his capital punishment finding by considering two separate years (1950 and 1960), two different functional forms (linear in his seven explanatory variables and linear in the tenth roots of those variables), and several alternative indicators of a state's involvement in executions. He interpreted the results as affirming the anti-deterrent conclusion of his 'best fit' analysis. In all of his models, however, he made a *homoscedasticity* assumption, under which all American states were given equal weight in the calibration of the regression model. Thus, getting a close match to the homicide rate of New Hampshire (with 8 killings in 1960) was given the same priority as achieving a close fit in Texas (with 837 killings that year).

Such even-handedness is not necessarily a virtue. A state's recorded homicide rate is not a perfect representation of its 'true' prevailing rate: some killings are misclassified as accidents, suicides, or natural deaths; some attempted murders yield injury rather than death; some assaults not intended to be lethal nonetheless are. Even in the absence of any trends, therefore, a locality will exhibit year-to- year fluctuations in its annual homicide rate. Yet such fluctuations do not affect all localities equally: in *percentage* terms, they should be especially large where the number of killings is low. (In such settings, one multiple murder could triple the year's murder rate.) The upshot is that annual per capita murder rates are far less stable in some American states than in others.

One could argue that a sensitivity analysis of Passell's findings should replace his homoscedasticity axiom with another that accords greater weight to states with many killings than to those with few [see Barnett, 1981]. When Passell's Equation (1) model was recalibrated under this principle, the coefficient of the execution- rate variable (a_3) changed from +4.8 to −15.5. While this revised analysis is itself far from perfect, it does imply a strong deterrent effect. At a minimum, it shows that Passell's results depend heavily on an equal-weighting assumption that is common to all the models in his sensitivity tests, that he did not justify, and that may not be implausible.

The larger point is that, when a sensitivity analysis is performed by those who created the original model, it is limited by any 'blind spots' in their perspective. Certain assumptions may be taken so much for granted that the thought of varying them along with others might not even occur to the analysts. Thus, a problem that damages the original model could easily disrupt all the alternatives with which it is compared.

5. Tests of structural validity

Even if a model appears faithfully to represent some process of interest, it might be doing well for the wrong reason. Devotees of *structural validity* argue for accompanying tests of a model's overall performance with tests of *each* of its primary assumptions. Influenced by this viewpoint, Green & Kolesar [1989] undertook extensive structural validity testing for a queuing-delay model about New York City police-cars.

Passing a gamut of structural tests is surely desirable; the question is whether it is necessary. Even major imperfections of apparently important assumptions might not render a model unable to perform its tasks. Because of its exceptional tractability, for example, the exponential probability distribution is routinely invoked by queuing theorists to model service-time variability. Other than radioactive decay, almost no process on earth is literally exponential. Yet it is well-known that, even when the exponential assumption is rather farfetched, descriptions of queuing behavior that depend on that assumption are sometimes uncannily accurate.

And if passing a series of structural tests is not always necessary, neither is it always sufficient. Structural-validity advocates correctly note that, even when a model functions as a perfect 'black box' in portraying current data, it could fall far short of duplicating that feat in another setting. But structural testing cannot fully dissipate that concern. Even if the data at hand support all of the model's key assumptions, how can one be certain that those assumptions would still hold in other situations? Structural validity tests, therefore, sometimes do less to dispel concerns about generalizability than to displace those concerns to another level.

The last paragraph may contain a touch of overstatement: there are some (and probably many) model assumptions that, if empirically validated in one setting, would be thoroughly believable elsewhere. The underlying point, though, is that structural testing is an uneven guide to model validity: it demands too much in some contexts yet asks too little in others.

Of course, not all attempts to demonstrate model validity fall neatly into the categories above. Another approach, somewhat akin to customized testing, sets important parameters at extreme values to see if the model reacts appropriately (e.g. does the population drop to zero in a world without oxygen?). But expanding the discussion thus far would not alter its main point: *whether singly or in combination, familiar model-validation procedures fall short of creating some all-purpose scanner that can make clear whether any given model can meet its objectives.*

Before grappling further with the general notion of successful modeling, it might help to consider two more specific cases. One leaps out as a classic case of a modeling failure, while the other has the scent of success.

6. A tale of two more models

6.1. Midway Airlines

An advertisement in late 1983 in *The New York Times* announced in large letters that '84% OF FREQUENT BUSINESS TRAVELERS TO CHICAGO PREFER MIDWAY TO AMERICAN, UNITED, AND TWA'. This statistic seemed surprising because, at the time, Midway's New York–Chicago flights were only half-full and only carried 8% of the route's passengers. Could there have been such a large discrepancy between what people preferred and what they actually did?

In small letters at the bottom of the advertisement, we were informed that the statistic arose from a survey 'conducted among Midway passengers between New York and Chicago'. Putting it less obliquely, the only ones eligible for inclusion in the sample were the small group of eccentrics who were already flying Midway! If there was any surprise at all in the results, it is that one of six Midway passengers would themselves prefer to be elsewhere.

This example is not intended to disparage Midway Airlines, a brave carrier that ceased operations in November 1991. But if the poll was meant as a modeling exercise to measure Midway's true popularity on the New York–Chicago route, it seems to epitomize a fatally flawed one.

6.2. Airline market-share changes

With the modesty characteristic of professors from Cambridge, Massachusetts, I turn to my own work for what seems an example of an successful model [Barnett & Lofaso, 1983]. An American Airlines DC-10 crashed on takeoff at Chicago in May, 1979, killing all 275 people on board. In an action unprecedented in the jet age, the F.A.A. thereafter decertified the entire DC-10 fleet and banned the plane from U.S. airspace for 37 days. It was widely predicted at the time that, even after the DC-10 was allowed to resume flying, it would never regain the confidence of the traveling public.

We decided to estimate empirically the extent of long-term DC-10 avoidance induced by the Chicago disaster. We chose to adopt a simple before/after quasi-experimental design based on Civil Aeronautics Board passenger-traffic data by city pair, airline, and quarter. We wanted to focus on specific routes served exclusively by two competing airlines, one of which used the DC-10 heavily while the other did not use it at all. The airlines would charge equal fares and offer unchanging schedules for a long period surrounding the May 1979 crash. (The disaster predated frequent flyer programs and deregulation-induced fare competition.) If the DC-10 carrier's share of passengers on the route consistently dropped between (say) the first quarter of 1979 and the first of 1980, the pattern would document public resistance to flying the DC-10 as well as suggest the magnitude of the effect.

It soon became clear, however, that the pristine experimental conditions of the last paragraph almost never prevailed literally. But there were a number of routes on which pre- and post-crash conditions were nearly the same. (For example, the only change on route X might be that Airline A's share of available seats rose from 45.1% in 1979's first quarter to 45.4% in 1980's first quarter.) This circumstance raised the issue of whether such small deviations from perfect before/after matchings were serious threats to the research design. The fear would be that, in the nonlinear style of catastrophe theory, slight relative changes in schedules or fares cause tumultuous shifts of passengers from one airline to another. In the latter case, distinguishing the effects of the DC-10 crash from those of other factors could be quite problematic.

To address the stability issue, we undertook a small modeling exercise. Using data for 45 illuminating two-airline routes and the first quarters of 1977 and 1978 (i.e. pre-crash periods), we calibrated via linear regression the first-order approximation formula:

$$\Delta(M) = a\Delta(S) + b\Delta(F) + c\Delta(N), \tag{4}$$

where

$\Delta(M)$ = change in the airline's market share (i.e. percentage of passengers on a route) between the first period and the second,

$\Delta(S)$ = change in the airline's proportion of nonstop seats on the route,

$\Delta(F)$ = change in the airline's proportion of nonstop departures,

$\Delta(N)$ = change in the airline's participation in discount night-coach service, as measured both in absolute terms and relative to its competitor.

Having argued that the 45 routes should be dichotomized into 'long' and 'short', we performed two separate regressions of form (4). Consistent with expectations, the absolute values of all three parameters were *below one* in both regressions. (Five of the six parameter estimates took the anticipated positive sign; the exception may have been caused by the high correlation of $\Delta(S)$ and $\Delta(F)$.) The results suggested that, when $\Delta(S)$, $\Delta(F)$, and $\Delta(N)$ are all small, $\Delta(M)$ will likewise be. Extrapolating this pattern to the relevant 1979 vs. 1980 comparisons, we concluded that 'what you see is what you get': on routes for which the DC-10 carrier's S, F, and N-values were nearly unchanged (i.e. on virtually all the routes we were comparing), its observed drop in market share is a reasonable proxy for its loss of traffic to DC-10 aversion.

7. A definition of sorts

Suppose that we describe a model as successful by the following standard:

A modeling effort is *successful* if there is no plausible reason to fear that it is unable to fulfil its purpose.

Such a definition might seem glib to the point of uselessness. In the context of models, one could argue, the word 'plausible' is no easier to define *a priori* than the word 'successful'. But before discarding the statement, we should recall the Supreme Court justice who said of pornography that he could not define it but knew it when he saw it. Assessing plausibility in specific situations might be easier than we might initially think, especially if we pay attention to a 'check list' of questions like the set below.

(1) What is the purpose of the modeling?

(2) What degree of descriptive accuracy is needed if the model is to accomplish its goal?

(3) Do the modelers give us enough information to compare the model's actual achievements with the requirements implied by (2)?

(4) Has the model been 'fleshed out' with reliable data that are invulnerable to dangerous selection biases?

(5) Does the model omit any variables that could well be highly relevant to describing the process under study?

(6) Does the model appear to have a sound logical structure? Do its key assumptions, even if not self-evidently true, at least avoid the appearance of absurdity?

(7) Is the description of the model reasonably comprehensive, or are any important issues treated with disconcerting brevity?

(8) What evidence do the modelers offer that their main conclusions are trustworthy? Do they treat model validity as a serious issue?

(9) Do the sensitivity analyses performed by the modelers reflect the range of serious alternatives to the primary model, or are certain realistic deviations not even considered?

(10) How carefully do the modelers frame the conclusions of their work? Do the inevitable qualifying remarks seem sincere, or do they appear intended mostly as 'preemptive strikes' at potential critics?

These questions somewhat overlap and are not terribly precise, and they can hardly generate some 'points score' that, in the tradition of discriminant analysis, would separate successful models from unsuccessful ones. They can, however, clarify our thinking in particular cases, as is suggested by returning to three models we have discussed: Passell's capital punishment analysis, the Midway Airlines poll, and the assessment of service-induced changes in DC-10 market shares.

Passell's capital punishment model would presumably be deemed unsuccessful because of issues related to questions (2), (3), (8), (9) and (10). Given the paucity of executions, any reliable inferences about capital deterrence are contingent on an extremely deep understanding of the determinants of homicide rates (question 2). Passell provided little useful information about the accuracy of his model in depicting state-by-state murder patterns (questions 3 and 8), nor did he vary his questionable homoscedasticity assumption in the course of sensitivity analysis (question 9). (As we have seen, further scrutiny of Passell's model uncovered evidence highly unfavorable to it.) His assertion that there is 'no reasonable way' to dispute his interpretation of the data suggests that he underestimated the analytic hazards of the enterprise on which he had embarked (10).

Likewise, the Midway Airlines analysis seems unsuccessful because of problems highlighted by questions (4), (6) and (10). The data collection was subject to startling selection biases (4). Taking the results seriously requires the strange assumption that the popularity of Midway Airlines among those who fly it is no higher than that among those who do not (question 6). Furthermore, the contrast between the screaming headlines announcing the poll's outcome and small print revealing the odd survey conditions is a legitimate contributor to a 'no confidence' vote on the work (question 10).

By contrast, the airline market-share model does not appear to stumble badly on any of the questions above. The model's goal was clearly limited: to support the intuitively appealing conjecture that an airline's market share is not thrown into tumult because of slight changes in schedule or in the fraction of seats offered at a discount. Because of the highly restricted circumstances in which the model was used (i.e. only when $\Delta(S)$, $\Delta(F)$ and $\Delta(N)$ were all small), it seems farfetched to claim that inaccuracies in the parameter estimates were of great consequence. Under the definition above as well as under commonsensical reasoning, this modeling exercise was presumably a success.

8. Final remarks

Modeling is a delicate business, in which strong simplification is essential but oversimplification can be lethal. Even our most meticulous and intellectually inspired efforts can fail to provide the information we need. If we practice 'denial' of this painful truth, we could pay a heavy price for our delusions.

I therefore believe that model validation should not be construed as a secondary and irksome task, the analytic equivalent of the sales tax. Intellectually complete modeling entails an unflinching review of what questions must be answered and how trustworthy are the answers the model provides. I would be happier if the same creativity and subtlety so often apparent in the construction of models were more evident in the attempts to validate them.

Our discussion should not be so lofty, however, as to miss a key practical point. If (as is probably true) model-builders routinely express undue confidence in the power of their formulations, much of the blame must go to the supervisors, clients, or tenure committees that the modelers are trying to please. Whether conscious or not, there is a tendency to equate the failure of a model with the failure of the modelers. When an unstated goal of a model's architects is their self-preservation, we should not be surprised if, sometimes, their assessments of model viability seem closer to salesmanship than to science.

References

Barnett, A. (1981). The deterrent effect of capital punishment: A test of some recent studies. *Oper. Res.* 29(2), 346–370.

Barnett, A., and A.J. Lofaso (1983). After the crash: The passenger response to the DC-10 disaster. *Management Sci.* 29(11), 1225–1236.

Farrington, D.P., and R. Loeber (1989). Relative improvement over chance (RIOC) and phi as measures of predictive efficiency and strength of association in 2×2 tables. *J. Quant. Criminol.* 5(3), 201–214.

Gass, S. (1983). Decision-aiding models: Validation, assessment, and related issues for policy analysis. *Oper. Res.* 31(4), 603–631.

Green, L., and P. Kolesar (1989). Testing the validity of a queueing model of police patrol. *Management Sci.* 35(2), 127–146.

Greenberg, D.F. (1991). Modeling criminal careers. *Criminology* 29(1), 17–46.

Passell, P. (1975). The deterrent effect of the death penalty: A statistical test. *Stanford Law Rev.* 28(1), 61–80.

Sobol, M. (1991). Validation strategies for multiple regression analyses: Using the coefficient of determination. *Interfaces* 21(6), 106–120.

Strauch, R.E. (1974). A critical essay of quantitative methodology as a policy analysis tool, RAND Report P-5282, The RAND Corporation, Santa Monica, CA.

S.M. Pollock et al., Eds., *Handbooks in OR & MS, Vol. 6*

Chapter 4

Military Operations Research

Alan Washburn

Naval Postgraduate School, Monterey, CA 93943, U.S.A.

1. Introduction

As an introduction to Military Operations Research (hereafter MOR – even the slightest acquaintance with the United States military causes the quick adoption of acronyms), this article has several predecessors. We will draw liberally from them. Morse & Kimball [1946], for example, is the source of many of our examples concerning measures of effectiveness. Section 5 below is simply a condensation of the section on wartime MOR that Clayton Thomas wrote for *Military Modeling* [Hughes, 1984], lifted almost verbatim. However, the imagined audience for this piece is analysts who are acquainted with the techniques of OR, and who perhaps have some civilian experience, but who are unfamiliar with the military or its problems. This audience, together with he academic proclivities of the (civilian) author, has caused the present work to be focused somewhat differently than the others. It has a philosophical bent, emphasizing the changes in one's point of view that are required by the bloody, competitive, ill-observed nature of combat. Our lack of understanding of the causes and goals of warfare forces some limitations on questions that should even be asked, let alone answered. It is well to understand these features of MOR at the outset, since it is easy to lose sight of them once one gets involved in the often fascinating details of constructing combat models. So, although the reader will find some detail here, the focus will be on fundamentals.

Military OR is concerned with the preparation for and the fighting of wars. Warfare differs qualitatively and quantitatively from more familiar economic human activity, and these differences influence the kind of OR that is applied. The main qualitative differences are the stakes (fate of nations, wastage of human life), the presence of a hostile and uncontrollable decision maker, and the fact that many major weapon systems are seldom tested in combat, if ever. Even in operations that at first hand might seem familiar, the scale on which major wars are fought often requires a different analytical point of view. Industrial mobilization, for example, strains the production and transport system of a nation to the point where commodity prices taken for granted in peacetime become meaningless, and more fundamental quantities such as national supplies or production capacities have to be dealt with.

Warfare values extreme capabilities. Thus military aircraft go faster than civilian aircraft, and military aircraft utilize inflight refueling while civilian aircraft do not. The question 'when and where should refueling take place?' is therefore peculiarly military, even though refueling is only indirectly related to combat. No imaginable civilian purpose would have jet aircraft trying to take off from ships, or people riding around in 100 ton, tracked, off-road vehicles. The fact that warfare is a fundamentally competitive activity has a heavy influence on the kind of weapon systems required, as well as the analysis needed to design them.

Military problems being different from those encountered in the commercial world, it is natural to expect that the mix of techniques that analysts customarily bring to bear will also differ. Military analyses carried out in peacetime are heavy users of the Theory of Probability, since many things about warfare are unknown or unknowable in the absence of the thing itself. The goals of warfare are multiple, so military analysts are often found groping for the right measure of effectiveness. The complexity and scale of military operations result in computer simulations of combat being heavily employed. The vital influence of the enemy's tactics often needs to be accounted for, either through Game Theory (an analytic technique) or Wargaming (a term we use here to imply the essential presence of humans as decision makers).

Sections 2–4 below describe certain problems arising in peacetime MOR, along with some of the techniques used to solve them. Emphasis is placed on material that illustrates unique aspects. This principle for selecting material is biased. Military organizations have vast logistics [Roehrkasse & Hughes, 1990], inventory [Sherbrooke, 1968], scheduling [Brown, Goodman & Wood, 1990], and personnel problems [Grinold & Marshall, 1977], for example, none of which will be dealt with below because combat is not explicitly involved. The Program Evaluation and Review Technique (PERT) was invented in the development of the POLARIS submarine [Pocock, 1962], but its wide use for complex projects in the civilian world is testimony to its essentially nonmilitary nature, and therefore its numerous applications will not be further discussed. Military exercises are the closest that many servicemen ever come to actual combat. Every exercise generates data that should be examined for clues about how well weapon systems and tactics would perform in combat. The associated data analysis problems are large and important, but none of them will be addressed in Sections 2–4. The fact that none of these application areas or techniques are discussed below does not mean that they are unimportant to military analysts, but only that problem formulation and solution follow relatively familiar lines.

2. Measures of effectiveness

If nation A and nation B engage in warfare, then, when all is said and done, roughly speaking, there are three things of importance to the two nations: A's losses, B's losses, and the political/territorial situation at the end of the war. Each of these three quantities is difficult to describe. A's losses might involve loss of life, loss of iron ore, loss of housing and loss of time for leading the good life. B's losses might be important to A, but in a different manner than are A's own losses, and certainly the situation at the end of the war is important to both A and B. Somehow all of these implications of warfare must be coalesced into a single measure of effectiveness (MOE) if conventional decision theory is to be employed. Since there is no universal way of doing this, MOE selection must inevitably be situation-dependent, and an experienced military analyst's almost reflex reaction to any statement that something is 'optimal' will be to ask 'in what sense?'

It does not help that even the identity of B may be unknown when A has to make decisions about force structure, or that more than two nations may be involved, or that losses to noncombatants or the environment might occur. This latter point is obvious in the case of nuclear warfare, but even conventional warfare has strong side effects, as the war in Kuwait has made clear. There were hundreds of oil tankers torpedoed by submarines in WWII. The resulting oceanic pollution was enormous, but imagine the effect if similarly unrestricted submarine warfare were carried out against today's much larger tankers. How should the contemplation of that disaster affect the Navy's decisions about whether to invest in antisubmarine warfare, which has the side effect of decreasing pollution through protecting tankers, or in submarines?

Although warfare in the large is hard to analyze on account of its multi-objective nature, in restricted circumstances a satisfactory MOE can frequently be found. The rest of this section outlines some of the possibilities.

The simplest situation is where A's losses in some local engagement are 0 or at least fixed, while B may or may not lose a single unit depending on the tactics or hardware employed. The natural MOE is the probability P that B's unit will be lost. Such situations may still be hard to analyze, since P may be a complicated function of tactics, but at least the MOE is clear. This MOE will be used in several examples in Section 3. Closely related is the situation where all of the variable losses are on one side. If B will lose a random number of identical units, then the expected value of that number will often[1] be a good MOE.

The assumption above that variable losses are confined to one side is important. Consider a situation where one A weapon is to attack one B target, but only after surviving the target's defenses. If S is the probability of surviving the defenses and K is the conditional probability of killing the target given survival, then the probability of killing the target is $P = SK$. Tactical or design questions may affect both S and K; for example it may be possible to introduce electronic countermeasures (ECM) into the weapon that increase S, but only at the expense of decreasing the weapon's payload and therefore K. If the data are as shown in Table 1, using P as the MOE leads to the decision not to employ ECM, since

---

[1] Even here one must know the context. If B's units are redundant parts of a communication system, then the probability of destroying all of them may be the right MOE, rather than the expected number.

Table 1
Electronic countermeasures analysis

	S	K	MOE = SK
No ECM	0.8	0.5	0.4
ECM	0.9	0.4	0.36

the increase in S is overpowered by the decrease in K. This is a reasonable conclusion as long as the weapon can only be used once, as would be the case if it were a missile of some sort since A's losses are fixed. If the weapon were an aircraft, however, then suddenly A's losses, as well as B's, are affected by the decision. Intuitively, S ought to receive more emphasis than it does in calculating P because a surviving aircraft can continue to attack other targets. The decision not to employ ECM should be suspect in this case.

As long as variable losses are confined to one side a 'weighted aggregate' MOE may still be satisfactory even when (say) B's losses involve units of different kinds. If L_i is the loss of type i units, then MOE = $\Sigma w_i L_i$, where $w_i > 0$ is the 'weight' for losses of type i. The technique of putting diverse quantities on a common scale by weighting them is an old one in MOR. Morse & Kimball [1946] describe how sunk and damaged cruisers were each weighted by 'cruiser months lost' to obtain a single aggregate measure of damage. The crucial question in WWII was often 'what is the scarce resource here?' It turned out that the same shipyards that produced cruisers were also used to repair them, hence the weights. In peacetime the weights often turn out to be monetary value, so that the weighted aggregate is just 'total cost'. Cost measures were sometimes employed even in WWII; Morse & Kimball tell of a decision not to deploy anti-torpedo nets on merchant vessels because they simply cost too much compared to the value of the ships and cargo that they saved.

The situation is more complicated when variable losses occur on both sides. The net difference of losses is sometimes used as a measure of effectiveness. The question of whether the losses should be weighted is sometimes sidestepped by employing the *ratio* of one side's losses to the other. Each of these measures has lying behind it the idea that the war will terminate when one side or the other runs out of resources, or at least when the ratio of resources remaining is such that further struggle by one side is clearly futile. 'Hurt the enemy more than he hurts you.' There is something to be said for the idea. Grant's campaigns at the end of the Civil War were conducted with this precept clearly in mind. Of course, the weighting issue must somehow be faced when taking differences, and in the case of ratios one always has to wonder whether the ratio 2/1 really means the same thing as 2000/1000. In spite of these potential difficulties, difference and ratio measures are frequently employed. Some examples follow.

Military OR problems frequently take the form of arranging some kind of defense to prevent a target from being attacked. The basic idea is to destroy the attacker, thereby preventing the target from being attacked. But destroying attackers is not always the same thing as saving targets. Morse & Kimball relate one incident where anti-aircraft (AA) guns were installed on merchant vessels in WWII despite the evidence that such guns hardly ever shoot down attacking aircraft. What those guns *did* do was to spoil the aim of the attacker, so that ships equipped with AA guns had a significantly better chance of making it across the Atlantic. Ravid [1989] gives a more modern example where the question is whether to conduct an anti-aircraft defense before or after the bomb release line (BRL). The advantage of defending before the BRL is that a successful defense will destroy the attacker early enough to prevent the target from being attacked. The advantage of defending after the BRL is that the probability of destroying the attacker (albeit after the bomb is released) is higher because the defenses can be located closer to the target. There seems to be a conflict between the goals of defending the target and shooting down aircraft. Ravid's point of view, however, is that the target can always be bombed if the attacker wishes to devote sufficient aircraft to the task; all the defense can do is make those attacks as expensive as possible in terms of aircraft lost. The MOE that reflects this point of view is 'number of bombs dropped on target per aircraft lost', to be minimized by the defender. This is an example of the use of a ratio MOE to escape the apparent dilemma of a conflict between goals.

The use of ratios can also be illustrated by continuing the ECM analysis. Consider a large number (say 1000) of similar attacks by aircraft. Ignoring statistical variability, the losses to side B will be 1000 P targets and the losses to A will be $1000(1 - S)$ aircraft. Using the loss ratio MOE $= P/(1 - S)$ amounts to making the ECM decision to maximize the number of targets killed per aircraft lost. A glance at Table 2 will reveal that the correct decision with this MOE is to employ ECM, exactly the opposite of the decision made earlier. Thus, it is reasonable to employ ECM on aircraft in the same circumstances where one would not employ ECM on a single-use weapon like a missile. Context is crucial.

Here are two more examples that illustrate the need for context. Consider the Army's Weapons Effectiveness Index/Weighted Unit Value (WEI/WUV) system for determining the fighting value of a division. Every component of the division (rifles, machine guns, tanks, etc.) is assigned a fighting value, and the fighting value of the division is then simply the weighted aggregate. A common use of such measures is in comparing the armies of different countries; simply counting divisions in that context could be seriously misleading because divisions can be remarkably different from each other, even within a given country. On the other hand, arguing that all tanks should be replaced with rifles because rifles have a better WEI-to-cost ratio is surely the wrong way to approach the question of how

Table 2
Another version of the ECM problem

	S	K	MOE $= SK/(1 - S)$
No ECM	0.8	0.5	2
ECM	0.9	0.4	3.6

a division ought to be armed, and in fact the Army employs extensive simulations of combat to help make such decisions. The same MOE that is useful for one purpose may be inappropriate for another. For another example, consider the Air Force's use of the Heavy Attack (HA) model. This model has been in use since 1974 [Clasen, Graves & Lu, 1974] in essentially the same form: fixed numbers of sorties by different kinds of aircraft are assigned to a collection of enemy targets in order to minimize surviving enemy target value. This is another use of a weighted aggregate MOE. Sound like a naive way to fight a war? It probably would be, but the Air Force has no plan to use HA to actually assign sorties in combat. It is used instead to help plan weapons inventories by converting sortie assignments into weapon usage. Weapons planning is an activity that must be conducted at such a distance from actual warfare that a simple aggregate MOE must suffice.

Raisbeck [1979] gives several other examples that illustrate the importance of MOE selection.

Warfare is an essentially two-sided activity, so it is of course possible that the two sides will have different MOEs, say MOE_A and MOE_B. MOE_B is immaterial if B has no decisions to make in the engagement being considered (or if B's decisions are for some reason known to A), but in the general case where both sides can affect the outcome, both MOEs should seemingly be considered in the analysis. In practice this seldom happens, for reasons that will be described later in Section 4. The most common approach is to simply postulate the enemy's actions as part of the 'scenario' being considered, after which the enemy's MOE is not needed (in practice it is not developed in the first place). For the most part military analyses consider only the goals and desires of whichever side is doing the analysis.

2.1. Cost-effectiveness

A large part of peacetime military OR is devoted to hardware acquisition. Cost must be considered, of course, as well as effectiveness. Figure 1 portrays a typical situation where effectiveness (E) increases with cost (c). Note that very small expenditures result in no effectiveness at all, and that very large expenditures also have a small marginal effect. The question is, is there any principle by which one might determine the best or most 'cost-effective' decision?

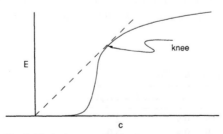

Fig. 1. Typical curve of effectiveness versus cost.

One point that stands out in Figure 1 is the one that maximizes the ratio of effectiveness to cost, sometimes called the 'knee'. It is the point that maximizes 'bang per buck'. There are circumstances where the knee is 'best' in a satisfying sense, but as usual context is important.

Suppose first that the object involved is a surveillance sensor that covers a certain area E, and that a system of many such sensors will be required to cover a much larger area A. To be precise, A/E of them will be required, so the total system cost will be $(A/E)c$. Clearly, the total system cost will be minimized when E/c is maximized, even if A is unknown. More generally, it can be said that maximizing the ratio E/c is the correct principle when many subsystems will have to be purchased, and when *total system cost and total system effectiveness are each proportional to the number purchased*. This is a rather narrow field of applicability, and even here one must be careful about how c is defined because shifts of the vertical axis in Figure 1 will affect the location of the knee. In the example, c must be the cost of buying, maintaining, and deploying the sensor, since otherwise the first proportionality assumption will not be true.

Now suppose instead that E is the probability of being able to communicate with a submerged, ICBM firing submarine in the midst of a nuclear attack, a crucial function if those submarines are to play their retaliatory role successfully. Such communication systems are not the kind of thing one can buy several of, at least not in the hope that total system effectiveness will be proportional to the number purchased. There is no simple principle that can be used to select the 'optimal' value of c in such circumstances.

Even in circumstances where the knee of the curve holds no particular attraction, quantification of effectiveness and cost is useful. Cost-effectiveness is not a quantity or even a well defined principle, but simply the attitude that cost and effectiveness should receive equal emphasis, and that tradeoffs will have to be made. In the words of Charles J. Hitch,

> ... the lesson of history is clear. Neither cost nor effectiveness alone is a sufficient basis upon which to choose a weapon system. Both must be considered simultaneously and in relation to each other.

Besides, 'merely' drawing curves such as Figure 1 certainly leaves MOR workers with enough to do. In practice one is often trying to estimate the cost of a system that has yet to be built, and which will be operated at considerable expense over decades. The attendant analytical and statistical issues are sufficient to justify journals devoted exclusively to cost estimation, and of course there is also the problem of estimating E.

3. Models and data

The Joint Chiefs of Staff (JCS) publishes *Catalog of Wargaming and Military Simulation Models*, part of the JCS purpose being to prevent redundant effort. Each model has only a bare description – proponent, purpose, computer language, etc. – but even so the book is a large one. The 11th (1989) edition includes over 300 models. Even so it is not exhaustive, since only large (in terms of computer code, inputs, and associated staff) models tend to be listed. The total number of models in use by military organizations is unknown, but certainly the JCS catalog represents only the tip of an iceberg. In the United States alone there are several major nonprofit organizations (Center for Naval Analyses, Institute for Defense Analyses, RAND, MITRE, Concepts Analysis Agency, and several military laboratories) staffed primarily by civilians who regularly create and manipulate military models. Major defense contractors invariably have a significant analytical arm, and there are several profit-making consulting organizations that specialize in military modeling. The military itself is also heavily engaged. The repetitive construction of the Single Integrated Operational Plan (the SIOP – this is the United States' major retaliatory plan in the event of nuclear war) alone requires hundreds of workers on a continuing basis, most of them in uniform, with combat models being central to the process. The construction, maintenance, and use of models of warfare is a major activity. The United States spends perhaps a billion dollars per year on it.

The models described in the JCS catalog generally represent combat in the large; a variety of forces are engaged on both sides, with many kinds of interactions and losses. Most of these models take the form of computer programs. One typically prepares inputs, runs the program, observes outputs, and revises inputs for the next run. Shubik & Brewer [1979] report that about half of the users of such models state that the major purpose is 'technical evaluation' (is tank A better than tank B?) with another quarter reporting 'force structure analysis' (do we have enough tanks?) and a smaller fraction 'doctrinal evaluation' (should we mass our tanks or spread them out?).

Large computer models are often justly criticized for their inflexibility, but analysts are sometimes able to bend them to serve unforeseen purposes. The U.S. Army developed the Concepts Evaluation Model to deal with a Warsaw Pact invasion of Europe, but in the last quarter of 1990 it was used to fight over 500 battles representing possibilities for what might happen in Kuwait. The environmental and logistical differences between Central Europe and the Middle East are substantial, so the adoption must have entailed great difficulties; nonetheless, lack of a tailor-made model left no alternative. Similarly, the U.S. Air Force adapted the Heavy Attack model mentioned earlier (another model developed with Central Europe in mind) to estimate Middle Eastern weapon requirements.

If the JCS catalog represents the tip of an iceberg, the rest of the iceberg consists of thousands of smaller models. Many of these smaller models are documented in technical reports, but many others are not documented at all. They are probably more concerned with tactics ('doctrinal evaluation') than are their larger counterparts, but otherwise it is difficult to say much about characteristics of the class. These smaller models will be the subject of most of the rest of this section, discussion of their larger brethren being prohibited by limitations on space and the reader's patience. Some of these small models are interesting in themselves, and some are interesting as extreme but insightful abstractions of larger ones. See also Hughes [1984].

3.1. Search models

Suppose that an object is hidden somewhere within an area A, and that a searcher examines an area a in an attempt to find it. What is the probability p that the object will be found? Some kinds of warfare are dominated by the search for targets (antisubmarine warfare being a notable example), so the question is frequently asked. The most natural response to the question, the *exhaustive search formula*, is $p = a/A$, the ratio of areas, or $p = 1$ if $a > A$. However, the value more often used in military analyses is $p = 1 - \exp(-a/A)$, the *random search formula*. One justifies this formula by arguing that the area a is in practice not examined as a single coordinated instantaneous *clump*, but rather by multiple searchers with imperfect navigation over a significant time period. The various parts of a may overlap, thus reducing the detection probability. The random search formula corresponds to a thought experiment where a is first cut up into confetti before being sprinkled inside of A. Obviously the searcher has no motive to *deliberately* attempt a tactic that would imitate the confetti experiment, but nonetheless the random search formula is not a bad approximation for many real searches. Its validity is a happy instance of real-world considerations actually simplifying the ensuing theory, since the random search formula has desirable analytic properties that the exhaustive search formula lacks. The main such property is that of interval independence: since $\exp(-a/A)\exp(-b/A) = \exp[-(a+b)/A]$, the probability of nondetection over an interval is the *product* (hence independence) of the nondetection probabilities over any partition.

The random search formula was known and employed by the Operations Evaluation Group in WWII. It led then and still leads to an interesting nonlinear optimization problem. Let q_i be the probability that the target of search is in area A_i; $i = 1, \ldots, n$, and let B be the total amount of search effort available. Then the static distribution of effort (SDOE) problem is to minimize the probability of nondetection:

$$\text{minimize} \quad \sum_{i=1}^{n} q_i \exp(-b_i/A_i)$$

$$\text{subject to} \quad \sum_{i=1}^{n} b_i = B, \quad b_i \geq 0.$$

The solution to SDOE has the feature that very little effort is applied when A_i is very large (no point in looking) or very small (no point in overkill); it is the medium-sized areas where q_i is not too small that get emphasized.

The SDOE problem is easily solved using modern computers, even when n is large, but this tractability has simply provided opportunities to formulate the search problem more realistically. Two difficulties with the SDOE model are that:

(a) In an extended search one must often account for unpredictable target motion even as the search proceeds.

(b) Transitions between cells in the SDOE model involve no cost to the searcher, whereas in reality they take time. Since search effort is essentially time in the first place, the SDOE model's predictions may be optimistic for the searcher.

Computationally effective methods have been developed to account for the possibility of target motion. As long as the motion is a Markov process, a nearly optimal search strategy can be found by an efficient iterative procedure, with each step requiring a solution of the SDOE. There has also been considerable theoretical work on the cell transition problem. Some of this work introduces cell-to-cell transition costs or constraints, and some of it simply abolishes *cells* and requires the searcher to have a continuous path. The computational problems in the latter case appear to be severe. Benkoski, Monticino & Weisinger [1991] give a recent review of the literature.

The U.S. Navy has deployed some tactical decision aids for submarine search. The main function of these aids is to simply display the current probability distribution of the target's position, conditioned on whatever results have been achieved (or not achieved) by past efforts. Computationally, these aids amount to repetitive applications of Bayes theorem; the user inputs a prior distribution[2], answers some questions about the type of target motion to be expected, plans a search, and then uses the software to produce a posterior distribution of the target's position that is then used as the prior distribution for the next stage, etc. Wagner [1989] describes the history, construction, and employment of such aids. Some of these aids incorporate optimization features, but optimization is never the main justification for the aid. Humans are good at seeing patterns in two dimensions, and bad at mentally going through Bayes' theorem to account for the effects of past actions. The computer's ability to apply Bayes' theorem and to instantly display the results as a pattern in two dimensions is thus a tremendous boon to human decision makers.

Software such as that described above has also been employed by the U.S. Coast Guard in searching for such things as drifting lifeboats. In fact, the case could be made that search and rescue is the more natural application, since lifeboats drift according to the whims of an unpredictable but at least indifferent Mother Nature, whereas the Navy's submarine target is motivated to choose some critical moment to stop moving in the manner that it has always used in the past and which the Navy has therefore come to rely on. An alternative would be to regard the Navy's search problem as a game (see Section 4), with the enemy submarine having options about motion that parallel the Navy's options about how to search. Unfortunately the computational problems associated with that point of view are currently insurmountable. The practical choice is between having a quantitative albeit essentially flawed Bayesian viewpoint on the one hand, and not having a quantitative viewpoint at all on the other hand. The former choice produces better

---

[2] Of course, one can not simply say 'input the prior distribution', when dealing with a sailor. The human interface is slighted here but actually crucial in an operational system.

operational results, and therefore it is the better viewpoint. The odd thing is that many analysts, although initially suspicious of describing the enemy's actions by postulating some kind of stochastic process, come eventually to regard the postulation as something real, rather than simply an analytic device that helps one to cope with a world that would otherwise be too complex. It seems that an assumption repeated often enough will eventually be believed, whatever the initial suspicions.

3.2. Lanchester's equations and generalizations

One of the major issues in defense procurement is the tradeoff between quality and quantity. Given a fixed budget, is one better off with a small number of capable systems, or a larger number of less capable systems? One way of illuminating the issue is to fight a notional battle between a hi-tech side and an initially more numerous lo-tech side, the idea being to see which side gets wiped out first. The simplest way to do this is to employ a pair of ordinary differential equations. Let $x(t)$ and $y(t)$ be the numbers of units remaining on the two sides at time t, and assume that:

$$dx(t)/dt = -by(t), \quad x(t) > 0,$$

$$dy(t)/dt = -ax(t), \quad y(t) > 0.$$

The constant a is the rate at which each x-type unit kills y-type units, and likewise b is y's lethality rate against x. The equations can be solved explicitly, but it is more insightful to eliminate time by taking the ratio of the two rates of change. The resulting equation is easily solved and one discovers:

$$a\,[x(0) - x(t)]^2 = b\,[y(0) - y(t)]^2$$

at all times for which $x(t) > 0$ and $y(t) > 0$. It follows that the side will first be wiped out that has the smaller *fighting strength*, where fighting strength is the product of lethality rate and the *square* of the initial number ($ax(0)^2$ for the x-side or $by(0)^2$ for the y-side). In this stark vision of warfare, one could compensate for being outnumbered by a factor of two only by having a lethality rate four times as large as the opponent. This heavy emphasis on numbers is called Lanchester's Square Law in honor of F.W. Lanchester [1916], who used ordinary differential equations to study aircraft attrition in WWI.

Engel [1954] was able to reproduce the battle of Iwo Jima after first using historical records to estimate lethality rates in a Square Law battle. He found that the defending Japanese forces caused casualties at almost five times the rate of the attacking U.S. forces. Nonetheless, U.S. casualties were comparatively light because U.S. forces initially outnumbered Japanese forces by about 3/1. The comparatively light U.S. casualties are consistent with Lanchester's Square Law. Figure 2 shows a time history of a Square Law battle where $x(0) = 60\,000$, $y(0) = 20\,000$, $a = 0.01$/unit per day, and $b = 0.05$/unit per day, numbers that

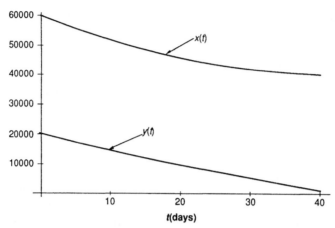

Fig. 2. Lanchester square law battle.

roughly characterized the battle of Iwo Jima. The actual battle had essentially no Japanese survivors.

There is also a 'Lanchester's Linear Law'. One discovers it by considering the possibility that attrition rates might be proportional to the number of targets, as well as the number of shooters. This would be the case if fire were simply directed into an area, rather than at specific targets, so the Linear Law is also sometimes referred to as *area fire* (the Square Law being *aimed fire*). In the Linear Law, fighting strength is simply the product of lethality rate (enemy losses per enemy unit per friendly unit per time unit) and initial number. The heavy emphasis on initial numbers disappears in the Linear Law. This should be plausible because an additional friendly unit in a Square Law battle has two advantages: the unit contributes to enemy attrition, and it also serves to dilute the enemy's fire. Only the first advantage is present in a Linear Law battle, hence the decreased emphasis on numbers.

Obviously, both of Lanchester's *laws* are highly simplified combat models, and yet they implicitly contain some important information about quality vs. quantity tradeoffs. Aimed and unaimed fire both occur in warfare, and quantity is more important in the former than in the latter. The Linear and Square laws do not exhaust the possibilities. Deitchman [1962] analyzed a guerrilla warfare model where one side employs aimed fire while the other employs area fire. There are also various fractional power laws. In many cases analytic solutions are possible for $x(t)$ and $y(t)$ [Taylor, 1983].

Lanchester's laws can clearly be generalized, since numerical solution of ordinary differential equations is easy on modern computers. Each side can consist of several types of units, coefficients can depend on time, logistics considerations can be included [as in Engel, 1954] by introducing positive right-hand-side terms, etc. Control terms can be introduced, so that questions like 'Should artillery fire at opposing troops or at opposing artillery?' can be posed. One can also force the integrality of the number of surviving units by making the results of individual engagements stochastic; this requires that the battle be replicated to get some idea of the variance of results, but still there is no conceptual problem in doing so. The U.S. Army relies heavily on Monte Carlo simulations of this sort. Many of the large-scale combat models listed in the JCS catalog can be thought of as generalizations or elaborations of Lanchester models. These can be quite complex, including such phenomena as the effects of terrain on lines of sight. Advances in computing power over the last several decades have permitted combat models to include increasing amounts of detail. The increased fidelity that these advances bring is of course welcome, but the associated trend toward greater complexity does have some associated difficulties that has caused considerable agonizing among MOR professionals. One difficulty is that complex models are difficult to describe. This is not just an inconvenience. The fact that there is very little real-world feedback about model verity in MOR means that the inherent plausibility of a model's structure must often substitute for verification. The plausibility of something that is difficult to describe is hard to judge. Also, the handover problem when one analyst relieves another becomes severe as describing the thing being handed over becomes difficult.

A second difficulty is that models can easily outrun the available data base as they become more complex. To some extent military judgment can be relied on for estimation of parameters, but it is not easy to keep track of sensitivity when dealing with a complex Monte Carlo simulation, and one would like to avoid situations where *crucial* inputs are supported only by military judgment. Military testing is expensive, occasionally destructive, and time-consuming, so the option of *not* relying on military judgment is not always feasible. The quality and extent of the data base is a continual item of concern [Stockfisch, 1975].

The gist of the above discussion is that large combat simulations, while useful, do not and should not displace smaller-scale efforts. There will always be a need for simple, aggregated models such as Lanchester systems that retain the essence of the situation while ignoring much of the detail. In fact, one good use for large, complex combat models is to generate data for the calibration of small, simple ones.

The monograph by Taylor [1980] is a good introduction to Lanchester Theory and its generalizations, including issues associated with complexity and aggregation.

4. Game theory and wargaming

John Maynard Keynes, in responding to critics of theoretical work in economics, stated that 'Practical men, who believe themselves to be quite exempt from any intellectual influences, are usually the slaves of some defunct economist...' Like economists, practitioners of MOR require a theory upon which to structure a view of a world where outcomes are affected by the choices of multiple agents, and, like economists, MOR practitioners suffer from the weakness and incompleteness of the currently available theories. Theoretical deficiencies are even more important for MOR than for economics, since the multiple agents involved in military problems tend to have strongly contrasting or even opposite goals.

The natural theoretical basis for MOR would seem to be the one that got its start in 1944 with the publication of *Theory of Games and Economic Behavior* (Von Neumann & Morgenstern). The authors of that seminal work intended their work to apply to games in the sense of chess and poker, but also more generally to practically any situation where multiple agents (*players*) affect an outcome and value it differently. The book got rave reviews, perhaps affected somewhat by the general ebullience of the time for things scientific. The May 1949 issue of *Fortune*, for example, contained a 20-page article describing the theory's accomplishments in WWII and projecting further successes in industry. The theory for two-person-zero-sum (TPZS) games (games with exactly two decision makers whose interests are perfectly opposed) had already been essentially worked out, and there was the promise of further successes for the other kind (which for brevity we will call *the general case*). It seemed to be merely a matter of working out some details and then undertaking the applications.

The initial enthusiasm was bound to be disappointed. The TPZS theory bore up under subsequent generalization and scrutiny, but the TPZS assumption of two completely opposed players turned out to be crucial. An adequate noncooperative decision-making theory for the general case has never really emerged. The reasons for this are well illustrated by one famous example, the Prisoner's Dilemma, which will be described in Section 4.1. As a result, it is no exaggeration to say that no widely accepted, normative theory for decision-making in the general case currently exists, a fact about the present that would have been surprising in 1944. It should therefore come as no surprise that game theory is not the intellectual foundation for MOR, in spite of its seemingly attractive framework for describing competitive problems.

The situation is different for the special case of TPZS games. Here the theoretical foundation is solid, but there are important practical difficulties of formulation and solution. Some of these will be described in Section 4.2.

A rival approach to competitive problems is to replace the abstract decision makers of game theory with role-playing humans. This is wargaming, the subject of Section 4.3. Wargaming gets around some of the difficulties associated with Game Theory, but only at the cost of introducing some new ones.

In practice, the most common approach to competitive situations in MOR is neither Game Theory nor wargaming. Instead, it is to maneuver them into being one-person decision problems for which an adequate theory exists (Keynes would be nodding his head at this point). Reasonable assumptions are made about the enemy's strategy, the sensitivity of outcomes to one's own decisions is determined for the case where the enemy's strategy is known, and then possibly the enemy's strategy is adjusted. There are dangers in this approach (try it on the D-Day game in Section 4.2), but there is sometimes no practical alternative.

4.1. The Prisoner's Dilemma

In a mathematical game all possible actions and all possible payoffs are known for each player. The Prisoner's Dilemma shown in Figure 3 is a famous example.

	C	D
C	(5,5)	(0,6)
D	(6,0)	(1,1)

Fig. 3. The Prisoner's Dilemma.

In that figure, players 1 and 2 choose the row or column, respectively, secretly, and independently of each other. The payoff is shown as a 2-vector, with the ith component being for the ith player. The Prisoner's Dilemma is saved from being a TPZS game by the fact that the sum of the payoffs is not constant, ranging from 2 to 10 in Figure 3.

The Prisoner's Dilemma exhibits the feature that being rational leads to an unattractive outcome. Each player can say to himself 'No matter what the other player chooses, I am better off choosing D (for 'Do not cooperate'), rather than C (for 'Cooperate').' That statement is easily verified, and it makes it very difficult to recommend choosing C unless there is some mechanism for enforcing agreements. The difficulty is that the (D,D) choice pair results in a payoff of 1 for each player, whereas the (C,C) pair results in the clearly superior payoff of 5 each. What should a theory recommend? There does not seem to be an answer. Books have been written on the Prisoner's Dilemma [Rapoport & Charmak, 1965], and game theorists have invented several notions of what *solution* should mean for such games, but none of these notions has taken on the stature of a widely accepted theory of decision-making.

The nuclear stalemate that existed for decades between the USA and the USSR has been described as a Prisoner's Dilemma where each side repeatedly chose C, so perhaps it is just as well that rationality occasionally fails. The whole idea of basing defense on retaliation is fraught with paradoxes. What is the point of retaliation if one has already lost everything? There is none, and yet deterrence relies on convincing the enemy that retaliation is sure even when seemingly irrational. In such circumstances it would be truly heroic for an analyst to announce confidently that an incremental unit of retaliation capability is *needed* or not, and yet judgments about exactly such questions must perforce be made. It is in such situations that the normative weakness of Game Theory is most strongly felt.

4.2. Two-person-zero-sum (TPZS) games

These are games with exactly two players whose interests are completely opposed, and for whom cooperation is therefore pointless. This is the part of Game Theory for which a widely accepted theory of decision-making has been worked out. We begin with an example: the D-Day game.

The Allies had to decide the place at which to invade France in 1944, while at the same time the Germans had to decide where to concentrate their defenses. The actual landing was in Normandy, but Calais was another possibility. In fact, Calais was arguably a better place to land for logistic reasons, being closer to

A. Washburn

Germany

		Calais	Normandy	Both
Allies	Calais	.7	1	.9
	Normandy	1	.4	.8

Fig. 4. The D-Day game.

Britain. Let us say that the Allies could land at either Calais or Normandy, and that the Germans had three choices about how to defend: (1) concentrate on Calais, (2) concentrate on Normandy, or (3) attempt to defend both places. There are thus $2 \times 3 = 6$ pairs of choices to be considered. For each of these pairs, the TPZS theory requires an assessment of the utility of the outcome to one of the players, the understanding being that the utility to the other player is exactly opposite. Now, the Allies' hopes were to establish a beachhead that would eventually grow to include some good port facilities. That was what actually happened, but it was by no means certain. The possibility that must have haunted Eisenhower, who was in practice the man who had to decide where and when the landing would take place, was that the still formidable German Army would quickly and completely wipe out the beachhead, with attendant large losses of men, materiel, and time. In other words, it is not much of an abstraction to argue that there were really only two possible outcomes: either the beachhead would survive its perilous infancy and subsequently expand into the sought after Second Front, or else it would be quickly and effectively wiped out. Since there are only two possibilities, the probability of one of them can serve as the utility or 'payoff' in the game. We will take the probability of a successful landing to be the payoff, in which case the Allies are maximizing and the Germans are minimizing. The probabilities shown in Figure 4 are hypothetical, but characteristic of the time. Note that Calais is a better place to land ($0.7 > 0.4$), and that the German 'defend both' option is not very effective (Allied control of the air made it difficult to move reserves around).

Every finite TPZS game can in principle be reduced to a payoff matrix like the one shown in Figure 4, although it will often be necessary to have a larger number of rows or columns to reflect a greater richness of tactical choice. The question is, 'Given that both sides know the entries in the payoff matrix, how should each side perform?' The answer depends on what intelligence each side has about the other's decision process, with three cases being distinguishable:

(1) The row player makes his choice in full knowledge of the column player's choice.

(2) The column player makes his choice in full knowledge of the row player's choice.

(3) Each player must choose in ignorance of the other player's choice.

Case 1 is the minimax case: the column player should choose the column for which the *largest* payoff in the column is as *small* as possible. In the D-Day game, the Germans should choose column 3, expecting the Allies to land in Calais with a payoff of 0.9. The Allies' strategy should be 'land in Normandy if they defend Calais, otherwise land in Calais'.

Case 2 is the maximin case: the row player should choose the row for which the *smallest* payoff in the row is as *large* as possible. In the D-Day game the Allies should land in Calais, expecting the payoff to be 0.7 (note that the payoff will be at least 0.7, no matter what the Germans do, so any surprise will be pleasant).

Neither case 1 nor case 2 is a good approximation to the actual situation in WWII. Both sides went to considerable trouble to conceal their true intentions by providing misleading intelligence to the other side. The net result of all these machinations was roughly case 3. At the time of invasion, the Germans were uncertain about where the Allies intended to land, and likewise the Allies were uncertain about what the German reaction would be when the shelling of the Normandy beaches began. Would German reserves be committed to Normandy, or, as actually happened, would Hitler keep them in reserve in the belief that the Normandy show was just a bluff? Thus case 3 is a better approximation of the actual situation than either case 1 or case 2.

Case 3 would seem to be troubled by the 'if he thinks that I think that he thinks. . .' difficulty, since guessing the opponent's choice seems central to making up one's own mind. In 1928 John Von Neumann proved a crucial theorem that satisfactorily deals with this apparently endless recursion. It turns out that the trick is not to find some clever way of predicting the opponent's behavior, but rather to behave in an unpredictable manner oneself. This is easily illustrated in the D-Day game. Given the assumptions made above there is practically no way to resist the following conclusion: in case 3 the Allies should choose an alternative randomly, with the probabilities for rows 1 and 2 being 2/3 and 1/3, respectively. To convince yourself of this, first note that the probability of success will be at least 0.8 under this randomization scheme, since $(2/3)(0.7) + (1/3)(1)$ $= 0.8$, $(2/3)(1) + (1.3)(0.4) = 0.8$, and $(2/3)(0.9) + (1.3)(0.8) > 0.8$. Even if the scheme were announced to the other side, the randomization would enforce a success probability of at least 0.8. Also note that the 0.8 success probability is not qualitatively different from the entries in the original payoff matrix, all of which are themselves success probabilities. The expectation operation does not change the meaning of the operand or imply the need for repeated trials. 'But why' you may ask, 'should the Allies be satisfied with 0.8, when half the numbers in the payoff matrix are larger than that?' The answer is that the Germans, by defending Calais with probability 2/3 and Normandy with probability 1/3 (they should never choose column 3) can ensure that the payoff will not exceed 0.8. Thus the two sides can guarantee the same success probability, even though their viewpoints are opposite. The number 0.8 is called the 'value of the game', and the whole situation can be summarized by saying that 'Provided both sides play rationally, the landing will succeed with probability 0.8.'

The solvability of the D-Day game in the sense described above is not a fluke. Von Neumann's theorem states that every finite matrix game has a solution in the same sense; that is, there always exists some number v such that each side can guarantee v regardless of the other side's behavior by using an appropriate randomization. Linear programming can be used to compute game solutions, so games where the numbers of rows and columns are on the order of 1000 are now solvable. Owen [1982] gives a good account of the relation between TPZS games and linear programming.

The fact that randomization seems to be required in order to describe rationality in competitive games is felt by some to be disappointing. Aside from the usual problems of interpreting expected values, the whole idea of Eisenhower deciding where the landing will take place by rolling a die is sort of repellent. In the actual event, most people prefer to wrestle with the 'if he thinks that I think that he thinks...' chain, rather than shortcut it by making the appropriate probabilistic choice. Hofstadter [1982] gives an entertaining account of his own personal disappointment upon discovering that von Neumann's result applied to a game he was interested in. But the introduction of random behavior is actually natural. Military thought has always emphasized the value of surprise, and abandoning control to a carefully chosen randomization device is simply a precise way of being unpredictable. If there is going to be a useful theory of decision-making for situations where unpredictability is important, it is almost inevitable that it must incorporate randomization.

Application of the TPZS theory requires a situation where cooperation is impossible; there must be exactly two players, and their interests must be completely opposed. This essentially restricts applications to certain kinds of warfare, sports and parlour games. Only the former concerns us here. Typical applications in the USA (the Soviet Union has also applied the theory to military problems [Suzdal, 1978]) include:

• *Search games* where side 1 assigns targets to cells, hoping side 2 will not detect them. Side 2 distributes search assets over the cells, in the hope of detecting as many targets as possible. How should the two sides distribute their assets? For example, 'targets' might be submarines and 'cells' might be a grid imposed on the ocean.

• *Strike games* involving aircraft on the two sides. Such a game might involve several consecutive days, with each side distributing aircraft over distinct roles (ground support, airbase defense, etc.) on each day. Aircraft that survive one day live to fight in the next. How should the aircraft be assigned to roles? An early reference is Berkovitz & Dresher [1959].

• *Guessing games* where each side names some physical quantity, with side 1 trying to guess the same thing (or nearly) as side 2 before taking some hostile action. For example, side 2 might be a submarine required to determine its own depth, and side 1 might have to determine the depth of a sensor that will hopefully locate the submarine. Or side 1 might be trying to guess the frequency being used by side 2 for communications in order to jam it.

• *Blotto games* are similar to search games except that assets assigned to each cell fight some kind of local battle. For example, 'targets' might be ICBM silos with side 1 defending them by allocating ABM's and side 2 attacking them by allocating nuclear weapons. The assignments determine the probability that each target survives, and the objective function is the sum of the survival probabilities.

• *Games of Pursuit and Evasion* are games where one vehicle (often an airplane or a missile) attempts to overtake another. The applicable part of Game Theory is Differential Games [Isaacs, 1965].

• *Games of Timing* where each side must determine the time at which to take some crucial action, hopefully just before the opponent's choice. The classic example is a duel. Dresher [1961] gives a good summary. Inspection games [Kilgour, 1990] could also be put in this category.

The main purpose of solving games such as those sketched above is usually not to obtain and record the optimal strategies. With rare exceptions, the U.S. military does not record tactical doctrine as probability distributions over actions.[3] The focus is usually on the game value, and then primarily to see how it depends on hardware (what if side 1 had more tanks, etc.).

The second category above (strike games) is the only one that involves losses on both sides. Since a TPZS game can have only one payoff, the question arises as to how these losses should be aggregated into a single number. One approach is to reason that the only real function of tactical aircraft is to provide ground support, with operations such as attacking enemy airbases having the ultimate objective of reducing the ground support carried out by the enemy. The natural TPZS payoff is then the net difference in ground support sorties over the length of a campaign. In actuality both sides might prefer an outcome with no ground support on either side to an outcome where (say) 100 sorties on each side cancel each other, even though the net difference is the same in each case, but such features must be ignored if the game is to be zero sum.

It should be emphasized that formulation of military problems as TPZS games is not in practice a major analytical technique, particularly for large problems with lots of data. None of the models in the JCS catalog, for instance, is a TPZS game. There are several reasons:

• It is not always possible to come to grips with what a *strategy* is, let alone list all the possibilities. The D-Day example did not include the German strategy 'Wait 5 hours after the first troops hit the beach and then send 80% of the reinforcements to that place as soon as dark falls and then the remaining 20% after another 24 hours unless the landing has already been repulsed, in which case withdraw half of the 80% to await a second attempt', and obviously a lot of others. The number of feasible strategies can be extremely large.

• Even when only moderately large sets of strategies capture the essence of the situation, the payoff must be evaluated for all possible combinations. In many military problems finding the payoff for even *one* combination of strategies can be a significant problem.

• One must be prepared for the possibility that the optimal strategy involves randomization. There is a certain amount of intellectual resistance to this idea in spite of its logical necessity.

At one time large matrix games also posed significant computational problems,

---

[3] However, the military does occasionally employ explicit randomixation. A WWII example would be randomly zigzagging convoys attempting to spoil the aim of torpedo-firing submarines.

but this difficulty has faded with modern advances in linear programming. The main impediments to application are now the ones listed above.

To summarize this section and the previous one: Game Theory might seem to be the natural foundation for MOR, but in practice it is not. It is a technique that is applied occasionally, rather than regularly. The main difficulty is in the modeling of the way in which humans make or should make decisions. A natural reaction to this theoretical failure is to replace the abstract decision maker of Game Theory with an actual human. This is wargaming, the subject of the next section.

4.3. Wargaming

A wargame is a more or less abstract model of warfare that permits humans to play the role of combatants. There are many forms. Commercial wargames often take the form of a playing board representing part of the Earth on which pieces representing military units are moved around. Military wargames (and to an increasing extent commercial wargames as well) often rely on computers to enforce realism in unit movements, assess damage, and display whatever parts of the game's status that the rules permit each player to see. Some wargames incorporate nonplaying humans (referees) to help control the game's evolution, and some do not. Some are very simple. Flood [1952] had pairs of humans repeatedly play the Prisoner's Dilemma; for him the wargame was essentially Figure 3. Some wargames are very complex, requiring several days to play.

While wargames can take many forms, the presence of human decision makers is essential. Usually the human players have at least partially conflicting goals, although the term *wargame* is increasingly being used to refer to situations where the strategies of all but one side have been automated, so that the remaining players (or player) are a team with a single goal.

Most wargames are played for recreation; the community of hobby wargamers is large and growing. Several companies publish wargames commercially and there are even magazines (*Fire and Movement, Moves, Strategy and Tactics*) devoted to the activity. There has been considerable interplay between hobby and professional wargamers, even though the audiences are distinct. Perla [1990] describes some of the innovations that both groups have introduced.

Professional wargaming (wargaming carried out by or for the military, for the most part) has two major purposes. The paramount purpose is education. Wargame participants must make decisions under stress with incomplete or even false information, and must cope with the capricious effects of luck and enemy action. These characteristics of warfare are difficult to simulate in any way other than in a dynamic, competitive simulation that involves humans. The experience of participating in a realistic wargame is often very intense, so that lessons learned are long remembered. At the end of WWII, Adm. Nimitz stated that

> 'The war with Japan had been re-enacted in the game rooms [at the Naval War College] by so many people and in so many different ways that nothing that happened during the war was a surprise – absolutely nothing except the Kamikaze tactics towards the end of the war; we had not visualized these.'

All three U.S. services, but particularly the Naval War College, place heavy emphasis on wargaming as an educational device.

The teaching power of wargaming has its dark side. There is a natural human tendency to emphasize strengths in wargaming, rather than weaknesses, whereas a real enemy can be expected to seek out weaknesses. Also, the wargame paradigm is sufficiently powerful to suppress some of the dissent from the official position that might otherwise occur. Bracken [1976] states that the initial German invasion of Russia in 1941 was so successful because the defense-in-depth tactics that the Russians needed were not available, and that these tactics were not available because Stalin had decreed that the only tactic that could be practiced in wargames (both sides wargamed the invasion beforehand) was a defense of the border. Russia eventually perfected defense-in-depth tactics, but the initial cost in terms of captured divisions was terrible. Finally, wargames will inevitably miss certain aspects of reality, and to some extent will thereby teach that those aspects are not present. Most wargames in the United States are carried out with all communications in English. That may not actually be the case, witness the 1991 war in Kuwait.

Wargaming can be used for analysis as well as education. Given the capability to fight abstract wars, it is tempting to test the effect of different weapons or tactics on the outcome. The tendency to use wargaming in this manner has fluctuated in the past. Wargaming's utility as an analytical tool is not as obvious as in the case of its use in education, so the technique will probably continue to come in and out of favor. The major recommendation for using wargaming as an analytical tool is that it gets around most of the difficulties mentioned earlier in discussing Game Theory. Game Theory requires that payoffs be explicit. The need to initially assess the payoff for all possible ways in which a battle might evolve is often so daunting as to either inhibit the exercise or lead to oversimplification. In wargaming, on the other hand, one can argue that the payoffs come with the players, so that a brief statement about goals ('Take Stalingrad, but whatever you do don't lose the Third Panzer Division') will suffice. Abstract games are often unsolvable, whereas questions of solvability do not arise in wargaming because 'optimal' tactics are not sought. Wars are fought by humans. Therefore it makes sense to use human players in wargaming, whatever their weaknesses and motivations. If the results reflect those weaknesses and motivations, then that, the argument goes, is as it should be.

The counterarguments are of two kinds, the first kind having to do with player motivation. A wargame is only a more or less accurate abstraction of the real world. Players sometimes express a felt conflict between making decisions as they would be made in the real world and making decisions in order to do well in the wargaming abstraction; these decisions may differ on account of readily perceived modeling deficiencies. How should those players be advised? The answer is not obvious, and the resulting murkiness does not augur well for making decisions about tactics or equipment based on the results of play. Player attitudes towards risk are particularly worrisome; there is a difference between having a blip labeled 'cv' disappear from a computer screen and having an actual aircraft carrier sunk.

In games where there are possibilities for coalition formation or cooperation, it is questionable whether the feelings of guilt that would accompany certain actions in the real world can be reproduced in an artificial situation. It is one thing to choose 'D' in the Prisoner's Dilemma played as a game ('game' in the sense of something trivial), and something else entirely to be selfish or shortsighted in the real world.

Even putting motivational questions aside, there are technical objections to using wargaming as a research technique. The idea that it is best to capture decision-making that is typical, rather than optimal, is particularly questionable in research games that represent an unfamiliar reality to the players. There is a natural tendency to overstate the effectiveness of new weapons or tactics when played against an inexpert enemy who has yet to develop countermeasures. The enemy might very well develop some tactical countermeasures in the process of repeatedly playing the wargame, but wargaming is a sufficiently time-consuming and expensive activity that repeated play of the same game by the same players is rare. To some extent this lack of repetition is deliberate, since research wargamers often try to avoid player learning because they fear that the learning will be about the wargame's artificialities. As a result questions of statistical validity are seldom dealt with. Besides, deliberately seeking enemy play that is typical, rather than optimal, violates a well-known military maxim by designing to the enemy's intentions instead of the enemy's capabilities. Typical play often differs substantially from optimal play in TPZS games for which the solution is known [Kaufman & Lamb, 1967]. Thomas & Deemer [1957] downplay the usefulness of wargaming as a tool for solving TPZS games, while at the same time admitting its usefulness for getting the 'feel' of a competitive situation. Berkovitz & Dresher [1959] state bluntly that 'In our opinion ... [wargaming] is not a helpful device for solving a game or getting significant information about the solution.'

The counter-counterargument, of course, is that, whatever the objections to it, research wargaming is usually the only feasible technique for taking a genuinely competitive look at genuinely competitive situations. We see through a glass darkly. Theoretical and experimental approaches each provide insights into combat, but a great deal of uncertainty must remain.

5. Operations research in combat

This section is a condensation of a similar chapter by Clayton Thomas in *Military Modeling* [Hughes, 1984].

Combat OR was first undertaken systematically in Britain and the U.S.A. in WWII. It achieved some important successes, particularly in situations where advanced sensors (radar, sonar) and weapon systems were involved. Combat OR is an essentially different activity than peacetime OR. It emphasizes tactical rather than strategic decision-making. Plenty of data are collected in combat, but the 'experiments' are unplanned and the trick is to find data that are meaningful.

The scientific outlook of WWII operations research pioneers was central to their success. Their primary emphasis was on devising measures of effectiveness and collecting data to find out how to improve operations. Statistical analysis, standard probability models, basic kinematic relationships, etc., were all important. Very few of the successes required anything beyond the above, though some advanced models were directly useful and others stimulated insights or postwar developments.

When one looks at reports of the combat operations research performed in WWII, Korea, Vietnam and Kuwait – four very different conflict situations – one is struck by how much they had in common. Each had its concern with logistics, radar performance, bombing accuracy, interdiction effectiveness, air-to-air exchange ratios, improvements in tactics, and responses to enemy innovations. Though the weapons differed, the reports were remarkably similar in their tabulations, plots, photographs of damaged targets, etc.

It is also very striking to note how such combat reports differ from the peacetime analyses performed in support of the planning, programming, and budgeting system. Outputs of combat analysis reports often look like inputs to some of the large simulations conducted in peacetime. Much that is parametrically varied in peacetime studies is known in war, and much that is the subject of anxious measurement in combat operations research is unconcernedly calculated in peacetime simulations.

Such differences were seen with special clarity by some of the talented pioneers. Thus, writing of his experiences as chief of British scientific intelligence in WWII, Jones [1978] observed:

> 'Despite any unpopularity, I survived because war is different from peace. In the latter fallacies can be covered up more or less indefinitely and criticism suppressed, but with the swift action of war the truth comes fairly quickly to light – as Churchill said, "In war you don't have to be polite, you just have to be right!"'

The swift action of war gives urgent emphasis to the 'here and now', which has many implications for combat operations research. For one thing, there is more emphasis on what can be done with the weapons in hand. One looks at the allocation of those weapons and the tactics of employment with the greatest of care. Maintenance and reliability are special concerns. Another consequence, as Koopman [in Koopman et al., 1978] recalled of WWII:

> 'Now, it's true that during the war, costs mean very little. The simple reason is that we couldn't buy something else. It simply took too long to develop a whole new system, so we had to use what we had.'

Koopman went on to point out that as costs became more important after the war, the term 'cost-effectiveness' came in, economists became more important, and mathematical physicists less so.

Another consequence of being in a war is to simplify and clarify much that had been unknown or ambiguous. Hitch [1955] points out how much more difficult it is to do a systems analysis of future systems, where no one scenario dominates, than it was to do operations research studies of weapons in WWII, where one knew the enemy and much about his equipment. Consider Pearl Harbor: a scenario that might have seemed unlikely a day or two earlier, suddenly, on December 7, 1941, became very compelling in the intensity of the interest it evoked.

This kind of learning applies not only to high-level scenarios but also to tactical details. H. Kahn [in MITRE, 1982] remarked:

> 'At one time I had been in the air defense business about 20 years. Many people here have been in it just as long. Not one of us thought a pilot could see a missile with his eyeballs. But one of the main defenses of our planes over Hanoi was a pilot seeing a Mach 2 missile coming at him and evading it. That was a totally unexpected tactic.'

The possibility of such revelations confers on war a reality that is unattainable by studies of possible wars. Much of the spirit of Blackett [1962] is conveyed by such words as 'actual', 'real', and 'fact'. Even the ability to know someday a yet unknown fact can contribute to this spirit. For example, in a wartime discussion of the effectiveness of bombing German cities, Blackett looked forward to the time after the war when certain facts would become known. In sharp contrast is our inability ever to know real facts about some of the futures postulated in peacetime.

With this emphasis on the actual and factual, it is not surprising that the operations research pioneers hoped that their profession would be 'commonsensical' and its practitioners 'hardheaded'. Solandt [1955] while recalling some of his wartime experiences, wrote:

> 'I for one hope that we shall never come to the day when a knowledge of the latest mathematical gadgets for war games, of communications theory, and so on becomes the badge of office of the operations research worker. I think the operations research worker should be known as a hardheaded experimental scientist, with a very broad vision, who trusts only what he can measure... If everyone sticks to these high ideals, I think ultimately operations research may come to justify what seems to me the most flattering, but, unfortunately, unreal definition of it; that is, that operations research is the systematic application of common sense.'

Dorfman [1951] wrote of the need for an analyst to be a 'a hardheaded staff member', though other staff members may see the analyst as 'a "long-hair" and a theoretician'. Dorfman's point was that while everyone acts on 'theory', the analyst must be aware of the theories on which he acts and test them against experience in a continual reexamination.

All of this serious emphasis on reality and hardheadedness reflects the serious nature of war itself. While the onset of war may strip away many spurious scenarios and reveal the identity of the enemy, that enemy will devote great energy to conceal his movements or to actively seek to mislead us. He is out to win, as are we. Thus, any serious war constitutes a great challenge, and a review of the setting as characterized above in this section shows a particular challenge to the ideal hardheaded scientist. WWII was a serious war in that sense, and there was a remarkable outpouring of scientific and analytical talent that led to well-known operations research successes. Despite having a much more limited scope, subsequent conflicts also elicited combat operations research in the mold of WWII. Here two observations may be made. The first is to note the greater menu of techniques available in later conflicts. Some technique developments, in fact, have been inspired by combat operations research problems but completed or popularized after conflict was over. Thus, planning problems of WWII led G. Dantzig to work on the simplex algorithm, and interdiction problems of Korea led L. Ford and D. Fulkerson to work on network flow algorithms.

The other observation is that what has been learned in an earlier conflict has sometimes not been known by later practitioners. Whitmore [1953] called attention to naval studies in WWI where Thomas Edison introduced methods much like those that were 'introduced' again in WWII. Later, Whitmore [1961] pointed out that even some of the better known results of WWII were not generally known to operations research workers in Korea and themselves had to be rediscovered. Perhaps such forgetting is a kind of retroactive inhibition that occurs in peace, making it necessary to rediscover many combat operations research 'truths' in the stark reality of war.

5.1. Methods of combat operations research

The greatest development of the methods of combat operations research came in the wartime setting of WWII. At the time there was no 'modeling community' in the modern sense, and, at the beginning of the war, very little even of an 'operations research community'.

As Morse recalled [in Koopman et al., 1978]:

> '... we were starting from scratch. We had to bring in and train people from all sorts of different backgrounds. We didn't have a supply of ... Ph.D.'s in operations research to pick up and try to retrain. We had to retrain physicists and mathematicians, biologists and so on... We had practically no background ... we had to build up our theory...'

One useful characterization of the combat operations research approach that eventually evolved is that of Dorfman [1951]. For expository purposes, he divides the approach to a problem into five stages:

> PERCEPTION
> FORMULATION
> OBSERVATION
> ANALYSIS
> PRESENTATION

These five stages will be used to organize the discussion in the remainder of this section. It should be emphasized, however, that what is convenient for exposition is not intended to suggest a simple step-by-step approach as normal procedure. Typically, there will be iteration of the steps and feedback from one step to another. One may start, for example, with crude *observations* which lead to the *perception* of a problem. This *perception* may lead to a formulation that involves more refined *observations* as a key step. Or, to go to the other end, when the *presentation* stage leads to the acceptance and implementation of a new procedure, there should be *observation* and *analysis* to see if it is working as well as expected. Keeping the importance of iteration in mind, it is now useful to say a little more about each of the five stages.

The whole process begins with the *perception* that a problem exists, and that there are alternatives for solution. This is not a trivial step, particularly in military organizations where for good reasons the ethic is to support 'the system', rather than to question it. The habitual skepticism of scientists may prove valuable in such circumstances. Newman [1956] states that

> 'What scientists brought to operational problems – apart from specialized knowl-
> edge – was the scientific outlook. This in fact was their major contribution. They
> tended to think anew, to suspect preconceptions, to act only on evidence.'

Sometimes, of course, the general nature of a problem (e.g., low bombing accuracy in the 8th Air Force in the early days of WWII) may be painfully evident.

The *formulation* stage is extremely important in that this is where measurement and hypotheses (including models) enter. Deciding what to use for a measure of effectiveness (MOE) is critical, as has been emphasized earlier. Whitmore [1961] gives an example that illustrates the importance of setting the right goals:

> '... there is still a place for the individual piece of deep insight, which sounds
> deceptively simple after it is first announced, but which transforms an entire
> analytical effort. One that has always stuck in my memory is Glen Camp's remark
> that the Navy's problem in protecting merchant shipping was not undersea warfare,
> but oversea transport. This did not diminish the strong emphasis on antisubmarine
> measures, but did effectively set them in a wider context. It suggested studies of
> methods of decreasing turnaround time in ports, placing of especially valuable
> cargoes in the least vulnerable positions in a convoy, analysis of unorthodox
> high-speed merchant ships, and the like.'

One danger should be remarked. Overt use of an MOE in combat by management may lead to unfortunate results. One example comes from the 8th Air Force bombing problem. A very useful MOE for analytical purposes was the percent of bombs dropped which fell within 1000 feet of an assigned 'point of impact'. This MOE was used in judging the efficacy of changes in tactics, and eventually it was also used to rate the performance of bomb groups. When group commanders learned that they were being scored on this basis, they sometimes, as Dorfman [1951] recalls, 'declined to release their bombs at assigned targets when visibility was only middling good'.

Once an MOE is formulated one may proceed to frame an hypothesis. A first step is to list, *a priori*, the main factors on which the MOE might depend. These factors may be divided into four sets according to 'control'. Those factors under friendly control for instance, make up the first set. These are the factors we can do something about. It is also important, however, to consider as a second set those factors under enemy control. Here the spirit, if not the techniques, of game theory may be glimpsed in the wings. Those factors not under either friendly or enemy control, which are 'uncontrollable but observable', Dorfman puts in a third set. One might say that these factors are under the control of 'nature'. In a fourth set are 'chance' factors that account for the variation in results even when all the other factors are held constant.

An hypothesis then makes a testable assertion about the role of the factors. It is here that models enter. As Dorfman [1951] puts it:

> 'The hypothesis takes the form, quite frequently, of a simplified mathematical model in which the measure of effectiveness is expressed as a function of the major influencing factors.'

When such a hypothesis is tested, there are various possible analytical results. The postulated function may be good enough for practical purposes. If so, one may estimate the numerical value of important operational parameters. It may even turn out that some of the factors included are not very important, so that one can find a simpler model. On the other hand, it may turn out that additional explanatory factors are needed. What is important in the formulation stage is the recognition that a useful hypothesis must lend itself to analysis.

The *observation* stage is of such importance that the entirety of the next part of this section is devoted to combat data. It must suffice here to note its criticality. Experience has shown that human observations and recollections must be very carefully checked and often supplemented. Observation is typically onerous, often dangerous, and as Dorfman notes, takes the analyst away from his desk, but it is indispensable.

The *analysis* stage, strictly speaking, tests hypotheses against the observed data, and if the fit is good, estimates the value of operational parameters. In actual fact it is often difficult to so confine analysis. If often leads to reformulation of hypotheses or modification of models, and may point the way to other data requirements.

The *presentation* stage is the destination that the operations research worker must keep in mind throughout. The presentation is not a report to be neatly filed but rather a recommendation for action. The recommendation may go to a high-level decision maker, but sometimes it is most effective when it is communicated to operators directly (as, e.g., when it concerns tactics under their control). Morse [in Koopman et al., 1978] points out that the recommended 'action' may very well be to retain present procedures unchanged.

In reflecting on all of the five stages discussed above, it is important to recall that their successful accomplishment in wartime depended, to a considerable extent, on the working mode of the operations research analysts. Morse [in Koopman et al., 1978] recalls:

> 'We did live with our problems and with our clients in a way that I don't think happens often nowadays. We worked pretty much seven days a week, 52 weeks a year. It wasn't a matter of a three-week or a three-month study and leaving a report which gets filed. We had to live with our successes as well as our failures.'

5.2. Combat data

It is not easy to get good data in war. We often lack data about our own operations because our own troops are typically too busy or preoccupied with combat to be concerned with data recording. To an even greater extent, we may lack good data about enemy operations because an enemy takes special precautions to conceal his movements and may actively seek to mislead us.

Analysts in WWII soon learned to be skeptical of data routinely collected. A typical experience is illustrated by Blackett [1962]. It was noted during WWII that coastal anti-aircraft batteries in Britain were apparently shooting down twice as many night bombers per shell fired as inland batteries. All kinds of explanations were suggested until:

> '... suddenly the true explanation flashed into mind. Over the land a battery, say, in the Birmingham area, which claimed an enemy aircraft destroyed, would have this claim checked by the search for and identification of the crashed machine. If no machine were found, the claim was disallowed. But, in general, no such check could be made of the claims of the coastal batteries, since an aircraft coming down at sea would not be traceable. The explanation of the apparent better shooting of the coastal batteries turned out to be due ... to an overestimate ... of their claims ... by a factor of about two.'

Jones [1978] gives a similar example where RAF fighter pilots claimed 186 killed but German records inspected after the war showed that the German losses were 62 aircraft. Jones observed that 'it was quite unreasonable to expect any pilot who thought that he had destroyed an enemy aircraft to follow it down... and watch it crash...' Hence overclaiming was inevitable.

Sometimes the realization of the low quality of certain kinds of data came only when an analyst got out into the field. Jones [1978] recalls an example where two operational research workers had the problem of deducing the characteristics of German magnetic mines laid at sea, 'especially the sensitivity and polarity of the firing mechanism'. The data from which the characteristics were to be deduced were the reports of our minesweepers as they exploded the mines, with positions of the explosions being reported as ranges and bearing from the minesweepers. One of the operational research workers took a few trips on a minesweeper to sample the data for himself and immediately found that 'the reports from the minesweeping crews were wildly inaccurate as regards both range and bearing, and the only item of data on which one could rely was whether the mine had exploded to port or starboard.' Interpreting the data with this limitation in mind, he did solve the problem, whereas another researcher stuck to his desk and never reached an answer.

Once it was realized that supplementary sources of data were needed, much more use of photography was made. Cameras were eventually installed in both fighters and bombers. H. Miser [in Koopman et al., 1978] recalled that in the 8th Air Force in Britain in WWII:

> '... the analysts discovered that ... there was a contingent of public relations people, and a few airplanes were carrying cameras for the purpose of taking

pictures to be sent back to the New York Times and other ... publications. These
were magnificent cameras; they took contact prints about 12 inches square ... the
analysts ... with a little bit of practice, discovered that you could do an incredible
amount of analysis from these photographs... So the next job was to see if you
could get the General ... to put cameras like that in at least one airplane in every
formation. Then you had to persuade the military that the analyst needed a copy
of those photographs as much as the New York Times. Well, that took a bit of
doing, but they got it done...'

Such data sources were much used in WWII, and retained in later conflicts.
During the Korean conflict the analysis of gun camera film was accompanied
by the analysis of supplemental combat information reports designed to give
information that could not be obtained from film. In instituting such reporting
systems, it is highly desirable for an analyst to explain in person why the data are
important and how they should be obtained.

By the time of Vietnam, there were many reporting systems, some in the form
of 'all-purpose' computerized data banks. These were not as useful as had been
hoped. In reporting on an Army Operations Research Symposium of 1969, which
was entirely devoted to problems of data collection, Greene [1969] commenced:

'"Data banks" are difficult to use for operations research, etc., because they are
not designed with specific problems or analyses in mind. We were admonished to
first plan an analysis, decide what to do with data, and then plan and design the
data collection.'

The amount of data collected routinely in combat continues to increase, largely
due to the still-ongoing microelectronic revolution in data storage capacity. The
brief war in Kuwait generated an order of magnitude more data than the
considerably longer Vietnamese War. But combat continues to be an unplanned
experiment with many unknown factors, and in data analysis quantity does not
compensate for quality. The need for insight will not disappear.

5.3. Data and models in combat analysis – examples

Analysis is, of course, the pivotal step in the five-stage process of problem
perception–formulation–data collection–analysis–presentation. It is by analysis
that one decides whether to accept the hypothesis conjectured in the formulation
stage, and press on towards recommendations for presentation to decision makers,
or whether the hypothesis should be rejected or refined, more data collected, etc.
If the hypothesis involved an explicit model, then that model will come to the fore
during analysis. This section will give a few examples of simple models, and a few
examples where no explicit model seems to enter.

The examples come from WWII, Korea and Vietnam. The focus is on the more
'real-time' analysis which most deserves to be called wartime combat operations
research. The emphasis, that is, must be on wartime analysis that is done in time
to have impact while the war is still going on.

Actually, considering the very different geographic extent of WWII, Korea and
Vietnam (and their different settings in time), combat analysis in the three conflicts

had a remarkably similar character. Silber [1953], for example, in a Korean study
(for the 5th Air Force of the United States Air Force) that computed force
requirements where bomber aircraft are to attack targets of different sizes, noted:

> '... that our assumptions and methods are similar to those used by many of
> the research organizations working on statistical and probability problems for the
> Services during World War II.'

An interesting parallel between WWII and Vietnam is shown by two following
observations. Summing up experience in Air Force analysis in WWII, Leach [1945]
wrote:

> 'The staple grist in all air forces was bombing accuracy, bomb selection and fuzing,
> gunnery and radar.'

In Vietnam, as combat began to heat up in 1962, analysts picked up very much
the same kind of problem. In a covering letter to an 'after action' report of analysis
[Starkey, 1962], it was noted that operations analysts and intelligence analysts:

> '... assumed the responsibility for weapon selection and physical vulnerability, and
> by recommending the introduction of different air ordnance into South Vietnam
> and matching the ordnance to the various target situations, increased the effec-
> tiveness of both VNAF and USAF air operations by some factor conservatively
> exceeding two.'

As noted earlier, WWII analysts introduced as an MOE the percent of bombs
falling within 1000 feet of a designated impact point, and they derived numerical
values of the MOE by analyzing photographs taken by bomb cameras. This simple
idea sometimes led to great improvements. Leach [1945] recalls a case where the
bombing data by themselves were conclusive:

> Some group commanders directed each bombardier to sight independently for
> range, i.e., along track (there could be only one sighting for deflection, i.e.,
> across track, since the bombers had to maintain formation and thus keep in
> a predetermined position with reference to the lead ship). Others ordered all
> bombardiers to drop when they saw the bombs leave the lead ship. Still others
> dropped on the squadron leaders. There were strong *a priori* arguments vigorously
> pressed for the validity of each of the three techniques. A comparison was now
> possible. Here is the result:

Technique of sighting	Bombs within 100 ft. of aiming point
On group leader	24.0%
On squadron leader	11.8%
Independent sighting for range	8.3%

That ended the argument! Sighting on the group leader became standard operating procedure.

In the previous example one had what was essentially an unplanned experiment.
Three different procedures were in use, and the data, once available, led directly
to a recommendation to select one of the three without further experimentation

or modeling (though data were used continuously, of course, to monitor accuracy and to provide the basis of other improvements). Leach [1945] gives a slightly more complicated example where data are again critical but no mathematical model was involved. In this example, however, the data led to rejection of an initial hypothesis and the need for a revised hypothesis before a recommendation was made:

'When the Eighth Air Force was small, it was confidently predicted that the larger formations would saturate enemy defenses and that the accuracy of bombing would rise sharply. The first groups, it was argued, would absorb the fighter attack and the fresh vigor of the flak; then later groups would have a field day. But when five or more groups were sent over the same target, bombing was worse than before! An OAS analysis of these strikes with references to the order in which each group went over the target told the story:

Order over target	Bombs within 1000 ft. of aiming point
1st	23.4%
2nd	16.3%
3rd	9.9%
4th	7.8%
5th and over	4.2%

The data show a difference in effectiveness between the first and last group of a factor exceeding five. Additional thought led to an explanation that appealed to two factors expressed by Leach as: (1) congestion of air traffic over the target and consequent interference with bombing runs; and (2) obscuration of the target by bomb falls from preceding groups.

Leach reports no model development but observes that:

'Conferences between OAS and command personnel brought a decision to space out combat wings over the target at intervals of 1 to 5 minutes. The results were shown in the following table, the payoff appearing in the last column:

Order over target	Bombs within 1000 ft. of aiming point		
	before change	after change	improvement
1st	23.4%	26.5%	13%
2nd	16.3%	19.8%	21%
3rd	9.9%	22.2%	124%
4th	7.8%	20.1%	158%
5th and over	4.2%	19.8%	370%

The 13% improvement for the first group was attributed to a general increase in effectiveness of bombing throughout the command, but the bulk of the improvement shown by the later groups seemed to be attributable to the new tactics.

It would be misleading to leave the impression that all improvements in bombing accuracy came with such seeming ease. The account of Brothers [1954] indicates that many factors had to be considered and intricate calculations were

involved. The effect of the analysis, which represented the work of many operations research scientists, was to increase the percent of bombs within 1000 feet
of the aiming point from about 15 in 1942 to about 60 in 1944. The point of the
examples above is to show that data, which are essential for analysis and the scientific use of models, may in themselves point the way to dramatic improvements in
effectiveness.

Because of the suggestive power of good data, compilations tend to be published
periodically during wartime by a variety of offices. This was true in both Korea
and Vietnam, although the war in Kuwait was too fast-moving to permit any
regular publication. The use of data and statistical analysis was very widespread
in the analysis of the Vietnam conflict, and it is interesting to note two extreme
examples, one from the Office of the Secretary of Defense and the other from the
field.

During the 1960s, systems analysis became an essential tool of the new planning,
programming, and budgeting system. It was institutionalized in the Office of the
Assistant Secretary of Defense (Systems Analysis), and its products were actively
used by the Secretary of Defense as a basis for many decisions. As the Secretary
became intimately involved in the conduct of the war in Southeast Asia, which saw
much more centralized direction from Washington than previous conflicts, it was
natural that the Systems Analysis office would play an important role.

One of the products of the office was a monthly publication of an analysis report
(for several years including the late 1960s and early 1970s [ODASD, 1969]). The
character of the analysis was quite similar to that of the WWII bombing problems
discussed earlier. The acquisition of data and its first-order analysis constituted
most of the quantitative analysis, with little elaborate modeling. Table 3 indicates
the kind of problem addressed, as illustrated by a sampling of 13 of the SEA
analysis reports.

The entries in Table 3 indicate some of the many concerns that lay outside
the scope of traditional military operations. There was deep concern with the
establishment of a viable government in South Vietnam, and such threats as
terrorism and economic instability were more worrisome than large concentrations
of opposing troops. Rather than fighting at a well-delineated front against masses
of enemy soldiers, the United States was fighting many local actions and often
saw the most challenging battle as that for the hearts and minds of Vietnamese
villagers.

For this kind of struggle there existed fewer combat models. A typical article in
the SEA analysis reports made its case with presentation of data – indicators and
MOEs – intended to show trends over time, comparisons of different troops, etc.
Most of this kind of analysis involved neither sophisticated statistics nor elaborate
model construction. There was, however, some regression analysis, both simple
and complicated in terms of the number of variables involved. An interesting
example is a model devised by Safeer of the Weapons Systems Evaluation Group
[TIA, 1968] to predict enemy-initiated attacks in South Vietnam. It represented
the number of such attacks in a given month as a linear function of two variables
– the total number of trucks sighted in Laos one and two months earlier and the

Table 3
Topics from Southeast Asia analysis report

Title or subject	April 1968	July 1968	October 1968	March 1969	April 1969	May 1969	July 1969	October 1969	January 1970	March 1970	Jun/Jul 1970	Sep/Oct 1970	Jan/Feb 1970
Deployments	×		×										
Friendly forces	×	×	×	×	×	×	×						
Revolutionary development	×												
Air operations	×	×	×	×		×	×				×		
Viet Cong/NV Army		×	×										
Pacification		×				×				×		×	
Economics		×							×				
Casualties				×	×	×	×	×		×	×		
Redevelopments							×	×	×				
Anti-infrastructure campaign								×					
Repub. VN Air Force								×	×	×			
Indicators of enemy activity									×				
Allied operations									×				
NVA/VC prisoners of war										×			
Hamlet evaluation system											×		×
Terrorism in SVN											×	×	
Phoenix												×	
The war in Cambodia													×
What the Viet peasant thinks													×
Standoff attacks													×
The herbicide issue													×

total number of trucks sighted in a particular area of North Vietnam two and three months earlier.

At the other extreme, as opposed to the centralized use of analysis in Washington, there was also some use of combat analysis in the field during the Vietnam conflict. Interesting examples are given by Ewell & Hunt [1974] of analyses conducted during 1968, 1969 and 1970 to improve operations of the 9th Infantry Division and II Field Force. Some indication of the diversity of applications is given by their chapter headings: unit management and personnel actions, Army aviation assets, battlefield analysis, intelligence, tactical refinements, pacification, etc. The subtitle of this publication is 'The Use of Analysis to Reinforce Military Judgment', and this indicates the character of the applications. The authors observe:

'Dr. Enthoven has stated in *How Much is Enough?* that operations research was used very little in Vietnam. He is probably correct if he was referring to systems analysis and cost-effectiveness... The Vietnamese war was so complex, so varied, and so changeable that these high-level approaches tended to be very difficult to use with any confidence. However, simple straightforward operations analysis, while not easy to use, ... was used extensively.'

'Straightforward operations analysis', as reported by Ewell and Hunt, made extensive use of data collection and presentation to indicate to commanders how operations were going. As the U.S.A. introduced improved tactics, the enemy reacted quickly so that after a few months further improvements were needed to retain the initiative. Computers were useful, but a 'general problem was the rigidity of computer data bases' that tended to become outdated.

The role of probability is broader than the foregoing references to statistics and regression may suggest. In this connection it is useful to apply what Koopman [1980] said of the role of probability in the theory of search, *mutatis mutandis*, to combat operations research generally:

'Every operation involved in search is beset with uncertainties; it can be understood quantitatively only in terms of the concepts and laws of the scientific theory of probability. This may now be regarded as a truism, but it seems to have taken the developments in operational research of World War II to drive home its practical implications. The reason for the lateness in taking full advantage of this theory has undoubtedly been the simple nature of most of the earlier operations of search, the short ranges involved, and the power of the human eye at such ranges. These factors made a "deterministic" approximation satisfactory: "When a thing is there and I look at it without anything in front of it, I see it; otherwise I don't." Approximations of this sort are still useful, but they must be validated by more realistic analysis, based on probability, among other things.'

For a variety of such reasons, therefore, many useful combat operations research models are largely applications of probability. These applications range over a wide spectrum from the simple to the extremely subtle. In his much quoted pioneering paper, Blackett [1962] spoke simply of 'a grasp of fluctuation phenomena (i.e., Poisson's Distribution)' as a requirement for an operational research practitioner. Similarly, Solandt [1955] recalled that:

'... we rarely used anything more elegant than some simple statistics and probability. I think our most spectacularly successful mathematical tool was the knowledge that in adding errors you do not add them arithmetically but add the squares and take the square root. This knowledge led to many important discoveries.'

On the other hand, Newman [1956] in characterizing the methods of early operations research workers observed:

'Their indispensable tool was the mathematics of probability and they made use of its subtlest theories and most powerful techniques.'

In some problems of wartime combat operations research one uses a model, or an *additional* model, because it supplements a previous approach. As often happens in mathematics or science, the availability of two or more ways of solving a problem greatly deepens our insight and adds to our confidence in the solution. As an illustration it is interesting to compare, in abbreviated versions, two approaches to the analysis of encounters between convoys of applied merchant vessels and packs of German submarines in World War II.

The first approach, reported by Morse & Kimball [1946], gave some interesting results that were derived by statistical analysis of data on encounters between convoys and submarines. Letting

M = the number of merchant vessels in a convoy,
K = the number of merchant vessels sunk,
C = the number of escort vessels protecting the convoy,
N = the number of submarines in a pack, and
L = the number of submarines sunk,

analysis of the data led to:

$$K = 5N/C$$

and

$$L = NC/100$$

as good approximations. From these expressions, one can derive the exchange ratio:

$$L/K = C^2/500.$$

Of even greater interest, however, was the observation that the equation for K is independent of M, so that the loss rate varies inversely with M. Contrary to a belief that the British Admiralty had held, it appeared that large convoys were safer than small convoys! Since operations analysis of the data had led to a result both unexpected and significant in its operational implications, it was natural to ask if the result could be corroborated by other approaches.

One such approach, reported by Blackett [1962], made use of a simple model. This model expressed the probability of sinking a merchant vessel in a convoy as a product of three probabilities:

$$\text{Pr (sinking)} = \underset{(a)}{\underset{\text{sighted)}}{\text{Pr (convoy}}} \times \underset{(b)}{\underset{\text{given sighting)}}{\text{Pr (penetration}}} \times \underset{(c)}{\underset{\text{penetration)}}{\text{Pr (sinking given}}}$$

Both theory and data suggested that the probability in (a) was independent of convoy size. It depended rather on the relationship of submarine search practices and convoy routes, speeds, etc. Simple models suggested that the probability in (b) depended on the linear density of escorts screening the convoy but not on the number of merchant vessels in the convoy. To obtain the probability in (c) it was noted that once a submarine had penetrated, its expected number of sinkings was independent of convoy size; thus the probability in (c) that a particular merchant vessel would be sunk varied inversely with convoy size. When the three probabilities on the right-hand side were multiplied together, the same inverse relationship extended to the overall Pr (sinking), which again leads to the conclusion that the number of merchant vessels sunk should be independent of convoy size.

There is an interesting postscript to the above account that has valuable lessons for operations research generally. Despite the statistical analysis and the plausibility of the results from the simple model, Blackett did not immediately urge the Admiralty to reverse its long-standing preference for small convoys. Only after convincing himself that his family would be safer in a large convoy were they to sail to Canada, did he report the result and point to its striking implications.

During the period of Vietnam analysis such 'dual' approaches continued to be used, now with the possibility of more complicated models executed on electronic computers. An example of an application of a computer model in Southeast Asia operations is given by Bortels & English [1968]. This example concerned the effect of aircraft formation size and configuration on the effect of their jammers in countering enemy radars. The computer was used, in effect, to speed the solution of the kind of geometry problem that in WWII would have required a more tedious approach.

There was another kind of model application, emphasized by Morse & Kimball [1946], that was introduced in World War II operations research, perhaps as a transplant of scientific and engineering practice. This was the comparison of an observed value of an operational parameter with a theoretical value of the parameter calculated for ideal conditions. An example given by Morse & Kimball involves 'sweep rates' calculated for aircraft, surface vessels, or submarines engaged in searching ('sweeping out') an area thought to contain enemy vessels or submarines. Operations research studies compared observed values of Q_{op} (the 'operational sweep rate') to ideal values of Q_{th} (the 'theoretical sweep rate').

The theoretical sweep rate was given by:

$$Q_{th} = 2RV \text{ (sq. mi./h)},$$

where

$R =$ effective lateral range of detection in miles,
$V =$ average speed of searching craft in mi./h.

If one searched with sweep rate Q_{th} for time T, then the expected number of contacts would be:

$$C_{th} = Q_{th}T(N/A),$$

where N is the number of enemy craft in area A, so that N/A represents an average density. Similarly, the observed number of contacts, C_{op}, would be given by:

$$C_{op} = Q_{op}T(N/A),$$

which gives

$$Q_{op} = (C_{op}T)(A/N).$$

From intelligence information on enemy operations, reasonably good values of A/N could often be inferred, so that from observed values of C_{op}, values of the Q_{op} could be calculated. By comparing these operational values with the theoretical values Q_{th}, operations research workers derived useful indications of operational effectiveness. When Q_{op} was substantially smaller than Q_{th}, for example, new enemy tactics or equipment were often the explanation.

Through the process illustrated above – comparison of observed operations with idealized models – and through the solution of many individual problems that pointed to common patterns, there came the recognition of some basic relationships and models as quite general and fundamental. As such models were introduced and related operational constants were measured, there developed the understanding of some operations that had many aspects of a scientific theory. Thus, in WWII operations research there came to be a 'theory of search', a 'theory of bombardment', etc.

As such bodies of knowledge were established, operations research workers gained confidence in using some models to estimate requirements, to indicate preferred allocations of effort, and to prescribe tactics. An example of a very simple relation that is found in several models is:

$$P = 1 - \exp(-a/A),$$

where a measure of effectiveness P is expressed in terms of input effort a, and a constant A with the same units. This expression was introduced in Section 3.1, where P denoted the probability of finding an object, a denoted the time of random search, and A was the area to be searched. A similar expression was used in gunnery (and bombardment) problems where P denoted the probability of destroying a target by expending a shells (or bombs). As such basic expressions became the cornerstones of developing theories, they were sometimes used as the point of departure for more involved mathematical developments such as the allocation of effort problem described in Section 3.1.

It is important to note that in keeping with the scientific outlook the validity of the applications of basic expressions, their extensions, and the body of theory generally must all be the subject of continuing scrutiny. The skeptical outlook is especially important when models derived from combat analysis are appropriated as building blocks for large computer simulation models.

5.4. Summary

The main examples of important combat analysis in wartime have come from World War II and, to a lesser extent, from later conflicts. These examples suggest that successful analysis usually owed remarkably little to sophisticated models, either mathematical or computer models. Instead, the operations research method depended strongly on the most fundamental aspects of the scientific outlook. Essential to the successes were skepticism, energy and ingenuity in digging for facts, deep thought and imagination in discerning the purpose of an operation and how to measure effectiveness, and persistence and caution in seeking operational improvements. These activities, as in scientific investigation generally, often led to model building, but the models tended to be much simpler than some of the large computer models developed in the last decade or two. The examples of wartime combat analysis described above serve to remind us of aspects of the scientific approach that are sometimes forgotten in peacetime MOR.

6. Further reading

Besides Morse & Kimball, the military OR textbooks by Chuyev [1965] and Venttsel [1964] contain introductory material on Measures of Effectiveness, as well as some instructive solutions of tactical problems. Hughes [1984] is a collection of articles on the philosophy and practice of MOR in the United States. The U.S. Army's Engineering Design handbook [U.S. Army, 1979] is a comprehensive 'pamphlet' (with 46 chapters!) covering many aspects of weapon systems analysis. It is of course biased towards land combat, but nonetheless contains much material useful for MOR in general. The reader who is interested in models of the process of employing multiple weapons against a target will find a thorough review of the subject, including some two-sided models, in Eckler & Burr [1972].

The sources mentioned above are worth hunting for, but are likely to be hard to obtain. The following books should be more readily available. Shephard et al. [1988] is a collection of case studies, each offered with a companion 'school solution'. Hoeber [1981] is a similar collection, but more oriented to strategic rather than tactical problems. U.S. Naval Academy [1977] is a textbook currently in use there. Przemieniecki [1991] is a collection of mathematical methods that will be of greatest use in problems involving aircraft, since the author is on the Air Force Institute of Technology faculty. The International Military and Defense Encyclopedia [Dupuy, 1993] is a good source for definitions of terms, armament statistics, and historical discussions. Finally, the Military Operations Research Society plans to issue a military analysis handbook in the near future.

References

Benkoski, S., M. Monticino and J. Weisinger (1991). A survey of the search theory literature. Special Issue on Search Theory. (L. Stone and A. Washburn, eds.), *Naval Res. Logist.* 38(4), 469–494.

Berkovitz, L.D., and M. Dresher (1959). A game-theory analysis of tactical air war. *Oper. Res.* 7(5), 599–624.

Blackett, P.M.S. (1950). The scope of operational research. *Oper. Quart.* 1(1), 6.

Blackett, P.M.S. (1962). *Studies of War*, Hill and Wang, New York.

Bortels, W.H., and J.A. English (1968). Computer program to aid in evaluation of ECM formations, Hq. PACAF Operations Analysis Note 68-5.

Bracken, P. (1976). Unintended consequences of strategic gaming, Hudson Inst., HI-2555-P, Croton-on-Hudson, NY.

Brothers, L.A. (1954). Operations analysis in the United States Air Force. *J. Oper. Res. Soc. Amer.* 2(1), 1–16.

Brown, G., C. Goodman and R. Wood (1990). Annual scheduling of Atlantic fleet naval combatants. *Oper. Res.* 38(2), 249–259.

Catalog of Wargaming and Military Simulation Models, 11th edition (1989). Joint Chiefs of Staff, AD-A213970.

Chuyev, Y., P. Mel'nikov, S. Petukhov, G. Stepanov and Y. Shor (1965). *Principles of Operations Research Involving Military Equipment*, U.S. Army translation J1445 of book originally published by Soviet Radio Publishing House, Moscow.

Clasen, R.J., G.W. Graves and J.Y. Lu (1974). Sortie allocation by a nonlinear programming model for determining a munitions mix, RAND R-1411-DDPAE, Santa Monica, CA.

Deitchman, S.J. (1962). A Lanchester model of guerrilla warfare. *Oper. Res.* 10(6), 818–827.

Dorfman, R. (1951). Work and method of operations analysis, Working Paper 17.1.2., Hq. U.S. Air Force, Directorate of Operations, Operations Analysis Division, Washington, DC.

Dresher, M. (1961). *Games of Strategy: Theory and Applications*, Prentice-Hall, Englewood Cliffs, NJ.

Dupuy, T. (ed.) (1993). *The International Military and Defense Encyclopedia, six volumes*, Brassey's, Washington, DC.

Eckler, A.R., and S. Burr (1972). Mathematical models of target coverage and missile allocation, Military Operations Research Society, Washington, DC.

Engel, J.H. (1954). A verification of Lanchester's law. *Oper. Res.* 2(2), 163–171.

Ewell, J.J., and I.A. Hunt Jr (1974). Sharpening the combat edge, Department of the Army, Washington, DC.

Flood, M. (1952). Some experimental games, RAND RM-789-1, Santa Monica, CA.

Freck, P.G. (1968). Analysis of combat aircraft losses in Southeast Asia, Weapons Systems Evaluation Group, Report 128, Washington, DC.

Greene, W.G. (1969). Army operations research symposium – 1969, Hq. U.S. Air Force Operations Analysis, AFGOAC Memorandum for Record.

Grinold, R.C., and K.T. Marshall (1977). *Manpower Planning Models*, Elsevier, New York.

Hitch, Ch.J. (1953). Suboptimization in operations research problems. *J. Oper. Res. Soc. Amer.* 1(3), 87–99.

Hitch, Ch.J. (1955). An appreciation of systems analysis. *J. Oper. Res. Soc. Amer.* 3(4), 466–481.

Hitch, Ch.J. (1965). *Decision Making for Defense*, Univ. of California Press, Santa Barbara, CA.

Hoeber, F. (1981). *Military Applications of Modeling: Selected Case Studies*, Gordon and Breach, New York.

Hofstadter, D. (1982). Mathemagical themas. *Sci. Amer.* August, 16–18.

Hughes, W.P. Jr (ed.) (1984). *Military modeling, 2nd edition*, Military Operations Research Society, Washington, DC.

Isaacs, R. (1965). *Differential Games*, Wiley, New York.

Jones, R.V. (1978). *The Wizard War – A Story of British Scientific Intelligence, 1939–1945*, privately published.

Kaufman, H., and J. Lamb (1967). An empirical test of game theory as a descriptive model. *Percept. Mot. Skills* 24, 951–960.

Kilgour, D.M. (1990). Optimal cheating and inspection strategies under a chemical weapons treaty. *Infor. Syst. Oper. Res.* 28(1), 27–39.

Koopman, B.O. (1980). *Search and Screening*, Pergamon Press, New York.

Koopman, B.O. et al. (1978). Panel discussion (World War II Operations Research, unedited transcript), Operations Research Society of America meeting, Los Angeles, 13 November 1978.

Lanchester, F.W. (1916). *Aircraft in Warfare: The Dawn of the Fourth Arm*, Constable & Co., London.

Leach, W.B. (1945). U.S. Army Air Forces, Professors of Air Combat, Hq. U.S. Army, Operations Analysis Section.

Leckie, R. (1981). *The Wars of America*, Harper and Row, New York.

MITRE (1982). National security issues symposium – 1981, MITRE Document M82-30, Bedford, MA.

Morse, Ph.M., and G.E. Kimball (1946). Method of operations research, OEG Report 54, Operations Evaluation Group, Office of the Chief of Naval Operations, Navy Department, Washington,

DC [Subsequently revised and printed by Wiley, New York, 1951].

Newman, J.R. (1956). *The World of Mathematics*, Simon and Schuster, New York.

ODASD [Office of the Deputy Assistant Secretary of Defense (Systems Analysis), Regional Programs] (1969). Southeast Asia Analysis Report.

Owen, G. (1982). *Game Theory*, Academic Press, New York.

Perla, P. (1990). *The Art of Wargaming*, Naval Institute Press, Annapolis, MD.

Pocock, J. (1962). PERT as an analytical aid for program planning – its payoff and problems. *J. Oper. Res. Soc. Amer.* 10(6), 893–903.

Przemieniecki, J.S. (1991). *Introduction to Mathematical Methods in Defense Analysis*, American Institute of Aeronautics and Astronautics, New York (the companion MS-DOS diskette is 'Defense Analysis Software').

Raisbeck, G. (1979). How the choice of measures of effectiveness constrains operations research. *Interfaces* 9(4), 85–93.

Rapoport, A., and A.M. Charmak (1965). *Prisoner's Dilemma*, Univ. of Michigan Press, Ann Arbor, MI.

Ravid, I. (1989). Defense before and after Bomb-Release-Line. *Oper. Res.* 37(5), 700–715.

Roehrkasse, R., and G. Hughes (1990). Crisis analysis: Operation Desert Shield. *OR/MS Today* December.

Schaffer, M.B. (1968). Lanchester models of guerrilla engagements. *J. Oper. Res. Soc. Amer.* 16(3), 457–488.

Shephard, R., D. Hartley, P. Haysman, L. Thorpe and M. Bathe (1988). Applied operations research, examples from defense assessment, Plenum, London.

Sherbrooke, C. (1968). METRIC: A multi-echelon technique for recoverable item control. *Oper. Res.* 16(1), 122–141.

Shubik, M., and G.D. Brewer (1979). *The War Game*, Harvard Univ. Press, Cambridge, MA.

Silber, J. (1953). Force requirements for fighter bombers, Hq. Fifth Air Force, Operations Analysis Office, Memorandum 59.

Solandt, O. (1955). Observation, experiment, and measurement in operations research. *J. Oper. Res. Soc. Amer.* 3(1), 1–14.

Starkey, L. (1962). End-of-tour report, Hq. Second ADVON Operations Analysis, June 1962 (with transmittal letter by Dr. Oldham, Hq. U.S. Air Force Operations Analysis, AFOCA, July 1962).

Stockfisch, J.A. (1975). Models, data, and war: A critique of the study of conventional forces, RAND R-1526-PR, Santa Monica, CA.

Suzdal, V. (1978). *Theory of Games for a Fleet*, Soviet Radio Publishing House, Moscow.

Taylor, J. (1980). Force-on-force attrition modeling, Military Applications Section of the Operations Research Society of America, Baltimore, MD.

Taylor, J. (1983). Lanchester models of warfare, Vols. I and II, Operations Research Society of America, Baltimore, MD.

Thomas, C., and W.L. Deemer Jr (1957). The role of operational gaming in operations research. *Oper. Res.* 5(1), 1–27.

TIA (Trends, Indicators, and Analyses) (1968). Hq. U.S. Air Force, DCS Plans and Operations, Directorate of Operations.

U.S. Army (1977). *Engineering Design Handbook, Vol. 1*, DARCOM pamphlets 706-101.

U.S. Army (1979). *Engineering Design Handbook, Vol. 2*, DARCOM pamphlets 706-102.

U.S. Naval Academy (1977). *Naval Operations Analysis, 2nd edition*, Naval Institute Press, Annapolis, MD (a 3rd edition is in preparation).

Venttsel, Y. (1964). *Introduction to Operations Research*, Soviet Radio Publishing House, Moscow.

Von Neumann, J., and O. Morgenstern (1944). Theory of games and economic behavior. Princeton Univ. Press, Princeton, NJ.

Wagner, D.H. (1989). Naval tactical decision aids, Report NPSOR-90-01, Naval Postgraduate School, Monterey, CA.

Whitmore, W.F. (1953). Edison and operations research. *J. Oper. Res. Soc. Amer.* 1(2), 83–85.

Whitmore, W.F. (1961). Military operations research – A personal retrospect. *Oper. Res.* 9(2), 258–265.

S.M. Pollock et al., Eds., *Handbooks in OR & MS, Vol. 6*

Chapter 5

Models in Urban and Air Transportation

Amedeo R. Odoni

Massachusetts Institute of Technology, Room 33-404, Cambridge, MA 02139, U.S.A.

Jean-Marc Rousseau

GIRO Enterprises Inc., 75 Port-Royal Street East, Suite 500, Montreal, Que. H3L 3T1, Canada

Nigel H.M. Wilson

Department of Civil and Environmental Engineering, Massachusetts Institute of Technology, Cambridge, MA 02139, U.S.A.

Introduction

Transportation undoubtedly ranks as one of the areas in which operations research is most intensively applied. The purpose of this chapter is to review briefly operations research models in two major sectors of transportation, urban transportation and aviation. The review is not exhaustive: for urban transportation, it is restricted to planning and operational problems in urban transit authorities while, in the case of aviation, only work related to the infrastructure of the air transportation system (airports and air traffic control) has been covered. These limitations in scope stemmed from the desire to strike a compromise between, on the one hand, providing a review of manageable length and, on the other, presenting our material at a reasonable level of detail. Nonetheless, it is clearly impossible, even under these constraints, to offer a truly comprehensive survey of the extensive literature that has appeared on our two subject areas in the course of the past 40 or so years. Instead, we have tried to offer (the first author on the subject of aviation infrastructure and the second and third on urban transit) an overall perspective on the state-of-the-art and to suggest areas which may require further research.

PART I. AVIATION INFRASTRUCTURE

1. Background

Airports and the air traffic control (ATC) system are the two principal types of infrastructure for the air transportation system. Airport services and facilities are further subdivided into 'airside' and 'landside'. Runways, taxiways, apron areas and hangars are the principal airside facilities and they are collectively referred to as the *airfield*. Landside facilities consist primarily of passenger and cargo terminal buildings, access roads on the airport proper and such supporting facilities as automobile parking areas, power generation stations, etc. Most existing operations research models deal with issues related either to the runway and taxiway systems of airports or to passenger terminals or to ATC. We shall review each one of these three areas of work in Part I.

2. Airport airside analysis

Airfields and, specifically, runway complexes have been for the past thirty years (and continue to be today) the principal bottlenecks of the entire ATC and airport system. The reason, quite simply, is that runways constitute the 'interface' between the three-dimensional airspace and a 'single-file-flow' traffic regime. Moreover, all too often, there are too few of them: runways are expensive to build, 'consume' a great amount of land area and, most important, have significant environmental and other external impacts that necessitate long and complicated review-and-approval processes with uncertain outcomes.

2.1. A model for estimating the capacity of a single runway

It is no accident then that the first important analytical model of airport operations, due to Blumstein [1959, 1960], dealt with the issue of estimating the capacity of a single runway. We shall present this model in considerable detail because it remains valid today, illustrates the effects of the principal factors that affect airport capacity and provides a fundamental building block for many of the computer-based models which are now widely used to estimate capacity and delays at runway complexes.

Consider then a single runway, as shown in Figure 1, which is used for landings only. To land on such a runway, aircraft must descend in single file along the final approach path (Figure 1) where they decelerate and exit onto the taxiway system. Thus, aircraft paths merge in the vicinity of the 'gate' to the final approach – typically 5–8 miles away from the runway threshold. Throughout the final approach, aircraft must, of course, maintain a safe longitudinal distance from each other; moreover, ATC requires 'single occupancy' of runways by landing aircraft, i.e., each aircraft must be safely out of the runway before the next landing can 'touch down'. These safety rules impose limits on the maximum 'acceptance rate' of the runway, i.e., on its 'capacity'.

Let us define the following quantities for an aircraft of type i:

n = the length of the common final approach path.

v_i = ground speed (i.e., 'net' of wind speed) on final approach assuming, as a reasonable approximation, that each aircraft maintains a constant speed throughout the approach.

o_i = runway occupancy time, i.e., the time that elapses from the instant when the aircraft touches down on the runway to the instant when it leaves the runway at one of the runway exits.

Consider then the case in which an aircraft of type i is landing, followed immediately by another aircraft of type j. Denote by s_{ij} the minimum separation required by ATC between the two aircraft, while they are both airborne. Let T_{ij} denote the minimum acceptable (in the sense of not violating any ATC separation requirements) time interval between the successive arrivals at the runway of aircraft i and j. We have [Blumstein, 1959]:

$$T_{ij} = \max\left[\frac{n + s_{ij}}{v_j} - \frac{n}{v_i}, o_i\right] \text{ for } v_i > v_j, \tag{1a}$$

$$T_{ij} = \max\left[\frac{s_{ij}}{v_j}, o_i\right] \qquad \text{for } v_i \leq v_j. \tag{1b}$$

The situation in which $v_i > v_j$ is known as the 'opening case' because the airborne distance between the two aircraft keeps increasing as they fly along the final approach path on the way to the runway. In this case, the two aircraft are closest to each other at the instant when the first of the two, aircraft i, is at the gate of the final approach path (Figure 1). If at that instant the final approach controller has managed to achieve the minimum allowable separation s_{ij} between the two aircraft, then the time interval between the successive landings of the two airplanes will be given by (1a). By contrast, in the 'closing case' ($v_i \leq v_j$) the two aircraft are closest to each other at the instant when the first aircraft is at the runway threshold; T_{ij} is then given by expression (1b).

Suppose now that the 'long-run' probability of a 'type i aircraft followed by a type j aircraft' is p_{ij}. Then, we have:

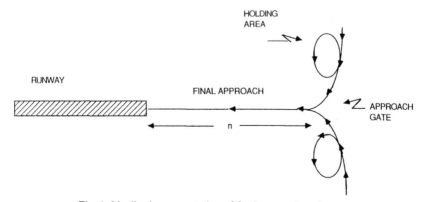

Fig. 1. Idealized representation of final approach and runway.

$$E\left[T_{ij}\right] = \sum_{i=1}^{K}\sum_{j=1}^{K} p_{ij} \times T_{ij}. \tag{2}$$

Example. A numerical example will be helpful at this point. The FAA subdivides aircraft into three classes with respect to the separations s_{ij} required on final approach: 'heavy' (H), defined as aircraft with a maximum take-off weight (MTOW) of 350 000 lbs. or more; 'large/medium' (L/M) with MTOW between 12 500 and 350 000 lbs.; and 'small' (S) with MTOW of 12 500 or less. Wide-body commercial jets generally belong to the H category; the L/M class includes practically all types of narrow-body commercial jets (L) as well as many of the non-jet airplanes typically used by regional or 'commuter' air carriers (M); finally, most small general aviation aircraft belong to the S class. Because the aircraft in class L/M have widely varying characteristics, it is customary in airport capacity analyses to subdivide this class into two more homogeneous subclasses, L and M. Let us denote the classes H, L, M and S with the indices 1 through 4, respectively.

Assume now that, at a major airport, a particular runway which is used for long periods of time for arrivals only (another runway(s) is presumably used for departures) serves an aircraft population with the following characteristics:

i (a/c type)	p_i (probability)	v_i (knots)	o_i (s)
1(H)	0.2	150	70
2(L)	0.35	130	60
3(M)	0.35	110	55
4(S)	0.1	90	50

1 knot = 1 nautical mile per hour $\approx$ 1.15 statute miles per hour $\approx$ 1.8 km per hour.

The probabilities, p_i, indicate the 'traffic mix' at this runway (e.g., 20% of the aircraft are of type H).

In instrument meteorological conditions (IMC) when aircraft are 'spaced' strictly according to the FAA's Instrument Flight Rules (IFR) the separation requirements, s_{ij}, used by ATC at several major airports in the United States are as follows:

Trailing aircaft

$$[s_{ij}] = \begin{array}{c} \\ \text{H} \\ \text{L/M} \\ \text{S} \end{array} \begin{array}{ccc} \text{H} & \text{L/M} & \text{S} \\ \left[\begin{array}{ccc} 4 & 5 & 6 \\ 2.5 & 2.5 & 4 \\ 2.5 & 2.5 & 2.5 \end{array}\right] \end{array}$$

Leading aircraft

[Separations specified in nautical miles].

Assuming now that the length, n, of the final approach path is equal to 5 n. miles and applying expressions (1a) and (1b) we find the following matrix, T, of minimum time separations, T_{ij} (in seconds) at the runway:

Trailing aircraft

$$
\begin{array}{c}
\text{Leading aircraft} \\
\\
T = \\
\\
\\
\end{array}
\begin{array}{cccc}
\quad 1(\text{H}) & 2(\text{L}) & 3(\text{M}) & 4(\text{S}) \\
\end{array}
$$

Leading aircraft	1(H)	2(L)	3(M)	4(S)
1(H)	96	157	207	240
2(L)	60	69	107	160
3(M)	60	69	82	160
4(S)	60	69	82	100

$$T = \qquad (3)$$

Air traffic controllers throughout the world currently use first-come, first-served (FCFS) sequencing of aircraft wishing to land at an airport. [In actual practice, at some busy airports, there are some occasional deviations from strict FCFS, for reasons to be discussed below.] For our example this makes it reasonable to assume that, given that an aircraft of type i has just landed at the runway, the probability that the next aircraft to land is of type j will be simply equal to the proportion p_j of type j aircraft in the aircraft mix. This means that

$$p_{ij} = p_i p_j. \qquad (4)$$

Thus, we obtain the following matrix, P, of aircraft-pair probabilities p_{ij}:

Trailing aircraft

Leading aircraft	1(H)	2(L)	3(M)	4(S)
1(H)	0.04	0.07	0.07	0.02
2(L)	0.07	0.1225	0.1225	0.035
3(M)	0.07	0.1225	0.1225	0.035
4(S)	0.02	0.035	0.035	0.01

$$P = \qquad \qquad \cdot$$

Multiplying the corresponding elements of the matrices T and P to apply (2) we find $E[T_{ij}] = 101.3$ s, i.e., if the ATC system could always achieve the minimum allowable separations between landing aircraft, the runway of this example could serve one arrival every 101.3 s, on average, or up to 35.5 arrivals per hour.

In practice, it is, of course, very difficult to achieve as perfect a level of precision in spacing successive landing aircraft on final approach as implied by the matrix T above. Since spacing in IMC is carried out 'manually' through instructions from air traffic controllers to pilots, it is natural to expect some deviations from the separations indicated by the elements T_{ij} of T. In fact, in view of the expected conservatism of both pilots and controllers, one would expect the separations between given pairs of aircraft types to be, on the average, larger than the corresponding values of T_{ij}. This is indeed the case in practice: for example, in the

United States average spacing under IMC seems to exceed the minimum allowable by ATC rules by about 10–15 s. This effect can be captured by Blumstein's model by modifying the matrix T through the addition of appropriate 'buffers' to each element T_{ij}, designed to account for the additional spacing which is added, intentionally or unintentionally, in practice. For instance, under a particularly simple but reasonable approximation, one could just add the same constant buffer, b, to all T_{ij}, obtaining a new matrix T' of average (not minimum) separations expected between pairs of aircraft, with

$$T'_{ij} = T_{ij} + b. \tag{5}$$

If, to continue our numerical example, we set $b = 10$ s in (5), we shall obviously obtain $E[T'_{ij}] = 111.3$ s, as the expected separation between successive landing aircraft. This leads to an expected service rate of $C = 32.3$ aircraft per hour, a number which is typical of the service rates that would be observed in today's ATC system in an airport in the United States with a traffic mix similar to that described above. The quantity C is referred to as the 'saturation capacity' or 'maximum throughput' by airport and ATC specialists. (Note that, technically, maximum throughput is truly achieved only when $b = 0$, in which case $E[T'_{ij}] = 101.3$ s and $C = 35.5$ aircraft per hour for this example.)

Despite its simplicity, Blumstein's model has proved extremely valuable as a planning tool in ATC and airport studies, especially in the context of assessing the effects of various procedural or ATC equipment changes on airport capacity. For example, it was not until recently that the FAA allowed controllers at certain major airports to use 2.5 n. miles separations for the L/M–H, L/M–L/M, S–H, S–L/M and S–S aircraft pairs. Until then the separations required for these aircraft pairs was 3 n. miles – and this is still the case at most airports. This change from 3 to 2.5 n. miles provides an increase of approximately 2.7 arrivals per hour (from $C = 29.6$ to $C = 32.3$) or 9.1% in the runway (saturation) capacity. Similarly, ATC controllers attempt to achieve more uniform final approach speeds at congested commercial airports, typically by recommending that pilots land the smaller and slower aircraft at speeds more similar to those of some of the commercial jets. For instance, if in the numerical example above, ATC could somehow achieve $v_3 = 130$ knots and $v_4 = 110$ knots by assigning higher final approach speeds to 'medium' and 'small' aircraft, we would obtain $C = 36.8$ arrivals per hour, a 13.9% increase over $C = 32.3$.

Other promising possibilities for increasing runway capacity also emerge from the study of the Blumstein model and of realistic examples of its application, such as the one above. For instance, inspection of the matrix T in (3) indicates that certain aircraft sequences may be more desirable than others (e.g., the sequence 1–4, or 'H–S', requires at least 4 min of separation between successive landings, while the sequence 4–1, or 'S–H', requires only a 1-min separation). This suggests the possibility of computer-aided sequencing of aircraft waiting to land at an airport, an idea that has been investigated in detail by several researchers [Dear, 1976; Psaraftis, 1980; Venkatakrishnan, Barnett & Odoni, 1993]. The 'runway sequencing problem' is typically formulated as a constrained optimization problem with the objective of finding sequences which maximize the service rate of runways (or some other aggregate measure of performance) while maintaining a certain level of 'fairness', so that some types of aircraft are not unduly penalized by being always relegated to the end of the queue of arrivals waiting to land. This approach is now reaching the stage of initial implementation through innovative terminal area ATC systems currently being installed in Germany, in France and in the United States. Note that, when sequences are in use which are not based on a FCFS discipline, expression (4) is no longer valid and must be replaced by an expression (or an algorithm for computing the probabilities p_{ij}) which reflects the sequencing scheme actually in use.

A number of improvements and extensions of the Blumstein model of a single runway used for arrivals only were proposed soon by early researchers. It is obvious, for example, that some of the parameters which are treated as constants in the Blumstein model (e.g., the approach speeds, v_i, and the runway occupancy times, o_i, of each type of aircraft) can be treated more realistically as random variables with associated probability distributions [Odoni, 1972]. The distances between successive aircraft on final approach can also be treated as random variables whose probability distribution depends on the required ATC separations and on the characteristics and performance of the terminal area ATC system, including the controllers and pilots [Harris, 1972].

Entirely analogous concepts can also be applied for estimating the capacity of runways used only for takeoffs, as well as of runways used for both landings and takeoffs. In the latter case, it is important to identify the strategy used by ATC controllers to sequence landings and takeoffs on the runway. Under the strategy most commonly used, controllers during peak demand periods may serve a long 'string' of successive arrivals (e.g., 5 to 10 arrivals in a row), then a long string of successive departures, then another string of arrivals, and so on. In this case the runway capacity can be approximated as a simple weighted average of C_a, the runway capacity when the runway is used only for arrivals, and of C_d, the runway capacity when the runway is used only for departures, the weights being equal to the fractions of time when the runway is used for serving arrivals and departures, respectively [Odoni, 1972]. However, at busy airports in the United States, controllers often use a strategy whereby arrivals alternate with departures on the runway, i.e., the separations on final approach between successive arriving aircraft are 'stretched', so that a departure can take place during the time interval between the two arrivals. This is a procedure that requires considerable skill but, if performed accurately, can increase considerably the total operations (landings and takeoffs) capacity of the runway. A model of this operating strategy was developed by Hockaday & Kanafani [1972] and was subsequently generalized by several researchers [see, e.g., Swedish, 1981].

2.2. More complex runway configurations

Many major airports operate with more than a single runway: some use two, three or four runways simultaneously, while the two busiest airports in the world,

Chicago's O'Hare (ORD) and Dallas/Ft. Worth (DFW) often operate with six simultaneously active runways. In fact, the number and identity of runways in use at any given time, as well as the allocation of types of aircraft and mix of operations to them, may change several times a day at many of these large airports. The selection of the specific runways to be operated at any one time depends on many factors: demand (e.g., during periods of low demand an airport may accommodate all its traffic on a single runway, even though more than one runways may actually be available); weather conditions, including visibility, precipitation and wind speed and direction; mix of traffic (e.g., during peak periods for flight arrivals, one or more runways may be dedicated to serving exclusively arrivals – and conversely for peak departure periods); and noise regulations which, for example, may prohibit or discourage the use of certain runways during the night or during certain parts of the year. For an airport with several runways, there can be a large number of combinations of weather (ranging from 'VFR-1' – good weather conditions – to 'IFR-3' – very limited visibility all the way down

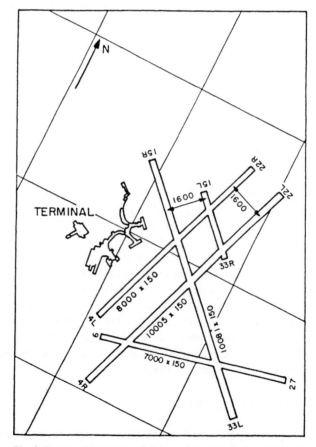

Fig. 2. Runway layout plan, Boston Logan International Airport.

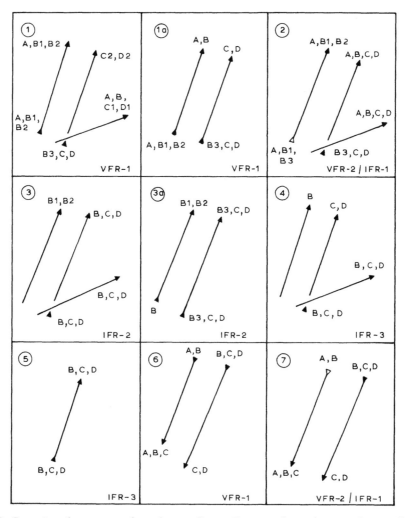

Fig. 3. Examples of runway configurations at Boston Logan under various weather conditions (VFR-1, VFR-2/IFR-1, etc.). Inbound arrows indicate direction of landings, outbound of take-offs. Aircraft types (A, B, B1, B2, ...) assigned to each runway are also indicated.

to the runway surface), active runways and allocation of traffic and operations to the runways. Each of these combinations is called a 'configuration'. For example, Boston's Logan International Airport (BOS) with five runways (Figure 2) can operate under 39 different configurations (Figure 3)!

For computing airport capacity and improving airport design and operations in such more complex cases, the use of OR approaches is a necessity. The specific tools that are used in practice can be analytical models or simulations. To start with, it is rather straightforward to extend the type of analytical model described in the previous section to airport configurations involving two simultaneously

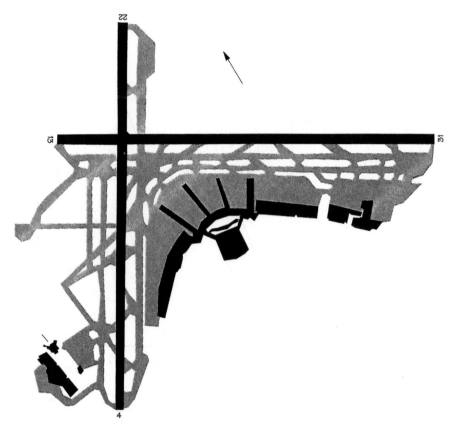

Fig. 4. LaGuardia Airport, New York.

active runways. Given a set of priority rules for sequencing operations on the two active runways, one can develop the usual time separation matrix for successive operations and compute quite accurately the available capacity. For example, New York's LaGuardia Airport (LGA) is usually operated with two intersecting runways, one for arrivals and the other for departures (Figure 4). Air traffic controllers will typically alternate arrivals and departures in this case (for instance, an arrival on runway 31, then a departure on 4, then an arrival on 31, etc.). Given the location of the runway intersection, it is easy to compute LGA's capacity using a Blumstein-like methodology. Note also that, depending on wind directions, the assignment of landings and takeoffs to runways at LGA may change, giving rise to additional configurations. Because of the change of the location of the runway intersection relative to the points where takeoffs are initiated or where landing aircraft touch down, the capacities of these various configurations at LGA (all involving two active runways) may not be equal. Similarly, in the case of two parallel runways the degree of interaction between the runways and the capacity of the airport depends on the distance between the runways.

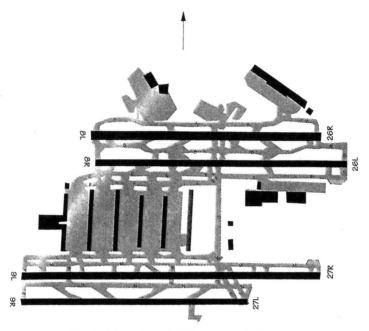

Fig. 5. Atlanta Hartsfield International Airport.

The application of analytical models to configurations involving three or more simultaneously active runways is more problematic, because of the large number of possible interactions among operations taking place at different runways and the complex operation-sequencing strategies that can be used. The typical analytical modeling approach taken in such cases is to approximate the representation of the airport's operation by 'decomposing' the airport into more easily analyzable components. For example, Atlanta's airport, one of the world's busiest, usually operates with two close pairs of parallel runways (Figure 5). One runway in each pair is used for arrivals and the other for departures. Since the two pairs of runways are at a sufficient distance from each other to be operated more or less independently for ATC purposes, one can approximate the capacity of the airfield by adding together the capacities of each individual close pair of runways. (Note that the capacities of the two individual pairs may not necessarily be equal – for instance, if the mix of traffic served by the 'North' pair happens to be different from that served by the 'South' pair.) The accuracy of such a decomposition approach depends, of course, on the geometry of the airfield, i.e., on how 'decomposable' the runways' layout is in the first place.

2.3. Simulation models

A second approach is the obvious one of simulating the airfield. Beginning in the early 1970's, a large number of general-purpose simulation packages have

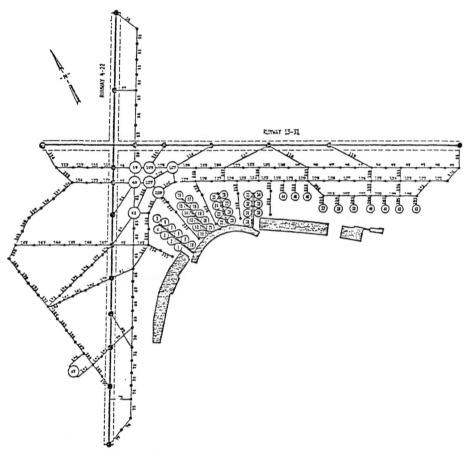

Fig. 6. Network representation of LaGuardia Airport. Line segments indicate network 'links', each of which can hold one aircraft at a time. Small circles indicate apron gates, larger ones key intersections on the airfield.

been developed for application to the analysis of airport airside operations, often covering not only runways but also aircraft movements on taxiways and aprons [for a review, see Odoni, 1991]. Some of these simulation packages are publicly available, while others are proprietary. Practically all of them represent the airfield as a network of nodes and links (see Figure 6 for an example). Aircraft move on this network along prescribed paths that consist of strings of nodes and links. Typically each link can be occupied by a single aircraft at a time. Thus a delay occurs whenever an aircraft attempts to use a link which is already occupied by another aircraft. Whenever two or more aircraft attempt to occupy a free link at the same time (e.g., two aircraft approach a taxiway intersection from different directions) the logic of the model resolves the conflict according to ATC priorities and assigns the free link to one of the candidate aircraft.

The network representation has both advantages and disadvantages. On the positive side, the network structure is intuitively appealing, can be used to develop a highly detailed representation of the airfield and provides a convenient base for collecting and reporting occupancy and delay statistics. On the negative side, the network structure can impose high set-up costs, reduce flexibility and slow down program execution. For example, the process of identifying the paths to be traversed by aircraft on the airport's surface is far from trivial and has major implications for the functionality of the simulation. In this respect, until recently, most available simulation packages required among their inputs a listing of assigned paths connecting each of the apron 'gates' (aircraft parking positions) with each runway end. For a large airport with 5 runways (i.e., 10 runway ends) and 100 gates, this meant listing 1000 different paths, each consisting typically of 30 or more links – or a total of 30 000 or more input numbers. Interestingly, the more sophisticated solutions to this particular problem that have been adopted by some modelers in the last few years, often have serious drawbacks as well. To avoid listing all paths, variations of shortest path algorithms have now been incorporated into some models: for each configuration of the airport they compute the paths that aircraft would travel between a gate and each active runway's end. (The 'variations' are needed to adopt the standard shortest path algorithms to the peculiarities of airfield traffic.) However, through this approach, the model still 'knows' of only a single best path between a gate and a runway. As a result, flexibility and realism suffer: the model does not react dynamically to operating conditions, as the ATC tower would in practice. For instance, if a major congestion problem develops at some location on the taxiway system, the model would continue to send aircraft to that location (since the aircraft paths are fixed) instead of routing them around the bottleneck to relieve congestion.

The above is but one example of the many – relatively minor but irritating – technical deficiencies with which users of existing airfield simulation models may still have to contend. A new generation of such models, currently under development at a number of organizations, will probably overcome such problems. Nevertheless, even the existing models are now meeting with growing acceptance and use for a variety of reasons, including the appeal of the traffic display capabilities of some of them. Two such models worth specific mention are the Airport Machine and SIMMOD, because they are extensively used by the FAA and several airport and ATC organizations overseas. The former is a simulation model that covers the airfield only (runways, taxiways, aprons) while SIMMOD is both an airspace and an airfield modeling tool and can, in fact, be used to simulate operations in a regional ATC system that may include several major airports. (It was used recently, for instance, to assess the impacts of a third major airport in the Chicago area.) SIMMOD enjoys strong and continued support from the FAA and has several companies involved in its application and further development, including a significantly improved forthcoming version. It is thus acquiring the status of the 'semi-official' model of the FAA and may become, at least for a while, the standard tool in highly detailed airfield and airspace analyses.

2.4. Delay analysis

A natural consequence of airport congestion is the widespread incidence of significant airport delays. Airport delays are generally considered as one of the most vexing (and apparently long-term) problems confronting air transportation in much of the world. Estimating airport delays, given actual or anticipated demand and capacity data, is thus a very important aspect of airport planning and design.

The estimation of airport delays poses an interesting challenge to operations researchers: it provides a prominent example of a practical congestion problem for which the results developed in the voluminous literature on classical steady-state queueing theory are largely irrelevant – at least, when it comes to the really interesting cases. The reason is that practically every closed-form expression developed in that body of work assumes (i) arrival and service rates at the queueing system which are constant over time, and (ii) arrival rates which are strictly less than service rates ($\rho < 1$). Both of these assumptions are generally false, often for extended periods of time, at busy airports. Figure 7 shows a typical example of a 24-hour demand profile for a major airport which illustrates this point. A number of authors [see especially Green, Kolesar & Svoronos, 1991; Odoni & Roth, 1983] have demonstrated in detail the poor performance of even sophisticated approximation schemes which try to estimate airport delays by judiciously applying steady-state expressions to the type of situation shown in Figure 7.

In the absence of reliable, closed-form analytical expressions, two approaches have been developed by now for computing airport delays: numerical solution of analytical models and simulation. The former of these approaches was pioneered by Koopman [1972]. His main argument was the following:

(i) The non-homogeneous Poisson process provides a reasonable approxima-

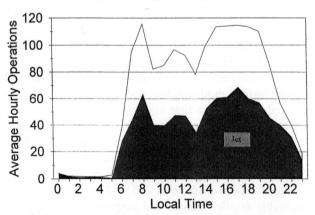

Fig. 7. A typical day's demand profile for Boston Logan.

tion of demand (arrivals and departures) for access to the runway systems of major airports.

(ii) The random variable which describes the duration of service times for arrivals and/or departures at an airport has a probability distribution which is 'less random' than the negative exponential and 'more random' than 'deterministic' (constant).

(iii) Hence, the queueing characteristics of an airport with k runways ('servers') must 'fall somewhere between' the characteristics of the $M(t)/M(t)/k$ and the $M(t)/D(t)/k$ queueing systems – with the two models providing 'worst case' and 'best case' results, respectively. (The t makes explicit the fact that these models allow for dynamic changes in the demand rates and service rates over time.)

Based on these premises, Koopman solved the Chapman-Kolmogorov equations describing the $M(t)/M(t)/k$ and the $M(t)/D(t)/k$ queueing systems, using airport demand profiles, such as the one shown in Figure 7, to depict demand rates and typical airport capacities, such as those discussed in Section 2.1, for the service rates. (These service rates can obviously be made to vary over time depending on the particular demand/capacity scenarios being analyzed.) For typical data specific to JFK International and to LaGuardia Airports in New York, Koopman plotted the expected queue length (expected number of aircraft waiting to use the airfield) as a function of time over a 24-hour period and showed that the results obtained from the two queueing systems were very close. He thus argued that queueing characteristics at airports are relatively insensitive to the precise form of the service time distribution.

Extending the work of Koopman, the $M(t)/E_k(t)/k$ queueing system was proposed by Kivestu [1976] as a model that could be used directly to compute approximate queueing statistics for airports – rather than solving separately an $M(t)/M(t)/k$ and an $M(t)/D(t)/k$ model and then 'interpolating' their results. The Erlang (E_k) family of random variables is indeed very flexible and can be used to represent: negative exponential service times (M) by setting $k = 1$; constant service times (D) by setting k to infinity; and 'inbetween' situations by selecting an appropriate value of k. Kivestu also developed an approximation scheme that solves numerically the Chapman-Kolmogorov equations for the $M(t)/E_k(t)/1$ system quickly and with high accuracy.

Recent research [Abundo, 1990; Horangic, 1990] has indicated that Kivestu's suggested approach is very practical computationally and produces realistic estimates of airport delays. In fact, a software package, DELAYS, that implements this approach on a range of personal computers is beginning to receive extensive use by a number of organizations, including the FAA.

The second approach, i.e., the use of simulation models to estimate airport delays, while straightforward conceptually, is less attractive than analytical methodologies for the usual reasons. To obtain results which are statistically meaningful, a large number of simulation experiments ('runs') is typically necessary; moreover, determining the correct number of required runs as well as the statistical significance of the results obtained from a simulation model is not an easy task for systems, such as airports, that operate under (and are simulated for) dynamic conditions that may vary greatly over the course of a typical day. An additional complication in the case of airports is that the user of the simulation model is usually interested in estimating distributions, not just averages. For example, a quantity of great interest to ATC and airport planners is the fraction of flights or operations delayed more than a certain amount of time, e.g., 15 or 20 minutes. This increases further computational requirements, as well as the need for sophisticated statistical analysis.

3. Airport passenger terminal design

While the airfield is the element that truly determines an airport's eventual capacity, as well as its land requirements, the passenger terminal plays a crucial role in defining the overall 'image' that most air travelers really associate with any individual airport. The passenger terminal is also a very expensive part of the airport, both absolutely and per gate of aircraft: typical recent fixed costs per gate of major international terminals are in the $15–25 million range, so that a large building with 30 gates could easily cost $600 million to build and equip.

Partly in response to these practical considerations and also because the modeling of passenger terminals offer some interesting challenges, a considerable amount of effort has been dedicated by operations researchers over the last 15 years to developing improved quantitative tools for supporting the design and operation of these large buildings. Much of this work is reviewed, in far more detail than is possible here, in two recent publications, a special issue of *Transportation Research* [1992, see especially Tosic, 1992] and a volume published by the Transportation Research Board [1987]. However, despite significant progress, it is fair to say that the 'state of the art' in this area still leaves much to be desired.

The 'elements' of a passenger terminal are generally classified into three categories: the terms *processing facilities* (e.g., ticket counters, check-in counters, security and passport controls, baggage carousels, customs counters, etc.), *holding areas* (e.g., lobbies, atria, gate lounges, etc.) and *passageways* (e.g., corridors, escalators, moving sidewalks, etc.) are often used to refer to servers or spaces where passengers and other airport users, respectively, (i) are processed or are offered a service, (ii) congregate while waiting for an event (such as initiation of boarding) or spend time voluntarily, and (iii) travel on foot. Holding areas also include ancillary facilities and concessions. In the case of processing facilities questions of interest include: the determination of the number of servers needed; the amount of linear frontage necessary (e.g., for check-in counters or for baggage claim devices); and the area that should be set aside for the servers and for the queues that form in front of them. For holding areas, the key issues concern the amount of space that should be reserved and the physical configuration of that space. This physical configuration is important, for example, in ensuring that occupants of the holding area (e.g., of a large lobby for departing passengers) have a good sense of orientation or are distributed quite uniformly within the holding area and are not all crowded in one or more parts of it. Finally, in the case of passageways, one is interested in the width or, more generally, the dimensions and physical configuration that would achieve certain flow requirements.

3.1. Standards for 'level of service'

None of these questions could be addressed in the absence of specified standards for desirable 'levels of service' (LOS). For example, in order to determine the required number of check-in counters, one must know what is considered an acceptable amount of waiting time for checking in; similarly, in determining how much space should be set aside for a departure gate lounge, one should have some idea of acceptable levels of 'crowding' (number of lounge occupants per unit area). As the reader would surmise, specifying such general-purpose LOS standards is far from simple. However, since 1981 a consensus of airlines and airport operators has been reached on a set of verbal definitions of LOS ranging from 'A' ('excellent level of service; conditions of free passenger flow; no delays; excellent level of comfort') to 'E' ('inadequate level of service; condition of unstable flow; unacceptable delays; inadequate level of comfort') – with 'F' labelled as 'entirely unacceptable LOS'. To be useful in guiding passenger terminal design and operations, it is, of course, necessary to 'translate' these verbal descriptions of LOS into quantitative sets of standards. Obviously, one such set should specify waiting time standards for processing facilities. Another set should specify 'space per occupant' standards for holding areas and for areas used for queueing in front of processing facilities. Yet a third set should refer to passenger and other flows in passageways.

To date, two such sets of standards have been proposed, one for space and the other for passageways, and seem to be gaining wide international acceptance. Table 1 lists the space LOS standards [AACI/IATA, 1981]. LOS standards for passageways [Benz, 1986; Fruin, 1971] are stated in terms of passengers per meter width (of the passageway) per minute with typical recommended values around 40 (LOS = C) or 54 (LOS = D).

Unfortunately, no similar progress has been made in the case of waiting time standards. Various airlines and airport operators have, however, developed their own standards in this regard. Ashford [1988] presents a good survey of the standards used by several major European Airport Authorities. As a typical

Table 1
LOS standards for holding areas

LOS	Wait circulate	Check-in bag claim	Holdroom inspection
A	2.7	1.6	1.4
B	2.3	1.4	1.2
C	1.9	1.2	1.0
D	1.5	1.0	0.8
E	1.0	0.8	0.6

example, the British Airports Authority specifies that: 95% of passengers should be processed at baggage check-in in less than 3 minutes overall and 80% of passengers in less than 5 minutes during peak traffic periods; or, that 95% of passengers on 'regular' flights should be screened for security in less than 3 minutes apiece, while for 'high security' flights 80% of passengers should be screened in less than 8 minutes. This illustrates the fact that many of the existing waiting time standards are distributive in nature ('$X\%$ wait less than Y minutes') and that different standards may be set for different processing facilities, to take into consideration the nature of the service rendered or factors related to the 'psychology of queueing'.

3.2. Models

As in the case of the airfield, both analytical models and simulations are available for passenger terminals. For questions involving individual elements of the passenger terminal, it is often quite easy to develop approximate analytical models that help resolve such issues as the capacity or the number of servers required at a processing facility, or the amount of space needed to reach a desirable LOS standard. These models are sometimes as simple as a 'back-of-the-envelope' formula. The following is a typical example.

Example. To estimate the amount of space to be provided for a departure lobby shared by several flights at a time, a model recommended by IATA [1981] states:

$$S = K_{LOS}(\lambda D + 2\sqrt{\lambda D}) \tag{6}$$

where

S = the amount of space needed (in m^2),
K_{LOS} = the appropriate LOS space coefficient (see Table 1),
λ = the number of passengers per hour flowing through the lobby during the terminal's period of peak demand,
D = the average 'dwell' time (in hours) of passengers in the lobby during this period of peak demand.

If, for instance, the rate of flow of passengers through the lobby during the peak period is $\lambda = 1200$ per hour, the average dwell time in the lobby is 20 minutes ($D = 1/3$) and the desired LOS is C ($K_{LOS} = 1.9$ from Table 1) then the space required is about 844 m^2 (or about 9000 square feet).

This example illustrates a number of general observations about this area of work. First, models, whether analytical or simulations, are very 'data intensive'. Any type of planning for passenger terminals requires quite extensive data (or, as an alternative, numerous assumptions) about passenger flows and passenger characteristics and behavior – in our example, how many passengers will be passing through the lobby and how long they will be staying there. Obviously, such data or assumptions are subject to massive uncertainty, especially when one is designing a terminal for a 'target date' which may easily be 10 years in the future.

It is important, therefore, to have models which are flexible and easy-to-use so that planners can perform extensive sensitivity analyses and come up with 'robust' operational designs.

Second, most models include some probabilistic considerations. In Equation (6), for instance, the underlying assumption is that the flow of passengers through the lobby can be approximated as a Poisson process and the term $2\sqrt{\lambda D}$ provides extra space to accommodate a '2-standard-deviations' fluctuation from the average rate of flow.

Finally, the application of these models relies heavily on the user's judgement and experience. An obvious example is the choice of the LOS factor, K_{LOS}, in (6) and the trade-offs it implies between passenger comfort during peak traffic periods, on the one hand, and utilization of the terminal during off-peak periods, on the other.

A few specific families of analytical models that have been applied to airport terminals and deserve mentioning are: (i) models based on classical steady-state queueing theory; (ii) graphical analyses using 'cumulative diagrams'; and (iii) 'macroscopic' models based on geometrical probability.

Models in (i) include some of the earliest applications of queueing theory, described in an outstanding early book by Lee [1966]. Unfortunately, the practical value of these models is quite limited, since most processing facilities in passenger terminals are essentially never in steady-state: they are almost always undergoing some kind of dynamic change. The only significant exceptions would seem to involve facilities involving several parallel servers shared by many flights (or by several airlines, as in the case of common check-in areas encountered at many European airports) where roughly steady rates of demand at high server utilization levels are achieved for significant periods of time.

To take into account dynamic phenomena, deterministic queueing models have been used extensively [Tosic, 1992]. The technique most often used is that of cumulative diagrams, i.e., graphical displays of the total number of arrivals and service completions over time at a processing facility [Newell, 1971]. This approach assumes that the patterns of demand over time, at least on average, are known. Thus, it is best suited for short-term planning, e.g., in reconfiguring a particular space within an existing structure.

A more recent family of models [Bandara & Wirasinghe, 1991, 1992] has attempted to develop approaches for optimizing the dimensions of passenger terminals and for selecting the most appropriate geometrical configuration among various alternatives (pier terminals, satellite-type terminals, etc.). The primary criterion used is a weighted objective function of average walking distance and average travel time on mechanical devices (e.g., people movers) for passengers, including those transferring between flights. To compute the relevant objective functions for any given configuration and allocation of flights to gates some use is made of geometrical probability concepts. A body of work with a related theme uses mathematical programming models (integer programming, the assignment problem, etc.) to allocate a day's schedule of arriving and departing flights to aircraft gates in such a way as to minimize expected passenger walking distances or, more generally, travel times in the terminal [Babic, Teodorovic & Tosic, 1984; Mangoubi & Mathaisel, 1985]. Obviously, these models must take into account the amount of time a gate will be occupied by an aircraft, as well as the fact that some gates may be able to accommodate only certain specific types of aircraft.

4. Air traffic control studies

Operations research models have also been used widely to analyze a number of problems arising in air traffic control (ATC). Probably the two principal areas of application are in estimating sector workload and in determining flow management strategies for air traffic. We shall discuss briefly below the first of these two topics.

One of the principal indicators of the workload of an ATC system is the frequency with which the system is required to resolve 'conflicts' between pairs of aircraft. Estimating this frequency is an important step in the process of either designing (i.e., specifying the dimensions and overall configuration) ATC 'sectors' (= local control regions) or of determining the personnel or equipment requirements of such sectors.

In attempting to estimate these conflicts a volume of *protected airspace* is defined around each flying aircraft. Typically this volume has the shape of a cylinder with radius r and height h. A conflict is then defined as the overlap of any two of these cylinders in airspace. (One can visualize the cylinders as flying ice-hockey 'pucks' – the flat sides of the pucks always parallel to the horizontal plane – and a conflict as the collision of two pucks.) Depending on the dimensions of the protected volume, a conflict then takes different interpretations. For example., when $2r$ and h are set, respectively, equal to the minimum horizontal and vertical ATC separation requirements between two aircraft (usually 3–5 n. miles and 1000 feet, respectively, for the airspace above the continental United States) a conflict is equivalent to a violation of ATC separation standards. In this case, each aircraft can be approximately represented by a point mass at the midpoint of its associated cylinder's axis. If, on the other hand, $2r$ and h correspond respectively to the wingspan and to the height of the hull of aircraft, a conflict is equivalent to a mid-air collision. In this latter case, representation of the aircraft as a cylinder is clearly an idealization that may necessitate some adjustments of the estimated probabilities and frequencies of conflicts.

Several authors have analyzed various types of conflicts arising in connection with the general situation described above. One such type is *overtaking conflicts*, which refer to cases involving aircraft flying on the same 'airway' (i.e., a straight-line path between two navaids) and in the same direction, but not at the same speed. Given the probability distribution of aircraft speeds, the traffic density on the airway and the length of the airway, Siddiqee [1974] and Dunlay [1975] have derived a simple expression for the expected number of overtaking conflicts per unit of time on the airway, assuming that aircraft enter the airway independently in a Poisson manner and that each maintains its preferred constant speed. This

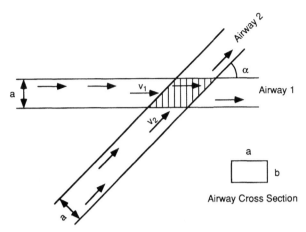

Fig. 8. Geometric model of the intersection of two airways.

expected number indicates how often the air traffic controller responsible for the airway will have to oversee the safe overtaking of one aircraft by another. It is interesting to note that the airspace model was developed independently of an essentially identical model in traffic flow theory which estimates the frequency with which a car, moving at a given constant speed on a lightly traveled stretch of highway, passes or is passed by other cars, given the overall probability distribution of car speeds.

A second fundamental model is the one that predicts the number of conflicts at the *intersection of two airways* (Figure 8). In its simplest form [Dunlay, 1975] this model assumes that the flows of traffic on each of the airways constitute independent homogeneous Poisson processes with intensities of f_1 and f_2 aircraft per unit of time. It is also assumed that the width and height of both airways (denoted by a and b in Figure 8) are equal to zero and that all aircraft on airways 1 and 2 travel at constant speeds V_1 and V_2, respectively. The model was subsequently extended to the more general geometry of Figure 8 by Endoh [1982] and to intersections of an arbitrary number of airways (not just two) and more generally distributed traffic flows (not just Poisson) by MacDonald [1987].

The third fundamental model in this area is the so-called *gas model*. As its name suggests, this uses the classic physical model of gas molecules in a heated chamber to estimate the number of conflicts between aircraft occupying some part of airspace. In its original form [Marks, 1963], the model assumes that aircraft are uniformly and independently distributed within an area, when movement is restricted to the horizontal plane (think of pucks on an ice-hockey rink) or a volume, when changes in aircraft altitude are permitted [see also Flanagan & Willis, 1969]. It is further assumed that aircraft travel in straight lines in directions which are independently and uniformly distributed between 0 and 2π and with speeds that are independent of the direction of travel and are drawn, independently for each aircraft, from a probability distribution $p_V(.)$.

Clearly this simple representation may be better suited to an uncontrolled part of airspace occupied by pleasure fliers who may indeed be flying in random directions. Nevertheless, estimates of frequencies of potential conflicts obtained through the gas model [Alexander, 1970; Graham & Orr, 1970] played an important role in the work of the Department of Transportation's ATC Advisory Committee which in 1969 charted much of the future of the ATC system in the United States. These estimates were used extensively in determining some of the computer specifications for the system. It was argued that estimates of the expected number of conflicts obtained through the model (i.e., assuming random directions of travel) are conservative upper bounds for the actual situation in controlled airspace where directions of travel are far from random. Indeed it was subsequently shown [Endoh, 1982; Endoh & Odoni, 1983] that, for any ensemble of aircraft flying in straight lines, the expected number of conflicts is maximized when the directions of aircraft travel are uniformly distributed between 0 and 2π, as assumed in the gas model. This may be a counter-intuitive result since it might seem that the expected number of conflicts would be maximum if half the aircraft were flying in one direction and the other half in exactly the opposite direction.

Another more obvious result can be proven easily: the distribution of aircraft with respect to *altitude* which *minimizes* the expected number of conflicts, everything else being equal, is the uniform distribution [Endoh, 1982; Ratcliffe & Ford, 1982]. Thus, the universal practice in ATC that concentrates aircraft around specific altitudes, typically at 500- or 1000- or 2000-feet intervals, increases the *potential* number of conflicts that must be resolved.

The assumption of uniformly distributed travel directions in the 2-dimensional and 3-dimensional gas models is unnecessarily restrictive. Endoh [1982] and Endoh & Odoni [1983] present a *generalized gas model* in which the probability distribution for the direction, θ, of travel can be arbitrary. For example, if for a given region we have

$$f_\theta(\theta) = K \times \delta(\theta - \gamma) + \frac{1 - K}{2\pi}, \quad \text{for } 0 \le \theta \le 2\pi \tag{7}$$

where $\delta(.)$ indicates the impulse function, then a fraction K of aircraft are flying in the same direction, γ, while the directions of the remaining aircraft are uniformly distributed between 0 and 2π. The generalized gas model can be used to derive expressions for the expected number of conflicts for several interesting traffic scenarios. In addition, it is shown in Endoh & Odoni [1983] that the overtaking conflicts model and the airways intersection model are but special cases of the generalized gas model.

All the models described above have one consistent aspect, namely they show that the expected number of conflicts per unit of time is proportional to the square of 'traffic density', with the constant of proportionality depending on the 'geometry' and other characteristics of the particular situation being modeled. The term traffic density may mean the number of aircraft per unit volume or per unit area of airspace in the case of 3-dimensional and 2-dimensional gas models, respectively, or the number of aircraft per unit length in the case of overtaking and intersection conflicts where traffic is restricted to move along straight line paths (airways).

PART II. URBAN TRANSIT

1. Background

The purpose of this section is to review how operations research techniques have been used to solve planning and operational problems in public transport authorities. This review is not exhaustive, but emphasizes operations research techniques that have been applied or that, in our opinion, have potential applications. A further limitation is that it examines public transport problems in isolation from two larger problems in which they are embedded. First, public transport is just one element of the larger urban transportation problem. Street congestion, availability of reserved lanes (road-space reserved for public transport), parking policy and pricing, and limits on private car utilization all have a significant impact on public transport planning and operations. Second, urban development plans may directly influence decisions concerning the location of major public transport infrastructure (e.g., subways, light rail) so as to encourage desired urban development. These important interrelations are not considered here.

2. The elements of transit problems

Figure 9 presents the various elements necessary for the planning and operation of public transport service from an operations research perspective. As can be seen, there are many interrelations between the elements of the problem. However, mathematically it is not feasible to take into account all these elements at the same time. It is part of the art of operations research to split large interconnected problems into pieces that are significant yet tractable. These pieces often correspond to the internal organization of public transport authorities. Generally strategic planning activities, such as designing new routes, or constructing new infrastructure, are separated from the timetabling and vehicle and crew scheduling elements, which are in turn separated from the day-to-day management of operations. We will describe these problems in more detail in the following sections together with the operations research techniques used in each context.

We classify public transport problems into those at the strategic, tactical and operational levels. Strategic planning is concerned with long-term development of the system including fixed investments such as subway and light rail facilities, and also in major modifications to the bus route network. Since it is difficult for the public to adapt to major revisions in the bus network, most changes of this type are the result of comprehensive studies and must stay in place for some time to achieve their full potential impact. As such, there is a stability to the bus network structure, making it appropriately part of the strategic planning problem.

The tactical planning problem includes minor route revisions, the structuring of routes in high ridership corridors and the assignment of service frequencies to routes. These aspects of the overall problem often do not receive much attention, with some of the attendant strategies being implicitly part of the planning

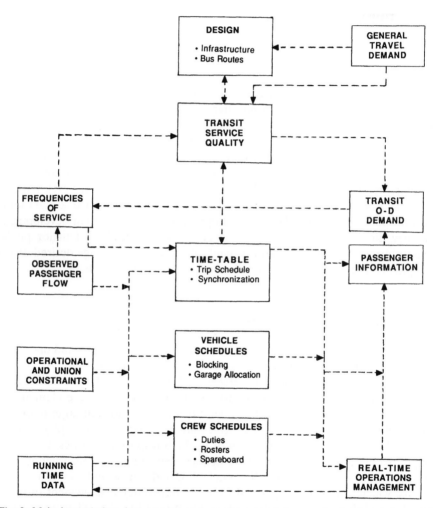

Fig. 9. Main interrelations between the various elements of the transit planning and operations problem.

department while others are included in the operational planning function. We will however discuss these problems independently because we believe that further research is warranted in this area.

Operational planning encompasses all scheduling-related activity, including the production of timetables, the scheduling of vehicles, the generation of daily duties for drivers, and the construction of rosters comprising the daily duties of individual drivers together with their days off and holidays.

Finally, we will briefly refer to the increasingly important topic of public transport operations control.

3. The strategic planning problem

The transit network design problem is one of a class of very difficult network design problems covering most scheduled carrier systems and including airlines and rail passenger systems. There are several reasons for this complexity. First is the existence of the route as an intermediate structure between the link and the full network. Second is the strong interdependence between the design of routes by the operator and the choice of travel itinerary carried out independently by users. We are in a user optimum context rather than a system optimum context because the network planning agency does not decide the actual routing (or routing strategies) of the traffic on its network (which is the case for telephone companies, pipelines, trucking, etc.). In addition, the objective function is ill-defined as in many design problems. The planner certainly wants to minimize the total travel time of the population, but he or she also wants to give 'equitable' access to the system to every taxpayer, design 'attractive routes' that will be 'easy' to use, maybe 'favor' the use of heavy infrastructure such as subways to minimize operating cost, while taking into account 'acquired rights' to certain services and dealing with political pressures for better services in individual political jurisdictions.

For all these reasons, it seems appropriate to favor an approach by which the design of new infrastructure or new bus routes is done interactively, with the planner choosing scenarios (route and network structures) while the computer performs the evaluation of these scenarios, providing the planner with information to help in the design of new scenarios, etc. Indeed, while many attempts have been made to design routes heuristically by computer [see, for example, Hasselström, 1981; Lampkin & Saalmans, 1967; Last & Leak, 1976; Mandl, 1980], all transit network models which have received widespread application are of an interactive type.

VIPS-II, developed jointly by VTS and Stockholm Transport, is the only one of these models which allows the automatic generation of transit routes, as described in Hasselström [1981]. This is essentially a typical location–allocation approach. It is first assumed that there is a direct transportation link between each pair of zones, and the frequency of service is calculated using a simple model of the type to be described in the following section. The algorithm allocates passengers to alternative paths between each origin–destination pair so as to minimize travel time. It sequentially drops from the network the least attractive routes, reallocating the passengers affected to the remaining routes and recalculating the frequency of services until a satisfactory solution is reached (see Figure 10). In addition to this automatic generation of routes, routes can be specified by the planner with the model then being used for network evaluation as in the approaches described below.

Several computer packages have been designed for transit network simulation and evaluation and so can be used in the interactive design of bus routes and transit infrastructure. Among these are Transcom [Chapleau, 1974], Transept [Last & Leak, 1976], NOPTS [Rapp, Mattenberger, Piguet & Robert-Grandpierre, 1976], VIPS [Andreasson, 1976] and its successor VIPS-II, U load [UMTA, 1977], TRANSPLAN [Osleeb & Moellering, 1976], IGTDS [General Motors, 1980], Ma-

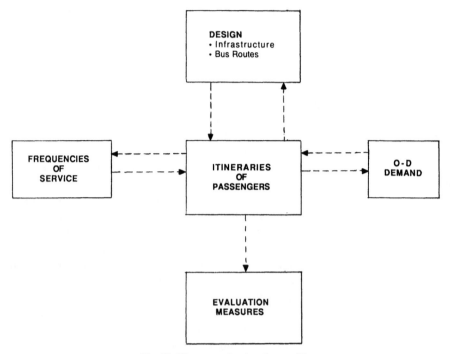

Fig. 10. The strategic planning problem.

dituc [Chapleau, Allard & Canova, 1982] and EMME/2 [Babin, Florian, James-Lefebvre & Spiess, 1982, 1984; Florian, 1985; Florian & Spiess, 1986]. Of these, VIPS-II and EMME/2 appear to be among the most sophisticated evaluation models. Both provide extensive graphical displays that assist the user in the evaluation of a transit network. In each, the planner can define scenarios interactively and the program then forecasts how the passengers will use the system, providing answers through a series of graphical and numerical outputs. Whereas VIPS-II is strictly a public transport planning tool, EMME/2 provides a multi-modal urban transportation planning environment letting the user define up to ten modes of transportation. Both systems have been used extensively around the world.

Any transit network evaluation tool supposes that the transit network is given, including the frequency of service on each route, and that total travel demand by transit between all zones is known (in some cases a modal split function is used to extract the transit demand from a total origin–destination travel matrix). From this information it calculates the itinerary of passengers and the transit flow on each line together with average trip duration between each O–D zone and other local and global measures. In this context, one feedback loop possible is the reevaluation of the matrix by using a mode choice function. The process may be repeated until a stable solution is obtained.

A key operations research problem in any public transport network evaluation model, as well as in any heuristic approach to network design, is to calculate the passenger assignment to routes in the network. The key behavioral principle is well-accepted; the transit user wants to travel at minimum 'inconvenience', this being a weighted combination of access time, waiting time, travel time, travel cost and transfer inconvenience. Any generalized cost functions can be calibrated and tested in each context assigning different weights to the various factors composing it.

However, even given this objective function, the solution of the passenger assignment problem is not as simple as it might appear at first sight. First, the O–D matrix is an aggregation at a zonal level; it will not always be true that persons living in the same zone and travelling to the same destination, will choose the same route. One reason for this is that their exact locations in the zone may dictate different choices, given the importance of access time. Second, several transit routes may serve a given street segment or a given intersection. The optimal choice of itinerary for a transit user may very well be dictated by the arrival of the first bus on any of these routes. In the same way, the transit user may well change his or her itinerary according to the presence of a given bus at a certain street intersection, etc.

The transit passenger assignment problem has been studied by many authors, either as a separate problem [see, for example, Andreasson, 1976; Chriqui, 1974; Chriqui & Robillard, 1975; Dial, 1967; Le Clerq, 1972; Marguier & Ceder, 1984; Rapp, Mattenberger, Piguet & Robert-Grandpierre, 1976; Spiess, 1983], or as a sub-problem of more complex models, such as transit network design [see, for example, Hasselström, 1981; Jansson & Ridderstolpe, 1992; Lampkin & Saalmans, 1967; Mandl, 1980; Schéele, 1977], or multimodal network equilibrium [Florian, 1977; Florian & Spiess, 1983].

Following Dial [1967], many of these algorithms are based on the assumptions of deterministic running times and exponentially distributed headways on all routes, in which case the market share for a particular route is simply its frequency share. Jansson & Ridderstolpe [1992] show that when headways are deterministic rather than exponential, the frequency share model does not always hold, with the result depending on the degree of schedule coordination. Chriqui & Robillard [1975] and Marguier & Ceder [1984] both examine route choice among routes on a common path. Chriqui & Robillard proposed a heuristic for selecting a set of acceptable paths among which the passenger would select the first bus to arrive so as to minimize the expected total travel time. They show that their heuristic is optimal when all routes have exponentially distributed headways and identical running times, but Marguier & Ceder showed that this heuristic is not optimal for all headway distributions. Jansson & Ridderstolpe present an alternative heuristic for this problem for the deterministic headway case.

Spiess [1983], Spiess & Florian [1989] and De Cea et al. [1988] present linear programming solutions to the transit path assignment problem as a relaxation of a mixed integer program under the assumption of exponentially distributed headways. There are two main differences between these models and other approaches. First and foremost, in these models the traveller does not simply choose a path, but rather selects a strategy. While in earlier methods the transit traveller's route choice is limited to one path, defined as a sequence of route segments, links or transfer points, the strategies considered in Spiess' approach allow the transit rider to select any subset of paths leading to the destination with the first vehicle to arrive, determining which of the alternative routes is actually taken on an individual trip. This concept of optimal strategies allows more realistic modelling of the traveller's behavior. Second, the resulting transit assignment problem, formulated as a mathematical programming problem, may be solved directly without recourse to heuristic approaches.

The principal difference between the approaches of Speiss and De Cea is in the representation of the problem in network form. Spiess' algorithm is in the form of a shortest-path problem, whereas de Cea's approach results in network search to define feasible paths, followed by Chriqui's heuristic to determine optimal paths. Spiess' algorithm solves the problem in polynomial time and so may be applied even to very large transit networks. This method is used in EMME/2. A method based on similar ideas has also been developed and implemented in Torino by Nguyen & Pallottino [1988].

In this general area of transit network design, additional development may come from the automatic generation of options or marginal improvements to systems that could be proposed to the planner. These suggestions could be generated through a set of rules gathered together in an expert system by the planners themselves. However, we do not envisage a totally automatic design tool for the transit network design problem in the near future, expert system or not.

4. Tactical planning

The tactical planning problem for transit has received relatively little serious attention. Figure 11 summarizes the various elements of this problem. The transit network is assumed known and the objective is to allocate the available resources (buses and drivers) in order to provide the best possible service at the least cost. Several problems can be studied at this level, including the transit assignment problem discussed at length in the previous section. Another problem that has received some attention [Fearnside & Draper, 1971; Last & Leak, 1976; Schéele, 1977], is that of choosing the optimal frequencies for bus routes, given a fixed fleet of vehicles, in order to minimize total travel time. The frequency of service influences the itinerary and duration of travel, which in turn may influence travel demand.

There are two fundamentally different ways of defining the frequency of service in a transit network. Most transit authorities set frequencies, or the number of vehicles required, so as to obtain a given number of passengers per vehicle at the peak loading point on each route, subject to a minimum frequency constraint. Typically both acceptable peak loads and minimum frequencies vary by time of day. This type of approach has been formulated (with extensions) by Ceder [1984]. An alternative approach treats the problem as one of resource allocation, with the resources, for example bus-hours, being allocated across routes and across time periods so as to maximize some objective subject to passenger loading constraints. Furth & Wilson [1981] showed that this problem could be

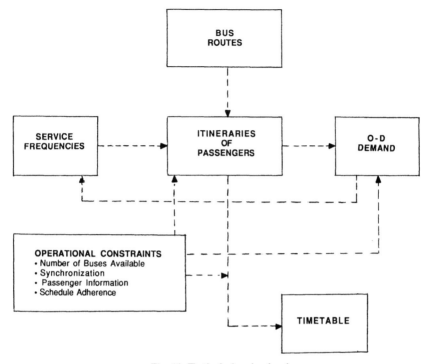

Fig. 11. Tactical planning level.

formulated either as a fixed demand minimization of total expected passenger waiting time, or as a variable demand consumer surplus maximization with very similar results. This work was extended by Koutsopoulos, Odoni & Wilson [1985] and later by Wilson & Banasiak [1984] to treat more complex objective functions and constraints. A similar approach was also taken by Hasselström [1981] for frequency determination in the VIPS model. Constantin in her thesis [Constantin, 1993] and in a subsequent paper [Constantin & Florian, 1993] use a non-linear bi-level programming approach to solve the problem of allocating the fleet of vehicles to bus routes in order to minimize passenger travel time given the passenger will travel according to the model of Spiess.

Another topic that falls within the tactical planning area is design of operating strategies in high ridership corridors which might be amenable to market segmentation techniques designed either to increase service quality or to increase productivity (or both). Turnquist [1979] formulated the design of zonal express service as a dynamic programming problem and this work was later extended by Furth [1986] to zonal design for bidirectional local service including light direction deadheading, and to branching as well as linear corridors. These models have received little application by transit planners largely because most real transit corridor planning situations have such limited design options that they can typically be solved by enumeration.

5. Operational planning models

In operational planning, we consider that the requirement for service on each route is known (frequency of service or number of buses), that the running times (to travel between various points on a route) are known for each period of the day, and all operating and crew contract constraints are fixed. We then have to define timetables, vehicle schedules and crew schedules. The determination of the number of spares drivers required and their schedules of work are also part of the operational plan.

5.1. Timetabling

Given a required frequency of service and the running times, the generation of trips is normally immediate. Combining trips into blocks is generally fairly trivial. After ensuring that a minimum layover is allowed to maintain the regularity of services [Wilson, 1986], a first-in first-out (FIFO) strategy is optimum on a route-by-route basis both for the number of vehicles necessary, and for the minimization of total duty times [Ceder, 1986; Saha, 1970]. A vehicle is freed as soon as it is no longer required or would have to wait an excessive amount of time for the next trip assignment. A vehicle is dispatched from the depot when needed for the trip schedule. However, it may be necessary in the timetabling problem to take into account crew scheduling constraints. For example, blocks of less than two hours may generate additional pay to the driver (because a piece of work for the driver must be at least two hours) and must thus be avoided as much as possible. It may also be useful to integrate a longer layover into a block that could be used later for a coffee break or lunch break for the driver. Some of these situations are described in Hamer & Séguin [1994].

There are few mathematical considerations in timetable preparation, but there is a need for a sophisticated management information system with graphic interfaces. Several bus scheduling software packages have been developed and are available commercially, most integrated with crew scheduling software [see Daduna & Wren, 1988; Desrochers & Rousseau, 1992; Paixao & Daduna, 1994; Rousseau, 1985; Wren, 1981].

However, when the service requirement is specified in terms of number of buses in service by time of the day, the problem of producing a smooth timetable is more complex, particularly at times when the number of buses required changes significantly [Ceder, 1986]. The adjustment of trip departure time can be difficult particularly when one is dealing with complex bus routes with several branches. One other topic which falls under the timetabling umbrella is the setting of timetables on connecting routes so that the service for transferring passengers is optimized [Bookbinder & Désilets, 1992]. While this topic is complex, particularly in the full network context, there may be scope for future application for route pairs involving large transfer volumes. Other references on the subject can be found in Desrochers & Rousseau [1992] and Paixao & Daduna [1994].

5.2. Vehicle scheduling problems

Vehicle scheduling refers to the class of problems in which vehicles must be assigned to timetabled trips or tasks, in such a way that each task is carried out by one vehicle, a given set of constraints is satisfied and cost is minimized. For simplicity here, the term 'trip' will be used to denote all vehicle tasks defined in the timetable (whether trips or blocks of trips). Very often, the cost structure reflects the fact that the number of vehicles must be minimized. We assume that for each trip, the departure time, trip duration, and origin and destination terminal are known. In addition to regular trips, we assume that deadheading trips are allowed between terminals. A survey paper and several papers on specific vehicle scheduling problems are published in Paixao & Daduna [1994].

5.2.1. The simple case

In this section we will discuss the problem as stated above with only one depot and no complicating constraints. The reader who requires more details on this problem could consult Ceder & Stern [1981], Bodin, Golden, Assad & Ball [1983], Carraresi & Gallo [1984b], and Scott [1986].

Desrosiers, Soumis & Desrochers [1982] presented a scheduling model which takes into account the use of a single vehicle to serve many chains of trips (see Figure 12). In this approach, each trip in the schedule is represented by an arc with a minimal and maximal flow of one, thus requiring a unit of flow to traverse it. There is no specific cost associated with the trips themselves because they all must be included in the solution. All feasible deadhead trips are also represented by arcs with a minimum flow of zero, a maximum flow of one and an associated cost c_{ij} corresponding to the cost of deadhead time and distance. Equivalently, a cost is associated with a deadhead trip to and from the garage $(c_{.i}, c_{i.})$. The originality of this formulation lies in the fact that the garage is not represented by a single node but by a sequence of time nodes. All buses in the garage can flow freely from one time node to the next time node without cost. A bound N_k on the maximum number of buses in the garage at time period k can be easily imposed on the solution. Finally, a return arc from the end of the day to the beginning of

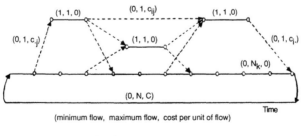

(minimum flow, maximum flow, cost per unit of flow)

○———○ : correspond to trips

------- : deadhead trip to or from the depot or between regular trips

Fig. 12. A time space network for the transit bus scheduling problem.

the day ensures the conservation of flow and counts the number of buses required to operate the schedule. The fixed cost C of a vehicle and an upper bound N on the number of vehicles can be imposed on this arc.

A standard minimum cost flow algorithm can be used to solve this problem. This formulation accurately takes into account the number of buses required without generating too many arcs. However, Scott [1986] demonstrated that if deadhead cost is proportional to travel time and waiting time, which is characteristic of a broad class of vehicle scheduling problems, there need not be any conflict between the two objectives of minimizing fleet size and minimizing the cost of operating a schedule. In other words, there is never, in general, any need for the application of a fleet size penalty to the creation of independent chains when one intends to find a minimum-cost scheduling solution which uses a minimal fleet.

5.2.2. Complicating constraints

We will consider here three types of complicating constraints that can destroy the structure of the basic vehicle schedule observed earlier. First, we may want to impose a minimum length or a maximum length on the duration of a vehicle duty (set of trips assigned to a vehicle between its visits to the garage). The minimum length constraint arises when there is a minimum duration of each piece of work assigned to a driver, for example two hours. In this context, a vehicle duty of less than two hours duration will cost at least two hours of paid time. It is thus advisable to try to minimize the number of such vehicle duties. The maximum duration constraint is in general related to the necessity to refuel vehicles.

Both of these problems have to be dealt with heuristically. In practice the following heuristics have been found useful:

Step 0. Solve the problem without these maximum or minimum length constraints.

Step 1. Split the day into a certain number of time periods.

Step 2. For each time period, split the vehicle duty into two partial duties: the set of trips finishing before or during the time period, and the set of trips finishing after the time period. Solve an assignment problem between the two sets of partial duties taking into account the cost of having vehicle duty durations below the lower limit, and prohibiting duties from being longer than the upper limit.

Step 3. Cycle through the time period or various sets of time periods until no improvement is possible.

The second set of complicating constraints arises because one may want to take advantage of possible flexibility in the timetable concerning the departure time of the trip (for example, trip departure time may vary within ±5 minutes of a desired time). Desrosiers, Soumis & Desrochers [1984] have described a combinatorial approach for this type of problem in which they solve a set-covering problem with column generation over all possible feasible vehicle duties respecting the time windows. These vehicle duties are not predefined but are generated as the algorithm progresses using shortest path or dynamic programming algorithms.

A third set of constraints occurs for companies that operate their fleets out of several garages such that each vehicle belongs to a single garage and must return to that garage at the end of its daily cycle. Each garage will typically have a capacity constraint and some garages may also have certain minimum usage levels, even if this is not cost-effective, for example in the case of a new garage located in an industrial rather than residential area. The company may also require that a certain number of vehicles be always out of the garage to facilitate maintenance activities. Finally for control reasons, the company may not allow vehicles assigned to a route to be split between several garages.

Various approaches have been proposed for this problem [Bodin, Golden, Assad & Ball, 1983; Carraresi & Gallo, 1984a; Mandl, 1980; Maze & Khasnabis, 1985; Rousseau, Lessard & Désilets, 1988]. Essentially, a choice must be made between clustering the trips and assigning them to the garage first, and then scheduling vehicles in each garage separately, or first scheduling the whole fleet as if there were only one garage and then assigning the resulting trips to each garage. If there are no constraints on separating a given route among several garages, Carraresi & Gallo [1984a] have proposed an approach based on a Lagrangean relaxation of the problem coupled with a subgradient optimization technique to find an optimal solution. On the other hand, Rousseau, Lessard & Désilets [1988] have proposed a simple clustering heuristic that can take into account all kinds of operational constraints. They sequentially assign all the trips of each route to the best garage and then search for a feasible solution by neighborhood exchange heuristics, moving routes from one garage to another in order to improve the cost or feasibility in relation to the various constraints. They then optimize the schedule for each garage. These methods can also be used to study the location of new garages and evaluate their impact on operational costs.

Although crew costs often represent more than 60% of operating costs, it does not appear useful to consider the crew scheduling constraints in preparing the vehicle schedule, except for the minimum length of a piece of work and some other similar constraints. For small problems with particular constraints it would also seem worthwhile to take these constraints into account [Scott, 1984]. Finally, in some contexts, it is necessary to schedule drivers and buses together because each driver is assigned to a given bus. This often happens in intercity contexts where deadheading drivers to a relief point is not practical. It also happens in some urban contexts where the authority wants to keep a given driver on a given bus in order that each driver takes better care of his/her bus.

5.3. Crew scheduling

Crew schedule planning in a transit company involves two different operations: the generation of the drivers' daily duties and the assignment of a set of daily duties (called a roster) to each driver. We will consider each of these problems in turn. The proceedings of the most recent workshops on computer scheduling of public transport constitute an excellent set of references on the subject [Daduna & Wren, 1988; Desrocher & Rousseau, 1992; Paixao & Daduna, 1994; Rousseau, 1985; Wren, 1981]. Wren & Rousseau [1994] also provides a survey of this problem.

5.3.1. Duty generation

The problem can be expressed simply as the creation of a set of duties of minimum cost, ensuring that each bus trip is covered by a driver (or crew), and that all union contract rules are respected. Several authors favor an approach based on the set-covering formulation of the problem. Theoretically, in this approach all feasible duties have to be generated according to union contract rules, and the least cost subset of duties that covers all bus trips is mathematically selected. The formulation is as follows:

$$\text{Min} \sum_j c_j x_j$$

subject to $\quad \sum_j a_{ij} x_j = 1$ $\hspace{4cm}$ (1)

$\hspace{3.4cm} \sum_i b_{ij} x_j \geq d$ $\hspace{4cm}$ (2)

$\hspace{3.4cm} x_j = 0 \text{ or } 1$

where x_j is the duty variable with cost c_j, $a_{ij} = 1$, if duty j performs the task (trip) i. Constraint (1) insures that all tasks will be performed by a duty, while constraint (2) imposes other constraints on the problem such as a minimum number of duties of certain types, etc.

If the operating or union rules restrict a driver to working on only one bus route, and if there are not too many feasible duties due to strict working rules, this approach may be feasible. Otherwise, if for example full interlining is permitted (meaning that drivers are allowed to work on several routes during a duty), the number of feasible duties is extremely large and simply cannot be generated. Advocates of the set-covering approach then either have to split the problem into several sub-problems (evening problem, morning problem, etc. [see Ward, Durant & Hallman, 1981]) or heavily restrict the generation of duties according to heuristic rules (for example by eliminating relief points that are unlikely to be useful). This is the case for Busman, Ramcutter, and Crewsched, among other software packages [see Rousseau, 1985, for several papers based on this approach].

The main difficulty with this approach is that there does not exist a good set of rules for identifying what are likely to be good feasible duties. A typical duty may be very efficient under certain operating and union rules while being very inefficient under another set of rules. Desrochers [1986] and Desrochers & Soumis [1989] used the set-covering approach to the problem, but sequentially generated only the duties useful to improve the solution at each step of the algorithm. Thus only a small subset of the duties have to be generated. It seems, however, that the technique will apply only to small to medium-size problems, but could be quite useful in the context where the drivers have to work on only one bus route. Rousseau, Desrosiers & Dumas [1994] have reported on the results obtained with this approach.

The most common approach to the transit crew scheduling problem, in both manual and computer-based methods, proceeds as follows:

First, the vehicle duties, called blocks (the itinerary of a vehicle between its departure from the garage and its return to the garage) in the literature, are split into pieces of work (the period of time during which a driver works continuously). Second, the pieces of work are grouped to form driver duties, and finally, the solution is improved heuristically and/or manually. A matching or an assignment problem formulation for the construction of duties is generally used. Various strategies are possible for splitting the blocks into pieces of work. Most approaches use heuristics adapted to the type of problem considered. In RUCUS [Wilhelm, 1975], the first general package developed for transit crew scheduling, a set of parameters enables the user partially to determine the method by which the pieces will be defined. In Sage runcutting and RUCUS II [Luedtke, 1985], an interactive system for transit crew scheduling, the user has direct control on the ways the pieces are identified. Hoffstadt [1981] and Parker & Smith [1981] include heuristic approaches adapted to their respective problems related to German and British working conditions. The HASTUS system uses a relaxation of the problem to determine how to define the pieces. Ball, Bodin & Dial [1981] form the pieces and blocks by sequentially matching the trips.

While using this general decomposition approach, HASTUS uses a mathematical model to split the blocks into pieces of work. A full description of the algorithm can be found in Rousseau, Lessard & Blais [1985]. The authors chose to solve a relaxation of the crew scheduling problem first, trying to keep the main features of the problem while relaxing all the details. The idea is to retain the essentials of the bus schedule structure and its impact on the contract rules and costs while greatly simplifying the precise bus schedule.

First the user must define periods, normally about 30 minutes in length, although they can vary, depending on the problem, from 15 to 60 minutes. The schedules of all buses are approximated so that all blocks both start and end at the beginning (or end) of a period. Reliefs (the times, and places, at which change of drivers is possible) can also occur only at the beginning of a period. Moreover, the problem is further relaxed by requiring that the duties selected be sufficient to cover the total requirement of drivers per period instead of requiring that they exactly cover all the blocks individually.

All feasible duties made up of two or three pieces of work covering an integer number of periods and satisfying the union contract are generated. The generating rules eliminate, under instructions from the user, duties which are of no interest or which do not correspond to unwritten rules or common practice (for example, a duty with a long break during a peak hour). All the duties are costed according to the union contract in use. A linear program then searches for the set of duties that will provide the number of drivers required during each period and satisfy other additional constraints at minimum cost.

One type of additional constraint is related to the union contract. All the constraints related to the total number of duties of a certain type are considered. These include constraints on the minimum or maximum number of duties without break and constraints on the maximum number of duties with certain undesirable characteristics like long spreads (the time between driver sign on and sign off for the day), small breaks, etc.

The relaxation is called HASTUS-macro and can also be used as a planning tool for the evaluation of the economic impact of changes in the union contract or in the service level. By changing the cost parameters or the service level, a new solution is obtained and can be compared with the current solution. The paper by Blais & Rousseau [1982] describes in detail the HASTUS-macro system and its use in that context. In practice, this relaxation has been found to be very accurate, producing cost estimates within 2% of the real operating costs for drivers.

The HASTUS-macro solution gives a guide to the number of duties of each type that should be constructed in a final solution. The next step uses this information to split the blocks into pieces of work that correspond as closely as possible to the ones generated in the HASTUS-macro relaxation.

Each block is sequentially split into pieces of work by solving a shortest path problem. It is interesting to note that the problem of splitting a block into pieces can be expressed as the problem of finding a path from the starting time of the block to its ending time using arcs that correspond to pieces of work. Figure 13 illustrates this concept with the feasible pieces of work (we are assuming here a minimum length of two hours) represented by arcs. We have assumed for simplicity that a relief opportunity exists at every hour in this example.

The cost associated with each piece of work in the flow formulation corresponds to a penalty indicating whether this given piece will increase or decrease the difference between the number of pieces of work of that type desired, and the number of pieces of work of that type already present in the current solution. We cycle through all blocks until no improvement can be achieved towards coming closer to the number of desired pieces of each type indicated by HASTUS-macro.

Once the blocks have been split into pieces of work, a matching algorithm is used to generate duties [Lessard, Minoux & Rousseau, 1989; Rousseau, Lessard & Blais, 1985] and several heuristics are used to improve the solution. The whole system is embedded in a software system [Rousseau & Blais, 1985] and is installed in more than seventy cities around the world (including Montréal, Québec, Calgary, Seattle, New York, Boston, Stockholm, Singapore, Newcastle and Barcelona). The savings of this system over a manual solution varies but is typically in the range of 15% to 20% of unproductive costs (unproductive time, overtime, special payments, etc.), which could represent 2–3% of total operating costs (for example, approximately 3 million dollars annual savings in Montréal). This application has been described in *Interfaces* [Blais, Lamont & Rousseau, 1990], where the mathematical model is also provided.

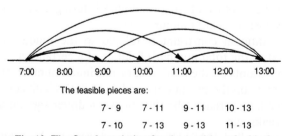

Fig. 13. The flow formulation for the partition of a block.

5.3.2. The rostering problem

A roster can be defined as the set of duties assigned to a particular driver. Making up rosters may be easy or difficult depending on the particular union contract. In most North American companies the assignment of duties is left to the drivers themselves and the decision is made on a seniority basis: this leaves no role at all for mathematical modelling! On the other hand, with many European companies, work load must be distributed evenly among the drivers. In fact, in these problems, few penalties are associated with unpleasant duties. Rather, these duties are evenly distributed among all drivers, who all receive approximately the same monthly pay. The rules for making monthly, weekly, or in some cases, several month rosters vary widely from one company to another. While there seem to be very few general packages available for rostering problems in transit, there is a consensus on the most efficient methods to be used to build such rosters. A more detailed description of the approach used can be found in Rousseau [1984], Belletti, Davini, Carraresi & Gallo [1985] and Hagberg [1985].

The basic method is a heuristic based on a construction phase and on a marginal improvement phase. The construction phase can be described as follows: given a set of partial rosters P_i constructed from day 1 to day i (initially the set of partial rosters is composed of all duties for day 1), construct P_{i+1} by defining an assignment problem between the partial rosters in P_i and the duties that have to be performed on day $i + 1$.

The assignment problem can be solved with standard well known algorithms. The objective function is a penalty function measuring how the resulting partial rosters will differ on various criteria from the ideal partial rosters. For example, if the main criterion is to equalize as much as possible the total number of driving hours among the rosters, the penalty incurred by assigning duty k to partial roster j might be the square of the difference between the number of driving hours in the resulting roster and the desired level for such a number after $i + 1$ days. A general penalty function is described in Nicoletti [1973, 1975] for the airline rostering problem.

Many kinds of exchange algorithms well known in routing and scheduling can be used to obtain marginal improvements. An interesting approach, however, has been applied by Carraresi & Gallo [1984a] for the transit crew rostering problem in which the objective is to minimize the maximum total driving time in the period considered. This problem is described as the multi-level bottleneck problem and it is shown that the problem is NP-complete. An asymptotically optimal algorithm is presented for this case. In general, the objective function is different, but their type of algorithm could easily be adapted to the general situation when starting from a feasible solution.

Sequentially consider each day i in the rostering period.

Option 1. Remove from each roster the duties of day i. Define and solve an assignment problem between the duties just removed and the partial rosters with the penalty function in use, allowing only feasible assignments.

Option 2. Define and solve an assignment problem with on one side the partial rosters composed of all the duties starting before day i, and on the other side the partial rosters composed of all the duties starting on or after day i. Of course, only feasible assignments are allowed and the same cost function as in the construction heuristic is used.

If no improvement in the objective function is obtained after all days in the rostering period have been considered, the process stops. If an improvement has been achieved, another iteration is performed on the period. Based on the results of Carraresi & Gallo on their specific problem, we can expect this algorithm to perform very well on all rostering types of problems even if the theoretical properties demonstrated by the authors may not hold in all situations. These methods obviously need to be adapted to particular situations, but they have been used successfully in several contexts.

5.4. Spare driver planning

A final aspect of operational planning which is now beginning to receive more serious attention is the determination and assignment of spare drivers (often referred to as the extraboard) who are required to be available both to fill in for absent regular drivers and to provide unscheduled extra service which is required from time to time. This problem can be viewed at both a strategic level and a tactical level, and both problems have received some attention in the past decade [Koutsopoulos & Wilson, 1987]. At the strategic level the principal problem is to find the optimal extraboard size which minimizes total operator cost while providing a given level of service reliability. This problem has been formulated as a non-linear program with the non-linearity arising from the nature of the overtime term in the total cost function [Hickman, Koutsopoulos & Wilson, 1988] and has also been solved heuristically [Shiftan & Wilson, 1993a,b].

The tactical problem is, given a certain size of extraboard on a particular day, how to schedule these spare drivers to provide the best coverage of the (uncertain) absences and extra work. This problem is more closely related to the driver scheduling problem discussed in the previous section, but has a much stronger flavor of scheduling under stochastic demands. It also has been approached both heuristically and optimally [Kaysi & Wilson, 1990; Koutsopoulos, 1990]. It is an area where future work is likely to have a real impact on practice.

6. The dispatching problem

In some respects dispatching problems are similar to operational planning problems. Vehicle schedules including additional or chartered trips must be planned, and spare drivers must be allocated to perform pieces of work left open by regular drivers on vacation or reporting sick. The same type of techniques as described earlier can be used in this context. Here again the technology is opening a whole new field related to the optimum control of vehicle schedules. With an automatic vehicle location and control system (AVLC), the dispatcher now has several strategies for dealing with a vehicle that is delayed: take measures to help the vehicle catch up with the schedule, or delay the following vehicles in order to insure an even frequency and prevent bunching. Priority for buses at intersections may be used to reduce delay and better control adherence to schedules. In fact, with all the information collected with an AVLC system, even the timetables may be calculated in order to facilitate adherence to schedules. In heavily congested cities (e.g., Shanghai) it is also possible to imagine some real time scheduling of buses [Li et al., 1992] where at each departure of a bus, it is decided which stops will be served or skipped. As we can see, there are new and challenging problems ahead in this field.

7. Conclusion

This review has been brief, with very little detail. We have demonstrated, however, that in the transit area, operations research techniques are alive and well. They are being used to assist in the planning and operation of many transit networks around the world. All the problems have not been solved, and even for the ones that have been solved, better techniques could be found. New problems are arising from the implementation of new technology in transit. Better information will be available from the in-vehicle microcomputer and better information will be required by the public in general. There will be plenty of challenging operations research problems in the transit area for many years to come.

References

Part I

AACI/IATA (Airport Associations Coordinating Council/International Air Transport Association) (1981). *Guidelines for Airport Capacity/Demand Analysis*, Montreal, Que., and Geneva.

Abundo, S. (1990). An approach for estimating delays at a busy airport, S.M. Thesis, Operations Research Center, Massachusetts Institute of Technology, Cambridge, MA.

Alexander, B. (1970). Aircraft density and midair collision. *Proc. IEEE* 58, 377–381.

Ashford, N. (1988). Level of service design concepts for airport passenger terminals – a European view. *Transportation Planning Tech.* 12, 5–21.

Babic, O., C. Teodorovic and V. Tosic (1984). Aircraft stand assignment to minimize walking. *ASCE J. Transportation Engrg.* 110, 55–66.

Bandara, S., and S.C. Wirasinghe (1991). Optimum geometries for pier type airport terminals. *ASCE J. Transportation Engrg*, 117.

Bandara, S., and S.C. Wirasinghe (1992). Walking distance minimization for airport terminal configurations. *Transportation Res.* 26A, 59–74.

Benz, G.P. (1986). *Pedestrian Time–Space Concept – A New Approach to the Planning and Design of Pedestrian Facilities*, Parsons, Brinckerhoff, Quade and Douglas, New York.

Blumstein, A. (1959). The landing capacity of a runway. *Oper. Res.* 7, 752–763.

Blumstein, A. (1960). An analytical investigation of airport capacity, Report TA-1358-G-1, Cornell Aeronautical Laboratory, Ithaca, NY.

Dear, R. (1976). The dynamic scheduling of aircraft in the near-terminal area, Technical Report R76-9, Flight Transportation Laboratory, Massachusetts Institute of Technology, Cambridge, MA.

Dunlay, W.J. (1975). Analytical models of perceived air traffic control conflicts. *Transportation Sci.* 9, 149–164.

Endoh, S. (1982). Aircraft collision models, Technical Report R82-2, Flight Transportation Laboratory, Massachusetts Institute of Technology, Cambridge, MA.

Endoh, S., and A.R. Odoni (1983). A generalized model for predicting the frequency of air conflicts. *Proc. Conf. Safety Issues in Air Traffic Systems Planning and Design*, Princeton University, Princeton, NJ.

Flanagan, P.D., and K.E. Willis (1969). Frequency of airspace conflicts in the mixed terminal environment, Report of Department of Transportation Air Traffic Control Advisory Committee, Vol. 2, U.S. Dept. of Transportation, Washington, DC.

Fruin, J.J. (1971). *Pedestrian Planning and Design*, Metropolitan Association of Urban Designers and Environmental Planners, New York.

Graham, W., and R.H. Orr (1970). Terminal air traffic flow and collision exposure. *Proc. IEEE* 58, 328–336.

Green, L., P. Kolesar and A. Svoronos (1991). Some effects of nonstationarity on multiserver Markovian queueing systems. *Oper. Res.* 39, 502–511.

Harris, R.M. (1972). Models for runway capacity analysis, Report No. FAA-EM-73-5, The MITRE Corporation, McLean, VA.

Hockaday, S.L.M., and A. Kanafani (1972). A methodology for airport capacity analysis. *Transportation Res.* 8, 171–180.

Horangic, B. (1990). Some queueing models of airport delays, S.M. Thesis, Operations Research Center, Massachusetts Institute of Technology, Cambridge, MA.

IATA (International Air Transport Association) (1981). Guidelines for airport capacity/demand management, Report AACC/IATA TRAP WG, Cointrin–Geneva, Switzerland.

Kivestu, P. (1976). Alternative methods of investigating the time-dependent M/G/K queue, S.M. Thesis, Department of Aeronautics and Astronautics, Massachusetts Institute of Technology, Cambridge, MA.

Koopman, B.O. (1972). Air terminal queues under time-dependent conditions. *Oper. Res.* 20, 1089–1114.

Lee, A.M. (1966). *Applied Queueing Theory*, Macmillan, London, St. Martin's Press, New York.

MacDonald, B. (1987). A generalized model for the prediction of controller intervention rates in the en route ATC system, Ph.D. Thesis, Operations Research Center, Massachusetts Institute of Technology, Cambridge, MA.

Mangoubi, R., and D.F.X. Mathaisel (1985). Optimizing gate assignments at airport terminals. *Transportation Sci.* 19, 173–188.

Marks, B.L. (1963). ATC separation standards and collision risk, Technical Note MATH 91, Royal Aircraft Establishment, Farnborough.

Newell, G.F. (1971). *Applications of Queueing Theory*, Barnes and Noble, Boston, MA, Chapman and Hall, London.

Odoni, A.R. (1972). Efficient operation of runways, in: A.W. Drake, R.L. Keeney and P.M. Morse (eds.), *Analysis of Public Systems*, MIT Press, Cambridge, MA.

Odoni, A.R. (1991). *Transportation Modeling Needs: Airports and Airspace*, U.S. Department of Transportation, Volpe National Transportation Systems Center, Cambridge, MA.

Odoni, A.R., and R. De Neufville (1992). Passenger terminal design. *Transportation Res.* 26A, 27–36.

Odoni, A.R., and E. Roth (1983). An empirical investigation of the transient behavior of stationary queueing systems. *Oper. Res.* 31, 432–455.

Psaraftis, H.N. (1980). A dynamic programming approach for sequencing groups of identical jobs. *Oper. Res.* 28, 1347–1359.

Ratcliffe, S., and R.L. Ford (1982). Conflicts between random flights in a given area. *J. Navigation* 35, 47–71.

Reich, P.G. (1966). Analysis of long-range air traffic systems: separation standards. *J. Navigation* 19, 88–98, 169–186, 331–347.

Siddiqee, W. (1974). Air route capacity models. *Navigation* 20, 296–300.

Swedish, W.J. (1981). Upgraded FAA airfield capacity model, Report MTR-81W16 (also Federal Aviation Administration Report FAA-EM-81-1), The MITRE Corporation, McLean, VA.

Transportation Research (1992). Special issue: Airport landside planning and operations, 26A, S.C. Wirasinghe and J.P. Braaksma, guest editors, pp. 1–92.

Transportation Research Board (1987). Measuring airport landside capacity, Special Report 215, National Research Council, Washington, DC.

Tosic, V. (1992). A review of airport passenger terminal operations analysis and modeling. *Transportation Res.* 26A, 3–26.

Venkatakrishnan, C.S., A.I. Barnett and A.R. Odoni (1993). Landings at Logan Airport: Describing and increasing airport capacity. *Transportation Sci.*, 211–227.

Part II

Andreasson, I. (1976). A method for the analysis of transit networks, in: M. Ruebens (ed.), *2nd European Congress on Operations Research,* North-Holland, Amsterdam.

Babin, A., M. Florian, L. James-Lefebvre and H. Spiess (1982). EMME/2: Interactive graphic method for road and transit planning. *Transportation Res. Record* 866, 1–9.

Babin, A., M. Florian, L. James-Lefebvre and H. Spiess (1984). EMME/2: Une méthode interactive graphique pour la planification du transport urbain multimodal. *Routes Transports* XIV(4), 22–31.

Ball, M.O., L.D. Bodin and R. Dial (1981). Experimentation with a computerized system for scheduling mass transit vehicles and crews, in: A. Wren (ed.), *Computer Scheduling of Public Transport: Urban Passenger Vehicle and Crew Scheduling,* North-Holland, Amsterdam, pp. 319–326.

Belletti, R., A. Davini, P. Carraresi and G. Gallo (1985). BDROP: A package for the bus drivers' rostering problem, in: J.-M. Rousseau (ed.), *Computer Scheduling of Public Transport 2,* North-Holland, Amsterdam, pp. 319–326.

Blais, J.-Y., J. Lamont and J.-M. Rousseau (1990). The HASTUS vehicle and manpower scheduling system at the Société de transport de la Communauté urbaine de Montréal. *Interfaces* 20(1), 26–42.

Blais, J.-Y., and J.-M. Rousseau (1982). HASTUS: A model for the economic evaluation of drivers' collective agreements in transit companies. *INFOR* 20, 3–15.

Bodin, L., B. Golden, A. Assad and M. Ball (1983). Routing and scheduling of vehicles and crews: The state-of-the-art. *Comput. Oper. Res.* 10(2), 65–211.

Bookbinder, J.H., and A. Désilets (1992). Transfer optimization in a transit network. *Transportation Sci.* 26(2), 106–118.

Carraresi, P., and G. Gallo (1984a). A multilevel bottleneck assignment approach to the bus drivers' rostering problem. *European J. Oper. Res.* 16(2), 163–173.

Carraresi, P., and G. Gallo (1984b). Network models for vehicle and crew scheduling. *European J. Oper. Res.* 16(2), 139–151.

Ceder, A. (1984). Bus frequency determination using passenger count data. *Transportation Res. A* 18A(5/6), 439–453.

Ceder, A. (1986). Methods for creating bus timetables. *Transportation Res. A* 21A(1), 59–83.

Ceder, A., and H. Stern (1981). Deficit function bus scheduling with deadheading trip insertions for fleet size reduction. *Transportation Sci.* 15, 338–363.

Chapleau, R. (1974). Réseaux de transport en commun: Structure informatique et affectation, Ph.D. Thesis, Dept. I.R.O., Univ. de Montréal, Que.

Chapleau, R., B. Allard and M. Canova (1982). Madituc: Un modèle de planification opérationnelle adapté aux entreprises de transport en commun de taille moyenne, Publication #265, Centre de Recherche sur les Transports, Univ. de Montréal, Que.

Chriqui, C. (1974). Réseaux de transport en commun: Les problèmes de cheminement et d'accès, Ph.D. Thesis, Dept. I.R.O., Univ. de Montréal, Que.

Chriqui, C., and P. Robillard (1975). Common bus lines. *Transportation Sci.* 9, 115–121.

Constantin, I. (1993). Optimisation des fréquences d'un réseau de transport en commun, Publication #881, Centre de Recherche sur les Transports, Univ. de Montréal, Que.

Constantin, I., and M. Florian (1993). Optimizing frequency in a transit network; A non-linear bi-level programming approach, Publication #914, Center for Research on Transportation, University of Montreal, Que.

Daduna, J.R., and A. Wren (eds.) (1988). *Computer-Aided Transit Scheduling*, Lecture Notes in Economics and Mathematical Systems 308, Springer-Verlag, Berlin.

De Cea, J. (1986). Rutas y strategias en modelos de asignacion a redes de transporte publico, *IV Congreso Panamericano de Ingenieria de Transito y Transporte*, Chile, December 1986.

De Cea, J., J.P. Bunster, L. Zubieta and M. Florian (1988). Optimal strategies and optimal routes in public transit assignment models: an empirical comparison. *Traffic Engrg. Control* 29(10), 520–526.

Desrochers, M. (1986). La fabrication d'horaires de travail pour les conducteurs d'autobus par une méthode de génération de colonnes, Publication #470, Centre de Recherche sur les Transports, Univ. de Montréal, Que.

Desrochers, M., and J.-M. Rousseau (eds.) (1992). *Computer-Aided Transit Scheduling*, Lecture Notes in Economics and Mathematical Systems 386, Springer-Verlag, Berlin.

Desrochers, M., and F. Soumis (1989). A column generation approach to the urban transit crew scheduling problem. *Transportation Sci.* 23(1), 1–13.

Desrosiers, J., F. Soumis and M. Desrochers (1982). Routes sur un réseau espace–temps. *Proc. of the Meeting of the Administrative Sciences Association of Canada*, Operations Research Section 3(28) [also Publication #236, Centre de Recherche sur les Transports, Univ. de Montréal, Que.].

Desrosiers, J., F. Soumis and M. Desrochers (1984). Routing with time windows by column generation. *Networks* 14, 545.

Dial, R.B. (1967). Transit pathfinder algorithm. *Highway Res. Record* 205, 67–85.

Fearnside, K., and D.P. Draper (1971). Public transport assignment – A new approach. *Traffic Engrg. Control*, November, 298–299.

Florian, M. (1977). A traffic equilibrium model of travel by car and public transit modes. *Transportation Sci.* 11(2), 166–179.

Florian, M. (1985). Le logiciel EMME/2 et son utilisation dans la région de Montréal. *Transports* 30, 141–148.

Florian, M., and H. Spiess (1983). On binary mode choice/assignment models. *Transportation Sci.* 17(1), 32–47.

Florian, M., and H. Spiess (1986). Models and techniques for the planning of urban and regional transportation networks, Publication #463, Centre de Recherche sur les Transports, Univ. de Montréal, Que.

Furth, P. (1986). Zonal route design for transit corridors. *Transportation Sci.* 20(1), 1–12.

Furth, P., and N.H.M. Wilson (1981). Setting frequencies on bus routes: Theory and practice. *Transportation Res. Record* 818, 1–7.

General Motors Transportation System Center (1980). Interactive graphic transit design system (IGTDS) demonstration study: Bellevue, Washington, Final Report, Vols. I and II (EP-80023A) (GMTSC, Warren, MI).

Hagberg, B. (1985). An assignment approach to the rostering problem: An application to taxi vehicles, in: J.-M. Rousseau (ed.), *Computer Scheduling of Public Transport 2*, North-Holland, Amsterdam, pp. 313–318.

Hamer, N., and L. Séguin (1994). The HASTUS vehicle and crew scheduling system: New version and features, in: J. Paixao, and J.R. Daduna (eds.), *Computer-Aided Transit Scheduling*, Springer-Verlag, Berlin, to appear.

Hasselström, D. (1981). Public transportation planning – A mathematical programming approach, Ph.D. Thesis, Department of Business Administration, University of Gothenburg, Gothenburg.

Hickman, M.D., H.N. Koutsopoulos and N. Wilson (1988). A strategic model for operator workforce planning in the transit industry. *Transportation Res. Record* 1165, 60–68.

Hoffstadt, J. (1981). Computerized vehicle and driver scheduling for Hamburg Hochbahn Aktiegesellschaft, in: A. Wren (ed.), *Computer Scheduling of Public Transport – Urban Passenger Vehicle and Crew Scheduling*, North-Holland, Amsterdam, pp. 35–52.

Jansson, K., and B. Ridderstolpe (1992). A method for the route-choice problem in public transport systems. *Transportation Sci.* 26(3), 246–251.

Kaysi, I., and N. Wilson (1990). Scheduling transit extraboard personnel. *Transportation Res. Record* 1266, 31–43.

Koutsopoulos, H. (1990). Scheduling for extraboard operations in transit systems. *Transportation Sci.* 24(2), 87–104.

Koutsopoulos, H., A. Odoni and N. Wilson (1985). Determination of headway as a function of time-varying characteristics on a transit network, in: J.-M. Rousseau (ed.), *Computer Scheduling of Public Transport 2*, North-Holland, Amsterdam, pp. 391–414.

Koutsopoulos, H., and N. Wilson (1987). Operator workforce planning in the transit industry. *Transportation Res. A*, 21A, 127–138.

Lampkin, W., and P.D. Saalmans (1967). The design of routes, service frequencies and schedules for a municipal bus undertaking: A case study. *Oper. Res. Q.* 18(4), 375–397.

Last, A., and S.E. Leak (1976). Transept: A bus model. *Traffic Engrg. Control* 17(1), 14–20.

Le Clerq, F. (1972). A public transport assignment method. *Traffic Engrg. Control* 14(2), 91–96.

Lessard, R., M. Minoux and J.-M. Rousseau (1989). A new approach to general matching problems using relaxation and network flow subproblems. *Networks* 19(4), 459–480.

Li, Y., J.-M. Rousseau and M. Gendreau (1994). Real-time scheduling for public transit operations with bus-location information, in: J. Paixao, and J.R. Daduna, *Computer Aided Transit Scheduling*, Springer-Verlag, Berlin, to appear.

Li, Y., J.-M. Rousseau and F. Wu (1992). Real-time scheduling on a transit bus route, in: M. Desrochers, and J.-M. Rousseau, *Computer Aided Transit Scheduling*, Springer-Verlag, Berlin.

Luedtke, L.K. (1985). Rucus II: A review of system capabilities, in: J.-M. Rousseau (ed.), *Computer Scheduling of Public Transport 2*, North-Holland, Amsterdam, pp. 61–110.

Mandl, C. (1980). Evaluation and optimization of urban public transportation networks. *European J. Oper. Res.* 5, 396–404.

Marguier, P., and A. Ceder (1984). Passenger waiting strategies for overlapping bus routes. *Transportation Sci.* 21(3), 207–230.

Maze, T.H., and S. Khasnabis (1985). Bus garage location planning with dynamic vehicle assignments: A methodology. *Transportation Res. B* 19B(2), 1–13.

Nguyen, S., and S. Pallottino (1988). Equilibrium traffic assignment for large scale transit networks. *European J. Oper. Res.* 37, 176–186.

Nicoletti, B. (1973). Automatic crew rostering. *AGIFORS Symp. Proc.*, Acapulco, pp. 157–182.

Nicoletti, B. (1975). Automatic crew rostering. *Transportation Sci.* 9, 33–42.

Osleeb, J.P., and H. Moellering (1976). TRANSPLAN: An interactive geographic information system for the design and analysis of urban transit systems, URISA 1976. *14th Annual Conference of the Urban and Regional Information Systems Association*, pp. 212–225.

Paixao, J., and J.R. Daduna (1994). *Computer-Aided Transit Scheduling*, Lecture Notes in Economics and Mathematical Systems, Springer-Verlag, Berlin, to appear.

Parker, M.E., and B.M. Smith (1981). Two approaches to computer crew scheduling, in: A. Wren (ed.), *Computer Scheduling of Public Transport – Urban Passenger Vehicle and Crew Scheduling*, North-Holland, Amsterdam, pp. 193–222.

Rapp, M.H., P. Mattenberger, S. Piguet and A. Robert-Grandpierre (1976). Interactive graphics system for transit route optimization. *Transportation Res. Record* 559, 73–88.

Rousseau, J.-M. (1984). Crew scheduling methods in the operation and planning of transportation systems, in: M. Florian (ed.), *Transportation Planning Models*, North-Holland, Amsterdam, 439–474.

Rousseau, J.-M. (ed.) (1985). *Computer Scheduling of Public Transport 2*, North-Holland, Amsterdam.

Rousseau, J.-M., and J.-Y. Blais (1985). HASTUS: An interactive system for buses and crew scheduling, in: J.-M. Rousseau (ed.), *Computer Scheduling of Public Transport 2*, North-Holland, Amsterdam, pp. 45–60.

Rousseau, J.-M., J. Desrosiers and Y. Dumas (1994). Results obtained with Crew-Opt, a column generation method for transit crew scheduling, in: J. Paixao, and J.R. Daduna (eds.), *Computer-Aided Transit Scheduling*, Springer-Verlag, Berlin, to appear.

Rousseau, J.-M., R. Lessard and J.-Y. Blais (1985). Enhancements to the HASTUS crew scheduling algorithm, in: J.-M. Rousseau (ed.), *Computer Scheduling of Public Transport 2*, North-Holland, Amsterdam, pp. 255–268.

Rousseau, J.-M., R. Lessard and A. Désilets (1988). Aliages: A system for the assignment of bus routes to garages, in: J.R. Daduna, and A. Wren (eds.), *Computer-Aided Transit Scheduling*, Springer-Verlag, Berlin, pp. 8–14.

Saha, J.L. (1970). Algorithms for bus scheduling problems. *Oper. Res. Q.* 21, 463–474.

Schéele, C.E. (1977). A mathematical programming algorithm for optimal bus frequencies, Institute of Technology, University of Linköping, Sweden.

Scott, D. (1984). A method for scheduling urban transit vehicles which takes account of operation labor cost, Publication #365, Centre de Recherche sur les Transports, Univ. de Montréal, Que.

Scott, D. (1986). Minimal fleet size in transhipment-type vehicle scheduling problems, Publication #487, Centre de Recherche sur les Transports, Univ. de Montréal, Que.

Shiftan, Y., and N. Wilson (1993a). Strategic transit workforce planning model incorporating overtime, absence and reliability relationships. *Transportation Res. Record* 1402, 98–106.

Shiftan, Y., and N. Wilson (1993b). Public transport workforce Sizing Recognizing the Service Reliability Objective, in: J. Paixao, and J.R. Daduna (eds.), *Computer Aided Transit Scheduling*, Springer-Verlag, Berlin, to appear.

Spiess, H. (1983). On optimal route choice strategies in transit networks, Publication #286, Centre de Recherche sur les Transports, Univ. de Montréal.

Spiess, H., and M. Florian (1989). Optimal strategies: A new assignment model for transit networks. *Transportation Res. B*, 23B(2), 83–102.

Turnquist, M. (1979). Zone scheduling of urban bus routes. *Transportation Engrg. J.* 105(1), 1–12.

UMTA/FHWA (1977). *UTPS Reference Manual*, U.S. Department of Transportation, Washington, DC.

Ward, R.E., P.A. Durant and A.B. Hallman (1981). A problem decomposition approach to scheduling the drivers and crews of mass transit systems, in: A. Wren (ed.), *Computer Scheduling of Public Transport – Urban Passenger Vehicle and Crew Scheduling*, North-Holland, Amsterdam, pp. 297–312.

Wilhelm, E. (1975). Overview of the Rucus package driver run cutting program, Preprints, in: L. Bodin, and D. Bergman (eds.), *Workshop on Automated Techniques for Scheduling of Vehicle Operators for Urban Public Transportation Services*, Chicago, IL.

Wilson, N. (1986). Bus operations planning, Preprints, *Management and Planning of Urban Transport Systems from Theory to Practice*, Montréal, Que.

Wilson, N., and M. Banasiak (1984). The role of computer models in transit service allocation decisions. U.S. Department of Transportation, Report MA-11-0041, Washington, DC.

Wren, A. (ed.) (1981). *Computer Scheduling of Public Transport – Urban Passenger Vehicle and Crew Scheduling*, North-Holland, Amsterdam.

Wren, A., and J.-M. Rousseau (1994). Bus driver scheduling, in: J. Paixao, and J.R. Daduna (eds.), *An Overview in Computer-Aided Transit Scheduling*, Springer-Verlag, Berlin, to appear.

S.M. Pollock et al., Eds., *Handbooks in OR & MS, Vol. 6*

Chapter 6

The Deployment of Police, Fire, and Emergency Medical Units

Arthur J. Swersey

Yale School of Management, Box 1-A, New Haven, CT 06520, U.S.A.

1. Introduction

A fire engine or ambulance speeding to the scene of an emergency, or a police car patrolling city streets are common images of daily life. Beginning in the mid-1960's operations researchers began studying the deployment of these emergency services and since then a very large body of OR literature has emerged. Police, fire, and emergency medical systems are all concerned with improving public safety, and share the common objective of responding to citizen calls for assistance as quickly as possible to reduce loss of life and injury. In each system, the primary problem is to decide the number and locations of emergency units, and which unit or units to dispatch to an incoming call for service.

Emergency services, like urban services in general, are highly labor-intensive, with personnel costs accounting for more than 90% of operating costs. The traditional approach to achieving productivity gains in the face of rising labor costs, is to substitute capital for labor, but this is hard to do in emergency service systems. (One attempt was the robot fire fighter developed by the Japanese, but because of the complex nature of the fire fighting environment, there is little likelihood that robots will be useful except in very specialized situations.) Given this difficulty, the role of OR models in productivity improvement becomes more important, either by making existing resources more effective, or by maintaining effectiveness with fewer units.

The challenge of implementation is particularly formidable in this field because emergency services operate in a highly politicized environment. For example, closing a fire station is difficult in the face of predictable opposition from militant unions, private citizens, and local politicians. In one noteworthy example in Trenton, N.J., a fire station location study showed it was possible to both reduce the number of fire companies and improve fire protection. At the last moment, the mayor gave in to political pressures in an election year and implementation plans were abandoned [Walker, 1978].

An essential part of any operations research study is determining appropriate measures of effectiveness. Ideally, the analyst would like to relate deployment decisions to final outcomes such as lives lost or property damage. As discussed in Section 4, in the emergency medical area beginning about 1980, some very useful results have been achieved in this regard, but in the fire and police areas, there has been less progress. Consequently, deployment studies have focused on surrogate performance measures such as response time.

In comparing alternative deployment policies, the OR analyst and the decision-maker need to consider issues of efficiency and equity. For example, on efficiency grounds (in order to minimize total losses), more fire units would be placed in the high fire incidence areas of a city, while equity considerations (giving each neighborhood its fair share) would emphasize spreading units evenly throughout the city. The problem is to arrive at an appropriate tradeoff or balance between these competing objectives. Many of the models discussed in this chapter are descriptive, allowing the decisionmaker to compare alternatives on the basis of the performance measure(s). The prescriptive (optimization) models usually choose an objective function that focuses either on efficiency (e.g., minimize average response time), or equity (e.g., insure that each demand region is within x miles of a server). In some cases, multi-objective techniques have been used to generate tradeoffs between equity and efficiency. Although the focus in emergency service modelling is on measures of service such as response time or patrol frequency, the workload of the service units is often considered as well.

In many situations, emergency service demand is low and deterministic models are adequate. This is true, for example, in most cities for the problem of locating fire stations. In other cases, servers are unavailable a substantial fraction of the time, and the stochastic nature of demand and service times must be accounted for.

In the mid to late 1960's operations research approaches to emergency service problems were given impetus by two significant activities: the Rand Fire Project in New York City and the police work for the Science and Technology Task Force of the President's Commission on Law Enforcement and the Administration of Justice.

The police work for the Science and Technology Task Force took place during 1966 and 1967. The most significant contributor was Richard Larson who documented these efforts and additional work in the Lanchester prize winning book, *Urban Police Patrol Analysis* [Larson, 1972b]. This fascinating volume is pioneering research that along with the Rand Fire Project (described below) set the stage for much of the work that was to follow. One interesting problem that Larson considered was inspired by Koopman's [1957] search theory modelling. He adopted Koopman's model to determine the likelihood that a patrol car on random patrol intercepts a crime in progress, and found the probability to be remarkably small over a range of reasonable assumptions about patrol frequency and crime incidence [see also Blumstein & Larson, 1967]. Subsequently, other authors [Chelst, 1978a,b; Olson & Wright, 1975; Rosenshine, 1969] addressed this issue of patrol strategy, but given the low intercept probabilities, these papers are of more theoretical then practical interest.

In another chapter of *Urban Police Patrol Analysis*, Larson used relatively simple probability arguments to estimate police car travel distances to calls for service for various patrol area geometries. These square root models will be discussed in Section 5.

The Rand Fire Project represented a unique example of urban operations research, bringing together the equivalent of about ten full-time researchers over the eight-year period from 1968 to 1976. In 1968, New York City Mayor John Lindsay asked the Rand Corporation, the California think tank which up to that time had been known primarily for its defense work, to open an office in New York City to study the city's problems, initially in the areas of fire, police, health care, and housing. The Fire Project was formed under the direction of Edward H. Blum, a Rand employee with a Ph.D. in chemical engineering. Blum recognizing the operational nature of the fire protection problem assembled a team of mainly operations researchers and computer specialists. The Fire Project benefitted from the top management support of the fire department and the participation of fire department personnel in the problem-solving process. The work was a joint effort in which the Rand analysts provided expertise in operations research while fire department officers provided the needed fire fighting and fire protection knowledge. The Rand team was close to the day-to-day operations of the Department but sufficiently removed to enable them to take a more strategic view.

The Fire Project researchers found that they had to break new ground in developing models that were useful to the largest and busiest fire department in the world which at the time of the study deployed about 375 fire companies throughout the city. The Fire Project budget of about $700 000 per year was roughly equivalent to the cost of operating a single fire company and the expectation was that spending this sum of money to make the existing fire fighting force more effective would bring returns far in excess of the benefit of adding one additional company.

The Fire Project was credited with monetary saving of more than $6 million per year, but more than that the work resulted in cultural and organizational changes that greatly affected the way the Department is run. The Rand Fire Project research is documented in a comprehensive book [Rand Fire Project, 1979], while a summary of the work is given in Ignall, Kolesar, Swersey, Walker, Blum, & Bishop [1975]. Also, Greenberger, Crenson & Crissey [1976] devote a chapter to a discussion of the project and its impact.

1.1. Outline of the chapter

In discussing the emergency services literature I divide the research into six areas:

– *The relationship between measures of effectiveness and system performance.* Here I briefly describe attempts to relate commonly used performance measures such as response time and patrol frequency to the actual quality of service provided.

– *The number of units needed in a region.* The concern of research in this area is with the macro problem of how many units to place in a region without solving the micro problem of selecting specific locations.

– *Deterministic location models*. The problem is to determine unit locations under the assumption that they are always available to respond. These deterministic, approximate models have been applied mainly to siting fire stations.

– *Probabilistic location, districting and dispatching models*. This research examines issues such as locating ambulances, designing police patrol beats or sectors, and deciding how many and which units to dispatch to an incoming call for service while making explicit allowance for the randomness in call arrivals and service times.

– *Staffing and scheduling*. In fire, police, and emergency medical operations, staffing is a critical issue. Is it better to have fewer fire companies with more firefighters per company? Is the degradation in response time offset by the improvements in firefighting effectiveness? In police, the question is whether to have one or two officers per patrol car, while in emergency medical operations, the question is not only how many persons to assign but also what level of training should each person have. Given staffing levels, an additional problem common to the three services is determining tours of duty.

– *Emergency service mergers*. As cities face increasing budgetary pressure it becomes natural to consider merging two or more emergency services to save money. But what are the service and political implications of doing so?

This chapter focuses on papers that apply operations research/management science. (See Chaiken & Larson [1972] and Kolesar & Swersey [1986] for two earlier surveys.) There is a large body of related literature in police, health and fire journals and in unpublished reports, that is not included here. Most of it can be found in the references given in the papers discussed. I also ignore the large literature on location problems except for those papers directly related to emergency services.

The remainder of the chapter is organized as follows. In Section 2, I describe the characteristics of fire, police, and emergency medical problems. The pitfalls of traditional approaches to these problems are discussed in Section 3, while literature on measures of effectiveness and system performance is discussed in Section 4. In Section 5, I discuss the literature on the number of units needed in a region, while in Section 6, I present deterministic location models. In Section 7, I report on probabilistic location, districting, and dispatching models while in Section 8, I discuss papers relating to staffing and scheduling. Section 9 covers the literature on mergers. I end the chapter (Section 10) with a general discussion of the models I have described and the likely direction of future work.

2. The characteristics of emergency service problems

2.1. Fire

An essential part of the fire deployment problem is to determine the number of units needed and their locations and the number of firefighters to assign to each unit. In most cities there are two types of units: engine companies whose trucks are equipped as pumpers and extinguish fires, and ladder companies which are responsible for lifesaving and removing toxic gases from a burning building. Given a basic allocation of resources, there is often a need for the temporary relocation of units when one or more units are sent from their home locations to replace others that are temporarily unavailable. These relocations improve coverage in response to changing conditions.

Given an incoming alarm, the fire department must decide how many and which units to dispatch. In the past, this problem was straightforward. If the alarm were reported by telephone, the dispatcher would send the resources that appeared to be needed based on the information received. If reported by street telegraph box, a predetermined fixed response judged sufficient to handle a serious incident was dispatched. In all cases, the closest units would respond. These approaches were reasonable and valid when originally designed. But at high call rates that occur in many regions of New York City, for example, these traditional rules break down. In some situations it may pay not to send the closest company [Carter, Chaiken & Ignall, 1972]. In other instances it makes sense to send a minimal response to an incident judged to have a small chance of being serious, holding back units for more serious fires in the future [Swersey, 1982].

One highly significant development in the fire protection area has been the dramatic increase in smoke detector usage in the last 10 years as the cost of these devices has fallen sharply. A study by the National Fire Protection Association (NFPA) found that the likelihood of a fire death was roughly halved in incidents in which a detector was present [Hall, 1991]. Halpern [1979] in a very interesting paper examined the tradeoff between smoke detectors and fire companies.

2.2. Police

In the police deployment problem, patrol vehicles and officers are assigned to subregions of the city usually called commands or precincts. A patrol vehicle is staffed by either one or two officers. Most cities have one system or the other while some may assign one-officer cars to low crime areas and two-officers cars elsewhere. Currently, the trend in many cities is toward one-officer patrol. Within a precinct, each patrol car is given a primary patrol area called a beat or sector. Calls originating in that area are assigned to the sector car if it is available. If not, a nearby car will usually be assigned, or if the call has a low priority, it may be held in queue. If all cars in a precinct are busy, the call will be queued or a special backup car sent. Generally police departments do not dispatch across precinct boundaries.

Priorities for incoming calls are especially important in the police area. Calls are generally dispatched in order of priority within several priority classes. Sectors are designed with an aim to balancing unit workloads, reducing response times, and providing for police patrol.

2.3. Emergency medical services (EMS)

Prior to about 20 years ago, an ambulance was mainly a vehicle for quickly transporting a patient to a hospital; it had little life-supporting equipment. Since then, most cities have implemented advanced life support (ALS) units, which consist of paramedics staffing vehicles equipped with appropriate drugs and life-stabilizing equipment. In contrast, a vehicle staffed by emergency medical technicians (EMT's) and without this specialized equipment is usually called a basic life support (BLS) unit. Some cities have all-BLS or all-ALS systems, while others mix the types of units. In some cities with both types of units, life-threatening emergencies would receive an ALS unit, while BLS units would be used for other emergencies. It is also common to dispatch the nearest fire department engine company (with its members trained in basic emergency medical care) to the most serious emergencies. Emergency medical services (EMS) are provided either by the fire department, or a separate service run by the city or county or by a private firm. There are many organizational variations. For example, the fire department may operate EMS units that provide care at the scene, but a private ambulance service would be called if transport to a hospital is required.

2.4. The dispatching office

Calls for emergency services are usually received in a central dispatching center, where queuing delays may occur in the processing of them. Larson [1972a] described a queuing model of police dispatching, while Swersey of the Rand Fire Project developed a simulation model of the fire dispatching system in the Brooklyn dispatching office. Swersey's analysis, which is discussed in Chapter 8 of Greenberger, Crenson & Crissey [1976] and used by Quade, in his book on systems analysis, to illustrate the process of building an OR model [Swersey, 1975], identified a critical bottleneck at the decision-making stage of the dispatching process. He recommended a short-term solution: splitting the borough in two for dispatching purposes. In the longer run, the analysis caused the Fire Department to abandon their plans to simply automate the existing system and instead to develop a new computerized system with multiple decision-making capability.

After a call for service is processed, unit(s) are notified to respond. The *travel time* of a unit is the interval between when the unit is dispatched until it arrives at the scene. In the police and emergency medical systems, a call may wait in queue for a unit to become available. For these systems, *response time* is the sum of this queuing delay and the travel time to the scene. In the papers I discuss, I will consistently use these definitions of travel time and response time.

3. The pitfalls of traditional approaches: two examples

The traditional approach to allocating police patrol units to geographical commands was to use either a hazard or workload formula. One approach

Table 1
An example of applying a hazard formula

Factor	Precinct A	Precinct B	Precinct C	Total
1. Violent outside crimes	280	500	900	1680
2. Other FBI index crimes	700	1400	2500	4600
3. Other calls for service	6000	20000	56000	82000

that has been widely used is the hazard formula developed by O.W. Wilson in the late 1930's. For each command, the user identifies factors which are considered important such as crimes of various types, number of arrests, number of street miles, and population. Weights which indicate relative importance are then assigned to each factor. For each command, a hazard index is then calculated as follows. For each factor, the total amount of the factor is determined for the entire city. Then the fraction of the factor occurring in the command being considered is determined. This fraction is multiplied by the hazard weight and the products for all the factors are summed. Chaiken [1975] showed how this simple hazard index can lead to very undesirable results. Consider his three-precinct, three-factor example shown in Table 1. Suppose the decisionmaker assigns equal hazard weights to each factor, that is $h_1 = h_2 = h_3 = 1$. In this case, the hazard index for Precinct C would be:

$$\frac{\frac{900}{1680} + \frac{2500}{4600} + \frac{56000}{82000}}{3} = 0.587.$$

Thus Precinct C would get 58.7% of all the officers.

Now suppose the decisionmaker considers violent outside crime as more important (a reasonable opinion), and assigns weights $h_1 = 7, h_2 = 2, h_3 = 1$. Then the assignment to Precinct C is:

$$\frac{7 \times \frac{900}{1680} + 2 \times \frac{2500}{4600} + 1 \times \frac{56000}{82000}}{10} = 0.552.$$

Although Precinct C has the largest number of both violent outside crimes and other FBI index crimes, the second allocation gives fewer patrol officers to it. Chaiken pointed out this happens because the ratio of the third factor (other calls for service) to the first factor (violent outside crimes) is larger in Precinct C than in the other precincts, while the ratio of the second factor (other index crimes) to the first factor is about the same for all precincts.

In New York City the traditional approach to meeting increasing fire company workload was to add fire companies. In 1966, two years before the start of the Rand Fire Project, Engine Company 82 in the South Bronx responded to over 6000 alarms, making it the busiest engine company in the City and, for that matter, in the world. To relieve its workload, the Fire Department in July of 1967, created a new company, Engine 85, and put it into the same firehouse as Engine 82. Its first full year of operation was in 1968. It was expected that Engine 82's workload would be cut in half. In fact, in 1968 Engine 82 was still the busiest company in the City and Engine 85 was the second busiest, responding to 9111 calls and 8386 calls, respectively. Instead of helping the busy unit, there were now two busy units.

Adding Engine 85 did not relieve the workload of Engine 82 because of the unexpected interplay of two seemingly logical dispatching rules which together comprised the traditional dispatching policy: (1) always dispatch the units closest to an alarm, and (2) send three engine companies and two ladder companies, if they are available, but send at least one engine and one ladder. The Fire Project analysis showed the Department that, since, in busy periods, many companies are not available, as few as one engine company and one ladder company are often sent. As a simulation model showed, the new company was drawn into the role of 'filling out' the response to alarms, primarily providing an unneeded second or third engine at trash fires and false alarms. As a result of the dispatch policy, instead of the same number of responses being spread over more companies, the total number of responses increased.

4. The relationship between measures of effectiveness and system performance

Ideally, in evaluating fire deployment options, it would be useful to know the relationship between fire losses and fire company response time. Unfortunately, the work on this question has yet to yield relationships that are generally useful. Using data from over 20 000 fires in the United Kingdom, Hogg [1971] did develop a relationship between fire damage (defined in terms of how far the fire has spread) and the time until the first fire company reaches the scene. However, there is some question about the validity of the results: Baldwin & Fardell [1970] examined the same data in a slightly different way and found no relationship between damage and response time. Hogg [1973] also developed a model that relates loss of life and property to response time. Although this was a pioneering effort, it is unclear whether the relationships are valid and reliable and if they apply outside of the United Kingdom (see Swersey, Ignall, Corman, Armstrong & Weindling [1975] for a fuller discussion of all three papers).

A study by Miller & Rappaport [1977] failed to establish a relationship between fire losses and response time, while Corman, Ignall, Rider & Stevenson [1976] using very extensive data uncovered only a weak relationship between fire casualties and response distance. More promising is the work of Halpern [1979] who studied 230 one- and two-family fires in Calgary, Canada. Halpern first separated the data according to the estimated state of the incident at the time the Fire Department was notified. The states were: fire confined to object of origin; fire confined to part of room of origin; fire confined to room of origin; fire confined to floor of origin and fire confined to building of origin. Relationships were then developed for the fires in each state. For each of the five states, Halpern found statistically significant linear relationships between property loss (measured as a percentage of the total value of building and contents) and response time.

For police deployment, an important issue is the relationship between response time and the probability of arrest. Clawson and Chang [1977] examined 5875 high-priority incidents occurring in Seattle over a one-year period. They *did* find a statistically significant relationship between both travel time and the sum of travel and dispatching times and the likelihood of an on-scene arrest. But as the authors noted, their results must be viewed with caution. It may be that the police respond faster if the dispatcher receives information indicating that an arrest is likely. For example, under such circumstances, the dispatcher may react more quickly or send the closest unit.

Tarr [1978] extended the work of Clawson & Chang [1977] by examining Seattle data for another year and finding a similar relationship between response time and travel time and the probability of arrest. Tarr also found that if the first-arriving unit was a two-officer car rather than a one-officer car, the probability of arrest increased by about 20%.

The Kansas City preventive patrol experiment [Kelling, Pate, Dieckman & Brown, 1974] was a comprehensive attempt to determine the effectiveness of police preventive patrol. The experimental area consisted of fifteen patrol beats. Five were designated control beats and received normal patrol. Five others were selected as reactive beats and were not patrolled, while the remaining five were designated proactive beats and received two to three times normal patrol. The experiments were run for one year starting in October 1972. The results showed that reported crime rates and citizens perceptions of police presence as well as other measures did not vary in a statistically significant way across the three types of beats. These findings do not seem surprising given the density of patrol vehicles in Kansas City. As Larson [1975b] pointed out in an extensive and excellent critique, in the control beats, a patrol car would pass a particular point once in about six hours. Thus removing patrol coverage should be (and was) difficult for the average citizen to perceive. Larson also indicated several shortcomings in the experimental design.

For the deployment of emergency medical service (EMS) units it is important to know how travel time and response time (which includes queuing delay) relate to survival probabilities for victims of medical emergencies. Mayer [1979] examined 525 cases of cardiac arrest occurring in Seattle over a one-year period. About 60% of the incidents were ventricular fibrillation (VF), a form of cardiac arrest consisting of totally disorganized electrical activity in the heart which precludes blood circulation. For the other three types of cardiac arrest which Mayer described, there is evidently little chance of living long enough to be discharged from the hospital [Pozen, Fried, Smith, Lindsay & Voigt, 1977]. Mayer found for VF patients a statistically significant relationship between both short-term survival (admittance to hospital) and longer-term survival (discharge from hospital) and paramedic travel time. For example, for travel times of three minutes or less, 77% of all victims were admitted to the hospital, while 48% of all victims were discharged from the hospital. For travel times of seven minutes or longer, the corresponding figures were 52% and 19%. The responding paramedics administer cardiac defibrillation, one or more electric shocks that often resuscitate the VF victim. Mayer also looked at survival rates versus the time until arrival for the first vehicle on the scene. In Seattle, the nearest fire department engine company whose personnel can administer cardiopulmonary resuscitation (CPR) and other basic emergency medical care, is sent to life-threatening emergencies and usually arrives before one of the city's four paramedic units. Mayer found evidence of a relationship between survival rates and the arrival of the first unit, although the results were not statistically significant.

Eisenberg, Hallstrom & Bergner [1981] examined data for 611 cardiac arrest cases in the suburban area of King County, Washington (outside Seattle) over a three-year period, and also found a statistically significant relationship between survival and paramedic travel time. They found that for VF patients, when travel times were less than four minutes, 56% of the victims were discharged from the hospital, for travel times of between four and eight minutes, 33% were discharged, while for travel times of more than eight minutes, 17% were discharged. The authors also found that if CPR was performed by a bystander the likelihood of survival was increased significantly. The cost-effectiveness of training citizens in CPR was examined by Gorry & Scott [1977]. A later study in Seattle by Weaver, Cobb, Hallstrom, Copass, Ray, Emery & Fahrenbruch [1986] analyzed 244 witnessed cases of cardiac arrest with VF. Because a witness was present, it was possible to estimate the time from victim collapse until initiation of CPR either by a bystander or first-arriving fire department unit and defibrillation by paramedics. Using logit regression, the authors found survival rates decreased about 3% with each minute of delay until CPR and continued to fall by about 4% per minute until the delivery of the first defibrillatory shock. Other studies [for example, Roth, Steward, Rogers & Cannon, 1984 in Pittsburgh and Olson, LaRochelle, Fark, Aprahamtan, Aufderheide, Mateer, Hargarten & Stueven, 1989 in Wisconsin] have confirmed the importance of both rapid initiation of CPR and defibrillation.

The work to date relating emergency medical response time and cardiac arrest survival rates is very useful for OR modellers and decisionmakers. It provides key input to the determination of appropriate objective functions and makes possible cost/benefit analyses of emergency medical systems. Urban, Bergner & Eisenberg [1981] performed such a cost/benefit study in King County, Washington. Currently, researchers [Eisenberg, Cummins, Damon, Larsen & Hearne, 1990] are calling for uniform reporting systems to provide even more valuable data about the effect of emergency medical deployment on cardiac arrest survival rates in an attempt to provide insights into reported differences in performance across cities (Eisenberg, Horwood, Cummins, Reynolds-Haertle & Hearne [1990]) summarize the results of published studies in 29 cities).

5. The number of units needed in a region

Except when server utilizations are very low, it is important to account for the stochastic nature of emergency service systems. Various queuing models are applicable. In deciding how many ambulances are needed under the restrictive assumption that all are located at a single garage, Bell & Allen [1969] viewed the ambulance system as an $M \mid G \mid \infty$ model, that is, Poisson arrivals, general service time distribution and an infinite number of servers. For such a system, the distribution of the number of busy servers (ambulances) is Poisson with mean λ/μ where λ is the average arrival rate of calls and μ is the average service rate. As long as the probability that all ambulances are busy is small, the $M \mid G \mid \infty$ model will be a good approximation and has the virtue of not requiring any particular specification for the distribution of service time; the model needs only μ. Using this model, the authors determined the number of ambulances required so that the probability that all ambulances are busy is less than or equal to some specified and very small probability.

A model developed by Chaiken [1971] has a similar objective: to determine the number of fire companies of a given type – engine or ladder – needed in a region so that the probability that they are all busy does not exceed a specified threshold. The problem is more complicated in the fire case, since several units are usually dispatched to fire alarms and the service time varies per unit depending on the order of arrival at the scene of the fire. Chaiken derived his results assuming Poisson arrivals and an infinite number of servers.

Taylor & Templeton [1980] developed a queuing model which is applicable to an ambulance system where the two classes of customers are emergency calls requiring immediate service and routine calls such as hospital transfers which can afford to wait. Low priority calls are 'cut off' (put in queue) whenever N_1 or more servers are busy, in order to keep $N - N_1$ servers free for high priority arrivals. Arrivals are Poisson, while service times are exponential with the same mean service time for high and low priority customers. The model calculates three performance measures: (1) the probability that an emergency will find B or fewer ambulances available, (2) the mean waiting time for routine calls, and (3) the probability that a routine call will have to wait more than T minutes. The authors described an application of the model to the central sector of Toronto.

5.1. Square root models

Another approach to determining the number of units to locate in a region is to estimate the average travel time as a function of the number of units and find the number of units needed to achieve a target average travel time. Larson [1972b] as well as Kolesar & Blum [1973] of the Rand Fire Project have shown that the average travel distance in a region is inversely proportional to the square root of the number of units per unit area. The constant of proportionality depends on street configuration and the placement of the units and can be determined by geographic arguments or via simulation. By combining this square root distance model with empirical data relating travel time to travel distance it is possible to estimate average travel time for a specified number of units (Figures 1 and 2). Papers by Kolesar, Walker & Hausner [1975] and Kolesar [1975] developed specific relationships between time and distance and hence between the number of units and travel time for fire engines in New York City. Using a queuing model

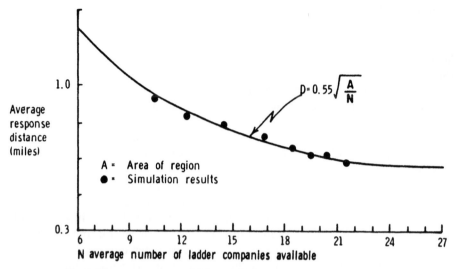

Fig. 1. The square root model for predicting average response distance.

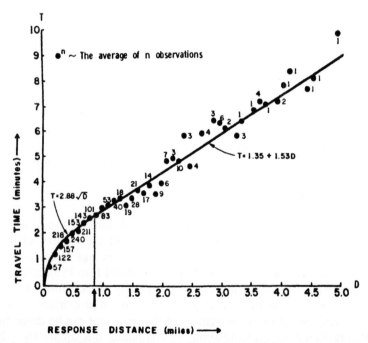

Fig. 2. An empirically determined function for relating travel time to response distance.

like those discussed above one can determine the average travel time in a region containing N units by first estimating the probability distribution of the number of busy units and then using the square root model to estimate distance (and time) for each possible system state. This approach was used by Larson [1972b]. Scott, Factor & Gorry [1978] used a similar approach but estimated the probability distribution of travel time rather than average travel time.

Kolesar & Blum [1973] used an even simpler method. They showed that the average travel distance is also approximately inversely proportional to the square root of the *average* number of available units per unit area. Then using the relationship between time and distance, they found the expected travel time in a region without the need of a queuing model.

The square root model was used extensively by the Rand Fire Project. In particular, in November 1972, the New York City Fire Department disbanded six fire companies and permanently relocated seven others. The analyses that led to these changes were based mainly on the square root model [Ignall, Kolesar, Swersey, Walker, Blum, Carter & Bishop, 1975]. Tien & Chiu [1985] used the square root model to evaluate the cost reduction options of closing fire companies from 2 a.m. to 10 a.m., and reducing fire company staffing (see Section 8 for a discussion of other papers on the staffing issue).

Also as part of the Rand Fire Project activities, Rider [1976] developed a method called the Parametric Allocation Model for allocating fire companies to regions of a city. Rider's model calculates the travel times in each region using the square root model. He then uses a tradeoff parameter that allows the user to strike a balance between potential demand (a region's hazard) and realized demand (a region's fire incidence). The Parametric Allocation Model has been used in a number of cities including Jersey City and Tacoma [Rand Fire Project, 1979, pp. 349–264 and pp. 681–588].

5.2. The Patrol Car Allocation Model (PCAM)

The Patrol Car Allocation Model (PCAM) has been widely used in determining the number of units to assign to police precincts [Chaiken, 1978; Chaiken & Dormont, 1978a,b]. PCAM extends and improves upon several earlier models, notably the work of Larson [1972b], and a package based upon work in St. Louis [IBM Program Product, n.d.], which are discussed in Chaiken & Dormont [1978a]. It utilizes an $M \mid M \mid c$ queuing model with priority classes, and estimates average travel time using the square root model discussed previously. For each precinct, the user specifies call rates by hour of the day and day of the week, the area of the precinct, number of street miles, response and patrol speeds of patrol cars, and crime rates. Given a specified number of units on duty, the program estimates performance measures such as the average number of units available, preventive patrol frequency, average travel time to incidents and average waiting time in queue for calls of each priority class. Saladin [1982] used PCAM within a goal programming framework to allocate patrol units, developing tradeoffs between various managerial, budgetary, and performance goals.

PCAM recognizes that a significant fraction of a patrol unit's time is spent on activities not related to calls for service (CFS) such as meals, auto repairs or transporting prisoners. The PCAM user estimates the fraction of time, U, spend on such non-CFS activities using a method described in Chaiken & Dormont [1978b]. The fraction of time available for CFS activities, $1 - U$ is then multiplied by the number of cars on duty to get the 'number of effective cars' which is then used for queuing purposes.

A revised version of PCAM incorporates the queuing model of Green that treats those situations in which more than one patrol car frequently responds to a call [Green, 1984; Green & Kolesar, 1984a]. Municipalities in which there is one-officer per patrol car are likely to send more than one car to potentially hazardous calls and are particularly suited to analysis by Green's model. The model has been used and tested in New York City to compare the effectiveness of one- or two-officer patrol cars. (See discussion of this application in Section 8 of this chapter.) The Green multiple car dispatch (MCD) model has calls arriving according to a Poisson process in varying severity and priority categories. Within each category there is a probability distribution of the number of patrol cars dispatched to an incident. Service times of cars are all independent identically distributed random variables and 'runs' only begin when all the required cars are available. The model aggregates behavior in a region such as a precinct and an efficient numerical algorithm calculates very detailed performance statistics including the mean delay to all cars dispatched, and the intervals between dispatches.

In PCAM each hour of the day is treated separately using a steady state $M \mid M \mid c$ model with time-dependent parameters that has been used by Kolesar, Rider, Crabill & Walker [1975] in the police context and by Ignall & Walker [1977] to deploy ambulances. The essential idea is to develop the set of differential equations that describe the dynamics of the system with time-dependent parameters and to use numerical integration to find the probability distribution of the number of busy units.

6. Deterministic location models

These models assume that the nearest unit to a call for service is always available. In most fire departments this is a reasonable assumption since the average availability of units is 95% or more. For EMS units, such low utilizations occur much less often. Consequently, these deterministic models have been applied mainly in the fire area.

6.1. Average travel time models

In the late 1960's in England, Hogg [1968a] developed an approach to the fire station location problem and applied it in a number of cities [Hogg, 1968a, 1970, 1973]. In Hogg's method: (1) the city is divided into m small sub-areas; the rate of fire incidence in each is determined from historical data or based on a model that relates fire incidence to population density, and all demands within an area are assumed to occur at a single representative point; (2) n potential company locations are specified; if a station is located in one of the sub-areas it is assumed to be at a major intersection near the center; and (3) travel times between sub-areas are determined by timing fire company responses or estimating travel speeds along the road network. The problem is solved separately and heuristically for engine and ladder companies. The objective for a specified number of companies is to find the locations that minimize the total travel time of all companies to all fire incidents.

ReVelle & Swain [1970] developed an ordinary linear programming formulation of a problem similar to Hogg's which minimizes the average distance or time people travel to a set of facilities. Apparently, their model was developed with hospitals, libraries or similar facilities in mind since there is no reference in their paper or in several related papers to emergency services in general or fire station location in particular. However, their model applies to the fire situation: if one replaces the number of people by the number of fires, then the problem is to minimize the average travel time to fires. The formulation is:

$$\text{minimize} \quad \sum_{i=1}^{n} \sum_{j=1}^{n} a_i d_{ij} x_{ij}$$

$$\text{subject to} \quad \sum_{j=1}^{n} x_{ij} = 1 \qquad i = 1, 2, \ldots, n,$$

$$x_{jj} \geq x_{ij} \qquad i, j = 1, \ldots, n \, ; i \neq j,$$

$$\sum_{j=1}^{n} x_{jj} = m$$

$$x_{ij} \geq 0 \qquad i, j = 1, 2, \ldots, n,$$

where

a_i = the demand population at node i. However, in a fire context it would be more appropriate for this to be the number of fires at node i.

d_{ij} = the shortest time (or distance) from node i to node j.

x_{ij} = 1 if a company at node j is assigned to respond to node i.

n = the number of nodes of the network.

m = the number of fire companies to be located.

If x_{ij} = 1, then a company is located at node j. The second set of constraints insure that each demand node is assigned to a node at which a company is in fact located. Since there are no workload balancing constraints in this formulation, each demand node will be assigned to the closest company.

Clearly, ReVelle & Swain's model is a relaxation of an integer program where x_{ij} = 0 or 1, and although there is no guarantee that the solution will always give integer valued variables, the authors reported that this was almost always the case in applications. However, solving the linear program may require extensive computational time for larger problems. This may have motivated Garfinkel, Neebe & Rao [1974] and Swain [1974] to devise faster decomposition methods for solving the LP.

The problem that ReVelle & Swain formulated, was first defined by Hakimi [1964, 1965] and is referred to in the literature as the *p*-median problem. Hakimi proved that there exists an optimal solution for which the facilities are located on the nodes rather than the arcs connecting the nodes.

A number of solution methods, in addition to the linear programming approaches described above, have been proposed for the *p*-median problem. The Teitz & Bart [1968] heuristic is essentially the same as Hogg's method. Jarvinen, Rajala & Sinervo [1972] and El-Shaieb [1973] developed branch and bound algorithms but they can only handle moderate-sized problems. Cornuejols, Fisher & Nemhauser [1977] and Narula, Ogbu & Samuelson [1977] used Lagrangian relaxation procedures, Galvao [1980] used a branch and bound method with the bounding procedure based on the dual of the LP relaxation of the integer programming formulation, while Hanjoul & Peeters [1985] compared the performance of two dual based procedures.

Toregas, Swain, ReVelle & Bergman [1971] recognized that the *p*-median problem as applied to public sector location problems has a serious deficiency: minimizing weighted travel time may leave some demand nodes with very unfavorable travel times. As they showed, it is easy to include a maximal travel time constraint, simply by not including any assignments which violate the constraint.

Khumawala [1973] developed a heuristic method for solving this problem and Rushton, Goodchild & Ostresh [1972] modified the Teitz & Bart [1968] heuristic to include a maximal travel time constraint.

6.2. Set covering models

Toregas, Swain, ReVelle & Bergman [1971] were the first to formulate the fire station location problem as a set covering problem. They assumed that there are *n* demand nodes and that a fire company may be located at any demand node.

The problem is to:

$$\text{minimize} \quad \sum_{j=1}^{n} x_j$$

$$\text{subject to} \quad \sum_{j \in N_i} x_j \geq 1 \quad i = 1, 2, \ldots, n,$$

$$x_j = 0, 1 \quad j = 1, 2, \ldots, n,$$

where

$$x_j = \begin{cases} 1 & \text{if a fire company is located at } j \\ 0 & \text{otherwise} \end{cases}$$

and $N_i = \{j \mid t_{ji} \leq s_i\}$, where t_{ji} is the travel time from j to i and s_i is the specified maximum travel time for node i; that is, a fire company must be within a travel time of s_i to i.

Although this problem is an integer program, the authors reported that in most cases, solution as a linear program yielded integer valued variables. In the few instances in which non-integer values resulted, the authors used a very ad-hoc type cutting plane method where an additional constraint is added to the linear program and it is re-solved. For example, suppose the initial solution has an objective function value of 12.2. Since the best integer solution is 13 or more, the following constraint is added:

$$\sum_{j=1}^{n} x_j \geq 13,$$

and the problem is re-solved. The authors reported that this procedure had always yielded an optimal integer solution.

Since in the set covering formulation the number of constraints in the LP is equal to the number of demand nodes, it is possible to solve quite large problems by this method within a reasonable computation time. In addition, a number of even faster methods have been devised [Balas & Ho, 1980; Fisher & Kedia, 1990; Toregas & ReVelle, 1972; Toregas, Swain, ReVelle & Bergman, 1971].

The set covering approach requires subjective specifications of the allowable maximum travel times and small changes in these specifications can result in large differences in the number of companies needed. By changing the specifications parametrically one obtains a range of solutions with varying numbers of companies. This gives a 'cost–benefit' curve that can be used to examine solution trade-offs. (Neebe [1988] developed a one-pass procedure for generating this curve.) However, for a given number of companies there may be many solutions that satisfy the coverage specifications and it is not easy to generate all such solutions. (One approach is to find the solution that minimizes the maximum time from any demand node to its nearest fire company. Minieka [1970] showed how that solution could be obtained by solving a sequence of set covering problems. Another approach by Daskin & Stern [1981] is discussed below). Since the set covering method does not consider average travel time, varying the coverage specifications can produce undesirable results: for example, the constraints may be slightly tightened yielding a solution with the same number of companies but a *higher* average travel time. Finally, the set covering approach does not consider the relative fire incidence at the demand nodes. Thus, for example, two demand nodes might have the same travel time specifications even though one of them has five times as many fires. (A fuller discussion of the set covering approach is given in a review written by J.M. Chaiken in Swersey, Ignall, Corman, Armstrong & Weindling [1975]).

Plane & Hendrick [1977] used the set covering model in their analysis of engine company locations in Denver. They modified the Toregas, Swain, ReVelle & Bergman [1971] formulation to maximize the number of already existing fire stations included in the solution, by adding a small penalty ε to the objective function coefficient for those variables that represent a new fire station location. The variables for new locations have coefficient $1 + \varepsilon$, where ε is any number between 0 and $1/n$, where n is the number of potential locations.

Although Plane & Hendrick reported that the covering model was a valuable tool in their analysis, their findings highlight an additional shortcoming of the model. Since the model only considers the travel time of the closest company, the solution provided for two new units in the downtown area where it is particularly important to have additional companies respond quickly.

The set covering model was used in New York City by Walker [1974] of the Rand Fire Project to locate specialized equipment called tower ladders. The Fire Department wanted to deploy the tower ladders so that at least one conventional ladder was assigned as one of the two closest ladder companies to every alarm box in the City. This specification led to the set covering formulation. Schreuder [1981] used the set covering model to locate fire stations in Rotterdam. Swersey & Thakur [1994] developed a variation of the model to locate vehicle emissions testing stations, while Belardo, Harrald, Wallace & Ward [1984] used a covering approach for siting resources used to respond to oil spills.

Church & ReVelle [1974], recognizing that the set covering model can lead to an excessive number of units if all demand nodes are covered, extended the set covering model by considering a problem they called the maximal covering location problem. The formulation is the following:

$$\text{maximize} \quad \sum_{i \in I} a_i y_i$$

$$\text{subject to} \quad \sum_{j \in N_i} x_j \geq y_i \quad i \in I,$$

$$\sum_{j \in J} x_j = P,$$

$$x_j, y_i = 0, 1 \quad i \in I, j \in J,$$

where a_i is the population or call rate at demand node i, P is the number of units to be located, I is the set of demand nodes, J is the set of possible facility locations, and x_j and N_i are as defined in the set covering problem. In contrast to the set covering problem, in which the objective is to find the minimum number of units such that all demand nodes are covered, here the problem is to maximize weighted coverage, given a fixed number of units. A difficulty with this approach is that the optimization does not consider by how much a node is uncovered: a particular node may have an associated travel time just above the specified standard or far above it.

Church & ReVelle [1974] reported that solving the maximal covering problem as a linear program yielded integer solutions about 80% of the time. The fractional solutions were resolved either by inspection or by a branch and bound method that reportedly only required a few iterations to yield an optimal integer solution. (ReVelle [1993] discussed formulations that generally yield integer solutions when solved as an LP, which he calls 'integer friendly'.) They also described two heuristic methods that generally produced near optimal solutions.

A simple extension to their formulation requires that every node be within some maximal travel time (or distance) by adding the constraint:

$$\sum_{j \in M_i} x_j \geq 1 \quad i \in I$$

where $M_i = \{j \mid t_{ji} \leq T\}$. In this problem, the solution will have as much of the population as possible within the tighter travel time, with everyone within the maximum travel time.

Eaton, Daskin, Simmons, Bulloch & Jansma [1985] applied the maximal covering location problem to locating EMS units in Austin, Texas. Their approach was to find the number of units needed so that 95% of the calls would be reached within five minutes, the response time goal that had been adopted by Austin's emergency medical officials.

How do allocations compare under the set covering model and the maximal covering model? For the same number of companies, the set covering model will cover all of the nodes but the travel time specification for coverage will be equal to or greater than the travel time specifications for the maximal covering problem. Neither allocation is preferred a priori. Each of the resulting configurations must be examined and a subjective choice made.

Several extensions to the maximal covering model have been developed by Schilling, Elzinga, Cohan, Church & ReVelle [1979]. In their approach primary and specialized units (e.g., engines and ladders) are allocated simultaneously. One model, the Facility-Location, Equipment-Emplacement Technique (FLEET) which has been applied in Baltimore, first locates a fixed number of fire stations, and then allocates a fixed number of engines and ladders to them. Each station may house an engine or a ladder or both. The model maximizes weighted coverage, where the weights may be population, number of structural fires, etc., and a node is covered if an engine and ladder are within prescribed travel times. A related model of Marianov & ReVelle [1991] extended the maximal covering model to maximize the number of fire calls that have at least three engine companies within an engine standard response distance and at least two truck companies within a truck standard response distance, given a specified number of fire stations and a specified total number of engine and truck companies. They applied the approach to a test network with the engine standard response distance of 1.5 miles and the truck standard response distance of 2.0 miles. For an eight-vehicle problem, the solution located three engines at one station, three engines at another station and two trucks at a third station, with the locations clustered near the center of the region presumably reflecting a higher call density in that area. This is an undesirable result from a firefighting standpoint: the expected travel times of first-, second- and third-due engine companies would be equal to all calls, while the expected travel times for first- and second-due trucks would also be equal to all calls. The problem is that the model does not recognize that the importance of a fire unit's travel time is directly related to its order of arrival with the first-arriving unit more important than the second-arriving and so forth. The coverage constraint requires that all three engines and both trucks be within specified distances. The authors modified their model to require that every demand node achieves first-due engine and truck coverage within specified travel distances. They did so because they observed that 'in some situations it is not possible to achieve the standard (three engine and two truck) coverage because of a limited number of companies or stations'. This latter model would result in some improvement, spreading the companies out more, increasing coverage of outlying demand nodes and reducing first-due travel distance.

In a paper that is related to the Marianov & ReVelle [1991] approach, Batta & Mannur [1990] extended the set covering and maximal covering models to situations in which more than one unit is needed to service a demand (e.g., a serious fire would require two or three engine companies). They specify coverage standards (maximum distance) for each arriving unit to a call requiring multiple units and used their models to solve a number of test problems.

The set covering model as originally formulated is applicable only to those emergency medical systems having very low server utilizations since it assumes that the closest unit to a call is always available. Berlin [1972] and Daskin & Stern [1981] treated the stochastic nature of the problem in an ad-hoc way by using an objective function that was designed to select from among alternative solutions that minimize the number of units, the one that maximizes the amount of multiple coverage in the system. A number of authors have developed extensions to this approach. Benedict [1983] and Eaton, Hector, Sanchez, Lantigua & Morgan [1986] maximized weighted multiple coverage; the number of additional coverers beyond the first for each demand node is weighted by the population of that node. Hogan & ReVelle [1986] also developed a formulation that maximizes weighted multiple coverage in a way that maximizes the population that has at least one backup coverer. In the same paper they devised a multiple objective approach that allows one to develop tradeoffs between the amount of first coverage and backup coverage. In other multiple objective approaches, Storbeck [1982] made it possible to tradeoff the population that receives at least one backup coverer and the population that is uncovered, while Charnes & Storbeck [1980] used goal programming to address the question of backup coverage.

In a later section of this chapter I will discuss a number of additional approaches that explicitly consider server unavailability in set covering models. An earlier approach to dealing with uncertainty by Berlin & Liebman [1974] first used the set covering model to suggest a set of alternative locations which were then evaluated by simulation.

In formulating location models such as the maximal covering, set covering, and p-median problems, the analyst specifies discrete locations for demands and potential server sites. The level of aggregation used affects computation times and the accuracy of the solutions. Daskin, Haghani, Khanal & Malandraki [1989] examined aggregation errors in the maximal covering model while Casillas [1987], Current & Shilling [1987], Goodchild [1979] and Hillsman & Rhoda [1978] considered the same problem in the context of the p-median problem.

6.3. A relocation problem

The set covering model also plays a role in the fire engine relocation algorithm devised by Kolesar & Walker [1974] of the Rand Fire Project in a paper that won the Lanchester prize. Under their method, analysis is done separately for engines and ladders. A call for relocation is made whenever some location in the city is 'uncovered'. For example, a typical definition of 'uncovered' is that both the closest and second closest units are unavailable and are expected to remain so for some extended period of time. In response to an uncovered situation, enough empty houses are filled to insure that no location remains uncovered, while moving as few companies as possible. The authors showed that this can be accomplished by solving a set covering problem but actually used a heuristic approach to reduce computation time because the algorithm is part of a real-time system. The companies chosen to relocate are those that incur the lowest 'cost' while not uncovering any of their home areas. 'Cost' is the average travel time (estimated by using the square root model described in Section 4) to alarms expected to occur in the area affected by the moves, during the time the moves are in effect. The question of to which house should a relocating company go is solved by minimizing the time relocating companies will spend travelling. The Kolesar & Walker algorithm is especially noteworthy because of its successful implementation: it is an integral part of the New York City Fire Department's computerized dispatching system. An earlier formulation by Swersey [1970] was based on average travel time rather than coverage. He formulated the relocation problem as an integer program in which given the current number of available fire companies, the problem is to determine in which firehouses to locate the companies, where the objective function minimizes the sum of average travel time to fires and fixed penalty costs for any units relocated.

6.4. Fire station location packages

The PTI [Public Technology, Inc., 1974] fire station location package is based on the work of a number of researchers, especially Toregas, Swain, ReVelle & Bergman [1971] and Toregas & ReVelle [1972]. In this approach: (1) the street map of a city is converted into a computer-readable network with intersections represented by nodes, and streets represented by arcs connecting the nodes; (2) travel speeds along arcs are estimated; (3) the city is divided into fire demand zones which are small areas of the city having relatively homogeneous land use: (4) all demands within the zone are assumed to come from a designated 'focal point'; these focal points also serve as potential fire station locations; and (5) for each focal point, the required travel time for the closest unit is specified.

Although the PTI package includes a set covering model, this optimization mode is not emphasized. Instead, the package is usually used to evaluate the consequences of alternative configurations. The output shows the uncovered zones, the overall average travel time, and the travel times of first-due, second-due and third-due companies to each demand zone.

The PTI package has a well-written user's manual and was used in more than 50 cities by 1977 [Wright, Hall & Hatry, 1978]. Unfortunately, developing the street network is a time consuming task, and in evaluating options explicit weight is not given to fire incidence (except insofar as fire incidence may enter subjectively into the travel time requirements). Also, the user may have difficulty comparing alternative site configurations. For example, one measure of effectiveness used is the average of the travel times to fire demand zones. But because the demand zones vary in size, this averaging gives more weight to travel times in areas where the demand zones are small, i.e., the travel times in these areas will be counted more times in computing the average. In general, smaller demand zones probably reflect greater hazards, so this method implies some weighting by hazard. But it is not clear that the relative size of the demand zone is the proper weight.

A number of cities have used the fire station location package developed by the Rand Fire Project [Dormont, Hausner & Walker, 1975; Hausner & Walker, 1975; Hausner, Walker & Swersey, 1974; Rand Fire Project, 1979; Walker, 1978] in which: (1) the city is divided into relatively homogeneous demand zones or hazard regions; (2) grid coordinates are determined for every alarm box (or, in some cases, groups of alarm boxes); (3) travel distance is estimated from either Euclidean distance or right-angle distance; (4) actual responses of fire apparatus are timed and compared to distance travelled; these data are used to develop a relationship between travel time and travel distance; and (5) a computer model is used to measure the travel time from any potential fire station location to any alarm box.

Given any deployment change, the travel time characteristics by hazard region and citywide can be evaluated. However, the model also provides output data concerning the region affected by the change. This is crucial since small changes in citywide travel time or travel time in a hazard region may mask large changes in the particular sub-region that is affected.

One of the most interesting applications of the package was to Trenton, New Jersy [Hausner & Walker, 1975]. In this case it was possible to locate engine companies so that seven companies provided better travel time compared to the original nine companies.

7. Probabilistic location, districting and dispatching models

In contrast to determining the number of units needed in a region, selecting particular locations or districts is more difficult since the responsibilities and behavior of individual units must be considered. Consequently, the model state space must be increased substantially to represent explicitly individual units at some level of detail. Given this, most of the research in the area used simulation or made simplifying assumptions. An exception is Larson's [1974, 1975a] hypercube model, a queuing approach that maintains the identity of individual servers.

7.1. Locating ambulances

Perhaps the first paper dealing with the probabilistic location problem was Savas' [1969] study of the deployment of ambulances in a single district in Brooklyn. The traditional approach was to locate all ambulances at the district's hospital. Using a simulation model developed by Gordon & Zelin [1968], Savas considered the benefits of moving some ambulances to a satellite garage close to the district's highest incidence of demand. Simulation results showed an improvement in response time – the interval from dispatch until arrival at the scene of the emergency – of about 10% by moving several ambulances to the satellite. The simulation was also used to examine wider dispersal of the ambulances throughout the district by stationing them at curbside locations. In addition, Savas considered the costs and benefits (in response time) of adding ambulances to the district. He also suggested the improvements possible by dispatching across district lines. The Savas study is important because it laid the groundwork for future EMS studies and because of its emphasis on policy implications.

Volz [1971] considered the problem of locating ambulances in semirural areas. His goal was to minimize the expected response time to calls while including a constraint on the maximum response time to any point. He simplified by assuming that available ambulances are located optimally; in effect, necessary relocations are made as required. In the Michigan County that Volz studied, there is a relocation policy in effect, although relocations would not be made as often as Volz's model prescribed. To calculate the expected response time, Volz estimated the probability distribution of the number of busy ambulances using the binomial distribution in a way that is equivalent to assuming an $M \mid G \mid \infty$ queuing model as used by Bell & Allen [1969]. Volz divided the county into one-mile squares, with calls within a square modelled as coming from a single central point. The collection of these points served as potential ambulance locations. Thus he in effect located vehicles on a simple network, an idea used in the police area as well. Volz determined the travel times from point to point by considering the type of road travelled and estimating travel speed on each type of road using actual data. The optimization used a steepest descent procedure.

Fitzsimmons [1973] also used the $M \mid G \mid \infty$ model to estimate the probability distribution of the number of busy ambulances. He then used simulation to estimate the probabilities of particular ambulances being busy given some total number of busy ambulances. (Volz [1971] avoided such calculations by assuming that relocations always bring the system to its optimal state.) Fitzsimmons then used a pattern search routine of Hooke & Jeeves [1961] to find locations that minimize average response time for a fixed number of ambulances. His method could include a constraint on the maximum allowable response time to any region. Fitzsimmons reported that his approach has been successfully applied in Los Angeles and in Melbourne, Australia. A similar approach was used by Siler [1979].

Swoveland, Uyeno, Vertinsky & Vickson [1973] studied the deployment of ambulances in Vancouver, Canada. They divided the city into regions that roughly equalize workload and assigned one ambulance to each region. The problem was then to find the specific locations within regions that minimized average response time. The authors determined for each demand node the probability that the qth closest ambulance serves a call from that node, that is, that the qth closest is the closest available ambulance at the time of the call. They hypothesized that these probabilities were roughly the same for any particular set of ambulance locations and used simulation to estimate them.

Hall [1971, 1972] also developed and applied a queuing approach in Detroit where station wagons modified as ambulances and manned by police officers respond to medical or police calls. There are also police patrol cars that respond only to police calls. Hall modelled a particular precinct with a maximum of four ambulances where each could be in one of the following states: idle, serving a police call, serving an ambulance call which requires less than 1 mile travel distance to the scene, serving an ambulance call which requires more than 1 mile travel distance to the scene. For each of the three 'busy' states, the service time is exponential with a state specific mean. The model calculated the steady-state probability that all ambulances in a precinct are busy. Because the state space grows rapidly with the number of ambulances, Hall's approach is limited to very small problems. As Hall noted, there are obvious advantages to pooling resources, i.e., dispatching across precinct boundaries. But doing so leads to problems that are too large to solve using his methodology.

Groom [1977] developed an approach to ambulance deployment that has been applied extensively in the United Kingdom. The task is to select ambulance locations from a number of potential sites to meet two criteria set by health authorities: response time must be x minutes or less for 50% of all calls and y minutes or less for 95% of all calls. He assumed Poisson call arrivals and considered two system designs. In the first all ambulances respond to emergency calls only. In the second some vehicles are designated to respond to emergency calls while the others handle non-emergency calls. In addition, the non-emergency vehicles substitute for the emergency vehicles as the latter become busy. As did Volz [1971], Groom simplified by assuming continual optimal relocations.

7.2. The hypercube model

An important probabilistic location method is Larson's [1974, 1975a] hypercube model. It has mainly been used to design police patrol sectors or beats, but has also been used to evaluate alternative ambulance locations [Brandeau & Larson, 1986]. The original model had the following major assumptions: (1) the service region is divided into sub-areas or 'atoms' (nodes); (2) within each atom calls for service occur according to a Poisson process; (3) service times are exponential with the same mean across all atoms; (4) exactly one unit is dispatched to each call; (5) associated with each atom is an ordered list of preferred units with the most preferred available unit dispatched to each call; (6) a unit's location or patrol beat is an atom or set of atoms; when available, the unit is located within each atom according to probabilities specified by the user; (7) the user either specified the travel times between atoms or the program calculates them based on right-angle distances and constant speeds in each coordinate direction which are supplied by the user.

The hypercube model is descriptive. After the user specifies for each unit its patrol beat in the case of police cars or its location for ambulances, and the preferred dispatch list for each atom, the program solves for the steady state probability distribution of busy units. It does so by assuming either (1) a 'loss' system (when all servers are busy, incoming calls are handled by units outside of the system), or (2) by allowing calls to queue. Larson [1974] has an exact method for problems with 15 or fewer units and an approximate but very accurate method for larger problems [Larson, 1975a]. The program provides a range of performance measures including travel time to incidents, workload of patrol units, fraction of dispatches that take a unit outside its beat, and patrol frequency.

The hypercube model does not explicitly consider non-calls for service (CFS) activities. They can be accounted for by inflating the arrival rate of CFS's, but this approach is imperfect since the mechanisms generating the two kinds of demands are different: a CFS occurs at a specific location while a non-CFS activity (a meal, car repair, etc.) is usually unit-specific and sometimes is scheduled rather than random.

The original hypercube model as applied to police patrol has been extensively field tested in an NSF-sponsored project [Heller, Stenzel, Gill & Kolde, 1977]. The evaluators concluded that the hypercube is a valuable tool for beat design, but cautioned that using the model may require considerable cost for data collection and staff training. Moreover, they found that the accuracy of the results is often limited by the model's assumptions and the reliability of input data. In comparing the model's predictions to actual performance in two departments, they found reasonably accurate estimates for workload and travel times, but rather poor estimates of the amount of cross-beat dispatching. The authors attributed these differences to several limitations of the original model: it does not explicitly account for non-CFS workload, multiple unit dispatches are not allowed, there is no allowance for call priorities, calls at the beat level cannot be held in queue until the beat car becomes available, and travel distance estimates may be inaccurate when there are barriers to travel, such as parks. As discussed below, subsequent work addressed a number of these issues. Also, it is likely that the assumptions of the original model are more consistent with reality in the case of EMS deployment than for police beat design.

There have been a number of extensions to the hypercube model. Chelst & Jarvis [1979] modified the hypercube to enable it to calculate the probability distribution of travel times, in addition to the mean travel time. Chelst & Barlach [1981] allowed sending two units to incoming incidents, recognizing that in many instances police departments do so. In addition, since fire departments generally send multiple units to incidents, this extension makes it possible to begin to apply the hypercube model to the deployment of fire vehicles.

Prior to the work of Chelst & Barlach, one approach to handling multiple dispatches using the hypercube model was to increase the hourly call rate by double-counting calls requiring two units. As Chelst & Barlach pointed out, this approach may roughly show the effect of multiple dispatches on unit workloads but it does not estimate travel time for first- and second-arriving units. These measures are particularly important in evaluating the effectiveness of one-officer versus two-officer patrol units (see Section 7).

Larson & McKnew [1982] extended the original hypercube model by allowing for so-called patrol-initiated activities which are not assigned by a dispatcher but result from something the patrol officer sees from the patrol car. Examples include traffic violations, building checks, and car checks. These activities are part of the total non-CFS workload, but do not include other non-CFS tasks such as auto repairs and meals. This variant of the hypercube model includes patrol-initiated activities as a third state for a patrol unit.

Other extensions to the hypercube model include a 'varying service times option', 'mean service time calibration', and a 'barriers algorithm'. The original version of the approximate hypercube model assumed that all units had the same average service time. An algorithm of Jarvis [1975] allows for different average service times by unit but can only be used when the hypercube is viewed as a loss system. 'Mean service time calibration' recognizes that average unit service times include average travel times which themselves depend on the location of services and service requests. The calibration is an iterative procedure by which the hypercube model loops through its computation process, replacing the input service times with the model-computed service times until they agree. The method is discussed by Brandeau & Larson [1986]. The barriers algorithm, developed by Larson & Li [1981], uses a right-angle travel metric as does the original hypercube but allows for barriers to travel such as parks.

Bodily [1978] applied multi-attribute utility theory to the police sector design problem. He identified three interest groups: citizens who desire equalization of mean travel times throughout the district, police officers who want equalization of unit workloads, and system administrators who seek system-wide efficiency, i.e., minimization of average system travel time. Bodily developed what he called a surrogate utility function which consists of a utility function for travel time determined by a citizen representative, a utility function for workload determined by a police representative, and a cross-product term whose coefficient is determined by the administrative representative who thereby makes inter-interest group tradeoffs between travel time and workload. This surrogate utility function is then used in conjunction with the hypercube model to determine a beat design.

7.3. Another approach to sector design

An alternative model to the hypercube for designing patrol beats was reported by Bammi [1975] and Bammi & Thomopoulos [1976]. The authors assumed Poisson arrivals and a general service time distribution, and modelled patrol car states as: busy answering calls for service; on preventive patrol; or occupied with non-patrol activities such as going for gasoline. Their model first treats each beat separately and then allows for interbeat dispatching by assuming that unit unavailabilities are independent. The model can be used descriptively or an optimization routine can be used that minimizes average citywide response time.

In cities like Aurora, Illinois where the model was applied, in which units are busy a small fraction of the time, the independence assumption is probably a reasonable one. In larger cities, it would be interesting to compare the results of the Bammi and Thomopoulos model to Larson's hypercube model. (For a further comparison of the two models, see Chaiken [1975].)

7.4. Always send the closest unit?

In deciding which emergency unit to send to an incoming call the conventional answer was the obvious one: send the closest. But three Rand Fire Project researchers, Carter, Chaiken & Ignall [1972] showed that under certain conditions it pays not to send the closest unit. The problem they considered is related to the question of beat design. Their queuing optimization model determines which of two emergency units stationed at fixed locations to send to an incoming call for service. Calls for service are Poisson and service times for all calls are identically distributed with mean $1/\mu$. The problem is to select a district or response area for each unit to serve. The unit responds to all calls inside its area unless it is busy serving another call. If both units are busy, it is assumed that the call is served by a unit outside of the region. Under these assumptions, they found that it is not always optimal to dispatch the closest unit. In particular, if the rate at which calls arrive in one region is significantly higher than the rate in the other, it can pay to shrink the response area of the busier unit and expand the region of the other. That is, the less busy unit will be assigned primary responsibility for some calls to which it is not closest. In this way average response time in the region can be improved and the workloads of the two units more nearly balanced. Figure 3 illustrates their result. The 'city' consists of two regions of equal area – 'A' a high alarm rate region and 'B' a low alarm rate region with an emergency unit stationed at the center of each region. Suppose a fire occurs at location X; company A would respond under the closest unit rule. Now assume while company A is out, another fire occurs. It is more likely to occur in the region of high demand; suppose it occurs at location Y. Now company B must respond. If the response boundary had been shifted to the left so that company B was assigned to fire 1 at location X, company A would have responded to Y and the total travel time would have been reduced, while shifting the line to the left also balances workload.

The Carter–Chaiken–Ignall model was motivated by the high workload of some New York City fire companies (recall the earlier discussion of Engine 82 and Engine 85), which led to union demands for more fire companies. But their insight is more widely applicable, because it suggests that in many situations – for example, in EMS dispatching – balancing workload by not sending the closest unit would result in only small increases in response time.

For determining which units to dispatch for the case of an arbitrary number of servers, Jarvis [1975] developed a Markov decision model. He generated results for up to 10 servers showing that optimal state dependent response boundaries improve average travel time and reduce workload imbalances.

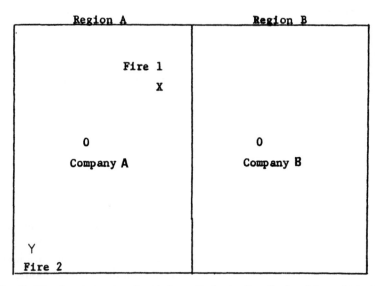

Fig. 3. Sending the closest company is not always the best policy. Region A has a high alarm rate. If company A is available, it responds first to the fires there. Region B has a low alarm rate. If company B is available, it responds first. In the example, a fire breaks out at location 1 first, and shortly thereafter a fire breaks out at location 2. Total response time would be reduced if we send company B rather than company A to fire 1, even though B is farther away.

7.5. How many units should be sent?

The model of Carter, Chaiken & Ignall and the model of Jarvis provide insights that are particularly useful in deciding which fire units to dispatch. Swersey [1982] of the Rand Fire Project considered the related problem of determining how many fire units to dispatch. His Markovian decision model tracks the number of busy units in a region but not their identity. Thus, his 'aggregated' approach resembles the work described in Section 5. For a given number of busy units, the model determines the number to dispatch depending on the probability that the incoming alarm represents a serious fire. Swersey then developed an approximation to the Markovian decision model and used it to derive a simple decision rule. The rule considers three key factors: (1) the probability that the incoming alarm is serious (the greater the probability the more units dispatched); (2) the expected alarm rate in the area surrounding the alarm (the greater the alarm rate, the fewer units dispatched); and (3) the number of units available in the area surrounding the alarm (the more units available, the more units dispatched). Recognizing that the most important factor is the probability that an alarm is serious, the Rand Fire Project and New York City Fire Department devised and implemented an adaptive response policy that dispatches more units to potentially more serious alarms [Ignall, Kolesar, Swersey, Walker, Blum, Carter & Bishop, 1975].

Ignall, Carter & Rider [1982] developed a practical algorithm for deciding how many and which units to send based upon Swersey's work and the paper of Carter,

Chaiken & Ignall [1972] on response areas discussed previously. Their procedure could substantially improve response time to serious fires while keeping total workload essentially unchanged.

Denardo, Rothblum & Swersey [1988] developed a model for deciding which units to send that would apply to the fire problem under extreme conditions in which a number of calls for service are waiting to be dispatched. The problem is to decide which units to send to which incidents and leads to an extension of the classic transportation problem in which the 'costs' depend on the order of arrival.

7.6. Probabilistic set covering models

There have been a proliferation of papers that extend the deterministic set covering models discussed in Section 6 to deal with a stochastic environment. The first was Daskin [1983] who, based on earlier unpublished work of S.C. Chapman and J.A. White, developed the maximal expected covering location model, an extension to the maximal covering location model. He assumes that p, the probability that a unit is busy, is the same for every unit and estimates it as the average server utilization. Assuming that the probabilities of individual units being busy are independent, then if a demand node i with call rate h_i is covered by m units, its expected coverage is $h_i(1 - p^m)$. Daskin's objective function maximizes the expected coverage over all the demand nodes given a specified number of servers. Fujiwara, Makjamroen & Gupta [1987] used Daskin's model to locate ambulances in Bangkok. They first used the model to generate alternative good solutions which were then evaluated via simulation.

Batta, Dolan & Krishnamurthy [1989] used Larson's hypercube model in conjunction with Daskin's maximal expected covering model. As noted above, Daskin assumes servers are busy independent of one another with identical busy probabilities. Batta and his co-authors used an iterative procedure which uses the hypercube to solve for individual server busy probabilities. The procedure starts with a set of server locations, then uses the hypercube to find the busy probabilities and based on these probabilities calculates the expected coverage. The authors use a single node substitution heuristic (equivalent to the method of Teitz & Bart, [1968]) to optimize the server locations. For each current server location (node) the procedure evaluates the effect on the expected coverage of moving the server to each of the other nodes. This entails $(N - 1)M$ iterations of the hypercube model at each iteration. The procedure continues until no further improvement in expected coverage is possible. The authors solved a 55-node, 3-server example and found that embedding the hypercube in the expected coverage model resulted in some differences in the estimated expected coverage but little difference in the locations of the servers.

Goldberg, Dietrich, Chen, Mitwasi, Valenzuela & Criss [1990b] made an observation about Daskin's expected covering model concerning Daskin's assumption that travel times are deterministic. Their point is best illustrated by an example. Suppose in order to be covered a demand zone must be within eight minutes of a server. Using deterministic travel times is equivalent to using the expected travel time since travel times are actually random variables. Under Daskin's approach, a server that is just under eight minutes from a demand zone, covers it as well as a server that is only one minute from the zone, but in reality the closer server will almost certainly arrive within eight minutes if it is available, while the server that has an expected travel time of just under eight minutes, when available will have only a 0.5 probability of arriving within eight minutes, assuming a symmetrical distribution of travel times. In their paper, Goldberg and his co-authors modify Daskin's approach by assuming travel times are random variables. They estimate for all pairs of demand nodes and locations the probability that a vehicle will arrive within eight minutes, when it is available. The objective function is the same as Daskin's expected covering model, to maximize the expected number of calls that are covered (i.e., reached within eight minutes). The difference is that in Daskin's model the objective function is actually the expected number of calls that on average are covered. Some apparently covered calls will actually have travel times greater than eight minutes. Goldberg and his co-authors view an arrival within eight minutes as a success and any longer travel time as a failure, while Daskin views the expectation of an arrival within eight minutes as sufficient. In this case the 8-minute criterion was based on the subjective judgment of the Tucson Fire Department. Since the criterion is subjective, it would be difficult to argue that 8 minutes is acceptable but 8.25 minutes (say) is not. It would have been interesting and useful for Goldberg, Dietrich, Chen, Mitwasi, Valenzuela & Criss [1990b] to compare the results of their model to Daskin's using the Tucson data. It could be that reducing Daskin's coverage criterion to an appropriate value below an average of eight minutes would lead to similar results or that there would still be significant differences in deployment and performance. The problem that Goldberg, Dietrich, Chen, Mitwasi, Valenzuela & Criss [1990b] raised, reflects the fact that covering models in general ignore average response time. The Goldberg, Dietrich, Chen, Mitwasi, Valenzuela & Criss [1990b] approach should tend to place units closer to demand zones, thereby improving average response time.

The work of Goldberg, Dietrich, Chen, Mitwasi, Valenzuela & Criss [1990b] noteworthy because it was applied to a real problem in Tucson and because of extensive efforts at validation. The authors used a simulation model, described in more detail in a companion paper [Goldberg, Dietrich, Chen, Mitwasi, Valenzuela & Criss, 1990a] to validate both their travel time model and their analytical covering model and then used actual data to validate the simulation. Solution methods for their model, which is a nonlinear program, are discussed in Goldberg & Paz [1991] and Goldberg & Szidarovsky [1991].

ReVelle & Hogan [1986] devised an approach that is somewhat different from the expected coverage method of Daskin. They find the minimum number of units subject to constraints that each node is covered with probability α. Like Daskin, they also assume that the probabilities of individual units being busy are independent, but develop region-specific estimates of the probability that a unit is busy. Variations on this model are discussed in ReVelle & Hogan [1989a].

In a related paper, ReVelle & Hogan [1989b] considered a problem they call the maximum availability location problem. The model positions p servers to maximize the population (or demand) that is covered with probability α, where covered means an emergency unit is within a specified time standard. (A comprehensive review of basic covering models and their extensions is given in ReVelle [1989].)

A problem with ReVelle & Hogan's approach is that it is very difficult to interpret the meaning of a node being covered with probability α. Surely $\alpha = 0.8$ is better than $\alpha = 0.7$, but without having a measure of the consequence of being uncovered it is difficult to make a comparison. In inventory models, a service level may be stated in terms of the probability of a stockout during a replenishment leadtime. The consequence of a stockout is fairly clear; the consequent of being uncovered is not. Also, the optimal solutions to the test problems that ReVelle & Hogan solved lead to putting two or more units at the same location which serves to increase average response time.

Two papers include workload capacities in maximal covering models. Pirkul & Schilling [1989, 1991] building on earlier work by Current & Storbeck [1986], extended the maximal covering location problem to include both backup service because the primary facility is utilized, and constraints on facility workload.

7.7. The p-median problem with unavailable servers

The p-median problem which is discussed in Section 6, seeks to locate p units on a network to minimize average travel time to a random service call, under the assumption that the closest server to a demand request is always available. In situations where servers are unavailable a significant proportion of the time, it is important to modify the deterministic p-median problem and there have been two different approaches for doing so. The first builds on the descriptive hypercube model discussed earlier. Recall that given a specified set of server locations, solving the hypercube gives the distribution of busy servers which is used to determine the average system-wide travel time and other performance measures. Jarvis [1975] developed an iterative optimization procedure that uses the hypercube model. His algorithm, which has also been used by Berman & Larson [1982], begins with a set of locations for the p servers, and solves the hypercube for the probability distribution of busy servers. The distribution is then used to determine the pattern of responses, i.e., the fraction of total responses from each server to each demand node. Next, each server is optimally located to respond to *its* demands. This requires solving for each of the servers, the 1-median problem, the one server version of the p-median problem. This is accomplished by solving a simple linear program or enumerating all of the alternative locations. This results in a new set of locations for the p servers. The hypercube is then solved to determine a new pattern of responses and the 1-median problem is solved again for each of the servers. The process terminates when the new locations are identical to the locations in the previous iteration, which results in achieving at least a local optimum.

Berman, Larson & Parkan [1987b] explored the use of a slightly different algorithm. Rather than solving the deterministic 1-median problem to improve the location of each server, they solved for the stochastic queue median. The stochastic queue median [see Berman, Larson & Chiu, 1985] is the location of a single server on a network that minimizes the expected response time to a random call for service. The response time is the sum of any queuing delay and the travel time to the call. Using simulation, the authors found that the two heuristics performed similarly with the more complicated stochastic queue median approach doing marginally better for arrival rates in the middle ranges. As the authors note, for a sufficiently low arrival rate each of the servers should be located at the 1-median.

The second approach to account for server unavailability in the p-median problem is the work of Weaver & Church [1985]. They call their method the vector assignment p-median problem. If p is the number of units to be located, the user specifies for each demand node the probability that the ith closest unit responds for $i = 1, \ldots, p$. In the simplest case, the probabilities would be the same for each demand node. One simple approach to determining these probabilities would be to calculate ρ, the average server utilization from the call rate and service rate data and to assume that the probability busy is equal to ρ for each server. Then assuming that servers are busy independent of one another, the required probabilities could be easily calculated. An alternative suggested by the authors would be to estimate the probabilities using actual data from the system being modelled. They also suggest using simulation, 'some complex analytical' model of the system or the subjective estimates of the decisionmaker.

Given these specified probabilities, they formulated as an integer program the problem of locating p servers on the nodes of a network to minimize total weighted distance. Although the weights they use are the populations at each demand node, these weights could be the number of total calls or serious calls for service. The authors reported that in most cases solving the integer program as a linear program yielded integer solutions but devised a faster method using Lagrangian relaxation. The authors applied their method to two test problems reported in the literature and showed that their results were significantly different from the solutions obtained by the deterministic p-median problem.

Neither of the two approaches to the p-median problem with unavailable servers consider service equity. In the case of the vector assignment p-median problem, although the authors do not do so, it would be possible and useful to add constraints that insure that the average travel time to each demand node is not greater than a specified value. For the iterative hypercube approach there is no obvious way to include such a constraint and it is possible that minimizing average response time could leave some areas with unacceptably poor service.

Blalock & Swersey [1993] developed an approach that joins the hypercube model to the vector assignment p-median problem and applied it to locating the four EMS units in New Haven. They first solved the vector assignment p-median problem assuming that each unit is busy independent of any other with the same busy probability equal to the average server utilization. For the locations found, the hypercube was then used to find the busy probabilities for each system state which were used as input to the vector assignment p-median problem. This iterative procedure continues until the locations do not change. In the New Haven application the procedure converged quickly, and the locations did not change from the initial vector assignment p-median solution. It would be interesting to test the performance of the vector assignment p-median approach further in a larger city such as Boston or Washington, DC, which have more EMS units.

Pirkul & Schilling [1988] developed a multi-objective siting model that seeks to minimize the sum of the fixed costs of opening facilities and first- and backup-unit travel times, subject to constraints on the workload of each facility, i.e., the total demand the facility can serve.

7.8. Other probabilistic models

Mirchandani & Odoni [1979] extended the p-median problem to a stochastic network, one in which the travel times on arcs and/or demands at nodes are discrete random variables, and showed that an optimal solution exists at nodes and that the problem can be formulated as an integer program. Weaver & Church [1983] developed computational approaches to solving the problem.

As noted earlier, Berman, Larson & Chiu [1985] used results from the $M \mid G \mid 1$ queuing system to find the stochastic queue median, the optimal location of a single server on a network subject to random demands and service time. Their work was extended by Chiu, Berman & Larson [1985], while Brandeau [1992] considered the stochastic queue median on a plane rather than a network.

In an earlier section, the work of Carter, Chaiken & Ignall [1972] was described which showed that under certain conditions it pays not to send the closest unit. This districting problem was also studied by Berman & Larson [1985] who use the $M \mid G \mid 1$ queuing model to find optimal districts for a 2-server problem. In contrast to the approach of Carter, Chaiken & Ignall [1972], Berman & Larson allow no cooperation between the two servers; if a call is received in the server's district when it is busy, it enters a queue. Berman & Mandowsky [1986] combined the results of the single server stochastic queue median model [Berman, Larson & Chiu, 1985] with the Berman & Larson [1985] districting approach to solve a problem they call location-allocation, which is to find both the locations of the servers and their districts. (In a related paper, Ahituv & Berman [1986, 1987] considered two adjacent service networks which may cooperate.) Benveniste [1985] also studied the location-allocation problem which she calls the combined zoning and location problem. She does allow cooperation between servers, making use of results of the $M \mid M \mid C$ queuing model. This is an ambitious approach that is modelled as a non-linear programming problem with an approximate solution method applied to test problems with three and four servers.

The relocation approach of Kolesar & Walker [1974] was discussed in Section 6.3. Berman [1981a,b] and Berman, Larson & Odoni [1981] devised a Markovian decision approach to deciding how free servers at any given time should be repositioned or relocated to compensate for servers which are busy, an approach that is potentially applicable to police and EMS problems.

Simulation models have played important roles in the deployment of emergency services and have often been used to examine the type of 'micro' location problems we have been discussing. In addition to the simulation model cited earlier, that was used by Savas [1969], Carter & Ignall [1970] of the Rand Fire Project built a detailed simulation of firefighting operations, Larson [1972a,b] and Kolesar & Walker [1975] developed simulations of police patrol, while Trudeau, Rousseau, Ferland & Choquette [1989] developed a simulation of an EMS system. The Carter & Ignall model was used to evaluate specific fire company deployment changes such as opening new companies, while the Kolesar & Walker model was used to test the effectiveness of an automatic car locator system. Simulation models were also used by Uyeno & Seeberg [1984] for locating ambulances in British Colombia, and by Heller, Cohon & ReVelle [1989] to validate a multi-objective model for locating EMS units.

8. Staffing and scheduling

In police patrol, an important issue is whether patrol cars should be staffed with on or two officers. Single-officer cars provide much more patrol presence for a fixed number of officers, but some argue against them citing safety considerations.

In cities where finances are tight, there is motivation to reduce the size of the patrol force by changing to one-officer cars. But how many one-officer cars are needed to provide similar service to the public and safety to the officers as a given number of two-officer cars? Thus, the one- versus two-officer issue has created a need for new deployment models. In evaluating one-officer cars, it is important to know the response times of both first- and second-arriving vehicles at a hazardous incident. The time between the arrival of the two vehicles, during which the first-arriving officer must deal with the emergency without any assistance, is especially important.

Kaplan [1979] used simple analytical models to compare one- and two-officer units by estimating the effect on coverage, response time, patrol frequency, visibility, crime detection and officer injury. Among his conclusions were that the reduction in expected travel time for the first-arriving unit may be quite large, while similar large reductions in response time, which includes queuing delay, are likely. For example, applying his model to San Diego, he estimated a decrease in response time of about 50% resulting from the use of two one-officer units patrolling a beat rather than a single two-officer unit.

Kaplan's response time model considers only the first unit dispatched to an incident. In contrast, Chelst [1981] estimated travel times for both first- and second-arriving units for one- and two-officer systems. His approach is similar in spirit to the work of Larson [1972b] and Kolesar & Blum [1973] discussed in Section 5. That is, rather than using a detailed queuing model, Chelst estimated travel distance in a region as a function of the region's area, the number of units assigned and the average unit availability. He considered two different models of dispatch operations. In the first, corresponding to a beat system, the unit that is actually closest to the incident may not be dispatched. In the second, it is assumed that a vehicle monitoring system is in operation so that the closest unit is always dispatched. Chelst found that a vehicle monitoring system can greatly enhance the effectiveness of one-officer units. Without such a system, a one-officer system is likely to have mixed results: shorter average travel times for the first-arriving officer and longer travel times for the second-arriving officer. With a vehicle monitoring system his results suggest that personnel levels can be reduced as well as the average travel times for both first- and second-arriving officers.

The MCD queuing model of Green [1984] discussed in Section 5 has been used by Green & Kolesar [1984b] to analyze the potential effectiveness of one-officer patrol in New York City. The question put to the researchers was: 'How many one-officer cars are needed to achieve equal dispatching delay to high priority calls at the current number of two-officer cars?' The researchers broadened the scope of their analyses to consider the impact on patrol officer safety as well as service to the public and reported on political aspects of the policy analysis which showed that while one-officer patrol had great potential, there were important managerial problems to resolve. A follow-up study of the validity of the model as a representation of the current New York City two-officer patrol car operations was reported in Green & Kolesar [1983].

The number of firefighters to assign to a unit is an important deployment question. Is it better to have fewer, better staffed units or more units with fewer firefighters per unit? To answer this question the effect of staffing level on firefighting operations needs to be understood. Halpern, Sarisamlis & Wand [1982] developed an approach which was used to measure the relationship between staffing levels and time needed to extinguish the fire for one- and two-family residential fires in Calgary, Canada. In their method which is based on the critical path technique, fireground operations are broken down into distinct and well-defined activities, and interviews with fire department officers are used to generate data concerning precedence relations among activities, their durations and their manpower requirements. Although, as the authors acknowledged, their results are preliminary, this is an interesting start toward answering an important deployment question.

Much work in the OR literature has addressed the scheduling of airline crews, nurses, and other personnel. Taylor & Huxley [1989] in an Edelman prize-winning paper devised a comprehensive approach that was used to schedule police officers in San Francisco. The Police Department was particularly interested in evaluating the effects of changing from five-day, eight-hour shifts to four-day, ten-hour shifts and deploying more one-officer cars. The problem begins with a forecast of the hourly number of police officers needed and determines the work group start times and number of officers in each work group. The non-linear multi-objective function seeks to minimize total shortages (fewer officers than are needed) and the maximum shortage in any hour of the week. The problem is solved by a heuristic search procedure.

Trudeau, Rousseau, Ferland & Choquette [1989] and Aubin [1992] reported on a method for scheduling emergency medical crews that has been successfully used in Montreal. The problem is formulated as an integer program with the objective to minimize personnel costs subject to meeting hourly requirements. Earlier work on scheduling police officers was done by Heller & Stenzel [1974].

9. Emergency service mergers

With cities and towns increasingly under budgetary pressures, some have sought to improve efficiency by merging services. Chelst [1987, 1988, 1990] has led the way in devising OR models for police/fire mergers which may be appropriate for towns and smaller cities, with populations under 100 000. Chelst [1990] modelled a police/fire merger in which the cross-trained officers normally are on police patrol until interrupted by a fire emergency. Chelst uses Green's [1984] multiple dispatch queuing model discussed earlier, to estimate the probability that there will be n service units available at the time of an incoming call. He then superimposes a binomial distribution on the basic queuing model to account for a serious fire call preempting police activities. He found that because typical police workloads are under 50%, while 80–90% of police calls are interruptible, that the probability of a manpower shortage at a fire is near zero.

Chelst [1988] completed a short (17 days) study of a potential police/fire merger in Grosse Pointe Park, Michigan, finding that a merger was feasible and appropriate. His findings were reported in the newspaper a week before a referendum vote on the merger which was carried by a 58% to 42% vote. The program has been running successfully since then.

But all such merger attempts have not been successful. In Roseville, Michigan in the midst of Chelst's analysis, the firefighter's union led a major political fight (Figure 4) and the concept was soundly defeated in a referendum [Chelst, 1990]. The merger supporters on the City Council lost their seats in subsequent elections and the city manager who championed the concept lost his job. At the present time, it appears that police/fire mergers hold promise only for towns and the smallest cities.

Swersey, Goldring & Geyer [1993] developed a plan for the New Haven Fire Department that had dual-trained fire-medics responding to medical emergencies or fire incidents. The approach was feasible and desirable because the authors found that fire units were busy only about 4% of the time, while emergency medical units were busy about 15% of the time. Under the plan, a team of two fire-medics and three firefighters would replace an emergency medical unit (with two emergency medical technicians) and a fire company (with four firefighters), thus saving one position. In response to an emergency medical call, the two fire-medics would be dispatched on the emergency medical vehicle, leaving three firefighters available to respond to a fire call. In response to a fire call with the entire team available, all five would respond on the fire truck. About 15% of the time (when the fire-medics were on an emergency medical call) only three firefighters would respond. But this small degradation in fire protection was more then offset by significant improvements in the response time to medical emergencies. This

Fig. 4. Poster used by opponents of the Roseville police-fire merger.

improvement was accomplished by having fire companies in outlying areas whose members were trained in CPR respond to emergency medical calls as well as fire incidents. The program ran successfully for a year and saved about 10% of the operating budget, but as a consequence of union opposition and other political considerations it was then abandoned. In spite of this implementation setback in New Haven, as Swersey, Goldring & Geyer [1993] noted an increasing number of fire departments across the country have begun to recognize the benefits of cross-trained personnel providing fire and emergency medical services.

10. Discussion

Over nearly three decades, an impressive body of literature has emerged on the deployment of emergency services. These works, which include two Lanchester prize recipients [Larson, 1972b; Kolesar & Walker, 1974], both further the development of location theory and provide practical tools for decisionmakers.

For deciding how many units to assign to a region, there are simple and easy to implement models including the square root model of Kolesar & Blum [1973], and the Patrol Car Allocation Model [Chaiken, 1978].

Among the deterministic location models, the descriptive fire station location packages [Dormont, Hausner & Walker, 1975; Public Technology, Inc., 1974] have great value for decisionmakers. They allow the user to evaluate quickly a range of options by considering travel time statistics, hazards, and fire incidence. There is potential value in using the p-median optimization model with constraints on maximum travel distance to suggest locations that could then be evaluated using one of the location packages. However, experience with these packages suggests that the analyst or decisionmaker can easily identify preferred locations by examining current and potential locations on a map in relation to demand rates and fire hazards.

Among probabilistic location models, the descriptive hypercube queuing model of Larson [1974, 1975a], which has been applied mainly to designing police patrol beats but also applies to EMS location [Brandeau & Larson, 1986], is a valuable tool for estimating response times and unit workloads. The prescriptive probabilistic location models also have high utility for decisionmakers. Jarvis' [1975] algorithm is a useful method which embeds the hypercube in an iterative optimization procedure that seeks to minimize average response time. Weaver & Church's [1985] vector assignment p-median model is especially valuable. In a very simple way it extends the p-median model to deal with server unavailability. As noted earlier, the model would be even more useful if constraints were added on maximum average travel distance to each demand node, which would be easy to do. It would be interesting to compare the prescriptions of the iterative hypercube procedure to those of the vector assignment p-median problem. In doing so, the hypercube model could be used to estimate the average travel time for locations chosen by the vector assignment p-median problem.

Daskin's [1983] maximal covering model is the most policy-relevant of the many optimization models that focus on coverage rather than average response time. But it is difficult to establish an appropriate coverage standard and maximizing coverage emphasizes equity with little weight given to efficiency. For example, in Austin, Texas [Eaton, Daskin, Simmons, Bulloch & Jansma, 1985], the goal was to find the number of units needed so that 95% of the calls could be reached within five minutes, while in Tucson, Arizona, Goldberg, Dietrich, Chen, Mitwasi, Valenzuela & Criss [1990b], using a model similar to Daskin's [1983], attempted to maximize the number of calls reached within eight minutes. Eaton and others have motivated the use of the maximal covering approach for locating EMS units by citing the Emergency Medical Services Act of 1973 which prescribes that urban EMS systems be able to cover 95% of all demand within ten minutes. This Act was established prior to the valuable and extensive research results discussed in Section 4 relating EMS response time to survival from cardiac arrest. These findings [Olson, LaRochelle, Fark, Aprahamtan, Aufderheide, Mateer, Hargarten & Stueven, 1989; Weaver, Cobb, Hallstrom, Copass, Ray, Emery & Fahrenbruch, 1986] show a declining survival rate as a function of response time and highlight the importance of reducing response time. In an EMS context, it would be useful to compare the prescriptions of Daskin's [1983] maximal expected covering model to those of Weaver & Church's [1985] vector assignment p-median problem.

The best of the OR research such as the Rand Fire Project work and the hypercube model are problem- and client-driven. Although there are numerous examples of applications to places that include Austin, Tucson, the Dominican Republic, and Bangkok, there are more papers in which models are only applied to test problems.

The extensive and relevant work relating mortality to EMS response time has been virtually ignored by OR modellers of the EMS deployment problem. Meaningful data is now available so that model objective functions can now focus on the probability of death rather than response time.

Even though the field has produced very impressive models and results there are opportunities for important future work. In the fire area, the tradeoff between the number of firefighters per company and number of companies remains an unsolved and important question. In recent years cities have reduced fire company staffing in the face of budgetary pressures as an alternative to the politically difficult task of closing fire stations.

In the EMS area there are a number of important research questions. The proper mix of basic life support (BLS) and advanced life support (ALS) units, and the best dispatching policy for these units (e.g., should ALS units be sent only to the most life-threatening emergencies) are two challenges issues. Also, attention should be given to how EMS services are organized. For example, some cities use their EMS units to transport patients to the hospital while others, like New Haven, use a private ambulance service. The New Haven System reduces the utilization of the City's EMS units, at the same time that the private ambulance service, which responds in nearby communities as well, is able to operate at a high utilization and thereby reduce the cost of their services. In all three emergency services, OR modellers will be challenged in the future to help communities under budgetary constraints find ways to maintain service with fewer resources.

Although some very interesting deployment problems still need to be addressed, in the future there should be a shift in focus to the consideration of broader emergency service questions. The study of the tradeoff between smoke detectors and fire companies [Halpern, 1979] is a good example of this kind of work. Two other studies also exemplify this broader research. One is Cretin's [1977] study of the costs and benefits of three approaches to the prevention and treatment of heart attack: hospital coronary care units, mobile coronary care units (ambulances with advanced life support equipment), and prevention by identifying and treating those with high levels of serum cholesterol. The other is the study by Urban, Bergner & Eisenberg [1981] of the costs and benefits of reducing deaths due to cardiac arrest in King County, Washington. In short, as operational problems are solved, the challenge of the future will be to address broader, more strategic issues.

Acknowledgements

The writing of this chapter was supported by the Yale School of Management Faculty Research Fund. I would like to thank Arnold Barnett, one of the editors of this volume for his helpful suggestions as well as Peter Kolesar who collaborated with me on a survey of this field in the mid-1980's. Most important, I would like to express my gratitude for the influence of my thesis advisor and friend, the late Edward J. Ignall, a leader of the Rand Fire Project whose contributions to urban operations research will also be remembered.

References

Ahituv, N., and O. Berman (1987). Devising a cooperation policy for emergency networks. *J. Oper. Res. Soc.* 38(11), 1015–1029.

Ahituv, N., and O. Berman (1986). Negotiating a coordination agreement between two adjacent service networks, in: A. Swersey, and E. Ignall (eds.), *Delivery of Urban Services, TIMS Studies in the Management Sciences*, 22, Elsevier, pp. 155–182.

Aly, A.A., and J.A. White (1978). Probabilistic formulation of the emergency service location problem. *J. Oper. Res. Soc.* 29, 1167–1179.

Anderson, L.R., and R.A. Fontenot (1992). Optimal positioning of service units along a coordinate line. *Transportation Sci.* 26(4), 346–351.

Aubin, J. (1992). Scheduling ambulances. *Interfaces* 22(2), 1–10.

Avi-Itzhak, B., and R. Shinnar (1973). Quantitave models in crime control. *J. Crim. Justice* 1(3), 185–217.

Baker, J.R., E.R. Clayton and L.J. Moore (1989). Redesign of primary response areas for county ambulance services. *European J. Oper. Res. Soc.* 41, 23–32.

Baker, J.R., and K.E. Fitzpatrick (1986). Determination of an optimal forecast model for ambulance demand using goal programming. *J. Oper. Res. Soc.* 37(11), 1047–1059.

Balas, E., and A. Ho (1980). Set covering algorithms using cutting planes, heuristics and subgradient optimization: a computational study. *Math. Programming* 12, 37–60.

Baldwin, R., and L.G. Fardell (1970). Statistical analysis of fire spread in buildings, Fire Research Note No. 848, Joint Fire Research Organization, Borehamwood.

Bammi, D. (1975). Allocation of police beats to patrol units to minimize response time to calls for service. *J. Comput. Oper. Res.* 2(1), 1–12.

Bammi, D., and N.T. Thomopoulos (1976). A predictive model for the police response function. *Oper. Res. Q.* 27(1), 15–30.

Barnett, A., and A.J. Lofaso (1986). On the optimal allocation of prison space, in: A. Swersey, and E. Ignall (eds.), *Delivery of Urban Services, TIMS Studies in the Management Sciences*, 22, Elsevier, pp. 245–268.

Batta, R., J. Dolan and N. Krishnamurthy (1989). The maximal expected covering location problem: Revisited. *Transportation Sci.* 23, 277–287.

Batta, R., and N.R. Mannur (1990). Covering-location models for emergency situations that require multiple response units. *Management Sci.* 36(1), 16–23.

Becker, L.B., M.P. Ostrander, J. Barrett and G.T. Kondos (1991). Outcome of CPR in a large metropolitan area – Where are the survivors? *Ann. Emergency Medicine* 20(4), 355–361.

Belardo, S., J. Harrald, W. Wallace and J. Ward (1984). A partial covering approach to siting response resources for major maritime oil spills. *Management Sci.* 30, 1184–1196.

Bell, C., and D. Allen (1969). Optimal planning of an emergency ambulance service. *J. Socio-Econom. Planning Sci.* 3(2), 95–101.

Benedict, J.M. (1983). Three hierarchical objective models which incorporate the concept of excess coverage to locate EMS vehicles or hospitals. M.S. Thesis, Department of Civil Engineering, Northwestern University, Evanston, IL.

Benveniste, R. (1985). Solving the combined zoning and location problem for several emergency units. *J. Oper. Res. Soc.* 36(5), 433–450.

Berlin, G. (1972). Facility location and vehicle allocation for provision of an emergency service, Ph.D. thesis. The Johns Hopkins University.

Berlin, G., and J. Liebman (1974). Mathematical analysis of emergency ambulance location. *J. Socio-Econom. Planning Sci.* 8, 323–388.

Berman, O. (1981a). Dynamic repositing of indistinguishable service units on transportation network. *Transportation Sci.* 15(2), 115–136.

Berman, O. (1981b). Repositioning of distinguishable urban service units on transportation networks. *Transportation Sci.* 8, 105–118.

Berman, O., and R.C. Larson (1982). The median problem with congestion. *J. Comput. Oper. Res.* 9(2), 119–126.

Berman, O., and R.C. Larson (1985). Optimal 2-facility network districting in the presence of queuing. *Transportation Sci.* 19(3), 261–277.

Berman, O., and R.R. Mandowsky (1986). Location-allocation on congested networks. *European J. Oper. Res.* 26, 238–250.

Berman, O., and E.H. Kaplan (1990). Equity maximizing facility location schemes. *Transportation Sci.* 24(2), 137–144.

Berman, O., R.C. Larson and S.S. Chiu (1983). Optimal server location on a network operating as an M/G/1 queue, Working Paper, September [*Oper. Res.* 33 (1985) 746–771].

Berman, O., R. Larson and N. Fouska (1992). Optimal location of discretionary service facilities. *Transportation Sci.* 26(3), 201–211.

Berman, O., R.C. Larson and A.R. Odoni (1981). Developments in network location with mobile and congested facilities. *European J. Oper. Res.* 6(2), 104–116.

Berman, O., R. Larson and C. Parkan (1987a). The median problem with congestion. *J. Comput. Oper. Res.* 9, 119–126.

Berman, O., R. Larson and C. Parkan (1987b). The stochastic queue *p*-median problem. *Transportation Sci.* 21, 207–216.

Blalock, G., and A.J. Swersey (1992). An iterative procedure for locating emergency medical units, Working Paper, June, Yale School of Management.

Blalock, G., and A.J. Swersey (1993). An iterative procedure for locating emergency medical units. *Working Paper.* Yale School of Management.

Blumstein, A., and R. Larson (1967). Crime and criminal justice, in: P. Morse, and L.W. Bacon (eds.), *Operations Research in Public Systems*, Massachusetts Institute of Technology, Cambridge, MA 159–180.

Bodily, S., (1978). Police sector design incorporating preferences of interest groups for equality and efficiency. *Management Sci.* 24(12), 1301–1313.

Brandeau, M.L. (1992). Characterization of the stochastic median queue trajectory in a plane with generalized distances. *Oper. Res.* 40(2), 331–341.

Brandeau, M., and R.C. Larson (1986). Extending and applying the hypercube queueing model to deploy ambulances in Boston, in: A. Swersey, and E. Ignall (eds.), *Delivery of Urban Services, TIMS Studies in the Management Sciences* 22, Elsevier, pp. 121–153.

Carson, Y.M., and R. Batta (1990). Locating an ambulance on the Amherst campus of the State University of New York at Buffalo. *Interfaces* 20(5), 43–49.

Carter, C., J. Chaiken and E. Ignall (1972). Response areas for two emergency units. *Oper. Res.* 20(3), 571–594.

Carter, G., and E. Ignall (1970). A simulation model for fire department operations: Design and preliminary results. *IEEE Trans. Syst. Sci. Cybernet.* SSC-6, 282–293.

Carter, G., and J. Rolph (1974). Empirical Bayes methods applied to estimating fire alarm probabilities. *J. Amer. Statist. Assoc.* 69(348), 880–885.

Casillas, P.A. (1987). Data aggregation and the *P*-median problem in continuous space, in: A. Ghosh, and G. Ruchton (eds.), *Spatial Analysis and Location-Allocation Models*, Van Nostrand Reinhold Co., New York, p. 327.

Chaiken, J. (1971). The number of emergency units busy at alarms which require multiple servers, R-531-NYC/HUD, The Rand Corporation, Santa Monica, CA.

Chaiken, J.M. (1975). Patrol allocation methodology for police departments, R-1852-HUD, The Rand Corporation, Santa Monica, CA.

Chaiken, J.M. (1978). Transfer of emergency service deployment models to operating agencies. *Management Sci.* 24(7), 719–731.

Chaiken, J., and P. Dormont (1978a). A patrol car allocation model: Background. *Management Sci.* 24(12), 1280–1290.

Chaiken, J., and P. Dormont (1978b). A patrol car allocation model: Capabilities and algorithms. *Management Sci.* 24, 1291–1300.

Chaiken, J., and E. Ignall (1972). An extension of Erlang's formulas which distinguishes individual servers. *J. Appl. Probab.* 9(1), 192–197.

Chaiken, J., E. Ignall, P. Kolesar and W. Walker (1980). Response to the Wallace communication of the Rand-HUD fire models. *Management Sci.* 26(4), 422–431.

Chaiken, J., and R. Larson (1972). Methods for allocating urban emergency units. *Management Sci.* 19(4), 110–130.

Chaiken, J., M. Lawless and K. Stevenson (1974). The impact of police activity on crime: Robberies on the New York City subway system, R-1424-NYC, The Rand Corporation, Santa Monica, CA.

Charnes, A., and J. Storbeck (1980). A goal programming model for the siting of multilevel EMS systems. *Socio-Econ. Plan. Sci.* 14, 155–161.

Chelst, K. (1978a). An algorithm for deploying a crime directed (tactical) patrol force. *Management Sci.* 24(12), 1314–1327.

Chelst, K. (1978b). The basis of search theory applied to police patrol, in: R. Larson (ed.), *Police Deployment*, Lexington Books, D.C. Heath & Co., Lexington, MA, Chapter 9.

Chelst, K.R. (1980). Paramedic-sheriffs vs. paramedic ambulances, in Kent County, Michigan: A study in cost effectiveness, in: *Proceedings of the International Conference on Systems in Health Care, held in Montreal* II (July 14–17) pp. 991–1000.

Chelst, K.R. (1981). Deployment of one- vs. two-officer patrol units: A comparison of travel times. *Management Sci.* 27(2), 213–230.

Chelst, K. (1987). Police–fire merger: A preimplementation analysis of performance and cost. *J. Urban Affairs* 9(2), 171–188.

Chelst, K. (1988). A public safety merger in Grosse Points Park, Michigan – a short and sweet study. *Interfaces* 18(4), 1–11.

Chelst, K. (1990). Queuing models for police–fire merger analysis. *Queuing Syst.* 7, 101–124.

Chelst, K.R., and Z. Barlach (1981). Multiple unit dispatches in emergency services: Models to estimate system performance. *Management Sci.* 27(12), 1390–1409.

Chelst, K.R., and J.P. Jarvis (1979). Estimating the probability distribution of travel times for urban emergency service systems. *Oper. Res.* 27(1), 199–204.

Chiu, S., O. Berman and R.C. Larson (1985). Stochastic queue median on a tree network. *Management Sci.* 31, 764–772.

Church, R.L., and M. Meadows (1979). Location modelling utilizing maximum service distance criteria. *Geographical Analysis* 11, 358–379.

Church, R., and C. ReVelle (1974). The maximal covering location problem. *Papers Regional Sci. Assoc.* 32, 101–120.

Church, R., and J. Weaver (1983). Computational procedures for location problems on stochastic network. *Transportation Sci.* 17, 168–180.

Clawson, C., and S.K. Chang (1977). The relationship of response delays and arrest rates. *J. Police Sci. Administration* 5(1), 53–68.

Cobham, A. (1954). Priority assignment in waiting line problems. *Oper. Res.* 2(1), 70.

Cohon, J.L. (1978). Multiobjective programming and planning. Academic Press, New York.

Corman, H. (1986). Costs and benefits of mandatory sentencing: Crime aversion through incarceration, in: A. Swersey, and E. Ignall (eds.), *Delivery of Urban Services, TIMS Studies in the Management Sciences*, 22, Elsevier, pp. 227–244.

Corman, H., E. Ignall, K. Rider and A. Stevenson (1976). Casualties and their relation to fire company response distance and demographic factors. *Fire Tech.* 12, 193–203.

Cornuejols, G., M.L. Fisher and G.L. Nemhauser (1977). Location of bank accounts to optimize float: An analytic study of exact and approximate algorithms. *Management Sci.* 23, 789–810.

Cretin, S. (1977). Cost/benefit analysis of treatment and prevention of myocardial infarction. *Health Services Res.* 12(2), 174–189.

Cretin, S., and T.R. Willemain (1979). A model of prehospital death from ventricular fibrillation following myocardial infarction. *Health Services Res.* 14(3), 221–234.

Cuninghame-Green, R.A., and G. Harries (1987). Nearest-neighbour rules for emergency services. *Z. Oper. Res.* 32, 299–306.

Current, J.R., and D.A. Schilling (1987). Elimination of source A and B errors in *P*-median location problems. *Geographical Analysis* 19, 95.

Daberkow, S.G. (1977). Location and cost of ambulances serving a rural area. *Health Services Res.* 12(3), 299–311.

Daskin, M.S. (1982). Application of an expected covering model to EMS system design. *Decision Sci.* 13(3), 416–439.

Daskin, M.S. (1983). A maximum expected covering location model: Formulation, properties and heuristic solution. *Transportation Sci.* 17(1), 48–70.

Daskin, M.S. (1987). Location, dispatching and routing models for emergency services with stochastic travel times, in: A. Ghosh, and G. Rushion (eds.), *Spiral Analysis and Location-Allocation Models*, Van Nostrand-Reinhold Co., New York, pp. 224–265.

Daskin, M.S., and A. Haghani (1984). Multiple vehicle routing and dispatching to an emergency scene. *Environment Planning A* 16, 1349–1359.

Daskin, M.S., A. Haghani, M. Khanal and C. Malandraki (1989). Aggregation Effects in Maximum Covering Models., *Ann. Oper. Res.* 18(February), 115–139.

Daskin, M.S., K. Hogan and C. ReVelle (1988). Integration of multiple, excess, backup, and expected covering models. *Environment Planning* 15, 15–35.

Daskin, M.S., and E.H. Stern (1981). A hierarchical objective set covering model for emergency medical service vehicle deployment. *Transportation Sci.* 15, 137–152.

Dearing, P.M., and J.P. Jarvis (1978). A location model with queuing constraints. *J. Comput. Oper. Res.* 5, 273–277.

Denardo, E., U. Rothblum and A.J. Swersey (1988). A transportation problem in which the costs depend on the order of arrival. *Management Sci.* 34(6), 774–783.

Doering, R. (1975). A systems analysis of police command control operations. *AIIE Trans.* 9(1), 21–28.

Dormont, P., J. Hausner and W. Walker (1975). Firehouse site evaluation model: Description and user's manual, Report E-1618/2, The Rand Corporation, Santa Monica, CA, June.

Eaton, D., and M.S. Daskin (1980). A multiple model approach to planning emergency medical service vehicle deployment, in: C. Tilquin (ed.), *Proceedings of the International Conference on Systems Science Health Care* (refereed), Pergamon Press, Montreal, Que, pp. 951–959.

Eaton, D.J., M.S. Daskin, D. Simmons, B. Bulloch and G. Jansma (1985). Determining emergency medical service vehicle deployment in Austin, Texas. *Interfaces* 15(1), 96–108.

Eaton, D.J., M.L. Hector, U. Sanchez, R.R. Lantigua and J. Morgan (1986). Determining ambulance deployment in Santo Domingo, Dominican Republic. *J. Oper. Res. Soc.* 37(2), 113–126.

Eisenberg, M.S., R.O. Cummins, S. Damon, M.P. Larsen and T.R. Hearne (1990). Survival rates from out-of-hospital cardiac arrest: Recommendations for uniform definitions and data to report. *Ann. Emergency Medicine* 19(11), 1249–1259.

Eisenberg, M., A. Hallstrom and L. Bergner (1981). The ACLS score, predicting survival from out-of-hospital cardiac arrest. *JAMA* 246(1), 50–52.

Eisenberg, M.S., B.T. Horwood, R.O. Cummins, R. Reynolds-Haertle and T.R. Hearne (1990). Cardiac arrest and resuscitation: A tale of 29 cities. *Ann. Emergency Medicine* 19(2), 179–185.

El-Shaieb, A. (1973). A new algorithm for locating sources among destinations. *Management Sci.* 20(2), 221–231.

Finnerty, J. (1977). How often will the firemen get their sleep. *Management Sci.* 23(11), 1169–1173.

Fisher, M.L., and P. Kedia (1990). Optimal solution of set covering/partitioning problems using dual heuristics. *Management Sci.* 36(6), 674–688.

Fitzsimmons, J.A. (1973). A methodology for emergency ambulance deployment. *Management Sci.* 19(6), 627–636.

Fitzsimmons, J.A., and B.N. Srikar (1982). Emergency ambulance location using the contiguous zone search routine. *J. Oper. Management* 2(4), 225–237.

Forter, S.T., and W.L. Gorr (1986). An adaptive filter for estimating spatially-varying parameters: Application to modelling police hours spent in response to calls for service. *Management Sci.* 32(7), 878–889.

Francis, R., L. McGinnis and J. White (1983). Locational analysis. *European J. Oper. Res.* 12, 220–252.

Fujiwara, O., T. Makjamroen and K.K. Gupta (1987). Ambulance deployment analysis: A case study of Bangkok. *European J. Oper. Res.* 31, 9–18.

Fyffe, D., and R. Rardin (1974). An evaluation of policy related research in fire protection service management, Georgia Institute of Technology, October (Available from the National Technical Information Service (NTIS) US Dept. of Commerce, Springfield, VA.)

Galvao, R.D. (1980). A dual-bounded algorithm for the *p*-median problem. *Oper. Res.* 28(5), 1112–1121.

Garfinkel, R., A. Neebe and M. Rao (1974). An algorithm for the *m*-median plant location problem. *Transportation Sci.* 8(3), 217–236.

Gass, S. (1968). On the division of police districts into patrol beats, *Proceedings of the 24rd National Conference of the ACM*, Brandon/Systems Press, Princeton, NJ, pp. 459–473.

Goldberg, J., R. Dietrich, J. Chen, M. Mitwasi, T. Valenzuela and E. Criss (1990a). A simulation model for evaluating a set of emergency vehicle base locations: Development validation and usage. *J. Socio-Econom. Planning Sci.* 24, 125–141.

Goldberg, J., R. Dietrich, J.M. Chen, M.G. Mitwasi, T. Valenzuela and E. Criss (1990b). Validating and applying a model for locating emergency medical vehicles in Tucson, AZ. *European J. Oper. Res.* 49, 308–324.

Goldberg, J., and L. Paz (1991). Locating emergency vehicle bases when service time depends on call location. *Transportation Sci.* 25(4), 264–280.

Goldberg, J., and F. Szidarovsky (1991a). Methods for solving nonlinear equations used in evaluating emergency vehicle busy probabilities. *Oper. Res.* 39(6), 903–916.

Goldberg, J., and F. Szidarovsky (1991b). A general model and convergence results for determining vehicle utilization in emergency systems. *Stochastic Models* 7, 137–160.

Goodchild, M.R. (1979). The aggregation problem in location-allocation. *Geographical Analysis* 11, 240.

Gordon, G., and R. Zelin (1968). A simulation study of emergency ambulance service in New York City, Technical Report No. 320–2935, March, IBM New York Scientific Center.

Gorry, G.A., and D.W. Scott (1977). Cost effectiveness of cardiopulmonary resuscitation training programs. *Health Services Res.* 12(1), 30–42.

Green, L. (1984). A multiple dispatch queuing model of police patrol operations. *Management Sci.* 30(6), 653–664.

Green, L., and P. Kolesar (1983). Testing the validity of a queuing model of police patrol operations, Working Paper No. 521A, Columbia University, New York.

Green, L., and P. Kolesar (1984a). A comparison of the multiple dispatch and M/M/C priority queuing models of police patrol. *Management Sci.* 30(6), 665–670.

Green, L., and P. Kolesar (1984b). The feasibility of one-officer patrol in New York City. *Management Sci.* 30(8), 964–981.

Greenberger, M., M. Crenson and B. Crissey (1976). *Models in the Policy Process*, Russell Sage Foundation, New York.

Gregg, S.R., J.M. Mulvey and J. Wolpert (1988). A stochastic planning for siting and closing public service facilities. *Environment Planning A* 20(1), 83–98.

Groom, K. (1977). Planning emergency ambulance services. *Oper. Res. Q.* 28(2), 641–651.

Hakimi, S. (1964). Optimum locations of switching centers and the absolute centers and medians of a graph. *Oper. Res.* 12, 450–459.

Hakimi, S. (1965). Optimum distribution of switching centers in a communications network and some related graph theoretic problems. *Management Sci.* 13, 462–475.

Hall, W.K. (1971). Management science approaches to the determination of urban ambulance requirements. *J. Socio-Econom. Planning Sci.* 5, 491–499.

Hall, W.K. (1972). The application of multifunction stochastic service systems in allocating ambulances to an urban area. *Oper. Res.* 20(3), 558–570.

Hall, Jr., J.R. (1991). U.S. experience with smoke detectors: who has them? How well do they work? When don't they work? *National Fire Protection Association*, Quincy, MA.

Halpern, J. (1977). The accuracy of estimates for the performance criteria in certain emergency service queuing systems. *Transportation Sci.* 11(3), 223–242.

Halpern, J. (1979). Fire loss reduction: Fire detectors vs. fire stations. *Management Sci.* 25(11), 1082–1092.

Halpern, J., E. Sarisamlis and Y. Wand (1982). An activity network approach for the analysis of manning policies in firefighting operations. *Management Sci.* 28, 1121–1136.

Hanjoul, P., and D. Peeters (1985). A comparison of two dual-based procedures for solving the *p*-median problem. *European J. Oper. Res.* 20(3), 387–396.

Hausner, J., and W. Walker (1975). An analysis of the deployment of fire-fighting resources in Trenton, NJ, Report R-1566/1, February, The Rand Corporation, Santa Monica, CA.

Hausner, J., W. Walker and A. Swersey (1974). An analysis of the deployment of fire-fighting resources in Yonkers, NY, Report R-1566/2, October, The Rand Corporation, Santa Monica, CA.

Heller, M., J.L. Cohon and C.S. ReVelle (1989). The use of simulation in validating a multiobjective EMS location model. *Ann. Oper. Res.* 18, 303–322.

Heller, N.B., and W.W. Stenzel (1974). Design of police work schedules. *Urban Analysis* 2, 21–49.

Heller, N.B., W.W. Stenzel, A.D. Gill and R.A. Kolde (1977). Field evaluation of the hypercube system for the analysis of police patrol operations: Final report, The Institute for Public Program Analysis, St. Louis, MO.

Hillsman, E.L., and R. Rhoda (1978). Errors in measuring distances from populations to service centers. *Ann. Regional Sci.* 12, 74.

Hogan, K., and C. ReVelle (1986). Concepts and applications of backup coverage. *Management Sci.* 32(11), 1434.

Hogg, J. (1968a). The siting of fire stations. *Oper. Res. Q.* 19, 275–287.

Hogg, J.M. (1968b). Planning for fire stations in Glasgow in 1980, Fire Research Report No. 1/68, Home Office Scientific Advisory Branch, London.

Hogg, J.M. (1970). Station siting in Peterborough and Market Deeping, Fire Research Report No. 7/70, Home Office Scientific Advisory Branch, London.

Hogg, J.M. (1971). A model of fire spread, Fire Research Report No. 2/71, Home Office Scientific Advisory Branch, London.

Hogg, J.M. (1973). Losses in relation to the fire brigade's attendance times, Fire Research Report No. 5/73, Home Office Scientific Advisory Branch, London.

Hogg, J.M., and D.M. Morrow (1973). The siting of fire stations in Northampton and Northamptonshire, Fire Research Report No. 4/73, Home Office Scientific Advisory Branch, London.

Hooke, R., and T.A. Jeeves (1961). Direct search solution of numerical and statistical problems. *J. Assoc. Comp. Mach.* 8(2), 212–229.

IBM Program Product (n.d.). LEMRAS application description manual, Document H20-0629; Law enforcement manpower resource allocation system, Program description manual, Program 5736-G21, Document SH20-6695-0.

Ignall, E., G. Carter and K. Rider (1982). An algorithm for the initial dispatch of fire companies. *Management Sci.* 28(4), 366–378.

Ignall, E., P. Kolesar, A. Swersey, W. Walker, E. Blum, G. Carter and H. Bishop (1975). Improving the deployment of New York City fire companies. *Interfaces* 2(2), 48–61.

Ignall, E., P. Kolesar and W. Walker (1978). Using simulation to develop and validate analytic models: Some case studies. *Oper. Res.* 26(2), 237–253.

Ignall, E.J., and W.E. Walker (1977). Deployment of ambulances in Washington, D.C. *Urban Analysis* 4, 59–92.

Jarvinen, P., J. Rajala and H. Sinervo (1972). A branch-and-bound algorithm for seeking the *P*-median. *Oper. Res.* 20(10), 173–178.

Jarvis, J. (1975). Optimization in stochastic systems with distinguishable servers, Technical Report 19-75, Operations Research Center, MIT, Cambridge, MA.

Jarvis, J.P., K.A. Stevenson and T.R. Willemain (1975). A simple procedure for the allocations of ambulances in semi-rural areas, Technical Report 13-75, Operations Research Center, MIT, Cambridge, MA.

Kaplan, E.H. (1979). Evaluating the effectiveness of one-officer versus two-officer patrol units. *J. Crim. Justice* 7, 325–355.

Kelling, G.L., T. Pate, D. Dieckman and C.E. Brown (1974). The Kansas City preventive patrol experiment, A Summary Report, October, Police Foundation, Washington, DC.

Kenney, R. (1972a). A method for districting among facilities. *Oper. Res.* 20(3), 613–618.

Kenney, R. (1972b). Utility functions for multiattributed consequences. *Management Sci.* 18(5), 276–287.

Khumawala, B. (1973). An efficient algorithm for the *P*-median problem with maximum distance constraints. *Geographical Analysis* 4, 309–321.

Kolesar, P. (1975). A model for predicting average fire engine travel times. *Oper. Res.* 23(4), 603–613.

Kolesar, P., and E. Blum (1973). Square root laws for fire engines response distances. *Management Sci.* 19(12), 1368–1378.

Kolesar, P., K. Rider, T. Crabill and W. Walker (1975). A queuing linear programming approach to scheduling police cars. *Oper. Res.* 23(6), 1045–1062.

Kolesar, P., and W. Walker (1974). An algorithm for the dynamic relocation of fire companies. *Oper. Res.* 22(3), 249–274.

Kolesar, P., and W. Walker (1975). A simulation model of police patrol operations, Executive summary and program description, Report R1625/1/2 HUD, The Rand Corporation, Santa Monica, CA.

Kolesar, P., W. Walker and H. Hausner (1975). Determining the relation between fire engine travel times and travel distances in New York City. *Oper. Res.* 23(4), 614–627.

Kolesar, P., and A.J. Swersey (1986). The deployment of urban emergency units: a survey, in: A. Swersey, and E. Ignall (eds.), *Delivery of Urban Services, TIMS Studies in the Management Sciences*, 22, Elsevier, pp. 87–119.

Koopman, B.O. (1957). The theory of search III. The optimum distribution of searching effort. *Oper. Res.* 5, 613.

Larson, R. (1972a). Improving the effectiveness of New York City's 911, in: A. Drake, R. Keeney and P. Morse (eds.), *Analysis of Public Systems*, MIT Press, Cambridge, MA, pp. 151–180.

Larson, R. (1972b). *Urban Police Patrol Analysis*, MIT Press, Cambridge, MA.

Larson, R. (1974). A hypercube queuing model for facility location and redistricting in urban emergency services. *J. Comput. Oper. Res.* 1(1), 67–95.

Larson, R. (1975a). Approximating the performance of urban emergency service systems. *Oper. Res.* 23(5), 845–868.

Larson, R. (1975b). What happened to patrol operations in Kansas City? A Review of the Kansas City preventive patrol experiments. *J. Crim. Justice* 4, 267–297.

Larson R. (ed.) (1978). *Police Deployment: New Tools for Planners*, Lexington Books, D.C. Heath and Co., Lexington, MA.

Larson, R.C. (1979). Structural system models for locational decisions: An example using the hypercube queuing model, in: K.B. Haley (ed.), *OR '78*, North-Holland, Amsterdam, pp. 1054–1091.

Larson, R.C., and V.O.K. Li (1981). Finding minimum rectilinear distance paths in the presence of barriers. *Networks* 11, 285–304.

Larson, R.C., and M.A. McKnew (1982). Police patrol-initiated activities within a systems queuing model. *Management Sci.* 28(7), 759–774.

Larson, R., and A. Odoni (1981). *Urban Operations Research*, Englewood Cliffs, NJ. Prentice-Hall.

Larson, R.C., and K.A. Stevenson (1972). On insensitivities in urban redistricting and facility location. *Oper. Res.* 20, 595–612.

Maranzana, F. (1964). On the location of supply points to minimize transport cost. *Oper. Res. Q.* 15(3), 261–270.

Marianov, V., and C. ReVelle (1991). The standard response fire protection sitting problem. *INFOR* 29(2), 116–129.

Martinich, J.S. (1988). A vertex-closing approach to the *p*-center problem. *Naval Res. Logist.* 35, 185–201.

Mayer, J.D. (1979). Paramedic response time and survival from cardiac arrest. *Social Sci. Med.* 13D(4), 267–271.

McEwen, T., and R. Larson (1974). Patrol planning in the Rotterdam police department. *J. Crim. Justice* 3, 85–110.

Miller, R., and A. Rappaport (1977). On the relationship between fire department response times and damages, Paper presented at the ORSA/TIMS National Meeting, November, Atlanta, GA.

Minieka, E. (1970). The M-center problem. *SIAM Rev.* 12(1).

Mirchandani, P.B., and A.R. Odoni (1979). Locations of medians on stochastic network. *Transportation Sci.* 13, 85–97.

Moore, G., and C. ReVelle (1982). The hierarchical service location problem. *Management Sci.* 28(7), 775.

Mukundam, S., and M.S. Daskin (1991). Joint location/sizing maximum profit covering models. *INFOR* 29(2), 139–152.

Narula, S.C. (1986). Minisum hierarchical location/allocation problems on a network. *Annals of Operations Research* 6, 257–272.

Narula, S.C., U.I. Ogbu and H.M. Samuelson (1977). An algorithm for the *p*-median problem. *Oper. Res.* 25, 709–713.

Neebe, A.W. (1988). A procedure for locating emergency service facilities for all possible response distances. *J. Oper. Res. Soc.* 39(8), 743–748.

Olson, D.G., and G.P. Wright (1975). Models for allocating preventive patrol effort. *Oper. Res. Q.* 26(4), 703–715.

Olson, D.W., J. LaRochelle, D. Fark, C. Aprahamtan, T.P. Aufderheide, J.R. Mateer, K.M. Hargarten and H.A. Stueven (1989). EMT-defibrillation: The Wisconson experience. *Ann. Emergency Medicine* 18(8), 806–811.

Pirkul, H., and D.A. Schilling (1988). The siting of emergency service facilities with workload capacities and backup service. *Management Sci.* 34(7), 896–908.

Pirkul, H., and D. Schilling (1989). The capacited maximal covering location problem with backup service. *Ann. Oper. Res.* 18, 141–154.

Pirkul, H., and D.A. Schilling (1991). The maximal covering location problem with capacities on total workload. *Management Sci.* 37(2), 233–248.

Plane, D., and T. Hendrick (1977). Mathematical programming and the location of fire companies for the Denver fire department, *Oper. Res.* 25(4), 563–578.

Pozen, M.W., D.D. Fried, S. Smith, L.V. Lindsay and G.C. Voigt (1977). Studies of ambulance patients with isochemic heart disease. *Amer. J. Public Health* 67(6), 527–541.

Press, S. (1971). Some effects of an increase in police manpower in the 20th precinct of New York City, Report R-704-NYC, The Rand Corporation, Santa Monica, CA.

Public Technology Inc. (1974). PTT station location package: Vol. 1, Executive summary; Vol. 2, Management report; Vol. 3, Operations guide; Vol. 4, Project leader's guide, Washington, DC.

Rand Fire Project (1979). W. Walker, J. Chaiken and E. Ignall (eds.), *Fire Department Deployment Analysis*, Elsevier North-Holland, New York.

ReVelle, C. (1987). Urban public facility location, in: E. Mills (ed.), *Handbooks of Urban and Regional Economics*, North-Holland, Amsterdam.

ReVelle, C. (1989). Review, extension and prediction in emergency service siting models. *European J. Oper. Res.* 40, 58–69.

ReVelle, C. (1993). Facility siting and integer-friendly programming. *European J. Oper. Res.* 65, 147–158.

ReVelle, C., D. Bigman, D. Schilling, J. Cohon and R. Church (1977). Facility location: A review of context-free and EMS models. *Health Services Res.* 12(2), 129–146.

ReVelle, C., and K. Hogan (1986). A reliability constrained siting model with local estimates of busy fractions. *Environment Planning B* 15, 143.

ReVelle, C., and K. Hogan (1989a). The maximum reliability location problem and reliable p-center problem: Derivatives of the probabilistic location set covering problem. *Ann. Oper. Res.* 18, 155–174.

ReVelle, C., and K. Hogan (1989b). The maximum availability location problem. *Transportation Sci.* 23(3), 192–200.

ReVelle, C., and V. Marianov (1991). A probabilistic FLEET model with individual vehicle reliability requirements. *European J. Oper. Res.* 53, 93–105.

ReVelle, C., D. Marks and J. Liebman (1970). An analysis of private and public sector location models. *Management Sci.* 16(11), 692–707.

ReVelle, C., and R. Swain (1970). Central facilities location. *Geographical Analysis* 2, 30–42.

Richard, D., H. Beguin and D. Peeters (1990). The location of fire stations in a rural environment. *Environment Planning A* 22(1), 39–52.

Rider, K. (1976). A parametric model for the allocation of fire companies in New York City. *Management Sci.* 23(2), 146–158.

Rider, K. (1979). The economics of the distribution of municipal fire protection services. *Rev. Econom. Statist.* LXI(2), 249–258.

Rosenshine, M. (1969). Contributions to a theory of patrol scheduling. *Oper. Res. Q.* 21(1), 99–108.

Roth, R., R.D. Steward, K. Rogers and G.M. Cannon (1984). Out-of-hospital cardiac arrest: Factors associated with survival. *Ann. Emergency Medicine* 13(4), 237–241.

Rushton, G., M. Goodchild and L. Ostresh (1972). Computer programs for location-allocation problems, Monograph No. 6, Department of Geography, University of Iowa, Iowa City, IA.

Saladin, B.A. (1982). Goal programming applied to police patrol allocation. *J. Oper. Management* 2(4), 239–249.

Savas, E. (1969). Simulation and cost-effectiveness analysis of New York's emergency ambulance service. *Management Sci.* 15(12), B608–627.

Savas, E. (1978). On equity in providing public services. *Management Sci.* 24(8), 800–808.

Saydam, C., and M. McKnew (1985). A separable programming approach to expected coverage: An application to ambulance location. *Decision Sci.* 16, 381–397.

Schilling, D., D.J. Elzinga, J. Cohan, R. Church and C. ReVelle (1979). The team/fleet models for simultaneous facility and equipment siting. *Transportation Sci.* 13(2), 163–175.

Schreuder, J.A.M. (1981). App,ıcation of a location model to fire stations in Rotterdam. *European J. Oper. Res.* 6, 212–219.

Scott, D.W., L.E. Factor and G.A. Gorry (1978). Predicting the response time of an urban ambulance system. *Health Services Res.* 13(4), 404–417.

Seward, S.M., D.R. Plane and T.E. Hendrick (1978). Municipal resource allocation: Minimizing the cost of fire protection. *Management Sci.* 24(16), 1740–1748.

Sforza, A. (1990). An algorithm for finding the absolute center of a network. *European J. Oper. Res.* 48, 376–390.

Shinnar, S., and R. Shinnar (1975). The effects of the criminal justice system on the control of crime: A quantitative approach. *Law Soc. Rev.* 9(4), 581–611.

Siler, K.F. (1979). Evaluation of emergency ambulance characteristics under several criteria. *Health Services Res.* 14(2), 160–176.

Stevenson, K. (1972). Emergency ambulance transportation, in: A. Drake, R. Keeney and P. Morse (eds.), *Analysis of Public Systems*, MIT Press,. Cambridge, MA, pp. 133–150.

Storbeck, K. (1982). Slack, natural slack, and location covering. *J. Socio-Econom. Planning Sci.* 16(3), 99–105.

Swain, R. (1974). A parametric decomposition approach for the solution of uncapacitated location problem. *Management Sci.* 21, 189–203.

Swersey, A. (1970). A mathematical formulation of the fire engine relocation problem, unpublished mimeograph. New York City Rand Institute.

Swersey, A. (1975). Reducing fire engine response time: A case study in modelling, in: E. Quade (ed.), *Analysis for Public Decisions*, Elsevier, New York, pp. 222–239.

Swersey, A.J. (1982). A Markovian decision model for deciding how many fire companies to dispatch. *Management Sci.* 28(4), 352–365.

Swersey, A.J., L. Goldring and E. Geyer (1993). Improving fire department productivity: Merging fire and emergency medical units in New Haven. *Interfaces* 23(1), 109–129.

Swersey, A., E. Ignall, H. Corman, P. Armstrong and J. Weindling (1975). Fire protection and local government an evaluation of policy-related research, Report R-1813-NSF, September, The Rand Corporation, Santa Monica, CA.

Swersey, A.J., and L. Thakur (1994). An integer programming model for locating vehicle emissions inspection stations. *Management Sci.*, to appear.

Swoveland, C., D. Uyeno, I. Vertinsky and R. Vickson (1973). Ambulance locations: A probabilistic enumeration approach. *Management Sci.* 29, 686–698.

Tarr, D.P. (1978). Analysis of response delays and arrest rates. *J. Police Sci. Administration* 6(4), 429–451.

Taylor, I.D.S., and J.G.C. Templeton (1980). Waiting time in a multi-server cutoff-priority queue, and its application to an urban ambulance service. *Oper. Res.* 28(5), 1168–1187.

Taylor, P.E., and S.J. Huxley (1989). A break from tradition for the San Francisco police: Patrol officer scheduling using an optimization-based decision support system. *Interfaces* 19(1), 4–24.

Teitz, M., and P. Bart (1968). Heuristic methods for estimating the generalized vertex median of a weighted graph. *Oper. Res.* 16(5), 901–1092.

Teodorovic, D., J. Rados, S. Vuuanovic and M. Sarac (1986). Optimal locations of emergency service depots for private cars in urban areas: Case study of Belgrade. *Transportation Planning Tech.* 11, 177–188.

Tien, J., and S. Chiu (1985). Impact analysis of some cost reduction options for a metropolitan fire department. *Fire Tech.* 21(1), 5–21.

Toregas, C., and C. ReVelle (1972). Optimal location under time or distance constraints. *Regional Sci. Assoc.* 28, 133–143.

Toregas, C., and C. ReVelle (1973). Binary logic solutions to a class of location problems. *Geographical Analysis* 5(2), 145–155.

Toregas, C., R. Swain, C. ReVelle and L. Bergman (1971). The location of emergency service facilities. *Oper. Res.* 19(6), 1363–1373.

Trudeau, P., J. Rousseau, J.A. Ferland and J. Choquette (1989). An operations research approach for the planning and operation of an ambulance service. *INFOR* 27(1), 95–113.

Urban, N., L. Bergner and M. Eisenberg (1981). The costs of a suburban paramedic program in reducing deaths due to cardiac arrest. *Medical Care* XIX(4), 379–392.

Uyeno, D.H., and C. Seeberg (1984). A practical methodology for ambulance location. *Simulation* 43(2), 79–87.

Valinsky, D. (1955). A determination of the optimum location of fire-fighting units in New York City. *Oper. Res.* 3(4), 494–512.

Volz, R.A. (1971). Optimum ambulance location of semi-rural areas. *Transportation Sci.* 5(2), 193–203.

Walker, W. (1974). Using the set covering problem to assign fire companies to fire houses. *Oper. Res.* 20(3), 275–277.

Walker, W. (1978). Changing fire company locations: Five implementation case studies, Stock No. 023-000-00456-9, Government Printing Office, Washington, DC.

Wallace, R., and D. Wallace (1977). Studies on the collapse of fire service in New York City 1972–1976, *The Impact of Pseudoscience in Public Policy* (pamphlet), University Press of America, Washington, DC.

Wallace, R., and D. Wallace (1980). Rand-HUD fire models, Communication-Letter to the Editor. *Management Sci.* 26(4), 418–421.

Weaver, J.R., and R.L. Church (1983). Computational procedures for location problems on stochastic networks. *Transportation Sci.* 17, 168–180.

Weaver, J.R., and R.L. Church (1985). A median location model with nonclosest facility service. *Transportation Sci.* 19, 58–71.

Weaver, W.D., L.A. Cobb, A.P. Hallstrom, M.K. Copass, R. Ray, M. Emery and C. Fahrenbruch (1986). Considerations for improving survival from out-of hospital cardiac arrest. *Ann. Emergency Medicine* 15(10), 1181–1186.

Willemain, R. (1974). Approximate analysis of a hierarchical queuing network. *Oper. Res.* 22(3), 522–544.

Willemain, T., and R. Larson (1978). *Emergency Medical Systems Analysis: The Planning and Evaluation of Services*, Lexington Books, D.C. Heath and Co., Lexington, MA

Wolkinson, B.W., K. Chelst and L.A. Shepard (1985). Arbitration issues in the consolidation of police and fire bargaining units. *Arbitration J.* 40(4), 43–54.

Wright, V., J.R. Hall Jr and H.P. Hatry (1978). *An Examination of Productivity Related Findings from the 'Four City' Projects and the RAND and PTI Deployment Analysis Approaches*, The Urban Institute, Washington, DC.

S.M. Pollock et al., Eds., *Handbooks in OR & MS, Vol. 6*

Chapter 7

Operations Research in Studying Crime and Justice: Its History and Accomplishments

Michael D. Maltz

Department of Criminal Justice and Department of Information and Decision Sciences, University of Illinois at Chicago, Chicago, IL, U.S.A.

1. Introduction

The application of operations research, in particular mathematical and statistical modeling, to crime, justice, and law enforcement has been an activity of long standing, and one that has benefited both operations research and criminal justice practice over the years. In terms of statistical theory, Poisson's analysis of criminal justice data led to his derivation of:

- the Poisson distribution [Stigler, 1986, p. 183][1]; and
- the law of large numbers [Hacking, 1990, p. 100].

Criminal justice practice has profited to an even greater extent from the mutual association. Mathematical and statistical modeling of criminal justice data has led to:

- the treatment of homicide of young urban African–American males as an epidemic;
- enhancing the fairness of the jury system;
- improved police scheduling;
- improvements in evaluating the effectiveness of correctional programs;
- increased knowledge of offender behavior; and
- improved methods of forecasting prisoner populations.

In short, the application of operations research in this field has been, by and large, a success. That this has been the case should not be surprising. The criminal justice system is an information-intensive public bureaucracy (or, rather, group of bureaucracies) that uses reams of paper and generates mountains of data. Its input includes reports that are generated by police officers; they are added up to generate statistics; offenders' records are summarized on 'rap sheets'; arrest reports lead to prosecutors' records, which lead to trial transcripts; probation and parole officers prepare reports on their clients' behavior; correctional institutions track the inmates in their care. The system's output is not a tangible product, but

---

[1] Poisson derived this distribution (as a limiting case of the binomial distribution) in the book *Recherches sur la probabilité des jugements en matière criminelle et en matière civile.*

decisions: where to patrol, who are probable suspects, who is to be arrested, who is adjudged guilty, what type of sentence to impose, who should be released. Thus, although not all of the information is accessible to researchers, the system is overflowing with data, providing excellent opportunities for studies aimed at detecting patterns in the data: how offenders flow through the system; how (and how often) they commit crimes; how the agencies deal with finding and processing offenders.

1.1. Mathematical modeling

There are also excellent opportunities for mathematical modeling, especially when it comes to inferring patterns of offender behavior. Unlike the officials in the criminal justice system who react to offenders, the offenders themselves do not ordinarily keep records or otherwise inform us about their activity. We have to assess their behavior from the rather limited information we do have about their activity, most notably the crimes for which they have been arrested. It is in that context that mathematical models of offender behavior are of great benefit.

Modeling the behavior of *individual* offenders has been going on for a long time. Sherlock Holmes epitomizes the deductive aspects of such modeling: starting with a clue and using it to identify the suspect. Most modern-day detectives, on the other hand, use induction to identify suspects, based on their knowledge of previously arrested persons. Yet for the most part they have not modeled *the general flow of offenses*, which might be of interest in developing strategies for crime prevention as distinct from offender apprehension.

1.2. Scope of this chapter

This chapter will describe how OR/MS has been used in studying crime and criminal justice. Not all OR/MS applications are covered in this chapter. In particular, police resource allocation methods and models are discussed elsewhere in this handbook. Nor is this the first time the application of OR to crime and justice has been reviewed. Tarling [1986] provides a useful overview of the application of statistical models and methods in criminology, and different OR or mathematical modeling techniques are compiled in Chaiken, Crabill, Holliday, Jaquette, Lawless & Quade [1975], Brounstein & Kamrass [1976], Greenberg [1979], and Fox [1981a,b].

Nor does this chapter cover applications of the more standard statistical techniques (i.e., those found in the SPSS, SAS, BMDP, or SYSTAT software packages), such as time series, regression, logit, LISREL, and the prediction techniques based on them; those who are interested in such techniques may wish to consult Finkelstein [1978], Greenberg [1979], Saks & Baron [1980], Monahan & Walker [1984], Farrington & Tarling [1985], Copas & Tarling [1986], DeGroot, Fienberg & Kadane [1986], S. Gottfredson & D. Gottfredson [1986], or M. Gottfredson & D. Gottfredson [1987].

The line has also been drawn to exclude some approaches that might well have been included in this chapter. In particular, the line of research initiated by Becker [1967], based on an economic approach to crime, is not included. Nor are all topics covered to the same depth. In part this is due to different priorities accorded different topics, in part to the incomplete knowledge of the author. It is not always possible to be sure of covering all sources of published material[2], so there are some gaps in this review.

The symbols used in this chapter are not always the same as those used in the papers cited. In a rapidly developing field, different authors writing on the same topic often use different symbols to represent the same variable. In the interests of clarity, I have taken some liberty with the notation used in the papers and employ symbols that have in some sense become standard, so that the reader is not confused (in this chapter, at least) by having one symbol defined in two different ways, or two symbols to denote the same phenomenon.

The beginnings of the intersection between operations research and issues of crime and justice are rooted in the works of early European statisticians, described in Chapter 1. Starting with that foundation, this chapter begins with a discussion of the modeling work of Poisson, but the greatest attention is given to the work that has taken place more recently, primarily in the past 25 years, and for the most part, in the published literature. It describes the work initiated by the President's Crime Commission [1967]. Subsequent sections describe the research that that effort spawned, in studies of criminal justice systems models, criminal careers, incapacitation, recidivism, deterrence, population forecasts, the jury system, and other areas.

2. A historical perspective

2.1. The nineteenth century

According to Chevalier [1973], crime was one of the most pressing social problems in Paris in the early nineteenth century. The misery of the working classes was captured in Hugo's *Les Misérables* as well as in contemporary data: Chevalier reports how concerned the police were about fluctuations in the price of bread because 'its curve followed the curve of all the ills that Paris was heir to' (p. 262).

The misery was also reflected in French statistics that described the relationship between literacy and crime, a topic that is still a matter of concern. For example, in 1828 Taillander wrote that '67 out of 100 (prisoners) are able neither to read nor write. What stronger proof could there be that ignorance, like idleness, is the mother of all vices?' [quoted in Porter, 1986].

Further, the Société Française de Statistique Universelle was deeply involved in the debate over the death penalty. In the first issue of its bulletin (1830–31) the

---

[2] For the most part, papers, reports and dissertations not in general circulation are not included in this review. Although citations to work outside of North America are few in this review, the reason may be due in part to there not being as much quantitative research in criminology and criminal justice in other countries [Cohn & Farrington, 1990].

Table 1
French conviction data

Year	Number accused	Number convicted	Conviction rate
1825	6652	4037	0.6069
1826	6988	4348	0.6222
1827	6929	4236	0.6113
1828	7396	4551	0.6153
1829	7373	4475	0.6069
1830	6962	4130	0.5932

Société announced a prize for the best analysis calling for its abolition:

> 'By attaining statistical certainty that fewer crimes are committed where the penalty of death has been abolished, the influence that a gentler and more genuinely philosophical legislation exerts on the criminality of human actions can better be appreciated.'

However, this call in France for a 'kinder and gentler nation' was not heeded at that time [Porter, 1986].

The availability of judicial data permitted the development of tools for statistical analysis of social problems. Adolphe Quetelet [1835] initiated this movement in France, using the criminal justice statistics that had begun to be collected in France in 1825 [Daston, 1988, p. 286], and Siméon-Denis Poisson began his studies soon after. Quetelet noted the relatively constant annual number of persons accused and the smooth but gradual decrease in the annual conviction rate of those accused, as shown in Table 1, excerpted from Stigler [1986, p. 189].[3]

Quetelet concluded that there was a general downward trend in the proportion of trials that resulted in conviction, which was based in part on his using incorrect numbers for 1825 (7234 and 4594, respectively; see Figure 1), but also because he did not consider the stochastic aspects of the data. This can be seen more clearly in Poisson's analysis of the correct data.

Poisson took a different analytic view of these statistics [Stigler, 1986, p. 186]. First, he developed a model of the trial process that assumed that jury behavior was constant over time, that the jury members made their decisions independently, and that each had the same probability (u) of reaching the correct verdict. Then the probability that no more than k of N jurors will decide correctly is:

$$B(k, N, u) = \sum_{i=0}^{k} \binom{N}{i} u^i (1 - u)^{N-i}.$$

In France before 1831, a majority of 7 of the 12 jurors were required for a determination of guilt, so the probability of conviction of a guilty defendant is $B(5, 12, 1-u)$ and of an innocent defendant is $B(5, 12, u)$. If G is the probability that the defendant is in fact guilty, then the probability of conviction P_C is

---

[3] This description is largely based on Stigler's account.

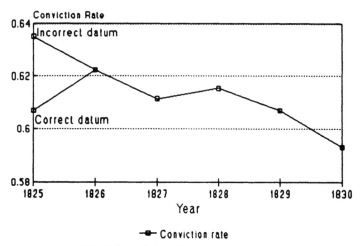

Fig. 1. Quetelet's analysis of conviction data.

$$P_C = G\, B(5, 12, 1 - u) + (1 - G)\, B(5, 12, u).$$

Poisson assumed that G and u are constant over time, so P_C is also constant over time. He could therefore model the juries' decisions as a binomial process and determined the stochastic variation in the data. Based on his estimates (Figure 2 shows the estimate ± 2 standard deviations), he found that the variation in rates over time were 'not so large as to support a belief that there has been a notable change in the causes' [quoted in Stigler, 1986, p. 190]. In other words, the year-to-year differences were small compared to the expected variation, or were not 'statistically significant'.

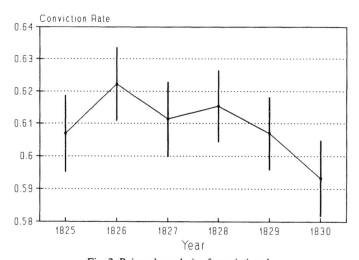

Fig. 2. Poisson's analysis of conviction data.

In comparing the French statistics with those of the Department of the Seine (Paris), however, Poisson did discern a significant difference in the conviction rate. As Hacking [1990, p. 101] put it, Poisson thought he had 'detected a real change in court behavior. 1830 was a year of revolution. Either the court was bringing too many criminals to trial in a draconian attempt to maintain order, or jurors were, in revolutionary spirit, declining to bring in convictions.'

Thus, Poisson did not just analyze the data as raw numbers but as outputs of a mathematical model of the jury process. Although his assumptions regarding the independence and constancy of jurors' decisions may have been in error[4], it put the analysis of jury behavior on a firm analytic footing, with his assumptions made explicit. Thus, his models may have been one of the first applications of operations research (at least as defined herein) to problems of crime and justice.[5] Accordingly, we may have the French Ministry of Justice and its *Compte général de l'administration de la justice criminelle en France* to thank for the birth of operations research.[6]

2.2. The early twentieth century

There appears to have been little OR related to problems of crime and justice between that time and the 1960s. Although models of offender behavior were developed during this period, none were the subject of the mathematical or statistical manipulation that normally characterizes OR models. Among the conceptual models that were developed during this period – models that still have relevance today – are the ecological models developed by Shaw & McKay [1969] and the models of delinquent behavior posited by Glueck & Glueck [1950].

That crime and justice were not the subject of operations research in this period, especially in the United States, is understandable for a number of reasons. In that era, criminologists were searching for the causes of criminality, and 'the criminal mind' (and physiognomy as well) were their primary focus. Thus, the criminal justice system (i.e., police, courts, corrections, and their interrelationship) was not then of great interest to criminologists; nor was it of great interest to operations researchers in that era.[7] In the United States, it was only when crime began to

---

[4] For example, his model assumes that each juror's reliability is the same regardless of the truth, that is, that P (guilty vote | actual guilt) = P (not guilty vote | actual innocence) = u. This would not ordinarily be the case, especially if the benefit of the doubt is given to one side, as in the presumption of innocence.

[5] Stigler (p. 186) refers to earlier models of jury behavior, by Condorcet and Laplace, but they are not described.

[6] Criminal justice statistics were also instrumental in Poisson's development of the law of large numbers. According to Hacking [1990, p. 101], 'Some jurors are more reliable than others. *Poisson's law of large numbers was devised in order to solve just this problem*. He studies as a model the situation in which reliability varies from juror to juror, but in which there is some law (Poisson's word) or probability distribution (our phrase) for reliability among French jurors' (emphasis in the original).

[7] This is, of course, a tautology, since operations research as a discipline did not exist at that time. I refer here to those who analyzed problems quantitatively, regardless of their professional affiliation.

increase rapidly that officials began to take notice of the relationship between crime and the criminal justice system. This happened twice during this period of time, immediately after Prohibition and again in the late 1960s. As a consequence of these increases, the United States Government did what it seems to do best in the face of pressing problems: it formed a commission to study them. The first commission, the National Commission on Law Observance and Enforcement (also known as the Wickersham Commission) published its findings in the early 1930s. One outcome of its work was the beginning of the systematic collection of police statistics (i.e., crimes reported to the police, arrests) by the International Association of Chiefs of Police, and subsequently, by the FBI [Maltz, 1977]. At this time prosecutorial, court, and correctional statistics were still not collected with any degree of uniformity.

Although France and other European countries had been collecting criminal justice data for years, similar statistics for the United States (as noted in Chapter 1) were not so easy to obtain: whereas France had (and has) a centralized criminal justice system, in the United States virtually every state, county, and municipality has its own criminal justice agency, making standardization of crime statistics a major obstacle to their collection, one that has not been overcome to this day. In fact, there are still enormous problems of criminal justice data collection that have to be surmounted; for example, in many jurisdictions it is extremely difficult to track an individual offender from the reporting of a crime s/he (allegedly) committed and his/her arrest – responsibilities of the police, a municipal agency – through to the prosecutorial and court dispositions – responsibilities of county prosecutors and county courts – and subsequently to the correctional disposition – a responsibility of a state agency if s/he was put in prison, or of yet another county agency if s/he was jailed or placed on probation.[8]

2.3. The 1960s and the President's Crime Commission

These problems of data collection and coordination were apparent from the start of one of the most significant investigations into problems of crime and justice in this century, the President's Commission on Law Enforcement and Administration of Justice [1967]. The President's Crime Commission, as it was known, spawned a number of task forces, among them a Task Force on Science and Technology, headed by Alfred Blumstein. The publication of the Science and Technology Task Force Report [1967] marks the beginning of the modern era of applying operations research to problems of crime and justice, an era that continues to the present day. The topics covered by that report set the priorities and direction for most subsequent operations research studies of the criminal justice system. They include:

---

[8] To show how current this problem is, a 1990 audit of the Illinois Computerized Criminal History system 'found that nearly 85 percent of the arrests sampled were missing one or both of the state's attorney or court dispositions, while nearly 60 percent were missing both' [Illinois Criminal Justice Information Authority, 1991, p. 3]. Yet the Illinois system is one of the better state systems.

- system-wide models and simulations;
- population projections (including the stability of punishment hypothesis);
- probability of arrest and response time.

In addition, a number of other topics have been the subjects of operations research investigations, based on research subsequent to that report. They include:
- models of criminal careers;
- incapacitation;
- recidivism;
- deterrence;
- crime measurement;
- white-collar and organized crime;
- jury scheduling.

The rest of this chapter examines the application of operations research to these topics.

3. System-wide models

One of the first 'facts of life' to confront the researchers of the Commission's Science and Technology Task Force (STTF) in their study of the criminal justice system was that there was no system. The separation of powers in governments at all levels in the United States, designed to ensure the independence of the executive, legislative, and judicial branches of government, also meant that the police paid little attention to the courts, which paid little attention to the correctional system, which paid little attention to the police. A primary task of the STTF, then, was to describe the system, or as it was often called, the 'non-system', in sufficient detail to permit decision-makers to see how problems in one part of the system affected the rest of the system. No one knew, for example, how a change in police resources (e.g., an increase in the number of police officers, shifting more patrol officers to the detective division) would affect:
- the workload of prosecutors (perhaps leading them to use plea bargaining more often);
- the number of judges and courtrooms needed;
- the number of new correctional institutions needed at different security levels;
- the number of probation or parole officers needed, etc.

Nor could anyone provide useful forecasts of the crime rate based on population statistics. The STTF therefore called for a 'systems analysis' of the criminal justice system, to determine how changes in criminality affected agency activity, or how changes in one criminal justice agency affected other agencies.

One of the first such systems analyses, designed to show how the parts were interrelated, was conducted by the New York State Identification and Intelligence System (NYSIIS) in its report entitled *NYSIIS: System Development Plan* [1967]. The first figure in that report was a six-foot-long foldout figure entitled 'The criminal justice process for adult felonies'. It detailed how a criminal case proceeds through the criminal justice system from the initial crime to the incarceration of an offender and his/her eventual discharge or release.[9] Its primary goal was to develop the specifications for a state-wide computerized information system that would collect, store and disseminate criminal justice information throughout the state. Its developers believed that, based on this information system, decisions would be made on a more rational basis; people and problems would no longer 'fall through the cracks'; and the total system would function more effectively and efficiently.

These beliefs in the ultimate triumph of technology in curing urban ills should be seen from the historical context of the era: we were about to put a man on the moon, and the cry from everyone was, 'If we can put a man on the moon, why can't we solve X?', where X was whatever urban problem was pressing at the moment. In addition, the war in Vietnam was still being fought, and there were a number of systems analysts who had developed command-and-control systems for the military who felt that the same techniques could be brought to bear on solving the crime problem. Furthermore, 'crime in the streets' had been a major focus of the Presidential campaign of 1964, and computers and other high-tech solutions were just beginning to be seen (often inappropriately, as it turned out) as the answer to social as well as technical problems.

Some aspects of the first analyses of the criminal justice system were quite dramatic to the general public. The 'funnelling effect' of the criminal process provided a graphic depiction of case attrition. At the top of the funnel were found 2 780 000 crimes that occurred in one year. At the bottom of the funnel were found the 63 000 individuals sent to prison, in what was seen as a 98% attrition rate.

Other systems analyses of criminal justice began to turn up in the academic and professional literature [e.g., Blumstein & Larson, 1967, 1969]. These analyses underscored the fact that offenders who wend their way through the criminal justice system (see Figure 3) often wend their way again and again through the same system. This observation that recidivism provides the positive feedback to the system [e.g., Blumstein & Larson, 1971] gave rise to studies to see how recidivism affected the criminal justice system [Belkin, Blumstein & Glass, 1973]. As seen in Figure 4, a very simplified system flow diagram, 'virgin' (i.e., first-time) arrestees, $V(t)$, and recidivating arrestees, $R(t)$, enter the criminal justice system. A fraction $1 - \Omega$ of them never recidivate, and the remaining Ω of them reenter the system after remaining free for a (mean) time delay τ.

Aside from explicitly recognizing the role of recidivism as a feedback loop to the system, this model also led to development of JUSSIM, a computerized simulation of the criminal justice system [Belkin, Blumstein, Glass & Lettre, 1972]. This system and its variants are still in use [e.g., Cassidy, 1985; Institute for Law and Justice, 1991; McEwen & Guynes, 1990]. Similar work has been carried out in the United Kingdom [Morgan, 1985; Pullinger, 1985; Rice, 1984].

Aggregate flow models of this sort (which can become quite complicated, given the complicated structure of the criminal justice system) are very useful in

---

[9] Figure 3, taken from the STTF [1967], is a similar depiction of the flow of criminal cases through the criminal justice system.

210

A general view of The Criminal Justice System

This chart seeks to present a simple yet comprehensive view of the movement of cases through the criminal justice system. Procedures in individual jurisdictions may vary from the pattern shown here. The differing weights of line indicate the relative volumes of cases disposed of at various points in the system, but this is only suggestive since no nationwide data of this sort exists.

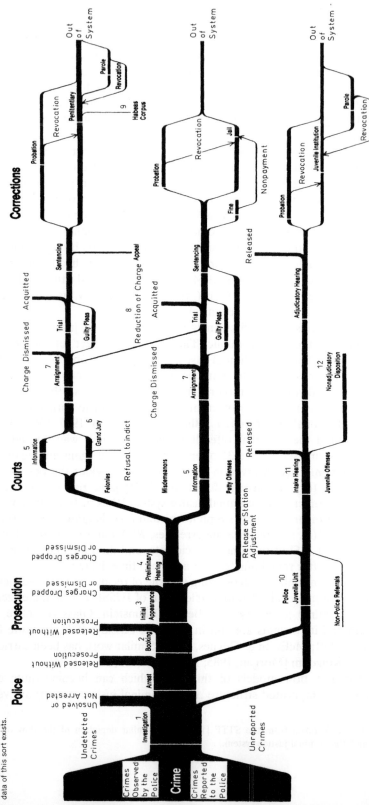

Fig. 3. A general view of the criminal justice system. [Source: Science & Technology Task Force, 1967, pp. 58–59.]

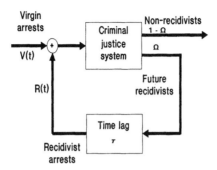

Fig. 4. A simplified criminal justice feedback model.

developing workload statistics that answer 'what if' questions relating to changes in either the input (e.g., the 'baby boom') or the system (e.g., elimination of plea bargaining). They are of limited value, however, in determining what the workload actually consists of. For example, study after study [e.g., Chaiken & Chaiken, 1982; Reiss & Farrington, 1991; Wolfgang, Figlio & Sellin, 1972] revealed that a surprisingly small fraction of all juveniles accounts for a very high proportion of all crimes and arrests. Models that relate the flow to *individual* offenders' behavior are required, to determine the effect of this subpopulation on the criminal justice system.

Attempting to identify the characteristics of this small subpopulation became the focus of much research. It was felt that their identification (prospectively, before they committed the bulk of their criminal acts) would mean that the more dangerous individuals could be identified for early intervention programs or, should intervention prove ineffective, could be incarcerated for longer periods of time than those offenders who are less dangerous.[10]

A first step in this direction was embodied in a very simple model proposed by Shinnar & Shinnar [1975; see also Avi-Itzhak & Shinnar, 1973]. Assume that a person commits crimes at a Poisson rate λ of per year. If not arrested, s/he would commit λT crimes during his/her career length T years. If the probability of arrest for each crime is q, the probability of imprisonment (given arrest) is Q, and the average sentence length (given imprisonment) is S, the offender would on average be free for $1/[\lambda q Q]$ years between the prison sentences of S years (see Figure 5 for a deterministic representation of such a career). Thus, the offender's *effective* crime rate, $\hat{\lambda}$, is $\lambda/[1 + \lambda q Q S]$, which provides a quantitative estimate of the incapacitative effect of prison. Although there are some gross simplifications

---

[10] Section 5, Incapacitation, discusses this line of research. There are some major ethical issues imbedded in it: first, it implies that it is proper to sentence an individual not only for the crime(s) already committed, but also for the crimes to come, which is antithetical to the philosophy of the U.S. criminal justice system; see Von Hirsch [1985]. Second, because no method of prediction is perfect, a sizable fraction of the predicted population would be punished for crimes they would not have committed, and a sizable fraction of the dangerous offenders would not be so labeled and would avoid the longer incarceration.

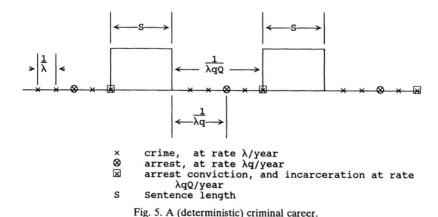

x   crime,   at rate λ/year
⊗   arrest, at rate λq/year
⊠   arrest conviction, and incarceration at rate
          λqQ/year
s   Sentence length

Fig. 5. A (deterministic) criminal career.

in this model, it encapsulates in one equation the effects of the primary elements of the criminal justice system: the offender, in λ, the offense rate; police, in q, the probability of arrest; the courts, in Q, the probability of commitment to prison; and the correctional system, in S, the sentence length.[11] Cohen [1978] reviewed this and other models of incapacitation, and provided some guidance for future research on modeling the incapacitative effect of imprisonment.[12]

The simple model of offender behavior depicted in Figure 5 produced a number of important and controversial lines of research. The first relates to the description of criminal careers; the second relates to the possibility of incapacitating high-rate offenders to reduce the crime rate. The next section describes some of the research in criminal careers.

4. Criminal careers

The criminal career paradigm was delineated in a series of reports and articles [Blumstein & Cohen, 1987; Blumstein, Cohen & Farrington, 1988a,b; Blumstein, Cohen, Roth & Visher, 1986]. It pointed to the utility of modeling an offender's career using four different dimensions:
  • participation, the probability that an individual will commit a crime;
  • frequency, the rate at which s/he commits crimes while criminally active;

[11] In this simple model the variable T can be argued away by assuming that the birth and death processes balance out. In other words, as each offender terminates his/her career, another offender arises to take his/her place. Other, more realistic, models are discussed below, which account for the problems this assumption poses if, for example, the offender terminates his/her criminal career while still incarcerated.

[12] Greenberg [1975] proposed a model of offender behavior that is conceptually similar but different in its details. Using aggregate statistics, his model permits the estimation of various criminal career parameters. See Cohen [1978] for a review and comparison of these and other models.

- seriousness, the nature of the crimes s/he commits; and
- length, the time interval between his/her first and last offenses.

Although it was certainly an oversimplification to assume that all offenders would fit the same model of behavior, one could apply this model to different sub-populations and aggregate them to come up with the overall characteristics of the population under study.

There is a difference between the concepts of the 'criminal career' and the 'career criminal', although the two are often confused. The *career crim nal* is an individual for whom crime is a profession. A *criminal career* is merely , pattern of offending, delineating the progression of incidents from the one that initiates the individual's career, through the last, at career termination. Having a criminal career, a property of everyone who commits at least one crime, does not imply that the individual is a career criminal.

One of the key variables relating to an offender is his/her rate of commission of offenses λ. This must ordinarily be inferred from his/her arrest rate $\mu = \lambda q$, where q is the probability of being arrested. The arrest rate μ is based on his/her 'rap sheet,' which is a listing of an individual's arrest, but not crime commission, history; and inferring his/her offense rate from this information is not a straightforward process – see Blumstein & Cohen [1979]. Some argue that arrests represent the crimes which the offenders failed to commit successfully, and therefore are a biased sample of the offender's crime history. Self-report studies, however [e.g., Chaiken & Chaiken, 1982], seem to indicate that the crimes for which an offender is arrested are generally indicative of the types of crimes s/he generally commits.

In the first studies it was assumed that λ was constant for all offenders during their period of active offending.[13] Later models included variations in offense rates [Copas & Tarling, 1988; Lehoczky, 1986; Maltz & Pollock, 1980b; Rolph, Chaiken & Houchens, 1981].

The distribution of λ, offenders' crime commission rates, is an important aspect of a criminal career. Although offenders are not all expected to have the mean crime commission rate, the particular distribution of rates does not fit a well-behaved parametric distribution, either. Using data collected from prisoners in three states [Chaiken & Chaiken, 1982], Rolph, Chaiken & Houchens [1981] developed a method to estimate the distribution of offense rates among offenders. They analyzed data provided by imprisoned offenders concerning the number of offenses they reported having committed while free (Figure 6), and then used Turnbull's [1976] method to estimate the empirical distribution of offense commission rates. In attempting to fit the data with various distributions they found that the thickness of the tail of the distribution made this process difficult (see Figure 6).

---

[13] This was assumed for mathematical tractability and convenience, not because analysts showed that this was actually the case. This concept, of a constant (Poisson) offense rate, has been misconstrued by some criminologists: they take this to mean that the model implies that offenders are very regular in their criminal activity, unaware, perhaps, that a Poisson process can be realized in an infinite variety of ways, most of which would not appear to be very regular.

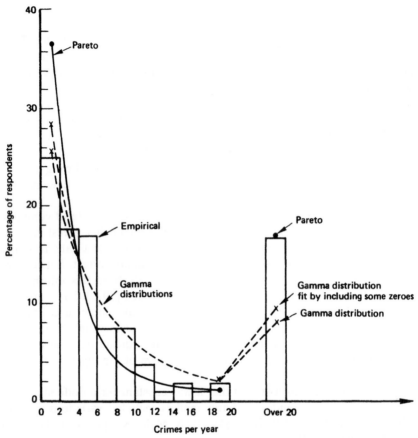

Fig. 6. Distribution of crime rates for business robberies. [Source: Rolph, Chaiken & Houchens, 1981, p. 28.]

Since the data were obtained from imprisoned individuals, certain biases were present. A sample of prisoners is not representative of the general offender population; for example, all other factors being equal, it contains ten times as many individuals imprisoned for ten years as it does individuals imprisoned for one year. For that reason, they developed a model-based method for extrapolating to other populations of interest. Using a number of simplifying assumptions, they estimated that the probability that an offender is in prison is $\lambda q Q S / (1 + \lambda q Q S)$ – see Figure 5 – then used the inverse of this probability as sampling weights. Although the assumptions were admittedly somewhat simplistic, the poor quality of the data militated against complicating the model with more realistic assumptions.

These methods were used to analyze data from a major study [Chaiken & Chaiken, 1982] that described the past criminal experience of convicted offenders in three states, in which sub-populations of offenders were identified based on their offending histories. In addition, prior longitudinal studies of prospective criminal activity were investigated to determine the characteristics of sub-populations and their career parameters [Barnett, Blumstein & Farrington, 1987, 1989; Blumstein & Cohen, 1987; Blumstein, Farrington & Moitra, 1985], including the use of hierarchical models [Ahn, Blumstein & Schervish, 1990].

A similar (hierarchical model) approach was taken by Blumstein, Canela-Cacho & Cohen (1993) to estimate the expected variation in λ of the population studied by the Chaikens. Because it is more likely to have high-rate offenders than low-rate offenders incarcerated due to their greater exposure to risk – a process they call 'stochastic selectivity' – modeling is needed to estimate the characteristics of the offending population from which the inmates were drawn. They posited that the incarcerated offenders committed offenses at an offense rate λ_i that was drawn from a probability distribution that is a mixture of r exponential distributions,

$$f(\lambda) = \sum_{k=1}^{r} p_k \beta_k e^{-\beta_k \lambda},$$

where the mixing parameters p_k sum to 1. Using maximum likelihood estimation, they show that the robbery offenses for the three states' offenders can be fit by a mixture of three exponentials: about 90% of the offenders have an expected robbery commission rate of one robbery per year; about 10% of the offenders have an expected rate of about nine offenses per year; and less than 1% have an expected rate of over 100 robberies per year. This distribution of robbery offenders 'in the wild' contrasts with the estimate it provides of incarcerated robbers: about half come from the low-rate sub-population, one-third from the middle-rate sub-population, and one-sixth from the high-rate sub-population.

4.1. A competing theory: the age–crime relationship

The criminal career paradigm was challenged by some researchers [e.g., Gottfredson & Hirschi, 1986, 1987, 1988, 1990; Tittle, 1988; for counterarguments see Blumstein, Cohen & Farrington, 1988a,b], who felt that it was unnecessarily complicated. They noted the long-term stability of the relationship between arrest rate and age (Figure 7). The stability of this relationship, they argued, is based on offenders' lack of self-control, which leads directly to criminality, and this lack of self-control increases through adolescence and then diminishes with age. They maintained that 'differences in the propensity to engage in criminal acts are established before the high-crime-rate years, persist during those years, and indeed maintain themselves throughout life' [Gottfredson & Hirschi, 1989]. They considered this formulation of a stable criminality equivalent to a natural law, making it superfluous to consider models of offender behavior that incorporate four different variables (i.e., participation, frequency, seriousness, and length) into a model. They argued that their cross-sectional approach to analysis of criminality held more promise than the longitudinal approach, especially considering the cost of longitudinal research.

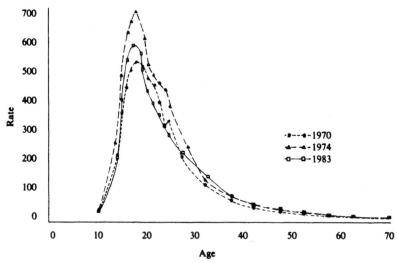

Fig. 7. Number of robbery arrests per 100 000 males. [Source: Gottfredson & Hirschi, 1986, p. 223.]

4.2. Arguments against the age–crime explanation

This reliance on a stable pattern of *aggregate behavior* to make inferences about *individual behavior* is reminiscent of the approach used by Quetelet and Durkheim [see Hacking, 1990, p. 158], who saw in the constancy of numbers (conviction rates and suicides, respectively) from year to year an innate *'penchant au crime'* or 'suicidogenetic currents'. The age–crime stability is, however, based on better empirical evidence than that used by Quetelet or Durkheim. In particular, not only are the patterns stable over time, but the relationship of these patterns to covariates (e.g., race, education, income) is also stable over time. Thus, there is much to be learned from the cross-sectional approach. Yet there are also some significant problems with this approach; inferring from a stable *aggregate* pattern a characteristic of *every member of a population* sweeps away the variation within that population and relegates it to 'error'.

This theory of criminality, based on an age–crime constancy, has been challenged on other grounds as well. Harada [1991] points out that the concept of a stable criminality implies that the hazard rate[14] of every individual in a group follows the same general course, the only difference between individuals being a constant of proportionality. He used arrest records of a sample of Japanese youth of junior high-school age to determine whether hazard rates actually followed this pattern. His findings do not support the stable criminality hypothesis. Furthermore, there is additional evidence [from Visher & Linster, 1990] (see Figure 8) that individuals with different characteristics have very different hazard rates. In

---

[14] The hazard rate at time t is the probability that an individual will fail (i.e., be arrested) in the time interval $(t, t + dt)$, conditioned on his/her not having failed up to time t.

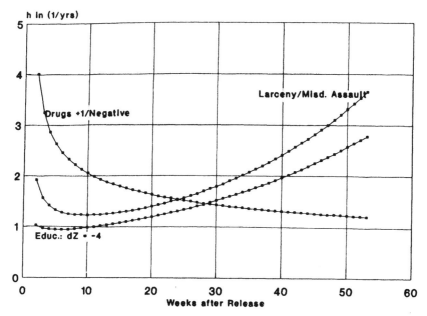

Fig. 8. Hazard rate for pretrial arrest, for individuals with different characteristics. [Source: Visher & Linster, 1990, p. 168.]

other words, the fact that a *group* exhibits a certain stability in its statistics does not guarantee that each *individual* in the group has the same general characteristic, which is implied by Gottfredson and Hirschi's theory. This may merely be a variant of the 'ecological fallacy' [Robinson, 1950]: in general, a pattern based on the aggregate behavior of a group does not hold for all individuals in the group.

The debate over the adequacy of different models of criminality does not seem to be diminishing. In fact, when a journal editor asked another researcher to compare the two approaches, that researcher posited a new model of offender behavior [Greenberg, 1991]. And when yet another journal editor found the controversy continuing between the developer of this new model and proponents of the criminal career paradigm [Barnett, Blumstein, Cohen & Farrington, 1992; Greenberg, 1992], another reviewer was asked to resolve this newer controversy – and this reviewer proceeded to posit yet another model [Land, 1992]! It brings to mind Persig's Postulate, one of Murphy's Laws [Bloch, 1977, p. 87]: 'The number of rational hypotheses that can explain any given phenomenon is infinite.'

In point of fact, the new models are not as well grounded as the ones developed using the criminal career paradigm, which are based on a much more thorough analysis of the data. It should also be noted that some of the insights possible using the longitudinal approach would not have been gained in a cross-sectional study of criminal careers. One of the more significant results is that, although *participation* in criminal activity is strongly correlated with race or ethnicity, the subsequent criminal careers of offenders of different racial and ethnic backgrounds are very similar: for example, although one study [Nagin & Smith, 1990] showed that participation and frequency appear to be closely associated, two other studies [Farrington & Hawkins, 1991; Shover & Thompson, 1992] indicate that participation and desistance are predicted by different characteristics. And a cross-sectional approach makes it difficult to disentangle the effects of age, period, and cohort on a group's criminal behavior [Mason & Fienberg, 1985].

Furthermore, some characteristics of an offender's career cannot be observed in a cross-sectional study. For example, Reiss & Farrington [1991] use longitudinal data to show that 'the incidence of co-offending[15] decreases with age primarily because individual offenders change and become less likely to offend with others rather than because of selective attrition of co-offenders or persistence of those who offend primarily alone' (p. 393). A cross-sectional study would not have been able to discern this pattern of behavior, since individual offenders are not tracked over time.

4.3. Specialization and offense switching

An interesting aspect of criminal careers is the extent to which offense switching occurs during an individual's career. However, offenders do not ordinarily provide us with their *offense* histories: arrest histories are, in most cases, the only indicators we have of an offender's degree of specialization, which permit the analysis of arrest transitions (or arrest switching), but not crime switching.

Cohen [1986] reviewed the literature and evidence relating to crime switching, specialization, and escalation. She investigated whether criminal careers can be modeled as a Markov process; specifically, consider the transition matrix $M(k, k+1)$, where each element $m_{ij}(k, k+1)$ represents the probability that an offender, whose kth arrest was for offense type i, will next be arrested for offense type j. That is, does the offender's present state alone (and not arrests prior to the present) determine future states? She showed that careers may not be modeled as a Markov process even in the short-term [Cohen, 1986, p. 406]; Stander, Farrington, Hill & Altham [1989] subsequently showed that the Markov model cannot be applied generally in modeling criminal careers because past offenses help to predict future offenses. And Figlio [1981] and Farrington, Snyder & Finnegan [1988] showed that some degree of specialization occurs among persistent juvenile offenders in later stages of their offending careers, so that for large k we would have:

$$m_{ii}(k+1, k+2) \geq m_{ii}(k, k+1).$$

Again, it should be noted that the data most often used in these studies are arrest data, not crime data, and that one cannot always infer criminal career parameters directly from such data.

---

[15] Co-offenders are persons who act together in a crime, as juvenile gang members are wont to do.

5. Incapacitation

The correctional system has many goals, among them deterrence, education, retribution, rehabilitation, and incapacitation. It is sometimes difficult to determine the extent to which these goals are met. Operations research and mathematical modeling have played a part in estimating the extent to which they are achieved. In this section models relating to incapacitation are explored.

Models of incapacitation are all based to some extent on those developed by Avi-Itzhak & Shinnar [1973] and Shinnar & Shinnar [1975]. Greenberg [1975] used aggregate data to develop estimates of the extent to which imprisonment affects the general population's crime rate through incapacitation. He also distinguished between *collective* incapacitation – the effect on the overall crime rate[16] of prison sentences in general – and *selective* incapacitation – the effect on the overall crime rate of giving longer sentences to selected individuals whose characteristics make them more likely to have a higher *individual* crime rate (i.e., λ) upon release.

5.1. Collective incapacitation

If incapacitation can reduce the overall crime rate, there should be a means of determining the extent to which different sentencing policies affect it: for example, is it better to sentence half as many offenders to twice the sentence, or twice as many to half the sentence? Such determinations depend on the characteristics of the offending population, and on the effect that prison is likely to have on their subsequent careers. Blumstein & Nagin [1978, 1981] developed a model that related the assumed characteristics of offenders to the sentencing process, in order to determine how sentencing policies might affect overall crime rates. It estimated the crime-control potential of different policies and the trade-off that can exist between mean sentence length and overall crime rate. This model appears to be in agreement with Langan's [1991] analysis that showed that the prison population, which had soared from the mid-1970s due to changes in sentencing practices, was accompanied by a reduction in crime, at least through the 1980s, that might have been due to the increased incapacitation of offenders.

5.2. Selective incapacitation

The proposal for serious consideration of selective incapacitation as a penal policy was put forward by Greenwood [1982]. It was based on combining the findings from two studies. The first study, an analysis of interviews of incarcerated offenders in California, Texas, and Michigan [Chaiken & Chaiken, 1982], calculated the individual offense rates (while free) for these individuals; they demonstrated that

---

[16] In the following discussion I distinguish between the overall crime rate, such as the number of crimes per year in a jurisdiction, and the individual crime rate λ, the estimated number of crimes per year committed by a given offender.

SALIENT FACTOR SCORE SHEET

Case Name _____ Register Number _____

Item A...
    No prior convictions (adult or juvenile) = 2
    One or two prior convictions = 1
    Three or more prior convictions = 0

Item B...
    No prior incarcerations (adult or juvenile) = 1
    One or two prior incarcerations = 1
    No prior incarcerations = 0

Item C...
    Age at first commitment (adult or juvenile): 18 years or older = 1
    Otherwise = 0

Item D...
    Commitment offense did not involve auto theft = 1
    Otherwise = 0

Item E...
    Never had parole revoked or been committed for a new offense
        while on parole = 1
    Otherwise = 0

Item F...
    No history of heroin, cocaine, or barbiturate dependence = 1
    Otherwise = 0

Item G...
    Has completed 12th grade or received GED = 1
    Otherwise = 0

Item H...
    Verified employment (or full-time school attendance) for a total of
        at least 6 months during last 2 years in the community = 1
    Otherwise = 0

Item I...

    Release plan to live with spouse and/or children = 1
    Otherwise = 0

TOTAL SCORE..

Fig. 9. Salient factor score sheet. [Source: Hoffman & Beck, 1974.]

rates for some offenders (called 'violent predators') were extremely high – see
Figure 6. The second study [Hoffman & Adelberg, 1980; Hoffman & Beck, 1974]
developed a 'Salient Factor Score', a relatively easy method of scoring risk levels
posed by offenders (Figure 9).

Greenwood [1982] analyzed data from the California high-rate offenders and found that a simplified Salient Factor Score was able to identify (retrospectively) a significant number of the high-rate offenders. He concluded that it might be possible to have an effect on the crime rate by identifying the high-rate offenders (prospectively) using the Salient Factor Score and then selectively incapacitating them by having them serve longer sentences than others not so identified. He estimated that a 20% reduction in California robberies would ensue if sentences for the scale-identified high-rate offenders were to approximately double while sentences for other offenders were held to one year.

In order to incapacitate those with high offense rates, it is necessary to estimate an individual's offense rate. Chaiken & Rolph [1980] explored how to develop this estimate so as to maximize the selective incapacitation effect. The maximum likelihood estimate of an individual's offense rate λ_i is:

$$\lambda_{i(\text{MLE})} = \frac{N_i}{T_i},$$

where N_i is the number of offenses individual i was observed to have committed during observation time T_i. However, using the one-time empirical realization to estimate his/her actual offense rate λ_i would be incorrect, since those with relatively many offenses in a short observation time would all be considered high-rate offenders. They showed that using a Bayesian estimator, based on *a priori* knowledge of the distribution of offense rates, would be a better estimator. If, for example, true offense rates are distributed as a gamma function with parameters α and β, the Bayesian estimate would be:

$$\lambda_{i(\text{Bayes})} = \frac{\alpha + N_i}{\beta + T_i}.$$

Using the Bayesian estimator the incapacitative effect is slightly greater, and it is slightly fairer in that it would be less likely to select low-rate offenders for higher sentences. However, the slight improvements do not alter the strong case against using such data for selective incapacitation purposes.

5.2.1. Utility of selective incapacitation

But however unbiased the estimator, data on past offenses cannot be assumed to be a good predictor of future offenses. Significant errors result; even on retrospective data, 55% of those identified as high-rate offenders were not in fact high-rate offenders, and 46% of true high-rate offenders were not so classified by the scale. This proposed policy had other difficulties as well [Blumstein, 1983; Cohen, 1983]. And Visher [1986] showed that applying the sentencing policy, based on Greenwood's analysis [1982] of California inmates, to Michigan's inmates would *increase* robberies by 30%.

In an effort to explore whether the prediction technique used by Greenwood would select high-rate offenders, Barnett & Lofaso [1985] tested it with data from a cohort of Philadelphia youths [Wolfgang, Figlio & Sellin, 1972]. They showed that the arrest rates among active delinquents do not vary that much – the most

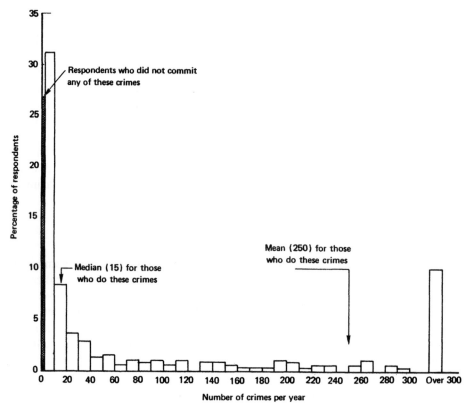

Fig. 10. Observed crime commission rate for burglary, robbery, assault, theft, auto theft, forgery, and fraud. [Source: Rolph, Chaiken & Houchens, 1981, p. 13.]

active have about 2.4 times the rate of the least active. Their study could not estimate the extent of Type 1 and Type 2 errors, because their data set was truncated when the youths reached 18 and there was no way of knowing the extent to which offense activity continued (or desisted) beyond that age.

Subsequently, Greenwood & Turner [1987] studied the offenders who had been labeled high-rate offenders in the first [Greenwood, 1982] study. They found that it was not possible to use the Salient Factor Score to provide a sufficiently accurate prediction as to who would continue to be a high-rate offender: offense rates may have highly dispersed distributions (such as in Figure 10, based on offender self-reports); arrest data do not exhibit the same dispersion.

Yet not all of the evidence is negative. Block & Van der Werff [1991], in their study of a cohort of individuals arrested in the Netherlands in 1977, found that they were able to identify, prospectively, the active and dangerous offenders who are responsible for a disproportionate number of serious offenses. They used only official data, but their data included juvenile records, which may limit the utility of such a method in the United States: currently in many jurisdictions, juvenile records may not be used in adult proceedings. But it does suggest that the goal of identifying those who may become dangerous offenders may be achievable to some extent.

5.2.2. Offender desistance and selective incapacitation

Identifying those *likely to become* high-rate offenders on the basis of juvenile and adult records is not equivalent to actually identifying these offenders. As discussed earlier, the variables associated with termination of a criminal career are not the same as those associated with its initiation, frequency, or seriousness. One means of investigating career termination is to obtain sufficiently detailed longitudinal data about a group of offenders so that their residual career length can be calculated. One can then analyze the data to determine the variables that appear to be associated with residual career length, to see the extent to which policy changes might affect it.

Toward this end, a reanalysis of a number of data sets was undertaken [Blumstein, Cohen, Roth & Visher, 1986; Blumstein, Farrington & Moitra, 1985; Blumstein & Moitra, 1980]. They contained information relating to the characteristics of the individuals and records of their contact with the criminal justice system.[17] Based on this information they calculated the probability of having $k + 1$ contacts, given k contacts (Figure 11).

This study did not disaggregate the data by offender characteristics, but it shows that after a small number of police contacts, regardless of the definition of contact,

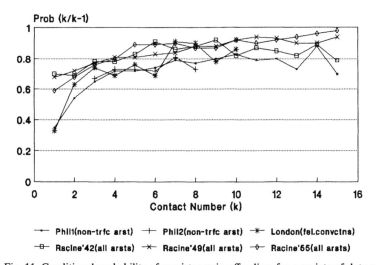

Probability of a kth Contact Given k-1

Fig. 11. Conditional probability of persistence in offending, for a variety of data sets.

---

[17] The definition of what constituted an event varied from study to study. In two, it was all non-traffic police contacts; in three it was all police contacts; in a sixth it was conviction.

the probability of additional contacts $[P(k + 1 | k)]$ is relatively constant and quite high – about 0.8.[18]

It is noteworthy that, using so many different definitions of contact, populations, and sources of data, the probability trajectories are so similar. However, it is difficult to infer very much from this figure. First, the observation times are different for each cohort, with the cutoff age ranging from 22 to 32 years of age. Should additional offenses occur after the cutoff age, they are not included in the data. This means that, if a person is arrested for a fifth crime at age 33, s/he would have been considered a person who desisted after his/her fourth contact.

Second, the seriousness of events varies considerably from study to study: the Racine cohorts include all offenses, traffic as well as non-traffic, under the rubric 'police contact', whereas the London cohort includes only convictions for indictable offenses. Because of this fact, it would be expected that both the time and the seriousness dimensions would be different for these cohorts. That is, a London youth incurring ten indictable offenses through age 25 (the cutoff for this cohort) has probably not committed offenses as serious as a London youth with two indictable offenses who is still incarcerated at age 25. Nor can they be compared directly with Racine youths who have committed up to fifteen offenses, many of which may be traffic offenses.

Research on the correlates of desistance is increasing [Farrington & Hawkins, 1991; Rhodes, 1989; Shover & Thompson, 1992]. Results to this point, however, do not indicate whether an exponential model of desistance (implied by the relative constancy of the probabilities in Figure 11) is warranted.[19]

5.3. Selective incapacitation and allocating prison space

Another use to which (a variant of) the Avi-Itzhak & Shinnar model has been put is in attempting to determine the extent to which early termination of criminal careers while they are in prison will 'waste' the space that might be occupied by a person who will still be criminally active, and therefore incapacitated, while in prison. If we assume that (1) offenders commit crimes during their criminal careers at rate λ, (2) their probability of arrest and subsequent conviction for an offense is $q Q$, (3) their career length is exponentially distributed with mean T, and (4) when incarcerated they receive a fixed sentence S, it can be shown [Avi-Itzhak & Shinnar, 1973; Barnett & Lofaso, 1986] that the number of crimes committed by an offender, N, is:

---

[18] Yet Broadhurst & Maller [1991] did not find the same constancy in their analysis of reconviction data from a large data base of Western Australian prisoners.

[19] Note that the abscissa in Figure 11 is number of police contacts, not time. Therefore, it is certainly not possible to infer an exponential model in time from these data. Note also that the offense histories represented in this figure are time-truncated at different times, depending on whether an individual was incarcerated when data collection stopped. Thus a person given a long sentence after two contacts (presumably because s/he is more dangerous) might be represented in this figure as someone who 'desisted' after $k = 2$ contacts.

$$N = \frac{\lambda}{\frac{1}{T} + \lambda q \, Q (1 - e^{S/T})} .$$

Even with this idealized model of offender behavior, Barnett & Lofaso show that it is not possible to develop clear-cut rules of thumb regarding allocation of prison space. Using a number of examples, they estimate the extent to which crimes are averted and conclude that using selective incapacitation for 'identifying the high-rate offenders and locking them up for enormous periods' is very wasteful of resources.

6. Recidivism

The offender is the *raison d'être* of the criminal justice system. S/He is also the linchpin of criminal career studies, since it is by virtue of his/her reappearance, at fairly regular intervals, in the arrest, conviction, and correctional processes that criminal careers can be studied. Thus, the recidivism of an offender, his/her continuing to commit crimes[20], is a crucial factor in criminal career research.

Recidivism has been analyzed in two ways in the literature. It is most often looked on as a failure that occurs at a specific point in time, interrupting the offender's time on the street. (This is especially true when reincarceration is the definition of recidivism.) It has also been investigated as a continuing process of being arrested, since arrests do not always interrupt a person's street time.

6.1. Recidivism as a failure event

Recidivism was originally measured for the purpose of evaluating correctional treatments. Two groups were given different treatments, and their post-release activity was monitored. The benchmark of comparison was the fraction of offenders who failed (e.g., were rearrested, had their parole revoked) during the first twelve months after release. A simple difference-of-proportions test was used to determine whether the difference was statistically significant.

However, individuals fail at different times, and comparing failure proportions at only one point in time is not warranted. As can be seen from Figure 12, although the 'satisfactory' group failed at lower rates than the 'unsatisfactory' group at all three measured points of time, a reasonable extrapolation beyond the given data would suggest that the 'unsatisfactory' group would ultimately have a lower fraction of failures. The risk of failure varies over time, and a benchmark at a single point in time can be misleading [Berecochea, Himelson & Miller,

---

[20] Although recidivism is considered to be 'the reversion of an individual to *criminal* behavior after he or she has been convicted of a prior sentence, sentenced, and (presumably) corrected' [Maltz, 1984, p. 1; emphasis added], we do not normally have unbiased indicators of criminal behavior. What we do have are arrest, conviction, or incarceration data, which is why recidivism is usually operationalized as 'rearrest, reconviction, or reincarceration after correctional treatment'.

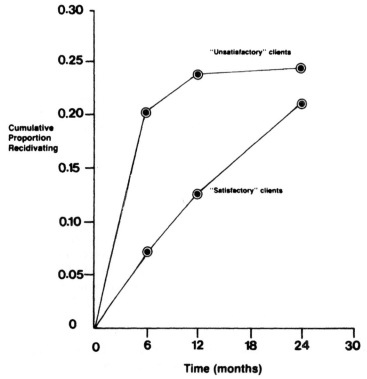

Fig. 12. Recidivism rates at three different times, for two groups of Minnesota halfway house releasees. [Source: Maltz, 1984, p. 73.]

1972]. Stollmack & Harris [1974; see also Harris & Stollmack, 1976] studied recidivism as a failure process over time and showed how to apply failure-rate techniques to study the effectiveness of correctional programs. In particular, they compared two different groups of releasees from DC prisons and showed that the (exponential) failure rates of the two groups were significantly different from each other. Models based on the reliability of electromechanical components [e.g., Barlow & Proschan, 1975; Kalbfleisch & Prentice, 1980] were thus invoked to study recidivism.

Reliability models, however, have their limitations. Whereas we can expect the eventual failure of every jet engine or hard disk drive[21], not every person can be expected to recidivate: some people do turn over new leaves, desist, and do not reappear in the criminal justice system. A new class of recidivism models was proposed [Maltz & McCleary, 1977; see also Carr-Hill & Carr-Hill, 1972; Greenberg, 1978; Partanen, 1969] that specifically include the possibility of non-failures.

In particular, the failure process can be modeled by an incomplete distribution (one whose cumulative probability of failure does not reach unity as time

---

[21] Even while writing this chapter, unfortunately.

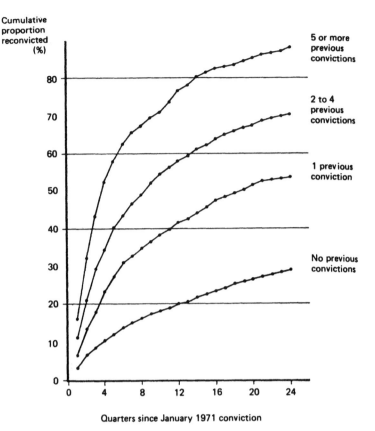

Fig. 13. Proportion reconvicted as a function of prior record. [Source: Philpotts & Lancucki, 1979, p. 23.]

approaches infinity). The cumulative distribution function for the incomplete exponential distribution (one that is suggested by Figures 12 and 13) is:

$$F(t) = \Omega(1 - e^{-\phi t}), \quad \text{where } 0 < \Omega \le 1.$$

This model of offender behavior is closely related to the 'innocents, desisters, and persisters' model of Blumstein, Farrington & Moitra [1985]. The desisters consist of the $1 - \Omega$ nonrecidivists, and the remaining Ω are persisters; the innocents, never having committed a crime in the first place, never have the opportunity to recidivate.

Maximum likelihood methods for estimating Ω and ϕ were developed[22] [Maltz & McCleary, 1977], and their empirical validity has been confirmed using data from a number of sources [Barnett, Blumstein & Farrington, 1987, 1989; Blumstein, Farrington & Moitra, 1985; Broadhurst, Maller, Maller & Duffecy, 1988;

[22] Note that ϕ in the above equation is equivalent to $1/\tau$ in Figure 1.

Maltz, 1984; Rhodes, 1989; Schmidt & Witte, 1988; Visher & Linster, 1990). They imply that the incomplete exponential distribution is an appropriate model when failure time is based on arrest, but that the incomplete lognormal distribution may be the model of choice when the failure time is based on return to prison.

6.1.1. Using the incomplete exponential distribution

There are strong statistical arguments for using the incomplete exponential distribution for modeling time to arrest and the incomplete lognormal distribution for modeling return to prison. In the former case, the time to failure is based on two processes, the offense process and the arrest process. Since the arrest process is a 'thinning' process, and since most of the (offense) points are thinned out – that is, most offenses do not result in arrest – then the resulting joint process approaches a Poisson process [Cox & Isham, 1980, p. 100]. For those who do not desist, then, the time to next arrest is exponentially distributed. Thus, there are both empirical and theoretical reasons for using the exponential distribution.

6.1.2. Using the incomplete lognormal distribution

When return to prison is the indicator of failure (and time between release and return is the time to failure), there are strong statistical arguments for using the incomplete lognormal distribution. Note that return to prison results from the concatenation of many processes: the offense process, the (thinning) arrest process, the prosecutorial decision to bring charges, the trial, the finding of guilt, the sentencing process, and the appeals process, if initiated. All processes subsequent to the arrest have significant time periods associated with them, so the time to reincarceration would not be expected to ever be close to 0. As Aitchison & Brown [1963] point out, the lognormal distribution is particularly appropriate when the end process is the result of the product of independent stochastic processes, each of which adds a contributory factor, as it is here. In addition, Schmidt & Witte [1988] show the empirical validity of this distribution in modeling time to return to prison.

Incomplete distributions are also used in biostatistics [e.g., Gross & Clark, 1975]. They were first used by Boag [1949], to estimate the proportion of patients expected to be cured of cancer. Maltz [1984, p. 81] lists other uses to which these models have been put in non-criminal justice areas, and Chung, Schmidt & Witte [1990, p. 61] suggest other uses to which they can be put in criminal justice contexts.

6.1.3. The proportional hazards method

Other methods have also been used for studying recidivism. Barton & Turnbull [1979, 1981] used Cox's proportional hazards method [Cox & Oakes, 1984]. This requires the hazard function $h_i(t;x)$ for individual i to be of the form:

$$h_i(t;x) = h_0(t) f_i(x),$$

where

$$\ln[f_i(x)] = \alpha_0 + \alpha_1 x_{i1} + \alpha_2 x_{i2} + \ldots + \alpha_k x_{ik}$$

and x_{ij} is the value of covariate j for individual i. If h_i is of this form, then the specific form h_0 of the hazard function does not enter into the likelihood maximization procedure, and the values of α_j that maximize the likelihood function can be readily determined.

Although this method is considered non-parametric [e.g., Copas & Tarling, 1988], it incorporates two assumptions, one reasonable, one questionable. The first assumption is embodied in the functional form of $f_i(x)$, that the covariates are loglinearly related; this is done for analytical tractability, so that the likelihood function can readily be maximized over the α-values.

The second assumption, however, is much more restrictive: specifically, all individuals are assumed to have the same basic hazard rate, a multiplicative constant being the only difference among them. For example, it assumes that hazard rates do not cross.[23] This assumption may in fact be suitable for some biostatistical applications, in which there is to be only one failure mechanism (a disease) that affects all individuals in the same way. However, there are indications that it is not true for correctional applications. Visher & Linster [1990] depict hazard distributions for some individuals in the cohort they studied; some of them have a high hazard of failing early in their careers, whereas others have low initial hazard rates that grow over time (Figure 8). Gruenwald & West [1989] also found the proportional hazards model unsuitable in studying juvenile delinquency.

6.1.4. Exponentially decreasing hazard rate

The proportion of individuals expected to fail and the parameters of their failure distribution are not the only characteristics of interest in studying recidivism. Different models can be posited that capture the same behavior, but in different ways. For example, noting that hazard rates for recidivism decline over time, Bloom [1979; Bloom & Singer, 1979] posited a hazard rate that declined exponentially with time:

$$h = h_0 \, e^{-\theta t}.$$

This resulted in an incomplete distribution similar in many respects to the incomplete exponential distribution. Similarly, Gerchak [1983, 1984] looked upon decreasing hazard rates as a indicative of a kind of inertia; i.e., the longer a person stays in an unfailed state, the more likely he/she is to remain in it.

Regardless of the model used, it seems clear that the models which best fit the data appear to be those with decreasing hazard rates. There is a theoretical explanation for this as well; since some offenders may have high hazard rates and others low rates, the resulting pooled data will always exhibit a decreasing hazard rate – those with high hazard rates fail early, so as time increases the remaining members have a lower and lower mean hazard rate [Proschan, 1963].

---

[23] Recall that this is equivalent to the assumption of 'stable criminality' proposed by Gottfredson & Hirschi [1990], and investigated by Harada [1991] – see Section 4.2 and Figure 8.

6.1.5. Population heterogeneity

The incomplete distribution represents but one class of models for studying recidivism. It implies that a group can be split into two sub-groups, one which does not recidivate, the other of which recidivates according to a particular distribution (e.g., exponential, Weibull, lognormal). There are, however, other modes of failure. For example, both groups may fail, but at different rates:

$$F(t) = \Omega f_1(t) + (1 - \Omega) f_2(t),$$

where f_1 and f_2 are two different probability density functions. Harris, Kaylan & Maltz [1981] investigated a mixture of exponentials (with three parameters, Ω, ϕ_1, and ϕ_2) and Broadhurst & Maller [1991] considered a mixture of two Weibull functions (with five parameters).

There are also other ways to model population heterogeneity. Lehoczky [1986] suggested the use of hierarchical models. Gerchak & Kubat [1986] considered the use of beta and gamma mixtures of exponentials. Schmidt & Witte [1988] performed a covariate analysis of recidivism data. (They found, however, that models using individual covariates are hardly better than models that do not use explanatory variables [Schmidt & Witte, 1988, p. 117].) And Ellerman, Sullo & Tien [1992] modeled population heterogeneity using a Burr model, a continuous mixture of Weibull distributions.

It is always difficult to decide how many parameters to use to model a process. Koopman [1986, p. 379] invoked the aphorism 'With six parameters I could model an elephant' to state his aversion for overly complicated models. Models with few parameters can provide a great deal of insight, at the expense of grouping many different phenomena together, while those with a greater number of parameters fit the data better, at the expense of providing less insight; and 'the more complex the model, the further do its data requirements outstrip the numbers that are readily available' [Barnett, 1987, p. 31]. The inclination to keep the number of parameters as small as possible, using the principle of Ockham's razor, seems to have some validity from a Bayesian standpoint [Jefferys & Berger, 1992].

6.2. Recidivism as a sequence of failures

The revolving door of recidivism seems to turn faster for juveniles than for adults, since penalties for juveniles are of considerably shorter duration than for adults. As a consequence, chronic juvenile delinquents may have a long record of arrests with little incarceration time after court intervention to interrupt them. Murray & Cox [1979] analyzed the police contact data for a group of chronic delinquents and found that the post-intervention police contact rates were substantially lower than their pre-intervention rates. They called this phenomenon the 'suppression effect', because offenses appeared to be suppressed by the court-mandated intervention (Figure 14). They argued that since arrests are a proxy for all crimes, a decrease in the arrest rate is tantamount to a decrease in the offense rate.

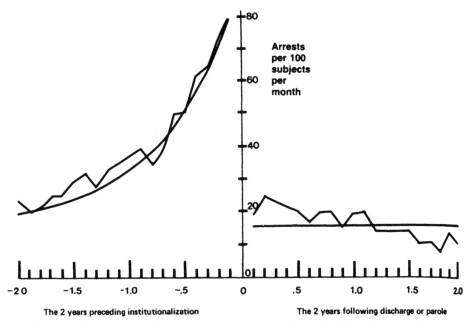

Fig. 14. Pre- and post-intervention police contact rates, superimposed with a Markov model of the intervention process. [Source: Maltz, 1984, p. 34.]

Maltz & Pollock [1980b] showed that this 'suppression effect' is probably not based on true suppression (that is, a person actually increasing his/her offense rate before court intervention and curtailing it afterward), but could be adequately explained by the 'regression to the mean' phenomenon.[24] They posited that since offenders' police contact rates are stochastic, the effect of conditioning an intervention on a police contact, or on a sequence of contacts, could generate the appearance of a steep rise immediately prior to the intervention.

They showed how this could be accomplished, *even with constant police contact rates both before and after intervention,* by either of two decision rules. In the first, offenders are assumed to commit crimes and incur arrests at a constant mean rate by jumping between two rates ('active' and 'quiescent') stochastically in a Markov process; in such a case, since the intervention is conditioned on an arrest, the arrest rate increases exponentially just prior to intervention. Specifically, let the 'active' arrest rate be μ_1 and the 'quiescent' arrest rate be μ_2; then if the transitions between these states are α (from state 1 to state 2) and β (from state 2 to state 1), the contact rate shows exponential growth just prior to intervention:

[24] Regression to the mean is caused by selection of the extreme cases. It can best be explained by a simple example. Suppose that 1000 fair coins are tossed three times each and 125 of them (or 1/8th, as expected) come up with all tails. We can call these coins 'delinquent' coins, subject them to a treatment, and reexamine them by tossing them three more times. Note that most of them now are 'cured'; only about 15 or so coins (1/8th) are still 'delinquent'.

$$\mu_{\text{eff}}(t \mid \text{intervention}) = \hat{\mu} + \frac{(\mu_1 - M_2)^2}{\hat{\mu}} \frac{\alpha\beta}{(\alpha + \beta)^2} \, e^{(\alpha+\beta)t},$$

where

$$\hat{\mu} = \frac{\mu_1\beta + \mu_2\alpha}{\alpha + \beta}.$$

The smooth curve on the left in Figure 14 is found with $\mu_1 = 0.8$, $\mu_2 = 0.02$, $\alpha = 0.063$ and $\beta = 0.007$.

The second process that could explain the 'suppression effect' is based on judicial selection criteria. If the process whereby offenders are selected for intervention is based generally on 'k arrests in the past M months', then a constant prior arrest rate will again generate a steep rise just prior to intervention. This is easily explained: if pre-intervention activity must exceed a threshold in order for intervention to occur, then average level prior to intervention will exceed the post-intervention level. This 'selection of the extreme' cases, followed by a 'regression to the mean' makes it appear that the rate has changed drastically between before and after [Hwang, 1990; Maltz, 1980; Maltz, Gordon, McDowall & McCleary, 1980; Pollock & Farrell, 1984; Tierney, 1983].

7. Deterrence

Two different types of deterrence are distinguished by Zimring & Hawkins [1973]: *special* (or individual) deterrence and *general* deterrence. Special deterrence is the reduction in criminal activity by known offenders, due to the criminal sanctions previously imposed on them or to the threat of similar penalties should they continue to break the law. Operationally, it cannot be distinguished from rehabilitation, since it is difficult to determine whether the carrot of rehabilitation or the stick of punishment caused the change. Measuring the extent of special deterrence is accomplished by investigating the recidivism behavior of the offenders being studied; the techniques used are described in Section 6.

7.1. General deterrence

General deterrence is the reduction in criminal activity by the general public (that is, actual and potential offenders) attributable to a given intervention. It is not associated with specific individuals, so it cannot be measured by tracing offenders' careers. Rather, it must be inferred from the available aggregate data. Some examples of interventions that may affect crime rates are the effect of the death penalty on homicide rates, or the effect that increased penalties for gun-related crimes might have on armed robbery.

Mathematical modeling plays an important role in the study of general deterrence, although all too often its role is ignored. Inferring that a change in offense rates is attributable to a particular intervention requires that the effects of other possible explanatory variables be accounted for, which means that their effect on the outcome must either be known or modeled, and that the measured change is sufficiently large that it can be distinguished from random variation.

One problem with inferring deterrence from data is that it can be confounded with an incapacitation effect: if a sizable fraction of the offending population is incarcerated, then offense rates will decrease due to incapacitation of the offenders, which cannot be distinguished from the reduction in offenses by those deterred. Cohen [1978, 1983] and Nagin [1978] used the Shinnar and Shinnar model to estimate the magnitude of the incapacitative effect on crime rates.

7.2. Linear models of deterrence

Nagin also reviewed a number of studies of general deterrence. Almost all of the studies used official data and were cross-sectional in nature; almost all used linear models of one form or another (correlation, regression, ordinary least squares, two-stage least squares) to 'control' for the effect of explanatory variables (such as income and age distributions of a jurisdiction, percent nonwhite, and education levels). The justification for using linear models to relate these variables apparently was not discussed in any of the studies, perhaps because linear models are tractable, and others have shown that such models are 'robust'. They are very often (implicitly) justified by virtue of the fact that, should a different relationship actually relate the variables, if that relationship is well-behaved, then the Taylor series expansion of the function in a small neighborhood around any point is linear to a first-order approximation.[25]

For the most part, these studies appealed only to audiences of academics who were trying to determine whether changes in arrest rates, sentencing patterns, or police resources affected crime rates. This changed, and the study of deterrence and deterrents took on a greater importance, after a paper by Ehrlich [1975] on the deterrent effect of the death penalty hit the headlines.

7.3. Deterrence and the death penalty

Ehrlich analyzed data on homicide rates and the death penalty, and concluded that the death penalty deterred homicide: his estimate was that every execution reduced the number of homicides by eight. This finding was not only published in an academic journal, it was cited by the US Supreme Court in *Fowler v. North Carolina* and featured in newspaper stories.

His analysis was based on an econometric model and used national data from the Uniform Crime Reports from the 1930s to the 1970s. The functional form he used was the Cobb-Douglass econometric model wherein his 'murder supply

---

[25] This approximation, of course, holds only for the immediate neighborhood of the point. However, this limitation has not stopped people from extrapolating the solution to regions of the solution space for which the approximation does not hold.

function' was:

$$M = k P_a^{\alpha_1} P_{c|a}^{\alpha_2} P_{e|c}^{\alpha_3} U^{\beta_1} L^{\beta_2} Y_p^{\beta_3} A^{\beta_4} e^{\nu}$$

where M is the murder rate, k is a constant, P_a is the probability of apprehension for a homicide, $P_{c|a}$ is the probability of being convicted of homicide given apprehension, $P_{e|c}$ is the probability of execution for homicide given conviction, U is the (civilian) unemployment rate, L is the fraction of adult civilians in the labor force, Y_p is an estimate of real per capita income, A is the fraction of the residential population between 14 and 24 years of age, and ν represents the noise or random fluctuations. Taking the logarithm of this equation results in an equation that is linear in the model's parameters (the α- and β-values). The probabilities were estimated by dividing, respectively, arrests for homicides by number of homicides, homicide convictions by homicide arrests, and executions for homicide by homicide convictions.

His finding was hotly contested as others found weaknesses in the model, the data, and the method of analysis he used [Barnett, 1978; Beyleveld, 1982; Bowers & Pierce, 1975; Fisher & Nagin, 1978; Klein, Forst & Filatov, 1978; Nagin, 1978; Passell, 1975]. Yet for the most part, his critics believed that the deterrent effect of executions on homicides could be modeled, should the problems with data, model, and analytic tools be cleared up. Some of the model's problems included the following [Barnett, 1978]:

• the Cobb-Douglas model may have been chosen more for its analytic tractability than its appropriateness;[26]

• how the variables were entered into the equation was not explained – Ehrlich used, for example, P_a and not $1 - P_a$ (the probability of *avoiding* arrest) in the equation, without justifying his choice;[27]

• the model was assumed to be time-invariant over four decades, implicitly ignoring the potential effects of a world war, civil rights legislation, the increasing availability of automobiles and guns, and other factors that might exert some influence on the homicide rate.

7.4. Stochastic modeling of homicide data

Yet there was an even more fundamental problem with Ehrlich's model. Like any other statistic, the homicide rate has a certain natural (stochastic) variation. Barnett [1978, 1981a,b; see also Barnett, 1983a,b] developed an estimate of the expected 'noise' in the homicide data. His approach is reminiscent of Poisson's

---

[26] 'Buttressed by an elegant theory and vast computer packages, regression models have great appeal in criminology and elsewhere. But mathematical models of a process ideally should arise from attempts to quantify reasonable assumptions about it, rather than from an excessive concern about tractability and familiarity' [Barnett, 1978, p. 302].

[27] Riccio [1974] makes a similar point, that deterrence may depend on the probability of getting away with the offense, not on the probability of failure. This is especially true when the probability of failure is small: a tenfold increase in the failure probability will have little effect on an offender if the increase is from 0.001 to 0.01, since the probability of success drops only from 0.999 to 0.990.

investigation of jury behavior (Section 2.1 above); Barnett modeled the stochastic process that results in homicide by investigating the structure of the data and making realistic assumptions about it.

Barnett assumes that there is a random variable h_i $(i = 1, \ldots, N)$ associated with each of the N persons in a jurisdiction, equal to the number of homicides he/she will commit in a given year. If p_{ij} is the probability that person i will commit j homicides (i.e., that $h_i = j$), then person i is expected to commit

$$E(h_i) = \overline{h_i} = \sum_{j=1}^{\infty} j p_{ij}$$

offenses with a variance of

$$\sigma^2(h_i) = \sum_{j=1}^{\infty} j^2 p_{ij} - \overline{h_i}^2.$$

Barnett then makes two assumptions: that $\overline{h_i}^2$ is negligible compared to $\overline{h_i}$, and that $\overline{h_i}$ is independent of $\overline{h_j}$ for $i \neq j$, both of which he shows to be reasonable. Then the expected number of total homicides in the jurisdiction for that year is:

$$E(H) = E\left(\sum_{i=1}^{N} h_i\right) = \sum_i \sum_j j p_{ij} = \sum_j \left[\sum_i p_{i1} + 2 \sum_i p_{i2} + \ldots\right]$$
$$= [q_1 + 2q_2 + 3q_3 + \ldots],$$

where q_j is the sum of the probabilities that individuals will commit j murders in a year, and therefore is the expected number of the N individuals who commit j murders in a year

$$q_j = \sum_i p_{ij}.$$

Using his assumptions, the variance can be approximated by:

$$\sigma^2(H) = \sum_i \sigma^2(h_i) = \sum_i (q_1 + 4q_2 + 9q_3 + \ldots).$$

Based on data from a number of states and cities on double, triple and quadruple murderers, he was able to develop the estimates $q_2/q_1 \approx 0.0046$, $q_3/q_1 \approx 0.00016$, $q_4/q_1 \approx 0.0005$, etc., so that

$$\sigma^2(H) \approx 1.04 E(H).$$

Barnett then showed that, for a typical state with 200 homicides per year (and an associated variance of about $200 \times 1.04 = 208$), even with the most

favorable assumptions about the validity of the deterrence model used, none of
the purported deterrent effects rise above the noise level inherent in the data.

7.5. Deterrence and other offenses

Research on deterrence is not restricted to investigations of the death penalty.
Other crimes are also subject to deterrence (and to studies of deterrence),
which would benefit from knowledge of the extent of variation in expected rates.
Extending his work on modeling the magnitude of fluctuations expected in the
homicide rate, Barnett [1981b] developed a model of robbery. In this section, we
extend his model and show how it can be used in developing program evaluation
guidelines.

Consider the case of an individual, say a chronic offender, who would, absent
police intervention, commit c crimes in a given year. His offense 'career' during
that year, however, might be interrupted by an arrest during any one of the crimes,
with probability q. Under the assumption that the offender is incapacitated for the
rest of the year after apprehension, the probability distribution of c_{eff}, the number
of crimes actually committed, is:

$$c_{\text{eff}} = \begin{cases} i \text{ with probability } q(1-q)^{i-1}, & i = 1, \ldots, c-1 \\ c \text{ with probability } (1-q)^c \end{cases}$$

This leads to the estimates of mean and variance of:[28]

$$E(c_{\text{eff}} \mid c) = \frac{(1-q)[1-(1-q)^c]}{q},$$

$$\sigma^2_{c_{\text{eff}} \mid c} = \frac{(1-q)[1-(2c+1)q(1-q)^c - (1-q)^{2c+1}]}{q^2}.$$

We will assume that, for these chronic offenders, c is normally distributed, with
a mean of κ and a variance of κ as well, which is a conservative assumption. This
produces a distribution with the following estimates for mean and variance of the
annual offense rate:

$$E(c_{\text{eff}}) = \frac{(1-q)[1-(1-q)^{\hat{\kappa}}]}{q},$$

$$\sigma^2_{c_{\text{eff}} \mid c} = \frac{(1-q)[1-(2\tilde{\kappa}+1)q(1-q)^{\hat{\kappa}} - (1-q)^{2\hat{\kappa}+1}]}{q^2},$$

where

$\tilde{\kappa} = \kappa[1 + \ln(1-q)],$
$\hat{\kappa} = \kappa[1 + \frac{1}{2}\ln(1-q)].$

For 'violent predators' who would average (if unconstrained by arrest), say, $\kappa = 200$ offenses a year, a probability of arrest, q, of 0.1 would result in an expected

---

[28] These estimates are slightly different than the ones derived by Barnett.

value of 9 offenses in a year, with a variance of 90; in general, for the range of offense rates and arrest probabilities expected, the number of offenses would average $(1 - q)/q$ with a variance of $(1 - q)/q^2$.

Suppose we were able to identify a group of 100 such offenders. They would be expected to produce 900 offenses each year with a variance of 9000 (and standard error of 95). To be 95% confident (one-tailed) that a program actually caused a reduction in offenses, there would have to be 156 fewer offenses, or a reduction of 17%.

Note that, absent arrest, these offenders would be expected to produce about 20 000 offenses, but only produce about 900 because of arrest and incarceration; and that the high intrinsic variance makes assessing change difficult: even for a very active group of offenders whose activity for the year was assumed to terminate after arrest, there would have to be a very large reduction in their activity if a program aimed at reducing their offense rate were to be distinguished from the natural variation in their offense activity.

8. Population projections

8.1. Prison population projections

Another area of importance to prison administrators is the projection of future populations of offenders. As discussed earlier, the fact that prison populations are determined by judges, who are generally unaware of prison resource constraints, means that rational planning for prisons could not be carried out effectively without the development of some sort of model. Although there are a number of time series and regression models for forecasting crime [e.g., Fox, 1978; Orsagh, 1981], Stollmack [1973] developed one of the first probabilistic models for projecting prison populations. If prison arrivals have a Poisson arrival rate A, and sentences are distributed exponentially with mean $1/\theta$, then the number of prisoners $N(t)$ in year t can be estimated as:

$$N(t) = A(1 - e^{-\theta})/\theta + e^{-\theta} N(t - 1).$$

A similar approach was used by Blumstein, Cohen & Miller [1980], who based their projection on Stollmack's model. They allowed A to vary over time according to the expected number of annual admissions for different age–race–crime categories. The number of admissions for each age–race category was estimated by using census data for the total population in each category, then multiplying this by the fraction of each category admitted to prison in the past for each offense type. They then aggregated the number for each category to produce their overall forecast.

In their basic form, such models suffer from the deficiency noted in Section 3, the inability to explore the characteristics of the workload. In addition, it presupposes that two of the reasons given for applying the criminal sanction, incapacitation and deterrence, do not work – or at least, do not vary from year to year in how they work. For example, individuals who flow through the system may be affected differentially by incarceration and return in greater or lesser numbers; or offenders may all be given twenty-year sentences and therefore the number of recidivists would be drastically reduced; or a shortage of prison space might reduce the sentence lengths for many prisoners, increasing the number of potential offenders out on the street and, therefore, the number of individuals at risk for prison. In other words, these models rely on history to forecast the number of prison admissions, rather than allowing for the possibility that policy changes may affect admissions.

Barnett [1987; see also Rich & Barnett, 1985] developed a model that takes a number of these considerations into account. His model is based on the criminal career paradigm. It incorporates offense and arrest activity by specifying a mean arrest rate, offender recidivism behavior by permitting specification of the age distribution of career termination, sentencing behavior by specifying an age-specific probability distribution of imprisonment given arrest, and correctional behavior by specifying an age-specific sentence length distribution.

Although this model substitutes one set of assumptions (past admission ratios are the best predictor of future admissions) with another (a constant arrest rate and stationarity in career termination and criminal justice behaviors), the new assumptions are more flexible and mirror reality more closely. This model, for example, shows how to incorporate the criminal career model into a population projection model. Second, this model accommodates offender characteristics and policy changes explicitly. Should changing employment patterns affect career termination, or should sentencing practices change[29], this model can show how they affect the prison population.

Lattimore & Baker [1992] developed a model conceptually similar to that of Barnett, but based it on characteristics specific to the recidivism process. For example, since first-time offenders and recidivists have different recidivism characteristics (e.g., see Figures 11 and 13), they disaggregated the prisoner population into 'first-timers' and recidivists.[30] In addition, their model explicitly accounts for prison capacity constraints. Furthermore, they use the incomplete lognormal distribution to model return to prison; as noted in Section 5.1, this distribution is especially suitable for describing recidivism when return to prison is the indicator of failure.

When dealing with forecasts, the proof of the pudding can be set as far in the future as one wants, but eventually comes due. Although the Lattimore and Baker model provides a good forecast of commitments to prison, it stumbles over a common problem in forecasting prison populations, the lack of a stable policy and social environment. The changes that have occurred in recent years

---

[29] Langan [1991] found that over half of the substantial growth in prison admissions over the past fifteen years is attributable to the increased use of prison at sentencing. He suggests that this may also have contributed to the gradual reduction in the crime victimization rate during this period.

[30] The models posited by Barnett and by Blumstein, Cohen and Miller can also accommodate such disaggregation.

have drastically changed the criminal justice context: the increased prevalence of crack cocaine in urban areas, with the high rate of addiction it engenders; the consequent increase in drug crimes and in drug enforcement activity; the increased availability of money to focus on drug enforcement (via asset forfeiture); the increased prison construction, to name but a few. As Cherlin [1991] points out, 'no demographic method can be used to predict future behavior during a period of great social change.'

8.2. The 'stability of punishment' hypothesis

This same lack of stable conditions has also affected a conjecture about prison populations, that there is a 'stability of punishment' in any given jurisdiction [Blumstein & Cohen, 1973]. Similar to Quetelet's *'penchant au crime'* (see Chapter 1), it was hypothesized that a state or nation would tolerate the imprisonment of a certain percentage of its citizens: once a threshold or trigger level above this percentage is reached, the imprisonment rate decreases until it falls within the appropriate limits; and, similarly, if the imprisonment rate falls below a certain threshold, events conspire to increase the percentage to fall within the limits. In short, it was hypothesized that a society operated much like a thermostat, increasing or decreasing the punishment rate to keep it within the threshold limits of a set point. This phenomenon appeared to be present in the imprisonment statistics of a number of states and countries through the early 1970s [Blumstein, Cohen & Nagin, 1976; Blumstein & Moitra, 1979].

Others disputed this interpretation of prison population statistics. They found different explanations that fit as well or found examples that did not fit the 'stability of punishment' hypothesis [e.g., Berk, Messinger, Rauma & Berecochea, 1983; Berk, Rauma, Messinger & Cooley, 1981; Blumstein, Cohen, Moitra & Nagin, 1981; Greenberg, 1977; Rauma, 1981a,b]. Since the time those articles were written, the growth in prison populations has been so high (Figure 15) that they appeared to be 'out of control' [Blumstein, 1988]. Considering the recent changes in the prevalence of drug activity and enforcement of drug laws, one would not expect much stability in recent incarceration rates.

8.3. Projecting the lifetime probability of arrest

Although not a projection of prison population that would be of much benefit to prison administrators, in 1967 Christensen made a forecast of the offender population that made people aware of the major part the criminal justice system was beginning to play in the life of every citizen. He used a stochastic model of the offending population to project estimates of the fraction of the population that might experience an arrest or conviction for a criminal offense sometime during their lifetimes. Using a steady-state assumption about trends, he found that over half of the male population was eventually likely to experience an arrest, a rate that rose to about 90% for nonwhite males. These statistics led others to explore the potential effect of high crime rates on prisons more closely.

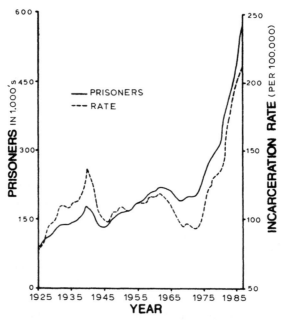

Fig. 15. Prison admissions and population in the United States. [Source: Blumstein, 1988.]

8.4. Projecting the lifetime risk of victimization

A line of research similar to that of Christensen's has focused on the probability that one would become a victim of crime. Using age-specific crime data from the New York City Police Department, Shinnar & Shinnar [1975] applied life table techniques to show that the risk of becoming a victim of crime had increased substantially between 1960 and 1970 (with robbery increasing tenfold during this period).

More recent work in this vein has focused on homicide. In a series of papers [Barnett, 1982; Barnett, Essenfeld & Kleitman, 1980; Barnett, Kleitman & Larson, 1975; Barnett & Schwartz, 1989], Barnett and his colleagues showed that the lifetime risk of homicide for an individual born in an urban area is one in 68 – and for a young urban African–American male the risk is far greater.

With statistics like these, economics can no longer claim to be the only 'dismal science'. Not only have they made headlines, these findings have led to policy changes as well. In part because of these studies, the Centers for Disease Control have recognized that homicides are the leading cause of death among young African–American adults and have begun to take an epidemiological approach to urban homicide.

8.5. Estimating the size of the criminal population

Using the official statistics of the time, in Paris in 1825 Balzac estimated that '40 000 rogues, 15 000 petty thieves, 10 000 burglars and 40 000 ingenuous females living at someone else's expense add up to some 110 to 120 000 persons who are a great handicap to efficient administration' [Chevalier, 1973, p. 71]. Although his estimate was based on faulty data and methods, the idea of expressing criminality in terms of such statistics brought a 'statistical mentality' to the description of crime and the criminal population. Such estimates are important for other reasons as well.

For a jurisdiction experiencing 365 robberies a year, it makes a huge difference in terms of criminal justice policy if that number is the result of one offender plying his/her trade daily or 365 people pulling one job a year. In the first case, locking up one person is tantamount to solving the entire problem (by incapacitation); in the second case, locking up one person would make little difference. It is therefore important to develop methods for estimating the extent of participation of individuals in criminal careers and their frequency of committing crimes during their careers.

Greene & Stollmack [1981] developed such methods using models based on capture–recapture studies in ecology. They assumed that every offender experiences arrests according to the same Poisson distribution with parameter μ, such that the probability of a person experiencing k arrests in a year is:

$$P(K = k) = \frac{\mu^k e^{-\mu}}{k!}.$$

(Unlike the capture–recapture models, there is an implicit assumption that only the *offender* population is of interest, not all individuals. That is, the fact that most of the population would have an arrest rate μ of 0 is not explicitly handled, and no distinction is made between individuals for whom $\mu = 0$ and those for whom $k = 0$ but $\mu > 0$.)[31]

Greene & Stollmack compared this with a model in which a fraction p is arrested at rate μ_1 and a fraction $1 - p$ is arrested at rate μ_2, such that the probability of a person experiencing k arrests is:

$$P(K = k) = \frac{p\mu_1^k e^{-\mu_1}}{k!} + \frac{(1 - p)\mu_2^k e^{-\mu_2}}{k!}$$

They used maximum likelihood estimation techniques to fit the model to data from Washington, DC, and found that the model that best fits the data is one that assumes that there are two sub-populations with different arrest rates: 4% of the population had a mean arrest rate of about 1.5 arrests per year (a mean time between arrests of eight months), whereas the other 96% (of offenders, not of the total population) had a mean arrest rate of about 0.2 per year (for a mean time between arrests of five years).

Greene [1984] reanalyzed the same data under a different set of assumptions, including disaggregating the data into different age categories. He found that the model did not provide as good a fit under these conditions. Riccio & Finkelstein [1985] used arrest data to estimate the size of the burglar population, and Rossmo & Routledge [1990] used similar techniques, but different distributions, to

---

[31] I thank Jacqueline Cohen for pointing this out.

estimate the size of the prostitute and fugitive population in Vancouver. Collins & Wilson [1990] used the Greene and Stollmack methods to estimate the number of automobile thieves in the Australian Capital Territory, and found that the model based on two sub-populations provides the best fit to the data.

As with all models, this is predicated on assumptions about the population under study. This model assumes that there are no 'births' or 'deaths,' i.e., the population is fixed, and the 'capture' and 'recapture' events occur independently of each other. Neither of these can be justified. The first assumption ignores the fact that in ecology the label 'trout' is permanently attached to the animal, which is always subject to capture; but the label 'criminal' applies only when the individual is active and subject to capture, at a rate dependent on his/her own λ, and ignores the possibility of his/her criminal career terminating between capture and recapture.

The second assumption, independence, cannot be justified for two reasons. First, most police departments maintain files on prior arrestees, including their addresses and their *modi operandi*, just so they can increase the probability of arrest of these offenders should they commit additional crimes. It can also be argued that the more a person has been arrested the more s/he is liable to arrest, if only because his/her prior record reflects a lack of skill at his/her chosen career. (Of course, a third argument is that in time offenders may improve their skills and thus lower their probability of arrest.) The extent to which these explanations hold has not been ascertained; regardless, they serve to show that capture and recapture events are not independent.

8.6. Estimating the number of narcotics users

Estimates of the prevalence of narcotics use in the United States vary widely, based on the political predilections of the estimators and on the methods they use as well. Hser, Anglin, Wickens, Brecht & Homer [1992] reviewed the different methods used to estimate the number of narcotics users. They distinguished between *static models* and *dynamic models*: static models are those that estimate the number of users at one point in time, while dynamic models generate estimates over time.

Among the static models they review are those based on straight-forward *population projections* and those based on *closed-population capture models*. The former merely assume that the usage patterns in an *unknown* population of known demographic characteristics are similar to those in a *known* population of known demographic characteristics, and estimate the number of users according to the relative demographic characteristics of the two populations.

The second static method, the closed-population capture model, is based on some of the same dubious assumptions that have been used to estimate the number of offenders: that capture samples are independent and that every individual has the same probability of capture. If n_{12} individuals are captured in each of two samples, then the population estimate is $n_1 n_2 / n_{12}$.

Among the dynamic models they review are the *open-population multiple capture* model, the *truncated Poisson estimation* model, *Markov open-population* models, and *system dynamics* models. The open-population multiple capture model is similar to the closed-population model, except that the population itself is not considered fixed in size but is integrated with a demographic birth and death process in which the population itself is changing its size and character.

The truncated Poisson model is based on the method used by Greene & Stollmack [1981] to estimate offender populations. In a given period of time some narcotics users are not arrested, while some are arrested once, some twice, some three times, etc. Based on the statistics of those arrested at least once, one can fit a Poisson distribution to the data and estimate the number of users who have avoided arrest. This method also is based on questionable assumptions, those of independence of arrests and homogeneity of users' arrest rates.

Markov open-population models consider the fact that individuals move into and out of different states; in some of those states they are at risk of capture, while in other states they are not. The model is calibrated using the statistics of known individuals and makes the implicit assumption that all individuals have the same transition probabilities.

System dynamics models have the advantage of incorporating feedback relationships among the variables, e.g., including the effect of increased enforcement on increasing arrest rates initially, on increasing prices, and on eventually reducing narcotics use (and therefore arrests) due to the increased prices. The difficulty with this method is that there are a great number of parameters to be estimated, and therefore it is difficult to ensure that the structure posited for the feedback relationships is correct, because so many different model structures could produce similar results.

9. Crime- and police-related studies

Operations research has also been used to study crime and how the police react to it. Some of these studies are described elsewhere in this handbook, especially those studies relating to allocation of police resources. This section describes some of the studies that have been made of crime and police patrol operations.

9.1. Crime measurement issues

The crime data we have available to work with is both detailed and extensive. Yet caution is advised nonetheless. Stamp [1929, p. 258] tells the story of a man who, while in India, quoted some statistics to a Judge, an Englishman, and a very good fellow. His friend said:

> 'Cox, when you are a bit older, you will not quote Indian statistics with that assurance. The Government are very keen on amassing statistics – they collect them, add them, raise them to the *n*th power, take the cube root and prepare wonderful diagrams. But what you must never forget is that every one of these figures comes in the first place from the *chowty dar* [village watchman], who just puts down what he damn pleases.'

9.1.1. Issues surrounding crime data

Although crime statistics in the United States are not as random as the Indian statistics apparently were sixty years ago, they are still subject to errors, and sometimes the errors can be substantial. This is especially true of police-collected crime statistics, which are subject to changes in police policies that may have the inadvertent (or intentional) effect of changing reporting behavior. Consider what can happen when a police official, concerned about the amount of time spent by patrol officers writing burglary and larceny reports, decides to restrict them to taking reports of only those thefts that exceed $200. This policy may be a direct result of an increased crime rate. Its effect may be to reduce the reported crime rate dramatically: making victims of less costly crimes go into the police station to report a crime may just convince them to forgo reporting it, especially if they are not insured or if their insurance deductible is $200. (This scenario is not hypothetical; it occurred in at least one city in the 1970s.)

More recently, major police departments have been found to have reduced the number of reported crimes by the simple expedient of unfounding them: after the initial report is filed by the patrol officer, a follow-up investigation is conducted by a detective. If, based on his/her judgment (or based on pressure from above), the detective feels that no crime took place or is unable to locate the victim or witnesses, that crime can be 'unfounded' or treated as if it did not occur.

Although these irregularities no longer take place beyond public scrutiny, an independent set of crime data is now available. It was to provide a set of data not subject to police reporting biases that the Justice Department funded the Census Bureau to begin to collect victimization data from the general public. Reconciling the two data sets requires knowledge of the different methods used to collect them. Comparing the two measurement processes, Maltz [1975b] showed how some of the differences in methodologies can lead to incorrect conclusions. Eck & Riccio [1979] also compared the two data sets, attempting to reconcile them by modeling the degree to which the extent of nonreporting (to the police) accounted for the discrepancies between them.

Another concern about crime statistics is that the FBI-reported statistics of crime are just the sum of the numbers of different crimes reported to the police. No weighting is given crimes according to their seriousness: robbing a bank adds one to the count, as does robbing a schoolchild of lunch money. It is for this reason that Sellin & Wolfgang [1964] developed a Crime Seriousness Index. Although this index is far superior to simple bean-counting, it has its own limitations. First, Blumstein [1974] showed that when the crime type mix is stable, the simple FBI index of crime is as good as a seriousness-weighted index. Second, Maltz [1975a] described some of the conceptual problems with the Crime Seriousness Index and proposed a vector measure of crime, which is also applicable to the measurement of organized crime [Maltz, 1990].

9.1.2. Geographical patterns of crime

The study of geographical patterns has played a prominent role in criminology since Shaw & McKay [1969] first studied them in Chicago sixty years ago, showing the way juvenile delinquency rates seemed to spread out from the center of the city in concentric rings. Not only social scientists but police departments as well have studied crime geographically, using pin maps to spot crime patterns. The problem with using such techniques in the past, for both the researcher and the police, was that they were very labor-intensive. Locating a few hundred events on a map is an arduous task. Even more difficult is attempting to determine what each pin represents. Although using different colored pins to represent different types of offenses can help, it can only do so much: on the next day, a person would have a hard time remembering whether a particular pin represents a nighttime robbery of an elderly latina on a Wednesday or the daytime robbery of a young African–American male last Friday.

These problems have been all but eliminated by two technological facts. First, more and more police departments have computerized data available for analysis; and second, mapping software is now available that permits researchers and/or the police to plot selected data (e.g., nighttime robberies of elderly women) automatically, making it possible to infer different kinds of patterns from the data. Maltz, Gordon & Friedman [1990] provide an overview of the potential uses of such patterning for police purposes. Block [1989] describes how the STAC (Spatial and Temporal Analysis of Crime) algorithm, developed by the Illinois Criminal Justice Information Authority for use by police departments, can be used to find crime 'hot spots'. Harries [1990; see also Harries, 1980] shows how mapping data can assist the police in other ways.

Such data lend themselves to geographic models that have been developed by geographers for other purposes. Brantingham & Brantingham [1984] describe a number of techniques and models that can be used to discern geographic patterns of crime. They show how patterns change as the unit of geographical analysis changes [Brantingham, Dyreson & Brantingham, 1976]. In addition, they discuss the utility of distance-decay modeling [Capone & Nichols, 1976], gravity potential modeling [Rossmo, 1990; Smith, 1976], graph theory, and diffusion modeling to the analysis of such patterns.

9.2. Response time and police patrol strategies

Not all of the initial operations research or management science done in the criminal justice field was useful or effective. Mistakes were made as analysts gradually learned the limitations of quantification and mathematical models. As previously mentioned, one of the areas in which quantitative analysis was seen to hold a great deal of promise was in command-and-control. Many operations researchers and systems analysts had worked on military command-and-control problems and felt that the same tactics and concepts, so 'successful' in Vietnam, could be imported lock, stock, and barrel into the 'war on crime'.[32]

---

[32] A personal note: I was not immune to this belief, but it was quickly dispelled in me in consulting for the Boston Police Department in the late 1960s and working for the National Institute of Law Enforcement and Criminal Justice (now the National Institute of Justice) in the

A key area in which this was felt was in the push to reduce police response time. The impetus for this was twofold. First, the empirical justification came from a study of the length of time between calls for police service and arrests in cases of emergency calls. It was found [STTF, 1967, p. 93] that higher probabilities of arrest were associated with lower response time. Second, we see the technological imperative at work here: if delay is a problem, let us put our minds to work and reduce it, preferably through the use of computers.[33]

One attempt to show how crime might be controlled by police use of computers was called 'random patrol' or 'intercept patrol' [Elliott & Sardino, 1971; see also Elliott, 1968]. It was based on a research project in Syracuse, New York. Its hypothesis was that, since certain crimes (e.g., auto theft) occur potentially in view of patrolling police officers, if the police are able to come upon the scene during the time it takes to commit the crime, then an arrest can be effected. If, in addition, their patrol procedures can be kept random, then the offenders will not be able to predict where the patrol officers might be and thus would be liable to arrest at a rate determined by the parameters of the situation.

For most crimes visible from the street (e.g., purse snatches, car thefts, street robberies), however, the time of commission is fairly short, resulting in a fairly low probability of on-site apprehension; based on New York City data, Riccio [1974] estimated it to be about 0.00004. Furthermore, a key assumption is that the commission of the crime and the arrival of the police car are independent events, which is not always the case: an offender may be able to see the patrol car from a distance, or s/he may alternatively wait until the patrol car has turned the corner before s/he begins to commit the crime.

Although computerization of the police command-and-control system (or police dispatch procedure) is both useful and appropriate for police departments – after all, policing is one of the most information-intensive enterprises – selling it primarily on the basis of increased arrest probabilities was not. The studies suggesting this connection ignored the fact that the calls were a biased sample[34], and that what is important is not necessarily dispatching an officer as quickly as possible so much as what he/she does upon arrival. For example, the data may have merely been showing that aggressive officers (who normally arrive at the scene more rapidly) also do a better job of making arrests; Clawson & Chang [1977] found a similar relationship in Seattle, but suggested that 'both police dispatchers and responding officers are able to instinctively sense which calls have

---

early 1970s. During a 1970 May Day protest in Washington, DC, I remember *looking down on* military helicopters from my vantage point on the tenth floor of an office building on Indiana Avenue, as they tried to herd protesters down the streets by spreading tear gas with their prop wash. Whatever its utility in the rice paddies of Vietnam, this tactic was neither appropriate nor effective in the concrete canyons of the nation's capitol.

[33] The authors of the study were aware of its limitations, stating that 'the evidence does not directly imply that faster response time will result in more arrests'; they called for a controlled experiment to test this hypothesis.

[34] The primary study refuting this connection, the Kansas City Response Time Analysis [Kansas City, 1977], criticized other studies for their data and analysis deficiencies, but this study also suffered from many of the same deficiencies [see Larson & Cahn, 1981].

a high probability of resulting in an arrest and thus react quicker to these calls'. These and other possible explanations of response-related findings helped to inject a note of reality into the claims made by hardware purveyors.

Another attempt to use stochastic methods in police departments was tried in Edina, Minnesota [Bennett, 1970]. Here, however, the goal was to reduce police response time by pre-positioning officers in various areas of the city using prior probabilities of having calls for service in different areas. An experimental design was employed (i.e., experimental and control beats were selected), the prior year's data provided a benchmark for average response time (about seven minutes for both experimental and control areas), and the experiment was run. In one sense the experiment was a success: the response time in the experimental areas dropped from seven to about three minutes. However, the same reduction in response time was recorded for the control areas! What this appeared to have proved is that, when unequivocal goals are given to police officers – reducing response time is much easier to operationalize and effect than 'serving and protecting' the public – they can meet them. It also pointed out one of the difficulties of doing true experiments in field settings, especially when competition may be engendered between the experimental and control groups.

Patrol strategies of this type have a number of limitations that can be clarified using appropriate models. One such model was developed by Larson [1975] in his critique of one of the most well-known experiments in police patrol, the Kansas City Preventive Patrol Experiment [Kelling, Pate, Dieckmann & Brown, 1974]. The fifteen beats in one section of the city were assigned to one of three conditions, five beats each: control, within which patrol would continue as in the past; reactive patrol, in which there would be no 'routine preventive patrol', cars entering these beats only in response to calls for service; and proactive patrol, which were to have two to three times the normal level of patrol visibility. The exhaustive analysis found that there was little difference among the three types of patrol, leading to a number of questions about the heretofore taken-for-granted effectiveness of preventive patrol.

Based on fairly simple assumptions, Larson developed an equation for the frequency f with which a patrol car would pass a randomly selected point in the beat:

$$f = Ns(1 - b)/D,$$

where N is the number of cars in the beat, s is the average speed of the car, b is the fraction of time the car is busy on calls for service, and D is the number of street miles in the beat. Based on this model, he estimated that the range of patrol coverage was too limited to actually test the efficacy of preventive patrol. He also estimated the number of miles that a reactive patrol car would spend servicing calls in its beat, and showed that during busy periods there is little difference in terms of patrol presence between a reactive beat and a control beat. Thus, the models showed that, although there was supposed to be a great deal of variation in the amount of time that officers spent in different beats, operational considerations limited this difference severely. We see, then, that models of the patrol process, based on realistic conditions, can be of significant benefit in developing and testing patrol strategies.

Models can also be used to determine the extent of crime deterrence provided by a patrol unit [Riccio, 1974] or to ensure that patrol units are deployed to reduce response time. In addition, they can be used to estimate the extent of patrol coverage provided different parts of the city if workloads of the beat cars are known. Larson [1972] uses a more sophisticated version of this model for that purpose.

Investigation of response time is also useful in a prison context. Dessent [1987] developed a model of the penetration of a prison perimeter which contains a number of different types of barriers or detection devices. Its primary benefit is in identifying combinations of barriers and devices that are worth more detailed examination.

9.3. The police investigation process

The police investigation process is far removed from the keen-eyed analytic activity portrayed in fiction. The sheer volume of cases makes it all but impossible for detectives to spend the time to investigate each case fully [Greenwood, Chaiken & Petersilia, 1977]. This is not to say that some cases are not investigated in the manner portrayed by fictional detectives. As suggested earlier, however, their approach is more inductive, based on empirical knowledge, rather than deductive.

In a seminal book, Willmer [1970] considered the investigation process as one of attempting to reduce the set of possible suspects by increasing the amount of information and therefore reducing the amount of uncertainty or entropy. He also introduced decision theory and game theory into the development of strategies for investigating crimes, and developed a Poisson formulation for individuals committing crimes, which he then used to estimate the number of offenders in a jurisdiction. Many of the models and methods described herein were built on these concepts. Both Greene & Stollmack [1981] and Riccio & Finkelstein [1985] based their estimation of the number of offenders on such models.

9.4. White-collar and organized crime

Relatively little work has been done in the application of operations research and management science to white-collar and organized crime. It would seem that this area would be quite fruitful, since OR and MS are both business-oriented, and these types of crimes are at the intersection of crime and business.

Maltz [1976] developed a model of the cigarette smuggling process to determine the effect of differential tax rates on the cigarette smuggling process. The model assumed that the amount of smuggling from state i to state j was based on the population of state j, the tax difference (smuggling occurs only if $t_j - t_i$ is positive), and the distance between their borders. This model was later applied [Maltz, 1981] to estimating the effect of a cigarette tax increase; since it estimated both the increase in revenue and the increase in smuggling, it showed how the state could in essence set the level of cigarette smuggling that would be generated by adjusting its tax rate.

The stochastic properties of bidding data were analyzed by Maltz & Pollock [1980a] to infer collusion among bidders. Although their study developed no models, it presented the data in such a way (by displaying the cumulative distribution of bids) that it graphically depicted clear evidence of collusion.

Maltz [1990] employed graph theoretic concepts in developing measures to evaluate organized crime enforcement efforts. Since the essence of organized crime is that individual crimes are in some way connected, the extent of their connectivity could be used to determine if there was sufficient evidence from separate crimes to warrant labeling the crimes as part of an organized crime enterprise.

Caulkins [1993] developed a model of patterns of consumption of illegal drugs to consider the efficacy of 'zero tolerance' to drug crimes, a policy that enforces the anti-drug laws irrespective of the quantity of drugs involved in the crime. Although this policy may be predicated on minimizing the number of users, Caulkins shows that a punishment policy that is proportional to quantity reduces overall drug consumption.

10. Jury fairness and administration

The Sixth Amendment of the US Constitution guarantees every person accused of a crime the right to a 'speedy and public trial, by an impartial jury of the State and the district wherein the crime shall have been committed'. But this rhetoric does not hold with the reality: in most jurisdictions, the great majority of criminal cases are disposed of through plea bargaining. Although the right still exists, it is used more as a bargaining chip than as a normal means of dealing with a criminal case. Defendants fear that standing on this right could result in a harsher penalty if convicted – or hope that relinquishing this right will result in a shorter penalty. Yet the court system must be ready to empanel juries for any given criminal trial, should a defendant so request it.

A number of problems related to juries have been investigated using operations research. These include the elimination of intentional bias in empaneling juries; considerations related to *increasing* bias in a jury by using peremptory challenges; and studies relating to the reduction of juror waiting time and the cost of empaneling juries.

10.1. Biases in empaneling the jury

In the past, jury duty was so onerous a burden that many people used whatever means they could to get out of it. Some individuals did not register to vote, so that their names would not appear on registers from which the names of prospective jurors were pulled. Others claimed hardships because of the low fees paid jurors and the long time they might have to sit: twenty years ago it was not uncommon to have terms of service for jurors that exceeded one month [Munsterman & Pabst, 1976]. The economic burden of jury service was considerable in some jurisdictions, which was the main reason that individuals tried to avoid jury service.[35]

The juries of that time, therefore, had certain biases built in, by virtue of the means people took to avoid serving. In some jurisdictions they had more insidious biases built in, by virtue of rules that had the effect of keeping blacks from serving. Challenges to the existing system of empaneling jurors led to a mandate for the development of new procedures that would be fair. In essence, the call was for a procedure that would ensure that every eligible citizen would have essentially the same probability of being called for jury service [Kairys, Kadane & Lehoczky, 1977]. Since no person is to be chosen twice for the same panel, a better plan would be to ensure that, if n names are to be selected from a master list of L individuals, then each subset of d names has a probability of selection of

$$\frac{\binom{n}{d}}{\binom{L}{d}}, \qquad d = 1, 2, \ldots, n.$$

Kadane & Lehoczky [1976] considered the problem of obtaining a master list of potential jurors by combining different overlapping lists – e.g., of voters, those holding drivers licenses, utility customers – into a master list such that each individual found on at least one of the lists would be as probable as any other individual to be selected, regardless of the number of lists on which each was found. The simplest method, of course, is merely to merge all lists into one and eliminate all duplicates. As they point out, however, this list would have to be updated whenever a new sample is required; and the individual lists become obsolete at different times, which may require frequent recompilation of the master list.

They investigated this method as well as a number of other methods for generating lists and estimated the costs and flexibility of each procedure. Based on their analysis, it appears that the following method holds the most promise if the cost of checking names is the same for all lists:

> The k lists are ordered by size, with $n_i > n_{i+1}$, where n_i is the number of names on list i. List i is selected with probability n_i/N (where N is the sum of the n_i-values). A name is randomly selected from this list, and frames $i - 1, i - 2, \ldots,$ 1 are checked sequentially. If the name is found on one of these lists, then it is discarded; otherwise it is added to the sample.

If the cost of checking a list varies from list to list, then this ordering of the lists does not result in the lowest cost. The optimal order cannot be calculated easily,

---

[35] Pabst & Munsterman [1978] cited the case of a woman in the District of Columbia who served six terms on a jury, while few of her friends had ever been called. Despite this apparent inequity, they showed that the statistics of jury service generally followed a Poisson distribution, because drawing a sample of jurors at the time was normally done with replacement.

but a rule of thumb appears to be to order the lists according to the unit cost of checking a name [Kadane & Lehoczky, 1976].

The problems inherent in implementing such a system in San Diego County are detailed in Munsterman, Mount & Pabst [1978].

10.2. Intentional biasing of juries: the peremptory challenge

The ability of both prosecution and defense lawyers to make peremptory challenges of jurors (i.e., arbitrarily exclude a prescribed number of prospective jurors from serving on the jury) leads directly to a sequential decision process: given the *a priori* probabilities of each potential juror voting for conviction (based on the two lawyers' estimates, which may be different), and given the characteristics of the process (how many challenges each side has, who goes first, etc.), what is the strategy that minimizes (for the defense; or maximizes, for the prosecutor) the *a priori* probability of conviction?

Brams & Davis [1978] considered the situation in which both sides have the same assessments of jurors' probabilities. The probability distribution for the population in question is known beforehand, but the value for each individual is not known until his/her interview. With this situation they show that both sides will never challenge the same person and that the defense is generally favored as the number of challenges and/or the size of the jury increases.

Roth, Kadane, & DeGroot [1977] assume that each side assigns a different probability to each prospective juror, but also that each side knows the value the other side has assigned. Both sides are also assumed to know the joint distribution of the two probabilities in the population. They show that optimal strategies exist for both sides, and that in some cases it does not matter which sides have the first challenge. They also provide an algorithm for finding the optimal strategy. In a related paper, DeGroot & Kadane [1980] show that there always exists an optimal sequence of decisions, and describe the circumstances under which it is and is not advantageous to go first.

10.3. Jury simulations

Waiting in a courthouse to be called to sit on a jury is greeted by most prospective jurors with the excitement usually reserved for visits to the dentist [Pabst, Munsterman & Mount, 1976]. In an effort to minimize the amount of waiting around, simulations of the jury selection process have been developed. Broadhurst [1977] used empirical data to fit parameters with different distributions. He approximated the duration of the *voir dire* (interview of jurors by attorneys from both sides) and the trial by lognormal distributions and the number of trial starts by a Poisson distribution, and then showed, for specific situations (e.g., number of courtrooms, number in the jury pool), the extent to which a reduction in the pool size affected the likelihood of a delay in starting a trial. A microcomputer-based jury management simulation was subsequently developed by Martin & Fuerst [1986].

11. Conclusion

This chapter has reviewed the many applications of operations research and management science to problems of crime and justice. As has been shown, the applications have been both considerable and successful. The systematic, quantitative thinking exemplified by these approaches to problem-solving has been very effective in helping to improve the administration of criminal justice, and it is likely that this effort will continue.

As more and more of the data problems are overcome in criminal justice, we will be awash in an even greater 'avalanche of printed numbers' remarked on by Hacking [1990], but numbers which will be far more amenable to analysis than in the past. It would appear most likely that the future for such analyses is very bright indeed, funding permitting.

This qualification is far from a minor concern. Although successes have been forthcoming, very little money has been devoted to this research. Politicians continue to seek votes by promising to 'get tough on crime', but what it usually translates to is adding another crime to the list of crimes for which the death penalty may be imposed, or increasing the sentences for other crimes; rare is the politician who says, 'What we have been trying does not seem to be working, since crime continues to increase; perhaps we should try to understand why this is so.'

The amount of money devoted to Federal research on crime and criminal justice, as Petersilia [1991] points out, is about thirteen cents per capita, compared to about $32 per capita for health. And the needs are great, not just for mathematical modeling, but for finding out what works (or more correctly, under what conditions and to what extent a program works). To study the effectiveness of a new police tactic or a new correctional program is a worthwhile activity, but research of this type costs a great deal of time and money, leaving even less for mathematical modeling or operations research. Considering these realities, it is even more impressive what OR/MS has accomplished in this field of inquiry.

Keeping this qualification in mind, one can foresee the need to develop better means of handling the streams of data. Mathematical models are one way of coming to grips with them [Hodges, 1991]. It might also be expected that, although analytic models will continue to be developed to provide the insight into crime and justice problems, more efforts will be devoted to understanding the data using maps and other graphical or pictorial techniques. The development of new analytic models might then be based on insights gained from being able to visually infer patterns in the data.

In addition, it is likely that more realistic models of offender behavior will be developed, recognizing that different offenders can be subject to different causal mechanisms. With the increases in data that are inevitable, it may be possible to develop multiple models, that would more closely reflect the multiplicity of human behaviors that manifest themselves criminally.

Patterns of offending may also reflect responses to criminal justice actions. Crime displacement [Barr & Pease, 1990; Maltz, 1972] may result from enforcement activity. More generally, it may be possible to model the decisions of offenders; Clarke & Cornish [1985] and Cornish & Clarke [1986] point the way to consideration of the 'rational offender' as a construct that may have some utility in crime-prevention research.

The implicit assumption in many prior studies of crime (and police deployment in response to crime) is that crimes and calls for service are stochastic processes. Although this model may serve adequately for many purposes, the validity of this assumption should be ascertained. As with organized crimes, it may well be that street crimes are interconnected in ways that would make them more amenable to prevention and/or deterrence. Investigating the 'fine structure' of criminal activity to find and model patterns may yield benefits in terms of crime reductions that are not possible using more traditional methods of analysis.

These other perspectives are bound to enrich criminological research. New insights, coupled with the expectation of increasing amounts of data, mean that one person, with one set of analytic tools and one disciplinary focus, will not be adequate to the task of model development. More and more will there be the necessity of team approaches to data analysis, so that teams of operations researchers, police, court and correctional personnel, social scientists, and administrators learn from each other and develop multi-disciplinary approaches and models that advance our understanding of one of the major social problems of our time.

Acknowledgements

I am indebted to Arnold Barnett, Jacqueline Cohen, David Farrington, Joseph Kadane, Richard Larson, Thomas Munsterman, Stephen Pollock and Roger Tarling, for directing me to relevant research and for their advice and comments on earlier versions of this chapter. Any mistakes and omissions in the chapter, however, remain mine.

References

Ahn, C.W., A. Blumstein, and M. Schervish (1990). Estimation of arrest careers using hierarchical stochastic models. *J. Quant. Criminol.* 6(2), 131–152.

Aitchison, J., and J.A.C. Brown (1963). *The Lognormal Distribution*, Cambridge University Press, Cambridge.

Avi-Itzhak, B., and R. Shinnar (1973). Quantitative models in crime control. *J. Crim. Justice* 1(3), 185–217.

Barlow, R., and F. Proschan (1975). *Statistical Theory of Reliability and Life Testing: Probability Models*, Holt, Rinehart and Winston, New York.

Barnett, A. (1978). Crime and capital punishment: Some recent studies. *J. Crim. Justice* 6, 291–303.

Barnett, A. (1981a). The deterrent effect of capital punishment: A test of some recent studies. *Oper. Res.* 29, 346–370.

Barnett, A. (1981b). Further standards of accountability in deterrence research, in: Fox [1981a], pp. 127–145.

Barnett, A. (1982). Learning to live with homicide. *J. Crim. Justice* 10(1), 69–72.

Barnett, A. (1983a). The capital punishment controversy: Part I. *Interfaces* 13(3), 24–28.

Barnett, A. (1983b). The capital punishment controversy: Part II. *Interfaces* 13(5), 35–39.

Barnett, A. (1987). Prison populations: A projection model. *Oper. Res.* 35(1), 18–34.

Barnett, A., A. Blumstein, J. Cohen and D. Farrington (1992). Not all criminal career models are equally valid. *Criminology* 30, 133–140.

Barnett, A., A. Blumstein and D. Farrington (1987). Probabilistic models of youthful criminal careers. *Criminology* 25, 83–108.

Barnett, A., A. Blumstein and D. Farrington (1989). A prospective test of a criminal career model. *Criminology* 27, 373–385.

Barnett, A., E. Essenfeld and D. Kleitman (1980). Urban homicide: Some recent developments. *J. Crim. Justice* 8, 379–385.

Barnett, A., D. Kleitman and R.C. Larson (1975). On urban homicide: A statistical analysis. *J. Crim. Justice* 3, 85–110.

Barnett, A., and A.J. Lofaso (1985). Selective incapacitation and the Philadelphia cohort data. *J. Quant. Criminol.* 1(1), 3–36.

Barnett, A., and A.J. Lofaso (1986). On the optimal allocation of prison space, in: A.J. Swersey (ed.), *Delivery of Urban Services*, TIMS Series in the Management Sciences, Vol. 22, Elsevier North-Holland, Amsterdam, pp. 245–268.

Barnett, A., and E. Schwartz (1989). Urban homicide: Still the same. *J. Quant. Criminol.* 5(1), 83–100.

Barr, R., and K. Pease (1990). Crime placement, displacement, and deflection, in: M. Tonry, and N. Morris (eds.), *Crime and Justice: A Review of Research, Vol. 12*, University of Chicago Press, Chicago, IL, pp. 277–318.

Barton, R.R., and B. Turnbull (1979). Evaluation of recidivism data: Use of failure rate regression models. *Evaluation Quart.* 3, 629–641.

Barton, R.R., and B. Turnbull (1981). A failure rate regression model for the study of recidivism, in: Fox [1981b], pp. 81–101.

Becker, G.S. (1967). Crime and punishment: An economic approach. *J. Political Econom.* 78, 526–536.

Belkin, J., A. Blumstein and W. Glass (1973). Recidivism as a feedback process: An analytical model and empirical validation. *J. Crim. Justice* 1, 7–26.

Belkin, J., A. Blumstein, W. Glass and M. Lettre (1972). JUSSIM, an interactive computer program and its uses in criminal justice planning. *Proc. Internat. Symp. Criminal Justice Information and Statistics Systems*, Project SEARCH, Sacramento, CA., pp. 467–477.

Bennett, W. (1970). *The Use of Probability Theory in the Assignment of Police Patrol Areas*, US Government Printing Office, Washington, DC.

Berecochea, J.E., A.N. Himelson and D.E. Miller (1972). The risk of failure during the early parole period: A methodological note. *J. Crim. Law, Criminol. Police Sci.* 63(1), 93–97.

Berk, R.A., S.L. Messinger, D. Rauma and J.E. Berecochea (1983). Prisons as self-regulating systems: A comparison of historical patterns in California for male and female offenders. *Law Soc. Rev.* 17(4), 547–586.

Berk, R.A., D. Rauma, S.L. Messinger and T.F. Cooley (1981). A test of the stability of punishment hypothesis: The case of California, 1851–1970. *Amer. Sociol. Rev.* 45, 805–829.

Beyleveld, D. (1982). Ehrlich's analysis of deterrence. *Br. J. Criminol.* 22, 101–123.

Bloch, A. (1977). *Murphy's Law and Other Reasons Why Things Go Wrong*, Price/Stern/Sloan Publishers, Los Angeles, CA.

Block, C.R. (1989). *Spatial and Temporal Analysis of Crime: Users Manual and Technical Manual*, Illinois Criminal Justice Information Authority, Chicago, IL.

Block, C.R., and C. Van der Werff (1991). *Initiation and Continuation of a Criminal Career: Who Are the Most Active and Dangerous Offenders in the Netherlands?* Ministry of Justice, WODC, The Hague.

Bloom, H.S. (1979). Evaluating human service and criminal justice programs by modeling the probability and timing of recidivism. *Sociol. Meth. Res.* 8, 179–208.

Bloom, H.S., and N.M. Singer (1979). Determining the cost-effectiveness of correctional programs: The case of patuxent institution. *Evaluation Quart.* 3(4), 609–627.

Blumstein, A. (1974). Seriousness weights in an index of crime. *Amer. Sociol. Rev.* 39, 854–864.

Blumstein, A. (1983). Selective incapacitation as a means of crime control. *Amer. Behavior. Scient.* 27, 87–108.

Blumstein, A. (1988). Prison populations: A system out of control? in: N. Morris, and M. Tonry (eds.), *Crime and Justice: An Annual Review of Research, Vol. 10*, University of Chicago Press, Chicago, IL, pp. 231–266.

Blumstein, A., J.A. Canela-Cacho and J. Cohen (1993). Filtered sampling from populations with heterogeneous event frequencies. *Management Sci.* 39(7), 886–899.

Blumstein, A., and J. Cohen (1973). A theory of the stability of punishment. *J. Crim. Law, Criminol. Police Sci.* 63(2), 198–207.

Blumstein, A., and J. Cohen (1979). Estimating of individual crime rates from arrest records. *J. Crim. Law Criminol.* 70(4), 561–585.

Blumstein, A., and J. Cohen (1987). Characterizing criminal careers. *Science* 238(4818), 985–991.

Blumstein, A., J. Cohen, S. Das and S.D. Moitra (1988). Specialization and seriousness during adult criminal careers. *J. Quant. Criminol.* 4(4), 303–345.

Blumstein, A., J. Cohen and D.P. Farrington (1988a). Criminal career research: Its value for criminology. *Criminology* 26(1), 1–35.

Blumstein, A., J. Cohen and D.P. Farrington (1988b). Criminal career research: Further clarifications. *Criminology* 26(1), 57–74.

Blumstein, A., J. Cohen and H. Miller (1980). Demographically disaggregated projections of prison populations. *J. Crim. Justice* 8(1), 1–25.

Blumstein, A., J. Cohen, S. Moitra and D. Nagin (1981). On testing the stability of punishment hypothesis: A reply. *J. Crim. Law Criminol.* 72(4), 1799–1808.

Blumstein, A., J. Cohen and D. Nagin (1976). The dynamics of a homeostatic punishment process. *J. Crim. Law Criminol.* 67(3), 317–334.

Blumstein, A., J. Cohen and D. Nagin (eds.) (1978). *Deterrence and Incapacitation: Estimating the Effects of Criminal Sanctions on Crime Rates*, National Academy of Sciences, Washington, DC.

Blumstein, A., J. Cohen, J.A. Roth and C.A. Visher (eds.) (1986). *Criminal Careers and 'Career Criminals', Vols. I and II*, National Academy Press, Washington, DC.

Blumstein, A., D.P. Farrington and S. Moitra (1985). Delinquency careers: Innocents, desisters, and persisters, in: M. Tonry, and N. Morris (eds.), *Crime and Justice: An Annual Review of Research, Vol. 6*, University of Chicago Press, Chicago, IL, pp. 187–219.

Blumstein, A., and R.C. Larson (1967). A systems approach to the study of crime and criminal justice, in: P.M. Morse, and L. Bacon (eds.), *Operations Research for Public Systems*, MIT Press, Cambridge, MA, pp. 159–180.

Blumstein, A., and R.C. Larson (1969). Models of a total criminal justice system. *Oper. Res.* 17(2), 219–232.

Blumstein, A., and R.C. Larson (1971). Problems in modeling and measuring recidivism. *J. Res. Crime Delinquency* 8, 124–132.

Blumstein, A., and S. Moitra (1979). An analysis of the time series of the imprisonment rate in the States of the United States: A further test of the stability of punishment hypothesis. *J. Crim. Law Criminol.* 70(3), 376–390.

Blumstein, A., and S. Moitra (1980). The identification of 'career criminals' from 'chronic offenders' in a cohort. *Law Policy Quart.* 2, 321–334.

Blumstein, A., and D. Nagin (1978). On the optimum use of incarceration for crime control. *Oper. Res.* 26(3), 381, 403. [reprinted (with modifications) in Fox [1981b], 39–59].

Boag, J.W. (1949). Maximum likelihood estimates of the proportion of patients cured by cancer therapy. *J. Roy. Statist. Soc.* 11, 15–53.

Bowers, W.J., and G.L. Pierce (1975). The illusion of deterrence in Isaac Ehrlich's research on capital punishment. *Yale Law J.* 85, 187–208.

Brams, S.J., and M.D. Davis (1978). Optimal jury selection: A game-theoretic model for the exercise of peremptory challenges. *Oper. Res.* 26, 966–991.

Brantingham, P., and P. Brantingham (1984). *Patterns in Crime*, Macmillan, New York.

Brantingham, P.J., D.A. Dyreson and P.L. Brantingham (1976). Crime seen through a cone of resolution. *Amer. Behavior. Scient.* 20, 261–273.

Broadhurst, R., and R. Maller (1991). Estimating the numbers of prison terms in criminal careers from the one-step probabilities of Recidivism. *J. Quant. Criminol.* 7, 275–290.

Broadhurst, R., R. Maller, M. Maller and J. Duffecy (1988). Aboriginal and non-aboriginal recidivism in Western Australia: A failure-rate analysis. *J. Res. Crime Delinquency* 25, 83–108.

Broadhurst, R.H. (1977). A simulation to improve juror utilization. *Jurimetrics J.* 17, 314–331.

Brounstein, S.H., and M. Kamrass (eds.) (1976). *Operations Research in Law Enforcement, Justice, and Societal Security*, Lexington Books, Lexington, MA.

Capone, D., and W.J. Nichols (1976). Urban structure and criminal mobility. *Amer. Behavior. Scient.* 20, 199–213.

Carr-Hill, G.A., and R.A. Carr-Hill (1972). Reconviction as a process. *Br. J. Criminol.* 12, 35–43.

Cassidy, R.G. (1985). Modelling a criminal justice system, in: Farrington & Tarling [1985], pp. 193–207.

Caulkins, J.P. (1993). Zero-tolerance policies: Do they inhibit or stimulate drug consumption? *Management Sci.* 39(4), 458–476.

Chaiken, J., T. Crabill, L. Holliday, D. Jaquette, M. Lawless and E. Quade (1975). Criminal justice models: An overview, Report R-1859-DOJ, The Rand Corporation, Santa Monica, CA.

Chaiken, J.M., and M.R. Chaiken (1982). Varieties of criminal behavior, Report R-2814-NIJ, The Rand Corporation, Santa Monica, CA.

Chaiken, J.M., and J.E. Rolph (1980). Selective incapacitation strategies based on estimated crime rates. *Oper. Res.* 28(6), 1259–1274.

Cherlin, A. (1991). Will young single women ever marry? The strange career of a statistical projection. *Chance* 4(1), 11–15.

Chevalier, L. (1973). *Laboring classes and dangerous classes in Paris during the first half of the nineteenth century*, Princeton University Press, Princeton, NJ. [Translation (by F. Jellinek) of *Classes Laborieuses et Classes Dangereuses à Paris Pendant la Première Moitié du XIXe Siècle*, Librairie Plon, Paris, 1958].

Christensen, R. (1967). Projected percentage of U.S. population with criminal arrest and conviction records, Appendix J (pp. 216–228) of Science and Technology Task Force Report (1967).

Clarke, R.V., and D.B. Cornish (1985). Modeling offenders' decisions: A framework for policy and research, in: M. Tonry, and N. Morris (eds.), *Crime and Justice: An Annual Review of Research, Vol. 6*, University of Chicago Press, Chicago, IL, pp. 147–185.

Clawson, C., and S.K. Chang (1977). The relationship of response delays and arrest rates. *J. Police Sci. Administration* 5, 53–68.

Chung, C.-F., P. Schmidt and A. Witte (1990). Survival analysis: A survey. *J. Quant. Criminol.* 7(1), 59–98.

Cohen, J. (1978). The incapacitative effect of imprisonment: A critical review of the literature, in: A. Blumstein, J. Cohen and D. Nagin (eds.), *Deterrence and Incapacitation: Estimating the Effects of Criminal Sanctions on Crime Rates*, National Academy of Sciences, Washington, DC, pp. 187–243.

Cohen, J. (1983). Incapacitation as a strategy for crime control: Possibilities and pitfalls, in: M. Tonry, and N. Morris (eds.), *Crime and Justice: An Annual Review of Research, Vol. 5*, University of Chicago Press, Chicago, IL, pp. 1–84.

Cohen, J. (1986). Research on criminal careers; Individual frequency rates and offense seriousness, Appendix B, in: Blumstein, Cohen, Roth & Visher [1986], Volume I, 292–418.

Cohn, E.G., and D.P. Farrington (1990). Differences between British and American criminology: An analysis of citations. *Br. J. Criminol.* 30, 467–482.

Collins, M.F., and R.M. Wilson (1990). Automobile theft: Estimating the size of the criminal population. *J. Quant. Criminol.* 6(4), 395–409.

Copas, J.B., and R. Tarling (1986). Some methodological issues in making predictions, in: Blumstein, Cohen, Roth & Visher [1986] Vol. II, pp. 291–313.

Copas, J.B., and R. Tarling (1988). Stochastic models for analyzing criminal careers. *J. Quant. Criminol.* 4(2), 173–186.

Cornish, D.B., and R.V. Clarke (1986). *The Reasoning Criminal*, Springer-Verlag, New York.

Cox, D.R., and V. Isham (1980). *Point Processes*, Chapman and Hall, London.

Cox, D.R., and D. Oakes (1984). *Analysis of Survival Data*, Chapman and Hall, London.

Daston, L. (1988). *Classical Probability in the Enlightenment*, Princeton University Press, Princeton, NJ.

DeGroot, M.H., S.E. Fienberg and J.B. Kadane (eds.) (1986). *Statistics and the Law*, Wiley, New York.

DeGroot, M.H., and J.B. Kadane (1980). Optimal challenges for selection. *Oper. Res.* 28, 952–968.

Dessent, G.H. (1987). Prison perimeter cost-effectiveness. *J. Oper. Res. Soc.* 38(10), 975–980.

Eck, J.E., and L.J. Riccio (1979). Relationship between reported crime rates and victimization survey results: An empirical and analytical study. *J. Crim. Justice* 7, 293–308.

Ehrlich, I. (1975). The deterrent effect of capital punishment: A question of life and death. *Amer. Econom. Rev.* 65, 397–417.

Ellerman, R., P. Sullo and J.M. Tien (1992). An alternative approach to modeling recidivism using quantile residual life functions. *Oper. Res.* 40, 485–504.

Elliott, J.F. (1968). Random patrol. *Police* 13(2), 51–55.

Elliott, J.F., and T. Sardino (1971). *Intercept Patrol*, Charles C. Thomas, Springfield, IL.

Farrington, D.P., and J.D. Hawkins (1991). Predicting participation, early onset and later persistence in officially recorded offending. *Crim. Behavior Mental Health* 1, 1–33.

Farrington, D.P., H.N. Snyder and T.A. Finnegan (1988). Specialization in juvenile court careers. *Criminology* 26, 461–487.

Farrington, D.P., and R. Tarling (eds.) (1985). *Prediction in Criminology*, State University of New York Press, Albany, NY.

Figlio, R.M. (1981). Delinquency careers as a simple Markov process, in: Fox [1981b], pp. 25–37.

Finkelstein, M.O. (1978). *Quantitative Methods in Law*, Free Press, New York.

Fisher, F.M., and D. Nagin (1978). On the feasibility of identifying the crime function in a simultaneous model of crime rates and sanction levels, in: Blumstein, Cohen & Nagin [1978], pp. 361–399.

Fox, J.A. (1978). *Forecasting Crime Data*, D.C. Heath, Lexington, MA.

Fox, J.A. (ed.) (1981a). *Methods in Quantitative Criminology*, Academic Press, New York.

Fox, J.A. (ed.) (1981b). *Models in Quantitative Criminology*, Academic Press, New York.

Gerchak, Y. (1983). Durations in social states: Concepts of inertia and related comparisons in stochastic models, in: S. Leinhardt (ed.), *Sociological Methodology 1983–1984*, Jossey-Bass, San Francisco, CA, pp. 194–224.

Gerchak, Y. (1984). Decreasing failure rates and related issues in the social sciences. *Oper. Res.* 32(3), 537–546.

Gerchak, Y., and P. Kubat (1986). Patterns and dynamics of population heterogeneity in mixtures models. *Quality Quantity* 120, 285–291.

Glueck, S., and E. Glueck (1950). *Unraveling Juvenile Delinquency*, Harvard University Press, Cambridge, MA.

Gottfredson, M., and T. Hirschi (1986). The true value of lambda would appear to be zero: An essay on career criminals, criminal careers, selective incapacitation, cohort studies, and related topics. *Criminology* 24(2), 213–234.

Gottfredson, M., and T. Hirschi (1987). The methodological adequacy of longitudinal research on crime. *Criminology* 25(4), 581–614.

Gottfredson, M., and T. Hirschi (1988). Science, public policy, and the career paradigm. *Criminology* 26(1), 37–56.

Gottfredson, M., and T. Hirschi (1989). A propensity-event theory of crime, in: W.S. Laufer, and F. Adler (eds.), *Advances in Criminological Theory*, Transaction Publishers, New Brunswick, NJ, pp.

57–67.

Gottfredson, M., and T. Hirschi (1990). *A General Theory of Crime*, Stanford University Press, Stanford, CA.

Gottfredson, M.R., and D.M. Gottfredson (1987). *Decision Making in Criminal Justice: Toward the Rational Exercise of Discretion, 2nd edition*, Plenum Press, New York.

Gottfredson, S.D., and D.M. Gottfredson (1986). Accuracy of prediction models, in: Blumstein, Cohen, Roth & Visher [1986] Vol. II, pp. 212–290.

Greenberg, D.F. (1975). The incapacitative effect of imprisonment: Some estimates. *Law Soc. Rev.* 9(4), 541–580.

Greenberg, D.F. (1977). The dynamics of oscillatory punishment processes. *J. Crim. Law, Criminol. Police Sci.* 68(4), 643–651.

Greenberg, D.F. (1978). Recidivism as radioactive decay. *J. Res. Crime Delinquency* 24, 124–125.

Greenberg, D.F. (1979). *Mathematical Criminology*, Rutgers University Press, New Brunswick, NJ.

Greenberg, D.F. (1991). Modeling criminal careers. *Criminology* 29(1), 17–46.

Greenberg, D.F. (1992). Comparing criminal career models. *Criminology* 30(1), 141–147.

Greene, M.A. (1984). Estimating the size of the criminal population using an open population approach. *Proceedings of the American Statistical Association*, Survey Research Methods Section, pp. 8–13.

Greene, M.A., and S. Stollmack (1981). Estimating the number of criminals, in: Fox [1981b], pp. 1–24.

Greenwood, P., and S. Turner (1987). Selective incapacitation revisited: Why the high-rate offenders are hard to predict, Report R-3397-NIJ, The Rand Corporation, Santa Monica, CA.

Greenwood, P.W., with A. Abrahamse (1982). Selective incapacitation, Report R-2815-NIJ, The Rand Corporation, Santa Monica, CA.

Greenwood, P.W., J.M. Chaiken and J. Petersilia (1977). *The Criminal Investigation Process*, Lexington Books, Lexington, MA.

Gross, A.J., and V.A. Clark (1975). *Survival Distributions: Reliability Applications in the Life Sciences*, Wiley, New York.

Gruenwald, P.J., and B. West (1989). Survival models of recidivism among juvenile delinquents. *J. Quant. Criminol.* 5(3), 215–229.

Hacking, I. (1990). *The Taming of Chance*, Cambridge University Press, Cambridge.

Harada, Y. (1991). Testing the 'stable criminality' hypothesis with Japanese data, Paper delivered at the 50th Meeting of the American Society of Criminology, San Francisco, CA, November 22, 1991.

Harries, K.D. (1980). *Crime and the Environment*, Charles C. Thomas, Springfield, IL.

Harries, K.D. (1990). *Geographic Factors in Policing*, Police Foundation, Washington, DC.

Harris, C.M., A.R. Kaylan and M.D. Maltz (1981). Recent advances in the statistics of recidivism measurement, in: Fox [1981b], pp. 61–79.

Harris, C.M., and S. Stollmack (1976). Failure-rate analysis in correctional systems, in: Brounstein & Kamrass [1976], pp. 143–153.

Hodges, J.S. (1991). Six (or so) things you can do with a bad model. *Oper. Res.* 39, 355–365.

Hoffman, P.B., and S. Adelberg (1980). The salient factor score: A nontechnical overview. *Federal Probation* 44, 44–52.

Hoffman, P.B., and J.L. Beck (1974). Parole decision-making: A salient factor score. *J. Crim. Justice* 2, 195–206.

Hser, Y.-I., M.D. Anglin, T.D. Wickens, M.-L. Brecht and J. Homer (1992). Techniques for the estimation of illicit drug-use prevalence, Research Report NCJ 133786, National Institute of Justice, Washington, DC.

Hwang, S.-A. (1990). Modeling the suppression effect of correctional programs on juvenile delinquency. *J. Quant. Criminol.* 6(4), 377–393.

Illinois Criminal Justice Information Authority (1991). Despite Improvements, Many Rap Sheets Still Missing Disposition Information. *Compiler*, spring issue, ICJIA, Chicago, IL, 3 pp.

Institute for Law and Justice (1991). *CJSSIM: Criminal Justice System Simulation Model*, Software and User Manual, Institute for Law and Justice, Alexandria, VA.

Jefferys, W.H., and J.O. Berger (1992). Ockham's razor and Bayesian analysis. *Amer. Scient.* 80, 64–72.

Kadane, J.B., and D. Kairys (1979). Fair numbers of peremptory challenges in jury trials. *J. Amer. Statist. Assoc.* 74, 747–753.

Kadane, J.B., and J.P. Lehoczky (1976). Random juror selection from multiple lists. *Oper. Res.* 24, 207–219.

Kairys, D., J.B. Kadane and J.P. Lehoczky (1977). Jury representativeness: A mandate for multiple source lists. *California Law Rev.* 65, 776–827 [reprinted in the record of a hearing before the Subcommittee on Improvements in Judicial Machinery of the Committee on the Judiciary, U.S. Senate, September 28, 1977].

Kalbfleisch, J.D., and R.L. Prentice (1980). *The Statistical Analysis of Failure Time Data*, Wiley, New York.

Kansas City, Missouri, Police Department (1977). *Response Time Analysis*, Kansas City, MO.

Kelling, G.L., T. Pate, D. Dieckmann and C.E. Brown (1974). *The Kansas City Preventive Patrol Experiment*, Police Foundation, Washington, DC.

Klein, L.R., B. Forst and V. Filatov (1978). The deterrent effect of capital punishment: An assessment of the estimates, in: Blumstein, Cohen & Nagin [1978], pp. 336–360.

Koopman, B.O. (1986). An empirical formula for visual search. *Oper. Res.* 34(3), 377–383.

Land, K.C. (1992). Models of criminal careers: Some suggestions for moving beyond the current debate. *Criminology* 30, 149–155.

Langan, P.A. (1991). America's soaring prison population. *Science* 251, 1568–1573.

Larson, R.C. (1972). *Urban Police Patrol Analysis*, MIT Press, Cambridge, MA.

Larson, R.C. (1975). What happened to patrol operations in Kansas City? A review of the Kansas City preventive patrol experiment. *J. Crim. Justice* 3, 267–297.

Larson, R.C., and M.F. Cahn (1981). Synthesizing and extending the results of police research studies, Final Project Report, Public Systems Evaluation, Inc. Cambridge, MA.

Lattimore, P.K., and J.R. Baker (1992). The impact of recidivism and capacity on prison populations: A projection model. *J. Quant. Criminol.* 8, 155–173.

Lehoczky, J.P. (1986). Random parameter stochastic-process models of criminal careers, in: Blumstein, Cohen, Roth & Visher [1986] Vol. II, pp. 380–404.

Maltz, M.D. (1972). *Evaluation of Crime Control Programs*, National Institute of Law Enforcement and Criminal Justice, US Department of Justice, Washington, DC.

Maltz, M.D. (1975a). Measures of effectiveness for crime reduction programs. *Oper. Res.* 23(3), 452–474.

Maltz, M.D. (1975b). Crime statistics: A mathematical perspective. *J. Crim. Justice* 3(3), 177–194.

Maltz, M.D. (1976). On the estimation of smuggling in a 'gray market' commodity. *Oper. Res.* 23(6), 1156–1163.

Maltz, M.D. (1977). Crime statistics: A historical perspective. *Crime Delinquency* 23(1), 32–40.

Maltz, M.D. (1980). Beyond suppression: More Sturm und Drang on the correctional front. *Crime Delinquency* 26(3), 389–397.

Maltz, M.D. (1981). Transportation modeling in analyzing an economic crime, in: Fox [1981a], pp. 77–97.

Maltz, M.D. (1984). *Recidivism*, Academic Press, Orlando, FL.

Maltz, M.D. (1990). *Measuring the Effectiveness of Organized Crime Control Efforts*, Office of International Criminal Justice, University of Illinois at Chicago, Chicago, IL.

Maltz, M.D., A.C. Gordon and W. Friedman (1990). *Mapping Crime in its Community Setting: Event Geography Analysis*, Springer-Verlag, New York.

Maltz, M.D., A.C. Gordon, D. McDowall and R. McCleary (1980). An artifact in pretest–posttest designs: How it can mistakenly make delinquency programs look effective. *Evaluation Rev.* 4(2), 225–240.

Maltz, M.D., and R. McCleary (1977). The mathematics of behavioral change: Recidivism and construct validity. *Evaluation Quart.* 1(3), 421–438.

Maltz, M.D., and R. McCleary (1978). Comments on 'stability of parameter estimates in the split-population exponential distribution'. *Evaluation Quart.* 2(4), 650–654.

Maltz, M.D., R. McCleary and S.M. Pollock (1979). Recidivism and likelihood functions: A reply to Stollmack. *Evaluation Quart.* 2(1), 124–131.

Maltz, M.D., and S.M. Pollock (1980a). Analyzing suspected collusion among bidders, in: G. Geis, and E. Stotland (eds.), *White-Collar Crime: Theory and Practice*, Sage Publications, Beverly Hills, CA, pp. 174–198.

Maltz, M.D., and S.M. Pollock (1980b). Artificial inflation of a delinquency rate by a selection artifact. *Oper. Res.* 28(3), 547–559.

Martin, M.P., and W.L. Fuerst (1986). A juror management simulation. *Justice Syst. J.* 11, 89–99.

Mason, W.M., and S.E. Fienberg (eds.) (1985). *Cohort Analysis in the Social Sciences: Beyond the Identification Problem*, Springer-Verlag, New York.

McEwen, J.T., and R. Guynes (1990). Criminal justice system simulation model (CJSSIM), Paper presented at the Annual Meeting of the American Society of Criminology, Baltimore, MD.

Monahan, J., and L. Walker (1984). *Social Science in Law: Cases and Materials*, Foundations Press, Mineola, NY.

Morgan, P.M. (1985). Modelling the criminal justice system, Home Office Research and Planning Unit Paper 35, Home Office, London.

Munsterman, G.T., C.H. Mount and W.R. Pabst (1978). *Multiple Lists for Jury Selection: A Case Study for the San Diego Superior Court*, US Government Printing Office, Washington, DC.

Munsterman, G.T., and W.R. Pabst Jr (1976). Differences in the economic burden of jury duty, in: Brounstein & Kamrass [1976], pp. 229–241.

Murray, C.A., and L.A. Cox Jr (1979). *Beyond Probation: Juvenile Corrections and the Chronic Delinquent*, Sage Publications, Beverly Hills, CA.

Nagin, D. (1978). General deterrence: A review of the empirical evidence, in: Blumstein, Cohen & Nagin [1978], pp. 95–139.

Nagin, D. (1981). Crime rates, sanction levels and constraints on prison population. *Law Soc. Rev.* 12(3), 341–366 [reprinted as: Methodological issues in estimating the deterrent effect of sanctions, in: Fox [1981b], pp. 121–140].

Nagin, D., and D.A. Smith. Participation in and frequency of delinquent behavior: A test for structural differences. *Criminology* 28, 335–356.

New York State Identification and Intelligence System (1967). *NYSIIS: System Development Plan*, NYSIIS, Albany, NY.

Orsagh, T. (1981). A criminometric model of the criminal justice system, in: Fox [1981b], pp. 163–187.

Pabst, W.R. Jr, and G.T. Munsterman (1978). Poisson distribution as a model of jury selection processes, Presented at the Meeting of the Criminal Justice Statistics Association, Minneapolis, MN, August 2–4.

Pabst, W.R. Jr, G.T. Munsterman and C.H. Mount (1976). The myth of the unwilling juror. *Judicature* 60, 164–171.

Partanen, J. (1969). On waiting time distributions. *Acta Sociologica* 112, 132–143.

Passell, P. (1975). The deterrent effect of the death penalty: A statistical test. *Stanford Law Rev.* 28, 61–80.

Petersilia, J. (1991). Policy relevance and the future of criminology. *Criminology* 29, 1–15.

Philpotts, G.J.O., and L.B. Lancucki (1979). *Previous Convictions, Sentence and Reconviction*, Home Office Research Study No. 53, Her Majesty's Stationery Office, London.

Pollock, S.M., and R.L. Farrell (1984). Past intensity of a terminated Poisson process. *Oper. Res. Lett.* 2, 261–263.

Porter, T.M. (1986). *The Rise of Statistical Thinking, 1820–1900*, Princeton University Press, Princeton, NJ.

President's Commission on Law Enforcement and Administration of Justice (1967). *The Challenge of Crime in a Free Society*, US Government Printing Office, Washington, DC.

Proschan, F. (1963). Theoretical explanation of observed decreasing failure rate. *Technometrics* 5, 375–383.

Pullinger, H. (1985). The criminal justice system model: The flow model, Home Office Research and Planning Unit Paper 36, Home Office, London.

Quetelet, L. Adolphe Jacques (1835). *A Treatise on Man* [Translated by S. Diamond, Scholars Facsimiles and Reprints, Gainesville, FL, (1969)].

Rauma, D. (1981a). Crime and punishment reconsidered: Some comments on Blumstein's stability of punishment hypothesis. *J. Crim. Law, Criminol. Police Sci.* 72(4), 1772–1798.

Rauma, D. (1981b). A concluding note on the stability of punishment: A reply to Blumstein, Cohen, Moitra and Nagin. *J. Crim. Law, Criminol. Police Sci.* 72(4), 1809–1812.

Reiss, A.J. Jr, and D.P. Farrington (1991). Advancing knowledge about co-offending: Results from a prospective longitudinal survey of London males. *J. Crim. Law Criminol.* 82, 360–395.

Rhodes, W. (1989). The criminal career: Estimates of the duration and frequency of crime commission. *J. Quant. Criminol.* 5(1), 3–32.

Riccio, L.J. (1974). Direct deterrence: An analysis of the effectiveness of police patrol and other crime prevention technologies. *J. Crim. Justice* 2(3), 207–217.

Riccio, L.J., and R. Finkelstein (1985). Using police arrest data to estimate the number of burglars operating in a suburban county. *J. Crim. Justice* 13, 65–73.

Rice, S. (1984). The criminal justice system model: Magistrates courts sub-model, Home Office Research and Planning Unit Paper 24, Home Office, London.

Rich, T., and A. Barnett (1985). Model-based U.S. prison population projections. *Public Administration Rev.* 45, 780–789.

Robinson, W.S. (1950). Ecological correlations and the behavior of individuals. *Amer. Sociol. Rev.* 15, 351–357.

Rolph, J.E., J.M. Chaiken and R.L. Houchens (1981). Methods for estimating crime rates of individuals, Report No. R-2730-NIJ, Rand Corporation, Santa Monica, CA.

Rossmo, D.K. (1990). Fugitive migration patterns, Paper presented at the Annual Meeting of the American Society of Criminology, Baltimore, MD.

Rossmo, D.K., and R. Routledge (1990). Estimating the size of criminal populations. *J. Quant. Criminol.* 6(3), 293–314.

Roth, A., J.B. Kadane and M.H. DeGroot (1977). Optimal peremptory challenges in trial by juries: A bilateral sequential process. *Oper. Res.* 25, 901–919.

Saks, M.J., and C.H. Baron (1980). *The Use/Nonuse/Misuse of Applied Social Science Research in the Courts*, Abt Books, Cambridge, MA.

Schmidt, P., and A.D. Witte (1988). *Predicting Recidivism Using Survival Methods*, Springer-Verlag, New York.

Science and Technology Task Force (1967). *Task Force Report: Science and Technology*, US Government Printing Office, Washington, DC.

Sellin, T., and M.E. Wolfgang (1964). *The Measurement of Delinquency*, Wiley, New York.

Shaw, C., and H. McKay (1969). *Juvenile Delinquency and Urban Areas*, University of Chicago Press, Chicago, IL.

Shinnar, R., and S. Shinnar (1975). The effects of the criminal justice system on the control of crime: A quantitative approach. *Law Soc. Rev.* 9(4), 581–611.

Shover, N., and C.Y. Thompson (1992). Age, differential crime expectations, and crime desistance. *Criminology* 30, 89–104.

Smith, T.S. (1976). Inverse distance variations for the flow of crime in urban areas. *Social Forces* 54, 804–815.

Stamp, Sir Josiah (1929). *Some Economic Factors in Modern Life*, P.S. King and Son, Ltd., London.

Stander, J., D.P. Farrington, G. Hill and P.M.E. Altham (1989). Markov chain analysis and specialization in criminal careers. *Br. J. Criminol.* 29(4), 317–335.

Stigler, S.M. (1986). *The History of Statistics: The Measurement of Uncertainty before 1900*, The Belknap Press of Harvard University Press, Cambridge, MA.

Stollmack, S. (1973). Predicting inmate population from arrest, court disposition, and recidivism rates. *J. Res. Crime Delinquency* 10, 141–162.

Stollmack, S., and C.M. Harris. Failure-rate analysis applied to recidivism data. *Oper. Res.* 22, 1192–1205.

Tarling, R. (1986). Statistical applications in criminology. *Statistician* 35, 369–388.

Tierney, L. (1983). A selection artifact in delinquency data revisited. *Oper. Res.* 31(5), 852–865.

Tittle, C.R. (1988). Two empirical regularities (maybe) in search of an explanation: Commentary on the age/crime debate. *Criminology* 26, 75–85.

Turnbull, B.W. (1976). The empirical distribution function with arbitrarily grouped, censored and truncated data. *J. Roy. Statist. Soc.* Series B 38(3), 290–295.

Visher, C.A. (1986). The rand inmate survey: A reanalysis, in: Blumstein, Cohen, Roth & Visher [1986], Vol. II, pp. 161–211.

Visher, C.A., and R.L. Linster (1990). A survival model of pretrial failure. *J. Quant. Criminol.* 6(2), 153–184.

Von Hirsch, A. (1985). *Past or Future Crimes: Deservedness and Dangerousness in the Sentencing of Criminals*, Rutgers University Press, New Brunswick, NJ.

Willmer, M.A.P. (1970). *Crime and Information Theory*, Edinburgh University Press, Edinburgh.

Wolfgang, M.E., R.M. Figlio and T. Sellin (1972). *Delinquency in a Birth Cohort*, University of Chicago Press, Chicago, IL.

Zimring, F.K., and G.J. Hawkins (1973). *Deterrence: The Legal Threat in Crime Control*, University of Chicago Press, Chicago, IL.

S.M. Pollock et al., Eds., *Handbooks in OR & MS, Vol. 6*
© 1994 Elsevier Science B.V. All rights reserved

Chapter 8

Energy Policy Applications of Operations Research

John P. Weyant

Department of Engineering - Economic Systems, Stanford University, Stanford, CA 94305-4025, U.S.A.

1. Introduction

World oil supply disruptions during the 1970s, deregulation of energy markets during the 1980s, and heightened environmental concerns during the 1990s have left us with a rich legacy of public sector applications of OR to energy sector issues. Moreover, the emergence of climate change as a critical global environmental concern and our unanticipated and unwanted experience with Desert Shield and Desert Storm ensure that energy/environmental policy will continue to be a rich and diverse OR application area.

This chapter is designed to provide the reader with an overview of the many applications of OR techniques to energy sector public policy issues. Although a number of individual policy issues and models will be mentioned, the objective here is to provide the reader with a feel for the types of analyses that have been completed, not the details of any one piece of analysis. Additional overviews of the energy policy modeling field include Manne, Richels & Weyant [1979], Moroney [1982] and Lev [1983].

There is also a liberal inclusion of economic concepts and analysis here. Some of the most interesting applications of OR methods in this area involve their use in combination with economic analysis. Analyses that are primarily economic in nature are not, however, included, as this would expand our scope greatly and could well take us outside the area of interest and expertise of our readers. Thus, analyses that primarily involve macroeconomic adjustments via unemployment and inflation or trade adjustments through terms of trade adjustments are not covered [see, e.g., EMF, 1984; Hickman, Huntington & Sweeney, 1987].

The chapter starts with a review of a number of basic concepts employed in many of the applications included in our review. The review itself is included in two main sections; one covering 'market models', the other covering 'decision-oriented' models. The market models section is in turn split into country and international models sections reflecting the differences in approaches required by those two types of models. The 'decision-oriented' models review is likewise divided into two sections; one covers models that optimize on a particular decision variable of interest and the other the use of market models in a decision analysis framework. We conclude the chapter with a discussion of emerging issues in energy policy and frontiers in energy policy modeling.

2. Basic concepts

In this section we describe seven basic concepts that are widely used in energy policy models. These concepts are employed in models used in most, if not all, of the application areas discussed subsequently. Thus, discussing these cross-cutting concepts first allows us to greatly economize on our model application review. The basic concepts discussed here are: (1) resource supply and depletion modeling; (2) price and non-price determinants of energy demand; (3) interfuel competition; (4) end-use modeling; (5) integrating energy supply and demand; (6) aggregate energy economy interactions; and (7) multi-sectoral energy economy interactions.

2.1. Resource supply and depletion

One concept represented in models that include resource supply is the idea of an upward sloping supply curve, representing the assumption that the lower-cost deposits of the resource will generally be found and produced before higher-cost deposits. Conceptually this relationship is represented with a long-run marginal cost curve for the resource like that shown in Figure 1a. In a one-period model, some estimate is made of how much of the resource will be used between now and the target year and a static supply curve like that shown in Figure 1a is derived from the long-run marginal cost curve.

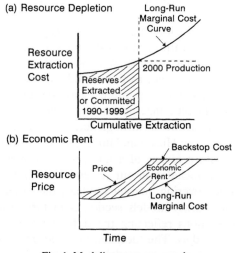

Fig. 1. Modeling resource supply.

Another feature often included in an intertemporal model with resource depletion is the capability to include an intertemporal resource rent, reflecting the propensity of resource owners to delay producing the resource if their net profit (resource price less production costs) is increasing faster than their rate of return on alternative investments (usually approximated by the rate of interest) and to produce it all immediately if their net profit is increasing more slowly than the rate of return on alternative investments. Together these two conditions require that the difference between the price and cost of the resource rise at the rate of interest as shown in Figure 1b. Hotelling [1931] derives the implied equilibrium conditions for the case of a depletable resource with zero extraction costs; Solow & Wan [1977] add results for the case where extraction costs are non-zero; and Nordhaus [1973] uses the concept of a 'backstop' technology, available in unlimited supply, but with high cost, as a natural terminal condition in the differential equations derived by Hotelling and Solow, leading to closed-form solutions. Oren & Powell [1985], Krautkramer [1986] and Powell & Oren [1989] analyze the implications of more complicated, but also more realistic, backstop specifications. For a good general overview of depletable resource theory and practice see Dasgupta & Heal [1979].

2.2. Price and non-price determinants of energy demand

The simplest models of energy demand project demand as a function of future prices and incomes. To summarize the relevant relationships economists often use elasticity estimates. The price elasticity of demand is the percentage reduction in energy demand in response to a one percent increase in energy prices after enough time has passed for the economy to adjust its energy using equipment and structures to the price change; the income elasticity of demand is the percentage increase in demand in response to a one percent increase in income. A simple back-of-the-envelope energy demand forecasting equation might be:

$$\% \text{ change in energy demand} = \text{income elasticity} \times \% \text{ change in GNP}$$
$$- \text{ price elasticity} \times \% \text{ change in energy price.} \qquad (1)$$

For example, suppose the long-run price elasticity for primary energy in the United States is 0.4 and the income elasticity is 1.0. Furthermore, suppose the U.S. economy is projected to grow at a rate of 2.4% per year, and it is desired to limit the growth of primary energy demand to 1% per year because of resource scarcity or environmental concerns. Then, energy prices would need to increase at $(2.4 - 1.0)/0.4 = 3.5\%$ per year in inflation-adjusted terms to meet the limit on energy demand growth (for more on aggregate energy price elasticities see EMF [1980]).

There is considerable debate about the extent to which factors other than price and income need to be considered in projecting energy demand. In aggregate models, a common practice in recent years has been to add a time trend to the simple forecasting equation given above, representing a gradual shift in energy use per unit of economic activity (energy efficiency) that is independent of prices.

If such a trend was an improvement in energy efficiency of 0.5% per year, the price increase in the above example would fall to only 2.25% per year in inflation-adjusted terms. In more disaggregated models various attempts have been made to measure causal determinants of energy demand other than price and income. Factors considered include: (1) changing industry structure (discussed below); (2) changes in productivity; and (3) technological innovation (discussed below).

Another complication to the simple aggregate demand forecasting equation shown above is the time lags in the adjustment of demand to price changes. Since energy using capital stock, e.g., industrial boilers, automobiles, is long-lived, the adjustment to sharp changes in energy prices can take many years to be completed. Models that attempt to capture these dynamics generally treat the existing capital stock as completely (or nearly completely) non-adjustable while new capacity (for replacement or to satisfy growth in demand) are completely flexible. Only 5–10% of the capital stock is typically assumed to be new each year (for a slightly more flexible formulation see Peck & Weyant [1985]).

2.3. Interfuel competition

Another key aspect of the demand for a particular fuel is interfuel competition. Capturing interfuel competition is of great importance in projecting the demand for an individual fuel, and can also improve any estimate of aggregate energy demand. One simple way to capture interfuel competition is through the use of own- and cross- price elasticities of demand; the own-price elasticity is the percentage reduction in the demand for a fuel in response to a one percent increase in its own price and the cross-price elasticity of a particular fuel with respect to the price of a competitive fuel is the percentage change in the demand for that fuel in response to a one percent change in the price of the competitive fuel. Own-price effects are generally negative and cross-price effects are generally positive.

As an example of the application of the cross-price elasticity concept, consider the demand for oil in the long run to be dependent on income, the price of oil and the price of competitive fuels. Then our simple demand forecasting equation becomes:

$$\% \text{ change in oil demand} = \text{income elasticity} \times \% \text{ change in GNP}$$
$$- \text{own-price elasticity} \times \% \text{ change in oil price}$$
$$+ \text{cross-price elasticity} \times \text{change in price of competitive fuel}. \qquad (2)$$

For example, suppose the income elasticity for oil demand is 1.0, the own-price elasticity is 0.6 and the cross-price elasticity with respect to the price of competitive fuels is 0.2. In addition, suppose the price of competitive fuels is expected to increase at 3% per year and energy security concerns lead policy makers to set no increase in oil consumption as an objective. Then oil prices would need to increase at a $[(1.0)(2.4) + (0.2)(3.0)]/0.6 = 5\%$ per year to keep oil consumption constant (see Sweeney [1984] for a good overview of energy demand modeling and Bohi [1981] for more on energy price elasticities).

2.4. Process engineering

Another concept employed in most energy models is process engineering estimates of the cost and efficiency of various energy conversion processes. For example, models that consider the supply and demand for all energy fuels generally include representations of one or more electric generation technologies that use fossil fuel combustion to run a turbine generator. Such a system generally has an energy conversion efficiency of 35–40%. Such characterizations are common in process analyses employed in applied mathematical programming and they are used in some models in precisely this way. In other models, however, process engineering modules are embedded in market equilibrium networks as discussed below.

Process engineering is widely used to model primary energy conversion owing to the large scale and homogeneous design of the facilities involved [see, e.g., EMF, 1980, 1987]. Although much more effort is required, the process engineering approach is increasingly being used to analyze energy demand technologies. By representing demand in terms of end-use energy services (e.g., industrial process heat, residential space heating, and automobile vehicle miles traveled), such models include representations of alternative technologies that can be used to satisfy those end-use demands. These technologies can have different costs, conversion efficiencies, and employ different input fuels. Thus different levels of home insulation and competition between gas combustion and electric heat-pumps can be explicitly considered, leading many to refer to this approach as a 'bottom up' approach to energy demand modeling, as contrasted with the 'top down' approach employed in many aggregate economic analyses. The advantages of the increased technological detail included in end-use energy modeling must be balanced against the increased data requirements and lack of behavioral response estimates at the appropriate level. For example, although many estimates of the price elasticity of the demand for electricity by consumers are available, not many estimates of the end-use price elasticity for residential space heating are available. This results from the existence of publicly available data on fuel purchases, but not on end-use energy use consumption. By including technological data in consumer choice models in recent years, econometricians have started producing credible estimates of end-use demand elasticities.

2.5. Integrating supply and demand

In models that cover both, energy supply and demand are balanced through the determination of a market clearing set of prices. These prices may be determined either through iteration or optimization. Figure 2 shows the equivalence between the two approaches for the case of a single energy product (originally shown by Samuelson [1952]; see also Scarf [1990] for a general discussion of the relationship between optimization and economic theory). In the iterative approach the equilibrium price and quantity are sought through a search procedure. In the optimization approach the maximand is the shaded area labeled

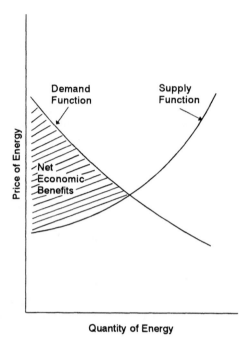

Fig. 2. Balancing supply and demand.

'net economic benefits', representing the difference between the value consumers place on the amount of energy supplied and what it cost producers to supply it. This area is maximized precisely at the market clearing price; if more energy is produced at that point, the cost of production will exceed its value to consumers. Although it is possible to approximate the equilibrium by using step function approximations to the supply and demand functions in a linear optimization formulation, this is usually awkward computationally, so non-linear programming or complementary formulations are often employed. Ahn & Hogan [1982] show conditions under which this process will converge when the demand system is linearized for a single-period formulation. Daniel & Goldberg [1981] extend these results to a multi-period optimization formulation. Greenberg & Murphy [1985] show how to compute regulated price equilibria using mathematical programming.

2.6. Aggregate energy–economy interactions

Thus far we have proceeded as if the level of economic activity has a strong influence on energy demand, but not vice versa. This is sometimes referred to as a partial equilibrium analysis. If a long time horizon must be considered to address the policy issue of interest or if energy prices are expected to increase dramatically, the impact of changes in energy prices on the level of economic activity needs

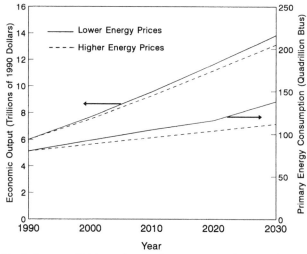

Fig. 3. Impact of higher prices on the economy and energy demand.

to be taken into account. This requires the use of a general equilibrium model in which the prices and quantities of all goods and services in the economy are allowed to vary. The simplest form of a such a model, and one that has been put to good use in energy analysis, splits all goods and services produced in the economy into just two categories – energy inputs and all other goods. Since energy and other goods are imperfect substitutes, both in production and consumption, when energy costs increase, more of the other goods are devoted to energy production *and* less energy inputs are consumed, as the substitution unfolds. Both of these effects reduce the total level of output of the economy. And less economic activity leads to less energy demand via Equation (1). The result of this 'feedback' is illustrated in Figure 3, where the impact of higher energy prices and lower economic growth on the trend projection of energy demand is illustrated. Since energy inputs represent only 5–10% of all inputs to the economy, the energy–economy feedback can usually be ignored for policy issues for which the appropriate evaluation period is less than 20 years, unless very large changes in energy prices are envisioned (see EMF [1977] and Hitch [1977] for more on energy/economy interactions).

2.7. Multi-sector energy–economy interactions

Although our simple back-of-the-envelope energy demand projection formulae treated the price sensitivity of energy demand to changes in energy prices as homogeneous across all sectors of the economy, the substitution potential varies widely from sector to sector. For some applications it may be very important to capture this heterogeneity. A first cut at the nature of these interactions can be gained through the use of standard fixed-coefficient input analysis, where the output of each sector of the economy is represented as being produced by a fixed fraction of the outputs of the other sectors and of the primary input factors. Thus, the instantaneous impact of a reduction in energy availability on the output of each sector can be estimated. Of course, if energy availability is reduced or energy prices increase, producers will substitute other goods in the production process and consumers will shift away from purchasing energy-intensive products. This realization lead to the development of interindustry models with input/output coefficients that depend on the relative prices of all intermediate goods and primary inputs [e.g., Hudson & Jorgenson, 1974]. In these models the price elasticity of each fuel depends on the existing industry structure and on the price elasticity within each sector of the economy. Thus, the price elasticities of the individual fuels and the degree of substitution between energy and other goods can shift substantially over time in such models. It is also possible to formulate single-sector models where energy demand depends on both fuel and non-fuel factor input prices. Such model can be used to study the dynamics of adjustment of the capital stock in that one sector to variations in all prices [see, e.g., Peck, Bosch & Weyant, 1988].

3. Market models

Market models are designed to project the supply, demand and pricing of energy fuels over time. Such models are used to forecast future market conditions for the fuels, to study the impacts of current and proposed regulations on those conditions, to evaluate the impact of new energy producing and consuming technologies on the market balances, and to guide international negotiations on energy policy. In our overview we distinguish between national and international models because differences in objectives for these two types of analyses lead to some differences in modeling philosophy and architecture.

To economize in this and subsequent sections we use final reports on the twelve Energy Modeling Forum studies completed to date as basic references on the models that have been employed and the issues that have been addressed with those models. This saves considerable effort, as each study includes about ten models and 100 references on models, methodologies, data, and the domain being modeled. For example, in virtually every study a model employed by the Energy Information Administration in the U.S. Department of Energy is included. These models are often documented with extensive technical report series published by the federal government. The same can be said to a lesser extent about the analytical tools developed by the Electric Power Research Institute, the Gas Research Institute, and (in recent years) the Environmental Protection Agency. Thus, by citing the EMF reports we implicitly refer the reader to a vast number of technical reports that have been compiled to document some of the best applied OR models ever developed. For a description of the Energy Modeling Forum, its objectives, format, process, and early results see Huntington, Weyant & Sweeney [1982].

3.1. National models

National models are concerned with the supply, demand and pricing for energy in a single country. International energy prices are typically treated as inputs to such models. We use the United States as the subject for national modeling here although excellent models have been developed for a large number of other countries. This strategy is pursued to economize on the length of the exposition, and because most of the relevant modeling techniques can be addressed even with the omission of country-specific modeling details. In addition, we divide our discussion of U.S. market models into two categories – single-fuel models and multi-fuel models. In general, focusing on a single fuel enables the analyst to include more detail on supply conditions for that fuel, but reduces the richness of the representation of interfuel competition between that fuel and other competitive fuels.

3.1.1. Single-fuel models

Single-fuel models generally consist of a resource supply module, a fuel demand module, and an integrating mechanism. For applications where the focus is clearly on the demand or supply response, however, the other two modules are sometimes omitted. Four fuels are considered here, the three primary fossil fuels – coal, oil and natural gas – and electricity, which is produced from the three fossil fuels and other primary energy resources like nuclear, hydro, and geothermal.

Oil and gas supply models are similar in structure. Such models typically include about a dozen supply regions within the U.S. Texas, a major supplier of both fuels, is divided into a number of subregions, Alaska is a major oil supply region, Oklahoma a major gas producing region and Colorado may have the potential to become a major gas supplier in the future. The supply of oil and gas is either modeled using an aggregate long-run supply (marginal cost) curve like that shown in Figure 1, or with a more detailed engineering approach. The engineering approach generally involves classifying the resource base by cost of recovery category. Undiscovered resources are then converted into discovered reserves and reserves to production based on discounted cash flow calculations. If the expected return to the required investment at each stage exceeds some risk-adjusted threshold value the investment is assumed to be made. To prevent unrealistic jumps in reserve additions when resource prices run up rapidly, increases in drill rig activity or in reserve additions from period to period are typically constrained (see EMF [1982a, 1988] and Clark, Coene & Logan [1981] for more on oil and gas supply modeling).

Coal supply is modeled using approaches similar to those used for oil and gas supply, although resource depletion for coal is much slower than for oil and gas, so great care must be taken to get estimates of the resource base by cost category to get a realistic pattern production. The major coal producing regions of the U.S. are the Appalachian Basin (dominantly in West Virginia and Kentucky), the Illinois Basin, the Powder River Basin (mostly in Wyoming) and the Colorado Basin. In addition, engineering models of coal supply typically allocate enough resources for the entire life of a mine (30 to 40 years) when new supply capacity is added [see EMF, 1979a].

Each of the three fossil fuels must be processed prior to consumption to remove impurities and, in the case of oil products, to alter its chemistry to enable it to be used in specialized applications like the use of gasoline to power automobiles and trucks. Oil refinery models are among the most successful applications of mathematical programming, but most focus on individual company or facility optimizations, and are proprietary. For an example of a global refining and oil transport model see Manne, Nelson, So & Weyant [1985]; see also Baker & Lasdon [1985], and Klingman, Phillips, Steiger, Wirth, Padman & Krishman [1987]. Oil refinery models generally include activities that represent the conversion of different types of crude oil into slates of oil products (e.g., gasoline, jet fuel, heating oil, residual fuel oil, etc.). These multi-product activities can be represented as being approximately linear in the output of each product per unit of crude oil input. The use of each activity is limited by the availability of the required equipment, which can be added to in longer-term models.

The three fossil fuels differ substantially in their transportation economics; its high energy density and viscosity make oil relatively inexpensive to transport, while gas has a lower energy density and coal lower viscosity and energy density.

Thus, the delivered price of oil to consumers has a small transportation component, while the cost of transporting natural gas or coal can easily be 25–35% of their costs delivered to consumers. Since these resources are generally produced far from the major demand centers, representing transportation economics is crucial in any attempt to project supply, demand and prices.

The demand module of single-fuel models generally use a demand curve to represent demand behavior in each consuming region (often using the nine census regions or the ten federal energy demand regions). Sometimes demand in each demand region is further disaggregated into demands by major consuming sectors – for example, residential, commercial, industrial, transportation, and electric utilities.

The most direct influence of Operations Research on the design of the single-country market models is in the design and implementation of the integrating mechanism used to balance supply and demand. As suggested in our discussion of Figure 2, the balancing occurs either directly through the solution of an optimization problem or through an iterative procedure governed by algorithmic steps very similar to those embodied in conventional optimization algorithms. Both approaches seek to find the solution to systems of non-linear, but they differ in the sequencing of the steps during each iteration and in what is fixed at each step. (For more on model integration see Nesbitt [1984], Hogan & Weyant [1982, 1983], Weyant [1985] and Murphy, Sherali & Soyster [1982].)

Oil market models are generally solved by iteration in order to allow for the allocation of available drilling capacity across regions with the response of reserve additions to incremental drilling effort in each region represented as being highly non-linear. Coal models are generally solved by optimization owing to the importance of transportation economics in the market balance for that fuel [see, e.g., Shapiro & White, 1982]. In fact, the relatively flat supply and demand curves for coal coupled with the importance of the transportation network has made this a rich area for decomposition approaches for both linear and quadratic programming formulations. Gas market models may be solved either by iteration or by optimization techniques depending on whether the analyst chooses to emphasize supply or transportation economics for the application being addressed.

Electricity market models generally take fossil fuel prices and electricity demand curves as given. Such models typically include a rich technological process analysis representation of the alternative methods available for generating electricity from fossil fuels, renewable resources, hydro-electric systems, nuclear fission, etc. If the time horizon is short the existing generation capacity is fixed leaving minimizing the cost of satisfying electricity demand as the objective of interest in models referred to as 'production simulation' models. If the focus is on market conditions over a longer period of time when new capacity can be installed, the cost minimization is over capacity as well as production decisions [see Bloom, 1983; Bloom, Caramanis & Charny, 1984; Borison, Morris & Oren, 1984; Sherali, Soyster, Murphy & Sen, 1984].

In the aggregate the laws of energy conversion and economics of electricity production allow electricity production to be described by sets of linear equations. Such constraints can be used to constrain the optimization of a number of simple convex specifications of objective functions representing the response of electricity demand to changing electricity prices. This approach may provide a reasonable approximation to system optimization at a national or even a regional level. At the level of individual utility service area analysis, however, non-linear reliability and plant operation constraints need to be added to the formulation. An example of the former are area reliability constraints which limit the electricity transmitted into a particular area to some fraction of total electricity consumption in that area; an example of the former would be ramp-up constraints reflecting the fact that it can take many hours if not days to get a large thermal plant up to full power output. Thus, service area models generally are simulation systems run within an optimizing framework with various types of approximation and decomposition methods used to facilitate the computation of an optimal solution (see Baughman & Joskow [1976], Baugman, Joskow & Kamat [1979] and EMF [1979b, 1990b] for more on electricity sector models).

3.1.2. Multi-fuel models

The supply of individual fuels – oil, gas, coal and electricity – in multi-fuel models is generally modeled with simplified versions of the single-fuel model representations. Other than joint constraints used on the availability of rigs that can do either oil or gas drilling, the fact that oil and gas are sometimes found together, and the use of the primary fossil fuels in electricity generation, there are not many interactions between the supplies of the various fuels. On the demand side of the market, though, the fuels are direct competitors in a number of markets; gas and electricity compete for the home heating market; oil, gas and electricity compete for the commercial building space conditioning market;

and coal, oil and gas compete for the industrial and utility boiler markets. This interfuel competition has been modeled with two different approaches: (1) using cross-price elasticities of the demand for the fuels, and (2) a process analysis of end-use technologies like space heating systems, boilers, etc. The cross-price elasticity and process analysis concepts were described above. Here we extend this discussion to the use of these techniques in multi-fuel market models.

The cross-price elasticity approach to interfuel competition is easy to use and can be applied at a very aggregate level when aggregate elasticities are based on aggregate fuel consumption and average prices paid by some class of consumers or perhaps even the whole economy. Again, it is necessary to include some estimate of the income elasticity of demand and of non-price induced energy efficiency changes in order to make credible demand projections. With multiple independent fuel demands, the equivalence between optimization and equilibrium shown in Figure 2 can only be employed under very restrictive assumptions on the demand elasticities. In general, either an direct iterative solution procedure or a computable general equilibrium approach could be employed. In practice, however, a blend of iterative equation solving algorithms and mathematical programming techniques are typically employed. For example, in the Project Independence Evaluation System (PIES) model (see Hogan [1975], and Hogan, Sweeney & Wagner [1978]; see also Daniel & Goldberg [1981] for an example of a multi-fuel multi-period national model), an approximation with zero cross-price elasticities to a fully specified fuel demand model is incorporated in a linear programming integrating model that includes fuel supply curves, transportation, energy conversion, and distribution to consumers. Fuel prices obtained from the dual of this model are then fed into the full demand model in order to obtain a new demand model approximation and this information is fed back to the integrating model until the fuel prices obtained on successive iterations are approximately equal, at which point the zero cross-price elasticity assumption used in the approximation is irrelevant. For a careful study of convergence criteria for this type of system when the demand equations are linear see Ahn & Hogan [1982].

In contrast, the Intermediate Future Forecasting System (IFFS) model (the successor to PIES; Murphy, Conti, Sanders & Shaw [1988]) employs a traditional equation solving approach to decompose the energy system and still allows embedded math programs to be used in areas where the optimization framework is natural and solution algorithms are efficient – like coal supply and electricity capacity expansion. Part of the IFFS procedure is to let cross-fuel price elasticities to be fixed entirely during each iteration of the system.

Finally, in the popular Fossil2 model [Applied Energy Services, 1990; U.S. Department of Energy, 1991] the time stability of a system of differential equations is exploited. In this model, a system of quarterly multi-fuel demand equations is executed to approximate annual average conditions. Although convergence is not tested for, this procedure may approximate the dis-equilibrium, but equilibrium-seeking behavior exhibited by most real world markets.

The second approach to modeling interfuel competition is to extend the type of process analysis approach typically applied to the electric utility sector to energy end-use technologies. For example, capital and fuel requirements for typical residential space heating systems would be included for gas, electric, and solar systems, with the minimum cost system selected to satisfy incremental demands in each region. This approach has the additional advantage of allowing the explicit representation of conservation via the use of technology options with higher capital costs and lower fuel costs like residential heating systems with greater levels of insulation. To be employed effectively, however, this approach does require a great deal of data at a relatively disaggregated level by location and consumer type. In addition, the response of consumer demand to changing prices must be measured in terms of end-use energy for which no direct transaction data exists. Finally, such models must either be solved by assuming purely optimizing behavior on the part of broad classes of consumers, or through iterative search procedures with market shares based on the relative prices of alternative technologies. For an excellent discussion of the use of the economic foundations for the latter approach see Nesbitt [1984].

3.1.3. Models with energy–economy feedback

For longer-run applications or those where substantial changes in energy prices are expected to occur, the feedback from the energy sector to the rest of the economy is generally represented in some way. Two basic approaches have been employed: (1) the use of an economy-wide production function using capital, labor and energy inputs; and (2) use of a GNP elasticity, representing the percentage reduction in GNP in response to a one percent increase in energy prices. Energy is disaggregated in many different ways in the models, but it enters into the feedback calculation only in the aggregate (see Hitch [1977] and EMF [1977] for more on modeling energy–economy interactions; see Rowen & Weyant [1982] for a simple application of the basic paradigm to international energy security).

3.1.4. Multi-sector models

Multisectoral models employ variable coefficient input–output analysis to project changes in industry structure. This allows energy demand, as well as capital and labor demand, to be projected on an industry by industry basis. The input–output analysis is often combined with an aggregate model of economic growth like those used in the aggregate economy feedback analysis to equalize the marginal productivity of capital across sectors in the long run. This can, however, lead to the aggregation of capital into a single aggregate implying that installed capital is free to flow from industry to industry. This malleability of capital assumption is probably not a good assumption for shorter-run analyses.

3.1.5. Policy applications

National models have been used in a wide variety of applications; from R&D planning [Chao, Peck & Wan, 1985; EMF, 1982b, 1992] to price and entry regulation [EMF, 1982a, 1990a; Higgins & Jenkins-Smith, 1985; Hobbs, 1986; Wolak & Kolstad, 1988], to energy security policy [EMF, 1982b, 1984, 1991], to environmental policy [EMF, 1979a, 1992]. Several modeling systems are updated annually and used as the basis for extensive sets of policy analyses. For example, the Energy Information Administration, an independent arm of the U.S. Department of Energy prepares an 'Annual Energy Outlook', which includes a reference model forecast, as well as a number of sensitivities over external conditions (e.g., economic growth, oil market behavior), and policy options [see, e.g., Hogan, 1975; Murphy, Conti, Sanders & Shaw, 1988]. Similarly, the Gas Research Institute prepares an annual 'baseline forecast' with sensitivities to be used in planning GRI's research and development program.

Extensive model development and use has also taken place during major energy and environmental policy studies like the Clean Air Amendments of 1990, National Acid Precipitation Assessment Program (NAPAP), the National Energy Strategy (both the Clean Air Act and the National Energy Strategy [National Research Council, 1992; U.S. Department of Energy, 1991] are subject to review and assessment every few years), and the Intergovernmental Panel on Climate Change.

There are a growing number of applications where fuel-by-fuel emissions of air pollutants from the energy sector are calculated so that the costs of imposing constraints on those emissions can be computed [see EMF, 1992].

3.2. International models

Two features of international energy trade distinguish international market models from national market models: (1) fuel transport distances are generally longer which favors international trade in oil over gas, coal, and electricity; and (2) multiple economies with different institutional structures and objectives interact to create market balances in all goods including energy.

3.2.1. Single-fuel models

Overland transport of oil, gas, coal and electricity from one country to another costs approximately the same per unit-mile as within-country transport. Therefore, it is not surprising that active trade in all fuels occurs between countries with contiguous or close-by borders. For example, Canada is a major source of natural gas for the United States, and a somewhat smaller source of coal and electricity. U.S. Canadian oil trade takes place in both directions. Similarly, the Netherlands has been a major source of gas supply for Western Europe, and France is becoming a major supplier of electricity. Where oceans must be negotiated, however, the transportation shifts decidedly in favor of oil because of its relatively high energy density. Coal is bulky and much more expensive to ship via rail than by barge and therefore trade is limited to transport from ports near mines to ports near demand centers; and gas must be liquefied (greatly increasing its energy density), which is very expensive, to make ocean transport feasible.

The other factor that makes international oil trade more prevalent than gas or coal trade is geological; most of the world's very low-cost oil reserves are concentrated in countries with relatively low populations and levels of economic output. In fact, most of these reserves are located in a single relatively isolated region of the world – the Persian Gulf. The concentration of low-cost reserves in the Persian Gulf creates a challenge for analysts and policy makers alike. While markets for most energy fuels in most world regions can be represented as approximately competitive so that equilibrium is characterized by the equilibration of the value of the last unit produced to consumers to the cost of the last unit consumed to producers, the supply of oil from the Gulf producers does not seem to follow this paradigm. The price received by the Gulf producers is and has been far above production costs for over 20 years. Unfortunately, the behavior of these producers does not seem to fit a pure monopoly formulation or any of the popular oligopoly formulations either. Rather, these producers appear to set production levels and prices according to a very complicated internal negotiating procedure that changes over time and is as often based on politics as economics. Analysts have developed dozens of formulations to the Gulf oil production problem; these range from pure monopoly and oligopoly approaches used to bound feasible outcomes, to constrained optimizations with the constraints representing political factors, to price reaction functions which relate changes in oil prices to the level of utilization of some externally specified level of available production capacity. The last approach is the most common and seems to work fairly well for making short-run projections. Over the longer term, however, it is not clear how to project the level of available capacity required to implement this method.

World oil models are typically composed of three main components: (1) an OPEC (or Persian Gulf) supply model like that discussed above; (2) a non-OPEC (or Persian Gulf) supply model that follows the design of the supply component of national models; and (3) a consumer demand module. Each module is disaggregated by region or in some cases even by country. The integration of the modules in each model vary according to the objectives of the modeler and available modeling technology. In general, there is a transportation network between supply and demand regions in each model. The models differ significantly in what is assumed the participants represented in one module know about the aggregate behavior of the participants represented in the other modules and in what they assume is done with that information. A number of the models progress iteratively with oil demand less production by non-OPEC producers in one period determining the change in price for the next period via an OPEC price reaction function like that described above. The new price is in turn input to the demand and non-OPEC supply modules to get the next periods net demand for OPEC oil and so on. This approach has proven to be useful for short- to intermediate-term projections. Models with a longer-term focus generally assume that one or more of the groups represented has foresight about future prices and possibly about the response of the other groups to price changes. The former allows investment decisions to be made in anticipation of future prices, and the latter allows for monopoly or monopsony behavior by producers or consumers respectively. For example, one world oil model assumes that all participants know future prices, and, in addition, that the OPEC producers known the response of consumers, and non-OPEC producers and picks production levels to maximize discounted profits (see EMF [1982b, 1991], Salant [1982] and Gately [1984, 1986] for more on world oil models). Work at Resources for the Future in the mid-1990s [Murphy,

Toman & Weiss, 1987, 1989] focused on the use of Nash versus Stackelberg equilibrium concepts in such models. This distinction is important because of the difficulty one encounters in identifying the leader in these situations. The Stackelberg 'leader–follower' formulations also typically suffer from 'dynamic consistency' problems because it is generally advantageous for the leader to announce a complete intertemporal strategy and then change tactics once the other players have committed. For the other players to take this possibility into account is inconsistent with their 'follower' role and can lead to multiple equilibria depending precisely on what is assumed about the correspondence between announced strategies and actual behaviors.

International market models have also been developed for gas [see Beltramo, Manne & Weyant, 1986] and coal [Kolstad & Abbey, 1984], although trade in these fuels is much less active than it is for oil. As mentioned above, this is because transportation, particularly via oceans, is more expensive for these fuels. Because of the importance of transportation costs, these models have generally been constructed within a transportation network with supply and demand curves for each region. Such models generally assume competitive markets, except for some coal models designed to look at potential market power on the part of coal producers.

3.2.2. Multi-fuel models

Multi-fuel international models generally use the same supply structures as the individual fuel models and represent interfuel competition in each demand region in the same way as in national models. In fact, a multi-fuel formulation is sometimes employed in world oil models to improve the representation of the response of oil demand to changes in oil prices [see EMF, 1982b, 1991; Pindyck, 1979].

3.2.3. Energy–economy feedback

It is more difficult to represent energy–economy feedback fully in international models because each nation has its own objectives, and international trade in non-energy goods has proven to be very difficult to model. Innovative iterative algorithms have been used to allow each region to maximize its own discounted consumption with international oil and capital transferred updated on successive iterations. This type of formulation can be solved directly within a computable general equilibrium framework with the optimality conditions for the individual countries (or regions) included as constraints on the equilibrium solution. This approach has been used for some time to solve multi-sectoral single-economy models.

3.2.4. Multi-sectoral models

Multi-sectoral international models are difficult to formulate and solve. The most promising approach has been the use of the type of computable general equilibrium formulation used for multi-sectoral country models. Adding individual country objectives and trade flows to this type of formulation complicates things significantly, though, and only a few examples of this type of model exist. One potential limitation of the existing models of this type is that they all use either static one-period formulations or a recursive scheme where each period is solved as if no one has any information about future prices (for more on model integration see Hogan & Weyant [1982, 1983] and Weyant [1985]).

3.2.5. Policy applications

International market models have also been used in a wide variety of applications; from understanding world energy markets [Beltramo, Manne & Weyant, 1986; EMF, 1982b, 1991; Gately, 1984, 1986; Kolstad & Abbey, 1984; Manne & Rothkopf, 1991; Salant, 1982], to international trade analyses [EMF, 1982b, 1991], to developing proposals for international negotiations on energy security [Rowen & Weyant, 1982] and the environment [Edmonds & Reilly, 1985; EMF, 1992; Manne & Richels, 1992]. Several modeling systems are updated annually and used as the basis for extensive sets of policy analyses. For example, the International Energy Agency in Paris periodically prepares a 'World Energy Outlook', which includes a reference model forecast, as well as a number of sensitivities over external conditions (e.g., economic growth, oil market behavior), and policy options. In addition the Organization for Economic Cooperation and Development (OECD) also located in Paris, the European Economic Community (EEC) in Brussels, and the International Institute for Applied Systems Analysis (IIASA) in Vienna regularly use energy-environmental analyses in their policy studies.

In addition, there are a growing number of applications where fuel-by-fuel emissions of air pollutants from the energy sector are calculated so that the costs of imposing constraints on those emissions can be computed [see, e.g., Edmonds & Reilly, 1985; EMF, 1992].

4. Decision-oriented models

The market models discussed so far are often used to calculate the impact of changing key policy parameters. For example, a tax could be placed on crude oil imports, on gasoline consumption, or carbon emissions from fossil fuels. These analyses provide information that is useful in the development of appropriate policies. In themselves, though, such calculations provide only a partial analytic guide to decisionmakers. The methodologies described in this section are designed to focus more comprehensively on a complex decision. Two basic approaches can be distinguished: (1) models that explicitly add one or more dimensions of complexity to the market models and can thus be used to optimize directly over the policy variable of interest; and (2) applications of decision analysis to the policy decision of interest, with market models used as a value function generator.

4.1. Policy optimization models

Policy optimization models generally try to incorporate uncertainty (multiple outcomes), multiple objectives, or multiple decision makers into the analysis of a particular policy option. This makes stochastic programming, stochastic dynamic programming, goal programming, and various game theoretic formulations. These models often build on market models directly or on simplified versions of them. Our goal here is to give a few examples of each approach rather than a comprehensive review.

4.1.1. Stochastic programming

An early application of stochastic programming to energy policy was the analysis of the breeder nuclear reactor program by Manne [1974]. In this analysis an aggregate multi-fuel model of the U.S. energy system with technology detail in the electricity production sector was modified to analyze uncertainty regarding the amount of low-cost uranium that would ultimately become available. This parameter affects the economic necessity of the breeder because its uranium efficiency relative to conventional nuclear reactors is its main advantage. It was assumed that total low-cost uranium supply is not known initially, but that it becomes known with certainty in ten years. Thus, for the first ten years (actually represented by two time periods in the model), a single set of decision variables representing the amount of electric generation technology of each type are included for each time period. After the uncertainty regarding uranium supply is resolved, however, three separate sets of variables are defined for each of the three possible outcomes regarding uranium supply. A separate constraint is defined for each contingency, and the contingent variables enter the objective function multiplied by their probability of occurrence.

A more recent application of stochastic programming is a global climate change study by Manne & Richels [1992, Chapter 4]. In this study, the objective is to reduce greenhouse gas emissions by controlling fossil fuel combustion. The extent of control required though is uncertain; there is some probability that very stringent controls will be required, some probability that a moderate degree of control will be required, and some chance that no control will be required. In this study the uncertainty regarding the level of control required is resolved in 2010, so decisions must be made in 1990 and 2000 before the uncertainty is resolved, and contingent decisions are made in 2010 through 2100 depending on the level of control required. This formulation results in an emissions trajectory over the period until 2010 that maximizes the expected discounted utility of consumption over the whole time horizon.

4.1.2. Dynamic programming

A major energy policy issue that has been effectively analyzed over the past decade via dynamic programming is the Strategic Petroleum Reserve. Since oil supply interruptions have been very costly to the economies of the oil importing countries, one possible policy response is to store oil when the market is stable and draw down the reserve when the interruptions occur. This policy is probably the most direct response to the threat of oil supply interruptions because it provides a direct substitute for the oil supplies lost during the disruption. An oil stockpile entails a number of costs (e.g., for site preparation, tied up capital and for upward pressure stock fill puts on the world oil market), however, so the issue of optimal size arises. A related issue is the optimal drawdown policy – if all the oil in the reserve is used up this year none will be left for further contingencies next year when things could be worse rather than better.

In one well known model [Teisberg, 1981; see also Chao & Manne, 1983] the evolution of the world oil market is modeled as a three-state Markov Chain, with normal, moderate disruption, and large disruption. Each state has its own probability of occurring, with the state next period depending on the state this period. As in any stochastic dynamic programming formulation, this structure allows a large number of plausible sequences of world oil states to be considered with appropriate probability measures. Thus, the cost of building a stockpile of any size can be weighed against its benefits in reducing the effective size of any disruption weighted by its probability of occurrence (for a discussion of how private stockpiles might react to changes in public stocks see Hubbard & Weiner [1986]; for a renewal process approach to stockpile management see Oren & Wan [1986]).

4.1.3. Goal programming

Charnes, Cooper, Gorr, Hsu & Von Rabenau [1986] formulate a number of stochastic goal programs for allocating limited gas supplies in times of supply shortages.

4.1.4. Game theory

Several researchers have added game theory features to the stochastic programming formulation of the oil stockpiling problem. For example, Hogan [1983] analyzes the 'free rider' benefit that accrues to those who fail to stockpile oil when others do. By dividing the OECD into two aggregate regions – the U.S. and all other OECD countries – the incentives for the two players are analyzed under alternative assumptions regarding the state of information and strategy of each player. A Nash equilibrium and two alternative Stackelberg 'leader–follower' assumptions are explored. The result of this analysis is that there are significant free-rider benefits to those who avoid the investment in an oil stockpile, but that everyone is better off if all nations participate in the stockpiling program.

4.2. Decision analysis applications

Decision analysis has been applied to a number of energy policy decisions. Two such applications – synthetic fuels and advanced nuclear reactors – are described here to give the reader a feel for the types of issues that have been addressed.

4.2.1. Synthetic fuels

The Synfuels Interagency Task Force was formed in 1975 to examine alternatives for implementing President Ford's goal of assuring early commercialization of synthetic fuels (dominantly oil and gas produced from coal or shale oil) in the United States. The problem was formulated in a decision analysis framework with the initial decision reduced to a choice among four alternative government-financed synthetic fuel programs: (1) no program; (2) a program designed to produce 350 000 barrels per day of synthetic fuels a day by 1985; (3) a program designed to produce 1 000 000 barrels a day by 1985; and (4) a program designed to produce 1 700 000 by 1985 [Synfuels Interagency Task Force, 1976; see also Harlan, 1982 for a more recent synfuels decision analysis].

This initial decision is followed by the resolution of three uncertainties that affect the profitability of synthetic fuels: (1) the U.S. energy industry's beliefs in 1985 about the cost of synthetic fuels in 1995; (2) the strength of the world oil cartel in 1985; and (3) the price of oil in 1985 which depends in part on the strength of the cartel. These conditions lead to an industry decision on the most profitable size of a commercial synthetic fuels industry by 1995. This decision is followed by the resolution in 1995 of actual 1995 synthetic fuels cost, 1995 cartel strength and 1995 oil price uncertainties.

After considerable interagency debate, the Task Force agreed to a nominal set of judgmental probabilities. Based on these estimates, the optimal initial decision turned out to be not to initiate any government-driven synthetic fuels program at all. Although this was not the recommendation that was ultimately adopted, the analysis is credited with persuading the Administration to cut back from President Ford's initial goal of one million barrels down to 350 000 barrels a day by 1985.

4.2.2. Advanced nuclear reactors

During the late 1970s, Manne & Richels [1978] conducted a number of decision analyses of the value of different types of advanced nuclear reactors. The most comprehensive of these analyses was an analysis of the breeder reactor program that focused sequential nature of the breeder development program as well as the necessity of making early investments in the program before important uncertainties are resolved. The analysis was performed in 1978 when an active government-sponsored development program for the Liquid Metal Fast Breeder Reactor (LMFBR) was underway. The breeder was viewed as essential to the long-run development of the nuclear industry because the limited supply of low-cost uranium available in the U.S. was projected to become exhausted early in the next century unless the breeder which is more than 100 times more efficient in its use of uranium than conventional reactors could be developed. Of course, the urgency of the breeder would depend on the rate of growth of energy demand, the availability of uranium, the availability of substitute fuels for electric generation like coal and shale oil, the cost of alternative fuels like solar heating and cooling and alternative ways of generating electricity like solar cells, and public acceptability of the breeder with its reliance on plutonium as a primary fuel cycle element. All these uncertainties were all explicitly incorporated into the Manne-Richels analysis in the same way as the key uncertainties were incorporated into the synthetic fuels analysis described above. What distinguishes the breeder analysis from the synthetic fuels program analysis is its explicit representation of the time phasing of the breeder development program. The program was to include a prototype breeder which would be only 10–15% of full commercial scale, a prototype that would be 30–50% of full scale and a full scale government-owned first commercial breeder. This development program was initially laid out over a 10–15 year development cycle. It was assumed that it would take this type of a program to stimulate commercial pursuit of the breeder option. The Manne-Richels analysis explicitly recognized that it would be possible to slow down or accelerate the development process should (1) the early experience with the breeder concept, or (2) information about the evolution of energy demand, success in developing alternative fuels, etc., dictate. Recognition that today's decision was not an all or nothing commitment to the whole program over a decade or more enabled Manne and Richels to consider various time phases of the three phases of the breeder development program depending on how conditions changed over time. Thus, if energy demand is high, uranium supply is low, alternative fuels turn out to be expensive, and the public accepts the breeder concept, it proves desirable to pursue the three phases of the development program in parallel where each subsequent phase is initiated before the results from the previous phase are complete. On the other hand, if energy demand is low, uranium supply is abundant, alternative fuels are inexpensive and public acceptability is questionable, it may prove desirable to delay the subsequent phases of the program for many years or even forever.

5. Emerging issues and modeling frontiers

The evolution of energy modeling over the next couple of decades will depend on the level of interest in current policy issues and the emergence of new ones, as well as the development and application of new modeling methodologies. Although it is difficult to predict exactly what the future will bring, several new policy areas and methodological developments seem certain.

5.1. Emerging policy issues

5.1.1. Trade issues

As the world economy has become more interdependent, it has become more important to model international trade and financial flows. This has proven difficult in the past because of data and methodological complications. New methods have been developed in recent years, and better data are now being collected. It will be especially important to be able to realistically model trade impacts if international energy security or carbon taxes are seriously considered because each country will be hesitant to implement such taxes without knowing the implications for its own trade balance.

5.1.2. Environmental policies

In addition to the emissions-oriented energy models described above, a few models that balance the costs and benefits of carbon emissions have been developed. These models explicitly consider the linkages between carbon emissions and concentrations of carbon dioxide in the atmosphere, between concentration levels and climate change, and between climate change and the economic losses that result from it. These models are generally solved by non-linear optimization or control theory techniques [see Nordhaus, 1990; Peck & Teisberg, 1993].

5.2. Modeling frontiers

5.2.1. Introduction of new technologies
One of the more difficult tasks in modeling the evolution of the energy system over the intermediate-to-long term is realistically representing the interplay between the cost and rate of introduction of new technologies. Most engineering cost estimates for new technologies assume that adequate supplies of the materials necessary to produce the technology and manufacturing capacity, including skilled labor, exist. If the technology is a fundamentally new one, though, it may take some time for the supplying industries to develop adequate production capacity, especially until the long-run stability of the new market demand is demonstrated. During the interim, one would expect both the inputs and the new technology to be more expensive than the engineering cost estimate. This phenomenon can be modeled in a number of ways including everything from the use of absolute introduction rate constraints to the explicit representation of conditions in the supplying industries. None of these approaches has proven completely satisfactory, however, so additional research and model development in this area are highly desirable.

5.2.2. Computable general equilibrium models
One way to improve the modeling of trade issues is to employ a computable equilibrium framework where the prices and quantities of all goods are solved for simultaneously. Thus far, only static and recursive models of this type have been employed. The development of a full intertemporal computable general equilibrium model with multi-sectoral trade is beyond the current state of the art, but within sight (see Murphy, Sherali & Soyster [1982] and Mathiesen [1985] for more on practical solution techniques for computable general equilibrium models).

5.2.3. Expert systems
One way to make energy models more useful is to make them more useable. Developments in experts systems theory make it possible to put a user-friendly front end on an integrated modeling system so resolution can be improved in the area of direct interest and summary representations of other affected systems can be employed. Such systems can also allow even the most inexperienced user to experiment with alternative model parameter values and in so doing gain confidence in the model and its operation.

5.2.4. Parallel processing
One way to improve the computability of modeling systems of any type is to employ parallel processing techniques which allow the multiple processing

capabilities of modern computers to be used to good advantage. This capability would be particularly valuable in stochastic programming formulations where dimensionality tends to become a limiting factor for realistic formulations [see Dantzig & Glynn, 1990].

References

Ahn, B., and W. Hogan (1982). On convergence of the PIES algorithm for computing equilibria. *Oper. Res.* 30, 281–300.

Applied Energy Services (1990). Overview of Fossil2, Working Paper, 1001 19th Street North, Arlington, VA.

Baker, T.E., and L.S. Lasdon (1985). Successive linear programming at Exxon. *Management Sci.* 31, 264–274.

Baughman, M., and P. Joskow (1976). The future of the U.S. nuclear energy industry. *Bell J. Econom.* 7, 3–31.

Baughman, M., P. Joskow and D. Kamat (1979). *Electric Power in the United States: Models and Policy Analysis*, MIT Press, Cambridge, MA.

Beltramo, M.A., A.S. Manne and J.P. Weyant (1986). A North American gas trade model: GTM. *Energy J.* 7, 15–32.

Bloom, J.A. (1983). Solving an electricity generating capacity expansion problem by generalized bender decomposition. *Oper. Res.* 31, 84–100.

Bloom, J.A., M. Caramanis and L. Charny (1984). Long-range generation planning using generalized benders decomposition: Implementation and experience. *Oper. Res.* 32, 290–313.

Bohi, D.R. (1981). *Analyzing Energy Demand Behavior: A Study of Energy Elasticities*, Johns Hopkins University Press for Resources for the Future, Baltimore, MD.

Borison, A.B., P.A. Morris and S.S. Oren (1984). A state-of-the-world decomposition approach to dynamics and uncertainty in electric utility generation expansion planning. *Oper. Res.* 32, 1052–1068.

Chao, H., and A.S. Manne (1983). Oil stockpiles and import reductions: A dynamic programming approach. *Oper. Res.* 31, 632–651.

Chao, H., S.C. Peck and Y. Wan (1985). LOAD: An electric technology R&D planning model with contingent decisions. *Resources and Energy* 7, 163–178.

Charnes, A., W.W. Cooper, W.L. Gorr, C. Hsu and B. Von Rabenau (1986). Emergency government interventions: Case study of natural gas shortages. *Management Sci.* 32, 1242–1258.

Clark, P., P. Coene and D. Logan (1981). A comparison of ten U.S. oil and gas supply models. *Resources Energy* 3, 297–335.

Daniel, T.E., and H.M. Goldberg (1981). Dynamic equilibrium modeling with the Canadian BALANCE model. *Oper. Res.* 29, 829–852.

Dantzig, G., and P. Glynn (1990). Parallel processors for planning under uncertainty. *Ann. Oper. Res.* 22, 1–21.

Dasgupta, P., and G. Heal (1979). *Economic Theory and Exhaustible Resources*, Cambridge University Press, Cambridge.

Edmonds, J., and J.M. Reilly (1985). *Global Energy: Assessing the Future*, Oxford University Press, Oxford.

Energy Modeling Forum (EMF) (1977). Energy and the economy, EMF 1 Summary Report, Vols. 1 and 2, Stanford University, Stanford, CA.

Energy Modeling Forum (EMF) (1979a). Coal in transition: 1980–2000, EMF 2 Summary Report, Vols. 1 and 2, Stanford University, Stanford, CA.

Energy Modeling Forum (EMF) (1979b). Electric load forecasting: Probing the issues with models, EMF 3 Summary Report, Vol. 1 [Vol. 2 (1980)], Stanford University, Stanford, CA.

Energy Modeling Forum (EMF) (1980). Aggregate elasticity of energy demand, EMF 4 Summary Report, Vol. 1. [Vol. 2 (1981)], Stanford University, Stanford, CA.

Energy Modeling Forum (EMF) (1982a). U.S. oil and gas supply, EMF 5 Summary Report, Vols. 1 and 2, Stanford University, Stanford, CA.

Energy Modeling Forum (EMF) (1982b). World oil, EMF 6 Summary Report, Vols. 1 and 2, Stanford University, Stanford, CA.

Energy Modeling Forum (EMF) (1984). Macroeconomic impacts of energy shocks, EMF 7 Summary Report, Vol. 1 [Vols. 2 and 3 (1987)], Stanford University, Stanford, CA.

Energy Modeling Forum (EMF) (1987). Industrial energy demand, EMF 8 Summary Report, Vol. 1 [Vol. 2 (1988)], Stanford University, Stanford, CA.

Energy Modeling Forum (EMF) (1988). North American natural gas markets, EMF 9 Summary Report, Vol. 1 [Vol. 2 (1989)], Stanford University, Stanford, CA.

Energy Modeling Forum (EMF) (1990a). Electricity market players report, A. Borison (ed.), EMF 10 Summary Report, Vol. 1, Stanford University, Stanford, CA.

Energy Modeling Forum (EMF) (1990b). The role of models in national electricity policy debates: Issues and frontiers, P. Blair (ed.), EMF 10 Summary Report, Vol. 2, Stanford University, Stanford, CA.

Energy Modeling Forum (EMF) (1991). International oil supplies and demands, EMF 11 Summary Report, Vol. 1 [Vol. 2 (1992)], Stanford University, Stanford, CA.

Energy Modeling Forum (EMF) (1992). Global climate change: Energy sector impacts of greenhouse gas emissions control strategies, EMF 12 Summary Report, Vol. 1, Stanford University, Stanford, CA.

Gately, D. (1984). A ten year retrospective: OPEC and the world oil market. J. Econom. Literature 22, 1100–1114.

Gately, D. (1986). Lessons from the 1986 oil price collapse. Brookings Papers Econom. Activity, pp. 237–271.

Greenberg, H.J., and F.H. Murphy (1985). Computing price equilibria with price regulations using mathematical programming. Oper. Res. 33, 935–954.

Harlan, J.K. (1982). Starting on Synfuels: Benefits, Costs, and Program Design Assessments, Ballinger, Cambridge, MA.

Hickman, B.G., H.G. Huntington and J.L. Sweeney (1987). Macroeconomic Impacts of Energy Shocks, North-Holland, Amsterdam.

Higgins, T., and H.C. Jenkins-Smith (1985). Analysis of the economic effect of the Alaskan export ban. Oper. Res. 33, 1173–1202.

Hitch, C. (ed.) (1977). Modeling Energy Economy Interactions: Five Approaches, Johns Hopkins University Press for Resources for the Future, Baltimore, MD.

Hobbs, B.F. (1986). Network models of spatial oligopoly with an application to deregulation of electricity. Oper. Res. 34, 395–409.

Hogan, W.W. (1975). Energy policy models for project independence. J. Comput. Oper. Res. 2, 251–271.

Hogan, W.W. (1983). Oil stockpiling: Help thy neighbor. Energy J. 4, 49–71.

Hogan, W., J. Sweeney and M. Wagner (1978). Energy policy models in the national energy outlook, in: J.S. Arnosky, A.G. Rao and M.F. Shakun (eds.), Energy Policy, North-Holland, Amsterdam, pp. 37–62.

Hogan, W.W., and J.P. Weyant (1982). Combined energy models, in: J.R. Moroney (ed.), Formal Energy and Resource Models, Advances in the Economy of Energy and Resources 4, JAI Press, Greenwich, CT, pp. 117–150.

Hogan, W.W., and J.P. Weyant (1983). Methods and algorithms for combining energy models; Optimization in a network of process models, in: B. Lev (ed.), Energy Models and Studies, Studies in Management Science and Systems 20, North-Holland, Amsterdam, pp. 3–43.

Hotelling, H. (1931). The economics of exhaustible resources. J. Political Econom. 39, 137–175.

Hubbard, R.G., and R.J. Weiner (1986). Inventory optimization in the U.S. petroleum industry. Management Sci. 32, 773–790.

Hudson, E.A., and D.W. Jorgenson (1974). U.S. energy policy and economic growth; 1975–2000. *Bell J. Econom. Management Sci.* 5, 461–514.

Huntington, H.G., J.P. Weyant and J.L. Sweeney (1982). Modeling for insights, not numbers; The experiences of the energy modeling forum. *OMEGA* 10, 449–462.

Klingman, D., N. Phillips, D. Steiger, R. Wirth, R. Padman and R. Krishman (1987). An optimization based integrated short-term refined petroleum product planning system. *Management Sci.* 33, 813–830.

Kolstad, C.D., and D.S. Abbey (1984). The effect of market conduct on international steam coal trade. *European Econom. Rev.* 24, 39–59.

Krautkramer, J.A. (1986). Optimal depletion with resource amenities and a backstop technology. *Resources Energy* 8, 109–132.

Lev, B. (ed.) (1983). *Energy Models and Studies*, Studies in Management Science and Systems 20, North-Holland, Amsterdam.

Manne, A.S. (1974). Waiting for the breeder, in: Symposium on the Economics of Exhaustible Resources, Special Issue. *Rev. Econ. Studies*, pp. 47–65.

Manne, A., C. Nelson, R. So and J.P. Weyant (1985). A contingency planning model of the international oil merket. *Appl. Management Sci.* 4, 1–35.

Manne, A.S., and R.G. Richels (1978). A decision analysis of the breeder reactor program. *Energy* 3, 747–768.

Manne, A.S., and R.G. Richels (1992). *Buying Greenhouse Insurance: The Economic Costs of CO_2 Emission Limits*, MIT Press, Cambridge, MA.

Manne, A.S., R.G. Richels and J.P. Weyant (1979). Energy policy modeling: A survey. *Oper. Res.* 27, 1–36.

Manne, A.S., and M.H. Rothkopf (1991). Analyzing US policies for alternative automotive fuels. *Interfaces* 21, 34–52.

Mathiesen, L. (1985). Computational experience in solving equilibrium models by a sequence of linear complementarity problems. *Oper. Res.* 33, 1225–1250.

Moroney, J.R. (ed.) (1982). *Formal Energy and Resource Models*, Advances in the Economy of Energy and Resources 4, JAI Press, Greenwich, CT.

Murphy, F.H., J.J. Conti, R. Sanders and S.H. Shaw (1988). Modeling and forecasting energy markets with the intermediate future forecasting system. *Oper. Res.* 36, 406–420.

Murphy, F.H., H.D. Sherali and A.L. Soyster (1982). A mathematical programming approach to determining oligopolistic market equilibria. *Math. Programming Stud.* 24, 92–106.

Murphy, F.H., E.A. Stohr and P. Ma (1992). Composition rules for building linear programming models from component models. *Management Sci.* 38, 948–963.

Murphy, F.H., M.A. Toman and H.J. Weiss (1987). A stochastic dynamic Nash game for managing the strategic petroleum reserves of consuming nations. *Management Sci.* 33, 484–499.

Murphy, F.H., M.A. Toman and H.J. Weiss (1989). A dynamic Nash game model of oil market disruptions and strategic stockpiling. *Oper. Res.* 37, 958–971.

National Research Council (1992). *The National Energy Modeling System*, Committee on the National Energy Modeling System, National Academy Press, Washington, DC.

Nesbitt, D.M. (1984). The economic foundation of generalized equilibrium modeling. *Oper. Res.* 32, 1240–1267.

Nordhaus, W.D. (1973). The allocation of energy resources. *Brookings Papers Econom. Activity* 3, 529–576.

Nordhaus, W.D. (1990). An intertemporal general-equilibrium model of economic growth and climate change, Presented at the Workshop on Economic/Energy/Environmental Modeling for Climate Policy Analysis, Washington, DC.

Oren, S.S., and S.G. Powell (1985). Optimal supply of a depletable resource with a backstop technology: Heal's theorem revisited. *Oper. Res.* 33, 277–292.

Oren, S.S., and S.H. Wan (1986). Optimal strategic petroleum reserve policies: A steady state analysis. *Management Sci.* 32, 14–29.

Peck, S.C., D.K. Bosch and J.P. Weyant (1988). Industrial energy demand: A simple structural approach. *Resources Energy* 10, 111–134.

Peck, S.C., and T.J. Teisberg (1990). Exploring intertemporal CO_2 control paths, Presented at the Workshop on Economic/Energy/Environmental Modeling for Climate Policy Analysis, Washington, DC.

Peck, S.C., and T.J. Teisberg (1993). Global warming uncertainties and the value of information: An analysis using CETA. *Res. Energy Econom.* 15, 71–98.

Peck, S.C., and J.P. Weyant (1985). Electricity growth in the future. *Energy J.* 6, 23–43.

Pindyck, R.S. (1979). *The Structure of World Energy Demand*, MIT Press, Cambridge, MA.

Powell, S.G., and S.S. Oren (1989). The transition to nondepletable energy: Social planning and market models of capacity expansion. *Oper. Res.* 37, 373–383.

Rowen, H.S., and J.P. Weyant (1982). Reducing the economic impacts of oil supply interruptions; an international perspective. *Energy J.* 6, 1–34.

Salant, S. (1982). Imperfect competition in the international energy market: A computerized Nash-Cournot model. *Oper. Res.* 30, 252–280.

Samuelson, P.A. (1952). Spatial price equilibrium and linear programming. *Amer. Econom. Rev.* 42, 283–303.

Scarf, H.E. (1990). Mathematical programming and economic theory. *Oper. Res.* 38, 377–385.

Shapiro, J.F., and D.E. White (1982). A hybrid decomposition method for integrating coal supply and demand models. *Oper. Res.* 30, 887–906.

Sherali, H.D., A.L. Soyster, F.H. Murphy and S. Sen (1984). Intertemporal allocation of capital in electric utility capacity expansion under uncertainty. *Management Sci.* 30, 1–19.

Solow, J.L., and F.Y. Wan (1977). Extraction costs in the theory of exhaustible resources. *Bell J. Econom.* 7, 359–370.

Sweeney, J.L. (1984). The response of energy demand to higher prices: What have we learned? *Amer. Econom. Rev.* 74, 31–37.

Synfuels Interagency Task Force (1976). *Recommendations for a Synthetic Fuels Commercialization Program*, U.S. Government Printing Office, Washington, DC.

Teisberg, T.J. (1981). A dynamic programming model of the U.S strategic petroleum reserve. *Bell J. Econom.* 12, 526–546.

U.S. Department of Energy (DOE) (1991). National energy strategy, Report DOE/S-0082P, Technical Annex 2.

Weyant, J.P. (1985). General economic equilibrium as a unifying concept in energy-economic modeling. *Management Sci.* 31, 548–563.

Wolak, F.A., and C.D. Kolstad (1988). Measuring relative market power in the Western U.S. coal market using Shapley values. *Resources Energy* 10, 293–314.

S.M. Pollock et al., Eds., *Handbooks in OR & MS, Vol. 6*

Chapter 9

Managing Fish, Forests, Wildlife, and Water: Applications of Management Science and Operations Research to Natural Resource Decision Problems

Bruce L. Golden

College of Business and Management, University of Maryland, College Park, MD 20742, U.S.A.

Edward A. Wasil

Kogod College of Business Administration, American University, Washington, DC 20016, U.S.A.

1. Introduction

Flood or drought. Overpopulated or endangered. Harvest or cut back. Too much or too little. The myriad of problems encountered in the management of fish, forests, wildlife, and water are essentially dichotomous and interrelated, and proposed solutions have far-reaching economic, social, and political consequences.

Take the case of flounder that is caught off the East Coast of the United States. In 1979, records for landings of flounder by commercial fishermen were set in all East Coast states (see Miller [1991] for additional details). Virginia fishermen alone landed more than 10 million pounds of flounder. A little more than a decade later, flounder landings have dropped dramatically. Landings in Virginia fell to 3.8 million pounds in 1986 and in 1989 the state adopted strict fishing regulations that banned trawlers from state waters and imposed a 10-fish per day limit for recreational anglers. However, landings of flounder in Virginia waters continued to drop and they plummeted to 2.1 million pounds in 1990. The situation was much the same for all East Coast states. A new flounder management plan for 1992 was proposed by the Mid-Atlantic Fishery Management Council. The plan called for an overall commercial limit of 11 million pounds with each East Coast state allotted a portion of the total amount. In addition, the length of the recreational fishing season would be reduced and limits would be imposed on the size and number of fish that could be caught by recreational fishermen in a day.

Take the case of the northern spotted owl and other threatened species that live in the forests of the Pacific Northwest. These birds live in ancient fir and hemlock trees. Current U.S. Forest Service practice allows four to five billion board feet of lumber to be sold annually from national forests – this is enough lumber to construct 500 000 new homes each year. Harvesting very large amounts of timber threatens the survivability of the forest and the birds that live there: new trees planted to replace the ancient timber cannot grow fast enough to sustain long-term timber yields or to maintain healthy bird populations. A draft report by four authoritative scientists commissioned by the U.S. Congress outlines 14 different options for managing forests (see *The Economist* [1991], Booth [1991], Berry [1991], and Gordon, Franklin, Johnson & Thomas [1991] for more details). One alternative would reduce the amount of timber harvested each year to less than 1.7 billion board feet. It is a costly move: 38 000 jobs could be lost as well as $1.8 billion in personal income.

Take the case of the California condor. At the turn of the 20th century only a few hundred of the birds were alive. In 1953, fewer than one hundred birds remained and these were accorded legal protection under California law. In 1967, the California condor appeared on the first list of endangered species in the United States. However, the population of birds kept dropping: the birds were still hunted and some were poisoned from eating carrion that contained lead pellets from hunters. In 1983, only 22 birds remained. In 1987, despite opposition from such wildlife groups as the National Audubon Society, the U.S. Fish and Wildlife Service rounded up the few remaining wild condors and began breeding them at the Los Angeles Zoo and at the San Diego Wild Animal Park (see Reinhold [1991a] for complete details). Since 1988, 25 chicks have been hatched (only one has died), so that there are now 52 birds alive. The project has been deemed a success: two condor chicks were to be released into the wild in the fall of 1991. Now, even the National Audubon Society believes that the 1987 roundup of condors was a wise action. However, the captive breeding project has been costly: over $10 million has been spent so far.

Take the case of the United States' largest water project: California's Central Valley Project. Since 1935, water from the Sacramento River, the San Joaquin River, and their tributaries (over 20% of California's water supply) is stored in reservoirs and then diverted to irrigate three million acres of farm fields (see Lancaster [1991] and Reinhold [1991b] for additional details). At the same time, over the last 50 years, the project has severely impacted fish and wildlife populations. Fish and wildlife habitats are parched or dried up. Dams block the paths of migrating fish and pumps kill millions of fish each year. The winter run of chinook salmon is on the U.S. Fish and Wildlife Service's list of endangered species and the delta smelt (at 10% of its 1980 population) could be added to the list. In the last 15 years, winter populations of waterfowl have been reduced to 3.5 million from 10 million. The 5-year drought in California has exacerbated the problem: fish, wildlife, and even cities need water but long-term contracts preclude diversion of the Project's water for needs other than agricultural. A battle between agricultural interests and environmental interests has ensued and court action or legislative action will follow.

Each of these cases illustrates a very difficult natural resource decision problem in the management of fish, forests, wildlife, and water. In each case, key decision makers must grapple with a wide variety of complex issues. They must address the concerns of diverse constituencies and they must make timely decisions in a highly charged political atmosphere. Sometimes the decision makers rely on mathematical models for guidance. In each case, decisions made today can have long-term impacts on the environment and on the well-being of society.

Overall, the four areas of natural resource management that are the focus of this chapter contain a wealth of important problems that affect significant numbers of people worldwide. We briefly present some of the modelling challenges found in each area and, in Exhibit 1.1, we summarize seven works that are noteworthy general references on natural resource management.

Fisheries management

In 1980, the commercial harvesting, processing, and marketing of fish contributed $7 billion to the gross national product of the United States (this is about 1% of the U.S.'s GNP). In Alaska, the fish industry accounts for about 13% of the state's gross product, while in California, Louisiana, Texas, Massachusetts, and other coastal states, fishing exerts a major influence on employment and on the state's gross product (see Portney [1982] for more details). In many foreign countries, including most of the less developed countries, fishing and related occupations employ large numbers of people, while a sizable percentage of protein in the diet is derived from consuming fish. Around the world, there is evidence of declining catch due to overfishing, disease, and other environmental factors. Many fisheries have fleets that are larger than necessary. The problems facing fisheries managers are especially challenging due to the complexity of the marine environment. The population dynamics, especially in the multiple-species case, are not clearly understood, and reliable and accurate data are typically difficult to obtain.

Forestry

Those of us who live in houses, purchase furniture, and read newspapers, books, and journals are dependent on wood products. The United States is the world's largest producer of forest products. The products are worth about $190 billion a year (about 1% of the U.S.'s 1990 GNP). Each year the timber industry seeks to cut as many acres of trees as is necessary to fulfill the demand for wood products. This means that new trees must be planted in anticipation of future demands for timber. In addition, the timber industry must also contend with environmentalists who are very critical of the effect that the logging industry has had on nature. Multiple objective management problems of this type are commonplace in forestry today.

Wildlife management

Biologists have identified about one and a half million species of animals and plants worldwide but they estimate that the total number of species might be closer to five million with most species residing in tropical forests. Furthermore, biologists estimate that 1000 species are disappearing each year due, in part, to the dominance of short-term economic factors over such long-term factors

Exhibit 1.1

The field of natural resource management not only deals with problems related to fish, forests, wildlife, and water but also deals with problems in such diverse areas as public lands, nonfuel minerals, and global climate. The seven works listed below serve as very good sources for background information on problem areas, modelling and solution methods, and policy-related issues.

Hilborn [1979]. *Some Failures and Successes in Applying Systems Analysis to Ecological Systems.* The author describes four efforts to apply management science and operations research methods (in particular, simulation) in real-world settings with the Canadian Fisheries Service, the Canadian Wildlife Service, and private consulting companies. These efforts involve salmon catch in British Columbia, sport fishing for salmon in the Gulf of Georgia near Vancouver, Canada, the impact of fires on the northern caribou, and the biological impact of oil exploration in the Beaufort Sea (Egan [1991] provides an up-to-date look at the struggle over the Arctic refuge). Hilborn was a member of the team that performed the systems analysis work in these four applications. For each application, Hilborn presents his observations in four key areas: (1) institutional structure and decision making; (2) modelling effort (that is, what the team did); (3) institutional response; and (4) failure or success. The author deemed two of the applications failures since the analysis did not make '... any significant impact on the decisions...,' while two of the applications were judged successes. In the case of the highly successful sport fishing project, Hilborn concludes: 'More importantly, the [simulation] methodology has gained wide acceptance within the fisheries service and it seems probable it will become extensively used in that office.'

Portney [1982]. *Current Issues in Natural Resource Policy.* This is an edited volume of nine easy-to-read chapters that is intended to inform the public of important policy issues in the management of natural resources. It is published by Resources for the Future, a Washington-based nonprofit organization committed to the study of energy, environment, and natural resource issues. Five of the chapters focus on areas that have not received a great deal of attention in the public policy arena: (1) public lands (how should public lands be allocated to competing uses? how much oil, gas, coal, and timber should be produced from those lands?); (2) nonfuel minerals (an examination of the U.S. dependence on such nonfuel minerals as manganese and cobalt); (3) global climate (discusses two serious threats to climate: carbon dioxide and the greenhouse effect, and the use of chlorofluorocarbons and the breakdown of the ozone layer); (4) agricultural land (a discussion of the adequacy of agricultural land in the U.S.); and (5) private forests (examines the importance of private forests in terms of land use and timber production). Three chapters are devoted to issues related to the areas of endangered species, marine fisheries, and water supplies.

Dykstra [1984]. *Mathematical Programming for Natural Resource Management.* The goal of this book is to expose readers (primarily students taking introductory

Exhibit 1.1 (continued)

---

courses) to those mathematical programming techniques that have proved useful in modelling and solving problems in the management of natural resources. Five chapters are devoted to linear programming including coverage of graphical solutions, the simplex method, and duality. The largest of the five chapters (it is over 70 pages long) provides the details of six applications of linear programming to problems in timber harvest scheduling, veneer production planning, agroforestry, wildlife management, land use planning, and soil loss. In addition to these areas, the book also includes examples and problems in outdoor recreation, ecology, water resources, range management, mining, and fisheries. Dykstra works through a formulation of each problem and then discusses the optimal solution in detail. The remaining chapters in the book cover network models, multi-objective programming, integer programming, and dynamic programming. Each chapter includes a useful set of literature citations and homework problems.

Mangel [1985]. *Decision and Control in Uncertain Resource Systems.* This book serves as an advanced introduction to resource exploitation and exploration under uncertainty. The first two chapters give a review of probability theory, an introduction to stochastic processes, and a discussion of optimal stochastic control and stochastic dynamic programming. The next five chapters contain various applications of these methods: key results in the deterministic theory of resource exploitation; exploration for and optimal utilization of exhaustible resources; exploration, observation, and assessment of renewable resource stocks; management of fluctuating renewable resource stocks; and management of mixed renewable and exhaustible resource systems. Examples are drawn from fisheries management and agricultural pest control. However, the author does not cover water resource systems. The book contains a reference list with more than 260 entries.

Kennedy [1986]. *Dynamic Programming: Applications to Agriculture and Natural Resources.* This book presents a comprehensive treatment of the basics of dynamic programming (about 40% of the book) and its application to natural resource management problems. There are five main sections with eleven chapters in all: (1) Introduction; (2) The Methods of Dynamic Programming—introduction to DP, stochastic and infinite-stage DP, and extensions to the basic DP formulation; (3) Dynamic Programming Applications to Agriculture—scheduling, replacement, and inventory management, crop management, and livestock management; (4) Dynamic Programming Applications to Natural Resources—land management, forestry management, and fisheries management; and (5) Conclusions. An appendix contains BASIC listings of several dynamic programming routines written by Kennedy. The book contains numerous large tables that nicely summarize some of the studies in which DP has been used. Each table gives the number of stages, the interval between stages, the states, the decision, the objective function, and some brief comments about each application. In these tables, Kennedy

Exhibit 1.1 (continued)

---

summarizes a total of 98 DP citations: 21 in water management, 10 in pesticide management, 10 in crop selection, 32 in livestock management (applications in the management of laying hens, grazing animals, dairy production, beef production, and intensive pig and broiler production), 14 in forestry management, and 11 in fisheries management.

Getz & Haight [1989]. *Population Harvesting: Demographic Models of Fish, Forest, and Animal Resources.* In this monograph, the authors present a framework for modelling populations that reproduce seasonally. One objective is to give a comprehensive review of the theory of discrete stage-structured models as found in fisheries, forestry, and wildlife management. A second objective is to provide a detailed account of the authors' own research into the theory of nonlinear stage-structured population harvesting models and the application of these models to problems in fisheries management and forest-stand management. The monograph contains six chapters: (1) Introduction; (2) Linear Models—life tables, population dynamics, harvesting theory, stochastic theory; (3) Nonlinear Models—density-dependent recruitment, nonlinear stage-class models, general harvesting theory, stochastic theory, aggregated age structure; (4) Fisheries Management—deterministic models, equilibrium yield analysis, deterministic dynamic harvesting, stochastic harvesting, aggregated catch-effort analysis, multi-species multi-participant fisheries; (5) Forest Management—models for predicting stand growth, evaluating harvest systems, nonlinear optimization, application to true fir, forest-level management; and (6) Other Resources and Overview—harvesting and culling large mammals, mass rearing insects, overview. In several places, the authors briefly discuss the theory of linear programming and highlight applications of LP to forest management (for example, the FORPLAN model). In addition, the authors review nonlinear optimization models, solution techniques such as the gradient method, and the application of nonlinear methods to problems in forest management. The monograph concludes with a solid reference list that contains nearly 220 entries.

Frederick & Sedjo [1991]. *America's Renewable Resources: Historical Trends and Current Challenges.* This book provides an interesting historical look at the use and management of renewable resources—water, forest, rangeland, cropland and soil, and wildlife—found in the United States. The focus of the book is to describe in detail how the quantity and quality of the U.S.'s resource base has changed over the last 300 years and also to describe how the management of each renewable resource has contributed to the changes. There are seven chapters written by acknowledged experts, including five senior researchers from the staff of Resources for the Future. The first chapter is an overview written by Frederick and Sedjo that covers trends in renewable resources. Each of the next five chapters traces the history of a renewable resource. For example, the chapter on forest resources covers how forests have changed over four time periods: 1600 to 1849,

Exhibit 1.1 (continued)

1850 to 1920, 1921 to the end of World War II, and 1945 to the late 1980s. In particular, this chapter examines such topics as public forests as common property, forest management, early conservation and preservation movements, changing land-use patterns, forest renewability, and the roles of the federal government and the private sector in forest renewal. The other four chapters are similarly structured. The final chapter cuts across several resources in its examination of the growing role of outdoor recreation in the United States.

---

as ecosystem balance, biodiversity, and the potential medicinal and industrial benefits of dying species. For example, the overexploitation of blue whales for their oil has resulted in their virtual extinction; smaller species of whales have also been overharvested. The effective management of endangered species and wildlife in general often requires the careful balancing of economic and biological considerations.

Water resources management

Worldwide, water is one of the most abundant, important, and versatile natural resources. Animals and plants require water to survive, while water is needed for manufacturing, farming, and generating electricity. The hydrological cycle makes water a renewable resource: surface water evaporates, rises as vapor into the atmosphere, and is precipitated as rain, snow, and hail. Water is usually plentiful but supply and demand do not always coincide perfectly. Too much water leads to flooding and too little water leads to drought. Water resource managers must be able to anticipate, plan for, and remedy these natural imbalances in a systematic way.

Over the last 40 years, policy makers and analysts associated with government agencies, consulting firms, research institutes, and universities throughout the world have relied upon a wide variety of management science and operations research (MS/OR) models to gain insights into important problems that deal with the management of fish, forests, wildlife, and water. MS/OR models incorporate elements of the physical system under study along with practical constraints into a mathematical representation that is then studied within an overall decision-making framework. In general, MS/OR models serve as powerful aids to decision-making and, in the decade ahead, they can play a major role in the management of natural resources.

Our goal in this chapter is to review the published literature on MS/OR modelling efforts in natural resource management and to report on the state of the art in applying MS/OR methods to problems in fisheries management, forestry, wildlife management, and water resources management. We do not seek to be encyclopedic since the open literature that comprises natural resource management is simply too vast. Rather, we focus on representative streams of applied research. We are especially interested in those applications in which modelling results were actually implemented and used by policy makers. We also highlight applications in which results from MS/OR models guided and shaped the decision-making process in a substantial way but final results may not have been implemented. For those applications that we discuss, we try to impart the institutional setting for the application and we try to bring out the challenges that are involved in modelling and solving complex problems and in implementing recommendations that are based on model results.

2. Fisheries management

2.1. Overview of MS/OR models in fisheries management

The use of mathematical methods to model fisheries began in the mid to late 1950s with the contributions of Ricker [1954] and Beverton & Holt [1957] to the famous problem of predicting the number of recruits (that is, the number of new fish that become vulnerable to fishing in a given season) that will be produced by a population for any given stock size. Ricker specifies a curvilinear density-dependent recruitment–stock relationship of the following form

$$R = \alpha S e^{-\beta S}, \tag{2.1}$$

where S is the stock and R is the recruitment. This functional form (known as a Ricker curve) predicts that recruitment maximizes for some intermediate stock size and that for high stock sizes recruitment will decline. The contrasting relationship (known as a Beverton and Holt curve)

$$R = S(AS + B)^{-1} \tag{2.2}$$

suggests that at high stock values recruitment approaches a maximum asymptotically. In both models, at low stock size, recruitment increases nearly in proportion to stock size. (The interested reader can consult Chapter 5 of Rothschild [1986] for more information on the recruitment–stock paradox.) The static and dynamic versions of the Gordon–Schaefer model (see Clark [1985] for details) focused on the relationships between catch and fishing effort and between revenue and fishing effort. These models, using elementary calculus, gave rise to the key concepts of maximum sustainable yield, maximum economic yield, and bionomic equilibrium. This type of mathematical modelling prevailed until the early 1970s when researchers began to apply methods from optimal control theory and mathematical programming to a wide variety of problems in fisheries management.

One of the first papers to apply linear programming to fisheries management and decision-making appeared in the journal *Fishery Bulletin* in 1971. Rothschild & Balsiger [1971] develop a linear program that is designed to help manage salmon. The traditional approach had been to allocate the salmon catch to the days of the run, based on the experience of management biologists. The primary (biological) objective had been the attainment of an escapement (post-harvest population) goal, resulting in economic inefficiencies. The LP seeks to maximize the value of the salmon catch subject to a variety of constraints including an escapement goal. In the LP model, fish are categorized by age and sex. The decision variables are defined to be the number of fish of category i caught on day j of the salmon run. There are two major sets of constraints. The first set ensures that the daily catch does not exceed the daily capacity of the canneries. The second set provides for adequate escapement for each category of fish. The proposed LP model is illustrated on the 1960 sockeye salmon run in the Naknek–Kvichak system of Bristol Bay, Alaska (this system is a chain of lakes and rivers connecting Bristol Bay to the sea). There are 18 days in the run and the LP model contains about 180 variables and 100 constraints. Rothschild & Balsiger experiment with three value functions which set the daily value of catch. The increased value of the optimally allocated catch ranges from $350 000 to $420 000, depending on the value function. In addition, the optimal solution enables the cannery to process the same number of fish in fewer days of operation. Finally, sensitivity analysis and interpretation of shadow prices are examined in detail.

Over the last 20 years or so, despite the great difficulty in obtaining reliable data, fisheries managers have used a variety of MS/OR methods to model and manage fisheries. For example, more recently, Lane [1988, 1989a] models the investment decision-making of fishermen as a Markov decision process. Walters & Collie [1989] use statistical analysis and simulation to develop a long-term strategy to manage Pacific groundfish. Gunn, Millar & Newbold [1991] use large-scale linear programming to coordinate harvesting, processing, and marketing in the Atlantic Canada groundfishery. Charles [1992] tries to understand the behavior of the Gulf of Carpenteria prawn fishery over a 50-year time horizon by using a Bayesian updating algorithm that is embedded within a bioeconomic simulation model. Crowley & Palsson [1992] describe the use of a statistical model and a linear programming model (models that were originally proposed by Clough [1980]) to determine optimal regulation enforcement policies in Canada's offshore fishery.

As you might imagine, the economies of the Scandinavian countries are highly dependent on the fishing industry. In fact, the first major conference on the use of MS/OR models in fishing (sponsored by NATO) was held in Trondheim, Norway in 1979. Exhibit 2.1 summarizes the volume that emerged from that conference, as well as five other works that survey the use of MS/OR models in fisheries management. One third of the lecturers at the more recent NATO-sponsored conference in Póvoa de Varzim, Portugal were from Scandinavia. With this as background, we summarize in Exhibit 2.2 three key MS/OR modelling efforts that have taken place in Scandinavia.

2.2. Estimating harvest capacity in a multiple-species fishery

The U.S. Fishery Conservation and Management Act of 1976 (FCMA) requires that regional fishery management councils specify the capacity of a fishing fleet.

Exhibit 2.1

A partial list of books and papers that survey the use of management science and operations research methods in modelling and solving problems in fisheries management.

Haley [1981]. *Applied Operations Research in Fishing.* This volume, which is one of the early books to document the use of MS/OR models in fisheries management, contains 35 papers that were presented at the NATO Symposium on Applied Operations Research in Fishing. The symposium was held in Trondheim, Norway in the summer of 1979. The book is organized into six major sections: (1) fish industry – scope, problem, and approaches; (2) resource management; (3) fishing operations; (4) the structure of fish industries; (5) integrated analysis; and (6) additional papers. A wide variety of MS/OR modelling efforts are described including: (1) the use of goal programming to determine the optimal composition of the fishing fleet for the municipality of Øksnes in northern Norway and the use of linear programming to determine the composition of the fleet for the United Kingdom demersal fishery; (2) using dynamic programming to determine the optimal harvesting in fisheries and then optimally allocate the harvest among vessels using linear programming; and (3) analyzing capacity adaptation in the Norwegian fish-meal industry by using a multi-objective simulation model in which the effects of alternative fleet/processing combinations on catching and processing operations can be modelled.

Clark [1985]. *Bioeconomic Modelling and Fisheries Management.* In this book, the author looks at the relationship between the economic forces that impact the commercial fishing industry and the biological factors that influence the production and supply of fish. The book would serve as an excellent textbook for a course in the economics of fisheries management. The primary quantitative tools involve continuous time optimization. In particular, calculus and optimal control theory are used throughout the book's six chapters. In the first chapter, the basic concepts of fisheries economics, including overfishing, maximum sustainable yield, maximum economic yield, and bionomic equilibrium, are defined. The sole owner fishery is also presented. In Chapter 2, the notion of fishing effort is clarified. Catch rates and the impact of stochastic fish concentrations are discussed as well. In Chapter 3, Clark presents a variety of interrelated deterministic single-species fisheries management models. Complicating factors such as government regulation, multiple species, and uncertainty are introduced in the last three chapters. The emphasis throughout is on the small fishing firm that takes prices as given.

Rothschild [1986]. *Dynamics of Marine Fish Populations.* This book conveys the state of the art in fisheries management. In particular, it focuses on the concept of variability in fish stock abundance. Based on empirical data from a variety of settings, the author points out that, not only is it impossible to predict stock

Exhibit 2.1 (continued)

abundance with confidence, it is often difficult even to explain fluctuations after the fact. A key challenge is to separate the effects of fishing from the effects of naturally induced variation. One obstacle is that interactions among species and life stages are poorly understood. Each life stage (egg, larvae, juvenile, and adult) implies its own set of biological variables for each species. The number of possible interactions therefore becomes quite large. A second obstacle is that understanding naturally induced variation and the impact of pollution requires a deep understanding of the marine ecosystem. The physics and chemistry of the sea imply a virtually infinite dimensional marine environment. However, researchers have only recently begun to recognize this complexity. Throughout the book, Rothschild describes a wide variety of problems in fisheries management and the state of current knowledge including recruitment–stock theory, the production of eggs, and the life and death of fish larvae. The importance of density-enhancing and density-dampening mechanisms at each life stage is emphasized. Finally, a foundation for an overall theory of fish stock variability is advanced.

Lane [1989b]. *Operational Research and Fisheries Management.* Lane [1992]. *Management Science in the Control and Management of Fisheries: An Annotated Bibliography.* In these two papers, Lane provides a comprehensive review of the historical development and use of MS/OR models in fisheries management. He begins by classifying the fundamental problems in fisheries management into two major areas – conservation and resource allocation. There are four major groupings of conservation problems: (1) population dynamics – studying reproduction, growth, mortality, and foraging and movement patterns; (2) stock assessment – provides longitudinal information so that inferences can be made about the status of the stock (such as number of fish and their weight); (3) environmental dependencies – determining the magnitude and direction of environmental effects (such as pollution or the effects of the El Niño current in the Pacific Ocean) on fisheries resources; and (4) stock interactions – studying ecosystem dynamics and analyzing the interactions of multiple species. Resource allocation problems focus on controlling the removal of a renewable resource (in this case, fish) for profit. There are three groups of resource allocation problems: (1) stock exploitation – measuring fishing effort and catching power, gathering information about the industry structure of the fisheries, and understanding harvesting operations; (2) harvest allocation – studying the accessibility of fish to capture by commercial harvesters and recreational anglers including the assignment of property rights and enforcement issues; and (3) socioeconomic issues – examining the economic and social impacts of management decisions. Next, Lane classifies papers that appear mostly in journals that specialize in fisheries, biology, and resource analysis into five areas of MS/OR modelling activities: (1) descriptive mathematical modelling – 38 citations covering efforts in economic systems, biological growth, spatial models, international jurisdiction, and linked biological and economic systems models; (2) mathematical programming – 51 citations in optimal control

Exhibit 2.1 (continued)

---

theory, dynamic programming, Markov decision processes, linear programming, and nonlinear programming; (3) statistical analysis and estimation procedures – 22 citations; (4) computer simulation – 7 citations; and (5) decision theory – 23 citations. Seven applied studies in fisheries management are briefly described and two modelling efforts that use actual data from fisheries are discussed in detail.

Guimarães Rodrigues [1990]. *Operations Research and Management in Fishing.* This book is a compilation of 21 papers that were presented at the NATO Advanced Study Institute on Operations Research and Management in Fishing. The conference was held in early spring 1990 in Póvoa de Varzim, Portugal. The two main sections of the volume focus on production functions and management (six papers) and marine fish stocks and fisheries models (nine papers). Many of the papers describe the application of a wide variety of MS/OR methods to diverse fisheries management problems including: (1) the construction of an expert system for use in fishery stock assessment and management on the Chesapeake Bay; (2) the application of vehicle routing heuristics to dispatch a fleet of fishing trawlers; (3) using large-scale linear programming as a tactical planning tool for a large integrated fishing firm; and (4) the use of queueing theory to evaluate the operational capacity of a fishing harbor.

Exhibit 2.2

Researchers in Scandinavian countries have applied MS/OR methods to a wide variety of problems in fisheries management. These three papers highlight the application of simulation, optimization, and decision analysis to problems found in Iceland and Norway.

Jensson [1981]. *A Simulation Model of the Capelin Fishery in Iceland.* Since the disappearance of the herring from Iceland's fishing waters in the late 1960s, the capelin has been the major industrial fish for the production of meal and oil in Iceland. The capelin fleet consists of about 80 boats which range in size from 130 to 1300 tons. Collectively, they catch 500 000 tons during the winter season (January through March). Each year, the capelin migrate along the coast of Iceland from north to east to south to west. There are 23 processing factories scattered along the same coastline. The factories vary significantly in terms of processing capacity. At the end of each fishing trip (several days), captains must bring their catch to a factory. Since most captains prefer the nearest harbor, the capelin fleet spends as much as 30% of its time waiting in harbors. In 1977, the author was asked to assess the costs and benefits of encouraging some captains to sail longer distances in order to reduce waiting and better utilize the available factories. The proposal was to announce a new price structure which would include an extra payment that was proportional to the distance sailed. In response,

Exhibit 2.2 (continued)

a detailed simulation model of the capelin fishery was designed. A key assumption was that each captain selects the harbor which maximizes his ratio of revenue to time. Data were available and the model was carefully validated. The results indicated that: (1) too much time was, indeed, spent waiting in harbor; (2) larger boats would be motivated to sail longer distances, leaving room at nearby harbors for the smaller boats; and (3) a maximum increase of 10% in total catch (worth $3 million) could be expected. The price restructuring proposal was rejected as too radical. However, the simulation model has been in use since 1977 to help answer a wide variety of what–if questions.

Flam & Storøy [1982]. *Capacity Reduction on Norwegian Industrial Fisheries.* In this paper, the authors examine the Norwegian industrial fisheries (primarily in the North Sea and Barents Sea) and find a relatively large amount of fishing effort (450 vessels), depressed stocks, and a low sustainable yield. Given these conditions, they set out to study the impact of capacity reduction. In particular, they formulate the management problem as a linear program which seeks to maximize profit subject to a variety of constraints concerning fleet capacities, capacities at the Norwegian factories where catch is processed into fish meal and oil, and catch limits. The time horizon is one year, and the model allows for multiple species, different types of boats, and numerous factories. By varying the fleet capacity constraints, the model can examine the impact of capacity reduction in a rather systematic way and find the most profitable fleet structure. Using 1977 data, the authors demonstrate that the current fleet's profit is −225 million Norwegian kroner whereas the most profitable fleet has an estimated profit of 185 million Norwegian kroner. In addition, the model reveals that factory processing capacity should be maintained in northern Norway, reduced by 40% in the south, and eliminated entirely from the middle region. These results were presented to the Norwegian Department of Fisheries to help with long-range planning. Despite the fact that the model ignores possible nonlinearities, stochastic effects, and multiple objectives, the model seems to give reasonable answers to vital questions regarding capacity adaptation in industrial fisheries.

Helgason & Olafsson [1988]. *An Icelandic Fisheries Model.* Fishing comprises the major economic activity in Iceland, accounting for 70% of exports. Most important are the demersal species which includes cod. In fact, cod accounts for 55% of the demersal catch. Prior to 1976, domestic and foreign fishing vessels competed for cod in Iceland's waters. Iceland gained full control over her fishing grounds in 1976 and foreign vessels were soon replaced by a domestic fleet of trawlers. Poor planning and overfishing resulted in cod catch declining precipitously in 1983. The authorities and the fishing industry began to recognize the need to restrain fishing effort. In earlier work (late 1970s), Helgason had used a dynamic optimization model to conclude that total effort should be cut in half. His model was criticized for being too simple, too linear, and for having a single objective. The Ministry

Exhibit 2.2 (continued)

---

of Fisheries established a working group to develop a more suitable model of the demersal fisheries. This paper describes that simulation-based model. Model parameters are obtained from a decade's worth of detailed data. The model predicts catch, earnings, and costs several years into the future. Fleet size and composition are major control variables. The model has been used for short-term management of quota systems and long-term investment planning. For example, the model was used to determine that the fishing fleet was far larger than it should be (that is, a 20% reduction could easily be justified).

Capacity is defined as the amount of fish (in pounds) that the fleet can be expected to harvest within a specified time interval using available vessels, gear, and technology, given catch quotas, processing capabilities, and market conditions. Estimates of capacity are especially important in determining allocations of catch between domestic and foreign fishing fleets.

Siegel, Mueller & Rothschild [1979] construct an LP model to estimate short-run capacity (output) in a multi-species fishery. Multi-species fisheries are significantly more complex than single-species fisheries due, in large part, to bycatch. Bycatch is the incidental catch of fish of other species that results from fishing for a particular (target) species. The LP model is presented in Exhibit 2.3.

The LP model is illustrated using data on the otter trawl fishery in New England. Landings of fish by otter trawl vessels in Maine, Massachusetts, and Rhode Island are known for the years 1955–1974. In addition, data on species, prices, bycatch ratios, and physical capacity estimates for both harvesting and processing are also available. Since harvesting costs are not readily available, Siegel, Mueller & Rothschild approximate the problem by maximizing gross revenues, rather than net revenues.

In the otter trawl example, there are 11 species of fish, one vessel category (all otter trawlers), a single time period of one year, and a single fishing area. Recent catch restrictions and bycatch ratios are used. Bycatch is further illustrated in Exhibit 2.4.

Exhibit 2.3

The objective function (1) of this linear program maximizes net revenue at the harvesting level. This includes the value of the target species as well as the bycatch. Constraints (2) enforce the total allowable catch (TAC) for each species and each area. These are key constraints since bycatch often accounts for a large percentage of the total catch. If bycatch is ignored or underestimated, then all of the TACs would be exceeded. Therefore, the bycatch ratios (that is, the a_{mijt} coefficients) must be estimated carefully. In constraints (3), an upper bound on the total amount of processing capacity that is available during each time period is

Exhibit 2.3 (continued)

imposed. Constraints (4) place a physical limit on the amount of fish that can be caught by the fleet in each area and time period.

Input parameters

p_{ijt} = revenue realized per pound of species i landed in a directed fishery for species i in area j during period t (includes value of bycatch)

c_{ijt} = cost associated with catching a pound of species i (and bycatch) in area j during period t in a directed fishery for species i

a_{mijt} = number of pounds of species m caught per pound of species i in a directed fishery for species i in area j during period t

t_{mj} = TAC for species m in area j for all periods

b_{ijt} = the number of pounds of processing capacity required when a pound of species i is caught in a directed fishery for species i in area j during period t

b_t = the number of pounds of processing capacity available during period t

d_{ijt} = the number of units of physical harvesting capacity required when a pound of species i is caught in a directed fishery for species i in area j during period t

f_{jt} = the total number of pounds of fish that a fleet consisting of a fixed size (given technology and gear) is physically capable of catching in area j during period t

Decision variables

l_{ijt} = pounds of species i in area j landed in a directed fishery for that species during period t

Linear programming model

$$\text{maximize} \quad \sum_i \sum_j \sum_t l_{ijt}(p_{ijt} - c_{ijt}) \tag{1}$$

$$\text{subject to} \quad \sum_i \sum_t a_{mijt} l_{ijt} \leq t_{mj} \qquad \text{for all } m \text{ and } j, \tag{2}$$

$$\sum_i \sum_j b_{ijt} l_{ijt} \leq b_t \qquad \text{for all } t, \tag{3}$$

$$\sum_i d_{ijt} l_{ijt} \leq f_{jt} \qquad \text{for all } j \text{ and } t, \tag{4}$$

$$l_{ijt} \geq 0.$$

Exhibit 2.4

In the New England otter trawl fishery, many different species of fish from Atlantic cod to squid can be targeted for fishing. However, even though one species is targeted, other species can also be caught incidentally. The incidental catch is termed bycatch. In the mid 1970s, we see that for every pound of haddock that was targeted and caught, 0.377 pounds of other species were also caught, that is, the bycatch was more than a third of a pound. The total catch of 1.377 pounds produced 52.7 cents in total revenue.

Species sought	Pounds of target species caught	Pounds of other species caught (bycatch)	Total pounds caught	Total revenue (in cents) per pound of target species caught (includes value of bycatch)
Atlantic cod	1	0.344	1.344	35.2
Haddock	1	0.377	1.377	52.7
Red fish	1	0.159	1.159	16.6
Silver hake	1	0.433	1.433	16.2
Red hake	1	1.112	2.112	20.3
Pollock	1	0.476	1.476	22.6
Yellowtail flounder	1	0.186	1.186	46.4
Other flounder	1	0.948	1.948	55.6
Other finfish	1	1.063	2.063	28.7
Atlantic mackerel	1	0.138	1.138	13.3
Squid	1	0.003	1.003	10.0

The optimal LP solution produces a gross revenue of $68.5 million. Since the FCMA requires that foreign fleets be allowed to target those stocks for which surpluses are anticipated, the optimal solution produced by the LP model can be used to provide this information (see Exhibit 2.5). In addition, the authors compute the shadow prices for binding constraints (see Exhibit 2.6).

In related work, Brown, Brennan & Palmer [1979] use both 1971 and 1973 bycatch ratios and other data to formulate an LP model to estimate the total 1975 catch of countries fishing in the Northwest Atlantic. The model assumes that each country attempts to maximize its total catch (in units of weight). Each country is handled separately. For each species j, the amount of species j caught over all fisheries must not exceed the quota for that country. The LP models are small, but the authors had to contend with rough (approximate) data and missing data. The results were quite interesting. Using 1971 and 1973 data, the key ratio of total directed catch (ignoring bycatch) to total catch (including bycatch) was determined for each country and for each species. Overall, it was about 70%. The difference between 1971-based and 1973-based LP solutions was minimal. We point out that Siegel, Mueller & Rothschild found the same ratio (233/325 = 71.7%) in their work. The authors concluded that in multiple-species fisheries, bycatch must be

Exhibit 2.5

The optimal solution produced by the linear programming model of the otter trawl fishery helps fisheries managers anticipate which species will be underfished. Foreign fleets will then be allowed to target those species for which the U.S. quota is not met. For example, the directed catch of Atlantic cod produced by the optimal LP solution is 27 pounds with another 28 pounds of bycatch. This meets the total catch quota of 55 pounds. Consequently, there is no estimated surplus. Thus, foreign fleets would not be allowed to fish for Atlantic cod. For this data set, the optimal solution to the LP indicates that Atlantic cod, haddock, red fish, pollock, yellowtail flounder, and other flounders should be reserved exclusively for exploitation by U.S. fishing fleets. The actual surplus, provided in the rightmost column, is based on real-world data.

Species sought	Directed catch	Bycatch	Total catch	Quota on total catch	Estimated surplus	Actual surplus
Atlantic cod	27	28	55	55	0	0
Haddock	8	5	13	13	0	0
Red fish	17	3	20	20	0	0
Silver hake	0	4	4	265	261	188
Red hake	0	2	2	97	95	77
Pollock	62	4	66	66	0	0
Yellowtail flounder	18	13	31	31	0	0
Other flounder	40	4	44	44	0	0
Other finfish	0	16	16	269	253	132
Atlantic mackerel	61	0	61	165	104	152
Squid	0	13	13	174	161	94
Total	$\overline{233}$	$\overline{92}$	$\overline{325}$	$\overline{1199}$	$\overline{874}$	$\overline{643}$

---

considered in the allocation of quotas to species and to elements of the fishery (such as quotas to a country). Otherwise, an unexpected overharvest of selected species may result.

More recently, Murawski & Finn [1986] described a linear programming approach to effort allocation among two or more fisheries that are exploiting several common species. Their LP model is illustrated for a multi-species fishery system in the Georges Bank region off the northeastern United States.

2.3. Managing Maryland's river herring fishery

Since 1929, river herring landings in Maryland have generally declined. Catch in recent years has gone from nearly four million pounds in 1968 to 133 000 pounds in 1984. Other indicators (including survival data) also suggest that the abundance of river herring in the Maryland portion of Chesapeake Bay has declined.

Exhibit 2.6

A nice byproduct of solving linear programs is the availability of shadow prices. The shadow prices in this application allow fisheries managers to observe how much the objective function will increase if the quota on the total catch of a species is loosened, that is, if the quota is increased. For example, if the Atlantic cod quota is increased by one pound, then the objective function value is expected to increase by $0.14. The shadow price for harvesting capacity is relatively low since increasing harvesting capacity would result in catching additional fish of lower-valued species. The shadow prices can be used to address the question: Which stocks in the otter trawl fishery should be rebuilt? Based on the output from the LP model for this application, it appears that Atlantic cod, haddock, and both categories of flounder would be likely candidates for rebuilding.

Resource	Shadow price (in $ per pound)
Atlantic cod	0.14
Haddock	0.32
Red fish	0.02
Pollock	0.01
Yellowtail flounder	0.30
Other flounder	0.19
Harvesting capacity	0.12

In 1985, faced with declining river herring catches and consistently poor recruitment (survival of a fish to maturity), the Maryland Department of Natural Resources (MDNR) contracted Martin Marietta Environmental Systems to define potential options for action. Three policies were considered: open access to the commercial river herring fishery, restricted access, and closure of the fishery (that is, a moratorium on river herring fishing). After careful analysis, the contractor recommended closure of the fishery. However, this option was never implemented. Fishermen viewed the closure policy as inconsistent. The striped bass fishery was already closed in Maryland. Striped bass that swam uncaught through Maryland waters could be fished in Virginia waters. Fishermen wondered: Would not the same situation exist for river herring? Faced with this unpopular sentiment, key decision makers who were seeking re-election or re-appointment were unwilling to act.

With this as background, DiNardo, Levy & Golden [1989] showed that the difficult decision concerning the river herring fishery that faced MDNR could be modelled using the analytic hierarchy process (AHP). (This is one of the first applications of the AHP to a problem in fisheries management. Other fisheries management applications are described by Imber, Wasil, Golden & Stagg [1991] and by Dzurek [1992]. Technical details about the AHP are discussed by Harker [1989], while applications are catalogued in Golden, Wasil & Levy [1989].) The

Exhibit 2.7

At the top level of the hierarchy is the overall goal of the decision problem. The goal is broken down into four key decision factors and each factor is further decomposed into important subfactors. In this application, there is a large number of subfactors and we do not show them in this partial hierarchy. The lines emanating from the bottom of each decision factor node represent the subfactors. (DiNardo, Levy & Golden [1989] give the complete hierarchy.) At the bottom level are the three policy alternatives that are to be ranked. The weight for each decision factor and each alternative is shown adjacent to each node of the hierarchy.

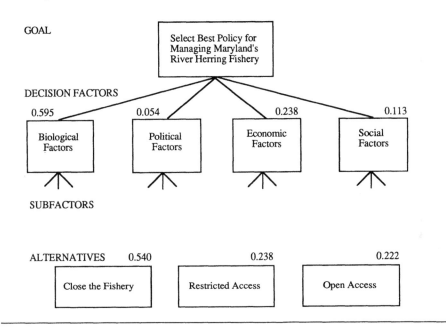

authors constructed a model (using the Expert Choice [1986] microcomputer software system) that sought to answer the question: Which policy should be implemented in order to protect the fish population and limit the negative effects of any regulation?

The hierarchy consisted of six levels and 57 nodes. A partial hierarchy is shown in Exhibit 2.7. The goal is broken down into four major decision factors: (1) biological factors that concern issues relating to the fish population and surrounding ecosystem; (2) political factors that deal with the perceived impact of the management policy; (3) economic factors that examine the economic impact of a policy on various segments of society and government; and (4) social factors that consist of qualitative benefits. Each of these factors is decomposed into subfactors. For example, the social factors branch is further broken down into two subfactors:

aesthetics and intergenerational equity. At the bottom level of the hierarchy are the three policy alternatives under consideration: (1) close the fishery – prohibit all fishing for the species; (2) restrict access to the fishery – the fishery remains open but some form of control, such as limiting the type of fishing gear or mesh used, is imposed; and (3) open access – the fishery remains open for fishing as usual.

To determine the overall importance of each decision factor and each alternative, the authors constructed 181 pairwise comparison matrices. The entries in these matrices allow decision makers to numerically trade off one factor against another. From these matrices it is possible to obtain a weight that indicates the overall importance of each factor or alternative. Some of the weights determined by DiNardo, Levy & Golden are shown in Exhibit 2.7. Thus, we see that the authors judged the biological considerations as the most important factor in determining which policy to implement (this factor received a weight of 0.595). Overall, the authors recommended closing the fishery (the weight of 0.540 was nearly twice as large as the weight given to the restricted access alternative). The authors also conducted an extensive sensitivity analysis of the weights that were produced for each decision factor. An example of this type of analysis is shown in Exhibit 2.8. The results of the sensitivity analysis indicated that the ranking of the alternatives is fairly robust since each individual weight would have to change significantly before the highest priority alternative changes.

Although this particular study did not influence MDNR's decision about the river herring fishery, the results from the AHP-based model coincided with the results reached by Martin Marietta and the work was shared with numerous fisheries scientists in Maryland.

2.4. Predicting salinity levels in the Chesapeake Bay

The effects of salinity on biological and chemical processes in the Chesapeake Bay have been a major concern of fisheries managers in recent years. For example, salinity levels greatly affect the Bay's oyster fishery. High levels of salinity favor the survival of the larval and spat stages of oysters (spats are small, recently born oysters resulting from larval settlement on substrate material such as fossil shell). Simultaneously, high salinity levels provide favorable conditions for the disease MSX which has greatly reduced the oyster population in the Bay. To combat the decline of oysters, the Maryland Department of Natural Resources distributes oyster shells to areas in the Bay where heavy spat settlement occurs (this provides the larvae with increased surface area for attachment) and also transplants oyster seed from congested areas to other areas in the Bay. The success of both activities relies in part on predicting the salinity level of various areas in the Bay that are to be used.

From 1984 to 1989, the United States Environmental Protection Agency collected data at 18 stations in the mainstem Chesapeake Bay and at 16 stations in tributaries of the Bay. At each station, samples were collected at different depths, and salinity, pH, dissolved oxygen, and temperature were measured. There is one

Exhibit 2.8

A sensitivity analysis performed on the major decision factors in the AHP involves varying a simple factor's weight from zero to one in increments of 0.1. The weights of the other major decision factors are adjusted accordingly (all weights must sum to one) and the overall weights for the decision alternatives are then determined. For the river herring problem, this analysis involves changing the weights of the four second-level factors (that is, the weights of biological, political, economic, and social factors). In the sensitivity analysis plot produced by Expert Choice for the biological factor, we see that the assigned weight of 0.595 (indicated by the dashed line) results in the current ranking (Close the Fishery > Restricted Access > Open Access). If the weight for the biological factor is increased, we see that the current ranking remains stable. Only when the weight is decreased, does the current ranking change. Expert Choice produces three other plots of this type associated with the sensitivity analysis on the political, economic, and social factors.

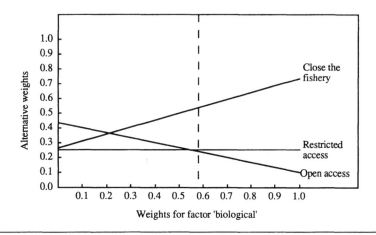

Weights for factor 'biological'

---

data record corresponding to each water sample and the entire data set for this time period contains 43 628 records.

Wang, Golden, Wasil & DiNardo [1992] use 36 258 records that contain salinity values to construct multiple regression models that predict salinity levels in the Maryland portion of the Chesapeake Bay and its tributaries. Salinity is taken as the dependent variable and four key independent variables are included in their models – latitude and longitude of the sampling station, depth, and day of the year on which the sample was taken. A few transformed independent variables, such as squared longitude, were also considered. The authors generated 10 regression models in all: separate models were built for the upper, middle, and lower Bay, lower tributaries, and the entire Bay using two data sets – one data set contained only measurements made at the bottom of the Bay while the other contained all

Exhibit 2.9

This multiple regression model is designed to predict salinity levels in the entire Chesapeake Bay. It was constructed using all of the data. The R-squared value of this model is 0.649. As depth increases, the salinity level should also increase. This is indicated in the model by the positive coefficient of the depth variable.

Independent variables
Day   = day of the year on which measurements were taken
Day1   = sine transformation of the Day variable
Day2   = sine transformation of the Day variable
Depth   = depth at which measurements were taken
Latitude = latitude at which sampling station is located
Longitude = longitude at which sampling station is located
Longitude1 = transformation (square) of the Longitude variable

Dependent variable
Salinity   = observed salinity

Multiple regression model
$$\text{Salinity} = 199.839 - 1.151\,\text{Day1} + 1.161\,\text{Day2} + 0.283\,\text{Depth}$$
$$- 4.863\,\text{Latitude} - 1.543\,\text{Longitude} - 13.402\,\text{Longitude1}$$

---

of the measurements that were gathered at various depths in the Bay. The bottom data models were especially important since that is where oyster larvae settle. One of the 10 regression models is shown in Exhibit 2.9.

Overall, the 10 models performed reasonably well. The models are simple to use and easily explained. They passed standard tests of significance and exhibited R-squared values that ranged from 0.56 to 0.81. In addition, each model used only six independent variables. The authors validated each model on a new data set and found that errors averaged less than 22% for all 10 models and under 14.1% for 8 of the 10 models. The results indicate that the regression models can be used by fisheries managers to easily obtain fairly accurate predictions of salinity levels throughout the Chesapeake Bay.

In subsequent work that uses the same set of data, DeSilets, Golden, Wang & Kumar [1992] construct a three-layer feedforward neural network with an input layer, a single hidden layer, and an output layer that is designed to predict salinity levels in the Bay. The neural network employs a supervised learning algorithm commonly referred to as the generalized delta rule (for a nice introduction to neural networks see Pao [1989]). The authors use only 100 to 300 observations to construct models for each of the five regions of the Bay (upper, middle, lower, lower tributaries, and entire Bay). Using new salinity data from the Bay, the authors test their neural network models against the regression models built by

Wang, Golden, Wasil & DiNardo [1992] and find that nine of their models are more accurate. This represents one of the first applications of neural networks to fisheries management.

With regard to this database, both the regression models and the neural network models provide robust, yet simple ways of predicting salinity levels over the entire Bay and over several regions of the Bay. One major advantage of the regression models is that they are easily explained. A major advantage of the neural network models is that they perform so effectively using very few observations.

In related work, Starfield, Farm & Taylor [1989] develop a rule-based ecological model to study the impact of salinity on plant and animal biomass (quantity) in a large, shallow lake (Lake St. Lucia in South Africa). The model involves discrete variables such as salinity level, lake level, season, plant biomass, and animal biomass. For example, when salinity is low and lake level is high, reeds and submerged plants will thrive and ducks will feed on underwater plants. When salinity is high, reed density tends to decline, fish leave the area, and flamingos feed upon zooplankton. Starfield, Farm & Taylor build a rule-driven simulation model consisting of six if–then rules. They then perform two experiments. In both experiments, salinity levels are increased first and then decreased. In the first case, these changes are slow, whereas in the second case the changes are faster. In each case, the rules are applied over time and both the plant and animal biomass are recorded for each time period. The results are both surprising and informative: faster (more dramatic) changes in salinity level lead to lower levels of submerged plants. In other words, the abundance of underwater plant biomass depends upon the rate of change of salinity more than the actual salinity level. This in turn impacts the level of animal biomass.

2.5. The chinook salmon commercial and sport fisheries in Georgia Strait

Despite their enormous potential, there are very few fisheries applications in which MS/OR models play a major role in policy decision-making. In Hilborn, Walters, Peterman & Staley [1984] a successful collaboration between a university-based research team and the Canadian Department of Fisheries and Oceans is traced over a period of 10 years. During this time, a simulation model developed by the team was used on a regular basis to evaluate policy alternatives with respect to the chinook salmon commercial and sport fisheries in Georgia Strait, British Columbia. Legislation to prevent overfishing was passed regulating these fisheries as a result of this joint effort. The chronology of key events is summarized in Exhibit 2.10.

Several important observations emerge from this modelling effort:

(1) In public-sector decision-making, the major obstacles are often political, rather than scientific.

(2) The role of the model was one of evaluation – it told the managers what would happen if they implemented certain policies.

(3) The primary decision maker came to the research team for help.

Exhibit 2.10

This time line traces the chronology of the development and use of a computer simulation model that was designed for a policy analysis of the sport and commercial salmon fisheries in British Columbia, Canada.

Date	Event
Early 1970s	Researchers at the University of British Columbia (UBC) began work on a simulation model of the Skeena River salmon fishery.
1974–1976	Researchers hold meetings and workshops with the Canadian Department of Fisheries and Oceans (DFO). DFO felt the UBC approaches were interesting, but the real world was too complicated for these models.
1977	A.W. Argue, chief management biologist for the south coast of British Columbia, became convinced that sport and commercial fishermen in Georgia Strait were seriously overexploiting chinook salmon. The sport fishery was essentially unregulated: no fishing license was required and fishing was permitted year round with a large daily catch limit. In addition, recent surveys had revealed the sport fishery to be three to four times larger than previously thought.
1977	Mr. Argue, charged with making recommendations to DFO, looked to the UBC researchers for help. The team met with Mr. Argue and began building a simulation model of the sport and commercial fisheries of Georgia Strait. Argue sought a set of regulations that would increase escapement (escape to rivers where fish can spawn) of resident fish in Georgia Strait from 36 000 to 72 000.
1977–1978	After a few weeks, the team had constructed a reasonable model of the fisheries. However, it took a year before the model looked good to Argue. He insisted that the model had to produce current values of catch and escapement using current regulations. When new policies were imposed in the model, Argue had to be able to understand why things changed as they did.
Mid 1978	The model had become the official tool to evaluate policies. Two-area licenses (large trolling vessels would choose the fish inside Georgia Strait or outside, but not both) and winter closure had already been evaluated. Argue's goal of 72 000 seemed unlikely. The model was being used in a direct fashion to evaluate a variety of regulations suggested by Argue.
August 1978	Argue left, but his replacement worked with the team and accepted the model.
Summer 1979	The model was again in active use. Managers at DFO settled on a two-area license for commercial fishermen and a 20-inch minimum fish length for sport fishermen.
Late 1979	Sport fishermen lobbied hard against the Summer 1979 plan and won. Many alternative proposals were run through the model.

Exhibit 2.10 (continued)

Spring 1980	A limit of 30 salmon per year for sport fishing was evaluated. A tentative agreement was reached which included the two-area license and the 30 salmon per year limit.
Summer 1980	Salmon stock and catch sank to new lows. Thus, the Spring 1980 agreement was viewed as too weak.
Early 1981	The Minister of Fisheries announced several restrictions on the commercial salmon fishery including a two-area license. Commercial fishermen wanted restrictions placed on the sport fishery. DFO announced winter closure, a one salmon per day limit, and a ban on certain gear types for the sport fishery.
Mid 1981	Intense lobbying followed. The Sport Fish Advisory Committee proposed a limit of 30 salmon per year, an 18-inch minimum length, and a two salmon per day limit in winter as an alternative. The simulation model indicated that this proposal was weaker than the original; nevertheless DFO accepted it.
May 1983	Regulations were in place for both the commercial and sport fisheries.

(4) The amount of time the research team spent on communication with managers was considerable.

(5) The project represented a long-term commitment.

We will revisit some of these points later in this chapter when we discuss successful efforts in natural resource modelling.

3. Forestry

3.1. Overview of MS/OR models in forestry

There has been a long and successful association between MS/OR models and problems in forestry that goes back to the mid 1950s. One of the earliest applications of an MS/OR method to a forestry problem was the use of linear programming to solve the paper trim problem, that is, the problem of how to best cut rolls from a machine into sizes that are demanded by customers (see Paull & Walter [1955]). This was followed by the famous Lanchester prize-winning work of Gilmore & Gomory [1961, 1963] in which the column generation technique was developed to solve the cutting stock problem.

Over the last four decades, MS/OR methods have been applied to a diverse set of problems in forest management and in the forest products industry. Optimization and simulation have been used to solve problems in two major areas: forest management (including problems in nursery operations, stand management, and the protection of forest stands) and forest products (including problems in harvesting trees, crosscutting trees into logs, transporting forest products, lumber manufacture, and manufacturing finished goods). The four works listed in Exhibit 3.1 give a comprehensive survey of MS/OR applications in both areas.

Although the focus of this section is on public-sector applications in forest management, we point out that large profit-making companies have been major users of MS/OR methods in both application areas. For example, from 1977 to 1985, the Weyerhaeuser Company, which is one of the largest forest products companies in the world, cited benefits of over $100 million due to improved operations from using an interactive, video-based training device known as VISION (see Lembersky & Chi [1986] for more details about this Edelman Prize winning application). VISION simulates the stem-cutting decisions that workers face on the floor of the forest. VISION has optimizing capabilities: a dynamic programming model embedded within the software finds the optimal cutting decision for each stem and compares the profit of the best solution to the profit that results from a forest worker's cutting decision. In this way, VISION serves as both a training device and a decision support system.

The remainder of this section describes the application of several MS/OR tools (that is, multiple objective linear programming, decision analysis, expert systems, separable goal programming, and large-scale linear programming) to problems in timber and habitat management, forest fire management, forest land management, and strategic planning for a nation's forestry sector that are faced by decision makers at the U.S. Forest Service, the U.S. Federal Emergency Management Agency, the Ontario Ministry of Natural Resources, and the Indonesian Directorate General of Forestry.

It is interesting to note that MS/OR models have been applied to natural resource problems that have very different ecological or geographical scales. For example, in forestry management, MS/OR applications span a wide continuum: models have been built for national forests, small groups of stands, and individual logs.

3.2. Pine forests and the red-cockaded woodpecker

The red-cockaded woodpecker is an endangered species that inhabits pine forests throughout the southern United States. These woodpeckers nest and roost in cavities that they have excavated in pine trees. The birds prefer decaying pine trees and it takes at least 95 years for longleaf pine trees and 75 years for other species of pine such as the loblolly pine to become potential cavity trees. Nearby their habitat of older trees, the woodpeckers require a foraging habitat containing pine trees that are at least 30 years old.

The simultaneous long-term management of the woodpeckers' habitat and the production of timber creates difficulties for foresters. On one hand, in order to maximize timber production, forest managers would prefer to cut pine trees long before they become cavity trees. On the other hand, managers also need to

Exhibit 3.1

Over the last 10 years or so, mainstream MS/OR publications have contained numerous papers that apply MS/OR methods to problems in forestry. Listed below are four works that, taken together, provide a solid overview of the field for researchers and practitioners: a special issue of *Interfaces* that focuses on MS/OR in forestry, a paper that gives a comprehensive review of the state of the art in the field from the 1950s until the early 1980s, an edited collection that illustrates forestry applications of MS/OR methods, and a forest management textbook that includes applications of LP, DP, and decision trees.

Harrison & de Kluyver [1984]. *MS/OR and the Forest Products Industry: New Directions.* Harrison & de Kluyver guest-edited a special issue of the MS/OR journal *Interfaces* that focuses on forestry and the forest products industry. The issue contains 12 papers in which a wide variety of MS/OR tools are applied including combining LP and DP to plan Weyerhaeuser's stump-to-product activities in two million acres of pine forests in the southern U.S., using inventory models to manage wood chip inventories at Weyerhaeuser, applying artificial intelligence to select timber stands for harvesting in the Chattahoochee National Forest, and modelling tree breeding using multiple objective linear programming. In the lead article, Harrison & de Kluyver review the 30-year history of MS/OR activity in forestry and identify new research and applications areas. They provide over 30 references of comprehensive review articles and of papers that use LP, NLP, DP, and GP to model and solve problems in forest management planning and in the manufacture of forest products.

Bare, Briggs, Roise & Schreuder [1984]. *A Survey of Systems Analysis Models in Forestry and the Forest Products Industries.* This paper serves as a well-written, comprehensive source of MS/OR modelling efforts. The authors start by tracing the history of MS/OR applications in forest land management and the forest products industry from the late 1950s to the early 1980s. The authors point out that, from 1960 until 1980, twelve conferences, symposia, and workshops were held on the use of MS/OR methods in forestry and nine surveys were written that catalogue developments in the field until 1982. (Bare [1991] notes that another 10 conferences or so, that are devoted to the same topic, were held during the 1980s and early 1990s.) Most of the paper is devoted to a review of MS/OR applications in two areas—forest management (timber production) and forest products (product yield models and process models). The authors provide over 170 references. Applications in forest management are broken down into five areas: (1) nursery operations—3 LP and simulation papers in the operation and maintenance of forest nurseries; (2) stand management—20 DP and NLP papers that address decisions about how many trees (by species) to plant per acre, how to control competing vegetation, and about a wide variety of other problems; (3) growth and yield—23 papers that mostly use simulation to predict the condition of forest stands under different management practices; (4) forest-

Exhibit 3.1 (continued)

---

wide management concerns—30 papers that use simulation, LP, IP, and GP to decide when, where, and how much to harvest; and (5) forest protection—16 papers that use simulation, LP, IP, NLP, and DP to determine how to best protect forests from fire, insects, and disease. Next, the authors examine product yield models. These models help determine how to best convert raw material (such as logs) into finished products. Product yield models are broken down into five areas: (1) paper trim problem—4 papers that use LP and heuristics; (2) crosscutting trees into logs—7 papers that use simulation, LP, and DP; (3) lumber manufacture—10 papers that use simulation, LP, and DP; (4) veneer manufacture—3 simulation papers; and (5) secondary manufacturing—2 papers that apply simulation and LP to millwork and furniture-making activities. Finally, the use of process models (models developed to optimize the activities of personnel and equipment involved in producing a specific forest product) is summarized in six areas: (1) harvesting activities—16 papers that apply simulation, LP, IP, NLP, DP, PERT, and CPM; (2) log allocation and procurement—3 simulation and LP papers; (3) sawmill models—11 papers that use simulation, queueing, and LP; (4) veneer and plywood manufacture—8 LP and NLP papers; (5) pulp and paper—12 papers that use simulation, LP, and NLP; and (6) secondary manufacturing—6 papers that use simulation, LP, and DP. The authors conclude: 'In summary, we believe that SA–OR [systems analysis–operational research] models still have an important role to play in the development of solutions to many of our forest resource management problems.'

Kallio, Andersson, Seppälä & Morgan [1986]. *Systems Analysis in Forestry and Forest Products*. This is an edited collection of 31 articles written by authors mostly from the U.S., U.S.S.R., and Scandinavia. After an introductory article that gives an overview of economic modelling in forestry, the book breaks down into six sections: International Issues, National and Regional Analysis, Timber Market, Long-Term Forestry Planning, Medium- and Short-Term Forestry Planning, and Forest Ecosystem Dynamics. A variety of MS/OR methods are used in the articles including multi-objective optimization for scheduling timber harvests, mixed integer programming for integrating transportation with timber management planning, decision analysis of forest fire management decisions, nonlinear programming for determining the optimal rotation age for a pine plantation, and linear programming for analyzing the impacts of woodfuel policy alternatives.

Davis & Johnson [1987]. *Forest Management*. In the preface of this book, Davis & Johnson observe that '... decision making guided by the forest owner's goals lies at the heart of forest management and that thinking about forest problems in terms of objectives and constraints provides a unifying analytical framework for decision making.' In addition to comprehensively covering standard forest management techniques (such as models for predicting growth and yield), the

Exhibit 3.1 (continued)

authors cover several MS/OR techniques that can be used by forest managers to quantitatively analyze problems dealing with commercial crops of timber and other forest outputs. The book is divided into four parts (Production of Timber from the Forest, Decision Analysis in Forest Management, Valuation, and Forest Management) that consist of 16 chapters. The book is intended as a college textbook so that it includes many numerical problems and exercises with answers. Chapter 6 serves mostly as an introduction to formulating and solving mathematical programs, although some material on decision-making under uncertainty is presented. In particular, two applications of linear programming taken from the forest management literature are presented. One application, adapted from Thompson, Halterman, Lyon & Miller [1973], models the management of timber harvesting and wildlife production in the Pocomoke State Forest in Maryland. The second application, taken from Teeguarden and Von Sperber [1968], focuses on a reforestation planning and budgeting problem for the Douglas fir in western Oregon. The authors also discuss the simplex algorithm, present output from the LINDO computing package (see Schrage [1991] for information about LINDO), and formulate a goal programming model that illustrates how to handle two outputs from a land resource. The authors return to linear programming in Chapter 15 which presents detailed material on forest management scheduling under constraints. In other chapters, the authors show an example of a dynamic programming approach for finding the combination of commercial thinnings (that is, deciding how much volume to harvest and when to harvest it) for a forest stand that best meets management's objective, and present several applications of decision trees. To supplement their presentations, Davis & Johnson provide references to papers in the open literature that apply or develop MS/OR techniques for forest management.

---

protect the woodpecker's habitat of older trees. (A similar problem involving the northern spotted owl in the Pacific Northwest was highlighted in the introduction.) A realistic model of habitat and timber management must consider long-term changes in forest age-class structure, that is, the location of the woodpecker's habitat must change over time. One would think that by simply increasing the longleaf pine's rotation time (say, to 100 years) and also increasing the rotation time for other pine species (say, to 80 years), the needs of the woodpecker population would be satisfied. However, simulation experiments reveal that, under such a policy, the woodpecker's habitat becomes very unstable: levels of habitat would increase dramatically over the next 50 years and then fluctuate between scarcity and abundance over the next 200 years.

Roise, Chung, Lancia & Lennartz [1990], supported in part by the U.S. Forest Service, model the conflicting objectives of maintaining a protected habitat for the woodpecker and maximizing revenue from timber production using multiple objective linear programming (MOLP). MOLP is applied in order to generate many efficient (noninferior) solutions from which the decision maker can make a choice. We point out that MOLP has been used extensively to model and solve multiple-use forest planning problems (for example, see Leuschner, Porter & Burkhart [1975], Steuer & Schuler [1978], and Kent [1980]).

The authors provide an illustrative application using data from the Savannah River Plant Forest in South Carolina. Two management regimes are under consideration: a 30-year rotation of trees for timber production and a 100-year rotation of trees for habitat preservation. Given the current condition and inventory of the forest, the authors use standard growth and yield equations to estimate pine yields over time (for example, cubic feet per acre and cords per acre over time). Their model is shown in Exhibit 3.2.

Roise, Chung, Lancia & Lennartz solve their model of the Savannah River Forest and discuss results in detail. For example, if the forester essentially ignores the habitat (that is, objective weights are set at $w_1 = 1$ and $w_2 = 0$), then the net present value of timber is \$229 million and the size of the protected habitat is 184 acres. If the forester shifts weights to $w_1 = 1$ and $w_2 = 3000$, then the net present value of timber decreases by only 9% but the size of the habitat dramatically increases to 19 524 acres. The authors find that, in general, when the ratio of w_1 to w_2 is large, short rotations will dominate; when the ratio is small, long rotations become more prevalent.

Increasing habitat acreage in the short run is easy, it just takes time (several decades). However, effective management of the forest must ensure that adequate habitat levels are sustained over time. Using graphical methods to evaluate four specific efficient points, Roise, Chung, Lancia & Lennartz demonstrate that stable levels of nesting habitat can be maintained when MOLP-generated harvest schedules are used by foresters.

Exhibit 3.2

This multiple objective linear program indicates how adequate and stable nesting habitat levels can be reached and maintained. The model, with a planning horizon of 200 years, examines 10-year periods and includes 1080 decision variables and 182 constraints. The objective function (1) is a linear combination of the net present value of timber in dollars and the size of the protected habitat in acres. The objective function weights may be varied by the decision maker to specify the efficient frontier. The individual objectives are defined by (2) and (3). In order to reduce the impact of initial conditions, the sustainable habitat constraint is not imposed until the seventh decade. Constraints (4) limit fluctuations in harvest volume from one period to the next. Constraints (5) limit fluctuations in acres of nesting habitat from one period to the next. Constraints (6) limit fluctuations in areas of foraging habitat from one period to the next. Land area constraints are provided in (7).

Exhibit 3.2 (continued)

Input parameters

$$a_{ijk} = \begin{cases} 1 & \text{if the age of trees at site type } i \text{ is 75 years or more for loblolly pine} \\ & \text{and 95 years or more for longleaf pine under regime } j \text{ in period } k, \\ 0 & \text{otherwise} \end{cases}$$

c_{ij} = the discounted net revenue associated with site type i under management regime j

$$f_{ijk} = \begin{cases} 1 & \text{if the age of trees at site type } i \text{ is 30 years or more under regime } j \\ & \text{in period } k, \\ 0 & \text{otherwise} \end{cases}$$

w_i = weight on objective i

AST_i = acres of site type i

HC_{ijk} = harvest volume from site type i under regime j in period k

α, β, γ = allowable variation constants

Decision variables

x_{ij} = the number of acres of site type i under management regime j

NPV = net present value

MH = minimum sustainable habitat

Multiple objective linear program

$$\text{maximize} \quad w_1\text{NPV} + w_2\text{MH} \tag{1}$$

subject to

$$\sum_i \sum_j c_{ij} x_{ij} = \text{NPV}, \tag{2}$$

$$\sum_i \sum_j a_{ijk} x_{ij} \geq \text{MH}, \qquad\qquad k = 7, \ldots, 20, \tag{3}$$

$$(1-\alpha)\sum_i \sum_j \text{HC}_{ijk} x_{ij} \leq \sum_i \sum_j \text{HC}_{ij(k+1)} x_{ij} \leq (1+\alpha)\sum_i \sum_j \text{HC}_{ijk} x_{ij},$$
$$k = 1, \ldots, 19, \tag{4}$$

$$(1-\beta)\sum_i \sum_j a_{ijk} x_{ij} \leq \sum_i \sum_j a_{ij(k+1)} x_{ij} \leq (1+\beta)\sum_i \sum_j a_{ijk} x_{ij},$$
$$k = 1, \ldots, 19, \tag{5}$$

$$(1-\gamma)\sum_i \sum_j f_{ijk} x_{ij} \leq \sum_i \sum_j f_{ij(k+1)} x_{ij} \leq (1+\gamma)\sum_i \sum_j f_{ijk} x_{ij},$$
$$k = 1, \ldots, 19, \tag{6}$$

$$\sum_j x_{ij} = \text{AST}_i, \qquad\qquad i = 1, \ldots, 54, \tag{7}$$

$$x_{ij} \geq 0.$$

3.3. Forest fire management

To a forest manager, fire represents both a management tool and a destructive force. As a management tool, fires can be ignited under controlled conditions (known as prescribed fires) in order to achieve a wide variety of land management objectives such as reducing the accumulation of hazardous fuels that might contribute to more intense wildfires (by burning wastes that remain after logging operations), enhancing wildlife habitat (by removing decadent vegetation and stimulating the growth of more palatable vegetation), clearing the way for seeding or the planting of seedlings, and controlling disease and insects. As a destructive force, once a forest fire has started (say, from a lightning strike or debris burning), forest managers need to make key decisions concerning fire suppression activities in such areas as mobilizing fire fighting crews and equipment, dispatching the initial attack force of fire fighting resources, and managing large fires that escape initial attack and burn for extended periods of time. Forest managers are also concerned with fire prevention programs and fire detection activities. We point out that Martell [1982] gives a comprehensive review of MS/OR efforts in forest fire management. Martell's survey covers the years 1961 to 1981 and contains nearly 200 references. In the three applications that follow, we describe recent efforts in planning and executing prescribed fires, in evaluating initial attack resources for fighting forest fires, and in predicting the outbreak of wildfires.

3.3.1. Prescribed fires

Consider the following problem faced by forest managers in the Prescott National Forest in Arizona. In order to reduce the hazard of wildfire in the forest, managers wish to remove large amounts of vegetation. The managers must make a number of decisions in three key areas: (1) treatment selection decisions (Should air-dropped herbicides be used? Or is prescribed fire the best alternative?); (2) planning decisions (When should the fires be scheduled? What type of equipment and crews are needed?); and (3) execution decisions (Given the weather forecast and site conditions, should the prescribed burn take place? Or should it be postponed?). In making these decisions, managers must carefully consider uncertainties in fire behavior, weather, and other factors in order to guard against a fire that spreads beyond the burn boundaries (an escaped fire could have disastrous effects – in the current case, there are about 2000 homes and other structures in the area).

The sequence of decisions surrounding the proposed burning program in the Prescott National Forest is modelled as a decision tree by Cohan, Haas, Radloff & Yancik [1984]. (This is one of the first applications of MS/OR to prescribed burning.) In Exhibit 3.3, we show the types of decisions and uncertainties that are faced by forest managers in general, and in Exhibit 3.4 we present a decision tree for a prescribed burn program under consideration by managers of a hypothetical national forest. This tree illustrates many of the features from the generic decision tree in Exhibit 3.3. Based on the decision tree analysis for the Prescott National Forest, the authors concluded that, over a 20-year period, total costs plus losses could be halved by implementing the burn program. The authors also use decision trees to model selection of a post-harvest treatment for the Tahoe National Forest in California and to model site preparation for replanting at the Gifford Pinchot National Forest in Washington.

3.3.2. Fighting forest fires

Once a forest fire has been detected, forest fire managers must move quickly to begin fire-suppression activities in order to contain fires while they are small. Managers must make timely decisions concerning the initial attack dispatch that could consist of a ground crew and an airborne attack force: What is the size of the fire-fighting crew? From which base is the crew dispatched? Is the crew transported by truck, fixed-wing aircraft, or helicopter? Are air tankers required to drop water on the fire? Many factors affect the decision-making process including the location of the fire, the fire's anticipated behavior and impact, and the availability of fire-fighting resources.

From 1973 to 1982, the Ontario Ministry of Natural Resources (OMNR) fought an average of 1925 fires per year with annual costs and losses from forest fires averaging 70 million Canadian dollars. In 1982, OMNR wanted to study different options for satisfying aircraft requirements to fight forest fires in Ontario. In particular, OMNR wanted to evaluate different initial attack system alternatives. Martell, Drysdale, Doan & Boychuk [1984] construct a simple deterministic simulation model of the annual operation of the initial attack system that takes into account the use of air tankers for fire bombing, the availability of fire fighters, the construction of a fire line, and the transportation of initial attack crews and their equipment to the scene of a fire. A flowchart of their single-day simulation model is shown in Exhibit 3.5.

The model's results indicated the primary importance of well-trained fire fighters equipped with adequate transport. For most fires, air tanker support would not be necessary. Some of the major recommendations put forth by Martell, Drysdale, Doan & Boychuk (including removing some aircraft that were used as water bombers and purchasing new water bombers) formed the basis of OMNR's Air Fleet Rationalization Plan (the first stage of this plan was implemented in 1983). The Director of OMNR's Aviation and Fire Management Centre noted that: 'In preparing the plan, the results of the study reported in the paper were used as the starting point ... The result, as noted in the paper, was a fleet that is little different than that suggested by the study...'

3.3.3. Predicting the outbreak of wildfires

The Federal Emergency Management Agency (FEMA) provides funds to states in cases of large wildfire emergencies. Simard & Eenigenburg [1990], working at the U.S. Forest Service and supported by FEMA, develop a PC-based executive information system that calculates a daily probability of a large wildland or forest fire for every climate division in the U.S. To qualify for federal funding, state officials must apply to FEMA and await a decision. More than for most natural disasters, a quick funding decision can result in the dramatic limitation

Exhibit 3.3

The general sequence of decisions and uncertainties faced by forest managers when considering whether or not to implement a burn program is illustrated. Square nodes represent decision points and circular nodes represent chance events. In moving from left to right, we see that the first decision managers face is whether or not to commit resources. There are two additional decisions to be made: whether to initiate a full burn and whether to continue, modify, or stop the burn once it has been initiated. Of course, these decisions must be made while there are uncertainties in the environmental conditions, the fire behavior, and the final effects of the fire.

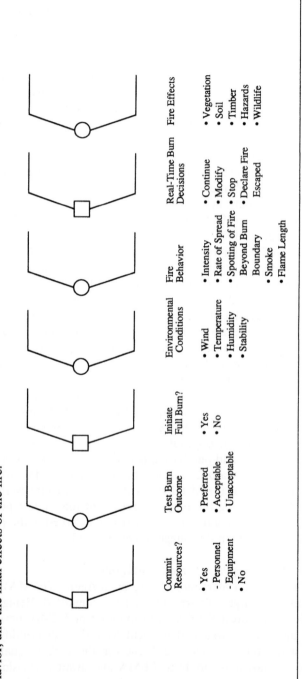

Commit Resources?	Test Burn Outcome	Initiate Full Burn?	Environmental Conditions	Fire Behavior	Real-Time Burn Decisions	Fire Effects
• Yes - Personnel - Equipment • No	• Preferred • Acceptable • Unacceptable	• Yes • No	• Wind • Temperature • Humidity • Stability	• Intensity • Rate of Spread • Spotting of Fire • Spotting of Fire Beyond Burn Boundary • Smoke • Flame Length	• Continue • Modify • Stop • Declare Fire Escaped	• Vegetation • Soil • Timber • Hazards • Wildlife

Exhibit 3.4

This decision tree models a prescribed fire decision problem on a site in a hypothetical national forest. Despite the uncertainty associated with the test burn outcome, the test burn should be performed. Unless the outcome is unacceptable, the full burn should then be initiated. The expected net benefit is $9047.

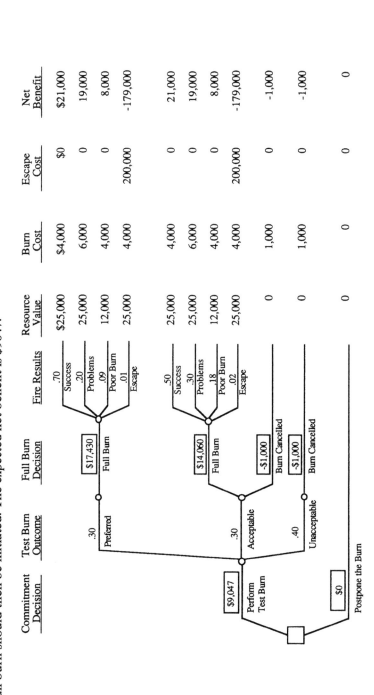

Commitment Decision	Test Burn Outcome	Full Burn Decision	Fire Results	Resource Value	Burn Cost	Escape Cost	Net Benefit
			.70 Success	$25,000	$4,000	$0	$21,000
			.20 Problems	25,000	6,000	0	19,000
		$17,430	.09 Poor Burn	12,000	4,000	0	8,000
	.30 Preferred	Full Burn	.01 Escape	25,000	4,000	200,000	-179,000
			.50 Success	25,000	4,000	0	21,000
			.30 Problems	25,000	6,000	0	19,000
		$14,060	.18 Poor Burn	12,000	4,000	0	8,000
	.30 Acceptable	Full Burn	.02 Escape	25,000	4,000	200,000	-179,000
		-$1,000 Burn Cancelled		0	1,000	0	-1,000
	.40 Unacceptable	-$1,000 Burn Cancelled		0	1,000	0	-1,000
$9,047 Perform Test Burn							
$0 Postpone the Burn				0	0	0	0

Exhibit 3.5

This flowchart depicts the deterministic model that is used by Martell, Drysdale, Doan & Boychuk [1984] to evaluate initial attack resources. The Fire File contains data on a stratified random sample of 80 days from the 1971 to 1980 fire seasons. The Aircraft File contains data on Ontario's fire management air fleet that, in 1982, consisted of 35 aircraft that could be used for transport or water bombing, 9 water bombers, and 17 transport helicopters. The Model Parameters File contains a variety of data including the number of fire fighters that are available for an initial attack. The simulation model was run under a number of simplifying assumptions. For example, the cost of transporting fire fighters and equipment between regions is ignored and it is assumed that each day begins with all aircraft and fire fighters available for immediate dispatch.

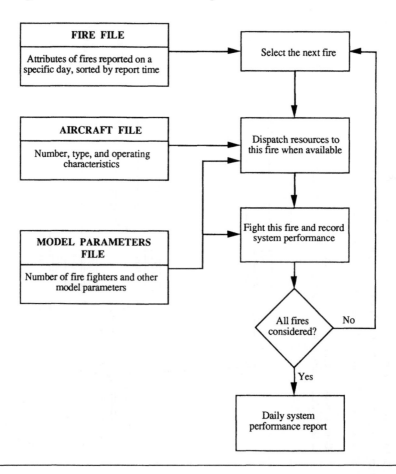

of damage. If one could forecast these large fires accurately, sizeable savings might be possible. The information system developed in this paper is designed to help state fire managers decide whether or not to submit an application for federal funding and to assist FEMA officials in disaster declaration decisions. The key idea is that if the information system is successful in predicting the outbreak of large wildfires, then it can be used with confidence by state and federal managers in order to speed up interagency coordination and cooperation. The system has been designed so that: (1) individual fires can be tracked across the nation; (2) at least 70% of all large fires can be predicted; and (3) it operates 365 days per year. The system, called METAFIRE, required nine-person years to develop and is currently in use. It relies on five types of weather-related data. In addition, a large-fire database was used to evaluate the system. Approximately 80% of all large fires occurring during the test period have been represented in this database. A mapping package and a statistical package are also part of METAFIRE. At the heart of the information system are three decision support models. The first is a weather-based severity index for each of the 390 climate divisions. Six categories of severity are used. The second model is an expert system which attempts to relate nonweather information to the probability of a large fire. The third model is used to actually compute the large-fire probabilities. During 29 months of testing, the system predicted 75% of all large fires. Simard [1991] reports that in the last four years, the system has predicted 83% of all large fires.

3.4. Modelling the Indonesian forestry sector

In work supported by the Food and Agriculture Organization of the United Nations and the Indonesian Directorate General of Forestry, Buongiorno & Svanqvist [1982] develop a separable goal programming model to help perform strategic planning for the forestry sector of Indonesia. Indonesia consists of 13 000 islands and has a population in excess of 140 million. Forests comprise about 60% of the usable land and log production has increased rapidly since around 1970. Nearly 70% of the logs are exported (mainly to Japan).

The mathematical programming model (see also Buongiorno, Svanqvist & Wiroatmodjo [1981]) can be used to address a variety of important questions such as: For which provinces is long-term forestry output most critical? Through which ports should most of the timber traffic flow? Which ports merit expansion? Which shipping routes (origin–destination pairs) are most valuable? Which provinces have the greatest potential as centers for timber manufacture? Rather than shipping to Japan through Singapore, what other port locations make sense from an economic point of view?

Buongiorno & Svanqvist derive the most cost-effective pattern of timber production, industrial processing, and transportation, given specific targets for domestic and foreign demands over a 20-year planning horizon. As many as 500 points are used to represent forests, ports, industrial sites, and demand sites in the underlying transportation network (see Exhibit 3.6 for a small example).

Exhibit 3.6

This type of transportation network is used in the strategic planning model of
the Indonesian forestry sector. Logs harvested and fuelwood at a forest location
are transported to a port or to a domestic industrial site. Logs can be shipped
from one port to another or to a demand destination. At industrial sites, logs
may be used to manufacture sawnwood and fuelwood (from residues). Sawnwood
and fuelwood are generally transported directly from their sources to a port or a
demand site. Ports and demand sites may be within Indonesia or they may be in
foreign countries.

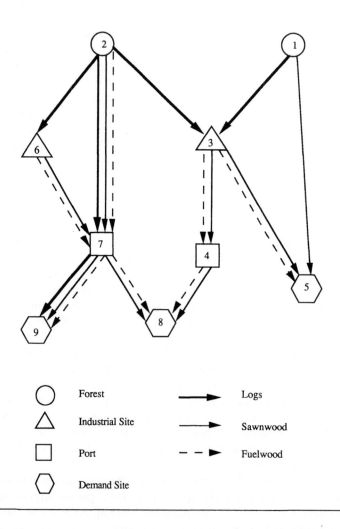

The objective function and constraints of the separable goal programming model are stated below.

(1) The objective function seeks to minimize total cost which includes transport cost, costs of industrial and port capacity expansion, and the cost of not satisfying domestic and foreign demands. Each port capacity expansion cost is a nonlinear function of expansion volume. It is approximated by three linear segments. All remaining terms in the objective function are linear.

(2) During a fixed period of time, the volume of logs or fuelwood leaving a supply point cannot exceed the maximum amount of logs or fuelwood that can be cut in the region represented by the supply point.

(3) At industrial sites, logs are used to manufacture sawnwood. Some of the wood residues that are generated during this process can be used as fuelwood.

(4) The volume of sawnwood manufactured at each industrial site must equal industry capacity, plus capacity expansion or minus underutilization.

(5) The volume of logs, sawnwood, and fuelwood in and out at each port must balance.

(6) The total volume of wood shipped through a port must equal the handling capacity of the port, plus capacity expansion or minus underutilization.

(7) Domestic and foreign demand targets for logs, sawnwood, and fuelwood should be met, or at least, approached.

The goal programming structure derives from variables which measure deviations from demand targets and other variables which measure deviations from current industrial and port capacities. The model has been run using the Functional Mathematical Programming System (FMPS) on a UNIVAC mainframe. Extensive sensitivity analysis has been performed.

Whereas Buongiorno & Svanqvist approximate the actual transportation network with a simple grid, Kirby, Hager & Wong [1986] use the actual road network and apply similar goal programming ideas to the management of national wildlands. Typically, a number of activities take place in a wildland such as tree planting, timber harvesting, recreation, fishing, and transportation amongst forest areas. A mixed integer goal program is developed to determine a least cost land allocation and transportation system. Cost savings for the Sierra Forest in northern California were about $12 million. The model has been used on 14 national forests (including forests in Alaska, California, Colorado, Idaho, Montana, Oregon, and Washington) to explore the impact of proposed actions. Results so far have been favorable and the model should be used more extensively in the future.

In other work, Kowero & Dykstra [1988] demonstrate how linear programming can be used as a long-term planning tool in the management of multiple-species plantation forests. Their model is run on a microcomputer and applied to the Meru Forest Project in northern Tanzania.

3.5. Forest planning at the forest and national levels

Over the last 20 years, the U.S. Forest Service has used a wide variety of MS/OR tools to perform forest-level planning. For example, in the early 1970s, the Forest

Service developed Timber RAM – a mathematical programming system designed to model and solve timber harvest scheduling problems. In 1976, Congress passed the National Forest Management Act which required the Forest Service to prepare comprehensive land management plans every 10 years for the 154 national forests in the U.S. Developing these plans is a formidable task, in part, due to the sheer size of the National Forest System and due to the multi-use capabilities of the nation's timberlands. Field [1984] points out that the national forests, which cover 191 million acres, annually produce 12 billion board feet of timber, 10 million animal unit months of grazing, 200 million visitor days of recreation, and 425 million acre-feet of water.

After regulations were issued in 1979, the Forest Service designated FORPLAN (FORest PLANning) as the primary analysis tool. FORPLAN is a large-scale LP system that consists of a matrix generator, an interface to a commercial mathematical programming package (FMPS), and a report writer. Field reviews much of the history surrounding the development of FORPLAN ($100 million was spent on this effort) and the use of MS/OR models at the Forest Service until the early 1980s. Kent, Bare, Field & Bradley [1991] evaluate nine years worth of U.S. Forest Service experience with an earlier version and an improved version of FORPLAN. The basic formulation that is used in FORPLAN to represent a forest land base is shown in Exhibit 3.7. As the nature of planning problems changes from one national forest to another, each version of FORPLAN can accommodate different types of constraints. Repeated solution of a sequence of FORPLAN models allows important what–if questions to be answered.

Kent, Bare, Field & Bradley point out three major technical difficulties with FORPLAN: (1) a single run of the model on a UNIVAC 1100/92 can be quite costly (costs range from $50 to $500 and some runs cost several thousand dollars); (2) due to problem size, not all problems can be solved; and (3) infeasibilities and fractional solutions are sometimes hard to resolve. In addition, many nontechnical questions on the role of FORPLAN analysis in forest planning have been raised: Should FORPLAN be used to guide strategic, tactical, or operational planning? Are planners seeking answers or insights from FORPLAN models? Is the model to be used as an optimizer or simulator?

Kent, Bare, Field & Bradley conclude that '... the use of FORPLAN (primarily Version 2) has been significant in helping managers translate multiple-use policies into action at the forest level... The agency can be proud of its accomplishments and is to be congratulated for undertaking such ambitious changes in its planning procedures – an effort unparalleled in modern times.' Finally, based upon their evaluation, the authors highlight three issues that need to be addressed if FORPLAN is to be successfully used in future forest planning activities: (1) a clearer understanding of the desired level of planning must be agreed upon; (2) more emphasis should be placed on insights instead of answers; and (3) rigorous training programs in planning and analysis need to be instituted.

In related work, Hof & Baltic [1991] analyze the multi-resource capabilities of the entire National Forest System using a multi-level optimization approach. The authors take the solutions that were generated by solving FORPLAN models in each of the 120 National Forest Planning Units and use them as choice variable options in a multi-level linear programming model of national forest production possibilities. Their analysis covers five 10-year time periods, eight National Forest

Exhibit 3.7

In all FORPLAN models, the analysis areas usually correspond to groupings of acres that respond similarly to a set of management practices. Management practices can include such activities as timber harvesting and recreation facility maintenance. One or more sets of management practices, known as prescriptions, are defined for each analysis area. The LP, shown below, is known as a Model 1 formulation and it is the most frequently used model. The objective function (1) seeks to maximize the total contribution. Constraints (2) are forest land base constraints that ensure that all of the acreage in an analysis area is prescribed. These constraints appear in every FORPLAN model that uses a Model 1 formulation. In addition, users can incorporate other types of constraints into a model. For example, users can include constraints on budget revenue and constraints on output production targets. In this LP, constraints (3) and (4) ensure that the forest-wide timber harvest volume never declines on a period-by-period basis. Constraints (5) restrict the amount of suitable wildlife habitat on a forest-wide basis. In practice, FORPLAN models can have planning horizons of 15 decades and can contain 1000 to 5000 rows and 15 000 to 120 000 columns.

Input parameters

A_i = the acreage of the ith analysis area

c_{ijk} = the per acre contribution to the objective function of the kth timing choice of the jth prescription defined for the ith analysis area

D = the number of periods in the planning horizon

H_d = the total timber volume harvested across the forest (in millions of cubic feet) in the dth period

H_{ijkd} = the per acre volume of timber harvested in period d for the kth timing choice of the jth prescription defined for the ith analysis area

I = the number of analysis areas defined for the forest

K_j = the number of timing choices of the jth prescription defined for the ith analysis area

P_i = the number of prescriptions defined for the ith analysis area

W_d = the minimum number of acres of suitable wildlife habitat required in period d

W_{ijkd} = the wildlife habitat index value in period d for the kth timing choice of the jth prescription defined for the ith analysis area

Decision variable

x_{ijk} = the acres allocated to the kth timing choice of the jth prescription defined for the ith analysis area

Exhibit 3.7 (continued)

Linear programming model

$$\text{maximize} \quad \sum_{i=1}^{I} \sum_{j=1}^{P_i} \sum_{k=1}^{K_j} c_{ijk} x_{ijk} \tag{1}$$

$$\text{subject to} \quad \sum_{j=1}^{P_i} \sum_{k=1}^{K_j} x_{ijk} = A_i \qquad \text{for } i = 1, \ldots, I, \tag{2}$$

$$\sum_{i=1}^{I} \sum_{j=1}^{P_i} \sum_{k=1}^{K_j} H_{ijkd} x_{ijk} = H_d \qquad \text{for } d = 1, \ldots, D, \tag{3}$$

$$H_{d+1} \geq H_d \qquad \text{for } d = 1, \ldots, D-1, \tag{4}$$

$$\sum_{i=1}^{I} \sum_{j=1}^{P_i} \sum_{k=1}^{K_j} W_{ijkd} x_{ijk} \geq W_d \qquad \text{for } d = 1, \ldots, D, \tag{5}$$

$$x_{ijk} \geq 0.$$

System regions, and as many as nine forest outputs. The outputs included the number of elk and deer, pounds of fish, cubic feet of timber, and number of acres of direct wildlife habitat improvement. Based upon the results of this modelling effort, Hof & Baltic conclude that '... it is not feasible for the National Forest System to supply a constant proportion of all projected resource needs. Furthermore, we found that even more conservative levels of output require significant increases in investment and management intensity.' The results from the analysis carried out by Hof & Baltic led planners at the Forest Service to conclude in their 1989 assessment of all forests and rangelands in the U.S. that expected future demands could not be adequately met by continuing the current management direction of the National Forest System. Thus, the Forest Service is considering strategies that involve more reliance on other forests and rangelands and more intensive multi-resource management of the National Forest System.

4. Wildlife management

4.1. Overview of MS/OR models in wildlife management

The use of mathematical models in wildlife management dates back to the 1920s. Lotka [1925] and Volterra [1926] examine the predator–prey relationship for the two-species case using simultaneous differential equations. If N_1 is the number of the prey and N_2 is the number of predators, then the conflict between species can be represented by:

$$\frac{dN_1}{dt} = r_1 N_1 - k_1 N_1 N_2 \tag{4.1}$$

and

$$\frac{dN_2}{dt} = k_2 N_1 N_2 - d_2 N_2, \tag{4.2}$$

where r_1 is the coefficient of population increase for the prey species, d_2 is the coefficient of population mortality for the predator species, and k_1 and k_2 are constants.

The Lotka-Volterra model is quite simple; real-world ecological systems are much more complex (see Holling [1977] for more on this). This line of research (for both the two-species and multi-species cases), however, has been extended by numerous researchers over the years to encompass concepts such as stability, instability, oscillation, and chaos. This work has been applied to wildlife, pest control, and fisheries (see Goh [1980] for details).

Leslie [1945] introduced a matrix model that takes into account the age structure of a population in order to accurately predict the population in each age class at some future time. Many enhancements to the basic model have been proposed since the 1940s and the method has been applied to wildlife, fisheries, forestry, and human demography (see Cullen [1985] for details).

Since the 1970s, standard MS/OR techniques, including simulation, linear programming, and decision analysis, have been applied regularly to wildlife management problems. In Exhibit 4.1, we summarize two books that are general references on modelling in wildlife management.

4.2. Controlling the lion population in a game park

Since lions are major predators of other species, it is of interest to examine strategies for controlling their population growth in order to promote a diverse mix of species in a large game park. Starfield, Shiell & Smuts [1981] describe a simulation model of lion culling operations at Kruger National Park in South Africa. Culling is the systematic removal of lions from the Park. The authors, who acknowledge the involvement of the Chief Director of National Parks in South Africa, set out to study the effects of five alternative culling strategies as applied to five of the 31 territories in the Park.

The model distinguishes between cubs, sub-adults, and adults. The key socio-biological unit for lions is the pride. Sub-adults aged two to three years are expelled from the pride. They form groups of nomadic lions and wander from one territory to the next. Female nomads are absorbed by nearby prides, but they are most likely to return to the pride into which they were born. When the time is right, male nomads challenge pride males. The result is either death or control of the pride.

Data on lion fertility, mortality, social and territorial behavior, and age distribution were available as the result of previous studies of lion culling operations at

Exhibit 4.1

A partial list of books that survey the use of management science and operations research methods in solving wildlife management problems.

Kingsland [1985]. *Modeling Nature: Episodes in the History of Population Ecology.* This book is about the history of population ecology. It is not about wildlife management per se, but it includes many topics which are related to or are a subset of wildlife management. The author traces the interface between the abstract mathematical realm and the biological real world from the early years of this century to the present. Population ecology is the study of how populations grow and decline and how they interact with their complex environment. The environment includes physical dimensions (for example, climate) as well as biological dimensions (for example, predators, preys, competitors). The mathematical topics discussed include contributions from Ludwig von Bertalanffy (the father of general systems theory), the Lotka-Volterra predator–prey differential equations, predator–prey oscillations, the Leslie matrix, the logistics population growth curve, and Robert MacArthur's examination of the tight packing of multiple species into a single environment.

Starfield & Bleloch [1991]. *Building Models for Conservation and Wildlife Management.* This is a book about mathematical modelling in wildlife management. The focus is on how to build and use lean and simple models in order to generate insights and make better decisions. While the modelling process is described in general and numerous modelling techniques are presented, the specific examples all come from conservation and wildlife management. Chapter 1 provides a brief introduction to modelling terminology. Key issues are illustrated via a small example. In Chapter 2, a single-species model is presented. The model addresses the population decline of wildebeest in an African game park. Since lions feed on wildebeest, predator–prey equations are derived. Coefficients are estimated from field data and the model is used to predict the size of the wildebeest population over time, under several scenarios. A stochastic simulation model is presented in Chapter 3. The roan antelope in Africa is vulnerable to a variety of adverse conditions. In particular, habitat, amount of rainfall, predation, and competition from other grazers have all led to population declines. Management seeks to implement policies that will protect the population against further declines. Detailed simulation experiments and sensitivity analyses are presented. Chapter 4 describes a simulation model for controlling the lion population in a game park (we discuss this model more fully in Section 4.2). In Chapter 5, a simulation model of a complex system of herbivores (for example, giraffe, zebra, and wildebeest) is presented. The various species feed upon grass, trees, and shrubs and compete for space and food, but there are no significant predators. Analytical models involving either differential equations or difference equations are covered in Chapter 6. In Chapter 7, linear programming is proposed to determine the maximum (herbivore) population size that ensures adequate vegetation. Next, the conflicting

Exhibit 4.1 (continued)

---

objectives of (1) maintaining the integrity of the vegetation and (2) increasing the population size are reconciled using goal programming. In Chapter 8, the Leslie matrix concept and enhancements are used to predict kudu population changes from one year to another (see Cullen [1985] for an excellent introduction to the Leslie matrix model). Decision trees and expert systems are explored in Chapter 9. The prescribed burning of wooded areas in a park is used as an example.

Kruger National Park. The simulation model was found to be both believable and internally consistent. By studying culling operations in five contiguous territories of the Park, the authors ensured that the simulation was run under conditions similar to those of ongoing field experiments.

The authors examined five culling strategies: no culling (benchmark case); cull entire pride; cull all nomads; cull half pride plus half nomads; cull pride males. One-time and sustained culling simulations were carried out. In the one-time culling simulation exercise, the lion population was monitored for a 4-year period with culling taking place during the first year only. A typical one-time culling simulation run is presented in Exhibit 4.2.

In the sustained culling simulation exercise, the population is exposed to culling for six consecutive years and is then monitored for another five years. A typical sustained culling simulation run is presented in Exhibit 4.3.

The authors propose a bang-for-buck measure of culling efficiency

$$CE = \frac{L_{i+1}^* - L_{i+1}}{c_i}, \tag{4.3}$$

where c_i = the number of lions removed in year i, L_{i+1} = the number of lions present one year later, and L_{i+1}^* = the estimated number of lions that would have been present had no removal taken place.

For sustained culling over n years, the cumulative culling efficiency is given by:

$$CCE = \frac{\sum_{i=1}^{n}(L_{i+1}^* - L_{i+1})}{\sum_{i=1}^{n} c_i}. \tag{4.4}$$

Whether cubs are included in the population size or not, culling pride males (that is, Strategy 4 in Exhibits 4.2 and 4.3) has a larger CCE than the other strategies, by a wide margin.

4.3. White-tailed deer in Ontario

Between 1951 and 1980, hunters in Ontario were allowed to shoot one deer of either sex during the hunting season. Since 1980 harvest quotas on antlerless

Exhibit 4.2

These are the results from a one-time culling simulation run carried out over a 4-year period for lions in Kruger National Park. Two observations emerge from these results. First, the long-term impact of culling in the first year only is negligible, regardless of the culling strategy. Second, it is important to focus on the social status of the culled lions. For example, Strategy 4 requires culling many fewer lions than the other culling strategies.

Strategy	Year			
	1	2	3	4
Strategy 0: No culling				
Adults plus sub-adults	63	67	52	53
Cubs	44	37	40	50
Strategy 1: Cull entire pride				
Adults plus sub-adults	71	35	44	58
Cubs	37	0	33	30
Number culled	76	0	0	0
Strategy 2: Cull all nomads				
Adults plus sub-adults	66	58	63	63
Cubs	42	47	64	50
Number culled	25	0	0	0
Strategy 3: Cull half pride and half nomads				
Adults plus sub-adults	74	53	54	58
Cubs	28	21	34	59
Number culled	50	0	0	0
Strategy 4: Cull pride males				
Adults plus sub-adults	75	52	44	43
Cubs	39	4	51	50
Number culled	13	0	0	0

(female) deer have been imposed in many parts of Ontario. In work performed for the Wildlife Branch of Ontario's Ministry of Natural Resources, Euler & Morris [1984] study the impact of the either sex quota in order to learn what kinds of limits on the harvesting of female deer made sense from an ecological point of view. The authors describe the use of a computer model (ONEPOP) that simulates the dynamics of the white-tailed deer populations in four areas of Ontario – Loring, Parry Sound, Manitoulin Island, and Bruce Peninsula. All four areas are similar in that the white-tailed deer are subject to long, cold winters and to predation by wolves and coyotes.

The computer model simulates the population dynamics of big game in order to assist natural resource managers in decision-making (Walters & Gross [1972] and Williams [1981] provide background information on the computer model). The model is essentially a bookkeeping simulation program in which animals are added

Exhibit 4.3

These are the results from a sustained culling simulation run carried out over an 11-year period for lions in Kruger National Park. Culling is performed in years 1 through 6 and the effects are then monitored in years 7 through 11. Two observations emerge from these results. First, Strategy 2 has no influence on the population in the target territories (Strategy 0 and Strategy 2 yield essentially the same number of lions). Second, Strategy 4 requires culling many fewer lions than the other culling strategies. Starfield, Shiell & Smuts [1981] go on to show that when Strategies 1 to 4 are applied to the five target territories there is a reduction in the total lion population (excluding cubs) over all 31 territories.

Strategy	Year										
	1	2	3	4	5	6	7	8	9	10	11
Strategy 0: No culling											
Adults plus sub-adults	62	67	52	53	61	62	51	64	61	47	57
Cubs	44	37	40	50	47	44	40	34	47	49	47
Strategy 1: Cull entire pride											
Adults plus sub-adults	62	41	24	17	32	24	15	24	33	26	32
Cubs	44	0	0	0	0	0	0	3	15	27	42
Number culled	83	28	19	14	20	20	0	0	0	0	0
Strategy 2: Cull all nomads											
Adults plus sub-adults	62	50	60	52	47	61	49	43	50	52	52
Cubs	44	38	55	47	51	30	44	32	44	40	45
Number culled	23	12	25	19	15	23	0	0	0	0	0
Strategy 3: Cull half pride and half nomads											
Adults plus sub-adults	62	48	45	31	29	29	47	32	57	47	47
Cubs	44	16	19	11	11	4	11	20	53	25	68
Number culled	4	32	30	21	20	16	0	0	0	0	0
Strategy 4: Cull pride males											
Adults plus sub-adults	62	56	55	39	42	43	38	37	42	47	46
Cubs	44	7	0	0	0	0	0	59	43	53	37
Number culled	11	6	8	6	6	8	0	0	0	0	0

or subtracted over time in response to events such as births, deaths, hunting, and severe winters.

The data sources for the simulation experiment include earlier work by conservation officers and field biologists, (faecal) pellet-group surveys, hunter check stations, and a mailed survey of licensed hunters. To test the model, observed data from the 10-year period extending from 1970 to 1980 were compared with model prediction for deer populations. The model was run one year at a time and seemed to work reasonably well. Simulation results are summarized in Exhibit 4.4. In general, the simulation tended to smooth some of the erratic population fluctuations.

Exhibit 4.4

The results of the simulation experiment performed by Euler & Morris [1984] show the impact of the number of female deer harvested on total population. For each site, the estimated population levels and percent of total females that are harvested each year are presented. Based upon the results of the experiment, Euler & Morris conclude that an average harvest of 10% to 13% of the herd's females is likely to ensure population stability, whereas a harvest in excess of 13% is likely to result in a population decline. The authors' final recommendations argue against a quota based on the number of deer of either sex in favor of a data-derived quota that is based on the number of female deer·harvested.

Site	Time period	Start population	End population	Range in % of total females harvested	Average % of total females harvested	Result for overall population
Loring	1967–1976	6400	8000	8–15	10.11	Growth
	1976–1979	8000	7400	11–16	13.00	Decline
Parry Sound	1968–1970	7000	9800	9–16	12.50	Growth
	1970–1979	9800	6000	11–23	18.44	Decline
Manitoulin	1967–1973	5000	3700	13–18	15.17	Decline
Island	1973–1979	3700	7500	6–13	9.00	Growth
Bruce Peninsula	1968–1979	3300	2100	8–20	14.73	Decline

4.4. Simulating the dynamics of barren-ground caribou, roe deer, and moose populations

There are a wealth of studies in wildlife management that use simulation as the primary analysis method. In fact, simulation seems to be the predominate MS/OR tool used by wildlife managers. To illustrate this point, we briefly describe three representative simulation studies taken from the wildlife literature.

4.4.1. Barren-ground caribou

Walters, Hilborn & Peterman [1975] describe a comprehensive simulation model of barren-ground caribou dynamics developed jointly by six biologists from the Canadian Wildlife Service and three researchers from the University of British Columbia. The model takes into account food types, the growth rate of food types, the probability of fire by age of the forest, weather conditions, feeding time, sex ratios, natural and hunting mortality, and other factors. Three specific management policies are evaluated. The model indicates that the population size could be increased by reducing the harvest temporarily. In addition, forest fires were found not to pose a threat to the caribou population.

4.4.2. Roe deer

Bobek [1980] models the population of roe deer in central Europe using simulation. The roe deer is a popular game animal and, without careful management, stock size will decrease rapidly. The model, which allows for 20 decision variables to be manipulated by the decision maker, has been implemented in the Niepolomicka National Forest in Poland. After three years of use, the population yield of roe deer in the forest showed a six-fold increase.

4.4.3. Moose

Crete, Taylor & Jordan [1981] study the dynamics of moose populations in southwestern Quebec. Computer simulation experiments are performed to evaluate the impact of different hunting regimes on populations. In particular, three pairs of nearly adjacent populations are examined. Each pair includes one lightly hunted area and one heavily hunted area. The model assumes that predation rather than food limitation is the major mortality factor, other than hunting. Natural mortality is modelled as density-dependent based on an analysis of the data. Aerial surveys by planes and helicopters are used to provide census estimates. Since all moose killed must be registered at a checking station, harvest data are readily available. The simulation's predictions are acceptable; the simulation is used to estimate the equilibrium density and allowable kill for maximum sustainable yield. The authors conclude that moose management in southwestern Quebec can be enhanced by: (1) increasing female vulnerability to hunting to equal that of males by delaying the start of the hunting season to mid-October; (2) maintaining moose density at 0.2 per km^2 by using regulatory hunting pressure; and (3) harvesting more calves by educating the hunting public.

5. Water resources management

5.1. Overview of MS/OR models in water resources management

One of the earliest applications of MS/OR methods to problems in the planning and management of complex water resources systems appeared in the mid 1950s. In an article that was published in the journal *Operations Research*, John D.C. Little [1955] considers the operation of a single water storage reservoir with a hydroelectric plant. Little wants to schedule storage water use so that the expected cost of supplemental energy is minimized. He constructs a discrete dynamic programming model and then applies his model to the Grand Coulee generation plant on the Columbia River using 39 years of historical flow data. The models are solved on a Whirlwind I computer with solution times between 5 minutes and 60 minutes. The resulting solutions produce annual savings of about $70 000. Yakowitz [1982] claims that Little's paper is the earliest reservoir operation study in the English language and calls Little's effort a '. . . computational tour-de-force.' Little demonstrated that MS/OR methods could be used to successfully model and solve water resource management problems and that significant financial benefits could accrue to the users of such models.

In the 35 years that have elapsed since Little's pioneering effort, a wide variety of powerful MS/OR methods (for example, linear programming, nonlinear programming, dynamic programming, and simulation) have been used to model and solve important water resource management problems such as operating a multipurpose, multi-reservoir water system, estimating freshwater inflow needs for estuaries and bays, evaluating investment alternatives in a water supply system, selecting, designing, and managing irrigation methods, expanding water supply capacity, and maximizing benefits in a hydroelectric power system. MS/OR methods have been applied to hundreds of problems in both developed countries and less developed countries throughout the world including the United States, Canada, Mexico, Chile, Brazil, Argentina, The Netherlands, Hungary, Spain, Israel, Pakistan, and Bangladesh.

During this 35-year period, it appears that water resources researchers and managers have openly embraced MS/OR methods: they seem to have recognized the value and importance of quantitative modelling in the overall decision-making process. This is reflected in the voluminous open literature on modelling water resource systems in which published papers number in the thousands. Of course, this precludes an exhaustive and comprehensive treatment in this chapter. Instead, we highlight key works that describe noteworthy MS/OR practice in the field of water resources planning and management. We focus on survey articles and books that can serve as valuable reference sources and, more importantly, we present a number of high-impact MS/OR modelling efforts in which results were actually implemented by decision makers or in which results substantially influenced the decision-making process. To impart the flavor of MS/OR applications in water resources management, we begin this section with a brief synopsis of an application that was a finalist in the competition for the 1985 Franz Edelman Award for Management Science Achievement (for more information about the Edelman Award see Rider, Kolesar & Lilien [1986]) and a description of one of the first MS/OR applications involving the operation of an aqueduct system.

5.1.1. A hydro-scheduling system for Pacific Gas and Electric

Imagine that it is early spring in eastern California. It has been a wet winter with an especially heavy snowfall. The snow has just begun to melt and will continue to melt for the next three months. Streams and rivers swollen by melting snow and spring rains feed reservoirs that store the water. At periodic intervals, the power company releases water from the reservoirs and allows it to flow through power plants to generate electricity. Exhibit 5.1 shows the major components of a hydroelectric system.

One group in the Hydro Generation Department at the Pacific Gas and Electric Company (PG&E) is responsible for developing monthly schedules that specify when to release water, how much to release, how much to store in each reservoir and power plant, and how to route the water through the hydroelectric system. The group must consider many complex factors when constructing these schedules. Exact quantities of rain and snowfall and the timing of the snowmelt are uncertain

Exhibit 5.1

A hydroelectric generation system consists of natural inflows of water, reservoirs for storage, power plants, diversion points, and pipes and rivers that interconnect the various points.

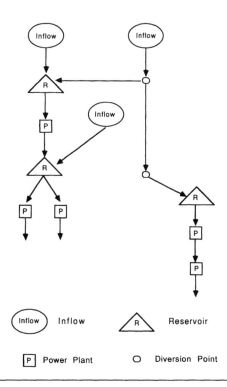

and are difficult to predict accurately. Physical limitations, such as the minimum and maximum storage capacities of each reservoir and the flow capacities of each interconnecting river, canal, or pipe, act as constraints. Operational and legal considerations also apply; state and local regulations specify the minimum downstream flow necessary to protect the environment and to maintain minimum storage levels in the reservoirs. The analysis must also reflect the impact of the demand for electricity which peaks during the summer months.

Prior to 1983, analysts at PG&E manually developed schedules for a hydroelectric system that consisted of 86 power plants, 23 river basins, and over 143 reservoirs. This was a time-consuming process: three analysts took three to five days to route the entire system.

Ikura & Gross [1984] and Ikura, Gross & Hall [1986] use a network flow structure to model PG&E's hydro-scheduling problem. Reservoirs, power plants, and diversion points form the set of nodes, and pipes, canals, and rivers form the set of directed arcs in the network. The decision variables specify the water flow from one facility to another during each time period.

The hydro-scheduling problem is first formulated as a deterministic optimization model with three types of constraints and a nonlinear objective function that maximizes the total benefit due to power generation. Many restrictions, such as conservation of flow and upper and lower bounds on flows and storage levels, are modelled by linear, network flow constraints. Linear, nonnetwork side constraints capture such physical, operational, and legal restrictions as an upper bound on the release of water from a reservoir. Nonlinear constraints model conditions when water must be spilled from a reservoir during periods when streamflows are high.

By using Lagrange multipliers, the authors reformulate this model by moving the nonlinear, forced-spill constraints to the objective function. The resulting NLP has a nonlinear objective function and linear constraints. For a hydroelectric system with nine reservoirs and eight power plants, the NLP for a two-year schedule requires 817 rows and 1272 columns.

The reformulated model is embedded in a decision support system known as HYSS (HYdro System Scheduler) that can produce a 12-month schedule for a medium-size river system in about 10 seconds on an NAS 9050 computer. A near-feasible starting solution is generated by using a specialized network flow algorithm to solve the sub-problem, which consists of the linear portion of the objective function and the network constraints. Using this starting point, a large-scale commercial code for solving NLPs is then used to solve the entire model.

Using HYSS over a 3-year period enabled PG&E to increase power generation and to increase the amount of water available for energy production during peak summer months. The authors estimate that producing schedules with HYSS has saved PG&E between $10 million and $45 million per year.

Gross [1989] confirmed that HYSS is still used extensively for scheduling by the Hydro Generation Department at PG&E. The output from HYSS is also used for fuel requirement forecasting by the Power Control Department. Staschus [1991] informed us that PG&E is working on a research and development project to include stochastic optimization (using Benders' decomposition) and more explicit coordination with thermal resources in its mid-term hydro scheduling.

The hydro-scheduling problem at PG&E is an illustrative example of a high-impact, very successful application of MS/OR methodology: a real-world problem was modelled and solved, the model-produced schedules were actually implemented, and PG&E saved a substantial amount of money each year.

5.1.2. Central Arizona Project

Authorized by Congress in 1968 after years of legislative and judicial debate, the Central Arizona Project (CAP) is a large aqueduct system which will deliver Arizona's remaining Colorado River water entitlement to urban, agricultural, and industrial water users in central and southern Arizona. Up to 3000 cubic feet per second of flow will be lifted 824 feet from Lake Havasu on the Colorado River and conveyed through a series of open channel aqueducts, tunnels, and inverted pipe siphons and raised another 465 feet by relift pumping plants. The CAP is composed of three major aqueducts: Granite Reef, Salt Gila, and Tucson. These aqueducts are all connected serially, stretching from the Colorado River at Lake Havasu to south of Tucson. Within their span there are 14 pumping plants using in excess of 500 megawatts of power, 38 check structures, and 33 turnouts. The check structures are located at periodic intervals along the aqueduct, breaking the aqueduct into numerous, independent reaches, called pools. The entire system is designed to be remotely operated from the Arizona Projects Office of the U.S. Bureau of Reclamation, located in Phoenix, Arizona.

Yeh, Becker, Toy & Graves [1980] describe the development of an optimization model that can be used to determine operating policies for the Granite Reef Aqueduct of CAP. The objective of the model is to minimize on-peak hour pumping while meeting downstream delivery and constraints. The section of aqueduct considered for optimization contains 4 pumping stations, 4 inverted siphons, 2 turnouts, 13 check structures, and 19 pools. Pump schedules and gate positions and flows are determined on the basis of steady-state linearized analysis of the hydraulics at a 2-hour interval for a week. Linear programming is used for the optimization with decomposition in time and along the aqueduct length. The linearized hydraulics are included in the constraint set. Therefore, the optimized results are hydraulically feasible. An iteration and updating procedure is used to reduce linearization errors.

Decision variables in the LP model are pump and gate flow. Model outputs include an optimal on-peak pumping policy over a week's duration and accompanying gate flows that will satisfy system constraints. The LP model was solved on an IBM 360/91 and, on the average, a weekly run required about 40 LP optimizations taking 750 seconds of execution time. By using the optimization procedure, the authors estimated that $5000 to $20 000 in pumping costs could be saved per week. The optimization model developed by Yeh, Becker, Toy & Graves was one of the first applications of mathematical programming to the optimal operation of a modern aqueduct system. In the next section, we review several books and articles that survey applications, MS/OR methods, and modelling issues.

5.1.3. Literature review of modelling efforts in water resources management

The open literature on the use of MS/OR methods in water resources management contains many books and articles that are intended to comprehensively survey the field. Exhibit 5.2 contains an annotated bibliography of references that catalogue MS/OR models and that also discuss water resource modelling issues. Based on our review of the literature, including the seven citations listed in Exhibit 5.2, we conclude the following.

(1) Over the last 35 years or so, there has been a dramatic increase in the application of management science and operations research models and solution methods to problems found in the field of water resources management. Researchers and practitioners have used a wide array of optimization-based (most notably LP, NLP, and DP), simulation-based, and statistical models to solve important problems (in particular, problems in reservoir operation, hydropower generation, and irrigation management). Willett & Sharda [1991]

Exhibit 5.2

A partial list of books and papers that survey the use of management science and operations research methods in modelling and solving problems in water resources management.

Loucks, Stedinger & Haith [1981]. *Water Resource Systems Planning and Analysis*. In this book, the authors present quantitative methods (mathematical programming and simulation, probability and statistics, cost–benefit analysis, and multi-objective modelling) that form the basis of water resource systems analysis. The book is written for students taking college-level introductory water resources courses in engineering schools and for practitioners who are planning and managing water resource systems. The book is divided into four parts: overview (planning and analysis of water resource systems), methods of analysis (identification and evaluation of water management plans, planning under uncertainty, and planning objectives), managing surface-water quantity (deterministic and stochastic river basin modelling, synthetic streamflow generation, and irrigation planning and operation), and water quality management (water quality prediction, simulation, and management).

Yakowitz [1982]. *Dynamic Programming Applications in Water Resources*. The author reviews the use of dynamic programming in a wide variety of water resource problems including water quality control in rivers and sewers, water resource project development (for example, allocation of capacity to reservoir sites and timing and sequencing of water supply projects), irrigation management, and reservoir operations for both the deterministic and stochastic cases. Yakowitz surveys a variety of techniques that have been used to solve problems including discrete DP, differential DP, and state incremental DP. Over 130 citations are provided. Yakowitz concludes that '... water resource problems serve as an excellent impetus and laboratory for dynamic programming developments; conversely, progress in making dynamic programming applications in water resources economically viable depends on further advances in theoretical and numerical aspects of dynamic programming. At the present time the influence of dynamic programming on water resource practice is modest.'

Loucks, Stedinger & Shamir [1984]. *Research in Water Resources and Environmental Systems Modeling: Some Historical Perspectives, Current Issues, and Future Directions*. Loucks, Stedinger & Shamir [1985]. *Modelling Water Resource Systems: Issues and Experiences*. In these two papers, the authors try to assess two decades worth of applications of optimization and simulation modelling to a variety of water resources and environmental management problems. Each paper briefly reviews the recent history of modelling in the field and then presents a representative sample of real-world water resources and environmental modelling applications. In the 1984 paper, 42 applications from around the world (including the High Aswan Dam in Egypt, the St. John River in Canada, and the Mu River in Burma) are summarized with respect to problem type, selected model, overall

Exhibit 5.2 (continued)

purpose of effort, outcomes, and results. In addition to discussing key factors that indicate the success or failure of modelling efforts (for example, commitment of the government agency), the authors discuss current modelling issues in three areas: (1) model appropriateness, complexity, and validity; (2) information needs and communication; and (3) model implementation, interaction, and technology transfer. The authors conclude that '... model development and use has become increasingly influential. This is especially true for engineering design and operation studies, and perhaps less so for more strategic regional development and policy studies.'

Friedman, Ansell, Diamond & Haimes [1984]. *The Use of Models for Water Resources Management, Planning, and Policy.* In 1982, the Office of Technology Assessment (OTA), reporting to the U.S. Congress, held two workshops on the use of mathematical models in water resources management and also surveyed water resource managers in 22 federal agencies and offices in all 50 states to determine how models are used and what are constraints and limitations on their use. In this paper, the authors summarize OTA's analysis and list nine major findings. In particular, OTA found that: 'Mathematical models have significantly expanded the nation's ability to understand and manage its water resources.' OTA also found that: 'Models have the potential to provide even greater benefits for water resource decisionmaking in the future.' Conversely, OTA discovered that most federal agencies have not developed an overall strategy for formulating and using models and that support for user training, technical assistance, maintenance, and dissemination of model information has been inadequate. The authors conclude the paper by discussing five major issues that need to be addressed in the future: (1) improving federal problem-solving capabilities; (2) meeting the needs of the states; (3) establishing appropriate modelling strategies within individual federal agencies; (4) providing potential users with information about existing models; and (5) federal support for model-related training.

Yeh [1985]. *Reservoir Management and Operations Models: A State-of-the-Art Review.* Yeh gives a comprehensive, critical, and historical review of linear programming models (including stochastic LP, chance-constrained LP, and linear decision rules – rules which relate water releases to storage, inflow, and decision parameters), nonlinear programming models, dynamic programming models (including incremental, stochastic, reliability-constrained, and differential DP), and simulation models as they are used to analyze problems concerning the optimal operations of reservoirs. He includes a bibliography of over 220 citations. Yeh also discusses the real-time reservoir operations of the California Central Valley Project, the Tennessee Valley Authority, and Hydro Quebec. Several recommendations are made for future research including developing and implementing LP decomposition schemes for practical application and developing accelerated NLP solution procedures.

Exhibit 5.2 (continued)

Rogers & Fiering [1986]. *Use of Systems Analysis in Water Management.* In contrast to the glowing report by OTA on the use of mathematical models in water resources management [Friedman, Ansell, Diamond & Haimes 1984], Rogers & Fiering paint a much different picture in a very provocative article. Based on their experiences and their survey of government agencies, water resources practitioners, and the open literature, the authors conclude that '... there is strong resistance to the use of systems analysis by many government agencies involved in water management both in developed and developing countries.' In their survey, three major federal water resources agencies (Tennessee Valley Authority, Soil Conservation Service of the Department of Agriculture, and Bureau of Reclamation) could not provide any study that would qualify as a systems analysis. For the authors, systems analysis implies optimization; for example, using a computer to simulate alternative designs of water systems would not qualify as a systems analysis. The authors also surveyed the U.S. Army Corps of Engineers. Nine generalizations about the Corps' use of systems analysis are offered, the most important of which is: '... the use of simplified decision or optimization models to guide in the selection of candidates for further detailed analysis, perhaps by simulation, has not been done, is not now being done, and under foreseeable conditions will not be done by the Corps.' The authors claim that federal agencies and major consultants have only used systems analysis on a very small number of projects. Furthermore, they claim that modelling inadequacies, deficient databases, and institutional resistance have limited the use of optimization models. We point out that some water resources researchers feel that Rogers & Fiering have overstated their case.

---

have recently applied the AHP to the study of flood protection alternatives.

(2) The applications exhibit a wide range of final outcomes and results. It is easy to identify papers in which the authors report that the modelling effort influenced the decision-making process. It is more difficult to find papers that are unqualified success stories (that is, papers in which the authors report that the model-generated solution was implemented and significant benefits resulted).

(3) MS/OR models and solution methods have the potential to become high-impact decision-making aids in the field of water resources management. However, many technical and institutional limitations must be overcome. For example, there is resistance to using these models on the part of federal and state agencies.

5.1.4. Successful modelling efforts in water resources management

In this section we describe several successful MS/OR applications in water resources management. We begin by briefly highlighting five well-known modelling efforts that have appeared in the MS/OR and water resources literature (see Exhibit 5.3). To give the reader an appreciation of the scope, magnitude, and

Exhibit 5.3

There are several well-known MS/OR modelling efforts that have appeared in the literature. These applications are some of the best examples of management science practice in water resources management: model results were actually implemented and significant benefits were produced. Several applications are prize winners or finalists in competitions that recognize outstanding theoretical contributions or important implementations of management science.

Goreux & Manne [1973]. *Multi-Level Planning: Case Studies in Mexico*. This book received the Lanchester Prize awarded by the Operations Research Society of America for the best English language publication in 1973. This monograph is a collaborative effort that consists of 22 papers written by 17 contributors. The book focuses on the problem of interdependence in planning for Mexico. A system of integrated optimizing models is developed to help analyze policy decisions at three levels. At the highest level of aggregation, there is a multi-sector model of the Mexican economy (DINAMICO is an LP with 316 rows and 421 columns). At the next level are models for Mexican agriculture (CHAC is an LP with 1500 rows and 3400 columns – nonlinear constraints and the objective function have been linearized – that describes the total national supply and use of 33 short-cycle crops) and for energy (ENERGETICOS is a mixed integer programming model for electric power planning). The agricultural models had to account for irrigation. For example, constraints that modelled the use of gravity-fed water and well water were included in the models. At the lowest level of aggregation are models for an agricultural district (BAJIO) and for electric plants and transmission lines (INTERCON).

Major & Lenton [1979]. *Applied Water Resource Systems Planning*. This book describes the 3-year collaborative effort begun in 1970 between the Ralph M. Parsons Laboratory for Water Resources and Hydrology at the Massachusetts Institute of Technology and the State Subsecretariat for Water Resources in Argentina to formulate a plan for the development of the Rio Colorado river basin. Development was to occur for two main purposes: irrigation water supply and electric power production. Over 20 potential irrigation sites along with 13 power sites in the river basin had been identified. A system of three models is constructed to generate alternative development plans for the river and to assess each plan's overall impact. First, a screening model is formulated and solved to produce initial plan configurations. The decision variables in this mixed integer programming model are the sizes of potential dam sites, irrigation areas, power stations, and import and export sites (water at these sites is exchanged with other river systems) on the river. There are seven classes of constraints including constraints on continuity of water flow, reservoir storage capacity, and hydroelectric energy. The objective function maximizes a weighted sum of net benefits from each planning objective. A deterministic hydrology is assumed; the historical mean flows are used in the model. The screening model contains about 900 decision variables (eight are 0–1 variables) and about 600 constraints.

Exhibit 5.3 (continued)

The most promising configurations produced by the screening model (that is, optimally sized works for power, irrigation, and imports and exports) are then passed to the simulation model. Each configuration is evaluated in terms of hydrologic reliability and net benefit and could then be altered to improve its performance. This model was run with 50 years of seasonal flows. The configurations that emerged from the simulation model are then optimally scheduled in four future time periods by the mixed integer sequencing model. This model contains about 180 variables (120 are integer) and 110 constraints. In 1976, based on the results of this study, Argentine officials agreed on a development plan for the Rio Colorado.

Goeller & the PAWN Team [1985]. *Planning the Netherlands' Water Resources.* This paper won the competition for the 1984 Franz Edelman Award for Management Science Achievement. Begun in 1977, the Policy Analysis for the Water Management of The Netherlands (PAWN) was conducted by the Rand Corporation, the Delft Hydraulics Laboratory, and the Rijkswaterstaat (the government agency responsible for water control and public works). The goal of the study was to develop a methodology for generating and then assessing alternative water management policies for The Netherlands. The effort of the PAWN team and the overall accomplishments are impressive. The project involved 125 man-years of effort in developing and applying an integrated system of 50 models that includes twelve simulations, six mathematical programs (including LP and NLP), two heuristic optimizations, and eleven fitted-function models such as multiple regression. The final report spans 21 volumes that contain 4,000 pages. Many of the policy recommendations suggested in the PAWN analysis were adopted and implemented by the Dutch government in its *Nota Waterhuishouding* (the national policy document on water management) which was approved by Parliament in 1984. The impact of PAWN has been far reaching. Goeller sums up: 'Analysis performed with the system resulted in a new national water management policy, saving hundreds of millions of dollars in investment expenditures and reducing agricultural damage by about $15 million per year, while decreasing thermal and algae population. The methodology ... has been used to train water resource planners from many nations.'

Terry, Pereira, Araripe Neto, Silva & Sales [1986]. *Coordinating the Energy Generation of the Brazilian National Hydrothermal Electrical Generation System.* This paper was a finalist in the competition for the 1985 Franz Edelman Award for Management Science Achievement. The authors describe the modelling effort that was undertaken to coordinate the operation of the large Brazilian multi-owned hydrothermal generating system. The bulk of the electric power in Brazil is generated by 18 utilities (four of which are controlled by the federal government and the remainder by state governments). The utilities use both thermoelectric plants (coal, gas, oil, and nuclear) and hydroelectric plants to meet the demand for electricity. The objective of the power system is to supply the demand for electrical

Exhibit 5.3 (continued)

power using both sources of power in the most economical and reliable way. The operation problem for hydrothermal systems has the following characteristics: (1) operating decisions today affect the future operating costs; (2) it is stochastic since there is uncertainty about future water inflows; and (3) there is a clear trade-off between operating cost and system reliability. A five-step solution process was used: (1) aggregate the system reservoirs into equivalent reservoir models; (2) aggregate the inflows to the system into equivalent energy inflows; (3) define a stochastic inflow model that represents the statistical characteristics of the inflow; (4) use a stochastic dynamic programming (SDP) model to obtain the optimal operating policy for the aggregate model; and (5) disaggregate the total hydro generation calculated in step 4 into generating targets for each of the hydro plants. A 5-year optimization takes about three minutes of CPU time on an IBM 4341. Model development started in mid-1975, lasted 18 months, and required 3.25 man-years. The model was officially adopted by the pool of utilities in 1979. We point out that the model was extensively validated and its performance was compared to that of a system rule-curve (a rule-curve is a recursive algorithm applied to a water inflow sequence that specifies at the beginning of a month the minimum storage level of a reservoir that ensures there will be no energy shortages during the planning period). The model projected a savings of $87 million over a 5-year period, a 28% reduction in operating costs. Actual savings from 1979 to 1984 were about $260 million. The model was also being used to help make generation expansion decisions.

Dembo, Chiarri, Martin & Paradinas [1990]. *Managing Hidroeléctrica Española's Hydroelectric Power System.* This paper was a finalist in the competition for the 1989 Franz Edelman Award for Management Science Achievement. In 1984, Hidroeléctrica Española (HIE) hired Algorithmics, Inc. (ALG) to develop a set of models to assist it in managing reservoirs to generate hydroelectric power. HIE gathered extensive data but performed very little modelling. It had no operations research staff and owned no optimization software. ALG developed a hierarchy of models to help HIE plan water releases to generate electricity. These models focus on short-, medium-, and long-term decisions. A relational database containing 20 years of information was used in hydrological forecasting, while adaptive filtering, Box-Jenkins, and multivariate analysis were used for forecasting energy demand. Much of the analysis centered on the Tajo river system with its three interconnected rivers and 10 reservoirs. The system was represented as a network of hydroelectric facilities (nodes) and various uses for the water (arcs). The short-, medium-, and long-term models attempted to maximize the benefit of hydro-generated power, while satisfying the network constraints. In particular, when power restrictions are moved into the objective function via a penalty, the short-term model becomes nonlinear with pure network constraints. The authors employed a scenario analysis using a detailed deterministic NLP model. These models were solved using the specialized network optimizer NLPNET.

Exhibit 5.3 (continued)

For example, for the Tajo system with 10 reservoirs and 50 time stages, a detailed optimization model (without aggregation) for a single scenario would contain approximately 1500 variables and 500 network flow constraints. The model forms the primary basis for setting hydro production levels. The authors successfully solved very large NLPs. For example, a 10-year planning model with 20 000 bounded variables, a nonlinear, nonconvex, and nonseparable objective function, and 5000 linear network constraints was solved in eight CPU hours. By using the models, HIE saved approximately $2 million annually. In addition, the models can be used to solve other problems in the field. (We point out that recent significant research on reservoir scheduling centers on applications of various stochastic programming techniques and includes work of Pereira & Pinto [1991].)

---

significance of MS/OR efforts, we provide extended descriptions of three high-profile applications in the sections that follow.

5.2. California Aqueduct

The California State Water Project (SWP) consists of reservoirs linked by rivers, pumping plants, canals, tunnels, and generating plants with the California Aqueduct being the principal water conveyance structure. The California Department of Water Resources (CDWR) is the steward of the SWP. In the early 1960s, CDWR entered into 75-year contracts to satisfy the water demands of 31 local agencies throughout California.

SWP requires a large amount of electrical energy to operate its pumps: the pumps account for about 3% of all electricity that is used in California. Some of the energy for the operation of the pumps is generated by SWP in its own plants on the aqueduct system, while energy in excess of that amount is purchased from four California utilities. In March 1983, low-cost contracts with the four utilities were terminated and CDWR found itself in the position of having to purchase energy at a substantially higher cost. CDWR now essentially acted as an electric utility. Since CDWR could control the timing of its hourly and seasonal loads through water storage and excess pumping capacity, it could produce electrical energy at its hydrogeneration plants during on-peak periods of demand and sell this energy at maximum revenue and, at the same time, use off-peak energy to operate its pumping plants. To take advantage of this opportunity, CDWR needed to develop efficient operating schedules for SWP.

Sabet, Coe, Ramirez & Ford [1985] and Sabet & Coe [1986] develop a set of models (network flow models, large-scale LPs, and simulation models) that determine the optimal flows throughout the California Aqueduct system taking into account water demands, energy generation capabilities, and energy demands for pumping. The models can be used to schedule both water and power on a yearly, weekly, or daily basis. Weekly or daily water scheduling is done prior to power scheduling by using a network flow model that is solved by a modified out-of-kilter algorithm. The solution from this network model provides the total flows at the pumping plants and generating plants in the aqueduct system over the time period under study. Electrical scheduling is then handled by solving a power allocation network (PAN) model. PAN models the power contracts that must be satisfied as a network flow model.

The daily or weekly operation of the 'core Aqueduct system' (that is, 57 aqueduct pools, seven pumping plants, and two generating plants) is modelled as a linear program. To reduce the computational effort, the authors divide the core system into 10 reaches (a reach is a series of consecutive aqueduct pools followed by a pumping plant, a generating plant, or a check structure). The complete LP for the daily scheduling of water is shown in Exhibit 5.4. The weekly LP model minimizes weekly on-peak energy use subject to constraints that are similar to those found in the daily model. Both models are solved in real time using XMP [see Marsten, 1981] either on a UNIVAC computer or on a CDC computer.

The authors conclude: 'The model is well-coordinated and can provide a practical and efficient schedule for water and power operation of the SWP. In addition to real-time operation, the model may be used for long-term studies with weekly or daily details. A sufficient link exists between the hydraulic networks, the LP optimization, and the PAN models to insure consistency and continuity in water and power operations.'

5.3. California Central Valley Project

The Central Valley Project (CVP) is a complex water resource system in California that consists of nine storage reservoirs, three canals, four pumping stations, and nine power plants. The functions served by each of these facilities include irrigation, flood control, navigation, power generation, recreation, water quality protection, water supply, regulation, and fish protection. The CVP is managed and operated by the Bureau of Reclamation, United States Department of the Interior.

Becker & Yeh [1974], Becker, Yeh, Fults & Sparks [1976], and Yeh [1979] describe the development of an on-line set of integrated optimization procedures that would assist the real-time operation of this multiple-reservoir system. These procedures are designed to help project managers construct monthly, daily, and hourly plans for the release and storage of water throughout the system. The water that is released is then used for a variety of purposes, including irrigation and hydroelectric power generation. In the current operation, the Bureau of Reclamation schedules water releases for the next day. This enables the major power customer, Pacific Gas and Electric Company, to develop hourly schedules of hydropower generation that are compatible with the releases.

The authors develop a set of three models: a monthly model over a 1-year period, a daily model over a 1-month period, and an hourly model over 24 hours. The overall structure of the CVP system model is shown in Exhibit 5.5. We point

Exhibit 5.4

This daily linear programming model is used by the operators for real-time scheduling purposes over 24 one-hour periods. The objective function (1) minimizes the net value of energy used. The first term in (1) gives the net value of energy used or produced by the pumping and generating plants and the second term in (1) gives the total weighted energy associated with storing water in the reaches. The last two terms in (1) are designed to prevent unnecessary changes in hourly plant flows. Constraints (2) set upper and lower bounds on the allowable flow through each reach while constraints (3) set upper and lower bounds on the storage capacity at each reach. Constraints (4) set an end of the day target storage for each reach. Note that the end of the day occurs when $j = 24$. The decrease in the quantity of water in storage must be constrained to protect the lining of the aqueduct pools from failure. Thus, constraints (5) limit the drawdown rate in each reach. Constraints (6a) and (6b) ensure that demands along the aqueduct are satisfied. Note that the local inflows (the l_{ij} terms) are assumed to be known quantities. Constraints (7) control the fluctuation in flow rate. Flow change may take place with no penalty at the beginning of the on-peak and off-peak periods, that is, when $j = 8$ or $j = 22$. Constraints (8) ensure that the total daily flow through a plant equals the required flow for that day as determined by the network flow programming model for the aqueduct.

Input parameters

c_{ij}	=	value of energy used or generated at pumping or generating plant i during period j (in kW-hr/acre-ft)
cs_{ij}	=	penalty associated with storing water in reach i during time period j (in kW-hr/acre-ft)
df_i	=	total required daily flow through reach i (in acre-ft)
dm_{ij}	=	water demand plus estimated seepage and evaporation at reach i during period j (in acre-ft/hr)
l_{ij}	=	local inflow to reach i during period j (in acre-ft/hr)
p_{ij}	=	unit cost assigned as penalty for any flow change from one period to another
pc_{ij}	=	maximum allowable flow through reach i during period j (in acre-ft/hr)
mpc_{ij}	=	minimum allowable flow through reach i during period j (in acre-ft/hr)
sc_{ij}	=	maximum storage capacity of reach i during period j (in acre-ft)
ms_{ij}	=	minimum storage capacity of reach i during period j (in acre-ft)
sh_{ij}	=	maximum allowable drawdown in reach i during period j (in acre-ft/hr)
s_{ie}	=	end of the day target storage at reach i
t_j	=	length of time period j (in hours)

Decision variables

q_{ij}	=	flow rate through reach i during period j (in acre-ft/hr)
s_{ij}	=	storage volume at reach i during period j (in acre-ft)
d_{ij}, f_{ij}	=	dummy variables to control flow changes

Exhibit 5.4 (continued)

Daily linear programming model

$$\text{maximize} \quad \sum_{i=1}^{m}\sum_{j=1}^{n}(t_j c_{ij} q_{ij} + cs_{ij}s_{ij} + t_j p_{ij}d_{ij} + p_{ij}f_{ij}) \tag{1}$$

subject to

$$mpc_{ij} \leq q_{ij} \leq pc_{ij} \qquad i = 1, 2, \ldots, m; \quad j = 1, 2, \ldots, n, \tag{2}$$

$$ms_{ij} \leq s_{ij} \leq sc_{ij} \qquad i = 1, 2, \ldots, m; \quad j = 1, 2, \ldots, n-1, \tag{3}$$

$$s_{ij} = s_{ie} \qquad i = 1, 2, \ldots, m; \quad j = 24, \tag{4}$$

$$s_{ij-1} - s_{ij} \leq t_j sh_{ij} \qquad i = 1, 2, \ldots, m; \ i \neq 10; \ j = 1, 2, \ldots, n, \tag{5}$$

$$t_j(q_{i-1j} - q_{ij} + l_{ij}) + s_{ij-1} - s_{ij} = t_j dm_{ij}$$
$$i = 1, 2, \ldots, m; \ i \neq 6; \ j = 1, 2, \ldots, n, \tag{6a}$$

$$t_j(q_{5j} - q_{6j} - q_{9j} + l_{6j}) + s_{6j-1} - s_{6j} = t_j dm_{6j}$$
$$j = 1, 2, \ldots, n, \tag{6b}$$

$$q_{ij} - q_{ij-1} + d_{ij} - f_{ij} = 0$$
$$i = 1, 2, \ldots, m; \ j = 1, 2, \ldots, n; \ j \neq 8, 22, \tag{7}$$

$$\sum_{j=1}^{n} t_j q_{ij} = df_i \qquad i = 1, 2, \ldots, m, \tag{8}$$

$$d_{ij}, f_{ij}, q_{ij}, s_{ij} \geq 0 \qquad i = 1, 2, \ldots, m; \ j = 1, 2, \ldots, n.$$

out that reservoir input flows are assumed to be deterministic. Monthly forecasts are based on a two-stage least-squares regression that uses snow water content, precipitation index, and previous streamflow as independent variables. Daily forecasts are generated by a computer simulation that models certain parts of the hydrologic cycle. Streamflow forecasts are frequently updated. Consequently, the optimization models are updated accordingly using the newest forecasts.

The monthly model requires a minimum of 22 decision variables and 48 constraints for each month over which the model is run. This model uses a combination of linear programming and dynamic programming to perform the required optimization. This approach makes the best use of LP and DP in that LP is used to perform the spatial optimization, and the optimized results are embedded in a one-dimensional forward DP to perform the sequential optimization in time. A monthly model solved over a 12-month span requires 55 seconds on an IBM 360/91. The best water release policies for the reservoirs,

Exhibit 5.5

The system that is used to produce optimal operations for the California Valley Project consists of three major models. The outputs from a more aggregated model are used as inputs into a less aggregated, more detailed model. For example, in the monthly model a number of LPs are solved to produce release policies and end-of-month storages for each month. A dynamic program is then used to select an optimal reservoir storage policy path through a specified number of months. The best release policy is then used as an input into the daily model.

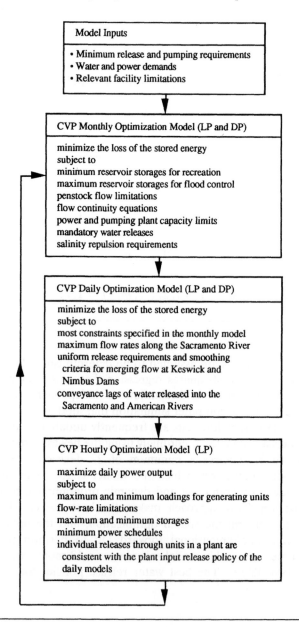

as determined by the monthly model, are then passed as inputs to the daily model. The CVP daily model requires a minimum of 22 decision variables and 70 constraints for each day over which the model is run. The daily model uses the same solution algorithm as the monthly model. A typical solution time is about one minute on the IBM 360/91. The optimal daily policy is then passed to the hourly model. The hourly model produces a detailed plan for the release of water through each generating unit throughout the system over a 24-hour period. This model requires a minimum of 144 decision variables and 341 constraints for the northern portion of the CVP. In the hourly model, an iterated LP is used to establish a set of initial solutions which are feasible. The initial solutions are improved by an incremental DP allied with successive approximations. This model runs in less than two minutes on an IBM 360/91. The monthly model was completed in 1973 and the daily and hourly models were completed in 1976 and 1978, respectively.

In his evaluation of the CVP models, Coleman [1979] concludes that the MS/OR modelling effort has resulted in the more efficient use of available water and an increase in power production. Specifically, he identifies three quantifiable benefits from using MS/OR models: (1) water savings are estimated at about 100 000 acre-feet annually; (2) improvement of power production is estimated at 1%, which represents a minimum of 50 to 100 gigawatt hours annually; and (3) a reduction of 1.5 staff positions at the Water Operations Branch within the Central Valley Operations Coordinating Office.

5.4. Tennessee Valley Authority

The Tennessee Valley Authority (TVA) has over 50 years of successful operating experience. TVA operates a system of 32 reservoirs as a portion of a large hydrothermal power system. In the early 1980s, the management of TVA felt the need to strengthen its use of reservoir operations models. TVA wanted to: (1) make more efficient use of historical data (including information on hurricanes, floods, and droughts) that it has gathered since 1903; (2) evaluate new operating requirements that better accommodate different interest groups such as electrical power, recreation, water quality, and farming; (3) improve long-range guidance; and (4) integrate weather forecasts with guidance models.

In two papers, Shane & Gilbert [1982] and Gilbert & Shane [1982] present the theoretical and applied aspects surrounding their development of a hydro system simulation model (HYDROSIM). HYDROSIM was designed by the authors in consultation with two groups: TVA Reservoir Operations and TVA Power System Operations. Both of these groups influenced model development in a major way (in fact, the authors spent several hundred hours with the branch chief of reservoir operations discussing results, limitations, and model use).

HYDROSIM is designed to: (1) evaluate the impact of new requirements on operating objectives; (2) check current reservoir status; (3) forecast reservoir system operation; and (4) develop new long-range operating guidance tools. The structure of HYDROSIM is shown in Exhibit 5.6. The optimization model is

Exhibit 5.6

The system developed to help managers at TVA operate the reservoir system has three major components. An interactive program, accessed via a CRT graphics terminal, allows the user to develop the data set for a run of the model. The system is run on an AMDAHL V8 with only a few seconds of CPU time required for the input development program and the graphical analysis output program. The scheduling program takes between one and five minutes of CPU time depending on the number of weeks and years that are modelled.

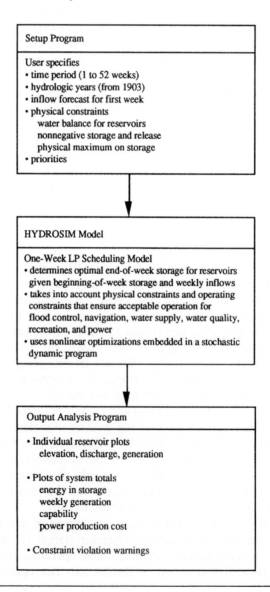

---

a stochastic dynamic program in which the basic steps are nonlinear optimizations. These optimizations produce weekly reservoir schedules that maximize hydropower benefit subject to preemptive priority constraints that reflect many multipurpose objectives including flood control and navigation.

The authors report that many man-hours were spent on model validation. This effort was directed at simulating current operating practices and then comparing model-produced schedules against both actual and simulated operations. The authors conclude that: 'Initial testing and evaluation have shown the model to be a practical tool for use in day-to-day planning of reservoir operations and policy and project studies.'

TVA has now accumulated 10 years of experience with continual heavy use of the model. This experience is summarized by Shane, Waffel, Parsly & Goranflo [1988]. The model has been used numerous times in different types of applications including reservoir operations planning, system forecasting, operating policy studies, and hydropower contract negotiations. Shane [1991] confirmed that, during this time period, the basic structure of the model remained virtually unchanged from the description shown in Exhibit 5.6. However, applications are now run on microcomputers instead of on a mainframe computer.

6. Conclusions

The applications that we reviewed in the previous sections demonstrate the pervasiveness of MS/OR methods in modelling and solving natural resource management problems. Many of the applications were major undertakings that involved teams of analysts, spanned many years, and produced significant benefits. Others were more modest efforts that, nevertheless, had an impact on the decision-making process. In all of these applications, there are several common characteristics which affect the success of the overall model development and implementation effort. Based on the key lessons that are summarized in Exhibit 6.1, we highlight the following five characteristics which are hallmarks of successful MS/OR applications in natural resource management: (1) *Find a high-level decision maker or manager who will champion the effort*; (2) *Use models that are understandable and familiar*; (3) *Pay close attention to the needs of users*; (4) *Communicate results of the modelling effort throughout the decision-making process*; and (5) *Let the model evolve by allowing decision makers and analysts to modify it even after implementation*.

Over the last 35 years, a wide variety of MS/OR methods have been applied to important problems in the management of fish, forests, wildlife, and water. We hope that the applications we presented in each of these four areas convince readers that MS/OR methods have greatly impacted the decision-making process of natural resource managers and that, in some cases, significant economic and social benefits emerged as a result of the modelling effort. After all, 'We live in a critical period when clear definition of the natural resources research objectives and the development plans for realizing them are of great importance to the

Exhibit 6.1

Researchers and practitioners have over 35 years worth of experience in managing fish, forests, wildlife, and water through the application of MS/OR methods. During this time period, they have written extensively about key lessons that can point the way to a successful application and they have also highlighted technical and institutional barriers that can block success.

Author(s)	*Key lessons*
Hilborn [1979]	• In order to be successful, an applied systems analysis effort must be requested by decision makers who have the power to insist that final results will actually be used by management.
	• Closing the gap between analysis and successful implementation requires a considerable amount of time devoted to communication.
	• Models should be easy to explain and easy to understand. Furthermore, models should be easy to defend against technical criticism.
Bare, Briggs, Roise & Schreuder [1984]	• Decision problems facing forest managers are complex. Because of the technological uncertainty surrounding problems, it is difficult for a model to capture all of the relevant decision factors.
	• By necessity, important qualitative decision factors are often omitted from models.
	• Analysts are more interested in building models than in implementing results. Oftentimes, key decision makers have not been included in the model formulation and development stages. These decision makers are then suspicious of models that are dumped on them when they have not provided input during model-building stages.
	• Many public-sector decision problems involve multiple goals and these goals must be satisfied in a setting that involves multiple decision makers.
	• Analysts like to build large data-intensive models that are linked to databases. This complicates implementation and application to new problem instances since most large models must be modified before they can be used. The trend is to build smaller modular models on microcomputers so that the time between problem identification and solution can be reduced.
Friedman, Ansell, Diamond & Haimes [1984]	• Successful applications of MS/OR models require trained personnel with highly developed technical capabilities. The appropriateness of a particular water resource model should be ascertained by a knowledgeable analyst.
	• Successful applications also require budgetary support for computer facilities, data gathering and processing, and user support services.

Exhibit 6.1 (continued)

	• Federal agencies need to: (1) formulate integrated plans for developing and supporting mathematical models and (2) establish a model clearinghouse that provides potential users with information about previously developed water resource models.
	• Decision makers at all levels of government must have training in the basic concepts of mathematical modelling including the interpretation of results.
Loucks, Stedinger & Shamir [1984, 1985]	• Successful applications of MS/OR models for policy and planning purposes require an institutional interest and commitment. Also critical to success is the establishment of modelling centers that develop, support, and maintain models.
	• Analysts are generally concerned with problem detail, while high-level policy makers are concerned with simplicity and generality. Thus, analysts might use complex models that are difficult for policy makers to understand. A spectrum of models that includes comprehendible and credible models is needed.
	• Analysts must be able to communicate technical information, as well as environmental, economic, and social information, in such a way that decision makers can easily assess the impact of these factors on the problem setting.
	• Key decision makers must know something about the model that was chosen. They must be able to run a model under a variety of conditions and examine the results that emerge.
Rogers & Fiering [1986]	• Systems analysis techniques have not been widely used in the management of water resources because there is: (1) institutional resistance in federal agencies; (2) unreliability in databases; and (3) an existence of conflicting objectives.
	• The stated goals and measures that are used in optimizing models do not reflect the true concern of decision makers. In fact, analysts do the wrong thing since '... models are not usually concerned with what decision makers care about!'
	• For a specific decision problem, the important point is that systems analysis techniques should be able to offer decision makers a number of alternative solutions from which to choose.
	• Consultants who perform systems analysis place too much emphasis on delivering a final model by a specified date. Very little attention is focused on issues that surround the continuing nature of problems, such as ensuring that the client staff is trained to run the model and interpret its results.

future and stability of mankind. Today the United States is able to enjoy a certain complacency concerning its short-range situation; but it faces a wider arena and a longer term in which complacency would be tragically dangerous.' This quote is as meaningful and appropriate today as it was when it appeared in a 1963 National Academy of Sciences report written by a team that included Philip Morse (see Morse [1977] for additional details including the Academy's 10 recommendations concerning research in natural resources). We hope that our review serves to focus the attention of MS/OR researchers and practitioners on the important role that they can play in the decades ahead in helping to manage the earth's precious natural resources.

Acknowledgements

We are very appreciative of the efforts of Qiwen Wang in helping us produce this manuscript. We also thank the following individuals who provided us with useful and timely comments: Jerald Ault, Bruce Bare, Gerard DiNardo, Dennis Dykstra, David Euler, John Gordon, George Gross, John Hof, Brian Kent, Malcolm Kirby, Dan Lane, Daniel Loucks, David Martell, Paul Schonfeld, Richard Shane, Albert Simard, Tony Starfield, Konstantin Staschus, Jery Stedinger, Carl Walters, and William Yeh.

References

Bare, B.B. (1991). Personal communication.
Bare, B.B., D.G. Briggs, J.P. Roise and G.F. Schreuder (1984). A survey of systems analysis models in forestry and the forest products industries. *European J. Oper. Res.* 18, 1–18.
Becker, L., and W.W.-G. Yeh (1974). Optimization of real time operation of a multiple-reservoir system. *Water Resources Res.* 10, 1107–1112.
Becker, L., W.W.-G. Yeh, D. Fults and D. Sparks (1976). Operations models for Central Valley project. *ASCE J. Water Resources Planning Management Division* 102(WR1), 101–115.
Berry, J.M. (1991). The owl's golden egg. *Washington Post* 242, August 4, H1–H4.
Beverton, R.J.H., and S.J. Holt (1957). *On the Dynamics of Exploited Fish Populations*, Investigation Series 2(19), Ministry of Agriculture, Fisheries and Food, London.
Bobek, B. (1980). A model for optimization of roe deer management in Central Europe. *J. Wildlife Management* 44, 837–848.
Booth, W. (1991). Study: Logging cut needed to save northwest forests. *Washington Post* 232, July 25, A3.
Brown, B.E., J.A. Brennan and J.E. Palmer (1979). Linear programming simulations of the effects of bycatch on the management of mixed species fisheries off the northeastern coast of the United States. *Fishery Bulletin* 76, 851–860.
Buongiorno, J., and N.H. Svanqvist (1982). A separable goal-programming model of the Indonesian forestry sector. *Forest Ecology and Management* 4, 67–78.
Buongiorno, J., N.H. Svanqvist and P. Wiroatmodjo (1981). Forestry sector development planning: A model for Indonesia. *Agricult. Syst.* 7, 113–135.
Charles, A.T. (1992). Uncertainty and information in fishery management models: A Bayesian updating algorithm. *Amer. J. Math. Management Sci.* 12, 191–225.

Clark, C.W. (1985). *Bioeconomic Modelling and Fisheries Management*, John Wiley & Sons, New York.

Clough, D.J. (1980). *Optimization and Implementation Plan for Offshore Fisheries Surveillance*, Department of Fisheries and Oceans, Ottawa, ON.

Cohan, D., S.M. Haas, D.L. Radloff and R.F. Yancik (1984). Using fire in forest management: Decision making under uncertainty. *Interfaces* 14(5), 8–19.

Coleman, D.G. (1979). Utilizing strategy models to assist in managing the Federal Central Valley Project, in: G.H. Toebes, and A.A. Shepherd (eds.), *Reservoir Systems Operations*, American Society of Civil Engineers, New York, pp. 209–216.

Crete, M., R.J. Taylor and P.A. Jordan (1981). Optimization of moose harvest in southwestern Quebec. *J. Wildlife Management* 45, 598–611.

Crowley, R.W., and H.P. Palsson (1992). Modeling offshore fishery regulation enforcement in Canada. *Amer. J. Math. Management Sci.* 12, 153–190.

Cullen, M.R (1985). *Linear Models in Biology*, Halsted Press, New York.

Davis, L.S., and K.N. Johnson (1987). *Forest Management, 3rd edition*, McGraw-Hill, New York.

Dembo, R.S., A. Chiarri, J.G. Martin and L. Paradinas (1990). Managing Hidroelétrica Española's hydroelectric power system. *Interfaces* 20(1), 115–135.

DeSilets, L., B. Golden, Q. Wang and R. Kumar (1992). Predicting salinity in the Chesapeake Bay using backpropagation. *Comput. Oper. Res.* 19, 277–285.

DiNardo, G., D. Levy and B. Golden (1989). Using decision analysis to manage Maryland's river herring fishery: An application of AHP. *J. Environmental Management* 29(2), 193–213.

Dykstra, D. (1984). *Mathematical Programming for Natural Resource Management*, McGraw-Hill, New York.

Dzurek, D.J. (1992). An analytical model for managing the Sea of Japan, Working Paper Number 31, Environment and Policy Institute, East–West Center, Honolulu, HI.

Economist (1991). 319(7712), June 22, 19–23.

Egan, T. (1991). The great Alaska debate: Can oil and wilderness mix?. *New York Times Magazine* CXL (48, 682), August 4, 20–49.

Euler, D., and M.M.J. Morris (1984). Simulated population dynamics of white-tailed deer in an any-deer hunting system. *Ecological Modelling* 24, 281–292.

Expert Choice 1986. Decision Support Software, Inc., McLean, VA.

Field, R.C. (1984). National forest planning is promoting US Forest Service acceptance of operations research. *Interfaces* 14(5), 67–76.

Flam, S.D., and S. Storøy (1982). Capacity reduction on Norwegian industrial fisheries. *Canad. J. Fisheries Aquatic Sci.* 39, 1314–1317.

Frederick, K.D., and R.A. Sedjo (eds.) (1991). *America's Renewable Resources: Historical Trends and Current Challenges*, Resources for the Future, Washington, DC.

Friedman, R., C. Ansell, S. Diamond and Y.Y. Haimes (1984). The use of models for water resources management, planning, and policy. *Water Resources Res.* 20, 793–802.

Getz, W.M., and R.G. Haight (1989). *Population Harvesting: Demographic Models of Fish, Forest, and Animal Resources*, Princeton University Press, Princeton, NJ.

Gilbert, K.C., and R.M. Shane (1982). TVA hydro scheduling model: Theoretical aspects. *ASCE J. Water Resources Planning Management Division* 108(WR1), 21–36.

Gilmore, P.C., and R.E. Gomory (1961). A linear programming approach to the cutting stock problem: Part I. *Oper. Res.* 9, 849–859.

Gilmore, P.C., and R.E. Gomory (1963). A linear programming approach to the cutting stock problem: Part II. *Oper. Res.* 11, 863–888.

Goeller, B.F., and the PAWN Team (1985). Planning the Netherlands' water resources. *Interfaces* 15(1), 3–33.

Goh, B.-S. (1980). *Management and Analysis of Biological Populations*, Elsevier, Amsterdam.

Golden, B.L., E.A. Wasil and D.E. Levy (1989). Applications of the analytic hierarchy process: A categorized, annotated bibliography, in: B.L. Golden, E.A. Wasil and P.T. Harker (eds.), *The Analytic Hierarchy Process: Applications and Studies*, Springer-Verlag, Berlin, pp. 37–58.

Gordon, J., J.F. Franklin, K.N. Johnson and J.W. Thomas (1991). Alternatives for management of late successional forests of the Pacific Northwest, Draft Report to the U.S. House of Representatives, Committee on Agriculture and Committee on Merchant Marine and Fisheries, Washington, DC.

Goreux, L.M., and A.S. Manne (eds.) (1973). *Multi-Level Planning: Case Studies in Mexico*, North-Holland, Amsterdam.

Gross, G. (1989). Personal communication.

Guimarães Rodrigues, A. (ed.) (1990). *Operations Research and Management in Fishing*, Kluwer, Dordrecht.

Gunn, E.A., H.H. Millar and S.M. Newbold (1991). Planning harvesting and marketing activities for integrated fishing firms under an enterprise allocation scheme. *European J. Oper. Res.* 55, 243–259.

Haley, K.B. (ed.) (1981). *Applied Operations Research in Fishing*, Plenum Press, New York.

Harker, P.T. (1989). The art and science of decision making: The analytic hierarchy process, in: B.L. Golden, E.A. Wasil and P.T. Harker (eds.), *The Analytic Hierarchy Process: Applications and Studies*, Springer-Verlag, Berlin, pp. 3–36.

Harrison, T.P., and C.A. de Kluyver (1984). MS/OR and the forest products industry: New directions. *Interfaces* 14(5), 1–7.

Helgason, T., and S. Olafsson (1988). An Icelandic fisheries model. *European J. Oper. Res.* 33, 191–199.

Hilborn, R. (1979). Some failures and successes in applying systems analysis to ecological systems. *J. Appl. Syst. Analysis* 6, 25–31.

Hilborn, R., C.J. Walters, R.M. Peterman and M.J. Staley (1984). Models and fisheries: A case study in implementation. *North Amer. J. Fisheries Management* 4, 9–14.

Hof, J., and T. Baltic (1991). A multilevel analysis of production capabilities of the national forest system. *Oper. Res.* 39, 543–552.

Holling, C.S. (1977). The curious behavior of complex systems: Lessons from ecology, in: H.A. Linstone, and W.H.C. Simmonds (eds.), *Futures Research: New Directions*, Addison-Wesley, Reading, MA, pp. 114–129.

Ikura, Y., and G. Gross (1984). Efficient large-scale hydro system scheduling with forced spill conditions. *IEEE Trans. Power Apparatus Syst.* PAS-103, 3502–3512.

Ikura, Y., G. Gross and G.S. Hall (1986). PG&Es state-of-the-art scheduling tool for hydro systems. *Interfaces* 16(1), 65–82.

Imber, S., E. Wasil, B. Golden and C. Stagg (1991). Selecting a survey design to monitor recreational angling for striped bass in the Chesapeake Bay. *Socio-Econom. Planning Sci.* 25(2), 113–121.

Jensson, P. (1981). A simulation model of the capelin fishery in Iceland, in: K.B. Haley (ed.), *Applied Operations Research in Fishing*, Plenum Press, New York, pp. 187–198.

Kallio, M., Å.E. Andersson, R. Seppälä and A. Morgan (eds.) (1986). *Systems Analysis in Forestry and Forest Industries*, TIMS Studies in the Management Sciences, Vol. 21, North-Holland, Amsterdam.

Kennedy, J.O.S. (1986). *Dynamic Programming: Applications to Agriculture and Natural Resources*, Elsevier, London.

Kent, B.M. (1980). Linear programming in land management planning on national forests. *J. Forestry* 78, 469–471.

Kent, B., B.B. Bare, R.C. Field and G.A. Bradley (1991). Natural resource land management planning using large-scale linear programs: The USDA Forest Service experience with FORPLAN. *Oper. Res.* 39, 13–27.

Kingsland, S.E. (1985). *Modeling Nature: Episodes in the History of Population Ecology*, University of Chicago Press, Chicago, IL.

Kirby, M.W., W.A. Hager and P. Wong (1986). Simultaneous planning of wildland management and transportation alternatives, in: M. Kallio, Å.E. Andersson, R. Seppälä and A. Morgan (eds.), *Systems Analysis in Forestry and Forest Industries*, TIMS Studies in the Management Sciences, Vol. 21, North-Holland, Amsterdam, pp. 371–387.

Kowero, G.S., and D.P. Dykstra (1988). Improving long-term management plans for a forest plantation in Tanzania using linear programming. *Forest Ecology Management* 24, 203–217.

Lancaster, J. (1991). Drought adds urgency to California water debate. *Washington Post* 220, July 13, A3.

Lane, D.E. (1988). Investment decision making by fishermen. *Canad. J. Fisheries Aquatic Sci.* 45, 782–796.

Lane, D.E. (1989a). A partially observable model of decision making by fishermen. *Oper. Res.* 37, 240–254.

Lane, D.E. (1989b). Operational research and fisheries management. *European J. Oper. Res.* 42, 229–242.

Lane, D.E. (1992). Management science in the control and management of fisheries: An annotated bibliography. *Amer. J. Math. Management Sci.* 12, 101–152.

Lembersky, M.R., and U.H. Chi (1986). Weyerhaeuser decision simulator improves timber profits. *Interfaces* 16(1), 6–15.

Leslie, P.H. (1945). On the use of matrices in certain population mathematics. *Biometrika* 33, 183–212.

Leuschner, W.A., J.R. Porter and H.E. Burkhart (1975). A linear programming model for multiple-use planning. *Canad. J. Forest Res.* 5, 485–491.

Little, J.D.C. (1955). The use of storage water in a hydroelectric system. *Oper. Res.* 3, 187–197.

Lotka, A.J. (1925). *Elements of Physical Biology*, Williams and Wilkins, Baltimore, MD. [Reprinted as *Elements of Mathematical Biology*, Dover, New York, 1956.]

Loucks, D.P., J.R. Stedinger and D.A. Haith (1981). *Water Resource Systems Planning and Analysis*, Prentice-Hall, Englewood Cliffs, NJ.

Loucks, D.P., J.R. Stedinger and U. Shamir (1984). Research in water resources and environmental systems modeling: Some historical perspectives, current issues, and future directions. *Natural Resources Forum* 8, 219–240.

Loucks, D.P., J.R. Stedinger and U. Shamir (1985). Modelling water resource systems: Issues and experiences. *Civil Engrg. Syst.* 2, 223–231.

Major, D.C., and R.L. Lenton (1979). *Applied Water Resource Systems Planning*, Prentice-Hall, Englewood Cliffs, NJ.

Mangel, M. (1985). *Decision and Control in Uncertain Resource Systems*, Academic Press, Orlando, FL.

Marsten, R.E. (1981). The design of the XMP linear programming library. *Trans. Math. Software* 7, 481–497.

Martell, D.L. (1982). A review of operational research studies in forest fire management. *Canad. J. Forest Res.* 12, 119–140.

Martell, D.L., R.J. Drysdale, G.E. Doan and D. Boychuk (1984). An evaluation of forest fire initial attack resources. *Interfaces* 14(5), 20–32.

Miller, S. (1991). New catch limits may save flounder. *Daily Press* 20, July 28, A1–A5.

Morse, P.M. (1977). *In at the Beginnings: A Physicist's Life*, The MIT Press, Cambridge, MA.

Murawski, S.A., and J.T. Finn (1986). Optimal effort allocation among competing mixed-species fisheries, subject to fishing mortality constraints. *Canad. J. Fisheries Aquatic Sci.* 43, 90–100.

Pao, Y. -H. (1989). *Adaptive Pattern Recognition and Neural Networks*, Addison-Wesley, Reading, MA.

Paull, A.E., and I.R. Walter (1955). The trim problem: An application of linear programming to the manufacture of newsprint paper. *Econometrica* 23, 336.

Pereira, M.V.F., and L.M.V.G. Pinto (1991). Multi-stage stochastic optimization applied to energy planning. *Math. Programming* 52, 359–375.

Portney, P.R. (ed.) (1982). *Current Issues in Natural Resource Policy*, Resources for the Future, Washington, DC.

Reinhold, R. (1991a). Savaged, then saved by man, condors to be sent into wild. *New York Times* CXL (48, 680), August 2, A1–B6.

Reinhold, R. (1991b). Drought taking its toll on California environment. *New York Times* CXL (48, 682), August 4, 21.

Ricker, W.E. (1954). Stock and recruitment. *J. Fisheries Res. Board Canad.* 11, 559–623.

Rider, K.L., P. Kolesar and G.L. Lilien (1986). Franz Edelman Award for management science achievement. *Interfaces* 16(1), 1–5.

Rogers, P.P., and M.B. Fiering (1986). Use of systems analysis in water management. *Water Resources Res.* 22, 146S–158S.

Roise, J., J. Chung, R. Lancia and M. Lennartz (1990). Red-cockaded woodpecker habitat and timber management: Production possibilities. *Southern J. Appl. Forestry* 14, 6–12.

Rothschild, B.J. (1986). *Dynamics of Marine Fish Populations*, Harvard University Press, Cambridge, MA.

Rothschild, B.J., and J.W. Balsiger (1971). A linear programming solution to salmon management. *Fishery Bulletin* 69, 117–140.

Sabet, M.H., and J.Q. Coe (1986). Models for water and power scheduling for the California State water project. *Water Resources Bulletin* 22, 587–596.

Sabet, M.H., J.Q. Coe, H.M. Ramirez and D.T. Ford (1985). Optimal operation of California aqueduct. *J. Water Resources Planning Management* 111, 222–237.

Schrage, L. (1991). *LINDO: An Optimization Modeling System*, Scientific Press, South San Francisco, CA.

Shane, R.M. (1991). Personal communication.

Shane, R.M., and K.C. Gilbert (1982). TVA hydro scheduling model: Practical aspects. *ASCE J. Water Resources Planning Management Division* 108 (WR1), 1–19.

Shane, R.M., H.D. Waffel, J.A. Parsly and H.M. Goranflo (1988). TVA weekly scheduling model application experience, in: J.W. Labadie et al. (eds.), *Computerized Decision Support Systems for Water Managers*, American Society of Civil Engineers, New York, pp. 426–438.

Siegel, R.A., J.J. Mueller and B.J. Rothschild (1979). A linear programming approach to determining harvesting capacity: A multiple species fishery. *Fishery Bulletin* 77, 425–433.

Simard, A.J. (1991). Personal communication.

Simard, A.J., and J.E. Eenigenburg (1990). An executive information system to support wildfire disaster declarations. *Interfaces* 20(6), 53–66.

Starfield, A.M., and A.L. Bleloch (1991). *Building Models for Conservation and Wildlife Management, 2nd edition*, Bellwether Press, Edina, MN.

Starfield, A.M., B.P. Farm and R.H. Taylor (1989). A rule-based ecological model for the management of an estuarine lake. *Ecological Modelling* 46, 107–119.

Starfield, A.M., J.D. Shiell and G.L. Smuts (1981). Simulation of lion control strategies in a large game reserve. *Ecological Modelling* 13, 17–38.

Staschus, K. (1991). Personal communication.

Steuer, R.E., and A.T. Schuler (1978). An interactive multiple-objective linear programming approach to a problem in forest management. *Oper. Res.* 26, 254–269.

Teeguarden, D.E., and H.-L. Von Sperber (1968). Scheduling Douglas fir reforestation investments: A comparison of methods. *Forest Sci.* 14, 354–368.

Terry, L.A., M.V.F. Pereira, T.A. Araripe Neto, L.F.C.A. Silva and P.R.H. Sales (1986). Coordinating the energy generation of the Brazilian national hydrothermal electrical generating system. *Interfaces* 16(1), 16–38.

Thompson, E.F., B.G. Halterman, T.J. Lyon and R.L. Miller (1973). Integrating timber and wildlife management planning. *Forestry Chronicle* 49, 247–250.

Volterra, V. (1926). Fluctuations in the abundance of a species considered mathematically. *Nature* 118, 558–560.

Walters, C.J., and J.S. Collie (1989). An experimental strategy for groundfish management in the face of large uncertainty about stock size and production, in: R.J. Beamish, and G.A. McFarlane (eds.), *Effect of Ocean Variability on Recruitment and an Evaluation of Parameters Used in Stock Assessment Models. Canad. Special Publication Fisheries Aquatic Sci.* 108, 13–25.

Walters, C.J., and J.E. Gross (1972). Development of big game management plans through simulation modelling. *J. Wildlife Management* 36, 119–128.

Walters, C.J., R. Hilborn and R. Peterman (1975). Computer simulation of barren-ground caribou dynamics. *Ecological Modelling* 1, 303–315.

Wang, Q., B. Golden, E. Wasil and G. DiNardo (1992). Modeling salinity dynamics in the Chesapeake Bay. *Amer. J. Math. Management Sci.* 12, 227–245.

Willett, K., and R. Sharda (1991). Using the analytic hierarchy process in water resources planning: Selection of flood control projects. *Socio-Econom. Planning Sci.* 25(2), 103–112.

Williams, G.L. (1981). An example of simulation models as decision tools in wildlife management. *Wildlife Soc. Bulletin* 9, 101–107.

Yakowitz, S. (1982). Dynamic programming applications in water resources. *Water Resources Res.* 18, 673–696.

Yeh, W.W-G. (1979). Real-time reservoir operation: The California Central Valley project case study, in: G.H. Toebes, and A.A. Shepherd (eds.), *Reservoir Systems Operations*, American Society of Civil Engineers, New York, pp. 217–227.

Yeh, W.W-G. (1985). Reservoir management and operations models: A state-of-the-art review. *Water Resources Res.* 21, 1797–1818.

Yeh, W.W-G., L. Becker, D. Toy and A.L. Graves (1980). Central Arizona project: Operations model. *ASCE J. Water Resources Planning Management Division* 106(WR2), 521–540.

S.M. Pollock et al., Eds., *Handbooks in OR & MS, Vol. 6*

Chapter 10

Models for Water and Air Quality Management

Charles ReVelle and J. Hugh Ellis

Department of Geography and Environmental Engineering, The Johns Hopkins University,
Baltimore, MD 21218, U.S.A.

Management models which address problems of water quality and those which address air quality have surprisingly similar forms. Although the basic descriptive models which underlie the management models reflect different mechanisms, the management models themselves tend to approach the public decision-making problems similarly. This chapter lays out the management models for water and air quality that have been developed over the last twenty-plus years. To provide these models in a comprehensible fashion, it is necessary to describe the fundamental models of pollutant transport and transformation in water and air. Thus, each of the sections includes a mathematical description of pollutant transport and transformation appropriate to the particular medium.

PART A. WATER QUALITY MANAGEMENT IN RIVERS AND ESTUARIES

1. The descriptive model for river water quality

The preservation of aquatic life is probably the principal concern of those who focus on river water quality. The aquatic life that we value includes such species as fish, mayflies, crayfish, and other of the freshwater aggregation that requires adequate dissolved oxygen content in the water. As a consequence, river water quality management focuses on maintaining a dissolved oxygen level in the stream that will support these species. Adequate oxygen level is achieved by the removal of organic wastes from wastewater; these organic wastes enter the river at the various points of municipal and industrial discharge. Organic wastes are of interest because the degradation of these wastes, by microbes and protozoa in the stream, cause the removal of oxygen.

The problem then becomes one of allocating the burden of treating organic wastes among the polluters along a river. The degree of treatment by each polluter, which is really the fraction of the organic wastes that each polluter removes, determines the contribution of that discharger toward the depletion of oxygen in the river. The constraint that forces the removal of organic wastes is the maintenance of a certain level of dissolved oxygen. The objective most commonly sought is the least total of costs over all dischargers, both municipal and corporate, since the least-cost solution places the least burden on society as a whole. Although 5 mg/l of oxygen is regarded as adequate to insure the survival of most species of fish, one can envision a tradeoff between system cost and the lowest level of dissolved oxygen over the entire length of the river. A number of researchers have attacked this basic problem, including Liebman & Lynn [1966], ReVelle, Loucks & Lynn [1967, 1968], Arbabi, Elzinga & ReVelle [1974], and Thoman & Sobel [1964].

The problem, while fairly simple to state, requires technical detail to state mathematically. In particular, the notion of organic wastes is not a precise idea, since organic wastes are of diverse origin and chemical composition. To measure the quantity of every organic substance in a waste stream is an exhausting, and perhaps impossible, job. Each substance present would first have to be identified. Next, once a substance has been shown to be present, the quantity of that substance would have to be measured. Then, if we also know the rate of oxygen consumption when bacteria oxidize each of the substances present, we could predict how much oxygen would be removed by oxidation of all the wastes in say a liter of the polluted water. Clearly such a process of predicting oxygen consumption is not feasible.

A much easier way to measure and state the concentration of organic wastes reveals not only the concentration of organics but the amount of oxygen that all the organic wastes, acting together, will eventually remove from the water. This measure is the *biochemical oxygen demand (BOD)*. BOD is the amount of oxygen, determined by testing, that would be consumed if all the organics in one liter of polluted water were oxidized in the presence of air by bacteria and protozoa. It is reported in number of milligrams of oxygen per liter.

Suppose we are studying a sample of polluted water discharged as a waste stream from a community into a river. The sample is reported to have a BOD of 120 mg/l. This means that bacteria and protozoa oxidizing all the organic substances in one liter of the water would consume 120 mg of oxygen. Now suppose that 50 ml (0.05 liter) of the polluted water were mixed with 950 ml of clean water; that is, the sample has been diluted to 50 parts in 1000 parts, or to 1/20 of the original concentration. The BOD of the mixture will be $(1/20) \times 120$ or 6 mg/l.

This dilution is similar to what happens when the flow of sewage from a community enters a watercourse that has a substantial water flow. Suppose the BOD in the discharge is the 120 mg/l we were discussing. Assume further that the community empties 1 million gallons of waste per day into the stream and that the clean stream is flowing at 19 million gallons per day past the outfall. The BOD of the mixture is diluted to 1/20 of the discharge value, or 6 mg/l. This number is the amount of oxygen that can be removed from every liter in the combined flow of stream and wastewater. Clean water, saturated with oxygen, can only possess oxygen up to about 9 mg/l, so if the BOD of the mixture is 6 mg/l, the oxygen in the mixture could potentially be reduced to close to 3 mg/l. How low it will actually go depends on many factors, but especially on the rate of oxidation by bacteria and on the natural rate of restoration of oxygen to the stream.

Thus, the BOD value tells a biologist the capability of the organic wastes in polluted water to deplete the oxygen resources in the stream. This is a valuable indicator of pollution, since the lack of oxygen is responsible for fish kills and also causes foul odors and the growth of populations of undesirable pollution-tolerant organisms. The BOD does not explain which organic substances are present in the water nor in what quantity they are present. Nonetheless, it provides a rapid and important insight into the maximum pollution damage the wastewater could cause.

The concentration of BOD does not by itself predict the amount of oxygen that will be removed from a river or stream. Thus the removal of oxygen and the degradation of BOD do not take place instantaneously but over a period of time during which other processes are operating. In particular, the water–air interface is in constant motion, causing the water to redissolve oxygen from the air. Thus, a complex interrelationship of BOD removal as well as oxygen removal and uptake needs to be modelled.

The removal rate of BOD with time (and time of flow downstream) is approximated most commonly as a first order chemical reaction – even though it is mediated by bacteria and protozoa. The differential and integral forms of the simplest model for removal of BOD with time are:

$$\frac{dL}{dt} = -kL \quad \text{and} \quad L = L_0 e^{-kt} \tag{1}$$

where

L = the concentration of BOD at time of flow t [mg/l];
k = a bio-oxidation rate constant [days^{-1}]; and
L_0 = the concentration of BOD at the top of the reach of the river,

i.e., at the point at which the wastewater was introduced and at which mixing took place.

In the above, and what follows, the units of parameters and variables are given in square brackets ([ ]). The removal and replenishment of dissolved oxygen is likewise modelled in differential equation form.

$$\frac{dC}{dt} = r(C_s - C) - kL$$

where

r = a reaeration coefficient [days^{-1}];
C = the concentration of dissolved oxygen at time of flow t [mg/l]; and
C_s = the maximum level of oxygen that can be dissolved in water [mg/l].

The first term of this dissolved oxygen equation suggests that the rate of reincorporation of oxygen is proportional to the additional oxygen that can be dissolved; that is, that the rate is proportional to $(C_s - C)$.

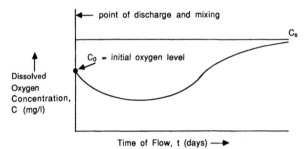

Fig. 1. The dissolved oxygen-sag curve.

The value of the proportionality constant r is a function of the rate at which the water is mixing, which depends on its velocity of flow, among other parameters.

The integrated form of the dissolved oxygen equation is:

$$C = C_s(1 - e^{-rt}) + C_0 e^{-rt} + \frac{k}{r - k}(e^{-rt} - e^{-kt})L_0 \qquad (2)$$

where C_0 = the concentration of dissolved oxygen at the top of the river. The integrated equation is often referred to as 'the oxygen-sag equation' because of the characteristic dip and recovery shown by the graphical form of this equation (see Figure 1). The equations were originally derived by Streeter & Phelps [1925].

From the above equation, we can see that the concentration at any point along the river is a linear function of initial conditions, as given here by initial dissolved oxygen (C_0) and initial BOD (L_0) level. This property, a property of all linear differential equations, is exploited in the building of a management model. In particular, we now discuss how these equations used in a mathematical program give rise to a first order linear optimal control problem – which is the focus of the remainder of this section.

2. The management model for water quality in rivers

2.1. The objective function

The annual cost of building and operating a wastewater treatment plant increases approximately linearly with the fractional removal of BOD (within a range of 35–90%). Non-linearities in costs may appear at levels of treatment above and below this range. In the upper range, convexities may occur. In the lower range, concavities are likely. For the model presented here, it is assumed that at least primary treatment (35% BOD removal) is required at each facility. Primary treatment or first-stage treatment consists of settling sewage solids out of the waste flow. This operation is performed in virtually all modern facilities, since it is needed to prevent the discharge of unsightly solids into the stream. In some third world countries, even this first stage of treatment may not be practiced.

The assumption of primary treatment removes the concave portion of the cost function, markedly simplifying analysis without a loss of realism. The introduction of tertiary treatment (greater than 90% BOD removal) adds convexities to the treatment cost function, which can be handled by piecewise approximation. For simplicity of description, however, we limit our attention to the range of treatment from 35 to 90%. In this range, linear costs can reasonably be assumed.

We assume that the river system being modelled consists of a sequence of waste dischargers on a single non-branched river system. Branched systems can be handled easily, but the mathematics is particular to the river topology being considered and introduces no new modelling concepts. To develop the objective function, we introduce the following notation:

n = the number of waste dischargers on the stream;

i = treatment plant index, $i = 1, 2, \ldots, n$;

y_i = annual cost of treatment for plant i [$];

g_i = slope of the linear portion of the cost curve [$/degree efficiency];

h_i = intercept of the linear portion of the cost curve (i.e., the cost at zero percent treatment using the linear cost curve) [$]; and

E_i = the efficiency of treatment plant i [% BOD removal $\div$ 100].

The cost as a function of percent treatment or efficiency is

$$y_i = g_i E_i + h_i$$

The objective function to be minimized is then

$$Z = \sum_{i=1}^{n} g_i E_i + \sum_{i=1}^{n} h_i \tag{3}$$

The second term is the sum of constants and hence does not depend upon the decision variables y_i. Equation (3) is the primary objective function for the cost allocation problem; but other objectives may also be of importance in determining politically acceptable allocations of cleanup burden. These other objectives are introduced at a later point in the chapter.

2.2. The constraint set

The first set of constraints comes from the range of allowable treatment efficiencies, namely:

$$0.35 \leq E_i \leq 0.90 \quad i = 1, 2, \ldots, n \tag{4}$$

In addition to the range of treatment which can be provided at each plant, there are three additional groups of constraints: (a) the relation between plant efficiency and BOD discharge, (b) internal 'inventory' equations to keep track of wastes and oxygen at points of mixture within the stream, and (c) restrictions on water quality.

The relation between plant efficiency and BOD discharge is simply given by the definition of efficiency.

The second type of constraint, an inventory equation, is essentially a mass balance. It is used to eliminate excessive algebraic manipulation. Consider a location where a treatment plant discharge mixes with the main stream. The BOD and deficit leaving this point of mixture are each related, by an inventory equation, to the BOD and deficit entering the point of mixture.

The last type of constraint is an explicit restriction on water quality, written in terms of the required level of oxygen in the river, and based on the oxygen-sag equation.

2.2.1. Plant efficiency and BOD discharged

The efficiency of a treatment plant is defined as the amount of BOD removed divided by the amount originally present. Thus, for plant i, efficiency is

$$E_i = \frac{P_i - M_i}{P_i},$$

where

P_i = concentration of BOD entering plant i [mg/l]; and
M_i = concentration of BOD leaving plant i [mg/l].

This can be written

$$P_i E_i + M_i = P_i \tag{5}$$

which is a linear equation in the (unknown) efficiency E_i and the effluent BOD, M_i. The relationship is enforced by writing the constraint of equation (5) for all dischargers $i = 1, 2, \ldots, n$.

2.2.2. Inventory constraints and water quality constraints

Inventory constraints and water quality constraints require that a set of new variables and terms be defined:

Q_0 = flow in the river above the first point of withdrawal [millions of gallons per day], known;
x_i = river flow removed for the use of community or corporate discharger i [millions of gallons per day], known;
q_i = wastewater flow from discharger i [millions of gallons per day], known;
Q_i = flow in the river in reach i [millions of gallons per day], known;
T = oxygen concentration in the discharge from polluter i (about 1 mg/l).
C_i = concentration of dissolved oxygen at the top of reach i, just after a waste flow mixes with the river flow [mg/l], unknown;
B_i = concentration of dissolved oxygen at the bottom (last point) of reach i [mg/l], unknown;
L_i = concentration of BOD at the top of reach i, just after a waste flow mixes with the river flow [mg/l], unknown; and

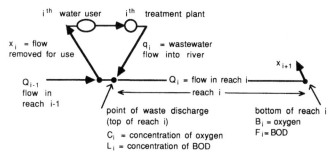

Fig. 2. Reach i and discharge i.

F_i = concentration of BOD at the bottom (last point) of reach i [mg/l], unknown.

We can now write mass balances for BOD and for dissolved oxygen at discharge point i. This is repeated for all dischargers:

$$\text{BOD mass balance:} \quad (Q_{i-1} - x_i) \cdot F_{i-1} + q_i M_i = Q_i \cdot L_i \tag{6}$$
$$i = 1, 2, \ldots, n$$

$$\text{oxygen mass balance:} \quad (Q_{i-1} - x_i) \cdot B_{i-1} + q_i T = Q_i \cdot C_i \tag{7}$$
$$i = 1, 2, \ldots, n$$

Both sets of equations are linear in the unknown variables. Placed in standard form in the final constraint set, the equations define the immediate water quality impact of successive pollutant additions and their impacts on water quality. (See Figure 2 for depiction of reach i.)

Since Q_i, the flow in reach i, is the initial flow less any removals plus any returns, an additional condition holds:

$$Q_i = Q_0 - \sum_{k=1}^{i} x_k + \sum_{k=1}^{i} q_k.$$

However, this calculation can be performed outside any mathematical program since it involves no decision variables.

Two types of water quality constraints are used to maintain dissolved oxygen levels above a standard, S. The first type requires the dissolved oxygen at the top and bottom of each reach to be greater than S:

$$C_i \geq S \quad i = 1, 2, \ldots, n \tag{8}$$

$$B_i \geq S \quad i = 1, 2, \ldots, n \tag{9}$$

The second constraint type, which follows, uses the sag curve of equation (1) to calculate dissolved oxygen levels at suitably spaced points in each reach. Each of these calculated values of dissolved oxygen are also constrained to be greater than or equal to the dissolved oxygen standard. The points are assumed to be spaced sufficiently closely that any violation of the standard between the points will be negligibly small [see ReVelle, Loucks & Lynn, 1967, for details].

Using j as the index of points in reach i and J_i as the set of points (other than the first and last), we can write

$$a_{ij}L_i + b_{ij}C_i + d_{ij} \geq S \quad i = 1, 2, \ldots, n; \quad j \in J_i \tag{10}$$

The coefficients a_{ij}, b_{ij}, d_{ij} are defined using t_{ij}, the time of flow from the top of reach i to the jth point in reach i:

$$a_{ij} = \frac{k_i}{r_i - k_i}(e^{-r_i t_{ij}} - e^{-k_i t_{ij}})$$

$$b_{ij} = (e^{-r_i t_{ij}})$$

$$d_{ij} = C_s(1 - e^{-r_i t_{ij}})$$

The inventory or mass balance constraints of equations (6) and (7) by themselves are insufficient to represent BOD and dissolved oxygen throughout the river. We need, in addition, equations for BOD and dissolved oxygen at the last point in each reach as a function of appropriate values at the top of each reach. Using the integrated forms of the differential equations for BOD (1) and dissolved oxygen (2), we can write the required relations:

$$F_i = (e^{-k_i m_i}) \cdot L_i \quad i = 1, 2, \ldots, n \tag{11}$$

$$B_i = \frac{k_i}{r_i - k_i}(e^{-r_i m_i} - e^{-k_i m_i})L_i + (e^{-r_i m_i})C - i + C_s(1 - e^{-r_i m_i}) \tag{12}$$

$$i = 1, 2, \ldots, n$$

where

m_i = the time of flow from the top of reach i to the last point in reach i;
k_i = the bio-oxidation rate constant characteristic of reach i; and
r_i = the reaeration coefficient characteristic of reach i.

Since the coefficients of L_i and C_i are in terms of known constants, these two equations can be rewritten as:

$$F_i = f_i \cdot L_i \tag{13}$$

$$B_i = a y_i^\circ L_i + b_i^\circ C_i + d_i^\circ \tag{14}$$

where the constant coefficients f_i, a_i°, b_i°, and d_i° are the coefficients of Equations (11) and (12).

The problem, finally, is one of choosing treatment efficiencies at each wastewater treatment plant which provide dissolved oxygen levels everywhere at or above a water quality standard. Intermediate decision variables representing BOD and dissolved oxygen at different points in the river are used to simplify the problem statement. The objective, the water quality constraints, definitions, and inventory equations can be summarized as follows:

$$\min Z = \sum_{i=1}^{n} g_i E_i q \quad \text{(Program WQ.1)}$$

subject to $\quad P_i E_i + M_i = P_i$

$$F_i - f_i L_i = 0$$

$$B_i - a_i^o L_i - b_i^o C_i = d_i^o$$

$$(Q_{l-1} - x_i) F_{i-1} + q_i M_i - Q_i L_i = 0 \quad i = 1, 2, \ldots, n$$

$$Q_i \cdot C_i - (Q_{i-1} - x_i) B_{i-1} = q_i T$$

$$C_i \geq S$$

$$B_i \geq S$$

$$a_{ij} L_i + b_{ij} C_i \geq S - d_{ij} \qquad i = 1, 2, \ldots, n \quad j \in J_i$$

$$0.35 \leq E_i \leq 0.90 \qquad i = 1, 2, \ldots, n$$

One of the most interesting aspects of this linear programming model is the use of many equality constraints in place of a fewer number of constraints that could be obtained by algebraic manipulation. It is possible (in a problem with up to, say, nine polluters) to reduce algebraically the water quality constraints from being functions of top-of-reach BOD and top-of-reach dissolved oxygen to being functions only of all the preceding removal efficiencies. The problem would then have *only* water quality constraints, and constraints on the range in which the efficiencies must lie. However, the manipulation needed to achieve this reduction in problem size quickly boggles the mind. Instead, we use the power of existing linear programming codes as linear algebra solvers, and thereby leave to the computer the enforcement of the needed algebraic relations. The prices are a larger problem and longer solution times, but the problems are still not large in any sense compared to capabilities of modern LP codes on modern machines. It is a tradeoff well worth making.

The results of applying this model could take many forms. Figure 3 displays a dissolved oxygen profile from a particular configuration of wastewater treatment plants. The break points in the curve represent the points of waste discharges to the river. The figure is hypothetical, but the form is entirely possible. This figure implies that only one of the water quality constraints is binding; in this case, it is the dissolved oxygen level at the top of the reach 3 that is at the standard. The drop in dissolved oxygen concentration at that point is due to the low level of oxygen in the wastewater discharged by treatment plant 3. Low dissolved oxygen in wastewater effluents are common. The water quality constraints could also bind somewhere in the middle of a reach, between treatment plants. Both types of binding have been observed. Surprisingly, not many constraints actually bind. One or two points of binding might occur in a 10-plant problem.

The need to write a number of closely spaced water quality constraints motivated Arbabi, Elzinga & ReVelle [1974] to examine the integrated form of the oxygen sag equation for properties which would admit fewer constraints on dis-

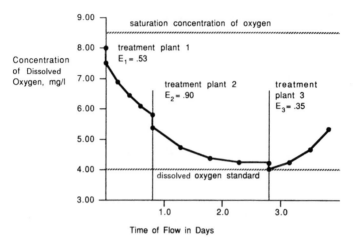

Fig. 3. Dissolved oxygen profile of a river basin.

solved oxygen. Setting the derivative of the oxygen sag equation to zero provides the time of flow at which the dissolved oxygen level reaches its lowest point in a reach. If this time of flow, which is called the critical time, is substituted in the equation for dissolved oxygen, an equation for the lowest concentration of oxygen results. This lowest level reflects the initial concentrations of BOD and dissolved oxygen as well as other parameters.

This lowest concentration of dissolved oxygen, called C_c, is an extremely complicated, non-linear function of the parameters C_o and L_o:

$$C_c = \frac{k}{r}L_o\left\{\frac{r}{k}\left[1-\left(\frac{r-k}{k}\right)\left(\frac{C_s-C_c}{L_o}\right)\right]\right\}^{-k/(r-k)} \tag{15}$$

Arbabi, Elzinga & ReVelle [1974] derived a linear (in the initializing parameters L_o and of C_o) approximation of the critical dissolved oxygen:

$$C_c = E + RL_o + A(C_s - C_o)$$

where the coefficients E, R, and A are presented in graphical form as a function of the parameters r and k. (Interestingly, the methodology utilized to derive this equation used a minimax error criterion and linear programming. Arbabi, Elzinga & ReVelle [1974] showed that the maximum error that could be expected from this approximation would be about 6%.) This equation can also be written in constraint form for each reach i in the problem

$$E + RL_i + A(C_s - C_i) \geq S \quad \text{or}$$

$$RL_i - AC_i \geq S - E - AC_s$$

As such, this constraint, written only once for each reach, could replace the multiple, closely spaced water quality constraints of Equation (10).

2.2.3. Other objectives

The water quality management problem admits of more objectives than simply minimum cost. An obvious additional objective is the maximization of water quality. That is, for the purpose of informed decision-making, an analyst would like to display the tradeoff between water quality and the system-wide cost of treatment.

Maximizing water quality requires the analyst to utilize a single concise measure of water quality. The integrated average dissolved oxygen is one such measure, but does not reflect the worst quality in the river, only the average quality. By shifting the standard, S, to the objective function as an unknown to be maximized, it is possible to trade off the water quality, as measured by the lowest dissolved oxygen anywhere in the river, against the total cost of treatment. The objectives then are

$$\max Z_1 = S$$

$$\min Z_2 = \sum_{i=1}^{n} q_i E_i$$

where S, the worst dissolved oxygen anywhere in the river, now appears on the left-hand side of the constraint equations since it is an unknown.

Other objectives may also be important. Prime among these is equity. An equitable standard of treatment means that a polluter is not assigned a cleanup burden, in terms of fractional removal of pollutants or cost, which differs radically from the burdens of other polluters in a similar category. To understand why equity is important, we explore a real situation in which a water quality management model was applied and in which the initial results were decidedly inequitable. The situation involved data from the Delaware River and its estuary in the late 1960s [see Brill, Liebman & ReVelle, 1976, and Smith & Morris, 1969]. A linear programming model, not unlike the one presented here, was used to determine the least-cost set of treatment efficiencies which maintain dissolved oxygen levels everywhere along the river at values greater than a standard.

Of the pollution removal efficiencies assigned to the 44 dischargers on the river, the smallest was 0.2 (which satisfied the particular constraints of the situation) and the largest 0.9. The price tag of this least-cost solution was $66.8 million. With such a wide disparity in required treatment efficiencies, even though the solution was the least-total-cost solution, imposition of this solution on the dischargers would likely lead to serious complaints. Indeed, a lawsuit based on inequity, never resolved because laws changed, prevented the solution from being implemented.

Nonetheless, the case was studied for insights into ways to achieve equity. The first method of achieving equity was to recast the problem into one in which the least-cost solution for maintaining dissolved oxygen is sought, subject to the constraint that all dischargers provide the same level of treatment. That is, the program WQ.1 is solved subject to the additional constraints

$$E_i - s = 0 \quad i = 1, 2, \ldots, n$$

where s is the unknown level of treatment, uniform across all dischargers. The result is that all dischargers each provided 78% removal efficiency and the total system cost escalated to \$195 million, nearly three times the price tag of the least-cost solution.

A second method of achieving equity was studied as well. This second method is referred to as the zoned uniform treatment program. In this program, dischargers are grouped into zones or classes. (The classes could, for example, be industrial waste dischargers and municipal waste dischargers. Or the zones could be geographical, e.g., lower estuary, upper estuary or a combination of the two.) The zoned uniform treatment program was solved subject to the additional constraints

$$E_i - s_z = 0 \quad z = 1, 2, \ldots, Z; \quad i \in I_z$$

where

s_z = the unknown uniform removal efficiency in zone z;
I_z = the set of dischargers i in zone z; and
Z = the number of zones.

The price tag of the least-cost solution using three classes of dischargers was \$108 million, 50% higher than the least-cost solution but almost half the uniform treatment solution.

In addition to the 'classes of discharger' programs for achieving equity, the ideal of equity can be approached by relaxing equal treatment requirements for the discharges to the status of an objective, namely the achievement of as equal treatment as possible given a cost constraint on total treatment. One translation of this goal is to minimize the range of assigned efficiency values given a cost constraint. To accomplish this, the following objective and constraints are added to the basic mathematical program:

$$\text{minimize} \quad E_{\max} - E_{\min}$$

$$\text{subject to} \quad E_i - E_{\max} \leq 0 \quad i = 1, 2, \ldots, n$$

$$E_i - E_{\min} \geq 0 \quad i = 1, 2, \ldots, n$$

The original objective of minimum cost now becomes a constraint:

$$\sum_{i=1}^{n}(g_i E_i + h_i) \leq C$$

where $E_{\max}$ and $E_{\min}$ are the (unknown) maximum and minimum treatment efficiencies. A tradeoff exists between the range of assigned efficiencies and the allowable level of investment C. As C grows, the range of efficiencies can be decreased. For the Delaware River example, when C reaches \$195 million, the range can be reduced to zero; that is, all efficiencies can be at the same level and the dissolved oxygen standard achieved everywhere in the system.

Another way to achieve equitable treatment efficiencies is to minimize the maximum efficiency necessary to meet the dissolved oxygen standard. Maximum efficiency is an interesting surrogate for equity in that the polluter faced with the largest level of treatment will view itself as being treated inequitably. Of course, as the maximum efficiency from the least-cost solution is pushed down, other efficiencies must increase in response, thereby increasing system cost. Again, there is a tradeoff between the highest efficiency in the system (being minimized) and the total costs of treatment.

The new objective and the constraints added to the base program are:

$$\text{minimize} \quad E_{max}$$

$$\text{subject to} \quad E_i - E_{max} \leq 0 \quad i = 1, 2, \ldots, n$$

and again the original objective becomes a constraint:

$$\sum_{i=1}^{n} (g_i E_i + h_i) \leq C$$

where all notation is as previously defined.

3. Regional treatment plant siting

Not long after the problem of finding the least-cost treatment efficiencies was first formulated, researchers began to focus on a second problem statement. In this second statement, removal efficiencies were put at relatively high levels and the sites for regional wastewater treatment plants were determined. The motivation behind this new problem setting was that economies of scale might be captured by regional treatment of wastewater. These scale economies were present in two areas. First, the treatment cost per-unit of wastewater flow declines as greater flows of wastewater are aggregated together. Second, as larger flows are collected in sewers, the per-unit piping and pumping costs from source to treatment plant decrease as well. Researchers thus pursued the problem of determining optimal levels of regionalization – since the costs of regional systems offered relatively large potential savings when compared to the traditional method of at-source treatment. In regional systems, wastes may be shipped, often in common pipelines, to a central or regional treatment plant or regional treatment plants. The problem is one of specifying where the regional plants should be sited and which wastewater sources should be assigned to each plant that is established.

The early published work on this problem, except for that of Converse [1972] who utilized a dynamic programming approach, can be characterized as applications of mixed-integer programming methods. Mixed integer programming was a natural approach to the problem because the economies of scale in treatment could be approximated as fixed charge cost functions, while other constraints resembled the linear assignment and capacity constraints of the transportation problem. As might be expected, these approaches were cumbersome, relying extensively on time-consuming branch-and-bound methodologies. To account for the economies of scale in pumping and piping would have required additional fixed charged approximations and even greater computer times. The fixed charge, branch-and-bound based approaches included works by Wanielista and Bauer

[1972], Joeres, Dressler, Cho & Falkner [1974], Jarvis, Radin, Unger, Moore & Schimpeler [1978], Hahn, Meier & Orth [1974], Brill & Nakamura [1978], Phillips, Beltrami, Carroll & Kellogg [1982], and Leighton & Shoemaker [1984]. One additional approach, that of Whitlatch and ReVelle [1976], used siting heuristics from the field of location analysis.

The work of Phillips, Beltrami, Carroll & Kellogg on a spatially dispersed system of sources was the first to see value in the fixed charge plant location model of Balinski [1965]. That model, initially proposed and quickly abandoned by Balinski, had been later studied extensively by Morris [1978] and shown to provide (0,1)-solutions with 96% regularity on some 600 random test problems. Phillips, Beltrami, Carroll & Kellogg were able to apply it in relatively the same form as originally proposed by Balinski, but their spatial setting was an unlikely one: central treatment plants with sources of wastes dispersed in a star pattern around the plants. In the star pattern for sources, joint flows of wastewater in the same pipe are less likely to be particularly advantageous.

In contrast, the most common setting for the regional treatment plant problem involves sources spaced along a river or estuary, with potential regional treatment plants also spaced along the river/estuary (see Figure 4). In this situation, in contrast to the setting considered by Phillips, Beltrami, Carroll & Kellogg wastewater flows are likely to join in common pipes to gain the economies of scale in piping and pumping. This latter situation is the one considered by Zhu and ReVelle [1988]. The Zhu and ReVelle model utilizes a restructured version of the Balinski plant location formulation. It captures economies of scale in treatment through a fixed charge cost function and it accounts for economies of scale in pumping and piping when the flows from waste sources are combined in a common pipe en route to the regional plant. This reformulation of the Balinski plant location problem for sources and treatment plants stretched along a river in a chain configuration has never failed to yield all zero–one solutions when the problem is attacked as a linear programming problem. Indeed, there appears to be theoretical justification for anticipating that it will *never* fail to provide all zero–one solutions.

The Zhu–ReVelle model deals with the situation (1) in which no treatment is presently provided by any of the existing waste dischargers, (2) in which bypass of waste flows around plants is not allowed, and (3) in which the same, fixed level of treatment is required at each regional treatment plant. Water quality constraints are honored by enforcing the same level of treatment of all waste flows prior to discharge into the river or estuary.

We begin by reviewing the plant location formulation of Balinski [1965] for the uncapacitated plant location problem:

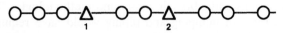

Fig. 4. A linear configuration of pollutant sources and potential regional treatment plants. A triangle denotes a potential regional plant site. A circke indicates a pollutant source.

$$\min Z = \sum_{i=1}^{m} \sum_{j=1}^{n} c_{ij} x_{ij} + \sum_{i=1}^{m} f_i y_i \tag{16}$$

subject to

$$(1) \quad \sum_{i=1}^{m} x_{ij} = 1 \quad j = 1, 2, \ldots, n$$

$$(2) \quad x_{ij} \le y_i \quad \begin{aligned} & i = 1, 2, \ldots, m \\ & j = 1, 2, \ldots, n. \end{aligned}$$

All x_{ij}'s ≥ 0 and $y_i = (0,1)$,

where

i = the index of plant sites, $i = 1, 2, \ldots, m$;
j = the index of demand points, $j = 1, 2, \ldots, n$;
x_{ij} = the fraction of the demand at point j supplied by a plant at site i;
c_{ij} = the cost of supplying the entire demand at point j from a plant at site i including both transportation and production costs;
y_i = 1 if a plant is established at site i and 0 otherwise; and
f_i = the cost to establish a plant at site i.

Constraints (1) require that each demand point j is fully supplied by all of the plants together. Constraints (2) enforce the logical condition that a plant must open at i if demand at point j is supplied from a plant at i, or that j cannot be served by i unless a plant opens at i. Based on the experience of Morris [1978], this formulation of the uncapacitated plant location problem due to Balinski can be conveniently solved by linear programming. That is, zero–one variables can be replaced simply by non-negative variables.

The siting model for regional wastewater treatment plants that we discuss here can be developed from the Balinski formulation. Figure 4 shows a linear system with eight pollutant sources and two potential regional treatment plant sites along a stream. It is assumed that a pollutant source can either treat its own wastes (at-source treatment) or transfer its wastes to a regional treatment plant, but it cannot split its flow in two.

Each pollutant source provides flow, either to treatment at that source or to a regional treatment plant. The same general kinds of constraints as are used in the Balinski plant location formulation are used in this problem. First, all of the flow from each pollutant source must be fully assigned somewhere, either to at-source treatment or to regional treatment. Second, if a waste source assigns its flow to a particular site, a regional treatment plant must open at that site. This second constraint is achieved by 'sequential priority constraints' which say that a source cannot assign its waste flow to a particular regional treatment plant unless all sources en route to that plant and closer to the plant than the source in question have fully assigned their waste flows to the plant. It will be found that the sequential priority constraints replace the equation (18) constraints of the Balinski formulation.

The generally accepted cost functions for treatment and transfer have decidedly non-linear forms:

$$C_{\text{treatment}} = aQ^b$$

$$C_{\text{transfer}} = \alpha Q^\beta \quad \text{(cost per unit distance)}$$

where a, b, α, and β are coefficients given by regressions of collected data and Q is the volume of wastewater flow being treated or transferred. The values of b and β are less than one, making both functions concave. A fixed charge function is used to approximate the concave cost of treatment:

$$\begin{aligned} C_{\text{treatment}} &= f + kQ \quad \text{if } Q > 0 \\ &= 0 \quad\quad\quad \text{if } Q = 0 \end{aligned} \quad \text{with } f \text{ and } k \text{ positive}$$

Surprisingly, no approximation is needed for the concave transfer costs.

The following notation is used for the regional treatment plant model:

m = number of the potential regional plants;

n = number of the pollutant sources;

i = indicator of sources, $i = 1, 2, \ldots, n$;

j = indicator of potential plants, $j = 0, 1, 2, \ldots, m$ (the plant indexed by 0 is at-source treatment);

x_{ij} = 1 if the ith source transfers its wastes to the jth plant and 0 otherwise (x_{i0} = 1 indicates at-source treatment by source i);

c_{ij} = the incremental cost (annualized) of treatment and transfer which accrues when the ith source joins the jth regional plant, (c_{i0} is the at-source treatment cost at source point i);

d_{ik} = distance of the transfer from source point i to site k, where k could be either a regional plant site or another source point;

y_j = 1 if a plant is established at site j and 0 otherwise;

f_j = opening cost (annualized) at site j (intercept of the linear approximation of the concave treatment cost function);

k_j = slope of the fixed charge function at the jth plant; and

Q_i = quantity of wastes originating at source i.

3.1. Calculation of assignment costs

Since c_{ij} is the cost of including source i in the set of assignments that are made to plant j, determining its value requires a calculation of the cost to assign source i to j in conjunction with the sources closer to j than i and en route from i to j.

Suppose source k is the closest source to j and i is the next closest source to j. Furthermore, source k is on i's route to j, so that the waste flow from i would join that from k in a common pipe to j (see Figure 5). Since source k must assign to j before i can assign to j, the cost of the regional plant would, at minimum, be

$$\alpha Q_k^\beta \cdot d_{ki} + (f_j + k_j Q_k)$$

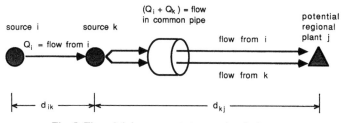

Fig. 5. Flows joining en route to a regional plant.

The first term is the cost of transfer of the waste flow from k to j. The second term, in parenthesis, is the fixed charge approximation of the cost of treatment of k's waste flow at j.

If i and k are both assigned to plant j, and no other waste sources are assigned to j, the cost of treatment and transfer would be

$$\alpha Q_i d_{ik} + \alpha (Q_i + Q_k)^\beta d_{kj} + k_j (Q_i + Q_k) + f_j$$

The first term is the cost of transferring the waste flow at i to source k. The second term is the cost of transferring in a common pipe both the waste flow from i and that from k to plant j. The third and fourth terms represent the fixed charge approximation of the treatment cost at j for both waste flows.

It follows that the additional cost to transfer the waste flow from i to j and treatment of that flow at plant j is the difference between the cost of treating/transferring both flows and the cost of treating/transferring only the waste flow from k. Thus, c_{ij}, the cost of including the flow from i in the set of assignments to plant j, is given by

$$c_{ij} = \alpha Q_i^\beta d_{ik} + \alpha [(Q_i + Q_k)^\beta - Q_k^\beta] d_{kj} + k_j Q_i$$

If there exists several intermediate waste sources between i and j, a similar computation can be performed.

The cost c_{i0} of at-source treatment by discharger i is simply:

$$c_{i0} = a Q_i^b$$

No fixed charged approximation is needed for at-source treatment.

All elements of the objective function have now been developed. All that remains is to create the constraint set. We indicated earlier that it would be necessary to structure sequential priority constraints, constraints which ensure that i assigns to j only if k assigns to j, and so on. Such constraints go hand-in-glove with the calculation of the costs, the c_{ij}, since the calculation of these costs presumes that only sequential assignments occur.

3.2. Sequential priority constraints

Suppose a, b, and c are the sources closest to j, on one side of j, and are ranked by distance from j as most distant, next most distant, and closest to j.

Then we can prevent a from assigning to j, unless b does, b from assigning to j, unless c does, and c from assigning to j unless a plant is open at j, by the following constraints:

$$x_{aj} \leq x_{bj}, \quad x_{bj} \leq x_{cj}, \quad \text{and} \quad x_{cj} \leq y_j.$$

Taken together, these constraints imply

$$x_{aj} \leq y_j$$

which is the Balinski constraint (18), suggesting that use of the sequential priority constraints duplicate the effect of the Balinski constraints.

If the ability of the Balinski model to yield zero–one solutions results from the 'can't unless' constraints as Morris has suggested, then it is also likely that the sequential priority constraints produce zero–one solutions with high frequency – because the sequential priority constraints duplicate the effects of the Balinski 'can't unless' constraints.

In fact, only zero–one solutions have thus far been obtained from linear programming solutions of this model [Zhu and ReVelle, 1988].

3.3. Summary of the regional treatment plant problem

$$\min Z = \sum_{i=1}^{n} \sum_{j=0}^{m} c_{ij} x_{ij} \sum_{j=1}^{m} f_j y_j \qquad \text{(Program WQ.2)}$$

subject to

(1) $\displaystyle\sum_{j=0}^{m} x_{ij} = 1$ $i = 1, 2, \ldots, n$

(2) $x_{cj} \leq y_i$ $j = 1, 2, \ldots, m$; c is the closest source to j on each side of j;

(3) $x_{aj} \leq x_{bj}$ $j = 1, 2, \ldots, m$; a and b, on the same side of j, are eligible to connect with j; source a is the next closest to j after b.

All x_{ij}'s and y_i's $\in (0,1)$.

In application, the assumption that each source is eligible to connect to every one of the potential plant sites is not realistic, and leads to an unnecessarily large number of assignment constraints. To address this concern we specify the following sets:

M_j = the set of sources i which are eligible to transfer wastes to plant j;
N_j = the set of sources i which are closest to j in M_j in either direction from j; and
L_i = the set of regional plants j which are eligible to be connected with source i, and each L_i at least includes $j = 0$, at-source treatment.

Then the model can be written as:

$$\min Z = \sum_{j=0}^{m} \sum_{i \in M_j} c_{ij} x_{ij} + \sum_{j=1}^{m} f_j y_j$$

subject to

(1) $\sum_{j \in L_i} x_{ij} - 1 \quad i = 1, 2, \ldots, n$;

(2) $x_{cj} \leq y_j \quad j = 1, 2, \ldots, m$; $\quad c \in N_j$;

(3) $x_{aj} \leq x_{bj} \quad j = 1, 2, \ldots, m$; $\quad a, b \in M_j$ and a is the next closest to j after b.

All x_{ij}'s and y_i's $\in (0,1)$.

Constraint set (1) indicates that each pollutant source disposes of its wastes either to a regional plant or by at-source treatment. Constraint set (2) says that if either of the closest sources to j assigns to j, the plant j must be open. This constraint parallels that of Balinski's formulation. Constraint set (3) says that source a cannot assign to plant j unless closer source b assigns to j.

4. Research remaining in water quality management systems

Our purpose in presenting finished material on this topic is not only to lay out the kinds of problems amenable to operations research, but at the same time to build up a foundation to describe research problems that remain. We have seen that two problems are largely well-formulated: (1) the allocation of treatment efficiencies to pollutant dischargers along a river in order to maintain at least a certain level of dissolved oxygen, and (2) the siting of regional treatment plants in a chain configuration along a river, where efficiencies are specified in advance at a level sufficient to sustain desired levels of dissolved oxygen.

At least three major problems flow from these formulations. The first problem deals again with the chain configuration. In its single objective version, without introducing notions of equity, the least-cost solution meeting dissolved oxygen standards would find both the locations of treatment and the degrees of treatment in order to simultaneously (a) obtain the optimal (least cost) mix of regional treatment plants and at-source treatment plants *and* (b) assign treatment efficiencies to both the regional treatment plants and at-source plants. No satisfactory approach to determining a solution to this problem has yet appeared in the literature, although early work by Graves, Hatfield & Whinston [1972] and Whitlatch & ReVelle [1976] approached the problem heuristically.

This proposed approach combines the efficiency determination model and regional location problem, but is specific for the chain configuration of sources and plants. In some cases, however, the configuration of sources and regional plants is not a chain. Instead, sources and plants may be dispersed on a branched river network. In such a situation, two or more waste flows may proceed in separate pipes for a portion of the distance to the regional plant and then merge at 'y' junctions to proceed the remaining distance to the plant. In this problem, in addition to determining assignments of dischargers to plants and location of plants, the locations of pipe junctions for merged flows need to be calculated. Although Phillips et al. considered dispersed sources and plants, they did not allow flows to merge en route to treatment plants, but assumed that each waste flow had its own separate pipe, thereby ignoring the issue of pipe configuration. Thus, the second new problem is one of siting regional treatment plants in a dispersed source or spur configuration setting. The problem remains open and challenging.

It follows that a third major problem setting remains: combining efficiency determination with regional treatment plant location in a dispersed source setting.

Other system problems of water quality management have been less well studied than efficiency determination and plant location. One of these is efficiency determination in a setting in which parameters of bio-oxidation, reaeration and river flow could be random variables [see Cardwell & Ellis, 1993; Ellis, 1987; Fujiwara, Gnanedran & Ohgahi, 1985; and Lohani & Than, 1978]. Another setting would consider these parameters as simply uncertain and would apply decision analysis to determine efficiencies.

The issues inherent in water quality management constitute classic forms in public sector problems. Efficiency objectives overlay standards which are required to be met, and equity challenges the derived solutions pushing policy toward feasible and just solutions. Finally, spatial characteristics as well as randomness and uncertainty complicate the problem forms and demand of analysts new research.

PART B. AIR QUALITY MANAGEMENT

1. Introduction

From a mathematical programming perspective, the fundamental issues in air quality management are, like water quality management, issues concerning the allocation of limited resources. Moreover, the physical and chemical processes that govern air pollutant transport and transformation are very similar and often identical to those for water-based pollutants. With these similarities very much in mind, our intent here is to sketch out some of the history and current modelling practices in air quality management.

2. Management model structure

Consider a rough depiction of the air pollution system that contains three major components. First are the sources, large and small, of the airborne pollutants of concern. Next are the physical and chemical processes through which these pollutants are transported and chemically transformed over distances from tens to many hundreds of miles. Finally, there is some preselected array of locations at which pollutant concentrations or deposition constitute an environmental concern. In this vastly oversimplified system then, a pollutant is emitted from a source, is transported and chemically transformed and subsequently either falls to earth, in both dry and wet forms, or exists suspended in air, with the result that humans or receiving ecosystems (water bodies or forests, or crops, or buildings) are subject to stress.

This description of air pollution can be described generally as looking forward, that is, from source to receptor in roughly the direction that the wind blows. Suppose mathematical models exist through which we can simulate the various components of this forward looking picture of air pollution. We now pose two central questions: are the levels of airborne pollutant stress excessive for human populations or sensitive receptors?; and, if so, how can that stress be reduced?

Answers to the first question require, at a minimum, computation of the concentrations or amount of pollution deposited which can then be compared with 'tolerable' levels of pollution. Forward-looking simulation models provide the first estimates – the spatial and temporal distribution of airborne pollutants. The tolerable (or allowable) concentrations or deposition limits can be developed from epidemiological studies, human exposure studies and/or specialized models designed to calculate ecosystem-specific maximum allowable deposition rates. (Most of our experience with such rates concerns acid rain [Likens, Wright, Galloway & Bulter, 1979] – in this case, these rates are usually referred to as critical loads.)

With these tools, we could assess where and to what extent airborne pollutants pose a human health or environmental threat. But now the second question: how to reduce that perceived threat?

By having a forward-looking mathematical model of the pollution transport system, we have the mechanism to invert the problem and look backward, i.e., to begin with, for example, desired ambient concentrations or critical loads at sensitive receptor locations and subsequently ascertain what modified (e.g., reduced) pollutant emission levels would be needed so that these concentrations or critical loads would not be exceeded. This step is most easily accomplished for the case of transport linearity, that is, transport and transformation processes represented by source–receptor-specific coefficients [Hidy, 1984] that are independent of source emission rate. If transport and transformation processes are not independent of emission rate – the system is non-linear and non-separable – then optimization approaches are still viable, but not all resulting models represent convex programming problems.

To reaffirm the important difference between forward-looking or simulation analyses and optimization analyses, recall the central decision problem: how to reduce emission levels so as to meet prespecified concentration or deposition limits? As one possibility, we could manually adjust pollutant emission levels to values that seem, a priori, to be consistent with a prescribed policy consideration and then re-simulate the system to determine whether the resultant concentration or deposition estimates satisfy our prescribed standards. In air pollution problems, however, such an approach is highly inefficient in that:

(1) There exists an enormous number of possible policy considerations and thus an enormous number of associated manually assignable sets of pollutant emission levels.

(2) In any given simulation, the prescribed pollutant standards may or may not be satisfied; that is not known until after the run has been performed.

In contrast, optimization methods that explicitly include pollutant standards have the desirable attribute that they can be restricted to identify only those control strategies that specifically meet the standards.

Both simulation-based and optimization approaches need basically the same information: current emission levels, transport estimates obtained from an air pollutant transport simulation model and concentration or deposition standards.

Mathematical models are thus a powerful, convenient means to explore inter-relationships between environmental standards and emission reduction decisions. Reaffirming this notion, the Clean Air Act Amendments passed in November 1990 [United States Congress, 1990] have an interesting provision relating to the important long-range pollution problem of acid rain. Section 404 – Acid Deposition Standards (paraphrased here) states that by November 15, 1993, the EPA must transmit '. . . a report on the feasibility and effectiveness of an acid deposition standard or standards to protect sensitive and critically sensitive aquatic and terrestrial resources. The study to include. . . '

(1) identification of sensitive resources in the U.S. and Canada;

(2) describe the nature and numerical value of a deposition standard;

(3) describe use of such standards by other Nations or by other States;

(4) describe measures to integrate such standards into title IV of the Clean Air Act;

(5) describe state-of-knowledge of source–receptor relationships and other ongoing research; what would be needed to make such a program feasible; and,

(6) describe impediments to implementation; cost-effectiveness of deposition standards compared to other control strategies, including ambient air quality standards, New Source Performance Standards, title IV requirements.

Mathematical programming methods constitute the most effective and efficient means through which many of these issues can be addressed.

3. Long-range transport modelling

Mathematical models for air pollution management yield control strategies that intimately depend upon and are influenced by our knowledge of pollutant transport and transformation – the so-called transfer coefficients mentioned earlier. Given the complexity of synoptic meteorology and chemical transformation, and the typical simplifications required to ensure modelling tractability, the estimation of transport coefficients often represents a weak link in the chain of strategy optimization. Nonetheless, a considerable amount of research has and is being conducted in an effort to improve the accuracy of long range transport modelling.

3.1. General review

Atmospheric dispersion and transport phenomena can be fundamentally represented by kinematic models. Typically, the motion of the atmosphere itself is not calculated, (i.e., meteorological measurements are employed as model input). The principal physical effects of concern are:
- advective motion of the atmosphere;
- dispersion caused by atmospheric turbulence;
- transformation of primary to secondary pollutants; and
- wet and dry deposition of pollutants.

Long range transport (LRT) models can be divided into two main types on the basis of their temporal resolution:

(1) Models which enable the calculation of concentrations and deposition rates on a daily (or shorter time period) basis (2) Models (usually statistical) which provide longer-term-averaged concentrations and deposition rates.

Within each model type, two approaches are commonly used to solve the general convective (parabolic) diffusion equation. The approaches are:

(1) integrate the equation in a (fixed) Eulerian grid,

(2) integrate the equation along conceptualized parcel trajectories in a Lagrangian framework.

Lagrangian (trajectory) solutions can be further subdivided into plume and puff models as will be shown later.

3.2. Daily basis models – general

Daily basis models typically involve the use of a single completely mixed boundary layer in which pollutant transport occurs. These models have proven satisfactory for transport distances greater than about 100 km. The general convection diffusion (GCD) equation for pollutants in the boundary layer is

$$\frac{\partial q}{\partial t} = -\nabla \cdot qv + E - R \tag{1}$$

where

q = concentration;
v = horizontal wind field;
E = emission; and
R = removal function. (E and R are functions of travel distance.)

Horizontal diffusion is neglected because E is usually given in terms of area sources on a scale of about 10^3 km^2 [Fay and Rosenzweig, 1980]. Transport through the top of the (assumed) completely vertically mixed boundary layer is ignored (the vertical transport velocity = 0). This represents an upper barrier impervious to transport, analogous to the lower (earth) boundary. Air density variations are similarly neglected. There are two possible approaches by which the equations can be integrated: Eulerian and Lagrangian.

3.2.1. Daily basis – Eulerian advection models

Solutions for models of this type are complicated by the presence of numerical dispersion which is closely related to the problem of closure when turbulent as well as mean flow properties are considered. One method to reduce numerical dispersion is to characterize the mass distribution of each grid element by a center of mass (1st moment), and radius of inertia (2nd moment) [Eliassen, 1980].

The model of Hidy et al. [1978] is an example of a daily basis-Eulerian advection model. Concentration variation is considered in three dimensions. The unsteady diffusion equation is averaged over 24 hours with depletion of pollutants modelled by a first-order concentration decay function. The solution technique is numerical and has had success in approximating the actual short-term-averaged wind field.

Another example is provided by the work of Gillani [1978]. A steady-state diffusion equation is used for transport scales of 1–100 km. The mean wind is uniform and horizontal cross-wind eddy diffusivity varies with downwind distance. As in almost all cases, primary pollutant loss (in this case, SO_2) was assumed to obey a first order decay function.

3.2.2. Daily basis – Lagrangian (trajectory) models

Lagrangian solutions imply integration along trajectories to obtain the concentration associated with moving air parcels, instead of working in a fixed Eulerian grid. For the case of acid rain, the individual contributions of SO_2 from different emissions along a trajectory are exponentially reduced with transport time between emission and arrival of the trajectory at the receptor. The total (net) concentration for a given trajectory is the sum of all emission concentrations along the trajectory. This type of general Lagrangian formulation has been used by the Norwegian Meteorological Institute to generate daily concentration estimates [Fay and Rosenzweig, 1980]. Another class of Lagrangian models exist which involve the concept of diffusing Gaussian puffs travelling along computed trajectories. The models of Pack et al. [1978] and Johnson et al. [1978] are of this type.

3.3. Longer-term models – General

The fundamental concepts inherent in the daily basis models apply equally to longer-term models. The major difference between the two is obviously the length of the averaging time scale. As would be expected, longer-term models are less sensitive to localized perturbations in time and space, hence are usually used to generate ambient concentration estimates. The choice of solution approaches, Eulerian or Lagrangian is, as with the daily basis models, available for longer-term models. With basic model mechanics having already been described, following are brief qualitative summaries of some Eulerian Lagrangian longer-term models.

3.3.1. Longer-term Eulerian models

Alam and Seinfeld [1981], developed analytical solutions of the steady-state three-dimensional atmospheric diffusion equation for SO_2 and SO_4^{2-} dispersion from point sources. The chemical transformation of SO_2 to SO_4^{2-} is included. Using an elevated continuous point source, the model enables generation of three dimensional concentration distributions with or without the presence of an elevated inversion layer.

Van Egmond et al. [1978], analysed SO_2 transport over distances of about 300 km. Vertical SO_2 distributions were deduced from horizontal ground level measurements. The effective mixing height of the boundary layer was generated with a two dimensional advection model. The results, generated for the Netherlands, indicated that the major part of the transport takes place above the surface layer, not affecting ground level concentrations. In addition, under special meteorological conditions, very high ground level concentrations can be experienced at large distances from the source areas.

3.3.2. Longer-term Lagrangian (trajectory) models

The model of Rodhe [1974], constructed for European conditions, considered major pollutant sources at four locations. The deposition from a source was calculated for each of eight conceptualized 45° sectors (in planview). For the ith sector, the deposition per unit area was defined as:

$$d_i(r) = \frac{8 f_i Q}{2\pi r_0 r} e^{-r/r_0} \tag{2}$$

where

Q = emission rate per unit time;
f_i = frequency of occurrence of trajectory end points within the sector;
r = distance from source; and
r_0 = constant 'turnover' distance.

Deposition within a sector, up to distance r was given by:

$$D_i(r) = \int_0^r \frac{2\pi r'}{8} d_i(r') \, dr' \tag{3}$$

$$= Q f_i \left[1 - e^{-r/r_0} \right] \tag{4}$$

Bolin and Persson [1975], utilized a two-dimensional distribution of trajectory end points around the mean displacement. Horizontal dispersion was assumed independent of vertical dispersion.

3.4. Current modelling efforts

The International Sulfur Deposition Model Evaluation [ISDME, 1987] documents eleven linear chemistry atmospheric models and rates their relative performance. The models were,
   • Atmospheric Environment Service (AES) Long-Range Transport Model
   ◦ Advanced Statistical Trajectory Regional Air Pollution Model (ASTRAP)

- Ontario Ministry of the Environment Long-Range Transport Model (MOE)
- Regional Impacts on Visibility and Acid Deposition Model (RIVAD)
- Regional Lagrangian Model of Air Pollution (RELMAP)
- Regional Transport Model (RTM-II)
- Statistical Estimates of Regional Transport and Acidic Deposition Model (SERTAD)
- Statistical Model (STATMOD) (2 versions)
- Tennessee Valley Authority Model-T (TVA)
- University of Michigan Contributions to Interregional Deposition Model (UMACID)

Some of these models were also part of the United States–Canada Memorandum of Intent [1990], a comprehensive study of the modelling and measurement of transboundary air pollutant transport related to acid rain.

Another useful source of long-range modelling efforts lies in the documentation of the National Acid Precipitation Assessment Program [NAPAP, 1989, 1991]. Much of NAPAP dealt with the development of the most sophisticated simulation model currently in existence: the Regional Acid Deposition Model, or RADM. RADM, however, differs in very important ways from the models listed above. It is inherently non-linear and thus does not directly yield transfer coefficients as do the previous linear chemistry-based models for long-range transport and transformation. A simplified (linearized) version of RADM, known as RELMAP, exists through which transfer coefficients are obtained directly.

4. Optimization models for air quality management

The first appearance of linear programming models for air quality management was in the mid-1960's. An interesting, but apparently little known paper by Teller [1968] used linear programming to estimate the cost of alternative air pollution strategies. The objective of the model was to minimize total fuel cost subject to a constraint on maximum allowable air pollutant concentration. Control strategies were restricted to fuel substitution, and the pollutant in question was sulfur dioxide. The basic model had the form,

$$\text{minimize} \quad \sum_{j=1}^{n} \left[C_{jb} T_{jb}^{v} + C_{ja} T_{ja}^{v} \right] \tag{5}$$

$$\text{subject to} \quad T_{ja}^{v} K_{ja} + T_{jb}^{v} K_{jb} \geq H_j \qquad j = 1, 2, \ldots, n \tag{6}$$

$$\sum_{j=1}^{n} M_{ij} \left[T_{ja}^{v} E_{ja} + T_{jb}^{v} E_{jb} \right] \leq S_i \quad i = 1, 2, \ldots, m \tag{7}$$

where

T_{ja} = number of tons of fuel A presently used by source J;

T_{ja}^{v} = (decision variable) number of tons of fuel A;

T_{jb}^v = (decision variable) number of tons of fuel B;
C_{ja} = cost per ton of fuel A;
C_{jb} = cost per ton of fuel B;
K_{ja} = BTU per ton of fuel A;
K_{jb} = BTU per ton of fuel B;
H_j = number of BTUs required by source J;
E_{ja} = emission per ton of fuel A from source J;
E_{jb} = emission per ton of fuel B from source J;
S_i = air quality standard at receptor I; and
M_{ij} = meteorological parameter relating emissions at source J to air quality at receptor I.

The transfer coefficients M_{ij} were obtained from Turner [1964]. We see here virtually all of the components of many future air quality management models to come.

At roughly the same time, models applied to the St. Louis airshed were developed by Kohn [e.g., Kohn, 1971, 1972, 1978] and Seinfeld and Kyan [1971]. The first models of Kohn were much broader in scope than Teller's, but the basic tools are the same. Kohn's [1972] effort extended costs to include those associated with labor displacement. Seinfeld and Kyan incorporated the notable development of decomposing the overall optimization problem into two problems: first, a linear program, then a dynamic program. Soon thereafter, Trijonis [1974] published a general least-cost air quality model, applied to the control of photochemical smog in Los Angeles. His model too had the basic framework involving cost minimization subject to environmental constraints. Additional papers in this time frame include Schweizer [1974] and Gipson, Freas & Meyer [1975].

In the mid 1970's, the subject of air quality optimization appeared in publications other than the traditional operations research and engineering science fields, specifically in applied economics, as exemplified by Atkinson and Lewis [1974, 1976], Downing and Watson [1974], Parvin and Grammars [1976], Fishelson [1976], Viscusi and Zeckhauser [1976], Adar and Griffin [1976], Yohe [1976], Mathur [1976], Dolde, Epple, Harris, Lave & Leinhardt [1977], Haimes, Nainis & Goldstone [1977], Cobb [1977], Harrison and Rubinfeld [1978], Hamlen [1978], Marin [1978] and Loehman et al. [1979].

The period from 1980 onward has seen yet another burst of activity in optimization of air quality management, much of it centering around acid rain control. This work includes Guldmann and Shefer [1980], Johnson [1983], Fortin and McBean [1983], Streets, Hanson & Carter [1984], Fronza and Melli [1984], Morrison and Rubin [1985], Streets, Lesht, Shannon & Veselka [1985], Ellis, McBean & Farquhar [1985a,b, 1986], Shaw [1986], Young and Shaw [1986], Guldmann [1986, 1988], Hordijk [1986], Fuessle, Brill & Liebman [1987], Ellis [1987, 1988a,b, 1990]. These papers cover a broad array of research directions, including those which focus on stochastic programming, industrial location, and multiobjective programming.

In the work dealing with stochastic programming, the source–receptor transfer coefficients are typically taken to be random variables. Both stochastic linear programming and chance constrained optimization techniques have been employed. The multiobjective programming models incorporate additional objectives beyond the traditional cost minimization, in order to include equity concerns, such as allocation of removal burdens across polluters. Multiobjective techniques have proven useful in models in which environmental standards are treated as targets that can be exceeded. The associated math programs then typically minimize some aggregate measure of standard exceedence, for example minimizing average or maximum violation of a stipulated target. In an extension of a minmax model for acid rain control, Ellis [1988b] includes as well the transfer coefficients from several long-range transport models simultaneously, and forms a model to minimize the maximum regret associated with the wrong choice of model.

Certain of these notions are described in greater detail in the following section. The intent here is to demonstrate the math programming formulations associated with different types of linear, non-linear, stochastic and multiobjective models. We use as a vehicle for this demonstration certain of the models described in Ellis, McBean & Farquhar [1985a,b, 1986] and Ellis [1987, 1988a,b, 1990].

4.1. Minimizing emission reductions or control costs

This model has a simple formulation: minimize emission reductions necessary to satisfy inviolate upper bounds on net deposition. It is written,

$$\text{minimize} \quad \sum_{k=1}^{n} E_k R_k \tag{8}$$

$$\text{subject to} \quad \sum_{k=1}^{n} E_k(1 - R_k)t_{jk} + B_j \leq D_j \tag{9}$$

$$R_k \leq R_k^u \tag{10}$$

where

E_k = SO$_2$ emission rate for source k;
R_k = removal level (i.e., the decision variables) with source-specific upper limits R_k^u;
t_{jk} = transfer coefficient relating emission at source k to deposition at receptor j;
B_j = background deposition rate at receptor j; and
D_j = maximum allowable deposition rate at receptor j.

A common variant on this model involves explicitly minimizing control cost instead of emission reductions. Given source-specific cost-removal functions $C_k(R_k)$ the objective function becomes,

$$\text{minimize} \quad \sum_{k=1}^{n} C_k(R_k) \tag{11}$$

In both versions, the D_j can be interpreted as maximum allowable ambient concentrations, or maximum deposition rates, depending upon the pollutant. It often occurs, however, that when the D_j are cast as inviolate upper bounds, such models are infeasible (i.e., the deposition constraints cannot be satisfied even with all pollutant removal levels (R_k) set to their upper limits (R_k^u)). Feasibility can be obtained by sequentially removing receptors from the model or, more commonly, relaxing concentration or deposition limits at those receptor locations where infeasibility occurs (the effect is the same).

4.2. Minimizing average violation

For the next model and its variants we adopt a somewhat softer interpretation for the D_j and now allow violations (i.e., exceedences of the D_j) to occur. We then trade off aggregate measures of violations against, for example, measures of the costs of control. The model shown below minimizes average constraint violation subject to a fixed aggregate emission reduction T (e.g., 10 million tons SO_2 per year in the U.S. for an acid rain control application) and is written,

$$\text{minimize} \quad \sum_{j=1}^{m} W_j V_j \tag{12}$$

$$\text{subject to} \quad \sum_{k=1}^{n} E_k(1 - R_k)t_{jk} + B_j + U_j - V_j = D_j \tag{13}$$

$$\sum_{k=1}^{n} E_k R_k = T \tag{14}$$

$$R_k \leq R_k^u \tag{15}$$

The decision variables V_j represent violations and are weighted by location, using weights W_j. A variant of this model normalizes violations and acts to minimize average violation expressed as a relative exceedence. The objective function then becomes,

$$\text{minimize} \quad \sum_{j=1}^{m} W_j \left(\frac{V_j}{D_j} \right) \tag{16}$$

From a mathematical programming perspective, the violation models described above are in essence, penalty models. More specifically, they are models with linear, asymmetric penalty functions. Other penalty function forms are certainly possible and if convex, will result in optimization problems that guarantee global optimality.

4.3. Minimizing maximum violation

A somewhat more conservative version is the model that minimizes the *maximum* violation (not knowing in advance, where that maximum violation will occur). Solutions using this approach can be interpreted as minimizing the worst concentration or deposition exceedence that could occur. This so-called minmax model is written,

$$\text{minimize} \quad MAXVIOL \tag{17}$$

$$\text{subject to} \quad \sum_{k=1}^{n} E_k(1 - R_k)t_{jk} + B_j + U_j - V_j = D_j \tag{18}$$

$$MAXVIOL - W_j V_j \geq 0 \tag{19}$$

$$\sum_{k=1}^{n} E_k R_k = T \tag{20}$$

$$R_k \leq R_k^u \tag{21}$$

When compared to models that minimize average violation, minmax solutions have a smaller maximum violation, but a slightly higher average violation, which is the tradeoff one would expect.

4.4. Two-objective model

The previous models are in fact multiple objective models [Ellis, 1988a] but of a specific kind. To recognize their multiobjective nature we note that the minmax model for example, could be repeatedly run for different values of aggregate emission reduction (T) thereby generating a tradeoff between maximum violation (objective one) and removal effort (objective two). This next model is again multiobjective but uses the weighting method [e.g., see generally Cohon, 1978]. It serves to minimize control cost and average violation and is written,

$$\text{minimize} \quad \alpha \cdot \sum_{k=1}^{n} C_k(R_k) + (1 - \alpha) \cdot \left(\sum_{j=1}^{m} W_j V_j \right) \tag{22}$$

$$\text{subject to} \quad \sum_{k=1}^{n} E_k(1 - R_k)t_{jk} + B_j + U_j - V_j = D_j \tag{23}$$

$$R_k \leq R_k^u \tag{24}$$

Here the weight α is arbitrary and functions only to generate the tradeoff between cost and average violation.

4.5. Multiple sets of inputs

A variant of the acid rain management model addresses certain of the problems posed when we encounter multiple sets of inputs with little or no guidance as to which set of inputs is likely and/or preferable. First consider the situation wherein we have different sets of deposition limits. A model that simultaneously incorporates all such sets involves minimizing maximum violation *regret*, given a fixed aggregate emission reduction and is shown as,

$$\text{minimize} \quad MAXVIOL \tag{25}$$

$$\text{subject to} \quad \sum_{k=1}^{n} E_k(1 - R_k)t_{jk} + B_j + U_j^s - V_j^s = D_j^s \tag{26}$$

$$j = 1, \ldots, m\,; s = 1, \ldots, S$$

$$MAXVIOL - W_j^s V_j^s \geq 0 \tag{27}$$

$$R_k \leq R_k^u \tag{28}$$

We first solve the minmax model separately for each s and identify the resulting optimal deposition rates. Next we combine all S optimal deposition rates and minimize the maximum violation with respect to these set-specific values. In effect then, we are comparing the best that we can do if we knew in advance what set of standards was 'right' against what we have to settle for, given that such foreknowledge is not available. The differences between these two situations is often called regret. This type of model can be applied to situations other than those involving multiple sets of critical loads, namely multiple sets of transfer coefficients from different long-range transport models [Ellis, 1988b] or alternatively, multiple sets of transfer coefficients from different meteorological years.

4.6. Minimizing number of violations

In the previous models, the extent of constraint violation plays a central role in shaping an abatement strategy. One model that represents a significant departure from this assumption treats violations in an 'on/off' manner. That is, we are concerned only whether a violation occurs or not, and not how large that violation might be. To model this attribute, we minimize the number of locations where violations occur, and do so by formulating a mixed integer programming model,

$$\text{maximize} \quad \sum_{j=1}^{m} Y_j \tag{29}$$

$$\text{subject to} \quad \sum_{k=1}^{n} E_k R_k t_{jk} \geq Y_j \cdot \left(\sum_{k=1}^{n} E_k t_{jk} + B_j - D_j \right) \tag{30}$$

$$R_k \leq R_k^u \tag{31}$$

$$Y_j \in [0, 1] \tag{32}$$

$$Y_j = \begin{cases} 1 & \text{if no violation occurs at receptor } j; \\ 0 & \text{otherwise.} \end{cases}$$

Such a model is appropriate when one is unwilling or unable to specify deposition-related penalty functions. In that sense, this model represents a significant departure from the explicit penalty-driven models described below.

4.7. Stochastic programs

While virtually all of the components of the management models discussed thus far can reasonably be considered random, attention has focused, for the most part, on the stochasticity of transfer coefficients. In the chance constrained technique of stochastic programming [Charnes and Cooper, 1959, 1962, 1963] applied to the problem to air quality management, the concentration or deposition constraints are recast in generalized form as

$$P\left[\sum_{k=1}^{K} a_{jk}x_k \le D_j\right] \ge \alpha_j \tag{33}$$

where

$P[\cdot]$ denotes probability; and
α_j = satisfaction level (i.e., reliability, $0 \le \alpha_j \le 1$) specified for constraint j.

These constraints can be interpreted as 'the probability of constraint satisfaction must be at least α_j'. In the context of air quality management, the a_{jk} represent the product of a transfer coefficient and an associated emission rate, while the x_k refer to emission removal fractions. If the a_{jk} are random variables (due to transfer coefficient stochasticity), and choice of x_k does not affect the densities of the a_{jk}, the resulting deterministic equivalent to (33) is

$$\sum_{k=1}^{K} E[a_{jk}]x_k + F^{-1}(\alpha_j)(\mathbf{x}^T\mathbf{V}^j\mathbf{x})^{1/2} \le D_j \tag{34}$$

where

$F^{-1}(\alpha_j)$ = inverse cumulative distribution function (CDF) value of the random variable $\sum a_{jk}x_k$ (i.e., the value of the random variable $\sum a_{jk}x_k$ that has non-exceedence probability α_j);
$\mathbf{V}^j$ = variance–covariance matrix of the random elements a_{jk}, for all $k = 1, \ldots, K$, within constraint j.

In a typical use of the model, the first and second moments of the transfer coefficients are obtained from a stochastic simulation model. If the simulation is conducted in a Monte Carlo fashion, that is, repeated simulations using random realizations obtained from a joint density of selected model inputs and/or parameters, then we have a traditional Type II-based chance constrained programming problem [e.g., see generally Ellis, 1987; Ellis, McBean & Farquhar, 1985b, 1986; Fronza and Melli, 1984; Fuessle, Brill & Liebman, 1987; Guldmann, 1986, 1988].

4.8. Two-stage programming

An interesting contrast to chance-constrained approaches involves models that explicitly incorporate penalty or loss functions in a two-stage programming framework [see, generally, Birge, 1982; Dantzig, 1955; Dantzig and Madansky, 1961; Ferguson and Dantzig, 1956; Walkup and Wets, 1967; and Wets, 1974, 1983]. Ostensibly these loss functions involve environmental disbenefits expressed as functions of concentration or deposition exceedences beyond a specified standard. A basic two-stage optimization model is,

$$\text{minimize} \quad c^T x + E\,[MIN\,\mathbf{dy}] \tag{35}$$

$$\text{subject to} \quad \mathbf{Ax} + \mathbf{By} = \mathbf{b} \tag{36}$$

$$\mathbf{x}, \mathbf{y} \geq \mathbf{0} \tag{37}$$

In this depiction, the first-stage costs $c^T x$ correspond to pollution control costs, where the pollutant removal levels are x; $\mathbf{Ax}$ represents pollutant concentration or deposition after emission reduction; $\mathbf{b}$ is the vector of concentration or deposition standards; y are the second-stage or penalty decision variables; $\mathbf{dy}$ are the second-stage or penalty costs; and, for the most common case of simple recourse, $\mathbf{B}$ is $[\mathbf{I}\,|\,-\mathbf{I}]$, that is, the second-stage penalties are absolute deviations between $\mathbf{Ax}$ and $\mathbf{b}$.

5. Future directions

Given the (arguable) assumption that the emissions and transport inputs to air quality management models are of sufficient quality to support decision making, the quantification of environmental loss functions appears to be the next major problem to resolve. As a case in point, consider acid rain and our current use of deposition limits (i.e., critical loads) as benchmarks of environmental quality. Moreover, recall the models that attempt to minimize some aggregate measure of critical load violation. Without environmental loss functions of some sort, how then do we evaluate, for example, two control strategies – one of which produces relatively large violations at few sensitive receptor locations; the other which produces relatively small violations at many locations? In other words, how do we best aggregate violations across space, and what do these violations mean? Models that minimize average or maximum violation certainly have utility, but one is left with the impression that we are not solving precisely the problem that needs to be addressed.

Another research direction involves the ever-present need to effectively communicate, to the decision making community, the fruits of large-scale air quality management modelling exercises. Experience has shown repeatedly that in order to be effective – to make a difference – mathematical modelling tools need to be employed interactively, with active collaboration between modeller and end-user.

Moreover, in many of these problems that involve public decision making, the end-users, i.e., the decision making community, are best positioned to know the right questions to ask.

References

Part A

Arbabi, M., J. Elzinga and C. ReVelle (1974). The oxygen sag equation: New properties and a linear equation for the critical deficit. *Water Resour. Res.* 10(5), 921.

Balinski, M.L. (1965). Integer programming: Methods, uses, computation. *Management Sci.* 12, 253.

Brill, E., J. Liebman and C. ReVelle (1976). Equity measures for exploring water quality management alternatives. *Water Resour. Res.* 12(5), 845.

Brill, E., and M. Nakamura (1978). A branch and bound method for use in planning regional wastewater treatment systems. *Water Resour. Res.* 14, 109.

Cardwell, H.E., and J.H. Ellis (1993). Stochastic dynamic programming models for water quality management. *Water Resour. Res.* 29(4), 803–813.

Converse, A.O. (1972). Optimum number and location of treatment plants. *J. Water Pollut. Control Fed.* 44(8), 1629.

Ellis, J.H. (1987). Stochastic water quality optimization using imbedded chance constraints. *Water Resour. Res.* 23(12), 2227.

Fujiwara, O., S. Gnanedran and S. Ohgahi (1986). River quality management under stochastic streamflow. *J. Environ. Engrg.* 112(2), 185.

Graves, G., G. Hatfield and A. Whinston (1972). Mathematical programming for regional water quality management. *Water Resour. Res.* 8(2), 273.

Hahn, H., P.M. Meier and H. Orth (1974). Regional wastewater management systems, in: R. Deininger (ed.), *Models for Environmental Pollution Control*, Ann Arbor Science Publishers, Ann Arbor, MI.

Jarvis, J., R. Radin, V. Unger, R. Moore and C. Schimpeler (1978). Optimal design of regional wastewater quality management systems: A fixed charge network flow model. *Oper. Res.* 26, 538.

Joeres, E., J. Dressler, C. Cho and C. Falkner (1974). Planning methodology for the design of regional wastewater treatment systems. *Water Resour. Res.* 10, 643.

Leighton, J., and C. Shoemaker (1984). An integer programming analysis of the regionalization of large wastewater treatment and collection systems. *Water Resour. Res.* 20, 671.

Liebman, J., and W. Lynn (1966). The optimal allocation of stream dissolved oxygen. *Water Resour. Res.* 2(3), 581.

Lohani, B., and N. Than (1978). Stochastic programming model for water quality management in a river. *J. Water Pollut. Control Fed.* 50, 2175.

Morris, J. (1978). On the extent to which certain fixed charge depot location problems can be solved by LP. *Oper. Res. Soc.* 29(1), 71.

Phillips, K., E. Beltrami, T. Carroll and S. Kellogg (1982). Optimization of areawide wastewater management. *J. Water Pollut. Control Fed.* 54, 87.

ReVelle, C., D. Louchs and W. Lynn (1967). A management model for water quality control, *J. Water Pollut. Control Fed.* 39(7), 1164.

ReVelle, C., D. Louchs and W. Lynn (1968). Linear programming applied to water quality management. *Water Resour. Res.* 4(1), 1.

Smith, E., and A. Morris (1969). Systems analysis for optimal water quality management. *J. Water Pollut. Control Fed.* 4(9), 1635.

Streeter, H., and C. Phelps (1925). A study of the pollution and natural purification of the Ohio River. *U.S. Public Health Bull.* 146 (February).

Thoman, R., and M. Sobel (1964). Estuarine water quality management forecasting. *J. Sanitary Engrg. Div., Amer. Soc. Civil Eng.* 90(SA5), 9

Wanielista, M., and C. Bauer (1972). Centralization of waste treatment facilities. *J. Water Pollut. Control Fed.* 44, 2229.

Whitlatch, E., and C. ReVelle (1976). Designing regionalized wastewater treatment systems. *Water Resour. Res.* 12, 581.

Zhu, Z., and C. ReVelle (1988). A siting model for regional wastewater treatment systems. *Water Resour. Res.* 24(1), 137.

Part B

Adar, Z., and J.M. Griffin (1976). Uncertainty and the Choice of Pollution Control Instruments. *J. Environ. Econ. Management* 3, 178–188.

Alam, M.K., and J.H. Seinfeld (1981). Solution of the steady state three dimensional atmospheric diffusion equation for sulfur dioxide and sulfate dispersion from point sources. *Atmos. Environ.* 15(7), 1221–1225.

Atkinson, S.E., and D.H. Lewis (1974). A cost-effectiveness analysis of alternative air quality control strategies. *J. Environ. Econ. Management* 1, 237–250.

Atkinson, S.E., and D.H. Lewis (1976). Determination and implementation of optimal air quality standards. *J. Environ. Econ. Management* 3, 363–380.

Birge, J.R. (1982). The value of the stochastic solution in stochastic linear programs with fixed recourse. *Math. Programming*, 24, pp. 314–325.

Bolin, B., and C. Persson (1975). Regional dispersion and deposition of atmospheric pollutants with particular application to sulfur pollution over Western Europe. *Tellus* 27(3), 281–310.

Charnes, A., and W.W. Cooper (1959). Chance-constrained programming. *Management Sci.* 6(1), 73–79.

Charnes, A., and W.W. Cooper (1962). Chance-constraints and normal deviates. *J. Amer. Stat. Soc.* 57(297), 134–148.

Charnes, A., and W.W. Cooper (1963). Deterministic equivalents for optimizing and satisficing under chance constraints. *Oper. Res.* 11(1), 18–39.

Cobb, S.A. (1977). Site rent, air quality, and the demand for amenities. *J. Environ. Econ. Management* 4, 214–218.

Cohon, J.L. (1978). *Multiobjective Programming and Planning*, Academic Press, New York.

Dantzig, G.B. (1955). Linear programming under uncertainty. *Management Sci.* 1(3), 197–206.

Dantzig, G.B., and A. Madansky (1961). On the solution of two-stage linear programs under uncertainty, in: *Proc. of the Fourth Berkeley Symposium on Mathematical Statistics and Probability*, Univ. of Calif. Press, Berkekey, CA, pp. 165–176.

Dolde, W., D. Epple, M. Harris, L. Lave and S. Leinhardt (1977). Dynamic aspects of air quality control costs *J. Environ. Econ. Management* 4, 313–334.

Downing, P.B., and W.D. Watson (1974). The economics of enforcing air pollution controls. *J. Environ. Econ. Management* 1, 219–236.

Eliassen, A. (1980). A review of long-range transport modelling. *J. Appl. Meteorol.* 19(3), 231–240.

Ellis, J.H. (1987). Optimization models for development of acid rain abatement strategies. *Civil Engrg. Systems* 4(2), 58–66.

Ellis, J.H. (1988a). Multiobjective mathematical programming models for acid rain control. *European J. Oper. Res.* 35(3), 365–377.

Ellis, J.H. (1988b). Acid rain control strategies: options exist despite scientific uncertainties. *Environ. Sci. Technol.* 22(11), 1248–1255.

Ellis, J.H. (1990). Integrating multiple long range transport models into optimization methodologies for acid rain policy analysis. *European J. Oper. Res.* 46(3), 313–321.

Ellis, J.H., E.A. McBean and G.J. Farquhar (1985a). Deterministic linear programming model for acid rain abatement. *J. Environ. Engrg. Div., Amer. Soc. Civil Eng.*, 111(2), 119–139.

Ellis, J.H., E.A. McBean and G.J. Farquhar (1985b). Chance-constrained, stochastic linear programming model for acid rain abatement, 1. Complete colinearity and noncolinearity. *Atmos. Environ.* 19(6), 925–937.

Ellis, J.H., E.A. McBean and G.J. Farquhar (1986). Chance-constrained, stochastic linear programming model for acid rain abatement, 2. Limited colinearity. *Atmos. Environ.* 20(3), 501–511.

Fay, J.A., and J.J. Rosenzweig (1980). An analytical diffusion model for long distance transport of air pollutants. *Atmos. Environ.* 14(3), 355–365.

Ferguson, A.R., and G.B. Dantzig (1956). The allocation of aircraft to routes – An example of linear programming under uncertain demand. *Management Sci.*, 3(1), 45–73.

Fishelson, G. (1976). Emission control policies under uncertainty. *J. Environ. Econ. Management* 3, 189–197.

Fortin, M., and E.A. McBean (1983). A Management Model for Acid Rain Abatement, *Atmos. Environ.* 17(11), 2331–2336.

Fronza, G., and P. Melli (1984). Assignment of emission abatement levels by stochastic programming. *Atmos. Environ.* 17(10), 2025–2029.

Fuessle, R.W., E.D. Brill and J.C. Liebman (1987). Air quality planning: a general chance-constraint model. *J. Environ. Engrg., ASCE* 113(1), 106–123.

Gillani, N.V. (1978). Project MISTT: Mesoscale plume modelling of the dispersion, transformation and ground removal of SO_2. *Atm. Environ.* 12(1/3), 569–588.

Gipson, G.L., W. Freas and E.L. Meyer (1975). Evaluation of techniques for obtaining least-cost regional strategies for control of SO_2 and suspended particulates. *Environ. Sci. Technol.* 9, 354–359.

Guldman, J.M. (1986). Interactions between weather stochasticity and the locations of pollution sources and receptors in air quality planning: A chance-constrained approach. *Geogr. Anal.* 18(3), 198–214.

Guldman, J.M. (1988). Chance-constrained dynamic model of air quality management. *J. Environ. Engrg., ASCE* 114(5), 1116–1135.

Guldmann, J.-M., and D. Shefer (1980). *Industrial Location and Air Quality Control.*, Wiley and Sons, New York.

Haimes, Y.Y., W.S. Nainis and S. Goldstone (1977). Cost- sharing approach for air quality control implementation. *J. Environ. Econ. Management* 4, 219–238.

Hamlen, W.A. (1978). The optimality and feasibility of uniform air pollution controls. *J. Environ. Econ. Management* 5, 301–312.

Harrison, D., and D.L. Rubinfeld (1978). The distribution of benefits from improvements in urban air quality. *J. Environ. Econ. Management* 5, 313–332.

Hidy, G.M. (1984). Source–receptor relationships for acid deposition: Pure and simple? *J. Air Pollut. Control Assoc.* 34, 518–531.

Hidy, G.M. et al. (1978). Spatial and temporal distributions of airborne sulfates in parts of the United States. *Atmos. Environ.* 12(1/3), 735–752.

Hordijk, L. (1986). Towards a targeted emission reduction in Europe. *Atmos. Environ.* 20(10), 2053–2058.

ISDME (1987). *International Sulfur Deposition Model Evaluation*, Rep. EPA-600/3-87-008, USEPA, Washington, DC.

Johnson, W.B. (1983). Interregional exchanges of air pollution: Model types and applications. *J. Air Pollut. Control Assoc.* 33, 563–574.

Johnson, W.B. et al. (1978). Long- term regional patterns and transformation exchanges of airborne sulfur pollution in Europe. *Atmos. Environ.* 12(1/3), 511–527.

Kohn, R.E. (1971). Application of linear programming to a controversy on air pollution control. *Management Sci.*, 17(10), B609-B621.

Kohn, R.E. (1972). Labor displacement and air pollution control. *Oper. Res.* 21(5), 1063–1070.

Kohn, R.E. (1978). *A Linear Programming Model for Air Pollution Control*, MIT Press, Cambridge, MA.

Likens, G.E., R.F. Wright, J.N. Galloway and T.J. Bulter (1979). Acid rain. *Sci. Amer.* 241, 43–51.

Loehman, E.T., et al. (1979). Distributional analysis of regional benefits and costs of air quality control. *J. Environ. Econ. Management* 6, 222–243.

Marin, A. (1978). The choice of efficient pollution policies: Technology and economics in the control of sulphur dioxide. *J. Environ. Econ. Management* 5, 44–62.

Mathur, V.K. (1976). Spatial economic theory of pollution control. *J. Environ. Econ. Management* 3, 16–28.

Morrison, M.B., and E.S. Rubin (1985). A linear programming model for acid rain policy analysis. *J. Air Pollut. Control Assoc.* 35(11), 1137–1148.

NAPAP (1989), *Models Planned for Use in the NAPAP Integrated Assessment*, National Acid Precipitation Assessment Program, Washington, DC.

NAPAP (1991). *Acidic Deposition: State of Science and Technology*, National Acid Precipitation Assessment Program, Washington, DC.

Pack, D.H. et al. (1978). Meteorology of long-range transport. *Atmos. Environ.*, 12(1/3), 425–444.

Parvin, M., and G.W. Grammars (1976). Optimization models for environmental pollution control: A synthesis. *J. Environ. Econ. Management* 3, 113–128.

Rodhe, H. (1974). Some aspects of the use of air trajectories for the computation of large scale dispersion and fallout patterns, in: *Advances of Geophysics*, 18B.

Schweizer, P.F. (1974). Determining optimal fuel mix for environmental dispatch. *IEEE Trans. Automat. Control* October, pp. 534–537.

Seinfeld, J.H., and C.P. Kyan (1971). Determination of optimal air pollution control strategies. *Socio-Econ. Planning Sci.* 5, 173–190.

Shaw, R.W. (1986). A proposed strategy for reducing sulphate deposition in North America, II. Methodology for minimizing costs. *Atmos. Environ.* 20(1), 201–206.

Streets, D.G., D.A. Hanson and L.D. Carter (1984). Targeted strategies for control of acidic deposition. *J. Air Pollut. Control Assoc.* 34(12), 1187–1197.

Streets, D.G., B.M. Lesht, J.D. Shannon and T.D. Veselka (1985). Climatological variability. *Environ. Sci. Technol.* 19, 887–893.

Teller, A. (1968). The use of linear programming to estimate the cost of some alternative air pollution abatement policies, in: *Proc., IBM Scientific Computing Symposium on Water and Air Resource Management*, pp. 345–353.

Trijonis, J.C. (1974). Economic air pollution control model for Los Angeles County in 1975. *Environ. Sci. Technol.* 8(9), 811–826.

Turner, D.B. (1964). A diffusion model for an urban area. *J. Appl. Meteorol.* 3, 83–91.

United States–Canada Memorandum of Intent (1982). *Memorandum of Intent on Transboundary Air Pollution, Atmospheric Sciences and Analysis*, Work Group 2, November, 1982.

United States Congress (1990). *Public Law 101-549: The 1990 Clean Air Act Amendments.*

Van Egmond, N.D. et al. (1978). Quantitative evolution of mesoscale air pollution transport. *Atmos. Environ.* 12(12), 2279–2287.

Viscusi, W.K., and R. Zeckhauser (1976). Environmental policy choice under uncertainty. *J. Environ. Econ. Management* 3, 97–112.

Walkup, D.W., and R.J.-B. Wets (1967). Stochastic programs with recourse. *SIAM J. Appl. Math.* 15(5), 1299–1314.

Wets, R.J.-B. (1974). Stochastic programs with fixed recourse: The equivalent deterministic problem. *SIAM Rev.* 16(3), 309–339.

Wets, R. (1983). Stochastic programming: Solution techniques and approximation schemes, in: A. Bachem, M. Grotschel and B. Korte (eds.), *Mathematical Programming: The State of the Art*, Springer- Verlag, New York, pp. 566–603.

Yohe, G.W. (1976). Substitution and the control of pollution – A comparison of effluent charges and quantity standards under uncertainty. *J. Environ. Econ. Management* 3, 312–324.

Young, J.W.S., and R.W. Shaw (1986). A proposed strategy for reducing sulphate deposition in North America, I. Methodology for minimizing sulphur removal. *Atmos. Environ.*, 20(1), 189–199.

S.M. Pollock et al., Eds., *Handbooks in OR & MS, Vol. 6*

Chapter 11

Siting of Hazardous Facilities

Paul R. Kleindorfer and Howard C. Kunreuther

Center for Risk Management and Decision Processes, The Wharton School, University of Pennsylvania, Philadelphia, PA 19104, U.S.A.

While OR methodologies ranging from risk assessment to decision analysis have helped to improve our understanding of the siting process, finding homes for hazardous facilities has remained a controversial area of public policy analysis. This chapter first describes the features of the siting problem which have made it difficult to find a home for noxious facilities and then proposes a set of guidelines for improving the process. In our view methodologies which are designed to improve siting outcomes must be coordinated carefully with a broader process view of siting. The remainder of the chapter summarizes recent research on the nature of the hazardous facility siting problem and related transportation problems with a focus on route-mode selection issues, facility location models and decision analysis for choosing between predetermined sites. This chapter concludes by raising open questions for future research.

1. Introduction

Rachel Carson's book *Silent Spring* [1962] first made the general public aware of environmental hazards by depicting the sudden and eerie disappearance of living creatures on earth as a result of toxic chemicals which poisoned the air, water, and soil. People's fears have been further honed by heavily publicized 'catastrophes' with the dumping of carcinogens at Love Canal and Times Beach, the nuclear power plant accidents at Three Mile Island and Chernobyl, and the chemical disasters at Seveso, Italy and Bhopal, India.[1]

This new climate of concern has consistently attached itself to waste-disposal facilities. Indeed, because of intense public opposition, it has become exceedingly difficult for government agencies and private developers to site landfills, incinerators, repositories, and other facilities that dispose of solid, hazardous or radioactive waste. For example, 28 of the 34 solid waste incinerators proposed for

---

[1] See Kleindorfer & Kunreuther [1987] for a review of these catastrophes and the public policy debate to which they gave rise.

California were either canceled or postponed in the late 1980s. Likewise, although the Environmental Protection Agency (EPA) has estimated that between 50 and 125 new sites would be needed for storing hazardous waste, no facilities were sited by 1986 and very few since then [Whitehead, 1991]. This inability to find successful sites for new waste facilities is part of a larger trend that extends to many other facilities that benefit society as a whole, but have undesirable impacts on the local community (e.g., AIDS treatment centers, halfway houses for parolees, and recycling plants to name a few). [Lake, 1987].

This chapter addresses these issues from two perspectives: descriptive and prescriptive. The next section provides an overview of characteristics of the siting process and describes examples of recent problems in finding acceptable locations for nuclear power plants, hazardous, and radioactive waste disposal facilities. We argue that, to be effective, OR methodologies which are designed to improve siting outcomes must be coordinated carefully with a broader process view of siting. By focusing on both process and outcome considerations a set of prescriptive guidelines for siting are presented in Section 3.

The remainder of the paper reviews the operations research methodologies for improving the siting process. Section 4 provides a formal statement of the siting problem. Section 5 reviews OR approaches for analyzing hazardous materials transportation problems. Sections 6 and 7 summarize the relevant OR literature on location theory and decision analysis as it relates to the siting of hazardous facilities. The chapter concludes by discussing several open questions and areas for future research.

2. Descriptive characteristics of hazardous facility siting

Hazardous facility siting involves a number of competing, interacting features. This section describes these features and illustrates them by examples as a prelude to our discussion of operations research methodologies for improving the siting process.

2.1. The problem: global benefits and local costs

Consider the siting problem for waste disposal. Society faces a dilemma in finding homes for different types of trash and waste. On the one hand, people demand the goods and services whose production yields waste as by-products. There appears to be widespread agreement by the public on the need for properly designed and managed disposal facilities, since, in the aggregate, their presence would yield benefits in excess of their risks and costs. On the other hand, opposition is vehement when mention is made of locating a trash disposal or hazardous waste facility at a specific site (i.e., in someone's backyard). A 1980 national opinion poll found that over 95% of respondents would actively protest against siting a hazardous materials facility near their home [U.S. Council on Environmental Quality, 1980]. Today we expect that opposition to be the same or even greater. This is a typical feature of hazardous facility siting: societal benefits from such facilities may be large, but the risks and costs to a host community are also perceived to be large.

2.2. Relevant interested parties

In any siting controversy there are a set of interested parties, each of whom has their own values and goals. There are those groups who would like to see the facility built because it yields sufficient benefits to them; others are likely to have serious concerns about the facility.

Some of the interested parties may feel the same way about the facility but for different reasons. For example, an environmental group may oppose the construction of a high-level nuclear waste repository primarily because they would like to end the use of nuclear power and recognize that this will happen if there is no place to store the waste. Citizens groups may oppose the facility due to strong fears of an accident either to themselves or future generations.

When one lines up all the different interested parties on a particular siting question there is likely to be considerable conflict on whether the facility is needed and, if so, where it should be placed. The fact that different groups may have the same attitude toward a proposed facility but for very different reasons suggests that it is important to understand the nature of the controversy before making policy recommendations. A closer look at the stakeholders who are involved in a given siting situation provides strong insights into why such controversies are likely to exist.

2.2.1. Applicant

The initiator of the siting effort is the applicant – the firm, agency, or other organization that is interested in seeing that a certain type of facility is built (or more generally, that a specific problem is solved). In siting problems related to solid or hazardous waste, the applicant is typically either a private corporation or the state.

For private firms to enter into the siting fray, they must first perceive that their economic benefits from the proposed facility (e.g., a new landfill for municipal waste or a hazardous waste incinerator) will be greater than the construction costs and operating expenses associated with the facility, as well as the transaction costs associated with convincing the community and regulatory agencies to grant a permit.

Governmental agencies have also been applicants, frequently out of necessity. For example, states bear ultimate responsibility for finding a means of disposal of low-level radioactive waste. Similarly for high-level radioactive waste, national legislation has established responsibility for oversight and siting of a repository with several federal agencies. The federal government assumed this role as a result of (a) the accumulation of high-level nuclear waste at its own weapons installations, and (b) legislation that explicitly transferred responsibility for civilian waste from the generators (i.e., public utilities) onto itself. Direct responsibility for the management of high-level nuclear waste has been assigned to the Department of Energy (DOE). DOE in turn has been active in evaluating sites such as the Yucca Mountain Nevada site for a geologic repository. We discuss this case in more detail below.

Whether the applicant is from the private or the public sector, there will be certain common concerns. The first concern, obviously, is to find some site where it is possible to build the facility. If the applicant is a private firm, this objective is accompanied by the need to find a site where the facility can be run in a cost-effective manner. All applicants must show some concern with protecting the public's health and safety, although this responsibility is generally made more explicit when the applicant is a government agency.

2.2.2. Affected constituency

This term refers to the individuals, groups and agencies directly impacted by the proposed facility. These residents and their political representatives often have a strong say over whether a facility can be built at the proposed site. Solid waste problems normally involve municipalities which must find a community willing to take their trash. At the other extreme is the high-level nuclear waste (HLNW) repository problem where the federal government must find a site where it is legally and politically able to license and construct the facility.

2.2.3. Public interest groups

In recent years, citizens groups and environmental groups have become increasingly active in siting debates. These organizations generally represent the interests and preferences of certain sectors of the public. For example, the Sierra Club and Natural Resources Defense Council are concerned with the short- and long-term effects that a proposed waste disposal facility will have on the environment. Local citizens groups are normally concerned with the health and safety of the local residents as well as with the impact that the facility will have on property values.

2.2.4. Regulatory bodies

Government agencies normally have well specified formal responsibilities in the siting process. Their roles are defined by legislation, the nature of the facility, and the type of applicant who plans to develop the facility. One of the key areas of interest in current siting debates is how the general public perceives these governmental bodies. For example, what values and goals do Nevadans assign to the Department of Energy in its attempt to study Yucca Mountain as a site for the HLNW repository?

2.3. Disagreements about facts and values

Different stakeholders may disagree about the merits of a proposed facility for a number of reasons. The most obvious cause of disagreement stems from differences in vested interests. For example, residents of an area in the proximity of an incinerator or landfill may be concerned with the impact on future property values should they wish to sell their property. The business community may be concerned with the potential negative impact that a waste repository may have on tourism or convention activity, but neither the regulatory agency nor the applicant may have this as a primary consideration. The regulatory agency is concerned primarily with ensuring that the applicable laws and regulations are likely to be satisfied, while the developer hopes to run a cost-effective operation that meets the letter of the law.

Even when stakeholders are talking about the same impact, they may disagree on their estimate of what it will be. Disagreement is especially common with facilities that handle hazardous or radioactive material. Part of this disagreement results from complexities in the causal chain of events. Kasperson, Renn, Slovic, Brown, Emel, Gobel, Kasperson & Ratick [1988] have pointed out that the consequences of risk events go far beyond direct harms to include many of the indirect impacts such as loss of confidence in institutions and the perceived fairness of the risk management process. They point to the accident at Three Mile Island which did not kill any individual but wrought enormous social consequences in the form of stricter regulations, greater opposition to nuclear power and an increased concern with other complex technologies such as chemical plants and genetic engineering. This potential social amplification of risk needs to be taken into account when designing the decision process and strategies for siting and managing new facilities.

Because of the wide range of potential impacts that might be considered, as well as the extensive uncertainty involved in predicting any specific impact, the evidence gathering process tends to be decentralized and conflictual. Each stakeholder group collects data on the facility in order to defend its position, satisfy its objectives and meet its responsibilities. To a large extent these data pertain to the issue of risk (either to health or the environment), although the different groups may vary significantly with respect to the nature of information they collect. At the most elementary level, different definitions of risk may be utilized. For example, one group may define risk in terms of the consequences of the worst-case scenario, while another stakeholder may disregard any possible event where the probability of its occurrence falls below a specific threshold.

Even if risk is defined in the same way by all the stakeholders, there are likely to be significant discrepancies in estimates. For new technologies there are limited statistical data on how well the facility is likely to perform in practice. In the case of the proposed HLNW repository, one has to rely entirely on theoretical or prototype analyses since there is no historical record to consult. Scientists may disagree on the assumptions on which their analysis is based, and thus come up with very different estimates of probabilities and consequences.

In many siting controversies, there arise issues where the available data are insufficient to determine whether a certain scientific statement is true or false. In fact, as many philosophers have argued, it is only possible to prove that a scientific statement may be false, *not* that it is correct. In the case of low probability events, there is inherently insufficient information to prove that a given risk estimate is incorrect due to the limited data on accidents. For this reason Weinberg [1972] proposed the term 'transcientific' to describe these risks. In other words, there is no practical basis for estimating the statistical chances and consequences of the occurrence of certain types of accidents. For such risks, risk assessment is an art rather than a science.

As a result of this indeterminacy, each stakeholder is likely to be able to find some expert to defend a particular point of view. It is often difficult to dispute or confirm this position with solid scientific evidence. For example, a private contractor or government agency anxious to site a waste facility will be able to identify scientific experts who claim the facility poses little risk to health and safety. Citizen groups can find other experts who paint a very different picture, claiming that the facility poses great hazards. To date, there have been no forums or science courts for examining the reasons for these differences but even if such institutions were established, there may be legitimate differences that are not reconcilable based on existing data.[2]

Even if there were general agreement on the size of the facility's risk (or other factual issues), the different interested parties are likely to disagree on values. This point has been clearly brought home by Von Winterfeldt & Edwards [1984] in a study of technological conflicts and disputes about risky technologies. By studying 162 different cases they developed a taxonomy for classifying different disputes based on conflicts over facts and values. They point out that in the case of siting new facilities, some disputes will arise over facts (as indicated above), but the debate between relevant stakeholders will revolve primarily around value and moral issues on which legitimate differences exist. For example, questions arise as to whether society should develop technologies that we cannot fully control and whether we should expose future generations to potential long-term risks which are not fully understood. These issues turn out to be of great concern to the public and affected constituencies when judging the attractiveness of a HLNW repository for long-term storage, but typically have *not* been considered as critical issues by the applicant.

Disagreements over both facts and values are more likely to occur in siting cases where the applicant has failed to cultivate the *trust* of the affected constituency. Firms and government agencies that have poor track records managing existing facilities, or that put forth a demeanor of arrogance or secretiveness in their dealings with the public, have an extremely difficult time gaining the confidence of local residents. In these cases, the motives, the data, and the conclusions of the applicant are likely to be met with a special breed of skepticism. This has in fact been the nature of the relationship between the Department of Energy and the states that have been identified as having potential HLNW repository sites, particularly Nevada [see Kunreuther, Easterling, Desvousges & Slovic, 1990; Slovic, Layman and Flynn, 1991].

---

[2] See Kunreuther & Linnerooth [1982] for a detailed case study of the siting of a liquified natural gas terminal showing the wide variety of risk assessments utilized by different stakeholder groups in the siting process.

2.4. Institutional arrangements

Understanding a siting case also requires an appreciation of the institutional arrangements. It is important to identify which parties have an interest in seeing that a facility is built, which parties have regulatory or statutory authority over the siting decision, and the overlap between these two sets. An especially key factor concerns the degree of control that the local 'community' can exert over the siting decision; in some cases, the decision must be approved by the town council or the zoning commission, while in other cases, the state preempts local authority.

It is interesting to compare the siting of a high-level radioactive waste facility to the low-level radioactive waste siting challenges in terms of the institutional arrangements facing individual states. In the high-level case, each state is represented in the forum that dictates siting policy (i.e., U.S. Congress), but the ultimate decision making authority rests at the federal level. Candidate states are assigned some special authority (e.g., oversight), but in general, they are subject to the discretion of a higher-order applicant. In contrast, for the low-level radioactive waste case, each state has the responsibility to find a suitable means of disposal. Hence, the state is the applicant.

2.5. Siting processes

The decision-making process associated with any particular siting problem depends to a large extent on the nature of the institutional arrangements between the different stakeholders. Legislation, regulation and cultural considerations all play a role in determining what type of process is likely to be put in place. Three illustrative approaches are described below.

2.5.1. Decide Announce Defend (DAD) approach

The traditional approach to siting, at least up until 1980, was the DAD approach. It is normally characterized by three sequential stages. In Stage 1 the applicant, normally the developer or contractor, makes a series of technological choices based on engineering analyses regarding the need for a facility, the type of facility to build, and where to locate it. These decisions are not discussed with the other concerned stakeholders, such as the local government or residents living near the proposed facility. In Stage 2, the developer publicly announces the proposed technological and siting package. Then in Stage 3 the developer defends his position amidst much conflict and opposition [O'Hare, Bacow & Sanderson, 1983].

This process has not worked in practice because it alienates many of the stakeholder groups, including those who have veto power over the siting decision. It also fosters an adversarial relationship between the developer and the local community. In effect, a DAD proposal constitutes a challenge for the affected groups to find fault with the proposal. O'Hare, Bacow & Sanderson [1983] provide several case studies illustrating the failure of the DAD procedure in practice.

2.5.2. Legislated siting processes

Due to the failure of the DAD process, there have been developments at both the state, regional, and federal levels to specify the siting process within legislation. These legislated processes generally call for formal negotiations between the various parties with a direct interest in a proposed facility.

For example, the Massachusetts Hazardous Waste Siting Act of 1980 is a state-initiated effort designed to stimulate negotiation between a developer and a host community. Several communities in Massachusetts have expressed an interest in hosting a waste disposal facility, but no siting agreements have been reached to date. In each case where it appeared that a facility might be sited, groups have raised the claim that the facility would pose an undue economic or psychological burden on local residents, and hence pose a *special risk*. In these situations, the Massachusetts legislation enables the community to exclude these waste facilities.

Legislated siting procedures have also been worked out at the regional level. The Low Level Radioactive Waste (LLRW) Policy Act of 1980 required that each state take responsibility for the LLRW generated within its borders, but also recommended that groups of states form compacts to deal with their disposal problems more efficiently. As of mid 1991, regional compacts have been formed for Appalachian, Central Interstate, Central Midwest, Midwest, Northwest, Rocky Mountain, Southeast, and Southwestern regions.

Those states that are selected to host a repository (or who elect to go on their own) must then find a suitable site for the facility. In many cases, the procedure for selecting this site is also specified through legislation. However, this does not necessarily guarantee that the procedure will play out according to plan.

In the high-level nuclear waste case, a legislated siting strategy was invoked at the federal level. In formulating the Nuclear Waste Policy Act of 1982, Congress recognized the need to find a site that would be both technically and politically acceptable. Thus, an intricate (and some might add fragile) arrangement which acknowledged the concerns of different stakeholders was negotiated. Under the act, strict safety standards would be employed, all potential sites would be considered, the site selection procedure would be systematic and fair, regional equity would be sought, and candidate states would have some degree of control over the decision making process. However, as discussed in Kunreuther, Easterling, Desvousges & Slovic [1990], many of the agreed upon provisions have unravelled in practice due to the problems noted above of value conflicts, scientific uncertainties, and related public perceptions of the risks of radioactive waste.

2.5.3. Voluntary siting agreements

The legislated process requires the host community to prove that the facility should not be built as proposed. Under voluntary siting, the objective is to construct a facility proposal that appears attractive enough to cause communities to consider becoming a partner in the effort to site it.

Communities will not even consider entering into a voluntary siting process unless they are assured that the facility will operate safely. Second, the need for the proposed facility must be widely recognized by demonstrating that the current or future costs associated with the status quo are unacceptable. Third, the applicant must construct a package of benefits that makes potential host communities feel that they are better off with the facility than without it.

Ideally, the potential benefits will be attractive enough that several communities will each make offers for the facility. The resultant competition is beneficial both in terms of economic efficiency and in generating a balanced debate regarding the actual risks and impacts associated with the facility. The ultimate goal of the voluntary siting process is to change the commonly observed NIMBY (Not In My Backyard) response to YIMBY (Yes in My Backyard).

2.6. Process and outcome considerations

The concepts of procedural and substantive rationality developed by Simon [1978] for structuring choice under uncertainty are useful for formulating prescriptive guidelines for siting a noxious facility. *Procedural rationality* refers to the decision processes utilized by the different interested parties concerned with a particular problem given inherent human limitations in collecting and processing information. *Substantive rationality* refers to the way an outcome(s) is chosen from a set of alternatives. It focuses on the types of benefit–cost criteria that are utilized and how specific policy tools can facilitate the final outcome.

A large literature has emerged that recognizes the importance of both these types of rationality in formulating siting strategies. The importance of process considerations has been emphasized by a number of social scientists given the failure of the traditional Decide Announce Defend (DAD) approach to siting which was common through the 1970s [Kunreuther & Linnerooth, 1982; Morell & Magorian, 1982; O'Hare, Bacow & Sanderson, 1983; Portney, 1991; Susskind & Cruikshank, 1987]. This research points out that the DAD process has not worked in practice because it alienates many of the interested parties, including those who have veto power over the siting decision. There is general agreement across all these studies that one needs to involve the interested parties in siting discussions even if this requires more time and effort than the DAD approach.

Outcome-based approaches to siting have also been developed which involve the use of multi-attribute utility models to choose between alternative sites [Keeney, 1980] and examine how compensation can play a role in encouraging communities or regions to accept a facility [Kunreuther, Easterling, Desvousges & Slovic, 1987; O'Hare, Bacow & Sanderson, 1983]. Today compensation or benefit-sharing is considered a legitimate policy tool for siting facilities. There is general agreement, however, that it should only be introduced as a part of the process after the affected public is convinced that appropriate mitigation and control measures will be in place so that the risk associated with the facility is considered to be acceptable [Carnes, Copenhaver, Sorensen, Soderstrom, Reed, Bjornstad & Peelle, 1983; Peelle, 1987; Gregory, Kunreuther, Easterling & Richards, 1991].

3. Improving the siting process

The siting process involves global benefits and local costs and, typically, considerable uncertainties. Potential host communities for hazardous facilities have therefore been very reluctant to site such facilities unless they expect to share in the benefits (e.g., through employment or tax relief), and only if they feel a sense of trust toward the applicant and developer and a sense that the siting process is equitable.

Given the relatively few hazardous facilities that have been sited in recent years there is a need to improve the process. The proposed procedure recognizes the importance of process and outcome considerations and is an outgrowth of a National Workshop on Facility Siting that brought practitioners and siting experts together to address the facility siting dilemma. The Facility Siting Credo was the principal product developed from this workshop. Some of the key steps for developing a workable siting process are summarized below.[3]

3.1. Step 1: Get agreement that the status quo is unacceptable

Unless the key stakeholders are convinced that maintaining the current situation is worse on key dimensions (e.g., cost, risk) than one of the other options it is highly unlikely that a new site will be chosen. By developing a set of objectives and performance measures one can examine the status quo in relation to the proposed alternatives.

One of the principal ways that the status quo will be shown to be unacceptable is if there is legislation passed requiring new facilities by prespecified dates. As pointed out in the introduction legislated siting procedures such as the Low Level Radioactive Waste Policy Act of 1980 have forced states to either find a site for their own waste or form a compact with other states.

3.2. Step 2: Guarantee stringent safety standards

No community should be asked or will want to trade off health or safety for economic benefits. All potentially hazardous facilities must be required to meet all legally established health and safety standards. The host site will want to have data assuring them that the organizations responsible for satisfying the safety standards of the facility have a proven track record. Candidates for a facility should also have an opportunity to specify any additional health, safety, and environmental standards that could be met through mitigation, such as changes in facility design, substitute technologies, operational modifications, and training of operators.

Swallow, Opaluch & Weaver [1992] suggest a procedure for screening all sites for technical suitability that meet a set of constraints associated with health, safety and environmental effects. For example, landfill sites must satisfy hydrologic and geologic constraints so that it is highly unlikely that pollutants will migrate off-site.

---

[3] For more details on the nature of the Facility Siting Credo and an empirical test of its principles see Kunreuther, Fitzgerald & Aarts [1993].

Gregory, Kunreuther, Easterling & Richards [1991] stress the importance of mitigation as a way of ensuring the public that a facility will be safe in the future. The public demands that the best available technology be utilized if there are health and environmental risks associated with the facility. U.S. Ecology learned this lesson with respect to a low-level radioactive waste facility, deciding to forego the extra protection offered by a double-walled barrier. The public, who had generally supported the facility, reacted very negatively to this decision.

Monitoring and control procedures are the key to minimizing risks, maintaining standards and reducing fears of the public regarding the operation of the facility. A written agreement should stipulate conditions for a facility's operation and the type of monitoring procedures that will be followed. For example, maximum thresholds for the facility (e.g., amount of waste, number of admittants) should be established.

Plans and restrictions for the use of the facility should be specified (e.g., restrict who is eligible to ship waste to a facility) and the community should be provided with the right to shut down the facility if certain conditions and standards are not met.

3.3. Step 3: Make the host community better off

A package of benefits should be put together by the applicant so that the proposed host community feels that it is better off with the facility than without it. There should be a way of 'taxing' the gainers from the facility to obtain these funds for reimbursing the potential losers.

A negotiated schedule of contingent compensation payments for any harmful effects should be described in a written siting agreement. Property value guarantees, as well as assessment of future liability to the relevant party (e.g., developer, waste disposers, government) in case of an accident need to be explicitly stated.

Specific property value guarantees need to be established so that residents who sell their homes can obtain a fair price. An illustrative example of this type of arrangement is the program established by Champion International Corp. when it established a landfill in an agricultural area 25 miles north of Cincinnati. Property owners received two appraisals of their property prior to the landfill being sited and used the sale prices of property in other parts of the county to determine any changes in value. If a sale price falls short of the latest countywide value figure, Champion makes up the difference [Ewing, 1990].

An explicit agreement needs to be specified in writing at the time the facility is sited as to who is responsible for the recovery costs following an accident. The nature of the liability payments from any environmental pollution should also be clearly delineated.

3.4. Step 4: Seek acceptable sites through a volunteer process

Avoid naming a 'technically best' site since siting criteria are subjective enough that it is impossible to rank sites with such precision. Look for volunteer sites that would meet minimal technical criteria.

Encourage communities, regions, or states to volunteer sites indicating that this is not an irreversible commitment and that there are potential benefits packages (e.g., new revenues, employment, tax reductions) that come with the facility.

By undertaking preliminary risk assessments one can determine whether the proposed location is feasible for a particular facility. These costs should be borne by the developer or relevant federal agency.

Start-up funds should be provided for potential host communities or states to evaluate their own needs in relation to the siting option. The public should be encouraged to participate in the process to determine the concerns of different groups and whether they can be addressed.

A voluntary approach has been developed in Canada [Rabe, 1991; Zeiss, 1991] and is now being applied in the United States [Rennick & Greyell, 1990; Ruckelshaus, 1989]. Under this siting approach, the developer does not unilaterally select a site, but rather invites all communities with technically suitable sites to enter into negotiations. The developer and community representatives together construct a mutually acceptable facility proposal (which includes benefits).

The key feature is that discretion over the siting decision rests with the communities rather than the developer. The facility will not be sited within a community that has qualms, because only volunteer communities are considered. The emphasis on community control is maintained throughout the entire siting process; a community that initially expresses interest is free to withdraw at any point along the way.

In addition, the strategy strives for a cooperative arrangement in which communities are asked to become partners in the development of the facility. The terms of the partnership are negotiated between community representatives and the developer. These terms may include such factors as the design and operation of the facility and the amount of revenue.

3.5. Step 5: Consider a competitive siting process

Assuming that multiple technically acceptable volunteer sites are found, facility sponsors should consider a competitive process of site selection. Potential host communities should have a chance to propose compensation or incentive packages for later consideration. The final choice of a facility will be a complicated one based on technical criteria, the nature of the benefits package and a comparison of costs and risks across sites. The advantage of having more than one site compete for the facility is that a particular region does *not* feel that it is singled out to house a facility that no one else wants.

If there is more than one site in contention then there are several different procedures that might be followed in choosing a final site. One could institute a lottery between the sites in contention and agree to pay the 'winner' a prespecified sum S. After the 'winner' is announced any of the other sites have the option of bidding for the site by offering a lower amount than S. This bidding could take the form of a sealed bid auction with each candidate specifying the minimum amount they would require to take the facility [Kunreuther & Portney, 1991]. It could also take the form of an open bidding system with the monetary offer continuing to drop until only one site remained. Alternatively, one could begin the bidding process with a low amount and raise it until one community agreed to host the facility. This reverse Dutch auction process has been proposed by Inhaber [1990].

An alternative procedure would be to ask each site to specify the benefits package it would require and then let the developer or government agency decide which location should be declared the 'winner'. The criteria for determining the host site would be based not only on the amount of compensation required but also risk, costs, and other economic factors.

These approaches are designed to encourage regions to think positively about the possibility of hosting a facility. In fact, by giving them an opportunity to specify a benefits package each candidate may think about how much they would *lose* if they were not chosen to host the facility – a strange reversal of the normal NIMBY reaction.

4. Operations research and hazardous facility siting

The methodologies on siting developed in the operations research literature are designed to find an optimal outcome (e.g., a site, set of transportation routes) based on a well-specified objective function and a set of constraints. The next four sections review some of these formal approaches and provide a general guide to the literature on the topic. A more comprehensive bibliography on any of these topics can be found in the papers referenced in this review. Our purpose in this paper is to summarize the principal questions addressed in the OR literature and specify the models utilized to answer them.

After providing a general statement of the siting problem below, we review the literature on transportation of hazardous materials (Section 5) and extensions of traditional facility location models to hazardous facilities (Section 6). In Section 7 we first explore decision analytic approaches to the evaluation of alternative sites and then illustrate the importance of process issues in determining an acceptable outcome. The challenges in finding a site for the first high-level nuclear waste repository in the United States offers a concrete example of the need to address procedural as well as substantive rationality questions when addressing the facility siting question.

It is useful to begin with a general statement of the siting problem. Let X be the set of feasible siting options, where each $x \in X$ represents a specific set of site locations, facility types at each location, technologies used, transportation routes used, and any other characteristics important to the costs and benefits of operations or to the perceived risks of the facilities to be sited. In the simplest problem of locating a single facility of specific size and technology within a region, X could just represent the coordinates of feasible locations for the facility.

Let the relevant stakeholders in the facility siting problem be denoted by Θ, where the typical $\theta \in \Theta$ might be a household generating waste or a household in the host community near x.

Let Y be the set of risk reduction and mitigation measures, where each $y \in Y$ represents a vector of individual and collective actions which might reduce the probability of an accident or mitigate the consequences of accidents if they occur. Such actions would include special safety equipment, monitoring and control procedures, insurance, investments in emergency response capability and so forth.

Let Z be a set of states of the world, with some distribution function $F(z)$ describing their relative likelihood of occurrence. For the moment, we will assume that all stakeholders agree on a common-knowledge distribution function $F(z)$.

To make matters transparent, we assume that risk preferences of stakeholders are representable by a utility function of the quasi-linear form

$$U(x, y, z, M; \theta) = V(x, y, z; \theta) + M, \tag{1}$$

where $V(x, y, z; \theta)$ is stakeholder θ's willingness-to-pay (which may be negative) for facility option x, when risk mitigation measures y are undertaken and state z occurs, and where M represents 'money' available to spend on other goods; M may incorporate compensation payments to stakeholder θ to assure that θ remains at or above some status quo utility level. We have assumed for simplicity here that income or wealth is separable in each stakeholder's preference function. Given this quasi-linear form of preferences, $V(x, y, z; \theta)$ is referred to as willingness-to-pay, since (from (1)) stakeholder θ would be indifferent between the option (x, y, z) and the compensation payment $M = V(x, y, z; \theta)$. In this sense, stakeholder θ should be willing to pay exactly $V(x, y, z; \theta)$ for (x, y, z). If this payment must be made before the state of the world z is known, then under the expected utility axioms, e.g., of Savage, stakeholder θ should be willing to pay exactly $E_z[V(x, y, z; \theta)]$ for the option (x, y). If $E_z[V(x, y, z; \theta)]$ is negative, then we interpret $-E_z[V(x, y, z; \theta)]$ as the necessary compensation to stakeholder θ to make θ just indifferent between implementing (x, y) and not doing so. Thus, if the expected value $E_z[V(x, y, z; \theta)]$ is negative, then stakeholder θ is 'inconvenienced' by the siting option (x, y), and some compensation might be required (i.e., M would have to be increased by a transfer payment to stakeholder θ) in order to make up for this inconvenience.

Denote by $C(x, y, z)$ the total out-of-pocket cost associated with option x, when y is chosen, and z occurs. C would include the costs of the facility, additional transportation infrastructure, risk mitigation measures and so forth. C would also include the costs of accidents in some states of the world z.

The siting problem which we consider is to determine the option (x, y) which maximizes total expected social benefits, i.e.:

$$\underset{x \in X, y \in Y}{\text{maximize}} \quad E_z \left\{ \sum_{\theta \in \Theta} V(x, y, z; \theta) - C(x, y, z) \right\} \tag{2}$$

$$\text{subject to} \quad E_z[V(x, y, z; \theta)] + T(\theta) \geq V_o(\theta), \qquad \forall x, y, \theta, \tag{3}$$

with

$$\sum_{\theta \in \Theta} T(\theta) = -E_z[C(x, y, z)] \qquad \forall x, y, \tag{4}$$

where E_z is expectation w.r.t. $F(z)$, where $T(\theta)$ is the transfer payment *to* stakeholder θ, and where $V_o(\theta)$ represents status quo utility for θ. If $T(\theta) < 0$, then stakeholder θ contributes $-T(\theta)$ to pay for the facility. If $T(\theta) \geq 0$, then θ receives $T(\theta)$ in compensation.

Expression (2) is the traditional efficiency criterion of maximizing total net benefits: i.e., the socially optimal choice of (x, y) is that which maximizes the ex ante expected total benefits, represented as the aggregate willingness-to-pay by stakeholders (the first term in (2)), minus the expected social cost of the option (x, y).[4] Equation (3) states that all stakeholders must be compensated at such a level to at least maintain their status quo utility level V_o. Equation (4) states that sufficient monies are collected to pay for the expected cost of the facility. We express this in ex ante terms, which would be appropriate if all risks from the facility were insurable, with insurance costs incorporated in $C(x, y, z)$.[5]

It is straightforward to characterize a formal solution to the siting problem, Equations (2)–(4). In effect, this problem embodies two separable problems. First is the problem of determining a net benefit maximizing option (x, y) which solves (2). Given the solution (x, y) to this problem, the optimal $T(\theta)$ are derived which solve (3) and (4) and perhaps other criteria relating to equity. There may be many feasible sets of transfer payments $(T(\theta): \theta \in \Theta)$, especially if the aggregate net benefits at the optimal (x, y) solving (2) are large. Alternative sets of transfer payments $T(\theta)$ will give rise to alternative Pareto solutions to the siting problem. By summing both sides of (3) and using (4), it can be seen that if there is no solution satisfying (3)–(4) at the optimal solution to (2), then none of the available options dominate the status quo. In that case, of course, no facility should be sited.

The formal approach just described for solving (2)–(4) does not indicate how the siting process should be managed nor how negotiations with various stakeholders should take place to ensure successful implementation. These process management issues are very important as noted in Section 3 above and as we will discuss further below. However, the formulation of the siting problem (2)–(4) does contain important insights on the overall siting problem:

(i) The socially optimal solution solving Equation (2) implies minimizing expected cost for a given level of risk as measured by aggregate willingness-to-pay (WTP). In particular, if it is assumed that $V(x, y, z; \theta)$ depends on (x, y, z) only through some facility parameter such as expected (or, alternatively, worst case) risk to stakeholder θ, then the solution to (2) can be represented as

---

[4] For a more detailed analysis of the foundations and implications of this kind of applied welfare analysis, see Crew & Kleindorfer [1986, Chapter 2]. There it is noted that the quasi-linear preferences assumed here (i.e., the willingness-to-pay form of preferences (1)) are a good approximation to more general preferences under fairly weak assumptions. For a general analysis of location problems in the context of spatial games, see Laing & Slotznick [1994].

[5] It is easy to represent governmental subsidies in this framework, e.g., to cover the costs or in the form of indemnity guarantees. One simply defines the government as a stakeholder with ex ante willingness-to-pay $V_o = -S$, where S is the maximum subsidy available.

minimizing expected cost subject to risk exposure constraints for each stakeholder θ and across all stakeholders. Transfer/compensation payments at the associated solution to this problem would then assure that (3) and (4) were satisfied. The OR literature we review below provides a framework for solving this class of problems. In particular, tracing out the solution to (2) for various individual and social risk levels allows the planner to determine the efficient risk–cost frontier. If aggregate WTP does depend on the assumed risk parameters, this is quite appropriate. Using this approach, the socially optimal solution to (2)–(4) is just the point on the efficient risk–cost frontier at which incremental costs and risks just balance one another, or equivalently at which the aggregate WTP for risk reduction just equals the incremental expected cost of such risk reduction.

(ii) It is important to note that solving Equation (2) explicitly requires that the siting planner understand the various stakeholders' WTP for various siting and transportation options, and related risk mitigation procedures. Because, as noted in Section 2 above, obtaining such information is difficult, it may be important to use a decentralized approach that allows communities to 'bid' for the right to be the host community for a facility having certain risk characteristics. Such decentralized negotiation and bidding processes work best for simple, single-facility siting problems. When multiple facilities or complex transportation problems are involved, the use of value-elicitation and OR-siting techniques to map out efficient solution possibilities along the lines of (i) become imperative, at least to structure the efficient options.

(iii) In Equation (2), we assume implicitly that stakeholders have common beliefs about the likelihood of occurrence of uncertain states of the world (E_z does not depend on θ). This formulation can be generalized to allow heterogeneous beliefs. In practice, the issue of determining stakeholders' ex ante beliefs and their impact on WTP is difficult, as discussed earlier.

(iv) Finally, it should be clear that (2) represents a first-best solution. Not only is the best facility $x^* \in X$ selected, but it is also assumed that the optimal risk mitigation option, i.e., the $y^* \in Y$ solving (2), can be implemented. In reality, this option may depend on individual actions by stakeholders and may not be centrally enforceable.

The above problems make clear why the siting problem, even in theory, is difficult. What is required is a *siting process* which encourages all stakeholders to understand their preferences and beliefs, together with the siting options available, and to work together to determine a feasible and cost-effective solution to (2), including compensation or transfer payments among stakeholders to ensure that all stakeholders gain from the siting option chosen. In this process, OR models can play an important role by structuring and evaluating the tradeoffs among various risk categories and across stakeholder groups.

In what follows, we consider the contributions of OR to the siting problem under three headings: transportation problems, extensions of facility location problems to deal with risk, and decision analysis methods for evaluating alternative sites. After a review of the contributions of OR modeling in these three areas, we return to process and legitimation issues in the final section of the chapter. There we examine recent research on coordinating risk analysis and cost reduction methods with negotiation processes for siting. Throughout, we emphasize the importance of OR models and support systems in improving the overall siting process by encouraging informed participation of all stakeholders and by assuring that cost-effective options are considered through use of appropriate OR methodologies to evaluate risk–cost tradeoffs.

5. Transportation of hazardous materials[6]

Hazardous materials transportation problems in the OR literature are concerned with determining the optimal routing and transport modes to minimize several criteria involving expected cost and consequences of accidents. Demands and supplies are usually taken as given, as are the sites of facilities involved (we will relax this last assumption later). The hazardous materials in question can be either dangerous goods (e.g., sulfuric acid or chlorine) or hazardous wastes (e.g., radioactive waste). Two, sometimes overlapping, perspectives are evident in the literature: a profit-maximizing firm's perspective [Kleindorfer & Vetschera, 1989; List & Mirchandani, 1991] or a regulator's perspective [Glickman, 1991: ReVelle, Cohon & Shobrys, 1991].[7]

The firm's problem. Which routes and modes should be chosen to minimize the expected costs of transporting the hazardous materials in question subject to observing various regulatory restrictions, e.g., avoiding various routes or transport modes?

Regulator's problem. Given predicted choices by firms, what are their consequences in terms of property damage, deaths and injuries caused by transportation accidents and which regulatory policies optimize some multi-criteria objective function defined in terms of these aggregate consequences for a given region and given hazardous substance?

Following the literature [e.g., Turnquist & Zografos, 1991], we consider a general problem encompassing both of the above problems. We assume the transport firm is an organization with a multi-criteria objective (which may involve profits, social objectives, equity objectives, risks, etc.) for evaluating its route and mode decisions, and we consider the problem of determining the set of nondominated solutions for this problem.

A typical methodology is to first model the consequences of a given accident (e.g., as in Kleindorfer & Vetschera [1989] and Institute for Risk Research [1986]) at a given location in the specified region. These models can be very detailed and are useful in investigating for a particular type of accident such issues as plume dispersion, paths of risk exposure, and so forth, together with implications for risk mitigation and emergency response. These location-accident-specific models

---

[6] This section is based in part on Kleindorfer & Vetschera [1989].

[7] As a reviewer points out, many OR models can be used to investigate both the firm's as well as the regulator's perspective, by customizing the optimization criterion or by exercising the model suitably.

are also useful as the starting point for modeling aggregate consequences along a route or across a set of routes, modes and locations [e.g., Glickman, 1991; List & Mirchandani, 1991]. Considerable complexity and uncertainty arises at all levels in this evaluation of transport risks because of the current inexact knowledge and available data concerning such risks. Nonetheless, the consequences of various scenarios can be evaluated in sufficient detail to perform useful policy evaluation.

The following major policy areas are related to hazardous materials transportation [cf. Hommel, 1983; O'Hare, 1987]:

• Definition and classification issues (e.g., wastes may be classified as toxic, corrosive, flammable, etc.);

  • Routing restrictions (e.g., transport on certain roads may be prohibited);
  • Mode restrictions (e.g., transport by truck may be prohibited);
  • Packaging regulations;
  • Frequency and hours of permitted carriage;
  • Liability rules and financial/insurance requirements;
  • Restrictions on who may carry the substance in question;
  • Labeling procedures and documentation;
  • Notification procedures in the event of an accident;
  • Emergency response procedures in the event of an accident.

Of the above policy options, the OR literature has been primarily concerned with evaluating alternative routing and mode selection issues to satisfy a scenario where a fixed amount of goods must be supplied to satisfy known demand. The evaluation of regulatory policy options to influence the decision processes of transport firms can then be evaluated in terms of their consequences on firms' route-mode decisions and resulting accident and economic consequences. We will only be concerned here with route-mode selection issues and marginally with liability and insurance.[8]

Route and mode decisions are represented in the following framework. Let X be a set of feasible transportation alternatives, i.e., various combinations of routes and modes in a given region. X can be influenced by regulatory policies, which for specific substances rule out one or another route or mode. Given X, one can represent the transport firm's choice process for determining its preferred alternative $x \in X$ as the solution to the multi-criteria minimization problem:

$$\operatorname*{minimize}_{x \in X} \quad [f_1(x), f_2(x), \ldots, f_n(x)]. \tag{5}$$

We illustrate (5) for the simple case in which the firm is only concerned with minimizing the expected cost of its transport activities, including liability

---

[8] As noted in Kleindorfer & Vetschera [1989], the other policy areas noted above can be dealt with by evaluating alternative scenarios as data input to routing and mode selection routines. Consider, for example, the area of container safety. Changes in container requirements can be expected to affect significantly the probability that a transport accident will lead to package ruptures and spillage. Impacts of container policy options can thus be represented by modeling the stochastic accident consequences of alternative packaging constraints along feasible route-mode choices. For an example, see Glickman [1991]. For a discussion of liability issues, see Watabe [1991].

costs from accidents. Let $L(x, I)$ be the expected net liabilities or monetary damages the firm believes it will incur when required insurance coverage is I and alternative x is chosen, and let $C(x)$ be the out-of-pocket transportation costs for using alternative x. The total expected cost for the carrier is the sum of transportation costs plus expected liabilities, i.e.:

$$TC(x) = L(x, I) + C(x). \tag{6}$$

The difficulties involved in evaluating hazardous transportation policies arise primarily in the evaluation of $L(x, I)$, a complex random variable which must be obtained through spatial integration of the consequences of accidents along the route-mode selection x [cf. Kleindorfer & Vetschera, 1989; List & Mirchandani, 1991]. In the simplest case where an accident can occur along only one segment of a route, say with probability $P(x)$, we can compute the expected liability of the firm from transport activities as follows:

$$L(x, I) = P(x) \times (\text{Max}[H(x) - I(x), 0]), \tag{7}$$

where $I(x)$ is the amount of insurance coverage for a carrier serving alternative x, and where $H(x)$ represents the value imputed by the firm to all economic, environmental and health effects of accidents along the given segment x.[9] These perceived costs may not coincide with actual assessed damages for property and health effects. They simply reflect what the firm believes will be its assessed damages, e.g., based on prevailing court awards for injuries and accidental deaths, if an accident occurs.[10]

Thus, for the expected cost minimizing transport firm, the following problem results:

$$\underset{x \in X}{\text{minimize}} \quad [L(x, I) + C(x)] = P(x) \times (\text{Max}[H(x) - I(x), 0]) + C(x). \tag{8}$$

Note that both the feasible set X and the perceived liabilities $L(x, I)$ faced by the firm depend on policy choices. We summarize in Figure 1 the various policy options and the logic by which these are translated into operational route and mode selection decisions. Note that the logic here is to determine the

---

[9] Note that if $I(x) \geq H(x)$, insurance coverage is sufficient to cover the total damages resulting from the accident and the firm therefore faces no residual liability, i.e., $L(x, I) = 0$. Note also that much more complex hazard distributions than our Bernoulli example could be considered [see, e.g., Kleindorfer & Vetschera, 1989], but the logic would be analogous. Note finally that we are treating insurance in this model as a fixed cost of doing business. Insurance decisions could also be treated as a decision variable, and these would likely depend on such matters as the firm's asset base, risk preferences and the existing transport risks as embodied in x and $L(x, I)$. For a discussion, see Kleindorfer & Kunreuther [1987] and Watabe [1991].

[10] The idea of perceived costs implies that there may be a wide variety of firm decision processes for route/mode selection. On the one extreme, the firm might only consider transport costs $C(X)$, making its decisions as if it believed $H(X)$ were identically zero. On the other extreme, a firm might impute very high values to health and environmental damages resulting from its decisions. See Kleindorfer & Kunreuther [1987] for further discussion.

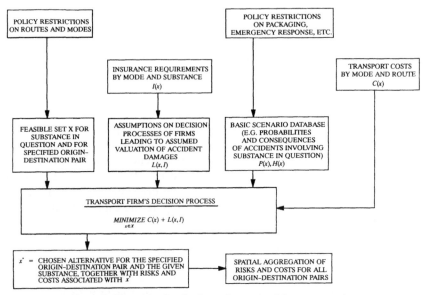

Fig. 1. Policy evaluation for hazardous materials transportation.

optimal route-mode for a single shipment between a given origin and destination. Aggregating these individual choices across all origin–destination pairs then yields the predicted consequences of the assumed supply–demand scenarios for the regulatory policies under study.

From the above description, we note that there are several levels of analysis related to hazardous materials transportation. These range from detailed location-specific models to aggregate models of the regional or national impacts of transport risks in a particular hazardous materials sector. We now consider a few of the OR contributions at several points along this spectrum.

5.1. Single-location accident evaluation models

At the very micro level of analysis is a description, typically in fault-tree form, of specific consequences of accidents resulting from route-mode choices, at specific locations, and with assumed weather and population exposure conditions (see Figure 2 for an illustration). This detailed level of analysis is especially useful for risk mitigation (e.g., improving emergency response programs or vehicular safety systems). For an introduction to risk management for hazardous materials transportation, see Yagar [1984], Institute for Risk Research [1986], and Saccomanno & Chan [1985].

5.2. Route-mode evaluation and choice models

At the next level of detail, route-mode evaluation models can be used to determine a good (undominated set of) route(s) for a given transport activity,

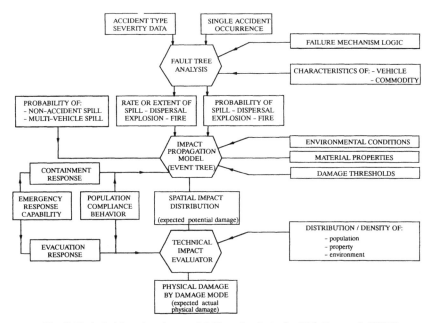

Fig. 2. Typical risk estimation model (from Institute for Risk Research [1986]).

characterized by the amount and type of substance involved and the fixed points of origin and destination. Typically, such models first generate a set of feasible transportation alternatives in terms of geographical routes, transport modes on sections of the routes and vehicles. A detailed cost and risk analysis is then performed for all alternatives and dominated alternatives are eliminated to arrive at (an appropriate subset of) undominated solutions to Equation (5).

The problem of determining efficient transport alternatives can formally be interpreted as a multi-criteria shortest path problem. Several algorithms were developed in the literature to solve this class of problems [cf. Corley & Moon, 1985; Habenicht, 1982; Hansen, 1980; Martins, 1984]. Generation of all efficient alternatives via these algorithms is, however, usually not practical and various heuristics have been developed. As an example, consider the 3-phase heuristic procedure developed by Kleindorfer & Vetschera [1989] (see Figure 3).

In the first phase, the heuristic generates a set of K alternative candidate paths (for the given origin–destination pair) in the underlying transport network[11], where each path is characterized by a route and the modes and vehicles used.

In the second phase of the heuristic, the risk and cost of each path generated in

---

[11] The transport network can be thought of as an undirected graph, consisting of arcs and nodes. Nodes represent geographical locations and points of interchange between arcs. Arcs represent transport possibilities between locations. To obtain a unified structure for analysis, all costs and risks considered are assumed to occur along the arcs. Therefore, arcs are used not only to represent physical transportation between different locations, but also for loading and mode change activities entailing risks or costs.

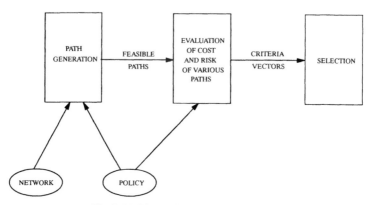

Fig. 3. Multi-criteria evaluation and choice.

the first phase is evaluated. This evaluation covers costs of physical transportation, insurance costs and liabilities as described above. The risk analysis evaluates both losses in the form of material damage and health risks to the population through injuries and fatalities. The evaluation covers the stochastic nature of losses (e.g., in terms of expected values, variances, and maximum probable losses) and could be extended to uncertainty analysis as well [e.g., Glickman, 1991].[12]

In the third phase of the heuristic, dominated alternatives are eliminated, using the criteria vector $f_1(x)$, $f_2(x)$, ..., $f_n(x)$ for each alternative generated in the evaluation phase. The result of the third phase is a set of undominated alternatives in terms of risk and cost criteria. A selection can be made directly from this set for a given origin–destination (O–D) pair, e.g., interactively by the decisionmaker. Alternatively, undominated sets for each O–D pair (and substance) can be input into an aggregate planning system for overall regional planning.

5.3. Regional transportation risk evaluation models

In the aggregate mode of analysis we are no longer directly concerned with route and mode selections for each transport activity and O–D pair, but with the aggregation of route-mode selections in a given region or market area, typically for a given hazardous substance. Several levels of complexity are possible here.

At the simplest level, assumptions are made about the volumes to be transported between each O–D pair and what choices transport firms will make from the undominated set of route/mode paths, e.g., minimizing total expected costs subject to regulatory constraints. This yields for each O–D pair and substance a specific route/mode outcome, which can be integrated spatially over all outcomes to yield aggregate outcomes for the region.

At the next level of complexity, the problem of minimizing the multi-criteria

---

[12] See List & Mirchandani [1991] for additional analytic models of integrated path costs and risks.

objective function (5) can be posed for a number of O–D pairs (e.g., the problem of satisfying chlorine demand within a region from a number of production sites, while minimizing a vector or risk–cost attributes).

For either of the above two problems, additional complexities arise in assuring equitable distribution of risks, e.g., minimizing the maximum exposure of any given segment of the population to mortality risks from accidents. This equity balancing might require choosing a number of paths between any given O–D pairs in order to reduce exposure to segments along, say, a major thoroughfare. See Lindner-Dutton, Batta & Karwan [1991].

At the next level of complexity, one can alter regulatory constraints on routing, modes, and other policy variables to mitigate aggregate risks, evaluated at the pattern of choices emerging from the above models. See Kleindorfer & Vetschera [1989].

We have taken siting decisions as fixed in the above discussion. It is clear that an additional level of complexity arises when some flexibility is possible for the sites of sources and sinks of the hazardous materials in question (e.g., when chlorine production sites or radioactive waste disposal sites can be determined as part of the analysis). Even more generally, one would like to integrate these siting and transportation problems to sectoral economic problems, such as solid waste management [e.g., Wilson, 1981]. These problems require at a minimum that we consider the general problem of simultaneous siting and transportation routing decisions.

6. Facility location models for hazardous facilities[13]

In this section, we review of the facility siting literature for hazardous or noxious facilities, including simultaneous choice of routing and facility choices. The problem of evaluating simultaneous siting and routing decisions is not that much different in principle from that of routing alone, especially in regard to building up from detailed location-specific modeling to more global, aggregate risk–cost tradeoffs. Of course, the simultaneous siting–routing problem can be much more complex, for both computation and ensuing policy analysis, when there are several potential sites for facilities.

Much of this literature on modeling hazardous facility location choices builds on the basic approach of solving multi-objective location models to determine the efficient risk–cost frontier. A policy decision can then be made as to the appropriate tradeoff on this frontier between risk and expected cost. To illustrate, we begin with the ReVelle, Cohon & Shobrys [1991] model for the routing and siting problem and build on this to discuss other contributions.

To make matters transparent, we will consider only two objectives in our formulation, a cost and risk objective. We will also state this problem in the

---

[13] This section is based in part on the excellent surveys available in Wilson [1981], Current, Min & Schilling [1990], and List, Mirchandani, Turnquist & Zografos [1991].

context where most work has been done, namely for hazardous wastes. In this context, we assume that there are a set of n possible origins with known locations and a set of m possible sites for waste disposal. The multi-objective (hazardous facility) siting problem can then be stated in the form of the classic warehouse location problem as follows:

$$\text{minimize} \quad \left\{ \sum_{j=1}^{m} \sum_{i=1}^{n} w_{ij}^{\lambda} x_{ij} + f_j y_j \right\} \tag{9}$$

$$\text{subject to} \quad \sum_{j=1}^{m} x_{ij} = 1, \qquad \forall i \tag{10}$$

$$x_{ij} \leq y_j, \tag{11}$$

$$x_{ij} \epsilon \{0, 1\}, \quad y_j \epsilon \{0, 1\}; \qquad \forall i, j \tag{12}$$

where

i = index of sources/origins: $i = 1, \ldots, n$;

j = index of eligible destinations, $j = 1, \ldots, m$;

w_{ij}^{λ} = $\lambda c_{ij} + (1 - \lambda) r_{ij}$, a weighted sum of the cost (c_{ij}) and risk (r_{ij}) of using destination j for source i wastes, where it is assumed that variable cost of using j for source i's wastes are included in c_{ij};

λ = weight between 0 and 1 associated with the cost objective versus the risk objective;

f_j = fixed cost, on say an annualized basis, for constructing, operating and maintaining facility j;

x_{ij} = a 0–1 variable: 1 if the destination j is used for source i and 0 if not;

y_j = a 0–1 variable: 1 if site j is selected to construct a facility and 0 if not.

Let us note a few characteristics of the above problem. First, it is assumed that the cost (c_{ij}) and risk (r_{ij}) of a particular origin–destination (O–D) pair are determined as an input to this optimization problem. This is accomplished by determining a set of feasible, candidate routes for each O–D pair using the detailed evaluation models described in Section 5 above [see Kleindorfer & Vetschera, 1989; List & Mirchandani, 1991]. In this sense, combined analysis of routing and siting builds on the more detailed cost and risk assessment models of hazardous materials transportation described earlier. Note that as the weighting constant λ varies from 0 to 1, alternative points on the efficient risk–cost frontier will be traced out, where risk in this model is assumed to be some additive measure of siting risk such as expected fatalities or expected number of individuals exposed to accidents along all routes.[14]

[14] Non-additive measures of risk such as worst case fatality or exposure risks could also be included, but these would be represented in minimax form across routes and facilities. Such non-additive measures are especially important in representing equity issues such as the maximum exposure or risk of any individual or group [see, e.g., List & Mirchandani, 1991].

Second, it should be noted from Equation (10) that the above model assigns only a single route to each O–D pair. More complex models are possible which would allow waste shipments from a given origin to be split among several disposal sites [e.g., List & Mirchandani, 1991; Wilson, 1981]. In the same spirit, we have suppressed the details of the amount of hazardous materials originating at source i. In the event of split shipments to multiple destinations, these details would have to be represented. This is accomplished in standard transportation model format by representing cost in a per unit fashion, with total cost for a given O–D pair then proportional to the number of tons shipped from i to j.

Third, the number of facilities j could also be constrained by appending an appropriate upper bound on the sum of the y_j's. In the simplest case, only a single facility might be allowed.

When used in association with an appropriately rich model of transportation risks, this class of models provides interesting insights into cost–risk tradeoffs. These models have been used for a host of planning problems (see Wilson [1981] for a review of the early literature), regional solid waste management models (see Gottinger [1988]), and for a number of environmental and cost–risk evaluation problems (see Current, Min & Schilling [1990] for a review). In the typical application, e.g., List & Mirchandani [1991], the weighting parameter λ is varied from 0 to 1 to assess the nature of jointly optimal facility siting and routing decisions for the pure cost-based solution ($\lambda = 1$), the minimum risk solution ($\lambda = 0$), and various middle-ground alternatives ($0 < \lambda < 1$).

The above problem statement is in the context of a single hazardous waste. This is easily extended to deal with multiple waste streams [e.g., Wilson, 1981]. Similarly, transfer stations and resource recovery facilities can be included with slightly more complex objective and constraint structures [e.g., Gottinger, 1988]. Such transfer facility problems require in particular the introduction of additional 0–1 location variables to represent the choice set for transfer/resource recovery facilities. This problem has been of special interest recently since many municipalities have found themselves short of solid waste disposal capacity and have therefore had to resort to using regional disposal alternatives. In this context, the economics of compaction, bulk transport and resource recovery are, of course, of considerable import.

A final related context worth noting is that of hazardous materials routing–siting problems in which destinations represent market areas (e.g., for chlorine or some other hazardous good) and origins represent supply points (e.g., plants producing chlorine). A very similar version of the above problem would then apply in trading off cost and risk of assigning various market areas to various supply facilities, with associated cost–risk efficient routing between supply and demand points [Batta & Chiu, 1988; List, Mirchandani, Turnquist & Zografos, 1991].

As noted, while risk is included in models such as the above, the assessment of risk (in the form of the r_{ij} parameters) is actually an input to this formulation. While this is arguably appropriate for aggregate routing and siting evaluation, it should also be clear that it neglects the details of risk perceptions and evaluation of risks across stakeholder groups. Only aggregate expected risk measures can be incorporated into the above type of formulation. For this reason, decision analysis has been applied to further analyze risk elements in more detail.

7. Siting facilities using decision analysis

Decision analysis (DA) has proven to be a useful approach for structuring the siting problem and has been applied in a number of different contexts (see Keeney & Raiffa [1976] and Keeney [1980] for illustrative examples). DA is a prescriptive approach which suggests a formal procedure for making good siting decisions. It requires the concerned parties to structure the problem so that they can compare a set of alternatives on the basis of a systematic analysis of the impact that the site will have on different performance measures. The DA approach to the problem has a well defined set of steps that are summarized and illustrated below. These steps may be viewed as providing a structured solution to the formal problem (1)–(4) stated above. We will use the notation introduced earlier.

7.1. Step 1: Specify the alternatives

The typical site selection problem involves the selection of a particular location x from a set X of different alternatives (including the status quo) using a number of different criteria to choose between them. In determining what alternative to choose, there are many concerns which play a role in the process. As pointed out in Section 2 there are likely to be conflicts between the objectives of the different interested parties which may be difficult to reconcile. Each proposed alternative will be attractive to some groups and is likely to be unattractive to others.

7.2. Step 2: Specify the set of objectives and measures of effectiveness

For the siting of noxious facilities the objectives normally revolve around economic considerations, health and safety features as well as environmental concerns. A growing literature has emerged in recent years as to how one structures objectives into a hierarchy so that one can better understand the key factors which guide the choice process [Keeney, 1992; Von Winterfeldt & Edwards, 1986]. Each objective $j = 1, \ldots, n$ is then translated into a performance measure that can be measured quantitatively using a specially constructed scale.

Let A_j represent a vector of performance measures related to objective j. An example of a quantitative performance measure would be the estimated cost of the facility (in dollars). A qualitative performance measure might be the environmental impact of a proposed site using a 0 to 6 scale (where 0 would be no impact and 6 significant damage to certain species). In terms of the problem (1)–(4), this step in DA is concerned with the structure of the WTP preferences in (1) and, in particular, with determining an operational set of measures A_j such that V in (1) can be expressed as:

$$V(x, y, z; \theta) = V[A_1(x, y, z), A_2(x, y, z), \ldots, A_m(x, y, z); \theta] \qquad (13)$$

7.3. Step 3: Specify a set of scenarios affecting the performance measures

The states of the world z in (1)–(4) are referred to as 'scenarios' in siting applications of DA. Constructing scenarios which depict a set of events that might occur at a particular site is a highly subjective process. It involves indicating the nature of specific risks that are associated with a particular site and the specification of the probabilities of such risks actually materializing.

Systematic procedures such as fault trees and event trees have been utilized for constructing scenarios for complex events [see Von Winterfeldt & Edwards, 1986]. However, there is often considerable variability across experts in characterizing the probabilities of these scenarios occurring due to the lack of past data and differences in assumptions which guide the analysis. For example, in the analysis of the risks associated with siting liquified natural gas facilities there was considerable discrepancy on the chances of specific accident scenarios by different experts [Kunreuther, Lathrop & Linnerooth, 1982]. There are also likely to be specific biases in estimating probabilities [Kahneman, Slovic & Tversky, 1982] that must be recognized when undertaking these analyses.

Ideally there will be a set of probabilities and outcomes associated with each scenario z for each specific site $x \in X$. These might be the result of consensual agreement if there is sufficient statistical data upon which to base these estimates. Let $P(A_1, \ldots, A_m \mid x, y, z)$ represent the probability that scenario z will occur at site x when control procedures y are used and yield outcomes A_j on each of the m performance measures associated with evaluating the site. In practice there will be significant differences between the experts for reasons stated above and it may be hard to reconcile these differences. In this situation it may be necessary to analyze the impact of different estimates of $P(A \mid x, y, z)$ on the performance of alternative sites, where $A = \{A_1, \ldots, A_m\}$.

The nature of the scenarios constructed by any one expert will differ depending on the nature of the siting questions being raised. For example, the key issue may be the uncertainty of the cost of specific siting proposals in which case a set of scenarios will be constructed which focus solely on this performance measure and assign different probabilities to different estimates of the costs for each site i. The other performance measures will either not be considered in this portion of the analysis or are set at some arbitrary level (e.g., mean outcome). Other scenarios will focus on the impact of different events that might occur at the site (e.g., an accident, leakage of toxic waste) and its impact on different measures. In this case the cost of facility i may be specified at some level (e.g., best estimate). If the probability of an accident occurring is affected by the cost of the facility then these interactions should be built into the scenario construction [Schoemaker, 1991].

7.4. Step 4: Assessing the values of different stakeholders

The relationship between different performance measures in constructing scenarios depends on the utility function of the different interested parties, i.e., on the structure of V in (13). There is a large literature on the assessment of multi-attribute utility functions or value functions for siting problems [Keeney, 1980]. Two extreme cases highlight some of the challenges associated with this step in the decision analysis process.

At one end of the spectrum is the case where there is a single stakeholder who has final authority to make a decision and attempts to reflect the concerns of all the relevant stakeholders in constructing a multi-attribute utility function. For example, if the state feels it has the authority to site a facility and can impose its will on the citizenry then one would want to assess the state's utility function (as represented by a policymaker) in undertaking a decision analysis. The key steps in such a process would be to determine the degree and nature of independence among the different performance measures [Keeney & Raiffa, 1976], assess the utilities for different measures (e.g., health effects, costs) and determining the scaling factors which reflect the relative importance of the different performance measures comprising the utility function.

At the other end of the spectrum is the case where many stakeholders are involved with a particular siting problem. It may then be useful to understand how $V(x, y, z; \theta)$ varies across stakeholders θ by developing utility functions for each important stakeholder group (i.e., for each $\theta \in \Theta$). A value tree is the elicitation or construction of a formal value structure by indicating the importance of different objectives and their performance measures. Value trees can be constructed for each individual stakeholder (or for a representative sample of stakeholders) and then combined into a joint value tree based on the concerns of all the parties [Von Winterfeldt, 1987]. At the end of this process there are still likely to be differences in the importance placed on specific performance measures by different stakeholders. This type of information will enable the parties to investigate alternative solutions to the siting problem to see if they can arrive at compromises.

7.5. Step 5: Evaluating alternative sites

In this stage of the process one can evaluate the expected net benefits of different sites. Although each siting problem has its own special characteristics there are two general approaches to the problem of determining the optimal site from a set X of possible alternatives.

7.5.1. Simultaneous selection process

If there are no fixed costs associated with obtaining detailed data on the site and interacting with the relevant stakeholders then it will always be optimal to consider the m different sites simultaneously and determine the one which maximizes expected net benefits where net benefits takes into account economic, health, safety, and environmental considerations. Let $E\{B(x)\}$ represent expected net benefits of site x, where $E\{B(x)\}$ is determined in theory as the solution to (2).[15] Figure 4 depicts a highly simplified decision tree for a siting problem where

---

[15] We neglect here the determination of site-specific mitigation measures $y(x)$.

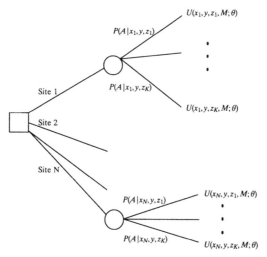

Fig. 4. Simultaneous characterization of sites.

there are N possible sites $x_1, \ldots, x_N$ so $X = \{x_1, \ldots, x_N\}$. As before, we assume a set Y of risk mitigation measures and a set of scenarios (or states of the world) $Z = \{z_1, \ldots, z_K\}$. We denote by $P(A \mid x, y, z)$ the probability of occurrence of the outcome vector $A = \{A_1, \ldots, A_m\}$, given the option (x, y). The resulting outcome on the different performance measures is evaluated using multi-attribute utility functions of the different stakeholders. As shown in Figure 4, if site x is selected and risk mitigation measures y are implemented, then the utility outcomes for the different stakeholders under scenario z are given by (1), that is:

$$U(x, y, z, M; \theta) = V(x, y, z; \theta) + M, \qquad (14)$$

where V is given in Equation (13) and M may be adjusted with compensation payments $T(\theta)$ as in (3) and (4).

There is limited discussion in standard DA as to how one combines these utility functions if there are significant differences between the stakeholders.[16] The use of value tree analysis is one approach for recognizing that the weights associated with different performance measures may differ across stakeholders and proposing compromise options that are attractive to the opposing stakeholders. In the end there may still be conflicts among the parties which may then require other procedures for attempting to resolve. Value trees may diagnose the nature of the conflicts but their usefulness in actual conflict resolution has still to be proven [Von Winterfeldt, 1987].

---

[16] Under the standard assumption of quasi-linear preferences (see (1)), aggregation across stakeholders is straightforward in theory. One needs only sum WTP across stakeholders, using transfer payments as in (3) to assure status quo levels of utility. In practice, of course, a host of complicating factors arise to hinder this process, not least of which is the determination of the WTP for each stakeholder, but also including considerations of equity as discussed above.

7.5.2. Sequential selection process

If there are substantial fixed costs[17] of characterizing each potential site, then it may be more desirable to sequentially examine the sites. Now one needs to define net benefits for any site before any information is collected on the details of the site. Let this be represented as $E\{B(x_i \mid 0)\}$. After characterization one may learn considerably more about the nature of the problems at this particular site. Cost estimates of the process will be more precise and the political dynamics may be clarified. This new state of knowledge for site i is represented by $E\{B(x_i \mid 1)\}$.

If F is the fixed cost associated with initiating the siting process in any location, then a sequential process will initially save $(N-1)F$ by only looking at one site. Suppose that the sites are ordered by when they will be characterized so that site 1 is initially selected, site 2 would be next in line and site N last in line. If some potential locations already have more noxious facilities in their vicinity than others then for equity reasons they may be placed towards the end of the line. Other locations which appear to be particularly well suited physically to host the facility may be towards the beginning of the line.

A second site would only be characterized if new information were collected after examining site 1 which indicates that $E\{B(x_2 \mid 0)\} - F > E\{B(x_1 \mid 1)\}$. Denote the probability of this occurring was q_1. Site 3 will only be characterized if site 2 is examined and it is determined that $E\{B(x_3 \mid 0)\} - F > E\{B(x_2 \mid 1)\}$.

Figure 5 depicts the sequential process and specifies the expected net benefits at each stage of the process. Note there is always some chance that a simultaneous

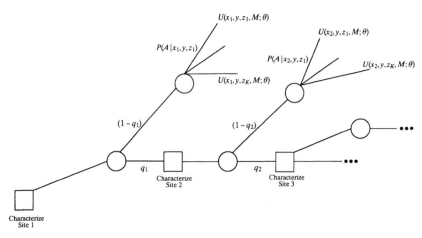

q_i = Probability that $E\{B(x_{i+1} \mid 0)\} > E\{B(x_i \mid 1)\} + F$

Fig. 5. Sequential site characterization.

---

[17] See Keeney [1992] for a discussion of some of the costs of site evaluation. See Kunreuther, Easterling, Desvousges & Slovic [1990] for a detailed discussion of these in the context of the Yucca Mountain site evaluation for a high-level nuclear waste repository.

process will discover a facility with a higher net benefit than if one followed the sequential process. However, if F is sufficiently high, then such a process cannot be justified *ex ante* if one used the criterion maximize expected net benefits. For example, Keeney [1987] has compared sequential and simultaneous procedures to determine which site(s) should be characterized for locating a high-level nuclear waste repository.[18] He recommended a sequential procedure due to the very high costs of characterization ($1 billion per site).

7.6. Process issues in siting facilities

Decision analysis can play an important role in clarifying the objectives of the relevant stakeholders concerned with a particular siting problem, characterizing their similarities and differences as well as evaluating the performance of different sites. At the end of the process it may reveal substantial conflicts between the groups which cannot be resolved through this type of formal analysis.

7.6.1. Siting the high-level nuclear waste repository

A case in point is the selection of a site for the first high-level nuclear waste repository. The search for a permanent means of disposing high-level nuclear waste originated in the mid 1950s when it became apparent to members of the Atomic Energy Commission that the temporary and makeshift methods of disposal were inadequate. The pressure to find a permanent means of disposal of civilian waste intensified in the 1970s and culminated in the passage of the Nuclear Waste Policy Act (NWPA) of 1982.

The NWPA recognized that a repository would not be politically acceptable to a host state unless the state had itself undertaken actions that assured citizens of the safety of the facility and the suitability of the local site [Colglazier & Langum, 1988]. The actual process of site selection has deviated considerably from the objectives of the NWPA. More specifically, the Department of Energy (DOE) developed a set of general guidelines for evaluating possible repository sites which explicitly consider public health and safety, environmental, and socioeconomic considerations.

On the basis of these guidelines DOE selected five sites as suitable for housing a repository. The procedures used by DOE were criticized by a number of groups including a letter from the National Academy of Sciences (NAS) calling their methods 'unsatisfactory, inadequate, undocumented and biased' [Merkhofer & Keeney, 1987]. As a result of these concerns, DOE elected to evaluate the five nominated sites based on multi-attribute utility analysis (MUA) in order to rank the top three sites.

---

[18] In this situation three sites were considered by the Department of Energy to be potential candidates because they appeared to be geologically safe. However, there was considerable uncertainty as to the costs of constructing the facility. Characterization involves construction of an exploratory shaft to the proposed repository area, subsurface excavation and tunneling as well as other activities.

In May 1986 DOE provided a different ranking of the proposed sites than the one suggested by the MUA. Some of the factors which were ignored in the MUA but may have been important to DOE in its consideration of which sites to consider are the degree of local opposition and risk factors such as fear and anxiety, equity concerns and equity considerations [Merkhofer & Keeney, 1987].

The controversy on where to locate the repository took another turn in December 1987 when Congress amended the NWPA of 1982 by selecting Yucca Mountain, Nevada as the site which should be characterized for the repository. In essence Congress changed its position on siting from one of simultaneously characterizing three sites to a process whereby Nevada would be the site for the repository unless geologic flaws were discovered in the more detailed characterization process. If Yucca Mountain was declared unsafe then one of the other two sites would be characterized. Note that this siting process differs from the sequential procedure discussed in the previous section where sites already characterized remain potential candidates for a facility at all stages.

The reaction to the Congressional ruling produced strong opposition to the repository in Nevada. Not only did state officials as well as the citizenry feel that the process was unfair, but they perceived the risks of the repository to be unacceptably high even though DOE claimed that the repository would pose no risk at all [Kunreuther, Easterling, Desvousges & Slovic, 1990]. Scientific evidence supporting the public's concern was provided by one of DOE's staff geologists in Las Vegas, Jerry Szymanski, who has promoted the theory that Yucca Mountain is subject to earthquakes which might create problems of radioactive waste leaking into the groundwater [Marshall, 1991]. This theory has been disputed by much of the scientific community but has fueled considerable opposition to the repository [Easterling & Kunreuther, 1994].

The search for a place for the HLNW repository illustrates the dilemma facing society in siting the entire set of potentially hazardous or noxious facilities ranging from landfills and trash disposal plants to radioactive waste facilities. Even if there is general agreement by scientific experts that a new facility will reduce the aggregate risk over the status quo (e.g., temporarily storing nuclear waste in many different places) this information may have no meaning to the residents of the community or state where the facility is being proposed. From their perspective the risk to them is increased over the status quo and for that reason they would prefer to have the facility located elsewhere.

Preemptive legislation which enables the appropriate legislative body (e.g., Congress, state legislature) to specify a site location does not appear to be an effective strategy for ensuring that objectionable facilities are built. Morell & Magorian [1982] point out that in almost any siting controversy at least one stakeholder group will have some degree of de facto veto power. If a preemptive strategy has succeeded in any state we are unaware of it. In fact, states such as Massachusetts that have considered adopting preemptive strategies for locating hazardous waste facilities have abandoned them because they have recognized the ability of local officials to defeat an unwanted facility [Bacow, 1980]. The recent experience of Clean Harbors trying to locate a hazardous waste incinerator in

Braintree, Massachusetts reveals the power of citizens groups to stop a project which has been viewed by experts as scientifically sound and one that promised to reduce risks over the status quo [Brion, 1991].

The rather extensive literature on siting potentially hazardous facilities that has emerged in recent years has stressed the importance of fear by communities as a principal reason for opposing the siting of facilities. There are two types of fear which need to be distinguished: fear associated with health and environmental effects of the facility to them personally as well as future generations and fear associated with economic impacts such as a decline in property values or unemployment.

Turning to concerns over health and environmental effects, studies of the public's perception of risks suggest that probabilities and loss magnitudes play a minor role in people's judgment of the severity of risks. Risk severity really depends on subjective features such as the voluntariness of exposure, familiarity, catastrophic potential and dread [Fischhoff, Slovic, Lichtenstein, Read & Combs, 1978; Slovic, 1987].

Nuclear waste repositories and hazardous waste facilities are perceived to be particularly dangerous because the public knows little about them and dreads the health impacts from any accident or leakage from the facility. A national survey of 1201 residents and a Nevada survey of 1001 individuals both revealed that average perceived risk from a HLNW repository as the more serious than any of five other risks [Kunreuther, Easterling, Desvousges & Slovic, 1990].[19] A national sample of 400 citizens throughout the U.S revealed that 1/3 of them were opposed to having a hazardous waste treatment facility in their backyard because they felt it was unsafe and dangerous [Portney, 1991].

With respect to economic impacts citizens in communities selected to host disposal facilities have expressed concern that the facility will lower property values. There is some evidence that these declines have occurred with some noxious facilities [Metz, Morey & Lowry, 1990]. McClelland, Schultze & Hurd [1990] did uncover evidence of depressed property values in the vicinity of an abandoned hazardous waste dump. Greater reductions in property value were observed in areas with a higher perceived risk. Interestingly enough the perceived risk was related to odors which were viewed by the scientific experts to be harmless.

A region may be concerned with the possibility of stigma effects from a proposed facility and hence oppose it on this ground. In the case of hazardous or nuclear waste the region may be concerned with having an image of a 'wasteland' that may discourage new businesses from entering the area or discourage consumers from buying products [Slovic, Layman, Kraus, Chalmers, Gesell & Flynn,

---

[19] Respondents were asked to rate the seriousness of the risks to them from six different sources on a scale of 1 (not at all serious) to 10 (very serious). The other 4 risks were home accident, job accident, nuclear power plants and nuclear weapons testing site. On the national level the nearby repository had an average perceived risk of 5.6 and an average rating of 5.2 for exposure to hazardous chemicals. Home accidents (the lowest rating) had a value of 3.9. The Nevada survey yielded perceived seriousness estimates that were slightly high for all risks.

1989]. In the case of a Multiple Retrievable Storage (MRS) facility, Tennessee refused to host the facility at Oak Ridge after considering the potential impact to economic development efforts in the eastern part of the state [Sigmon, 1987]. Agricultural communities in eastern Washington state opposed a nuclear waste repository at Hanford claiming that it would be perceived by the consuming public as contaminating fruits and wines grown in the area and hence cause a decline in the economy [Dunlap & Baxter, 1988]. The stigma and perceived risk of an HLNW repository (should it be constructed at Yucca Mountain) was viewed as adversely affecting future convention business [Easterling & Kunreuther, 1994] and tourism [Slovic, Layman & Flynn, 1991] in Las Vegas, 100 miles away from the proposed site.

7.7. Importance of equity and legitimacy

The siting of a noxious facility will have important distributional effects since certain groups and individuals will gain while others will lose. These equity considerations play an important role in selecting the alternative sites as well as in deciding what type of siting process to follow.

In addition to the perceived costs and benefits of a given facility that can be evaluated by a DA framework there are often strong feelings as to whether it is fair to place the facility in my backyard. Morell & Magorian [1982] point out that people do not want to feel that they are being taken advantage of when asked to host a facility. One example which they provide to illustrate this point is the case of Starr County, Texas which refused to accept a hazardous waste landfill even though they agreed that it did not pose any risks. The residents in the community were poor and felt they had been exploited by wealthier areas of the state.

O'Hare, Bacow & Sanderson [1983] have argued that the different parties in the siting debate, in particular the proposed communities, must be convinced that the status quo is unacceptable. Easterling [1992] has suggested that residents of a community, region or state would be inclined to feel that the siting process was fair if they believed that the local site is the safest one available. For the affected public to feel this way, the developer of a facility must have a reputation for assessing risk accurately, for constructing the facility according to rigorous standards and for managing the facility competently. Credibility and trust in the process is particularly relevant for new facilities since there is no past history on which to base relevant estimates.

8. Concluding comments

The above review points to a number of important implications for the use of OR methodologies in support of siting of hazardous facilities. First, our general model of Section 4 points to the interlinking of values and beliefs with siting, transport and risk mitigation options for efficient siting of hazardous facilities. In particular, OR methods are clearly important in evaluating options for transportation, siting and technology selection and in incorporating these into appropriate decision support systems to allow efficient risk–cost tradeoffs to be determined. Second, compensation (in-kind or monetary) to promote equity and to share benefits across stakeholders may be essential to enable implementation of efficient siting alternatives. Third, risk mitigation and control are central aspects of efficient siting. Finally, the information and equity issues associated with the siting of hazardous facilities make it imperative to understand siting as a process in which OR methods can contribute to determining efficient risk–cost tradeoffs, but in which the central problem is helping stakeholders to determine their values and beliefs relative to the siting options.

In particular, while operations research can contribute significantly to understanding and mitigating the multi-stakeholder risks associated with hazardous transportation and facility siting, it should be clear from the above that OR modeling is but one element of the complex process of assessing costs and risks in support of decision making in the siting process.

In our opinion, the key to the future success of siting problems will be integrating OR methods more closely with host community decision processes, to allow host communities to assess and to understand both the costs and the benefits they would be assuming in hosting a hazardous facility. This is clearly where the challenges for future research lie.

Acknowledgements

This paper was developed for the Handbook of Operations Research. We would like to thank Kevin Fitzgerald and Tom Aarts for their helpful comments and research assistance. The helpful comments of Ralph Keeney and two anonymous reviewers on a previous draft are gratefully acknowledged. This research was supported in part by the National Science Foundation (#SES 8809299) and by the William and Flora Hewlett Foundation (Grant # 5-26021).

References

Bacow, L.S. (1980). Mitigation, compensation, incentives and preemption, Monograph prepared for the National Governors' Association.

Batta, R., and S. Chiu (1988). Optimal obnoxious paths on a network: Transportation of hazardous materials. *Oper. Res.* 36, 84–92.

Brion, D.J. (1991). *Essential Industry and the NIMBY Syndrome*, Quorum Books, New York.

Carnes, S.A., E.D. Copenhaver, J.H. Sorensen, E.J. Soderstrom, J.H. Reed, D.J. Bjornstad and E. Peelle (1983). Incentives and nuclear waste siting: Prospects and constraints. *Energy Syst. Policy* 7(4), 324–351.

Carson, R. (1962). *Silent Spring*, Fawcett Publications, Greenwich, CT.

Colglazier, E.W., and R.B. Langum (1988). Policy conflicts in the process for siting nuclear waste repositories. *Annu. Rev. Energy* 11, 317–357.

Corley, H.W., and I.D. Moon (1985). Shortest paths in networks with vector weights. *JOTA* 46, 79–85.

Crew, M., and P. Kleindorfer (1986). *The Economics of Public Utility Regulation*, M.I.T. Press, Cambridge, MA.

Current, J., H. Min and D. Schilling (1990). Multiobjective analysis of facility location decisions. *European J. Oper. Res.* 49(3), 295–307.

Dunlap, R.E., and R.K. Baxter (1988). *Public Reaction to Siting a High-level Nuclear Waste Repository at Hanford: A Survey of Local Area Residents*, Report prepared for Impact Assessment, Inc. by the Social and Economic Sciences Research Center, Washington State University, Pullman, WA.

Easterling, D. (1992). Fair rules for siting a high level nuclear waste repository. *J. Policy Analysis Management* 11(3), 442–475.

Easterling, D., and H. Kunreuther (1994). *The Dilemma of Siting a High Level Nuclear Waste Repository*, Kluwer, Boston, MA.

Ewing, T.F. (1990). Guarantees near a landfill. *New York Times*, July 8.

Fischhoff, B., P. Slovic, S. Lichtenstein, S. Read and B. Combs (1978). How safe is safe enough? A psychometric study of attitudes toward technological risks and benefits. *Policy Sci.* 9, 127–152.

Glickman, T.S. (1991). An expeditious risk assessment of the highway transportation of flammable liquids in bulk. *Transportation Sci.* 25(2), 115–123.

Gottinger, H.W. (1988). A computational model for solid waste management with application. *European J. Oper. Res.* 35, 350–364.

Gregory, R., H. Kunreuther, D. Easterling and K. Richards (1991). Incentives policies to site hazardous waste facilities. *Risk Analysis* 11(4), 667–675.

Habenicht, W. (1982). Efficient routes in vector-valued graphs, in: J. Mühlbacher et al. (eds.), *Proc. 7th Conf. on Graphtheoretic Concepts in Computer Science*, Muenchen.

Hansen, P. (1980). Bicriterion path problems, in: G. Fandel, and T. Gal (eds.), *Multiple Criteria Decision Making, Theory and Application*, Springer-Verlag, Berlin, pp. 109–127.

Hommel, G. (1983). *Handbuch der gefaehrlichen Gueter*, Springer-Verlag, Heidelberg.

Inhaber, H. (1990). Hands up for toxic waste. *Nature* 347, 611–612.

Institute for Risk Research (IRR) (1986). Risk management in the handling and transportation of dangerous goods, Phase II Report, University of Waterloo, Waterloo, Ont.

Kahneman, D., P. Slovic and A. Tversky (eds.) (1982). *Judgement under Uncertainty: Heuristics and Biases*, Cambridge University Press, Cambridge.

Kasperson, R.E., O. Renn, P. Slovic, H.S. Brown, J. Emel, R. Gobel, J.X. Kasperson and S. Ratick (1988). The social amplification of risk: A conceptual framework. *Risk Analysis* 8(2), 177–197.

Keeney, R.L. (1980). *Siting Energy Facilities*, Academic Press, New York.

Keeney, R.L. (1987). An analysis of the portfolio of sites to characterize for selecting a nuclear repository. *Risk Analysis* 7, 195–218.

Keeney, R.L. (1992). *Value-Focused Thinking*, Harvard University Press, Cambridge, MA.

Keeney, R.L., and H. Raiffa (1976). *Decisions with Multiple Objectives*, Wiley, New York.

Kleindorfer, P.R., and H.C. Kunreuther (eds.) (1987). *From Seveso to Bhopal: Managing and Insuring Hazardous Risks*, Springer-Verlag, Berlin.

Kleindorfer, P.R., and R. Vetschera (1989). HASTM: Modelling hazardous materials transportation decisions, Working Paper 89-12-09, Decision Sciences Department, University of Pennsylvania, PA.

Kunreuther, H.W., Desvousges and P. Slovic (1988). Nevada's predicament: Public perception of risk from the proposed nuclear waste repository. *Environment* 30, 17–20, 30–33.

Kunreuther, H., D. Easterling, W. Desvousges and P. Slovic (1990). Public attitudes toward siting a high-level nuclear waste repository in Nevada. *Risk Analysis* 10(4), 469–484.

Kunreuther, H., K. Fitzgerald and T. Aarts (1993). The facility siting credo: Theoretical and empirical evidence. *Risk Analysis* 13(3), 301–318.

Kunreuther, H., J. Lathrop and J. Linnerooth (1982). A descriptive model of choice for siting facilities. *Behavioral Sci.* 27, 281–297.

Kunreuther, H., and J. Linnerooth (1982). *Risk Analysis and Decision Processes: The Siting of Liquified Energy Facilities in Four Countries*, Springer-Verlag, Berlin.

Kunreuther, H., and P. Portney (1991). Wheel of fortune: A lottery auction mechanism for the siting of noxious facilities. *J. Energy Engrg.* 117(3), 125–132.

Laing, J.D., and B. Slotznick (1994). On collective goods, private wealth, and the core solution of simple games with sidepayments. *Public Choice*, in press.

Lake, R. (ed.) (1987). *Resolving Locational Conflict*, Center for Urban Policy Research, New Brunswick, NJ.

Lindner-Dutton, L., R. Batta and M.H. Karwan (1991). Equitable sequencing of a given set of hazardous materials shipments. *Transportation Sci.* 25(2), 124–137.

List, G.F., and P.B. Mirchandani (1991). An integrated network/planar multiobjective model for routing and siting for hazardous materials and wastes. *Transportation Sci.* 25(2), 146–156.

List, G.F., P.B. Mirchandani, M.A. Turnquist and K.G. Zografos (1991). Modeling and analysis for hazardous materials transportation: Risk analysis, routing/scheduling and facility location. *Transportation Sci.* 25(2), 100–114.

Marshall, E. (1991). The geopolitics of nuclear waste. *Science* 251, 864–867.

Martins, E.Q.V. (1984). On a multi-criteria shortest path problem. *European J. Oper. Res.* 16, 236.

McClelland, G.H., W.D. Schultze and B. Hurd (1990). The effect of risk beliefs on property values: A case study of a hazardous waste site. *Risk Analysis* 10(4), 485–497.

McGlennon, J. (1983). The Alberta experience . . . Hazardous wastes? Maybe in my backyard. *Environmental Forum* 2, 23–25.

Merkhofer, M.W., and R.L. Keeney (1987). A multiattribute utility analysis of alternative sites for the disposal of nuclear waste. *Risk Analysis* 7, 173–194.

Metz, W.C., M. Morey and J. Lowry (1990). Hedonic price theory: Concept and applications, Conference Paper, Presented at the 1st Annu. Internat. High-Level Radioactive Waste Management Conf., Las Vegas, April 8–12.

Morell, D., and C. Magorian (1982). *Siting Hazardous Waste Facilities: Local Opposition and the Myth of Preemption*, Ballinger, Cambridge, MA.

O'Hare, M. (1987). Bargaining and negotiation in risk management: Hazardous materials transportation, in: P.R. Kleindorfer, and H.C. Kunreuther (eds.), *From Seveso to Bhopal: Managing and Insuring Hazardous Risks*, Springer-Verlag, Berlin, pp. 186–205.

O'Hare, M., L. Bacow and D. Sanderson (1983). *Facility Siting and Public Opposition*, Van Nostrand Reinhold, New York.

Peelle, E. (1987). Hazardous waste management outlook: Are there ways out of the 'not-in-my-backyard' impasse? *Forum for Applied Research and Public Policy* 2, 68–88.

Portney, K.E. (1991). *Siting Hazardous Waste Treatment Facilities: The NIMBY Syndrome*, Auburn House, New York.

Rabe, B. (1991). Beyond the NIMBY syndrome in hazardous waste facility siting: The Alberta breakthrough and the prospects for cooperation in Canada and the United States. *Governance* 4, 184–206.

Rennick, P.H., and R.L. Greyell (1990). Opting for cooperation: A voluntary approach to siting a low-level radioactive waste facility, Working Paper, Siting Task Force on Low-Level Radioactive Waste Management, Energy, Mines and Resources Canada, Ottawa, Ont.

ReVelle, C., J. Cohon and D. Shobrys (1991). Simultaneous siting and routing in the disposal of hazardous wastes. *Transportation Sci.* 25(2), 138–145.

Ruckelshaus, W.D. (1989). The politics of waste disposal. *Wall Street J.* September 5.

Saccomanno, F., and A. Chan (1985). Economic evaluation of routing strategies for hazardous road shipments. *Trans. Res. Rec.* 1020, 12–18.

Schoemaker, P. (1991). When and how to use scenario planning: A heuristic approach with illustration. *J. Forecasting* 10, 549–564.

Sigmon, E.B. (1987). Achieving a negotiated compensation agreement in siting: The MRS case. *J. Policy Analysis Management* 6, 170–179.

Simon, H. (1978). Rationality as process and as product of thought. *Amer. Econom. Rev. Papers Proc.* 68, 1–16.

Slovic, P. (1987). Perception of risk. *Science* 236, 280–285.

Slovic, P., M. Layman, N.N. Kraus, J. Chalmers, G. Gesell and J. Flynn (1989). Perceived risk, stigma, and potential economic impacts of a high-level repository in Nevada, Report prepared by Decision Research for Nevada Nuclear Waste Project Office, Carson City, NV.

Slovic, P., M. Layman and J. Flynn (1991). Risk perception, trust and nuclear waste: Lessons from Yucca mountain. *Environment* 33, 6–11, 28–30.

Susskind, L., and J. Cruikshank (1987). *Breaking the Impasse*, Basic Books, New York.

Swallow, S., J. Opaluch and T. Weaver (1992). Siting noxious facilities: An approach that integrates technical, economic and political considerations. *Land Econom.* 68(3), 283–301.

Turnquist, M.A., and K.G. Zografos (eds.) (1991). Transportation of Hazardous Materials. *Transportation Sci.* Spec. Iss. 25(2), May.

U.S. Council on Environmental Quality (1980). *Public Opinion on Environmental Issues: Results of a National Public Opinion Survey*, Washington, DC.

Verhovek, S. (1991). Judge delays toxic dump town wants. *New York Times*, September 18, B1, B4.

Von Winterfeldt, D. (1987). Value tree analysis, in: P.R. Kleindorfer, and H.C. Kunreuther (eds.), *From Seveso to Bhopal: Managing and Insuring Hazardous Risks*, Springer-Verlag, Berlin, Chapter 11.

Von Winterfeldt, D., and W. Edwards (1984). Patterns of conflict about risky technologies. *Risk Analysis* 4(1), 55–68.

Von Winterfeldt, D., and W. Edwards (1986). *Decision Analysis and Behavioral Research*, Cambridge University Press, Cambridge.

Watabe, A. (1991). Liability rules and hazardous materials transportation. *Transportation Sci.* 25(2), 157–168.

Weinberg, A.M. (1972). Science and trans-science. *Minerva* 10, 209–222.

Whitehead, B. (1991). Who gave you the right? Mimeo, J.F. Kennedy School of Government, Harvard University, Cambridge, MA.

Wilson, D.C. (1981). *Waste Management: Planning, Evaluation and Technology*, Clarendon Press, Oxford.

Yagar, S. (1984). *Transport Risk Assessment*, University of Waterloo Press, Waterloo, Ont.

Zeiss, C. (1991). Community decision-making and impact management priorities for siting waste facilities. *Environmental Impact Assessment Rev.* 11, 231–255.

S.M. Pollock et al., Eds., *Handbooks in OR & MS, Vol. 6*

Chapter 12

Estimation and Management of Health and Safety Risks

Lester B. Lave

Carnegie-Mellon University, Schenly Park, Pittsburgh, PA 15213, U.S.A.

1. Introduction

Until recently, companies neglected health, safety, and environmental risks. While managers care about the safety of their workers and the quality of the environment, they tended not to think of these effects and the company bore little or none of the consequences of their actions. If a worker was injured in a coal mine, there was another waiting for the job. If the river became polluted, those downstream could worry about it. The company could curse the poor quality of water it received while neglecting the water pollution it discharged. Largely as a result of these effects being 'external' to the firm, there were no systematic methods developed to treat them, even when they impacted the firm.

Managers are not monsters, but there are many issues competing for their attention. If the only cost to the company is hiring a replacement worker, the company is likely to place a lower value on preventing injury than if they knew a fatality would cost the company several million dollars. When the company is run by competent managers, placing a low value on injury prevention will lead to more injuries.

To achieve public desires for lower health and safety risks and to lower needless costs, a more systematic approach is needed to estimate and manage risks. The approach must sort out factors due to individual preferences, social preferences, externalities, and inept management. There are numerous disputes, such as about the nature of technology. I will identify the most important disputes and show their consequences. In the next section, I explore the nature of individual preferences and spillover effects. In the following two sections, I discuss the methods used to estimate risks qualitatively and quantitatively and then manage them. Following that will be a section illustrating the estimation and management of risks with several controversial examples. The final section is a conclusion.

1.1. Individual preferences regarding risk

Occasionally, some people decide to put their lives at risk for no purpose other than the thrill of risking their lives, as with Russian roulette. In contrast, even individuals who pursue dangerous sports seek equipment that increases their safety, e.g., safer bindings for skiers. Thus, with an occasional exception, needless health and safety risks are undesirable, and often unintended consequences of activities [Fischhoff, Lichtenstein, Slovic, Derby & Keeney, 1981]. The person killed in an auto crash sought to get to his destination faster, and may even have desired the thrill of speed, but did not want a crash. The plant spewing toxic chemicals into the environment is disposing of the material at least (private) cost; the plant manager regrets any health risks or environmental degradation that results. Human activities, including all production and consumption activities, generate increased health and safety risks as an undesired side effect. Especially in the past two decades and for those with high income, people throughout the world have been willing to give up desired activities and consumption in order to lower risks.

Often the risks are personal and their consequences known, at least qualitatively. For example, deciding to drive in a snow storm or dense fog is known to the driver and other occupants to increase the risk of property damage, injury, and even death. Although they might protest that they did not know precisely how dangerous was the behavior, occupants certainly knew that it was more dangerous than driving on a sunny, dry day. For example, driving between 2 and 3 AM Sunday morning is 140 times more dangerous per person–mile than driving between 11 AM and noon [Schwing & Kamerud, 1988].

When the risks are personal and the consequences are known, society generally allows each individual to make a personal decision. Often society will attempt to provide additional information and regulate the safety of a product (such as an automobile or powered mower), but the decision is fundamentally personal. Not everyone agrees that the decision ought to be personal, as explored below.

Some decisions involve risks to others, often where the risks are so diffuse that there is no way to identify the individual who will be harmed. For example, the sulfur dioxide emitted by a coal burning electricity generation plant likely will damage the environment and human health [Lave & Seskin, 1970, 1977; Lave & Upton, 1988]. But who is damaged and the extent of damage are unknown. In some instances, the victims are known after the trauma, e.g., a vehicle crash; in cases such as air pollution, the victims may never be known.

People tend to assign lower value to 'statistical lives' than to identified ones [Schelling, 1968]. If Baby Jane falls into an abandoned mine, society will go to great lengths to rescue her, even after it is likely she has died. The public is adamant, although somewhat less so, when an automobile model has a safety defect. Although no one knows who will be injured or killed, there is certainty that someone will be and we will know who the victim was when the inevitable crash occurs. One stage more removed from Baby Jane is exposure to some environmental toxicant, where there is uncertainty both about how many (or even whether) people will be injured and we will never know whether anyone ever was injured. For example, exposure to radon in buildings can lead to lung cancer, but there is no way of knowing whether a particular victim got the cancer from radon exposure.

When the production or consumption decisions of Jones impose risk on Smith, without Smith's consent, there is an 'externality'. Unless something is done to force Jones to get Smith's consent or to take account of the risks to Smith, in optimizing his personal decisions, Jones will not be optimizing society's decision. The most direct way to internalize the externality is to require Jones to get Smith's permission before the production or consumption can take place. Jones might, for example, change the production or consumption process to remove, or at least decrease, the risk to Smith. Or Jones might get Smith to accept the increased risk by compensating Smith, who can then take other actions to lower other risks or increase her consumption.

One indirect way of internalizing the risk is to proscribe inherently dangerous activities, e.g., keeping Siberian tigers in your back yard or shooting firearms on the street. For some inherently dangerous activities, the law allows the individual to engage in them, but warns that the owner does so at his own risk. For ordinary activities, such as operating an automobile, someone who is injured must first prove that my car caused the injury and then prove that I was operating the car in an unsafe fashion. For an inherently dangerous activity, such as keeping tigers in my backyard, a victim need merely prove that he was injured by the tigers; the law assumes that having the tigers is inherently unsafe. This doctrine of 'strict liability' warns the individual keeping tigers in his yard that he must pay for any damage the tigers do, without the need for the victim to prove that the risk was unreasonable [Baram, 1982].

Another indirect way to lower risk is to 'regulate' the way in which activities can be conducted. For example, automobiles must be manufactured with seat belts, steel mills must have air pollution control equipment, and automobile occupants must wear seat belts [Evans, 1990; Graham, 1988]. Until recently, most Americans did not want the government to tell them what they must or must not do. They believed that workers and consumers should be vigilant in protecting their own interests.

During this century, particularly during the past two decades, the public has become more conscious of health and safety risks and increasingly has sought to reduce them. The result has been myriad new regulations of health and safety risks [Asch, 1988]. Regulators have banned some products, e.g., three-wheeled all terrain vehicles and asbestos insulation. They have changed the design of other products, such as the distance between slats in baby cribs and the design of automobile dash boards to eliminate protruding objects and cushion hard surfaces. They have banned production facilities, such as beehive coke ovens. Regulations are rarely cost-effective; for example, EPA and the Nuclear Regulatory Commission have tightened standards for public exposure to the nuclear fuel cycle at great cost while all but ignoring large exposures to radon in buildings, even though exposure could be reduced more cheaply by focusing on radon [Marnicio, 1982].

2. Setting safety goals

Managing health and safety risks requires answering the question: 'How Safe Is Safe Enough?' Either a quantitative safety goal or a process is required. If the goal is vague, decision makers will be inconsistent. Since the previous section points out inconsistencies in health and safety regulation, we can infer that, in general, quantitative safety goals do not exist and that the processes are ill-specified.

Congress has hesitated to set quantitative safety goals. For example, the Food, Drug and Cosmetic Act directs FDA to ban 'unreasonable risks'. Who can argue that 'unreasonable' risks should be tolerated? The problem is that what is unreasonable will depend on the individual, circumstances, and the time. For example, guidelines for tolerable concentrations of toxic substances in the work place have continually been lowered during the past fifty years; almost all of these guidelines are considered insufficiently stringent to serve as guidelines for public exposure. A vague injunction such as banning unreasonable risks gives great flexibility to Congress and the agency; there is little they must do and little they are banned from doing. This approach seems designed to protect Congress against criticism rather than to provide concrete guidance to the FDA as to how the agency is to act.

In contrast to Congress, several regulatory agencies have decided they would manage risks better if they have quantitative safety goals. Unfortunately, there is no agreement among agencies. As shown in Table 1, safety goals for protecting the public from cancer vary by a factor of 600. Using risk analysis methods that they considered to be conservative, the FDA decided that a risk of less than one additional cancer per one million individuals exposed constituted a trivial risk. FDA determined that so small a risk is beneath their notice.

The U.S. Environmental Protection Agency [1989] went through a rule making process, asking for public comment, to set a safety goal. They proposed four possible rules: (1) a goal of no more than one additional cancer per million individuals exposed, (2) a goal of no more than one additional cancer per 10 000 individuals exposed, (3) a goal of no more than one additional cancer per year among those at risk, and (4) no quantitative standard. After sifting through public comment, EPA embraced all four rules. The agency said that they would like to reduce cancer risks to one in one million, but that was not presently possible. They said that, ordinarily, they would act on risks greater than one in ten thousand. They also said that, ordinarily, they would act in cases where more than one additional cancer each year was expected. Finally, they said that none of these standards would prevent EPA from acting as they deemed necessary in specific

Table 1
Agency risk goals

Agency	Cancers per 1 million lifetimes
FDA	1
EPA	1–100
Nuclear Regulatory Commission	300–600
California Proposition 65	10

Table 2
Expected deaths among one million Americans

Cancer deaths	190 000
Cancer incidence	300 000
FDA risk goal	300 001
Total deaths	1 000 000

cases. In other words, the EPA rule provides little or no guidance to individuals and companies.

The Nuclear Regulatory Commission set a safety standard that the mortality rate increase no more than 0.1% among the population living around a nuclear reactor. This goal was based on the lowest population death rate, that for young girls. This goal is equivalent to about 300–600 deaths per million people exposed. Thus, the NRC goal is less safe than even the EPA's proposal of one death in 10 000.

The California agency implementing Proposition 65 has set a safety level of one in 100 000.

Only one of these safety levels is offered with any justification: the NRC goal related to the lowest death rate observed among any group in the population. All the other goals are expected to be intuitively appealing.

Byrd & Lave [1987] and Cross, Byrd & Lave [1991] have proposed that a risk be deemed 'trivial' if it could not be observed in an epidemiology study. They argue that a risk that society could never be sure exists is trivial.

One way to put these safety goals into perspective is shown in Table 2. Consider one million Americans born in 1992. Eventually, all of them will die. The only questions are when they will die and from what they will die. About 30–35% of them will be expected to have cancer and about 19% can be expected to die of cancer. Thus, the FDA considers that increasing the number of cancers from 300 000 to 300 001 would be a trivial increase.

Doll & Peto [1981] estimate that about 1/3 of cancers are due to cigarette smoking and 1/3 to diet. Environmental exposure to carcinogens causes perhaps 1–2% of cancers. Certainly, there is a good deal of judgment in the Doll and Peto estimates. However, they are remarkably similar to estimates based on toxicology [Gough, 1988]. Gough also finds that EPA would be able to regulate away less than 1% of cancers [1990].

Americans could reduce their likelihood of getting cancer by more than 50% just by not smoking and eating a more healthful diet. Government actions to discourage smoking and limit exposure of nonsmokers to cigarette smoke have probably prevented more cancers than all of the environmental regulation of toxic chemicals. While the government can undertake actions that would lower cancer incidence from 350 000 per million Americans to perhaps half that level, I am baffled by why there are so many resources and so much attention is being devoted to toxic chemicals in the environment and so little to smoking cessation and improving diet.

These facts have not been ignored by the health professionals. Public health and other health professionals lobby for smoking cessation. The U.S. National Cancer Institute [1986] has set a goal of halving the number of cancer deaths in the USA by the end of the century. Their report focuses on smoking prevention and changing diet; environmental carcinogens are not even mentioned. While the misallocation of resources is not as bad as a decade ago, it is still shameful.

By using a safety goal of no more than one additional cancer per million people, FDA is wasting resources and misleading the public. Even a safety goal three orders of magnitude less stringent is likely to be lost in the noise of individual habits and exposures. Good management calls for focusing on the most important risks and using cost-effectiveness in managing them. This does not mean that carcinogenic chemicals in the environment should be forgotten, but it does mean that EPA Administrator O'Reilly was correct is asking Congress for the ability to shift EPA resources toward more cost-effective programs.

3. Methods for estimating health and safety risks

The archetypical safety risk is one where a healthy individual is subject to a traumatic event that causes injury or death, e.g., a highway crash. These safety risks can also include acute health risks such as exposure to an acutely toxic chemical, such as methyl-isocyinate in Bhopal. In contrast, chronic health risks result from long term exposure to a toxic agent, even where there is little or no immediate indication of harm. For example, women who painted radium on watch faces to make them glow in the dark were at high risk for bone cancer two or more decades later. The acute versus chronic nature of the risks leads to quite different methods for identifying the qualitative and quantitative risks.

3.1. Safety risks

Trauma occurs when the normal operation of a system fails, resulting in an undesired event, e.g., a car crash or boiler explosion. Risk analysts attempt to discover the consequences of various deviations from normal operation and the causes of the deviations.

3.1.1. Investigation of individual crashes
Crash investigators examine undesired events to discover their cause. For example, The National Safety Transportation Board (NTSB) investigates all aircraft, train, and commercial bus crashes. The investigation team attempts to determine the cause of the crash and what might have prevented it. For aircraft crashes, the most frequent cause is pilot error, although often new procedures and instruments will be prescribed to avoid this situation or to prevent future crashes in this situation, e.g., radar that automatically warns a pilot that another aircraft is near.

Just as the NTSB attempts to determine the causes of air crashes, so police attempt to determine the causes of fatal highway crashes. For example, the National Highway Transportation Safety Administration gathers data on all fatal automobile crashes (the Fatal Accident Reporting System (FARS)) and a sample of nonfatal automobile crashes (National Accident Severity System (NASS)) to determine the causes and describe the crash. The methods used tend to be informal, based on experience. After a fatal crash, the investigator attempts to determine speed, weather and other environmental conditions, experience and other attributes of the driver, and possible failure of some mechanical part or system.

3.1.2. Statistical analysis of crashes

A more systematic investigation of crashes involves statistical analysis of data bases tabulating individual crashes, e.g., the FARS and NASS data [Evans, 1990]. These statistical investigations seek factors that are common to many crashes. Unlike the investigation of individual crashes, these statistical endeavors attempt to quantify the affects of a given risk factor, such as a driver having a high level of alcohol in his blood.

One difficulty with investigating individual crashes is that there is little or no ability to discover patterns and subtle or contributing causes. The NTSB seeks to discover the cause of each crash and how to prevent it. There is no mechanism for seeing that one cause is common and another rare; thus, there is no way to focus prevention efforts on the common causes.

Unless there are data on the underlying incidence of causes, the statistical analysis has difficulty in isolating the conditions of concern [Evans, 1990]. For example, suppose the FARS data showed that 100 drivers over age 69 were killed in night crashes. If older drivers were as likely to be on the road at night as during the day, this result would have no significance. However, if only 400 older drivers had been out on the road at night during this period, the statistic would imply that older drivers are at extraordinarily high risk when they drive at night. Evans develops extraordinarily clever ways to utilize data where the population at risk is not known. For example, to estimate whether women are more likely than men to be killed in a crash of equal force, he selects crashes in which either a driver, passenger or both were killed. For crashes with female drivers and male passengers, he calculates the ratio of killed drivers to killed passengers. He calculates the same ratio for male drivers and male passengers. In dividing the first ratio by the second, he derives an estimate of the fatality risk to female relative to males, controlling for driving frequency and speed.

3.1.3. Event-tree and fault-tree analyses

In contrast to these two methods used to determine the cause of a crash, event-tree and fault-tree analyses seek to estimate factors leading to a crash before it occurs [Linneroth-Bayer & Wahlstrom, 1991]. For example, Rasmussen and colleagues attempted to isolate all causes of failure in the operation of a nuclear power reactor that would result in immediate or later injury to workers or the public [Rasmussen, 1981; U.S. Nuclear Regulatory Commission, 1975]. They first identified the events that would release a large amount of radioactive material from its prescribed location in the reactor, those that would breach the containment vessel for the reactor, and those that would scatter millions of curies of radioactivity to the environment.

A key event is allowing the reactor core to overheat to the point of melting, which frees the radioactive fuel from the fuel rods and core, releases hydrogen and leads to elevated pressure that might rupture containment or produce a chemical explosion. This event might be caused by operator error, a break in a cooling pipe, pump failure, sabotage, a flood, an earthquake, etc.

The next step was to isolate the events that would lead to core melt, such as loss of coolant because of the rupture of a major steam line. The possible causes of rupture of a major steam line were investigated, etc. The investigation identified the types of failure that could lead to breaching containment and the individual events that might cause them. For each sequence, the analysis attempted to identify the probability that this sequence would occur. For example, if failure of a coolant pump caused one sequence, Rasmussen and colleagues attempted to estimate the probability that this pump would fail.

The next step was to investigate each of the sequences to find ways to lower the probability of the undesired occurrence. For example, if pump failure caused core melt with a high probability, a backup pump could be installed to take over in case of failure of the primary pump. If loss of power to the control room caused core melt, a backup power system could be installed that was independent of the primary system and not subject to the same causes of failure.

The Reactor Safety Study proved to be extremely controversial [U.S. Nuclear Regulatory Commission, 1975]. Critics disagreed with the failure probabilities assigned to individual components, e.g., cooling pumps, claimed that some failure modes had not been identified or analyzed, e.g., fire due to a technician inspecting wiring with a candle, and claimed that safety had been overestimated due to 'common mode' failure. The painstaking process of specifying each event sequence leading to catastrophe and estimating the likelihood of each event is extraordinarily difficult and inherently arbitrary.

The major complaint has been that common-mode failure was not handled adequately. Reactors achieve high reliability by having backup systems, e.g., a second cooling pump. If each pump has a daily failure probability of 10^{-5}, the probability of both failing together is 10^{-10}, assuming their failure probabilities are independent. However, if the event that causes the primary pump to fail also causes the secondary pump to fail, the probability of both failing is not much greater than 10^{-5}. For example, if the voltage is so high that it burns out the first pump, it will also burn out the backup pump.

Additional operating experience has allowed the accumulation of operating data that quantifies the failure rate of components and the identification of some neglected paths. However, new components will have different failure rates or change the failure probabilities of other system components. Experience and systematic thought has identified common mode failures, from a defective batch of steel leading to the failure of several components, to floods and earthquakes that cause multiple failures. Nonetheless, identifying extremely infrequent failures before they occur is inherently difficult.

It may not be possible to engineer complicated systems that have failure rates of 10^{-5} per year or smaller. For example, Perrow [1984] argues that large, tightly coupled systems are inherently subject to high failure rates because of the interconnections. If Perrow is correct and there was a significant increase in the size or tight-connectedness of industrial facilities, there should be an increase in the proportion of losses in catastrophic events, compared to minor mishaps. From 1974 through 1988, Wulff [1991] found no increase in the proportion of fire loss due to the ten largest fires, implying that both major and minor fire losses seem to be increasing in proportion.

Even if systems could be built that are this safe, it may not be possible to demonstrate their safety, even if millions of years of operating experience can be accumulated. Equipment is constantly being modified to take advantage of new materials, new designs, and new manufacturing processes. Even small differences in components change their reliability. Thus, even if a new model is designed to fail no more often than once every million hours, rather than 10^5 hours for previous models, there may never be sufficient experience with this model to demonstrate the level of reliability has increased.

For example, Resendiz-Carrillo & Lave [1987] attempt to estimate the like-lihood of a flood that would cause catastrophic failure of a dam. The event is believed to have less than a 1/10 000 likelihood of occurring each year. Unfortunately, for U.S. locations, less than 100 years of data are available on the largest flood each year. Alternative, equally plausible, functional forms for the frequency distribution give return periods that differ by several orders of magnitude. It is hardly surprising that a 10 000 year event cannot be estimated with confidence from 67 years of data. However, the return period for all the functional forms is greater than 10 000 years. Thus, contrary to expert judgment, the design safety criterion appears to be satisfied for this dam and no safety improvements were required.

3.2. Health risks

Isolating the causes of chronic disease is inherently more difficult than identifying the cause of a traumatic event. The chronic disease is caused by exposure over a long period of time. Myriad insults, or the interaction among insults, might be the cause or aggravating factors.

3.2.1. Epidemiology: analysis of disease incidence

Until recently, the principal approach to identifying toxic agents has been the analysis of disease incidence [Schottenfeld & Fraumani, in press]. Most investigations have been informal attempts to identify the cause in a particular case. More formal statistical studies include (1) cohort analysis of the experience of a group from the beginning of their exposure, (2) case control analysis where the prior exposures of those with the disease are compared to the prior exposures of a sample of people who do not have the disease, and (3) statistical analysis of existing data to search for common factors.

Case control studies rely on a statistical comparison of a group of individuals who manifest the disease with a group of controls. The method assumes the two groups are comparable, save for the fact that one group has the disease and for the exposures that caused the disease. However, the analysis could reveal many differences between the two groups unrelated to the cause of the disease. For example, if the control group were from a different area, there might be lifestyle differences related to the different areas, but not to the disease. A careful analysis done by a master can reveal the causes of rare diseases, but a less careful analysis can lead to entirely erroneous results, such as that coffee causes prostate cancer.

Epidemiologists are inherently suspicious of statistical analyses of existing data. A data set with several diseases and many measures of exposure will have many statistically significant associations. Are these chance associations or do they indicate a causal effect? Epidemiologists point out that the analysis can discover associations, but cannot prove cause and effect. The statistical analysis can control for some of the factors that might lead to an increase in cancer incidence, but often they do not control for important personal habits, such as smoking.

A cohort study begins by enrolling a population before they are exposed to an environmental insult. For example, a famous study of steelworkers used all workers who were hired after a specified date [Mazumdar, Redmond, Sollecito & Sussman, 1975]. This study followed the workers for decades, attempting to discover which workers died and what they died of. Since tens of thousands of workers were enrolled and the study went on for decades, the study was expensive and a management nightmare. Furthermore, to make comparisons, cohort studies require a control population that is similar to the study population, except that they are not exposed to the agents of interest. For example, the control population for an occupational study must be a group of other workers, since workers are known to be healthier than the average person in the community (the 'healthy worker' effect).

Cohort studies are inherently time consuming and expensive. A large number of people must be enrolled in the study. These individuals must be followed over time, sometimes for several decades for a chronic disease. Heroic efforts are needed to locate individuals who leave the area so that few, if any, are lost to the study. To locate individuals lost to the study, death certificates throughout the United States must be examined, an exhausting, expensive process. If cause of death is the end point of interest, care is needed that cause of death was determined with care, by autopsy if possible.

Even when all of these conditions are fulfilled, the study may be worthless if the researchers have not identified, and measured, important confounding variables. For example, the study of coke oven workers found that cancer, particularly of the respiratory system, was the end point of interest [Mazumdar, Redmond, Sollecito & Sussman, 1975]. However, the study was not able to get data on the smoking habits of the coke oven workers. Gathering data on individuals is sufficiently expensive that studies rarely select a control group and follow them. Instead, they use disease incidence rates from a comparison group. However, the group used can be noncomparable in subtle ways. Many studies that use the general population as the control group find that exposure to toxic substances results in lower cardiovascular disease and cancer death rates — they are simply rediscovering the healthy worker effect.

Epidemiology research is inherently difficult, time consuming, and expensive. Epidemiologists are continually attempting to infer exposures, sometimes 40 years in the past. For example, exposure to asbestos among shipyard workers from 1940 to 1945 has been shown to elevate the risk of lung cancer, but no measurements were taken of worker exposure [Mossman, Bignon, Corn, Seaton & Gee, 1990; Royal Commission, 1984; Weill & Hughes, 1986]. When the chronic disease essentially never occurs in the absence of a particular toxicant, e.g., angiosarcoma of the liver from vinyl chloride monomer [Doniger, 1978], isolating the cause is much easier than if the disease can be caused by multiple toxicants, e.g., lung cancer might be caused by cigarette smoke, radon, asbestos — even by someone else's cigarette smoke [Greenberg, Bauman, Stretch, Keyes, Glover, Haley, Stedman & Loda, 1991; Stone, 1992].

The differences in genetic susceptibility among individuals, differences in lifestyles and consumption habits and differences in exposure to myriad toxicants mean that relatively large samples are required in order to draw a confident conclusion. The result is that only about three dozen substances have been shown to be human carcinogens by epidemiologists [IARC]. The current emphasis on prevention means that suspected carcinogens are banned or exposures are minimized; as a result epidemiologists may not ever be able to demonstrate that a new agent has caused cancer in humans.

3.2.2. Toxicology

Toxicology is the science studying poisons. The father of toxicology, Paracelsus, wrote that any substance is toxic in high enough doses and no substance is a poison in a sufficiently small dose [Gallo, Gochfeld & Goldstein, 1987]. Thus, toxicology is focused on finding the nature of the health effects and at what dose they occur.

Toxicology is a laboratory based science, examining the effects of chemicals on rodents or other laboratory animals in order to develop animal models for the human effects. In some cases the models are extremely simple, as with the assumption that any substance causing an increase in tumors (benign or malignant) in a mammalian species should be regarded as a human carcinogen. However, the simple models are generally inadequate and must be replaced by more complicated ones as the mechanisms of action become known. For example, d-limonene is a chemical that gives lemons their special flavor. It causes kidney tumors in male rats [Detrich & Swenberg, 1991]. But toxicologists were surprised that it did not cause tumors in female rats or other rodents. D-limonene has great health and economic significance since it is used in almost all soft drinks, in many other foods, and large quantities of citrus fruit with d-limonene are consumed by people. An intensive investigation revealed that the male rat has a hormone that reacts with d-limonene to produce a carcinogen. Since the female rat, mouse, and human do not have this hormone, there is no evidence that d-limonene would be carcinogenic in humans.

The classic National Toxicology Program rodent cancer bioassay is a relatively simple test. Sixteen groups of 50 animals are used: both sexes of two rodent species (usually rats and mice) exposed at the maximum tolerated dose, 1/2 the MTD, 1/4 the MTD, and the control group at zero dose. The animals are exposed to the test chemical beginning a few weeks after weaning and for the next 50 weeks, at which time they are sacrificed. An extensive pathological examination is made of each animal to determine if there are tumors. The test attempts to determine if there are more tumors in the test animals than in the controls. The biological plausibility of the results are the primary basis for accepting or rejecting statistically significant results. For example, do the number of tumors rise with the dose?

This lifetime rodent bioassay has been the focus of much criticism [Ames and Gold, 1990; Lave & Omenn, 1986; Lave, Ennever, Rosenkranz & Omenn, 1988]. Ames charges that using the MTD results in promotion of cancer, leading to a result different than would be obtained if lower doses, such as those experienced by humans, were used. Lave, Ennever, Rosenkranz & Omenn argue that the test is not likely to predict human carcinogenicity better than much less expensive and time consuming in vitro tests. Salsburg [1977] charges that the method of analysis overstates the statistical significance of the tests, leading to the conclusion that most chemicals tested give rise to a 'statistically significant' increase in tumors.

The two largest challenges in toxicology are: (1) devising an animal model that will predict human responses, and (2) predicting human responses at low doses from those at high doses. Both challenges require knowing the mechanisms of action, the way the chemicals are metabolized and detoxified, and the way the chemicals arrive at the target organ. Great progress has been made in toxicology during the last decade with regard to carcinogenesis. Toxicologists now routinely examine pharmacokinetics and mechanisms of action rather than just counting tumors in the rodents. They are willing to classify some chemicals as rodent carcinogens, but comment that they are not likely to be human carcinogens. Methods now exit to determine that some chemicals have thresholds in causing cancer.

3.2.3. Carcinogenic risk analysis

In contrast to the analysis of what caused existing diseases, carcinogenic risk analysis attempts to determine the causes of cancer and prevent it by removing or decreasing exposure [Travis, 1988]. For example, ionizing radiation is a known human carcinogen [National Research Council, 1980, 1988]. Carcinogenic risk analysis attempts to estimate the incidence of cancer that would be expected from low levels of exposure.

Prevention requires determining which agents are likely to be human carcinogens and then preventing or at least mitigating exposure. Thus, toxicologists work with in vivo and in vitro test systems to discover probable human carcinogens.

Because of its preventive nature, risk analysis relies more on toxicology with its animal experiments and analysis of chemical structure than on epidemiology with its analysis of the incidence of disease in humans. In the past decade, toxicology has taken over from epidemiology the principal role of identifying possible risks to humans [National Research Council, 1983].

While there are many charges and countercharges, the preventive approach is firmly anchored in current regulation. No one wants to return to the 'bad old days' when carcinogenicity was discovered by counting human cancers. However, current analysis involves needless controversy.

For example, the approaches of epidemiology, in vivo and in vitro testing, and analysis of the structure of the chemicals should not be thought of as competitors. Rather, they are different approaches that each have their comparative advantage. Test strategies need to identify the comparative advantages of each approach and to use each appropriately [Lave & Omenn, 1986].

Although risk analysis was designed to be conservative, to overstate risk, there is no proof that it does so in all cases. Bailar, Crouch, Shaikh & Spiegelman [1989] find data indicating that risks analysis is not necessarily conservative. Graham, Green & Roberts [1988] explore many of the conservative biases in risk analysis showing that often risk analysis would be expected to overstate the risk by several orders of magnitude. However, no one can guarantee that risk analysis is biased to showing greater risk in each case.

4. Risk management tools

A fundamental question to be answered is whether the goal is to reduce risks or to optimize them. The former is much easier than the latter. However, attempting to reduce all risks makes no sense. All activities involve risk. Lowering all risks in a setting can only be done at the cost of eliminating the activity or spending inordinate amounts of resources, e.g., eliminating carcinogens from the food supply.

In some cases, Congress enacted legislation that seeks to lower risks, no matter what costs are incurred, e.g., the Delaney Clause in the Food, Drug, and Cosmetic Act bans adding carcinogens to food [Lave, 1981]. More generally, Congress has written statutes that ask for some balancing of the costs and benefits of risk reduction, e.g., the Federal Insecticide, Fungicide, and Rodenticide Act that instructs EPA to balance the good of a pesticide against its harm. Risk analysis is the primary mechanism for quantifying risk and therefore is a necessary step in optimizing safety.

Even when, as in the Delaney Clause, Congress desires only the reduction of risk, no matter what the consequences, the analysis is difficult. For example, some essential nutrients are also carcinogens [Scheuplein, 1990]. The current theory of carcinogenicity is that even a single molecule of a carcinogen conveys a tiny risk of developing cancer. Thus, for a region where these nutrients were absent from the diet, the Delaney Clause would prevent adding them to food, with the probable result being a serious increase in disease or death. [See also Moolgavkar & Knudson, 1981.]

A more general example concerns the use of fungicides, all of which are toxic to some degree. Spraying fungicides on grain conveys some risk to the consumer but helps to prevent the development of some fungi that produce carcinogens.

Still another example is that construction has a high injury and death rate. Thus increasing the amount of construction in order to increase a facility's safety has the effect of increasing the injury and death of workers. Thus, major construction that would lower risk by a tiny amount can be calculated to reduce net safety, since the increased injury and death of workers will more than outweigh the tiny increase in safety.

In one of his first official acts, President Reagan promulgated Executive Order 12291 requiring regulatory agencies to estimate the costs and benefits of proposed major regulations. For all regulations involving risk, the executive order requires quantification of the risk increase or reduction along with the other benefits and costs. Even if it can only be done crudely, risk optimization is the goal.

4.1. Design standards

If a press can crush the arms of the operator, an obvious remedy is to require a design change to prevent the trauma [Baram, 1982]. For example, the press can be fitted with a switch that does not permit the press to close until both hands of the operator are on the switch. When individuals who have worked as safety consultants or worked for firms making safety equipment become regulators, they are tempted to specify the solution in the regulation. If a GT model 407b switch will stop the operator from being injured, why not require it to be used?

Design standards are the norm for environmental regulation. Congress ordered EPA to set technology standards for the 'best available control technology', etc. In general EPA specifies a particular technology, thus setting a design standard.

Design standards often are not efficient or effective. A cheaper switch might fulfill the same function or a guard that pushes the operator's hand out of the press might be as effective but be cheaper or lead to less productivity loss. Even for design standards that are efficient at the time they are promulgated, technological progress is likely to produce more efficient solutions in response to this stated need.

Design standards are inflexible; the standard must be changed whenever there is a new technology. Perhaps the most important point is that there are dozens of different types of presses and types of applications. No one solution is likely to work well in all applications. If so, a design standard that works well in one circumstance will be ineffective or inefficient in another.

Design standards appear to be simple and direct, with little need for arguing about the details. However, often the argument about the detail is necessary to discover the best current solution and to allow new solutions to emerge.

4.2. Performance standards

Performance standards specify what is to be accomplished and leave it to the individual responsible for compliance to come up with a solution. For example, a design standard might require the press to be designed so that it prevents injury to the operator's hands. How that is done is up to the designer. As another example, the National Highway Transportation Safety Administration required that occupants of automobiles must be protected in crashes without having to buckle their seat belts [Graham, 1988]. Auto manufacturers then came up with several ways to meet the standard, including air bags, seat belts on a motorized system in the ceiling, and fixed passive belts. There has been great controversy about the effectiveness, cost, and potential dangers of each system, but the standard spurred a search for superior technology that a design standard, such as an air bag requirement, would have cut off.

Occasionally, EPA has set performance rather than design (technology) standards. For example, the New Source Performance Standard was specified to be emissions of no more than 1.2 pounds of sulfur dioxide per one-million btu of energy from coal. This performance standard allowed utilities the flexibility to select low sulfur coal, cofiring, or other options instead of flue gas desulfurization.

Performance standards give more flexibility to producers. In doing so, they enable producers to achieve the standards at lower cost. For example, Tietenberg [1992, p. 403] estimates substantial difference in implementation cost between design (technology based) and performance standards.

The problem with performance standards is that the regulators have to specify precisely the outcome they desire. For example, the National Ambient Air Quality Standards specify that the concentration of sulfur dioxide cannot exceed a certain level. The cheapest way of meeting this standard in many cases is to build a tall stack to carry away the sulfur emissions. The tall stack ensures that the sulfur will not reach ground level in the immediate area, and so the performance standard is satisfied. However, tall stacks turn a local problem into a regional problem [Raufer & Feldman, 1987; Regens & Rycroft, 1988]. They send the sulfur oxides to other areas, allow the sulfur to remain in the atmosphere longer so that it is transformed into sulfates, and do nothing to decrease the sulfur loading in the atmosphere. The performance standard worked, but it created a problem that might be worse than the one it sought to alleviate.

4.3. Regulatory frameworks

Health and safety issues are highly emotional ones [Efron, 1984; Epstein, 1978; Fischhoff, 1981; National Research Council, 1989b; Whelan, 1985]. When Congress has attempted to grapple with food safety or toxic substances in the environment, it has found itself in 'no win' debates [Consumers Research, 1989; Merrill, 1978; Miller & Skinner, 1984]. On the one hand, health and safety advocates demand stringent standards. On the other hand, manufacturers claim that it is not feasible to achieve the most stringent standards and that moderately stringent standards are expensive to attain. Manufacturers may also point out that regulation is not cost-effective, with vast resources being devoted to one area, such as toxic waste dumps, while almost no resources go to much more important environmental problems, such as radon in buildings [U.S. Environmental Protection Agency, 1987, 1990].

Congress has learned that it cannot please the advocates on either side, or hope to educate the public quickly about the nature of the tradeoffs and uncertainties. Consequently, Congress typically charges a regulatory agency with responsibility for handling a problem, but often withholds a large part of the authority necessary to accomplish the task. More importantly, Congress enacts legislation with contradictory instructions to the regulatory agency. For example, the Occupational Safety and Health Administration is charged with protecting the worker over his or her working lifetime so that there is no diminution in function [Mendeloff, 1988]. OSHA is also charged with not promulgating regulations unless they are 'feasible' meaning feasible in both an economic and technical sense.

Congress can be seen as providing some rough guidelines to the regulator [Lave, 1981]. In particular, Congress has specified a number of frameworks for use in legislation. In choosing a framework for a particular bill, Congress is specifying how the regulatory agency is to act.

A first framework used by Congress is 'no risk'. For example, the Delaney Clause in the Food, Drug and Cosmetic Act instructs the FDA to ban any food additive that is a carcinogen. The instruction is clear, simple, and leaves no doubt about what Congress desired.

A second framework specified by Congress is 'risk–risk' analysis. When the FDA ponders whether to license a drug, they understand that almost all drugs have undesirable side effects in some people. Thus, almost all drugs pose a risk. However, there can be no benefit from the drug without taking the risk. Thus, the FDA examines the risk of taking the drug and attempts to balance that against the risk of not having access to the drug. Where death is likely to result without intervention, and where no less toxic drug is available, the FDA is willing to license known carcinogens, as for chemotherapy for cancer.

A third framework is 'technology based standards'. The language of the clean air and water pollution acts state that a company must install the 'best available control technology' (BACT), 'best practical technology' (BPT) or that its control technology must meet 'new source performance standards' (NSPS) or achieve the 'least achievable emissions rate' (LAER). None of the phrases can be taken literally; all involve a tradeoff between cost and level of control. For example, NSPS is more stringent than BACT but less stringent than LAER. Deciding among control technologies involves judgments about what tradeoff between control and costs is reasonable and what technologies are 'available'. BACT requires that the technology be demonstrated on a commercial scale — thus availability is not an issue. However, the tradeoff between control and cost is assumed to be at a reasonable level, i.e., it cannot cost ten times as much to get 1% additional control as it has cost to get the control up to this point. In contrast, LAER implies a willingness to spend much more to get additional control. The term also implies that the technology need not be fully proven at a commercial scale.

These technology based standards have put EPA and the Office of Management and Budget continually in conflict. EPA interprets the various phrases as implying more control while OMB interpret them as implying greater consciousness to cost. Congress has tended to stay out of the conflict, save for direct interventions in favor of some plant in a particular congressional district.

The fourth framework used by Congress is 'cost-effectiveness' analysis. This framework assumes that a goal is specified and instructs the regulatory agency to achieve this goal at least cost. This framework was refined for the military as a way of suboptimizing, given the defense mission. Having specified the defense mission, cost-effectiveness analysis is used to decide what mix of weapons systems will achieve this mission at least cost. The Nuclear Regulatory Commission has also used this framework in regulating exposures to ionizing radiation. 'As low as reasonably achievable' is interpreted to mean that companies should continue to abate exposure to ionizing radiation as long as the cost per rem averted is less than $1000 [Pochin, 1983].

The fifth framework is 'risk–benefit analysis' [Starr, 1969]. Congress asks the regulatory agency to weigh the benefits of a technology against its risks. The difference between the risk–benefit and risk–risk frameworks is that the latter includes only health risks while the former includes the whole ranges of benefits, rather than being limited to health. For example, a risk–benefit analysis of electricity generation would seek to weigh the additional risks to health against all of the benefits of having the electricity, from health benefits to greater enjoyment from television.

The sixth framework, 'benefit–cost analysis', attempts to evaluate the full social benefits and full social costs in deciding what regulatory action to take. Benefit–cost analysis differs from risk–benefit analysis by considering all the social costs, not just health costs. As noted above, Executive Order 12291 requires each agency to do a benefit–cost analysis of each 'major' regulation and to select the option with the greatest net benefit, unless precluded by law.

These frameworks are arrayed in terms of increasing difficulty in getting the data required for the analysis, in terms of the amount of analysis required, and in terms of the difficulty of required value judgments. The Delaney Clause is simple to apply, requires only one datum, and requires no value judgments from the regulatory agency. At the other end of the spectrum is benefit–cost analysis, which requires full scale analysis and quantification of every aspect of the decision. All of the aspects must not only be quantified, they must be translated into a common metric: dollars. Not only is the analysis difficult, it requires myriad value judgments about what is important and how much society values each aspect. Benefit–cost analysis is extremely difficult to do well. Even for the best analysis, differences in values can lead to opposite conclusions.

4.4. Nonregulatory alternatives

Scholars have long recognized that centralized command and control regulation (hereafter called simply 'regulation') is far from the perfect solution to complicated issues. Regulation is a blunt instrument. Formulating a new regulation takes years and thousands of professional work hours. Guarantees of due process mean that those with a stake in the issue can attempt to change the outcome; failing that, they can delay promulgation of the regulation and then delay its enforcement by legal and political challenges.

Regulation is not capable of optimizing nor is it capable of dealing with ' less important' issues — it is simply too costly and clumsy.

Recognition of these facts has tended to promote the search for nonregulatory alternatives, such as insurance or the legal system [Huber & Litan, 1991]. Each of these alternatives has received vast criticism for being inefficient, costly, or not getting at the central issues. While this criticism is true, often it is irrelevant. Regulation is also inefficient, costly, and often focuses on the wrong issues. What is relevant is finding which alternative or combination of alternatives manages to achieve the social goals best. In some cases, the legal system or arbitration is likely to lead to superior outcomes.

Labeling and the provision of information more generally are the focus of many efforts at increasing health and safety [Hadden, 1986; Viscusi & Magat, 1987]. For example, California's Proposition 65 requires that products be labeled if they present a nontrivial risk of cancer or birth defects [Roberts, 1989]. Alcoholic beverages and cigarettes contain prominent warnings. For these products, there is no adjustment that the manufacturer can make that will obviate the need for labeling. However, for other products manufacturers have changed the formulation of the product in order to avoid a warning label. For example, Gillette changed the formulation of Liquid Paper to eliminate a solvent that is a carcinogen. While there is controversy about the extent to which warning labels on cigarette and liquor containers deter consumption, there is no doubt that reformulating products lowers exposures.

The Occupational Safety and Health Administration has mandated labeling when carcinogenic chemicals are used; they require warning posters [Mendeloff, 1988]. Similarly, Congress inserted a provision in the Superfund Amendments and Reauthorization Act requiring plants to report their total discharges of more than 300 toxic chemicals each year. These reports are made available to the public and were the source of extensive media coverage. To avoid malpractice, physicians are advised to inform patients fully about the possible risks of a treatment regime. Numerous requirements have been established for informing people of health and safety risks directly or through labeling products. Although it is far from clear that all or even most people understand these warnings, they provide significant information.

4.4.1. Market incentives

Economists have discussed the use of market incentives to solve environmental problems for almost a century [Baumol & Oates, 1975; Pigou, 1920]. Particularly in the last two decades, economists have asserted that market incentives will speed compliance as well as lessening the cost [Hahn & Hester, 1989; Hahn & Hird, 1991; Kneese & Schultze, 1975; Stavins, 1988].

A particular market alternative that is receiving a great deal of attention is focused on improving enforcement. The use of 'market incentives' can simplify enforcement and even simplify setting the regulatory goals [Gruenspecht & Lave, 1991]. For example, a great deal of work has been done to relate the quantity of emissions of air pollutants to the resulting ambient air quality [Portney, 1990a,b].

A target air quality is set, this quality goal is then translated into a target emissions level. For standard regulation, current emission levels are estimated. Abatement targets are established and regulations are designed to reduce emissions to these targets.

For example, if current emissions are 500 and the target emissions level is 100, 80% abatement is required. A technology based standard could be specified to attain this abatement level. However, the emissions estimate might be wrong or the technologies might not give 80% abatement. An alternative approach would be to establish discharge licenses for emissions of 100. These discharge licenses could be sold or given to current polluters as a proportion of their emissions. Anyone emitting more than his discharge licenses would be shut down or given a large fine.

The advantage of the discharge licenses is that the regulators do not have to estimate current emissions levels or find what technology or regulations will reduce emissions an average of 80%. A second advantage should be ease of enforcement. Regulators can be challenged on their estimates of current emissions or their estimates about what regulations will achieve 80% abatement. These challenges make it less likely that a judge will insist that a polluter really adhere to the regulations or be forced to shutdown or pay a large fine. The use of discharge licenses chops two important, controversial steps from the regulatory process.

Similarly, if there is a determination that sulfur oxide emissions cost society $0.50 per pound, an effluent fee of $0.50 per pound could be set. No determination needs to be made of the inventory of current emissions or some target emissions goal set. Enforcement consists simply of measuring total sulfur oxide emissions from each polluter and charging $0.50 per pound.

The case for economic incentives is usually made on the ground that they are cost-effective, i.e., they provide the agreed upon amount of abatement at the lowest cost. For example, if the discharge license approach is taken, these discharge licenses can be bought and sold. The market determines the value of a license to discharge one pound of sulfur dioxide per day. If a firm can abate pollution for less than the cost of this discharge license, it will do so. If a firm cannot cover its costs, including the cost of the abatement and discharge license, it will go out of business and sell its discharge licenses. The system provides flexibility for firms to minimize their costs, given the emissions goals.

Similarly, effluent fees provide a strong incentive to provide the 'proper' (in the sense of least costly) level of emissions. Firms will abate emissions as long as that is the least cost means of lowering their costs, pay an effluent fee, or go out of business if the business is so marginal that it cannot cover its pollution control costs. At $500 per ton of sulfur dioxide, the typical coal burning utility would abate 90–95% of sulfur oxide emissions for this effluent fee, and pay the effluent fee for the remainder. At this effluent fee, some firms, such as old foundries, would cease to operate. In theory, this effluent fee would be efficient in the sense of producing the amount of pollution abatement at least cost.

Another current example is the use of effluent fees for reducing the production of CFCs [EPA]. In addition to legislation phasing out the production of CFCs,

Congress imposed a fee of about $1 per pound on the producer. The precise fee is related to the ozone destroying potential of each CFC [Orlando, 1990].

An example of the use of marketable discharge allowances is the 1990 Clean Air Act. In order to abate sulfur dioxide, an emissions limit is set for each electricity generation plant [Goldberg & Lave, 1992]. Plants that abate more than the target are allowed to sell the additional allowances to plants that have not abated the target amount. The result is additional flexibility that is estimated to lower the cost of abating sulfur dioxide by more than 20% compared to centralized command and control regulation.

5. Case studies of managing health and safety risks

To illustrate the frameworks, I develop two examples and then apply the concepts. One example is an accident where the effect is immediate. The other is a chronic disease where the effect does not occur for two or more decades after initial exposure.

5.1. Managing carcinogenic chemicals

As discussed above, toxic substances, particularly carcinogenic chemicals in food or the environment, have elicited great concern from Americans [Cross, Byrd & Lave, 1991; Lave & Upton, 1988]. In some context or at one time, Congress has used each of the decision frameworks to regulate toxic substances.

Congress has been concerned with preventing disease, even for new chemicals. The Delaney Clause is an expression of Congressional concern that no American get cancer from food additives. When Congress specifies a 'no risk' framework (Delaney Clause), the regulatory agency has little discretion. The agency need merely discover whether a chemical is carcinogenic. However, thousands of chemicals have been found to be mutagens and about 2/3 of those tested in the lifetime rodent bioassay have been found to be rodent tumorigens. These substances include essential nutrients and many cooked foods. It would be almost impossible to have an adequate diet without consuming some carcinogens. Thus, the no risk framework is not a reasonable possibility if it were applied to all foods; it is possible, although not very sensible, when applied only to food additives.

'Technology based standards' have been used to require a particular control device or process. For example, the best available machinery could be used to separate nuts and grains with aflatoxin so they are not consumed by people. Another possible interpretation is that carcinogens can not be present in detectable amounts in food. Congress actually wrote this interpretation into the Food, Drug and Cosmetic Act. However, as analytical chemistry has been able to detect ever more minuscule amounts, this interpretation has come to mean that no amount of the carcinogen can be present.

All of the other frameworks require some quantification of the risk of carcinogenicity. This means that the carcinogenic potency of the chemical must be estimated as well as the number of people exposed at each level. The latter can be estimated from the rodent bioassay; the former is estimated from discharges of the chemical into the environment, dispersion modeling via air or water, possible biological reconcentration, and then human exposure.

Once the number of human cancers has been estimated, risk–risk analysis would weigh the number of cancers against the health effects of having more expensive, less available food or of denying some essential minerals. For the essential minerals that are carcinogens, the decision would presumably to permit people to consume the required amount, but no more. In a time or place when food was in short supply, foods with small risks of causing cancer would be tolerated.

The risk–benefit framework would compare the estimated number of cancers to the benefit from being exposed. For example, the FDA sets a tolerance level for aflatoxin in peanuts and peanut products by some sort of informal risk–benefit calculus. Peanuts are a cheap source of protein and a popular food. Setting a stringent tolerance level would mean that much of the peanut crop could not be available for human consumption, raising the price of peanuts and peanut products. The FDA permits rich deserts to be sold despite the heart disease and cancer risks. The judgment is that consumers choose the benefits of consumption over the risks of disease.

A cost-effectiveness analysis would have FDA set the aflatoxin tolerance level at a point where the cost per cancer prevented was about the same as cancer prevention decisions for other carcinogenic substances. Since many of these substances are not in food, FDA, EPA, OSHA and other agencies would have to coordinate their decisions.

A benefit–cost analysis would set the tolerance level at the point where the incremental benefit was just equal to the incremental cost (assuming that, in the neighborhood of this standard, more stringent standards increase incremental cost and decrease incremental benefit).

Note that the 'no risk' and technology based standard frameworks requires much less information and analysis than the other decision frameworks: the only relevant attribute is whether the substance is a carcinogen. All of the other frameworks require a quantification of the disease resulting from exposure. The risk–risk framework trades off the disease risk from exposure to the health risk from not having the food. The risk–benefit and cost-effectiveness frameworks require still more information. For the former, benefits must be described so that risks can be traded off against benefits. For the latter, the cost per cancer prevented must be estimated for a number of programs to set the abatement level. Benefit–cost analysis requires the greatest amount of data and analysis since the benefits and costs must be described, quantified, and translated into dollars in order to determine the abatement level where incremental benefits equal incremental costs.

The nonregulatory alternatives provide a rich array of approaches. A believer in the free market need merely decide on whether to use an effluent fee or tradable allowance approach. A lawyer would specify a tort-liability approach. There is an extremely heavy burden of analysis in attempting to decide which of the regulatory or nonregulatory frameworks to use. In few cases should anyone attempt to examine the full menu of possibilities. For better or worse, when Congress chooses a regulatory or nonregulatory framework, they are making an important decision, even if they do not specify an explicit health, safety, and environmental goal.

5.1.1. Interpreting test information

An important issue has to do with which tests should be used to determine whether a chemical is a carcinogen. The general answer from toxicologists is that the test that is most accurate should be selected. In fact, neither the most accurate nor the least cost test is necessarily the best [Lave, Ennever, Rosenkranz & Omenn, 1988; Lave & Omenn, 1986].

Shown in Figure 1 is a simplified representation of the testing decision. The chemical either is or is not a carcinogen (the simplification does not change the nature of the conclusions); the test is either positive or negative. The test would be perfect if it was positive whenever the chemical was a carcinogen and negative whenever the chemical was not. Unfortunately, there are false negatives and false positives, instances where the test is negative for a carcinogen or positive for a noncarcinogen.

Assume that the cost of testing a chemical is c, the social cost of a false positive is x and the social cost of a false negative is bx. Now suppose that the a priori likelihood this chemical is a carcinogen is 0.1 and that the test is 80% sensitive and 60% specific. If so, there will be 0.02 false negatives and 0.36 false positives.

The social cost of testing 100 chemicals of this sort is $100c + 36x + 2bx$. The social cost of classifying all chemicals as noncarcinogens without testing (the policy prior to the preventive approach) is $10bx$. The social cost of classifying all chemicals as carcinogens without testing is $90x$. Whether to test is determined by the alternative with the lowest social cost. For example, if the cost of testing were $1 000 000 (the cost of a lifetime rodent bioassay), the cost of a false positive were $1 000 000 and the cost of a false negative were $10 000 000, the cost of the three alternatives in millions of dollars would be: test, $100 + 36 + 20 = 156$; do not test

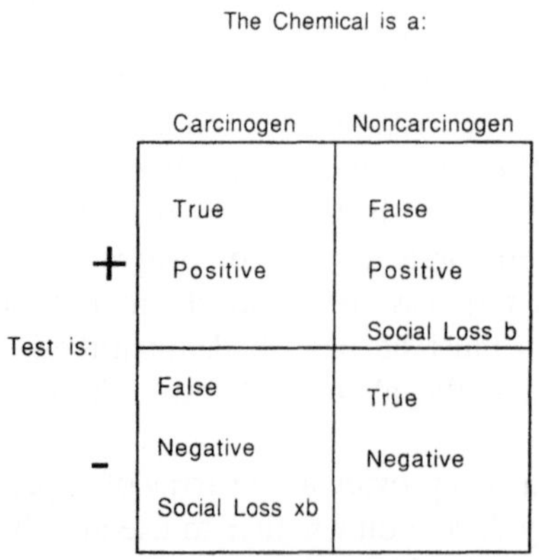

The Chemical is a:

	Carcinogen	Noncarcinogen
+	True Positive	False Positive Social Loss b
−	False Negative Social Loss xb	True Negative

Test is: (shown to the left)

Fig. 1. Social cost of testing (in millions of dollars): $100 + 36x + 2bx = 100 + 36 + 20$ when $x = 1$ and $b = 10$.

noncarcinogens, 100; do not test carcinogen, 90. Since 'do not test and classify all chemicals as carcinogens' has the least cost under these assumptions, it is the dominant strategy.

An alternative test could be compared to the rodent bioassay, knowing the other test's cost, sensitivity and specificity. Society ought to select the test with the lowest social cost. For example, an Ames test costs $2000 and is perhaps 55% sensitive and 45% specific. The cost of the three alternatives is: test, $0.2 + 40.5 + 45 = 85.7$; do not test noncarcinogen, 100; do not test carcinogen, 90. In this case, the Ames test has the lowest social cost. Even though it is less sensitive and less specific than the lifetime rodent bioassay, its test cost is low enough to offset the decreased accuracy.

These calculations can be done for other proposed tests or for chemicals whose costs of misclassification or likelihood of carcinogenicity are different. For example, for chemicals with a 0.5 likelihood of being carcinogens, 'do not test carcinogen' is likely to be the best alternative.

5.2. Highway safety

About 45 000 Americans are killed on highways each year. Highway crashes are the leading cause of death of children and young adults. Since 1965 when Congress passed the Highway Transportation Safety Act and created the National Highway Transportation Safety Administration to administer the law, the United States has displayed a high level of concern for highway safety [Graham, 1988].

One of the major issues has been the effect of automobile size and weight on safety [Evans, 1990; Graham, 1988]. In reaction to the OPEC oil embargo and sharp increase in petroleum prices, Congress enacted fuel economy standards for automobiles in 1975. The standard required that the average new car sold in 1985 would have to get 27.5 miles per gallon, almost double the 1974 average. As a result, automobiles were 'down sized', becoming both lighter and smaller.

Data on two car crashes has shown that lighter, smaller cars are much more likely to involve a fatality in a crash. However, the data do not allow control for vehicle speed and other factors. It is known that smaller, lighter cars tend to be driven by young adults who are more likely to be involved in crashes and to drive at greater speeds.

A further controversy involved the assertion that Detroit did not design cars that stressed safety. Rather, the cars were designed for speed or attractive appearance, with little consideration for safety. Safe cars could be designed, even light cars could be designed to be safe.

Evans [1990] finds that 500–900 kg cars are much more likely to result in the death of the driver or passengers in a crash than would an 1800–2400 kg car. This is especially true in a collision between cars of different sizes. In a crash between cars of these two size classes, the driver in the lighter car is 16.5 times more likely to be killed than the driver of the heavier car. If both cars in a collision weight 1800–2400 kg, the likelihood that the occupants will be killed is 3.5 times as great as if the car were hit by a 500–900 kg car. Finally, if two small cars collide, the occupants are twice as likely to be killed as if they were in two large cars that collided. Thus, Evans demonstrates that being in a car with greater mass in a crash is highly beneficial.

If Congress had written a 'no risk' decision framework into traffic safety law, all motor vehicles would be banned. Even though society regrets the 45 000 premature deaths each year, everyone appears to agree that having the freedom and access of automobiles is worth it.

Some individuals believe that wearing a safety belt would increase their chance of being injured in a crash, as for example in slowing their exit from a burning car after a crash. A risk–risk analysis shows that seat belts do occasionally increase risk, but that in general they are extremely helpful.

A technology based standard decision framework would lead to adding all safety devices that appear to offer any increase in safety. The result would be an extremely expensive vehicle that was clumsy and fuel inefficient.

Risk–benefit analysis would examine the nonhealth consequences of wearing a seat belt. If the belt were uncomfortable or was difficult to buckle or unbuckle, the benefit of the belt might be negative.

A cost-effectiveness framework would attempt to save lives at least cost, whatever the safety device. The NHTSA analysis suggests that improved traffic signals, increasing seat belt use, and other activities are more cost-effective than adding additional safety devices to cars. For cars already equipped with seat belts, it is highly cost-effective to get people to buckle their belts.

Benefit–cost analysis attempts to quantify both benefits and costs and set incremental benefit equal to incremental cost. This framework requires a dollar estimate for the social value of preventing a premature death. While there is little agreement on this figure, benefit–cost analysis has provided some insights. For example, seat belts have a high net benefit when they are worn. But at the usage rate in the early 1980s (about 10%), the safety devices were not worth having. At the same time, with seat belts in all cars, the cheapest way of increasing highway safety is to increase belt usage. This was done by nearly all states imposing mandatory belt use laws and campaigning to increase belt use, a highly successful (and cost-effective) campaign.

6. Conclusion

The formal analysis of risks to health and safety has contributed much to decreasing risks. An array of analytic tools are available to address a wide variety of concerns. The further development of these tools and their application to improving the management of death and safety risks has much to offer the nation.

References

Ames, B.N., and L.S. Gold (1990). Too many rodent carcinogens: Mitogenesis increases mutagenesis. *Science* 249, 970–971.

Ames, B.N., and L.S. Gold (1991). Reply to Rall. *Science* 251, 11–12.

Asch, P. (1988). *Consumer Safety and Regulation: Putting a Price on Life and Limb*, Oxford University Press, New York.

Bailar, J.C. III, E.A.C. Crouch, R. Shaikh and D. Spiegelman (1989). One-hit models of carcinogenesis: Conservative or not? *Risk Analysis* 8, 485–497.

Baram, M.S. (1982). *Alternatives to Regulation*, Lexington Books, Lexington, MA.

Baumol, W., and W. Oates (1975). *The Theory of Environmental Policy*, Prentice-Hall, Englewood Cliffs, NJ.

Berg, E.N. (1988). Asbestos buildings go begging; Now harder to sell, lease, or finance. *New York Times* 137, 25, April 28.

Byrd, D.M. III, and L.B. Lave (1987). Significant risk is not the antonym of de minimis risk, in: C. Whipple (ed.), *De Minimis Risk, Contemporary Issues in Risk Analysis, Vol. 2*, Plenum, New York, pp. 41–60.

Consumers Research (1989). Does everything cause cancer? 72, 11.

Cross, F.B. (1989). *Environmental Induced Cancer and the Law: Risks, Regulation, and Victim Compensation*, Quorum Books, New York.

Cross, F.B., D.M. Byrd III and L.B. Lave (1991). Discernible risk — A proposed standard for significant risk in carcinogen regulation. *Administrative Law Rev.* 43, 61–88.

Detrich, D.R., and J.A. Swenberg (1991). The presence of a2u-globulin is necessary for d-limonene promotion of male rat kidney tumors. *Cancer Res.* 51, 3512–3521.

Doll, R., and R. Peto (1981). The cause of cancer: Quantitative estimates of avoidable risks of cancer in the United States today. *J. National Cancer Institute* 66, 1193–1308.

Doniger, D. (1978). *The Law and Policy of Toxic Substances Control: A Case Study of Vinyl Chloride*, Johns Hopkins, Baltimore.

Efron, E. (1984). *The Apocalyptics: How Environmental Politics Controls what we Know about Cancer*, Simon and Schuster, New York.

Epstein, S. (1978). *The Politics of Cancer*, Sierra Club Books, San Francisco, CA.

Evans, L. (1990). *Traffic Safety and the Driver*, Van Nostrand-Reinhardt, New York.

Fischhoff, B., S. Lichtenstein, P. Slovic, S.L. Derby and R.L. Keeney (1981). *Acceptable Risk*, Cambridge University Press, New York.

Gallo, M., M. Gochfeld and B.D. Goldstein (1987). Biomedical aspects of environmental toxicology, in: L. Lave, and A. Upton (eds.), *Toxic Chemicals, Health, and the Environment*, Johns Hopkins, Baltimore, MD.

Goldberg, C.B., and L.B. Lave (1992). Trading sulfur dioxide allowances. *Environmental Sci. Tech.* 26, 2076.

Gough, M. (1988). Estimating 'environmental' carcinogenesis: A comparison of divergent approaches, Discussion Paper CRM 89-01, Resources for the Future, Washington, DC.

Gough, M. (1990). How much cancer can EPA regulate away? *Risk Analysis* 10, 1–6.

Graham, J.D. (1988). *Preventing Automobile Injury: New Findings for Evaluation Research*, Auburn House, Dover, MA.

Graham, J.D., L.C. Green and M.J. Roberts (1988). *In Search of Safety: Chemicals and Cancer Risk*, Harvard University Press, Cambridge, MA.

Greenberg, R.A., K.E. Bauman, V.J. Stretch, L.L. Keyes, L.H. Glover, N.J. Haley, H.C. Stedman and F.A. Loda (1991). Passive smoking during the first year of life. *Amer. J. Public Health* 81, 850–853.

Gruenspecht, H.K., and L.B. Lave (1991). Increasing the efficiency and effectiveness of environmental decisions: Benefit–cost analysis and effluent fees: A critical review. *J. Air Waste Management Assoc.* 41, 680–693.

Hadden, S.G. (1986). *Read the Label: Reducing Risk by Providing Information*, Westview Press, Boulder, CO.

Hahn, R.W., and G.L. Hester (1989). Marketable permits: Lessons for theory and practice. *Ecology Law Quart.* 16, 361–406.

Hahn, R.W., and J.A. Hird (1991). The costs and benefits of regulation: Review and synthesis. *Yale J. Regulation* 8, 233–278.

Huber, P.W., and R.E. Litan (eds.) (1991). *The Liability Maze: The Impact of Liability Law on Safety and Innovation*, Brookings Institution, Washington, DC.

Hutt, P.B. (1978). Food regulation. *Food, Drug, Cosmetics Law J.* 33, 505–592.

IARC *Monographs on the Evaluation of Carcinogenic Risk of Chemicals to Humans*, World Health Organization, Geneva.

Kneese, A.V., and C.L. Schultze (1975). *Pollution, Prices, and Public Policy*, Brookings Institution, Washington, DC.

Lave, L.B. (1981). *The Strategy of Social Regulation*, Brookings Institution, Washington, DC.

Lave, L.B., F.K. Ennever, H.S. Rosenkranz and G.S. Omenn (1988). Information value of the rodent bioassay. *Nature* 336, 631–633.

Lave, L.B., and G.S. Omenn (1986). Cost-effectiveness of short-term tests of carcinogenicity. *Nature* 324, 329–334.

Lave, L.B., and E.P. Seskin (1970). Air pollution and human health. *Science* 69, 723–733.

Lave, L., and E. Seskin (1977). *Air Pollution and Human Health*, Johns Hopkins University Press, Baltimore, MD.

Lave, L.B., and A.C. Upton (eds.) (1988). *Toxic Chemicals, Health, and the Environment*, Johns Hopkins University Press, Baltimore, MD.

Linnerooth-Bayer, J., and B. Wahlstrom (1991). Applications of probabilistic risk assessments: The selection of appropriate tools. *Risk Analysis* 11, 249–254.

Marnicio, R. (1982). Regulation of ionizing radiation, in: L. Lave (ed.), *Quantitative Risk Assessment in Regulation*, Brookings Institution, Washington, DC.

Mazumdar, S., C. Redmond, W. Sollecito and N. Sussman (1975). An epidemiological study of exposure to coal tar pitch volatiles among coke oven workers. *J. Air Pollution Control Assoc.* 25: 382–289.

Mendeloff, J.M. (1988). *The Dilemma of Toxic Substance Regulation*, MIT Press, Cambridge, MA.

Merrill, R.A. (1978). Regulating carcinogens in food: A legislator's guide to the Food Safety Provisions of the Federal Food, Drug, and Cosmetic Act. *Michigan Law Rev.* 77, 171–250.

Miller, S.A., and K. Skinner (1984). The nose of the camel: The paradox of food standards. *Food, Drug, Cosmetics Law J.* 39, 99–108.

Milvy, P. (1986). A general guideline for management of risk from carcinogens. *Risk Analysis* 6, 60–80.

Moolgavkar, S.H., and A.G. Knudson (1981). Mutation and cancer: A model for human carcinogenesis. *J. National Cancer Institute* 66, 1037–1052.

Mossman, B.T., J. Bignon, M. Corn, A. Seaton and J.B.L. Gee (1990). Asbestos: Scientific developments and implications for public policy. *Science* 247, 294–301.

National Research Council (1978). *Saccharin: Technical Assessment of Risks and Benefits*, National Academy Press, Washington, DC.

National Research Council (1979). *Food Safety Policy*, National Academy Press, Washington, DC.

National Research Council (1980). *The Effects on Populations of Exposures to Low Levels of Ionizing Radiation*, National Academy Press, Washington, DC.

National Research Council (1983). *Risk Assessment in the Federal Government: Managing the Process*, National Academy Press, Washington, DC.

National Research Council (1988). *Health Risks of Radon and Other Internally Deposited Alpha-Emitters (BEIR IV)*, National Academy Press, Washington, DC.

National Research Council (1989a). *Diet and Health: Implications for Reducing Chronic Disease Risk*, National Academy Press, Washington, DC.

National Research Council (1989b). *Improving Risk Communication*, National Academy Press, Washington, DC.

Oi, W. (1974). On the economics of industrial safety. *Law Contemporary Problems* 38, 538–555.

Ontario Royal Commission (1984). *Report on Matters of Health and Safety Arising from the Use of Asbestos in Ontario*, Ontario Ministry of the Attorney General, Toronto.

Orlando, G.A. (1990). Understanding the excise tax on ozone-depleting chemicals. *Tax Executive*, 359–363.

Perrow, C. (1984). *Normal Accidents*, Basic Books, New York.

Pigou, A.C. (1920). *The Economics of Welfare*, Macmillan, London.

Pochin, E. (1983). *Nuclear Radiation: Risks and Benefits*, Oxford University Press, New York.

Portney, P.P. (ed.) (1990a). *Public Policies for Environmental Protection*, Resources for the Future, Washington, DC.

Portney, P.P. (1990b). Air pollution policy, in: Portney [1990a].

Public Citizen v. Young, Supra (1987). 831 F.2d at 1123 U.S. Court of Appeals for the District of Columbia Circuit, October 23, 1987.

Rall, D.P. (1991). Comment on Ames and Gold. *Science* 251, 10–11. Rasmussen, N.C. (1981). The application of probabilistic risk assessment techniques to energy technologies, in: J.M. Hollander, M.K. Simmons and D.O. Wood (eds.), *Annual Review of Energy*, Annual Reviews, Palo Alto, CA, pp. 123–138.

Raufer, R.K., and S.L. Feldman (1987). *Acid Rain and Emissions Trading: Implementing a Market Approach to Pollution Control*, Towman and Littlefield, Totowa, NJ.

Regens, J.L., and R.W. Rycroft (1988). *The Acid Rain Controversy*, University of Pittsburgh, Pittsburgh, PA.

Resendiz-Carrillo, D., and L.B. Lave (1987). Optimizing spillway capacity with an estimated distribution of floods. *Water Resources Res.* 23, 2043–2049.

Roberts, L. (1989). A corrosive fight over California's toxics law. *Science* 243, January 20, 306–309.

Royal Commission on Matters of Health and Safety, Canada (1984). *Report on Matters of Health and Safety Arising from the Use of Asbestos in Ontario*, Ontario Ministry of Government Services, Toronto.

Salsburg, D.S. (1977). Use of statistics when examining lifetime studies in rodents to detect carcinogenicity. *J. Toxicology Human Health* 3.

Schelling, T.C. (1968). The life you save may be your own, in: S. Chase (ed.), *Problems in Public Expenditure Analysis*, Brookings Institution, Washington, DC.

Scheuplein, R.J. (1990). Perspectives on toxicological risk — An example: Food-Borne carcinogenic risk, in: D.B. Clayson, I.C. Munro, P. Shubik and J.A. Swenberg (eds.), *Progress in Predictive Toxicology*, Elsevier, New York.

Schottenfeld, D., and J.F. Fraumani Jr. *Cancer Epidemiology and Prevention, 2nd edition*, Oxford University Press, Oxford, in press.

Schwing, R.C., and D.B. Kamerud (1988). The distribution of risks: Vehicle occupant fatalities and time of the week. *Risk Analysis* 8, 127–133.

Slovic, P. (1987). Perception of risk. *Science* 236, 280–286.

Starr, C. (1969). Social benefits versus technological risk. *Science* 165, 1232–1238.

Stavins, R.N. (ed.) (1988). *Project 88: Harnessing Market Forces to Protect Our Environment — Initiatives for the New President*, A Public Policy Study Sponsored by Senator Timothy E. Wirth, Colorado and Senator John Heinz, Pennsylvania. Washington, DC. Kennedy School, Harvard University, 1988.

Stone, R. (1992). Bad news on second-hand smoke. *Science* 257, July 31, 607.

Tietenberg, T. (1992). *Environmental and Natural Resource Economics*, Harper and Collins, New York.

Travis, C.C. (ed.) (1988). *Risk Analysis*, Plenum, New York.

Travis, C.C., and H.A. Hattemer-Frey (1988). Determining an acceptable level of risk. *Environmental Sci. Tech.* 22, 873–876.

U.S. Environmental Protection Agency (1987). *Unfinished Business: A Comparative Assessment of Environmental Problems*, U.S. Environmental Protection Agency (EPA-450/1-85-001), Washington, DC.

U.S. Environmental Protection Agency (1989). Final rule on risk goals. *Federal Register* 54, 38 044–38 058.

U.S. Environmental Protection Agency (1990). Reducing risk: Setting priorities and strategies for environmental protection, Report of the Relative Risk Reduction Strategies Committee, Science Advisory Board, SAB-EC-90-021.

U.S. National Cancer Institute (1986). *Cancer Control Objectives for the Nation: 1985–2000*, National Cancer Institute, Bethesda, MD.

U.S. Nuclear Regulatory Commission (1975). *Reactor Safety Study: WASH 1400*, Government Printing Office, Washington, DC.

U.S. Nuclear Regulatory Commission (1978). *Risk Assessment Review Group Report, NUREG/CR 0400*, Government Printing Office, Washington, DC.

Viscusi, W.K., and W.A. Magat (1987). *Learning About Risk: Consumer and Worker Responses to Hazard Information*, Harvard University Press, Cambridge, MA.

Weill, H., and J.M. Hughes (1986). Asbestos as a public health risk: Disease and policy, in: L. Breslow, J. Fielding and L. Lave (eds.), *Annual Review of Public Health*, 7, Annual Reviews, Palo Alto, CA, pp. 171–192.

Weinberg, A.M. (1972). Science and trans-science. *Minerva* 10, 202–222.

Whelan, E.M. (1985). *Toxic Terror*, Jameson Books, Ottawa, IL.

Whipple, C. (1987). *De Minimis Risk*, Plenum, New York.

Wulff, P. (1991). More large accidents through complexity? *Risk analysis* 11, 249–253.

S.M. Pollock et al., Eds., *Handbooks in OR & MS, Vol. 6*

Chapter 13

Applications of Operations Research in Health Care Delivery

William P. Pierskalla

Anderson School of Business, University of California, Los Angeles, CA 90024-1481, U.S.A.

David J. Brailer

Care Management Science Corporation, Philadelphia, PA 19104, U.S.A.

This chapter reviews the body of work in operations research in recent years which is devoted to health care delivery. Two important observations should be stated at the outset. First, although many problems faced by operations researchers in health care are not analytically different from problems in other industries, many others are quite unique due to certain characteristics of health care delivery systems. Some of these are the possibilities of death or low quality of remaining life, the difficulty in measuring quality and value of outcomes, the sharing of decisions among several decision makers (physicians, nurses and administrators), third party payment mechanisms for diagnoses and treatments, and the concept of health care access as a right of citizens in society. This chapter attempts to focus on areas involving these unique characteristics. Second, the breadth and richness of this field cannot be covered in the limited space here. Therefore problems, issues and principles are discussed with references provided for the inquisitive reader.

This chapter is separated into three major sections. First is system design and planning, which deals with large allocation decisions, both at the policy level and at the operational level. Second is management of operations, which examines monitoring and control methodologies at the operational and tactical levels. Third is medical management, which involves patient disease detection and treatment at the policy and at the patient levels.

1. System design and planning

1.1. Planning and strategy

In most industrially developed nations and in many developing nations, health care system design and planning occurs principally at the federal or regional level.

For the developed nations, with the exception of the United States, the interplay between history, culture, economics, politics, and other factors result in remarkably similar strategies for providing universal access and cost control, including some form of social insurance, common fee schedules for all payors, and formal or informal national budget caps. Because of these strategic choices, the federal and regional design and planning process largely determines the type and levels of facilities and technologies and frequently (perhaps implicitly) the levels of health care manpower and levels of services received by the population. This section covers the analytic tools developed in operations research to support these areas, such as regionalization, health districting and the expansion and contraction of services.

Regionalization of health care services is an important component of system planning and is common in countries such as the United Kingdom or Italy, but not in the United States due, in part, to the U.S. reliance on private markets for financing and delivery of health services. However, the operations research methodologies which underlie regionalization are robust and can be useful in the operation of multi-institutional systems, distribution of high technology equipment, and in other health care issues which could be useful in all health systems. Because regionalization is frequently sought to improve the cost or quality of a health care system through more effective distribution of services, regionalization questions are often optimal clustering problems (the decision maker attempts to partition the set services so that some objective is optimized) or resource allocation problems (the central authority must plan for and allocate scarce resources to regions or districts).

At the national planning level, Rizakow, Rosenhead & Reddington [1991] develop a decision support system, AIDSPLAN, which is a spreadsheet model to plan for the resources needed for HIV/AIDS related services in the United Kingdom. The model incorporates demand forecasting by patient categories, care protocols and resource and budget needs for central and local planners in the British National Health Service. It can also be used with the planning efforts of earlier math programming balance of care (BOC) models incorporated in micro-computer software to determine resource needs and allocations for entire health service regions and districts [Boldy, 1987; Bowen & Forte, 1987; Coverdale & Negrine, 1978].

Pezzella, Bonanno & Nicoletti [1981] provide an example of health service districting. In this paper, the authors develop a model by which local health departments in Italy are assigned into regional health structures. Dimensions of the analysis include an analysis of the demand for health services based on demographic, socio-economic, and geographical information, interviews with experts and surveys of special disease populations, and an analysis of available hospital services, which are considered in the proposed mathematical model for optimal districting. The authors note previous attempts to perform such regionalization by set partitioning, generalized assignment models, location and allocation models, and other linear programs. The authors use a linear program which has two objectives: to minimize the average distance of individuals from the nearest center, which improves access, and to minimize the deviation between proposed and existing districting which improves political acceptability. The model achieves the objectives by assigning hospitals to nuclei and then building reduced graphs in such a way that these distances are minimized. The authors apply the model to a case study of the Cosenza province in Italy and discuss two formulations of the optimal districting solution.

Another example of a regionalization question, the regionalization of CT scanners, is addressed by Bach & Hoberg [1985]. The authors consider total cost per year of a regional system of CT scanner operation, cost per scan, utilization levels, and average and maximum distance travelled by patients. They use a linear programming model which considers the total cost of operations for the CT scanner system as the sum of transportation costs (determined by patient travelling) and operational costs, such as staffing, supplies and facility support. The operational costs include fixed, threshold, and variable costs. The objective of the program is to minimize total cost. The authors apply the model to the Baden-Württemberg region in Germany. They consider a number of alternatives and rank-order them on the basis of total cost. They find that an increase in the number of CT scanners in a regional system does not necessarily increase the total cost of operation due to decreased travel costs.

Or & Pierskalla [1979] consider the problem of determining the optimal number and location of facilities in a region. Because the facilities involved are central blood banks, the researchers model the optimal allocation of specific hospital blood product needs to the central blood banks and the optimal number of routes of special delivery vehicles needed to make regular (routine) and emergency deliveries to hospitals. The unique characteristics of this problem involve the perishability of the various blood products. They present algorithms and models to decide how many blood banks to set up, where to locate them, how to allocate hospitals to the banks, and how to route the supply operation of vehicles so that the total system costs are minimized, and the hospital needs are met. With data from blood centers throughout the U.S., Cohen, Pierskalla & Sassetti [1987] demonstrate significant economies of scale within operating areas (such as laboratories, storage and administration) in central blood banks. Combining these results with actual transportation costs data, the authors evaluate site location and vehicle scheduling in the Chicago metropolitan area.

Many studies are conducted at the institutional level to plan the addition, expansion or contraction of services and facilities. In health care, this problem is complicated by the interdependence among services and among institutions created by crisscrossing physician privileges, patient comorbidities, unknown levels of latent demand, and potential creation of demand. To avoid these issues, most studies deal with self-contained services such as obstetrics, pediatrics, and psychiatry, or with broad-based workforce planning models. Schneider [1981] examines the question of how the closure of obstetric services might affect the case load and profitability of hospitals in three communities. He models three factors: comparability of services, patient load redistributions, and financial measures. Comparability of services determines if closures of services in some locations changes the overall regional level of service as measured by staffing, bed requirements, number of delivery rooms, and outcomes measures (including still births, neonatal mortality, percent primary Caesarian sections, and percent of breach deliveries). Patient load redistribution examines how the underlying patient volume is redistributed among remaining units after some units close and how this affects the service at related institutions. Financial analysis determines how direct, service-specific, and marginal costs are used to determine the net savings under closure conditions and the costs of increased services at remaining units that increase in volume. The author finds that most hospitals in the three communities would face significant losses on existing obstetric services, that five of seven hospitals would improve financial performance if their obstetric services closed, and that if one obstetric service were closed per community, overall costs would be reduced by 7–15% with comparable levels of service quality.

The opening of new services is also addressed. Romanin-Jacur & Facchin [1982] examine the effect of opening an independent pediatric semi-intensive care unit in a pediatric hospital. The unit would have its own rooms, staff, and instruments and be devoted to the care of severely ill patients. The question they raise is one of distribution of current capacity, in which the question is the reallocation of beds from the general ward to the new unit rather than addition to total capacity. The authors consider several classes of case arrival sources, including urgencies from the floors and the surgical ward, emergent admissions, and planned admissions. Each class is modeled with Poisson inter-arrival times for all services, except planned surgical operations, which are deterministic. Using length of stay from historical data, a simulation model is used to determine the optimal number of beds for the unit. The authors present a staffing schedule to optimize nurse distribution, based on optimal number of beds.

An important and frequently encountered question in service planning is whether a new service can improve productivity, quality, or cost performance in such a way that it is a desirable addition to other services offered by an institution or a health care system. In this setting, analysis with production functions can be of limited value and simulation models are frequently employed. For example, Hershey & Kropp [1979] analyze the productivity potential of physician's assistants. They observe that previous models predict that physician's assistants will expand service productivity. Although the authors acknowledge that there might be many non-economic arguments which explain this, their concern is that prior studies used production function analysis and perhaps, therefore, could have included systematic biases and flaws which overestimate the productivity potential of these professionals by underestimating costs such as congestion and supervision time of physicians. They develop a computer simulation model that incorporates more features and more complex details than had previous attempts. These include daily operating hours of the facilities, physical resources available, schedules of patients' appointments, patient arrival patterns, required services and service times, and sequencing of tasks to meet patient service requirements. The authors run the same information in a linear programming model and demonstrate that 393 patients can be seen per week in a practice with a physician's assistant, compared to 208 without one, and that net income and productivity will increase over time. However, because physician supervision time and congestion would increase during the initial periods of using a physician's assistant, there would be a significant short-term deterioration in patient waiting time without significant income increases. Thus, the authors conclude that although in the long term, full capacity utilization of physician assistants would increase productivity of physicians' practices, the short run costs may prohibit physicians from using them, probably because of initial losses in patient volume and the costs of supervisory time.

In a related application, Denton, Gafni, Spencer & Stoddart [1983] examine the savings from the adoption of nurse practitioners in Canada. The authors develop a cost model in order to estimate the costs of a parallel nurse practitioner–physician primary care model strategy, simulated over a 70 year period, 1980–2050, by using output of a demographic projection model. They find that nurse practitioners could reduce expenditures by 10–15% for all medical services and 16–24% for all ambulatory services in 1980, with increased savings over time. A sensitivity analysis demonstrates that these results were insensitive to age mix in the Canadian population.

1.2. Demand forecasting

Aggregate demand forecasting and daily census prediction is important in improving the efficiency of capital resource use in health care. Health services research tends to employ existing and well known operations research algorithms from other industries to perform forecasting rather than make new contributions to this literature. Because demand forecasting is a fundamental input to many other analyses in health care operations research, it is briefly included in this chapter. For example, demand forecasting is an important component of capacity utilization and service quality in hospitals, nursing homes, outpatient practices, and in nearly every other component of the health care system. Forecasting demand has two roles, the determination of aggregate need for services (the demand side), and census planning (the supply side). Analysis of demand on a daily basis drives hospital-wide decisions, including staffing, ancillary services, elective admission scheduling, and support services (including cleaning, food service, and linens), as well as decisions regarding new and contemplated services in the health care environment. Demand forecasting in health care resembles the structure of the aggregate planning problem in the manufacturing environment.

In excellent reviews of forecasting techniques, Harrington [1977] and Hogarth & Makridakis [1981] review the major techniques which are used in health care settings. First are qualitative approaches such as historical analysis, which employ analysis of similar settings or an organization's own institutional history to determine future demand. This technique, while inexpensive and easy to use, ignores environmental changes and does not support the analysis of new venture decisions. Another qualitative approach is the Delphi technique, in which future predictions are extracted from experts. The process is repeated until a consensus emerges. The Delphi technique is susceptible to ideological biases which make it difficult to use in settings where predictions may not conform to standard views of system operation. The other major areas of demand forecasting, which is the focus of this section, are techniques for demand forecasting which are analytically based. These techniques are illustrated by the following articles.

Kamentzky, Shuman & Wolfe [1982] use least squares regression analysis to determine the demand for pre-hospital care in order to make ambulance staffing decisions. The authors employ several independent variables, including area population, area employment, and indicators of socio-economic status, and control variables, including operational and clinical categories. The socio-economic variables include demographic variables such as persons per household, mean age, and ratio of blue collar to white collar workers, and indicators of social well-being such as median family income and percent of families with female heads. Operational classifications include emergent cases, transport to hospitals, inter-hospital transport, standby, and volume. Clinical characteristics include cardiac status, trauma, life threatening emergency, or minor care. Using data from Pennsylvania, the authors find that the socio-economic, operational, and clinical variables are all significant in predicting unmet need, and they validate the model so that the transport system could be improved.

Kao & Tung [1980] use demand forecasting for inpatient services in the British health service. They employ an auto-regressive, integrated moving average (ARIMA) time series model to forecast demand for inpatient services. The procedure for model development, parameter estimation, and diagnostic checking involves the use of deterministic trends with regular differencing between periods so that the basic trend is changed from period to period. This model is stratified by patient service and month of year, so that monthly admissions and patient days can be forecasted by service and length of stay estimates can be made. Compared to actual data, the model produces forecast errors ranging from 21.5% (deviation from the predicted) in newborn nursery to 3.3% in psychiatry. The authors suggest that the demand forecasting system can be used for bed allocation and aggregate nurse planning.

Johansen, Bowles & Haney [1988] demonstrate a model for forecasting intermediate skilled home nursing needs which combines elements of simple observational models and complex statistical approaches, and was utilization-based rather than population-based. The authors restrict their model to outpatient variables that were uniformly, clearly, and consistently collected and coded, including principal and secondary diagnoses, patient disposition, nature of admission, hospital size, metropolitan area, and marital status. Medical and demographic factors describe four risk categories into which patients could be assigned, indicating their overall risk for intermittent home care services. The authors first perform two-way tabulations on patients on the basis of these variables, then determine the predicted number of patients in each category using weighted averages. The expected cost per skilled nursing service is obtained by multiplying the expected number of patients in each category by the mean cost per patient. Sensitivity analyses determine the effects of changes in the health care system on these estimates. The authors determine the probability of need for service given the risk level of the patient, which ranges from a probability of 5% for a low risk patient to 80% for a very high risk patient. The authors note that this model incorporates easily observable characteristics, and provides good performance accuracy when compared with real data.

Kao & Pokladnik [1978] describe adaptive forecasting of hospital census, demonstrating how institutional and exogenous variables can be used in forecasting models to improve accuracy longitudinally. The authors argue that such models should be analytically credible, yet simple and easy to use. In their model, the census on any given day is a function of a constant component, a linear trend factor, and random disturbances, which are minimized by a discounted least squares analysis. The authors then observe that, in addition to the basic pattern of census at many institutions, there are internal and external factors which could explain additional census variations. For example, renovations, holidays, and administrative actions may close units from time to time; utilization review programs could change length of stay; natural disasters or epidemics could change demand for a short time. The authors use tracking signals, rather than smoothing, to improve hospital forecasting and trigger different rates of parameter updating. In a case study, these techniques are used to improve forecasting decisions by including adjustment factors for holidays, adding, opening and closing nursing units, and unexpected events.

Demand forecasting is important for many aspects of health care operations research and management. The chief difference between techniques is the degree to which subjective judgement influences the model. Some models, such as the Delphi technique, attempt to formalize explicit expert judgement. Others, such as econometric modelling, have implicit judgements (e.g., specification of the model). This impact of judgement, whether explicit or implicit, on the results of demand forecasting, can be strong, as Hogarth & Makridakis [1981] describe in their review of models. In choosing forecasting models, the degree of judgement should be considered, and various approaches to modelling and sensitivity analysis should be tried.

1.3. Location selection

Location of health care delivery facilities and services has much in common with the location aspects of many types of facilities or services which have a geographically dispersed customer base, and where there is a need to be close enough to customers for ease of access and/or speed of access, as well as a need for low cost of siting and operations. Health care facilities and services are different because they may be subject to public control laws and, in the case of emergency vehicle locations where there are maximum response time requirements, may need to balance closeness to customers and facilities.

Siting or location problems usually fall into one of five categories with somewhat distinctive characteristics.

The first category is the regionalization of health care facilities (see Section 1.1).

The second category is the siting or removal of a single facility, such as an acute care hospital or a central blood bank which needs to be geographically close to its customer bases (also see Section 1.1). Here the customers are the patients and their physicians, and (to a lesser extent) hospital employees. Generally, mathematical programming or heuristic approaches are used to determine optimal or near-optimal locations. Major consideration is given to the current location of similar institutions in the region.

The third category is the location of ambulatory neighborhood clinics, which are primarily used for routine outpatient medical and/or surgical care and for preventive care. Again, proximity to patients is an important criterion in the location decision, as are network linkages to the general and specialized hospitals in the region. The location of health maintenance organization facilities, surgi-centers, diagnostic centers such as CT-scanner centers and poly-clinics fall into this category (see Section 1.1). Sometimes network mathematical programming is used for this analysis. For example, in order to locate ambulatory medical service centers for the independently living elderly, a planning strategy advocated by Cromley & Shannon [1986] incorporates the concept of aggregate activity spaces used by the target population in the criteria for determining the facility location. This approach is particularly suited to services for the elderly, who tend to restrict activity to familiar areas of the community. A similar idea could be used for the location of pediatric health service centers near schools and/or recreation areas.

The fourth category comprises the location of specialized long-term care facilities. The primary criteria for these location decisions are not so much closeness to customer bases but costs of site acquisition and construction, cost of operation, and (to some extent) speed of access to acute care facilities. The types of facilities involved in this category are nursing homes, psychiatric hospitals, skilled nursing facilities, and rehabilitation centers.

The fifth category of health care location problems is the siting of emergency medical services (EMS). This problem involves determination of the number and placement of locations, number and types of emergency response vehicles and of personnel. This problem is similar to the location of fire stations, equipment and crews, in which speed of response is a primary criterion (see Chapter 5). Speed of response includes distance to the problem occurrence location, but also the distance from the occurrence location to the treatment facility. In this latter regard, the problem differs from fire stations, where the occurrence location and the treatment location coincide. For example, if the health care treatment location is near the edge of a populated region, it is probably not optimal to locate the EMS at the midpoint of the region or close to the treatment center, whereas it may be optimal to locate a firestation there. The EMS location problem receives the most attention from operations researchers. It is rich in problem structure, having sufficient technical complexity yet minimal political and sociological constraints. The primary methods used to solve this problem are mathematical programming, queueing analysis and simulation. The solutions may then be modified heuristically to satisfy non-quantitative constraints.

Fitzsimmons & Sullivan [1979] combine a deployment model with varying fleet sizes to determine the appropriate level of ambulance service. The Computerized Ambulance Location Logic (CALL) simulation program combines the Hooke–Jeeves optimum seeking search routine with an EMS queueing model. Fitzsimmons & Srikar [1982] enhance the CALL approach by adding a contiguous zone search routine that relocates all deployed vehicles sequentially to zones contiguous to each vehicle's starting location. Individual and cumulative vehicle response times are then determined, until a cumulative minimum value is identified. Model outputs include demand for hospital emergency services, ambulance utilization and workload, mean response time, probability of all vehicles being idle, distribution of response time, mean response time by zone, and dispatch guidelines. Objective criteria used to evaluate siting alternatives include service equity, fleet size, and workload equity.

Brandeau & Larson [1986] describe an enhancement of the hypercube queueing model for studying an emergency medical service system. The model does not select an optimal emergency service configuration, but instead provides a variety of performance measures for any given configuration. The user must decide which configuration represents the best trade-off of the performance parameters. The model is used to configure the EMS system in Boston.

Daskin & Stern [1982] develop a hierarchical objective set covering (HOSC) model to find the minimum number of vehicles required to cover all zones while maximizing multiple coverage of zones within performance standards. Daskin [1981] describes a derivative of the maximum expected covering location model (MEXCLP) which accounts for vehicle busy periods. The model estimates the number of vehicles needed based on daily average calls. Eaton, Daskin, Simmons, Bulloch & Jansma [1985] describe the implementation of the maximum covering model in Austin, Texas. Eaton, Sanchez, Lantigua & Morgan [1986] incorporate weighted demand into the HOSC approach, and develop recommendations for ambulance deployment in Santo Domingo, Dominican Republic. Fujiwara, Makjamroen & Gupta [1987] use the maximum covering location model to identify 'good' solutions for ambulance deployment in Bangkok, Thailand. Each of these solutions is then analyzed by a Monte Carlo simulation. Model outputs include response time, service time, round trip time, and workload. Bianchi & Church [1988] combine the MEXCLP with another covering model, the Facility Location and Equipment Emplacement Technique, to develop an ambulance location pattern which places multiple homogeneous units at one location. Integer programming is used to determine the optimal solution. The benefits of this approach include easier dispatching, reduced facility costs, and better crew balancing, without altering the service level.

Facility location is a complex and data-hungry problem. Some of the greatest application successes have been in the EMS category. Developments in this area are stimulated by the establishment of standards of performance by which public or contract services can be held accountable, improvements in information systems which support EMS operations management, and by special federal legislation in the U.S. which help pay for the establishment and operation of EMS systems.

1.4. Capacity planning

Capacity planning relates to those decisions regarding the appropriate levels of facilities, equipment and personnel for some demand. In health care, capacity planning usually focuses on decisions such as total bed capacity, surgical system capacity, bed capacity allocation to different services, capital equipment capacities, ancillary service capacity, and factors which affect capacity utilization such as patient flow, staffing levels and staff skill mix. In examining these factors, providers are seeking ways to increase the productivity of existing assets and improve service quality. Many of the studies drive the capacity planning process with an underlying queueing system and use simulation to obtain solutions.

The allocation of bed capacity within a hospital is a critical factor in operating efficiency. Dumas [1984, 1985] develops a simulation which incorporates diagnostic categories of patients based on sex, admission type, time of demand, four categories of beds, and physician type (attending or resident). Outcome measures include percent occupancy, average daily census, annual patient-days, and misplaced-patient days (when the patient was not on the intended unit). Secondary measures include requests for admission, reservations, refusals due to inability to schedule a satisfactory admission date, wait list reneging, transfers and proxy measures for opportunity costs of these events. The simulator provides a method for evaluating a variety of patient placement rules. When applied to actual hospital data, the study results in a reallocation of beds, the creation of a new service, fewer misplacements, and reduced misplaced-patient days, but also resulted in increased transfers. The model does not incorporate costs for misplacement, transfers, and delayed admissions. The model can be used for the planned expansion, contraction or reallocation of beds as demand changes.

Similarly, Vassilacopoulos [1985] describes a general priority queueing simulation model that could be used to determine the number of hospital beds necessary to meet demand for inpatient services. The objectives of high occupancy, immediate admission of emergency patients, and a small waiting list for elective admissions were sought simultaneously.

Hospital waiting lists are investigated by Worthington [1987] to assess bed capacity and other characteristics of the British Health System. He uses a modified M/G/S queueing model which includes costs for patients who balk at long queues which, in turn, influence the length of the queue. The model tests the predicted responses to the long waiting list problem, such as increasing staffed beds, decreasing length of stay, combining waiting lists for different services, and introducing earlier feedback to general practitioners about the size of the queue.

Simulation models are widely used in capacity planning. Mahachek & Knabe [1984] simulate the flow of patients through two outpatient clinics, obstetrics and gynecology, which were to be combined. A simulation of surgical bed occupancy related to surgeon's schedule and category of the procedure (major, intermediate, or minor) is developed by Harris [1985]. A radiology service model developed by Sullivan & Blair [1979] predicts longitudinal workload requirements for radiology from medical services. The model is used to address the impact on capacity of centralization versus decentralization of radiology equipment and services. Ladany & Turban [1978] describe a simulation of an emergency room service. A simulation developed by Hancock & Walter [1984] evaluates the effects of inpatient admission policies and outpatient scheduling on the future workloads of ancillary services such as laboratory, physical therapy, and respiratory therapy.

Semi-Markov process models are also used to examine bed allocation and capacity questions, particularly in progressive patient care facilities. Hershey, Weiss & Cohen [1981] demonstrate, by using transitional probabilities for patient movements throughout the hospital, that the expected level of utilization can be modeled as a system with one unit with finite capacity. If the equilibrium rate of arrival at each unit, mean holding time at each unit, and the probability that the finite unit is at full capacity are known, then the utilization and service rate of the system can be determined. If multiple units are being considered for capacity changes, the authors recommend using simulation, with their model used for validating the simulation.

On a regional scale, Lambo [1983] uses optimization and simulation to improve efficiency and effectiveness in a network of rural Nigerian clinics. Optimization is used to establish an upper bound on the potential efficiency of a regional health center. Misallocation of personnel is the major constraint identified. Simulations at levels of both the center and individual clinics is used to evaluate operating policies and to determine the maximum capacity of the center.

Schmee, Hannan & Mirabile [1979] also address a broader regional capacity and services evaluation problem. They use a discrete-time semi-Markov process to describe the movement of a patient from one care level to another within a progressive patient care system. The system includes four levels of hospital care, extended care in a nursing home, and home care. Well-being and death are considered absorbing or terminal states. The optimum, non-dominated solution(s) are then found using linear programming, seeking the patient movement in the system which achieves a high probability of patient recovery, while minimizing cost.

As shown in the preceding examples, capacity planning usually deals with bed or procedure capacity. The objective is usually to maximize the use of finite capital equipment resources or to minimize inefficiencies and delays in delivering health care service. While substantial work has been done on capacity planning in health care, the relative cost and effectiveness of altering key variables affecting capacity and the system interactions among the many aspects of care delivery remain a fertile area for further work. In addition, in none of these studies are the capacity relationships studied with regard to economies of scale or scope and to quality levels of scale and congestion. Better models of patient flow and improved understanding of the delivery system for care hold promise as means to improve capacity planning.

2. Management of operations

2.1. Management information systems

Management information systems (MIS) are usually required to implement operations research models in health care management. There is a very large amount of literature on designing, planning, installing, and evaluating MIS systems. This literature will not be discussed here. Only a few brief comments will be made and some references given which can lead the interested reader into a range of writings on this topic. In combination with decision- and model-based support systems, MIS's have the potential to improve decision-making responsiveness, quality of patient care, and productivity. Quality of care improvements can result from reduced waiting time for physicians' orders to be carried out and results to become available, elimination of unnecessary services, reduction of errors, and increased provider and patient satisfaction. Productivity is improved by appropriate data availability for decisions about staffing patterns, scheduling, use of equipment and materials, and by elimination of redundant systems and actions. These benefits of MIS are succinctly summarized by Moidu & Wigertz [1989].

The elements of the hospital or office MIS for medical decision-making, billing, and planning as well as other activities are keyed to the patient identification number (PID) and the medical record (MR) [Pierskalla, Brailer & McVoy, 1990]. From the entire patient case mix, severity and resources consumed can be identified. Other MIS elements of importance are employee data, competitors' case mixes and resources, present and future regional demographics, income and resource cost patterns, market survey results of patient attitudes and preferences, private physician specialties, location and practice in the region, and competitors' known plans for the future. Using this information, different units at the management and care delivery levels construct models using statistics, operations research, management science and expert systems to make and support decisions. These decisions may involve expansion, contraction, new technology, mergers and acquisitions, and diversification. Operating decisions involve payroll and accounting systems, budget planning and analysis, admissions, discharge and transfer (ADT) systems, surgery and recovery room scheduling [Lowery & Martin, 1989], nurse staffing and scheduling, outpatient scheduling and appointment systems, purchasing, inventory control and maintenance, administrative personnel systems, and medical management of patients.

2.2. Patient scheduling

Controlling demand for services via scheduling can be very effective as a method of matching demand with the supply of services available. Outpatients frequently dislike waiting for service, and consequently balk or renege on appointments if waiting time is considered excessive. Inpatients, likewise, are dissatisfied with slow hospital service. Consequently, the problem of satisfying both patients and health care providers is a challenging one and most scheduling systems attempt to optimize the combined objectives of satisfaction of patients, satisfaction of physicians, and utilization of facilities.

Patient scheduling has many benefits which include reduced staffing costs and reduced congestion in the hospital and clinics. Appropriate supply of personnel, facilities, equipment and services can be more effectively provided to meet the smoothed flow of demand. An area of benefit that is just beginning to be addressed is the improvement in quality of care (in addition to patient satisfaction) that comes from reduction of congestion via effective demand and supply scheduling. Quality could be improved by providing the appropriate amounts and kinds of care at the appropriate times.

There are problems, however, in devising and implementing scheduling systems which meet the primary goals of minimizing staff and/or staff idle time (primarily physicians) and equipment idle time while maximizing or strongly satisfying patient needs. Some of these problems stem from inadequate information systems, others from resistance to change by staff or authorities who demand uniformity of approaches across institutions, and others from failing to capture key linkages and system interactions because of the complexity of the core delivery processes. This last set of problems occurs more frequently in hospital inpatient settings in situations where complex progressive patient care is needed rather than in outpatient settings.

2.2.1. Outpatient scheduling

Effective scheduling of patients in clinics for outpatient services is one of the earliest documented uses of operations research in improving health care delivery. Bailey [1975] applies queueing theory to equalize patients' waiting times in hospital outpatient departments. He observes that many outpatient clinics are essentially a single queue with single or multiple servers. The problem then becomes one of building an appointment system to minimize patient waiting time and keeping the servers busy. The appointment system must be designed to have the inter-arrival times of patients somewhat smaller than, or equal to, the service time. Unfortunately, outside the laboratory, the service system is more complicated. Some patients arrive late or not at all; some physicians arrive late; service times are not homogeneous but vary by the type and degree of illness; diagnostic equipment is not always available; there are unplanned arrivals of emergent patients and so forth. For these and other reasons many of the early outpatient scheduling models were not widely adopted.

However, more recent models and methodologies for effective outpatient scheduling show promise for successful implementation. The three most commonly used systems involve variations on block scheduling, modified block scheduling and individual scheduling. In block scheduling, all patients are scheduled for one appointment time, for instance 9:00 AM or 1:00 PM. They are then served on a first-come–first-service (FCFS) basis. Clearly, this approach has long patient waiting times, high clinic congestion and minimal staff idle time. Modified block scheduling breaks the day into smaller blocks (e.g. the beginning of each hour) and schedules smaller blocks of patients into those times. It has many of the characteristics of the block systems but patient waiting time is lowered. On the other hand, individual scheduling systems schedule patients for individual times throughout the day often in conjunction with staff availabilities. If scheduled inter-arrival times are not significantly shorter than service times, patient waiting time is reduced and staff idle time can be kept small. However, these systems require much more information on patients' illnesses and needs, triaging may be necessary by the appointment scheduler, and unforeseen events can cause severe scheduling problems. In spite of these potential drawbacks, individualized scheduling systems are most widely used in the United States.

The literature on outpatient scheduling is extensive, beginning in the 1950's and peaking in the 1960's and 1970's. Since much of it is based on queueing or simulation, studies were done to determine parametric distributions for patient service times. Scheduling schemes to reduce patient waiting time, while not increasing physician idle time, were analyzed using these distributions as inputs.

O'Keefe [1985] gives a very good description of the waiting times, congestion, and bureaucracy in consultative clinics in the British Health Service. A modified block system is used. Using heuristic methods he shows that some improvement can be made in spite of overwhelming resistance to change and extensive system constraints. Satisfying the scheduling system's non-patient stakeholders requires implementation of a policy that is clearly suboptimal for patients. The work is interesting in that it implicitly shows that, to effect change in a bureaucratic system, it is essential to address and/or change the incentives of the stakeholders running the system.

Fries & Marathe [1981] evaluate several approximate methods to determine the optimal variable-size multiple block (VSMB) appointment system. Patient waiting time, physician idle time, and physician overtime are the criteria used to compare various methods. The weights assigned these three criteria greatly affect the optimal appointment system choice. Simulation is used by Vissers & Wijngaard [1979] to produce a general method for developing appointment systems for single server outpatient clinics at a hospital. They demonstrate that the key variables in the simulation of a single server system are: the mean consultation time, the coefficient of variation of the consultation time, the mean system earliness, the standard deviation of patients' punctuality, and the total number of appointments. Simulations using various values for the five variables allow design of an appointment method which meet predetermined standards for waiting time and idle time. Callahan & Redmon [1987] devise a combined time-based and problem-based scheduling system for a pediatric outpatient clinic. Two types of time slots are designed: short times for routine patient exams and long times for extensive exams. Time slots for different patient problems are allocated to specific presenting problems. The problem-based scheduling system improves staff utilization and patient satisfaction, suggesting that additional development of this triaging and time-slotting approach may be beneficial.

Outpatient scheduling will require further refinement in the future, as the emphasis on this mode of care delivery increases. Scheduling models need to include performance measures reflecting the costs and benefits for all participants. Segmentation of patients into categories with significantly different requirements for service can also enhance the performance characteristics of patient-scheduling systems. In clinics where emergent patients are reasonably frequent each day, the classification scheme must separate these patients from non-emergent other patients. Work by Shonick [1972] for emergent patients in acute care general hospitals, and by other authors in other settings, demonstrates that a truncated Poisson distribution provides a good fit for the arrival process of such patients.

An outpatient scheduling system which considers the stochastic variation of emergency patients separately from the stochastic variation of no shows and late arrivals of scheduled patients will better achieve minimal waiting time and minimal staff idle time.

2.2.2. Inpatient scheduling

There are three major dimensions of inpatient scheduling. First is the scheduling of elective admissions together with emergent admissions into appropriate units of the hospital each day (admissions, A). Second is the daily scheduling of inpatients to the appropriate care units within the hospital for treatment or diagnoses throughout their stay (transfers, T). Third is the scheduling of the discharges of patients to their homes or other care delivery institutions (discharges, D). Clearly, these scheduling activities (ATD) are linked and depend upon many characteristics of the patients and hospital.

The models used for inpatient scheduling are more complex, and require more data and better information systems than those for outpatients. Many different methodologies are proposed involving queueing models as represented by Markov and semi-Markov processes, mathematical programming, heuristic and expert systems, and simulation. There are also less formal modelling approaches more traditionally associated with rules-of-thumb and charting models. Because of the complexities of inpatient scheduling problems and because of relatively poor internal forecasting and information systems, most hospitals use informal or ad hoc methods. Consequently, neither the size of the facilities, staffing, nor facility utilization are well planned, resulting in inefficiencies caused by peaks and valleys of occupancy. The valleys create a situation of excess contracted labor. The peaks create congestion and, because of difficulties of finding appropriately trained personnel on short notice at typical wages, can lead to patient dissatisfaction, lower quality and higher operating costs. Those problems can occur throughout the institution, involving physicians, residents, nurses, aides, and ancillary, support and administrative services personnel. On the other hand, analytic inpatient scheduling can ameliorate many of these problems and improve effective and efficient (optimizing) use of hospital resources.

As with outpatient scheduling, the inpatient scheduling literature began to appear in the early 1950's and peaked in the 1960's and 1970's. Most of the studies on admission scheduling divide the patients into two categories: waiting list and emergency. Furthermore, most of these studies only cover admissions to a single service in the hospital (such as surgery, obstetrics, pediatrics or another single ward). The idea underlying these scheduling systems is to compute the expected number of available beds for the next day (or longer). The schedule system would then reserve a block of beds for the emergent patients randomly arriving in the next 24 hours and then fill the remaining beds from the waiting list of patients for elective admission. Typically, the amount of reserve beds for emergency will be based on the means and variances or probability distribution of their arrival patterns (usually a truncated or compound Poisson would be used) and on some measure of 'over-run of demand' such as 95% or 99% of the emergent demand would be satisfied daily or over some longer period. This variation on the classic inventory control problem is usually solved by simulation rather than analytic methods.

In computing the anticipated bed availability for the next day, many authors attempt to estimate the length of stay of current patients and then forecast expected discharges. Due to lack of severity of illness information and other factors and because there is no incentive to discharge patients on a systematic basis in pre-DRG days, these forecasts were not very accurate. Furthermore, none of the studies look at the hospital as a total system in that there may have been other bottlenecks in the institution such as radiology, laboratory, personnel staffing or transport which are adding unnecessary days to length of stay or causing other bed utilization effects.

For admissions scheduling, queueing and simulation models are most often used. This is true also for inpatient flows within the hospital. The most common scheduling rule is to compute the number of beds needed to accept a given portion of emergent patients and then to fill any remaining available beds with waiting list patients. Variations on this rule are used in most admissions scheduling systems today. Some studies try to optimize on the tradeoff between patients' satisfaction as to when they were scheduled for admission, treatment and discharge versus some measures of hospital efficiency such as minimization of deviation from some desired hospital census level.

Kuzdrall, Kwak & Schnitz [1981] model five operating rooms and a twelve-bed, post-anesthesia care unit. Each operating room and PACU bed are treated as a separate facility. Paralleling results found in job shop scheduling, the authors find that a policy which schedules the longest surgeries first resulted in a 25% savings in operating room time compared with a policy of random scheduling.

Trivedi [1980] describes a stochastic model of patient discharges which could be used to help regulate elective admissions and achievement of occupancy goals. He also discusses the advantages of incorporating discharge forecasting, occupancy level management, and nurse staffing management.

Several authors construct patient flow models in hospitals as patients move progressively through different therapeutic or diagnostic units to obtain the appropriate treatment. The primary methodology used is to model the progressive care as a semi-Markov process where patients move randomly and progressively (depending on their conditions) from one unit to another and remain in each unit for a random period of time. Kao [1974] models the progression of coronary care patients, and Hershey, Weiss & Cohen [1981], Cohen, Hershey & Weiss [1980] and Weiss, Cohen & Hershey [1982] model the progressive care for obstetric patients. Kostner & Shachtman [1981] use a Markov chain analysis for patients with nosocomial infections. The primary purpose for modelling the progressive care in these studies are for bed planning (capacity) decisions, personnel scheduling decisions and care delivery decisions. However, it is also clear that these patient movements can be used for inpatient admission scheduling decisions and for other aspects of care evaluation, technology procurement and quality and cost control. Because of the lack of adequate data and information systems and complexity of these models, they have yet to be used in hospital settings. However, as cost pressures continue to grow, more effective patient scheduling methods will be needed to balance and plan staffing, facilities, equipment procurement and services. Much more research and applications need to be studied to link these systems for higher quality lower cost care.

2.3. Work force planning and scheduling

The management of human resources is a major activity in health care organizations. Because staffing costs usually represent the majority of the operating budget, this area will become even more important in the future as health costs are subject to increasingly tighter public scrutiny or regulation. Like many service organizations, the ability to match staffing resources to a fluctuating demand directly affects operating efficiency and the quality of service. The development of innovative approaches to the organization and management of nursing and other human resources holds great promise for further cost savings in the delivery of health services.

Although the planning and scheduling of health care personnel is not conceptually different than that of other personnel (one needs the right persons in the right places at the right times) there are several factors which make the problem in health care more complex. First, there is the interrelation among various highly trained and skilled personnel that must be available at the appropriate times for different patients. These personnel include different specialty categories of nurses, therapists, physicians, medical technicians and others. Staffing must be available 24 hours a day on all days, during which demand varies considerably. Personnel have preferences and requests for types of schedules and working conditions. Many function as relatively independent professionals with regard to the level and scope of tasks. Second, it is frequently difficult to measure quality of work, especially as it pertains to successful patient outcomes. This measurement difficulty presents problems in determining the mix of types and skill levels of personnel which are needed to obtain a given level of quality. Third, for most personnel categories there is a 'flat' organizational structure with few career paths available. As a consequence, human resource management must continually cope with ways to maintain personnel satisfaction and enjoyment for highly capable individuals over the period of many years, even decades, or face the high costs of absenteeism, turnover, and general dissatisfaction. Indeed, many debates about professional nursing activities are direct outgrowths of basic nurse staffing problems.

Most of the research in staffing and scheduling for health care organizations focuses on nursing. However, personnel availability and utilization in the laboratory, emergency department, respiratory therapy, HMO's, and other locations are also being examined.

Hershey, Pierskalla & Wandel [1981] conceptualize the nurse staffing process as a hierarchy of three decision levels which operate over different time horizons and with different precision. These three decision levels are called corrective allocations, shift scheduling, and workforce planning. Corrective allocations are done daily, shift schedules are the days on/days off work schedules for each nurse for four to eight weeks ahead, and workforce plans are quarterly, semiannual, or annual plans of nursing needs by skill level.

On any given day within a shift, the staff capacities among units may be adjusted to unpredicted demand fluctuations and absenteeism by using float, part-time, relief, overtime, and voluntary absenteeism. These 'corrective allocations' depend upon the individuals' preferences, their availabilities, and capabilities. Shift scheduling is the matching of nursing staff availabilities to expected workload among units on a daily basis for a four to eight week period in the future. For each employee days on and off, as well as shift rotation, are determined. The individual's needs and preferences must be considered to bring about high personnel satisfaction. The above two scheduling levels are tactical, in that they concern the utilization of personnel already employed within the organization with their known mix of specializations and experiences. Workforce planning is the long-term balance of numbers and capability of nursing personnel among units obtained by hiring, training, transferring between jobs, and discharging. Because of the time-lags involved, workforce-planning actions must be taken early to meet anticipated long-term fluctuations in demand and supply. Very few studies address this decision level.

The interdependence of the three levels must be recognized to bring about systematic nurse staffing improvements. Each level is constrained by available resources, by previous commitments made at higher levels, and by the degrees of flexibility for later correction at lower levels. Therefore, each decision level is strongly dependent on the other two. For best performance, one level cannot be considered in isolation.

The final component of the model is the coordination of staffing management activities with other departments. For example, if a nursing unit is short staffed, ancillary departments could transport patients. Shift scheduling should be coordinated with scheduled admissions and surgeries. Collart & Haurie [1980] evaluate the relative efficiency of three controls applied to the supply and demand system of inpatient nursing care: regulating admission of elective patients, allocation of a floating pool of nursing personnel, and assignment of the unit's nursing personnel to various tasks. They conclude that the float pool is only slightly superior to admissions control for matching supply and demand for care, while task assignment is not an efficient means of controlling the adjustment of supply to meet demand. Shukla [1985] also examines admissions monitoring and scheduling to improve the flow of work in hospitals.

The earliest OR work on work force planning and scheduling in hospitals began with measuring the needs of patients for various types of care. Over time, such needs have come to include physical, hygienic, instructional, observational, emotional, and family counseling needs of patients. These types and amounts of care are quantified in patient classification systems and then related to the hours of different skilled personnel needed to meet them [CASH, 1967; Connor, 1961; Jelinek, 1964]. Models for corrective allocations are given by Warner & Prawda [1972], and Hershey, Abernathy & Baloff [1974].

Longer-term workload forecasting (one to two months) by skill level is needed for shift scheduling. Most forecasting in use merely extrapolates recent experience using adjustments for seasonal and weekend variations. Often the models used are simple moving averages, but occasionally regression and ARIMA time series models have been used. Helmer, Opperman & Suver [1980] use a multiple regression approach to predict nursing labor-hour requirements by ward, shift, day of the week, and month of the year. Pang & Swint [1985] also used multiple regression to predict daily and weekly laboratory workloads for scheduling purposes. Other forecasting models and applications are discussed in Section 1.2.

Shift scheduling which is effective (i.e., meets the health care needs of patients and the preferences of nurses at minimal cost) is a complex problem that attracts the interest of operations researchers. The earliest and simplest scheduling model is the cyclic schedule. This schedule repeats a fixed pattern of days on and off for each nurse indefinitely into the future. This type of schedule cannot adjust for forecasted workload changes, extended absences, or the scheduling preferences of individual nurses. Such rigid schedules place heavy demands on the corrective allocations and workforce planning levels. Hence, corrective allocation must be extremely flexible and workforce planning must more precisely forecast long-term workforce needs to avoid excessive staffing [Hershey, Pierskalla & Wandel, 1981].

The two most frequently cited and applied approaches to flexible scheduling [Miller, Pierskalla & Rath, 1976; Warner, 1976] include the preferences of staff in the scheduling decision. Miller, Pierskalla & Rath [1976] develop a mathematical programming system using a 'cyclical coordinate descent' algorithm. The model incorporates two types of constraints. The feasibility constraints consist of hospital policies that must be met (for example minimum and maximum length of a work shift ('stretch'). The second type comprises non-binding constraints that can be violated (for example, minimum staffing levels or undesirable schedule patterns determined by the staff nurses). When a non-binding constraint is violated, a penalty cost is assigned. Each staff nurse is allowed to assign relative weights to various violations of her/his non-binding constraints. The problem is formulated to minimize penalty costs of the scheduling patterns. Benefits of this approach include decreased difference between actual and desired staffing, higher average personnel satisfaction, and lower staffing costs than manual or semi-automated systems. In a commercial implementation, this model is modified to include variable length shifts and goal optimization to meet staffing needs and to satisfy nurse preferences.

For scheduling personnel other than nurses, Vassilacopoulos [1985] simulates as an $M/G/m(t)$ system the allocation of physicians to shifts in an emergency department. Tzukert & Cohen [1985] describe a mixed-integer program that assigns patients to dental students in a clinic. Issues of efficiency, varied educational experiences, facility and faculty constraints, and continuity of care are incorporated in the model.

Workforce planning takes a longer time perspective and includes hiring, training, transferring between positions, and discharging employees. A variety of quantitative models of workforce planning appear in the literature. Worthington

& Guy [1988] describe a quarterly system of workforce allocations based on patient classification data for the previous three months. Baker & Fitzpatrick [1985] develop an integer programming model for the problem of reducing staff in a recreation therapy department with the objective of maximizing the effectiveness of staff retained. Multi-attribute utility theory is used to integrate performance and experience attributes, so as to obtain a utility surface for evaluating effectiveness. Shimshak, Damico & Burden [1981] use three queueing models to determine the effects of pharmacy staffing on prescription order delays.

Kao & Tung [1981] present a case study of long-range staffing planning. Their model is a combination of a linear program and an ARIMA forecasting system. The forecast is integrated with institutional constraints and patient care requirements in a linear program for assessing the need for permanent staff, overtime pay, and temporary help (differentiated by medical service, nursing skill level, and time period) and for evaluating the size of a float pool.

Cavaiola & Young [1980] develop an integrated system of patient classification, nurse staff planning, and staff budgeting for a long-term care facility. The basic staffing model uses mixed integer linear programming to solve the staffing allocation problem for the best assignment of nursing personnel based on a criterion called 'appropriateness' which served as a surrogate for quality of care.

Simulation is applied to a variety of workforce planning problems. Kutzler & Sevcovic [1980] develop a simulation model of a nurse-midwifery practice. Hashimoto, Bell & Marshment [1987] use a Monte Carlo simulation in an intensive care setting to evaluate cost, number of voluntary absences, staff call-ins, and total cost for a year at different staffing levels (FTEs per shift). Duraiswamy, Welton & Reisman [1981] develop a simulation for a similar problem, including seasonal variations in patient demand and staffing supply. They simulated a twenty-bed Medical Intensive Care Unit, including patient census, patient acuity and required staffing on a daily basis, for one year. A simulation of obstetric anesthesia developed by Reisman, Cull, Emmons, Dean, Lin, Rasmussen, Darukhanavala & George [1977] enables them to determine the optimal configuration of the anesthesia team. Magazine [1977] describes a patient transportation service problem in a hospital. The solution involves queueing analysis and simulation to determine the number of transporters needed to ensure availability 95% of the time. A mixed-integer program determines the required number of shifts per week.

In addition to the three personnel decision levels, nursing management must also make policy and/or budgetary decisions which inevitably restrict alternative actions at the tactical levels. Trivedi [1981] develops a mixed-integer goal programming model based on financial data and staffing standards in the preparation of the nursing budget. The model allows examination of consequences of changes in understaffing, wage levels, impact of changing skill substitution rules, personnel policies, and forecasted patient volume and mix. Model objectives include minimization of expenditures, of understaffing, and of the number of part-time employees. Looking at a similar problem, Hancock, Pollock & Kim [1987] develop a mathematical model to determine the cost effects of productivity standards and optimal staffing policies. One source of variation in productivity is the ability of the work force to absorb variations in workload. They recommend the establishment of optimal productivity levels and staffing, and determine the resulting budgets so that, if true potential productivity is known, the costs of productivity compromises needed to gain staff and management acceptance will also be known. The model also provides information for determining the costs of management policies about overtime, full and part-time staff, the quality of worker selection, and other related decisions.

Leiken, Sexton & Silkman [1987] use a linear program to find the minimum cost staffing pattern of RNs, LPNs, and nurse aides that meets patient needs in a nursing home. The model's decision variables are the number of hours of each skill level to employ and number of hours each skill level should devote to each task.

In the three preceding examples the authors suggest policies to improve the overall long-term productivity of the nursing (and other) staff while reducing or minimizing costs. Implementation often encounters primary or secondary impacts caused by the suggested changes on organizational characteristics that are hard to observe objectively. One such attribute is changes (if any) in the quality of health outcomes, which may occur if skill levels are downgraded or time available to complete tasks is significantly reduced. Other such attributes include employee morale, turnover, absenteeism, training costs and other effects. In spite of these difficulties, long-term personnel policies must be examined along the lines suggested by these models in order to bring about improved productivity and reduced costs in health care delivery and future research should expand the breadth of existing models.

3. Medical management

3.1. Screening for disease

The introduction of, and improvements in, tests which detect diseases have resulted in advances in medical diagnosis and disease detection. These tests may be applied to an individual ('individual screening') or to large subsets of the population ('mass screening'). These cases are different modelling problems because the objectives of the decision makers frequently differ, and the constraints and parameters affecting the decisions may vary. For example, in mass screening the objective may be to minimize the prevalence of a contagious disease in the population subject to resource constraints and compliance levels, expressed as parameters for subpopulations. For an individual, the objective may be to prolong life (or the quality of life) and the constraints may be related to the individual's ability or willingness to pay and the parameters to the individual's characteristics. In each case the decision makers are also usually different persons, e.g., the public health official or HMO director for mass screening and the patient or patient's physician for individual screening.

Currently, mass screening programs are under discussion for the detection and control of HIV (Human Immuno-Deficiency Virus), the infectious virus which causes the Acquired Immuno-Deficiency Syndrome (AIDS). Mass screening programs are also used for hepatitis A, B, nonA-nonB, tuberculosis, syphilis, and other infectious diseases. In some countries, mass screening protocols for non-contagious as well as contagious diseases have been established for national health programs. In the U.K, for example, there is a mass screening protocol for the early detection of cervical cancer, intended to reduce the prevalence of the disease and save lives.

Mass screening programs, however, are expensive. Direct quantifiable costs of mass screening, such as those of the labor and materials needed to administer the testing are large, but indirect costs may be much greater. Indirect costs, for example, include the inconvenience and possible discomfort necessitated by the test, the cost of false positives which entails both emotional distress and the need to do unnecessary follow-up testing, and even the risk of physical harm to the testee (e.g., the cumulative effect of X-ray exposure or harm from unnecessary surgery).

The policy maker must consider several factors in choosing a mass screening protocol. First, mass screening programs have to be designed in light of the tradeoff between the testing cost, which increases both with the frequency of test applications and with the accuracy of the test used, and the testing benefits to be achieved from detecting the defect in an earlier stage of development. Second, such a design must determine which kind of testing technology should be used, as different technologies may have different reliability characteristics (false positive and false negative levels) and costs. Third, the frequency of testing must be decided. Fourth, because different subpopulations may have different susceptibility to the disease, the problem of optimal allocation of a fixed testing budget among subpopulations must be considered. Fifth, behavioral problems of attendance at the testing location and compliance with treatment after disease discovery must be included in the analysis. Many of these factors apply to models for individual screening as well.

The literature on screening models has a long history, but the last two decades have seen its greatest growth. Two major streams of knowledge contribute to this area. The first, and perhaps larger stream, is the work in epidemiology and biology. This work focuses primarily on descriptive modelling of disease processes, progression and causal factors. In the case of contagious diseases, very complex simultaneous differential equation and/or statistical models are frequently used to describe the growth, maturity and decline of various specific or general types of diseases. Interventions in the disease propagation are often modelled as changes in the progression parameters rather than as explicit decision variables. An early work, by ReVelle, Feldman & Lynn [1969], uses these approaches and models the epidemiology of tuberculosis under different scenarios and types of interventions. Under simplifying assumptions, the authors derive a linear program which can be optimized to determine the minimum cost solution for screening and treatments. An also excellent, but somewhat dated, book in this area is by Bailey [1975]. More recent work which gives a good flavor of this work in epidemiology and biology modelling literature includes the papers by Dietz [1988], Hethcote, Yorke & Nold [1982], Hyman & Stanley [1988] and May & Anderson [1987].

The second stream of research related to screening models is the work in maintainability (i.e., the modelling of decisions for inspection and maintenance of units or systems subject to deterioration or obsolescence). This literature contains the application of a large variety of decision models, including mathematical programming, Markov decision, and simulation. Simulation is frequently used in the epidemiological literature also. Two somewhat dated literature reviews in maintainability are contained in Pierskalla & Voelker [1976] and McCall [1965].

Much of the recent work on screening has been driven by the increased emphasis on major serious chronic diseases. In the case of non-contagious diseases, these have been cancer, heart disease and malaria. For contagious diseases, they are diseases that are largely sexually transmitted (STDs), most notably HIV and hepatitis B.

Models of screening programs for an individual frequently incorporate information on the disease's progression and then try to minimize the expected detection delay (the time from disease incidence until its detection) or maximize the lead time (the time from detection by screening until self-detection or until symptomatic). Characteristically, these models take a longitudinal time frame for the individual, because an individual, through his/her lifetime, is subject to different conditional probabilities of incurring the disease. Thus, screening schedules are determined sequentially by utilizing prior testing results, or simultaneously for an entire lifetime, such as every X years.

Using the etiology and progress of a disease and its relationship to screening effectiveness, the reliability of test and the lead time gained from detection can be modelled as a function of the state of the disease rather than the time since the defect's incidence, e.g., Prorok [1976a,b], Thompson & Doyle [1976], Schwartz & Galliher [1975], Thompson & Disney [1976] and Voelker & Pierskalla [1980]. Bross & Blumenson [1976] develop a mathematical model to evaluate a screening strategy, termed a 'compromise screening strategy', which consists of two stages of screening examinations with different harmful effects as well as reliabilities. The model is also applied to evaluate different screening intervals for breast cancer detection. Schwartz [1978b] develops a mathematical model of breast cancer, and then uses it later to evaluate the benefits of screening [Schwartz, 1978a]. Again the rate of disease progression was explicitly included as a factor affecting the probability of the disease detection.

Eddy [1980], well aware of the complexity of relationships among test reliabilities, disease development, and prognosis of breast cancer, develops the most comprehensive breast cancer screening model by focusing on two attributes that carry information about the effectiveness of the screening tests: the mammogram interval and the patient's age. By modelling these two factors as random variables, Eddy is able to derive analytical expressions for the sensitivity (true-positive rate) and specificity (true-negative rate) of test procedures, utilizing repeatedly the Bayesian statistical approach. The design of screening strategies to optimally allocate fixed resources, however, is only briefly discussed by Eddy. He uses the basic model to evaluate screening for other cancers, such as colorectal and cervical, as well as non-cancerous, non-contagious diseases. Eddy's work is very important, as it has been implemented by health agencies in national policy recommendations for screening intervals based on the individual's age, sex and prior histories. Eddy [1983] gives a good exposition on the importance of screening, the critical factors and parameters necessary for screening models, and a comprehensive sensitivity analysis of his model to various assumptions and parameters.

Kolesar [1980], using integer mathematical programming, constructs an optimal screening procedure to test for vision loss in suspected glaucoma patients. This model assumes perfect test reliabilities. The screening is done by choosing a subset of a grid of points covering the eye.

Less work has been done on mass screening models than on individual screening. Kirch & Klein [1974a] address a mass screening application that seeks an inspection schedule to minimize expected detection delay. The methodology is then applied to determining examination schedules for breast cancer detection [Kirch & Klein, 1974b]. Pierskalla & Voelker [1976] and Voelker & Pierskalla [1980] develop analytical models of a mass screening program and analyze them for both cases where the test procedures are perfect or imperfect. Optimal allocation of a fixed budget to different sub-populations is given in the perfect test case, whereas optimal decision rules concerning the best choice and frequency of testing are derived for the imperfect case.

Lee & Pierskalla [1988a] describe the stochastic processes underlying the progression of a disease in a population when mass screening programs and compliance regimens are instituted. The resulting models are useful for the analysis of the optimal design of mass screening programs for a country or agency which is attempting to control or eradicate a contagious or non-contagious disease. In the model, non-contagious diseases are shown to be special cases of contagious diseases when certain distribution parameters are held constant. In a later paper, Lee & Pierskalla [1988b] present a simplified model describing the stochastic process underlying the etiology of contagious and non-contagious diseases with mass screening. Typical examples might include screening of tuberculosis in urban ghetto areas, venereal diseases in the sexually active, or HIV in high-risk population groups. The model is applicable to diseases which have zero or negligible latent periods (the latent period is the time from disease incidence until it becomes infectious to others). In the model, it is assumed that the reliabilities of the screening tests are constant, and independent of how long the population unit has the disease. Both tests with perfect and imperfect reliabilities are considered. A mathematical program for computing the optimal test choice and screening periods is presented. It is shown that the optimal screening schedule is equally spaced for tests with perfect reliability. Other properties relating to the managerial problems of screening frequencies, test selection, and resource allocation are also presented.

In England and Wales, various health authorities and medical societies have proposed different national policies to screen for cervical cancer. Parkin & Moss

[1986] use a computer simulation to evaluate nine such policies and their cost-effectiveness. They conclude that the original mass screening policy based on five-yearly testing of women aged over 35 years appears to be the most cost-effective for the National Health Service.

Most recently, many operations researchers and others have been involved in research to reduce the prevalence via prevention or ameliorate the effects of HIV and AIDS in individuals and populations. Notably, the queueing and differential equation models by Kaplan [1989] and Caulkins & Kaplan [1991] have been instrumental in the implementation of needle distribution, cleansing and information programs for intravenous drug users (IVDU) in New Haven, CT and New York, NY. Homer & St. Clair [1991], with a differential equations model, also examine the policy implications of clean needle efforts to reduce the rate of incidence and prevalence of HIV in IVDU. The simulation modelling efforts of Brandeau, Lee, Owens, Sox & Wachter [1991] greatly clarify the policy discussions concerning legislation such as testing high-risk women to reduce the birthrate of HIV-infected infants, contact tracing of sexual partners of HIV infected persons and screening of applicants for marriage licenses. By and large, their work shows that these types of programs for most populations are not cost-effective and do not significantly affect the course of the HIV epidemic. In an excellent review paper, Brandeau, Lee, Owens, Sox & Wachter [1990] also discuss and evaluate the structure and other issues involved in models for policy analysis of HIV screening and intervention. They also highlight gaps in current research and important policy questions for further analysis.

In a variant and extension of the idea of screening individuals for HIV, Bosworth & Gustafson [1991] develop a microcomputer-based decision support system for persons with HIV or who are at some risk to contract HIV to obtain anonymous, current and nonjudgemental information on personal behavior, social support, referral services, and medical advances to treat HIV. The intent of the DSS is to help people cope with the very difficult situations they face if seropositive, or understand their risks if not. In addition, it is hoped that the information would lead to personal behavioral changes to reduce the future incidence of HIV.

Operations researchers have been attracted to the problem of screening for disease due to its importance, close ties to maintenance problems, and rich structure. More work is needed on the linkages to the epidemiology literature and to the construction and evaluation of models which can aid in decisions that are often based on sparse or incomplete data and incomplete knowledge of the disease etiology and propagation.

3.2. Clinical decision-making

The contributions of operations research methodologies to disease prevention and the management of ill persons constitute a large and growing area of both health services research and operations research. This area is a hybrid which draws upon the mathematics and structural analysis of operations research and solution approaches including optimization and simulation, as well as a deep knowledge of biological, economic, and sociological aspects of patient care. This section will review medical management in three areas. First is the use of *decision analysis* to aid in the structuring of medical decisions. Second is *performance improvement*. In this area, operations research methodologies which improve the accuracy of diagnoses, the ability to diagnose under uncertainty, and the performance of testing or treatment strategies are reviewed. This area is particularly relevant to current concerns about quality of care and practice efficiency. Third is the use of operations research techniques and *cost effectiveness* analysis (CEA) to analyze health care policies and those policies that affect large populations.

Decision analysis has become widespread in analyzing medical decisions, policies, and practice efficiency. One of the first principles of approaching a decision in which there is risk and uncertainty is to determine the attributes, structure, and outcomes of those decisions, along with their concomitant probabilities. Pauker & Kassirer [1987] provide an excellent review of decision analysis in health care and describe three important areas. First is the use of decision trees to show probabilities, outcomes, chance nodes, and decision nodes for complex problems, such as thyroid irradiation treatment during childhood or coronary artery disease treatment. These principles have been used in numerous health services research articles. The key part of this process of decision tree structuring is identification of critical nodes or those decision variables which are important to outcomes or which the decision-maker wants to modify. Second is sensitivity analysis, where the parameters, particularly *ex ante* probabilities of chance events, are manipulated to determine the effect on the resultant decision to either errors in data or uncertainty itself. Third is identification of unambiguous outcomes. This facet is a weakness of most medical decision analytic research, because outcomes, or end points of treatment, are sometimes difficult to determine. For example, although death itself is a clearly identified state, it is rarely clear that the decision in question can be implicated in a death which is proximal to the decision. This ambiguity is the basis for so-called severity correction or risk adjustment for mortality. Beyond mortality, however, other indicators, such as life expectancy, quality of life, satisfaction, morbidity, or complications, are more difficult to determine and more ambiguous to structure. The current state of the decision analysis literature regarding outcomes is encouraging however. Wasson, Sox, Neff & Goldman [1983] report that in a survey of published prediction rules for clinical decision-making, 85% of articles clearly identify and appropriately define outcomes.

Many decisions faced by the clinician or the health services researcher are either too complex or contain states which are highly interdependent. Traditional, normal-form decision trees or other closed-form approaches are not easily applied, which consequently leads to a situation where simulation models are useful. One such approach to this problem is simulation of logical networks (SLN). In a 1984 article, Roberts & Klein review the application of network modelling to endstage renal disease, chronic stable angina, renal artery stenosis, and hypercholesterolemia. They then describe a technique by which modelling for other areas can be done. These diseases tend to be chronic and involve multi-component analysis.

Medical decision *performance improvement* applications are seen in two areas. First is in improving diagnostic accuracy for chronic and acute conditions. Second is in improving performance of testing strategies. This latter area usually uses tree structuring and network modelling, but involves analysis aimed at optimization or efficiency improvement.

A good example of this work is by Fryback & Keeney [1983] in which a complex judgmental model predicting the level of severity of a trauma patient is reported. The assessment of a trauma patient is confounded by rapidly changing physiologic states, multiple conflicting indicators, frequent erroneous normal physical examinations, and a high incidence of fatalities. To develop the model, the authors first elicit trauma surgeon expert opinions to develop seven specific concerns about trauma, such as ventilation systems or circulation systems. The experts rank-order these concerns into a hierarchy of trauma severity. They then develop a function in which the severity of a patient was a function of age, co-morbidities, and the measures of the seven severity indicators. Because severity scores were not additive, and since any measure alone could result in death, the severity conditions are considered multiplicative. It is further determined that many of the attributes were non-monotonic, indicating that they each have optimal ranges, and that deviations on either side represented deteriorations. From this information a trauma score index is developed which predicts level of severity for all trauma patients. The authors then perform a validation of the index on patients retrospectively.

Demonstrating an application of operations research techniques to chronic disease decisions, Moye & Roberts [1982] model the pharmacologic treatment of hypertension. The authors develop a stochastic representation of hypertension treatment that predicts the outcome of hypertensive treatment regimens which were observed in clinical situations. The authors do this by using expert input to determine different treatment protocols and the outcomes which were associated with them. The authors include compliance, effectiveness of the treatment regimen, side effects, cost, and symptoms of hypertension, and used traditional cut-offs for normal blood pressure (140/90) as an outcome measure. From this, probabilistic statements about whether a patient had controlled blood pressure on a given visit are developed. The authors then use consensus input from experts about compliance, probabilities that patients do not return for visits when their blood pressure is not controlled, and probabilities that patients are lost to care. These parameters are then subjected to a 13-step algorithm which determines optimal treatment, given the outcomes and cost information. These results are validated by comparison to studies reported in the literature about treatment outcomes.

In another application regarding live organ transplantation, David & Yechiali [1985] use a time-dependent stopping process to match donor kidneys to recipients. The authors note that at any given time, donor kidneys become available but, on the basis of histo-compatibility, rarely match any recipient perfectly in a regional pool. Thus, the degree of match is frequently imperfect, which usually determines the survival of the graft over the post-transplant period. The problem here is to determine at any given time whether an organ should be accepted or passed over to allow for another potential donor in the future. The authors formulate a general setting for optimal stopping problems with a time-dependent failure rate and model the arrival of offers as a renewal process. They show that the lifetime distribution of the underlying process of mismatches has an increasing failure rate. The authors then examine heterogeneous Poisson arrivals and derive a differential equation for the optimal control function, which leads to a tractable equation particularly suited to this problem. The authors apply the solution to the problem using observed data from the clinical literature.

The third area where operations research has made substantial contributions to medical management is in *cost effectiveness analysis* (CEA), or *cost benefit analysis* (CBA). The general framework of the CEA, as reviewed by Weinstein & Stason [1977], includes the following elements. First is net health care cost. The net costs of health care include direct health care and medical costs for any given condition, to which are added the costs of adverse side effects of any treatment and from which is subtracted the cost of morbidity, since these are the savings which health care accrues from the prevention of disease. Second is the net health effectiveness, the increase in life years which result from the treatment, to which are added the increased number of years gained from the elimination of morbidity. The number of life years lost to side effects are then subtracted. These years are frequently adjusted for quality of life (quality-adjusted life years, or QALY). The ratio of net costs to net effects is the cost effectiveness ratio. CBA, on the other hand, sets a value on the net effects and then seeks to determine if the value of the benefits outweigh the net costs. However, this requires assignment of value to life, which is frequently a controversial topic. Despite this shortcoming, several methodologies of life valuation, including willingness to pay and human capital, consumption, and production valuation, have been developed. CEA expresses the relative efficiency of a given treatment, and by comparison of treatments for similar diseases or conditions, an efficiency frontier can be identified and an 'optimal' treatment selected. However, comparison of multiple treatments is frequently precluded because they have different structures of care or outcomes, and hence, are difficult to compare. Therefore, most decisions are aimed at efficiency improvement rather than optimality.

Beyond providing the decision analysis framework by which CEA decisions can be structured and analyzed, operations research contributes to CEA in other ways, particularly in the development of computer simulations which allow analysis of decisions where data are sparse, where waiting periods for outcomes are long, or where different treatments result in widely differing levels of effectiveness. Habbema, Lubbe, Van Ortmarssen & Van der Maas [1985] demonstrate this approach in making cost effective decisions for the screening of cervical carcinoma. The authors develop a program which uses a Monte Carlo simulation to determine the effects of various screening protocols on the morbidity and mortality of a typical population. Because of the long period over which cervical carcinoma develops (lag time) and over which it could recur if treated (recurrence lag), simulation modelling is well suited to this problem. The authors generate distributions of cancer rates under various screening strategies, and then, by using standard assumptions about costs and effectiveness, determine the cost effectiveness of these scenarios.

In a related application, Kotlyarov & Schniederjans [1983] simulate a stochastic equipment utilization function to assist in the cost benefit analysis of capital investment in nuclear cardiology instruments, including the nuclear stethoscope, mobile camera, and fixed cardiac computer. The authors again use a Monte Carlo simulation technique to generate the stochastic behavior of utilization of the equipment, and use standard economic information about reimbursement rates and acquisition costs to determine under what utilization patterns it is cost effective to invest in such technology.

The extensive work which is being performed in expert systems and artificial intelligence cannot be reviewed in this chapter. The reader should refer to the work of: Greenes & Shortliffe [1990]; Langlotz, Shortliffe & Fagan [1988]; Langlotz, Fagan, Tu, Sikic & Shortliffe [1987]; Rennels, Shortliffe & Miller [1987]; Shortliffe [1987]; Rennels, Shortliffe, Stockdale & Miller [1987]; Gabrieli [1988]; Perry [1990]; Miller & Giuse [1991]; Hasman [1987]; and Steinwachs [1985] for examples of important research about expert systems and artificial intelligence.

Finally, it should be mentioned that data technology is opening up many more modelling opportunities for operations researchers. Some hospitals are experimenting with the installation of bedside terminals. These terminals are used primarily for bed-side admitting, transferring and discharging, nurse and physician order entry, and chart documentation. Other clinical departments making significant use of new data technologies are the medical and radiation laboratories, pharmacy, infectious disease control, and respiratory and physical/occupational therapies. These departments use systems to automate scheduling, testing, reporting, and recording of sessions and/or results. The systems check for errors, test duplication, wrong test/treatment time, allergic reactions, and incompatible drug protocols, and often state the correct actions to be taken or procedures to be followed and may suggest alternatives. Modelling these systems can enable hospital personnel to reduce errors, increase timeliness, reduce costs, and make appropriate diagnostic and treatment decisions, thereby reducing risk and increasing satisfaction and successful outcomes.

The management of medical patients has been enhanced greatly by the application of operations research. Of all areas of operations research applications in health care delivery, this area is perhaps the fastest growing. These models form the basis of artificial intelligence, management information systems, and decision support systems applications. However, clinicians still hesitate to use expert systems or other DSS models for diagnosis or treatment. Of course, there are many possible reasons why some innovations are adopted while others may only stay in the research mode. It is a goal of present and future research to study this clinician-system process in order to understand the dynamics of adoption and diffusion. As this knowledge grows, operations research-based knowledge systems will become more useful to the practicing physician.

References and bibliography

Planning and Strategy

Bach, L., and R. Hoberg (1985). A planning model for regional systems of CT scanners. *Socio-Econom. Planning Sci.* 19, 189–199.

Bahnson, H.T., T.R. Hakala, T.E. Starzl, R.L. Hardesty, B.P. Griffith and S. Iwatsuki (1986). Development and organization of a multiple organ transplantation program. *Ann. Surgery* 203(6), 620–625.

Boldy, D. (1987). The relationship between decision support systems and operational research: Health care examples. *European J. Oper. Res.* 29, 1128–1134.

Bowen, T., and P. Forte (1987). The balance of care microcomputer system, *Proc. 2nd Internat. Conf. of Systems Science in Health and Social Services for the Elderly and Disabled*, Curtin University of Technology, Perth.

Cohen, M.A., W.P. Pierskalla and R. Sassetti (1987). Economies of scale in blood banking, in: G.M. Clark (ed.), *Competition in blood services*, American Association of Blood Banks Press, New York, pp. 25–37.

Coverdale, I.L., and S.M. Negrine (1978). The balance of care project: Modelling the allocation of health and personal social services. *J. Oper. Res. Soc.* 29(11), 1043–1054.

Daskin, M.S., and E.H. Stern (1982). Application of an expected covering model to emergency medical service system design. *Decision Sci.* 13, 416–439.

Denton, F.T., A. Gafni, B.G. Spencer and G.L. Stoddart (1983). Potential savings from the adoption of nurse practitioner technology in the Canadian health care system. *Socio-Econom. Planning Sci.* 17, 199–209.

Fitzsimmons, J.A., and R.S. Sullivan (1982). The Post-industrial Era, *Service Operations Management*, McGraw Hill, New York, pp. 3–4.

Granneman, T.W., R.S. Brown and M.V. Pauly (1986). Estimating hospital costs: A multiple output analysis. *J. Health Econom.* 5, 107–127.

Hershey, J.C., and D.H. Kropp (1979). A re-appraisal of the productivity potential and economic benefits of physician's assistants. *Medical Care* 17, 592–606.

Hodgson, M.J. (1986). An hierarchical location-allocation model with allocations based on facility size. *Ann. Oper. Res.* 6, 273–289.

Hodgson, M.J. (1988). A hierarchical location-allocation model for primary health care delivery in a developing area. *Social Sci. Medicine* 26, 153–161.

Hughes, R.G., S.S. Hunt and H.S. Luft (1987). Effects of surgeon volume on quality of care in hospitals. *Medical Care* 25(6), 489–503.

Kao, E.P.C., and G.G. Tung (1981). Bed allocation in a public health care delivery system. *Management Sci.* 27, 507–520.

Kelly, J.V., and F. Hellinger (1986). Physician and hospital factors associated with mortality of surgical patients. *Medical Care* 24(9), 785–800.

Luft, H.S., J. Bunker and A. Enthoven (1979). Should operations be regionalized? An empirical study of the relation between surgical volume and mortality. *New Engl. J. Medicine* 301, 1364.

Maerki, S.C., H.S. Luft and S.S. Hunt (1986). Selecting categories of patients for regionalization: Implications of the relationship between volume and outcome. *Medical Care* 24(2), 148–158.

Or, I., and W.P. Pierskalla (1979). A transportation location-allocation model for regional blood-banking. *AIIE Trans.* 11, 86–95.

Pezzella, F., R. Bonanno and B. Nicoletti (1981). A system approach to the optimal health-care districting. *European J. Oper. Res.* 8, 139–146.

Price, W.L., and M. Turcotte (1986). Locating a blood bank. *Interfaces* 16, 17–26.

Rizakow, E., J. Rosenhead and K. Reddington (1991). AIDSPLAN: A decision support model for planning the provision of HIV/AIDS related services. *Interfaces* 21(3), 117–129.

Robinson, J.C., and H.S. Luft (1985). The impact of hospital market structure on patient volume, average length of stay, and the cost of care. *J. Health Econom.* 4(4), 333–356.

Romanin-Jacur, G., and P. Facchin (1982). Optimal planning for a pediatric semi-intensive care unit via simulation. *European J. Oper. Res.* 29, 192–198.

Schneider, D. (1981). A methodology for the analysis of comparability of services and financial impact of closure of obstetrics services. *Medical Care* 19(4), 393–409.

Todd, J.N., and A. Coyne (1985). Medical manpower: A district model. *Br. Medical J.* 291, 984–986.

Demand forecasting

Harrington, M.B. (1977). Forecasting area-wide demand for health care services: A critical review of major techniques and their application. *Inquiry* 14, 254–268.

Hogarth, R.M., and S. Makridakis (1981). Forecasting and planning: An evaluation. *Management Sci.* 27(2), 115–138.

Johansen, S., S. Bowles and G. Haney (1988). A model for forecasting intermittent skilled nursing home needs. *Res. Nursing Health* 11, 375–382.

Kamentzky, R.D., L.J. Shuman and H. Wolfe (1982). Estimating need and demand for pre-hospital care. *Oper. Res.* 30, 1148–1167.

Kao, E.P.C., and F.M. Pokladnik (1978). Incorporating exogenous factors in adaptive forecasting of hospital census. *Management Sci.* 24, 1677–1686.

Kao, E.P.C., and G.G. Tung (1980). Forecasting demands for inpatient services in a large public health care delivery system. *Socio-Econom. Planning Sci.* 14, 97–106.

Lane, D., D. Uyeno, A. Stark, E. Kliewer and G. Gutman (1985). Forecasting demand for long term care services. *Health Services Res.* 20, 435–460.

Trivedi, V., I. Moscovice, R. Bass and J. Brooks (1987). A semi-Markov model for primary health care manpower supply prediction. *Management Sci.* 33, 149–160.

Location selection

Benveniste, R. (1985). Solving the combined zoning and location problem for several emergency units. *J. Oper. Res. Soc.* 36, 433–450.

Bianchi, G., and R.L. Church (1988). A hybrid fleet model for emergency medical service system design. *Socio-Econom. Planning Sci.* 26, 163–171.

Brandeau, M.L., and R.C. Larson (1986). Extending and applying the hypercube queueing model to deploy ambulances in Boston, in: *TIMS Studies in the Management Sciences*, 22, Elsevier, Amsterdam, pp. 121–153.

Charnes, A., and J. Storbeck (1980). A goal programming model for the siting of multilevel EMS systems. *Socio-Econom. Planning Sci.* 14, 155–161.

Cohen, M.A., W.P. Pierskalla and R. Sassetti (1987). Economies of scale in blood banking, in: G.M. Clark (ed.), *Competition in blood services*, American Association of Blood Banks Press, New York, pp. 25–37.

Cromley, E.K., and G.W. Shannon (1986). Locating ambulatory care for the elderly. *Health Services Res.* 21, 499–514.

Daskin, M.S. (1981). An hierarchical objective set covering model for emergency medical service vehicle deployment. *Transportation Sci.* 15, 137–152.

Daskin, M.S., and E.H. Stern (1982). Application of an expected covering model to emergency medical service system design. *Decision Sci.* 13, 416–439.

Eaton, D.J., M.S. Daskin, D. Simmons, B. Bulloch and G. Jansma (1985). Determining emergency medical service vehicle deployment in Austin, Texas. *Interfaces* 15, 96–108.

Eaton, D.J., H.M.U. Sanchez, R.R. Lantigua and J. Morgan (1986). Determining ambulance deployment in Santo Dominga, Dominican Republic. *J. Oper. Res. Soc.* 37, 113–126.

Fitzsimmons, J.A., and B.N. Srikar (1982). Emergency ambulance location using the contiguous zone search routine. *J. Oper. Management* 2, 225–237.

Fitzsimmons, J.A., and R.S. Sullivan (1979). Establishing the level of service for public emergency ambulance systems. *Socio-Econom. Planning Sci.* 13, 235–239.

Fujiwara, O., T. Makjamroen and K.K. Gupta (1987). Ambulance deployment analysis: A case study of Bangkok. *European J. Oper. Res.* 31, 9–18.

Groom, K.N. (1977). Planning emergency ambulance services. *Oper. Res. Q.* 28, 641–651.

Hodgson, M.J. (1986). An hierarchical location-allocation model with allocations based on facility size. *Ann. Oper. Res.* 6, 273–289.

Hodgson, M.J. (1988). A hierarchical location-allocation model for primary health care delivery in a developing area. *Social Sci. Medicine* 26, 153–161.

Or, I., and W.P. Pierskalla (1979). A transportation location-allocation model for regional blood-banking. *AIIE Trans.* 11, 86–95.

Pezzella, F., R. Bonanno and B. Nicoletti (1981). A system approach to the optimal health-care districting. *European J. Oper. Res.* 8, 139–146.

Pirkul, H., and D.A. Schilling (1988). The siting of emergency service facilities with workload capacities and backup service. *Management Sci.* 34(7), 896–908.

Storbeck, J. (1982). Slack, natural slack, and location covering. *Socio-Econom. Planning Sci.* 16, 99–105.

Uyeno, D.H., and C. Seeberg (1984). A practical methodology for ambulance location. *Simulation* 43, 79–87.

Capacity planning

Dumas, M.B. (1984). Simulation modeling for hospital bed planning. *Simulation* 43, 69–78.

Dumas, M.B. (1985). Hospital bed utilization: An implemented simulation approach to adjusting and maintaining appropriate levels. *Health Services Res.* 20, 43–61.

George, J.A., D.R. Fox and R.W. Canvin (1983). A hospital throughput model in the context of long waiting lists. *J. Oper. Res. Soc.* 34, 27–35.

Hancock, W.M., and P.F. Walter (1984). The use of admissions simulation to stabilize ancillary workloads. *Simulation* 43, 88–94.

Harris, R.A. (1985). Hospital bed requirements planning. *European J. Oper. Res.* 25, 121–126.

Hershey, J.C., E.N. Weiss and M.A. Cohen (1981). A stochastic service network model with application to hospital facilities. *Oper. Res.* 29, 1–22.

Ittig, P.T. (1985). Capacity planning in service operations: The case of hospital outpatient facilities. *Socio-Econom. Planning Sci.* 19, 425–429.

Jones, L.M., and A.J. Hirst (1987). Visual simulation in hospitals: A managerial or a political tool? *European J. Oper. Res.* 29, 167–177.

Kao, E.P.C., and G.G. Tung (1981). Bed allocation in a public health care delivery system. *Management Sci.* 27, 507–520.

Kapadia, A.S., Y.K. Chiang and M.F. Kazmi (1985). Finite capacity priority queues with potential health applications. *Comput. Oper. Res.* 12, 411–420.

Kotlyrov, E.V., and M.J. Schniederjans (1983). Cost/benefit analysis and capital investment decisions in nuclear cardiology. *Socio-Econom. Planning Sci.* 17, 177–180.

Ladany, S.P., and E. Turban (1978). A simulation of emergency rooms. *Comput. Oper. Res.* 4, 89–100.

Lambo, E. (1983). An optimization-simulation model of a rural health center in Nigeria. *Interfaces* 13, 29–35.

Mahachek, A.R., and T.L. Knabe (1984). Computer simulation of patient flow in obstetrical/gynecology clinics. *Simulation* 43, 95–101.

O'Kane, P.C. (1981). A simulation model of a diagnostic radiology department. *European J. Oper. Res.* 6, 38–45.

Schmee, J., E. Hannan and M.P. Mirabile (1979). An examination of patient referral and discharge policies using a multiple objective semi-Markov decision process. *J. Oper. Res. Soc.* 30, 121–130.

Sullivan, W.G., and E.L. Blair (1979). Predicting workload requirements for scheduled health care services with an application to radiology departments. *Socio-Econom. Planning Sci.* 13, 35–59.

Vassilacopoulos, G. (1985). A simulation model for bed allocation to hospital inpatient departments. *Simulation* 45, 233–241.

Worthington, D.J. (1987). Queuing models for hospital waiting lists. *J. Oper. Res. Soc.* 38, 413–422.

Management information systems

Glaser, J.P., E.L. Drazen and L.A. Cohen (1986). Maximizing the benefits of health care information systems. *J. Medical Syst.* 10, 1.

Huang, Y.G. (1989). Using mathematical programming to assess the relative performance of the health care industry. *J. Medical Syst.* 13, 3.

Lowery, J.C., and J.B. Martin (1989). Evaluation of an advance surgical scheduling system. *J. Medical Syst.* 13, 1.

Moidu, K., and O. Wigertz (1989). Computer based information systems in health care — Why? *J. Management Syst.* 13, 2.

Pierskalla, W.P., D.J. Brailer and T. McVoy (1990). Current information systems applications in U.S. health care delivery. *Proc. European Oper. Res. Soc.* 8, 146–159.

Outpatient scheduling

Bailey, N.T.J. (1975). *The Mathematical Theory of Infectious Disease and Its Applications*, Charles Griffin and Co. Ltd., London.

Callahan, N.M., and W.K. Redmon (1987). Effects of problem-based scheduling on patient waiting and staff utilization of time in a pediatric clinic. *J. Appl. Behavior Analysis* 20, 193–199.

Cohen, M.A., J.H. Hershey and E.N. Weiss (1980). Analysis of capacity decisions for progressive patient care hospital facilities. *Health Services Res.* 15, 145–160.

Fries, B.E., and V.P. Marathe (1981). Determination of optimal variable-sized multiple-block appointment systems. *Oper. Res.* 29, 324–345.

Hershey, J.C., E.N. Weiss and M.A. Cohen (1981). A stochastic service network model with application to hospital facilities. *Oper. Res.* 29, 1–22.

Hodgson, M.J. (1988). A hierarchical location-allocation model for primary health care delivery in a developing area. *Social Sci. Medicine* 26, 153–161.

Kao, E.P.C. (1974). Modelling the movement of coronary care patients within a hospital by semi-Markov processes. *Oper. Res.* 22, 683–699.

Kostner, G.T., and R.J. Shachtman (1981). A stochastic model to measure patient effects stemming from hospital acquired infections, in: *Institute of Statistics Mimeo Series* 1364, University of North Carolina, Chapel Hill, NC, pp. 1209–1217.

Kuzdrall, P.J., N.K. Kwak and H.H. Schnitz (1981). Simulating space requirements and scheduling policies in a hospital surgical suite. *Simulation* 36, 163–171.

O'Keefe, R.M. (1985). Investigating outpatient department: Implementable policies and qualitative approaches. *J. Oper. Res. Soc.* 36, 705–712.

Shonick, W. (1972). Understanding the nature of the random fluctuations of the hospital daily census: An important health planning tool. *Medical Care* 10(2), 118–142.

Trivedi, V.M. (1980). A stochastic model for predicting discharges: Applications for achieving occupancy goals in hospitals. *Socio-Econom. Planning Sci.* 14, 209–215.

Vissers, J., and J. Wijngaard (1979). The outpatient appointment system: Design of a simulation study. *European J. Oper. Res.* 3, 459–463.

Weiss, E.N., M.A. Cohen and J.C. Hershey (1982). An interactive estimation and validation procedure for specification of semi-Markov models with application to hospital patient flow. *Oper. Res.* 30, 1082–1104.

Work force planning and scheduling

Baker, J.R., and K.E. Fitzpatrick (1985). An integer programming model of staff retention and termination based on multi-attribute utility theory. *Socio-Econom. Planning Sci.* 19, 27–34.

CASH (1967) (Commission for Administrative Services in Hospitals). Staff utilization and control program, Orientation Report, Medical/Surgical, revised, Los Angeles, CA.

Cavaiola, L.J., and J.P. Young (1980). An integrated system for patient assessment and classification and nurse staff allocation for long-term care facilities. *Health Services Res.* 15, 281–306.

Collart, D., and A. Haurie (1980). On the control of care supply and demand in a urology department. *European J. Oper. Res.* 4, 160–172.

Connor, R.J. (1961). Hospital work sampling with associated measures of production. *J. Indust. Engrg.* 12, 105–107.

Duraiswamy, N.G., R. Welton and A. Reisman (1981). Using computer simulation to predict ICU staffing. *J. Nursing Administration* 11, 39–44.

Hancock, W.M., S.M. Pollock and M. Kim (1987). A model to determine staff levels, cost, and productivity of hospital units. *J. Medical Syst.* 11, 319–330.

Hashimoto, F., S. Bell and S. Marshment (1987). A computer simulation program to facilitate budgeting and staffing decisions in an intensive care unit. *Critical Care Medicine* 15, 256–259.

Helmer, F.T., E.B. Opperman and J.D. Suver (1980). Forecasting nursing staffing requirements by intensity-of-care level. *Interfaces* 10, 50–59.

Hershey, J.C., W.J. Abernathy and N. Baloff (1974). Comparison of nurse allocation policies — A Monte Carlo model. *Decision Sci.* 5, 58–72.

Hershey, J., W. Pierskalla and S. Wandel (1981). Nurse staffing management, in: D. Boldy (ed.), *Operational Research Applied to Health Services*, Croon Helm, London, pp. 189–220.

Jelinek, R.C. (1964). Nursing: The development of an activity model, Ph.D. Dissertation, University of Michigan, Ann Arbor.

Kao, E.P.C., and G.G. Tung (1981). Aggregate nursing requirement planning in a public health care delivery system. *Socio-Econom. Planning Sci.* 15, 119–127.

Kutzler, D.L., and L. Sevcovic (1980). Planning a nurse-midwifery caseload by a computer simulated model. *J. Nurse-Midwifery* 25, 34–37.

Leiken, A., T.R. Sexton and R.H. Silkman (1987). Modelling the effects of price competition on the utilization of health workforce. *Socio-Econom. Planning Sci.* 21, 19–24.

Magazine, M.J. (1977). Scheduling a patient transportation service in a hospital. *INFOR* 15, 242–254.

Miller, H.E., W.P. Pierskalla and G.J. Rath (1976). Nurse scheduling using mathematical programming. *Oper. Res.* 24, 856–870.

Pang, C.Y., and J.M. Swint (1985). Forecasting staffing needs for productivity management in hospital laboratories. *J. Medical Syst.* 9, 365–377.

Reisman, A., W. Cull, H. Emmons, B. Dean, C. Lin, J. Rasmussen, P. Darukhanavala and T. George (1977). On the design of alternative obstetric anesthesia team configurations. *Management Sci.* 23, 545–556.

Shimshak, D.G., D.G. Damico and H.D. Burden (1981). A priority queuing model of a hospital pharmacy unit. *European J. Oper. Res.* 7, 350–354.

Shukla, R.K. (1985). Admissions monitoring and scheduling to improve work flow in hospitals. *Inquiry* 22, 92–101.

Trivedi, V.M. (1981). A mixed-integer goal programming model for nursing service budgeting. *Oper. Res.* 29, 1019–1034.

Tzukert, A., and M.A. Cohen (1985). Optimal student–patient assignment in dental education. *J. Medical Syst.* 9, 279–290.

Vassilacopoulos, G. (1985). Allocating doctors to shifts in an accident and emergency department. *J. Oper. Res. Soc.* 36, 517–523.

Warner, D. (1976). Scheduling nursing personnel according to nursing preference: A mathematical programming approach. *Oper. Res.* 24, 842–856.

Warner, D., and J. Prawda (1972). A mathematical model for scheduling nursing personnel in a hospital. *Management Sci.* 19, 411–422.

Worthington, D., and M. Guy (1988). Allocating nursing staff to hospital wards — A case study. *European J. Oper. Res.* 33, 174–182.

Additional references on work force planning and scheduling

Arthur, J.L., and A. Ravindran (1981). A multiple objective nurse scheduling model. *AIIE Trans.* 13, 55–60.

Cleland, V. (1982a). Relating nursing staff quality to patient's needs. *J. Nursing Administration* 12, 32–37.

Cleland, V. (1982b). Dialogue in print: Relating nursing staff quality to patient's needs. Response from the Author. *J. Nursing Administration* 12, 29–31.

Connor, R.J. et al. (1961). Effective use of nursing resources — A research report. *Hospitals* 35, 30–39.

Cooper, R.C. (1981). A linear programming model for determining efficient combinations of 8-, 10-, and 12-hour shifts. *Respiratory Care* 26, 1105–1108.

Feldman, J., and M. Hundert (1977). Determining nursing policies by use of the nursing home simulation model. *J. Nursing Administration* 7, 35–41.

Jelinek, R.C. (1967). A structural model for the patient care operations. *Health Services Res.* 2, 226–242.

Khan, M.R., and D.A. Lewis (1987). A network model for nursing staff scheduling. *Z. Oper. Res.* 31, B161–B171.

Nutt, P.C. (1984). Decision-modelling methods used to design decision support systems for staffing. *Medical Care* 22, 1002–1013.

Smith, P. (1982). A model of a hospital anaesthetic department. *Omega* 10, 293–297.

Screening for disease

Bailey, N.T.J. (1975). *The Mathematical Theory of Infectious Disease and Its Applications*, Charles Griffin and Co. Ltd., London.

Bosworth, K., and D.H. Gustafson (1991). CHESS: Providing decision support for reducing health risk behavior and improving access to health services. *Interfaces* 21(3), 93–104.

Brandeau, M.L., H.L. Lee, D.K. Owens, C.H. Sox and R.M. Wachter (1990). Models for policy analysis of human immunodeficiency virus screening and intervention: A review. *AIDS Public Policy J.* 5(3), 119–131.

Brandeau, M.L., H.L. Lee, D.K. Owens, C.H. Sox and R.M. Wachter (1991). Models for policy analysis of human immunodeficiency virus screening and intervention. *Interfaces* 21(3), 5–25.

Bross, I.D.J., and L.E. Blumenson (1976). Screening random asymptomatic women under 50 by annual mammographies: Does it make sense. *J. Surgical Oncology* 8, 437–445.

Caulkins, J.P., and E.H. Kaplan (1991). AIDS impact of the number of intravenous drug users. *Interfaces* 21(3), 50–63.

Dietz, K. (1988). On the transmission dynamics of HIV. *Math. Biosci.* 90, 397–414.

Eddy, D.M. (1980). *Screening for Cancer: Theory, Analysis and Design*, Prentice-Hall, Inc., Englewood Cliffs, NJ.

Eddy, D.M. (1983). A mathematical model for timing repeated medical tests. *Medical Decision Making* 3(1), 45–62.

Hethcote, H.W., J.A. Yorke and A. Nold (1982). Gonorrhea modelling: A comparison of control methods. *Math. Biosci.* 58, 93–109.

Homer, J.B., and C.L. St. Clair (1991). A model of HIV transmission through needle sharing. *Interfaces* 21(3), 26–49.

Hyman, J.M., and E.A. Stanley (1988). Using mathematical models to understand the AIDS epidemic. *Math. Biosci.* 90, 415–473.

Kaplan, E.H. (1989). Needles that kill: Modelling human immunodeficiency virus transmission via shared drug injection equipment in shooting galleries. *Rev. Infectious Diseases* 11, 289–298.

Kirch, R., and M. Klein (1974a). Surveillance schedules for medical examinations. *Management Sci.* 20, 1403–1409.

Kirch, R., and M. Klein (1974b). Examination schedules for breast cancer. *Cancer* 33, 1444–1450.

Kolesar, P. (1980). Testing for vision loss in glaucoma patients. *Management Sci.* 26(5), 439–450.

Lee, H.L., and W.P. Pierskalla (1988a). Theory and general models of mass screening for contagious and non-contagious diseases, in: G.K. Rand (ed.), *Operational Research '87*, Elsevier, Amsterdam, pp. 852–890.

Lee, H.L., and W.P. Pierskalla (1988b). Mass screening models for contagious diseases with no latent period. *Oper. Res.* 36(6), 917–928.

May, R.M., and R.M. Anderson (1987). Transmission dynamics of HIV infection. *Nature* 326, 137–142.

McCall, J. (1965). Maintenance policies for stochastically failing equipment: A survey. *Management Sci.* 493–524.

Parkin, D.M., and S.M. Moss (1986). An evaluation of screening policies for cervical cancer in England and Wales using a computer simulation model. *J. Epidemiology Community Health* 40, 143–153.

Pierskalla, W.P., and J.A. Voelker (1976). A survey of maintenance models: The control and surveillance of deteriorating systems. *Naval Res. Logist. Quart.* 23(3), 353–388.

Pierskalla, W.P., and J.A. Voelker (1978). A model for optimal mass screening and the case of perfect test reliability, Technical Report 3, Department of Industrial Engineering and Management Sciences, Northwestern University, Evanston, IL.

Prorok, P. (1976a). The theory of periodic screening I: Lead time and proportion detected. *Adv. Appl. Probab.* 8, 127–143.

Prorok, P. (1976b). The theory of periodic screening II: Doubly bounded recurrence times and mean lead time and detection probability estimation. *Adv. Appl. Probab.* 8, 460–476.

ReVelle, C., F. Feldman and W. Lynn (1969). An optimization model of tuberculosis epidemiology. *Management Sci.* 16(4), B190–B211.

Schwartz, M., and H. Galliher (1975). Analysis of serial screening in an asymptomatic individual to detect breast cancer, Technical Report, Department of Industrial and Operations Engineering, College of Engineering, University of Michigan, Ann Arbor.

Schwartz, M. (1978a). An analysis of the benefits of serial screening for breast cancer based upon a mathematical model of the disease. *Cancer* 41, 1550–1564.

Schwartz, M. (1978b). A mathematical model used to analyze breast cancer screening strategies. *Oper. Res.* 26(6), 937–955.

Thompson, D.E., and T.C. Doyle (1976). *Analysis for Screening Strategies for Colorectal Cancer: A Description of an Approach*, Michigan Cancer Foundation, Detroit, MI.

Thompson, D.E., and R. Disney (1976). *A Mathematical Model of Progressive Diseases and Screening*, Vector Research, Inc., Ann Arbor, MI.

Voelker, J.A., and W.P. Pierskalla (1980). Test selection for a mass screening program. *Naval Res. Logist. Quart.* 27(1), 43–56.

Clinical decision making

Blum, B.I. (1986). *Clinical Information Systems*, Springer-Verlag, New York.

David, I., and U. Yechiali (1985). A time dependent stopping problem with application to live organ transplants. *Oper. Res.* 33, 491–504.

England, W.L. (1988). An exponential model used for optimal threshold selection on ROC curves. *Medical Decision Making* 8, 120–131.

Fryback, D.G., and R.L. Keeney (1983). Constructing a complex judgmental model: An index of trauma severity. *Management Sci.* 29, 869–883.

Gabrieli, E.R. (1988). Computer-assisted assessment of patient care in the hospital. *J. Medical Syst.* 12(3), 135–146.

Greenes, R.A., and E.H. Shortliffe (1990). Medical Informatics — An emerging academic discipline and institutional priority. *JAMA* 263(8), 1114–1120.

Habbema, J.D.F., J.T.N. Lubbe, G.J. Van Ortmarssen and P.J. Van der Maas (1985). A simulation approach to cost–effectiveness and cost–benefit calculations of screening for the early detection of disease. *European J. Oper. Res.* 29, 159–166.

Hasman, A. (1987). Medical applications of computers: An overview. *Internat. J. Biomed. Comput.* 20(4), 239–251.

Kost, S., and W. Schwartz (1989). Use of a computer simulation to evaluate a seminar on child abuse. *Pediatric Emergency Care* 5(3), 202–203.

Kotlyarov, E.V., and M.J. Schniederjans (1983). Cost/benefit analysis and capital investment decisions in nuclear cardiology. *Socio-Econom. Planning Sci.* 17, 177–180.

Langlotz, C.P., L.M. Fagan, S.W. Tu, B.I. Sikic and E.H. Shortliffe (1987). A therapy planing architecture that combines decision theory and artificial intelligence techniques. *Comput. Biomed. Res.* 20(3), 279–303.

Langlotz, C.P., E.H. Shortliffe and L.M. Fagan (1988). A methodology for generating computer-based explanations of decision-theoretic advice. *Medical Decision Making* 8(4), 290–303.

Leonard, M.S., and K.E. Kilpatrick (1978). Treatment planning models: An application. *Decision Sci.* 9, 246–258.

Luft, H.S. (1976). Benefit–cost analysis and public policy implementation: From normative to positive analysis. *Public Policy* 24(4), 437–462.

McCann-Rugg, M., G.P. White and J.M. Endres (1983). Using goal programming to improve the calculation of diabetic diets. *Comput. Oper. Res.* 10, 365–373.

Miller, R.A., and N.B. Giuse (1991). Medical knowledge bases. *Acad. Medicine* 66(1), 15–17.

Molino, G., M. Ballare, P.E. Aurucci and V.R. Di Meana (1990). Application of artificial intelligence techniques to a well-defined clinical problem: Jaundice diagnosis. *Int. J. Biomed. Comput.* 26(3), 189–202.

Moye, L.A., and S.D. Roberts (1982). Modeling the pharmacologic treatment of hypertension. *Management Sci.* 28, 781–797.

Pauker, S.G., and J.P. Kassirer (1987). Decision analysis. *New Engl. J. Medicine* 316(5), 250–271.

Perry, C.A. (1990). Knowledge bases in medicine: A review. *Bulletin Medical Libr. Assoc.* 78(3), 271–282.

Rennels, G.O., E.H. Shortliffe and P.L. Miller (1987). Choice and explanation in medical management: A multiattribute model of artificial intelligence approaches. *Medical Decision Making* 7(1), 22–31.

Rennels, G.O., E.H. Shortliffe, F.E. Stockdale and P.L. Miller (1987). A computational model of reasoning from the clinical literature. *Comput. Methods Programs Biomedicine* 24(2), 139–149.

Roberts, S.D., and R.W. Klein (1984). Simulation of medical decisions: Applications of SLN. *Simulation* 43, 234–241.

Schwartz, W. (1989). Documentation of students' clinical reasoning using a computer simulation. *Amer. J. Dis. Children* 143(5), 575–579.

Shortliffe, E.H. (1987). Computer programs to support clinical decision making. *JAMA* 258(1), 61–66.

Sonderman, D., and P.G. Abrahamson (1985). Radiotherapy treatment design using mathematical programming models. *Oper. Res.* 33, 705–725.

Steinwachs, D.M. (1985). Management information systems — New challenges to meet changing needs. *Medical Care* 23(5), 607–622.

Wasson, J.H., H.C. Sox, R.K. Neff and L. Goldman (1983). Clinical prediction rules: Applications and methodological standards. *New Engl. J. Medicine* 313(13), 793–799.

Weinstein, M.C., and W.B. Stason (1977). Foundations of cost–effectiveness analysis for health and medical practices. *New Engl. J. Medicine* 296(13), 716–739.

S.M. Pollock et al., Eds., *Handbooks in OR & MS, Vol. 6*

Chapter 14

Operations Research in Sports

Yigal Gerchak

Department of Management Sciences, University of Waterloo, Waterloo, Ont. N2L-3G1, Canada

1. Introduction

Spectator sports are pervasive in society. The worldwide TV viewing audience of certain events in recent Olympic Games and the World Cup Soccer Tournament is estimated at 2–3 billion people, about half of the world population. The major U.S. networks televise more than 1400 hours of sports per year, and cable and pay TV stations in North America more than 8000. The total annual attendance of 11 major spectator sports in North America exceeded 427 million by the late 80's [McPhearson, Curtis & Loy, 1989]. Major league baseball attendance in 1990 was 55 million, twice as many as 20 years ago. Even some sports in which the real competition is almost unobservable, like the Tour de France and other long bicycle and automobile races are extremely popular in Europe and elsewhere.

Professional sports teams, events, venues and related gambling constitute major business activities that permeate the economy and society in many ways. Sports are a source of civic pride and loyalty. In the U.S., college sports, besides being big business on their own right, are the focus of campus culture and the identification of students and alumni with an institution.

Sports are structured, goal-oriented, contest-based and competitive. As such, they provide a natural setting for interesting decision making before and during the contest. Live spectators as well as 'armchair quarterbacks' often take active and vocal interest in some of these decisions: They urge football coaches to 'go-for-it' (i.e., attempt to get a first down) on fourth-down-and-short (third-down in Canadian football), attempt to steal second (or third) base in baseball, make certain substitutions during a basketball game, and draft/trade certain players.

The first applications of OR/MS thinking to sports issues seem to have occurred in the 50's. Their progress and acceptance in the 50's and 60's to a large extent paralleled the applications of such techniques to other fields of human endeavor. Their progress also reflects the gradual development of OR/MS techniques like linear programming, expected utility analysis, dynamic programming, control theory, combinatorics and game theory. Indeed, due to sports issues being familiar to so many, some of the inventors or popularizers of the above methods have used sports examples to demonstrate them [e.g., Howard, 1960, Chapter 5;, Bellman, 1964].

Many of the early applications were in baseball, a sport particularly suitable for OR approaches because the action occurs in discrete events and because the 'state' of the game is simple to specify [e.g. Allen, 1959; Cook & Garner, 1964; Lindsey, 1959, 1961, 1963]. American and Canadian football's discreteness also makes it popular with analytical types [e.g. Carter & Machol, 1971; Porter, 1967]. Sequential athletic events like high and long jump, pole vault and weightlifting are also natural [e.g. Ladany, 1975a; Ladany, Humes & Sphicas, 1975; Lilien, 1976]. Scheduling, rule-making, tournament design, and fairness issues related to various sports were also investigated since the 70's. Interest in OR/MS in sports seem to have peaked in the mid 70's, culminating in the two edited volumes by Machol, Ladany & Morrison [1976] and Ladany & Machol [1977] (henceforth MLM and LM, respectively). These volumes and other work by their editors were instrumental in consolidating the field.

An extensive pre-1976 annotated bibliography of the area is included in LM. We will not repeat these references, unless we have some specific comments to make on their subject matters. We give extra weight to more recent, and thus not previously surveyed/evaluated work. We do not discuss purely statistical issues, micro-economic aspects, issues of negotiation (like final-offer arbitration in baseball), business decision problems faced by sports venues, marketing issues, coaching techniques, or anything related to gambling. We also do not discuss kinetic issues (see Townend [1984], for various such topics, including a calculation of the optimal angle for releasing a shotput or hammer).

2. Strategies in team sports

2.1. Strategies in baseball

Decisions faced by baseball managers, such as whether to issue an intentional walk, when to have a batter try to sacrifice, when to have a runner try to steal a base, and what is the best batting order, have been the most widely discussed strategy issues in sports by fans and professionals for many decades. The popularity of baseball in the Western Hemisphere and Japan, its stop-and-go nature, and the century-old tradition of keeping and displaying keen interest in extensive statistics on all facets of the game, explains why this game was so extensively analyzed. Even several books have been published on the subject [Allen, 1959; Cook & Fink, 1972; Cook & Garner, 1964 (the latter two are summarized in LM]); Thorn & Palmer, 1989].

A particularly important contribution to understanding strategic issues in baseball was made by Lindsey [1959, 1961, 1963, with summary in LM]. Lindsey used historical data to compute the empirical probability distribution of the number of runs scored in the remainder of a half-inning when a new batter comes to the plate, for all combinations of number of men out and the occupation state of the bases.

These probabilities enabled Lindsey to examine the issue of when an intentional walk strategy is beneficial. If the batters are equally skilled, then an intentional walk is beneficial (in a statistically significant manner) in the bottom of the last inning only if there is one out, runners on second and third, and the fielding (visiting) team is leading by one run. In the top of the last inning, an intentional walk is beneficial only if the batting (visiting) team has runners on second and third with one out and the score is tied. In other last-inning situations an intentional walk is either not significantly beneficial, or is even significantly detrimental to the fielding team. Of course, if the current batter is particularly dangerous, and the following one is less so, an intentional walk can be beneficial in a wider class of situations.

Another conclusion Lindsey drew is that, with average batters, the strategy of sacrificing with a runner on first base is not a good one. With a runner on third base, a sacrifice is a good choice if one run is badly needed. Lindsey also addressed base-stealing strategies, and various statistical issues. One of his basic premises was that the probability of winning the game, and not just the immediate outcome of the present choice, is what should be considered.

Concerning the still controversial issue of the best batting order, Cook & Garner [1964], examining statistical data, arrived at the conclusion that the batting lineup should be arranged in decreasing order of productivity, with the team's best batters in the first positions, rather than in their traditional 'cleanup' positions. He estimated a small but measurable improvement in team performance (of the order of 11 runs per season) from such change. Simulations conducted in Cook & Fink [1972] seem to have pointed at the opposite conclusion. Freeze [1974, reprinted in LM] conducted a large simulation study of this issue. His conclusions were that batting order exerts only a small influence on the outcomes of baseball games. The traditional lineup, wherein a team's strongest batters hit in the third through fifth positions, was superior to a lineup in which batters are arranged in decreasing order of productivity. Yet another simulation, ran by Peterson [1977], concluded that the best-first order was slightly more productive than the traditional order. It seems that this issue is still unsettled, although all studies indicated that the batting order is not really that important.

The issue of when exactly has a team been eliminated from playoff consideration has been explored by several authors [see references in Robinson, 1991b]. This exact time usually occurs considerably sooner than baseball's popular 'magic number'. A recent linear programming solution to this problem, with application to 1987 major leagues standings, was given by Robinson [1991a]. In that season, for example, in the American League East, one team was really eliminated five games earlier than the 'magic number' would have indicated.

2.2. The value of field position in football

In order to evaluate key football strategy questions, like whether to 'go for it' on particular fourth down situations, it is essential to have means of comparing the value to one's team of them, or their opponents, having a first down at a certain spot on the field. Towards that goal, Carter & Machol [1971, reprinted in LM] have computed the empirical expected value of possession of the football, with first down and ten yards to go, at any particular point on the playing field, using data from the 1969 NFL season.

The field was divided into ten strips (with more extensive data the procedure can be extended to all 99 one yard marks). A possession can result in 14 different outcomes: a touchdown (approximately +7 points), a field goal (+3), a safety (−2), an opponent's touchdown due to a fumble or an interception (approximately −7 points), and eventually giving possession to the other team at any of the 10 strips. Multiplying the empirical probability of each outcome, when starting from a given location, by the consequence, provides the expected value of the position in terms of expected values to your team of the other team starting from various positions. Writing such an equation for each location results in ten equations in 10 unknowns. Solving these equations, Carter and Machol obtained the following results:

Center of the ten-yard strip (yards from the target goal line)	Expected point value
95	−1.245
85	−0.637
75	+0.236
65	0.923
55	1.538
45	2.392
35	3.167
25	3.681
15	4.572
5	6.041

Thus first and ten on one's own 20 (after a touchback) has an expected value very close to zero, which indicates wisdom on part of the rules makers. Other than at the extremes, the payoff is quite linear, about 0.0726 points per yard.

As an example of the implications of these numbers, Carter and Machol consider a fourth-and-goal situation on the opponent's two or three yard line, a situation in which the conservative strategy is a field goal attempt. The expected value of the kick is less than 3 points, because it may be missed, in which case the ensuing possession by the opponents has a negative value for the first team. If one *rushes*[1] instead, there is some probability, say p, of scoring 7 points, and if one fails to score one has achieved about 1.5 points by putting the opponent 'in a hole' (since opponent must start from very close to their goal line). Thus if $7p + 1.5(1 - p) \geq 3$, i.e., $p \geq 3/11$, which is quite plausible, a rushing attempt, rather than a field goal attempt, is called for.

---

[1] Here and in the remainder of this section rushing/running is to be understood as any attempt to move the ball, including passing.

In a subsequent note, Carter & Machol [1978] considered optimal strategy in fourth down situations in more detail. Data from the 1971 NFL season has shown that the probability of converting on fourth down and one yard to go is similar to that of converting on third down and one yard to go (an attempt occurring much more often), about 0.715. With two yards to go it was 0.569, and with three 0.410. Then, making the (very) conservative assumption that a successful run always gains exactly the required yards (no more), Carter and Machol were able, using the above table of expected vales, to compute the expected point value of a run attempt on fourth down from 5–35 yard distances from the opponents' goal line. This was compared to the expected point value of a field goal attempt (using 1972–1976 NFL data), and assumed (conservative) values for 'coffin-corner' punt attempts from the 35 yard distance.

The conclusion was that, assuming an average kicker, a run is a vastly superior option to a field goal attempt or a punt with one or two yards to go. With three yards to go, and perhaps even with four or five, a run is still superior inside the 10-yard line. From 35 yards away and four or five yards to go, a punt is the best choice. Carter and Machol comment that these conclusions were remarkably different from prevailing practice. Perhaps risk aversion plays a role here.

The fourth-down problem was recently reexamined by Schaefer, Schaeffer & Atkinson [1991], who used as an objective the maximization of probability of winning the game, rather than just maximizing the expected number of points scored. Their rich model considered the current relative scores, the relative strength of the two teams, and the time remaining in the game.

2.3. The value of a tie and extra-point strategy in football

In U.S. College Football, as well as in Canadian Football, a team which scores a touchdown (6 points) has the choice of attempting to score an additional point by kicking the ball, or attempting to score two additional points by 'running' (running or passing) the ball. The probability of a kick to be successful, k, is of course higher than the success probability of a run r. Suppose that late in a game a team which was behind 14 points just scored a touchdown, thereby reducing its deficit to 8 points. What should they do next, assuming that they will score another touchdown in the game and prevent the other team from scoring?

Porter [1967] alludes to a 1962 College game between Yale and Colgate in which Yale chose to run in such a situation, failed, but tied the game on a run following its next touchdown. In a similar situation during a 1967 Harvard–Cornell game, Cornell attempted a run, failed, and lost the game despite scoring another touchdown [Bierman 1968].

In a letter to *Management Science*, Bierman [1968] has considered the situation assuming that Cornell wanted to play to win the game, and thus, if they decided to kick now and were successful, they will attempt a run after the next touchdown. Thus if they kick first, the resulting probabilities are kr for a win and $(1 - k)r$ for a tie. If they run first instead, the probability of a win remains kr, but that of a tie increases to $(1 - k)r + (1 - r)r$. Thus they should run now. Brieman indicated that the situation might be different if Cornell 'played for a tie', thus planning to follow a successful kick by another kick.

In a follow-up letter, Means [1968] has argued that if the probabilities satisfy certain conditions, playing for a tie cannot be optimal in the first place. Kicking first and playing for a tie has a loss probability of $(1-k)(1+k-r)$ and no possibility of a win, as compared to a loss probability of $(1-r)^2$ when playing for a win (and thus, by above argument, running first). Thus if $(1-k)(1+k-r) > (1-r)^2$, i.e. if $r/k > (k-r)/(1-r)$, Cornell should 'play for a win by going for two points first'.

In a concurrent and independent attack on the problem, Porter [1967, reprinted in LM] has approached the issue from an expected utility perspective. Letting the utility of a win be one, of a loss zero, and of a tie t, $0 \le t \le 1$, the expected utilities of the three candidate strategies are:

(i) 'Run; if successful – kick, if failed – run' has an expected utility of $rk + \{r(1-k) + r(1-r)\}t$.

(ii) 'Kick; if successful – kick, if failed – run' (i.e. play for a tie), has an expected utility of $\{k^2 + r(1-k)\}t$.

(iii) 'Kick now, and regardless of result run next time' (i.e. play for a win), has an expected utility of $rk + r(1-k)t$.

The first thing Porter notes is that the expected utility of strategy (i) is higher than that of (iii) *regardless* of the utility of a tie. This conclusion is really the same one reached by Brieman. Porter comments that this conclusion seems not to be consistent with the intuition of many fans, which like strategy (iii). Strategy (i) is better than strategy (ii) if and only if $t < rk/\{k^2 - r(1-r)\}$, which is plausible unless a tie is almost as good as a win, and a run very unlikely to succeed. Thus the idea of 'always play for a win' may actually follow from expected utility maximization, rather than from the (low) value of t alone.

The value of a tie is also critical if a team, which trails by three points very late in the game, finds itself in a fourth (third in Canada)-and-short situation close to the opponents goal line. A successful field-goal will tie the game, while successfully 'going for it' will win it. Hurley [1989] attempted to quantify the relative benefit of a tie versus a win in an early season Canadian college game. The objective was to reach the playoffs, hopefully with a home field advantage.

2.4. When to pull the goalie in hockey

When a hockey team is down by one goal late in the game, they may decide to replace their goalie with an additional attacking skater, thereby increasing their scoring chances. Of course, this practice, called 'pulling the goalie', increases the chances that the other team will score by even more, but generally losing by two goals is no worse than losing by one. So the question is how late in the game to pull the goalie, if at all?

This problem was analyzed by Morrison & Wheat [1986]. They assumed that goals are scored according to independent Poisson processes. The Poisson nature of scoring was statistically documented by Mullet [1977], and the independence assumption was rationalized by hockey's very frequent team change in puck possession. The basic scoring rate λ of the team pulling the goalie increases to λ_A, while that of the other team increases from λ to λ_B, $\lambda_B > \lambda_A$ (the 1979-80 season estimates were $\lambda = 0.06$, $\lambda_A = 0.16$, and $\lambda_B = 0.47$ per minute).

With T minutes remaining, the probability of achieving a tie if the goalie is pulled t minutes before the end is

$$\frac{1}{2}\left\{1 - e^{-2\lambda(T-t)}\right\} + e^{-2\lambda(T-t)}\frac{\lambda_A}{\lambda_A + \lambda_B}\left\{1 - e^{-(\lambda_A + \lambda_B)t}\right\}.$$

The first term is the probability that a goal will be scored before the goalie is pulled, and the scoring team will be A. The second term is the probability that no goals will be scored before the goalie is pulled, a goal will be scored after the goalie is pulled, and the scoring team will be team A. The parameter T will drop out in the optimization, provided that the optimal t does not exceed it. The resulting optimal time to pull the goalie is

$$t^* = -\frac{\log\{\lambda(\lambda_A - \lambda_B)/\lambda_A(2\lambda - \lambda_A - \lambda_B)\}}{\lambda_A + \lambda_B}.$$

With the above estimates, $t^* = 2.34$ minutes remaining, with a tie probability of 0.196, while the prevailing practice was to pull the goalie about one minute before the end, which has a tie probability of 0.175.

Erkut [1987] has extended the analysis to situations of non-evenly matched teams. He provided a table giving the optimal pulling time for any combination of scoring rates. Erkut assumed that the pulled-goalie scoring rates are proportional to the normal (uneven) scoring rates of the teams. Nydick & Weiss [1989] have recalculated the tie probabilities assuming that the pulled-goalie scoring rates, unlike the normal scoring rates, are independent of the teams' abilities. All the analyses indicate that coaches are too conservative, and should be pulling goalies sooner than they do.

Washburn [1991] argued that while all previous works assumed an objective function of maximizing the probability that the trailing team would succeed in scoring before the other team, the 'complete' objective is to maximize the probability of winning the game. Thus one needs to consider what happens if and after one of the teams scores, including the possibility of overtime, assuming that the currently leading team will act optimally if they find themselves trailing later on. Thus Washburn proposed and analyzed a dynamic programming formulation as follows. Let $\lambda(\mu)$ be the respective relevant scoring rates, and let (x, t) be the state of the game with t time remaining and x as the relative score. When $x < 0$ the trailing team D must decide whether (λ, μ) should be (λ_0, μ_0) corresponding to the normal allingment, or (λ_D, μ_D) corresponding to D pulling their goalie. Similarly, if $x > 0$, the trailing team C has a choice between (λ_0, μ_0) and (λ_C, μ_C). Thus if $F(x, t)$ is the probability that D wins when both sides follow optimal policies, and δ is a small increment of time, the recursive equation is

$$F(x, t + \delta) = \max(\min)_{(\lambda,\mu)} \{(\lambda\delta) F(x + 1, t) + (\mu\delta) F(x - 1, t)$$
$$+ (1 - \lambda\delta - \mu\delta) F(x, t)\},$$

where max applies for $x < 0$, min for $x > 0$, and $(\lambda, \mu) = (\lambda_0, \mu_0)$ for x=0. The boundary conditions are $F(x, 0) = 0$ for $x < 0$ and $F(x, 0) = 1$ for $x > 0$, while $F(0, 0)$ depends on the tie-breaking mechanism.

Washburn computed the optimal strategy for some realistic numerical values, using both Erkut's and Nydick and Weiss' assumptions, and concluded that the goalie should be pulled even earlier (by approximately a minute) than the previous analyses indicated.

3. Other issues in team sports

3.1. Are streaks real?

There is a widespread belief among basketball fans, journalists and players that after a player hits several shots in a row, he 'gets in a groove' and thus subsequent success becomes more likely. This 'hot hand' phenomenon, if true, has potential coaching implications. To test for the presence of streaks, Tversky and Gilovich [1989] have computed the empirical conditional probabilities of a hit after various numbers of hits or misses for each player in 48 home games of the Philadelphia 76ers during the 1980-81 NBA season. The average hit probabilities following 1, 2 and 3 hits were 0.51, 0.50, and 0.46 respectively, and after 1, 2 and 3 misses 0.54, 0.53 and 0.56. Thus the streaks theory is not supported by the data. Other tests conducted by Tversky and Gilovich also confirmed that a player's chances of hitting are largely independent of the outcomes of his previous shots.

A similar issue in *baseball* – whether batters hit in streaks or suffer through slumps – has been recently investigated by Albright [1992]. Various statistical tests were run on complete major leagues 1987–1990 data, including logistic regression incorporating various situational variables. The results again provided very little support for the streakiness hypothesis.

3.2. Does divisional play lead to more pennant races?

When major league baseball split each twelve-team league into two six-team leagues in 1969, the primary reason given was that such a structure would provide closer pennant races. A pennant race occurs if the top two teams in a league finish 'very close' to each other. The issue is also relevant in other sports which do, or could, split leagues in that manner. In European leagues (e.g. soccer), it is relevant also to 'races' not to finish in the last place, an outcome which results in a demotion to a lower division.

Winston and Soni [1982] have addressed the issue of whether splitting a league indeed increases the expected number of pennant races. A pennant race is of closeness m in a league of size n if the two largest order statistics of a sample of size n differ by at most m. Winston and Soni assumed that the number of games won by each team during a season constitute independent, as well as identically distributed and continuous, variables. The probability of a pennant race of closeness m then turns out to be

$$P(Y_1 - Y_2 \le m) = 1 - n \int_m^1 f(y)F(y-m)^{n-1} \, dy$$

where F and f are, respectively, the cumulative distribution and density of number of games won. Realizing that the independence assumption is formally incorrect, they first compared the resulting model's predictions to extensive historical major-league baseball data. The fit turned out to be very good.

Under some empirically verifiable assumptions on the distribution of the fraction of games won, Winston and Soni then proved that when a league of 4 or more teams is split into leagues of at least two teams each, the expected number of pennant races cannot decrease. Thus splitting a 12-team league into two 6-team ones indeed increases the expected number of pennant races (and 1969–1980 major league baseball data bears this out, for various m's). Note that this result does not tell us whether two 6-team leagues will have more, or less, pennant races than three 4-team leagues. This analysis implicitly assumes that the schedule (how often particular teams play each other) is unaffected by league splitting. It is of interest to observe that it may be preferable to define a pennant race with reference to the standings several (say, ten) games before the end of the season, rather than at its very end. But this should not affect the analysis. Another observation is that the standings' proximity of *three* (or more) teams, rather than just two, may be relevant. After all, if 10 games before the end of the season the standings (number of games won) at the top of some league are 109, 107, 107, 107, things might potentially be at least as, or more, exciting than when they are 109, 108, 83, 79, since if in the latter case the runner-up team falters, the race is over.

3.3. Draft issues

In the draft system used in several North American professional sports, the teams having the worst win–loss records in the previous season get first pick of the new players in the draft. The worst teams gets first choice, the next-worst team second, and so on. After each team has made one draft choice, this procedure is repeated, round by round, until every team has exhausted its choices. The rationale of this system is to give the teams which were weak one season a chance to become stronger in subsequent seasons, thereby making the league more competitive.

While the idea seems fine, and in a rough sense is achieving its goals, Brams and Straffin [1979] have shown that the procedure might have some unexpected and highly undesirable consequences. Consider a simple example of three teams,

A, B and C, drafting in that order a total of six players, 1,..., 6. The preference orderings of the teams over the players are as follows:

A	B	C
1	5	3
2	6	6
3	2	5
4	1	4
5	4	1
6	3	2

'Sincere' choices, i.e. each team in turn drafting its most preferred player available, would result in the allocation $\begin{Bmatrix} 1 & 5 & 3 \\ 2 & 6 & 4 \end{Bmatrix}$. It can be shown that sincere choices always lead to Pareto-optimal allocations, namely ones where no team can do better without another team doing worse.

But if A and B's initial choices are 1 and 5 respectively, C will have an incentive to be insincere, and choose 6 rather than 3, since that results in the allocation $\begin{Bmatrix} 1 & 5 & 6 \\ 2 & 4 & 3 \end{Bmatrix}$, in which C does better (indeed, best possible) for itself. Knowing that C will do this, causing B to end up with 5 and 4, B can do better by choosing 2 in the first round, for then C will have to choose 3 and the resulting allocation is $\begin{Bmatrix} 1 & 2 & 3 \\ 4 & 5 & 6 \end{Bmatrix}$. Knowing that B will do this, A can do better than $\begin{Bmatrix} 1 \\ 4 \end{Bmatrix}$ by choosing 3 first. This results in the allocation $\begin{Bmatrix} 3 & 5 & 6 \\ 1 & 2 & 4 \end{Bmatrix}$.

Comparing this 'sophisticated' outcome to the sincere one, we see that all three teams end up strictly worse off(!) – a Prisoner's Dilemma situation. Furthermore, team A would have been better off drafting last rather than first, since then the sincere, as well as sophisticated, allocation is $\begin{Bmatrix} B & C & A \\ 5 & 3 & 1 \\ 6 & 4 & 2 \end{Bmatrix}$, so A ends up with its preferred players. This last observation implies that awarding the weakest team (A) the first draft choice may actually hurt that team – the exact opposite of the draft's philosophy.

In reality, the computation of sophisticated drafting strategies is practically impossible. For one thing, the problem size is very large, and for another, a team is unlikely to know the other teams' preferences beyond perhaps the one or two most preferred players. For that reason, teams value drafting early very highly. This situation seems to present 'moral hazards' for teams to whom it is clear several games before the end of the regular season that they are not going to make the playoffs.

To counteract that problem, the National Basketball Association has introduced in 1985 a first-round draft lottery among the teams which did not qualify for that season's playoffs, or the teams to which they have traded their first draft picks. In its first two years, the lottery was a simple one, giving each of the seven non-playoff teams equal chance to any of the first seven draft positions. More recently, the NBA, realizing that such a scheme may result in not sufficiently strengthening the weakest teams, decided to bias the lottery in favour of teams with poor regular season records. From 1987 to 1989 only the first three draft positions have been awarded to three non-playoff teams using a fair lottery. The rest of the teams drafted in a reverse order of their standing, thereby guaranteeing the team with the worst record at least a fourth draft position.

In 1990, a further bias in favour of weak teams was introduced. The rules of the 1990, 1991 and 1992 lotteries, which due to recent league expansion involved eleven teams, were as follows. Let team '1' be the one with the worst regular-season record, team '2' be the one with second-worst record, and so on through team '11' being the one with the best regular season record among the non-playoff teams. Then eleven '1' balls, ten '2' balls, and so on through one '11' ball were placed in an urn, and a ball was drawn at random. The ball drawn first awarded the team to which it belonged a first draft choice. The other balls belonging to that team were then removed, or their subsequent drawings were just ignored. The ball drawn second awarded the team to which it belonged a second draft choice (and its other balls were then removed or ignored), and the ball drawn third awarded a third draft choice. The teams which did not win any of the first three choices draft in a reverse order of their standings. Thus there are now two levels of bias in favour of weaker teams – the weighted draw for the first three positions, and the reverse order of drafting for the rest of the positions.

Gerchak and Mausser [1992] have computed the expected draft positions for the single-bias (87–89) as well as double bias (90–92) lotteries. The results are given in the following table.

	End of season standing (from end)										
Scheme	1	2	3	4	5	6	7	8	9	10	11
No lottery (pre-85)	1	2	3	4	5	6	7	8	9	10	11
Fair lottery (85–86)	6	6	6	6	6	6	6	6	6	6	6
Single-bias (87–89)	3.45	3.96	4.47	4.98	5.49	6.00	6.51	7.02	7.53	8.04	8.55
Double-bias(90–92)	3.04	3.39	3.79	4.26	4.82	5.47	6.23	7.10	8.10	9.25	10.54

It is evident that a double, or even a single, bias lottery gives the teams which finish last a very significant advantage. Nevertheless, the double-bias (90–92) scheme has a rather desirable property. The *difference* in expected drafting position of consecutive teams grows as the standing improves: by becoming last, the second last team can improve its expected draft position by only 0.35, while by becoming tenth, the eleventh can improve it by 1.29. Thus the double-bias lottery provides a limited 'incentive' for lowering end-of-season position for those teams who have no chance to make the playoffs. The teams on the other end of the spectrum are likely to be fighting for a playoff berth anyways.

3.4. Scheduling problems[2]

A recurring problem in planning a season's games schedule in various team sports is how to minimize travelling distance. Campbell and Chen [1976] addressed this issue in the context of a U.S. college basketball ten-team conference. Each team must play every other team twice, once at home and once away, and all games need to be played on ten consecutive Saturdays and Mondays. A tour (road trip) should not consist of more than one 'extended weekend'. The algorithm they proposed reduced the traveling distance in the 1973-4 Southeastern conference season by 29.3%, and the number of tours from 78 to 50, vis-a-vis the actual schedule. The same problem was independently addressed by Ball and Webster [1977], who tested their results on the 1974-5 Southeastern, and 1975-6 Big Eight conferences, again with very favorable results. Related work was also done by Liittschwager and Haagenson [1978].

Scheduling of major-league baseball was addressed by Cain [1977]. Bean and Birge [1980] explored scheduling issues in the NBA. A rather entertaining writeup on a husband and wife team of Henry and Holly Stephenson, who schedule major league baseball and (indoor) soccer since 1981 (and had previously scheduled NBA and NASL seasons) is provided by Kim [1991]. The writeup lists in detail the requirements and preassignment that need to be observed when scheduling baseball seasons, and various unexpected events which can impinge on the schedule.

De Werra [1979, 1980] introduced a graphical approach for solving the sports scheduling problem to minimize breaks, subject to a constraint requiring the games to constitute a round-robin. This method was used by Schreuder [1980] to develop an algorithm with a view towards scheduling the Dutch soccer league.[3]

Coppins and Pentico [1981] considered the problem of developing schedules for the NFL so as to minimize the discrepancies in teams' schedules difficulty. Tan and Magazine [1981] have addressed scheduling issues faced by the Canadian Football League, where preassignments, i.e. hard requirements on some pairs of teams to play on a certain date, are present.

More recently, the emphasis in the sports scheduling literature is on interactive, computer based, decision support systems. Such a system was developed by Evans [1988] to schedule umpires in the American Baseball League, and by Ferland and Fleurent [1991] to schedule games in the National Hockey League and the Quebec Major Junior Hockey League.

---

[2] I wish to thank Mike Magazine for bringing to my attention various unpublished articles in this area.

[3] I have been told that recent work on scheduling the Dutch soccer league had as its major objective the minimization of the number of game days in which more than one 'problematic' game (in terms of potential hooliganism) is played, as well as reducing the chance that fans of rival teams will meet on the same train . . .

4. Decision making in individual sports

4.1. Maximizing expected achievement in athletic events of increasing difficulty

In the athletic events of high jump, pole vault and weightlifting, a competitor starts at some level of difficulty, and, if (s)he clears it, proceeds to a higher level; the level of difficulty cannot be lowered (in weightlifting the above holds separately for the two categories, 'snatch' and 'clean-and-jerk'). If the criterion is the maximization of expected personal achievement, the question is at what level of difficulty to start, and, if the choice is available, what subsequent levels of difficulty to select.

Lilien [1976] has considered this problem in the context of weightlifting, where a competitor is allowed a maximum of three lift attempts in each category. The final score is the total of the highest weights lifted in the two categories. Each level of difficulty is associated with a probability of success, and the outcomes of successive lifts were assumed independent. If the criterion is the maximization of expected achievement or utility ('weight-range'), each category can be treated separately. Because of the increasing-level-of-difficulty constraints, Lilien considered a dynamic programming approach to be awkward, and used a numerical non-linear programming code to solve several examples. The weight selection policies turned out to be quite sensitive to the lifter's objectives and utilities.

Ladany [1975a] considered the problem in the context of pole vaulting, where the number of heights successfully attempted is unlimited. Fatigue is, however, a major factor, so starting at low heights with small increments may not be a good strategy. At the time that work was done, a competitor chose the initial height, but after clearing that one he had to vault at all levels to which the bar was raised (at constant steps). Up to three vaults to clear each height were allowed, and a failure at all attempt at some height terminated that vaulter's attempts. Thus the only decision by the vaulter concerned the initial height, and Ladany formulated a model for choosing that height to maximize expected personal achievement.

Ladany comments that the model can also be used to determine the optimal step-by-step increase in the height of the bar, which officials select before the competition. He also viewed the model as applicable to high jumping.

More recently, some of the rules of pole-vaulting competitions were changed. A competitor is now allowed to vault at any height not lower than his previous attempt, provided that he has not accumulated three successive failures. Thus he is not required to vault at all subsequent heights following his starting level, and even if he were to fail at a given height he may elect to attempt his next trial at a higher level. Hersh and Ladany [1989] have formulated a model taking into account these new rules. Now not only the starting height, but also subsequent increments contingent on previous outcomes, need to be planned in advance, giving rise to a dynamic programming model. The numerical examples they ran showed that, using the respective optimal policies, the new rules increase the maximal expected height by at least 2 cm, and possibly considerably more.

4.2. Competitive games of boldness

The competitive aspect of several athletic events can be described as follows. Each competitor, in turn, chooses a level of difficulty, and makes an attempt at that level once, or several times in a row. There might be just a single round (e.g. horse jumping, figure skating, gymnastics [in the same event]), or, perhaps if more than one competitor was successful, several rounds (e.g. high-jump, pole-vault, weight-lifting). The winner is the competitor who was successful in the hardest task, or had the best score, possibly taking level of difficulty into account. Henig and O'Neill [1990] coined the term 'games of boldness' for such competitions.

Consider a single-round success/failure game of boldness. Such a game may be summarized as follows: Each player chooses a probability, and performs a single (or several consecutive) Bernoulli trial(s) with this probability of success. The winner is the successful player whose probability of success was the lowest. A player's objective is to maximize his win probability.[4] These types of competitions have been recently analyzed by Gerchak and Henig [1986], Henig and O'Neill [1992] and Gerchak and Kilgour [1992].

Gerchak and Henig have addressed the format of a 'basketball shootout' competition staged by the Continental Basketball Association in 1985. A lottery had determined the order of the 14 participants, and each one, in turn, fully aware of previous participants' choices and their outcomes, selected a distance from the basket and attempted a shot from there. Assuming equal abilities, it was shown that the optimal probability of the nth last player is $1/n$ if none of the preceding players were successful, and slightly higher probability than chosen by predecessor if there was a previous success.[5] The resulting win probability of the 14th player is 8.5 times larger than that of the 1st player.

Henig and O'Neill have addressed the issue of whether the rules can be redesigned so that victory depends less on shooting order and more on skill. They considered a variety of rules and analyzed their consequences:

(1) Simultaneous choice of probability by all players.

(2) A continuously rising probability, where players choose when to act; the first successful one is then the winner.

(3) A continuously falling probability, where players choose when to act; the last successful one is then the winner.

(4) Order determined by lottery, players aware of previous players' outcomes, but not of their chosen probabilities.

(5) Order determined by lottery, players aware of previously chosen probabilities, but not of outcomes.

Henig and O'Neill showed that the last format has an equilibrium where the mth player out of n chooses a probability of $1/(n - m + 1)$, and has a win probability

---

[4] If a tie is a real possibility, its utility versus that of a win need to be specified.

[5] In the actual 14-players shootout, as reported by Scott and Sherman [1988], the distances and outcomes, success (S) vs. failure (F), were as follows: 24′ S, 24+′ F, 28′ S, 28+′ F, 32′ S, (32+′ F) × 9.

of $1/n$. This equilibrium is subgame-perfect[6] for $n = 2$ and $n = 3$, but it is not clear whether it is perfect for larger n's. Thus despite the seeming informational advantage of later players, all have the same win probability at that equilibrium.

Gerchak and Kilgour retained the lottery-based complete information structure of the basketball shootout, but imposed the restriction that the sequence of probabilities be non-increasing regardless of outcomes; Henig and O'Neill refer to this as the 'excelsior' rule. This rule was inspired by high-jump and pole-vault competitions, where the height of the bar is never lowered during the competition. The optimal strategies turned out as follows. When the number of players is three or five, the first player selects a probability of one, 'gambling' on the others failing. The first of two players, or the second of three, selects probability $1/2$. The third of three selects a probability just less than $1/2$. The first of four, or the second of five, picks probability $16/27$, and all three subsequent players then select probabilities not exceeding $1/3$, each just less than the previous player's choice. The first of six, seven and eight players select probabilities of 0.92, 0.41 and 1.00 respectively. A player's probability of winning does *not* always improve as the player moves back in the sequence; when it does, the improvement is much less dramatic than in the basketball shootout game. Gerchak and Kilgour also analyzed a three-player game where a tie, which occurs if all players fail, has a strictly higher utility than a loss. The first player's optimal strategy turned out to depend on the utility of a tie in a surprising and rather irregular way.

A striking demonstration of how crucial the starting height decision in pole-vault could be was provided in the 1992 U.S. Olympic Track and Field Trials [Moore, 1992]. Dan O'Brien, arguably the world's best decathlete in the early 90's, chose to start his vaulting at $15'9''$, and failed all three attempts. The loss of the several hundred points that caused, erased his considerable previous lead, and prevented him from securing one of the first three places, thereby excluding him from the U.S. Olympic team. It is no wonder that Sergei Bubka, the greatest pole-vaulter ever, referred to vaulting as a 'Professor's sport', where strategy is equally important to physical ability (which accounted for this sport's appeal to him).

4.3. Handicapping issues

Most sports hold separate competitions and keep separate records for men and women. Some sports, in which weight is considered to confer a significant advantage, like wrestling, weight-lifting and boxing, hold separate competitions in each weight category. An alternative to holding separate competitions or separately scoring different groups, is handicapping. Handicapping means adjusting individuals' scores according to some scheme based on the relevant attributes, or simply by past achievements. While this is not used in any olympic sports, the United States Golf Association has a scheme based on recent achievements [Pollock, 1974, reprinted in LM; and Scheid, 1977], which is used for amateur

---

[6] A subgame perfect equilibrium is one in which there is no gain from deviating even in subgames that would never be played when the players follow that equilibrium.

competitions. Friendly bowling competitions also occasionally use such handicaps.

One potential problem with handicapping by attributes, is that a small group may gain an unfair advantage if their previous record is coincidentally relatively low. For example, the record for 33 year old males in 5 km road races was slower than of 34–40 year olds, as well as younger, males [Camm and Grogan, 1988]. To counteract that, Camm and Grogan have proposed to use (efficient) frontier analysis. Specifically, they used the frontier function $f(i) = A + Bi + Ci^2 + D/i$ of age i, and estimated the parameters of this function by solving the linear program

$$\min \sum_{i \in I} U_i$$

subject to $f(i) + U_i = T_i$; $\quad U_i \geq 0 \quad i \in I$

where T_i is the record of age i. The U_i's represent the inefficiency, if any, of the record for age i; that is, how much slower the record is than it 'should' be. Camm and Grogan found the frontier functions for males and females, and used them to compute handicaps (time to be deducted) for selected ages, as well as for females vs. males. The system was applied in a 1987 5 km road race in Cincinnati.

In principle, one could use handicapping to combine men and women competitions/'records', eliminate bodyweight categories in weight lifting, and combine junior/senior competitions with mainstream ones. The downside of this would be the blurring of 'races' for fans and athletes alike. Competition needs to be exciting, not only fair.

5. Concluding remarks

During the period from the late 60's to the mid 70's, the 'golden era' of OR/MS in sports, there was a high degree of excitement and optimism about the viability of analytical approaches to sports issues. Brieman [1968] predicted that 'The day is rapidly approaching when the decision theorist... will be sitting on the player's bench.' In their introduction to Ladany and Machol [1977], the editors write 'We believe that managers are eventually going to read these articles and improve their strategies...'. They pointed out that, for example, Carter and Machol's [1971] suggestions for football coaches that time-outs be called later in the last two minutes, and that coffin-corner punts be attempted more often, already had an effect on practice. Schutz [1980], a physical education professor, who studied the relevant OR/MS literature, made a very strong case for the use of analytical approaches to sports.

From today's (mid 1992) perspective, it is debatable whether OR/MS had, or is having, the impact on sports that these pioneers had predicted. In major team sports, especially baseball[7], teams seem to over-collect data and then under-

---

[7] There is a voluminous, and occasionally quite sophisticated, work on baseball player's ratings, published regularly by The Society for American Baseball Research, but essentially the only decisions it might support are personnel moves.

analyze them, although one occasionally hears of 'decision support systems' like the one supposedly used by Oakland A's manager Tony La Russa. In a comment on the hockey Note by Nydick & Weiss [1989], Don Morrison states that 'I only wish that the hockey establishment had taken the same interest in this problem as my fellow academics have.' He did see some hope, however, in getting the attention of the NHL's LA Kings to this issue. Don Morrison also informed me that the UCLA football team has some well thought out strategies on 1 vs. 2 point attempts, fourth down strategies, etc.

Some OR/MS analyses in less main-stream sports, performed by or for various sports organizations, seem to have been successful in the 80's, as several publications in the journal *Interfaces* indicate. The work of Golden & Wasil [1987] on ranking outstanding sports records has been featured in the widely-read weekly *Sports Illustrated*. What seem to be lacking are publication outlets in academic or trade *sports* magazines, which could give these analyses visibility among sports administrators and coaches.

Future research is likely to address issues brought about by new rule changes, new tournament formats (or advocacy thereof), and adoption of new sports by some countries. For example, the 80's saw a change in awarding points for soccer wins in the U.K. and other countries – three, rather than two, points for a win, to increase its desirability vis-a-vis a tie, which receives one point – the effect of which was explored by Mehrez, Pliskin & Mercer [1987]. A draft lottery has been instituted, and evolved, by the NBA, the consequences of which were explored by Gerchak & Mausser [1992]. Testing athletes for drug use also emerged as an issue [Feinstein, 1990]. The growth in popularity in the U.S. of Jai Alai and dressage horseriding competitions since the late 70's led to their respective analyzes by Moser [1982] and Skiena [1988], and Shirland [1983]. The aging of American road runners, have led Camm & Grogan [1988] to devise a clever handicapping scheme, based on efficient frontier analysis. The need to stage large sports events in different cities also generates some interesting problems. An example is a DSS for scheduling the 1992 Summer Olympic Games in Barcelona [Andreu & Corominas, 1989].

While the sports issues which are the most obvious candidates for OR/MS, especially in baseball and football, have by now been well researched, some 'classical' issues are yet to be explored analytically. Two examples are substitutions strategy in basketball (taking into account the foul situation), and refueling strategies in various automobile races. A specific, and more recent, issue which had not yet been investigated analytically is the effect on players' risk-taking behavior of the unique non-linear scoring rules used by the *International* Golf Tournament in Colorado since the mid 80's.

The last issue we want to mention is government sports funding. One approach is to well-fund a small 'elite' group of promising athletes. The other approach is to provide basic funding for large numbers of potential athletes. Which approach is 'better' can only be determined if the objectives are clearly defined, which in national sports policy, unlike in research and development funding, is seldom the case. In the U.S., there is an ongoing debate whether college sport scholarships constitute an effective means of preparing international-calibre athletes. The system seems to be successful in swimming and some track events, but not in middle and long distance races.

Acknowledgements

I wish to thank Marc Kilgour, Mike Magazine, Don Morrison and Editor Steve Pollock for useful comments on previous drafts.

References

Albright, C. (1992). Streaks and slumps. *OR/MS Today* April, pp. 94–95.

Albright, S.C., and W. Winston (1978). A probabilistic model of winners' outs versus losers' outs in basketball. *Oper. Res.* 26, 1010–1019.

Allen, E. (1959). *Baseball Play and Strategy*, The Ronald Press.

Andreu, R., and A. Corominas (1989). SUCCESS 92: A DSS for scheduling the Olympic Games. *Interfaces* 19, 1–12.

Assad, A., J. Yee and B. Golden. (1982). *Scheduling Players in Team Competition: Theory and Computational Results*, W.P. MS/S #82-011, College of Business and Management, University of Maryland.

Atkinson, W.M., and M.K. Schaefer (1990). First down vs. field goal decisions in football. Presented at ORSA/TIMS Joint National Meeting, Philadelphia, October 1990.

Ball, B.C., and D.B. Webster (1977). Optimal scheduling for even-numbered team athletic conferences. *AIIE Trans.* 9, 161–167.

Bean, J.C., and J.R. Birge (1980). Reducing travelling costs and player fatigue in the National Basketball Association. *Interfaces* 10, 98–102.

Bellman, R.E. (1964). Dynamic programming and Markovian decision processes with particular application to baseball and chess, in: E. Beckenbach (ed.), *Applied Combinatorial Mathematics*, Wiley, New York, Chapter 7.

Bierman, H. (1968). A Letter to the Editor. *Management Sci.* 14, B281–282.

Blackman, S.S., and J.W. Casey (1980). Developing of a rating system for all tennis players. *Oper. Res.* 28, 489–502.

Brams, S.J., and P.D. Straffin, Jr. (1979). Prisoner's Dilemma and professional sports drafts. *Amer. Math. Monthly* 86, 80–88.

Cain, W.O., Jr. (1977). A computer-assisted heuristic approach used to schedule the major league baseball clubs, in: S.P. Ladany and R.E. Machol (eds.), *Optimal Strategies in Sports*, North-Holland, Amsterdam, pp. 32–41.

Camm, J.D., and T.J. Grogan (1988). An application of frontier analysis: Handicapping running races. *Interfaces*, 18, 52–60.

Campbell, R.T., and D.S. Chen (1976). A minimum distance basketball scheduling problem, in: R.E. Machol, S.P. Ladany and D.G. Morrison (eds.), *Management Science in Sports*, North-Holland, Amsterdam, pp. 15–25.

Carrol, B., P. Palmer and J. Thorn (1988). *The Hidden Game of Football*, Warner Books, New York.

Carter, V., and R.E. Machol (1971). Operations research in football. *Oper. Res.* 19, 541–544 (reprinted in: S.P. Ladany and R.E. Machol (eds.), *Optimal Strategies in Sports*, North-Holland, Amsterdam (1977)), pp. 94–96.

Carter, V., and R.E. Machol (1978). Optimal strategies on fourth down. *Management Sci.* 24, 1758–1762.

Clarke, S.R. (1979). Tie point strategy in American and international squash and badmington. *Res. Q.* 50, 729–734.

Clarke, S.R. (1988). Dynamic programming in one-day cricket – optimal scoring rates. *J. Oper. Res. Soc.* 39, 331–337.

Clarke, S.R., and J.M. Norman (1979). Comparison of North American and international squash scoring systems – analytical results. *Res. Q.* 50, 723–728.

Cook, E., and D.L. Fink (1972). *Percentage Baseball and the Computer*, Waverly Press.

Cook, E., and W.R. Garner (1964). *Percentage Baseball*, MIT Press, Cambridge, MA.

Cook, W.D., I. Golan and M. Kress (1988). Heuristics for ranking players in a round robin tournament. *Comput. Oper. Res.* 15, 135–144.

Cook, W.D., and M. Kress (1987). Tournament ranking and score difference. *Cah. Centre Etudes Rech. Oper.* 29, 215–222.

Coppins, R.J.R. and D.W. Pentico (1981). Scheduling the National Football League, Presented at CORS/TIMS/ORSA Conference, Toronto, Ont.

Cover, T.M. (1989). Do longer games favor the stronger player? *Amer. Stat.* 43, 277–278.

Cover, T.M., and C.W. Keilers (1977). An offensive earned-run average for baseball. *Oper. Res.* 25, 729–740; Erratum, *Oper. Res.* 27, 207.

De Werra, D. (1979). *Scheduling in Sports*, O.R. Working Paper 45, Department de Mathematiques, Ecole Polytechnique Federale de Lousanne.

De Werra, D. (1980). Geography, games and graphs. *Discrete Appl. Math.* 2, 327–337.

Eilon, S. (1986). Note: Further gymnastics. *Interfaces* 16, 69–71.

Ellis, P.M., and R.W. Corn (1984). Using bivalent integer programming to select teams for intercollegiate women's gymnastics competition. *Interfaces* 14, 41–46.

Erkut, E. (1987). More on Morrison and Wheat's 'pulling the goalie revisited'. *Interfaces* 17, 121–123.

Evans, J.R. (1988). A microcomputer-based decision support system for scheduling umpires in the American Baseball League. *Interfaces* 18, 42–51.

Farina, R., G.A. Kochenberger and T. Obremski (1989). The computer runs the bolder boulder: A simulation of a major running race. *Interfaces* 19, 48–55.

Feinstein, C.D. (1990). Deciding whether to test student athletes for drug use. *Interfaces* 20, 80–87.

Ferland, J.A., and C. Fleurent (1991). Computer aided scheduling for a sports league. *INFOR*, 29, 14–24

Ferland, J.A., and C. Fleurent (1992). *Game Allocation for a Major Sport League Undergoing Expansion*. Université de Montréal.

Fredricksen, J.S., and R.E. Machol (1988). Reduction of paradoxes in subjectively judged competitions. *European J. Oper. Res.* 35, 16–29.

Freeze, R.A. (1974). An analysis of baseball batting order by Monte Carlo simulation. *Oper. Res.* 22, 728–735.

Gerchak, M., and Gerchak Y. (1987). The effect of game sequencing on playoff-series duration. *Appl. Probab. Newslett.* 11, 1–3.

Gerchak, Y., and M. Henig (1986). The basketball shootout: Strategy and winning probabilities. *Oper. Res. Lett.* 5, 241–244.

Gerchak, Y., and M. Kilgour (1992). Sequential competitions with nondecreasing levels of difficulty. *Oper. Res. Lett.* to appear.

Gerchak, Y., and H.E. Mausser (1992). The NBA draft lottery in the 90's: Back to moral hazard? Working Paper, Department of Management Sciences, University of Waterloo.

Golden, B.L., and E.A. Wasil (1987). Ranking outstanding sports records. *Interfaces* 17, 32–42.

Hamilton, J., and R. Romano (1992). *Equilibrium Assignment of Players in Team Matches: Game Theory for Tennis Coaches*, WP 1992-26, Graduate School of Industrial Administration, Carnegie Mellon University

Hannan, E.L. (1979). Assignment of players to matches in a high school or college tennis match. *Comput. Oper. Res.* 6, 21–26

Henig, M., and B. O'Neill (1992). Games of boldness, Where the player performing the hardest task wins. *Oper. Res.* 40, 76–87.

Hersh, M., and S.P. Ladany (1989). Optimal pole-vaulting strategy. *Oper. Res.* 37, 172–175.

Horen, J., and R. Riezman (1985). Comparing draws for single elimination tournaments. *Oper. Res.* 33, 249–262.

Howard, R.A. (1960). *Dynamic Programming and Markov Processes*, MIT Press, Cambridge, MA.

Hurley, W. (1989). Should we go for the win or settle for a tie? Private communication.

Janssen, C.T.L., and T.E. Daniel (1984). A decision theory example in football. *Decision Sci.* 15, 253–259.

Kentarelis, D., and E.C.H. Veendorp (1991). A maximum likelihood ranking of American College football teams. Presented at the Western Economic Society Meeting, Seattle, WA, July 1991.

Kim, A. (1991). Popes, blizzards and walleyed pike. *Sports Illustrated*, April 8.

Ladany, S.P. (1975a). Optimal starting height for pole vaulting. *Oper. Res.* 23, 968–978.

Ladany, S.P. (1975b). Optimization of pentathlon training plans. *Management Sci.* 21, 1144–1155.

Ladany, S.P., J.W. Humes and G.P. Sphicas (1975). The optimal aiming Line. *Oper. Res. Q.* 26, 495–506 (reprinted in: S.P. Ladany and R.E. Machol (eds.), *Optimal Strategies in Sports*, North-Holland, Amsterdam (1977)), pp. 156–161.

Ladany, S.P., and R.E. Machol (eds.) (1977). *Optimal Strategies in Sports*, North-Holland, Amsterdam [LM].

Ladany, S.P., and J. Singh (1978). On maximizing the probability of jumping over a ditch. *SIAM Rev.* 20, 171–177.

Land, A., and S. Powell (1985). More gymnastics. *Interfaces* 15, 52–54.

Liittschwager, J.M., and J.R. Haagenson (1978). The round robin athletic sceduling problem. Presented at ORSA/TIMS Joint Meeting, Los Angeles, CA.

Lilien, G.L. (1976). Optimal weightlifting, in: R.E. Machol, S.P. Ladany and D.G. Morrison (eds.), *Management Science in Sports*, North-Holland, Amsterdam, pp. 101–112.

Lindsey, G.R. (1959). Statistical data useful for the operation of a baseball team. *Oper. Res.* 7, 197–207.

Lindsey, G.R. (1961). The progress of the score during a baseball game. *J. Amer. Stat. Assoc.* 56, 703–728.

Lindsey, G.R. (1963). An investigation of strategies in baseball. *Oper. Res.* 11, 477–501.

Machol, R.E., S.P. Ladany and D.G. Morrison (eds.) (1976). *Management Science in Sports*, North-Holland, Amsterdam [MLM].

Maltz, M.D. (1983). Management science in the long run. *Interfaces* 13, 40–45.

McPherson, B.D., J.E. Curtis and J.W. Loy (1989). *The Social Significance of Sports*, Human Kinetics Books, Toronto.

Means, E.H. (1968). More on football strategy. *Management Sci.* 15, B15–16.

Mehrez, A., and S.P. Ladany (1987). The utility model for evaluation of optimal behavior of a long jump competitor. *Simulation and Games* 18, 344–359.

Mehrez, A., J.S. Pliskin and A. Mercer (1987). A new point system for soccer leagues: Have expectations been realized?. *European J. Oper. Res.* 28, 154–157.

Moore, K. (1992). Dan & Dave: Not. *Sports Illustrated* July 6, pp. 14–18.

Morrison, D.G., and R.D. Wheat (1986). Pulling the goalie revisited. *Interfaces* 16, 28–34.

Moser, L.E. (1982). A mathematical analysis of the game of Jai Alais. *Amer. Math. Monthly* 89, 292–300.

Mullet, G.M. (1977). Simeon Poisson and the National Hockey League. *Amer. Stat.* 31, 8–12.

Musante, T.M., and B.A. Yellin (1979). The USA/equitable computerized tennis ranking system. *Interfaces* 9, 33–37.

Nagaraja, H.N., and W.T. Chan (1989). On the number of games played in a best of $(2n - 1)$ series. *Naval Res. Logistics* 36, 297–310.

Norman, J.M. (1985). Dynamic programming in tennis: When to use a fast serve. *J. Oper. Res. Soc.* 36, 75–77.

Nydick, R.L., Jr., and H.J. Weiss (1989). More on Erkut's 'More on Morrison and Wheat's 'pulling the goalie revisited'. *Interfaces* 19, 45–48.

Pankin, M.D. (1978). Evaluating offensive performance in baseball. *Oper. Res.* 26, 610–619.

Peterson, A.V., Jr. (1977). Comparing the run-scoring abilities of two different batting orders: Results of a simulation, in: S.P. Ladany and R.E. Machol (eds.), *Optimal Strategies in Sports*, North-Holland, Amsterdam, pp. 86–88.

Pollock, S.M. (1974). A model for evaluating golf handicapping. *Oper. Res.* 22, 1040–1050 (reprinted, in revised form, in: S.P. Ladany and R.E. Machol (eds.), *Optimal Strategies in Sports*, North-Holland, Amsterdam (1977), pp. 141–150).

Porter, R.C. (1967). Extra-point strategy in football. *Amer. Stat.* 21, 14–15 (reprinted in: S.P. Ladany and R.E. Machol (eds.), *Optimal Strategies in Sports*, North-Holland, Amsterdam), pp. 109–111.

Robinson, L.W. (1991a). Baseball playoff eliminations: An application of linear programming. *Oper. Res. Lett.* 10, 67–74.

Robinson, L.W. (1991b). Erratum: Baseball playoff eliminations: An application of linear programming. *Oper. Res. Lett.* 10, 429.

Schaefer, M.K., E.J. Schaefer and W.M. Atkinson (1991). *Fourth Down Decisions in Football*, Working Paper, Department of Mathematics, College of William and Mary, Williamsburg.

Schreuder, J.A.M. (1980). Constructing timetables for sports competitions. *Math. Programming Stud.* 13, 58–67.

Schutz, R.W. (1980). Sports and mathematics: A definition and delineation. *Res. Q. Exercise Sport* 51, 37–49.

Schwertmann, N.C., and L. Howard (1990). Probability models for the Australian Football League Grand Final Series. *Amer. Math. Soc. Gazette* 17, 89–94.

Schwertman, N.C., T.A. McCready and L. Howard (1991). Probability models for the NCAA regional basketball tournaments. *Amer. Stat.* 45, 35–38.

Scott, D.M., and G. Sherman (1988). The great shootout. *SIAM Rev.* 30, 492–497.

Shirland, L.E. (1983). Computerized dressage scheduling. *Interfaces* 13, 75–81.

Skiena, S.S. (1988). A fairer scoring system for Jai-Alais. *Interfaces* 18, 35–41.

Tan, Y.Y., and M.J. Magazine (1981). *Solving a Sports Scheduling Problem with Preassignments*, Department of Management Sciences, University of Waterloo.

Thorn, J., and P. Palmer (eds.) (1989). *Total Baseball*, Warner Books.

Townend, M.S. (1984). *Mathematics in Sport*, Ellis Horwood.

Tversky, A., and T. Gilovich (1989). The cold facts about the 'hot hand' in basketball. *Chance* 2, 16–21.

Washburn, A. (1991). Still more on pulling the goalie. *Interfaces* 21(2), 59–64.

Weiss, H.J. (1986). The bias of schedules and playoff systems in professional sports. *Management Sci.* 32, 696–713.

Winston, W., and A. Soni (1982). Does divisional play lead to more pennant races?. *Management Sci.* 28, 1432–1440.

Wright, M.B. (1988). Probabilities and decision rules for the game of squash rackets. *J. Oper. Res. Soc.* 39, 91–99.

S.M. Pollock et al., Eds., *Handbooks in OR & MS, Vol. 6*

Chapter 15

Apportionment *

M.L. Balinski

C.N.R.S., Laboratoire d'Econométrie de l'Ecole Polytechnique, 1 rue Descartes, 75005 Paris, France

H.P. Young

School of Public Affairs, University of Maryland, College Park, MD 20472, U.S.A.

1. Introduction

The apportionment problem is stated in Article 1, Section 2 of the United States Constitution:

> 'Representatives and direct Taxes shall be apportioned among the several States which may be included in this Union, according to their respective Numbers ... The Number of Representatives shall not exceed one for every thirty thousand but each State shall have at least one Representative.'

The phrase 'according to their respective numbers' conveys the general intent of proportionality, but no rule is specified. How to formulate such a rule has vexed noted statesmen and mathematicians for some two centuries. For, while proportionality is clearly the ideal, it cannot be met in practice. The problem is what to do about fractions, since no State's fair share is likely to be a whole number of seats. Nor is the 'rounding' problem merely academic: one seat more or less has provoked fierce political controversies throughout the nation's history – for representation is the very substance of political power.

Our approach to this problem is a marriage of history, political analysis, and mathematics. History provides a rich menu of methods. Political and scholarly debate – together with common sense – suggests the relevant principles that should apply. Finally mathematics, through the axiomatic method, gives a precise statement about the consistency or inconsistency of these principles – and thus ultimately provides a sensible basis for choosing which method seems right for a given application.

While we discuss the problem in the context of apportioning representation, the

---

* This paper is a revised and slightly expanded version of: M.L. Balinski and H.P. Young (1985) The apportionment of representation, in: H.P. Young (ed.), *Fair Allocation*, Proceedings of Symposia in Applied Mathematics, Vol. 33, American Mathematical Society, Providence, R.I.

theory is really one of discrete allocation, and has numerous other applications. How should a fixed total be allocated in whole numbers 'proportionally' to some criterion? For example, how should statistical data be rounded to sum to 100%? How should a number of discrete facilities be allocated to different regions according to needs or demands? How should manpower be allocated among different job categories or to satisfy specified quotas? These questions fit into the general framework of apportionment, and the politically inspired methods and principles are appropriate for their solution.

The intent of proportionality, of 'one person, one vote', is directly tied to the idea of obtaining an equitable distribution of voting 'power' among the citizens of the nation. The concept of power is an elusive one however. Stripped down to its essentials, voting power refers to the probability that a citizen's vote will make a difference – that his vote will decide the outcome. Of course, when there are many voters, the likelihood that any one person's vote will in fact make a difference is very small. Nevertheless, one might be interested in apportioning representation so that everyone's vote is *equally likely* to make a difference. Allocating seats in proportion to state populations does not achieve this result. Indeed the integer nature of the problem means that no method can achieve this result. One might try instead to make the voting power of citizens in different states as nearly *equal* as possible. This requires adopting a precise measure of power. Two measures that are often cited are the Banzhaf [1965] and Shapley & Shubik [1954] indices; unfortunately they can give quite different results. In any event, the United States Constitution asks for allocations that are proportional to populations, not to some abstract concept of 'power'.

The problem of apportionment is often confused with that of 'districting' or 'redistricting'. Apportionment determines the number of seats each state will receive. Redistricting refers to the drawing of congressional district boundaries within a state, one for each representative. Ideally the districts should have approximately 'equal populations'. Strict standards have been established by the Supreme Court of the United States on making district populations within a state as close to one another as is possible. In 1973, in *White* v. *Weiser* (412 U.S. 783), the Court overturned a Texas congressional district plan because the deviations 'were not "unavoidable" and the districts were not as mathematically equal as reasonably possible'. The maximum deviation of a district from the ideal was 2.4% by this plan. In addition to seeking districts of equal population, most states require that districts also be 'compact' [Young, 1988b]. They should not be gerrymandered; at least they should avoid the *appearance* of being gerrymandered. These considerations place severe restrictions on the districting plans, and makes of districting a quite difficult (and interesting) computational problem.

2. Formulation of the problem

An apportionment problem is given by a vector of *populations* $p = (p_1, p_2, \ldots, p_n)$ of n *states* and a total number of seats h (the *house size*) to be distributed among them. An *apportionment of h* is a vector $a = (a_1, a_2, \ldots, a_n)$ of nonnegative integers whose sum is h, $\sum a_i = h$. Very often, minima and maxima are imposed on the apportionment. Let $f = (f_1, f_2, \ldots, f_n)$ and $c = (c_1, c_2, \ldots, c_n)$ be prescribed *floors* and *ceilings* on the states' permissible allotments: $f_i \leq a_i \leq c_i$ for all i. In the U.S. for example, all $f_i = 1$; in France all $f_i = 2$; in other cases, such as Canada or the European Parliament, f_i depends on i. Variable ceilings are implied by the U.S. Constitutional statement but they are so large as to be moot. A *method* of apportionment M is a multiple-valued function that assigns *at least one* apportionment to every *feasible problem* (f, c, p, h), that is, for which $\sum f_i \leq h \leq \sum c_i$. M may be multiple-valued due to the possibility of 'ties'.

The *quota* of a state is the exact share of h to which its population would be entitled, irrespective of floors or ceilings. Given a problem (f, c, p, h), the quota of state i is $q_i = p_i h / \sum p_j$. If the q_i do not lie between the floors and ceilings, then the notion of quota must be modified. The 'fair shares' of the states are the exact amounts to which they would be entitled if noninteger representation were allowed, taking into account the constraints imposed by f and c. Accordingly, the shares are defined so that those that touch neither floor nor ceiling remain in the same proportions as the populations: i's *fair share* $s_i = \text{med}\{f_i, \lambda q_i, c_i\}$ is the median of the three numbers $f_i, \lambda q_i, c_i$, where λ is chosen so that $\sum s_i = h$. If the shares are all integers, then they must constitute the unique acceptable apportionment.

To illustrate the distinction between quota and fair share, consider a hypothetical country with four states having populations 580, 268, 102, and 50 (thousand), a house of 10 seats to apportion and floors of 1 seat per state. The raw quotas are 5.80, 2.68, 1.02, and 0.50. Since the latter is entitled to at least 1 seat, its fair share is 1 exactly. After setting this state aside, 9 seats remain to be divided among the rest. Their raw quotas of 9 are 5.49, 2.54 and 0.97. Since the latter is entitled to 1 seat, this leaves 8 seats for the first two. Their quotas of 8 are 5.47 and 2.53. Since these are higher than the floors, they represent the fair shares: the states' exact entitlements.

Solutions to the apportionment problem are not obvious. To see why, the reader is invited to study Table 1. What is the most reasonable apportionment of 36 seats

Table 1
A sample apportionment problem (no
floors or ceilings)

State	Population	Fair share
A	27 744	9.988
B	25 178	9.064
C	19 951	7.182
D	14 610	5.260
E	9 225	3.321
F	3 292	1.185
Total	100 000	36.000

Table 2
The 1976 apportionment of the European Parliament

Country	Population (thousands)	Quota	Floor	Fair share	Negotiated apportionment
Germany	62041	98.229	36	95.120	81
U.K.	56056	88.753	36	85.944	81
Italy	55361	87.652	36	84.878	81
France	53780	85.149	36	82.454	81
Netherlands	13450	21.295	14	20.621	25
Belgium	9772	15.472	14	14.982	24
Denmark	5052	7.999	10	10	16
Ireland	3086	4.886	10	10	15
Luxembourg	357	0.565	6	6	6
Total	258955	440	198	410	410

among these six states (assuming zero floors), and what 'method' produces this solution?

In the absence of floors and ceilings the fair shares in Table 1 are identical to the quotas. It would seem to the naked eye that A 'should' receive 10 seats, its fair share rounded up, whereas the other states 'should' receive their fair shares rounded down. But, then, only 35 seats are apportioned: so, which state 'should' be given the last seat? The reader will be able to verify anon that six different seemingly plausible methods resolve this conundrum in the six different possible ways.

Table 2 shows an example with real data: the populations and floors used to apportion the European Parliament in 1976. The reader is invited to compare the fair shares with the 'negotiated' solution shown in Table 2.

The Appendix gives two more examples with real data: the populations of the states by the censuses of 1980 and 1990 together with apportionments found by the six best known methods. It should be noticed that only 20 of the 50 states are allocated exactly the same number of seats by all 6 methods for the 1980 problem, and the same is true for only 21 of the 50 states for the 1990 problem: ample room, it seems, for heated debate.

3. Textbook methods

A currently fashionable approach to problem solving in applied mathematics is constrained optimization. Not surprisingly it has been advocated for apportionment. The constraints are that the numbers a_i must be *integers* satisfying $f_i \leq a_i \leq c_i$ for all i and $\sum a_i = h$. The objective is to find a vector a that most closely approximates the vector of fair shares s. But specifically what objective function is to be optimized?

One plausible choice is to minimize $\sum (a_i - s_i)^2$. It is easy to see that this yields the same result as minimizing the ℓ_p-norm or indeed any reasonable notion of 'distance' between *a* and *s*. The reason is that the solution is found by the following algorithm:

> Give each state the integer part of s_i and then award the
> remaining $\sum s_i - \lfloor s_i \rfloor$ seats one each to the states having largest   (1)
> remainders.[1] (Ties in remainders may give multiple solutions.)

Of course the 'error' in an apportionment could be measured differently. One could consider the total variance of the implied district sizes p_i/a_i from the ideal district size $\sum p_i/h$ and minimize $\sum a_i(p_i/a_i - \sum p_i/h)^2$. Or one could minimize the total variance in per capita representation from the ideal: $\sum p_i(a_i/p_i - h/\sum p_i)^2$. Yet again why not choose a minimax approach such as $\max_a \min_i a_i/p_i$? The difficulty with this general approach is that the choice of objective function remains *ad hoc*.

Another popular approach to fairness is lotteries. In theory the following gambling man's method is perfectly fair: construct a roulette wheel having *n* slots with widths proportional to the states' populations. Spin the wheel and drop a ball on it: the state on which it comes to rest wins a seat. After *h* 'plays' the house is apportioned. A better variant would be to give each state the integer part of its fair share and then use the roulette wheel to allocate the left-over seats, with the slot widths proportional to the states' remainders.

Such solutions are not acceptable in practice because what appears fair *a priori* seldom seems so *a posteriori*. A small state could get more seats than a large state: a state with fair share 1.1 might get 2 seats and another with fair share 1.9 get only 1 seat. The intriguing question is: what constitutes fairness in such a problem? The answers are found in history, political debate, decisions of the Supreme Court, and scholarly (and other) articles that have accumulated over some 200 years.

4. Historical methods

History is rife with the mathematical inventions of politicians when the apportionment of legislatures is at stake. In the United States the matter has concerned many of its greatest statesmen, including George Washington, Alexander Hamilton, Thomas Jefferson, John Quincy Adams, and Daniel Webster. The involvement of these eminent thinkers (and in more recent times of such mathematical luminaries as Edward V. Huntington, John von Neumann, Marston Morse, and, latterly, Garrett Birkhoff) attests both to the complexity of the problem and its profound political consequences. Some of the greatest contests over method have been fought over the disposition of a single seat.

When first confronted with an apportionment problem, most people suggest the rule (1) given in the preceding section. In fact that rule was first proposed by

---

[1] $\lfloor x \rfloor$ is the largest integer less than or equal to x, and $\lceil x \rceil$ is the smallest integer greater than or equal to x.

Alexander Hamilton (1792) to rebut a competing proposal of Thomas Jefferson. Curiously, the habit of thought in those days was not first to determine the house size and then to distribute them with an eye on the quotas. Rather one fixed upon some 'ratio of representation'; that is, one representative for every x persons, then divided x into the states' populations to obtain *quotients*. These quotients were rounded by some rule to determine the apportionment, and the house size fell where it may. Such an x came to be called a '*divisor*' and methods of this general type 'divisor methods'.

The first divisor method was stated in 1792 by Thomas Jefferson, then Secretary of State, in response to the results of the 1791 census. For a problem without ceilings or floors, a is a Jefferson apportionment[2] if and only if

$$\text{For all } i, \, a_i = \lfloor p_i/x \rfloor \text{ where } x \text{ is chosen so that } \sum_{i=1}^{n} a_i = h. \tag{2}$$

In the presence of floors and ceilings (2) would be modified to read as follows: a is a Jefferson apportionment for the problem (f, c, p, h) if and only if

$$\text{For all } i, \, a_i = \text{med}\{f_i, \lfloor p_i/x \rfloor, c_i\} \text{ where } x \text{ is chosen so that } \sum a_i = h. \tag{3}$$

This is equivalent to: a is a Jefferson apportionment for (f, c, p, h) if and only if $f \le a \le c, \sum a_i = h$, and for some x

$$\max_{i \, : \, a_i < c_i} p_i/(a_i + 1) \le x \le \min_{j \, : \, a_j > f_j} p_j/a_j. \tag{4}$$

Table 3 shows the 1792 apportionment populations, fair shares, and the solution by Jefferson's method for $h = 105$ (the number proposed in the Senate's 1792 apportionment bill). The Hamilton solution is given for comparison.

Jefferson's argument for dropping the fractions, i.e., for rounding the quotients *down*, was that the Constitution had left them 'unprovided for'. In a letter to George Washington he lambasted Hamilton's 'doctrine of fractions':

> '[The Constitution] could not but foresee that fractions would result, and it meant to submit to them. It knew they would be in favor of one part of the Union at one time and of another at another, so as, in the end, to balance occasional irregularities. But instead of such a *single* common ratio, or uniform divisor, as prescribed by the Constitution, the bill has applied *two* ratios. . . and if *two* ratios be applied, then *fifteen* may, and the distribution becomes arbitrary.'

Closer inspection of Table 3 reveals the true political import of Jefferson's ingenious proposal: Virginia has a fair share of only 18.310 but gets 19 seats. Delaware's share is 1.613 but it gets only 1 seat.

---

[2] To be strictly correct $\lfloor x \rfloor$ must be defined to be the largest integer less than x if x is not an integer, and otherwise is either x or $x - 1$.

Table 3
The 1792 problem: Jefferson and Hamilton apportionments

State	Population	Quotient ($x = 33\,000$)	Jefferson	Share	Hamilton
Conn.	236 841	7.177	7	6.877	7
Del.	55 540	1.683	1	1.613	2
Ga.	70 835	2.147	2	2.057	2
Ky.	68 705	2.082	2	1.995	2
Md.	278 514	8.440	8	8.088	8
Mass.	475 327	14.404	14	13.803	14
N.H.	141 822	4.298	4	4.118	4
N.J.	179 570	5.442	5	5.214	5
N.Y.	331 589	10.048	10	9.629	10
N.C.	353 523	10.713	10	10.266	10
Penn.	432 879	13.118	13	12.570	13
R.I.	68 446	2.074	2	1.988	2
S.C.	206 236	6.250	6	5.989	6
Vt.	85 533	2.592	2	2.484	2
Va.	630 560	19.108	19	18.310	18
Total	3 615 920	109.573	105	105	105

In the original House version of the bill, which used a divisor of 30 000, 112 seats were apportioned and Jefferson's method gave Virginia 21 seats with a share of 19.531, as the reader may verify.

Hamilton's method does not exhibit such startling departures from the fair shares. In general, a method *stays within fair share* if every apportionment a satisfies $\lfloor s_i \rfloor \leq a_i \leq \lceil s_i \rceil$, that is, if $|a_i - s_i| < 1$ for every i. Jefferson's method does not stay within fair share. It may be shown, however, that it only violates fair share on the high side.

To see this, suppose that Jefferson's method violates lower share. If $a_k < \lfloor s_k \rfloor$ then $a_k \leq s_k - 1$, since a_k is integer. Because $\sum s_i = \sum a_i = h$, there must be some $j \neq k$ such that $a_j > s_j$. Moreover $s_k > f_k$ (its floor) and $s_j < c_j$ (its ceiling), so $s_k = \lambda p_k$ and $s_j = \lambda p_j$ for some scalar $\lambda > 0$. Thus $a_k + 1 \leq \lambda p_k$ and $a_j > \lambda p_j$. Consider the common divisor $x = 1/\lambda$. Then $a_k + 1 \leq p_k/x$ whereas $a_j > p_j/x$. But this violates the minmax inequality (4), so a is not a Jefferson apportionment. This contradiction proves that Jefferson's method never violates lower share. In general, a method M does not *violate lower share* if all of its apportionments a satisfy $a_i \geq \lfloor s_i \rfloor$ for all i. Similarly M does not *violate upper share* if $a_i \leq \lceil s_i \rceil$ for all i.

For the record, Jefferson – backed by the Virginia contingent – won the day in 1792 and his method was used until 1840. During this period evidence accumulated that Jefferson's method strongly favors the large states. In the five censuses from 1790 to 1830 Delaware's shares were 1.61, 1.78, 1.95, 1.68, and 1.52 but in every case except 1810 it got only 1 seat. By contrast, New York received 10 seats with share 9.63 in 1790, 17 with share 16.66 in 1800, 27 with share 26.20 in 1810, 34 with share 32.50 in 1820, and 40 with share 38.59 in

1830! In the 1830's these injustices finally raised a great hue and cry from the smaller states – particularly those in New England, who saw their representation declining sharply. It especially aroused John Quincy Adams, then Representative from Massachusetts. After spending an 'entirely sleepless night... meditating in search of some device... to avert the heavy blow from the state of Massachusetts', he concocted a method that cleverly turned the tables on Jefferson: instead of rounding all quotients down, round them up. Not surprisingly, this method favors the small states as much as Jefferson's favors the large (see the sample apportionments in the Appendix). Formally, a is an Adams apportionment[3] for (f, c, p, h) if and only if

$$\text{For all } i, a_i = \text{med}\{f_i, \lceil p_i/x \rceil, c_i\}, \text{ where } x \text{ is chosen so that } \sum a_i = h, \tag{5}$$

equivalently if and only if $f \le a \le c$, $\sum a_i = h$, and for some x

$$\max_{i\,:\,a_i < c_i} p_i/a_i \le x \le \min_{j\,:\,a_j > f_j} p_j/(a_j - 1). \tag{6}$$

Adams' method is thus the mirror image of Jefferson's. The reader is invited to verify that Adams apportionments never violate upper share (just as Jefferson apportionments never violate lower share).

Daniel Webster, Senator from Massachusetts, took a more principled stance. He argued eloquently that the fair shares represent the true standard by which to judge an apportionment. Inspection of the Jefferson solution for 1830 (see Table 4) confirms the Senator's claim that it fails to meet this standard as near as may be:

> 'Now two things are undeniably true: first, that to take away the fortieth member from New York would bring her representation nearer to her exact proportion than it stands by leaving her that fortieth member; second, that giving the member thus taken from New York to Vermont would bring her representation nearer to her exact right than it is by the bill. And both these propositions are equally true of a transfer to Delaware of the twenty-eighth member assigned by the bill to Pennsylvania, and to Missouri of the thirteenth member assigned to Kentucky.' (From an address to the Senate by Daniel Webster, April 5, 1832.)

For any real number z let $[z]$ denote the integer closest to z. If the fractional part of z is one-half, then $[z]$ has two possible values. Formally, Webster's method may be stated as follows:

$$\text{For all } i, a_i = \text{med}\{f_i, [p_i/x], c_i\} \text{ where } x \text{ is chosen so that } \sum a_i = h. \tag{7}$$

This is equivalent to: a is a Webster apportionment for (f, c, p, h) if and only if

---

[3] To be strictly correct $\lceil x \rceil$ must be defined to be the smallest integer greater than x if x is not an integer, and otherwise x or $x + 1$.

Table 4
Apportionments for nine selected states, 1830

State	Population	Share	Adams	Dean	Webster	Jefferson
N.Y.	1918578	38.593	37	38	39	40
Penn.	1348072	27.117	26	27	27	28
Ky.	621832	12.509	12	12	12	13
Vt.	280657	5.646	6	6	6	5
La.	171904	3.458	4	4	3	3
Ill.	157147	3.161	4	3	3	3
Mo.	130419	2.623	3	3	3	2
Mich.	110358	2.220	3	2	2	2
Del.	75432	1.517	2	2	2	1
Total	4814399	96.844	97	97	97	97

$f \leq a \leq c, \sum a_i = h$ and for some x

$$\max_{i:a_i<c_i} \frac{p_i}{(a_i + 1/2)} \leq x \leq \min_{j:a_j>f_j} \frac{p_j}{(a_j - 1/2)}. \tag{8}$$

The Webster apportionment for 1830 is shown in Table 4 for nine selected states. It seems to give a more reasonable, middle-of-the-road answer than either the Jefferson or Adams solutions.

The essential property stated above by Webster may be formalized as follows. An apportionment is *near fair share* if no transfer of a seat between two states brings both of them nearer their fair shares. That is, there are no states i and j such that

$$s_i - (a_i - 1) < a_i - s_i \quad \text{and} \quad a_j + 1 - s_j < s_j - a_j.$$

The reader may verify that this must hold for any Webster apportionment, and so the Webster method is *near fair share*.

During this controversy Webster had received another proposal from one James Dean, formerly a professor at Webster's *alma mater*, Dartmouth. It was to take a divisor x and assign each state i that number of representatives a_i which makes p_i/a_i (the average district size in state i) as close as possible to x, and choose x so that $\sum a_i = h$.

Thus, a is a Dean apportionment (ignoring floors and ceilings) if

$$p_i/a_i - x \leq x - p_i/(a_i + 1)$$

and

$$x - p_i/a_i \leq p_i/(a_i - 1) - x,$$

which is equivalent to

$$\frac{a_i(a_i - 1)}{a_i - 1/2} \leq p_i/x \leq \frac{a_i(a_i + 1)}{a_i + 1/2} \quad \text{for all } i,$$

that is,

$$\max_{i} \frac{p_i}{\mathrm{d}(a_i)} \le x \le \min_{j} \frac{p_j}{\mathrm{d}(a_j - 1)}. \tag{9}$$

where for any integer a, $\mathrm{d}(a)$ is the *harmonic mean* of a and $a + 1$: $\mathrm{d}(a) = a(a + 1)/(a + 1/2)$. In general a is a Dean apportionment if and only if $f \le a \le c$, $\sum a_i = h$, and for some x

$$\max_{i\,:\,a_i < c_i} \frac{p_i}{\mathrm{d}(a_i)} \le x \le \min_{j\,:\,a_i > f_j} \frac{p_i}{\mathrm{d}(a_j - 1)} \tag{10}$$

The Dean apportionment for 1830 is shown in Table 4.

Formula (10) shows that Dean's method is of the same general type as those of Jefferson, Adams, and Webster. They are particular examples of the general class of 'divisor methods'. Let $\mathrm{d}(a)$ be a strictly increasing function (called a *rounding criterion*) defined on all integers $a \ge 0$, satisfying $a \le \mathrm{d}(a) \le a + 1$ and $\mathrm{d}(b) = b$, $\mathrm{d}(c) = c + 1$ for no pair of integers $b \ge 1$ and $c \ge 0$. Each rounding criterion d defines a 'rounding rule' as follows: for any real number $z \ge 0$, where $a \le z \le a + 1$ (an integer), round z *down* to a if $z < \mathrm{d}(a)$ and round z *up* to $a + 1$ if $z > \mathrm{d}(a)$, and round either way if $z = \mathrm{d}(a)$. The result is an integer $[z]_d$ (single-valued unless $z = \mathrm{d}(a)$) called a *d-rounding of z*.

The *divisor method* M *based on* d is defined for each problem (f, c, p, h) to be the apportionment(s) a satisfying

$$\text{For all } i, a_i = \mathrm{med}\{f_i, [p_i/x]_d, c_i\},$$

where x is chosen so that $\sum a_i = h$. Alternatively, a is an M-apportionment if and only if $f \le a \le c$, $\sum a_i = h$ and

$$\max_{i\,:\,a_i < c_i} \frac{p_i}{\mathrm{d}(a_i)} \le \min_{j\,:\,a_j > f_j} \frac{p_j}{\mathrm{d}(a_j - 1)}. \tag{11}$$

Thus all of the major historical methods except Hamilton's fall into the specific computational framework implied by a common divisor. Are there other important methods – not uncovered by history – that suggest themselves within this class? This question will be taken up again in Section 6. Already, however, we are in a position to prove several significant results.

Theorem 1. *Jefferson's method is the unique divisor method that never violates lower share.*

Proof. We have already established that Jefferson's method never violates lower share. Conversely, let M be a divisor method, based on divisor criterion $\mathrm{d}(a)$, that is *different* from Jefferson's. By (11) there must exist some two populations $p, q > 0$ and integers a, b such that $p/a < q/(b + 1)$ but (a, b) is an M-apportionment for the 2-state problem (p, q) with $h = a + b$ and a is not at its floor nor b at its ceiling.

Choose an integer $t \geq q/(qa - p(b+1))$. Consider the $(t+1)$-state problem of form $(p, p, \ldots, p, q)$ and $h = ta + b$. Evidently $p/a < q/(b+1)$ still holds, so in particular the minmax inequality (11) holds, and therefore $(a, a, \ldots, a, b)$ is an apportionment for this problem by the method M.

However, the share of state $t+1$ is (by choice of t)

$$\frac{qh}{tp+q} = \frac{q(ta+b)}{tp+q} \geq \frac{tp(b+1) + q(b+1)}{tp+q} = b+1.$$

Therefore, state $t+1$ with b seats violates its lower share. $\square$

A similar line of argument establishes the following:

Theorem 2. *Adams' method is the unique divisor method that never violates upper share.*

From these two theorems (and the fact that the Adams and Jefferson methods are distinct) we deduce the following impossibility result.

Theorem 3. *There is no divisor method that stays within fair share.*

Nevertheless, we have:

Theorem 4. *Webster's is the unique divisor method that is near fair share.*

Proof. We already know that Webster's method is near fair share. The proof of the converse is similar to that of Theorems 1 and 2. If M is a divisor method different from Webster's, then for $p_1, p_2 > 0$, (a_1, a_2) is an M-apportionment for (p_1, p_2) and $h = a_1 + a_2$, where $a_1 > 0$ and $a_2 < h$ but

$$\frac{p_1}{(a_1 - 1/2)} < \frac{p_2}{(a_2 + 1/2)}.$$

At $h = a_1 + a_2$ the share of state 1 is:

$$s_1 = \frac{p_1 h}{p_1 + p_2} = \frac{p_1(a_1 - 1/2 + a_2 + 1/2)}{p_1 + p_2} < a_1 - 1/2.$$

The share of state 2 is $s_2 > a_2 + 1/2$. But then $(a_1 - 1, a_2 + 1)$ is nearer fair share than (a_1, a_2). $\square$

The reader may verify that for two- and three-state problems, Webster's method does stay within fair share, and is the unique divisor method that does so. For larger numbers of states, Webster's method can violate fair share, but does so very infrequently. For the 1980 distribution of state sizes and 435 seats, for example, a Monte Carlo simulation shows that Webster's method can be expected to violate the fair share less than once in every 200 apportionments (or about once every 2000 years). The Jefferson and Adams methods violate fair share with near certainty.

5. Hamilton's method

Despite Webster's eloquent pleas in the 1830's, his method was not adopted until ten years later and then only for a decade. In 1850 it was deposed, by a curious quirk of fate, in favor of a 'new' proposal of Representative Samuel F. Vinton of Ohio which came to be known as 'Vinton's Method of 1850'. In fact it was none other than Hamilton's method, though largely unrecognized as such at the time. It remained on the statutes for over half a century, although it was never strictly followed. Indeed the manipulations of representation were so egregious in the post-Reconstruction era that they were directly responsible (through the effect of apportionment on the Electoral College) for the election of a minority-vote President (Rutherford B. Hayes in 1876). (For a detailed account see Balinski & Young [1982a, pp. 37–38 and the note on p. 180]).

In time, certain fundamental flaws in Hamilton's method began to emerge. The most notorious was the discovery of the so-called *Alabama paradox* in which Alabama by the census of 1880 would have received 8 seats in a House of 299 but only 7 in a House of 300. How could this happen? The answer lies in the peculiar way that remainders change as the house size changes. Table 5 shows the 1880 data: as the House increases by 1, Alabama's remainder increases, but not by enough to avoid being bumped for an extra seat by the interposition of two other states – Texas and Illinois.

The 'Alabama paradox' is no isolated phenomenon. In 1901 it was so outrageous that Maine's allocation fluctuated up and down five times between house sizes 382-391 – an event that led one member to exclaim, 'In Maine comes and out Maine goes – God help the State of Maine when mathematics reach for her to strike her down.' The case also sealed the fate of the Hamilton method, and in 1911 it was replaced with Webster's method.

In general a method M is *house monotone* if whenever a is an M-apportionment for (f, c, p, h) then there is some M-apportionment a' for $(f, c, p, h + 1)$ such that $a_i' \geq a_i$ for all i.

The question immediately arises: is there any way of doctoring Hamilton's method to make it house monotone? More generally, is there any method that is house monotone and stays within fair share? The answer is affirmative. Moreover, all such methods can be characterized by a simple recursive procedure. For simplicity of exposition let all floors be 0, and all ceilings be h. The idea is to increase the house size one seat at a time, beginning from zero, at each stage awarding the additional seat to some carefully selected state. The state selected is one for which upper quota is not violated by giving it an extra seat, *and* for

Table 5

The Alabama paradox under Hamilton's method, 1880 census data

State	Quota at 299	Quota at 300	% Increase	Absolute increase
Ala.	7.646	7.671	0.33	0.025
Tex.	9.640	9.672	0.33	0.032
Ill.	18.640	18.702	0.33	0.062

which lower quota will soon be violated if it is not given an extra seat. A particular example is the *Quota method*. It is defined by:

(i) $a = 0$ for house size $h = 0$,

(ii) if a is an apportionment for h, then a' is an apportionment for $h+1$ where a'_k $= a_k + 1$ for some k maximizing $p_j/(a_j + 1)$ over all j satisfying $a_j < p_j(h + 1)/p$, and $a'_i = a_i$ for $i \neq k$.

The choice guarantees that upper quota is not violated; it must be shown that lower quota is not violated. (For details see Balinski & Young [1982a], *Fair Representation*, Appendix, Section 7. A 'dual' procedure in which one decreases states' allocations has been treated by Mayberry [1978a].)

6. Pairwise comparisons

The decade 1910 to 1920 saw the number of states reach 48 and the number of seats 435. But no apportionment of seats was ever to be made on the basis of the 1920 census. Instead, the distribution determined in 1910, with the addition of one seat each to Arizona and New Mexico when they achieved statehood, remained in force for twenty years. The reason for this was political: the explosive growth in the populations of the industrial states at the expense of the agricultural states threatened to shift the balance of power. The rural states found arguments to cast doubt on the accuracy of the census, and their numbers in Congress were sufficient to enforce their point of view. Not unexpectedly this brought on a tide of protest both in Congress and in the grossly underrepresented states, and again made of the problem of fair representation a much debated issue of national importance.

The mathematical establishment of the day played a major role in this debate. Two reports commissioned by the National Academy of Sciences were crucial in supporting the method that was eventually chosen. One, released in 1929, was signed by G.A. Bliss, E.W. Brown, L.P. Eisenhart and Raymond Pearl. The other, written in 1948, carried the names of Marston Morse, John von Neumann and Luther P. Eisenhart.

Edward V. Huntington, Professor of Mechanics and Mathematics at Harvard, and a vice-president of the American Mathematical Society, took the lead. In January, 1921, he wrote the Chairman of the House Committee on the Census as follows: '. . . I have finished the formal exposition of my method and its application to the 1920 census. . . Statistical experts in the University who have examined my plan have pronounced it the only scientific method and have given me permission to state so.' Huntington's 'plan' – in fact, Joseph A. Hill, Chief Statistician of the Bureau of the Census had proposed it in 1911 – gave an apportionment that differed in six states from Webster's method (see Table 6). This uniquely 'scientific method' causes a change that takes seats away from larger states and gives them to smaller ones. Does it do so fairly? Certainly not if one accepts the idea of staying near to the fair share, for every one of the three possible transfers of a seat from a larger state to a smaller state results in both states having an apportionment further from their respective fair shares. So, why do it?

Table 6
Differences between Hill and Webster apportionments, 1920

State	Population	Share	Hill apportionment	Webster apportionment
N.Y.	10 380 589	42.824	42	43
N.C.	2 559 123	10.557	10	11
Va.	2 309 187	9.526	9	10
R.I.	604 397	2.493	3	2
N.M.	353 428	1.458	2	1
Vt.	352 428	1.454	2	1

Huntington's claim rested on an approach to apportionment by *pairwise comparisons* that was first suggested by Hill [1911] and fully developed by Huntington [1921, 1928a, 1940]:

> 'Between any two states, there will practically always be a certain inequality which gives one of the states a slight advantage over the other. A transfer of one representative from the more favored state to the less favored state will ordinarily reverse the *sign* of this inequality, so that the more favored state now becomes the less favored, and vice versa. Whether such a transfer should be made or not depends on whether the "amount of inequality" between the two states after the transfer is less or greater than it was before; if the "amount of inequality" is reduced by the transfer, it is obvious that the transfer should be made. The fundamental question therefore at once presents itself, as to how the "amount of inequality" between two states is to be measured.' [Huntington, 1928a]

It is unambiguous to say that i is *favored relative to* j if and only if $a_i/p_i > a_j/p_j$. One natural 'amount of inequality' between i and j is the difference $a_i/p_i - a_j/p_j$. Transferring one seat from the more favored state to the less favored state would result in an amount of inequality $|(a_j + 1)/p_j - (a_i - 1)/p_i|$. No transfer should be made if this difference is larger. The apportionment a is *stable* by this measure of inequality if for all pairs i and j with $a_i/p_i \geq a_j/p_j$ and $a_i > f_i, a_j < c_j$,

$$\frac{a_i}{p_i} - \frac{a_j}{p_j} \leq \frac{a_j + 1}{p_j} - \frac{a_i - 1}{p_i}. \tag{12}$$

It is by no means obvious that such an apportionment exists. By recombining terms it may be shown that (12) is equivalent to

$$\frac{p_i}{a_i - 1/2} \geq \frac{p_j}{a_j + 1/2},$$

and therefore

$$\min_{a_i > f_i} \frac{p_i}{a_i - 1/2} \geq \max_{a_j < c_j} \frac{p_j}{a_j + 1/2}. \tag{13}$$

But his means a must be a Webster apportionment. Moreover, every Webster apportionment satisfies (13) and so satisfies the transfer test for the measure of inequality $|a_i/p_i - a_j/p_j|$.

Another approach, paralleling the above, is to measure inequality by $a_i/a_j - p_i/p_j$ (where i is favored relative to j) and to ask for a stable solution for this test. But in this case stable solutions do not necessarily exist. A counterexample is given by $p = (762, 534, 304)$ and $h = 16$.

Huntington found 32 different ways of expressing the inequality $a_i/p_i > a_j/p_j$ (e.g., $p_i/a_i < p_j a_j$, $a_i p_j/a_j p_i - 1$, $a_i > a_j p_i/p_j$, etc.) and for each such measure he investigated the existence of stable solutions. He showed that, while some are 'unworkable' in the sense that stable solutions do not exist, all others result in one of five 'workable' methods – those of Adams, Dean, Webster, Jefferson, and his 'own' method. He preferred the fifth. In this he followed Hill's reasoning (1911) who had said,

> 'We might subtract one ratio from the other, measuring the divergence by the resulting arithmetical difference; or we might consider how many times greater one ratio is than the other, measuring divergence on a percentage basis, and expressing it as a percentage or relative difference instead of an arithmetical or absolute difference. This (latter) is believed to be the correct method.'

Hill pointed out that the arithmetical difference between two states with average constituencies 100 000 and 50 000, and two with 75 000 and 25 000, was the same but the degree of inequality in the second case seems worse. So he proposed that the apportionment be made so that no transfer of any one seat can reduce the percentage difference in representation between those states. Here the percentage difference between x and y is defined to be $|x - y|/\min(x, y)$. In fact the percentage difference between the two sides of the inequality $p_i/a_i > p_j/a_j$ is the same no matter which way the inequality is expressed by cross-multiplication.

Hill's method can therefore be expressed as a stable solution for many different (relative) measures of inequality. It also happens to be a divisor method with rounding criterion $d(a) = \sqrt{a(a+1)}$, the geometric mean of a and $a + 1$. Formally, a is a *Hill apportionment* if and only if with $d(a) = \sqrt{a(a+1)}$

$$\text{For all } i, \ a_i = \text{med}\{f_i, [p_i/x]_d, c_i\}, \text{ where } x \text{ is chosen so that } \sum_i a_i = h.$$

An argument similar to that used in deriving (13) does the trick.

Huntington's pairwise comparison approach yields five 'workable' methods. The corresponding measures of inequality are given in Table 7.

Table 7
Pairwise comparison tests (where $a_i/p_i \geq a_j/p_j$)

	Method				
	Adams	Dean	Hill	Webster	Jefferson
Measure	$a_i - a_j \left(\dfrac{p_i}{p_j} \right)$	$\dfrac{p_j}{a_j} - \dfrac{p_i}{a_i}$	$\dfrac{a_i/p_i}{a_j/p_j} - 1$	$\dfrac{a_i}{p_i} - \dfrac{a_j}{p_j}$	$a_i \left(\dfrac{p_j}{p_i} \right) - a_j$

7. Bias

Each of the five 'workable' methods that devolve from the pairwise comparisons approach is a divisor method. Which is preferable? Huntington had no difficulty with this question. Assuming that *only* these five methods are worthy of consideration he argued passionately on behalf of the 'method of equal proportions' – his carefully chosen new name for Hill's method – throughout a more than twenty-year period. His position was based on two principal tenets. First, 'it is clearly the relative or percentage difference, rather than the mere absolute difference, which is significant.' Second, of the five methods, Adams's clearly favors the small states most, Jefferson's the large states most, Webster's has a 'distinct bias in favor of the larger states' whereas Dean's has a 'similar bias in favor of the smaller states'. But between both pairs of these methods stands the method of Hill 'which has been mathematically shown to have no bias in favor of either the larger or the smaller states'. [Huntington, 1928b, p. 581]. The proof consisted in the observation that 'his' method was the 'middle' of the five. It was fortunate for this logic that the number of methods was odd. In fact, neither Huntington nor his mathematical allies put forward a definition of what 'bias' means. Nevertheless, these claims, buttressed by the 1929 National Academy of Sciences report, helped to persuade Congress. In 1941 Hill's method was enacted and has remained in force since that time. Political expediency also played a role: the effect of the change in 1941 was to shift one seat from a generally Republican state (Michigan) to a safe Democratic one (Arkansas). All Democrats in the House (except those from Michigan) voted in favor of the change.

That the method of Jefferson is exaggerated in its bias toward large states and that of Adams toward small is evident from looking at only a small sample of problems. In fact, in the order Adams to Jefferson, as listed in Table 7, the methods increasingly favor the large states. Say that a method M' *favors small states relative to* M, written $M' > M$, if, for every M-appointment a and M'-appointment a' of h seats for populations p

$$p_i < p_j \text{ implies either } a'_i \geq a_i \text{ or } a'_j \leq a_j.$$

Theorem 5. *If M and M' are divisor methods with rounding criteria d and d' satisfying* $d'(a)/d'(b) > d(a)/d(b)$ *for all integers* $a > b \geq 0$, *then* $M' > M$.

The proof is left to the reader. A corollary of the theorem is that Adams $>$ Dean $>$ Hill $>$ Webster $>$ Jefferson. So Huntington was right enough about the extremes, but what about the middle?

Bias has an absolute as well as a relative meaning. Compare two states with populations $p_1 > p_2 > 0$ and apportionments a_1, a_2. The apportionment *favors the larger state over the smaller* if $a_1/p_1 > a_2/p_2$ and *favors the smaller over the larger* if $a_1/p_1 < a_2/p_2$. As a practical matter any apportionment necessarily favors some states at the expense of others. Intuitively 'bias' means that the larger (or smaller) states are favored *over many problems*.

This point of view was developed by a distinguished scholar from Cornell, Walter F. Willcox. He had the distinction of having been elected at different times President of the American Economic Association, of the American Statistical Association and of the American Sociological Association. A pioneer in the use of statistics in demography, public health, and the law, he became the first serious student of apportionment [Willcox, 1910, 1916, 1952]. He believed that of the five traditional methods that of Webster was the correct choice, for two main reasons. First, because 'the history of reports, debates, and votes upon apportionment seems to show a settled conviction in Congress that every major fraction gives a valid claim to an additional representative.' Second, and in direct contradiction to the mathematicians, the method of Hill would defeat the main object of the Constitution '... which is to hold the scales even between the small and the large states. For the use of [Hill's method] inevitably favors the small states' [Willcox, 1916]. Willcox approached the analysis of bias in what must have been viewed by the theoreticians as quaint and old-fashioned: he studied historical data. For example, he prepared bar charts showing by how much each state was either favored or disfavored by each method for all previous census populations. He observed that Webster's method was by and large even-handed, whereas Hill's was not. Accused of 'crass misstatements of mathematical facts' and 'evasive and misleading arguments' in the National Academy of Science Reports, he was run off the mathematical plantation. But facts are often stranger than mathematics.

There are many possible ways to define the historical bias of a method. We will describe one. Given an apportionment a for populations p, let L and S be any two disjoint sets of states such that $a_i > a_j$ for every $i \in L$ and $j \in S$. L is a set of 'large' states and S a set of 'small' states. In general, let $k_E = \sum_E a_i / \sum_E p_i$ be the average number of representatives per person in each set of states E. Then a *favors the smaller states* if $k_S > k_L$ and *favors the larger states* if $k_L > k_S$.

One reasonable way of analyzing bias is the following choice of S and L: first, eliminate from consideration any state with quota less than $1/2$ since these must receive one seat and their inclusion would introduce an 'artificial' bias into the computation; then, take S to be the smallest one third (rounded down) of the remaining states and L the largest one third. Now count the *number of problems in which the smaller are favored* over the 19 problems from 1790 to 1970, for each method. The results are: Adams 19 (always), Dean 15, Hill 12, Webster 7, Jefferson 0 (never).

More insight is obtained by calculating the *percentage bias* between smaller and larger, that is the percentage difference between k_S and k_L, $100(k_S/k_L - 1)$. One finds that in *every* case the percentage bias of Webster's method is no larger than that of the other methods. (Sometimes apportionments by different methods are identical.) The average of the percentage biases of each method is given in Table 8. Other approaches give qualitatively similar results. Willcox seems to have had a point.

This approach to measuring bias suggests a mathematical model for theoretical analysis. The idea is to consider a fixed apportionment a and to look at the set of

Table 8
Average percentage bias, 1790–1970 censuses

	Method				
	Adams	Dean	Hill	Webster	Jefferson
Average bias	18.3	5.2	3.4	0.3	−15.7

all populations $p > 0$ whose M-apportionment is a. A difficulty is that this set of populations is unbounded. To define a bounded sample space in a natural way, we make use of the fact that M is a divisor method. Fix a divisor $x > 0$ and define

$$R_x(a) = \{p > 0; \, d(a_i) \geq p_i/x \geq d(a_i - 1)\}$$

where $d(-1) = 0$. Each $R_x(a)$ is a parallelepiped in the nonnegative orthant of R^n. A divisor method M is *unbiased* if for every $a > 0$, every divisor $x > 0$, and every pair of disjoint sets of larger and smaller states L and S, the probability given $p \in R_x(a)$ that (p, a) favors the larger states equals the probability that it favors the smaller states. Note that the condition holds for some x if and only if it holds for all x. In effect this model assumes that the populations p are *locally* uniformly distributed (in the vicinity of a), so no global distribution on p needs to be postulated.

It is easy to verify that Webster's method is unbiased. But many other rather bizarre methods are too. Consider, for example, the divisor method with criterion $d(2a) = 2a+1/5$, $d(2a+1) = 2a+9/5$, which rounds at $1/5$ and at $4/5$ in alternate integer intervals. This method is unbiased. It is also quite peculiar: consider two states with populations 30 000 and 40 000; by the 1/5–4/5 method they would split 6 seats as 3 and 3, but would share 4 seats as 1 and 3.

In general, a method M is *exact* if: (i) whenever an apportionment a is exactly proportional to p, then a is the unique M-apportionment for $\sum_i a_i$, and (ii) if a is an M-apportionment for p and αa is integer for some α, $0 < \alpha < 1$, then αa is the unique M-apportionment for $\alpha \sum_i a_i$. It can be shown that if M is an exact divisor method, then its divisor criterion satisfies

$$\frac{d(b)}{d(b-1)} \geq \frac{d(b+1)}{d(b)} \quad \text{for all } b > 0. \tag{14}$$

The '1/5–4/5' divisor method is not exact.

Theorem 6. *Webster's is the unique unbiased, exact divisor method.*

Proof. Suppose that M is an exact divisor method. Given $a > 0$ and $x > 0$, let L and S be any disjoint sets of larger and smaller states. The hyperplane $\{p : \sum_L p_i / \sum_L a_i = \sum_S p_i / \sum_S a_i\}$ divides $R_x(a)$ into the populations favoring L and those favoring S. These have equal measure if and only if the hyperplane passes through the center c of $R_x(a)$, $c_i = (d(a_i - 1) + d(a_i))/2$. So M is unbiased if and only if for all $a > 0$

Table 9
Expected percentage bias in favor of small states
(based on the actual 1970 apportionment)

Adams	Dean	Hill	Webster	Jefferson
28.2	7.0	3.5	0.0	−20.8

$$\frac{\sum_L a_i}{\sum_L d(a_i - 1) + d(a_i)} = \frac{\sum_S a_i}{\sum_S d(a_i - 1) + d(a_i)}. \tag{15}$$

If M is a Webster method, $d(a) = a + 1/2$, so satisfies (15) and is unbias ed.

Conversely, suppose M satisfies (15) for all $a > 0$. Then it must hold for a two state problem as well:

$$\frac{d(a_1 - 1) + d(a_1)}{d(a_2 - 1) + d(a_2)} = \frac{a_1}{a_2} \text{ for all } a_1 > a_2 > 0.$$

Setting $a_1 = a \geq 2$ and $a_2 = 1$, $(d(a - 1) + d(a))/a = d(0) + d(1)$, and letting $a \to \infty$, $d(0) + d(1) = 2$ and so

$$d(2a) = 2a + d(0), \quad d(2a + 1) = 2a + 2 - d(0).$$

Using (14) with $b = 2a + 1$ and the above identities

$$\frac{2a + 2 - d(0)}{2a + d(0)} \geq \frac{2a + 2 + d(0)}{2a + 2 - d(0)},$$

or $4a + 4 \geq (8a + 6)d(0)$. Letting $a \to \infty$ shows that $d(0) \leq 1/2$. The same derivation with $b = 2a$ yields $(8a + 2)d(0) \geq 4a)$, so $d(0) \geq 1/2$. Therefore $d(0) = 1/2$ and $d(a) = a + 1/2$, as was to be shown. □

The local probability model described above may be used to estimate the expected percentage bias of any divisor method when the number of states is large [see Balinski & Young, 1982a]. The results when a is taken to be the actual 1970 apportionment, S the 16 smallest states and L the 16 largest are given in Table 9.

8. Population monotonicity

Huntington's pairwise comparisons approach foundered on a muddle over middle. No one in the mathematical establishment bothered to analyze the historical data, no one even attempted to give a precise definition of bias. But the approach had another inherent flaw: no compelling reason was given as to *why* one test of inequality between a pair of states' representation should be chosen rather than another. Why, for example, compare the numbers a_i/p_i among each other rather than the numbers p_i/a_i? Indeed, one of the arguments for the relative difference measure was that it gave a result independent of the choice of a_i/p_i as versus p_i/a_i. But what, in the *context* of the problem itself, makes the choice of the relative difference the 'right' one? Virtually nothing: the choice is arbitrary, the argument for it *ad hoc*.

Yet the pairwise comparisons approach contains the germ of a much more fundamental idea, so obvious that it seems to have escaped the notice of earlier students. Another way to view pairwise comparisons is to ask: as the population of one state increases relative to another at what point should it gain a seat from the other? Each of Huntington's tests is, in effect, a specification of such a boundary point. Underlying this view is the *assumption* that, as populations change, a state that is growing will never give up a seat to a state that is shrinking. This innocuous 'population monotonicity' idea, which is basic to the very idea of proportionality and fairness, is not satisfied by all methods.

One example of a method that is not population monotone is Hamilton's. To estimate the frequency with which population monotonicity is violated, extrapolate the populations of the states for each year between censuses using compound growth state by state. The 19 censuses from 1791 to 1970 provides a sample of 180 apportionment problems. Had Hamilton's method been used, population monotonicity would have been violated 10 times, showing that the phenomenon is no isolated quirk. One instance of it is given in Table 10.

The 'population paradox' occurs because North Dakota, whose population is declining, gains a seat from Illinois, whose population is growing. The reader may find it instructive to devise a four state example for which Hamilton's method admits the paradox.

The Quota method is also not population monotone. Table 11 gives an example where only one state's population changes, namely, B's, which increases, but this leads to a loss of one seat from B to C.

How, precisely, *should* the idea of population monotonicity be defined? The second example (Table 11) indicates one way: if p_i increases and all other p_j ($j \neq i$) remain the same, then state i's apportionment does not decrease. This is a mathematically appealing definition, but a little thought shows that it is not really relevant to the context of the problem. Such comparisons can hardly be expected to occur in practice. The types of comparisons that actually occur are typically as

Table 10
The population paradox 1960–1961, Hamilton's method

State	Population		Growth rate (%)	Quota		Apportionment	
	1960	1961		1960	1961	1960	1961
Calif.	15 717 204	16 108 493	2.49	38.290	38.733	38	39
Ill.	10 081 158	10 186 391	1.04	24.559	24.493	25	24
Penn.	11 319 366	11 374 631	0.49	27.576	27.350	28	27
N.D.	632 446	631 615	−0.13	1.541	1.519	1	2
Total U.S.	178 559 219	180 912 144	1.32	435	435	435	435

Table 11
The population paradox, Quota method

State	Population	Quota appt.	State	Population	Quota appt.
A	501	6	A	501	6
B	394	5	B	400	4
C	156	1	C	156	2
D	149	1	D	149	1
Total	1200	13		1206	13

in the first example (Table 10), where the populations of all states change. A more useful and more realistic definition of population monotonicity is that *no state that is growing gives up a seat to a state that is shrinking*.

We need two other innocuous conditions to state the most important result in the theory of apportionment. A method M is *homogeneous* if the M-apportionments for p and h are the same as those for λp and h, $\lambda > 0$. A method M is *true* if whenever an apportionment a is exactly proportional to p then a is the unique apportionment for p when $h = \sum a_i$. These are rock-bottom requirements that must be satisfied by any method worthy of consideration.

Consider any two problems $p = (p_1, \ldots, p_n)$ with house size h and $p' = (p'_1, \ldots, p'_n)$ with house size h'. Suppose a method M gives to a pair of states with populations (p, q) from p the apportionment (a, b), and to a pair with populations (p', q') from p' the apportionment (a', b'). Then M is *population monotone* if, for every choice of pairs, $p' \geq p$ and $q' \leq q$ implies that either: (i) $a' \geq a$; (ii) $b' \leq b$; or (iii) $p' = p$, $q' = q$ and the solutions are tied, i.e., both (a, b) and (a', b') are solutions for (p, q). It may be verified that any divisor method is population monotone.

Theorem 7. *A true and homogeneous method M is population monotone if and only if it is a divisor method.*

Proof. We give the proof in the case of two states. Fix $h' = h \geq n = n' = 2$. Let $P = \{p = (p_1, p_2) > 0 : p_1 + p_2 = h\}$ be the set of all normalized populations. Suppose M is a population monotone method. For each $a = (a_1, a_2)$, $a_1 + a_2 = h$, define $P(a)$ to be the set of populations $p \in P$ such that a is an M-apportionment of h for p. By population monotonicity each $P(a)$ is an interval of the line P. Since M is true, a is the unique M-apportionment of h when $p = a$, and must be interior to the line segment $P(a)$. Moreover, $P(a)$ is a closed interval whenever $a = (a_1, a_2) > (1, 1)$. The intervals $P(1, h - 1)$ and $P(h - 1, 1)$ are either closed or half-open, whereas $P(0, h)$ and $P(h, 0)$ are either half-open (since $p > 0$) or empty. Finally, the intervals can overlap only at their endpoints, since otherwise population monotonicity would be violated.

To show that M is a divisor method we must establish the existence of a monotone increasing rounding criterion $d(a)$. Let $(d(a_1 - 1), d(a_2))$ be the left-hand endpoint of the interval $P(a_1, a_2)$ and $(d(a_1), d(a_2 - 1))$ be the right-hand endpoint for all $a_1 \geq a_2 > 0$, $a_1 + a_2 = h$. This defines $d(a)$ for $0 \leq a \leq h$, and shows $d(a)$ is monotone increasing in a. Moreover, since a belongs to $P(a)$, $a \leq d(a) \leq a + 1$. Finally,

$$\frac{d(a_1 - 1)}{d(a_2)} \leq \frac{p_1}{p_2} \leq \frac{d(a_1)}{d(a_2 - 1)} \qquad \text{if } a_1, a_2 \geq 1,$$

$$\frac{p_1}{p_2} \leq \frac{d(0)}{d(h - 1)} \qquad \text{if } a_1 = 0, \ a_2 = h,$$

$$\frac{d(h - 1)}{d(0)} \leq \frac{p_1}{p_2} \qquad \text{if } a_1 = h, \ a_2 = 0.$$

Equivalently,

$$\min_{a_i > 0} \frac{p_i}{d(a_i - 1)} \geq \max_{a_j \geq 0} \frac{p_j}{d(a_j)},$$

and so M can only be a divisor method.   □

In fact, the rounding criterion constructed in this manner holds for problems with any numbers of states, but a complete proof would carry us too far afield (for a stronger version of the theorem see Balinski & Young [1982a, p. 117]).

Several observations are in order. First, population monotonicity implies house monotonicity. Second, not only do the Hamilton and Quota methods violate population monotonicity, so does *any* method that satisfies quota. Third, we have resolved the difficulty concerning how to choose 'the middle'. There are not just five 'workable' methods, but a continuum of them.

9. Conclusion

The concepts advanced over the years by practical, political men have been distilled into axioms that express principles of fairness, and their logical implications have been explored. The force of this approach depends on the extent to which the axioms reflect the realities of the problem. For the theory to be useful, the axioms must be strong enough to meaningfully narrow the choice, yet not so strong as to eliminate all possible methods. The role of mathematics is to replace a choice of arithmetic formula by a choice of principles of fairness that determine a specific method.

The context of apportionment imposes two technical axioms that are the heart of proportionality: homogeneity and exactness. Common sense, history, and the investigation of numerical examples have suggested five fundamental axioms.

(1) *Population Monotonicity*: no state that gains population gives up a seat to one that loses population.

(2) *No Bias*: on average, over many problems, every state receives its fair share.

(3) *House Monotonicity*: as the total number of house seats increases, with populations fixed, no state's allocation decreases.

(4) *Fair Share*: no state's allocation deviates from its fair share by one whole seat or more.

(5) *Near Fair Share*: no transfer of a seat from one state to another brings both nearer to their fair shares.

There is no one method that satisfies all of these axioms, for there is none that is both population monotone and satisfies fair share. But population monotonicity singles out the class of divisor methods and guarantees house monotonicity as well. And adjoining to population monotonicity either no bias, or near fair share, narrows the choice of method down to one: Webster's. Moreover, it may be shown that, among divisor methods, Webster's is the least likely to violate fair share. When the number of states is large, the probability that it does violate fair share is negligibly small. All of this argues strongly for Webster's method. But there is an unbiased method that satisfies fair share (Hamilton's), albeit at the cost of losing house and population monotonicity. There are methods that satisfy fair share and are house monotone (the Quota methods), but at the cost of population monotonicity and simplicity of computation.

What do these results imply for the way Congress apportions its membership? History teaches that a change requires two ingredients: an interested party and principled arguments by which to advance its cause. The principles have clearly dominated the historical debates and provided the reasons for which methods are adopted and which rejected. Barring the discovery of some entirely new and compelling axioms, it seems that Webster's has the strongest claim. Indeed, Representative John A. Anderson of Kansas was already convinced when he addressed the House in 1882:

> 'Since the world began there has been but one way to proportioning numbers, namely, by using a common divisor, by running the 'remainders' into decimals, by taking fractions above .5, and dropping those below .5; nor can there be any other method. This process is purely arithmetical... If a hundred men were being torn limb from limb, or a thousand babes were being crushed, this process would have no more feeling in the matter than would an iceberg; because the science of mathematics has no more bowels of mercy than has a cast-iron dog.'

10. The 1991 debate

As this manuscript goes to press a new chapter in the history of apportionment is beginning to unfold. Ever since the reapportionment based on the census of 1910 the state of Montana has had 2 seats. However, on the basis of the 1990 census and by the method currently used by law to apportion the seats of the House of Representative – the method of Hill – it would receive only 1 seat. The Governor, the Attorney General, the two Senators and two representatives of Montana recently brought suit to declare the method of Hill unconstitutional. They advocate the method of Dean or that of John Quincy Adams (neither of

Table 12
Partial data from 1990 census and apportionments

State	Population	Fair share	Dean	Hill	Webster
Mass.	6 029 051	10.526	10	10	11
Wash.	4 887 941	8.533	8	9	9
Okla.	3 157 604	5.513	6	6	5
Mont.	803 665	1.404	2	1	1

which has ever been used in the United States). Both methods would allot to Montana the 2 seats it has enjoyed during the greater part of the century. In October 1991 a panel of three Federal judges in Montana ruled on this suit, declared that the present method is unconstitutional, and issued an injunction forbidding reapportionment based upon it.

And so one sees repeated an ever recurrent event of the history of apportionment: a local or partisan interest provokes action and what usually follows is a serious debate on the merits of the various methods. Indeed, as we have seen, the method of Hill does *not* fulfil the promises which were claimed for it when it was adopted as law in 1941, but of course neither do the methods of Adams and of Dean.

The apportionments given in the Appendix tell the tale. Montana's representation drops from 2 to 1 according to all the methods except those of Adams and Dean. To see the situation clearly all of the states for which there is a difference in the Dean, Hill and Webster apportionments are given in Table 12. Hill's method would give to Massachusetts 10 seats, one less that it received in 1980. If Montana and Massachusetts were to split a total of 12 seats between them what is the fair share of each? Montana's population represents 11.8% of the total and Massachusetts' 88.2%, so Montana's fair share of 12 is 1.411 and Massachusetts' 10.589. Between them it seems intuitively reasonable that Massachusetts should receive 11 and Montana 1. The same analysis between Massachusetts and Oklahoma sharing 16 seats gives Massachusetts a fair share of 10.50054 and Oklahoma 5.49946 – a very close call! So by the method of Webster Massachusetts gets 11 and Oklahoma gets 5. But, of course, we know that by the method of Webster this same property will hold for *every* pair of states, and Webster's is the *only* method that always will assure this. On these very grounds the state of Massachusetts has filed suit in federal court to overturn Hill's method and to adopt Webster's instead. The outcome of this suit has not yet been decided but it – and the Montana case – will almost certainly be ruled on by the Supreme Court in 1992. See *Note added in proof* at the end of this chapter.

11. A short guide to the literature

This paper is based on the book of Balinski & Young, *Fair Representation* [1982a], which contains a complete account of the mathematical theory and the history of apportionment in the United States. The theory is developed in Balinski & Young [1974, 1975, 1977a,b, 1978a,b, 1979a,b, 1980]. An expository outline of the axiomatic approach is given in Balinski & Young [1983a].

The problem has a rich political and mathematical background. Schmeckebier [1941] gives an early review of apportionment in the United States. The closely related problem – how to allocate seats among political parties on the basis of their vote totals – is discussed in the books of Cotteret & Emeri [1970], d'Hondt [1878, 1882], Rae [1971], and the paper by Rokkan [1968].

Optimization approaches may be found in Saint-Laguë [1910], Owens [1921] and Burt & Harris [1963]. The 'pairwise comparisons' approach is described in E.V. Huntington's papers [1921, 1928a, 1940]. Erlang [1907] discusses the idea of encouraging coalitions in the context of proportional representation, an idea fully developed in Balinski & Young [1978b]. Mayberry [1978a,b], Still [1979] and Balinski & Young [1979b] study house monotone methods that satisfy fair share.

A major scientific dispute over methods in the 1920's and 1930's pitted E.V. Huntington and the mathematical community, who argued for the method of Hill, against W.F. Willcox, who was for Webster's method. This debate is found in Huntington's papers, particularly [1928b], the papers of Willcox [1910, 1916, 1952], as well as a series of exchanges between Huntington and Willcox that appeared in *Science* in 1928, 1929 and 1942. This dispute brought forth two separate reports to the President of the National Academy of Sciences, one written by Bliss, Brown & Eisenhart [1929], the other by Morse, von Neumann & Eisenhart [1948].

Applications of the theory to Canada are given in Balinski & Young [1981, 1983b] and Balinski & Adamson [1985], and to the European Parliament in Balinski & Young [1982b]. Congressional testimony on the United States problem may be found in Young [1981, 1989].

The underlying ideas have been developed in several different directions. The problem of fair taxation is treated by Young [1987, 1988a]. The 'matrix' apportionment problem, where seats are to be allocated fairly to regions according to their populations and to political parties according to their votes simultaneously, is developed by Balinski & Demange [1989a,b]. These papers also treat axiomatically the problem of finding a matrix whose row and column sums are constrained, that is 'close' to a given matrix. This is a simplification of the matrix apportionment problem that has applications in economics and statistics [see Aït-Sahalia, Balinski & Demange, 1988].

References

Aït-Sahalia, Y., M. Balinski and G. Demange (1988). Le redressment des tables de contingence: Deux nouvelles approches, in: *Mélanges Economiques. Essais en l'Honneur de Edmond Malinvaud*, Economica, Paris, pp. 897–914.

Balinski, M.L., and A. Adamson (1985). How to make representation equal. *Policy Options* 6, November, 10–14.

Balinski, M.L., and G. Demange (1989a). An axiomatic approach to proportionality between matrices. *Math. Oper. Res.* 14, 700–719.

Balinski, M.L., and G. Demange (1989b). Algorithms for proportional matrices in reals and integers. *Math. Programming* 45, 193–210.

Balinski, M.L., and S.T. Rachev (1993). Rounding proportions: rules of rounding. *Numerical Functional Analysis and Optimization* 14, 475–501.

Balinski, M.L., and H.P. Young (1974). A new method for congressional apportionment. *Proc. National Academy Sci., USA* 71, 4602–4206.

Balinski, M.L., and H.P. Young (1975). The quota method of apportionment. *Amer. Math. Monthly* 82, 701–730.

Balinski, M.L., and H.P. Young (1977a). Apportionment schemes and the quota method. *Amer. Math. Monthly* 84, 450–455.

Balinski, M.L., and H.P. Young (1977b). On Huntington methods of apportionment. *SIAM J. Appl. Math. Part C* 33(4), 607–618.

Balinski, M.L., and H.P. Young (1978a). The Jefferson method of apportionment. *SIAM Rev.* 20(2), 278–284.

Balinski, M.L., and H.P. Young (1978b). Stability, coalitions and schisms in proportional representation systems. *Amer. Political Sci. Rev.* 72(3), 848–858.

Balinski, M.L., and H.P. Young (1979a). Criteria for proportional representation. *Oper. Res.* 27(1), 80–95.

Balinski, M.L., and H.P. Young (1979b). Quotatone apportionment methods. *Math. Oper. Res.* 4(1), 31–38.

Balinski, M.L., and H.P. Young (1980). The Webster method of apportionment. *Proc. National Academy Sci., USA* 77(1), 1–4.

Balinski, M.L., and H.P. Young (1981). Parliamentary representation and the amalgam method. *Canad. J. Political Sci.* XIV, 797–812.

Balinski, M.L., and H.P. Young (1982a). *Fair Representation: Meeting the Ideal of One Man, One Vote*, Yale University Press, New Haven, CT.

Balinski, M.L., and H.P. Young (1982b). Fair representation in the European Parliament. *J. Common Market Studies* XX, 361–373.

Balinski, M.L., and H.P. Young (1983a). Apportioning the United States House of Representatives. *Interfaces* 13(4), 35–43.

Balinski, M.L., and H.P. Young (1983b). Fair electoral distribution. *Policy Options* 4, July–August, 30–32.

Banzhaf, J.F. (1965). Weighted voting doesn't work; a mathematical analysis. *Rutgers Law Rev.* 19, 317–343.

Birkhoff, G. (1976). House monotone apportionment schemes. *Proc. National Academy Sci., USA* 73, 684–686.

Bliss, G.A., E.W. Brown, L.P. Eisenhart and R. Pearl (1929). Report to the President of the National Academy of Sciences, February 9, in: *Congressional Record*, 70th Congress, 2nd Session, 70, March 2, 4966–4967 [Also in US Congress, House, Committee on the Census, *Apportionment of Representatives: Hearings*, 76th Congress, 3rd Session, 1940].

Burt, O.R., and C.C. Harris Jr (1963). Apportionment of the US House of Representatives: A minimum range, integer solution, allocation problem. *Oper. Res.* 11, 648–652.

Cotteret, J.M., and C. Emeri (1970). *Les Systèmes Électoraux*, Presses Universitaires de France, Paris.

D'Hondt, V. (1878). *La Représentation Proportionnelle des Partis par Électeur*, Ghent.

D'Hondt, V. (1882). *Système Pratique et Raisonné de Représentation Proportionnelle*, Murquardt, Brussels.

Diaconis, P., and D. Freedman (1979). On rounding percentages. *J. Amer. Statist. Assoc.* 74, 359–364.

Erlang, A.K. (1907). Flerfordsvlag efter rene partilister. *Nyt Tidskr. Matematik*, Afd. B, 18, 82–83.

Hill, J. (1911). Letter to William C. Huston, Chairman, House Committee on the Census, dated April 25, in: US, Congress, House, *Apportionment of Representatives*, House Report 12, 62nd Congress, Session, April 25.

Huntington, E.V. (1921). The mathematical theory of the apportionment of representatives. *Proc. National Academy Sci., USA* 7, 123–127.

Huntington, E.V. (1928a). The apportionment of representatives in Congress. *Trans. Amer. Soc.* 30, 85–110.

Huntington, E.V. (1928b). The apportionment situation in Congress. *Science* 14, December, 579–582.

Huntington, E.V. (1940). *A Survey of Methods of Apportionment in Congress*, US Congress, Senate Document No. 304, 76th Congress, 3rd Session.

Hylland, A. (1975). En merknad til en artikkel fra 1907 om forholdsvalg. *Nordisk Matematisk Tidskr.* 23, 15–19.

Hylland, A. (1978). Allotment methods: procedures for proportional distribution of indivisible entities, Doctoral Dissertation, Harvard University, Cambridge, MA.

Leyvraz, J.P. (1977). Le problème de la répartition proportionnelle, Thèse de Docteur en Sciences, Ecole Polytechnique Fédérale de Lausanne, Département de Mathématiques, Lausanne.

Mayberry, J.P. (1978a). Quota methods for congressional apportionment are still non-unique. *Proc. National Academy Sci., USA* 75, 3537–3539.

Mayberry, J.P. (1978b). A spectrum of quota methods for legislative apportionment and manpower allocation, Brock University, St. Catharines, Ontario (mimeographed).

Morse, M., J. von Neumann and L.P. Eisenhart (1948). Report to the President of the National Academy of Sciences, May 28, Princeton, NJ.

Owens, F.W. (1921). On the apportionment of representatives. *Quart. Publ. Amer. Statist. Assoc.*, December, 958–968.

Rae, D.W. (1971). *The Political Consequences of Electoral Laws, revised edition*, Yale University Press, New Haven, CT and London.

Rokkan, S. (1968). Elections: Electoral systems, in: *International Encyclopedia of the Social Sciences* 5, Macmillan and Free Lance Press, New York, pp. 6–12.

Sainte-Laguë, A. (1910). La représentation et la méthode des moindres carrés. *C. R. l'Académie Sci.* 151, 377–378.

Schmeckebier, L.F. (1941). *Congressional Apportionment*, The Brookings Institution, Washington, DC.

Shapley, L.S., and M. Shubik (1954). A method of evaluating the distribution of power in a committee system. *Amer. Political Sci. Rev.* 48, 782–792.

Still, J.W. (1979). A class of new methods for congressional apportionment. *SIAM J. Appl. Math.* 37(2), 401–418.

Straffin, P.D. (1988). The Shapley-Shubik and Banzhaf power indices, in: *The Shapley Value: Essays in Honor of Lloyd S. Shapley*, Cambridge University Press, New York.

Willcox, W.F. (1910). Letter to E.D. Crumpacker dated December 21, in: US, Congress, House, *Apportionment of Representatives*, H. Rept. 1911, 61st Congress, 3rd Session, January 13, 1911.

Willcox, W.F. (1916). The apportionment of representatives. *Amer. Econ. Rev.* 6(1), Suppl., 3–16.

Willcox, W.F. (1952). Last words on the apportionment problem. *Law Contemporary Problems* 17, 290–302.

Young, P. (1981). Testimony, Census Activities and the Decennial Census. Hearing before the Subcommittee on Census and Population of the Committee on Post Office and Civil Service, House of Representatives, 97th Congress, 1st Session on H.R. 190, Serial No. 97-18, US Government Printing Office, Washington, DC.

Young, P. (1987). On dividing an amount according to individual claims or liabilities. *Math. Oper. Res.* 12, 398–414.

Young, P. (1988a). Distributive justice in taxation. *J. Econom. Theory* 44, 321–325.

Young, P. (1988b). Measuring the compactness of legislative districts. *Legislative Studies Quart.* 13, 105–115.

Young, P. (1989). Testimony, 1990 Census Oversight, Hearing before the Subcommittee on Government Information and Regulation of the Committee on Governmental Affairs, United States Senate, 101st Congress, 1st Session, US Government Printing Office, Washington, DC.

Appendix – Apportionments based on 1980 and 1990 census

1980 apportionments obtained with six different methods. The divisors for the five divisor methods are: Adams, 547 000; Dean, 524 100; Hill, 524 000; Webster, 522 000; Jefferson, 490 700

State	Population	Quota	Fair share	Adams	Dean	Hill	Webster	Jefferson	Hamilton
CA	23 688 562	45.584	45.548	44	45	45	45	48	46
NY	17 557 288	33.814	33.787	qb33	34	34	34	35	34
TX	14 228 383	27.403	27.381	27	27	27	27	28	27
PA	11 866 728	22.854	22.836	22	23	23	23	24	23
IL	11 418 461	21.991	21.974	21	22	22	22	23	22
OH	10 797 419	20.795	20.779	20	21	21	21	22	21
FL	9 739 992	18.758	18.744	18	19	19	19	19	19
MI	9 258 344	17.831	17.817	17	18	18	18	18	18
NJ	7 364 158	14.183	14.172	14	14	14	14	15	14
NC	5 874 429	11.314	11.305	11	11	11	11	11	11
MA	5 737 037	11.049	11.040	11	11	11	11	11	11
IN	5 490 179	10.574	10.565	11	10	10	11	11	11
GA	5 464 265	10.524	10.515	10	10	10	10	11	10
VA	5 346 279	10.296	10.288	10	10	10	10	10	10
MO	4 917 444	9.471	9.463	9	9	9	9	10	9
WI	4 705 335	9.062	9.055	9	9	9	9	9	9
TN	4 590 750	8.841	8.834	9	9	9	9	9	9
MD	4 216 446	8.120	8.114	8	8	8	8	8	8
LA	4 203 972	8.096	8.090	8	8	8	8	8	8
WA	4 130 163	7.954	7.948	8	8	8	8	8	8
MN	4 077 148	7.852	7.846	8	8	8	8	8	8
AL	3 890 061	7.492	7.486	8	7	7	7	7	7
KY	3 661 433	7.052	7.046	7	7	7	7	7	7

State	Population							
SC	3 119 208	6.007	6.003	6	6	6	6	6
CT	3 107 576	5.985	5.980	6	6	6	6	6
OK	3 025 266	5.826	5.822	6	6	6	6	6
IA	2 913 387	5.611	5.607	6	6	6	6	5
CO	2 888 834	5.564	5.559	6	6	6	6	5
AZ	2 717 866	5.234	5.230	5	5	5	5	5
OR	2 632 663	5.070	5.066	5	5	5	5	5
MI	2 520 638	4.855	4.851	5	5	5	5	5
KS	2 363 208	4.551	4.548	5	5	5	5	5
AR	2 285 513	4.402	4.398	4	4	4	4	4
WV	1 949 644	3.755	3.752	4	4	4	3	3
NB	1 570 006	3.024	3.021	3	3	3	3	3
UT	1 461 037	2.814	2.812	3	3	3	3	3
NM	1 299 968	2.504	2.502	3	3	3	3	2
ME	1 124 660	2.166	2.164	2	2	2	2	2
HI	965 000	1.859	1.857	2	2	2	2	2
RI	947 154	1.824	1.823	2	2	2	2	2
ID	943 935	1.818	1.817	2	2	2	2	2
NH	920 610	1.773	1.772	2	2	2	2	2
NV	799 184	1.539	1.538	2	2	2	2	2
MT	786 690	1.515	1.514	2	2	2	2	2
SD	690 178	1.329	1.328	1	1	1	1	1
ND	652 659	1.257	1.256	1	1	1	1	1
DE	595 225	1.146	1.145	1	1	1	1	1
VT	511 456	0.985	1	1	1	1	1	1
WY	470 816	0.907	1	1	1	1	1	1
AK	400 481	0.772	1	1	1	1	1	1
Total	225 867 174	435	435	435	435	435	435	435

1990 apportionments obtained with six different methods. The divisors for the five divisor methods are: Adams, 605 450; Dean, 578 057; Hill, 575 820; Webster, 574 143; Jefferson, 544 514

State	Population	Quota	Fair share	Adams	Dean	Hill	Webster	Jefferson	Hamilton
CA	29 839 250	52.124	52.094	50	52	52	52	54	52
NY	18 044 505	31.521	31.502	30	31	31	31	33	31
TX	17 059 805	29.801	29.783	29	30	30	30	31	30
FL	13 003 362	22.715	22.701	22	23	23	23	23	23
PA	11 924 710	20.830	20.818	20	21	21	21	21	21
IL	11 466 682	20.030	20.019	19	20	20	20	21	20
OH	10 887 325	19.018	19.007	18	19	19	19	19	19
MI	9 328 784	16.296	16.286	16	16	16	16	17	16
NJ	7 748 634	13.536	13.528	13	13	13	13	14	14
NC	6 657 630	11.630	11.623	11	12	12	12	12	12
GA	6 508 419	11.369	11.362	11	11	11	11	11	11
VA	6 216 568	10.859	10.853	11	11	11	11	11	11
MA	6 029 051	10.532	10.526	10	10	10	11	11	11
IN	5 564 228	9.720	9.714	10	10	10	10	10	10
MO	5 137 804	8.975	8.970	9	9	9	9	9	9
WI	4 906 745	8.571	8.566	9	9	9	9	8	9
TN	4 896 641	8.554	8.549	9	9	9	9	8	9
WA	4 887 941	8.538	8.533	9	8	9	9	8	9
MD	4 798 622	8.382	8.377	8	8	8	8	8	8
MN	4 387 029	7.663	7.659	8	8	8	8	8	8
LA	4 238 216	7.403	7.399	8	7	7	7	7	7
AL	4 062 608	7.097	7.093	7	7	7	7	7	7
KY	3 698 969	6.461	6.458	7	6	6	6	6	6
AZ	3 677 985	6.425	6.421	7	6	6	6	6	6

	Population							
SC	3 505 707	6.124	6.120	6	6	6	6	6
CO	3 307 912	5.778	5.775	6	6	6	6	6
CN	3 295 669	5.757	5.754	6	6	6	6	6
OK	3 157 604	5.516	5.513	6	6	5	5	5
OR	2 853 733	4.985	4.982	5	5	5	5	5
IO	2 787 424	4.869	4.866	5	5	5	5	5
MS	2 586 443	4.518	4.515	5	5	4	4	4
KA	2 485 600	4.342	4.339	4	4	4	4	4
AR	2 362 239	4.126	4.124	4	4	4	4	4
WV	1 801 625	3.147	3.145	3	3	3	3	3
UT	1 727 784	3.018	3.016	3	3	3	3	3
NB	1 584 617	2.768	2.766	3	3	3	3	2
NM	1 521 779	2.658	2.657	3	3	3	3	2
ME	1 233 223	2.154	2.153	3	3	2	2	2
NV	1 206 152	2.107	2.106	2	2	2	2	2
HA	1 115 274	1.948	1.947	2	2	2	2	2
NH	1 113 915	1.946	1.945	2	2	2	2	2
ID	1 011 986	1.768	1.767	2	2	2	2	2
RI	1 005 984	1.757	1.756	2	2	2	2	2
MT	803 655	1.404	1.403	2	2	1	1	1
SD	699 999	1.223	1.222	2	1	1	1	1
DE	668 696	1.168	1.167	2	1	1	1	1
ND	641 364	1.120	1.120	2	1	1	1	1
VT	564 964	0.987	1	1	1	1	1	1
AK	551 947	0.964	1	1	1	1	1	1
WY	455 975	0.797	1	1	1	1	1	1
Total	249 022 783	435	435	435	435	435	435	435

Note added in proof

The case *United States Department of Commerce et al., appelants v. Montana et al.* was argued before the Supreme Court of the United States on March 4 and decided on March 31, 1992. The Montana suit was dismissed in a decision written by Justice J. Stevens. It rejected the argument that the Constitution calls for adherence to the criterion of Dean – that 'the greatest possible equality in size of congressional districts, as measured by absolute deviation from ideal district size' should be enjoined – but it refused to make a choice as to which measure of inequality is best. It expressed a deference to Congress in making an 'apparently good faith choice of a method of apportionment' and expressly supported the right of Congress to legislate the automatic application of a specific method. However, the Court rejected the argument advanced by the Department of Commerce that apportionment is a purely political question which is beyond the purvue of the Court.

S.M. Pollock et al., Eds., *Handbooks in OR & MS, Vol. 6*

Chapter 16

Voting Theory

Lowell Bruce Anderson

Institute for Defense Analyses, 1801 N. Beauregard Street, Alexandria, VA 22311-1772, U.S.A.

1. Voting theory and paired comparisons

Many decision-making techniques require, desire or (in some meaningful sense) 'work better' if they are provided with consistent inputs. For example, if there is one decision-maker, then decision-making techniques function more reasonably if that person is consistent in always preferring option A to option C whenever there is another option, say B, such that the decision-maker both prefers option A to option B and prefers option B to option C. If there are multiple decision-makers, then these techniques function more reasonably if the decision-makers can reach a consistent consensus concerning their preferences.

Voting theory and the theory of paired comparison are quite different from such techniques in that both are designed to reach decisions when there are conflicts or certain types of inconsistencies among the inputs provided.

In particular, voting theory generally requires each voter to have internally consistent preferences, but it does not require all of the voters to agree with each other on one set of preferences. That is, while the voters may have to agree to accept the outcome of an election, they do not have to agree on one set of preferences concerning the candidates in order to hold the election. Thus, voting theory is specifically designed to address cases wherein there are multiple decision-makers (voters) who have distinctly conflicting preferences concerning the relevant options (candidates).

Paired comparison theory is directly concerned with developing a ranking (e.g., best to worst) of a set of items based on the outcomes of a set of comparisons involving pairs of those items, where a 'better item' is not necessarily selected over a 'worse item' in any given comparison. An example involves a set of teams that play various numbers of games against each other, and each game results in one team winning and one team losing that game. A paired comparison technique could then be used to rank those teams based on the outcomes of those games. Extensions that allow for ties are frequently (but not always) considered. Extensions that determine ranks based on magnitudes associated with the comparisons (e.g., on the scores of the games) rather than just on who (or what) won and who (or what) lost occasionally are considered.

561

In terms of ranking teams by game results, if each team plays against each other team the same number of times, and if one team (say team A) wins all of its games, while a second team (say team B) wins all of the rest of its games (i.e., all except its games against team A), and so forth, then developing a suitable ranking is trivial. However, there are many cases wherein the schedules or outcomes of the games do not satisfy this simple structure. To be useful, a paired comparison technique must be able to rank teams in more general cases. For example, it must be able to produce reasonable rankings in (many) cases in which every team has won some of its games, but has lost others. With a finite number of teams, this means that there is at least one subset of the teams, say $T_1, \ldots, T_n$, such that team T_i has defeated team T_{i+1} for $i = 1, \ldots, n - 1$, yet team T_n has defeated team T_1. Thus, paired comparison theory is designed to address cases in which the outcomes (in terms of wins and loses) of individual paired comparisons are not consistent in that there can be at least one set of options, say $T_1, \ldots, T_n$, such that option T_1 is preferred to option T_2, T_2 is preferred to T_3, and so on through T_n, yet option T_n is preferred to option T_1.

Some general points to note here are as follows. If each decision-maker involved has internally consistent preferences over the relevant options, and if these preferences are in agreement with those of all other decision-makers involved, then neither voting theory nor the theory of paired comparisons have anything very special to offer. Other decision-making techniques, which may have been designed to exploit such situations, would be much more appropriate. However, if these conditions do not hold, and major incompatibilities exist among the preferences of the decision-makers involved, then it may be quite useful to cast the relevant opinions and decisions into either a voting context or a paired comparison context (or both) for resolution.

Relatively brief descriptions of voting theory and the theory of paired comparisons are given in Section 2 and Chapter 17, respectively.

2. Basic aspects of voting theory

At the outset it should be noted that the goal of this section is to provide a general description of several major aspects of voting theory. Precise descriptions, which would require precise (and correspondingly complex) notation, are not given, and not all aspects of voting theory are discussed.

2.1. Background and motivation

Consider a situation in which v voters are presented with a alternatives, where v and a are strictly positive (finite) integers.[1] Since the cases in which $a = 1$

---

[1] A generalization here would be to assign weights to each voter (i.e., voter i would be assigned weight w_i where $0 < w_i < \infty$ for $i = 1, \ldots, v$), and the outcome of the vote would depend on these weights as well as on the voters' preferences. Unless explicitly stated otherwise, in the discussions below all voters are assumed to have equal voting power (i.e., $w_i = 1$ for all relevant i).

(for any v) and $v = 1$ (for any a) are clearly degenerate, assume that $a \geq 2$ and $v \geq 2$.[2] The goal of the vote is either to produce a ranking from 1 (most preferred) through a (least preferred) of these alternatives, perhaps with ties being allowed, or to select a' alternatives as being 'winners' (where a' is an integer between 1 and $a - 1$, inclusive). Frequently, $a' = 1$.[3]

Many different schemes have been proposed to elicit preferences from voters and to determine rankings of alternatives based on those preferences. Even in the case in which $a = 2$, there are several theoretically possible voting schemes that may reasonably apply in certain special cases. However, when $a = 2$, there is one generally applicable voting scheme – that of simple majority. To wit, each voter selects (votes for) exactly one of the two alternatives. The alternative receiving the majority of these votes is ranked ahead of the other, with a tie being declared if each alternative receives exactly the same number of votes. Two limitations could be raised concerning this simple majority voting scheme. First, it does not provide a method for breaking ties. Second, it applies only when $a = 2$.

For good reasons, voting theory is not directly concerned with what to do about ties in cases like this (e.g., cases in which v is even, and exactly $v/2$ of the voters prefer each of the two alternatives over the other). Such ties are not major theoretical problems in the sense that there is little that further theoretical development can contribute here. In large-scale elections (i.e., voting situations with large numbers of voters), such ties are unlikely to occur and thus should not present major practical problems, provided some plausible tie-breaking procedure is agreed upon in advance. In elections involving small numbers of voters, such ties may occur relatively frequently, but the small numbers involved may allow a flexibility (or inherent tie-breaking procedure) not present in large elections. In any event, there are several practical ways to break such ties, the choice of which may depend on the order of magnitude of the number of voters and the details of the situation.

While voting theory is not directly concerned with exact ties as just described, it is directly concerned with voting situations involving three or more alternatives. Simple majority rule, which is eminently appropriate for the $a = 2$ case, has no natural analog when $a \geq 3$. As a result, several plausible structures for

[2] Note that an election that considers one 'candidate', and allows each voter to either 'accept' or 'reject' that candidate, constitutes a vote in which $a = 2$.

[3] There are somewhat subtle differences between attempting to select a set of winners (even if $a' = 1$) and attempting to develop a full ranking. If the set of alternatives being considered is finite (which is the case addressed here), then the latter gives the former. (This is not true when there are infinitely many alternatives.) However, there are particular voting structures that can select winners (ties must be allowed in these structures) but cannot be reasonably extended to produce what are normally considered as being full rankings. A careful discussion of these matters is given in Sen [1970] (see Section 3.2.1.). However, Sen essentially shows that, given a finite number of alternatives, any characteristic of one of these goals (either selecting winners or developing a ranking) for all practical purposes can be converted into a similar characteristic of the other. Given this practical equivalence, no distinction is made in this overview between the theoretical properties of methods designed to develop full rankings and those designed only to select one or more winners.

obtaining voters preferences and several desirable properties for converting these preferences into a ranking of the alternatives have been postulated, and many different voting schemes have been devised. The specification and analysis of voting methods when $a \geq 3$ has produced meaningful problems that, in general, do not have obvious or trivially appropriate solutions. The essence of voting theory is to address these problems, and the rich structure of this problem area has led to many research papers and books on voting theory.

Of course, rich theory does not imply significant importance, and one aspect of the practical importance of voting theory is debatable. This aspect concerns the likelihood of changing current voting methods.

On one side, the people most directly involved are interested in winning elections, not in changing voting methods. Accordingly, there can be little motivation for people in power to change an existing voting system to a new (and perhaps somewhat more complex) voting system based on what are essentially altruistic grounds, such as attempting to improve general fairness and reasonability. This is true especially when such changes are quite likely to affect the outcomes of future elections, but in unknown directions. In addition, only recently have computational capabilities become sufficiently powerful to calculate results of large-scale elections when using all but the simplest of voting techniques; it has been argued that the computational aspects of converting to more sophisticated voting methods would make such changes far too expensive to seriously consider. Finally, theoretical work has shown that all voting methods are flawed in some sense when $a \geq 3$.

Of course, this is not to say that no changes should be made in voting methods; it does say, however, that for any proposed change, opponents can argue that the flaws in the proposed method will make that change not worthwhile. Also, proponents of some changes, but not of the particular change in question, can always argue, that, while changes should be made, the flaws of the proposed change means that it is not the right one to make. (In general, such arguments can be made about any change to any system.) The point is that theoretical work on voting already has established many relevant arguments and corresponding flaws, and so relatively little effort is needed to prepare the specifics of such arguments against any particular change proposed for any particular voting system.

On the other side, the rationale for taking a vote in the first place is related to the desire to reach what is, in some sense, a fair decision based on the preferences of the voters. Thus, there should be some motivation to examine the relative strengths and flaws of whatever voting method is being used in any given voting situation and, if a different voting system is found to be more appropriate and change is practical, then the voting method in question should be changed. In any given voting situation, some responsible set of officials should be interested in such matters. Also, since inexpensive but extremely powerful computers are now readily available, the computational complexity argument would appear no longer valid. Thus, the selection of a voting method for any particular voting situation now can depend on the inherent strengths and flaws of the relevant possible methods for the situation in question, not on historical limitations concerning the capability to collect and process voters' preferences.

While the likelihood of changing voting methods in any particular voting situation is debatable, there is little disagreement that the impacts of such changes (if made) often would be quite significant. Roughly speaking, in order for the choice of voting system to be significant, there must be more than two alternatives with no single alternative being preferred by a strict majority of the voters.

Real decision processes certainly involve cases in which there are more than two meaningfully different alternatives. However, to structure the voting in such cases, one could propose converting a vote involving a alternatives into a set of $a - 1$ pairwise votes. The winner of each pairwise vote (according to the simple majority rule discussed above) would remain viable, while the loser would be eliminated. After $a - 1$ such pairwise votes, one overall winner would remain. This proposal suffers from two flaws. First, it may be hard to implement in many voting situations: that is, while such a structure might be relatively easily implemented in some situations (e.g., committees voting on amending and passing bills), it can be practically unimplementable in other situations (such as in large-scale elections). Second, voting theory shows that the agenda by which these pairwise comparisons are made can strongly affect (to the extent of completely determining) the result. There may be special cases in which this characteristic is not considered to be a major flaw: for example, if a strict majority of the voters agree on a particular agenda, then the characteristic that the agenda determines the winner may be quite reasonable. However, it may be exactly for those cases that the voters would not agree on the agenda. Also, if (for some reason) the only other voting methods available for use in a particular situation are believed to have even worse flaws, then this agenda-based pairwise voting method might be useful, at least until a more desirable method can be made available. (This pairwise method does have some positive characteristics; the major one will be discussed later.) As stated above, the basic rationale for voting concerns the desire to reach a decision based on the preferences of the voters. Using a voting method that (potentially) allows the agenda-maker to determine the outcome clearly violates this rationale.

In voting situations, there frequently are more than two alternatives available with no single alternative being preferred by a strict majority of the voters; thus the choice of the voting system to be used can significantly affect the outcome of those voting situations. This applies to a vote by a social committee concerning what to serve at an upcoming banquet as well as to a vote by the citizens of a country concerning the election of a President. In terms of the likelihood of changing the current system, the former may precede the later. However, the latter example better exemplifies the potential importance of the selection of voting systems to be used.

A frequently cited example concerning the importance of the voting system used is the 1970 election for Senator from New York. In that election, James R. Buckley received about 40% of the vote while his two opponents, Charles E. Goodell and Richard L. Ottinger, split the remaining 60%. As a result, Buckley was elected according to the plurality rules (i.e., each voter votes for exactly one candidate and whichever candidate receives the most votes wins, even if that candidate does not receive a strict majority of the votes cast). However, it is widely believed that Buckley would have lost to Goodell and he would have lost to Ottinger had he faced either in a head-to-head contest. The same observation with the same results applies to the 1983 Democratic primary for Mayor of Chicago; in that election, Harold Washington beat Jane Byrne and Richard M. Daley in a plurality contest, yet probably would have lost to either in a head-to-head election. Other examples abound. Perhaps the most important concerns the 1966 Democratic primary for Governor of Maryland. In that race, George P. Mahoney received about 40% of the vote while his two opponents, Thomas Finan and Carlton Sickles, each received about 30%, and so Mahoney was declared the winner under the plurality system being used. Both Finan and Sickles are relatively liberal, and Maryland is a very liberal state. Mahoney is an unabashed ultraconservative, and it is extremely unlikely that he could have beaten either Finan or Sickles in a one-on-one contest. Maryland is a heavily Democratic state. However, in the main election, many Democrats could not support the ultraconservative Mahoney, and sufficiently many crossed over to vote Republican that the Republican candidate won. It is widely believed that, had either Finan or Sickles won the Democratic primary, then he would have beaten the (at that time, relatively obscure) Republican candidate, Spiro T. Agnew, in the main race. Agnew won, was later elected Vice President, and then resigned under pressure. Richard Nixon nominated Gerald Ford in Agnew's place and, when Nixon resigned, Ford became President. While this certainly is not a formal proof of importance, it is reasonable to believe that, had any of several different voting systems been used in that Maryland gubernatorial primary, then either Finan or Sickles would have been nominated instead of Mahoney, Agnew would never have been Governor much less Vice President, and the Presidency of the United States would have been different.

2.2. A numerical example

The following example is intended to help explain some of the general claims made above and to provide a setting for the following discussions of the specifics of several particular voting methods. Consider an election in which there are three candidates, A, B, and C, one of which is to be elected. Let $[x, y, z]$ denote a preference for x over y, y over z, and x over z, where x, y, z is any particular permutation of A, B, C. Suppose that the voters preferences can be described as follows:

Preferences	Percentage of voters with this preference
$[A, B, C]$	20
$[A, C, B]$	15
$[B, C, A]$	40
$[C, A, B]$	25
All others	0

With these preferences, note that all of the voters are consistent in that, if a particular voter prefers x to y and y to z, then that voter necessary prefers x to z. Note, however, that a strict majority of the voters (60%) prefers A to B, a strict majority (60%) prefers B to C, and a strict majority (65%) prefers C to A. The property that consistent individual preferences can lead to inconsistent group preferences is a fundamental characteristic of voting theory (and of the study of group decision-making in general). This property is frequently called the Condorcet paradox in the voting theory literature. The simplest example that exhibits this paradox is when there are three voters, one of which has preference $[A, B, C]$, one has preference $[B, C, A]$, and one has preference $[C, A, B]$. However, this simple example is a special case in the sense that it involves an exact tie (exactly one third of the voters have each of three different and incompatible preferences). In the example above, each of the voters' preferences is individually consistent and no ties (or other 'gimmicks') are involved.

This example also serves to demonstrate several other dilemmas concerning the choice of voting systems. For instance, it was stated above that if a particular voting situation were to be resolved by a set of pairwise votes according to a particular agenda, then it is possible that the agenda-maker has the power to determine the overall winner. In the example above, if the agenda-maker matches A against B with that winner facing C, then C is elected; if instead B is first matched against C with that winner facing A, then A is elected; and if C is first matched against A with the winner facing B, then B is elected. Thus, three different agendas produce three different winners even though the voters preferences remain the same throughout.

It was also stated above that, given a particular set of preferences, different voting systems could produce different winners. Three commonly proposed voting systems are as follows: plurality – elect whoever receives the most first place votes; runoff – match the top two candidates as measured by the number of first place received, and elect the majority rule winner of the pairwise match; Borda (named after its inventor) – award each candidate one point for each opposing candidate ranked below that candidate on each voters preference list, and elect the candidate that receives the greatest number of these points. For simplicity, assume that there are 100 voters in the example above. Then the plurality method would count 35 first place votes for A, 40 for B and 25 for C. Accordingly, the plurality method would elect candidate B. The runoff method would match B (with 40 firsts) against A (with 35 firsts) in a two-candidate majority rule runoff. Since 60 voters prefer A to B while only 40 prefer B to A, the runoff would elect candidate A. The Borda method would give 95 points to A (2 points for each of A's 35 first place rankings plus 1 point for each of A's 25 second place rankings), it would give 100 points to B (2 points for each of 40 firsts plus 1 for each of 20 seconds), and it would give 105 points to C (2 points for 25 firsts plus 1 point for 55 seconds). Accordingly, the Borda method would elect candidate C.

2.3. Some alternative voting methods

As stated above, many different voting methods have been devised. Several of the more common are described after the following brief discussion concerning ties.

Roughly speaking, two types of ties can occur in any of the voting methods described here, and a third type can occur in some (but not all) of them. One type is an input tie. This occurs when any given voter is absolutely indifferent over a subset of the available alternatives. All but one of the voting methods described here can be modified, at the cost of some increased complexity but with no additional theoretical difficulties, to handle such input ties; further, the one exception (approval voting) automatically handles such ties and so needs no such modification. For simplicity only, it is assumed here that no such input ties occur.

The second type of tie that can occur in any of these methods is an exactly tied outcome, namely, a tie in the results of the voting that could be broken (or changed) by any one voter if that voter (and no others) changed preferences. For example, an exactly tied vote would occur in plurality voting if the number of voters, v, divided by the number of alternatives, a, is an integer, and exactly v/a of the voters vote for each of the a alternatives. As stated above, reasonable methods exist to break such ties for each of the voting methods discussed here, where the specific details of the tie-breaking procedures can depend on the voting method and on the application involved. For simplicity, the discussions below implicitly assume that suitable tie-breaking procedures are used to break any exact ties that might occur, and, with two exceptions, no specific mention of such ties is made in these discussions. (The two exceptions concern methods that are also subject to a third type of tie.)

The third type of tie is a methodological tie in that it is created by the details of the voting method being used. Such ties can occur in voting methods that, in some sense, group the voters together. These methodological ties have the property that, in general, no single voter (acting alone) can break the tie by changing preference. Some specifics concerning methodological ties are discussed in conjunction with the descriptions of those voting methods subject to such ties.

The first three voting methods described below have commonly used descriptive names. The remaining methods are most frequently referred to by the name of their (best known) developer, and this convention is followed here.

2.3.1. Plurality voting

Suppose that, for a given election, one alternative is to be declared the winner (i.e., $a' = 1$). Plurality voting asks each voter to select exactly one alternative from the set of available alternatives and to cast a vote for that alternative (and only that alternative). The alternative that receives the most votes wins, whether or not it receives more than half of the votes cast (i.e., whether or not it was selected by a strict majority of the voters).

If $a' \geq 2$, then plurality voting asks each voter to select a' alternatives, for any a' between 1 and a' (inclusive), and to cast one vote for each of the a' alternatives so selected (and to cast no other votes). Plurality voting then ranks the alternatives in order according to the number of votes received and the top a' alternatives are declared to be the winners. Of course, if each voter has ranked all a alternatives from 1 (most preferred) through a (least preferred), then plurality voting can be implemented for any a' by casting a vote for each alternative in one of the first a' places in each voter's rankings.

2.3.2. Approval voting

Approval voting asks each voter to select a subset (of any size) from the set of available alternatives and to cast a vote for each alternative in that subset. That is, each voter votes 'yes' (casts a vote) or 'no' (does not cast a vote) for each alternative in the set. Approval voting then ranks the alternatives in order according to the number of 'yes' votes they receive. If one alternative is to be declared the winner (i.e., $a' = 1$), then the alternative that receives the most votes wins, whether or not that alternative was selected by a majority of the voters, and if it was so selected, whether or not some other alternatives were also selected by a majority of the voters. If $a' \geq 2$, then the top a' alternatives (in terms of votes received) are declared to be the winners.

2.3.3. Runoff voting

There are significant theoretical and practical reasons for considering runoff voting when exactly one winner is desired ($a' = 1$), and this is the only case considered here. In this case, runoff voting can be implemented in one of two equivalent ways. Either each voter can be asked to select exactly one alternative from the set of available alternatives (as in plurality voting), or each voter can be asked to rank the alternatives from 1 (most preferred) through a (least preferred), where a is the number of alternatives under consideration.

In the first implementation, if one alternative receives more than half the votes cast, then that alternative wins. If no alternative receives more than half the votes cast, then the voters are asked to participate in a second voting. This second voting matches the top two alternatives as measured by the number of votes received in the first voting (and it includes no other alternatives). In this second voting, each voter is asked to select exactly one of two alternatives being matched, and to cast a vote for that alternative. The alternative that receives the most votes in this second voting is then declared the winner.

In the second implementation, if one alternative is ranked first by more than half the voters, then that alternative wins. If no alternative is ranked first by more than half the voters, then the top two alternatives in terms of the number of first place rankings are compared against each other. Of these two alternatives, the alternative that ranks higher than the other on a majority of the voters' rankings is declared the winner.

2.3.4. Borda voting

As in the second implementation, Borda voting asks each voter to rank the alternatives from 1 (most preferred) through a (least preferred), where a is the number of alternatives under consideration. Each alternative receives $a - 1$ points for each voter that ranks that alternative first, it receives $a - 2$ points for each second place ranking, and so forth (receiving 1 point for each next-to-the-last place ranking and no points for being ranked last). That is, each alternative receives one point for each competing alternative ranked below it on each voter's preference list. The alternatives are then ranked in order, according to the number of points they receive. If $a' = 1$, then the alternative receiving the most points wins. If $a' \geq 2$, then the top a' alternatives (in terms of points received) are declared to be the winners.

2.3.5. Hare voting

Hare voting was designed to directly address elections in which $a' \geq 2$. Of course, it can also be used when $a' = 1$ and, for expository purposes, the $a' = 1$ case is described first below. Following this description, the Hare voting method for general a' is described. For any value of a', the Hare voting method asks each voter to rank the alternatives from 1 through a, as described above.

Suppose $a' = 1$. Then Hare voting proceeds as follows. If one alternative is ranked first by more than half of the voters, then that alternative wins. Otherwise, the alternative that receives the fewest first place votes is deleted from every voter's rankings, so that each voter now has a ranking of $a - 1$ alternatives, and those voters that previously had the deleted alternative in first place now have a new first place alternative. In these new rankings, if an alternative is now ranked first by more than half of the voters, then that alternative wins. If not, then the process is continued by deleting from every ranking the alternative that received the fewest first place votes in the rankings of the $a - 1$ alternatives that survived the first deletion. This second deletion results in each voter having a ranking of $a - 2$ alternatives. The process continues until one alternative receives a strict majority of the first place votes. In the extreme, the process could continue until only two alternatives remain, in which case simple majority rule would determine the winner. Note that, if $a = 3$ and $a' = 1$, then Hare voting is identical to runoff voting.

A three-part rationale for Hare voting when considering general values of a' (i.e., $1 \leq a' \leq a$) is as follows. First, if $a' = 1$ and some particular alternative receives more than one half of the first place votes cast, then no other alternative can receive as many first place votes as that alternative; thus the Hare rationale argues that the alternative in question should be chosen. Similarly, if $a' = 2$ and a particular alternative receives more than one third of the first place votes cast, then, at most, one other alternative can receive as many or more first place votes as that alternative and so, at most, one other alternative has a stronger claim to be chosen than that alternative. Since two alternatives are to be chosen, Hare argues that the alternative in question should be one of them. If there were another alternative that received more than one third of the first place votes cast, then that other alternative also would be chosen by Hare. If no other alternative received more than one third of first place votes, then the alternative in question (the one that did receive more than one third of the first place votes) is chosen and the process is continued to find a second alternative. If $a' = 3$, the same logic leads to the selection of any alternative that receives more than 25% of the first place votes cast, and so on. In general, if there are v voters, then any alternative that receives $q(v, a')$ or more first place votes is selected, where

$$q(x, y) = \lfloor x/(y+1) \rfloor + 1,$$

and $\lfloor x \rfloor$ denotes the largest integer less than or equal to x.

The second part of the Hare rationale is based on the general premise that, once an alternative has been selected, its supporters have had (at least some of) their say and their voting power should be reduced by some appropriate amount. If q votes are needed for selection, the Hare rationale argues that the supporters of the selected alternative have used up q votes worth of voting power. This premise is implemented in the following manner. Each voter starts with an initial voting power of 1.0. If a particular alternative, say alternative i, receives $q'_i \geq q(v, a')$, then: (1) that alternative is selected, (2) that alternative is deleted from the individual rankings of all of the voters, and (3) the voting power of those voters that ranked that alternative first is reduced (i.e., weighted) by a factor of $1 - q(v, a')/q'_i$. (the rationale for this weighting factor is discussed in the next paragraph). Let n_1 denote the number of alternatives selected here, i.e.,

$$n_1 = \text{card}\{i : q'_i \geq \lfloor v/(a'+1) \rfloor + 1\} = \text{card}\{i : q'_i \geq q(v, a')\}.$$

Note that $0 \leq n_1 \leq a'$. If $n_1 = a'$, then these a' alternatives are the winners by the Hare voting method. If $n_1 = 0$, then the next step in Hare voting involves the third part of the Hare rationale, which will be discussed below. Here, suppose that $0 < n_1 < a'$. Let

$$v_1 = v - n_1 q(v, a')$$

and

$$a'_1 = a' - n_1,$$

so that v_1 votes-worth of voting power remain to be used and there are a'_1 positions left to be filled. If, as a result of deleting the n_1 alternatives just selected, one or more new alternatives now receive at least $q(v_1, a'_1)$ first place votes (where the vote of each supporter of a selected alternative is reduced as described above), then those new alternatives are also selected, they are deleted from the individual voter's rankings, and the voting power of each of their supporters is reduced. In particular, if alternative j is selected here, and if alternative j received q'_{1j} (weighted) first place votes in the revised rankings, then the voting power of each supporter of alternative j is reduced by a weighting factor of $1 - q(v_1, a'_1)/q'_{1j}$. In general, at this stage some voters can have their voting power reduced by $1 - q(v, a')/q'_i$ for some i selected in the 'first round', some by $1 - q(v_1, a'_1)/q'_{1j}$ for some j selected in the 'second round', some by the product

$$(1 - q(v, a')/q'_i)(1 - q(v_1, a'_1)/q'_{1j}),$$

and some voters can still have full (1.0) voting power. This process continues until either a' alternatives have been selected or no alternative receives enough first place votes to be selected. If a' alternatives have been selected, the selection process is over. If (at this point in the selection process) fewer than a' alternatives have been selected and no remaining (unselected) alternative has enough first place votes to be selected according to the (revised and weighted) voters rankings, then the third part of the Hare rationale is applied.

Before discussing this third part, the reason for using $1 - q(v, a')/q_i'$ as a weighting factor should be noted. As stated above, the basic rationale here is that, if alternative i is selected (in the first round), then the supporters of that alternative are assumed to have used up $q(v, a')$ votes worth of voting power in selecting this choice. However, they should not lose more than this amount of voting power. That is, these supporters should not have reason to believe that they are wasting their voting power when more than $q(v, a')$ of them rank alternative i first. Given that q_i' voters have ranked that alternative first and that $q(v, a')$ of these votes are to be considered as having been expended, these q_i' voters should have a total of $q_i' - q(v, a')$ votes worth of voting power remaining. Distributing this remaining voting power uniformly over the q_i' voters in question means that each such voter should retain a voting power of

$$(q_i' - q(v, a'))/q_i' = 1 - q(v, a')/q_i'.$$

If, in tabulating the results of Hare voting, no remaining alternatives receives enough first place votes to be selected, yet there are still positions left to be filled, then the third part of the Hare rationale is employed. This third part is that the remaining alternative with the weakest claim to be selected is the alternative that is receiving the least number of first place votes in the current rankings. Accordingly, if, in these (revised and weighed) rankings, no alternative is receiving enough first place votes to be selected and one or more positions remain to be filled, then the alternative with the least number of first place votes is deleted from the rankings of all voters, thereby (in general) creating some new first place alternatives. (If not, then the alternative with the next fewest first place votes is removed from all of the rankings, and so on, thereby ensuring that new first place alternatives will eventually be created.) This creation of new first place alternatives allows the process to continue until a' alternatives have been selected.

The Hare voting method is the logically straightforward (but notationally complex) implementation of this three-part rationale.

2.3.6. Copeland voting

Copeland voting asks each voter to rank the alternatives from 1 through a as described above. For $i = 1, \ldots, a$ and $j = 1, \ldots, a$, let

$$w_{ij}' = \begin{cases} 1 & \text{if } i \neq j \text{ and a strict majority of the voters rank alternative } i \text{ ahead of} \\ & \text{alternative } j \\ 0 & \text{otherwise} \end{cases}$$

and

$$l'_{ij} = \begin{cases} 1 & \text{if } i \neq j \text{ and a strict majority of the voters rank alternative } j \text{ ahead of} \\ & \text{alternative } i \\ 0 & \text{otherwise.} \end{cases}$$

For $i = 1, \ldots, a$, let

$$w_i = \sum_{j=1}^{a} w'_{ij},$$

$$l_i = \sum_{j=1}^{a} l'_{ij},$$

$$t_i = a - 1 - (w_i + l_i),$$

and

$$s_i = w_i - l_i.$$

Copeland voting then ranks the alternatives in order according to s_i as just defined. That is, for all relevant i and j, alternative i is ranked ahead of alternative j if and only if $s_i \geq s_j$, and alternative i is tied with alternative j if $s_i = s_j$.

Note that, if a tie-breaking procedure is being used to break exact ties (where exact ties are as defined at the beginning of Section 3 above), then $t_i = 0$ for all relevant i. However, Copeland voting also can result in methodological ties (which occur if $s_i = s_j$ for any $i \neq j$). Under Copeland voting, such methodological ties are not necessarily rare (even in large-scale elections), and there is no intrinsic method for breaking such ties. Of course, there are many extrinsic methods that can be used to break such ties; for example, Borda voting or Hare voting, appropriately modified, could be used to break any methodological ties that occur within Copeland voting.

Note also that, whether or not t_i and t_j are zero,

$$s_i > s_j,$$

if and only if

$$\frac{w_i + t_i/2}{a - 1} > \frac{w_j + t_j/2}{a - 1},$$

and these inequalities hold if and only if

$$2w_i + t_i > 2w_j + t_j.$$

In particular, Copeland voting can be viewed as matching alternative i against alternative j for each pair of distinct alternatives i and j. With this viewpoint, each alternative participates in $a - 1$ matches, one each against of the other $a - 1$ alternatives, with the results being that alternative i wins w_i of these matches, loses l_i of these matches, and ties its opponent in t_i of these matches. If a tie is counted as half of a win half of a loss, then

$$\frac{w_i + t_i/2}{a - 1}$$

gives the winning percentage of alternative i in these matches. Accordingly, Copeland ranking (i.e., ranking by wins minus losses) is identical to ranking by winning percentage (counting ties as a half win and a half loss), which is the ranking method used by most team-sport leagues. (Instead of calculating a winning percentage, ice hockey typically gives each team 2 points for each win and 1 point for each tie, and uses total points to rank the teams. This clearly results in the same ranking as using winning percentage or using wins minus losses to rank the teams when the teams involved have all played the same number of games.)

Finally, it should be noted that if the voters rankings are such that there is one alternative that would win each one-on-one match against each other alternative (i.e., for some particular i, $w_{ij} = 1$ for all $j \neq i$), then that candidate is called a Condorcet winner in the voting theory literature. As the example in Section 2 above shows, voters can have individually consistent rankings on a set of alternatives, yet, based on those rankings, no alternative is a Condorcet winner. However, if a Condorcet winner exists, it is unique. A relevant property concerning voting systems is whether or not a given voting system will always rank a Condorcet winner first (i.e., declare it the winner if $a' = 1$) whenever the individual voters' rankings are such that a Condorcet winner exists. Copeland voting clearly has this property, and it is the only voting system of those discussed thus far in this section that necessarily selects a Condorcet winner if one exists. However, there are many other voting systems that also have this property, one of which is discussed next.[4]

2.3.7. Kemeny voting

Kemeny voting asks each voter to rank the alternatives from 1 through a as described above. Kemeny's approach is to define a metric over the possible rankings (i.e., over permutations of $\{1, \ldots, a\}$), and to find a 'consensus' ranking that minimizes the sum of the distances between this consensus ranking and each of the voter's rankings. Specifically, let $p = (p_1, \ldots, p_a)$ and $q = (q_1, \ldots, q_a)$ be any two permutations of $\{1, \ldots, a\}$: i.e., for all relevant i and j, $p_i \in \{1, \ldots, a\}$ and $p_i \neq p_j$ if $i \neq j$, and the same conditions apply to q. Accordingly, p and q can be viewed as being two (not necessarily distinct) voter's rankings of the alternatives involved. For all relevant i and j, let

$$d'_{ij}(p,q) = \begin{cases} 0 & \text{if } i = j \text{ or } i \neq j \text{ and either alternative } i \text{ is ranked ahead of alternative } j \text{ by both } p \text{ and } q \text{ or alternative } i \text{ is ranked behind alternative } j \text{ by both } p \text{ and } q \text{ (i.e., } p \text{ and } q \text{ agree when comparing } i \text{ with } j) \\ 1 & \text{otherwise (i.e., and } p \text{ and } q \text{ disagree when comparing } i \text{ with } j), \end{cases}$$

---

[4] Another voting system that has this property is taking pairwise votes according to a fixed agenda, as described in Section 1 above. That is, if a Condorcet winning alternative exists, then this alternative will be the overall winner of any sequence of pairwise votes in which it participates.

and define the function d on pairs of rankings (i.e., on the Cartesian product of permutations of $\{1, \ldots, a\}$ by

$$d(p, q) = \sum_{i=1}^{a-1} \sum_{j=i+1}^{a} d'_{ij}(p, q).$$

It is not difficult to show that d is a metric on rankings as defined here. (It also is not difficult to extend this structure to allow any voter to be indifferent over several alternatives, i.e., to allow input ties, which is how Kemeny suggests that this method be used. As above, it is assumed for simplicity here that no such input ties occur.) Assign each voter a distinct numeric label between 1 and v. For $k = 1, \ldots, v$, let

$$p^k = (p_1^k, \ldots, p_a^k)$$

be the preference ranking of voter k. Call q a consensus ranking if q is a permutation of $\{1, \ldots, a\}$ such that

$$\sum_{k=1}^{v} d(p^k, q) \le \sum_{k=1}^{v} d(p^k, q')$$

for every possible ranking q' (i.e., for every q' that is a permutation of $\{1, \ldots, a\}$). Since a is finite, there is always at least one such consensus ranking. If the voter's preferences are such that there is only one such ranking, then Kemeny voting ranks the alternatives in order, according to that unique consensus ranking. If there are multiple consensus rankings, then Kemeny voting ranks each alternative as being (in general, tied) at the smallest (closest to first) place in which that alternative appears in any of those consensus rankings. Accordingly, as with Copeland voting, Kemeny voting can result in methodological ties. However, also as with Copeland voting, if a Condorcet winning alternative exists, then Kemeny voting will rank that alternative uniquely in first place.

2.3.8. Other voting methods

As stated above, many other voting systems have been devised. These range from straightforward modifications of the methods described above – e.g., for Kemeny voting,

$$\sum_{k=1}^{v} [d(p^k, q)]^2 \le \sum_{k=1}^{v} [d(p^k, q')]^2$$

for every possible ranking q' – to qualitatively different systems.

As an example of a qualitatively different type of system, consider the following structure. Each voter is asked to rate each alternative on a scale from 0 to 100 (i.e., on a scale from 0 to 1 to two decimal places), and each alternative receives a number of points equal to its rating by each voter. The alternatives are then ranked in order by the total number of points they receive from all of the voters.

Interested readers should consult the rather extensive voting theory literature for descriptions of other voting methods.

2.4. Axioms and Arrow's Impossibility Theorem

In addition to defining voting methods, papers on voting theory literature often construct one or more sets of axioms and discuss: (a) whether or not any voting system can satisfy a given set of axioms, (b) if so, whether or not there is a unique voting system that satisfies that set of axioms, and (c) if not, then given a set of voting systems, which systems satisfy which axioms, and what constitutes counterexamples for those that do not.

Perhaps the best known and most significant such axiomatic structure is that of Arrow's Impossibility Theorem (for which, in part, Kenneth J. Arrow won a Nobel Prize). This theorem can be stated and proved in several different (but essentially equivalent) ways, and precise statements and proofs of it can be found in most texts that address voting theory. A brief statement of the relevant axioms and resulting theorem is as follows.

Axiom 1. A voting method satisfies Axiom 1 if that method accepts as input any finite set of voter's rankings of any finite set of alternatives, and produces a group ranking of these alternatives. (Ties can, but need not, be allowed in either the group or the voter's rankings. Inconsistencies are not allowed in either set of rankings.)

Axiom 2. A voting method satisfies Axiom 2 if, whenever all of the voters rank any given alternative ahead of any other alternative, that method also ranks that given alternative ahead of that other alternative.

Axiom 3. A voting method satisfies Axiom 3 if it does not allow the existence of an individual voter such that, whenever that voter ranks any given alternative ahead of any other alternative, that voting method also ranks that given alternative ahead of that other alternative.

Axiom 4 Let V be a set of voters' rankings of the alternatives, and let x be any one of those alternatives. Construct a revised set of rankings, $\overline{V}^x$, by moving x up in one of the voters' rankings, but making no other changes. Then a voting method satisfies Axiom 4 if, for any alternative y, that voting method necessarily ranks x ahead of y according to $\overline{V}^x$ whenever that method ranks x ahead of y according to V.

Axiom 5. Let V be a set of voters' rankings of the alternatives, and let s be any nonempty subset of those alternatives. Construct a revised set of voters rankings, $\overline{V}^s$, by allowing the voters to change their rankings in any manner whatsoever provided only that, for all x and y in s, those voters that ranked x somewhere ahead of y still do so, those voters that ranked y somewhere ahead of x still do so, and those voters that were indifferent between x and y still are so. Then a voting method satisfies Axiom 5 if that voting method necessarily ranks x ahead of y according to $\overline{V}^s$ whenever x and y are in s and that method ranks x ahead of y

according to V and is indifferent between x and y according to $\overline{V}^s$ when x and y are in s and it is indifferent between x and y according to V.

Arrow's Impossibility Theorem states that no voting method can satisfy all five of these axioms if there are three or more alternatives. In addition to formally stating and proving this theorem, texts on voting theory often discuss alternative forms and interpretations of these axioms and of this result. A very brief such discussion is as follows.

Axiom 1, or something similar, is needed to define the structure being considered. Occasionally this structure is defined in a preamble to the other axioms, not as a separate axiom. However, it can be useful to present this structure as an axiom both for clarity and because there are several voting methods that do not satisfy it.

Axiom 2 is needed to prevent an external (non-voting) dictator from determining the result (no matter what the voters' preferences are), and Axiom 3 is needed to prevent an internal (voting) dictator from determining the result (no matter what the other voters' preferences are). Note that, if a voting method bases its results on such a dictator, then that method satisfies Axioms 1, 4, and 5, and either 2 or 3 depending on whether the dictator is internal (thus violating 3) or external (thus violating 2), respectively.

Axiom 4 is redundant in the sense that it is not needed; no voting method can satisfy Axioms 1, 2, 3, and 5. While not needed, it is useful to state Axiom 4 as a separate axiom for (at least) the following reason. Many voting methods satisfy Axioms 1, 2, 3, while none can satisfy all five. Accordingly, it can be useful and important to have objective criteria that discriminate among the methods that satisfy 1, 2, and 3. Axiom 4 provides one such criterion (i.e., does any such voting method also satisfy Axiom 4?). For example, plurality voting, Borda voting, Copeland voting, and Kemeny voting all satisfy Axiom 4, whereas Hare voting does not.

Axiom 5 may be the culprit – it sounds somewhat reasonable, but it is just too hard to satisfy. Axiom 5 is frequently referred to using the phrase 'independence of irrelevant alternatives'. In many voting situations there will be what might be called minor, nuisance, unimportant, and/or insignificant alternatives (e.g., weak third-party candidates). Clearly, one does not want the results concerning the other (i.e., major, primary, important, or significant) alternatives to depend on how (or whether) these minor, etc. alternatives are considered. But this is not (only) what Axiom 5 forbids. Axiom 5 also forbids the results of the vote concerning any alternatives to ever depend on how any other alternatives are considered, no matter how meaningful, important, or significant those other alternatives are. Viewed in this light, it may not be surprising that no voting method can satisfy Axioms 1, 2, 3, and 5.

2.5. National security applications

Voting theory may well have the property that, where it can (reasonably) be applied, it is *obviously* applicable; no ingenuity is needed to determine whether or not voting theory is applicable in a particular situation. How to apply voting theory (where it is applicable) is, in general, very complex and can require considerable knowledge and ingenuity. Accordingly, the interested reader may want to concentrate on developing an understanding of the details and interpretations of various aspects of voting theory, as opposed to searching for unconventional applications.

Two standard applications of voting theory concern (1) determining how citizens elect representatives in a representative democracy, and (2) if some of those representatives are to make group decisions, determining how those decisions are to be reached. Established democracies have established procedures for making these decisions, and voting theory may be best applied in such democracies by suggesting (perhaps a series of) marginal changes to those procedures, where appropriate. Voting theory might be applied more quickly and more extensively in new (emerging) democracies, which do not have well established procedures. Such applicability could have a significant impact on (and so be quite important to) the people in those new democracies. However, this impact is not necessarily important (other than in a humanitarian sense) for people in other countries because those new democracies may be small countries that have little influence or effect on people outside their borders.

If one views the former Soviet Union and Warsaw Pact countries of central and eastern Europe as being emerging democracies in the 1990s, the last comment above does not apply. Indeed, it can be argued that the success of the democratization of these countries is extremely important to the national security of the United States (and all other countries). It also can be argued that democracy in the United States succeeds in spite of, not because of, the particular voting structures it currently uses. Accordingly, it may be quite important for the United States to help other countries (such as those in central and eastern Europe) to establish strong democracies, but it may not be wise for the United States to try to do so by recommending the adoption of the systems, structures, or methods currently in use in the United States. Instead, helping to enhance the understanding and implementation of appropriate aspects of voting theory in other countries could be quite important to those countries in the near future, and be quite important to the national security of all of the countries thereafter.

3. Annotated bibliography

3.1. Monographs

An inexpensive, entertaining, and very informative monograph on voting is:

Straffin, P.D. (1980). *Topics in the Theory of Voting*, UMAP Expository Monograph Series, Barkhäuser, Boston, Basel and Stuttgart.

The interested reader may want to purchase this monograph directly. A related monograph in the same series is:

Brams, S.J. (1979). *Spatial Models of Election Competition*, UMAP Expository Monograph Series, Barkhäuser, Boston, Basel and Stuttgart.

3.2. Books

3.2.1. Recent books on voting theory

The books listed below are some relatively recent texts that directly concentrate on aspects of voting that are described above (several are available in paperback).

Brams, S.J., and P.C. Fishburn (1982). *Approval Voting*, Barkhäuser, Boston, Basel and Stuttgart.

Fishburn, P.C. (1973). *The Theory of Social Choice*, Princeton University Press, Princeton, NJ.

Kelly, J.S. (1987). *Social Choice Theory, An Introduction*, Springer-Verlag, Berlin.

Mueller, D.C. (1989). *Public Choice II*, Cambridge University Press, Cambridge.

Schwartz, T. (1986). *The Logic of Collective Choice*, Columbia University Press, New York.

Sen, A.K. (1970). *Collective Choice and Social Welfare*, Elsevier, New York.

3.2.2. Books relating voting and game theory

The books listed below discuss aspects of game theory and voting theory, and the relationship between them. All are relatively recent, and all have been published in paperback.

Brams, S.J. (1975). *Game Theory and Politics*, The Free Press, New York.

Brams, S.J. (1978). *The Presidential Election Game*, Yale University Press, New Haven, CT.

Ordeshook, P.C. (1986). *Game Theory and Political Theory, An Introduction*, Cambridge University Press, Cambridge.

3.2.3. Books with chapters on voting theory

Several more generally oriented textbooks contain chapters devoted to voting theory. Two examples are listed below.

Malkevitch, J., and W. Meyer (1974). *Graphs, Models and Finite Mathematics*, Prentice-Hall, Englewood Cliffs, NJ.

Roberts, F. (1976). *Discrete Mathematical Models, with Applications to Social, Biological and Environmental Problems*, Prentice-Hall, Englewood Cliffs, NJ.

3.2.4. Books of historical interest

The books listed below were written a (relatively) long time ago, but are worthwhile to note for their historical contributions.

Arrow, K.J. (1963). *Social Choice and Individual Values, 2nd edition*, Yale University Press, New Haven and London.

Black, D. (1958). *The Theory of Committees and Elections*, Cambridge University Press, Cambridge.

Buchanan, J., and G. Tullock (1962). *The Calculus of Consent, Logical Foundations of Constitutional Democracy*, John Wiley & Sons, Rexdale, CA.

Farquharson, R. (1969). *Theory of Voting*, Yale University Press, New Haven, CT.

Luce, R.D., and H. Raiffa (1957). *Games and Decisions, Introduction and Critical Survey*, John Wiley & Sons, New York.

3.2.5. Books of related interest

The following book is a fascinating text on a closely related subject.

Balinski, M., and H.P. Young (1982). *Fair Representation, Meeting the Ideal of One Man, One Vote*, Yale University Press, New Haven, CT and London.

The following book discusses a potpourri of topics related to voting theory.

Brams, S.J., W.F. Lucas and P.D. Straffin (eds.) (1983). *Political and Related Models*, Springer-Verlag, New York.

The following books discuss relationships between voting theory and multicriterion decision-making.

Arrow, K.J., and H. Reynaud (1986). *Social Choice and Multicriterion Decision-Making*, The MIT Press, Cambridge, MA.

Hwang, C.L., and M.J. Lin (1987). *Group Decision Making under Multiple Criteria*, Springer-Verlag, Berlin.

3.3. Papers

A characteristic of papers on voting theory is that they appear in a wide variety of journals. For example, voting theory papers appear in journals on mathematics, applied mathematics, operations research, management science, econometrics, economics, political science and behavioral science. They also appear in specialized journals (such as *Public Choice*) and in popular journals (such as *Scientific American*). A representative but far from exhaustive bibliography of papers on voting theory is given in Section 3.3.2 below. The interested reader might want to begin examining this literature by starting with the particular papers in Section 3.3.1 in the order that these papers are listed.

3.3.1. Selected papers

Niemi, R.G., and W.H. Riker (1976). The choice of voting systems. *Sci. Amer.* 234(6), 21–27.

Fishburn, P.C. (1977). Condorcet social choice functions. *SIAM J. Appl. Math.* 33, 469–486.

Hertzberg, H. (1987). Let's get representative. *New Republic* 29, June, 15–18.

Fishburn, P.C., and S.J. Brams (1983). Paradoxes of preferential voting. *Math. Magazine* 56(4), 207–214.

Doron, G. (1979). Is the Hare voting scheme representative? *J. Politics* 41, 918–922.

Niemi, R.G. (1984). The problem of strategic behavior under approval voting. *Amer. Political Sci. Rev.* 58, 952–958.

Brams, S.J., and P.C. Fishburn (1985). Comment on the problem of strategic voting under approval voting. *Amer. Political Sci. Rev.* 79, 816–818.

Niemi, R.G. (1985). Reply to Brams and Fishburn. *Amer. Political Sci. Rev.* 79, 818–819.

Young, H.P. (1975). Social choice scoring functions. *SIAM J. Appl. Math.* 28(4), 824–838.

Young, H.P., and A. Levenglick (1978). A consistent extension of Condorcet's election principle. *SIAM J. Appl. Math.* 35(2), 285–300.

Saari, D.G. (1982). Inconsistencies of weighted summation voting systems. *Math. Oper. Res.* 7(4), 479–490.

Fishburn, P.C. (1981). Inverted orders for monotone scoring rules. *Discrete Appl. Math.* 3, 27–36.

Fishburn, P.C. (1974). Paradoxes of voting. *Amer. Political Sci. Rev.* 68, 537–546.

Fishburn, P.C. (1974). On the sum-of-ranks winner when losers are removed. *Discrete Math.* 8, 25–30.

Fishburn, P.C. (1971). A comparative analysis of group decision methods. *Behav. Sci.* 16, 538–544.

3.3.2. Representative bibliography

Ali, I., W.D. Cook and M. Kress (1986). Ordinal ranking and intensity of preference: A linear programming approach. *Management Sci.* 32(12), 1642–1647.

Armstrong, R.D., W.D. Cook and L.M. Seiford (1982). Priority ranking and consensus formation: The case of ties. *Management Sci.* 28(6), 638–645.

Barton, D.M. (1973). Constitutional choice and simple majority rule: Comment. *J. Political Econom.* 81(2), 471–479.

Barzilai, J., W.D. Cook and M. Kress (1986). A generalized network formulation of the pairwise comparison consensus ranking model. *Management Sci.* 32(8), 1007–1014.

Benneche, J., and B. Wing (1984). A study of approval voting, Student Paper for OR 291, December, George Washington University, Washington, DC.

Birnberg, J.G., L.R. Pondy and C.L. Davis (1970). Effect of three voting rules on resource allocation decisions. *Management Sci.* 16(6), B356–B372.

Blair, D.H., and R.A. Pollak (1983). Rational collective choice. *Sci. Amer.* 249(2), 88–95.

Blin, J.M., and A.B. Whinston (1975). Discriminant functions and majority voting. *Management Sci.* 21(5), 557–566.

Bowman, V.J., and C.S. Colantoni (1973). Majority rule under transitivity constraints. *Management Sci.* 19(9), 1029–1041.

Bowman, V.J., and C.S. Colantoni (1974). Transitive majority rule and the theorem of the alternative. *Oper. Res.* 22, 488–496.

Brams, S.J. (1980). Approval voting in multicandidate elections. *Policy Studies J.* 9(1), 102–108.

Brams, S.J. (1982). Strategic information and voting behavior. *Society* 19, 4–11.

Brams, S.J., and P.C. Fishburn (1978). Approval voting. *Amer. Political Sci. Rev.* 72, 831–847.

Brams, S.J., and P.C. Fishburn (1979). Reply to Tullock. *Amer. Political Sci. Rev.* 73, 552.

Brams, S.J., and P.C. Fishburn (1985). Comment on the problem of strategic voting under approval voting. *Amer. Political Sci. Rev.* 79, 816–818.

Campbell, D.E. (1981). Some strategic properties of plurality and majority voting. *Theory Decision* 13, 93–107.

Caplin, A., and B. Nalebuff (1985). On 64% majority rule, Dept. of Economics, Harvard University, Cambridge, MA (Caplin) and Dept. of Economics, Princeton University, Princeton, NJ (Nalebuff), September.

Cave, J.A.K. (1987). A median choice theorem, Rand P-7333, April, The Rand Corporation, Santa Monica, CA.

Cook, W.D., and M. Kress (1985). Ordinal ranking with intensity of preference. *Management Sci.* 31, 26–32.

Cook, W.D., and L.M. Seiford (1978). Priority ranking and consensus formation. *Management Sci.* 24(16), 1721–1732.

Cook, W.D., and L.M. Seiford (1982). On the Borda-Kendall consensus method for priority ranking problems. *Management Sci.* 28(6), 621–637.

Davis, O.A., M.J. Hinich and P.C. Ordeshook (1970). An expository development of a mathematical model of the electoral process. *Amer. Political Sci. Rev.* 64, 426–448.

Denzau, A., W. Riker and K. Shepsle (1985). Farquharson and Fenno: Sophisticated voting and home style. *Amer. Political Sci. Rev.* 79, 1117–1134.

Doron, G. (1979). Is the Hare voting scheme representative?. *J. Politics* 41, 918–922.

Dyer, J.S., and R.F. Miles (1976). An actual application of collective choice theory to the selection of trajectories for the Mariner Jupiter/Saturn 1977 Project. *Oper. Res.* 24(2), 220–244.

Fishburn, P.C. (1970). Arrow's impossibility theorem: Concise proof and infinite voters. *J. Econom. Theory* 2, 103–106.

Fishburn, P.C. (1970). The irrationality of transitivity in social choice. *Behav. Sci.* 15, 119–123.

Fishburn, P.C. (1970). Intransitive indifference with unequal indifference intervals. *J. Math. Psychology* 7, 144–149.

Fishburn, P.C. (1970). Comments on Hansson's group preferences. *Econometrica* 38(6), 933–935.

Fishburn, P.C. (1971). A comparative analysis of group decision methods. *Behav. Sci.* 16, 538–544.

Fishburn, P.C. (1972). Conditions on preferences that guarantee a simple majority winner. *J. Math. Sociology* 2, 105–112.

Fishburn, P.C. (1974). On the sum-of-ranks winner when losers are removed. *Discrete Math.* 8, 25–30.

Fishburn, P.C. (1974). Social choice functions. *SIAM Rev.* 16, 63–90.

Fishburn, P.C. (1974). Subset choice and the computation of social choice sets. *Quart. J. Econom.* 88, 320–329.

Fishburn, P.C. (1974). Aspects of one-stage voting rules. *Management Sci.* 21(4), 422–427.

Fishburn, P.C. (1974). Paradoxes of voting. *Amer. Political Sci. Rev.* 68, 537–546.

Fishburn, P.C. (1977). Condorcet social choice functions. *SIAM J. Appl. Math.* 33, 469–486.

Fishburn, P.C. (1977). Multicriteria choice functions based on binary relations. *Oper. Res.* 25(6), 989–1012.

Fishburn, P.C. (1978). Axioms for approval voting: Direct proof. *J. Econom. Theory* 19, 180–185.

Fishburn, P.C. (1978). A strategic analysis of nonranked voting systems. *SIAM J. Appl. Math.* 35(3), 488–495.

Fishburn, P.C. (1981). Inverted orders for monotone scoring rules. *Discrete Appl. Math.* 3, 27–36.

Fishburn, P.C. (1984). Discrete mathematics in voting and group choice. *SIAM J. Alg. Disc. Meth.* 5(2), 263–275.

Fishburn, P.C. (1989). Foundations of decision analysis: Along the way. *Management Sci.* 35(4), 387–405.

Fishburn, P.C., and S.J. Brams (1981). Approval voting, Condorcet's principle, and runoff elections. *Public Choice* 36, 89–114.

Fishburn, P.C., and S.J. Brams (1983). Paradoxes of preferential voting. *Math. Magazine* 56(4), 207–214.

Fishburn, P.C., and W.V. Gehrlein (1976). An analysis of simple two-stage voting systems. *Behav. Sci.* 21, 1–12.

Fishburn, P.C., and W.V. Gehrlein (1976). Borda's rule, positional voting, and Condorcet's simple majority principle. *Public Choice* 28, 79–88.

Fishburn, P.C., and W.V. Gehrlein (1977). Towards a theory of elections with probabilistic preferences. *Econometrica* 45(8), 1907–1924.

Fishburn, P.C., and J.D.C. Little (1988). An experiment in approval voting. *Management Sci.* 34(5), 555–568.

Flood, M.M. (1980). Implicit intransitivity under majority rule with mixed motions. *Management Sci.* 3, 312–321.

Gardner, M. (1974). Mathematical games. *Sci. Amer.* 231(4), 120–125.

Gardner, M. (1980). Mathematical games. *Sci. Amer.* 243(4), 16–26B.

Gehrlein, W.V., and P.C. Fishburn (1976). Condorcet's paradox and anonymous preference profiles. *Public Choice* 26, 1–18.

Gehrlein, W.V., and P.C. Fishburn (1976). The probability of the paradox of voting: A computable solution. *J. Econom. Theory* 13, 14–25.

Gehrlein, W.V., and P.C. Fishburn (1978). The effects of abstentions on election outcomes. *Public Choice* 33(2), 69–82.

Gibbard, A. (1973). Manipulation of voting schemes: A general result. *Econometrica* 41(4), 587–601.

Gladwell, M. (1990). When voix are in, have the people spoken? *Washington Post,* June 4, A3.

Glasser, G.J. (1958). Game theory and cumulative voting for corporate directors. *Management Sci.* 5, 151–156.

Greenberg, J., and S. Weber (1985). Multiparty equilibria under proportional representation. *Amer. Political Sci. Rev.* 79, 693-703.

Hansson, B. (1969). Group preferences. *Econometrica* 37(1), 50–54.

Hertzberg, H. (1987). Let's get representative. *New Republic,* June 29, 15–18.

Hinich, M.J., J.O. Ledyard and P.C. Ordeshook (1972). Nonvoting and the existence of equilibrium under majority rule. *J. Econom. Theory* 4, 144–153.

Hinich, M.J., and P.C. Ordeshook (1969). Abstentions and equilibrium in the electoral process. *Public Choice* 7, 81–106.

Hoffman, D.T. (1982). A model for strategic voting. *SIAM J. Appl. Math.* 42(4), 751–761.

Hoffman, D.T. (1983). Relative efficiency of voting systems. *SIAM J. Appl. Math.* 43(5), 1213–1219.

Hwang, C.L., and M.J. Lin (1987). *Group Decision Making under Multiple Criteria,* Springer-Verlag, Berlin.

Kellett, J., and K. Mott (1977). Presidential primaries: Measuring popular choice. *Polity* 9, 528–537.

Kemeny, J.G. (1959). Mathematics without numbers. *Daedalus* 88, 577–591.

Kiewiet, D.R. (1979). Approval voting: The case of the 1968 election. *Polity* 12, 170–181.

Levenglick, A. (1975). Fair and reasonable election systems. *Behav. Sci.* 20, 34–46.

Little, J.D.C. (1985). An experiment in approval voting. *OR/MS Today* 12(1), 18–19.

Mas-Colell, A., and H. Sonnenschein (1972). General possibility theorems for group decisions. *Rev. Econom. Studies* XXXIX (2), 118, 185–192.

May, R.M. (1971). Some mathematical remarks on the paradox of voting. *Behav. Sci.* 16, 143–151.

McKelvey, R.D. (1981). A theory of optimal agenda design. *Management Sci.* 27(3), 303–321.

McKelvey, R.D. (1983). Constructing majority paths between arbitrary points: General methods of solution for quasi-concave preferences. *Math. Oper. Res.* 8(4), 549–556.

McKelvey, R.D., P.C. Ordeshook and P. Ungar (1980). Conditions for voting equilibria in continuous voter distributions. *SIAM J. Appl. Math.* 39(1), 161–168.

McKelvey, R.D., and R.E. Wendell (1976). Voting equilibria in multidimensional choice spaces. *Math. Oper. Res.* 1(2), 144–158.

Merchant, D.K., and M.R. Rao (1976). Majority decisions and transitivity: Some special cases. *Management Sci.* 23(2), 125–130.

Merrill, S. (1979). Approval voting: A 'best buy' method for multi-candidate elections? *Math. Magazine* 52, 98–102.

Merrill, S. (1981). Strategic decisions under one-stage multi-candidate voting systems. *Public Choice* 36, 115–134.

Niemi, R.G. (1984). The problem of strategic behavior under approval voting. *Amer. Political Sci. Rev.* 58, 952–958.

Niemi, R.G. (1985). Reply to Brams and Fishburn. *Amer. Political Sci. Rev.* 79, 818–819.

Niemi, R.G., and W.H. Riker (1976). The choice of voting systems. *Sci. Amer.* 234(6), 21–27.

Nitzan, S. (1981). Some measures of closeness to unanimity and their implications. *Theory Decision* 13, 129–138.

Nurmi, H. (1983). Voting procedures: A summary analysis. *Br. J. Political Sci.* 13, 181–208.

Ray, D. (1984). More voting paradoxes. *Math. Magazine* 57(1), 57.

Saari, D.G. (1982). Inconsistencies of weighted summation voting systems. *Math. Oper. Res.* 7(4), 479–490.

Satterthwait, M.A. (1975). Strategy-proofness and Arrow's conditions: Existence and correspondence theorems for voting procedures and social welfare functions. *J. Econom. Theory* 10, 187–217.

Schwartz, T. (1972). Rationality and the myth of the maximum. *Nous* 6, 97–117.

Sen, A. (1977). Social choice theory: A re-examination. *Econometrica* 45(1), 53–89.

Shenoy, P.P. (1980). On committee decision making: A game theoretical approach. *Management Sci.* 26(4), 387–400.

Smith, J.H. (1973). Aggregation of preferences with variable electorate. *Econometrica* 41, 1027–1041.

Staring, M. (1986). Two paradoxes of committee elections. *Math. Magazine* 59(3), 158–159.

Stearns, R. (1959). The voting problem. *Amer. Math. Monthly* 66, 761–763.

Tullock, G. (1973). Constitutional choice and simple majority rule: Reply. *J. Political Econom.* 81(2), 480–484.

Tullock, G. (1979). Comment on Brams and Fishburn. *Amer. Political Sci. Rev.* 73, 551–552.

Young, H.P. (1974). A note on preference aggregation. *Econometrica* 42(6), 1129–1131.

Young, H.P. (1974). An axiomatization of Borda's rule. *J. Econom. Theory* 9, 43–52.

Young, H.P. (1975). Social choice scoring functions. *SIAM J. Appl. Math.* 28(4), 824–838.

Young, H.P., and A. Levenglick (1978). A consistent extension of Condorcet's election principle. *SIAM J. Appl. Math.* 35(2), 285–300.

S.M. Pollock et al., Eds., *Handbooks in OR & MS, Vol. 6*

Chapter 17

Paired Comparisons

Lowell Bruce Anderson

Institute for Defense Analyses, 1801 N. Beauregard Street, Alexandria, VA 22311-1772, U.S.A.

1. Introduction

Consistent with the goal of Section 2 of Chapter 16, the goal of this chapter is to provide a general description of the major aspects of paired comparison theory. Precise descriptions of these aspects are not always given, and not all aspects of paired comparison theory are discussed.

Paired comparison theory concerns the following situation. A set of objects is to be ranked from first (best) to last (worst), with (in general) ties being allowed in this ranking. This ranking is to be based on a set of comparisons of pairs of these objects where, in the simplest case, the outcome of each such comparison is that one of the two objects involved is strictly preferred over the other, with the degree of preference being irrelevant or immeasurable. Extensions that allow the comparisons to result in a tie (equal preference) are regularly considered, and will be discussed below. Extensions that consider a measure of the degree by which one object is preferred over the other are infrequently addressed, and will not be considered here. In general, not all pairs of objects are compared (i.e., each object is not necessarily compared with each other object), and some pairs of objects might be compared more than once. Further, when two objects are compared more than once, one of those objects does not necessarily win all of those comparisons.

The objects involved can be abstract objects (e.g., stability, deterrence, or social values), medical treatments, sensual stimuli, people, or teams (e.g., the training, readiness, or quality of these people or teams). The method of comparison can be based on qualitative judgments, on quantitative measurements or scores, or on a combination of both. A natural setting for a discussion of paired comparisons involves ranking a set of teams that compete against each other in some sport, and the discussion below will use this terminology. The reader should be aware that many other applications exist. Indeed, paired comparison theory was originally developed and has been primarily applied by people interested in such other applications, and it has largely been ignored by sports enthusiasts. Sports terminology, however, is quite useful for explaining the concepts involved.

Suppose that there are n teams, labeled $T_1, T_2, \ldots T_n$, that play a set of games against each other, where each game involves two teams and results in one of those teams winning and the other losing that game, or (optionally) in a draw (i.e., a tied game). For $i \neq j$, let m_{ij} denote the number of games that T_i plays against T_j (so that $m_{ij} = m_{ji}$). Let r_{ij} denote the number of these m_{ij} games that T_i wins plus, if ties can occur, one half of the number of these m_{ij} games that result in a tie. Thus for $i \neq j$,

$$r_{ij} + r_{ji} = m_{ij} = m_{ji}.$$

For simplicity, set $r_{ii} = m_{ii} = 0$ for all i. The goal of paired comparison theory is to develop an appropriate ranking of the teams based on the schedule (m_{ij}) and the results (r_{ij}).

The discussion below gives general descriptions of various approaches that have been considered in the paired comparison literature – these discussions do not necessarily contain precise definitions or descriptions of the techniques involved, and full historical credit is not carefully delineated. The rather extensive paired comparison literature should be consulted for such details. A very recent and relatively complete treatise on the theory of paired comparisons is given by David [1988]. In particular, David describes in some detail most of the approaches discussed below, and he references almost 300 publications concerning paired comparisons. (While these references constitute an extensive bibliography on the subject, a few recent and quite relevant papers are not referenced there – these omissions are listed in Section 6.2, below.)

Two basically different types of approaches to determine rankings have been discussed in the paired comparison literature. One type consists of deterministic combinatorial approaches; the other type consists of approaches that pose some type of probability model of the competition and then determine rankings based on the schedule, results, and model so posed. The deterministic combinatorial methods are described first, followed by a description of the methods based on probability models.

2. Deterministic combinatorial methods

2.1. Winning percentage

Perhaps the simplest and most straightforward method to rank teams is according to their winning percentage. Let

$$g_i = \sum_{j=1}^{n} m_{ij} \quad \text{and} \quad w_i = \sum_{j=1}^{n} r_{ij},$$

so that g_i is the total number of games played by T_i, and w_i is the number of those games won by T_i (counting a tie as a half win and a half loss). Assume that $g_i > 0$ for all i. Then the winning percentage of T_i, say p_i, is given by

$$p_i = w_i / g_i.$$

Ranking by winning percentage places T_i ahead of T_j if and only if $p_i > p_j$. If $p_i = p_j$ then T_i and T_j are tied in these rankings.

In symmetric round robin competitions (i.e., for all distinct i and j, $m_{ij} = \overline{m}$ for some positive integer $\overline{m}$), this is a quite reasonable and quite commonly used method. Three points should be noted here. First, in some applications, there may be more desirable methods for addressing ties. For example, tied games could simply be ignored (as if they never occurred), which would reduce g_i by the number of tied games involving T_i, and would reduce w_i by one half of this number of tied games. Second, as reasonable and as popular as this approach is for determining rankings in symmetric round robin competitions, other methods have been seriously proposed, and these other methods can produce different rankings than ranking by winning percentage, even if (in the competition being considered) no ties can occur. Two such methods are discussed below. Third, and perhaps most importantly, the reasonableness of ranking by winning percentage is strongly based on the round robin property that each team plays each other team an equal number of times. When some teams do not play some other teams ($m_{ij} = 0$ for some i and j), and/or they play different numbers of games against various other teams, then the 'strength-of-the-schedule' becomes an important factor to consider in determining rankings. Indeed, one reason for studying paired comparison theory is to find methods that are appropriate for general schedules (i.e., no restrictions are placed on m_{ij} other than that m_{ij} is a nonnegative integer, $m_{ij} = m_{ji}$ for all distinct i and j, and $m_{ii} = 0$ for all i), yet these methods reduce to ranking by winning percentage in the special case of symmetric round robin competitions.

Many of the papers on paired comparisons mention ranking by winning percentages in some manner. Some do so to demonstrate that their methods differ from this ranking; others do so to show that their methods reduce to this ranking for symmetric round robins. Rubenstein [1980] addresses ranking by winning percentage directly in that he posits three very general and quite plausible axioms, and he proves that ranking by winning percentage is the only ranking method that always satisfies these axioms for competitions in which tied games are not possible and $m_{ij} = 1$ for all distinct i and j. See also David [1971].

2.2. The Kendall–Wei method

This section gives a brief description of what is frequently called the Kendall–Wei method for determining rankings based on paired comparisons. Specific details can be found in the references cited below.

As background for the Kendall–Wei method, note that in symmetric round robins g_i is a constant, independent of i, and so ranking by winning percentage is equivalent to ranking by w_i. For simplicity, assume that tied games are not possible (i.e., all games result in a win for one team and loss for the other), and give each team one 'victory point' for each game it wins. Then ranking by winning percentage is equivalent to ranking by wins or by victory points as just defined.

The Kendall–Wei method argues that ranking solely by the number of games won is inappropriate because winning against stronger teams should count more than winning against weaker teams. Further, one measure of the strength of an opposing team is the number of games that the opposing team has won. To implement this measure, suppose that $m_{ij} = 1$ for all distinct i and j (i.e., each team plays each other team exactly once and, since ties are not allowed, $r_{ij} = 1$ if T_i beats T_j and $r_{ij} = 0$ otherwise). Then, instead of giving a team one victory point for each win, this measure of strength could be reflected in the rankings by giving each team one victory point for each win by each opponent that the team in question has beaten.

For example, if T_1 beats T_2 and T_3 but no other teams, and if T_2 wins 4 games and T_3 wins 2 games, then T_1 would be given 6 victory points, not 2. Note that this implementation would treat the second-level teams (e.g., the teams beaten by T_2 and T_3) as counting equally. Instead, a third level could be considered in which, in this example, T_i is given one victory point for each team beaten by each of the 4 teams beaten by T_2 plus one victory point for each team beaten by each of the 2 teams beaten by T_3. Normalizing the resulting vector of victory points allows this process to continue indefinity. Given certain restrictions on the matrix $r = [r_{ij}]$, it has been shown that, in the limit as this process goes to infinity, the normalized vector of victory points approaches the vector v that satisfies the matrix equation

$$rv = \lambda v,$$

where λ is the largest positive eigenvalue of r. (The restrictions on r are easily addressed, and the vector v is unique up to the normalization technique being used; the paired comparison literature should be consulted for details.) Teams are than ranked according to v, where T_i is ranked ahead of T_j if and only if $v_i > v_j$. (Note that this ranking is independent of the normalization technique used.)

The rationale above assumes that $m_{ij} = 1$ for all i and j, $i \neq j$. However, the equation

$$rv = \lambda v$$

can be solved for v without this restriction and without the restriction that tied games are prohibited (the aforementioned easily addressed restrictions on r still apply). Again, see the literature on the Kendall–Wei method for details. The important points to note here are as follows. The Kendall–Wei method can be extended in a consistent manner to allow ties. That is, the rationale for using the Kendall–Wei method (and the relevant numerical techniques) can easily be adapted to allow ties – this is discussed in the relevant literature. However, while the Kendall–Wei method can also be numerically extended to consider schedules other than symmetric round robin tournaments (i.e., to consider cases in which teams play different numbers of games, including possibly no games, against various other teams), there seems to be no particularly good rationale or logical basis for doing so.

Two important characteristics of the Kendall–Wei method are as follows.

First, the Kendall–Wei method can produce a different ranking than that produced by winning percentages, even in the simple case in which there are no ties and $m_{ij} = 1$ for all i and j, $i \neq j$. For example, if $n = 5$ and

$$
r_{ij} = \begin{cases}
1 & i < j \text{ and } (i, j) \neq (1, 5) \\
1 & (i, j) = (5, 1) \\
0 & \text{otherwise,}
\end{cases}
$$

then T_3 has 2 wins (over T_4 and T_5) and 3 losses, while T_5 has 1 win (over T_1) and 4 losses, yet the Kendall–Wei method ranks T_5 over T_3.

Second, it is not at all clear that wins against stronger teams should count more heavily than wins against weaker teams when losses to weaker teams are not also counted more heavily than losses to stronger teams. For example, in a symmetric round robin tournament with no ties, if T_i and T_j have the same win–loss record and if T_i has k more wins than T_j over some set of strong teams, then (calling the other teams weak) T_j must necessarily have k fewer losses than T_i against weak teams. In such a case, the Kendall–Wei method would rank T_i over T_j; yet it is plausible here that these two teams should be ranked equally. In a similar vein, it has been shown that, in the Kendall–Wei method, changing all wins to losses and all losses to wins does not necessarily reverse a ranking.

Variations of the Kendall–Wei method have been proposed that more heavily consider both wins over strong teams and losses to weak teams and, not surprisingly, these methods can reduce to simply ranking by winning percentages for symmetric round robin tournaments. See the literature for details.

In addition to David [1988], various properties, limitations, and extensions of the Kendall–Wei method are discussed in David [1971], Goddard [1983], Kendall [1955], Moon [1968], Ramanujacharyulu [1964], and Stob [1985].

2.3. The minimum violations method

The minimum violations method for paired comparisons is a logical analog of the Kemeny method for voting. Specifically, consider a symmetric round robin tournament with n teams in which $m_{ij} = 1$ for all distinct i and j and ties are not allowed. Accordingly, $r_{ij} = 1$ if T_i beat T_j in the game they played, and $r_{ij} = 0$ otherwise. Let S denote the set of all permutations of $(T_1, \ldots, T_n)$, so that S consists of all possible rankings (i.e., standings) of the teams in question. For any given ranking $s \in S$, let $\bar{r}^s = [\bar{r}^s_{ij}]$ be the 'perfect prediction' results based on s in that $\bar{r}^s_{ij} = 1$ if T_i is ranked ahead of T_j according to s, and $\bar{r}^s_{ij} = 0$ otherwise. Let

$$
d(s, r) = \sum_{\substack{i,j \\ i \neq j}} \bar{r}^s_{ij}(1 - r_{ij}),
$$

so that $d(s, r)$ is the number of pairs (i.e., distinct but unordered i and j) in which the ranking s rates T_i over T_j when, in their game, T_j beat T_i. In other words, given a ranking s and actual game results r, $d(s, r)$ is the number of upsets (according to s) that occurred in those games.

As an example, consider the example given in Section 2.2 above, namely $n = 5$

and

$$r_{ij} = \begin{cases} 1 & i < j \text{ and } (i, j) \neq (1, 5) \\ 1 & (i, j) = (5, 1) \\ 0 & \text{otherwise.} \end{cases}$$

Let

$$s^1 = (T_1, T_2, T_3, T_4, T_5),$$
$$s^2 = (T_1, T_2, T_3, T_5, T_4), \text{ and}$$
$$s^3 = (T_1, T_2, T_5, T_3, T_4).$$

Then

$$d(s^1, r) = 1,$$
$$d(s^2, r) = 2, \text{ and}$$
$$d(s^3, r) = 3.$$

Given r, a ranking is a minimum violations ranking if it minimizes $d(s, r)$ over all $s \in S$.

The minimum violations method has the following characteristics. First, it is relatively difficult to compute. Powerful algorithms (which have recently been developed) and modern (very fast) computers can mitigate problems caused by this characteristic, but it is still worth noting.

Second, like the Kendall–Wei method, the minimum violations method can be extended in a consistent manner to allow tied games. It can also be numerically extended to consider more general schedules than symmetric round robin tournaments; however, as with Kendall–Wei, there seems to be no particularly good rationale or logical basis for doing so.

Third, again like Kendall–Wei, the minimum violations method can produce a different ranking than that produced by winning percentages, even in the simple case in which there are not ties and $m_{ij} = 1$ for all i and j, $i \neq j$. An example is as follows. Let $n = 7$,

$$r_{ij} = \begin{cases} 1 & i < j \text{ and } (i, j) \notin \{(1, 2), (2, 5), (2, 6), (3, 7)\} \\ 1 & (i, j) \in \{(2, 1), (5, 2), (6, 2), (7, 3)\} \\ 0 & \text{otherwise,} \end{cases}$$

$$s^1 = (T_1, T_2, T_3, T_4, T_5, T_6, T_7),$$

and

$$s^2 = (T_2, T_1, T_3, T_4, T_5, T_6, T_7).$$

Then $d(s^1, r) = 4$ and $d(s^2, r) = 3$. Thus s^2, which ranks T_2 ahead of T_1, has fewer violations than s^1, which ranks T_1 ahead of T_2. However, T_1 has 5 wins and 1 loss in this example while T_2 has 4 wins and 2 losses.

Fourth, the minimum violations method as described here (and as described in the majority of the references) treats every violation in exactly the same way when evaluating a ranking, no matter how close together or how far apart the teams involved are in that ranking. However, it has been argued that teams that are, in fact, close in quality to each other are likely to win some games and lose others to each other, and so violations involving such teams should not be treated in the same manner as violations involving teams that are far apart in quality. According to this argument, a ranking that has six violations, all of which involve teams that are close to their opponents in that ranking, could well be a more reasonable ranking than one that has four violations all involving teams that are ranked far apart from each other.

For further discussions of the minimum violations method, see Ali, Cook & Kress [1986], David [1971], Goddard [1983], Harary & Moser [1966], Slater [1961], Stob [1985], and Thompson [1975].

3. Probabilistic methods

The probabilistic approaches discussed here all (in some sense) involve calculating probabilities, say p_{ij}, that T_1 will win a game played against T_j for all relevant i and j. These probabilities can be interpreted as estimates, based on game results, of true but unknown probabilities. They can also be interpreted as summary output measures that can be used for ranking teams based on (in general, intransitive) game results. These probabilities are determined by making a set of assumptions (different assumptions are made for different methods) and then calculating values for these probabilities that are consistent with these assumptions and with the game results in question. Two points should be noted here. First, the various assumptions made for these probabilistic methods seem to fit within an overall, integrated structure. This structure is presented below. Second, different assumptions do not necessarily lead to different results in that one set of assumptions can be equivalent to another set. Such equivalencies occur here and will also be discussed below. First, some relevant notion is introduced.

3.1. Notation

As above, suppose that there are n teams under consideration ($n \geq 2$), and that these teams are labeled $T_1, \ldots, T_n$. For $i = 1, \ldots, n$, $j = 1, \ldots, n$, and $i \neq j$, let m_{ij} denote the number of games that T_i plays against T_j, and let r_{ij} denote the number of these games that T_i wins plus one-half of the number of these games that result in a tie. For $i = 1, \ldots, n$, let $m_{ii} = r_{ii} = 0$. Note that $m_{ij} = m_{ji}$ and that $r_{ij} + r_{ji} = m_{ij}$ for all $i = 1, \ldots, n$ and all $j = 1, \ldots, n$. Call the matrix $m = [m_{ij}]$ the schedule matrix and the matrix $r = [r_{ij}]$ the results matrix. For $i = 1, \ldots, n$, let

$$g_i = \sum_{j=1}^{n} m_{ij}, \quad \text{and} \quad w_i = \sum_{j=i}^{n} r_{ij}.$$

Some new notation is as follows. Let P denote the set of all n by n matrices $p = [p_{ij}]$ such that, for all i and j from 1 through n,

$$0 \leq p_{ij} \leq 1 \quad \text{and} \quad p_{ij} + p_{ji} = 1.$$

Given $p \in P$, let

$$x_{ij} = x_{ij}(p_{ij}) = \begin{cases} p_{ji}/(1 - p_{ij}) = p_{ij}/p_{ji} & p_{ij} < 1 \\ \infty & p_{ij} = 1. \end{cases}$$

Also for $p \in P$, let

$$L(p) = \begin{cases} \displaystyle\prod_{i=1}^{n-1} \prod_{j=i+1}^{n} \binom{m_{ij}}{r_{ij}} p_{ij}^{r_{ij}} p_{ji}^{r_{ji}} & \text{if no game between any two teams ends in a tie} \\[3ex] \displaystyle\prod_{i=1}^{n-1} \prod_{j=i+1}^{n} \binom{2m_{ij}}{2r_{ij}} p_{ij}^{2r_{ij}} p_{ji}^{2r_{ji}} & \text{otherwise.} \end{cases}$$

and, for $p \in P$ and $\rho \geq 1$, let

$$O_\rho(p) = \sum_{i=1}^{n-1} \sum_{j=i+1}^{n} |r_{ij} - m_{ij} p_{ij}|^\rho .$$

Let R_1 denote the set of all n by n matrices such that, given any two different i and j in $\{1, \ldots, n\}$, there exists some $k \geq 2$ such that $r_{i_1 i_2}, r_{i_2 i_3}, \ldots, r_{i_{k-1} i_k}$ are strictly positive and either $i_1 = i$ and $i_k = j$ or $i_1 = j$ and $i_k = i$. Let R_2 denote the set of all n by n matrices such that, given any two different i and j in $\{1, \ldots, n\}$, there exists some $k \geq 2$ such that $r_{i_1 i_2}, r_{i_2 i_3}, \ldots, r_{i_{k-1} i_k}$ are strictly positive and $i_1 = i$ and $i_k = j$. That is, if $r \in R_1$, then there must be at least one 'one-way beats-or-ties' path between any two teams; and if $r \in R_2$, then there must be at least one such path in each direction between any two teams. For example, if $r \in R_1$, then the teams cannot be partitioned into two sets such that both no team in the first set beats or ties any team in the second set and no team in the second set beats or ties any team in the first set. Similarly, if $r \in R_2$, then the teams cannot be partitioned into two sets such that no team in the first set beats or ties any team in the second set. Note that $R_2 \subset R_1$.

3.2. An integrative structure for assumptions underlying these probabilistic methods

Ignoring ties, each of the various papers that propose probabilistic methods for ranking alternatives seems to make two basic assumptions (as opposed to making just one such assumption or to making three or more such assumptions). The particular assumptions that are made can differ from paper to paper, but each such paper seems to need to make two of them in order to allow the development of a structure sufficiently rich that values for the relevant probabilities can be calculated. Furthermore, ignoring the treatment of ties, each such paper seems to take one of its assumptions from 'Group A' and one from 'Group B' as listed in Table 1.

Some comments on the structure proposed in Table 1 are as follows.

First, a formal structure like that of Table 1 does not seem to appear in the literature, although the discussions in David [1988] and Stob [1984] come quite close. The interested reader may want to test the hypothesis presented in Table 1 by examining various publications on paired comparisons. Table 2 presents a start in this direction by relating several such publications to the structure given in Table 1. Note that, while all of the publications listed in Table 2 consider assumptions in pairs as indicated in Table 1, several of these publications consider more than one such pair of assumptions. David [1988] and Stob [1984] consider so many of the possible pairs that it would be pointless to list these publications in Table 2. The interested reader here should certainly consider examining these two publications.

Second, note the following distinction between the assumptions in Group A and those in Group B. Each assumption in Group A essentially defines a model in that each requires some particular relationship among the p_{ij}'s to hold. However, none of the assumptions in Group A concern calculating numbers for these p_{ij}'s in that none concern the relationship between these p_{ij}'s and the results matrix r. Conversely, each of the assumptions in Group B determines a relationship that must hold between the probabilities p_{ij} and the outcomes given by the schedule matrix m and the results matrix r. However, none of the assumptions in Group B relate the p_{ij}'s to each other outside of relationships involving m and r, and, in particular, none of the assumptions in Group B place sufficient restrictions on the p_{ij}'s to allow values for these p_{ij}'s to be calculated as functions of m and r. The paired comparison literature shows that values for the p_{ij}'s can be computed as meaningful functions of m and r if (in general) one assumption from each group in Table 1 is made and if $r \in R_1$.

Third, the roles played by R_1 and R_2 here are as follows.

R_1 concerns whether or not teams can be compared by any of these methods. If $r \in R_1$, then all of the teams can be compared with each other. If $r \notin R_1$, then there are at least two teams that cannot be compared by any of these methods. For example, one way (but not the only way) that this ($r \notin R_1$) could occur is as follows. Suppose m and r are such that it is possible to partition the teams into four groups, say G_a, G_{b_1}, G_{b_2}, and G_c, such that each team in G_a (if any) has won all of its games against teams not in G_a, each team in G_c (if any) has lost all of its games against teams not in G_c, and no team in G_{b_1} plays any games against any team in G_{b_2}. Then no method described here can compare any team in G_{b_1} with any team in G_{b_2}. Accordingly, whether or not $r \in R_1$ is important concerning whether or not any of these probabilistic methods can be applied, but it is not relevant for distinguishing among these methods.

If $r \in R_1$ but $r \notin R_2$, then all teams are comparable, but some comparisons are 'too easy' in that there are (at least) two teams, say T_i and T_j, such that the only reasonable value for p_{ij} based solely on m and r is $p_{ij} = 1$. For example, suppose m and r are such that it is possible to partition the teams as described in the last paragraph above, that G_a, G_{b_1}, and G_c are not empty, but G_{b_2} is empty,

Table 1

An hypothesized structure for integrating the assumptions underlying probabilistic methods for ranking alternatives

Select one assumption from Group A and one assumption from Group B. Then, given m and r, find $p \in P$ satisfying the two selected assumptions.

GROUP A (Modeling assumptions)

A1.1: Strong stochastic transitivity

For all i, j, k, if $p_{ij} \geq 1/2$ and $p_{jk} \geq 1/2$, then $p_{ik} \geq \max\{p_{ij}, p_{jk}\}$.

A.1.2: Moderate stochastic transitivity

For all i, j, k, if $p_{ij} \geq 1/2$ and $p_{jk} \geq 1/2$, then $p_{ik} \geq \min\{p_{ij}, p_{jk}\}$.

A1.3: Weak stochastic transitivity

For all i, j, k, if $p_{ij} \geq 1/2$ and $p_{jk} \geq 1/2$, then $p_{ik} \geq 1/2$.

A2: Odds multiply

$x_{ik} = x_{ij} x_{jk}$ for all i, j, k such that neither

$$p_{ij} = 1 \text{ and } p_{jk} = 0$$

nor

$$p_{ij} = 0 \text{ and } p_{jk} = 1;$$

equivalently,

$$p_{ij}\, p_{jk}\, p_{ki} = p_{kj}\, p_{ji}\, p_{ik}$$

for all i, j, and k.

A3: Odds are proportional to deterministic strengths

If $r \in R_2$ then n positive numbers, say

$$s_1, \ldots, s_n,$$

exist such that

$$p_{ij} = s_i / (s_i + s_j),$$

or, equivalently,

$$x_{ij} = s_i / s_j,$$

for all i and j.

A4: Wins are determined by random strengths

Let F_μ denote the (cumulative) distribution function of a continuous random variable with mean μ. Given F_μ, if $r \in R_2$ then n real numbers, say

$$\mu_1, \ldots, \mu_n,$$

and n independent random variables, say

$$s_1, \ldots, s_n,$$

exist such that s_i has distribution F_{μ_i} and

$$p_{ij} = \text{Prob}(s_i > s_j)$$

for all i and j, where:

A4.1: Strengths have extreme value distributions

$$F_\mu(x) = \exp\left[-e^{-[x-(\mu-\gamma)]}\right]$$

where $\gamma = 0.5772\ldots$ is Euler's constant.

A4.2: Strengths are normally distributed with common variance

$$F_\mu(x) = \frac{1}{\sqrt{2\pi}} \int_{-\infty}^{x} e^{-(y-\mu)^2/2} \, dy.$$

A4.3, A4.4, …: Strengths have other distributions

A4.(l): Specify $F_\mu(x)$ for $l = 3, 4, \ldots$

GROUP B (Estimation assumptions)

B1: Expected wins equal actual wins

$$\sum_{j=1}^{n} p_{ij} m_{ij} = w_i, \quad i = 1, \ldots, n.$$

B2: Maximum likelihood

$$L(p) \geq L(q) \quad \text{for all } q \in P.$$

B3 (ρ): Minimum deviation

For a selected value of $\rho \geq 1$ (e.g., $\rho = 2$),

$$O_\rho(p) \leq O_\rho(q) \quad \text{for all } q \in P.$$

Table 2
The relationship between the structure proposed in Table 1 and
some seclected papers on paired comparison theory

Publication	Assumptions as listed in Table 1	
	Group A	Group B
Bradley [1976]	A3	B2
Bradley [1976]	A4.1	B2
Bradley & Terry [1952]	A3	B2
David [1971]	A1.1	B2
David [1971]	A1.3	B2
Dykstra [1960]	A3	B2
Feinberg & Larntz [1976]	A2	B2
Feinberg & Larntz [1976]	A3	B2
Ford [1957]	A3	B2
Jech [1983]	A2	B1
Moon [1968]	A3	B2
Mosteller [1951]	A4.2	B3(2)
Stefani [1977]	A4.2	B3(2)
Stob [1985]	A1.1	B1
Stob [1985]	A3	B2
Thompson [1975]	A4.2	B2
Zermelo [1929]	A3	B2

and $r \in R_1$. Let $G_b = G_{b_1}$. Then, based on m and r, it is reasonable to conclude that each of the teams in G_a is better than any team in G_b or G_c, each team G_b is better than any team in G_c, and that for any probabilistic model

$$p_{ij} = 1, \quad p_{jk} = 1, \quad \text{and} \quad p_{ik} = 1$$

for all $T_i \in G_a$, $T_j \in G_b$, and $T_k \in G_c$. In this case, the interesting questions reduce to determining how the teams in G_a rate against each other, how those in G_b rate against each other, and how those in G_c rate against each other. In specific, if $r \in R_1$ but $r \notin R_2$, then the teams can be partitioned into subsets such that the restrictions of r to these subsets have the property that each restricted r belongs to the correspondingly restricted R_2. Accordingly, whether or not $r \in R_2$ is important concerning whether or not any of these probabilistic methods yield values for p_{ij} satisfying

$$0 < p_{ij} < 1$$

for all i and j, but it is not relevant for distinguishing among these methods.

Fourth, if (and, of course, only if) these games (i.e., comparisons) can end in ties, then the manner in which these ties are treated can be quite important.

As stated above, sports leagues tend to consider ties by treating them as half a win and half a loss (or in some essentially equivalent manner). Note that, in terms of Table 1, treating ties this way corresponds to treating ties under Group B (by adjusting r), not by changing the model postulated in Group A. For simplicity,

Table 1 is structured to treat ties this way, which is why $L(p)$ counts each game twice if ties can occur. If ties count as half a win and half a loss then r_{ij} need not be an integer, but $2r_{ij}$ will always be integral. The interested reader should note that this is not a standard approach in the paired comparison literature, but it does allow all of the combinations pairs of assumptions from Group A and B in Table 1 to be implementable when ties can occur. Another way to make the structure in Table 1 directly implementable when ties are possible is to treat tied games as if they never occurred (instead of treating ties as half a win and half a loss). That is, if t_{ij} of the m_{ij} games between T_i and T_j result in ties, then replace the schedule and results matrices m and r with $\tilde{m}$ and $\tilde{r}$, respectively, where

$$\tilde{m}_{ij} = m_{ij} - t_{ij} \quad \text{and} \quad \tilde{r}_{ij} = r_{ij} - t_{ij}/2,$$

and rate the teams based on $\tilde{m}$ and $\tilde{r}$. Of course, ignoring ties can yield different rankings than treating ties as half a win and half a loss – a somewhat interesting example is given in Section 4, below.

A different general approach for considering ties in probabilistic models is to change the specifications of the model as determined under Group A by introducing a second matrix of probabilities, say $\tilde{p} = \tilde{p}_{ij}$, where $\tilde{p}_{ij}$ is the probability that a game between T_i and T_j ends in a tie. If this is done, then p and $\tilde{p}$ must have the properties that:

$$0 \le p_{ij} \le 1, \quad 0 \le \tilde{p}_{ij} \le 1,$$

$$\tilde{p}_{ij} = \tilde{p}_{ji}, \quad \text{and} \quad p_{ij} + p_{ji} + \tilde{p}_{ij} = 1$$

for all relevant i and j.

For example, A3 could be changed so that

$$p_{ij} = \frac{s_i}{s_i + \theta s_j}$$

for some $\theta \le 1$, which gives that

$$\tilde{p}_{ij} = \frac{(\theta^2 - 1)s_i s_j}{(s_i + \theta s_j)(s_j + \theta s_i)};$$

or it could be changed so that

$$p_{ij} = \frac{s_i}{s_i + s_j + \nu(s_i s_j)^{1/2}}$$

for some $\nu \ge 0$, which gives that

$$\tilde{p}_{ij} = \frac{\nu(s_i s_j)^{1/2}}{s_i + s_j + \nu(s_i s_j)^{1/2}}.$$

Alternatively, A4 could be changed by introducing threshold parameters, e.g.,

$$p_{ij} = \text{Prob}\left\{s_i > s_j + \eta\right\}$$

for some $\eta \geq 0$, which gives that

$$\tilde{p}_{ij} = \text{Prob}\left\{|s_i - s_j| \leq \eta\right\}.$$

Instead of threshold parameters, discontinuous distribution functions could be considered under A4, in which case $\tilde{p}$ could be defined by

$$\tilde{p}_{ij} = \text{Prob}\left\{s_i = s_j\right\}.$$

Introducing $\tilde{p}$ into the model in the specifications under Group A necessitates making the corresponding changes to the restrictions under Group B. In particular, B1 as stated in Table 1 would change to

$$\sum_{j=1}^{n} p_{ij}m_{ij} = \tilde{w}_i \quad \text{and} \quad \sum_{j=1}^{n} \tilde{p}_{ij}m_{ij} = \tilde{t}_i$$

where

$$\tilde{t}_i = \sum_{j=1}^{n} t_{ij} \quad \text{and} \quad \tilde{w}_i = w_i - \tilde{t}_i/2$$

for $i = 1, \ldots, n$. B2 and B3 remain as stated in Table 1; however, the definition of $L(p)$ and $O_\rho(p)$ would change to

$$L(p) = \prod_{i=1}^{n-1} \prod_{j=i+1}^{n} \binom{m_{ij}}{\tilde{r}_{ij}} \binom{m_{ij} - \tilde{r}_{ij}}{t_{ij}} p_{ij}^{\tilde{r}_{ij}} \tilde{p}_{ij}^{t_{ij}} p_{ji}^{\tilde{r}_{ji}}$$

and

$$O_\rho(p) = \sum_{i=1}^{n-1} \sum_{j=i+1}^{n} \left(|\tilde{r}_{ij} - m_{ij}p_{ij}| + |t_{ij} - m_{ij}\tilde{p}_{ij}|\right)^\rho$$

respectively. The interested reader should consult the paired comparison literature for details, references, and further discussions of treating ties by explicitly incorporating the probabilities of ties into probabilistic models.

Finally, and perhaps most importantly, different assumptions can (and here frequently do) lead to the same result. Indeed, much of the paired comparison literature on probabilistic methods concerns showing that, under some set of conditions, making one particular pair of assumptions from Table 1 is completely equivalent to making another pair of such assumptions. Indeed, under fairly robust conditions, making any one of assumptions A2, A3, or A4.1 together with making either one of assumptions B1 or B2 is completely equivalent to making any other pair of assumptions in this subset of assumptions from Table 1. See the paired comparison literature, especially David [1988], and Stob [1984, 1985], for details.

3.3. An archetypical probabilistic method

Since several of the various possible pairs of assumptions from Table 1 turn out to be practically equivalent to each other, only one probabilistic method will be discussed in greater detail here. In terms of Table 1, the assumptions underlying this method are assumptions A2 and B1, and the discussion below is based on Jech [1983]. The notation introduced above will be used here (definitions for this notation will not necessarily be repeated below); assumptions A2 and B1 will be repeated and explained below.

3.3.1. Assumptions and goals

Given values for the schedule matrix m and the results matrix r (with ties counting as half a win and half a loss), one goal here is to find values for a matrix p such that:

(1) $p \in P$,

(2) $\displaystyle\sum_{j=1}^{n} p_{ij}m_{ij} = w_i \quad i = 1, \ldots, n$, and

(3) for all relevant i, j, and k, if neither

$$p_{ij} = 1 \quad \text{and} \quad p_{jk} = 0$$

nor

$$p_{ij} = 0 \quad \text{and} \quad p_{jk} = 1,$$

then

$$x_{ik} = x_{ij}x_{jk}$$

where

$$x_{ij} = p_{ij}/(1 - p_{ij}) = p_{ij}/p_{ji}$$

(if p_{ij} is the probability that T_i would beat T_j in any given game between them, then x_{ij} is the expected number of games between T_i and T_j that T_i would win per each such game that T_j would win). A second goal here is to determine a ranking (say from best to worst) given that values for the p_{ij}'s have been found satisfying the conditions just stated.

3.3.2. Discussion of assumptions

The first condition above, that $p \in P$, is just a way of stating the assumption that a probabilistic method is to be used.

The second condition above is, of course, assumption B1 in Table 1. With p_{ij} being the probability that T_i wins any given game against T_j, the sum

$$\sum_{j=1}^{n} p_{ij}m_{ij}$$

gives the expected number of games that T_i would win against all other teams if it were to play m_{ij} games against T_j for all other j. But it did play m_{ij} such games, it won w_i of them (counting a tie as half win), and the p_{ij}'s are assumedly to be based on these results. Accordingly, if games are not to be discounted by some external criteria (such as weighting games played earlier in a season less than games played more recently), then it seems quite reasonable to require that the p_{ij}'s satisfy the property that, for each team, its expected number of wins based on the schedule matrix m equals its actual number of wins according to that schedule, i.e. that assumption B1 holds.

The third condition above is, of course, assumption A2 in Table 1. As noted above, x_{ij} can be interpreted as the expected number of games between T_i and T_j that T_i would win for each such game that T_j wins. Thus, the assumption that $x_{ik} = x_{ij} x_{jk}$ can be interpreted as assuming that the expected number of wins by T_i per win by T_k in games between them equals the product of the expected number of wins by T_i per win by T_j (in games between T_i and T_j) times the expected number of wins by T_j per win by T_k (in games between T_j and T_k). Jech [1983] gives the following argument to justify the validity of assumption A2.

> Suppose we can compare the objects T_i and T_k only indirectly by comparing T_i with T_j and T_j with T_k and we do it a large number of times, say M. In $M \cdot p_{ij}$ cases, T_i looks better than T_j, and of these $M \cdot p_{ij}$ cases, T_j looks better than T_k exactly $M \cdot p_{ij} \cdot p_{jk}$ times and worse $M \cdot p_{ij} \cdot (1 - p_{jk})$ times. Whenever we find T_i better than T_j and T_j better than T_k we conclude that T_i is better than T_k, but when T_i is found better than T_j and T_j worse than T_k we reserve our judgment about T_i and T_k.
>
> A similar situation arises in the $M \cdot (1 - p_{ij})$ cases when T_j is deemed better than T_i. Thus we have $M \cdot p_{ij} p_{jk}$ cases when T_i is declared better than T_k and $M \cdot (1 - p_{ij}) \cdot (1 - p_{jk})$ cases when T_k is considered better. It follows that
>
> $$x_{ik} = \frac{M \cdot p_{ij} \cdot p_{jk}}{M \cdot (1 - p_{ij}) \cdot (1 - p_{jk})} = x_{ij} \cdot x_{jk}.$$

3.3.3. Two theorems

Jech [1983] proves several theorems based on the assumptions above. His Theorem 1 is stated as Theorem 1 below, and a slightly specialized version of his Theorem 3 is stated as Theorem 2 below.

Theorem 1. *If $r \in R_1$, then there exists one and only one probability matrix p whose entries, p_{ij}, satisfy assumptions B1 and A2.*

Theorem 2. *If $r \in R_1$, if assumptions B1 and A2 are made, and if the schedules for T_i and T_j are such that $m_{ik} = m_{jk}$ for all k other than $k = i$ or $k = j$, then the probability matrix p which is uniquely determined according to Theorem 1 has the properties that:*

$$p_{ij} > 0.5 \text{ (or equivalently, } x_{ij} > 1) \text{ if and only if } w_i > w_j,$$

and

$$p_{ij} = 0.5 \text{ (or, equivalently, } x_{ij} = 1) \text{ if and only if } w_i = w_j.$$

3.3.4. Discussion and implications of these theorems

Throughout this subsection, assume that $r \in R_1$ and let p denote the unique probability matrix that follows from making assumptions B1 and A2 according to Theorem 1 above.

First, note that assumption A2 implies assumption A1.1 and so p determines a unique ranking. To see this, add the teams one-at-a-time to an ordered list in the following manner. Order T_1 and T_2 in the obvious manner (with T_1 and T_2 being tied in this order if $p_{12} = 0.5$). Add T_3 ahead of both T_1 and T_2 if $p_{31} > 0.5$ and $p_{32} > 0.5$, add T_3 behind both T_1 and T_2 if $p_{31} < 0.5$ and $p_{32} < 0.5$, and add T_3 to the list in a tied position with T_i if $p_{3i} = 0.5$ for either $i = 1$ or $i = 2$ (by assumption A2, if both $p_{31} = 0.5$ and $p_{32} = 0.5$ then $p_{12} = 0.5$, so this addition is unambiguous). Finally, if $p_{3i} > 0.5$ but $p_{3j} < 0.5$, where (i, j) is either $(1, 2)$ or $(2, 1)$, then add T_3 above T_i but below T_j (if $p_{3j} < 0.5$ then $p_{j3} > 0.5$ and, by A1.1, if $p_{j3} > 0.5$ and $p_{3i} > 0.5$ then $p_{ji} > 0.5$ and so $p_{ij} < 0.5$; thus this addition is also unambiguous). Adding the remaining teams to this list in the same manner produces a unique ranking in which T_i is ranked ahead of T_j if and only if $p_{ij} > 0.5$ and T_i is ranked as being tied with T_j if and only if $p_{ij} = 0.5$.

Second, it can be shown that an equivalent ranking can be obtained in the following manner. Let

$$\bar{p}_i = \left(\sum_{\substack{j=1 \\ j \neq i}}^{n} p_{ij} \right) \bigg/ (n - 1) \quad i = 1, \dots, n.$$

Then $\bar{p}_i$ is the expected winning percentage of T_i in a symmetric round robin tournament (i.e., a tournament in which each team plays each other team the same number of times). Ranking the teams by these winning percentages yields the same ranking as the ordered list approach described just above.

Third, note that the ordered list approach above produces a unique ranking, but it does not produce (meaningful) cardinal ratings for the teams according to that ranking. The expected-round-robin-wins approach produces the same ranking, and also produces cardinal ratings (namely, those winning percentages) associated with that ranking. If $r \in R_2$, then it can be shown that another way to produce cardinal ratings for the teams according to this ranking is as follows. Let j_o be such that $p_{ij_o} \geq 0.5$ for all $i \neq j_o$ – that is, j_o is (one of) the team(s) ranked last by the ordered list approach above. Suppose that $r \in R_2$. Then $1 \leq x_{ij_o} < \infty$ for all i. Let $s_{j_o} = 1$ and let

$$s_i = x_{ij} s_{j_o} = x_{ij_o} \quad i = 1, \dots, n.$$

Call s_i the strength of T_i, rank T_i ahead of T_j if and only if $s_i > s_j$, and rank T_i as being tied with T_j if $s_i = s_j$. Then ranking by these strengths is identical to ranking by round robin winning percentages and to ranking by the ordered list approach described above. Additionally, it can be shown that these strengths have the property that

$$p_{ij} = \frac{s_i}{s_i + s_j}$$

for all i and j, and so assumption A3 in Table 1 is also satisfied.

In summary, the method proposed by Jech has the following properties. (1) It turns out to be equivalent to several other methods previously proposed in the paired comparison literature [see Stob, 1984], and so a justification for any of these methods is a justification for all of them. (2) It is not restricted to applying only to symmetric round robin comparisons – it can address any schedule matrix m, and it will produce a unique (ordinal) ranking with meaningful cardinal ratings for any m if $r \in R_1$. (3) It allows the result of any comparison to be a tie, not just a win or a loss, and it can address ties in either one of two distinct ways (either by ignoring all tied comparisons or by treating a tie as half a win and half a loss). This can be beneficial because different applications may have different logical bases for treating ties. (4) Finally, by Theorem 2 above, this method necessarily produces the 'standard' ranking according to winning percentages whenever it is applied to a symmetric round robin set of comparisons (i.e., one in which $m_{ij} = \overline{m}$ for some positive constant $\overline{m}$ and all i and j such that $i \neq j$).

4. Examples

The reader not interested in ties should skip directly to Section 4.2, below.

4.1. Some hypothetical examples involving ties

4.1.1. Some alternative approaches for treating ties

Two general approaches for considering tied games were described above; namely, either treat ties as half a win and half a loss, or simply ignore all games that result in ties by treating these games as if they were never played. Each of these general approaches are implementable (in some form) in each of the paired comparison methods discussed above, although some of these methods need slight adjustments to treat ties using these approaches (e.g., counting each game as two separate games for methods that use maximum likelihood functions).

Before presenting examples involving ties, two additional approaches that could be used to consider ties are defined as follows. First, ties could be treated as being almost as good as a win. That is, each tied game could count as $1 - \varepsilon$ of a win and as ε of a loss for both of the teams in that game, where ε is a sufficiently small positive real number such that using any smaller such number would not change the resultant rankings. (Given the assumptions that only a finite number of teams are being considered and that they play only a finite number of games, only extremely perverse ranking techniques would be able to rank the teams counting ties as $1 - \varepsilon$ of a win and ε of a loss yet not admit the existence of an ε' such that the rankings remain constant for all ε such that $0 < \varepsilon < \varepsilon'$. Of course, ε' could depend on the number of teams n, the schedule m, and, perhaps, the ranking method involved.) Symmetrically, ties could be treated as being almost as bad as a loss. That is, each tied game could count as ε of a win and as $1 - \varepsilon$ of a loss for both of the teams in that game, where again ε is some sufficiently small positive real number such that any smaller such number would not change the resultant rankings.

Given ε sufficiently small (in the sense discussed just above), let

$$\hat{w}_i = w_i + (1 - \varepsilon) \sum_{j=1}^{n} t_{ij}, \quad \hat{l}_i = g_i - \hat{w}_i,$$

$$\ddot{w}_i = w_i + \varepsilon \sum_{j=1}^{n} t_{ij}, \quad \text{and} \quad \ddot{l}_i = g_i - \ddot{w}_i$$

for $i = 1, \ldots, n$. Thus, $\hat{w}_i$ and $\hat{l}_i$ are the resulting number of wins and losses, respectively, if ties count almost as much as a win, and $\ddot{w}_i$ and $\ddot{l}_i$ are these wins and losses if ties count almost as much as a loss. Clearly

$$\hat{w}_i + \hat{l}_i = g_i \quad \text{and} \quad \ddot{w}_i + \ddot{l}_i = g_i$$

for each i, and

$$\sum_{i=1}^{n} (\hat{w}_i + \hat{l}_i) = 2\overline{g} \quad \text{and} \quad \sum_{i=1}^{n} (\ddot{w}_i + \ddot{l}_i) = 2\overline{g}$$

where $\overline{g}$ is the total number of games played, i.e.,

$$\overline{g} = \sum_{i=1}^{n-1} \sum_{j=i+1}^{n} m_{ij}.$$

Of course, corresponding forms of these equations also hold if ties are treated as half a win and half a loss, or if all tied games are completely ignored. However, the following inequalities are strict here if any games end in a tie:

$$\sum_{i=1}^{n} \hat{w}_i > \overline{m}, \quad \sum_{i=1}^{n} \hat{l}_i < \overline{m},$$

$$\sum_{i=1}^{n} \ddot{w}_i < \overline{m}, \quad \text{and} \quad \sum_{i=1}^{n} \ddot{l}_i > \overline{m},$$

whereas the corresponding relationships are all strict equalities either if ties are counted as half a win and half a loss, or if all tied games are completely ignored. Due to these inequalities just above, some of the ranking methods described in

Sections 2 and 3 are not directly implementable if ties are counted as almost a win or are counted as almost a loss (although some of these methods – and perhaps all of them – could be implemented if suitably significant adjustments to them were made).

Note, however, that ranking by winning percentage is always implementable. Also, if each team plays the same number of games ($g_i = \bar{g}$ for all i and some $\bar{g}$), then counting ties as almost a win and ranking by winning percentage is the same as simply ranking by fewest (actual) losses, where if two teams have the same number of losses then the team with fewer ties (and hence more wins) is ranked ahead of the other. (Teams are equally ranked if they have same numbers of wins, of ties, and of losses.) Likewise, if each team plays the same number of games, then counting ties as almost a loss and ranking by winning percentage is the same as ranking by most (actual) wins, where if two teams have the same number of wins then the team with more ties (and hence fewer losses) is ranked ahead of the other. (Again, teams are equally ranked if they have the same numbers of wins, of ties, and of losses.)

The reason for introducing alternative approaches for considering ties here is certainly not to suggest changes in the way that sports leagues treat tied games. Counting ties as half a win and half a loss has been found to be quite reasonable for sports. Instead, the reason for introducing these alternatives is as follows. Paired comparison theory has largely been developed and applied outside of the sports realm. Many additional applications of this theory (outside of sports) may exist, and it does not necessarily follow that the way that sports treats ties is appropriate for applications outside of sports. Accordingly, to assist in examining the possible merits of future applications, it is useful to have several alternative approaches for treating ties available for consideration.

For example, counting ties as almost a win might turn out to be appropriate in applications where consensus is valuable. Converting the terminology away from sports, suppose that paired comparisons of several alternatives are being made by several judges according to several criteria. If each alternative is involved in the same number of comparisons, then an alternative that wins or ties more of these comparisons than any other (and hence losses fewer comparisons than any other) might be viewed as being preferred on a consensus basis over the other alternatives, even if some of these other alternatives won some more but lost many more (and so tied much fewer) of these comparisons. Similarly, if the judging is being done to select an alternative to face some adversaries in future competitions, then it may be desirable to select a robust alternative – one that has fewer defects for those adversaries to exploit. Such a 'safe and sure' (or satisfying) goal might lead to counting each tie as almost a win. Finally, if the judging is being done to weed out inferior alternatives, then ties might not be considered to be much worse than wins.

Conversely, ties might be considered as being indicative of possessing a blandness which may be almost as bad as being inferior. That is, it may be that being 'just as good as...' is not good enough – the selected alternative might have to face adversaries where the only hope of succeeding is to be strictly better in some

Table 3
An example yielding four different rankings from four different ways to treat ties in calculating winning percentages

Team	Opponent (wins/losses/ties)						Totals		
	T_1	T_2	T_3	T_4	T_5	T_6	Wins	Losses	Ties
T_1	–	0/0/6	0/0/6	0/0/6	5/0/1	3/3/0	8	3	19
T_2	0/0/6	–	0/0/6	0/0/6	2/0/4	4/2/0	6	2	22
T_3	0/0/6	0/0/6	–	0/0/6	0/0/6	2/1/3	2	1	27
T_4	0/0/6	0/0/6	0/0/6	–	0/0/6	3/3/0	3	3	24
T_5	0/5/1	0/2/4	0/0/6	0/0/6	–	6/0/0	6	7	17
T_6	3/3/0	2/4/0	1/2/3	3/3/0	0/6/0	–	9	18	3

Team	Rankings by winning percentage when considering each tie as			
	Almost a win	1/2 Win + 1/2 loss	Almost a loss	If tied games never occurred
T_1	3	1	2	2
T_2	2	2	3	1
T_3	1	3	6	3
T_4	4	4	5	4
T_5	5	5	4	5
T_6	6	6	1	6

Standings by winning percentage when considering each tie as			
Almost a win	1/2 Win + 1/2 loss	Almost a loss	If tied games never occurred
T_3	T_1	T_6	T_2
T_2	T_2	T_1	T_1
T_1	T_3	T_2	T_3
T_4	T_4	T_5	T_4
T_5	T_5	T_4	T_5
T_6	T_6	T_3	T_6

ways, even if it is strictly worse in many other ways. For example, the developers of new products may want to be able to carve out sufficiently large shares of the market by being better than the competition according to the criteria important for those market shares, even if those products are worse everywhere else (which could be many more places). Blandness might also be considered as being bad in artistic judging or in places where major breakthroughs are being sought. In these cases, it might be reasonable to count each tie as being almost a loss.

4.1.2. Numerical examples involving ties

As can be inferred from the discussions above, the four ways considered here for treating ties (almost a win, half win plus half loss, almost a loss, and ignore the game completely) can produce different rankings from each other. The hypothetical example in Table 3 illustrates this outcome. In that example, $n = 6$ and $m_{ij} = 6$ for all distinct i and j from 1 through 6, so that each team plays 6 games against each of the other 5 teams for a total of 30 games.

Some points to note concerning the example of Table 3 are as follows. First, it involves a symmetric round robin competition (i.e., it does not yield different rankings because some teams play different teams or different numbers of games than other teams). Second, each team wins at least one game and loses at least one game (i.e., it does not yield different rankings due to zeros in numerators or denominators). Third, each team occupies its own place in each ranking (i.e., none of the rankings result in a tie for any position in any ranking). Fourth, not only are the four rankings different, each ranking produces a different winner.

Two of the techniques to treat ties (half win plus half loss, and ignore tied games) are quite robust in the example of Table 3 in that (1) the winner by either comes in second by the other, and (2) these two winners come in second or third in the two cases structured to give different winners for the other two techniques. Thus, in addition to the general acceptance and general applicability of these two techniques, they may be generally robust. This would give another general argument for using them in applications other than those for which there are specific arguments to the contrary.

One such argument to the contrary can be made in voting theory. By making pairwise comparisons of each alternative with each other alternative, a rank-order-input voting process can be viewed as being a symmetric round robin tournament among the alternatives in which each alternative is matched (i.e., plays a game) against each other alternative exactly once. Indeed, if ties are treated as half a win plus half a loss, this is exactly what Copeland's voting method does (see Chapter 16, Section 2.3.6). One way to paraphrase an argument made in voting theory is as follows. If, in this 'voters tournament', T_i beats or ties every alternative that T_j beats or ties, and T_i beats or ties T_j, then T_i should be ranked at least as high as T_j.

To help see the implications of the argument, consider the hypothetical example in Table 4. In that example, $n = 6$, $m_{ij} = 1$ for all distinct i and j from 1 through 6, and the terms 'team' and 'alternative' are used synonymously. It is not hard to construct a set of voter's preferences (i.e., individual voter's rankings of the six

Table 4
example involving ties and arguments from voting theory

Team	Opponent (W = win by team, L = loss to opponent, T = tie)						Totals		
	T_1	T_2	T_3	T_4	T_5	T_6	Wins	Losses	Ties
T_1	–	L	W	W	W	L	3	2	0
T_2	W	–	T	T	T	L	1	1	3
T_3	L	T	–	W	L	W	2	2	1
T_4	L	T	L	–	W	W	2	2	1
T_5	L	T	W	L	–	W	2	2	1
T_6	W	W	L	L	L	–	2	3	0

Team	Rankings by winning percentage when considering each tie as				Standings by winning percentage when considering each tie as			
	Almost a win	1/2 Win + 1/2 loss	Almost a loss	If tied games never occurred	Almost a win	1/2 Win + 1/2 loss	Almost a loss	If tied games never occurred
T_1	2	1	1	1	T_2	T_1	T_1	T_1
T_2	1	2	6	2t	T_1	T_2	$T_3 T_4 T_5$	$T_2 T_3 T_4 T_5$
T_3	3t	3t	2t	2t	$T_3 T_4 T_5$	$T_3 T_4 T_5$	$T_3 T_4 T_5$	$T_2 T_3 T_4 T_5$
T_4	3t	3t	2t	2t	$T_3 T_4 T_5$	$T_3 T_4 T_5$	$T_3 T_4 T_5$	$T_2 T_3 T_4 T_5$
T_5	3t	3t	2t	2t	$T_3 T_4 T_5$	$T_3 T_4 T_5$	T_6	$T_2 T_3 T_4 T_5$
T_6	6	6	5	6	T_6	T_6	T_2	T_6

alternatives T_1 through T_6) that result in the outcome displayed in Table 4. In the example in that table, T_1 is ranked first by three of the four tie treating techniques tabulated there. However, T_2 beats or ties every alternative that T_1 beats or ties and, not only does T_2 beat or tie T_1, T_2 beats T_1. Therefore, by this paraphrased voting theory argument, T_2 should be ranked at least as high as T_1. Further, since T_2 beat T_1, it can be argued that a tie in ranking between them should be broken in T_2's favor. Indeed, note that if T_i beats or ties every alternative that T_j beats or ties, and T_i beats T_j, then T_i will necessarily be ranked above T_j when these rankings are determined by winning percentages with ties being counted as almost a win. Accordingly, the fourth tie treating technique tabulated in Table 4 ranks T_2 in first place, ahead of T_1, and T_2 can be viewed as being a consensus alternative in the sense described above.

Thus, treating ties by counting them as almost a win may be quite appropriate in 'voter's tournaments'. However, one should be careful about applying arguments taken from voting theory (which may turn out to not actually have meaningful applications within voting theory). For example, another paraphrased (and slightly modified) argument from voting theory is that if every alternative that beats or ties T_i also beats or ties T_j, and T_i beats T_j, then T_i should be ranked ahead of T_j. This corresponds to treating each tie as being almost a loss. In the example in Table 4, every alternative that beats or ties T_6 also beats or ties T_2, and T_6 (strictly) beats T_2. Accordingly, treating a tie as almost a loss would rank T_6 ahead of T_2, which may not be what is actually desired.

4.2. A realistic example involving college football

The examples in Section 4.1 are hypothetical, are concerned with the treatment of ties, are symmetric round robins, and form rankings using winning percentages (which is quite reasonable for symmetric round robins). The example here is realistic, only incidentally involves ties, is not a symmetric round robin, and illustrates the use of the method described in Section 3.3 above. This example concerns the 1989 college football season, which ended with seven bowl games played on January 1, 1990.

Collecting and entering into a computer data for every game played by every college football team in the 1989 season is beyond the intent of this overview. However, a reasonably interesting and useful example can be constructed by considering individually only the fourteen teams that played on January 1, 1990, and aggregating all of the other teams into one notional opponent team, labeled 'All Others' in this example. (This is the same approach used by Jech [1983] to consider National Collegiate Athletic Association (NCAA) Division II and Division III teams.) In addition to this major simplifying assumption, the following two assumptions are also made. First, each game is to be counted equally no matter when it was played – who played against whom can make a difference, but whether two teams played each other on the first day of the season or on New Years Day is to make no difference. Second, only the results of the games in terms of who won, who lost, or whether it was a tie, is to be considered – neither the

L.B. Anderson

Table 5
A summary of the common games involving teams that played in New Years Day (1990) bowls

	MIA	NDU	FSU	COL	TEN	AUB	MIC	USC	ALA	ILL	NEB	ARK	UVA	OSU	Other	Totals
Miami	–	W	L	–	–	–	–	–	W	–	–	–	–	–	9-0	11-1
Notre Dame	L	–	–	W	–	–	W	W	–	–	–	–	W	–	8-0	12-1
Florida State	W	–	–	–	–	W	–	–	–	W	W	–	–	–	7-2	10-2
Colorado	–	L	–	–	–	–	–	–	L	W	–	W	–	–	9-0	11-1
Tennessee	–	–	–	–	–	L	–	–	W	L	–	–	–	W	9-0	11-1
Auburn	–	–	L	–	W	–	W	L	–	L	–	–	–	–	8-0	10-2
Michigan	–	L	–	–	–	L	–	W	–	–	–	–	–	W	8-0	10-2
U. South. Calif.	–	L	–	–	–	W	L	–	–	–	–	–	–	W	7-0-1	9-2-1
Alabama	L	–	–	W	L	–	–	–	–	–	–	–	W	–	9-0	10-2
Illinois	–	–	L	L	W	W	–	–	–	–	W	–	–	W	7-0	10-2
Nebraska	–	–	L	–	–	–	–	–	–	L	–	–	–	–	10-0	10-2
Arkansas	–	–	–	L	–	–	–	–	–	–	–	–	–	–	10-1	10-2
Virginia	–	L	–	–	–	–	–	–	L	–	–	–	–	–	10-1	10-3
Ohio State	–	–	–	–	L	–	L	L	–	L	–	–	–	–	8-0	8-4
All others	0W 9L	0W 8L	2W 7L	0W 9L	0W 9L	0W 8L	0W 8L	0W 7L 1T	0W 9L	0W 7L	0W 10L	1W 10L	1W 10L	0W 8L	–	4-119-1
Totals:																
Wins	11	12	10	11	11	10	10	9	10	10	10	10	10	8	4	146
Losses	1	1	2	1	1	2	2	2	2	2	2	2	3	4	119	146
Ties	0	0	0	0	0	0	0	1	0	0	0	0	0	0	1	2
Games	12	13	12	12	12	12	12	12	12	12	12	12	13	12	124	294
	MIA	NDU	FSU	COL	TEN	AUB	MIC	USC	ALA	ILL	NEB	ARK	UVA	OSU	Other	Totals

Table 6
Several alternative rankings of teams that played in New Years Day (1990) bowls

Jech	Kendall–Wei	AP	UPI
1 Notre Dame	1 Notre Dame	1 Miami(39)	1 Miami(36)
2 Miami	2 Miami	2 Notre Dame(19)	2 Florida State(7)
3 Colorado	3 Colorado	3 Florida State(2)	3 Notre Dame(6)
4 Tennessee	4 Tenessee	4 Colorado	4 Colorado
5 Illinois	5 Florida State	5 Tenessee	5 Tenessee
6 Michigan	6 Illinois	6 Auburn	6 Auburn
7 Alabama	7 Michigan	7 Michigan	7 Alabama
8 Auburn	8 Alabama	8 S. Calif.	8 Michigan
9 S. Calif.	9 Auburn	9 Alabama	9 S. Calif.
10 Florida State	10 S. Calif.	10 Illinois	10 Illinois
11 Nebraska	11 Nebraska	11 Nebraska	12 Nebraska
12 Ohio State	12 Arkansas	13 Arkansas	13 Arkansas
13 Arkansas	13 Virginia	18 Virginia	15 Virginia
14 Virginia	14 Ohio State	24 Ohio State	21t Ohio State
15 All others	15 All others		

points scored nor any other measure of how well any team played in any game is to be considered (other than through wins, losses, and ties). Table 5 summarizes the 1989 college football season based on these assumptions. The teams are listed in that table in order according to their relative position in the final Associated Press (AP) sports writers opinion poll, with All Others listed last. Data for the schedule matrix, m, and results matrix, r, can be taken directly from Table 5.

Table 6 gives the relative rankings of these teams according to the AP poll, the United Press International (UPI) coaches opinion poll, the Kendall–Wei method as described in Section 2.2 above, and Jech's method as described in Section 3.3 above. Note that Jech's method is equivalent to that proposed by Zermelo [1929], Bradley & Terry [1952], and Ford [1957].

The integers on the left side of the AP and UPI polls give the absolute position of the corresponding teams in those polls (e.g., Clemson came in 12th in the AP poll, between 11 Nebraska and 13 Arkansas, and Clemson came in 11th in the UPI polls between 10 Illinois and 12 Nebraska, but Clemson played on New Years Eve, not New Years Day (1990), and so is not individually identified in these rankings). The number in parentheses on the right gives the number of first place votes that these teams received in these polls (only the top three teams received any first place votes). The ranking in each of these polls is determined using a truncated Borda voting method. Each AP voter selects 25 teams to rank order, and each such voter's first place choice receives 25 points, each voter's second place choice receives 24 points, and so on through each 25th place choice which receives 1 point. Each UPI voter selects 20 teams to rank order in the same manner (except that the points awarded range from 20 points for each first place through 1 point for each 20th place).

The rankings for Jech's method and the Kendall–Wei method are determined using values for m and r obtained from Table 5 (the tie involving USC is counted as half a win and half a loss). A modified version of a computer program originally developed by Miller & Palocsay [1985] was used to perform the calculations. Note that $r \in R_2$ in this example, so these are the unique rankings produced by these methods.

Some points to note concerning this example are as follows.

First, the relative rankings of these fourteen teams by the Jech or Kendall–Wei method could change if all of the college football teams were individually considered. This is not unlikely for lower-ranked teams or for closely ranked teams – the relative strengths according to Jech's method (denoted by s_i for $i = 1, \ldots, n$ in Section 3.3), renormalized so that Notre Dame has a strength of 1.000, are given in Table 7. (That table also repeats the rankings by the Kendall–Wei method and gives the relative AP and UPI rankings of the fourteen individual teams.) As can be seen from Table 7, neither Miami nor Colorado are close to Notre Dame in relative strength by Jech's method (similar data applies for the Kendall–Wei method). Also, none of these three teams lost any games to any of the also-rans aggregated into the notional All Others team. Thus, with one exception, it seems quite unlikely that these top three places would change if every college football team were individually considered – the one exception is that Miami and Colorado might switch places (moving Miami to third and Colorado to second) since they are very closely ranked to each other.

Second, it was noted above that the Kendall–Wei method considers the strength-of-schedule as it concerns wins over strong teams versus wins over weak teams, but not as it concerns losses to weak teams versus losses to strong teams. In comparison, Jech's method considers all aspects of the strength of the

Table 7
Normalized strengths by Jech's method and relative rankings from Table 6

Team	Normalized strengths	Relative ranking			
		Jech	Kendal	AP	UPI
Notre Dame	1.000	1	1	2	3
Miami	0.580	2	2	1	1
Colorado	0.553	3	3	4	4
Tennessee	0.195	4	4	5	5
Illinois	0.169	5	6	10	10
Michigan	0.168	6	7	7	8
Alabama	0.138	7	8	9	7
Auburn	0.113	8	9	6	6
S. Calif.	0.108	9	10	8	9
Florida State	0.093	10	5	3	2
Nebraska	0.052	11	11	11	11
Ohio State	0.027	12	14	14	14
Arkansas	0.022	13	12	12	12
Virginia	0.021	14	13	13	13
All Others	0.002	15	15	(12)	(11)

schedule. This characteristic is evident in Tables 5, 6, and 7 in that the differences between their rankings involve Kendall–Wei's higher ranking (compared to Jech) of one team (Florida State) that lost two games to the notional 'weak' opponent team, and Jech's higher ranking (compared to Kendall–Wei) of one team (Ohio State) that lost no games to the notional 'weak' opponent.

Third, a common argument concerning mathematical techniques is that a (usually more complex) new technique might be theoretically better, but it might yield results that are insignificantly different from those produced by the current approach. This is clearly not the case here. Of course, just because a new technique produces significantly different results in a sports application does not necessarily mean that it even has appropriate applications outside of sports, let alone has meaningful applications that would produce significantly different results than currently used approaches. However, the real issue here may be the existence of appropriate applications, not the significance of the impact of using these techniques if such applications were found.

Fourth, a common argument concerning all modeling and abstract representation techniques is that a major purpose of these techniques is to gain insight and understanding, as opposed to obtaining a definitive answer from (say) one computer run using such a technique. This being the case, one might question whether ranking techniques are too sterile to provide any additional insight or understanding. In general, one might be able to gain such insight or understanding by doing sensitivity analyses. For example, what would happen if the outcome(s) of one (or a few) of the paired comparisons were reversed (winner-to-loser and vice versa)? In the particular example here, one could try to isolate (and support or discredit) possible reasons why the opinion polls differ so much from, say, Jech's ranking, which takes full account of the strength of the schedule.

Was it because the voters in the polls placed greater weight on more recent games? This could be tested by making relatively simple modifications to Jech's method to place unequal weights on different games and then trying to find a plausible time-discounting scheme that produces results comparable to the polls.

Was it because the voters in the polls considered the scores of the games rather than just who won or who lost? This could be tested by modifying Jech's method to consider game scores and/or by comparing the polls with results produced by other methods that directly consider such scores.

Was it because those voters felt that Notre Dame received unfair rewards in previous years, which they were not going to allow to happen that year? Voters' feelings are hard to test, especially after the fact. However, results and polls from past years could be analyzed to see if any given team, or set of teams, were generally overrated or underrated in those polls as compared to the more objective rankings produced by Jech's method (or by other methods described above).

Or was it because the polls ranked Colorado first, Miami second, Michigan third, and Notre Dame fourth before the New Year Day bowl games, and the voters did not consider Notre Dame's victory over Colorado in their bowl game to be significant enough to move Notre Dame ahead of Miami? This conjecture

Table 8
Pre-bowl and final 1990 college football rankings (Jech and AP)

Team	Pre-bowl record	Pre-bowl		Bowl result (opponent)	Final	
		Jech rank	AP rank		Jech rank	AP rank
Colorado	11-0	1	1	Lost (NDU)	3	4
Nebraska	10-1	2	6	Lost (FSU)	11	11
Notre Dame	11-1	3	4	Won (COL)	1	2
Michigan	10-1	4	3	Lost (USC)	6	7
Illinois	9-2	5	11	Won (UVA)	5	10
Miami	10-1	6	2	Won (ALA)	2	1
Alabama	10-1	7t	7	Lost (MIA)	7	9
Tennessee	10-1	7t	8	Won (ARK)	4	5
Auburn	9-2	9	9	Won (OSU)	8	6
S. Calif.	9-2-1	10	12	Won (MIC)	9	8
Florida State	9-2	11	5	Won (NEB)	10	3
Ohio State	8-3	12	21	Lost (AUB)	12	24
Arkansas	10-1	13	10	Lost (TEN)	13	13
Virginia	10-2	14	15	Lost (ILL)	14	18

has two parts: the first concerns the significance of Notre Dame bowl victory over previously unbeaten and top-ranked Colorado, and the second concerns the appropriateness of the pre-bowl polls, which can be tested by comparing these polls to rankings that Jech's method would produce given the games up to but not including the bowls. Such a comparison is shown in Table 8. Since Colorado was undefeated, and since Nebraska's one pre-bowl loss was to Colorado, Jech's method necessarily ranks Colorado first and Nebraska second (note that if r^- is the corresponding pre-bowl results matrix, then $r^- \in R_1$ but $r^- \notin R_2$). Clearly, more analysis could be done concerning this example. However, the point here is not to reach a conclusion as to why the polls ranked Miami ahead of Notre Dame, nor who really should have been No. 1 (according to various criteria) in college football that year, nor even that this is an important issue in the first place. Instead the point is that paired comparison methods are not so sterile as to preclude using them in comparative analyses, and the example here shows (at a minimum) how such an analysis could be begun.

Finally, as an aside, college football was used as an example both here and in Jech [1983]. One should not conclude that this means that one of the most appropriate applications of paired comparison theory in sports is to the post bowl determination of college football rankings. Indeed, one could argue that no post (complete) season application could be as important as an application that would affect who would (continue) to play in what games. For example, paired comparison theory could have a quite useful and relatively quite important application in determining which college teams (e.g., in basketball) should be selected to participate in the NCAA post (regular) season tournaments, and to help determine how such teams should be seeded. This theory could also be used to help determine which of, say, several National Football League teams with identical won–lost records should make the playoffs when, as frequently happens, more teams are tied with identical records than there are (wild card) places to be filled by these teams.

5. Some characteristics concerning general applicability with emphasis on combat analyses

Like voting theory, paired comparison theory does not appear to have been applied in major defense analyses. Unlike voting theory, it may not be immediately obvious whether, in any particular situation, paired comparison theory can be profitably applied. However, increased dissemination of the existence of this theory combined with sufficient ingenuity in structuring analyses may lead to such applications. To assist in finding such applications, the following framework is proposed.

5.1. A general framework for applying paired comparison theory

Paired comparison theory involves making and evaluating comparisons in situations that have the following four characteristics. First, each comparison is made between two alternatives (not among three or more). Second, different pairs of alternatives can (optionally) be compared different numbers of times, including (optionally) no comparisons being made of some pairs. Third, only which alternative won and which lost each comparison (if a tie did not occur) is important, the size of the victory in terms of any magnitude that could be associated with the comparison is irrelevant. Fourth, the comparisons need not be consistent either in that alternative A could win a comparison over B, B over C, yet C could win over A, or in that if A and B are compared several times, A might win some of these comparisons but lose others.

In a reasonable sense, this fourth characteristic either holds or it does not, and paired comparison theory has very little to offer concerning the analyses of situations for which it does not hold. However, these four characteristics are clearly not independent, and situations possessing the first and third characteristics above are likely to have the fourth also.

The third characteristic is not necessarily a 'definitely holds or definitely does not hold' characteristic. It clearly holds if the comparisons have no magnitudes associated with them. However, many comparisons have (and many of the rest can be easily modified to have) such magnitudes. The issue therefore concerns the relative significance of these magnitudes in the analysis being made. If the relative sizes of these magnitudes across comparisons are quite important, then paired comparison theory (as described here) may have little to offer. If the sizes of these magnitudes provide insight and explanation, but only within any given comparison, and they are not necessarily meaningful across comparisons, then paired comparison theory might be a useful tool.

The second characteristic clearly either holds or does not hold. If it holds, then paired comparison theory is relatively more likely to be applicable (but it is not necessarily so); while if it does not hold, paired comparison theory is relatively less likely to be applicable (but it still might be so).

The first characteristic may be more important than it first appears concerning the applicability of paired comparison theory. For example, it might seem unimportant because any ranking of a alternatives (perhaps with associated magnitudes) can be converted into $a(a-1)/2$ comparisons, one each for each different pair of alternatives. More generally, v rankings of a alternatives can be converted into $va(a-1)/2$ comparisons, where each different pair of alternatives is compared v times (this is essentially what Copeland's method does in voting theory). However, if this is done when $v = 1$, then characteristics 2 and 4 do not apply, and paired comparison theory has essentially nothing to offer. (If characteristic 3 applies, then the situation is trivial – the ranking gives the answer. If characteristic 3 does not apply, then analyses that directly address the relevant magnitudes may be useful. However, either way, paired comparison theory as described above would contribute nothing here.) If this is done when $v > 1$, then characteristic 2 does not apply, and voting theory (but not paired comparison theory) could apply, depending on characteristic 3.

5.2. Discussion of potential combat applications in terms of this framework

The purpose of this section is to discuss potential applications of paired comparison theory to combat related analyses in terms of the four characteristics described in Section 5.1 above. Non-combat defense applications are, of course, possible, and the interested reader could structure such applications in terms of these characteristics if desired. Some of the comments below apply to both combat and non-combat applications.

5.2.1. Making comparisons in pairs

At the outset it should be noted that the standard procedure of comparing a set of alternative forces by evaluating each force against a canonical enemy threat does not constitute making paired comparisons as defined here. That is, while each alternative force can be evaluated by pairing it in simulated combat against the canonical enemy force, the alternatives being compared in such an analysis are the different friendly forces, not a friendly alternative and an enemy alternative.

However, it may be that, due to personnel, time, equipment, and/or range constraints, the alternatives must be evaluated in separate groups, that not more than a certain (maximum) number of alternatives can be evaluated in any one group, and that cross-group comparisons are not valid. (Such cross-group comparisons might not be valid due to changes in personnel, equipment, and/or range conditions between groups.)

For example, if eight alternatives are to be evaluated, but no more than four can be evaluated in any one comparable group, then the following procedure is possible. Alternatives 1, 2, 3, and 4 could be evaluated in one group, alternatives

5, 6, 7, and 8 could be evaluated in a second group, and then two from each, say 3, 4, 5, and 6, could be evaluated in a third group. Such an approach would produce the following paired comparisons:

Pair of alternatives	Number of comparisons made	Pair of alternatives	Number of comparisons made
1.2	1	4.5	1
1.3	1	4.6	1
1.4	1	5.6	2
2.3	1	5.7	1
2.4	1	5.8	1
3.4	2	6.7	1
3.5	1	6.8	1
3.6	1	7.8	1
		All other pairs	0

This same point clearly applies if the alternatives are being compared purely by human judgments and the situation is sufficiently complex that no one judge can adequately address all of the alternatives. The example just above would apply if there were three judges, eight alternatives, and each judge could address any four but no more than four of these alternatives. In the extreme, each judge may not be able to address more than two alternatives, which would satisfy the first condition directly.

Finally, while war games and computer models frequently have been used to evaluate alternative forces and tactics against canonical threats, the lack of such threats in the future may preclude use of this technique. Of course, the goal of spending defense dollars wisely remains. However, testing the wisdom of such spending by evaluating alternatives against an arbitrarily specified threat (or a small set of such threats) may no longer be reasonable. Instead, alternatives could be evaluated by matching alternatives in pairs directly against each other using a war game or computer model. This approach is somewhat novel, but it has been suggested before, Grotte & Brooks [1983], and it may prove to be an appropriate threat-independent way to evaluate alternative future defense expenditures.

5.2.2. Unequal numbers of comparisons

Analyzing comparisons in groups as described above would generally result in unequal numbers of comparisons of various pairs of alternatives. In the example above, the pairs (3, 4) and (5, 6) are compared twice, the pairs (1, 2), (1, 3), (1, 4), (2, 3), (2, 4), (3, 5), (3, 6), (4, 5), (4, 6), (5, 7), (5, 8), (6, 7), (6, 8) and (7, 8) are compared once, and the remaining 12 pairs are not compared at all.

If comparisons are being made in pairs by matching two alternatives against each other in a fully automated combat model, then there is no inherent reason why all pairs would not be compared an equal number of times. However, if such comparisons are being made in an interactive war game, a field exercise, or any other human-intensive processes, then limitations on personnel, time, equipment, and/or range facilities, or (conversely) special interest by the personnel involved in repeating comparisons of selected pairs, could lead to unequal numbers of comparisons of pairs of alternatives.

5.2.3. Irrelevance of associated magnitudes

If comparisons are made in groups as described above, then cross-group comparisons would not be valid precisely when associated magnitudes are not comparable across groups. As indicated above, such magnitudes may not be comparable across groups because key personnel (players, judges/controllers, etc.) change between groups, or because there are sufficient changes in the setting (equipment, range conditions, etc.) that cross-group comparisons are not valid. Note that an important special case here occurs when these groups are all of size two; that is, the alternatives are being compared in pairs and, due to changes in the personnel or conditions involved, magnitudes associated with a comparison of one pair of alternatives are not necessarily commensurable with magnitudes associated with another comparison of that pair or with any comparison of any other pair.

There are several other conditions that would lead to considering only wins, losses, and ties, but not associated magnitudes, in making comparisons. For example, the goal in a war game may be to hold the enemy's advance to a certain amount, or to penetrate the enemy's defenses in at least a certain number of places. That is, the goal is to satisfy a set of criteria, not to maximize any particular war game output. In such a case, the magnitudes of associated outputs would not be directly relevant to any comparisons being made.

A related set of examples concerns Monte Carlo models. One might desire to run sufficiently many trials of a Monte Carlo model in order to achieve a certain level of statistical confidence in the results. One way to do this is to set a goal (e.g., to keep major bases or ships from being put out of action with probability greater than some specified amount) and to run sufficiently many trials to have high confidence in knowing whether or not a particular defense against a particular attack was capable of meeting that goal. In such a case, the comparisons should depend on whether or not that goal was achieved, not on associated magnitudes (such as how many attacking and defending weapons systems were killed).

Finally, if the associated magnitudes (or measures of the importance of these magnitudes) are determined directly by human judgment, then differences in magnitudes that seem large at the beginning of a set of comparisons may seem small at the end, and (in different cases) vice versa. Such order effects can be addressed by doing many more comparisons; but they are not important (and so need not be addressed) if only the direction (i.e., bigger, smaller, or the same) is to be counted, not the size of the differences in magnitudes.

5.2.4. Inconsistent comparisons

A comparison between alternative A and alternative B that favors alternative A is clearly inconsistent with another such comparison that favors alternative B, and can be said to be inconsistent with two comparisons, one between B and C and one between C and A, if those two comparisons favor B and C, respectively. As stated above, paired comparisons theory is designed to handle such inconsistencies; the question is whether such inconsistencies would occur so that paired comparisons theory would be a useful tool.

Such inconsistencies might occur, for example, if the comparisons were made in groups (including groups of size 2) as described above, and if the changes in personnel and/or conditions involved were sufficiently significant to reverse the outcomes of some comparisons.

Such inconsistencies might also occur in the following situation. Suppose a Monte Carlo model is used and insufficiently many trials for statistical significance are run. (For example, using Monte Carlo models in interactive war games frequently involves making only one trial per identical set of conditions.) The inherent randomness involved in such a use of Monte Carlo models could easily lead to the inconsistencies described here.

6. Annotated bibliography

6.1. Recommended reading

The following references, in the following order, are recommended for those who want to read into the literature on paired comparisons.

A good place to start is:

> Jech, T. (1983). The ranking of incomplete tournaments: A mathematician's guide to popular sports. *Amer. Math. Monthly* 90, 246–266.

In this paper, Jech presents a clean and clear exposition of the method described in Section 3.3. Theorems are well explained and proofs are nicely set off to assist the reader in understanding the concepts without getting lost in the details or rigor. However, one reason that this paper may be so clean is that it contains no references to any previous work nor does it mention any other non-trivial analytical methods; this is noted by:

> Stob, M. (1984). A supplement to 'A mathematician's guide to popular sports'. *Amer. Math. Monthly* 91, 277–282,

which should be read second. By relating Jech's paper to previous research, Stob provides a brief but useful and coherent overview of probability models in paired comparison theory.

Third, the interested reader should examine:

> Stob, M. (1985). Rankings from round-robin tournaments. *Management Sci.* 31, 1191–1195.

In this paper, Stob provides a brief but useful overview of deterministic combinatorial methods in paired comparison theory, and he points out that this is only one of two general approaches – the probability model approach being the other. Curiously, in this paper, Stob references neither his previous paper (cited just above) nor Jech's paper, and he does not reference Ford [1957], which is one of the (at least) three previously published research papers that contain results that Jech rediscovered. (He does cite the other two, but there is a typographical error in the reference to Zermelo – the correct date of that publication is 1929, not 1926.) Since this paper by Stob is oriented toward deterministic combinatorial methods, not probability models, these omissions are quite understandable, but they inhibit exploration of the literature by a new reader. In this paper, Stob reviews a paper by Goddard [1983], but that paper is not a prerequisite for Stob's paper. Another feature of Stob's paper is that it points out some characteristics of deterministic combinatorial methods that can reasonably be viewed as also being major flaws of those methods.

Fourth, the interested reader should examine:

> David, H.A. (1971). Ranking the players in a round robin tournament. *Rev. Internat. Statist. Inst.* 39, 137–147.

This paper also points out some questionable characteristics (i.e., flaws) of deterministic combinatorial methods, it points out a potentially serious problem with probability models that use maximum likelihood values, and it provides a nice transition from the other recommended references to:

> David, H.A. (1988). *The Method of Paired Comparisons, 2nd edition, revised*, Oxford University Press, London.

which should be (at least) skimmed and judiciously examined next. This text seems to be the only recent book on the subject, it is quite good, it covers a broad range of topics concerning paired comparison theory, and, with a few notable exceptions (listed in Section 6.2, below), it contains an outstanding bibliography for paired comparisons.

After examining this book, the reader might continue in any of several different directions. One such direction is to consider probability models based on random strengths with distributions other than the extreme value distribution or the normal distribution. An excellent start in this direction is given in:

> Frey, M.R. (1984). Predicting the outcome of sporting events: An application of probability theory, Student Paper for OR 291, George Washington University, Washington DC, April.

A reader particularly interested in sports should see:

> Ladany, S.P., and R.E. Machol (eds.) (1977). *Optimal Strategies in Sports*, North-Holland, Amsterdam, and
> Machol, R.E., S.P. Ladany and D.G. Morrison (eds.) (1976). *Management Science*, North-Holland, Amsterdam,
> and should consider the papers listed under Recreation and Sports (classification category 840) in the Subject Index of
> Marshall, K.T., and F.P. Richards (eds.) (1978). *The OR/MS Index 1952–1976*, The Institute of Management Sciences, Providence, RI, and Operations Research Society of America, Baltimore, MD,

Tolle, J.W. (ed.) (1988). *The OR/MS Index 1982–1987*, The Institute of Management Sciences, Providence, RI, and Operations Research Society of America, Baltimore, MD.

Tolle, J.W. and R.E. Stone (eds.) (1983). *The OR/MS Index 1976–1981*, The Institute of Management Sciences, Providence, and Operations Research Society of America, Baltimore, MD.

6.2. Omissions from David's references

In his book, David [1988] cites almost 300 references, one of which [Davidson & Farquhar, 1976] gives an extensive bibliography up to 1976. Accordingly, one might expect every major paper on paired comparison theory published between 1976 and 1988 to be cited there. The following are not.

Ali, I., W.D. Cook and M. Kress (1986). On the minimum violations ranking of a tournament. *Management Sci.* 32, 660–672.

Goddard, S.T. (1983). Ranking in tournaments and group decisionmaking. *Management Sci.* 29, 1384–1392.

Jech, T. (1983). The ranking of incomplete tournaments: A mathematician's guide to popular sports. *Amer. Math. Monthly* 90, 246–266.

Stob, M. (1984). A supplement to 'A mathematician's guide to popular sports'. *Amer. Math. Monthly* 91, 277–282.

Stob, M. (1985). Rankings from round-robin tournaments. *Management Sci.* 31, 1191–1195.

6.3. References and representative bibliography

The publications listed below include all those cited in this chapter, and include a representative sample of related publications.

Ali, I., W.D. Cook and M. Kress (1986). On the minimum violations ranking of a tournament. *Management Sci.* 32, 660–672.

Andrews, D.M., and H.A. David (1990). Nonparametric analysis of unbalanced paired-comparison or ranked data. *J. Amer. Statist. Assoc.* 85, 1140–1146.

Bradley, R.A. (1976). Science, statistics, and paired comparisons. *Biometrics* 32, 213–232.

Bradley, R.A., and M.E. Terry (1952). The rank analysis of incomplete block designs, I. The method of paired comparisons. *Biometrika* 39, 324–345.

David, H.A. (1971). Ranking the players in a round robin tournament. *Rev. Internat. Statist. Inst.* 39, 137–147.

David, H.A. (1988). *The Method of Paired Comparisons, 2nd edition, revised*, Oxford University Press, London.

Davidson, R.R. (1970). On extending the Bradley-Terry model to accommodate ties in paired comparison experiments. *J. Amer. Statist. Assoc.* 65, 317–328.

Davidson, R.R., and P.H. Farquhar (1976). A bibliography on the method of paired comparisons. *Biometrics* 32, 241–252.

Dykstra, O. (1960). Rank analysis of incomplete block designs method of paired comparisons employing unequal repetitions on pairs. *Biometric* 16, 176–188.

Feinberg, S.E., and K. Larntz (1976). Log linear representation for paired and multiple comparisons models. *Biometrika* 63, 245–254.

Ford, L.R. (1957). Solution of a ranking problem from binary comparisons. *Amer. Math. Monthly* 64, 28–33.

Frey, M.R. (1984). Predicting the outcome of sporting events: An application of probability theory, Student Paper for OR 291, George Washington University, Washington, DC, April.

Goddard, S.T. (1983). Ranking in tournaments and group decisionmaking. *Management Sci.* 29, 1384–1392.

Grotte, J.H., and P.S. Brooks (1983). Measuring naval presence using blotto games. *Internat. J. Game Theory* 12, 225–236.

Harary, F., and L. Moser (1966). The theory of round robin tournaments. *Amer. Math. Monthly* 73, 231–246.

Harville, D.A. (1978). Football ratings and predictions via linear models, in: Proceedings of the Social Statistics Section, *Amer. Statist. Assoc.*, pp. 74–82.

Horen, J., and R. Riezman (1985). Comparing draws for single elimination tournaments. *Oper. Res.* 33, 249–262.

Jech, T. (1983). The ranking of incomplete tournaments: A mathematician's guide to popular sports. *Amer. Math. Monthly* 90, 246–266.

Keener, J.P. (1993). The Perron–Frobenius theorem and the ranking of football teams. *SIAM Rev.* 35, 80–93.

Kendall, M.G. (1955). Further contributions to the theory of paired comparisons. *Biometrics* 2, 43–62.

Koehler, K.J., and H. Ridpath (1982). An application of a biased version of the Bradley-Terry-Luce model to professional basketball results. *J. Math. Psychology* 25, 187–205.

Ladany, S.P., and R.E. Machol (eds.) (1977). *Optimal Strategies in Sports*, North-Holland, Amsterdam.

Machol, R.E., S.P. Ladany and D.G. Morrison (eds.) (1976). *Management Science in Sports*, North-Holland, Amsterdam.

Miller, A., and S. Palocsay (1985). A comparison of ranking methods in pairwise competitions, Student Paper for OR 291, George Washington University, Washington, DC, December.

Moon, J.W. (1968). *Topics on Tournaments*, Holt, Rinehart and Winston, New York.

Mosteller, F. (1951). Remarks on the method of paired comparisons, I. The least squares solution assuming equal standard deviations and equal correlations. *Psychometrika* 16, 3–9.

Ramanujacharyulu, C. (1964). Analysis of preferential experiments. *Psychometrika* 29, 257–261.

Rubinstein, A. (1980). Ranking the participants in a tournament. *SIAM J. Appl. Math.* 38, 108–111.

Sagarin, J.S., and W.L. Winston (1983). The use of exponential smoothing to forecast the outcome of basketball and football games, School of Business, Indiana University, Bloomington IN, October, pp. 1–9.

Slater, P. (1961). Inconsistencies in a schedule of paired comparisons. *Biometrica* 48, 303–312.

Smith, J.H. (1956). Adjusting baseball standings for strength of teams played. *Amer. Statist.* 10, 23–24.

Stefani, R.T. (1977). Football and basketball predictions using least squares. *IEEE Trans. Syst., Man, Cybernet.*, February, 117–121.

Stob, M. (1984). A supplement to 'A mathematician's guide to popular sports'. *Amer. Math. Monthly* 91, 277–282.

Stob, M. (1985). Rankings from round-robin tournaments. *Management Sci.* 31, 1191–1195.

Thompson, M. (1975). On any given sunday: Fair competitor orderings with maximum likelihood methods. *J. Amer. Statist. Assoc.* 70, 536–541.

Tryfos, P., S. Casey, S. Cook, G. Leger and B. Pylypiak (1984). The profitability of wagering on NFL games. *Management Sci.* 30, 123–135.

Vergin, R.C., and M. Scriabin (1978). Winning strategies for wagering on national football league games. *Management Sci.* 24, 809–818.

Zermelo, E. (1929). Die Berechnung der Turnier-Ergebnisse als ein Maximumproblem der Wahrscheinlichkeitsrechnung. *Math. Z.* 29, 436–460.

S.M. Pollock et al., Eds., *Handbooks in OR & MS, Vol. 6*

Chapter 18

Limitations on Conclusions Using Scales of Measurement

Fred S. Roberts

Department of Mathematics and Center for Operations Research, Rutgers University, New Brunswick, NJ 08903, U.S.A.

1. Introduction

In almost every practical use of the methods of operations research, something is measured. Yet in many cases, little attention is paid to the limitations that the scales of measurement being used might place on the conclusions which can be drawn from them. Scales may to some degree be arbitrary, involving choices about zero-points or units or the like. It would be unwise to make decisions which could turn out differently if the arbitrary choice of zero-point or unit is changed in some 'admissible' way. We shall be interested in exploring the extent to which this can happen, and to lay down guidelines for what conclusions based on scales of measurement are allowable. These guidelines have implications for many applications of operations research. It is our main purpose to make our readers aware of the need for such guidelines. We hope that the readers will be influenced to the point that they will not want to use scales of measurement without thinking about whether or not the use of those scales leads to meaningful conclusions.

While this chapter will provide guidance on the types of conclusions which can be drawn from scales of measurement, it will not provide guidance for determining whether a scale of measurement is appropriate for the applied problem in question. The chapter will emphasize the mathematical form acceptable conclusions can take or that scales can take if we want to be able to make certain kinds of assertions from them. The approach presented will tell us, for example, whether or not it is appropriate to compare the arithmetic means of two given sets of performance scores. However, it will not tell us if the performance scores are measuring the right thing. The latter is something that is more appropriately left to a particular applied context.

The literature of measurement theory shows how much our confidence in conclusions can or should depend on the properties of the scales of measurement used to derive those conclusions. We start by giving some examples to illustrate this point. In many practical problems we are searching for an optimal solution. However, little attention is paid to the possibility that the conclusion that a particular solution is optimal might be an accident of the way that things are measured. For instance, many optimization problems can be formulated as linear programming problems. Yet, as we point out in Sections 9.1 and 9.2, the conclusion that z is an optimal solution in a linear programming problem can depend on the arbitrary choice of some parameters. For instance, if the cost parameters are measured on an *interval scale*, a scale which (like temperature) is unique up to specification of a unit and of a zero-point, the conclusion that z is optimal can be true with one choice of these parameters and false with another. Below, we shall say that in this case the conclusion of optimality is *meaningless*. To make a similar point, we note that many practical problems can be formulated as problems of quadratic optimization. In quadratic optimization, we maximize or minimize a quadratic polynomial function of some independent variables. These variables are often measured using a *ratio scale*, a scale which (like time or length) is unique up to specification of a unit. However, we point out in Section 9.2 that the conclusion that alternative z is optimal can be meaningless in quadratic optimization over ratio scales. A systematic study of the limitations that scale types impose on the meaningfulness of conclusions about optimization is called for. Roberts [1990a] gives a very elementary beginning to such a study. We return to this subject in greater detail in Section 9.

To give a second example, suppose different 'experts' are asked to give their judgements of the relative value or importance or potential of different alternatives, e.g., alternative strategies, alternative new technologies, alternative diagnoses, etc. Suppose the choice of alternative will depend on the 'average' of the experts' judgements, with the alternative having the highest average being chosen. If all the experts use a ratio scale, i.e., if only their units change, then which alternative has the highest *arithmetic mean* depends on the choice of these units (if they can be chosen independently). However, the alternative with the highest *geometric mean* is invariant. Thus, it is 'safer' to use the geometric mean. We shall demonstrate these observations in Section 5.1. The observation that the use of the geometric mean in averaging problems is often 'safer' than the use of the arithmetic mean has been part of the 'folklore' of scaling for a long time. However, Aczél & Roberts [1989] have recently put this on a firm mathematical foundation by showing that under certain reasonable assumptions about the averaging or merging procedure, it is not only the case that the arithmetic mean is unacceptable and that the geometric mean is acceptable, but that the geometric mean is the *only* averaging procedure which is acceptable. On the other hand, Aczél and Roberts identify other situations in which other averaging procedures are acceptable and the geometric mean is not. Similar averaging problems arise when we study the performance of a new technology such as a computer system or a communications system, or of a person such as a student or a job applicant, and we measure or score this performance on a number of different benchmarks and then merge the score into one overall score. They also arise when we study economic phenomena, and we take individual measurements, such as prices of different commodities, and then seek to merge or combine these individual measurements into one overall measure or index number. They also arise in decision support systems, when we rate the value of alternative solution strategies on the basis of several criteria and then choose a strategy by using some combined or merged rating. The work of Aczél & Roberts is part of a systematic attempt to identify different acceptable averaging procedures in different situations. We return to it and to related work in Section 5. Specifically, we discuss importance ratings and arithmetic means in Section 5.1 and index numbers (for consumer price, consumer confidence, and pollution) in Section 5.2. In Sections 5.3 through 5.6, we formulate the general problem of identifying different acceptable averaging procedures and describe various attempts to solve it. In Section 5.7, we summarize some basic guidelines for how to find appropriate averaging procedures. These guidelines apply more generally to many of the topics discussed in this chapter and provide a good summary of the spirit of the approach we will be developing in the chapter.

To give a third example, we note that in comparing the performance of alternative technologies such as new computer systems or new communications systems, we often measure or score the performance of each candidate technology on different benchmarks. We then normalize relative to the scores of one of the technologies and find some average or aggregate or merged overall score based on these normalized or *relative scores*. Fleming & Wallace [1986] make a point that is very similar to the one we have made in the previous paragraph. They point out (using real data from performance analysis of computer systems) that the widely used procedure of taking arithmetic means of these relative scores can lead to inappropriate statistics and misleading conclusions because the alternative having highest arithmetic mean relative score can depend on the choice of alternative used as the basis for the normalization. They argue that the geometric mean is the more appropriate averaging procedure to use. We discuss the Fleming–Wallace example in Section 6. Roberts [1990b] considers the general question of how to merge or average or aggregate relative performance scores into one overall score. Developing several invariance criteria, Roberts identifies the possible averaging procedures which are appropriate under the various criteria, under several reasonable assumptions. Aczél [1990] solves some of the open problems posed by Roberts [1990b] and extends the theory. The results of Fleming & Wallace, of Roberts, and of Aczél have applications to other problems as well as to choices of alternative technologies. For instance, the same problems arise if we are measuring the performance of alternative heuristics for solving the searching problems which 'intelligent' computational systems will have to solve [cf. Gaschnig, 1979] and we normalize relative to the scores of a particular heuristic. They also arise if we are measuring performance of different candidates for a job or of different students, we give them a battery of tests, and we normalize scores relative to those of a particular candidate. They also arise in the theory of index numbers, such as price indices or reliability indices, when we normalize relative to prices or reliabilities at a given time.

To give a fourth example, let us note that models which are used to solve decisionmaking problems often use subjective judgements, and one would like to know to what extent the conclusions based on such models are independent of arbitrary or accidental properties of the scales underlying these judgements. As a case in point, consider the structural models which are based on weighted digraphs or cross-impact matrices and are used to study problems of energy, transportation, technology assessment, health care delivery, water resources, personnel planning, communications, etc. These models play a central role in the 'computer-assisted analysis' of Greenberg & Maybee [1981] and play an important role in 'learning' to solve problems [Warfield, 1981]. (See Linstone [1978], Linstone, Lendaris, Rogers, Wakeland & Williams [1979], Roberts [1976, 1978], and Tanny & Zuker [1987, 1988] for surveys of applications). Typical conclusions from such models are that some variables will grow without bound; such conclusions are sometimes called *value instability*. Roberts [1979b] studies conclusions from structural modelling and considers their meaningfulness in the sense of the term introduced in our first example. He shows that the conclusion of value stability under a pulse process (a particular kind of structural model) is meaningful if all of the subjectively determined variables are measured on interval scales, but not if some of these variables are measured on *ordinal scales*, scales which (like hardness) are unique only up to order. We return to this and similar points in Section 8.

In this chapter, we present a variety of results and guidelines about the extent to which properties of scales of measurement place limitations on conclusions using such scales, limitations of the sorts illustrated by these four examples.

To understand the issues we have raised requires a fundamental understanding of the properties of scales of measurement and of the sensitivity of conclusions based on scales to changes in those scales. We shall take the point of view about measurement described in the books by Krantz, Luce, Suppes & Tversky [1971], Pfanzagl [1968], Fishburn [1970, 1988], Roberts [1979a], Narens [1985], Suppes, Krantz, Luce & Tversky [1989], and Luce, Krantz, Suppes & Tversky [1990]. In Section 2, we provide some background on this point of view about measurement. There are certainly other points of view about measurement. Some alternative points of view are summarized in Mitchell [1986, 1990]. In Section 3 we start with some very simple examples of meaningful and meaningless statements. Section 4 is devoted to descriptive statistics such as the arithmetic and geometric means above. In Section 5, we discuss the possible merging functions, as mentioned in our second example. As we noted earlier, the basic guidelines for how to find appropriate merging functions, summarized in Section 5.7, apply more generally to many of the topics discussed in this chapter and provide a good summary of the spirit of the approach we will be developing. Section 6 discusses merging relative scores, as mentioned in our third example. In Section 7, we explore the extent to which restrictions placed on descriptive statistics have analogues for inferential statistics, i.e., we ask to what extent the properties of scales of measurement used influence the meaningfulness of conclusions from statistical tests. Section 8 is devoted to structural modelling, as discussed in our fourth example, and Section 9 to optimization, as discussed in our first example. In Section 10, we discuss the implications of limitations on conclusions obtained from scales in the clustering and blockmodelling methods widely used in operations research. Section 11 is devoted to attempts to elicit expressions of preference and indifference and to calculate utility functions. In Section 12, we discuss the measurement of loudness and other related problems of psychophysical scaling, mention their significance in such operations research applications as measurement of noise near airports and buildings, and then discuss the limitations the theory described might place on the general forms attainable in scientific laws. Section 13 has concluding remarks.

2. Background: The theory of measurement

Our approach to scales of measurement is based on the notion, going back to Stevens [1946, 1951, 1959], that the properties of a scale are captured by studying *admissible transformations*, transformations that lead from one acceptable scale to another. Assuming that a scale assigns a real number to the object being measured, we call a scale a *ratio scale* if the admissible transformations are of the form $\varphi(x) = \alpha x, \alpha > 0$, an *interval scale* if the admissible transformations are of the form $\varphi(x) = \alpha x + \beta, \alpha > 0$, and an *ordinal scale* if the admissible transformations are the (strictly) monotone increasing transformations. For definitions of other scale types, see Roberts [1979a]. Thus, in the case of ratio scales, the scale value is determined up to choice of a unit; in the case of interval scales, it is determined up to choices of unit and of zero point; and in the case of ordinal scales, it is determined only up to order. Mass is an example of a ratio scale. The transformation from kilograms into pounds, for example, involves the admissible transformation $\varphi(x) = 2.2x$. Length (inches, centimeters) and time intervals (years, seconds) are two other examples of ratio scales. Temperature (except where there is an absolute zero) defines an interval scale. Thus, transformation from centigrade into Fahrenheit involves the admissible transformation $\varphi(x) = (9/5)x + 32$. Time on the calendar is another example of an interval scale (to say that this happened in the year 1992 involves not only a choice of unit but a choice of the zero year). An example of an ordinal scale is any scale in which we give grades of materials, such as leather, lumber, wool, etc. Expressed preferences sometimes lead only to ordinal scales, if we know our preferences only up to order.

For many scales, the scale type can be determined by showing that the scale arises from a (numerical) representation. In the rest of this paragraph, we say a word or two about how this is done in the theory in such books as Pfanzagl [1968], Krantz, Luce, Suppes & Tversky [1971], and Roberts [1979a], though the details will not be needed for what follows. Specifically, one studies certain *observed relations* on a set of objects of interest, relations such as '*a* is longer than *b*', '*a* is louder than *b*', 'I think the worth of *b* is between the worth of *a* and the worth of *c*', etc. One identifies corresponding *numerical relations*, relations on a set of real numbers, for instance the 'greater than' relation or the 'betweenness' relation. Then one studies mappings which take each object of interest into a number so that objects related in a certain way in an observed relation correspond to numbers related in the same way in the corresponding numerical relation. For example, one seeks to assign numbers to objects so that *a* is judged louder than *b* if and only if the number assigned to *a* is greater than the number assigned to *b*. Such a mapping from objects to numbers is called a *homomorphism* from the observed relation to the numerical relation. In measurement theory, scales are identified with homomorphisms. Formally, an *admissible transformation* of a scale is then a transformation of the numbers assigned so that one gets another homomorphism. For details on how to formalize these ideas, see Roberts [1979a].

(An alternative approach to defining an admissible transformation of scale, again one which we do not need in what follows, is to simply consider the numerical relations corresponding to the observed relations. Then one thinks of admissible transformations as transformations on the numbers so that numbers standing in a given numerical relation are transformed into other numbers standing in that numerical relation. Such transformations are called *automorphisms* of the 'image' numerical relational system. Related to this idea are the approaches to scale type of such authors as Alper [1985, 1987], Luce [1986, 1987], Luce & Narens [1983, 1984, 1985, 1986, 1987], Narens [1981a,b], and Roberts & Rosenbaum [1985, 1988]. Luce & Narens [1984, 1986, 1987] and Roberts [1989b] are expository papers, and Luce, Krantz, Suppes & Tversky [1990] contains a good summary of this work.)

It should be remarked that many scales based on subjective judgements cannot be derived from a (numerical) representation (or formalized as automorphisms of a relational system). Then, we must use the principle that the admissible transformations are those which preserve the information carried by the scale. Knapp [1990] and Thomas [1985] emphasize the difficulties involved in identifying scale type. As Stevens [1968] argues, it is often a matter of empirical judgement to determine the admissible transformations and hence the scale type. Sometimes the admissible transformations can be described on the basis of some procedure which is used in the gathering of data. Knapp [1990] gives advice on how to identify scale type using empirical methods. He suggests that you ask such questions as: Is there anything in the raw score scale that resembles a unit of measurement? If you get an answer of '3', can you ask the question '3 what?'. Is there a zero point? How arbitrary is that point? Are order-preserving transformations of scale acceptable? How about linear transformations $\varphi(x) = \alpha x + \beta, \alpha > 0$? Are any transformations acceptable? To this advice we could add the comment that if the scale type is not known, the conclusions should be analyzed under several different possible scale type assumptions and perhaps the most conservative assumption of all should be used. To summarize the situation: The place where the analysis in this chapter is most vulnerable is in the need to know what kind of scale you have in order to use this analysis.

One of the goals of research in the theory of measurement is to develop a collection of tools which can be used to determine what assertions can meaningfully be made and what conclusions can meaningfully be drawn, using scales of measurement. A statement involving scales of measurement is called *meaningful* if its truth value is unchanged whenever every scale in the statement is modified by an admissible transformation. This definition goes back to Suppes [1959] and Suppes & Zinnes [1963]. (While it is not mentioned explicitly in the work of Stevens, it is inherent in his treatment of admissible transformations; see Mundy [1986].) For example, the statement 'I am older than my son' is true, independent of which admissible transformations are applied to the way I measure age, and hence is meaningful. Similarly, the statement 'I weigh more than my car' is false, independent of which admissible transformations are applied to the scale I use to measure weight, and hence it is meaningful. The notion of meaningfulness is concerned with which assertions it makes sense to make, and which ones are just artifacts of the particular version of the scale of measurement that happens to be in use. This notion of meaningfulness is closely related to the concept of invariance in classical geometry. See Falmagne & Narens [1983], Narens [1988], and Luce, Krantz, Suppes & Tversky [1990]. Roberts & Franke [1976] point out that the definition of meaningfulness needs to be modified if the scales of measurement arise from so-called *irregular representations*, ones in which not every acceptable scale can be obtained from another acceptable scale by an admissible transformation. We give an example of such a situation in Section 11. In the case of irregular scales, we need to modify the definition to the following more general form: A statement involving scales of measurement is *meaningful* if its truth value is unchanged whenever every scale is replaced by another acceptable scale. For general discussions of the concept of meaningfulness and its wide variety of applications, see Luce, Krantz, Suppes & Tversky [1990, Chapter 22] and Roberts [1985].

The definitions we have given are reasonably well accepted, at least to the extent that it is widely agreed that 'invariance' is a desirable condition and that it is implied by 'meaningfulness'. Not everyone likes the term meaningfulness. Mitchell [1986], for example, argues that the very term encourages us to disregard meaningless statements, when in fact there are occasions when we should not. Others, for example Falmagne & Narens [1983], argue that the general definition is somewhat imprecise. For instance, it is not always clear what we mean by a 'statement involving scales'. There have been a variety of alternative formulations of the definition. Other definitions can be found in Adams, Fagot & Robinson [1965], Falmagne & Narens [1983], Luce [1978], Luce, Krantz, Suppes & Tversky [1990], Mundy [1986], Narens [1981a], Pfanzagl [1968], Roberts [1979a, 1980], Roberts & Franke [1976], and Robinson [1963]. In certain situations, in particular if a statement involves 'dimensional constants' which enter into scales and which change with changes of scale, the definition we have given certainly needs to be modified. Examples of dimensional constants given by Luce [1962] are the velocity of light, the density of a substance, the viscosity of a fluid, and the gravitational constant. These are adjusted with changes of scale. For instance, Luce gives the example of the law of radioactive decay, $q = q_0 e^{-kt}$, where t is the time elapsed since some event, q is the quantity of a material at time t, q_0 is the quantity at time 0, and k is a constant. This constant k is a dimensional constant. If for a particular material it is 0.14 if time is measured in seconds, then for that material it is 504 = 0.14(3600) if time is measured in hours. In this chapter, we shall disregard complications such as those introduced by dimensional constants and adopt the rather informal definition of meaningfulness we have given in this section. The only complication we shall not entirely disregard is that which arises when we have irregular scales.

3. Some simple examples of meaningful and meaningless statements

Since the concept of meaningfulness will play such a central role here, let us illustrate it with some simple examples. Consider the statement that project a will take three times as long to complete as project b. This is the statement that

$$f(a) = 3f(b), \tag{1}$$

where f is a scale measuring completion time. This statement is meaningful since f is a ratio scale. To see why, note that (1) is meaningful provided it holds if and only if

$$\varphi[f(a)] = 3\varphi[f(b)]. \tag{2}$$

Since admissible transformations are of the form $\varphi(x) = \alpha x, \alpha > 0$, (2) is just the statement

$$\alpha f(a) = 3\alpha f(b), \tag{3}$$

and (1) holds if and only if (3) holds since $\alpha > 0$. We conclude that (1) is meaningful. In general, for ratio scales, it is meaningful (as here) to compare ratios, i.e., to say that

$$f(a)/f(b) > f(c)/f(d).$$

For interval scales, however, this is not meaningful. For instance, it is easy to find α and β so that (1) holds but

$$\alpha f(a) + \beta = 3[\alpha f(b) + \beta] \tag{4}$$

fails. For instance, it is quite possible that the temperature of a is three times the temperature of b when measured in centigrade, but not when measured in Fahrenheit. For interval scales, it is easy to see that it is meaningful to compare intervals, i.e., it is meaningful to say that

$$f(a) - f(b) > f(c) - f(d). \tag{5}$$

For ordinal scales, it is meaningful to compare size, i.e., to say that

$$f(a) > f(b). \tag{6}$$

Incidentally, it is meaningful to say that I am 500 times as tall as the World Trade Center. This is because the statement is false no matter how I measure height, height being a ratio scale. Meaningfulness is not the same as truth. As we have said before, it has to do with what kinds of assertions it makes sense to make, which assertions are not accidents of the particular choice of scales (of units, zero points, etc.) in use.

4. Descriptive statistics

Let us discuss an example which is a bit more subtle than the simple examples of the previous section. Suppose that we study two groups of individuals under different experimental conditions. Let $f(a)$ be a measure of the performance of individual a and suppose for concreteness that $f(a)$ is the weight of the output produced by individual a in some task. Suppose that data suggests that the average performance of individuals in the first group is better than the average performance of individuals in the second group. It this a meaningful conclusion? Suppose that $a_1, a_2, \ldots, a_n$ are the individuals in the first group and $b_1, b_2, \ldots, b_m$ the individuals in the second group. (Note that m could be different from n.) Then we are (probably) asserting that

$$\frac{1}{n} \sum_{i=1}^{n} f(a_i) > \frac{1}{m} \sum_{i=1}^{m} f(b_i). \tag{7}$$

We are comparing arithmetic means. The statement (7) is meaningful if and only if under admissible transformation φ, (7) holds if and only if

$$\frac{1}{n} \sum_{i=1}^{n} \varphi[f(a_i)] > \frac{1}{m} \sum_{i=1}^{m} \varphi[f(b_i)] \tag{8}$$

holds. Now the weight of the output defines a ratio scale. Hence (8) is the same as

$$\frac{1}{n} \sum_{i=1}^{n} \alpha f(a_i) > \frac{1}{m} \sum_{i=1}^{m} \alpha f(b_i), \tag{9}$$

for some positive α. Certainly (7) holds if and only if (9) does, so (7) is meaningful.

Note that (7) is still meaningful if f is an interval scale. For instance, suppose the task is to heat something and a measure of performance is not the weight of the output but instead the temperature increase produced. It is still meaningful to assert that the average performance of the first group is higher than the average performance of the second group. To see why, note that (7) is equivalent to

$$\frac{1}{n} \sum_{i=1}^{n} [\alpha f(a_i) + \beta] > \frac{1}{m} \sum_{i=1}^{m} [\alpha f(b_i) + \beta], \tag{10}$$

where $\alpha > 0$.

However, (7) is easily seen to be meaningless if f is just an ordinal scale. To see that the latter holds, suppose $f(a)$ is measured on the common 5-point scale where 5 = excellent, 4 = very good, 3 = good, 2 = fair, 1 = poor. In such a scale, the numbers do not mean anything; only their order matters. Suppose that group 1 has three members with scores of 4 each, while group 2 has three members with scores of 5, 4, and 1. Then the average score in group 1 is 4 and this is higher than the average score in group 2, which is 3.33. On the other hand, suppose we consider the admissible transformation φ defined by $\varphi(5) = 200$, $\varphi(4) = 100$, $\varphi(3) = 50$, $\varphi(2) = 20$, $\varphi(1) = 3$. Then after transformation, each member of group 1 has a score of 100, for an average of 100, while the scores in group 2 are 200, 100, and 3, for an average of 101, which is higher. Which group had a higher average score? The answer clearly depends on which version of the scale is used. Of course, one can argue against this kind of example. As Suppes [1979] remarks in the case of a similar example having to do with grading apples in four ordered categories, 'surely there is something quite unnatural about this transformation' φ. He suggests that 'there is a strong natural tendency to treat the ordered categories as being equally spaced'. However, if we require this, then the scale is not an ordinal scale according to our definition. Not every strictly monotone increasing transformation is admissible. Moreover, there is no reason, given the nature of the categories, to feel that this is demanded in our example. In any case, the argument is not with the precept that we have stated, but with the question of whether the 5-point scale we have given is indeed an ordinal scale as we have defined it. To complete this example, let us simply remark that comparison of medians rather than arithmetic means is meaningful with ordinal scales: The statement that one group has a higher median than another group is preserved under admissible transformation.

The kinds of conclusions we have described in this section stem from the basic work of Stevens [1946, 1951, 1959, and elsewhere], who developed the classification of scales of measurement that we have been discussing and then provided guidelines about the kinds of descriptive statistics which are 'appropriate' for different kinds of scales. Ideas going back to Stevens, such as the one that arithmetic means are appropriate statistics for ratio and interval scales, but not for ordinal scales, for which medians are appropriate statistics, were developed and popularized by Siegel [1956] in his well-known book *Nonparametric Statistics*. They have become rather widely accepted. Siegel and others have attempted to apply Stevens' approach not only to descriptive statistics, but also to inferential statistics. Here, there is considerable disagreement, which we discuss in some detail in Section 7. However, even for descriptive statistics, the Stevens–Siegel approach is not without its critics.

For instance, in a well-known satirical article, Frederic Lord [1953] gave the example of the Freshman football players who discover that the average of the numbers on their uniforms is smaller than the average of the numbers on the uniforms of the other players. They go to complain and are told by the person assigning the numbers that they should not worry: Since assignment of numbers is not a ratio or an interval scale, but only a scale where any one to one transformation is admissible, one cannot take an arithmetic mean of the numbers. However, the number assigner has self-doubts and consults a statistician. The statistician simply averages the numbers, to the assigner's dismay, and then shows that the probability of obtaining such a low average would be very small indeed had the assignment of numbers been made randomly. At the assigner's protestation, the statistician argues that we should always be able to average the numbers, for after all, 'the numbers don't remember where they came from'. How does one resolve this conflict? A natural resolution seems to be the following. It is *always* appropriate to calculate means, medians, and other descriptive statistics.

However, it may not always be appropriate to make certain statements using these statistics. In particular, it is appropriate to make a statement using descriptive statistics only if the statement is meaningful. A statement which is true but meaningless gives information which is an accident of the scale of measurement used, not information which describes the population in some fundamental way. Hence, it is appropriate to calculate the mean of ordinal data, it just is not appropriate to say that the mean of one group is higher than the mean of another group. In the case of the football players, if indeed any one to one transformation is admissible, it is meaningless to assert that the mean of one group is higher than the mean of another. However, one can still meaningfully say that the probability of obtaining a particular mean is very small. For more on this topic, see Marcus-Roberts & Roberts [1987]. Other interesting papers and books on the subject are Knapp [1990], Mitchell [1986, 1990], Stine [1989], and Townsend & Ashby [1984], to name just a few. We give more references in Section 7.

5. The possible merging functions

5.1. Importance ratings and arithmetic means

Let us consider a variant of the example given in Section 4. Suppose that each of n different experts is asked to rate each of a collection alternatives as to its importance, value, significance, loudness, ... Let $f_i(a)$ be the rating of alternative a by expert i. Is it meaningful to assert that the average rating of alternative a is higher than the average rating of alternative b? We are now considering the statement

$$\frac{1}{n}\sum_{i=1}^{n} f_i(a) > \frac{1}{n}\sum_{i=1}^{n} f_i(b). \tag{11}$$

Note in contrast to statement (7) that we have the same number of terms in each sum and that the subscript is now on the scale value f rather than on the alternative a or b. If each f_i is a ratio scale, we then ask whether or not (11) is equivalent to

$$\frac{1}{n}\sum_{i=1}^{n} \alpha f_i(a) > \frac{1}{n}\sum_{i=1}^{n} \alpha f_i(b), \tag{12}$$

$\alpha > 0$. This is clearly the case.

However, we have perhaps gone too quickly. What if $f_1, f_2, \ldots, f_n$ have independent units? In this case, we want to allow independent admissible transformations of the f_i. Thus, we must consider

$$\frac{1}{n}\sum_{i=1}^{n} \alpha_i f_i(a) > \frac{1}{n}\sum_{i=1}^{n} \alpha_i f_i(b), \tag{13}$$

all $\alpha_i > 0$. It is easy to find α_i's for which (11) holds but (13) fails. Thus, (11) is meaningless. Does it make sense to consider different α_i? It certainly does in some contexts. For instance, suppose the alternatives are different arrangements for access to a central computing facility. Suppose that the first expert measures the value of the arrangement in terms of the amount of storage space provided and the second measures it in terms of the amount of computer time provided. Then (11) says that the average of a's storage space and time is greater than the average of b's storage space and time. This could be true with one combination of space and time, but false with another. A similar example would be the case if alternatives are animals and one expert measures their improved health in terms of their weight gain while a second measures it in terms of their height gain.

The conclusion is that we need to be careful when comparing arithmetic mean ratings, even when we are using ratio scales. Norman Dalkey [1969] was the first person to point out to the author that in many cases, it is safer to use geometric means, a conclusion which by now is 'folklore'. For consider the comparison

$$\sqrt[n]{\prod_{i=1}^{n} f_i(a)} > \sqrt[n]{\prod_{i=1}^{n} f_i(b)}. \tag{14}$$

If all $\alpha_i > 0$, then (14) holds if and only if

$$\sqrt[n]{\prod_{i=1}^{n} \alpha_i f_i(a)} > \sqrt[n]{\prod_{i=1}^{n} \alpha_i f_i(b)}. \tag{15}$$

Thus, if each f_i is a ratio scale, then even if experts change the units of their rating scales independently, the comparison of geometric means is meaningful even though the comparison of arithmetic means is not. An example of an application of this observation is the use of the geometric mean by Roberts [1972, 1973]. The problem arose in a study of energy use in commuter transportation. A preliminary step in the model building involved the choice of most important variables to consider in the model. Each member of a panel of experts estimated the relative importance of variables using a procedure called magnitude estimation. There is a strong body of opinion that magnitude estimation leads to a ratio scale, much of it going back to Stevens [see the discussion in Roberts, 1979a, pp. 179–180]. There is even some theoretical evidence [see Krantz, 1972; Luce, 1990; Shepard, 1978, 1981]. How then should we choose the most important variables? By the discussion above, it is 'safer' to combine the experts' importance ratings by using geometric means and then to choose the most important variables as those having the highest geometric mean relative importance ratings, than it is to do this by using arithmetic means. That is why Roberts [1972, 1973] used geometric means.

5.2. Index numbers: Indices of consumer price, consumer confidence, pollution

The discussion above is relevant to the computation of index numbers such as consumer price indices, indices of consumer confidence or productivity, pollution indices, etc. (Here we follow Roberts [1979a, Section 2.6] and Roberts [1985].) For instance, consider the consumer price index. Our discussion here is based on that in Fisher [1923, p. 40], Pfanzagl [1968, p. 49], and Roberts [1979a, Section 2.6.2]. Suppose the consumer price index is based on n fixed commodities and let $p_i(t)$ be the price of commodity i at time t, with $t = 0$ being some reference time. The Bradstreet–Dutot consumer price index is given by

$$I(t) = I[p_1(t), p_2(t), \ldots, p_n(t)] = \sum_{i=1}^{n} p_i(t) \Big/ \sum_{i=1}^{n} p_i(0). \tag{16}$$

Variants on this index might have different commodities weighted differently, using weighting factors λ_i, giving for instance

$$K(t) = K[p_1(t), p_2(t), \ldots, p_n(t)] = \sum_{i=1}^{n} \lambda_i p_i(t) \Big/ \sum_{i=1}^{n} \lambda_i p_i(0). \tag{17}$$

$K(t)$ is called the Laspeyres index, after Laspeyres [1871]. However, the Bradstreet–Dutot index will suffice to make the points we wish to make at first. Prices are measured in dollars, cents, pounds, yen, etc., and so define ratio scales. If we can change the unit of each price independently, then an analysis like that of the previous section shows that it is even meaningless to say that the consumer price index increased in the past year, i.e., that $I(t+1) > I(t)$. However, if all prices are measured in the same units, then it is easy to see that it is even meaningful to say, for example, that the consumer price index went up by $r\%$ in one year, for it is meaningful to say that $I(t+1) = (1 + r/100)I(t)$. A consumer price index for which comparisons of size are meaningful even if we measure different prices in different units is the index

$$J[p_1(t), p_2(t), \ldots, p_n(t)] = \left[\prod_{i=1}^{n} p_i(t) \Big/ \prod_{i=1}^{n} p_i(0) \right]^{1/n},$$

which is related to the geometric mean and is discussed in Boot & Cox [1970, p. 499]. Of course, it is not sufficient that comparisons of the type we would like to make be meaningful in the sense we have defined. We must also insist that an index number such as this one be meaningful in an economic sense. The judgement of whether this is meaningful in an economic sense is not something that measurement theory can answer, and is best left to experts in the applications area.

A closely related index number is the index of consumer confidence. Suppose we identify n variables which are relevant to consumer confidence and $p_i(t)$ is some measure of attitude toward variable i at time t. Then we can use a measure such as $I(t)$ of Equation (16) or $K(t)$ of Equation (17) to measure consumer confidence. In one study of consumer confidence, Pickering, Harrison & Cohen [1973] identified 23 variables and measured attitude toward variable i by using a 7-point 'semantic differential' scale, using the numbers 1 to 7. Then $p_i(t)$ was obtained by averaging the answers given by individuals in a poll. Of course, if the 7-point semantic differential scale is an ordinal scale (much like the 5-point scale discussed in Section 4), then it is even meaningless to assert that $p_i(t+1) > p_i(t)$. However, let us disregard that point. Pickering, Harrison & Cohen used the Laspeyres index $K(t)$ as their index of consumer confidence, where the weights λ_i were determined using a principal components analysis. Unfortunately, it is easy to show that the statement that $K(t+1) > K(t)$ is meaningless here, assuming that averaging ordinal scales gives no more than an ordinal scale. So not even comparisons of size of consumer confidence can be made in this situation, let alone statements to the effect that the consumer confidence increased by a certain percentage.

Still a third example of an index number is a pollution index. A typical question here is: How would one measure with one index number the quality of the air if there are different pollutants present? A simple way of producing a single, combined pollution index is to measure the total weight of emissions of each pollutant (say over a fixed time period) and then to sum up these weights. Suppose that we let $p_i(t, k)$ be the total weight of emissions of the ith pollutant in the tth time period due to the kth source. Then our pollution index is simply

$$I(t, k) = \sum_{i=1}^{n} p_i(t, k),$$

if there are n pollutants under consideration. Using this measure, Walther [1972] reaches such conclusions as: The largest source of air pollution is transportation and the second largest is stationary fuel combustion. These conclusions are meaningful if we measure all $p_i(t, k)$ in the same units of mass, since they are just statements like

$$I(t, k) > I(t, k').$$

However, although this is meaningful in the technical sense, we have to ask whether $I(t, k)$ is a reasonable measure. Since a unit of mass of carbon monoxide, for example, is far less harmful than a unit of mass of nitrogen oxide [cf. Babcock & Nagda, 1973], we might wish to consider weighting factors λ_i which weight the effect of the ith pollutant and then using a weighted sum

$$\sum_{i=1}^{n} \lambda_i p_i(t, k).$$

(This conclusion is not one to which the methods of this chapter would lead.) Such a weighted sum, sometimes known as *pindex*, has been used as a combined pollution index. (Early attempts at determining appropriate weighting factors λ_i can be found in Babcock & Nagda [1973], Babcock [1970], Walther [1972], and Caretto & Sawyer [1972].) Using pindex, Walther [1972] argues that transportation is still the largest source of pollution. However, stationary sources are now fourth. Again, this conclusion is meaningful if we use the same units of mass in each case. In early uses of this measure in the San Francisco Bay Area (see Bay Area Pollution Control District [1968] or Sauter & Chilton [1970]) and elsewhere, λ_i

is the reciprocal of the amount of emissions in a given period of time needed to reach a certain danger level. With these weighting factors, although comparisons using pindex are meaningful in our technical sense, the index does not seem to give meaningful numbers in any real sense. For reaching 100% of the danger level in one pollutant would give the same pindex value as reaching 20% of the danger level on each of five pollutants. (Again, this conclusion is not one to which the methods of this chapter have led.) In conclusion, we should stress again that there is a distinction between meaningfulness in the technical sense, which is the sense we are stressing in this chapter, and meaningfulness in other senses.

5.3. *The possible merging functions*

The problem of whether to use arithmetic mean, geometric mean, median, or some other method of combining judgements can be stated much more generally than it has been stated so far. As we pointed out in Section 1, in many choice situations, we obtain a number of individual measurements and then combine them by some merging or averaging or aggregation or consensus procedure. As we noted, this is the case with expert judgements, measures of the performance of a new technology, decision support systems, index numbers for economic phenomena, etc. Here we shall ask the general question: What merging procedures are appropriate in different situations?

Suppose A is a set of objects or alternatives or individuals about which we have obtained different measurements. Say $f_i(a)$ is the score of $a \in A$ by the ith procedure, $i = 1, 2, \ldots, n$. This could be the ith individual's judgement of the importance or quality or value of a, it could be a measure of the performance of a on the ith benchmark, it could be the price of the ith commodity at time a, and so on. Then we can think of each f_i as a function defined on the set A. In much of the literature, the function has been thought of as having as its range an appropriate subset R_i of the set of real numbers $\mathbb{R}$ (or of the set of positive real numbers $\mathbb{R}^+$). We seek a new function u on A, which depends on the functions $f_1, f_2, \ldots, f_n$, and which is the result of merging the individual judgement functions. We denote this new function by $u(f_1, f_2, \ldots, f_n)$. It is natural to assume that $u(f_1, f_2, \ldots, f_n)(a) = u[f_1(a), f_2(a), \ldots, f_n(a)]$, and we shall do so. Is there some systematic way in which we can determine the functions which are legitimate candidates for u? We shall seek to answer this question in the rest of Section 5. The question has been asked in other forms by various authors. For instance, Aczél & Saaty [1983], Aczél [1984], and Aczél & Alsina [1986] seek reasonable assumptions which determine the geometric mean as a merging or 'synthesizing' function or determine the synthesizing function as a member of a family of functions which contains the geometric mean.

5.4. *Luce's method*

In a foundational paper, Luce [1959] observed that the general form of the functional relationship between variables is greatly restricted if we know the *scale type* of the dependent and independent variables, where the scale type is defined by the class of admissible transformations. The restrictions are discovered by formulating a functional equation from knowledge of these admissible transformations. Solution of this equation then gives the set of allowable functional relationships. In Luce's case, the functional relationship of primary interest was the psychophysical function which relates a physical variable to a psychological one. We discuss this in more detail in Section 12 when we discuss the measurement of loudness. In our case, the functional relationship being sought is the merging function u. Luce's basic approach has been formulated, critiqued, extended, and clarified in Luce [1962, 1964, 1990], Rozeboom [1962a,b], Osborne [1970], Roberts & Rosenbaum [1986], Aczél, Roberts & Rosenbaum [1986], Kim [1990] and Aczél & Roberts [1989]. In particular, it seems to be well accepted that the method does not apply in general if there are 'dimensional constants' which enter the function u and cancel out the effects of transformations.

Luce's method is based on the principle, called the *principle of theory construction*, that an admissible transformation of the independent variable should lead to an admissible transformation of the dependent variable. Luce no longer refers to this as a 'principle' and, following criticisms of Rozeboom [1962a,b], points out [e.g., Luce, 1962] that it is not universally applicable. Luce [1985] now argues that this should not be an assumption, but it should be derived from deeper principles of theory construction. Attempts in this direction, at least for the related concept of dimensional invariance, are described in Krantz, Luce, Suppes & Tversky [1971, Chapter 10], Luce [1978], and Luce, Krantz, Suppes & Tversky [1990, Chapter 22].

To illustrate Luce's method, let us take the simplest situation in which one has one independent variable, $f_1 = f$, and $g(a) = u[f(a)]$. Suppose that both f and g define ratio scales. Applying the principle of theory construction, we observe that multiplying f by a positive constant α (an admissible transformation of a ratio scale) should lead to a multiplication of g by a positive constant $K(\alpha)$ (an admissible transformation). Thus, we derive the function equation

$$u(\alpha x) = K(\alpha)u(x), \qquad \alpha > 0, \qquad K(\alpha) > 0. \tag{18}$$

Luce [1959] then assumes that u is continuous. (The strong assumption of continuity can be replaced by a much weaker assumption, for instance that u is continuous at a point, that u is bounded on a closed real interval, etc. In any of the latter cases, we say that u is *regular*. See Aczél, Roberts & Rosenbaum [1986].) He then shows that all the solutions to Equation (18) are given by the functions of the form

$$u(x) = \gamma x^\delta, \qquad \gamma > 0, \tag{19}$$

for some constants γ, δ. These functions thus describe the only possible merging functions in our simple situation. Thus, in this situation, we know that $g(a)$ must be given by

$$g(a) = \gamma[f(a)]^\delta, \qquad \gamma > 0,$$

and it is only a matter of choosing appropriate constants γ and δ. (Technically, this result requires the assumption that the domain of u is the positive reals and the range is contained in the positive reals, and this in turn implies certain restrictions on the ranges of f and g. See Roberts [1979a] for details. In the rest of this chapter, we shall not be careful about specifying the domain and range under which similar conclusions hold. For precise statements, we refer the reader to the references given in the literature.)

A similar analysis can be applied if $g(a) = u[f(a)]$ and f is a ratio scale and g an interval scale. Then by the principle of theory construction, we derive the functional equation

$$u(\alpha x) = K(\alpha)u(x) + C(\alpha), \qquad \alpha > 0, \qquad K(\alpha) > 0. \tag{20}$$

Again assuming regularity, Luce [1959] obtains the solutions to this functional equation. They are

$$u(x) = \gamma \ln x + \delta \quad \text{or} \quad u(x) = \gamma x^\delta + \lambda. \tag{21}$$

Luce [1959] performs similar analyses in other cases where $n = 1$ and the independent and dependent variables are ratio or interval scales (as well as several other kinds). Luce [1964] extends the results to $n > 1$. Osborne [1970] and Kim [1990] study other scale types such as ordinal scales. Aczél, Roberts & Rosenbaum [1986] study the case $n > 1$, and allow scale transformations of the independent variables to depend upon one another in various ways. We close this section by illustrating one case where $n > 1$.

Suppose that $g(a) = u[f_1(a), f_2(a), \ldots, f_n(a)]$. Suppose that g is a ratio scale and that $f_1, f_2, \ldots, f_n$ are all ratio scales, with the units chosen independently. Then by the principle of theory construction, we get the functional equation

$$u(\alpha_1 x_1, \alpha_2 x_2, \ldots, \alpha_n x_n) = K(\alpha_1, \alpha_2, \ldots, \alpha_n)u(x_1, x_2, \ldots, x_n), \tag{22}$$

$$\alpha_i > 0, \qquad K(\alpha_1, \alpha_2, \ldots, \alpha_n) > 0.$$

Luce [1964] and Mohr [1951] show that if u is regular, then the solutions to (22) are given by

$$u(x_1, x_2, \ldots, x_n) = \gamma x_1^{\delta_1} x_2^{\delta_2} \ldots x_n^{\delta_n}, \qquad \gamma > 0, \tag{23}$$

which has the geometric mean as a special case where $\gamma = 1$ and $\delta_i = 1/n$, for all i. (Luce assumes continuity.) Aczél, Roberts & Rosenbaum [1986] show that without any assumption of regularity, the solutions are given by

$$u(x_1, x_2, \ldots, x_n) = \gamma M_1(x_1)M_2(x_2)\ldots M_n(x_n), \tag{24}$$

where $\gamma > 0$ and each $M_i(x)$ is an arbitrary function satisfying $M_i > 0$ and

$$M_i(xy) = M_i(x)M_i(y). \tag{25}$$

5.5. Replacing scale type with meaningfulness

One of the problems with applying Luce's approach in practice is that one often does not have a complete enumeration (description) of the class of transformations admissible for each variable, at least for the dependent variable. Roberts & Rosenbaum [1986] observe that, while we might not be able to determine or care to specify by assumption the entire class of admissible transformations of the dependent variable, we might eventually want to make certain assertions using the merging function u, and therefore we will want to require that these assertions can be meaningfully made. They observe that, in Luce's method, one can replace an enumeration or description of the class of admissible transformations of the dependent variable by an assumption that certain statements involving that variable are meaningful. Then it is the (presumably) known scale types of the independent variables and the statements which we wish to make using the merged values which determine the possible forms of the merging function.

To illustrate this idea, suppose we consider again the situation where $g(a) = u[f(a)]$. Suppose that we wish to be able to assert, for any $k > 0$, that

$$g(a) = kg(b), \tag{26}$$

equivalently

$$u[f(a)] = ku[f(b)]. \tag{27}$$

(That is the assertion, for instance, that the consumer price index went up by a certain percentage in the past year.) Assume that assertion (26) (equivalently (27)) is meaningful for all $k > 0$ and that f is a ratio scale. Then an admissible transformation of f should preserve the truth value of (26) (equivalently (27)), i.e., we should have

$$u[f(a)] = ku[f(b)] \longleftrightarrow u[\alpha f(a)] = ku[\alpha f(b)],$$

any $\alpha > 0, k > 0$, i.e.,

$$u(x) = ku(y) \longleftrightarrow u(\alpha x) = ku(\alpha y), \tag{28}$$

any $\alpha > 0, k > 0$. From (28) we can show that (18) holds, and so reduce the problem to the one considered by Luce [1959] in the case where f and g are ratio scales.

Analyzing this reasoning, Roberts & Rosenbaum [1986] show that there is a close relationship between scale types of various common kinds on the one hand and meaningfulness of certain statements on the other hand. They show, for instance, that if g is any function from A into a subset of the positive reals, then the statement (26) is meaningful for all $k > 0$ if and only if g is a ratio scale or stronger. (We say that a scale of type S is *stronger than* a scale of type T if the class of admissible transformations of a scale of type S is a proper subset of the class of admissible transformations of a scale of type T.) Combining this observation with Luce's solution (19) to Equation (18), Roberts & Rosenbaum formulate their basic conclusion as follows: Suppose f is a ratio scale and $g(a) = u[f(a)]$. Then the regular functions u making statement (26) meaningful for all $k > 0$ are exactly the functions given by Equation (19).

Similarly, Roberts & Rosenbaum [1986] show that g is an interval scale or stronger if and only if the following two statements are meaningful for all $k > 0$:

$$g(a) - g(b) = k[g(c) - g(d)], \tag{29}$$

$$g(a) > g(b). \tag{30}$$

(Statement (29) is, for instance, the statement that the increase in the consumer price index from year 1991 to year 1992 was twice as large as the increase from year 1981 to year 1982.) Similarly, g is an ordinal scale or stronger if and only if (30) is meaningful. The first result, combined with Luce's solution (21) to Equation (20), leads to the following conclusion: Suppose f is a ratio scale and $g(a) = u[f(a)]$. Then the regular functions u making statements (29) and (30) both meaningful, (29) for all $k > 0$, are exactly the functions given by Equation (21).

The results stated for $n > 1$ in Luce [1964] and Aczél, Roberts & Rosenbaum [1986] can also be formulated in this form, as the latter authors note. For instance, using the Luce [1964] and Mohr [1951] solution to Equation (22) given in Equation (23), we can say the following: Suppose $f_1, f_2, \ldots, f_n$ are ratio scales with independent units and $g(a) = u[f_1(a), f_2(a), \ldots, f_n(a)]$. Then the regular functions u making statement (26) meaningful for all $k > 0$ are exactly the functions given by Equation (23).

5.6. The possible merging functions under additional conditions such as agreement and symmetry

Aczél & Roberts [1989] carry this analysis further. They start with the requirement that certain statements involving the merging function u (based on the merging function u) be meaningful, statements like (26), (29), or (30). They then consider additional elementary assumptions about u which vary according to the application one has in mind. The assumptions they consider are:

> *agreement:* $u(x, x, \ldots, x) = x;$
>
> *symmetry:* $u(x_1, x_2, \ldots, x_n) = u(x_{\sigma(1)}, x_{\sigma(2)}, \ldots, x_{\sigma(n)})$
>   for all permutations σ of $\{1, 2, \ldots, n\}$;

and

> *linear homogeneity:* $u(rx_1, rx_2, \ldots, rx_n) = ru(x_1, x_2, \ldots, x_n),$
>   all $r > 0$.

They show that knowing the scale types of the independent variables, i.e., of the individual scales f_i, and making one or two of these elementary assumptions, then if one requires that certain statements involving u be meaningful, one can severely restrict the possible merging functions. Indeed, they show that in many cases, the merging function must be either the arithmetic mean or the geometric mean.

A sample theorem which illustrates the type of result Aczél & Roberts [1989] obtain is the following: Suppose $f_1, f_2, \ldots, f_n$ are ratio scales with independent units and u is a merging function which satisfies agreement and symmetry. Then it is meaningful to assert, for any $k > 0$, that (26) holds if and only if u is the geometric mean.

To state another result, if we omit the assumption of symmetry in the previous result, but assume that u satisfies some form of regularity (such as boundedness on an open interval), then Aczél & Roberts [1989] show that the only function u making statement (26) meaningful for all $k > 0$ is the weighted geometric mean $u(x_1, x_2, \ldots, x_n) = \prod x_i^{c_i}$, where the c_i are arbitrary constants which sum to 1.

Under different but analogous assumptions, u turns out to be the arithmetic mean. Specifically, suppose that $f_1, f_2, \ldots, f_n$ are interval scales with the same unit but independent zeroes (a very unusual case), and u is a merging function which satisfies agreement and symmetry. Then Aczél & Roberts [1989] show that the only function u making statements (29) and (30) both meaningful, (29) for all $k > 0$, is the arithmetic mean.

5.7. *General guidelines on how to find appropriate merging functions*

Let us summarize how to use the results of this section. The following discussion, appropriately modified, applies more generally to many of the topics discussed in this chapter, and gives a summary of how one might use the ideas of this chapter in practical applications. First, the user must specify the types of scales of the independent variables. This may be routine if the scales measure well-known variables. In some cases, as discussed in Section 2, this is difficult. In Section 2, we gave a few pointers on how to determine scale type in non-routine situations. Second, the user must determine to what extent admissible transformations of the different independent variables are independent. Third, it is necessary to specify the types of assertions the user will want to be able to make with the dependent variable. Fourth, the user will need to decide if the merging function has other special properties such as symmetry or agreement. On the basis of these four decisions, one can, hopefully, derive a general form for the merging function. The general form will have some parameters which will have to be chosen on the basis of the application. This is a little like 'calibrating' a measurement device. Choosing the appropriate parameters may already be difficult even for simple general forms such as the power functions of Equation (19). Sometimes one can develop 'test examples' to help in making the choice. For examples of how this is done, see for example Stevens [1955] in a psychophysical context and Norman & Roberts [1972] in a sociological context; the latter has a whole section on the use of test examples.

6. Merging relative scores

6.1. Choosing a computer system

As we have said in Section 1, in comparing the performance of alternative technologies such as new computer systems, we often measure the performance of each candidate technology on different benchmarks. We then normalize relative to the scores of one of the technologies and find some average or aggregate or merged overall score based on these normalized or relative scores. Fleming & Wallace [1986], using real data from performance analysis of computer systems, point out that if the averaging procedure is the arithmetic mean, then the statement that one system has a higher arithmetic mean normalized score than another system is meaningless in the sense that the system to which scores are normalized can determine which has the higher arithmetic mean. However, if the geometric mean is used, this problem does not arise.

Let us illustrate this point with the Fleming–Wallace example. Suppose that we have three systems, each tested on five benchmarks. Let us suppose that the scores on the tests are given in Table 1. Suppose that all scores are normalized relative to system a, i.e., all entries in the ith row of the table are divided by the entry in the ith row, first column. If we then compute the arithmetic mean of these relative or normalized scores in each column, i.e., for each system, we obtain the arithmetic means $M(a) = 1.00$, $M(b) = 1.01$, $M(c) = 1.07$. For instance, $M(b)$ is calculated as

$$\frac{1}{5}\left(\frac{244}{417} + \frac{70}{83} + \frac{153}{66} + \frac{33527}{39449} + \frac{368}{72}\right)$$

The arithmetic means lead us to choose system c. However, if we normalize all scores relative to system b, i.e., divide by the entries in the second column, then we obtain the arithmetic means $M'(a) = 1.32$, $M'(b) = 1.00$, $M'(c) = 1.08$, which leads us to choose system a. The geometric means of the relative scores in each column are, in the first case, $G(a) = 1.00$, $G(b) = 0.86$, $G(c) = 0.84$, and in the second case, $G'(a) = 1.17$, $G'(b) = 1.00$, $G'(c) = 0.99$. In both cases, we choose system a.

Table 1
Scores of different computer systems on various benchmarks

| | System | | |
Benchmark	a	b	c
1	417	244	134
2	83	70	70
3	66	153	135
4	39 449	33 527	66 000
5	72	368	369

Fleming & Wallace show that under certain assumptions, the geometric mean is the only possible averaging function. Their assumptions are that u satisfies agreement and symmetry (see Section 5.6) and the assumption that the average of the products is the product of the averages:

$$u(x_1 y_1, x_2 y_2, \ldots, x_n y_n) = u(x_1, x_2, \ldots, x_n) u(y_1, y_2, \ldots, y_n).$$

The third assumption is a little difficult to explain or justify and it may be that there are cases when we can argue with symmetry, as for instance when some benchmarks are more important than others. In this section, we consider an alternative approach. Motivated by the discussion in Sections 5.5 and 5.6, where we required that certain assertions be meaningful, we shall think in terms of requiring that certain assertions be invariant.

Before formulating the alternative approach, we mention a contrary idea. Smith [1988] agrees with Fleming & Wallace that relative scores can lead to inconsistencies. However, he questions whether taking the geometric mean of these scores leads to a reasonable performance measure. For instance, in the case where performance is measured as time to complete a computation, the geometric mean relative scores are not proportional to the time consumed when running the different benchmarks. The point, as we have said before, is that meaningfulness in the sense of measurement theory is not the same as meaningfulness in the sense of an application. Smith recommends that normalization be avoided (at least until after the averaging) and then argues that the arithmetic mean of the non-normalized scores is a perfectly reasonable averaging procedure if performance is measured as time to complete a computation. (He concludes that harmonic mean is the preferred averaging procedure if performance is measured as a rate such as mflops, millions of floating point operations per second.) Smith's conclusions are to a large extent based on matters of opinion and the essence of them is that normalization is not a good idea in the first place. However, normalization preceding averaging is a widespread procedure, not just in the choice of alternative technologies such as computer systems but in a variety of other applications, as we noted in Section 1. Hence, it seems worthwhile to try to lay down some guidelines for averaging relative or normalized scores.

In the next section, we consider the general question of how to merge or average or aggregate relative performance scores into one overall score. As we have just observed, we noted in Section 1 that this question arises in a variety of applications other than the choice of an alternative technology such as a computer system. Specifically, the same problems arise if we are measuring the performance of alternative heuristics for solving the searching problems which 'intelligent' computational systems will have to solve and we normalize relative to the scores of a particular heuristic; if we are measuring performance of different candidates for a job or of different students, we give them a battery of tests, and we normalize scores relative to those of a particular candidate; and in the theory of index numbers, such as price indices or reliability indices, when we normalize relative to prices or reliabilities at a given time.

6.2. A general formulation: Invariance conditions

Formally, suppose A is a set of alternatives (times), and $f_i(a)$ is the score of a on the ith benchmark (price at time a of the ith product). We assume that $f_i(a) > 0$. We normalize scores (prices) relative to those of an alternative x (to those at time x). Thus we seek a function u so that $u[f_1(a)/f_1(x), \ldots, f_n(a)/f_n(x)]$ merges the relative scores $f_i(a)/f_i(x)$. Under the assumption (implicit in Fleming & Wallace [1986]) that u is defined on all of $\mathbb{R}_n^+$, the set of n-tuples of positive reals, we call u a *relative merging function* or *RM function* for short.

Treating matters more generally, one can consider even the normalization procedure as subject to derivation. In this case, we consider a function v so that the merged score of a relative to x is given by $v[f_1(a), \ldots, f_n(a), f_1(x), \ldots, f_n(x)]$. Under the assumption that v is defined on all of $\mathbb{R}_{2n}^+$, we call v a *generalized relative merging function* or *GRM function* for short.

It seems reasonable to ask that conclusions drawn from merging relative scores be invariant under change of the alternative (or year) used as the basis for the normalization. The notion of invariance is closely related to the concept of meaningfulness. The types of conclusions we would like to draw from merging relative scores are analogous to those (like (26), (29), and (30)) which we would like to draw using merged scores in general. Invariance of these types of conclusions led Roberts [1990b] to define four invariance conditions. A typical one, *ordinal invariance*, can be defined for a GRM function by the condition

$$v(a_1, \ldots, a_n, x_1, \ldots, x_n) > v(b_1, \ldots, b_n, x_1, \ldots, x_n)$$

$$\longleftrightarrow v(a_1, \ldots, a_n, y_1, \ldots, y_n) > v(b_1, \ldots, b_n, y_1, \ldots, y_n). \tag{31}$$

Similarly, *ratio invariance* holds for v if for all $k > 0$,

$$v(a_1, \ldots, a_n, x_1, \ldots, x_n) = kv(b_1, \ldots, b_n, x_1, \ldots, x_n)$$

$$\longleftrightarrow v(a_1, \ldots, a_n, y_1, \ldots, y_n) = kv(b_1, \ldots, b_n, y_1, \ldots, y_n).$$

In this section, we shall discuss the question: What merging functions satisfy different invariance conditions? Some results along these lines are given by Roberts [1990b] and Aczél [1990]. For instance, Roberts characterizes the *ratio invariant RM functions*. These are exactly the functions of Equation (24), where $\gamma > 0$ and each M_i is an arbitrary function satisfying $M_i(x) > 0$ and Equation (25). If in addition we assume that u is regular, then he notes that it follows that

$$u(x_1, x_2, \ldots, x_n) = \gamma \prod_{i=1}^n x_i^{\delta_i},$$

and this is closely related to the geometric mean. Aczél [1990] shows that the continuous ordinally invariant RM functions are given by

$$u(x_1, x_2, \ldots, x_n) = \gamma \prod_{i=1}^n x_i^{\delta_i} + \lambda$$

or

$$u(x_1, x_2, \ldots, x_n) = \sum_{i=1}^{n} \gamma_i \log x_i + \delta.$$

Roberts [1990b] shows that for RM functions, under one additional assumption which we called agreement in Section 5.6, four different invariance conditions (including ordinal invariance and ratio invariance) are all equivalent. He characterizes those RM functions satisfying these four invariance conditions under the assumption of agreement. If in addition to agreement one assumes that the RM function is symmetric as defined in Section 5.6, he shows that all these invariance conditions are equivalent to u being the geometric mean. Similar results are being obtained for GRM functions.

To give another sample result, let us consider the GRM functions under the assumption called *identity*, which says that $v(a_1, a_2, \ldots, a_n, a_1, a_2, \ldots, a_n) = 1$. Aczél [1990] shows that the ratio invariant GRM functions satisfying identity are characterized as the functions which have the form

$$v(a_1, a_2, \ldots, a_n, x_1, x_2, \ldots, x_n) = F(a_1, a_2, \ldots, a_n)/F(x_1, x_2, \ldots, x_n),$$

where F is an arbitrary function from $\mathbb{R}_n^+$ to $\mathbb{R}$.

Guidelines on how to use the results in this section are similar to the ones given in Section 5.7. The user must choose an invariance requirement — this is a little like choosing what assertion will be allowed. The user must also decide if some additional properties of the RM or GRM function are reasonable to require, properties such as symmetry or agreement. On the basis of these assumptions, one can, hopefully, derive the general form of the RM or GRM function. Finally, parameters must be chosen, much as in the case of possible merging functions, as discussed at the end of Section 5.7.

7. Meaningfulness of statistical tests

7.1. Some general principles

In Section 4, we have discussed the idea that certain descriptive statistics are appropriate for certain types of scales. Following the influence of Siegel [1956], Senders [1958], and others, many authors have attempted to extend the same reasoning to inferential statistics. However, there has been considerable disagreement on the limitations that scales of measurement impose on the statistical procedures that we may apply. Indeed, while there is rather widespread (though certainly not universal) acceptance of the kinds of conclusions we have described with respect to descriptive statistics, the application of them to inferential statistics has been called a 'misconception' by such authors as Armstrong [1981] and Gaito [1980]. Recent surveys of the literature of this topic can be found in Knapp [1990], Marcus-Roberts & Roberts [1987], Mitchell [1986, 1990], Stine [1989] and Thomas

[1985], and Knapp [1985] has prepared an excellent annotated bibliography on the subject. In this section and Section 7.2, we follow the approach of Marcus-Roberts & Roberts.

Examples of the general principles espoused by Siegel and others which we would like to analyze in this section are the following: (1) classical parametric tests (such as the t-test, Pearson correlation, and analysis of variance) are not appropriate for ordinal scales but should only be applied to interval or ratio scale data; (2) for ordinal scales, non-parametric tests (such as Mann–Whitney U, Kruskal–Wallis, and Kendall's tau) are appropriate.

7.2. Measurement models, statistical models, and meaningless hypotheses

To discuss these principles, let us consider inferences about an unknown population P. Some assumptions must be made about the scale type of the scale which is used to describe the elements of P, i.e., about the admissible transformations. We call these assumptions the *measurement model* for P. In statistical inference, we are testing some null hypothesis H_0 about P. If we apply an admissible transformation φ to the scale values, we transform the population P to a transformed population

$$\varphi(P) = \{\varphi(x) : x \in P\}.$$

We then get a transformed null hypothesis $\varphi(H_0)$ obtained from H_0 by applying φ to all scales and scale values in H_0. For instance, suppose the population P is the set $\{-1, 0, 1\}$, the measurement model is that P is given on an ordinal scale, and the null hypothesis H_0 is the hypothesis that the mean of P is 0. This hypothesis is true, but it is meaningless. For the exponential transformation of the data, $\varphi(x) = e^x$, is an admissible transformation. However, $\varphi(P) = \{e^{-1}, 1, e\}$ and $\varphi(H_0)$ says that the mean of this population is $\varphi(0) = 1$. This hypothesis is false. The null hypothesis is meaningless. It seems to us that the major restriction measurement theory should place on inferential statistics is to place a restriction on what hypotheses are worth testing. Why should we bother testing a meaningless hypothesis? Much the same position is taken by Luce, Krantz, Suppes & Tversky [1990].

Can we test meaningless hypotheses? Yes, we can. We shall argue this point shortly. However, the information we get from testing a meaningless hypothesis is just information about the population as measured, and not some intrinsic information. Similar ideas are expressed by Adams, Fagot & Robinson [1965] and Luce [1967], as well as Marcus-Roberts & Roberts [1987].

How does one test a meaningless hypothesis? In the same way that one tests any hypothesis. Testing a hypothesis H_0 about a population P involves drawing a random sample S from P, calculating a test statistic based on S, calculating the probability that the test statistic is what was observed given that H_0 is true, and accepting or rejecting on the basis of this probability. The calculation of the probability depends on information about the distribution of P and about the sampling procedure. We shall call these two things the *statistical model*. However, the validity of the test does not depend on assumptions about the admissible transformations, i.e., on the measurement model. Thus, one can apply parametric tests to ordinal data. The only question is whether the statistical requirements for the test to work are satisfied, and those requirements have nothing to do with the scale type. One of the crucial assumptions needed to apply parametric tests, i.e., part of the statistical model, is that the data be normally distributed. Thomas [1982] shows that ordinal data can be normally distributed (it is a misconception that it cannot). Thus, we can apply parametric tests such as the t-test to ordinal data to test if the mean is 0. The trouble is that the result of the test only gives us information about a population measured under one choice of scale, and gives us no fundamental information about the population. What is wrong with applying the t-test to ordinal data to test the hypothesis that the mean is 0 is not that the test does not apply (though often it does not), but that the hypothesis is meaningless.

In sum, we hope that the reader will stop to check if hypotheses are meaningful before applying statistical tests to test them.

7.3. Additional observations on the testing of meaningful hypotheses

Let us make some additional observations on the testing of meaningful hypotheses. If a hypothesis is meaningful, it can be tested in various ways. We cannot expect that two different tests of the same hypothesis will necessarily lead to the same conclusion, even forgetting about change of scale. For instance, the t-test could lead to rejection and the Wilcoxon test to acceptance. But what happens if we apply the same test to data both before and after admissible transformation? In the best situation, the results of the test are always invariant under admissible changes in scale. To explain this more precisely, let us consider a meaningful hypothesis H_0 about a population P which satisfies a given measurement model. We test the hypothesis by drawing a (random) sample S. We shall denote by $\varphi(S)$ the set of all $\varphi(x)$ for x in S. We would like a test T for hypothesis H_0 which has the following properties:

(a) The statistical model for T is satisfied by P and also by $\varphi(P)$ for all admissible transformations φ as defined by the measurement model for P.

(b) T accepts H_0 with sample S at level of significance α if and only if T accepts $\varphi(H_0)$ with sample $\varphi(S)$ at level of significance α.
There are many examples in the statistical literature where conditions (a) and (b) hold. We give two examples.

Consider first data measured on an interval scale. Then the hypothesis H_0 that the mean is μ_0 is meaningful. It can be tested by the t-test. The statistical model for this test is that the population is normally distributed. Now every admissible φ is of the form $\varphi(x) = \alpha x + \beta, \alpha > 0$, and, as is well known, such φ take normal distributions into normal distributions. Hence, for a normally distributed population, condition (a) holds. To demonstrate condition (b), let us consider the test statistic t based on a sample S of size n. Let $\bar{x}$ be the sample mean and s^2 the sample variance. Then t is given by

$$t = \frac{\overline{x} - \mu_0}{s/\sqrt{n}}.$$

If the sample S is transformed by admissible transformation $\varphi(x) = \alpha x + \beta$, then the sample mean is now $\alpha\overline{x} + \beta$, and the sample variance is $\alpha^2 s^2$. Moreover, the new hypothesis $\varphi(H_0)$ says that the mean is $\varphi(\mu_0) = \alpha\mu_0 + \beta$. Hence, the new test statistic is

$$\frac{\alpha\overline{x} + \beta - (\alpha\mu_0 + \beta)}{\alpha s/\sqrt{n}} = \frac{\overline{x} - \mu_0}{s/\sqrt{n}}$$

i.e., we have the same t. Condition (b) follows.

As a second example, let us consider data measured on an ordinal scale, and consider the hypothesis H_0 that the median is M_0. This is meaningful. It can be tested by the sign test. The literature of nonparametric statistics is somewhat unclear on the statistical model needed for the sign test. Most books say that continuity of the probability density function is needed. In fact, it is only necessary to assume that $\Pr\{x = M_0\} = 0$ [see Gibbons, 1971]. For a population satisfying this statistical model, condition (a) is satisfied, for

$$\Pr\{x = M_0\} = 0 \text{ if and only if } \Pr\{\varphi(x) = \varphi(M_0)\} = 0.$$

The test statistic for a sample S is the number of sample points above M_0 or the number below M_0, whichever is smaller. Since this test statistic does not change when a (strictly) monotone increasing transformation φ is applied to the sample and M_0 is replaced by $\varphi(M_0)$, condition (b) holds.

Having conditions (a) and (b) hold is only one of the things that could happen. It is certainly the nicest situation and one which, luckily, is frequently the case. If condition (a) holds but condition (b) fails, we might still find test T useful, just as we sometimes find it useful to apply different tests with possibly different conclusions to the same data. However, it is a little disturbing that seemingly innocuous changes in how we measure things could lead to different conclusions under the 'same' test.

What happens if H_0 is meaningful, but condition (a) fails? This could happen, for instance, if P violates the statistical model for T. It might still be possible to test the hypothesis using the test T. This can happen if one can find an admissible φ such that $\varphi(P)$ satisfies the statistical model for T, and then apply T to test $\varphi(H_0)$. Since H_0 is meaningful, H_0 holds if and only if $\varphi(H_0)$ holds, and so T applied to $\varphi(P)$ and $\varphi(H_0)$ gives a test of H_0 for P. For instance, if the hypothesis is meaningful, then even for ordinal data, we can seek a transformation which normalizes the data and allows us to apply a parametric test. This situation could conceivably occur if the hypothesis is not about a property of the scale. A similar point is made by Luce [1967].

What happens if conditions (a) or (b) fail, but we still apply test T to test (meaningful) H_0? As Thomas [1982] points out, when we do this, we hope that the effect of misapplying the test will not especially alter the conclusions or implications of the study. There is a great deal of empirical work which is relevant to the issue of when misapplying a test like this will not alter the conclusions. This work emphasizes the case where conditions (a) and (b) fail because we have an ordinal scale, but we treat the scale like an interval scale, for which (a) and (b) hold. The results are not definitive: Some papers illustrate the danger of treating ordinal scales as interval scales while others minimize the danger. See papers by Baker, Hardyck & Petrinovich [1966], or Labovitz [1967, 1970], or O'Brien [1979], or Trachtman, Giambalvo & Dippner [1978] as examples, and see the criticisms of Labovitz' papers in *Social Forces* 46 [1968], 541–542 and *American Sociological Review* 35 [1970], 916–917 and 36 [1971], 517–520. Abelson & Tukey [1959, 1963] have attempted to formalize the risk involved in applying a test in a situation when it is inappropriate. However, little other theoretical work has been done that is relevant, and this should be an important area for research in the future.

8. Structural models

As we pointed out in Section 1, subjective judgements are used as input in models for solving problems in a wide variety of fields. Since the inputs to models are so often subjective, one must ask whether the conclusions from these models are meaningful. Roberts [1979b] considers the meaningfulness of conclusions from so-called structural modelling, which we discussed in example 4 of Section 1. Structural modelling has many other uses which are mentioned in Section 1, where we also gave a variety of references to the literature.

As we noted in Section 1, in his analysis of structural modelling, Roberts [1979b] demonstrates, for instance, that the conclusion of value stability under a pulse process (a particular kind of structural model) is meaningful if all the subjectively-determined variables are measured on interval scales, but not if some of them are only ordinal in nature. We explain this point in more detail here.

Structural modelling (SM) is a term used for a variety of techniques developed to understand the properties of complex systems or complex decisionmaking problems. In SM, we (1) identify variables relevant to a problem at hand, (2) pinpoint (binary) cross-impact relationships between these variables, and then (3) make predictions on the basis of these cross-impact relations. The example of the use of geometric mean to find most important variables to use in an energy modelling study, to which we referred in Section 5.1, was the first step in an SM study. The second step often uses subjective judgements, and might use a panel of experts to obtain a matrix a_{ij} of cross-impacts, where a_{ij} is the impact on variable j of (a change in) variable i. One particular technique of SM is called the pulse process method and was first introduced in Roberts [1971]. In this method, the variables become vertices of a signed or weighted digraph and the cross-impacts determine the existence of arcs between vertices and the signs or weights on arcs. Each variable i is thought of as achieving a certain *value* or level $v_i(t)$ at time t, with values measured only at discrete times $t = 0, 1, \ldots$ Initial values (values at time 0) are given and an initial, externally generated, change is introduced at some or all of the variables. From then on, it is assumed that whenever i goes up by u units at time t, then as a result, j goes up by ua_{ij} units at time $t + 1$. (This is only one of many possible assumptions to make in SM.) In the third step of SM, we make predictions about $v_i(t)$ as t changes. A typical prediction is that $v_i(t)$ remains bounded (in absolute value) over time. We then say that i is *value stable*. If the scales used to measure the values $v_i(t)$ are changed, can such conclusions as value stability change? Roberts [1979b] shows that if all $v_i(t)$ are interval scales (with independent units and zero points) and the a_{ij} are rescaled consistently with any changes in v_i and v_j, then the conclusion that $v_i(t)$ is value stable is meaningful. However, if some $v_i(t)$ are only ordinal, this conclusion is meaningless. In model building, we must be careful to analyze the conclusions from models to see if they are meaningful. This message is more important than the specific example used to present it, and it is the main message of this section.

In building signed and weighted digraphs to be analyzed using structural models and pulse processes, Roberts [1971, 1973, 1975] uses the opinions of experts and then consensus methods to obtain a consensus signed or weighted digraph. Bogart & Weeks [1979] point out some of the unpleasant properties of the consensus method used in Roberts [1973]. They introduce a distance measure between two signed or weighted digraphs and use the distances to define a consensus signed or weighted digraph given different digraphs constructed by different experts. They find the consensus by generalizing the Kemeny [1959] and Kemeny & Snell [1962] notions of median and mean of a collection of relations. (Recent work on the Kemeny–Snell consensus methods is summarized by Barthélemy [1989] and Barthélemy & Monjardet [1981, 1988]. These methods have had a variety of interesting applications, for example to the choice of alternative sites for commuter parking in Geneva [Ebenegger, 1988].) All of these consensus methods are sensitive to changes in scales used to define the signed and weighted digraphs. That suggests that one should investigate the meaningfulness of conclusions that a given digraph (relation) is a median or mean of a collection of digraphs or relations. The problem is analogous to the problem of identifying possible merging functions which we have studied in Section 5.

9. Optimization

9.1. Some examples

As we pointed out in Section 1, many practical decisionmaking problems involve the search for an optimal solution. In spite of the large literature on optimization, little attention has been paid to the possibility that the conclusion that a particular solution is optimal might be an accident of the way that things are measured. Here we shall discuss the meaningfulness of conclusions about optimization, with an emphasis on methods often called combinatorial optimization.

Let us give some simple examples to illustrate the ideas. A problem which is very important in applications of operations research is the shortest path problem. Indeed, according to Goldman [1981], it is perhaps the most widely encountered combinatorial problem in government. Goldman estimates that in the late 1970's, the shortest path algorithm developed by just one government agency, the Urban Mass Transit Agency in the U.S. Department of Transportation, was regularly applied *billions* of times a year. However, we wonder how often people stopped to ask whether the conclusions obtained from using such an algorithm were meaningful? To illustrate the point, suppose we have a network with three vertices, x, y, and z, and there are weights of 2 on the edge $\{x, y\}$, 4 on the edge $\{y, z\}$, and 15 on the edge $\{x, z\}$. Then the shortest path from x to z is the path going from x to y to z. But what if weights are measured on an interval scale (e.g., if they are temperature increments)? The transformation $\varphi(x) = 3x + 100$ takes the weights into 106 on $\{x, y\}$, 112 on $\{y, z\}$, and 145 on $\{x, z\}$. Now the shortest path from x to z is to go directly from x to z. The original conclusion was meaningless. It is meaningful if the weights are measured on a ratio scale.

The shortest path problem can be formulated as a linear programming problem. The above example thus illustrates the following point: The conclusion that z is an optimal solution in a linear programming problem can be meaningless if the cost parameters are measured on an interval scale.

Another very important practical problem in applications of operations research is the minimum spanning tree problem. Given a connected, weighted graph or network, we ask for the spanning tree with total sum of weights as small as possible. This problem has applications in the planning of large-scale transportation, communication, and distribution networks, as well as more unusual applications such as the one at the National Bureau of Standards which involves measuring the homogeneity of bimetallic objects [cf. Filliben, Kafadar & Shier, 1983; Goldman, 1981; Shier, 1982]. Graham & Hell [1985] is a survey which mentions many applications of this problem. Again, it is natural to ask if the conclusion that a given set of edges defines a minimum spanning tree is meaningful. It is surprising to observe that even if the weights on the edges define only an ordinal scale, then the conclusion is meaningful. This is not a priori obvious. However, it follows from the fact that the well-known algorithm known as Kruskal's algorithm or the greedy algorithm gives a solution. In Kruskal's algorithm [Kruskal, 1956; Papadimitriou & Steiglitz, 1982], we order edges in increasing order of weight and then examine edges in this order, including an edge if it does not form a cycle with edges previously included. We stop when all vertices are included. Since any admissible transformation will not change the order in which edges are examined in this algorithm, the same solution will be produced.

9.2. A general formulation

Let us try to formulate the issues we have been discussing in general terms, in particular for the optimization problems frequently called combinatorial. Much of what we say here applies to a much broader class of optimization problems. In the generic optimization problem, we are trying to optimize a function $t = f(x)$ for x ranging over a set A called the *feasible set*. Here, $f(x)$ measures the cost of x, the time involved in carrying out x, the profit with x, the utility or expected utility of x, etc. In considering the meaningfulness of statements which arise from such a problem, we have to decide where admissible transformations should be applied, and to what extent these admissible transformations should be applied independently of each other. Usually t will be measured on some scale and we shall need to consider admissible transformations of this scale. Moreover, the function f might be defined by several parameters which arise from a measurement process and we shall then need to consider the possibility of admissible transformations of scale being applied to these parameters and the question of whether these transformations can be applied independently. We might also think of measuring the elements x in the set A, and if this is the case, we will want to apply admissible transformations to the scale measuring x. Moreover, x might in fact consist of several measurable variables, as in multidimensional problems, and we shall then have to decide whether to apply admissible transformations independently to each of these variables. Finally, it might be that membership in the set A is determined by measuring some parameters which describe A, and then transformations of these parameters will have to be considered. To summarize, in analyzing a particular statement about an optimization problem and attempting to apply the theory of meaningfulness, a crucial step will be to decide what kinds of transformations should be allowed.

Roberts [1990a] considers, at a quite elementary level, the beginnings of a theory of meaningfulness of conclusions under (combinatorial) optimization. He limits the discussion to one kind of change at a time, a change in the scale used to measure t, a change in the scale(s) used to measure parameters associated with f, a change in scales which measure or describe elements x of A, or a change in scales used to determine membership in A. He analyzes such statements as:

(a) z is an optimal (maximal) solution in A;

(b) the optimal value $f(z_1)$ to instance I_1 of problem $\mathcal{P}$ is larger than (is k times as large as) the optimal value $f(z_2)$ to instance I_2 of problem $\mathcal{P}$;

(c) the value $f(z_1)$ produced as a solution to instance I_1 of problem $\mathcal{P}$ by algorithm G is larger than (is k times as large as) the value $f(z_2)$ produced as a solution to instance I_2 of problem $\mathcal{P}$ by algorithm G;

(d) the value $f(z)$ produced as a solution to instance I of problem $\mathcal{P}$ by algorithm G is within r percent of the optimal value.

In this section and Section 9.3, we mention some of Roberts' results, with an emphasis on statement (a) since not much has been done as yet with the other statements.

To give an example, suppose that only x may change, i.e., that no changes are allowed in the measurement of t, or of parameters in the function f, or of parameters determining membership in A. Suppose also that x is measured on a ratio scale, as for example when x is time or profit or length or mass. Now statement (a) says that

$$f(z) \geq f(x) \text{ for all } x \text{ in } A. \tag{32}$$

This statement is meaningful if it is equivalent to the statement

$$f[\varphi(z)] \geq f[\varphi(x)] \text{ for all } x \text{ in } A. \tag{33}$$

Then if f is linearly homogeneous ($f(\alpha x) = \alpha f(x)$ for all $\alpha > 0$), it is clear that (32) and (33) are equivalent, so statement (32) is meaningful. Similarly, if x is measured on an interval scale, statement (32) is meaningful if $f(\alpha x + \beta) = \alpha f(x) + \tau(\alpha, \beta)$, where τ is an arbitrary function of α and β. This property holds in linear optimization, but fails in such practically important situations as quadratic optimization (such as under $f(x) = x^2$). As a result, in the case of quadratic optimization, it is easy to give examples in which statement (32) can be meaningless.

Roberts [1990a] also studies conclusion (a) if only parameters associated with f may vary. For instance, in linear programming, these parameters are the cost parameters. Let us take the simplest example where we are maximizing a function $f(x) = cx$ subject to the constraint that $0 \leq x \leq b$. The conclusion (a) is now translated into the statement

$$cz \geq cx \text{ for all } x \in [0, b]. \tag{34}$$

In the present context (34) is considered meaningful if it is equivalent to

$$\varphi(c)z \geq \varphi(c)x \text{ for all } x \in [0, b]. \tag{35}$$

But (35) and (36) are not equivalent if c is measured on an interval scale. For instance, take $c = 2$ and $\varphi(c) = c - 10$. Then cx is maximized at $x = z = b$ but $\varphi(c)x$ is maximized at $x = 0$. Thus, in the case of linear programming, conclusion (a) is meaningless if the cost parameters are measured on an interval scale. We have already observed this by observing above that the conclusion that a given path is a shortest path from x to z in a weighted network is a meaningless conclusion if the edge weights are measured on an interval scale.

Roberts [1990a] also studies conclusion (a) in the case where only the scale measure t can vary. We note that many practical decisionmaking problems reduce to the determination of an alternative or strategy which optimizes utility. Roberts observes that if $f(x)$ measures the utility of x and we are interested in optimal utility, conclusion (a) can be meaningless. This is the case if indifference is not transitive and preference defines a semiorder. We expand on this point in Section 11.

In the case where only t can vary, Roberts [1990a] has also studied statement (d). This is a particularly important statement given the current emphasis in the optimization literature on approximation; we often make such a statement in the analysis of the performance of heuristics for problem solving. In this case, we are considering the assertion

$$f(z) \leq kf(x) \text{ for all } x \in A, \tag{36}$$

where z is the solution produced by algorithm G and $k = 1 + r/100$. Now if only t can vary, (36) is meaningful if it is equivalent to

$$\varphi[f(z)] \leq k\varphi[f(x)] \text{ for all } x \in A. \tag{37}$$

If f is a ratio scale, then this is true. However, if f is an interval scale, then it is easy to see that (36) can hold while (37) fails. This implies that in considering certain types of conclusions about how good an approximation is obtained through a heuristic, we usually do not want to be dealing with anything less than a ratio scale. We are safe with cost, profit, time, or weight; however, we might not be safe with utility, since that may only be measured on an interval or weaker scale.

9.3. Error evaluation functions or performance measures

Suppose $z \in A$ is a candidate solution to the problem $\mathcal{P}$ of maximizing the function $f(x)$ for x in the set A. Let $E(z, \mathcal{P})$ be a measure of the error in candidate solution z, with a higher value of E meaning a larger error. E is sometimes called an *error evaluation function (EEF)* and sometimes called a *performance measure*. Suppose that problem $\mathcal{P}$ is transformed into a new problem $\mathcal{P}'$ by some transformation which sends f into f' and A into A'. For every candidate solution z to problem $\mathcal{P}$, let z' denote the solution to problem $\mathcal{P}'$ obtained from z by applying the transformation which sends f to f' and A to A'. We would like to know if it is meaningful to say that candidate solution z to problem $\mathcal{P}$ is a better solution than candidate solution w. Thus, we would like to know whether

$$E(z, \mathcal{P}) < E(w, \mathcal{P}) \longrightarrow E(z', \mathcal{P}') < E(w', \mathcal{P}') \tag{38}$$

for all candidate solutions z and w to problem $\mathcal{P}$.

A commonly used EEF is the *percentage error* or *relative error*

$$E_1(z, \mathcal{P}) = \frac{f(u) - f(z)}{|f(u)|},$$

where u is an optimal solution to problem $\mathcal{P}$. Using E_1, Zemel [1981], Cornuejols, Fisher & Nemhauser [1977], and Korte [1979] analyze the following statement which is closely related to (38):

$$E(z, \mathcal{P}) = E(z', \mathcal{P}') \tag{39}$$

for all candidate solutions z to problem $\mathcal{P}$. Zemel analyzes this for certain 0–1 integer programming problems such as the binary knapsack problem, Cornuejols, Fisher & Nemhauser for certain problems of the plant location variety, and Korte for the maximum weighted acyclic subgraph problem. Note that statement (39) for all z implies statement (38) for all z and w, and these authors feel that even the stronger statement (39) is desirable as a property of EEFs. These authors analyze statement (39) for various transformations $\mathcal{P}$ into $\mathcal{P}'$, and give examples in which (39) fails. They do not consider transformations $\mathcal{P}$ into $\mathcal{P}'$ which arise from admissible transformations of scale. The arguments against (39) can of course be interpreted as arguments against (38). (By way of contrast, Magnanti & Wong [1984] argue that E_1 is a good performance measure for a large class of network design problems.)

What happens if the transformation $\mathcal{P}$ into $\mathcal{P}'$ arises from a scale transformation? For the sake of discussion, let us consider only the simplest case where only the scale t changes, where $t = f(x)$, and let us assume that $E = E_1$. (For other cases, see Roberts [1990a].) In this case, z' is z. It is clear that both (39) (for all z) and (38) (for all z and w) hold when t is measured on a ratio scale but fail when it is measured on an interval scale. To see the former, note that

$$E_1(z', \mathcal{P}') = [\alpha f(u') - \alpha f(z')]/\alpha f(u')$$
$$= [\alpha f(u) - \alpha f(z)]/\alpha f(u)$$
$$= [f(u) - f(z)]/f(u)$$
$$= E_1(z, \mathcal{P}).$$

Thus, it is meaningful to say that solution z is better than solution w if the function being optimized is measured on a ratio scale, but not if it is measured on an interval scale. Here there is one other interesting scale to consider, one we have not mentioned elsewhere in this chapter. It is a *difference scale*, a scale where the admissible transformations are functions φ of the form $\varphi(t) = t + \beta$. Difference scales arise, for instance, if we have ratio scale data but record it logarithmically. Cornuejols, Fisher & Nemhauser [1977] give examples of 0–1 integer programming problems where changes in some of the cost parameters lead to changes of this form. They point out, as is clear, that (39) fails with this kind of φ. It is also clear that (38) fails here. However, if we have a difference scale, both (39) and (38) hold if we use a different EEF,

$$E_2(z, \mathcal{P}) = f(u) - f(z),$$

where $f(u)$ is a maximum. However, both Zemel [1981] and Cornuejols, Fisher & Nemhauser [1977] criticize E_2. Zemel says that 'the difference in the objective values is meaningless by itself, and can be gauged only relative to some normalization factor', while Cornuejols, Fisher & Nemhauser say that it is sensitive to scale changes in the data (though not, of course, to the admissible transformations corresponding to difference scales). Zemel's comment is important because it again illustrates the comment that we have made that a statement which is meaningful in a measurement-theoretic sense, or a score or index which leads to statements meaningful in a measurement-theoretic sense, might not be meaningful in the sense of the intended application. In this sense, it seems more reasonable (as Cornuejols, Fisher & Nemhauser observe for certain facility location problems) to use an EEF like

$$E_3(z, \mathcal{P}) = [f(u) - f(z)]/[f(u) - f(a)],$$

where $f(u)$ is a maximum and $f(a)$ a minimum. Note that with E_3, both (39) and (38) hold even if t is an interval scale.

In summary the point of this section is that choice of an error evaluation function should be made on the basis of an assessment of several factors: the types of changes allowed in the problem $\mathcal{P}$, the admissible transformations allowed for each type of change, and the kinds of assertions to be made with the EEF. One should develop candidate EEFs on the basis of the application, but one should also evaluate candidate EEFs on the basis of such measurement-theoretic considerations as described in this section.

9.4. T-coloring

We present here one more detailed example of an application of the ideas of this section to an optimization problem. Both the domestic and military airwaves are becoming increasingly crowded, and numerous government agencies have been studying methods for optimizing the use of the available spectrum in assigning channels to transmitters. One method for dealing with the channel assignment problem is to formulate it as a graph coloring problem. The following formulation was developed by Hale [1980] and by Cozzens & Roberts [1982], and this and related methods have been in use at such agencies as the National Telecommunications and Information Administration, the U.S. Air Force Frequency Management Office, and NATO. Let $G = (V, E)$ be a graph consisting of a set V of *vertices* and a set E of pairs of vertices called *edges*. In the channel assignment problem, the vertices are transmitters and the edges represent pairs of transmitters which conflict. Let T be a set of nonnegative integers thought of as disallowed separations for channels assigned to conflicting transmitters. If a channel is thought of as a positive integer, then we seek a function f on V into the positive integers so that

$$\{x, y\} \in E \longrightarrow |f(x) - f(y)| \notin T.$$

Put in words, this says that if transmitters x and y conflict, then their channels $f(x)$ and $f(y)$ have a separation which is not disallowed. Such an assignment f is called a *T-coloring* of G. T-colorings have been studied extensively over the past decade. For instance, five Ph.D. theses have been written about them [Bonias, 1991; Liu, 1991; Raychaudhuri, 1985; Tesman, 1989; Wang, 1985]. See Roberts [1991a,b] for recent surveys of the subject.

Perhaps the problem which has received the most interest in the literature has been to find a T-coloring f which minimizes the *span* or maximum separation between channels which are used, i.e., $\max_{x,y} |f(x) - f(y)|$. This is a difficult problem in general, and even for such a simple graph as the complete graph K_n with n vertices all of which are joined by edges to each other, the optimal span is not known for all sets T. Another major open question is for what graphs a simple greedy algorithm, which always chooses the first available channel, obtains the optimal span. To give an example, suppose $T = \{0, 1, 4, 5\}$ and we are trying to T-color the complete graph K_n when $n = 3$. Then the greedy algorithm starts with channel 1, goes to channel 3 (since $1 - 1$ and $2 - 1$ are disallowed) and finally goes to channel 9 (since $1 - 1, 2 - 1, 3 - 3, 4 - 3, 5 - 1, 6 - 1, 7 - 3, 8 - 3$ are disallowed). This T-coloring has span $9 - 1 = 8$. However, an optimal T-coloring uses the channels 1, 4, and 7, giving a span of $7 - 1 = 6$.

In the years that these questions have been studied, no one has thought to ask whether they were meaningful questions to ask. What if the numbers in T change by a scale transformation? Does the fact that the greedy algorithm obtains the optimal span change? Is this a meaningful conclusion? Recently, Cozzens & Roberts [1991] have investigated this question.

Suppose that elements of T define a ratio scale. Then it is easy to see that the conclusion that the greedy algorithm obtains the optimal span is meaningless even for a complete graph. For instance, as we have observed, if $G = K_3$ and $T = \{0, 1, 4, 5\}$, then the greedy algorithm does not obtain the optimal span. However, if all elements of T are multiplied by 2, giving the set $T' = \{0, 2, 8, 10\}$, then the greedy algorithm does obtain the optimal span for $G = K_3$.

To give a somewhat more difficult example, suppose that $G = K_6$ and that

$$T = \{0, 1, 2, 3, 4\} \cup \{8\} \cup \{10, 11, 12\} \cup \{32\}.$$

Then the greedy algorithm obtains the optimal span for G. However, if all elements of T are multiplied by 2, giving the set T', then the greedy algorithm does not obtain the optimal span for $G = K_6$. This is proved by Cozzens & Roberts [1991] (and is the smallest example they could find in which the greedy algorithm obtains the optimal span with T but does not find it after multiplication of all elements of T by a positive integer).

What Cozzens and Roberts do prove is that the conclusion that the greedy algorithm obtains the optimal span for *all* complete graphs is a meaningful conclusion if elements of T are measured on a ratio scale. In other words, if the greedy algorithm obtains the optimal span for all complete graphs with the set T, then it does so for all complete graphs with the set $\alpha T = \{\alpha t : t \in T\}$.

Before closing this section, we should add another comment which points up the subtle issues involved in applying the methods described in this chapter. Hansen [1991] has pointed out that it is not clear that multiplication of all elements of T by a positive constant is always an admissible transformation and we might not have a ratio scale. For instance, suppose $T = \{0, 1\}$ and frequencies are measured in kiloHertz (kHz). Frequencies at distance 1 kHz are not allowed on conflicting transmitters and neither are frequencies at distance 1/2 kHz, because channels must be integers. However, if we change units and multiply by $\alpha = 1000$, then $\alpha T = \{0, 1000\}$ and the new units are Hertz (Hz). But now frequencies at distance 500 Hz = 1/2 kHz are allowed on conflicting channels, so we have changed the problem.

10. Clustering and blockmodelling

In many practical problems of detection, decisionmaking, or pattern recognition, we seek methods for clustering alternatives into groups. Clustering methods aim at finding within a given set of entities subsets called clusters which are both homogeneous and well-separated. Clustering problems are important in medicine [see for example Godehart, 1990], in genetics [see for example Arratia & Lander,

1990], and in the theory of social networks [see for example Johnsen, 1989]. In social network theory, the elements being clustered are individuals in an organization or group, clusters are called *blocks*, and the process of clustering alternatives into groups is called *blockmodelling*. There are a variety of concepts of clustering and a variety of algorithms for clustering have been developed. Among the more interesting recent algorithms are those in the papers by Guénoche, Hansen & Jaumard [1991], Hansen & Jaumard [1987], and Hansen, Frank & Jaumard [1989]; different clustering concepts are also described in these papers and below. The reader might be interested in the recent survey on clustering in Russia by Mirkin & Muchnik [1991].

One often bases the grouping into clusters or blocks on judgements of similarity or dissimilarity. Suppose $S = (s_{ij})$ is a matrix whose i, j entry gives a scaling of the similarity between elements i and j. Batchelder [1989] has observed that unless attention is paid to the types of scales used to measure similarity, the conclusions about clusters or blocks can be meaningless. He illustrates this point by considering the widely used blockmodelling algorithm called CONCOR. (For information on this algorithm, see Breiger, Boorman & Arabie [1975] and Arabie, Boorman & Levitt [1978].) CONCOR starts with the matrix S and uses it to obtain a measure of closeness c_{ij} between elements i and j. Closeness is measured by using either column by column or row by row product moment correlations. The partition into clusters or blocks is then based on the measure c_{ij}. Batchelder asks, for instance, what happens to the closeness measures if the similarities are measured on ratio scales. He assumes that the entries of each row are obtained on a ratio scale, but the units in each row might differ. This is a reasonable assumption in many practical applications. For instance, suppose the elements to be clustered are individuals in an organization, and s_{ij} is a measure of how similar i believes he is to j. Then it is reasonable to treat the scales as having independent units. Batchelder gives the following example. Suppose the similarities are given by the matrix

$$S = \begin{bmatrix} 0 & 7 & 2 & 1 \\ 2 & 0 & 6 & 3 \\ 2 & 4 & 0 & 5 \\ 1 & 1 & 3 & 0 \end{bmatrix}$$

Suppose that we obtain the transformed matrix S' by the transformation $s'_{ij} = \alpha_i s_{ij}$. For concreteness, take $\alpha_1 = \alpha_2 = \alpha_3 = 1$, $\alpha_4 = 3$. Then if one uses the Pearson column by column product moment correlation to define c_{ij}, one has $c_{12} = 1$ and $c'_{12} = -1$. Not only is it meaningless to say that alternatives i and j are positively correlated, but the change in correlation can be as dramatic as possible! It is not surprising that if the measures of closeness can change so dramatically, so can the blocks produced by the CONCOR algorithm. Hence, a given clustering or partition into blocks produced by this algorithm is not meaningful.

On the other hand, as Batchelder also observes, if c_{ij} is given by the row by row product moment correlation, things are different. Indeed, even if the rows of S define interval scales with independent units and zero points, i.e., if $s'_{ij} = \alpha_i s_{ij} + \beta_i$, then $c'_{ij} = c_{ij}$. Thus, the measure of closeness is invariant and hence so are the clusters or blocks produced by the CONCOR algorithm. Conclusions about blocks based on this version of CONCOR are meaningful.

Hansen [1992] identifies four types of clustering concepts or criteria based on a matrix of dissimilarities (rather than similarities as in the previous discussion). Based on these dissimilarities, one partitions the entities being clustered into sets or clusters according to some criterion. A *threshold type clustering criterion* is based on one overall value. To give an example, define the *diameter of a cluster* as the largest dissimilarity between two entities in the cluster and the *diameter of a partition* as the largest diameter of its clusters. Then a threshold criterion is to find a partition into a fixed number of clusters so that the diameter of the partition is as small as possible. A second criterion is a *threshold sum type clustering criterion*, which is based on combining one value from each cluster. An example is to minimize the sum of the diameters of the clusters in a partition into a certain number of clusters. A *sum type clustering criterion* is based on combining values given by dissimilarities within clusters. Thus, one sometimes seeks to minimize the largest sum of dissimilarities within a cluster. This is the classical p-median max problem of clustering. A fourth criterion is a *sum–sum type clustering criterion*, which is based on combining combined values, and using all dissimilarities. An example is to minimize the within clusters variance. It is important to develop concepts of clustering which are invariant under various transformations of data and to derive conditions under which different clustering algorithms lead to conclusions which are invariant in this sense. Hansen observes that as a general rule, threshold type clustering criteria lead to solutions which are invariant under monotone transformation of the dissimilarities. Thus, the partition into M clusters which minimizes the diameter does not change if the dissimilarities are on an ordinal scale, and hence statements based on this clustering are meaningful. This is an example of the type of result which is needed. While little theoretical work has been done in this direction and therefore few theoretical tools are available to help the user, we hope that the reader will at least be aware of the need for care in selecting clustering concepts and in applying clustering algorithms.

11. Judgements of preference and indifference

A great deal of applied operations research involves obtaining expressions of preference and/or indifference from individuals. Let us suppose for concreteness that we have a set A of alternatives. Suppose that for every x, y in A, an individual tells us one and only one of the following: he prefers x to y (abbreviated xPy), he prefers y to x (yPx), or he is indifferent between x and y (xIy). When we measure preferences, we usually seek a function f which gives the higher value to the preferred object, i.e., which satisfies

$$xPy \longleftrightarrow f(x) > f(y). \tag{40}$$

Such a function is often called an *(ordinal) utility function*. Of course (40) implies that

$$xIy \longleftrightarrow f(x) = f(y). \tag{41}$$

We can find a function f satisfying (40) only if the preferences satisfy certain conditions. (See Roberts [1979a] for a discussion of such conditions.) One necessary condition, which follows from (41), is that the relation I of indifference be *transitive*, i.e., that is, if we are indifferent between x and y and indifferent between y and z, then we should be indifferent between x and z. Arguments against the transitivity of indifference go back as early as Poincaré in the 19th century and became prominent in the economic literature through the work of Armstrong [1939, and elsewhere]. Many of these arguments arise from the fact that if two alternatives are sufficiently close but not equal, we are still indifferent between them. However, if x is sufficiently close to y and y is sufficiently close to z, this does not imply that x is sufficiently close to z. If judgements of indifference are not transitive, we cannot find a function f satisfying (40). There are now three kinds of approaches to consider. The 'descriptive' approach is to find an alternative model which better fits the data. The 'prescriptive' or 'normative' approach is to develop methods which will help a decisionmaker fit a desired model such as (40). A third approach combines the first two by developing a model which can still be useful in practice but is closer to what actual decisionmakers do, and then developing methods to help a decisionmaker fit that model. The first approach is described in Roberts [1979a] and the second in Keeney & Raiffa [1976]. We give an example of the third approach here.

As we noted above, arguments against the transitivity of indifference often are based on the idea that judgements of 'sufficiently close' violate transitivity. These kinds of arguments led Luce [1956] to suggest that a better model for preference might be the model which says that we prefer x to y if and only if x is not only better, but 'sufficiently better' than y. In terms of measurement, Luce suggests that we seek a function f which satisfies

$$xPy \longleftrightarrow f(x) > f(y) + \delta, \tag{42}$$

where δ is a positive real number measuring threshold or just-noticeable difference, to use terms psychologists like to use. A binary preference relation P on a finite set A for which we can find a function f satisfying (42) is called a *semiorder*. Since Luce's paper, there have been dozens of articles about semiorders, including the seminal article by Scott & Suppes [1958]. For extensive references on the subject, see for instance Roberts [1979a, 1989a], Fishburn [1985], and Trotter [1988]. While there has been a great deal of work on the development of procedures which elicit preferences satisfying the model (40), there has been little work on the development of procedures which elicit preferences satisfying the semiorder model (42). Such work is needed.

If preferences are elicited to satisfy either model (40) or model (42), it is of interest to ask what statements about the corresponding utility functions can be meaningfully made. If nothing is demanded of a utility function other than one of these models, then 'complex' assertions such as

$$f(a) = \alpha f(b)$$

or

$$f(a) - f(b) > f(c) - f(d)$$

are in general not going to be meaningful. If all we demand is (40), then f defines an ordinal scale and assertions like the above are of course meaningless. However, assertions like $f(a) > f(b)$, a has higher utility than b, are meaningful. That is because if φ is a (strictly) monotone increasing transformation, then

$$f(a) > f(b) \longleftrightarrow \varphi[f(a)] > \varphi[f(b)].$$

It is now also meaningful to assert that alternative z has the optimal utility of all alternatives in a set A. This is a statement we were considering in Section 9.2.

The assertions we can meaningfully make if f satisfies model (42) are also of interest to analyze. Suppose that we call a function f satisfying (42) a δ-*utility function*. Now it is interesting to observe that it can be meaningless to assert that alternative a has higher δ-utility than alternative b. Hence, it can also be meaningless to assert that alternative z has the optimal utility of all alternatives in a set A. To give an example, suppose that $\delta = 1$, the set of alternatives A is the set $\{u, v, w\}$, and that wPv and wPu, but uIv. Then one δ-utility function f is given by $f(u) = 0.1$, $f(v) = 0$, $f(w) = 2$. For this f, we have $f(u) > f(v)$. However, another δ-utility function f' is given by $f'(u) = 0$, $f'(v) = 0.1$, $f'(w) = 2$. For this f', $f'(u) > f'(v)$ fails. While we have not given a class of admissible transformations in this situation, we have given two acceptable scales, and shown that the statement that u has a higher δ-utility holds with one of these scales and fails with the other. This, as we discussed near the end of Section 2, suffices to demonstrate the meaningfulness of the statement in question. Indeed, for δ-utility functions, it can be shown that it is not always possible to obtain one δ-utility function from another by an admissible transformation of scale. To illustrate this, consider the same example and let the δ-utility function g be defined by $g(u) = g(v) = 0$, $g(w) = 2$. There is no function φ so that $f(x) = \varphi[g(x)]$ for all x in A, since $f(u) \neq f(v)$ while $g(u) = g(v)$. This kind of example, originally discussed by Roberts & Franke [1976], leads to the modification of the notion of meaningfulness from the one defined in terms of admissible transformations to the more general one defined near the end of Section 2 in terms of replacing one acceptable scale by another.

Continuing the discussion of δ-utility functions with $\delta = 1$, let us consider the case where $A = \{u, v, w\}$, and uPv, uPw, vPw. Then the statement $f(a) > f(b)$ is meaningful for all a, b in A whenever f is a δ-utility function. For it is easy to see that $f(u) > f(v) + 1 > f(w) + 2$ and hence $f(u) > f(v) > f(w)$ for all δ-utility functions f. Roberts [1984a] gives conditions under which a semiorder P on a set A has the property that the statement $f(a) > f(b)$ is meaningful for all δ-utility functions and all a, b in A.

The discussion for δ-utility functions, which emphasize the preference relation, has an analogue for indifference relations. Just as (40) implies (41), (42) implies

$$xIy \longleftrightarrow |f(x) - f(y)| \le \delta. \tag{43}$$

Indifference relations satisfying (43) are called *indifference graphs* and were first characterized by Roberts [1969]. The many papers on indifference graphs are surveyed in the references cited for semiorders earlier in this section. In the case of a function f satisfying (43), it is certainly meaningless to assert that $f(a) > f(b)$, since whenever f satisfies (43), then $-f$ does also. One of the conclusions which can be meaningful is that the value $f(b)$ lies between the values of $f(a)$ and $f(c)$. The meaningfulness of this conclusion is studied in Roberts [1984a].

There are many alternative models for preference and for utility functions. We have presented two in this section, (40) and (42). The judgement $f(a) > f(b)$ has been studied for some of these models by Roberts [1984b], Harvey & Roberts [1989], and Roberts & Rosenbaum [1994]. While few theoretical results are available about the meaningfulness of other types of judgements using utility functions, either in the models (40) and (42) or in others, we can still leave the reader with this message: Before making assertions about utilities, check how the utilities were derived, analyze what transformations of utilities are admissible, and be careful not to make assertions whose truth value can change under admissible transformations.

12. Psychophysics and the measurement of loudness

12.1. The psychophysical function

Psychophysics is the field which is concerned with the relationship between a physical stimulus and a psychological response. This field had much of its motivation from the study of sounds, and psychophysical research is very important in such operations research applications as measurement of noise near airports and in buildings. Here, we present a brief introduction to the subject of psychophysics and the role of measurement theory in it, following Roberts [1979a, 1985]. A much more detailed introduction can be found in such books as Falmagne [1985].

A sound has a variety of physical characteristics, such as its physical intensity, its frequency, its duration, etc. The same sound has various psychological characteristics: How loud does it sound? What emotional meaning does it portray? The *loudness* of a sound is not the same as its disturbing effect, which is called *noise*. Loudness is a psychological variable which we would like to be able to measure, and it is one of the critical determining factors in noise. We concentrate here on how one measures loudness. For more detailed discussion of how one does this, see Kryter [1970] or Stevens [1969].

The loudness of a sound is related to various physical characteristics of that sound, including its intensity, frequency, duration, etc. The simplest approach to measuring loudness is to fix all of the physical factors but one and to vary that one, seeing how the sensation of loudness changes. For instance, suppose we concentrate on the physical intensity. We study *pure tones*, sounds of constant intensity at one fixed frequency, and we present them for a fixed duration of time.

Let $I(a)$ denote the physical intensity of pure tone a, usually taken to be a number proportional to the square of the root-mean-square pressure of the tone. We often use the *decibel* (dB) to measure intensity. We use the formula

$$dB(a) = 10 \log_{10}[I(a)/I_0], \tag{44}$$

where I_0 is the intensity of a reference sound. A one decibel sound (at an 'average' frequency) is essentially the lowest audible sound.

Let $L(a)$ denote the loudness of pure tone a. We know that $L(a)$ is some function $\psi[I(a)]$. The function ψ is the *psychophysical function*, the function relating the physical variable $I(a)$ to the psychological one $L(a)$. The fundamental problem of psychophysics is to find this function for different physical and psychological variables. This problem goes back to Fechner [1860]. Stevens [1957, 1960, 1961a,b,c, and elsewhere] has argued that the fundamental psychophysical function for many psychological variables, and in particular for loudness, is a power function $\psi(x) = \alpha x^\beta$, $\alpha > 0$. This conclusion, based on a great deal of empirical evidence, is widely (though not universally) accepted. (For a summary of criticisms of the conclusion, see Roberts [1979a, p. 156], and see also Pradhan & Hoffman [1963] and Savage [1970].) Here we shall investigate one approach to deriving the 'power law' theoretically.

Once we know this general form of the psychophysical function, we can estimate the parameters α and β from data. In the case of loudness as a function of intensity, the parameter β is estimated to be approximately 0.3. Thus, approximately,

$$L(a) = \alpha I(a)^{0.3}. \tag{45}$$

On the basis of this, one would predict that an increase of 10 decibels in the physical intensity of a sound should lead to approximately a doubling in the loudness. For we have $\beta \approx \log_{10} 2$ and if $dB(b) = dB(a) + 10$, one can show from (44) and (45) that $L(b) = 2L(a)$. This prediction is well-verified by empirical data.

While the power law of Stevens is based on a great deal of empirical evidence, one would like to derive it from theoretical principles. One approach to doing so has its origins in a very widely quoted paper by Luce [1959], to which we have already referred in Section 5.4. As we pointed out there, Luce observed that the general form of the functional relationship between variables is greatly restricted if we know the scale type of the dependent and independent variables. The restrictions are discovered by formulating a functional equation from knowledge of these admissible transformations. Solution of this equation then gives the set of allowable functional relationships. As we have noted, Luce formulated and solved this equation in various cases, for instance where the dependent and independent variables are both ratio scales, where one is ratio and one is interval, and where both are interval scales. In our case, the functional relationship being sought is the psychophysical function ψ. In the case of loudness scaling, we have a ratio scale (the physical intensity) and we want to relate it to a psychological scale, the loudness scale, which, according to numerous experimenters, can be assumed on the basis of a large body of empirical evidence to be a ratio scale. This is argued in numerous publications of Stevens [e.g., 1968]. Now in the case where both the dependent and independent variables are ratio scales, one can prove that the only possible functional relationship between these variables is a power law. We sketched the proof of this result in Section 5.4.

As we have pointed out in Section 5.5, applying Luce's method, to loudness scaling and elsewhere, has a serious drawback. It assumes knowledge of the scale type of the dependent variable. However, if we are trying to use the method to determine how to measure something like loudness, it seems to be begging the question to make assumptions about the scale type of the resulting scale. Because of this, as we noted, Roberts & Rosenbaum [1986] developed a modification of Luce's method. They assumed knowledge of the scale type of the independent variable. In the case of the dependent variable, they pointed out that usually we will want to be able to make certain statements with this variable, and we will want them to be meaningful. They showed that we can derive the possible functional relationships if we know the scale type of the independent variable and we want to be able to make certain assertions with the dependent variable. In the specific case of loudness, we would like to be able to meaningfully assert that the loudness of sound a is k times the loudness of sound b. Roberts & Rosenbaum's results discussed in Section 5.5 show that if $L(a) = \psi[I(a)]$, ψ is continuous (or regular as defined in Section 5.4), $I(a)$ is a ratio scale, and the statement $L(a) = kL(b)$ is meaningful for all positive k, then again one can prove that ψ is a power function.

Although we have emphasized loudness here, similar results apply to such other psychological variables as brightness and sensations of temperature, duration, heaviness, etc.

Luce's work and the subsequent literature is just one example of the influence of measurement methods on psychophysics. Measurement theory, and in particular meaningfulness considerations, have been used in various situations to narrow down the class of numerical functions which can be used to describe a body of psychophysical data. For instance, Falmagne & Narens [1983] and Roberts [1985] describe the use of meaningfulness methods in a psychoacoustic experiment by Pavel [1980] and Iverson & Pavel [1981]. These methods were used to find a general model for observed data, and this general model was then used to make useful predictions which could be checked with experimental data.

12.2. The possible scientific laws

While Luce's method was developed to deal with the problem of describing the laws of psychophysics, it can be viewed much more generally. Indeed, we have developed it more fully in Section 5 in connection with the possible merging functions. More generally, one can use it to try to delimit the general forms of laws in science.

For instance, it is interesting to note that various laws of physics are of the form one would predict, a power law, if both independent and dependent variables are ratio scales. To give an example, consider Ohm's Law: Voltage is proportional to current (if resistance is fixed).

Similarly, various laws of geometry are of the expected power law form. For a sphere, $V = 4/3(\pi r^3)$, where V is the volume and r the radius. For a square, $A = s^2$, where A is the area and s is the side length.

If the independent variable is a ratio scale and the dependent variable is an interval scale, various laws of physics also have the desired form, that derived in Equation (21). Consider for example the law that if H is the entropy of a perfect gas and p is the pressure, then under constant temperature, $H = \alpha \log p + \beta$, where α and β are constants. Also, consider the law which says that if a body of constant mass is moving at a velocity v, then its energy E is given by $E = \alpha v^2 + \delta$, where α and δ are constants.

A considerable literature about the forms of the possible scientific laws derives from Luce's original article. Rozeboom [1962a,b] and Luce [1962] make explicit comments about the limitations in the approach. References to the subsequent literature can be found in any of the papers cited above as critiquing or extending Luce's original paper, and in particular in Luce [1990]. It is fair to say that the conclusions from Luce's method are widely believed to apply only in rather limited circumstances and in particular where there are no dimensional constants which enter the unknown law and cancel out the effects of various transformations.

As an aside, we comment that the reader might be interested in the problem of machine learning of functional descriptions of scientific laws. A discussion of the relevance of meaningfulness to this problem, with an emphasis on laws in engineering, can be found in Kokar [1985, 1986a,b].

13. Conclusion

In this chapter, we have presented in broad outline a methodology based on measurement theory. We have tried to show how methods of measurement theory, and in particular the notion of meaningfulness, puts limitations on the general forms of functional relationships between variables and puts restrictions on the assertions we may want to make using scales, index numbers, and the like. We have given a variety of examples to illustrate these limitations and restrictions and to show how to apply the theory to practical problems. At the same time, we have emphasized what the theory cannot do: determine if a particular measure is appropriate for a particular application.

The theory presented here is not well enough developed to cover many of the practical situations to which the reader might wish to apply it. We hope that the theory will continue to be developed at an increasing rate of speed and have tried to indicate in several places in this chapter where pressing theoretical breakthroughs are needed. However, it is reasonable to hope that if the reader cannot find theoretical results of use in his or her problem, he or she will have gained enough of a healthy skepticism about the use of scales of measurement so as to apply the general lessons of this chapter.

Acknowledgements

The author gratefully acknowledges the support of the National Science Foundation under grant number IRI-89-02125 to Rutgers University. He also thanks Denise Sakai for her helpful comments.

References

Abelson, R.P., and J.W. Tukey (1959). Efficient conversion of non-metric information into metric information. *Proc. Statist. Assoc., Social Statist. Sect.*, 226–230.

Abelson, R.P., and J.W. Tukey (1963). Efficient utilization of non-numerical information in quantitative analysis: General theory and the case of simple order. *Ann. Math. Statist.* 34, 1347–1369.

Aczél, J. (1984). On weighted synthesis of judgements. *Aequationes Math.* 27, 288–307.

Aczél, J. (1990). Determining merged relative scores. *J. Math. Anal. Applic.* 150, 20–40.

Aczél, J., and C. Alsina (1986). On synthesis of judgements. *Socio-Econom. Planning Sci.* 20, 333–339.

Aczél, J., and F.S. Roberts (1989). On the possible merging functions. *Math. Social Sci.* 17, 205–243.

Aczél, J., F.S. Roberts and Z. Rosenbaum (1986). On scientific laws without dimensional constants. *J. Math. Anal. Applic.* 119, 389–416.

Aczél, J., and T.L. Saaty (1983). Procedures for synthesizing ratio scale judgements. *J. Math. Psychol.* 27, 93–102.

Adams, E.W., R.F. Fagot and R.E. Robinson (1965). A theory of appropriate statistics. *Psychometrika* 30, 99–127.

Alper, T.M. (1985). A note on real measurement structures of scale type $(m, m + 1)$. *J. Math. Psychol.* 29, 73–81.

Alper, T.M. (1987). A classification of all order-preserving homeomorphism groups of the reals that satisfy finite uniqueness. *J. Math. Psychol.* 31, 135–154.

Arabie, P., S.A. Boorman and P.R. Levitt (1978). Constructing blockmodels: How and why. *J. Math. Psychol.* 17, 21–63.

Armstrong, G.D. (1981). Parametric statistics and ordinal data: A pervasive misconception. *Nursing Res.* 30, 60–62.

Armstrong, G.D. (1984). Letter to the Editor. *Nursing Res.* 33, 54.

Armstrong, W.E. (1939). The determinateness of the utility function. *Econom. J.* 49, 453–467.

Arratia, R., and E.S. Lander (1990). The distribution of clusters in random graphs. *Adv. Appl. Math.* 11, 36–48.

Babcock, L.R. (1970). A combined pollution index for measurement of total air pollution. *J. Air Pollution Control Assoc.* 20, 653–659.

Babcock, L.R., and N. Nagda (1973). Cost effectiveness of emission control. *J. Air Pollution Control Assoc.* 23, 173–179.

Baker, B.O., C.D. Hardyck and L.F. Petrinovich (1966). Weak measurement vs. strong statistics: An empirical critique of S.S. Stevens' proscriptions on statistics. *Educational Psychological Measurement* 26, 291–309.

Barthélemy, J.P. (1989). Social welfare and aggregation procedures: Combinatorial and algorithmic aspects, in: F.S. Roberts (ed.), *Applications of Combinatorics and Graph Theory to the Biological and Social Sciences*, IMA Volumes in Mathematics and its Applications, Vol. 17, Springer-Verlag, New York, pp. 39–73.

Barthélemy, J.P., and B. Monjardet (1981). The median procedure in cluster analysis and social choice theory. *Math. Social Sci.* 1, 235–268.

Barthélemy, J.P., and B. Monjardet (1988). The median procedure in data analysis: New results and open problems, in: H.H. Bock (ed.), *Classification and Related Methods of Data Analysis*,

North-Holland, Amsterdam.

Batchelder, W.H. (1989). Inferring meaningful global network properties from individual actors' measurement scales, in: L.C. Freeman, D.R. White and A.K. Romney (eds.), *Research Methods in Social Network Analysis*, George Mason University Press, Fairfax, VA, pp. 89–134.

Bay Area Pollution Control District (1968). Combined pollutant indexes for the San Francisco Bay Area, Information Bulletin 10-68, San Francisco, CA.

Bogart, K., and J.R. Weeks (1979). Consensus signed digraphs. *SIAM J. Appl. Math.* 36, 1–14.

Bonias, I. (1991). *T*-colorings of complete graphs, Ph.D. Thesis, Department of Mathematics, Northeastern University, Boston, MA.

Boot, J.C.G., and E.B. Cox (1970). *Statistical Analysis for Managerial Decisions*, McGraw-Hill, New York.

Breiger, R.L., S.A. Boorman and P. Arabie (1975). An algorithm for clustering relational data, with applications to social network analysis and comparison with multidimensional scaling. *J. Math. Psychol.* 12, 328–383.

Caretto, L.S., and R.F. Sawyer (1972). The assignment of responsibility for air pollution, Presented at the Annual Meeting of the Society of Automotive Engineers, Detroit, MI, January 10–14.

Cornuejols, G., M.L. Fisher and G.L. Nemhauser (1977). Location of bank accounts to optimize float: An analytic study of exact and approximate algorithms. *Management Sci.* 23, 789–810.

Cozzens, M.B., and F.S. Roberts (1982). *T*-colorings of graphs and the channel assignment problem. *Congressus Numerantium* 35, 191–208.

Cozzens, M.B., and F.S. Roberts (1991). Greedy algorithms for *T*-colorings of complete graphs and the meaningfulness of conclusions about them. *J. Comb. Inform. Syst. Sci.* 16, 286–299.

Dalkey, N. (1969). Personal communication.

Ebenegger, C. (1988). Personal communication.

Falmagne, J.-C. (1985). *Elements of Psychophysical Theory*, Oxford University Press, New York.

Falmagne, J.-C., and L. Narens (1983). Scales and meaningfulness of quantitative laws. *Synthese* 55, 287–325.

Fechner, G., (1860). *Elemente der Psychophysik*, Breitkopf and Hartel, Leipzig.

Filliben, J.J., K. Kafadar and D.R. Shier (1983). Testing for homogeneity of two-dimensional surfaces. *Math. Modelling* 4, 167–189.

Fishburn, P.C. (1970). *Utility Theory for Decision Making*, Wiley, New York.

Fishburn, P.C. (1985). *Interval Orders and Interval Graphs*, Wiley-Interscience, New York.

Fishburn, P.C. (1988). *Nonlinear Preference and Utility Theory*, Johns Hopkins University Press, Baltimore, MD.

Fisher, I. (1923). *The Making of Index Numbers*, Houghton Mifflin, Boston, MA.

Fleming, P.J., and J.J. Wallace (1986). How not to lie with statistics: The correct way to summarize benchmark results. *Commun. ACM* 29, 218–221.

Gaito, J. (1980). Measurement scales and statistics: Resurgence of an old misconception. *Psychol. Bull.* 87, 564–567.

Gaschnig, J. (1979). Performance measurement and analysis of certain search heuristics, Ph.D. Thesis, Computer Science Department, Carnegie-Mellon University, Pittsburgh, PA.

Gibbons, J.D. (1971). *Nonparametric Statistical Inference*, McGraw Hill, New York.

Godehart, E. (1990). *Graphs as Structural Models, 2nd edition*, Friedr. Vieweg, Braunschweig.

Goldman, A.J. (1981). Discrete mathematics in government, Lecture presented at SIAM Symposium on Applications of Discrete Mathematics, Troy, NY, June.

Graham, R.L., and P. Hell (1985). On the history of the minimum spanning tree problem. *Ann. History Comput.* 7, 43–57.

Greenberg, H.J., and J.S. Maybee (eds.) (1981). *Computer-Assisted Analysis and Model Simplification*, Academic Press, New York.

Guénoche, A., P. Hansen and B. Jaumard (1991). Efficient algorithms for divisive hierarchical clustering with the diameter criterion. *J. Classification* 8, 5–30.

Hale, W.K. (1980). Frequency assignment: Theory and applications. *Proc. IEEE* 68, 1497–1514.

Hansen, P. (1991). Personal communication.

Hansen, P. (1992). Recent results in clustering, Presentation at Office of Naval Research Workshop on Discrete Structured Classification, Herndon, VA, May.

Hansen, P., O. Frank and B. Jaumard (1989). Maximum sum of splits clustering. *J. Classification* 6, 177–193.

Hansen, P., and B. Jaumard (1987). Minimum sum of diameters clustering. *J. Classification* 4, 215–226.

Harvey, L.H., and F.S. Roberts (1989). On the theory of meaningfulness of ordinal comparisons in measurement II. *Annals N.Y. Acad. Sci.* 555, 220–229.

Iverson, G.J., and M. Pavel (1981). Invariant properties of masking phenomena in psychoacoustics and their theoretical consequences, in: S. Grossberg (ed.), *Symposium in Applied Mathematics of AMS-SIAM*, Vol. 13, American Mathematical Society, Providence, RI, pp. 17–24.

Johnsen, E.C. (1989). The micro–macro connection: Exact structure and process, in: F.S. Roberts (ed.), *Applications of Combinatorics and Graph Theory to the Biological and Social Sciences*, IMA Volumes in Mathematics and its Applications, Vol. 17, Springer-Verlag, New York, pp. 169–201.

Keeney, R.L., and H. Raiffa (1976). *Decisions with Multiple Objectives: Preferences and Value Tradeoffs*, Wiley, New York.

Kemeny, J.G. (1959). Mathematics without numbers. *Daedalus* 88, 575–591.

Kemeny, J.G., and J.L. Snell (1962). *Mathematical Models in the Social Sciences*, Blaisdell, New York; reprinted: MIT Press, Cambridge, MA, 1972.

Kim, S. (1990). On the possible scientific laws. *Math. Social Sci.* 20, 19–36.

Knapp, T.R. (1984). Letter to the Editor. *Nursing Res.* 33, 54.

Knapp, T.R. (1985). Treating ordinal scales as interval scales: An annotated bibliography of selected references, Mimeographed, Graduate School of Education and Human Development, University of Rochester, Rochester, New York.

Knapp, T.R. (1990). Treating ordinal scales as interval scales: An attempt to resolve the controversy. *Nursing Res.* 39, 121–123.

Kokar, M.M. (1985). Coper: A methodology for learning invariant functional descriptions, in: R.S. Michalski, J.G. Carbinell and T.M. Mitchell (eds.), *Machine Learning: A Guide to Current Research*, Kluwer Academic Publishers, Boston, MA.

Kokar, M.M. (1986a). Determining arguments of invariant functional descriptions. *Machine Learning* 1, 11–46.

Kokar, M.M. (1986b). Discovering functional formulas through changing representation base, *Proc. of AAAI-86, Fifth National Conference on Artificial Intelligence*, Morgan–Kaufmann, Philadelphia, PA, pp. 455–459.

Korte, B. (1979). Approximative algorithms for discrete optimization problems. *Ann. Discrete Math.* 4, 85–120.

Krantz, D.H. (1972). A theory of magnitude estimation and cross-modality matching. *J. Math. Psychol.* 9, 168–199.

Krantz, D.H., R.D. Luce, P. Suppes and A. Tversky (1971). *Foundations of Measurement*, Vol. I, Academic Press, New York.

Kruskal, J.B. (1956). On the shortest spanning tree of a graph and the traveling salesman problem. *Proc. Amer. Math. Soc.* 7, 48–50.

Kryter, K.D. (1970). *The Effects of Noise on Man*, Academic Press, New York.

Labovitz, S. (1967). Some observations on measurement and statistics. *Social Forces* 46, 151–160.

Labovitz, S. (1970). The assignment of numbers to rank order categories. *Amer. Sociological Rev.* 35, 515–524.

Laspeyres, E. (1871). Die Berechnung einer Mittleren Warrenpreissteigerung. *Jahrb. Nationalökonom. Statist.* 16, 296–314.

Linstone, H.A. (ed.) (1978). The use of structural modeling for technology assessment, Report to National Science Foundation, Systems Science Ph.D. Program, Portland State University, Portland, OR, February.

Linstone, H.A., G.G. Lendaris, S.D. Rogers, W.W. Wakeland and M. Williams (1979). The use of structural modeling for technology assessment. *Tech. Forecasting Social Change* 14, 291–327.

Liu, D.D. (1991). Graph homomorphisms and the channel assignment problem, Ph.D. Thesis, Department of Mathematics, University of South Carolina, Columbia, SC.

Lord, F.M. (1953). On the statistical treatment of football numbers. *Amer. Psychologist* 8, 750–751.

Luce, R.D. (1956). Semiorders and a theory of utility discrimination. *Econometrica* 24, 178–191.

Luce, R.D. (1959). On the possible psychophysical laws. *Psychol. Rev.* 66, 81–95.

Luce, R.D. (1962). Comments on Rozeboom's criticisms of 'On the possible psychophysical laws'. *Psychol. Rev.* 69, 548–555.

Luce, R.D. (1964). A generalization of a theorem of dimensional Analysis. *J. Math. Psychol.* 1, 278–284.

Luce, R.D. (1967). Remarks on the theory of measurement and its relation to psychology, in: *Les Modèles et la Formalisation du Compartement*, Editions du Centre National de la Recherche Scientifique, Paris, pp. 27–42.

Luce, R.D. (1978). Dimensionally invariant numerical laws correspond to meaningful qualitative relations. *Philos. Sci.* 45, 1–16.

Luce, R.D. (1985). Personal communication, August 20.

Luce, R.D. (1986). Uniqueness and homogeneity of ordered relational structures. *J. Math. Psychol.* 30, 391–415.

Luce, R.D. (1987). Measurement structures with Archimedean ordered translation groups. *Order* 4, 165–189.

Luce, R.D. (1990). 'On the possible psychophysical laws' revisited: Remarks on cross-modal matching. *Psychol. Rev.* 97, 66–77.

Luce, R.D., D.H. Krantz, P. Suppes and A. Tversky (1990). *Foundations of Measurement*, Vol. III, Academic Press, New York.

Luce, R.D., and L. Narens (1983). Symmetry scale types, and generalizations of classical physical measurement. *J. Math. Psychol.* 27, 44–85.

Luce, R.D., and L. Narens (1984). Classification of real measurement representations by scale type. *Measurement* 2, 39–44.

Luce, R.D., and L. Narens (1985). Classification of concatenation measurement structures according to scale type. *J. Math. Psychol.* 29, 1–72.

Luce, R.D., and L. Narens (1986). Measurement: The theory of numerical assignments. *Psychol. Bull.* 99, 166–180.

Luce, R.D., and L. Narens (1987). Measurement scales on the continuum. *Science* 236, 1527–1532.

Magnanti, T.L., and R.T. Wong (1984). Network design and transportation planning: Models and algorithms. *Transportation Sci.* 18, 1–55.

Marcus-Roberts, H.M., and F.S. Roberts (1987). Meaningless statistics. *J. Educ. Statist.* 12, 383–394.

Mirkin, B.G., and I.B. Muchnik (1991). Clustering and multidimensional scaling in Russia (1960–1990), Review, Mimeographed, Department of Informatics and Applied Statistics, Central Economics-Mathematics Institute, Krasikova, 32, Moscow, 117418.

Mitchell, J. (1986). Measurement scales and statistics: A clash of paradigms. *Psychol. Bull.* 100, 398–407.

Mitchell, J. (1990). *An Introduction to the Logic of Psychological Measurement*, Lawrence Erlbaum Associates, Hillsdale, NJ.

Mohr, E. (1951). Bemerkungen zur Dimensionsanalysis. *Math. Nachr.* 6, 145–153.

Mundy, B. (1986). On the general theory of meaningful representation. *Synthese* 67, 391–437.

Narens, L. (1981a). A general theory of ratio scalability with remarks about the measurement-theoretic concept of meaningfulness. *Theory Decision* 13, 1–70.

Narens, L. (1981b). On the scales of measurement. *J. Math. Psychol.* 24, 249–275.

Narens, L. (1985). *Abstract Measurement Theory*, MIT Press, Cambridge, MA.

Narens, L. (1988). Meaningfulness and the Erlanger Program of Felix Klein. *Math. Inform. Sci. Humaines* 101, 61–71.

Norman, R.Z., and F.S. Roberts (1972). A measure of relative balance for social structures, in: J. Berger, M. Zelditch and B. Anderson (eds.), *Structural Theories in Progress, II*, Houghton-Mifflin, New York, pp. 358–391.

O'Brien, R.M. (1979). The use of Pearson's *r* with ordinal data. *Amer. Sociological Rev.* 44, 851–857.

Osborne, D.K. (1970). Further extensions of a theorem of dimensional analysis. *J. Math. Psychol.* 7, 236–242.

Papadimitriou, C.H., and K. Steiglitz (1982). *Combinatorial Optimization: Algorithms and Complexity*, Prentice-Hall, Englewood Cliffs, NJ.

Pavel, M. (1980). Homogeneity in complete and partial masking, Ph.D. Thesis, Department of Psychology, New York University, New York.

Pfanzagl, J. (1968). *Theory of Measurement*, Wiley, New York.

Pickering, J.F., J.A. Harrison and C.D. Cohen (1973). Identification and measurement of consumer confidence: Methodology and some preliminary results. *J. Roy. Statist. Soc.* A, 43–63.

Pradhan, P.L., and P.J. Hoffman (1963). Effect of spacing and range of stimuli on magnitude estimation judgments. *J. Exp. Psychol.* 66, 533–541.

Raychaudhuri, A. (1985). Intersection assignments, *T*-coloring, and powers of Graphs, Ph.D. Thesis, Department of Mathematics, Rutgers University, New Brunswick, NJ.

Roberts, F.S. (1969). Indifference graphs, in: F. Harary (ed.), *Proof Techniques in Graph Theory*, Academic Press, New York, pp. 139–146.

Roberts, F.S. (1971). Signed digraphs and the growing demand for energy. *Environment Planning* 3, 395–410.

Roberts, F.S. (1972). Building an energy demand signed digraph I: Choosing the Nodes, Report 927/1-NSF, The RAND Corporation, Santa Monica, CA, April.

Roberts, F.S. (1973). Building and analyzing an energy demand signed digraph. *Environment Planning* 5, 199–221.

Roberts, F.S. (1975). Weighted digraph models for the assessment of energy use and air pollution in transportation systems. *Environment Planning* 7, 703–724.

Roberts, F.S. (1976). *Discrete Mathematical Models, with Applications to Social, Biological, and Environmental Problems*, Prentice-Hall, Englewood Cliffs, NJ.

Roberts, F.S. (1978). *Graph Theory and its Applications to Problems of Society*, CBMS-NSF Monograph No. 29, SIAM, Philadelphia, PA.

Roberts, F.S. (1979a). *Measurement Theory, with Applications to Decisionmaking, Utility, and the Social Sciences*, Addison-Wesley, Reading, MA.

Roberts, F.S. (1979b). Structural modeling and measurement theory. *Tech. Forecasting Social Change* 14, 353–365.

Roberts, F.S. (1980). On Luce's theory of meaningfulness. *Philos. Sci.* 47, 424–433.

Roberts, F.S. (1984a). Applications of the theory of meaningfulness to order and matching experiments, in: E. DeGreef, and J. Van Buggenhaut (eds.), *Trends in Mathematical Psychology*, North-Holland, Amsterdam, pp. 283–292.

Roberts, F.S. (1984b). On the theory of ordinal comparisons in measurement. *Measurement* 2, 35–38.

Roberts, F.S. (1985). Applications of the theory of meaningfulness to psychology. *J. Math. Psychol.* 29, 311–332.

Roberts, F.S. (1989a). Applications of combinatorics and graph theory to the biological and social sciences: Seven fundamental ideas, in: F.S. Roberts (ed.), *Applications of Combinatorics and Graph Theory to the Biological and Social Sciences*, IMA Volumes in Mathematics and its Applications, Springer-Verlag, New York, pp. 1–37.

Roberts, F.S. (1989b). Meaningless statements, matching experiments, and colored digraphs (applications of graph theory and combinatorics to the theory of measurement), in: F.S. Roberts (ed.), *Applications of Combinatorics and Graph Theory to the Biological and Social Sciences*, IMA Volumes in Mathematics and its Applications, Springer-Verlag, New York, pp. 277–294.

Roberts, F.S. (1990a). Meaningfulness of conclusions from combinatorial optimization. *Discrete Appl. Math.* 29, 221–241.

Roberts, F.S. (1990b). Merging relative scores. *J. Math. Anal. Applic.* 147, 30–52.

Roberts, F.S. (1991a). From garbage to rainbows: Generalizations of graph coloring and their applications, in: Y. Alavi, G. Chartrand, O.R. Oellermann and A.J. Schwenk (eds.), *Graph*

Theory, Combinatorics, and Applications, Vol. 2, Wiley, New York, pp. 1031–1052.

Roberts, F.S. (1991b). *T*-Colorings of graphs: Recent results and open problems. *Discrete Math.* 93, 229–245.

Roberts, F.S., and C.H. Franke (1976). On the theory of uniqueness in measurement. *J. Math. Psychol.* 14, 211–218.

Roberts, F.S., and Z. Rosenbaum (1985). Some results on automorphisms of ordered relational systems and the theory of scale type in measurement, in: Y. Alavi, G. Chartrand, L. Lesniak, D.R. Lick and C.E. Wall (eds.), *Graph Theory and its Applications to Algorithms and Computer Science*, Wiley, New York, pp. 659–669.

Roberts, F.S., and Z. Rosenbaum (1986). Scale type, meaningfulness, and the possible psychophysical laws. *Math. Social Sci.* 12, 77–95.

Roberts, F.S., and Z. Rosenbaum (1988). Tight and loose value automorphisms. *Discrete Appl. Math.* 22, 69–79.

Roberts, F.S., and Z. Rosenbaum (1994). The meaningfulness of ordinal comparisons for general order relational systems, in: P. Humphreys (ed.), *Patrick Suppes: Scientific Philosopher*, Vol. 2, Kluwer, Dordrecht, pp. 251–274.

Robinson, R.E. (1963). A set-theoretical approach to empirical meaningfulness of empirical statements, Technical Report No. 55, Institute for Mathematical Studies in the Social Sciences, Stanford University, Stanford, CA.

Rozeboom, W.W. (1962a). The untenability of Luce's principle. *Psychol. Rev.* 69, 542–547.

Rozeboom, W.W. (1962b). Comment. *Psychol. Rev.* 69, 552.

Sauter, G.D., and E.G. Chilton (eds.) (1970). Air improvement recommendations for the San Francisco Bay Area, The Stanford–Ames NASA/ASEE Summer Faculty Systems Design Workshop, Final Report, Published by School of Engineering, Stanford University, Stanford CA, under NASA Contract NGR-05-020-409, October.

Savage, C.W. (1970). *Measurement of Sensation*, University of California Press, Berkeley, CA.

Scott, D. (1964). Measurement models and linear inequalities. *J. Math. Psychol.* 1, 233–247.

Scott, D., and P. Suppes (1958). Foundational aspects of theories of measurement. *J. Symbolic Logic* 23, 113–128.

Senders, V.L. (1958). *Measurement and Statistics*, Oxford University Press, New York.

Shepard, R.N. (1978). On the status of 'direct' psychophysical measurement, in: C.W. Savage (ed.) *Minnesota Studies in the Philosophy of Science*, Vol. 9, University of Minnesota Press, Minneapolis, MN, pp. 441–490.

Shepard, R.N. (1981). Psychological relations and psychophysical scales: On the status of 'direct' psychophysical measurement. *J. Math. Psychol.* 24, 21–57.

Shier, D. (1982). Testing for homogeneity using minimum spanning trees. *UMAP J.* 3, 273–283.

Siegel, S. (1956). *Nonparametric Statistics for the Behavioral Sciences*, McGraw-Hill, New York.

Smith, J.E. (1988). Characterizing computer performance with a single number. *Commun. ACM* 31, 1202–1206.

Stevens, S.S. (1946). On the theory of scales of measurement. *Science* 103, 677–680.

Stevens, S.S. (1951). Mathematics, measurement, and psychophysics, in: S.S. Stevens (ed.), *Handbook of Experimental Psychology*, Wiley, New York, pp. 1–49.

Stevens, S.S. (1955). The measurement of loudness. *J. Acoust. Soc. Amer.* 27, 815–829.

Stevens, S.S. (1957). On the psychophysical law. *Psychol. Rev.* 64, 153–181.

Stevens, S.S. (1959). Measurement, psychophysics, and utility, in: C.W. Churchman, and P. Ratoosh (eds.), *Measurement: Definitions and Theories*, Wiley, New York, pp. 18–63.

Stevens, S.S. (1960). The psychophysics of sensory function. *Amer. Scientist* 48, 226–253.

Stevens, S.S. (1961a). The psychophysics of sensory function, in: W.A. Rosenblith (ed.), *Sensory Communication*, Wiley, New York, pp. 1–33.

Stevens, S.S. (1961b). To honor Fechner and repeal his law. *Science* 133, 80–86.

Stevens, S.S. (1961c). Toward a resolution of the Fechner-Thurstone legacy. *Psychometrika* 26, 35–47.

Stevens, S.S. (1968). Ratio scales of opinion, in: D.K. Whitla (ed.), *Handbook of Measurement and Assessment in Behavioral Sciences*, Addison-Wesley, Reading, MA.

Stevens, S.S. (1969). Assessment of noise: Calculation procedure mark VII, Paper 355-128, Laboratory of Psychophysics, Harvard University, Cambridge, MA, December.

Stine, W.W. (1989). Meaningful inference: The role of measurement in statistics. *Psychol. Bull.* 105, 147–155.

Suppes, P. (1959). Measurement, empirical meaningfulness and three-valued logic, in: C.W. Churchman, and P. Ratoosh (eds.), *Measurement: Definitions and Theories*, Wiley, New York, pp. 129–143.

Suppes, P. (1979). Replies, in: R.J. Bogdan (ed.), *Patrick Suppes*, Reidel, Dordrecht, pp. 207–232.

Suppes, P., D.H. Krantz, R.D. Luce and A. Tversky (1989). *Foundations of Measurement*, Vol. II, Academic Press, New York.

Suppes, P., and J. Zinnes (1963). Basic measurement theory, in: R.D. Luce, R.R. Bush and E. Galanter (eds.), *Handbook of Mathematical Psychology*, Vol. 1, Wiley, New York, pp. 1–76.

Tanny, S.M., and M. Zuker (1987). The sensitivity of eigenvalues under elementary matrix perturbations. *Lin. Alg. Applic.* 86, 123–143.

Tanny, S.M., and M. Zuker (1988). A further look at stability notions for pulse processes on weighted digraphs, Mimeographed, Department of Mathematics, University of Toronto, Toronto, Ont.

Tesman, B. (1989). *T*-colorings, list *T*-colorings, and set *T*-colorings of graphs, Ph.D. Thesis, Department of Mathematics, Rutgers University, New Brunswick, NJ.

Thomas, H. (1982). IQ, interval scales and normal distributions. *Psychol. Bull.* 91, 198–202.

Thomas, H. (1985). Measurement structures and statistics, in: S. Kotz, and N.L. Johnson (eds.), *Encyclopedia of Statistical Sciences*, Vol. 5, Wiley, New York, pp. 381–386.

Townsend, J.T., and F.G. Ashby (1984). Measurement scales and statistics: The misconception misconceived. *Psychol. Bull.* 96, 394–401.

Trachtman, J.J., V. Giambalvo and R.S. Dippner (1978). On the assumptions concerning the assumptions of a *t* test. *J. Gen. Psychol.* 99, 107–116.

Trotter, W.T. (1988). Interval graphs, interval orders and their generalizations, in: R.D. Ringeisen, and F.S. Roberts (eds.), *Applications of Discrete Mathematics*, SIAM, Philadelphia, PA, pp. 45–58.

Walther, E.G. (1972). A rating of the major air pollutants and their sources by effect. *J. Air Pollution Control Assoc.* 22, 352–355.

Wang, D. (1985). The channel assignment problem and closed neigborhood containment graphs, Ph.D. Thesis, Department of Mathematics, Northeastern University, Boston, MA.

Warfield, J.N. (1981). Learning through model building, in: H.J. Greenberg, and J.S. Maybee (eds.), *Computer-Assisted Analysis and Model Simplification*, Academic Press, New York, pp. 69–78.

Zemel, E. (1981). Measuring the quality of approximate solutions to zero–one programming problems. *Math. Oper. Res.* 6, 319–332.

S.M. Pollock et al., Eds., *Handbooks in OR & MS, Vol. 6*

Chapter 19

Models of Auctions and Competitive Bidding

Michael H. Rothkopf

Rutgers Center for Operations Research, Rutgers University, P.O. Box 5062, New Brunswick, NJ 08903-5062, U.S.A.

1. Introduction

1.1. Why auctions?

There are many different ways a society can allocate and transfer goods and services.[1] Governments often rely upon economic competition for this purpose. As opposed to common transfer methods such as negotiations and posted prices, auctions and competitive bidding are particular *formalized* forms of economic competition. This formality is of special interest in the public sector and in other situations where there may not be sufficient trust or coincidence between the goals of the selling or purchasing agent and those of the owner or buyer. It also serves a need for fairness and for avoiding even the appearance of prejudice. Since the term 'bidding' is sometimes used when what is meant is deregulation with reliance upon market forces, it is worth emphasizing that bidding is far from the only form of competition and does not, in general, have a convincing claim to being the most efficient form.

The formal nature of auctions and bidding is also of special interest to analysts including operations researchers.[2] Those interested in the general topic of decision-making in the face of both competition and uncertainty have found auctions and bidding a fruitful area of study precisely because of the added structure imposed by the formality as well as because of the availability of added data (e.g. on unsuccessful bids).

1.2. Types of auctions

There are many different forms of auctions and bidding and several useful ways of classifying these variants. An obvious, but relatively unimportant, distinction

---

[1] See Shubik [1970] for an encompassing discussion of the many alternatives that have been used.

[2] Indeed, the first Ph.D. in operations research was granted to a student whose dissertation was on competitive bidding [Friedman, 1957]).

is between high-bid-wins auctions, typically involving bidding by potential buyers, and low-bid-wins auctions, typically involving bidding by potential sellers. A more significant distinction is between 'first-price' and 'second-price' auctions. Standard sealed bidding is a closed first-price procedure. The phrase 'first-price' means that the winning bidder pays or gets paid the amount of his or her bid, the best price. In sealed second-price bidding, an unusual procedure[3] sometimes called a Vickrey auction after the economist who first proposed its use and analyzed it [Vickrey, 1961], the bidder offering the best price wins but pays (or is paid) the amount of the second best bid. For example, if three bidders competing to buy a single item make bids of $75, $90 and $100, then the bidder who offered $100 wins but pays only $90. If there is to be more than one winner in such an auction, the auction is 'nondiscriminatory', and the price for each winner is set by the best losing bid. If two identical items were to be sold by this method to the bidders in the previous example, the bidder offering $90 would also win, and each winner would pay $75. On the other hand, standard sealed bidding is normally discriminatory when multiple identical objects are sold; in other words, each bidder pays the amount he or she bid.

For each of these sealed bid procedures, there is an oral procedure that is at least somewhat analogous with respect to bidding strategy and results. The analog for sealed bidding is the 'Dutch auction' in which a selling auctioneer (or, in the Dutch flower auctions, a mechanical device) announces successively lower prices until a bidder makes a bid. That bidder then becomes the winner at the price he or she offered. As with standard sealed bidding, bidders have incentive to behave strategically, i.e. to trade off the chance of losing the auction against extra profit if they win.

In some ways, the common progressive (or 'English') auction is analogous to the Vickrey auction if one conceives of the strategies of bidders in oral auctions as limits up to which they will bid. In the progressive oral auction, under commonly met assumptions, each bidder has a dominant strategy[4] of bidding up to exactly the amount he or she values the object for sale.[5] If all bidders do this, then the object will always be sold to the bidder valuing it most. However, if it is to be analogous strategically to the English auction, the Vickrey auction requires bidders to reveal their true valuations and to trust the bid taker. The analogy breaks down if bidders are resistant to revealing their valuations or if they fear cheating by the bid taker [see Rothkopf, Teisberg & Kahn, 1990; Engelbrecht-Wiggans & Kahn, 1991].

Bidding may be on total price or, especially when the quantity involved is not known with certainty at the time the winning competitor is selected, on one or more unit prices. This distinction can become important when the winning bidder can exercise some control over the quantity or when there are multiple unit prices involved with the winner being selected based upon an estimate of quantities.

---

[3] See Rothkopf, Teisberg & Kahn [1990] for a discussion of the usage of this kind of auction and the reasons for it being unusual.

[4] A dominant strategy is one that it pays to follow irrespective of what competitors do.

[5] If the bidder bids more and wins or bids less and loses, he or she will regret it.

1.3. Alternative sources

There is a large, highly dispersed literature on competitive bidding. However, there are a few concentrated sources of wide interest worth mentioning. These include Cassady's book [1967] describing the wide usage of auctions and variety of oral auction practices, a comprehensive but early and unannotated bibliography by Stark & Rothkopf [1979], two survey papers (an early, but wide ranging one by Engelbrecht-Wiggans [1980] and a more recent one restricted to game theoretic models of single isolated auctions by McAfee & McMillan [1987]), two edited volumes of papers (Amihud [1976] and Engelbrecht-Wiggans, Shubik & Stark [1983]), a 'Symposium' of four papers in an issue of the *Journal of Economic Perspectives* (Vol. 3, No. 3, 1989), a book by Smith [1990] giving a sociological interpretation of oral auctions, and material by Wilson [1987, 1993]

1.4. This chapter

There are two remaining parts to this chapter. The first of these (Section 2) surveys a wide variety of mathematical models of auction phenomena. The final part of the chapter (Section 3) discusses the design of competitive systems. It discusses the objectives involved in such a design process, how process design decisions relate to other decisions, the various methodologies that can contribute to the design process and, finally, a number of different application areas and some of the issues that arise in them. As will become apparent, the answers to questions commonly asked about bidding are quite sensitive to the particulars of the bidding model. It will also become apparent that there are a number of phenomena and issues discussed in the final part that are not adequately represented in much of the theory discussed in the next part. These observations should serve as both a caution flag to those interested in applying the theory and as a welcome mat to those interested in extending the theory in fruitful directions.

2. Models of auction phenomena

2.1. Models of single isolated auctions

The bulk of the analytical literature on auctions deals with models of individual auctions. In these models, one or all of the bidders attempt to maximize their expected profit (or their von Neumann-Morgenstern utility) in the single auction. Sometimes, this is a realistic assumption. In many other important situations, it is clearly incorrect. However, single auction models can sometimes serve as useful building blocks or starting points for analyses that take account of the effects of other transactions.

Note that there is an almost perfect duality between auctions in which the highest payment offered wins and auctions in which the lowest cost offered wins. The major caution with respect to this duality is the potential role of zero as an implicit limit on acceptable bids. In what follows, we will normally not comment further on the difference between high-bid-wins and low-bid-wins auctions.

2.1.1. Decision theory models

We consider first models in which a single bidder maximizes its gain. The earliest such models [see Friedman, 1956, 1957] assumed or calculated a probability distribution, $F(x)$, for the best competitive bid, x, and then had the bidder choose the bid, b, that maximized its expected profit,

$$E(b) = \int_0^b (v - b) \mathrm{d}F(x) = (v - b)F(b),$$

relative to a *known* expected value, v, for what is being sold.[6] Where $F(b)$ was calculated, it was normally calculated as the distribution of the maximum of independent draws from the bid distributions of each competitor, i.e.

$$F(b) = \prod_j F_j(b),$$

where j indexes competitors and $F_j(b)$ is the cumulative distribution of competitor j's bid. Such models have come to be called independent private value models. They have been used by some bidders, in particular by some bidders for federal oil leases in the 1960s and, in some cases, even later.[7] One characteristic of such models is that they lead to more aggressive optimal bids when the level of competition is increased.

In a key paper, Capen, Clapp & Campbell [1971] argued for an alternative approach. They attacked the assumption, implicit in the models of Friedman and most of his many followers, of statistical independence between the best competitive bid and the value of what is being sold. They argued persuasively that, at least in the context of oil lease bidding, the best competitive bid was a good predictor of the value of what was being sold. They proposed, instead, a 'common value model' in which the value V, of what was being sold was the same for all bidders, but unknown to them. Bidders were assumed to make statistically independent estimating errors, e_i, where i indexes all bidders including the one for whom the analysis is being done. The result of such a model is that bidders who make unbiased estimates of the value of what is being sold will tend to be disappointed in the value of what they win, especially if the competition is heavy, since they will tend to win auctions in which their estimate was optimistic and lose ones in which it was pessimistic. Bidders who do not correct sufficiently

---

[6] If v is not known, then its expectation may be substituted for it, *provided* v and b are independent variables.

[7] See Keefer, Smith & Back [1991]. It is difficult to find out what bidders are doing since they usually have strong incentives to be secretive. Some bidders may have used a model proposed by Arps [1965] that maximized the probability of winning (or, equivalently, the expected reserves won) subject to the constraint that expected profit be nonnegative.

for this selection bias will be impoverished by what Capen, Clapp & Campbell termed 'the winner's curse'. In particular, the approach of Capen, Clapp & Campbell leads to less aggressive bidding when competition increases (beyond the level approximated by two equivalent competitors) or when estimating accuracy decreases. Oren & Williams [1975] proved the generality of the approach of Capen, Clapp & Campbell.

Stark [1974] showed that bidders faced with the problem of selecting a set of unit prices for a single contract can maximize their expected profit by solving a simple linear programming problem. Stark's concern was road building contracts, and the unit prices covered items such as cubic yards of earth moved and number of signs. However, as discussed below, his analysis is directly relevant to federal timber bidding where the unit prices are for board feet of various species of timber.

Suppose that i indexes the elements of the bid, that the bidder bids a unit price of p_i on the ith element, that the bid taker's quantity estimate for that element to be used in evaluating bids is q_i while the bidder's unbiased quantity estimate of it is Q_i and that D_i is a discount factor to be applied by the bidder in evaluating payments for element i. The bid taker's evaluation of the bid, B, is given by

$$B = \sum_i q_i p_i. \tag{1}$$

For any level of competitiveness, B, the bidder uses, its expected profit will be maximized if it chooses its values of p_i so as to maximize

$$Z = \sum_i D_i Q_i p_i$$

subject to (1) and

$$l_i \le p_i \le u_i,$$

where l_i and u_i are any lower or upper bounds, respectively, imposed by law, regulation or bidder policy on the unit price it bids for element i. When bidders do this, the result is 'skewed' or 'unbalanced' bids in which the unit prices are adjusted as much as possible to take advantage of differences between the way the price will be viewed by the bid taker and by the bidder. Differences in quantity estimates as well as in the timing of payments can be exploited. Diekmann, Mayer & Stark [1981] have generalized Stark's result, getting a quadratic program to be solved by risk averse bidders.

Rothkopf [1991] develops formulas for optimal strategies for bidders who can submit two or more bids in an auction and then, after the bids are opened, withdraw any bid not necessary in order to win, perhaps paying a withdrawal penalty. The formulas depend upon the number of bids that are possible, the size and nature (i.e. fixed or proportional) of the penalty, if any, for withdrawing a bid, and form of the distribution for the best competitive bid. For example, if the bidders probability distribution for the best competitive bid is distributed uniformly on a range, $[a, b]$, that includes the bidder's value, v, and if the bidder can submit K bids and withdraw bids without penalty, the optimal set of bids is

$$b_k^* = v - \frac{k(v-a)}{K+1}, \quad k = 1, 2, ..., K,$$

and the bidder's expected profit using these bids is

$$E^* = \frac{(v-a)^2 K}{2(K+1)(b-a)}.$$

With the same distribution, but with only two bids allowed and a penalty q for withdrawing a bid, the optimal bids are

$$b_1^* = \frac{2v+a-q}{3},$$

$$b_2^* = \frac{v+2a-2q}{3},$$

provided $q < (v-a)/2$. With these bids, the expected profit is given by

$$E^* = \frac{(v-a-q)^2 + q(v-a)}{3(b-a)}.$$

2.1.2. Game theory models

We now consider game theory models of single auctions.[8] Most of these assume a fixed set of bidders and find Nash equilibria in which every bidder optimizes its behavior with respect to the actions of every other bidder. There are also a few models that find Nash equilibria with respect to limited strategy sets.

The simplest case without limited strategy sets to analyze makes the following four assumptions:

(1) There is a fixed set of bidders.

(2) The independent private values assumption discussed above in Section 2.1.1 applies.

(3) The bidders are risk neutral.

(4) Before the bidders draw their private value from a commonly known distribution, they are symmetric with respect to value and information, knowing the number of competitors and their risk neutral rationality.

Several interesting results hold under these assumptions. First, in an oral auction each bidder's *dominant* strategy is to bid up to its value. When all bidders follow such strategies, the item for sale is sold to the bidder valuing it most for a price at or marginally above the second highest value attached to it by any bidder. This is perfectly efficient economically.

A similar result holds for sealed second-price auctions. This time it is the best bids rather than the 'strategies' that equal the bidders' values. As with oral auctions, the item is sold to the highest valuer at the second highest valuer's value.

---

[8] Note that game theory is discussed in a completely different context in this handbook's chapter on military applications (Chapter 4).

Both Dutch and standard sealed bidding call for identical strategies in which, using the decision theory approach for independent private values discussed above, the bidders select bids by balancing the risk of losing against the profit of winning. Since each optimal bid is an increasing function of the bidder's private valuation, sale to the highest valuer is assured. Furthermore, the difference between the value and the optimal bid of the highest valuer turns out on the average to be exactly equal to the difference between the highest and the second highest valuation. The somewhat surprising result of this is that *the expected revenue of the bid taker is identical for all four kinds of auctions.*[9]

When we relax the symmetry part of assumption (4), some of these results break down. Cases exist in which first-price auctions produce, on the average, more revenue, and other cases exist in which second-price auctions do [see Griesmer, Levitan & Shubik, 1967; Maskin & Riley, 1983; Vickrey, 1961]. Second-price procedures, both oral and sealed, continue to guarantee that the item sold goes to its highest valuer, but first-price procedures no longer do so.

Next, we restore the symmetry assumption and, instead, relax the risk neutrality of assumption (3). We now find that with risk averse bidders, the seller's expected revenue is greater with first-price bidding than with second-price bidding [see Harris & Raviv, 1981; Holt, 1980; Maskin & Riley, 1984]. However, this result becomes somewhat less widely applicable than it first seems when it is recalled that, in the independent private values context it assumes, the only risk facing bidders is the risk of losing the auction; hence, risk averse bidders are not 'cautious', but anxious to win.

Next, we relax the assumption of independent private values. Milgrom & Weber [1982] have defined a class of value functions they called 'affiliated values'. This class has independent private values as one extreme case and common values as another. They showed that when bidders' values are affiliated, the expected revenue received by the bid taker from an oral auction in which bidders can observe each other drop out is at least as great as that in a sealed second-price auction. The expected revenue from a second-price auction is at least as great as that from a sealed bid auction, which in turn has the same revenue as a Dutch auction. Lack of statistical independence and a bidder's lack of certainty about its true value each play a role when the independent private values assumption is relaxed. Table 1 gives more details about the effects on bidder strategy and on expected bid taker revenue. In addition, Harstad & Rothkopf [1991] have shown that the higher revenue from English auctions in Milgrom & Weber's model depends critically upon the assumption that bidders can observe when other bidders drop out. If bidders can hide their intentions about further bidding, they have incentive to do so, and the equilibrium expected revenue falls towards that in a sealed second-price auction.

---

[9] Such results, termed revenue neutrality theorems, date to Vickrey [1961]. For a more general treatment see Myerson [1981]. Rothkopf, Teisberg & Kahn [1990] point out that if some third party captures a fraction of the economic rent revealed by a second-price auction procedure, the 'neutrality' theorem still holds, but it applies to the bidders rather than the bid taker, i.e. on an expected value basis all of the rent captured by third parties comes from the bid taker.

Table 1
The effect on expected revenue in equilibrium and on bidder strategy in second-price auctions of
the nature of the uncertainty about values

	Statistical independence	Semi-strict affiliation
Bidders have no residual value uncertainty	English, 2nd-price strategies: Dominant strategy to bid value	English, 2nd-price strategies: Dominant strategy to bid value.
	Equilibrium expected revenue: Complete revenue equivalence.	Equilibrium expected revenue: Revenue (M-W English) = revenue (2nd-price) > revenue (1st-price)
Bidders have residual value uncertainty	English, 2nd-price strategies: Depends upon rivals' strategies; in equilibrium, uses information revealed by rivals' bids.	English, 2nd-price strategies: Depends upon rivals' strategies; in equilibrium, uses information revealed by rivals' bids.
	Equilibrium expected revenue: Complete revenue equivalence.	Equilibrium expected revenue: Revenue (M-W English) > revenue (2nd-price) > revenue (1st-price)

Source: Harstad & Rothkopf [1991]. 'Semi-strict affiliation' is affiliation without statistical independence in any subset of variables. 'M-W English' refers to the version of the English auction
analyzed by Milgrom & Weber [1982] in which bidders can observe the point at which each of
their competitors drop out of the bidding. References to first-price auctions apply to both standard
sealed bidding and Dutch auctions.

Another interesting result indicates the importance to a bidder of the privacy of
its information. Engelbrecht-Wiggans, Milgrom & Weber [1983] showed that, with
affiliated values, a bidder's expected profit from the auction is zero if its private
information is known to even one other bidder.

Game theoretic bidding models of first-price auctions do not usually yield
analytic formulas. Instead, they yield differential equations that must be solved
numerically. However, there are a few interesting exceptions. One of these is for
a game involving n bidders drawing independent private values from a uniform
distribution on $[0, 1]$ and then submitting standard sealed bids. Vickrey [1961]
showed that it is a Nash equilibrium strategy for each bidder to submit bid $b(v)$
$= v(n - 1)/n$, where v is the bidder's private value. Before drawing a value, each
bidder has a probability $1/n$ of winning the auction. The average profit of the
winner is $1/(n + 1)$. After drawing value v, a bidder has a probability of v^{n-1} of
earning a profit of v/n. The bid taker's expected revenue is $(n - 1)/(n + 1)$.

Another situation in which analytical solutions can be obtained occurs when
bidding strategies are restricted to multiples of estimated value in a particular
class of common value auctions. (Multiplicative strategies may be behaviorally
reasonable and they may approximate optimal policies especially in the limit
as the amount of common prior information becomes small, but there is no
useful model for which they are exactly optimal. See Rothkopf [1980a,b] and

Engelbrecht-Wiggans & ˙.Veber [1979a].) Rothkopf [1969] showed that when n bidders estimate a common cost, c, with estimates, c_i, $i = 1, 2, ..., n$, drawn independently from a Weibull probability distribution[10] with density

$$f(c_i) = amc_i^{m-1} \exp(-ac_i^m),$$

where m is the parameter that controls the standard deviation to mean ratio of the distribution and a is chosen so as to make the estimate unbiased, i.e.

$$a = \left[\frac{\Gamma(1 + 1/m)}{c} \right]^m,$$

the equilibrium multiplier is given by

$$P^* = \frac{m(n-1)n^{1/m}}{m(n-1) - 1}, \tag{2}$$

and when all bidders use this strategy the expected profit of each bidder is given by

$$E = \frac{c}{n[m(n-1) - 1]}. \tag{3}$$

In addition, Rothkopf [1969] presents closed form results for models with two bidders with costs that are different but in a known ratio and for a mirror image highest-bid-wins model in which the value estimate is drawn from a Gumbel distribution. (The Gumbel distribution is the distribution of the reciprocal of a Weibull distributed variable.) Rothkopf [1980b] also gives analytic results for equilibrium strategies for a case in which bids are restricted to being a general linear (i.e. affine) function of the estimate.

The game theory literature contains a number of papers containing results on the design of 'optimal', i.e. revenue maximizing, auctions in which the bid taker may set a reservation price and even charge fees to losing bidders.[11] However, the results so far seem to be of extremely limited practical significance. The cited models do not seem to be realistic enough. For example, they may not give bidders any ability to decide whether to participate.[12] In addition, the 'optimal' auctions are sometimes rather complex, and there is no evidence for their use in practice.

---

[10] The Weibull distribution arises in the statistics of extreme values. The minimum of any number of independent draws from a Weibull distribution itself has a Weibull distribution and the minimum of draws from any distribution bounded below approaches a Weibull distribution as the number of draws becomes large. See Gumbel [1958].

[11] See for example Laffont & Maskin [1980], Harris & Raviv [1981], Myerson [1981], Riley & Samuelson [1981], Matthews [1983, 1984], Maskin & Riley [1984] and Moore [1984].

[12] It is becoming clear to auction theorists that auction designers cannot afford to ignore the bidders' decisions to participate. See Engelbrecht-Wiggans [1987a]. Recently game theory models have started to appear that allow bidder participation to vary with the form of the auction. See Harstad [1990].

2.2. Models that include the decision to prepare a bid

The costs of preparing a bid are normally sunk costs when a bid is submitted. They are incurred when a decision is made to prepare a bid. Formal decision theoretic treatments of the decision to prepare a bid for a single auction date back to Flueck [1967] and Engwall [1976] and are unsurprising. Simmonds & Slatter [1978] approach the problem somewhat more broadly by analyzing the firm's decision on how large a staff it should have for preparing bids and, thus, how many of its bidding opportunities it should accept.

Hausch & Li [1991] consider game theoretic models of independent-private-value auctions in which the bidders decide how much costly information to gather. They find that when the accuracy of the information a bidder acquires is private to that bidder, the revenue equivalence of first-price and second-price auctions holds, but that when that accuracy is publicly observable, revenue equivalence fails.

Harstad [1990] presents a game theoretic model of a common value auction in which bidder participation is endogenously determined rather than predetermined. He finds symmetric Nash equilibria in which a large group of potential bidders select a probability of participating by observing their private value (at a cost) and submitting a bid. The result is that the expected number of bidders increases until it is no longer profitable for bidders to raise their participation probabilities. Since there are participation costs and bidders make no expected profit after paying them, the bid taker pays them and the best economic result for the bid taker occurs, somewhat paradoxically, when there is the smallest expected number of bidders. Hausch & Li [1990] consider a somewhat similar model that also entails endogenous decisions on information acquisition.

Bid takers desiring to purchase multiple items sometimes split the award, buying some items from one or more bidders asking a higher unit price. This practice has typically been viewed as a (costly) way of improving competition in future procurements [e.g., see Anton & Yao, 1987] or occasionally as justified by diseconomies of scale [see Anton & Yao, 1989]. However, Klotz & Chatterjee [1991] have developed a model of a single auction in which entry decisions by potential bidders with linear costs and risk aversion combine to make it profitable for a bid taker to precommit to a split procurement.

2.3. Auctions in context: models of multiple transactions

Auctions that are part of an important stream of commerce are not likely to be isolated. Various kinds of interrelationships may arise. There may be several simultaneous sales. These may be accomplished in a single auction as with Treasury bills, or there may be simultaneously opened bids in separate auctions as in the sales of outer continental shelf oil leases. There may be a sequence of interrelated auctions or of auctions and non-auction transactions. A wide variety of interrelationship between different auctions have been modeled. The next two subsections describe models of simultaneous sales and of sequential sales. However, there are many open research questions in this area. For example, what is the effect of an auctioneer selling sequentially the right to choose from among unsold items rather than selling individual items and how should bidders bid in such auctions?

2.3.1. Models of simultaneous auctions

The simplest simultaneous sale situation arises when the items to be sold are identical and freely interchangeable as with Treasury bills. If each bidder desires only one item, then a second price auction produces 'truth revealing' bids. However, any bidder who desires more than one item and submits multiple bids has incentive to bid less than his value for any item other than the last since there is some chance that his bid on one item will set the price for one upon which he has offered to pay the same price or a higher price. Dubey & Shubik [1980] have proposed a sale mechanism involving differentiated prices that restores incentive for truth revealing bids, essentially by paying off buyers for the monopsony power inherent in their having more than a marginal demand.

In general, the guidance from game theory for the revenue maximizing choice between discriminatory and nondiscriminatory sales of identical items is unclear. On the one hand, with affiliated values, symmetry and no risk aversion the uniform price auction will yield at least as much expected revenue. On the other, with independent private values, symmetry and risk aversion, the discriminatory auction will yield at least as much revenue [see Weber, 1983].

A number of papers dating back to Friedman [1956] have considered the situation faced by bidders who wish to bid on more than one of a number of differentiated items that are to be sold with simultaneously opened bids but who face a constraint upon the total of their bids. This is a situation often faced by oil company executives preparing bids for offshore oil tracts. Stark & Mayer [1971] pointed out that the problem of optimally allocating the scarce resource of bidding dollars over the competing opportunities provided by different sales did not have a concave objective function and, hence, could not be solved in general by means of marginal adjustment of proposed bids. They provided a computationally tractable dynamic programming approach for solving the problem. If there are n simultaneous auctions, $E_i(B_i)$ denotes the expected profit in auction i with bid B_i, $V_i(B)$ is the maximum expected profit that can be obtained from auctions 1 through i with a total bid limit for these auction of B and where a bid of 0 is understood to mean no bid at all, the relevant dynamic programming recursion is given by

$$V_0(B) = 0$$

$$V_i(B) = \max_{0 \le B_i \le B} [E_i(B_i) + V_{i-1}(B - B_i)], \quad i = 1, 2, ..., n.$$

Rothkopf [1977] showed that a modified marginal adjustment process could obtain a bounded, near optimal allocation of bidding dollars when the expected return from each auction as a function of the amount bid had a typical form involving an initial convex region followed by a concave one. He also showed that at most one auction could have an optimal bid in the convex region and gave conditions under which there could be none.

Engelbrecht-Wiggans [1987b] uses a principal agent model to show that constraining a bidder in simultaneous auctions who wants to maximize expected winnings on expected expenditures does not lead to different bidding from that of a bidder trying to maximize expected profits subject to the same constraint. However, a more workable constraint, one on total bids, does lead to different behavior.

Engelbrecht-Wiggans & Weber [1979b] have solved a particular, simple game theoretic model in which bidders participate through agents in n simultaneous oral auctions for identical items. Each bidder is assumed to have value for only one item; any items beyond one bought and paid for are worthless to their winner and not resalable.

Wilson [1979] and Maskin & Riley [1987] have constructed game theory models of the auctioning of shares in a combined asset rather than its separate parts. Wilson has results for auctions in which all shares are sold at the same price, while Maskin and Riley consider discriminatory share auctions.

Smith & Rothkopf [1985] consider the situation faced by a bidder bidding in simultaneous auctions who will incur a single fixed charge if and only if one or more of the auctions is won. They present a single state variable dynamic programming formulation applicable when the auctions are statistically independent and computationally helpful conditions for the general case. Cohen & Loeb [1990] consider the accounting implications of a similar situation.

2.3.2. Models of sequential auctions

Some models of a sequence of related auctions consider the interrelationships between the values to the bidder of the items for sale; others focus on the interrelationship between a bid in one auction and competitive behavior in subsequent auctions. Kortanek, Soden & Sodaro [1973] deal with the former. They consider a variety of models in which bidders are bidding in a sequence of auctions to sell products that use common scarce resources such as production capacity. While the particulars differ from model to model, the optimal strategy can always be characterized by the relationship:

$$\text{optimal bid price} = \text{direct costs} + \text{opportunity costs}$$
$$+ \text{competitive advantage fee.}$$

Oren & Rothkopf [1975] consider the effect of bids on future competitive behavior. They develop a general model in which there is a scalar characterizing the state of competition and a 'reaction function' relating a bidder's bid to changes in that state. They provide a general dynamic programming approach for finding the optimal bidding strategy. They then specialize this approach, applying it with a particular reaction function to Rothkopf's [1969] multiplicative strategy equilibrium model for lowest-bid-wins auctions described above. Note that because they use a reaction function their model is not a dynamic game, but rather a static game in which each bidder takes into account his estimate (which is not necessarily correct) of the effect of his present bid upon the future behavior of his competitors. A reaction function they consider is

$$Q_i(t+1) = Q_i(t) + ap_i(t)[P_i(t) - Q_i(t)],$$

where $P_i(t)$ is bidder i's multiplicative strategy in auction t, $Q_i(t)$ and $Q_i(t+1)$ are the strategies used by bidder i's competitors in auctions t and $t+1$, respectively, $p_i(t)$ is the probability that bidder i wins auction t (it is a function of P_i and Q_i), and a is a constant that determines the strength of the estimated competitive reaction. With this reaction function, the equilibrium strategies and the expected profits per auction their use results in, are given by

$$P^* = \frac{m(n-1)n^{1/m}}{m(n-1) - 1 - F},$$

and

$$E = \frac{c(1+F)}{n[m(n-1) - 1 - F]},$$

where D is the discount factor between auctions and $F \equiv aD/(1-D)$ is a factor indicating the effect of the sequential nature of the auction. Note that when $F = 0$, P^* and E revert to the expressions given in Section 2.1.2 above in Equations (2) and (3). As the strength of the competitive reaction increases and as the discount factor between auctions nears unity, F increases causing the bids and the expected profits to increase

There are a number of pure game theory models of sequential auctions. These models differ in the nature of the individual auctions (e.g. first-price vs. second-price and independent private values vs. common value vs. general affiliated values) and in the relationship between the auctions (e.g. bidders drop out after purchasing one item vs. continued participation and independent values in successive auctions vs. values in one auction contain information on values in later auctions).

Hausch [1986] compares selling a group of items using sequential auctions to selling them using simultaneous auctions. He considers a context in which information about the value of one object conveys information about the value of others. There are potential benefits to the bid taker from bidders in later auctions having information from earlier ones, and in some cases this can be the dominant effect. However, in many cases this effect is dominated in equilibrium by a deception effect: bidders have incentive to bid less aggressively in earlier auctions so as to avoid increasing the subsequent valuations and bids of their competitors. This result was foreshadowed by a simple two-stage, two-object, two-bidder signaling model of Ortega-Reichert [1968].

Weber [1983] reports that in a symmetric, affiliated values model the prices of sequential sales when each bidder wishes to win at most one of the identical items will exhibit a upward drift in equilibrium. Engelbrecht-Wiggans [1994] offers a model that drops the assumption of identical items with the result that, for many distributions, prices drift downward on average. Within this model, the auctioneer's expected revenue increases if objects with higher expected profit to bidders are offered earlier in the sequence. Engelbrecht-Wiggans argues that this may provide a rationale for the practice of some real estate auctioneers to auction off the right to choose among unsold items (e.g. condominiums in a large building) rather than the individual items.

Bikhchandani [1986, 1988] considers a model in which two bidders participate in a series of second-price auctions. The auctions are common-value auctions except for the existence of a (very) small probability that one of the bidders has a slightly higher valuation. He finds a nonsymmetric equilibrium in which one of the bidders establishes a reputation for aggressive bidding and thus forces the other to bid quite unaggressively in order to avoid the 'winner's curse'. Due to the second-price nature of the auctions, this equilibrium is quite unfavorable to the bid taker.

Bikhchandani & Huang [1989] have constructed a model of a common-value auction combined with a resale market. They consider the effect in the resale market of information on bids and derive conditions under which uniform-price auctions produce more expected revenue than discriminatory auctions.

Rothkopf, Teisberg & Kahn [1990] include an effect of information revelation in one auction on subsequent transactions. In comparing the expected revenue from standard sealed bidding and publicly opened second-price sealed bidding, they consider a model in which third parties will capture a fraction of the revealed economic rent (i.e. the amount above the lowest bid that the winning seller is paid in the second-price procedure). They point out that in equilibrium, on average, all of the cost of this payment to third parties will be borne by the bid taker. Engelbrecht-Wiggans & Kahn [1991] offer an example of this kind of behavior in which the winning bidder's labor union is a player in the second stage of a two-stage game. Motivated by the concern about the effect of information revelation, Nurmi & Salomaa [1993] suggest a cryptographic version of the sealed second-price auction to limit the information revealed.

2.4. Models of cheating in auctions

There are a few models of cheating in auctions. Comanor & Schankerman [1976] examine the role of identical bids in easing the coordination problem of an ongoing conspiracy to allocate market shares by rigging bids. Robinson [1985] and Graham & Marshall [1987] point out that conspiracies to collude are stable in oral auctions, since the conspirators can observe a violation of the agreed upon course of action in time to react to it, but are not stable in standard sealed bidding.

The role of the fear of cheating by bid takers in explaining the rarity of Vickrey auctions was discussed by Rothkopf, Teisberg & Kahn [1990] and modeled by Rothkopf & Harstad [1992].

Kuhlman [1974], Comanor & Schankerman [1976], Rothrock [1976, 1978] and Maltz & Pollock [1979, 1980] have reported on ways of detecting bid rigging from the examination of bidding history. However, some of the work on this topic has been kept confidential to avoid making bid rigging easier to conceal.

3. The design of competitive systems

3.1. Design objectives and politics

Sometimes, economists are tempted to assume that the bid taker chooses the form of auction unilaterally and in a way that will maximize his or her expected revenue. The first part of this assumption is often incorrect in competitive situations in which bidders can choose between participating in a particular auction or in other potential transactions. Governmental bid takers also may at times need to be concerned about bidders' willingness to participate, and they normally have concerns beyond revenue maximization. Because democratic governments normally operate under open and potentially adversarial scrutiny, they are concerned about the 'fairness' of the process and the appearance of fairness. Indeed, the openness and formality of auctions may be used to legitimize the assignment of rights to particular individuals or companies.[13]

Government sellers are representatives of the society as a whole and, thus, are appropriately concerned with the economic efficiency of the sale or procurement process as well as with maximizing the revenue received by the government or minimizing its payments. This concern with efficiency includes concerns about the costs to the government and to the bidders of the sale process and especially concerns about effects of any undesirable incentives imposed by the sale format. For example, there is concern that a sale format for rights to federal mineral deposits that requires large royalty payments on mineral production could lead to the premature abandonment of the extraction venture.

Sometimes concern about economic efficiency can serve as an excuse for politically expedient policies that transfer government assets cheaply to a particular industry.[14] However, in a context in which reduced revenue in government sales must be replaced with increased tax revenue, failure to collect revenue is a major source of economic inefficiency [see Rothkopf & Harstad, 1990]. In many situations, Congress prohibits resource sales for less than 'fair market value'. However, this requirement is less restrictive than it first sounds. Government officials speak of *a* fair market value, not *the* fair market value, and courts have generally been

---

[13] One of the points made by Dam [1976] in a critical analysis of the British government's decision to allocate most North Sea oil tracts noncompetitively is that it led to subsequent tax increases on profits from North Sea oil operations. In other words, the political legitimacy of North Sea oil tract control and profits was not established as it would have been in a formal competitive sale.

[14] Such transfers are normally politically expedient because the beneficiaries of them are few and well informed while the taxpayers are a diffuse, and usually uninformed, group each with relatively little at stake. A high level federal civil servant recently wrote me that 'As far as I know, no [high-level, nonpolitical program manager] has ever gotten a promotion, a raise, or more staff or responsibility because they helped produce more receipts. However, some careers have blossomed as a result of contribution to the re-allocation of significant numbers of leases from the Federal to the private sector.' The issue raised here extends to enforcing policies (e.g. collecting royalties) as well as enunciating them. See, for example, Eisendrath's attack [1987] on the performance of the U.S. Department of the Interior in this regard.

unwilling to block transactions subject to a fair market value restriction in the absence of proof of actual corruption.

Bidders faced with a set of auction rules and practices may try to 'beat the system' by taking advantage in unanticipated ways of aspects of it.[15] They may also try to get the system changed.[16] Finally, they may violate the rules surreptitiously, sometimes in criminal ways[17], in hopes of gain. It has been argued that resistance to cheating is a better predictor of choice of auction format than expected revenue to the bid taker on the assumption that the rules will be followed [see Robinson, 1984, 1985]. It is certainly an appropriate design criterion.

3.2. Decisions other than sale mechanism

While this chapter focuses on the design of the sale mechanism, it is important to note that many other decisions about the sale may affect the design objectives. For example, the decision of what to sell and when to sell it can have a major impact. The 'area-wide' leasing of federal offshore oil tracts carried out under Interior Secretary Watt in the early 1980s, changed previous policy in a way that lowered government revenues by billions of dollars. (See Moody & Kruvant [1990] as well as Stiglitz [1984] and Rothkopf & Harstad [1990].)

It is also true that some of these other decisions may affect the appropriateness of alternative sale mechanisms. For example, if many mineral leases are offered for sale at once, the increased chance that a particular lease will receive only one bid might justify higher minimum bid requirements. Also, if many leases are offered at once, the limited ability of bidders to finance multiple purchases could increase the relative attractiveness of sequential sales compared to simultaneous sales. It could also suggest that contingent bidding schemes might be worth considering.

Other important sale-related decisions include how to charge (e.g. per unit royalty, one time bonus, annual rent, profit share, etc.)[18], who may bid (e.g. citizenship requirements, financial responsibility requirements, joint bidding bans[19], etc.), special advantages (e.g. for small business, minority business, etc.), and strat-

---

[15] Rothkopf [1991] discusses an auction in which the winning bidder paid a penalty to withdraw an apparently winning bid in order to allow a less aggressive bid by an associate to win. Skewed bidding discussed above in Section 2.1.1 and below in Section 3.4.3 is a better known example of such a practice. Of course, when ways of 'beating the system' become widely known, they are no longer unanticipated, and bid takers must accept them or change the system.

[16] Rothkopf [1983] describes a situation in which Shell Chemical Company made a contingent bid not allowed by the rules originally specified by Congress in the hope, eventually realized, that Congress would agree to change the rules and accept the offer.

[17] Bid rigging, i.e. a conspiracy among supposedly competing bidders, is, of course criminal. In spite of this, it is not uncommon in some areas. See, for example, the condensed transcript of an interview with a convicted bid rigger and two attorneys involved in prosecuting bid rigging in the A.S.C.E. newsletter [American Society of Civil Engineers, 1985].

[18] See Mead, Moseidjord & Muraoka [1984], Rothkopf & Engelbrecht-Wiggans [1992], and Rothkopf & Harstad [1990].

[19] See Kobrin, Canes & Murphy [1977], Debrock & Smith [1983] and Rothkopf & Engelbrecht-Wiggans [1993].

egy related to multiple sourcing in order to avoid the risks and future monopoly problems of becoming dependent upon a single supplier.[20]

3.3. Methodologies available

Auction designers have several different methodologies available to them. In addition to the direct use of formal models, auction designers can call upon informal observation, interpretation and analysis, upon econometrics and upon experimental gaming. However, each of the other options, to some degree, uses models of auctions. While the main thrust of this chapter is formal models, it is appropriate to devote a brief description to each of these other approaches and, especially, to the role of models in them.

Informal observation, interpretation and analysis is the prevailing method in use for auction design. This can range from the most casual what-did-we-do-last-time approach, to sophisticated and detailed analyses of alternatives with initial results published in the federal register and final results determined after revisions in response to the comments of industry and, at times, other interested parties. Usually, even the more detailed and sophisticated of these analyses are buried in the unpublished staff papers of government agencies, but occasionally they surface.[21] When not dominated by political considerations, these analyses are usually in close touch with many of the detailed empirical realities of the sale situation. The complicated factual situations they involve often mean that preexisting modeling efforts are not definitive with respect to the policy choices under consideration. However, the open adversarial nature of the debate surrounding some of these policy choices can provide an opportunity for such analytical input as is available if the staff involved has missed it.

Econometrics has been applied as a tool both for comparing particular auction design alternatives and for comparing alternative auction models. Examples of the former use include Wiener [1979] and Hansen [1985], both of which examine the question of whether sealed bids or oral auctions produced more revenue in federal timber rights auctions [see also Rothkopf & Engelbrecht-Wiggans, 1993]. An example of the latter is Gilley & Karels [1981], a paper that shows statistically the presence of a tendency of bidders to bid less aggressively in offshore oil lease auctions involving heavy competition – a behavior called for, as discussed above, by certain bidding models and not by others. See also Hendricks & Porter [1988] and Hendricks, Porter & Boudreau [1987].

Econometrics is not as powerful a tool for use in auction design in practice as one might anticipate. There are several problems. First, the data are historical, i.e. restricted to past situations. Second, the variations between the effects of

---

[20] Seshadri, Chatterjee & Lilien [1991].

[21] See for example the Report of Commission by the U.S. Commission on Fair Market Value Policy for Federal Coal Leasing [1984], particularly Chapter 5: Coal Lease Sale Procedures. Other examples that have surfaced include U.S. Federal Energy Regulatory Commission, Offices of Pipeline and Producer Regulation and of Economic Policy [1987] and U.S. General Accounting Office [1983].

mechanisms may be small compared with other sources of variation. Third, the data often contain only one of the several auction mechanism alternatives that we would like to compare. Fourth, auctions are normally not exact repetitions of the same random process. When the data do contain more than one mechanism, often there are a variety of other uncontrolled or semi-controlled factors that have also varied with the mechanism change. Adding data from additional auctions may also add new factors in need of control. Finally, sometimes data is not released or not complied effectively.[22]

Partly because of the difficulties with econometric measurement, economists have begun doing laboratory experiments. See Plott [1982] and Smith [1982, 1987] for discussions of the role of laboratory experimentation in economics and Roth [1988] for a methodological critique. In most of these experiments, human subjects are given the opportunity to earn money by making decisions in a simulated economic situation. Many of these experiments have involved competitive bidding.

Some of these experiments are designed to check the predictive properties of Nash equilibrium solutions to game theoretic models of auction behavior. Often, the experimental subjects converge upon the equilibrium with great speed. See for example Smith [1967] and Plott & Smith [1978]. On the other hand, Kagel & Levin [1986] and Lind & Plott [1991] were able to find a particular kind of persistent disequilibrium behavior even when they repeated their experiments using experienced businessmen as subjects.

Some of the bidding experiments are designed not to test mathematically precise theories, but rather to test proposed new market mechanisms. Grether, Isaac & Plott [1979, 1981] and Rassenti, Smith & Bulfin [1982], for example, ran experiments to test proposed schemes for auctioning off landing rights at congested airports.

3.4. Application areas

This section discusses some of the better known and documented areas in which formal analysis has been applied to the design of auctions. These areas include state and federal oil leasing, federal coal leasing, federal logging rights sales, the sale of treasury bills, the purchase by electric utilities of power from cogenerators and other nonutility sources, military and other government procurement, road construction, and the allocation of capacity in space stations and in regulated pipelines.

3.4.1. Oil leasing

The sealed bid sales of U.S. offshore oil leases are among the most spectacular competitive sales and have attracted substantial analytical attention. The amounts at stake are large; a number of times, individual tracts have received bonus bids in

---

[22] Regression, however, has proven to be a key tool in detecting collusion in bidding and in estimating its economic effects [Rothrock, 1991].

excess of $100 000 000. The uncertainties and risks are also usually large; equally informed serious competitors may differ in their assessments of the value of tract by a factor of 10 or more. See Capen, Clapp & Campbell [1971] for a realistic description of the situation as well as for the best public description of the kind of analysis undertaken by some of the sophisticated bidders. Keefer, Smith & Back [1991] is also a useful description of a company's analytical efforts.

Capen, Clapp & Campbell also highlight a striking aspect of the offshore oil sales: in spite of the great uncertainty about a tract's value, that value is roughly the same to whichever competitor wins it. The amount of oil and its price will be the same, and the costs of extracting it will be extremely similar. This gives rise to a phenomenon termed by Capen, Clapp & Campbell 'the winner's curse'. In such auctions, even with unbiased estimating the winner will normally be the bidder who most overestimated the tract value. This effect grows larger with greater uncertainty and with larger numbers of bidders. Because of it, rational bidders must make an allowance for the overestimates in the tracts they win. However, such corrections are often counterintuitive, and in addition to the persuasive anecdotal report of Capen, Clapp & Campbell [1971], experimental economics provides evidence of persistence of a disequilibrium undercorrection [see Kagel & Levin, 1986, 1991; Lind & Plott, 1991].

Formal competitive sales of significant oil leases have normally been by standard sealed bidding. However, a number of different issues related to auction form have been analyzed. The issues include whether to hold sequential or simultaneous sales[23], whether to sell shares in large tracts rather than all of current sized tracts[24], how to decide whether to reject the best bid[25], whether to allow bidders to bid jointly[26], how to charge (i.e. cash bonus, production royalty, land rent, profit share, etc.)[27] and where more than one method of charging is used, which of the charges shall be fixed and which specified by the bid.[28]

3.4.2. Coal leasing

Federal coal leasing is quite different from federal oil leasing. The resource is not as valuable and the extent of the resource can be closely determined before leasing. One striking aspect of federal coal leasing is the prevalence, due to the history of 'checkerboard' control of land in the U.S. west, of tracts in which a single bidder controls adjacent coal and is, hence, the only party that can afford

---

[23] See for example Rothkopf, Dougherty & Rose [1986] and, for a theoretical treatment, Hausch [1986].

[24] See for example Wilson [1979].

[25] Department of the Interior staff work on this question has used simple cut off levels and at least considered using an algorithm by Dougherty & Lohrenz [1976] for eliminating 'nonserious bids' in order to use the 'serious bids' to update the Department's own estimate of 'fair market value'.

[26] See for example Kobrin, Canes & Murphy [1977], Debrock & Smith [1983] and Rothkopf & Engelbrecht-Wiggans [1993].

[27] See for example Mead, Moseidjord & Muraoka [1984] and Rothkopf & Engelbrecht-Wiggans [1992].

[28] See for example Rothkopf & Engelbrecht-Wiggans [1992].

to develop the resource. The Linowes Commission report (U.S. Commission on Fair Market Value Policy for Federal Coal Leasing [1984]) gives a comprehensive picture of the economics of federal coal leasing.

A key issue in federal coal leasing is dealing with one-bidder tracts. How can the government obtain 'fair market value' when there is only one 'competitor'? McGuire [1978] proposed an innovative approach termed 'intertract competition' in which the government would offer more tracts for sale than it intended to sell and then consummate the sale of only the tracts receiving the higher bids per estimated ton of coal.[29] Several other suggestions for innovations in auction form are contained in Rothkopf & Engelbrecht-Wiggans [1992].

3.4.3. Timber leasing

The U.S. Forest Service sells the right (and duty) to log within a time limit (often three years) all of the marketable timber in tracts in national forests. There are also some similar sales of logging rights by states and the federal Bureau of Land Management. In these sales, the government usually bears the quantity risk by selling the timber based upon a unit price for each species (e.g. $60 per thousand board feet of Douglas fir) to be applied to the measured quantity of timber actually harvested. Since tracts normally have more than one species of marketable timber, however, there is usually more than one unit price, and the winner is determined by weighting the unit prices by the selling agency's *estimate* of the quantities. Because the government bears this quantity risk, small logging operations without any timber mill, termed 'gypo loggers', are sometimes able to participate in the bidding.

The auction form issues that have received analytical attention include oral versus sealed bidding[30], auction design to resist collusion[31], and the treatment of 'skewed bidding' in which a bidder 'unbalances' its bid by offering an extremely high unit price for a species for which it believes the seller has overestimated the quantity and very low prices on the other species.[32]

3.4.4. Sale of federal debt

The U.S. Treasury regularly auctions off the short- and long-term debt of the United States government. For many years, the auction was a standard sealed bid discriminatory auction. After a trial period during 1973 and 1974 with a nondiscriminatory auction, the Treasury has returned to discriminatory auctions, but with a provision that small bidders may bid 'noncompetitively'. Such small bidders bids, which have always totaled well under half of the total amount of debt

---

[29] This approach is opposed politically by the coal industry. Also see Rothkopf & McGuire [1986] for a formalized round-robin negotiation approach intended to achieve the same results.

[30] See Mead [1967], Miller [1972], Wiener [1979], Craig [1979], Hansen [1985] and Rothkopf & Engelbrecht-Wiggans [1993].

[31] See Froeb & McAfee [1988].

[32] See U.S. General Accounting Office [1983], U.S. Forest Service [1983, 1984, 1985a,b] and Wood [1989]. Bidders have incentive to use such unbalanced bids because the winner is determined using the estimated quantity but the eventual payment is based upon the measured quantity.

offered, always win and pay the average price paid by the other, competitive bids. In September 1992, in the wake of the Salomon Brothers scandal, the Treasury again began trying nondiscriminatory auctions. See Chari & Weber [1992] for a recent economic analysis.

3.4.5. Electricity purchases

In recent years, state public utility commissions have been trying to define the competitive mechanisms under which electric utilities will purchase power from cogenerators and independent power producers. Different states are following different approaches. The issues being debated include the use of formal auctions versus RFP processes and/or informal negotiations, first-price versus second-price auctions, what kind of projects may compete, whether a utility's unregulated affiliates may compete in its auctions, what other factors besides price (if anything) are to be considered in evaluating bids, and how these factors will be evaluated.[33]

3.4.6. Other applications

Other public sector application areas include government purchases, especially federal military procurement[34] and state road construction [see Stark, 1974], detection of collusion [see State of Florida, 1978], and allocation of government assets, such as airport landing rights [see Grether, Isaac & Plott, 1979, 1981; Rassenti, Smith & Bulfin, 1982], and space on space shuttles [Plott, 1991]. Analysis is under way of the provisions in the 1990 Clean Air Act calling for auctions of emission rights. Other applications related to regulated public utilities include sale of debt [see Christianson, 1965] and allocation of space in gas transmission lines [see U.S. Federal Energy Regulatory Commission, 1987].

A recent paper used auction theory in analyzing the regulation of corporate takeovers [Cramton & Schwartz, 1991].

Acknowledgements

Over the years, many people have gone out of their way to help me appreciate better the issues involved in analyzing competitive bidding. Among these are Edward Capen, Richard Engelbrecht-Wiggans, Ronald Harstad, John Lohrenz, C. Bart McGuire, Charles Plott, Thomas P. Rothrock, Robert M. Stark, Thomas Teisberg and Robert B. Wilson. Engelbrecht-Wiggans, Harstad, Lohrenz and Stephen Pollock have supplied helpful comments on drafts of this chapter. Mistakes, of course, are mine alone.

---

[33] Plummer & Troppmann [1990] pulls together diverse materials dealing with these and some other issues. Specific modeling is contained in Rothkopf, Kahn, Teisberg, Eto & Nataf [1987] and Kahn, Rothkopf, Eto & Nataf [1990]. A recent overview is in Rose, Burns & Eifert [1991]. Recent material on the problems of evaluating bids are in Stoft & Kahn [1991] and Kahn, Marnay & Berman [1991].

[34] There are several articles in the volumes edited by Amihud [1976] and by Engelbrecht-Wiggans, Shubik & Stark [1983].

References

American Society of Civil Engineers (1985). Bid rigging: An inside story. *Civil Engrg.* 55, March, 60–63.

Amihud, Y. (ed.) (1976). *Bidding and Auctioning for Procurement and Allocation*, New York University Press, New York.

Anton, J., and D. Yao (1987). Second sourcing and the experience curve: Price competition in defense procurement. *Rand J. Econom.* 18, 57–76.

Anton, J., and D. Yao (1989). Split awards, procurement, and innovation. *Rand J. Econom.* 20, 538–552.

Arps, J.J. (1965). A strategy for sealed bidding. *J. Petroleum Tech.* 17, 1033–1039.

Bikhchandani, S. (1986). Market games with few traders, Ph.D. Dissertation, Graduate School of Business, Stanford University, Stanford, CA.

Bikhchandani, S. (1988). Reputation in repeated second-price auctions. *J. Econom. Theory* 46, 97–119.

Bikhchandani, S., and C.-F. Huang (1989). Auctions with resale markets: An exploratory model of treasury bill markets. *Rev. Financial Studies* 2, 311–339.

Capen, E., R. Clapp and W. Campbell (1971). Competitive bidding in high risk situations. *J. Petroleum Tech.* 23, 641–653.

Cassady, R. Jr (1967). *Auctions and Auctioneering*, University of California Press, Berkeley, CA.

Chari, V.V., and R.J. Weber (1992). How the U.S. treasury should auction its debt, Quarterly Review, Federal Reserve Bank of Minneapolis, Fall, pp. 3–12.

Christianson, C. (1965). *Strategic Aspects of Competitive Bidding for Corporate Securities*, Division of Research, Graduate School of Business Administration, Harvard University, Cambridge, MA.

Cohen, S.I., and M. Loeb (1990). Implicit cost allocation and bidding for contracts. *Management Sci.* 36, 1133–1138.

Comanor, W.S., and M.A. Schankerman (1976). Identical bids and cartel behavior. *Bell J. Econom.* 7, 281–286.

Craig, G.A. (1979). Comment on 'Sealed bids or oral auctions: Which yield higher prices?'. *J. Forestry* 77, 357–358.

Cramton, P., and A. Schwartz (1991). Using auction theory to inform takeover regulation. *J. Law, Econom. Organization* 7, 27–53.

Dam, K.W. (1976). *Oil Resources: Who Gets What How?*, University of Chicago Press, Chicago, IL.

Debrock, L.M., and J.L. Smith (1983). Joint bidding, information pooling, and the performance of petroleum leases. *Bell J. Econom.* 14, 395–404.

Diekmann, J.E., R.H. Mayer Jr and R.M. Stark (1981). Coping with uncertainty in unit price contracting, Preprint 81-541, American Society of Civil Engineers, New York, NY.

Dougherty, E.L., and J. Lohrenz (1976). Statistical analysis of bids for federal offshore leases. *J. Petroleum Tech.* 28, 1377–1390.

Dubey, P., and M. Shubik (1980). A strategic market game with price and quantity strategies. *Z. Nationalökonom.* 40, 25–34.

Eisendrath, J. (1987). You think that the NSC is screwed up? Take a look at Washington's worst run program. *Washington Monthly*, April, 13–16.

Engelbrecht-Wiggans, R. (1980). Auctions and bidding models. *Management Sci.* 26, 119–142.

Engelbrecht-Wiggans, R. (1987a). On optimal reservation prices in auctions. *Management Sci.* 33, 763–770.

Engelbrecht-Wiggans, R. (1987b). Optimal constrained bidding. *Internat. J. Game Theory* 16, 115–121.

Engelbrecht-Wiggans, R. (1994). Sequential auctions of non-identical objects. *Econom. Lett.*, to appear.

Engelbrecht-Wiggans, R., and C.M. Kahn (1991). Protecting the winner: Second-price versus oral auctions. *Econom. Lett.* 35, 243–248.

Engelbrecht-Wiggans, R., P.R. Milgrom and R.J. Weber (1983). Competitive bidding and proprietary information. *J. Math. Econom.* 11, 161–169.

Engelbrecht-Wiggans, R., M. Shubik and R.M. Stark (eds.) (1983). *Auctions, Bidding, and Contracting: Uses and Theory*, New York University Press, New York.

Engelbrecht-Wiggans, R., and R.J. Weber (1979a). On the nonexistence of multiplicative equilibrium strategies, Cowles Foundation Discussion Paper No. 523, Yale University, New Haven,
CT.

Engelbrecht-Wiggans, R., and R.J. Weber (1979b). An example of a multi-object auction game.
Management Sci. 25, 1272–1277.

Engwall, L. (1976). To bid or not to bid. *Omega* 3, 396–401.

Flueck, J.A. (1967). A statistical decision theory approach to a seller's bid pricing problem under
uncertainty, Ph.D. Dissertation, School of Business, University of Chicago, Chicago, IL.

Friedman, L. (1956). A competitive bidding strategy. *Oper. Res.* 4, 104–112.

Friedman, L. (1957). Competitive bidding strategies, Ph.D. Dissertation, Case Institute of Technology, Cleveland, OH.

Froeb, L., and P. McAfee (1988). Detering bid rigging in forest service timber auctions, Report EAG
88-5, Economic Analysis Group, Antitrust Division, U.S. Department of Justice, Washington,
DC.

Gilley, O.W., and G.V. Karels (1981). The competitive effect in bonus bidding: New evidence. *Bell
J. Econom.* 12, 637–648.

Graham, D., and R. Marshall (1987). Collusive bidder behavior at single-object second-price and
English auctions. *J. Political Econom.* 95, 1217–1239.

Grether, D., M. Isaac and C. Plott (1979). Alternative methods of allocating airport slots: Performance and evaluation, CAB Report, Polynomics Research Laboratories, Inc., Pasadena, CA.

Grether, D., M. Isaac and C. Plott (1981). The allocation of landing rights by unanimity among
competitors. *Amer. Econom. Rev.* 71, 166–171.

Griesmer, J.H., R.E. Levitan and M. Shubik (1967). Towards a study of bidding process, 4: Games
with unknown costs. *Naval Res. Logist. Quart.* 14, 415–433.

Gumbel, E.J. (1958). *Statistics of Extremes*, Columbia University Press, New York.

Hansen, R.G. (1985). Sealed bids versus open auctions: The evidence. *Econom. Inquiry* 24, 125–142.

Harris, M., and A. Raviv (1981). Allocation mechanisms and the design of auctions. *Econometrica*
49, 1477–1499.

Harris, M., and A. Raviv (1984). A theory of monopoly pricing schemes with demand uncertainty.
Amer. Econom. Rev. 71, 347–365.

Harstad, R.M. (1990). Alternative common-value auction procedures: Revenue comparisons with
free entry. *J. Political Econom.* 98, 421–429.

Harstad, R.M., and M.H. Rothkopf (1991). Models of information flows in English auctions, Report
RRR 6-91, RUTCOR, Rutgers University, New Brunswick, NJ.

Hausch, D.B. (1986). Multi-object auctions: Sequential vs. simultaneous sales. *Management Sci.* 32,
1599–1610.

Hausch, D.B., and L. Li (1990). A common value auction model with endogenous entry and
information acquisition, Working Paper, School of Business, University of Wisconsin, Madison.

Hausch, D.B., and L. Li (1991). Private values auctions with endogenous information: Revenue
equivalence and non-equivalence, Working Paper, School of Business, University of Wisconsin,
Madison.

Hendricks, K., and R. Porter (1988). An empirical study of an auction with asymmetric information.
Amer. Econom. Rev. 78, 865–883.

Hendricks, K., R. Porter and B. Boudreau (1987). Information, returns and bidding behavior in
OCS auction: 1954–1969. *J. Indust. Econom.* 35, 517–542.

Holt, C.A. Jr (1980). Competitive bidding for contracts under alternative auction procedures. *J.
Political Econom.* 88, 433–445.

Kagel, J.H., and D. Levin (1986). The winner's curse and public information in common value
auctions. *Amer. Econom. Rev.* 76, 894–920.

Kagel, J.H., and D. Levin (1991). The winner's curse and public information in common value auctions: Reply. *Amer. Econom. Rev.* 81, 362–369.

Kahn, E.P., C. Marnay and D. Berman (1991). Evaluating dispatchability features in competitive bidding, Paper 91 JPGC 558-7 PWRS, IEEE/PES 1991, International Joint Power Generation Conference and Exposition, San Diego, CA, October 6–9.

Kahn, E.P., M.H. Rothkopf, J. Eto and J.-M. Nataf (1990). Auctions for PURPA purchases: A simulation study. *J. Regulatory Econom.* 2, 129–149.

Keefer, D.F., B. Smith Jr and H.B. Back (1991). Development and use of a modeling system to aid a major oil company in allocating bidding capital. *Oper. Res.* 39, 28–41.

Klotz, D.E., and K. Chatterjee (1991). Variable split awards in a single-stage model, Working Paper 91-6-1, Graduate School of Business Administration, Fordham University, New York.

Kobrin, P.M., M. Canes and P. Murphy (1977). Is the ban on joint bidding by major oil companies warranted? Report 002, American Petroleum Institute, Washington, DC.

Kortanek, K.O., J.V. Soden and D. Sodaro (1973). Profit analyses and sequential bid pricing models. *Management Sci.* 20, 396–417.

Kuhlman, J.M. (1974). Inferring conduct from performance: An analysis of a price fixing Case, Working Paper, Department of Economics, University of Missouri–Columbia.

Laffont, J.-J., and E. Maskin (1980). Optimal reservation price in the Vickrey auction. *Econom. Lett.* 6, 309–313.

Lind, B., and C.R. Plott (1991). The winner's curse: Experiments with buyers and sellers. *Amer. Econom. Rev.* 81, 335–346.

Maltz, M.D., and S.M. Pollock (1979). An empirical investigation of bid-rigging, Working Paper, Center for Research in Criminal Justice, University of Illinois at Chicago Circle.

Maltz, M.D., and S.M. Pollock (1980). Analyzing suspected collusion among bidders, in: G. Geis, and E. Stotland (eds.), *White Collar Crime: Theory and Research*, Sage Publications, Beverly Hills, CA, pp. 174–198.

Maskin, E.S., and J.G. Riley (1983). Auctions with asymmetric beliefs, Working Paper #254, University of California, Los Angeles, CA.

Maskin, E.S., and J.G. Riley (1984). Optimal auctions with risk averse buyers. *Econometrica* 52, 1473–1518.

Maskin, E.S., and J.G. Riley (1987). Optimal multi-unit auctions, Working Paper, Harvard University, Cambridge, MA.

Matthews, S.A. (1983). Selling to risk averse buyers with unobservable tastes. *J. Econom. Theory* 30, 370–400.

Matthews, S.A. (1984). On the implementability of reduced form auctions. *Econometrica* 52, 1519–1523.

McAfee, R.P., and J. McMillan (1987). Auctions and bidding. *J. Econom. Literature* 25, 699–738.

McGuire, C.B. (1978). Intertract competition and the design of lease sales for western coal lands, Report, Graduate School of Public Policy, University of California, Berkeley, CA, Presented June 25 at the 53rd annual Western Economics Association Conference.

Mead, W.J. (1967). Natural resource disposal policy – Oral auction vs. sealed bid. *Natural Resources J.* 7, 194–224.

Mead, W.J., A. Moseidjord and D. Muraoka (1984). Alternative bid variables as instruments of OCS leasing policy, in: *Contemporary Policy Issues: The New Resource Economics, Land, Timber, and Energy*, No. 5, Western Economic Association International, Huntington Beach, CA, pp. 30–43.

Milgrom, P.R., and R.J. Weber (1982). A theory of auctions and competitive bidding. *Econometrica* 50, 1089–1122.

Miller, E.M. (1972). Oral and sealed bidding, efficiency versus equity. *Natural Resources J.* 12, 330–353.

Moody, C.E., and W.J. Kruvant (1990). OCS leasing policy and lease prices. *Land Econom.* 66, 30–39.

Moore, J. (1984). Global incentive constraints in auction design. *Econometrica* 52, 1523–1536.

Myerson, R.B. (1981). Optimal auction design. *Math. Oper. Res.* 6, 58–73.

Nurmi, H., and A. Salomaa (1993). Cryptographic protocols for Vickrey auctions. *Group Decision and Negotiation* 4, 363–373.

Oren, M.E., and A.C. Williams (1975). On competitive bidding. *Oper. Res.* 23, 1072–1079.

Oren, S.S., and M.H. Rothkopf (1975). Optimal bidding in sequential auctions. *Oper. Res.* 23, 1080–1090.

Ortega-Reichert, A. (1968). Models of competitive bidding under uncertainty, Technical Report No. 8, Department of Operations Research, Stanford University, Stanford, CA.

Plott, C.R. (1982). Industrial organization theory and experimental economics. *J. Econom. Literature* 20, 1485–1527.

Plott, C.R. (1991). Personal communication.

Plott, C.R., and V.L. Smith 1978). An experimental examination of two exchange institutions. *Rev. Econom. Studies* 45, 133–153.

Plummer, J., and S. Troppmann (eds.) (1990). *Competition in Electricity: New Markets and New Structures*, Public Utilities Reports, Inc., Arlington, VA.

Rassenti, S.J., V.L. Smith and R.L. Bulfin (1982). A combinatorial auction mechanism for airport time slot allocation. *Bell J. Econom.* 13, 402–417.

Riley, J.G., and W. Samuelson (1981). Optimal auctions. *Amer. Econom. Rev.* 71, 381–392.

Robinson, M.S. (1984). Oil lease auctions: Reconciling economic theory with practice, Working Paper, Department of Economics, University of California, Los Angeles, CA.

Robinson, M.S. (1985). Collusion and the choice of auction. *Rand J. Econom.* 16, 141–145.

Rose, K., R.E. Burns and M. Eifert (1991). Implementing a competitive bidding program for electric power supply, Report NRRI 90-15, The National Regulatory Research Institute, Columbus, OH.

Roth, A. (1988). Laboratory experimentation in economics: A methodological overview. *Econom. J.* 98, 974–1031.

Rothkopf, M.H. (1969). A model of rational competitive bidding. *Management Sci.* 15, 362–373.

Rothkopf, M.H. (1977). Bidding in simultaneous auctions with a constraint on exposure. *Oper. Res.* 25, 620–629.

Rothkopf, M.H. (1980a). On multiplicative bidding strategies. *Oper. Res.* 28, 570–575.

Rothkopf, M.H. (1980b). Equilibrium linear bidding strategies. *Oper. Res.* 28, 576–583.

Rothkopf, M.H. (1983). Bidding theory: The phenomena to be modeled, in: R. Engelbrecht-Wiggans, M. Shubik and R. Stark (eds.), *Auctions, Bidding and Contracting: Uses and Theory*, New York University Press, New York, pp. 105–120.

Rothkopf, M.H. (1991). On auctions with withdrawable winning bids. *Marketing Sci.* 10, 40–57.

Rothkopf, M.H., E. Dougherty and M. Rose (1986). Comment on 'Multi-object auctions: Sequential vs. simultaneous sales'. *Management Sci.* 32, 1611–1612.

Rothkopf, M.H., and R. Engelbrecht-Wiggans (1992). Innovative approaches to competitive mineral leasing. *Resources and Energy* 14, 233–248.

Rothkopf, M.H., and R. Engelbrecht-Wiggans (1993). Misapplication Reviews: Getting the model right – The case of competitive bidding. *Interfaces* 23(3), 99–106.

Rothkopf, M.H., and R. Harstad (1990). Reconciling efficiency arguments in taxation and public sector resource leasing, Report RRR 66-90, RUTCOR, Rutgers University, New Brunswick, NJ.

Rothkopf, M.H., and R. Harstad (1992). Two models of bid-taker cheating in Vickrey auctions, Working Paper No. 165, School of Business, Rutgers University, New Brunswick, NJ.

Rothkopf, M.H., E.P. Kahn, T.J. Teisberg, J. Eto and J.-M. Nataf (1987). Designing PURPA power purchase auctions: Theory and practice, Report LBL-23906, Lawrence Berkeley Laboratory, University of California, CA; reprinted by Office of Policy, Planning and Analysis, U.S. Department of Energy as Report DOE/SF/00098-H1, November 1987; reprinted, in part, in: Plummer & Troppmann [1990], pp. 139–193.

Rothkopf, M.H., and C.B. McGuire. Assessment of negotiation options for coal lease sales, Report LBL-22501, Lawrence Berkeley Laboratories, Berkeley, CA.

Rothkopf, M.H., T.J. Teisberg and E.P. Kahn (1990). Why are Vickrey auctions rare?. *J. Political Econom.* 98, 94–109.

Rothrock, T.P. (1976). Competition in sealed bid markets: An application of a statistical bidding model, Ph.D. Dissertation, University of Missouri, Columbia.

Rothrock, T.P. (1978). Statistical analysis of sealed tender markets using a firm bidding model. *J. Econom.* 4, 34–39.

Rothrock, T.P. (1991). Private communication.

Seshadri, S., K. Chatterjee and G. Lilien (1991). Multiple source procurement competitions. *Marketing Sci.* 10, 246–263.

Shubik, M. (1970). On different methods for allocating resources. *Kyklos, Internat. Z. Sozialwissenschaften* 23, 332–337.

Simmonds, K., and S. Slatter (1978). The number of estimators: A critical decision for marketing under competitive bidding. *J. Marketing Res.* 15, 203–213.

Smith, C.W. (1990). *Auctions: The Social Construction of Value*, University of California Press, Berkeley, CA.

Smith, S.A., and M.H. Rothkopf (1985). Simultaneous bidding with a fixed charge if any bid is successful. *Oper. Res.* 33, 28–37.

Smith, V.L. (1967). Experimental studies of discrimination versus competition in sealed bid markets. *J. Business* 40, 56–84.

Smith, V.L. (1982). Microeconomic systems as an experimental science. *Amer. Econom. Rev.* 72, 923–955.

Smith, V.L. (1987). Auctions, in: J. Eatwell, M. Milgate and P. Newman (eds.), *The New Palgrave: A Dictionary of Economics, Vol. 1*, The Macmillan Press Ltd., London, pp. 138–144.

Stark, R.M. (1974). Unbalanced highway contracting. *Oper. Res. Q.* 25, 373–388.

Stark, R.M., and R.H. Mayer Jr (1971). Some multi-contract decision theoretic competitive bidding models. *Oper. Res.* 19, 469–483.

Stark, R.M., and M.H. Rothkopf (1979). Competitive bidding: A comprehensive bibliography. *Oper. Res.* 27, 364–390.

State of Florida, Attorney General's Office, Civil Division, Department of Legal Affairs, Antitrust Unit (1978). *A Computerized Economic and Statistical Analysis of the Florida School Bread Market*; summarized in T.P. Rothrock, J.T. McClave and J.P. Ailstock, *Southeastern Antitrust Rev.* 1, Autumn.

Stiglitz, J. (1984). Affidavit on reduced bonus receipts under area-wide leasing transmitted to William Clark, Secretary of the Interior, by Mark White, Governor of Texas, May 25, 1984.

Stoft, S., and E.P. Kahn (1991). Auction markets for dispatchable power: How to score the bids. *J. Regulatory Econom.* 3, 275–286.

U.S. Commission on Fair Market Value Policy for Federal Coal Leasing (1984). *Report of the Commission*.

U.S. Federal Energy Regulatory Commission, Offices of Pipeline and Producer Regulation and of Economic Policy (1987). Gas transportation rate design and the use of auctions to allocate capacity, Staff Discussion Paper FERC-0121.

U.S. Forest Service (1983). National forest timber sales; Control of skewed bidding; Procedures. *Federal Register* 48(128), July 1, p. 30417.

U.S. Forest Service (1984). National forest timber sales; Control of skewed bidding; Procedures. *Federal Register* 49(137), July 16, p. 28748.

U.S. Forest Service (1985a). Sale and disposal of national forest system timber. *Federal Register* 50(157), August 14, p. 32694.

U.S. Forest Service (1985b). Sale and disposal of national forest system timber; Downpayment and bid monitoring. *Federal Register* 50(198), October 11, p. 41498.

U.S. General Accounting Office (1983). Skewed bidding presents costly problems for the Forest Service timber sales program, Report GAO/RCED-83-87.

Vickrey, W. (1961). Counterspeculation, auctions and competitive sealed tenders. *J. Finance* 41, 8–37.

Weber, R.J. (1983). Multiple object auctions, in: R. Engelbrecht-Wiggans, M. Shubik and R.M. Stark (eds.), *Auctions, Bidding, and Contracting: Uses and Theory*, New York University Press,

New York, pp. 165–191.

Wiener, A.A. (1979). Sealed bids or oral auctions: Which yields higher prices?. *J. Forestry* 77, 353–358.

Wilson, R.B. (1979). Auctions of shares. *Quart. J. Econom.* 93, 675–690.

Wilson, R.B. (1987). Bidding, in: J. Eatwell, M. Milgate and P. Newman (eds.), *The New Palgrave: A Dictionary of Economics, Vol. 1*, Macmillan, London, pp. 238–242.

Wilson, R.B. (1993). Strategic analysis of auctions, in: R. Aumann, and S. Hart (eds.), *The Handbook of Game Theory*, North-Holland, Amsterdam, pp. 227–279.

Wood, D.J. (1989). A study of multiplicative-strategy equilibria in second-price multi-component auctions, Ph.D. Dissertation, Department of Industrial Engineering and Operations Research, University of California, Berkeley, CA.

Biographical Information

Lowell Bruce ANDERSON received a Bachelor's degree in Electrical Engineering from The Johns Hopkins University, a Master's in Industrial Engineering and Management Science from Northwestern University, and a Ph.D. in Applied Mathematics from Northwestern. He served as a Lieutenant on the Department of the Army Staff in the Pentagon, and as a Captain on the Army Staff in Vietnam. Since 1971 he has been on the research staff at the Institute for Defense Analyses, where he has designed, built, and performed analyses involving various models of land, air, and sea combat. He served as an Associate Editor of *Operations Research* from 1979 through 1985. He won the ORSA/MAS Prize in 1979, and IDA's Andrew J. Goodpaster Award for excellence in research in 1985. He has been a Professorial Lecturer at The George Washington University. Voting Theory and the Theory of Paired Comparisons have long been among his non-defense interests. (Chapters 16, 17.)

Michel BALINSKI is Directeur de Recherche (de classe exceptionnelle) of the C.N.R.S. (Centre National de Recherche Scientifique) in France, Director of the Laboratoire d'Économétrie of the École Polytechnique in Paris, and co-Director of the joint University of Paris 1 (Pathéon-Sorbonne) and École Polytechnique doctoral program, 'Models and mathematical methods in economics: optimization and strategic analysis'. Before, he held positions in mathematics, economics and/or administrative sciences at Princeton, Pennsylvania, the Graduate Center of C.U.N.Y., I.I.A.S.A., Yale, and S.U.N.Y. Stony Brook. He is a winner of the Lanchester Prize of the Operations Research Society of America for work in integer programming and of a Lester R. Ford Award of the Mathematical Association of America 1975 for joint work with H.P. Young on apportionment. He is the Founding Editor-in-Chief of the journal *Mathematical Programming*. His research interests have centered on combinatorial optimization, mathematical programming and the use of the axiomatic method in diverse applied settings such as voting, apportionment and how to 'best' round data. (Chapter 15.)

Arnold BARNETT is Professor of Operations Research at MIT's Sloan School of Management. He holds a B.A. In Physics from Columbia College and a Ph.D. in Applied Mathematics from MIT. His main research speciality is applied probabilistic and statistical modeling related to issues of public health and safety. But he also worries about the health and safety of mathematic models, as evidenced by his decade-long authorship of the Misapplications Reviews column in *Interfaces*. Dr. Barnett has served as Departmental Editor for Public Sector Applications at *Management Science*, has authored or co-authored over 80 published papers, and has consulted for more than two dozen public or private organizations. (Chapter 3, Editor.)

David J. BRAILER, M.D., Ph.D. is an adjunct Professor of Health Care Systems at The Wharton School of Business and at the University of Pennsylvania Medical Center and a senior fellow at the Leonard Davis Institute of Health Economics. Dr. Brailer is President of Care Management Science Corporation and of the Center for Health Choice. Dr. Brailer completed his B.S. and M.D. degrees at West Virginia University and his Ph.D. in operations management and health care economics at The Wharton School. Dr. Brailer was a Charles A. Dana Scholar at the University of Pennsylvania

School of Medicine, and was the first recipient of the National Library of Medicine Martin Epstein Award for his work on health care information systems. He completed medical residency at the Hospital of the University of Pennsylvania and became board certified in internal medicine along the clinical investigator pathway. Dr. Brailer was then named a Robert Wood Johnson Clinical Scholar at the University of Pennsylvania. Dr. Brailer teaches health care operations, health care quality management, and managed care in Wharton's M.B.A. program. (Chapter 13.)

Hugh ELLIS received his Bachelor of Applied Science (1979), Master of Applied Science (1981) and Ph.D. (1984) degrees in Civil Engineering from the University of Waterloo. He joined The Johns Hopkins University in July 1984 as an Assistant Professor in the Systems Analysis Group of the Department of Geography and Environmental Engineering, and is now Associate Professor. His research interests involve environmental systems analysis with emphasis on the development and application of stochastic and multiobjective programming methods. Current work includes the development of regret-based models for decision-making under uncertainty, models for optimizing the design of groundwater and air pollution monitoring networks, surface water quality optimization studies, and stochastic analyses of structural system reliability. (Chapter 10.)

Saul I. GASS, received a B.S. in Education and an M.A. in Mathematics from Boston University, and a Ph.D. in Engineering Science/Operations Research from the University of California, Berkeley. He is a Professor of Management Science and Statistics, College of Business and Management, University of Maryland, College Park. Dr. Gass began his career in operations research with the Directorate of Management Analysis, Headquarters, U.S. Air Force. He was Manager of the Project Mercury man-in-space program for IBM, and Manager of IBM's Federal Civil Programs. Included in his many publications are the books *Linear Programming, An Illustrated Guide to Linear Programming*, and *Decision Making, Models and Algorithms*. Dr. Gass was President of the Operations Research Society of America and Omega Rho, the international operations research honorary society. He was the 1991 recipient of the Operations Research Society of America's George E. Kimball Medal for distinguished service to the society and the profession. (Chapter 2.)

Yigal GERCHAK received his Ph.D. in management science from the University of British Columbia in 1980. His early research was in mathematical models in the social sciences, statistical manpower planning in organizations and applied probability. His main current research interests are: operations management in production and service organizations, health management, and in decision analysis and the economics of uncertainty, and, as a hobby, OR in sports. He is with the Management Sciences Department of the University of Waterloo. He serves as the Department Editor for Inventory at *IIE Transactions*, and an Associate Editor of *Operations Research*. (Chapter 14.)

Bruce L. GOLDEN is a Professor in the College of Business and Management at the University of Maryland. He has served as Chairman of the Department of Management Science and Statistics since 1980. His research interests include network optimization, distribution management, natural resource management, and applied operations research, and he has published many technical articles in these and related fields. In addition, he has edited numerous volumes on vehicle routing, computing in operations research, and public sector OR. Some of Dr. Golden's recent research has been funded by the Maryland Department of Natural Resources, the U.S. Agency for International Development, Westinghouse, and the U.S. Census Bureau. He has consulted for a wide variety of organizations including the American Red Cross, the National Soft Drink Association, MidAtlantic Toyota, Airco Industrial Gases, the Military Airlift Command, and Amerigas Corporation. Dr. Golden is Editor of the *American Journal of Mathematical and Management Sciences*, Editor of the *ORSA Journal on Computing*, and Departmental Editor of *Management Science*, and he has served as Area Editor of *Operations Research*. He received his bachelor's degree in mathematics from the University of Pennsylvania and his masters and doctoral degrees in operations research from MIT. (Chapter 9.)

Paul KLEINDORFER is the Universal Furniture Professor of Decision Sciences and Economics at the Wharton School of the University of Pennsylvania. Dr. Kleindorfer graduated with distinction (B.S.) from the U.S. Naval Academy in 1961, followed by doctoral studies at Carnegie Mellon University, from which he received his Ph.D. in 1970 in Systems and Communication Sciences at the Graduate School of Industrial Administration. Dr. Kleindorfer has held university appointments at Carnegie Mellon University (1968–1969), Massachusetts Institute of Technology (1969–1972), The Wharton School (1973 – Present), and several international research institutes, including IIASA and The Science Center – Berlin. Dr. Kleindorfer is the author or editor of numerous books and research publications on topics such as quality, competitive strategy, energy policy, technology choice, and regulatory governance. In the past decade, Dr. Kleindorfer has focused his research on energy and the environment, with research topics ranging from global environmental issues, such as climate change and the implementation of the Montreal Protocol, to regional issues, such as airborne pollution, to local issues, including total environment quality and product/process design for environmental effectiveness. Dr. Kleindorfer is Co-Director of the Wharton Center for Risk Management and Decision Processes. (Chapter 11.)

Howard KUNREUTHER is the Celia Koo Professor of Decision Sciences and Public Policy & Management, as well as Co-Director of the Wharton Risk Management and Decision Processes Center at the University of Pennsylvania. In 1988–1989 he served as Director of the Decision Risk and Management Science Program at the National Science Foundation. During 1980–1982 he was Task Leader of the Risk Group at the International Institute for Applied Systems Analysis. His current research is concerned with the role of insurance compensation, incentive mechanisms, and regulation as policy tools for dealing with technological and natural hazards. He is author and co-author of numerous scientific papers concerned with risk and policy analysis, decision processes, and protection against low-probability/high-consequence events, as well as numerous books and monographs, including *Decision Sciences: An Interactive Perspective* (Cambridge University Press, 1993) with Paul Kleindorfer and Paul Schoemaker and *The Dilemma of Siting a High Level Nuclear Waste Repository* with Doug Easterling (Kluwer Academic Publishers, 1994). Dr. Kunreuther has a Ph.D. in Economics from the Massachusetts Institute of Technology. (Chapter 11.)

Lester B. LAVE is Higgins Professor of Economics at the Graduate School of Industrial Administration and University Professor at Carnegie Mellon University. He is also a professor in the Heinz School of Public Management and Policy and in the Department of Engineering and Public Policy. Dr. Lave received his B.A. from Reed College and his Ph.D. from Harvard University. From 1978–1982 he was a Senior Fellow at the Brookings Institution. He has acted as a consultant to many government agencies including the federal departments of Health and Human Services, Labor, Transportation, Defense, and Justice and the Environmental Protection Agency, Office of Technology Assessment, Government Accounting Office, and Congressional Research Service, as well as a large number of companies. He has received research grants from NIH, NIMH, NSF, EPA, OSHA, and other government agencies as well as many foundations and nonprofit organizations. His research has focused on public policy, exploring a wide range of issues from the effect of air pollution on human health to the economic capacity of a waterway, public policy toward the storage of helium, the information value of the cancer rodent bioassay, whether insulin-using diabetics should be allowed to drive trucks, to modeling global climate change. (Chapter 12.)

Michael D. MALTZ is Professor of Criminal Justice and of Information and Decision Sciences at the University of Illinois at Chicago. His undergraduate degree is from Rensselaer Polytechnic Institute, and his M.S. and Ph.D. are from Stanford University, all in electrical engineering. His training in operations research was acquired on the job, working with George Kimball, Bernard Koopman, and others at Arthur D. Little, Inc., from 1964 to 1969. Since then he has been active in applying OR techniques to problems of crime and justice, first as an operations analyst with the National Institute of Justice (1969–1972) and since then in his research at UIC. His book, *Recidivism*, won ORSA's Lanchester Prize for its contributions to operations research, as well as the Wilkins Award for its contributions to criminal justice and criminology. His more recent research has focused on the application of computer mapping to crime data and on the analysis of longitudinal 'life course' histories, as a means of inferring patterns of criminal behavior in both space and time. (Chapters 1, 7.)

Amedeo R. ODONI is Professor of Aeronautics and Astronautics and of Civil and Environmental Engineering at the Massachusetts Institute of Technology (MIT). He holds S.B. and S.M. degrees in Electrical Engineering (MIT 1965, 1967) and a Ph.D. in Operations Research (MIT 1969). His research interests are in applied probability and the modeling of large-scale systems, especially in air transportation. From 1986 to 1991 he served as Co-Director of the Operations Research Center at MIT, as well as Editor-in-Chief of *Transportation Science*. Dr. Odoni has been a consultant to many airports and government ATC organizations around the world and received the 1991 FAA Administrator's National Award for Excellence in Aviation Education. He has authored or co–authored four technical books and approximately 40 refereed articles and book chapters on airport planning, ATC, location theory, probabilistic combinatorial optimization and Markov decision processes. (Chapter 5.)

William P. PIERSKALLA, Ph.D., is the John E. Anderson Professor and Dean of the John E. Anderson Graduate School of Management at the University of California at Los Angeles. He holds B.A. in economics and M.B.A. degrees from Harvard University, an M.A. in mathematics from the University of Pittsburgh, and a M.S. in statistics and a Ph.D. in operations research from Stanford University. His current research interests include operations research, operations management, issues of global competition and the management aspects of health care delivery. Dr. Pierskalla is Past President of the International Federation of Operational Research Societies, 1992–1994, is on the Editorial Advisory Board of *Production and Operations Management*, is a Past President of the Operations Research Society of America, and is past Editor of *Operations Research*. He recently was the Deputy Dean for Academic Affairs, the Director of the Huntsman Center for Global Competition and Leadership, the Chairman of the Health Care Systems Department and the Ronald A. Rosenfeld Professor at The Wharton School. He has given numerous lectures and seminars at universities and organizations in the United States, Europe, and Japan and has over fifty refereed articles in mathematical programming, transportation, inventory and production control, maintainability and health care delivery. (Chapter 13.)

Stephen M. POLLOCK is Professor of Industrial and Operations Engineering at the University of Michigan. He has been involved in applying operations research methods to the analysis of a variety of operational situations, including submarine search, allocation of sewage treatment resources, the analysis of criminal recidivism, machine monitoring and understanding the behavior of networks of queues. After receiving his Ph.D. at MIT in 1964 he worked at Arthur D. Little, Inc. before going to the U.S. Naval Postgraduate School, and from there to the University of Michigan. He was President of the Operations Research Society of America in 1986. (Chapter 1, Editor.)

Charles REVELLE was educated as a chemical engineer (B.Ch.E.) and as an environmental systems engineer (Ph.D.) at Cornell University. He began his teaching and research in the Department of Environmental Systems Engineering at Cornell University in 1967 and has continued his work for the past 20 years at The Johns Hopkins University in the Department of Geography and Environmental Engineering. His present curricular involvement is with the Program in Systems Analysis and Economics, a program that emphasizes quantitative methods for public decision making on environmental resource and urban problems.

Professor ReVelle teaches courses on optimization and on public sector applications of optimization methods. His areas of teaching and research competence include: (1) the design of locational systems for such facilities as fire stations, ambulance dispatch sites, power plants, waste water treatment plants, and manufacturing plants, (2) the modelling of water quality systems both from a descriptive and management perspective, and (3) the management of water resources as embodied in reservoir design and operation policy. He serves on the editorial board of the *European Journal of Operational Research* and is an Associate Editor of *Management Science*.

With his wife Penelope, he has written three textbooks on environmental issues, the latest of which is *The Global Environment: Securing a Sustainable Future*, Jones & Bartlett Inc., 1992. (Chapter 10.)

Fred S. ROBERTS received his A.B. in mathematics from Dartmouth College in 1964 and his M.S. and Ph.D. in mathematics from Stanford University in 1967 and 1968. After a postdoctoral fellowship at the University of Pennsylvania, he joined the professional staff of the RAND Corporation in 1968. He was a postdoctoral fellow at the Institute for Advanced Study in Princeton in 1971–1972, and then joined the faculty at Rutgers University, where he has been Director of RUTCOR, the Rutgers Center for Operations Research, and DIMACS, the Center for Discrete Mathematics and Theoretical Computer Science and a consortium of Princeton and Rutgers Universities, AT&T Bell laboratories, and Bellcore. He is currently a Professor of Mathematics and a Fellow of RUTCOR.

Professor Roberts' major research interests are in mathematical models in the social, behavioral, and environmental sciences and of problems of communications and transportation; graph theory and combinatorics and their applications; measurement theory, utility, decisionmaking, and social choice; and operations research. His first book, *Discrete Mathematical Models, with Applications to Social, Biological, and Environmental Problems*, has been called a classic in the field, and was translated into Russian in 1986. He has also authored three other books: *Graph Theory and its Applications to Problems of Society*; *Measurement Theory, with Applications to Decisionmaking, Utility, and the Social Sciences*; *Applied Combinatorics*. Professor Roberts is also the editor of eleven other books and the author of some 122 scientific articles.

Professor Roberts is currently on the editorial board of eight scientific journals. He has been the organizer of 21 scientific conferences. He has been an active member of a variety of professional organizations, and has held such positions as Vice President of SIAM, Secretary and Member of the Board of the Societal Institute for the Mathematical Sciences, member of the COMAP Consortium Council, member of the Committee on Applications of Mathematics of the National Research Council, and member of the Board of Visitors of the Office of Naval Research. (Chapter 18.)

Michael H. ROTHKOPF is a modeler. He was the founding area editor for OR Practice of *Operations Research* and recently became the editor of *Interfaces*. After earning a Ph.D. in operations research from MIT, he spent 18 years in private industry with Shell Development Company, Shell International's Group Planning, and Xerox's Palo Alto Research Center. From 1982 to 1988, he was at the University of California's Lawrence Berkeley Laboratory where he headed the Energy Analysis Program. He has taught at the University of California, Stanford University, California State University and the University of Santa Clara. Since 1988, he has been a professor in RUTCOR and the School of Business at Rutgers University. He has published 17 papers on competitive bidding and 31 others on such diverse topics as scheduling, energy economics, modeling, applied stochastic processes, engineering applications of operations research, medical policy analysis, and market models. He has won an honorable mention in the Edelman Prize competition run by the College on the Practice of Management Science. He has served on the ORSA Council and is a TIMS vice-president. (Chapter 19, Editor.)

Dr. Jean-Marc ROUSSEAU is currently Vice President of GIRO Inc. and President of LO-GIROUTE Inc. He is a professor of Computer Science and Operations Research at the University of Montreal since 1973 (currently adjunct professor). Dr. Rousseau was Director of the University's Centre for Research in Transportation (C.R.T.) from 1979 to 1987. Specializing in the areas of crew and vehicle scheduling and routing problems, he has directed numerous research projects in these fields. (Chapter 5.)

Arthur J. SWERSEY is Professor of Operations Research at the Yale School of Organization and Management where, from 1986 to 1988, he was Associate Dean. He is co-editor (with Edward

Ignall) of the book *Delivery of Urban Services*, Vol. 22 in the TIMS Studies in the Management Sciences series. For his work on merging fire and emergency medical services in New Haven, he received a 1992 Elm and Ivy Award for Town-Gown relations, and was a finalist in the 1992 Edelman Prize Competition. In 1989, he received the Excellence in Teaching Award from his School's alumni Association.

Before coming to Yale in 1976, he spent eight years at the Rand Corporation, where he directed fire and police projects in New York City. For the fire project work, he was a recipient of the 1976 NATO Systems Science prize, and a finalist in the 1974 Edelman Competition.. He has developed methods for scheduling school buses and for locating vehicle emissions testing stations, and has studied urban homicide. He has ten years of experience in statistical process control and quality management. He has consulted to many organizations including the Pennsylvania Department of Transportation, Xerox Corporation, and Uniroyal Chemical Co. Professor Swersey has a B.S. from MIT and M.S. and Doctor of Engineering Science degrees from Columbia. (Chapter 6.)

Alan WASHBURN is a Professor in the Department of Operations Research at the Naval Postgraduate School. He has served as department chairman, and has recently completed an assignment as Associate Dean of Faculty. He pursued his undergraduate and graduate education in Electrical Engineering at Carnegie Institute of Technology, after which he was employed by the Boeing Company before accepting employment by the Navy. He has maintained a lifelong interest in Military Operations Research, particularly problems of decision making in conflict situations. He has served as Associate Editor for *Operations Research*, and publishes regularly in that journal as well as others. (Chapter 4.)

Edward Andrew WASIL, Jr. is an Associate Professor of Management Science in the Kogod College of Business Administration at American University in Washington, D.C. He received his Ph.D. in 1984 from the University of Maryland at College Park and currently teaches graduate courses in applied business statistics and production and operations management. His research interests include network optimization, the application of microcomputer software to decision problems, and the use of management science models in natural resource management, and he has published more than 35 technical articles in these and related fields. His publications include a special issue of the journal *Socio-Economic Planning Sciences* on public-sector applications of the analytic hierarchy process, a special issue of the journal *Computers & Operations Research* devoted to microcomputers, a book published by Prentice Hall titled *Excellence in Management Science Practice*, and a book published by Springer-Verlag titled *The Analytic Hierarchy Process: Applications and Studies*. He is the Feature Article Co-Editor of the *ORSA Journal on Computing*, an Associate Editor of *Management Science*, and a member of the editorial board of the *American Journal of Mathematical and Management Sciences*. (Chapter 9.)

John P. WEYANT is Professor of Engineering-Economic Systems and Director of the Energy Modeling Forum (EMF) at Stanford University. Established in 1976, the EMF conducts model comparison studies on major energy/environmental policy issues by convening international working groups of leading experts on mathematical modeling and policy development. Prof. Weyant earned a B.S./M.S. in Aeronautical Engineering and Astronautics, and an M.S. in Operations Research and Statistics from Rensselaer Polytechnic Institute, and a Ph.D. in Management Science with a minor in Economics from U.C., Berkeley. Before coming to Stanford, he held positions at the Rand Corporation and at Harvard University's Kennedy School of Government. Weyant has been a consultant to the Department of Energy, the Department of Defense, the Arms Control and Disarmament Agency, the Environmental Protection Agency, and the Office of Technology Assessment, as well as a dozen major corporations and institutes. His current research focuses on global climate change, energy and national security, Japanese energy policy, and models for strategic planning. (Chapter 8.)

Nigel H.M. WILSON is a Professor of Civil and Environmental Engineering at the Massachusetts Institute of Technology and the leader of the Transportation Group within the department. His research and teaching is focused on urban public transportation, including topics related to the operation, analysis, planning and management of transit systems. Specific research activities he has directed include workforce planning in the transit industry, short range transit planning methods, the role of private operators in public transportation and the potential for computers and communication systems to improve the performance of transit systems. He has authored more than sixty papers covering a wide range of transportation topics and has co-authored chapters of several books dealing with the role of analysis methods in public transportation. He is a past Associate Editor of *Transportation Science* and a member of the Editorial Advisory Board for *Transportation Research* (Part B) and currently serves on the Editorial Advisory Board for the *UITP Revue*.

He received his bachelors degree in civil engineering from Imperial College, University of London (1965) and the masters and doctoral degrees in civil engineering and transportation systems respectively from the Massachusetts Institute of Technology (1967 and 1970). Since 1970 he has been a faculty member at MIT and has also had visiting faculty appointments at Stanford University (1977–1978) and University College London (1993). He was instrumental in the creation of the interdepartmental Master of Science in Transportation program at MIT in 1978 and served as chairman of the standing faculty committee responsible for the program for twelve out its first fifteen years of existence. (Chapter 5.)

H. Peyton YOUNG is Professor of Economics and Public Policy at the University of Maryland. He received his B.A. from Harvard University and his Ph.D. in Mathematics from the University of Michigan. From 1976 to 1981 he was at the International Institute for Applied Systems Analysis in Austria where he was Deputy Chairman of the System and Decision Sciences Area. He has held visiting appointments at the University of Bonn, the University of Paris, the University of Chicago, and the Brookings Institution.

He has written on a variety of subjects in political science and economics, including the design of voting procedures, the apportionment of representation, districting, rate-setting by public utilities, the distributive effects of income tax policy, game theory, and bargaining. His books include *Fair Representation* (Yale University Press, 1982, with M.L. Balinski), *Fair Allocation* (Ed., American Mathematical Society, 1985), *Cost Allocation: Methods, Principles, Applications* (Ed., North-Holland, 1985), *Negotiations Analysis* (Ed., University of Michigan, 1991), and *Equity in Theory and Practice* (Princeton University Press, 1993). He is currently an associate editor of *Games and Economic Behavior* and *Social Choice and Welfare*. He lives with his wife and two children in Washington, DC. (Chapter 15.)

Subject Index

Handbooks in Operations Research
and Management Science
Contents of Previous Volumes

Volume 1. Optimization
Edited by G.L. Nemhauser, A.H.G. Rinnooy Kan and M.J. Todd
1989. xiv + 709 pp. ISBN 0-444-87284-1

Volume 2. Stochastic Models
Edited by D.P. Heyman and M.J. Sobel
1990. xv + 725 pp. ISBN 0-444-87473-9

Printed and bound by CPI Group (UK) Ltd, Croydon, CR0 4YY

08/05/2025

01865023-0002